CLASSICAL AND MEDIEVAL LITERATURE CRITICISM

Guide to Gale Literary Criticism Series

For criticism on	Consult these Gale series
Authors now living or who died after December 31, 1959	*CONTEMPORARY LITERARY CRITICISM (CLC)*
Authors who died between 1900 and 1959	*TWENTIETH-CENTURY LITERARY CRITICISM (TCLC)*
Authors who died between 1800 and 1899	*NINETEENTH-CENTURY LITERATURE CRITICISM (NCLC)*
Authors who died between 1400 and 1799	*LITERATURE CRITICISM FROM 1400 TO 1800 (LC)* *SHAKESPEAREAN CRITICISM (SC)*
Authors who died before 1400	*CLASSICAL AND MEDIEVAL LITERATURE CRITICISM (CMLC)*
Authors of books for children and young adults	*CHILDREN'S LITERATURE REVIEW (CLR)*
Black writers of the past two hundred years	*BLACK LITERATURE CRITICISM (BLC)*
Short story writers	*SHORT STORY CRITICISM (SSC)*
Poets	*POETRY CRITICISM (PC)*
Dramatists	*DRAMA CRITICISM (DC)*
Major authors from the Renaissance to the present	*WORLD LITERATURE CRITICISM, 1500 TO THE PRESENT (WLC)*

For criticism on visual artists since 1850, see

MODERN ARTS CRITICISM (MAC)

ISSN 0896-0011

Volume 12

CLASSICAL AND MEDIEVAL LITERATURE CRITICISM

Excerpts from Criticism of the Works of World Authors from Classical Antiquity through the Fourteenth Century, from the First Appraisals to Current Evaluations

Jelena O. Krstović
Editor

Michael Magoulias
Zoran Minderović
Anna J. Sheets
Brian J. St. Germain
Associate Editors

Gale Research Inc. • DETROIT • WASHINGTON, D.C. • LONDON

STAFF

Jelena Krstović, *Editor*

Alan Heblad, Michael Magoulias, Zoran Minderović, Anna J. Sheets, Brian St. Germain, Joseph C. Tardiff, *Associate Editors*

Sean McCready, *Assistant Editor*

Jeanne A. Gough, *Permissions & Production Manager*
Linda M. Pugliese, *Production Supervisor*
Donna Craft, Paul Lewon, Maureen Puhl, Camille P. Robinson, Sheila Walencewicz, *Editorial Associates*
Jill Johnson, *Editorial Assistant*

Sandra C. Davis, *Permissions Supervisor (Text)*
Maria L. Franklin, Josephine M. Keene, Michele M. Lonoconus, Shalice Shah, Kimberly F. Smilay, *Permissions Associates*
Jennifer A. Arnold, Brandy C. Merritt, *Permissions Assistants*

Margaret A. Chamberlain, *Permissions Supervisor (Pictures)*
Pamela A. Hayes, Arlene Johnson, Keith Reed, *Permissions Associates*
Susan Brohman, Barbara A. Wallace, *Permissions Assistants*

Victoria B. Cariappa, *Research Manager*
Maureen Richards, *Research Supervisor*
Robert S. Lazich, Mary Beth McElmeel, Donna Melnychenko, Tamara C. Nott, Jaema Paradowski, *Editorial Associates*
Maria Bryson, Julie Leonard, Stefanie Scarlett, *Editorial Assistants*

Mary Beth Trimper, *Production Director*
Catherine Kemp, *Production Assistant*

Cynthia Baldwin, *Art Director*
Barbara J. Yarrow, *Graphic Services Supervisor*
C. J. Jonik, *Desktop Publisher*
Willie Mathis, *Camera Operator*

Library of Congress Catalog Card Number 88-658021
ISBN 0-8103-2433-4
ISSN 0896-0011

Printed in the United States of America
Published simultaneously in the United Kingdom
by Gale Research International Limited
(An affiliated company of Gale Research Inc.)
10 9 8 7 6 5 4 3 2 1

I(T)P

The trademark **ITP** is used under license.

Contents

Preface

Since its inception in 1988, *Classical and Medieval Literature Criticism* has been a valuable resource for students and librarians seeking critical commentary on the writers and works of these periods in world history. Major reviewing sources have assessed *CMLC* as "useful" and "extremely convenient," noting that it "adds to our understanding of the rich legacy left by the ancient period and the Middle Ages," and praising its "general excellence in the presentation of an inherently interesting subject." No other single reference source has surveyed the critical reaction to classical and medieval literature as thoroughly as *CMLC*.

Scope of the Series

CMLC is designed to serve as an introduction for students and advanced readers of the works and authors of antiquity through the fourteenth century. The great poets, prose writers, dramatists, and philosophers of this period form the basis of most humanities curricula, so that virtually every student will encounter many of these works during the course of a high school and college education. By organizing and reprinting an enormous amount of commentary written on classical and medieval authors and works, *CMLC* helps students develop valuable insight into literary history, promotes a better understanding of the texts, and sparks ideas for papers and assignments. Each entry in *CMLC* presents a comprehensive survey of an author's career, an individual work of literature, or a literary topic, and provides the user with a multiplicity of interpretations and assessments. Such variety allows students to pursue their own interests; furthermore, it fosters an awareness that literature is dynamic and responsive to many different opinions.

CMLC continues the survey of criticism of world literature begun by Gale's *Contemporary Literary Criticism (CLC), Twentieth-Century Literary Criticism (TCLC), Nineteenth-Century Literature Criticism (NCLC), Literature Criticism from 1400 to 1800 (LC),* and *Shakespearean Criticism (SC)*. For additional information about these and Gale's other criticism series, users should consult the Guide to Gale Literary Criticism Series preceding the title page in this volume.

Coverage

Each volume of *CMLC* is carefully compiled to present:

- criticism of authors and works who represent a variety of genres, time periods, and nationalities
- both major and lesser-known writers and works of the period (such as non-Western authors and literature increasingly read by today's students)
- 4-6 authors or works per volume
- individual entries that survey the critical response to each author or work, including early criticism, later criticism to represent any rise or decline in the author's reputation, and current retrospective analyses. The length of each author or work entry also indicates relative importance, reflecting the amount of critical attention the author or work has received from critics writing in English, and from foreign criticism in translation.

An author may appear more than once in the series if his or her writings have been the subject of a substantial amount of criticism; in these instances, specific works or groups of works by the author will be covered in separate entries. For example, Homer will be represented by three entries, one devoted to the *Iliad,* one to the *Odyssey,* and one to the Homeric Hymns.

Starting with Volume 10, *CMLC* will also occasionally include entries devoted to literary topics. For example, *CMLC*-10 focuses on Arthurian Legend and includes general criticism on that subject as well as individual entries on writers or works central to that topic—Chrétien de Troyes, Gottfried von Strassburg, Layamon, and the Alliterative *Morte Arthure.*

Organization of the Book

An author entry consists of the following elements: author heading, biographical and critical introduction, principal English translations or editions, excerpts of criticism (each preceded by an annotation and followed by a bibliographic citation), and a bibliography of further reading.

- The **Author Heading** consists of the author's most commonly used name, followed by birth and death dates. If the entry is devoted to a work, the heading will consist of the complete title, followed by the most common form of the title in English translation (if applicable), and the original date of composition. Located at the beginning of the introduction are any name or title variations.

- A **Portrait** of the author is included when available. Many entries also feature illustrations of materials pertinent to the author or work, including manuscript pages, book illustrations, and representations of people, places, and events important to a study of the author or work.

- The **Biographical and Critical Introduction** contains background information that introduces the reader to an author or work and to the critical debate surrounding that author or work.

- The list of **Principal English Translations** or **Editions** is chronological by date of first publication and is included as an aid to the student seeking translated versions or editions of these works for study. The list will focus primarily on twentieth-century translations, selecting those works most commonly considered the best by critics.

- **Criticism** is arranged chronologically in each entry to provide a useful perspective on changes in critical evaluation over the years. All titles by the author featured in the critical entry are printed in boldface type to enable the user to ascertain without difficulty the works being discussed. Also for purposes of easier identification, the critic's name and the publication date of the essay are given at the beginning of each piece of criticism. Anonymous criticism is preceded by the title of the journal in which it appeared. Publication information (such as publisher names and book prices) and parenthetical numerical references (such as footnotes or page and line references to specific editions of works) have been deleted at the editors' discretion to provide smoother reading of the text. Many critical entries in *CMLC* also contain translations to aid the users.

- Critical excerpts are prefaced by **Annotations** providing the reader with information about both the critic and the criticism, the scope of the excerpt, the growth of critical controversy, or changes in critical trends regarding an author or work. In some cases, these notes include cross-references to excerpts by critics who discuss each other's commentary. Dates in parentheses within the annotation refer to a book publication date when they follow a book title, and to an essay date when they follow a critic's name.

- A complete **Bibliographic Citation** designed to facilitate the location of the original essay or book follows each piece of criticism.

- An annotated bibliography of **Further Reading** appears at the end of each entry and lists additional secondary sources on the author or work. In some cases it includes essays for which the editors could not obtain reprint rights. When applicable, the Further Reading is followed by references to additional entries on the author in other literary reference series published by Gale.

Topic Entries are subdivided into several thematic rubrics in which criticism appears in order of descending scope.

Cumulative Indexes

Each volume to *CMLC* includes a cumulative index listing all authors who have appeared in *Contemporary Literary Criticism, Twentieth-Century Literary Criticism, Nineteenth-Century Literature Criticism, Literature Criticism from 1400 to 1800, Classical and Medieval Literature Criticism,* and *Short Story Criticism,* along with cross-references to the Gale series *Children's Literature Review, Authors in the News, Contemporary Authors, Contemporary Authors Autobiography Series, Dictionary of Literary Biography, Concise Dictionary of American Literary, Something about the Author, Something about the Author Autobiography Series,* and *Yesterday's Authors of Books for Children.* Useful for locating an author within the various series, this index is particularly valuable for those authors who are identified with a certain period but who, because of their death date, are placed in another, or for those authors whose careers span two periods, For example, Geoffrey Chaucer, who is usually considered a medieval author, is found in *Literature Criticism from 1400 to 1800* because he died after 1399.

Beginning with the tenth volume, *CMLC* includes a cumulative index listing all topic entries that have appeared in the Gale Literary Criticism Series *Classical and Medieval Literature Criticism, Contemporary Literary Criticism, Literature Criticism from 1400 to 1800, Nineteenth-Century Literature Criticism,* and *Twentieth-Century Literary Criticism.*

Beginning with the second volume, *CMLC* also includes a cumulative nationality index. Authors and/or works are grouped by nationality, and the volume in which criticism on them may be found is indicated.

Title Index

Each volume of *CMLC* also includes an index listing the titles of all literary works discussed in the series. Foreign language titles that have been translated are followed by the titles of the translations—for example, *Slovo o polku Igorove (The Song of Igor's Campaign).* Page numbers following these translated titles refer to all pages on which any form of the title, either foreign language or translated, appears. Titles of novels, dramas, nonfiction books, and poetry, short story, or essay collections are printed in italics, while those of all individual poems, short stories, and essays are printed in roman type within quotation marks. In cases where the same title is used by different authors, the author's name or surname is given in parentheses after the title, e.g. *Collected Poems* (Horace) and *Collected Poems* (Sappho).

Critic Index

An index to critics, which cumulates with the second volume, is another useful feature of *CMLC.* Under each critic's name are listed the authors and/or works on whom the critic has written and the volume and page number where criticism may be found.

A Note to the Reader

When writing papers, students who quote directly from any volume in the Literary Criticism Series may use the following general forms to footnote reprinted criticism. The first example pertains to material drawn from a periodical, the second to material reprinted from books.

Rollo May, "The Therapist and the Journey into Hell," *Michigan Quarterly Review,* XXV, No. 4 (Fall 1986), 629-41; excerpted and reprinted in *Classical and Medieval Literature Criticism,* Vol. 3, ed. Jelena O. Krstović (Detroit: Gale Research, 1989), pp. 154-58.

Dana Ferrin Sutton, *Self and Society in Aristophanes* (University of Press of America, 1980); excerpted and reprinted in *Classical and Medieval Literature Criticism,* Vol. 4, ed. Jelena O. Krstović (Detroit: Gale Research, 1990), pp. 162-69.

Suggestions Are Welcome

Readers who wish to suggest authors to appear in future volumes, or who have other comments regarding the series, are cordially invited to write or call the editors.

Acknowledgments

The editors wish to thank the copyright holders of the excerpted criticism included in this volume, the permissions managers of many book and magazine publishing companies for assisting us in securing reprint rights, and Anthony Bogucki for assistance with copyright research. We are also grateful to the staffs of the Detroit Public Library, the Library of Congress, the University of Detroit Library, Wayne State University Purdy/Kresge Library Complex, and the University of Michigan Libraries for making their resources available to us. Following is a list of the copyright holders who have granted us permission to reprint material in this volume of *CMLC.* Every effort has been made to trace copyright, but if omissions have been made, please let us know.

COPYRIGHTED EXCERPTS IN *CMLC,* VOLUME 12, WERE REPRINTED FROM THE FOLLOWING PERIODICALS:

Critical Inquiry, v. 13, Spring, 1987 for "The Scrutiny of Song: Pindar, Politics, and Poetry" by Anne Burnett. Copyright © 1987 by The University of Chicago. Reprinted by permission of the publisher and the author.—***The Germanic Review,*** v. XLII, May, 1967. Copyright 1967 by Helen Dwight Reid Educational Foundation. Reprinted by permission of the publisher.—***MLN,*** v. 97, April, 1982. © copyright 1982 by The Johns Hopkins University Press. All rights reserved. Reprinted by permission of the publisher.—***Proceedings of the British Academy,*** v. LXVIII, 1982. © The British Academy 1983. Reprinted by permission of the publisher.

COPYRIGHTED EXCERPTS IN *CMLC,* VOLUME 12, WERE REPRINTED FROM THE FOLLOWING BOOKS:

Barfield, Owen. From "Imagination and Inspiration," in ***Interpretation: The Poetry of Meaning.*** Edited by Stanley Romaine Hopper and David L. Miller. Harcourt Brace Jovanovich, 1967. Copyright © 1967 by Drew University. Reprinted by permission of Harcourt Brace Company.—Barnstone, Willis. From ***The Poetics of Ecstasy: Varieties of Ekstasis from Sappho to Borges.*** Holmes & Meier, 1983. Copyright © 1983 by Willis Barnstone. All rights reserved. Reprinted by permission of the publisher.—Bonner, Anthony. From ***Selected Works of Ramon Llull (1232-1316), Vol. II.*** Edited and translated by Anthony Bonner. Princeton University Press, 1985. Copyright © 1985 by Princeton University Press. All rights reserved. Reprinted by permission of the publisher.—Bowra, C. M. From ***Pindar.*** Oxford at the Clarendon Press, 1964. © Oxford University Press 1964, renewed 1992. Reprinted by permission of the publisher.—Carne-Ross, D. S. From ***Pindar.*** Yale University Press, 1985. Copyright © 1985 by Yale University. All rights reserved. Reprinted by permission of the publisher.—Eliade, Mircea. From ***A History of Religious Ideas: From Gautama Buddha to the Triumph of Christianity, Vol. 2.*** Translated by Williard R. Trask. University of Chicago Press, 1982. © 1982 by Mircea Eliade. All rights reserved. Reprinted by permission of The University of Chicago Press.—Finley, John H., Jr. From ***Pindar and Aeschylus: Martin Classical Lectures, Vol. XIV.*** Cambridge, Mass.: Harvard University Press, 1955. Copyright, 1955 by the Board of Trustees of Oberlin College. Renewed 1983 by John Houston Finley, Jr. Excerpted by permission of the publisher.—Fränkel, Hermann. From ***Early Greek Poetry and Philosophy: A History of Greek Epic, Lyric, and Prose to the Middle of the Fifth Century.*** Translated by Moses Hadas and James Willis. Basil Blackwell, 1975. Copyright © Basil Blackwell 1975. All rights reserved. Reprinted by permission of the publisher.—Hatto, A. T. From "An Introduction to a Second Reading," in ***The Nibelungenlied.*** Translated by A. T. Hatto. Penguin Books, 1965. Copyright © A. T. Hatto, 1964. Reproducted by permission of Penguin Books Ltd.—Haymes, Edward R. From ***The "Nibelungenlied": History and Interpretation.*** University of Illinois Press, 1986. © 1986 by the Board of Trustees of the University of Illinois. Reprinted by permission of the publisher and the author.—Highet, Gilbert. From ***The Classical Tradition: Greek and Roman Influences on Western Literature.*** Oxford University Press, 1949. Copyright 1949 by Oxford University Press, Inc. Renewed 1976 by Gilbert Highet. Reprinted by permission of

Oxford University Press. In the U.S. by Oxford University Press, Inc.—Hillgarth, J. N. From ***Ramon Lull and Lullism in Fourteenth-Century France.*** Oxford at the Clarendon Press, 1971. © Oxford University Press 1971. Reprinted by permission of the publisher.—Hutson, Arthur E., and Patricia McCoy. From ***Epics of the Western World.*** J. B. Lippincott Company, 1954. Copyright, 1954, by Arthur E. Hutson and Patricia McCoy. Renewed 1982 by Eleanor Hutson. Reprinted by permission of HarperCollins Publishers, Inc.—Huxley, Aldous. From an introduction to ***The Song of God: Bhagavad-Gita.*** Translated by Swami Prabhavananda and Christopher Isherwood. New American Library, 1954. Copyright 1944, 1951, by The Vedanta Society of Southern California. Renewed 1972. All rights reserved. Reprinted by permission of The Vedanta Society of Southern California.—Jump, John D. From ***The Ode.*** Methuen & Co. Ltd., 1974. © 1974 John D. Jump. Reprinted by permission of the publisher.—Leech, Kenneth. From an introduction to ***The Book of the Lover and the Beloved.*** By Ramon Lull, edited by Kenneth Leech and translated by E. Allison Peers. Revised edition. Sheldon Press 1978. Copyright © SPCK. All rights reserved. Reprinted by permission of the author.—Lesky, Albin. From ***A History of Greek Literature.*** Translated by James Willis and Cornelis de Heer. Methuen, 1966. Copyright © Methuen & Co. Ltd., 1966. All rights reserved. Reprinted by permission of the publisher.—Mascaró, Juan. From an introduction to ***The Bhagavad Gita.*** Translated by Juan Mascaró. Penguin Books, 1962. Copyright © Mascaró, 1962. Renewed 1990 by Kathlin M. Mascaró. Reproduced by permission of Penguin Books Ltd.—Miller, Barbara Stoler. From "The 'Bhagavad-Gita', Context and Text," in ***The Bhagavad-gita: Krishna's Counsel in Time of War.*** Translated by Barbara Stoler Miller. Bantam, 1991. English translation copyright © 1986 by Barbara Stoler Miller. All rights reserved. Reprinted by permission of Bantam, a division of Bantam Doubleday Dell Publishing Group, Inc.—Moorman, Charles. From ***Kings & Captains: Variations on a Heroic Theme.*** University Press of Kentucky, 1971. Copyright © 1971 by The University Press of Kentucky. Reprinted by permission of the publisher.—Mowatt, D. G., and Hugh Sacker. From ***The Nibelungenlied: An Interpretative Commentary.*** University of Toronto Press, 1967. © University of Toronto Press 1967. Reprinted by permission of the publisher.—Nisetich, Frank J. From an introduction to ***Pindar's Victory Songs.*** Translated by Frank J. Nisetich. Johns Hopkins University Press 1980. Copyright © 1980 by The Johns Hopkins University Press. All rights reserved. Reprinted by permission of the publisher.—Norwood, Gilbert. From ***Pindar.*** University of California Press, 1945. Copyright, 1945, 1973, by The Regents of the University of California. Reprinted by permission of the publisher.—Podlecki, Anthony J. From ***The Early Greek Poets and Their Times.*** Vancouver: UBC Press, 1984. © The University of British Columbia. All rights reserved. Reprinted by permission of the publisher.—Prabhavananda, Swami, and Christopher Isherwood. From a preface to ***The Song of God: Bhagavad-Gita.*** Translated by Swami Prabhavananda and Christopher Isherwood. New American Library, 1945. Copyright 1944, 1951 by The Vedanta Society of Southern California. Renewed 1972. All rights reserved. Reprinted by permisson of The Society of Southern California.—Rexroth, Kenneth. From "The 'Bhagavad-gita' " in ***More Classics Revisited.*** Edited by Bradford Morrow. New Directions, 1989. Reprinted by permission of New Directions Publishing Corporation.—Ryder, Frank G. From ***The Song of the Nibelungs: A Verse Translation from the Middle High German "Nibelungenlied."*** Wayne State University Press, 1962. Copyright © 1962 by Wayne State University Press. Renewed 1990 by Frank G. Ryder. All rights reserved. Reprinted by permission of the publisher and the author.—Sargeant, Winthrop. From "Cosmology and Psychology," in ***The Bhagavad Gita.*** Translated by Winthrop Sargeant. Doubleday & Company, Inc., 1979. Copyright © 1979 by Winthrop Sargeant. Copyright © 1984 State University of New York. All rights reserved. Reprinted by permission of State University of New York Press.—Segal, Charles. From ***Pindar's Mythmaking: The Fourth Pythian Ode.*** Princeton University Press, 1986. Copyright © 1986 by Princeton University Press. All rights reserved. Reprinted by permission of the publisher.—Steiner, Rudolf. From ***The Occult Significance of the Bhagavad Gita.*** Translated by George Adams and Mary Adams. Anthroposophic Press, 1968. Copyright © 1968 by Anthroposophic Press, Inc. Reprinted by permission of the publisher.—West, M. L. From "Other Early Poetry," in ***Ancient Greek Literature.*** By K. J. Dover and others, edited by K. J. Dover. Oxford University Press, Oxford, 1980. © K. J. Dover, E. L. Bowie, Jasper Griffin, M. L. West 1980. All rights reserved. Reprinted by permission of Oxford University Press.—Zimmer, Heinrich. From "The Philosophies of Eternity: Brahmanism," in ***Philosophies of India.*** Edited by Joseph Campbell. Princeton University Press, 1969. © 1969 by Princeton University Press. Reprinted with permission of the publisher.

PHOTOGRAPHS AND ILLUSTRATIONS APPEARING IN *CMLC*, VOLUME 12, WERE RECEIVED FROM THE FOLLOWING SOURCES:

Copyright Sharma Picture Publications: **pp. 14, 72;** Illustration by Shirley Triest: **p. 45;** Illustration by Alois Kolb: **p. 182;** Drawing by Josef Hegenbarth: **p. 204;** Alinari/Art Resource: **pp. 256, 327;** Mansell Collection, London: **p. 275;** The British Museum: **p. 318;** Louvre Museum, Paris: **p. 335;** Museo Nazionale, Naples: **p. 342;** Glyptothek, Munich: **p. 367;** American School of Classical Studies at Athens: Agora Excavations: **p. 377.**

Bhagavad Gītā

c. First Century B.C.–c. First Century A.D.

Indian poem.

INTRODUCTION

Regarded as one of the great religious documents of humankind, the *Bhagavad Gītā* (*Song of God*), a poem about a hero's encounter with the awesome majesty of God, is also known for its philosophical depth and outstanding literary value. In India the *Gītā* is revered as the fundamental book of Hinduism; in the West, the *Gītā* not only exemplifies Indian spirituality, but also, owing to a passionate, love-inspired theism spiritually akin to Christianity, represents an affirmation of spiritual truths transcending the boundaries of religion, language, and tradition.

Consisting of less than 700 verses divided into eighteen chapters, the *Gītā* is one of the books comprising the *Mahābhārata,* India's gigantic epic poem about the apocalyptic war between two branches (the Pāṇḍavas and the Kauravas) of the Hastinpura royal family. A minute episode in the *Mahābhārata,* the *Gītā* depicts a crucial moment: a hero's despair before the great battle. The semidivine Arjuna, son of the war-god Indra, is about to lead the Pāṇḍavas to victory and glory. But Arjuna hesitates, horrified by the prospect of killing human beings and overcome by sorrow as he sees kinsmen, friends, and teachers among the enemy ranks; in utter confusion—unwilling to fight, torn between duty and compassion—he turns to Kṛṣṇa, his friend and charioteer, for advice. But Arjuna's charioteer is not an ordinary mortal. Not only does Kṛṣṇa appear as the incarnation of the cosmic god Viṣṇu, but he eventually reveals himself as God, Creator of the Universe. Kṛṣṇa understands the warrior's predicament, but nevertheless proceeds to convince him that a just war must be executed in accordance with one's *dharma,* or sacred duty. Furthermore, Kṛṣṇa explains that, since physical death does not affect our true being, which is spiritual and eternal, Arjuna's anguish at killing his enemies springs from a delusion. Finally, Arjuna, convinced by Kṛṣṇa's reasoning and overwhelmed by the presence of God, follows the call of destiny and completes the warrior's holy mission.

Scholars have asserted that as a poetic compendium of Hindu theology and philosophy, the *Gītā* incorporates the principal tenets of Hinduism, creating a brilliant synthesis in which various, even seemingly incompatible, traditions are successfully reconciled. For example, from the *Upaniśads,* which along with the *Vedas* record the spiritual worldview of the Aryans who conquered India between 1500 and 500 B.C, the *Gītā* takes the idea of *atman,* or self, which anticipates the potential, but also necessary, union between the human, individual self and the Supreme Self, or God. Yet in contrast to the Vedic, eminently monistic,

Krsna and Arjuna.

world-view derived from the *Upaniśads,* the *Gītā* also embraces the dualistic, pre-Aryan Sāṅkhya philosophy which divides all reality into *puruṣa* (life monads) and *prakṛti* (lifeless matter). Yoga, the practical and theoretical path to enlightenment which figures prominently in the *Gītā,* also espouses a dualistic conception of the universe, in apparent discord with the poem's God-centered monism. However, the *Gītā,* as commentators have maintained, correctly employs yoga as a path to God. This path, as Kṛṣṇa tells Arjuna, is threefold: salvation comes through *karma* (action), *jñāna* (knowledge), and *bhakti* (devotion). Thus, as critics have observed, the *Gītā,* by affirming the apparently paradoxical fact that different roads to God are essentially identical, effectively reconciles disparate worldviews. Furthermore, by incorporating the Buddhist idea of *ahiṁsa* (non-violence), the poem reaches beyond Hinduism and boldly juxtaposes the peaceful ethos of Buddhism and the relentless, sometimes violent, activism of the Vedic perspective. The *Gītā*'s strongly theistic conception of the world has led some scholars to compare the poem's religiosity with Christianity. Despite its wealth of conflicting and even self-negating ideas, the *Gītā* offers, in a "master stroke," as Heinrich Zimmer declared, a unified and convincing spiritual synthesis of India's rich and intricate religious legacy.

As scholars have observed, the *Gītā*'s lofty style is in remarkable harmony with the poem's subject: the poetic images and diction are noble and exalted. Also characterized by paradoxes, conundrums, and daring verbal constructions, this style, particularly in the sections where poetry and philosophy blend, challenges the Western belief in the logical principle of non-contradiction. Since the *Gītā* is deemed a divinely inspired text, its underlying thought patterns are held to originate from supernatural spheres and should not be judged by mundane criteria. A telling example of divine thought is provided by Kṛṣṇa's closing lines in Chapter XV of the *Gītā:* "There are two kinds of personality in this world, the mortal and the immortal. The personality of all creatures is mortal. The personality of God is said to be immortal. It is the same for ever. But there is one other than these; the Impersonal Being who is called the supreme Atman. He is the unchanging Lord who pervades and supports the three worlds. And since, I, the Atman, transcend the mortal and even the immortal, I am known in this world and in the *Vedas* as the supreme Reality." The vehicle of God's enigmatic message, however, is human: Sanskrit, the highly inflected and hypnotically sonorous language of classical Indian literature. With its vast poetic resources, hallucinatory imagery, and dizzying verbal creativity, Sanskrit splendidly serves the intent of the *Gītā*'s author, as scholars and translators have noted. When the intellect is paralyzed by clashing concepts in the *Gītā,* the spirit is led to further insights by the power of the poem's highly suggestive similes. For instance, Kṛṣṇa promises to lift his worshippers from the "ocean of death." And knowledge, according to the *Gītā* is like a fire: "The blazing fire turns wood to ashes: / The fire of knowledge turns all karmas to ashes." Finally, the famous simile of the lotus adumbrates a feeling of absolute peace attained through knowledge and detachment from material concerns: "He puts away desire, / Offering the act to Brahman. / The lotus leaf rests unwetted on water: / He rests on action, untouched by action."

There is a bewildering assortment of manuscripts of the *Gītā* (as part of the *Mahābhārata*) including transcripts of different versions of the epic in the numerous languages of India. Scholars have not yet identified an original version, and authorship, traditionally ascribed to the mythological seer Vyasa, as well as the exact time of composition, are unknown. It is believed that the poem came into being around the first century B.C. or the first century A.D. The first Sanskrit edition of the *Mahābhārata* is the 1834-39 Calcutta Edition, and the first English translation of the entire epic is that of Kisari Mohan Ganguli, published in 1884-96. The first English translation of the *Gītā* alone, by Charles Wilkins, appeared as early as 1785—an indicator of the poem's exceptional appeal.

By the time the first notable Western interpretations of the *Gītā* appeared, around 1800, Indian thinkers had been pondering and writing commentaries on their sacred book for at least a millennium. For example, the great medieval philosopher Śaṅkara identified knowledge as the principal path to God in the *Gītā.* Rāmānuja, another important medieval thinker who did not share Śaṅkara's rationalism, gave devotion the highest status in the poem. In the West, the poem was received with immense enthusiasm by German linguists and philosophers of the Romantic period. Infatuated by the wisdom of the *Gītā,* these scholars proceeded to translate and interpret the work in an effort to grasp its hidden meaning. August Wilhelm von Schlegel, the first professor of Sanskrit at the University of Bonn, translated the *Gītā* into Latin in 1823 because he believed that that language was best suited to convey the abstract concepts in the *Gītā.* Wilhelm von Humboldt, sharing Schlegel's enthusiasm, hailed the *Gītā* as the greatest philosophical poem of Antiquity. There was also a dissenting voice: the philosopher Georg Wilhelm Hegel, whose view of Eastern thought was generally negative, rejected the poem's idea of total contemplation as intellectual surrender. But the nineteenth-century reception of the *Gītā,* which enthralled many of the period's eminent writers and thinkers, is best summed up by Henry David Thoreau, who in his *Walden* (1854) described the poem, his frequent companion, as "stupendous." In the twentieth century, as the work became more accessible to readers, the *Gita* assumed the status of a great classic of world literature. Thus T. S. Eliot, in a 1929 essay on Dante Alighieri, pronounced the *Gītā* "the next greatest philosophical poem to the *Divine Comedy.*" In India the poem has retained the exalted status of a sacred book. Such thinkers as Śrī Aurobindo have lauded its philosophical depth and such humanists as Mahatma Gandhi have found solace in the poem's wisdom.

More recent criticism, particularly by philosophers, has focused on various aspects of the *Gītā,* examining the poem's many ethical, psychological, and logical puzzles. Comprehensive views of the work are generally the domain of religious scholars. Thus, for example, Mircea Eliade has credited the *Gītā* with having "effected the resacralization of the cosmos, of universal life, and even of man's *historical existence.*" In Eliade's view, the God of the *Gītā,* just like the biblical God Yahve, never abandons humankind, announcing his presence in times of crisis. The *Gītā,* Eliade has contended, magnificently expresses the omnipresence of God, even in evil times. The "message of the *Bhagavad Gītā,*" Eliade concludes, "was addressed to all categories of [human beings] and encouraged all religious vocations. This was the privilege of devotion paid to a God who was at once personal and impersonal, creative and destructive, incarnate and transcendent."

PRINCIPAL ENGLISH TRANSLATIONS

The Bhăgvăt-gēētā; or, Dialogues of Krēēshnă and Ărjŏŏn in Eighteen Lectures (translated by Charles Wilkins) 1785

The Song Celestial; or, Bhagavad-Gîtâ (translated by Edwin Arnold) 1885

Bhagavad-Gita: The Book of Devotion Dialogue between Krishna, Lord of Devotion, & Arjuna, Prince of India (translated by William Q. Judge) 1891
Bhagavad Gita: The Songs of the Master (translated by Charles Johnston) 1908
Srimad-Bhagavad-gita; or, The Blessed Lord's Song (translated by Swami Paramananda) 1913
The Bhagavadgītā (translated by W. Douglas P. Hill) 1928
The Bhagavad Gītā (translated by Franklin Edgerton) 1944
Bhagavad-Gita: The Song of God (translated by Swami Prabhavananda and Christopher Isherwood) 1944
The Bhagavadgītā (translated by Sarvepalli Radhakrishnan) 1948
Bhagavad Gita (translated by Juan Mascaró) 1962
The Bhagavad Gītā (translated by Eliot Deutsch) 1968
The Bhagavad-Gītā (translated by R. C. Zaehner) 1969
The Bhagavad Gita (translated by Geoffrey Parrinder) 1974
The Bhagavad Gītā (translated by Winthrop Sargeant) 1984
The Bhagavad-Gītā (translated by Barbara S. Miller) 1986
The Bhagavad Gītā (translated by David White) 1989

CRITICISM

Rāmānuja (essay date c. 11th–12th century)

[Rāmānuja was one of the great figures of medieval Indian philosophy. A theist, he postulated that self and ultimate reality could not be identical, for if self and God are identical, devotion would be rendered meaningless. In the following excerpt from his commentary on the Gītā *written in the eleventh to twelfth century, he examines the poem's conception of God, explaining that, according to the* Gītā, *God exists in a supersensible realm and can be reached only through devotion.]*

GOD IS INACCESSIBLE TO NATURAL PERCEPTION.

Question. The words by which God has revealed to Arjuna that most profound mystery of the ātman [self] in order to show his favour to Arjuna when he was bewildered by the misconception that the ātman is the body, these words have dispelled his misconception. Arjuna has also heard that the origination and dissolution of all beings depend on God who is the Supreme Ātman, that God's eternal greatness consists in this that all spiritual and non-spiritual entities constitute a śeṣa [cosmic serpent] of God, that God is the supreme One because of his beautiful qualities, that God is the foundation of all and that God is the inner actuator of all beings. Now Arjuna desires to have direct presentation of God in his forms of sovereign, creator, maintainer and dissolver of all entities as well as in his form of absolute superiority. Therefore he beseeches God to reveal Himself completely to him in these forms, if that could be possible.

Answer. Quoth God, Behold my various forms which are the foundation of all, which are constituted by a plurality of modifications and which are supernatural, multicoloured and multiformed. Behold in this one form of Mine all things of which direct experience may be had as well as all things which can only be known from the śāstras [sacred books], as well as the many marvelous things which are never yet witnessed before either in the entire universe or in the entire śāstra. Behold the entire universe with its mobile and immobile beings concentrated in this one body of Mine and behold therein everything thou wishest to see. But thine eye cannot behold Me such as I am, different in kind from everything else and infinite: by thy natural eye thou canst perceive but things finite and subject to My dominion. Therefore I bestow on thee a supernatural eye by which thou mayest perceive Me. So do now behold My yoga which is association with beautiful qualities and endless supernal manifestations.

GOD'S MAJESTY.

Then, Saṃjaya relates, God showed Arjuna his supremely majestic form which is the foundation of the entire universe manifold and multiform, and which governs everything. That form or body was splendid and unlimited by space and time, facing all directions and adorned with behoving garments, perfumes, garlands, ornaments and weapons. In that body of the God of gods, infinite in all dimensions, with numberless trunks, mouths and eyes, of unimaginable splendour, equipped with innumerable weapons etc., Arjuna—who by divine Grace had been granted supernatural vision—beheld the entire universe with all its various subdivisions, crowded by the various kinds of classes of experiencing beings—gods, men, animals, immovables etc. of all sorts and forms—and by places, objects and means of experiences—such as earth, ether, heaven, pātāla, atala, sutala etc.—and consisting of puruṣa [self] and prakṛti [matter]; this entire universe was concentrated in one single point of God's body. Arjuna was struck with amazement at perceiving the entire universe in one single point of God's body and, while beholding God himself who is the foundation of the entire universe, the actuator of all and the possessor of marvelous beautiful qualities, he was so transported that his hairs bristled. He prostrated himself before God and exclaimed with folded hands,

God, I behold in Thy body all gods and all classes of living beings among whom Brahmā himself and He who liveth in Brahmā's mind, and all ṛṣis [sages] and the splendid snakes. I behold Thee everywhere with Thy numberless members and endless forms. Thy body is formed by all beings and it shows neither end nor beginning nor middle, for Thou art unending. Thou art a mass of tejas [spiritual energy] which is of immeasurable splendour. Thou art the supreme Akṣara [Being], the chief foundation of all. In Thine avatāras, one of which is this present incarnation, Thou art the protector of the everlasting Vedic dharma. I know Thee to be the eternal Personality. Thou art without beginning, middle and end, and Thou art a treasury of boundless knowledge, power, force, dominion and tejas.

Innumerable are Thine arms, feet, bellies etc. All Thine eyes are serene like the moon and glaring like the sun. Thou dost govern the universe by Thy tejas. Thou dost pervade all worlds, high and low, and the space in which they are situated. When beholding Thy marvelous awe-inspiring form the three worlds are appalled, mahātman! Yonder hosts of divinities approach Thee, at beholding Thee who art the foundation of all. Some of them are awed and praise Thee according to their knowledge. Others, maharsis and siddhas, glorify Thee as the venerable Lord with beseeming hymns. Rudras, ādityas etc. and pitaras do now behold Thee and they are stricken with amazement.

ARJUNA'S TERROR.

Now while beholding Thine exceedingly terrifying form all three worlds and I myself are panic-stricken. While I behold Thee touching the Supreme Heaven, glaring, multicoloured, with yawning mouth and wide fiery eyes, my heart is terrified and I am unable to find support for my body or rest for my mind and senses, O Pervader! Looking at Thy horrid faces which are operant in destroying everything like the Fire of Time at the end of the yuga, I am led astray and find no happiness. Overlord of all lords, of Brahmā himself and all others, do show me Thy favour and restore my old self!

All the sons of Dhṛtarāṣṭra and the sūta's son Karṇa, are, together with their partisans and even some chief warriors of our army, entering Thy terrifying mouth to be destroyed: they hasten to their end of their own accord. Thou hast revealed this appalling form to me when I besought thee to show Thine eternal ātman so that I could cognize Thine unlimited dominion. But who art Thou who hast such a horrible form? To what end does it serve Thee? Be gracious to me and tell me the reason why Thou hast revealed this form of destroyer and tell me what actions Thou proposest to perform in this form.

THE MEANING OF GOD'S TERRIBLE ASPECT.

Quoth God, While calculating the end of the lives of all beings, among whom Dhṛtarāṣṭra's warriors are the first, I appear in this horrible shape which causes their destruction, in order to annihilate these beings. Therefore, even if thou, O Arjuna, refusest the help of thine energy, the hostile warriors will of a certainty be destroyed; so rise to fight them and do by defeating them obtain the fame of victory and enjoy righteous kingship. I am the One who doom those who have sinned: thou art but the instrument by which I have chosen to kill them. Slay Droṇa, Bhīma, Karṇa etc. whom I have doomed because of their sins, and do not suffer thine anxiety about dharma and adharma and thy love and compassion for thy relatives to worry thee. I have doomed them because they are sinners; do therefore not hesitate and fight them, for thou shalt defeat thy rivals. No cruelty is to be found at all in this battle: on the contrary, thou shalt win the victory.

ARJUNA'S EXALTATION.

Then, Saṃjaya proceeds, Arjuna was over-awed and prostrating himself before God he exclaimed,

Justly does this universe of gods, gandharvas and the like which has foregathered to see the battle and has by Thy divine Grace beheld Thee now, delight in Thee, love Thee and glorify Thee; and justly do the rākṣasas run away in terror, and justly do all siddhas pay homage to Thee! Why indeed should Hiraṇyagarbha and all others not pay homage to Thee who art superior to them and art the creator even of Brahmā Hiraṇyagarbha? Thou art the jīvātman [immortal soul], Thou art the prakṛti, whether existing as cause or as effect, and Thou art the released ātman. Therefore Thou art the primeval God, the Person, the ancient One. Thou art the supreme foundation, for Thou art the ātman of all and sundry beings which constitute Thy body. Thou art all knowledge and all that can be known; so Thou art the highest end. Thou dost pervade the entire universe consisting of cit [the spiritual] and acit [the non-spiritual]. Thou art to be called by the names of everyone and everything because Thou art their ātman. Thy valour is boundless!

Question. Being ignorant of Thy qualities and urged upon by perplexity and life-long familiarity, I have always considered Thee my equal and friend. So I came to address Thee simply as Kṛṣṇa, or Yadu's son, or friend, and in jest I have not shown Thee the reverence that is due to Thee. For all this I beseech Thy forgiveness. Thou art father and guru of this world, and therefore Thou art most venerable. No one in the entire universe equals Thee, how then could one surpass Thee? Thus, most venerable Lord, I prostrate myself before Thee and implore Thy mercy. Just as a father or a friend, when fittingly entreated, will show mercy to his son or his friend if he have been at fault, so, most compassionate Lord, abide me in all things, like a lover abides his beloved. Having seen Thy most marvelous and awe-inspiring form, I am transported by love and my mind is panic-stricken. So reveal to me Thy first, most gracious form, Lord of the gods!

Answer. Quoth God, Herewith I have revealed to thee My majestic form, which no one before thee has ever beheld, because thou art my devotee. I could do so because it is in My nature that all that I will comes true. In this form, in which I exist just as I am, I am visible but to one who has perfect and complete bhakti [devotion] toward Me, not to one who merely follows the Veda, performs sacrifices etc. Thy terror and bewilderment caused by My terrifying form which thou hast seen may cease now, for I show thee the benign shape to which thou wert accustomed before: look at it!

Then, Saṃjaya proceeded, God showed Arjuna his familiar fourarmed body and reassured him; and Arjuna said,

Now I have come to my senses again, now I behold once more this lovable beautiful body of Thine, peculiar to none but Thee which has the generic structure of a common human being and is most benevolent.

PRESENTATION OF GOD'S PROPER FORM IS ONLY POSSIBLE BY BHAKTI.

God states that the form which Arjuna has witnessed a moment before cannot be seen by anyone, not even by gods: for it is not through *Vedas,* sacrifices, charity etc. that God can be seen, for all those are destitute of bhakti. It is only through bhakti that God may be either known by the śāstras, or experienced directly, or approached as He really is. Only when a man performs all acts—studying *Vedas,* performing sacrifices etc.—, when all his enterprises serve one purpose: the supreme end: God, when he is God's devotee because he loves God so much that he cannot sustain his ātman unless he glorifies God and therefore performs all acts to one end: God, when he is attached to God alone, when he fosters no hatred for any being because he has no reason to do so since to him all happiness and unhappiness naturally coincide with union with and separation from God and since he realizes that all beings depend on the Supreme Person,—only then he will attain God as He really is, that is, all his defects—ignorance etc.—will vanish and he will cognize God alone. (pp. 126-32)

Rāmānuja, in J. A. B. Van Buitenen, Rāmānuja on the Bhagavadgītā: A Condensed Rendering of His Gītābhāsya, *1953. Reprint by Motilal Banarsidass, 1968, 187 p.*

Swami Vivekananda (lecture date 1900)

[*Vivekananda was a respected Indian thinker and religious leader who lectured widely on Hinduism in India and abroad. In the following excerpt from a lecture delivered in 1900, he comments on the* Gītā's *spiritual message, remarking that the poem exhorts the reader to relinquish any allegiance to the material world and embrace a purely spiritual life.*]

The ***Gita*** requires a little preliminary introduction. The scene is laid on the battle-field of Kurukshetra. There were two branches of the same race fighting for the empire of India about five thousand years ago. The Pandavas had the right, but the Kauravas had the might. The Pandavas were five brothers, and they were living in a forest. Krishna was the friend of the Pandavas. The Kauravas would not grant them as much land as would cover the point of a needle.

The opening scene is the battle-field, and both sides see their relatives and friends—one brother on one side and another on the other side; a grandfather on one side, a grandson on the other side. . . . When Arjuna sees his own friends and relatives on the other side and knows that he may have to kill them, his heart gives way and he says that he will not fight. Thus begins the ***Gita.***

For all of us in this world, life is a continuous fight. . . . Many a time comes comes when we want to interpret our weakness and cowardice as forgiveness and renunciation. There is no merit in the renunciation of a beggar. If a person, who can [give a blow], forbears, there is merit in that. If a person, who has, gives up, there is merit in that. We know how often in our lives thorugh laziness and cowardice we give up the battle and try to hypnotise our minds into the belief that we are brave.

The ***Gita*** opens with this very significant verse: "Arise, O prince! Give up this faintheartedness, this weakness! Stand up and fight!" Then Arjuna, trying to argue the matter [with Krishna], brings higher moral ideas, how non-resistance is better than resistance, and so on. He is trying to justify himself, but he cannot fool Krishna. Krishna is the higher Self, or God. He sees through the argument at once. In this case [the motive] is weakness. Arjuna sees his own relatives and he cannot strike them. . . .

There is a conflict in Arjuna's heart between his emotionalism and his duty. The nearer we are to [beasts and] birds, the more we are in the hells of emotion. We call it love. It is self-hypnotisation. We are under the control of our [emotions] like animals. A cow can sacrifice its life for its young. Every animal can. What of that? It is not the blind, birdlike emotion that leads to perfection. . . . [To reach] the eternal consciousness, that is the goal of man! There emotion has no place, nor sentimentalism, nor anything that belongs to the senses—only the light of pure reason. [There] man stands as spirit.

Now, Arjuna is under the control of this emotionalism. He is not what he should be—a great self-controlled, enlightened sage working through the eternal light of reason. He has become like an animal, like a baby, just letting his heart carry away his brain, making a fool of himself and trying to cover his weakness with the flowery names of "love" and so on. Krishna sees through that. Arjuna talks like a man of a little learning and brings out many reasons, but at the same time he talks the language of a fool.

The sage is not sorry for those that are living, nor for those that die. [Krishna says:] "You cannot die nor can I. There was never a time when we did not exist. There will never be a time when we shall not exist. As in this life a man begins with childhood, and [passes through youth and old age, so at death he merely passes into another kind of body]. Why should a wise man be sorry?" And where is the beginning of this emotionalism that has got hold of you? It is in the senses. "It is the touch of the senses that brings all this quality of existence: heat and cold, pleasure and pain. They come and go." Man is miserable this moment, happy the next. As such he cannot experience the nature of the soul. . . .

"Existence can never be non-existence, neither can non-existence ever become existence. . . . Know, therefore, that that which pervades all this universe is without beginning or end. It is unchangeable. There is nothing in the universe that can change [the Changeless]. Though this body has its beginning and end, the dweller in the body is infinite and without end."

Knowing this, stand up and fight! Not one step back, that is the idea. . . . Fight it out, whatever comes. Let the stars move from the spheres! Let the whole world stand against us! Death means only a change of garment. What of it? Thus fight! You gain nothing by becoming cowards. . . . Taking a step backward, you do not avoid any misfortune. You have cried to all the gods in the world. Has misery ceased? The masses in India cry to sixty million gods, and still die like dogs. Where are these gods? . . . The gods come to help you when you have succeeded. So what is the use? Die game. . . . This bending the knee to superstitions, this selling yourself to your own mind does not befit you, my soul. You are infinite, deathless, birthless. Because you are infinite spirit, it does not befit you to be a slave. . . . Arise! Awake! Stand up and fight! Die if you must. There is none to help you. You are all the world. Who can help you?

"Beings are unknown to our human senses before birth and after death. It is only in the interim that they are manifest. What is there to grieve about?

"Some look at It [the Self] with wonder. Some talk of It as wonderful. Others hear of It as wonderful. Others, hearing of It, do not understand."

But if you say that killing all these people is sinful, then consider this from the standpoint of your own caste-duty. . . . "Making pleasure and misery the same, making success and defeat the same, do thou stand up and fight!"

This is the beginning of another peculiar doctrine of the ***Gita***— the doctrine of non-attachment. That is to say, we have to bear the result of our own actions because we attached our selves to them. . . . "Only what is done as duty for duty's sake . . . can scatter the bondage of Karma." There is no danger that you can overdo it. . . . "If you do even a little of it, [this Yoga will save you from the terrible round of birth and death]."

> Know, Arjuna, the mind that succeeds is the mind that is concentrated. The minds that are taken up with two thousand subjects [have] their energies dispersed. Some can talk flowery language and think there is nothing beyond the *Vedas.* They want to go to heaven. They want good things through the power of the *Vedas,* and so they make sacrifices.

Such will never attain any success [in spiritual life] unless they give up all these materialistic ideas.

That is another great lesson. Spirituality can never be attained unless all material ideas are given up. . . . What is in the senses? The senses are all delusion. People wish to retain them [in heaven] even after they are dead—a pair of eyes, a nose. Some imagine they will have more organs than they have now. They want to see God sitting on a throne through all eternity—the material body of God. . . . Such men's desires are for the body, for food and drink and enjoyment. It is the materialistic life prolonged. Men cannot think of anything beyond this life. This life is all for the body. "Such a man never comes to that concentration which leads to freedom."

"The *Vedas* only teach things belonging to the three Gunas, to Sattva, Rajas, and Tamas." The *Vedas* only teach about things in nature. People cannot think anything they do not see on earth. If they talk about heaven, they think of a king sitting on a throne, of people burning incense. It is all nature, nothing beyond nature. The *Vedas,* therefore, teach nothing but nature. "Go beyond nature, beyond the dualities of existence, beyond your own consciousness, caring for nothing, neither for good nor for evil."

We have identified ourselves with our bodies. We are only body, or rather, possessed of a body. If I am pinched, I cry. All this is nonsense, since I am the soul. All this chain of misery, imagination, animals, gods, and demons, everything, the whole world—all this comes from the identification of ourselves with the body. I am spirit. Why do I jump if you pinch me? . . . Look at the slavery of it. Are you not ashamed? We are religious! We are philosophers! We are sages! Lord bless us! What are we? Living hells, that is what we are. Lunatics, that is what we are!

We cannot give up the idea [of body]. We are earth-bound. . . . Our ideas are burial grounds. When we leave the body we are bound by thousands of elements to those [ideas].

Who can work without any attachment? That is the real question. Such a man is the same whether his work succeeds or fails. His heart does not give one false beat even if his whole life-work is burnt to ashes in a moment. "This is the sage who always works for work's sake without caring for the results. Thus he goes beyond the pain of birth and death. Thus he becomes free." Then he sees that this attachment is all delusion. The Self can never be attached. . . . Then he goes beyond all the scriptures and philosophies. If the mind is deluded and pulled into a whirlpool by books and scriptures, what is the good of all these scriptures? One says this, another says that. What book shall you take? Stand alone! See the glory of your own soul, and see that you will have to work. Then you will become a man of firm will.

Arjuna asks: "Who is a person of established will?"

[Krishna answers:] "The man who has given up all desires, who desires nothing, not even this life, nor freedom, nor gods, nor work, nor anything. When he has become perfectly satisfied, he has no more cravings." He has seen the glory of the Self and has found that the world, and the gods, and heaven are . . . within his own Self. Then the gods become no gods; death becomes no death; life becomes no life. Everything has changed. "A man is said to be [illumined] if his will has become firm, if his mind is not disturbed by misery, if he does not desire any happiness, if he is free of all [attachment], of all fear, of all anger. . . ."

"As the tortoise can draw in his legs, and if you strike him, not one foot comes out, even so the sage can draw all his sense-organs inside," and nothing can force them out. Nothing can shake him, no temptation or anything. Let the universe tumble about him, it does not make one single ripple in his mind.

Then comes a very important question. Sometimes people fast for days. . . . When the worst man has fasted for twenty days, he becomes quite gentle. Fasting and torturing themselves have been practised by people all over the world. Krishna's idea is that this is all nonsense. He says that the senses will for the moment recede from the man who tortures himself, but will emerge again with twenty times more [power]. . . . What should you do? The idea is to be natural—no asceticism. Go on, work, only mind that you are not attached. The will can never be fixed strongly in the man who has not learnt and practised the secret of non-attachment.

I go out and open my eyes. If something is there, I must see it. I cannot help it. The mind runs after the senses. Now the senses must give up any reaction to nature.

"Where it is dark night for the [sense-bound] world, the self-controlled [man] is awake. It is daylight for him. . . . And where the world is awake, the sage sleeps." Where is the world awake? In the senses. People want to eat and drink and have children, and then they die a dog's death. . . . They are always awake for the senses. Even their religion is just for that. They invent a God to help them, to give them more women, more money, more children—never a God to help them become more godlike! "Where the whole world is awake, the sage sleeps. But where the ignorant are asleep, there the sage keeps awake"—in the world of light where man looks upon himself not as a bird, not as an animal, not as a body, but as infinite spirit, deathless, immortal. There, where the ignorant are asleep, and do not have time, nor intellect, nor power to understand, there the sage is awake. That is daylight for him.

"As all the rivers of the world constantly pour their waters into the ocean, but the ocean's grand, majestic nature remains undisturbed and unchanged, so even though all the senses bring in sensations from nature, the ocean-like heart of the sage knows no disturbance, knows no fear." Let miseries come in millions of rivers and happiness in hundreds! I am no slave to misery! I am no slave to happiness! (pp. 48-58)

Swami Vivekananda, in his Thoughts on the Gita, *fifth edition, Advaita Ashrama, 1963, 84 p.*

Rudolf Steiner (lecture date 1913)

[*Known as the founder of Waldorf Education, Steiner was a noted Austrian philosopher, literary scholar, educator, social reformer, and critic. His numerous writings, which deal with a wide variety of subjects, elucidate the principles of Steiner's anthroposophy, or spiritual science. In the following excerpt from a lecture delivered in 1913, he extols the* Gītā *as a work which enchants the reader by its great poetic beauty while proclaiming the eternity of the spirit.*]

We are going to speak of one of the greatest and most penetrating manifestations of the human spirit—the ***Bhagavad Gita,*** which, ancient as it is, yet in its foundations comes before us with renewed significance at the present time. A short time ago the peoples of Europe, and those of the West generally, knew little of the ***Bhagavad Gita.*** Only during the last century has the fame of this wonderful poem extended to the West. Only lately have Western peoples become familiar with this marvellous song. But . . . a real and deep knowledge of this poem, as against mere familiarity with it, can only come when its occult foundations are more and more revealed from an age. . . . The mighty sentiments, feelings and ideas it contains had their origin in an age that was still illumined by what was communicated through the old human clairvoyance. One who tries to feel what this poem breathes forth page by page as it speaks to us, will experience, page by page, something like a breath of the ancient clairvoyance humanity possessed.

The Western world's first acquaintance with this poem came in an age in which there was little understanding for the original clairvoyant sources from which it sprang. Nevertheless, this lofty song of the Divine struck like a wonderful flash of lightning into the Western world, so that a man of Central Europe, when he first became acquainted with this Eastern song, said that he must frankly consider himself happy to have lived in a time when he could become acquainted with the wondrous things expressed in it. This man was not one who was unacquainted with the spiritual life of humanity through the centuries, indeed through thousands of years. He was one who looked deeply into spiritual life—Wilhelm von Humboldt, the brother of the celebrated astronomer. Other members of Western civilization, men of widely different tongues, have felt the same. What a wonderful feeling it produces in us when we let this ***Bhagavad Gita*** work upon us, even in its opening verses! (pp. 2-3)

A poem is here before us that from the very first sets us in the midst of a wild and stormy battle. We are introduced to a scene of action that is hardly less wild than that into which Homer straightway places us in the *Iliad.* We go further and are confronted in this scene with something which Arjuna—one of the foremost, perhaps the foremost of the personalities in the ***Song***—feels from the start to be a fratricidal conflict. He comes before us as one who is horror-stricken by the battle, for he sees there among the enemy his own blood relations. His bow falls from his grasp when it becomes clear to him that he is to enter a murderous strife with men who are descended from the same ancestors as himself, men in whose veins flows the same blood as his own. We almost begin to sympathize with him when he drops his bow and recoils before the awful battle between brothers.

Then before our gaze arises Krishna, the great spiritual teacher of Arjuna, and a wonderful, sublime teaching is brought before us in vivid colors in such a way that it appears as a teaching given to his pupil. But to what is all this leading? That is the question we must first of all set before us, because it is not enough just to give ourselves up to the holy teaching in the words of Krishna to Arjuna. The circumstances of its giving must also be studied. We must visualize the situation in which Krishna exhorts Arjuna not to quail before this battle with his brothers but take up his bow and hurl himself with all his might into the devastating conflict. Krishna's teachings emerge amid the battle like a cloud of spiritual light that at first is incomprehensible, and they require Arjuna not to recoil but to stand firm and do his duty in it. When we bring this picture before our eyes it is almost as though the teaching becomes transformed by its setting. Then again this setting leads us further into the whole weaving of the *Song of the Mahabharata,* the mighty song of which the ***Bhagavad Gita*** is only a part.

The teaching of Krishna leads us out into the storms of everyday life, into the wild confusion of human battles, errors and earthly strife. His teaching appears almost like a justification of these human conflicts. If we bring this picture before us quite dispassionately, perhaps the ***Bhagavad Gita*** will suggest to us altogether different questions from those that arise when—imagining we can understand them—we alight upon something similar to what we are accustomed to find in ordinary works of literature. So it is perhaps necessary to point first to this *setting* of the ***Gita*** in order to realize its world-historic significance, and then be able to see how it can be of increasing and special significance in our own time.

I have already said that this majestic song came into the Western world as something completely new, and almost equally new were the feelings, perceptions and thoughts that lie behind it. For what did Western civilization really know of Eastern culture before it became acquainted with the ***Bhagavad Gita***? Apart from various things that have only become known in this last century, very little indeed! If we except certain movements that remained secret, Western civilization has had no direct knowledge of what is actually the central nerve impulse of the whole of this great poem. When we approach such a thing we feel how little human language, philosophy, ideas, serving for everyday life, are sufficient for it; how little they suffice for describing such heights of the spiritual life of man upon earth. We need something quite different from ordinary descriptions to give expression to what shines out to us from such a revelation of the spirit of man.

I should like first to place two pictures before you so you may have a foundation for further descriptions. The one is taken from the book itself, the other from the spiritual life of the West. This can be comparatively easily understood, whereas the one from the book appears for the moment quite remote. Beginning then with the latter, we are told how, in the midst of the battle, Krishna appears and unveils before Arjuna cosmic secrets, great immense teachings. Then his pupil is overcome by the strong desire to see the form, the spiritual form of this soul, to have knowledge of him who is speaking such sublime things. He begs Krishna to show himself to him in such manner as he can in his true spirit form. Then Krishna appears to him (later we shall return to this description) in his form—a form that embraces all things, a great, sublime, glorious beauty, a nobility that reveals cosmic mysteries. We shall see there is little in the world to approach the glory of this description of how the sublime spirit form of the teacher is revealed to the clairvoyant eye of his pupil.

Before Arjuna's gaze lies the wild battlefield where much blood will have to flow and where the fratricidal struggle is to develop. The soul of Krishna's disciple is to be wafted away from this battlefield of devastation. It is to perceive and plunge into a world where Krishna lives in his true form. That is a world of holiest blessedness, withdrawn from all strife and conflict, a world where the secrets of existence are unveiled, far removed from everyday affairs. Yet to that world man's soul belongs in its most inward, most essential being. The soul is now to have knowledge of it. Then it will have the possibility of descending again and re-entering the confused and devastating battles of this our world. In truth, as we follow the description of this picture we may ask ourselves what is really taking place in Arjuna's soul? It is as though the raging battle in which it stands were forced upon it because this soul feels itself related to a heavenly world in which there is no human suffering, no battle, no death. It longs to rise into a world of the eternal, but with the inevitable force that can come only from the impulse of so sublime a being as Krishna, this soul must be forced downward into the chaotic confusion of the battle. Arjuna would gladly turn away from all this chaos, for the life of earth around him appears as something strange and far away, altogether unrelated to his soul. We can distinctly feel this soul is still one of those who long for the higher worlds, who would live with the Gods, and who feel human life as something foreign and incomprehensible to them. In truth a wondrous picture, containing things of sublime import!

A hero, Arjuna, surrounded by other heroes and by the warrior hosts—a hero who feels all that is spread before him as unfamiliar and remote—and a God, Krishna, who is needed to direct him to this world. He does not understand this world until Krishna makes it comprehensible to him. It may sound paradoxical, but I know that those who can enter into the matter more deeply will understand me when I say that Arjuna stands there like a human soul to whom the earthly side of the world has first to be made comprehensible.

Now this ***Bhagavad Gita*** comes to men of the West who undoubtedly *have* an understanding for earthly things! It comes to men who have attained such a high degree of materialistic civilization that they have a very good understanding for all that is earthly. It has to be understood by souls who are separated by a deep gulf from all that a genuine observation shows Arjuna's soul to be. All that to which Arjuna shows no inclination, needing Krishna to tame him down to earthly things, seems to the Westerner quite intelligible and obvious. The difficulty for him lies rather in being able to lift himself up to Arjuna, to whom has to be imparted an understanding of what is well understood in the West, the sense matters of earthly life. A God, Krishna, must make our civilization and culture intelligible to Arjuna. How easy it is in our time for a person to understand what surrounds him! He needs no Krishna. It is well for once to see clearly the mighty gulfs that can lie between different human natures, and not to think it too easy for a Western soul to understand a nature like that of Krishna or Arjuna. Arjuna is a man, but utterly different from those who have slowly and gradually evolved in Western civilization.

That is one picture I wanted to bring you, for words cannot lead us more than a very little way into these things. Pictures that we can grasp with our souls can do better because they speak not only to understanding but to that in us which on earth will always be deeper than our understanding—to our power of perception and to our feeling. Now I would like to place another picture before you, one not less sublime than that from the ***Bhagavad Gita*** but that stands infinitely nearer to Western culture. Here in the West we have a beautiful, poetic picture that Western man knows and that means much for him. But first let us ask, to what extent does Western mankind really believe that this being of Krishna once appeared before Arjuna and spoke those words? We are now at the starting-point of a concept of the world that will lead us on until this is no mere matter of belief, but of knowledge. We are however only at the beginning of this anthroposophical concept of the world that will lead us to knowledge. The second picture is much nearer to us. It contains something to which Western civilization can respond.

We look back some five centuries before the founding of Christianity to a soul whom one of the greatest spirits of Western lands made the central figure of all his thought and writing. We look back to Socrates. We look to him in the spirit in the hour of his death, even as Plato describes him in the circle of his disciples in the famous discourse on the immortality of the soul. In this picture there are but slight indications of the beyond, represented in the "daimon" who speaks to Socrates.

Now let him stand before us in the hours that preceded his entrance into the spiritual worlds. There he is, surrounded by his disciples, and in the face of death he speaks to them of the immortality of the soul. Many people read this wonderful discourse that Plato has given us in order to describe the scene of his dying teacher. But people in these days read only words, only concepts and ideas. There are even those—I do not mean to censure them—in whom this wonderful scene of Plato arouses questions as to the logical justification of what the dying Socrates sets forth to his disciples. They cannot feel there is something more for the human soul, that something more important lives there, of far greater significance than logical proofs and scientific arguments. Let us imagine all that Socrates says on immortality to be spoken by a man of great culture, depth and refinement, in the circle of his pupils, but in a different situation from that of Socrates, under different circumstances. Even if the words of this man were a hundred times more logically sound than those of Socrates, in spite of all they will perhaps have a hundred times less value. This will only be fully grasped when people begin to understand that there is something for the human soul of more value, even if less plausible, than the most strictly correct logical demonstrations. If any highly educated and cultured man speaks to his pupils on the immortality of the soul, it can indeed have significance. But its significance is not revealed in what he says—I know I am now saying something paradoxical but it is true—its significance depends also on the fact that the teacher, having spoken these words to his pupils, passes on to look after the ordinary affairs of life, and his pupils do the same. But Socrates speaks in the hour that immediately precedes his passage through the gates of death. He gives out his teaching in a moment when in the next instant his soul is to be severed from his bodily form.

It is one thing to speak about immortality to the pupils he is leaving behind in the hour of his own death—which does not meet him unexpectedly but as an event predetermined by destiny—and another thing to return after such a discourse to the ordinary business of living. It is not the words of Socrates that should work on us as much as the situation under which he speaks them. Let us take all the power of this scene, all that we receive from Socrates' conversation with his pupils on immortality, the full immediate force of this picture. What do we have before us? It is the world of everyday life in Greek times; the world whose conflicts and struggles led to the result that the best of the country's sons was condemned to drink the hemlock. This noble Greek spoke these last words with the sole intention of bringing the souls of the men around him to believe in what they could no longer have knowledge; believe in what was for them "a beyond," a spiritual world. That it needs a Socrates to lead the earthly souls until they gain an outlook into the spiritual worlds, that it needs him to do this by means of the strongest proofs, that is, by his *deed,* is something that is indeed comprehensible to Western souls. They can gain an understanding for the Socratic culture. We only grasp Western civilization in a right sense when we recognize that in this respect it has been a Socratic civilization throughout the centuries.

Now let us think of one of the pupils of Socrates who could certainly have no doubt of the reality of all that surrounded him, being a Greek, and compare him with Krishna's disciple Arjuna. Think how the Greek has to be introduced to the supersensible world, and then think of Arjuna who can have no doubt whatever about it but becomes confused instead with the sense-world, almost doubting the possibility of its existence. I know that history, philosophy and other branches of knowledge may say with apparently good reason, "Yes, but if you will only look at what is written in the ***Bhagavad Gita,*** and in Plato's works, it is just as easy to prove the opposite of what you have just said." I know too that those who speak like this do not want to feel the deeper impulses, the mighty impulses that arise on the one hand from that picture out of the ***Bhagavad Gita,*** and on the other from that of the dying Socrates as described by Plato. A deep gulf yawns between these two worlds in spite of all the similarity that can be discovered. This is because the ***Bhagavad Gita*** marks the end of the age of the ancient clairvoyance. There we can catch the last echo of it; while in the dying Socrates we meet one of the first of those who through thousands of years have wrestled with another kind of human knowledge, with those ideas, thoughts and feelings that, so to say, were thrown off by the old clairvoyance and have continued to evolve in the intervening time, because they have to prepare the way for a new clairvoyance. Today we are striving toward this new clairvoyance by giving out and receiving what we call the anthroposophical conception of the world. From a certain aspect we may say that no gulf is deeper than the one that opens between Arjuna and a disciple of Socrates.

Now we are living in a time when the souls of men, having gone through manifold transformations and incarnations in the search for life in external knowledge, are now once more seeking to make connection with the spiritual worlds. . . . You are seeking the connection that will lead you up in a new way to those worlds so wondrously revealed to us in the words of Krishna to his disciple Arjuna. So there is much in the occult wisdom on which the ***Bhagavad Gita*** is founded that resounds to us as something responding to our deepest longings. In ancient times the soul was well aware of the bond that unites it with the spiritual. It was at home in the supersensible. We now are at the beginning of an age wherein men's souls will once more seek access in a new way to the spiritual worlds. We must feel ourselves stimulated to this search when we think of how we once had this access, that it once was there for man.

Indeed, we shall find it to an unusual degree in the revelations of the holy song of the East.

As is generally the case with the great works of man, we find the opening words of the ***Bhagavad Gita*** full of meaning. (Are not the opening words of the *Iliad* and the *Odyssey* most significant?) The story is told by his charioteer to the blind king, the chief of the Kurus who are engaged in fratricidal battle with the Pandavas. A blind chieftain! This already seems symbolical. Men of ancient times had vision into the spiritual worlds. With their whole heart and soul they lived in connection with Gods and Divine Beings. Everything that surrounded them in the earthly sphere was to them in unceasing connection with divine existence. Then came another age, and just as Greek legend depicts Homer as a blind man, so the ***Gita*** tells us of the blind chief of the Kurus. It is to him that the discourses of Krishna are narrated in which he instructs Arjuna concerning what goes on in the world of the senses. He must even be told of those things of the sense-world that are projections into it from the spiritual. There is a deeply significant symbol in the fact that old men who looked back with perfect memory and a perfect spiritual connection into a primeval past, were *blind* to the world immediately around them. They were seers in the spirit, seers in the soul. They could experience as though in lofty pictures all that lived as spiritual mysteries. Those who were to understand the events of the world in their spiritual connections were pictured to us in the old songs and legends as blind. Thus we find this same symbol in the Greek singer Homer as in that figure that meets us at the beginning of the ***Bhagavad Gita.*** This introduces us to the age of transition from primeval humanity to that of the present day.

Now why is Arjuna so deeply moved by the impending battle of the brothers? We know that the old clairvoyance was in a sense bound up with external blood relationship. The flowing of the same blood in the veins of a number of people was rightly looked upon as something sacred in ancient times because with it was connected the ancient perception of a particular group-soul. Those who not only felt but knew their blood-relationship to one another did not yet have such an ego as lives in men of the present time. Wherever we look in those ancient times we find everywhere groups of people who did not at all feel themselves as having an individual "I" as man does today. Each felt his identity only *in the group,* in a community based upon the bloodbond.

What does the folk-soul, the nation-soul, signify to a man today? Certainly it is often an object of the greatest enthusiasm. Yet we may say that, compared with the individual "I" of a man, this nation-soul does not really count. This may be a hard saying but it is true. Once upon a time man did not say "I" to *himself* but to his tribal or racial *group.* This group-soul feeling was still living in Arjuna when he saw the fratricidal battle raging around him. That is the reason why the battle that raged about him filled him with such horror.

Let us enter the soul of Arjuna and feel the horror that lived in him when he realized how those who belonged together are about to murder each other. He felt what lived in all the souls at that time *and is about to kill itself.* He felt as a soul would feel if its body, which is its very own, were being torn in pieces. He felt as though the members of one body were in conflict, the heart with the head, the left hand with the right. Think how Arjuna's soul confronted the impending battle as a battle against its own body, when, in the moment he drops his bow, the conflict of the kinsmen seems to him a conflict between a man's right hand and his left. Then you will feel the atmosphere of the opening verses of the ***Bhagavad Gita.***

[The] *Bhagavad Gita* marks the end of the age of the ancient clairvoyance.

—Rudolf Steiner

When Arjuna is in this mood he is met by the great teacher Krishna. Here we must call attention to the incomparable art with which Krishna is pictured in this scene: The holy God, who stands there teaching Arjuna what man shall and will discard if he would take the right direction in his evolution. Of what does Krishna speak? Of *I,* and *I,* and *I,* and always only of *I.* "I am in the earth, I am in the water, I am in the air, I am in the fire, in all souls, in all manifestations of life, even in the holy Aum. I am the wind that blows through the forests. I am the greatest of the mountains, of the rivers. I am the greatest among men. I am all that is best in the old seer Kapila." Truly Krishna says nothing less than this, "I recognize nothing else than myself, and I admit the world's existence only in so far as it is *I!* " Nothing else than *I* speaks from out the teaching of Krishna.

Let us once for all see quite plainly how Arjuna stands there as one not yet understanding himself as an ego but who now has to do so. How the God confronts him like an all-embracing cosmic egoist, admitting of nothing but himself, even requiring others to admit of nothing but themselves, each one an "I." Yes, in all that is in earth, water, fire or air, in all that lives upon the earth, in the three worlds, we are to see nothing but Krishna.

It is full of significance for us that one who cannot yet grasp the ego is brought for his instruction before a Being who demands to be recognized only as his own Self. Let him who wants to see this in the light of truth read the ***Bhagavad Gita*** through and try to answer the question, "How can we designate what Krishna says of himself and for which he demands recognition?" It is *universal egoism* that speaks in Krishna. It does indeed seem to us as though through the whole of the sublime ***Gita*** this refrain resounds to our spiritual hearing, "Only when you recognize, you men, my all-embracing egoism, only then can salvation be for you!"

The greatest achievements of human spiritual life always set us riddles. We only see them in the right light when we recognize that they set us the very greatest riddles. Truly, a hard one seems to be given us when we are now confronted with the task of understanding how a must sublime teaching can be bound up with the announcement of universal egoism. It is not through logic but in the perception of the great contradictions in life that the occult mysteries unveil themselves to us. (pp. 3-15)

The more deeply we penetrate into the occult records of the various ages and peoples, that is to say, into the truly occult records, the more we are struck by one feature of them which meets us again and again. . . . I refer to the fact that on looking deeply into any such occult record it becomes ever clearer that it is really most wonderfully composed, that it forms an artistic whole. I could show, for instance, how *St. John's Gospel,* when we penetrate into its depths, reveals a wonderful, artistic composition. With remarkable dramatic power the story is carried up stage by stage to a great climax, and then continues from this point onward with a kind of renewal of dramatic power to the end. You can study this in the lectures I gave at Cassel on *St. John's Gospel* in relation to the three other Gospels, especially to that according to St. Luke.

Most impressive is the gradual enhancement of the whole composition while the supersensible is placed before us in the so-called miracles and signs; each working up in ever-increasing wonder to the sign that meets us in the initiation of Lazarus. It makes us realize how we can always find artistic beauty at the foundation of these occult records. I could show the same for the structure of *St. Mark's Gospel.* When we regard such records in their beauty of form and their dramatic power, we can indeed conclude that just because they are *true* such records cannot be other than artistically, beautifully composed, in the deepest sense of the word. (pp. 16-17)

Now it is remarkable that the same thing meets us again in the ***Bhagavad Gita.*** There is a wonderful intensification of the narrative, one might say, a hidden artistic beauty in the song, so that if nothing else were to touch the soul of one studying this sublime ***Gita,*** he still could not help being impressed by its marvellous composition. Let us begin by indicating a few of the outstanding points—and we will confine ourselves . . . to the first four discourses—because these points are important both for the artistic structure and the deep occult truths that it contains.

First of all Arjuna meets us. Facing the bloodshed in which he is to take part, he grows weak. He sees all that is to take place as a battle of brothers against brothers, his blood relations. He shrinks back. He will not fight against them. While fear and terror come over him and he is horror-stricken, his charioteer suddenly appears as the instrument through which Krishna, God, is to speak to him. Here in this first episode we already have a moment of great intensity and also an indication of deep occult truth. Anyone who finds the way, by whatever path, into the spiritual worlds, even though he may have gone only a few steps—or even had only a dim presentiment of the way to be experienced—such a person will be aware of the deep significance of this moment.

As a rule we cannot enter the spiritual worlds without passing through a deep upheaval in our souls. We have to experience something which disturbs and shakes all our forces, filling us with intense feeling. Emotions that are generally spread out over many moments, over long periods of living, whose permanent effect on the soul is therefore weaker—such feelings are concentrated in a single moment and storm through us with tremendous force when we enter the occult worlds. Then we experience a kind of inner shattering, which can indeed be compared to fear, terror and anxiety, as though we were shrinking back from something almost with horror. Such experiences belong to the initial stages of occult development, to entering the spiritual worlds. (pp. 17-18)

With wonderful truth the ***Bhagavad Gita*** sets such a moment of upheaval at the starting-point of Arjuna's experience, only he does not go through an occult training but is placed into this moment by his destiny. He is placed into the battle without being able to recognize its necessity, its purpose or its aim. All he sees is that blood relations are about to fight against each other. Such a soul as Arjuna can be shaken by that to its innermost core, for he has to say to himself,

> Brother fights against brother. Surely then all the tribal customs will be shaken and then the tribe itself will wither away and be destroyed, and all its morality fall into decay! Those laws will be shaken that in accordance with an eternal destiny place men into castes; and then will everything be imperilled—man himself, the law, the whole world. The whole significance of mankind will be in the balance.

Such is his feeling. It is as though the ground were about to sink from under his feet, as though an abyss were opening up before him. (p. 20)

There is another feeling that Arjuna has absorbed, on which for him the whole well-being of human evolution depends. He feels that the forefathers of the tribe, the ancestors, are worthy of honor. He feels that their souls watch over the succeeding generations. For him it is a sublime service to offer up fires of sacrifice to the Manes, to the holy souls of the ancestors. But now what must he see? Instead of altars with sacrificial fires burning on them for the ancestors, he sees those who should join in kindling such fires assailing one another in battle. If we would understand a human soul we must penetrate into its thoughts. Above all we must enter deeply into its feelings because it is in feeling that the soul is intimately bound up with its very life. Now think of the great contrast between all that Arjuna would naturally feel, and the bloody battle of brother against brother that is actually about to take place. Destiny is hammering at Arjuna's soul, shaking it to its very depths. It is as though he had to gaze down into a terrible abyss. Such an upheaval awakens the forces of the soul and brings it to a vision of occult realities that at other times are hidden as behind a veil. That is what gives such dramatic intensity to the ***Bhagavad Gita.*** The ensuing discourse is thus placed before us with wonderful power, as developing of necessity out of Arjuna's destiny, instead of being given us merely as an academic, pedantic course of instruction in occultism.

Now that Arjuna has been rightly prepared for the birth of the deeper forces of his soul, now that he can see these forces in inward vision, there happens what everyone who has the power to behold it will understand: His charioteer becomes the instrument through which the god Krishna speaks to him. In the first four discourses we observe three successive stages, each higher than the last, each one introducing something new. Here in these very first discourses we find an accent that is wonderful in its dramatic art, apart from the fact that it corresponds to a deep occult truth. The first stage is a teaching that might appear even trivial to many Westerners in its given form. (pp. 21-2)

To begin with then we find a teaching that might easily appear trivial, especially to a philosophical mind. For what is the first thing that Krishna says to Arjuna as a word of exhortation for the battle? "Look there," he says,

> at those who are to be killed by you; those in your own ranks who are to be killed and those who are to remain behind, and consider will this one thing. What dies and what remains alive in your ranks and in those of the enemy is but the outer physical body. The spirit is eternal. If your warriors slay those in the ranks over there they are but slaying the outer body, they are not killing the spirit, which is eternal. The spirit goes from change to change, from incarnation to incarnation. It is eternal. This deepest being of man is not affected in this battle. Rise, Arjuna, rise to the spiritual standpoint, then you can go and give yourself up to your duty. You need not shudder nor be sad at heart, for in killing your enemies you are not killing their essential being.

Thus speaks Krishna, and at first hearing his words are in a sense trivial, though in a special way. In many respects the Westerner is short-sighted in his thinking and consciousness. He never stops to consider that everything is evolving. If he says that Krishna's exhortation, as I have expressed it, is trivial, it is as though one were to say, "Why do they honor Pythagoras as such a great man when every schoolboy and girl knows his theorem?" It would be stupid to conclude that Pythagoras was not a great man in having discovered his theorem just because every schoolboy understands it! We see how stupid this is, but we do not notice when we fail to realize that what any Western philosopher may repeat by rote as the wisdom of Krishna—that the spirit is eternal, immortal—was a sublime wisdom at the time Krishna revealed it. Souls like Arjuna did indeed feel that blood-relations ought not to fight. They still felt the common blood that flowed in a group of people. To hear it said that "the spirit is eternal" (spirit in the sense of what is generally conceived, abstractly, as the center of man's being)—the spirit is eternal and undergoes transformations, passing from incarnation to incarnation—this stated in abstract and intellectual terms was something absolutely new and epoch-making in its newness when it resounded in Arjuna's soul through Krishna's words. All the people in Arjuna's environment believed definitely in reincarnation, but as Krishna taught it, as a general and abstract *idea,* it was new, especially in regard to Arjuna's situation. This is one reason why we had to say that such a truth can only be called "trivial" in a special sense. That holds true in another respect as well. Our abstract thought, which we use even in the pursuit of popular science, which we regard today as quite natural—this thinking activity was by no means always so natural and simple. (pp. 22-3)

Ideas arise in the soul through exactly the same process as what gives rise to its highest powers. It is immensely important to learn to understand that clairvoyance begins in something common and everyday. We only have to recognize the supersensible nature of our concepts and ideas. We must realize that these come to us from the supersensible worlds; only then can we look at the matter rightly. (pp. 25-6)

It is from those worlds that concepts and ideas come into the human soul, not from the world of the senses. In the 18th century what was considered a great word was uttered by a pioneer of thinking, "O, Man, make bold to use thy power of reason!" Today a great word must resound in men's souls, "O, Man, make bold to claim thy concepts and ideas as the beginning of thy clairvoyance." What I have just expressed I said many years ago, publicly in my books *Truth and Science* and *The Philosophy of Freedom,* where I showed that human ideas come from supersensible, spiritual knowledge. It was not understood at the time. . . . We must realize that at the moment when Krishna stands before Arjuna and gives him the power of abstract judgment, he is thereby giving him, for the first time in the whole of evolution, the starting-point for the knowledge of higher worlds. The spirit can be seen on the very surface of the changes that take place within the external world of sense. Bodies die; the spirit, the abstract, the essential being, is eternal. The spiritual can be seen playing on the surface of phenomena. This is what Krishna would reveal to Arjuna as the beginning of a new clairvoyance for men.

One thing is necessary for men of today if they would attain to an inwardly-experienced truth. They must have once passed through the feeling of the fleeting nature of all outer transformations. They must have experienced the mood of infinite sadness, of infinite tragedy, and at the same time the exultation of joy. They must have felt the breath of the ephemeral that streams out from all things. They must have been able to fix their interest on this coming forth and passing away again, the transitoriness of the world of sense. Then, when they have been able to feel the deepest pain and the fullest delight in the external world, they must once have been absolutely alone—alone with their concepts and ideas. They must have had the feeling, "In these concepts I grasp the mystery of the worlds; I take hold of the outer edge of cosmic being,"—the very expression I once used in my *Philosophy of Freedom*! This must be experienced, not merely understood intellectually, and if you would experience it, it must be in deepest loneliness. Then you have another feeling. On the one hand you experience the majesty of the world of ideas that is spread out over the *All.* On the other hand you experience with the deepest bitterness that you have to separate yourself from space and time in order to be together with your concepts and ideas. Loneliness! It is the icy cold of loneliness. Furthermore, it comes to you that the world of ideas has now drawn together as in a single point of this loneliness. Now you say, I am alone with my world of ideas. You become utterly bewildered in your world of ideas, an experience that stirs you to the depths of your soul. At length you say to yourself, "Perhaps all this is only I myself; perhaps the only truth about these laws is that they exist in the point of my own loneliness." Thus you experience, infinitely enhanced, utter doubt in all existence.

When you have this experience in your world of ideas, when the full cup of doubt in all existence has been poured out with pain and bitterness over your soul, then only are you ripe to understand how, after all, it is not the infinite spaces and periods of time of the physical world from which your ideas have come. Now only, after the bitterness of doubt, you open yourself to the regions of the spiritual and know that your doubt was justified, and in what sense it was justified. For it had to be, since you imagined that the ideas had come into your soul from the times and spaces of the physical world. How do you now feel your world of ideas having experienced its origin in the spiritual worlds? Now for the first time you feel yourself inspired. Before, you were feeling the infinite void spread around you like a dark abyss. Now you begin to feel that you are standing on a rock that rises up out of the abyss. You know with certainty, "Now I am connected with the spiritual worlds. They, not the world of sense, have bestowed on me my world of ideas."

This is the next stage for the evolving soul. It is the stage where man begins to be deeply in earnest with what has today come to be a trivial, commonplace truth. To bear this feeling in your heart will prepare you to receive in a true way the first truth that Krishna gives to Arjuna after the mighty upheaval and convulsion in his soul: The truth of the eternal spirit living through outer transformations. To abstract understanding we speak in concepts and ideas. Krishna speaks to Arjuna's heart. What may be trivial and commonplace for the understanding is infinitely deep and sublime to the heart of man.

We see how the first stage shows itself at once as a necessary consequence of the deeply moving experience that is presented to us at the start of the ***Bhagavad Gita.*** (pp. 26-9)

[We] can feel it natural that Krishna, having brought Arjuna into the world of ideas and wishing to lead him on into the occult world, now goes on to show him the next stage, how every soul can reach that higher world if it finds the right starting-point. Krishna then must begin by rejecting every form of dogmatism, and he does so radically. Here we come up against a hard saying by Krishna. He absolutely rejects what for centuries had been most holy to the highest men of that age—the contents of the *Vedas.* He says, "Hold not to the *Vedas,* nor to the word of the *Vedas.* Hold fast to Yoga!" That is to say, "Hold fast to what is within thine own soul!"

Let us grasp what Krishna means by this exhortation. He does not mean that the contents of the *Vedas* are untrue. He does not want Arjuna to accept what is given in the *Vedas dogmatically* as the disciples of the *Veda* teaching do. He wants to inspire him to take his start from the very first original point whence the human soul evolves. For this purpose all dogmatic wisdom must be laid aside. We can imagine Krishna saying to himself that even though Arjuna will in the end reach the very same wisdom that is contained in the *Vedas,* still he must be drawn away from them, for he must go his own way, beginning with the sources in his own soul. Krishna rejects the *Vedas,* whether their content is true or untrue. Arjuna's path must start from himself, through his own inwardness he must come to recognize Krishna. Arjuna must be assumed to have in himself what a man can and must have if he is really to enter into the concrete truths of the supersensible worlds. Krishna has called Arjuna's attention to something that from then onward is a common attribute of humanity. Having led him to this point he must lead him further and bring him to recognize what he is to achieve through Yoga. Thus, Arjuna must first undergo Yoga. Here the poem rises to another level.

In this second stage we see how the ***Bhagavad Gita*** goes on through the first four discourses with ever-increasing dramatic impulse, coming at length to what is most individual of all. Krishna describes the path of Yoga to Arjuna. . . . He describes the path that Arjuna must take in order to pass from the everyday clairvoyance of concepts and ideas to what can only be attained through Yoga. Concepts only require to be placed in the right light; but Arjuna has to be *guided* to Yoga. This is the second stage.

The third stage shows once more an enhancement of dramatic power, and again comes the expression of a deep occult truth. Let us assume that someone really takes the Yoga path. He will rise at length from his ordinary consciousness to a higher state of consciousness, which includes not only the ego that lies between the limits of birth and death but what passes from one incarnation to the next. The soul wakens to know itself in an expanded ego. It grows into a wider consciousness. The soul goes through a process that is essentially an everyday process but that is not experienced fully in our everyday life because man goes to sleep every night. The sense world fades out around him and he becomes unconscious of it. Now for every human soul the possibility exists of letting this world of sense vanish from his consciousness as it does when he goes to sleep, and then to live in higher worlds as in an absolute reality. Thereby man rises to a high level of consciousness. . . . But when man gradually attains to where he no longer, consciously, lives and feels and knows *in himself,* but lives and feels and knows *together with the whole earth,* then he grows into a higher level of consciousness where the things of the sense world vanish for him as they do in sleep. (pp. 29-31)

The path of Yoga, especially in its modern sense, leads to this expansion of consciousness, to the identification of our own being with a more comprehensive being. We feel ourselves interwoven with the whole earth. Then as men we no longer feel ourselves bound to a particular time and place, but we feel our humanity such as it has developed from the very beginning of the earth. We feel the age-long succession of our evolutions through the course of the evolution of the earth. Thus Yoga leads us on to feel our at-one-ment with what goes from one incarnation to another in the earth's evolution. That is the third stage.

This is the reason for the great beauty in the artistic composition of the ***Bhagavad Gita.*** In its climaxes, its inner artistic form, it reflects deep occult truths. Beginning with an instruction in the ordinary concepts of our thinking it goes on to an indication of the path of Yoga. Then at the third stage to a description of the marvellous expansion of man's horizon over the whole earth, where Krishna awakens in Arjuna the idea, "All that lives in your soul has lived often before, only you know nothing of it. But I have this consciousness in myself when I look back on all the transformations through which I have lived, and I will lead you up so that you may learn to feel yourself as I feel myself." A new moment of dramatic force as beautiful as it is deeply and occultly true!

Thus we come to see the evolution of mankind from out of its everyday consciousness, . . . from the particular world of thoughts and concepts that are a matter of everyday life in any one age, up to the point from where we can look out over all that we really have in us, which lives on from incarnation to incarnation on the earth. (pp. 32-3)

Rudolf Steiner, in his The Occult Significance of the Bhagavad Gita, *translated by George Adams and Mary Adams, Anthroposophic Press, Inc., 1968, 142 p.*

Krsna shows Arjuna his divine splendor.

S. Radhakrishnan (essay date 1923)

[*Radhakrishnan was a prominent Indian philosopher and statesman whose writings include* Contemporary Indian Philosophy *(1936),* Religion and Society *(1947), and* The Brahma Sutra: The Philosophy of Spiritual Life *(1960). In the following excerpt, he provides an exhaustive analysis of the* Gītā's *conception of God, with particular emphasis on the essentially divine foundations of the individual's self-knowledge and understanding of reality.*]

THE BHAGAVADGITA

The ***Bhagavadgītā*** which forms part of the Bhīṣma parva of the *Mahābhārata* is the most popular religious poem of Sanskrit literature. [Wilhelm von Humboldt called it] "the most beautiful, perhaps the only true philosophical song existing in any known tongue." It is a book conveying lessons of philosophy, religion and ethics. It is not looked upon as a śruti, or a revealed scripture, but is regarded as a smṛti, or a tradition. Yet if the hold which a work has on the mind of man is any clue to its importance, then the ***Gītā*** is the most influential work in Indian thought. Its message of deliverance is simple. While only the rich could buy off the gods by their sacrifices, and only the cultured could pursue the way of knowledge, the ***Gītā*** teaches a method which is within the reach of all, that of bhakti, or devotion to God. The poet makes the teacher the very God descended into humanity. He is supposed to address Arjuna, the representative man, at a great crisis in his life. Arjuna comes to the battle-field, convinced of the righteousness of his cause and prepared to fight the enemy. At the psychological moment he shrinks from his duty. His conscience is troubled, his heart is torn with anguish and his state of mind, "like to a little kingdom, suffers then the nature of an insurrection." If to slay is to sin, it is a worse sin to slay those to whom we owe love and worship. Arjuna typifies the struggling individual who feels the burden and the mystery of the world. He has not yet built within himself a strong centre of spirit from which he can know not only the unreality of his own desires and passions, but also the true status of the world opposing him. The despondency of Arjuna is not the passing mood of a disappointed man, but is the feeling of a void, a sort of deadness felt in the heart, exciting a sense of the unreality of things. Arjuna is ready to repudiate his life if necessary. He does not, however, know what is right for him to do. He is faced by a terrible temptation and passes through an intense inward agony. His cry is a simple yet tremendous one, significant of the tragedy of man, which all who can see beyond the actual drama of the hour can recognise. The mood of despair in which Arjuna is found in the first chapter of the ***Gītā*** is what the mystics call the dark night of the soul, an essential step in the upward path. The further stages of illumination and realisation are found in the course of the dialogue. From the second chapter onwards we have a philosophical analysis. The essential thing in man is not the body or the senses, but the changeless spirit. The mind of Arjuna is switched on to a new path. The life of the soul is symbolised by the battle-field of Kurukṣetra, and the Kauravas are the enemies who impede the progress of the soul. Arjuna attempts to recapture the kingdom of man by resisting the temptations and controlling the passions. The path of progress is through suffering and self-abnegation. Arjuna tries to evade the rigorous ordeal by subtle arguments and specious excuses. Kṛṣṇa stands for the voice of God, delivering his message in thrilling notes, warning Arjuna against dejection of spirit. The opening chapter shows great insight into the heart of man, its conflict of motives, the force of selfishness and the subtle whisperings of the Evil One. As the dialogue proceeds the dramatic element disappears. The echoes of the battle-field die away, and we have only an interview between God and man. The chariot of war becomes the lonely cell of meditation, and a corner of the battle-field where the voices of the world are stilled, a fit place for thoughts on the supreme.

The teacher is the favourite god of India, who is at once human and divine. He is the god of beauty and love, whom his devotees enthrone on the wings of birds, on the petals of flowers, on whatever they most delight in of all that lives on earth. The poet vividly imagines how an incarnate God would speak of Himself. There is support for the poet's device to make Kṛṣṇa say that he was Brahman. In the *Vedānta Sūtras,* the Vedic passage where Indra declares himself to be Brahman is explained on the hypothesis that Indra is only referring to the philosophical truth that the Ātman in man is one with the Supreme Brahman. When Indra says "Worship me," he means "worship the God I worship." On a similar principle Vāmedeva's declaration that he is Manu and Sūrya is explained. Besides, the ***Gītā*** teaches that an individual freed from passion and fear and purified by the fire of wisdom attains to the state of God. Kṛṣṇa of the ***Gītā*** stands for the infinite in the finite, the God in man concealed within the folds of flesh and the powers of sense.

The message of ***Gītā*** is universal in its scope. It is the philosophical basis of popular Hinduism. The author is a man of deep culture, catholic rather than critical. He does not lead a missionary movement; he addresses no sect, establishes no school, but opens the way to all the winds that blow. He sympathises with all forms of worship, and is therefore well fitted for the task of interpreting the spirit of Hinduism which is unwilling to break up culture into compartments and treat other forms of thought and practices in a spirit of negation. The ***Gītā*** appeals to us not only by its force of thought and majesty of vision, but also by its fervour of devotion and sweetness of spiritual emotion. Though the ***Gītā*** did much to develop spiritual worship and undermine inhuman practices, still on account of its non-critical attitude it did not destroy altogether false modes of worship.

The tone of the ***Gītā*** is dogmatic, and its author does not suspect that it is possible for him to err. He gives the truth as he sees it, and he seems to see it in its entirety and many-sidedness, and to believe in its saving power. "In the ***Gītā*** there is a sage that speaks in the fullness and enthusiasm of his knowledge and of his feelings, and not a philosopher brought up in any school who divides his material in conformity to a settled method and arrives at the last steps of his doctrines through the clue of a set of systematic ideas" [Richard von Garbe, "Introduction to the ***Bhagavadgītā,***" *Indian Antiquary,* 1918]. The ***Gītā*** stands midway between a philosophical system and a poetic inspiration. We do not have here the illimitable suggestiveness of the *Upaniṣads,* since it is a deliberately intellectual solution of the problem of life. It is designed to meet a situation complicated by troubles of conscience and confusion of mind.

The main spirit of the ***Gītā*** is that of the *Upaniṣads;* only there is a greater emphasis on the religious side. The thin abstractions of the *Upaniṣads* could not satisfy the many-sided needs of the soul. The other attempts to solve the secret of life were more theistic in their texture. The author of the ***Gītā*** found that men could not be made to love logic. So he took his stand on the *Upaniṣads,* drew out their religious implications, galvanised them into a living system by incorporating with them popular mythology and national imagination. (pp. 519-22)

RELATION TO OTHER SYSTEMS

Almost all the views which prevailed in the age [the fifth century B.C.] influenced the author of the ***Gītā,*** who brings to a focus the rays of religious light cast at random in the world about him. It is necessary for us to note the exact relations between the ***Gītā*** on the one hand and the *Vedas,* the *Upaniṣads,* Buddhism, the Bhāgavata religion and the systems of Sāṁkhya and Yoga on the other.

The ***Gītā*** does not throw overboard the authority of the *Vedas.* It considers the Vedic injunctions to be quite valid for men of a particular cultural status. One cannot attain perfection, according to the ***Gītā,*** without obeying the ordinances of the *Vedas.* Sacrificial acts are required to be performed without any expectation of reward. After a particular stage, the performance of Vedic rites tends to become an obstacle to the attainment of supreme perfection. The exalted character of the Vedic gods is not accepted. Though the Vedic obervances secure for us power and wealth, they do not take us straight to freedom. Deliverance can be found by the discovery of self. When the secret of salvation is in our possession there is no need for the performance of Vedic karmas.

The philosophic background of the ***Gītā*** is taken from the *Upaniṣads.* Some verses are common to the *Upaniṣads* and the ***Gītā.*** The discussions of Kṣetra and Kṣetrajña, Kṣara and Akṣara are based on the *Upaniṣads.* The account of the supreme reality is also derived from the same source. Bhakti is a direct development of the upāsana of the *Upaniṣads.* The love for the supreme involves the giving up of all else. "What shall we do with progeny, when we have got this being, this world to live in?" Ideas of devotion to the supreme, the conquest of self and the attainment of a condition of peace and serenity are in the atmosphere of the period. Disinterested work is defended even in the *Upaniṣads.* That non-attachment results from an elevated state of mind is brought out in the *Upaniṣads.* The practical and the religious tendencies of the *Upaniṣads* are so developed as not to supersede the teachings of earlier thinkers. The cold flawless perfection was no doubt a magnificent explanation of the world, but it was not quite suited to be a transforming power of life. The vogue of the Bhāgavata religion inclined the author of the ***Gītā*** to give a glow and a penetrating power to the absolute of the *Upaniṣads.* He made it into a personal Īśvara, called by the different names of Śiva, Viṣṇu, etc. All the same, the author is aware that he is only revivifying a dead past and not propounding a new theory. "This imperishable yoga I declared to Vivasvat, and he taught it to Manu, Manu to Ikṣvāku," and this secret is now revealed to Arjuna by Kṛṣṇa. This passage indicates that the message of the ***Gītā*** is the ancient wisdom taught by Viśvāmitra, the seer of Gāyatrī, and the ṛṣi of the third cycle of the *Ṛg-Veda* and Rāma, Kṛṣṇa, Gautama Buddha, and other teachers of the Solar line. The full name of the ***Gītā,*** as it is evident from the colophon at the end of each chapter, is the Upaniṣad of the name of the ***Bhagavadgītā.*** The traditional account of the relation between the ***Gītā*** and the *Upaniṣads* is contained in the passage now almost too familiar for quotation, that "the Upaniṣads are the cows, Kṛṣṇa is the milker, Arjuna the calf, and the nectar-like ***Gītā*** is the excellent milk."

The Bhāgavata religion was the immediate stimulus to the synthesis of the ***Bhagavadgītā.*** It is actually suggested that the teaching of the ***Gītā*** is identical with the doctrine of the Bhāgavatas. It is sometimes called the Harigītā.

There is no mention of Buddhism, though some of the views of the ***Gītā*** are like those of Buddhism. Both protest against the absolute authority of the Vedas and attempt to relax the rigours of caste by basing it on a less untenable foundation. Both are the manifestations of the same spiritual upheaval which shook the ritualistic religion, though the ***Gītā*** was the more conservative, and therefore less thoroughgoing protest. Buddha announced the golden mean, though his own teaching was not quite true to it. To prefer celibacy to marriage, fasting to feasting, is not to practise the golden mean. The ***Gītā*** denounces the religious madness of the hermits and the spiritual suicide of saints who prefer darkness to daylight and sorrow to joy. It is possible to attain salvation without resorting to the cult of narrowness and death. The word nirvāṇa occurs in the ***Gītā,*** but this does not show any borrowing from Buddhism, since it is not peculiar to it. In the descriptions of the ideal man the ***Gītā*** and Buddhism agree. As a philosophy and religion, the ***Gītā*** is more complete than Buddhism, which emphasises overmuch the negative side. The ***Gītā*** adopts the ethical principles of Buddhism, while it by implication condemns the negative metaphysics of Buddhism as the root of all unbelief and error. It is more in continuity with the past, and therefore had a better fortune than Buddhism in India.

According to Garbe, "the teachings of the Sāṁkhya-Yoga constitute almost entirely the foundation of the philosophical observations of the ***Bhagavadgītā.*** In comparison with them the Vedānta takes a second place. Sāṁkhya and Yoga are often mentioned by name, while the Vedānta appears only once (*Vedāntakṛt,* xv. 15), and then in the sense of Upaniṣad or treatise. Accordingly, when we think merely of the rôle which the philosophical systems play in the ***Gītā*** as it has been handed down to us, and when we consider the irreconcilable contradictions between the Sāṁkhya-Yoga and the Vedānta, which can only be done away with by carefully distinguishing between the old and the new, the Vedāntic constituents of the ***Bhagavadgītā*** prove not to belong to the original poem. Whether we investigate the ***Gītā*** from the religious or the philosophical side, the same result is reached." The terms Sāṁkhya-Yoga when they occur in the ***Gītā*** do not represent the classical schools of Sāṁkhya and Yoga, but only the reflective and the meditative methods of gaining salvation. Besides, during the period of the ***Gītā*** there was no clear-cut distinction between the Sāṁkhya-Yoga on one side and the Vedānta on the other, which alone can justify Garbe's interpretation. Fitz-Edward Hall is more correct when he says [in his preface to *Sāṁkhyasāra*]: "In the *Upaniṣads,* the ***Bhagavadgītā,*** and other ancient Hindu books, we encounter, in combination, the doctrines, which after having been subjected to modifications that rendered them as wholes irreconcilable, were distinguished at an uncertain period into what have for many ages been styled the Sāṁkhya and the Vedānta." The psychology and the order of the creation of the Sāṁkhya are accepted by the ***Gītā,*** though the metaphysical implications of the Sāṁkhya are rejected by it. Kapila's name is mentioned, though not that of Patañjali. We cannot, however, be sure that this Kapila is the founder of the Sāṁkhya system. Even if it be so, it does not follow that the system in all its details was elaborated by that time. The terms buddhi or understanding, ahaṁkāra or self-sense, and manas or mind, occur, though not always in their Sāṁkhya significations. The same is true of prakṛti. While the Sāṁkhya deliberately avoids the question of the existence of God, the ***Gītā*** is most anxious to establish it.

Though the distinction between puruṣa and prakṛti is recognised, the dualism is overcome. Puruṣa is not an independent element, but only a prakṛti or form of God. The physical intelligence is the higher nature. . . . Though prakṛti or nature is unconscious, its activities are purposive, meant as they are for the freedom of the soul. The teleological character of its activities is not in accord with its alleged unconsciousness. In the ***Gītā*** the difficulty is overcome. There is a spiritual fact behind the play of prakṛti or nature. Puruṣa or soul is not the independent reality which it is in the Sāṁkhya system. Its nature is not mere awareness, but bliss also. The ***Gītā*** does not recognise any ultimate distinctness of individual souls. It also believes in the existence of an Uttamapuruṣa, or supreme soul. Yet the character of the individual soul and its relation to nature as given in the ***Bhagavadgītā*** show the influence of the Sāṁkhya theory. Puruṣa is the spectator, and not the actor. Prakṛti does everything. He who thinks "I act" is mistaken. To realise the separateness of puruṣa from prakṛti, soul from nature, is the end of life. The theory of the guṇas or qualities is accepted. "There is no entity on earth or heaven among the devas that is free from the three qualities born of prakṛti." The guṇas constitute the triple cord of bondage. So long as we are subject to them we have to wander in the circuit of existence. Freedom is deliverance from the guṇas. The physiological account of the internal organs and the senses is found here as in the Sāṁkhya.

The ***Gītā*** refers to yoga practices also. When Arjuna asks Kṛṣṇa as to how mind, which is admittedly fickle and boisterous, can be brought under control, Kṛṣṇa answers by saying that abhyāsa, or practice, and vairāgya, or indifference to worldly objects, should be acquired.

THE TEACHING OF THE GITA

At the time of the ***Gītā*** many different views about ultimate reality and man's destiny prevailed. There were the *Upaniṣad* traditions based on the intuition of the soul, the Sāṁkhya doctrine that liberation can be obtained by freeing oneself from contact with nature, the Karma Mīmāṁsā view that by fulfilling our duties we attain perfection, the way of devotional feeling which holds that by attaining exaltation of the heart, the gladness of freedom can be obtained, and the Yoga system, which declares that man is free when the quiet life of the soul takes the place of the vari-coloured light of the world. The supreme spirit is viewed either as an impersonal absolute or a personal lord. The ***Gītā*** attempts to synthesise the heterogeneous elements and fuse them all into a single whole. (pp. 524-29)

The ***Gītā*** is an application of the *Upaniṣad* ideal to the new situations which arose at the time of the ***Mahābhārata.*** In adapting the idealism of the *Upaniṣads* to a theistically minded people, it attempts to derive a religion from the *Upaniṣad* philosophy. It shows that the reflective spiritual idealism of the Upaniṣads has room for the living warm religion of personal devotion. The absolute of the *Upaniṣads* is revealed as the fulfilment of the reflective and the emotional demands of human nature. This change of emphasis from the speculative to the practical, from the philosophical to the religious, is also to be found in the later *Upaniṣads,* where we have the saviour responding to the cry of faith. The ***Gītā*** attempts a spiritual synthesis which could support life and conduct on the basis of the Upaniṣad truth, which it carries into the life-blood of the Indian people. (pp. 530-31)

The context in which the ***Gītā*** is said to be delivered points out how its central purpose is to solve the problem of life and stimulate right conduct. It is obviously an ethical treatise, a yoga śāstra. The ***Gītā*** was formulated in a period of ethical religion and so shared in the feeling of the age. Whatever peculiar adaptations the term yoga may have in the ***Gītā,*** it throughout keeps up its practical reference. Yoga is getting to God, relating oneself to the power that rules the universe, touching the absolute. It is *yoking* not merely this or that power of the soul, but all the forces of heart, mind and will to God. It is the effort of man to unite himself to the deeper principle. We have to change the whole poise of the soul into something absolute and uncompromising and develop the strength to resist power and pleasure. Yoga thus comes to mean the discipline by which we can train ourselves to bear the shocks of the world with the central being of our soul untouched. It is the method or the instrument, upāya, by which the end can be gained. Patañjali's yoga is a system of psychic discipline by which we can clear the intellect, free the mind of its illusions and get a direct perception of reality. We can discipline the emotions and realise the supreme by a soul-surrender to God. We can train our will so as to make our whole life one continuous divine service. We can also perceive the divine in the nature of our being, watch it with ardent love and aspiration, till the spark grows into an infinite light. All these are different yogas or methods leading to the one supreme yoga or union with God. But no ethical message can be sustained if it is not backed up by a metaphysical statement. So the yoga śāstra of the ***Gītā*** is rooted in brahmavidyā, or knowledge of the spirit. The ***Gītā*** is a system of speculation as well as a rule of life, an intellectual search for truth as well as an attempt to make the truth dynamic in the soul of man. This is evident from the colophon at the end of each chapter, which has come down to us from a date which is unknown, that it is the yoga śāstra, or religious discipline of the philosophy of Brahman, "brahmavidyānāṁ yogaśāstre."

ULTIMATE REALITY

The problem of ultimate reality is here approached, as in the *Upaniṣads,* by the two ways of an analysis of the objective and of the subjective. The metaphysical bent of the author is clearly revealed in the second chapter, where he gives us the principle on which his scheme is based: "Of the unreal there is no being, and of the real there is no non-being." The objective analysis proceeds on the basis of a distinction between substance and shadow, the immortal and the perishable, the akṣara and the kṣara. "There are these two beings in the world, the destructible kṣara and the indestructible akṣara. The unchanging one is the akṣara." We cannot say that the "unchanging one" here referred to is the supreme reality, for in the very next verse the ***Gītā*** declares that "the supreme being is another called the highest self, Paramātman, who as the inexhaustible Lord pervading the three worlds supports them." The author first distinguishes the permanent background of the world from its transitory manifestations, the prakṛti from its changes. Within this world of experience, "imau loke," we have the perishable and the permanent aspects. Though prakṛti is permanent when compared with the changes of the world, still it is not absolutely real, since it depends on the supreme Lord. This supreme spirit is the true immortal, the abode of the eternal. Rāmānuja, to suit his own special theory, makes kṣara stand for the principle of prakṛti, and akṣara for the individual soul, and regards Puruṣottama, or the supreme self, as superior to both these. It is possible for us to interpret the conception of Puruṣottama as that of the concrete personality which is superior to the false abstractions of the infinite and the finite. The only difficulty is that Brahman, declared to be the basis of the finite, cannot be looked upon as a mere abstraction. The ***Gītā*** distinguishes between the finite or the impermanent, and the infinite or the permanent. Whatever is limited or transitory is not real. All becoming is an untenable contradiction. That which becomes is not being. If it were being, it would not become. Since the things of the world are struggling to become something else, they are not real. Transitoriness marks all things on earth. In the background of our consciousness, there is the conviction that there is something that does not pass away. For nothing can come out of nothing. That ultimate being of reality is not the everchanging prakṛti. It is the supreme Brahman. It is the eternal or rock-seated being, *kūṭasthasattā,* while the world is only timeless, endless existence, *anādipravāhasattā.* "He sees truly who sees the supreme Lord abiding alike in all entities and not destroyed though they are destroyed." This eternal spirit dwells in all beings, and is therefore not a qualitatively distinct other to the finite. The ***Gītā*** believes in the reality of an infinite being underlying and animating all finite existences.

The individual self is ever unsatisfied with itself and is struggling always to become something else. In its consciousness of limitation, there is a sense of the infinite. The finite self which is limited, which ever tries to rise beyond its sad plight, is not ultimately real. The true self has the character of imperishableness. The ***Gītā*** tries to find out the element of permanence in the self, that which is always the subject and never the object. Kṣetra is the place or the object, and Kṣetrajña is the knower of the object or the subject. What is known is not a property of the knower. In the self of man, there is the element of the knower that remains constant behind all changes. It is the eternal, immutable, timeless self-existence. Breaking up the individual self into its component parts of body, mind, soul, the ***Gītā*** tries to discover the element which *is* always. The body is not the permanent subject, for it has an end, being only a fleeting frame. The sense life is brief and mutable. The empirical mind is ever changing. All these are only objects for a subject, the instruments through which the soul works. They have no existence in their own right. The inner principle, the source of all knowledge, is in the words of the ***Gītā,*** "greater than the senses, the mind and the understanding." It is the element which combines and is present throughout even in deep sleep. This function of combination cannot be attributed to the senses or the understanding or a combination of these. The principle of the subject is the indispensable basis on which the object world, including the empirical self, is based. If we drop the subject, the object vanishes. But the subject does not vanish even though the object disappears. The ***Gītā*** gives eloquent descriptions of this undying element. It is the lord of the body. "He is not born nor does He die, nor having been, does He cease to be any more. Unborn, eternal, everlasting, ancient, He is not slain when the body is destroyed." "Weapons do not reach it, flame does not burn it nor water wet it. Wind does not dry it. It is impenetrable, uncombustible . . . perpetual, all pervading, stable, immovable, ancient."

About the nature of the supreme self, the ***Gītā*** account is rather puzzling. "This inexhaustible supreme self, being without beginning and without qualities, does not act and is not tainted, though stationed in the body." It is viewed as a mere spectator. The self is akartṛ, non-doer. The whole drama of evolution belongs to the object world. Intelligence, mind, senses are looked upon as the developments of the unconscious prakṛti, which is able to bring about this ascent on account of the presence of spirit. The subject self is within us calm and equal, uncaught in the external world, though its support, source and immanent witness.

We have in the actual individuals of the world combinations of subject and object. The empirical individuals are the divine principle of subject limited by contexts of object. In the world the subject and the object are always found together. Only the object has not an ultimate transcendental existence. The subject superior to the object is the basis of the object. "When a man sees all the variety of existence as rooted in one and all as emanating from that, he becomes one with the supreme." When the confusion with the object terminates, the subject in all is found to be the same. When Kṛṣṇa urges Arjuna not to grieve for the dead, he says that death is not extinction. The individual form may change, but the essence is not destroyed. Until perfection is obtained, individuality persists. However repeatedly the mortal frame is destroyed, the inner individuality preserves its identity and takes on a new form. Buoyed up by this faith, man has to work for self-knowledge. Our imperishableness is guaranteed either by way of endlessness or perfection. It is the unfolding of our implicit infinitude. It is by this affirmation of the soul, by this vindication of the intuition of the *Upaniṣads,* that the Ātman, or the pure subject, remains unaffected, even though our body be "dust returning unto dust," that Kṛṣṇa stills the unrest of Arjuna's mind.

> Never the spirit was born; the spirit shall cease
> to be never,
> Never was time it was not; end and beginning
> are dreams;
> Birthless and deathless and changeless remai-
> neth the spirit for ever,
> Death hath not touched it at all, dead though the
> house of it seems.

In the spirit of the *Upaniṣads* the ***Gītā*** identifies the two principles of the Ātman and the Brahman. Behind the fleeting senses and the body there is the Ātman; behind the fleeting objects of the world there is Brahman. The two are one, being of identical nature. The reality of this is a matter of each man's experience to be realised for himself. Any endeavour to define the unchanging in terms of the changing fails. There is, however, no attempt in the ***Gītā*** to prove that the absolute discerned by intuition is the logical foundation of the world, though this is implied. If the world is to be an experience and not a chaotic confusion, then we require the reality of an unconditioned absolute. We should, however, be very careful not to oppose the infinite and the finite as two mutually exclusive spheres. This will lead us to a false view of the infinite. What strikes us at first is the distinction between the passing finite and the real infinite. But if this were all, then the infinite becomes finitised, converted into something limited, since the opposed and the excluded finite becomes the limit of the infinite. It is wrong to conceive the infinite as something pushed out of the being of the finite. It is the finite itself in its truth. It is the infinitised finite, the real in the finite, and not something lying side by side with it. If we overlook the infinite in the finite, we get an endless progress peculiar to the world of finitude or saṁsāra. This very endlessness is the sign of the infinite within the sphere of the finite. The finite reveals itself as nothing more than the infinite made finite. The distinction between the infinite and the finite is only a characteristic of loose thinking. In truth there is only the infinite, and the finite is nothing more than the finitisation of the infinite. It follows that terms like transcendence and immanence are inapplicable, since these assume a distinct "other" to the absolute. Any category of thought is inadequate for the purposes of the absolute. It is described as neither being nor non-being, neither formed nor unformed. The ***Gītā*** reiterates the *Upaniṣad* principle that the real is the immutable self-existence behind the cosmic world, with its space, time and causality.

The ***Gītā*** asserts the truth of an advaita or non-dualism in philosophy. The supreme Brahman is the immutable self-existence "of which the Vedāntins speak, to which the doers of the austerities attain." It is the highest status and supreme goal of the soul's movement in time, though it is itself no movement, but a status original, eternal and supreme. In the unalterable eternity of Brahman, all that moves and evolves is founded. By it they exist; they cannot be without it, though it causes nothing, does nothing and determines nothing. The two, Brahman and the world, seem to be opposed in features. Even though we repudiate the reality of saṁsāra and look upon it as a mere shadow, still there is the substance of which it is the shadow. The world of saṁsāra shows its unreality by its constant struggle to overreach itself, but the absolute Brahman is its own end, and looks to no end beyond itself. Since the world of saṁsāra is based on the absolute, the latter is sometimes said to be both the changeless and the changing. The endless details and the oppositions of the saṁsāra are there just to turn the mind in the direction where all oppositions are overcome and successions are embraced in a successionless consciousness. While all possible relatives and opposites are only based on it, it is not opposed to them, being their very substratum. We do not know how exactly the world of saṁsāra is based on the absolute Brahman, though we are sure that without the absolute there would be no saṁsāra. There is the silent sleeper as well as the seething sea. We do not know how exactly the two are related. We conceal our ignorance by the use of the word māyā. The two are one, yet they seem different, and the seeming is due to māyā. The transcendental reality, though untouched by the changes, still determines them. From the philosophical point of view we are obliged to stop here. "Who could perceive directly and who could declare whence born or why this variegated creation?"

The same problem when applied to the individual self becomes one of the relation of the free subject to the object. The bond between the immortal witness self and the flowing changes of consciousness, we do not know. Śaṁkara in this difficulty adopts the hypothesis of adhyāsa or superposition. The two, subject and object, cannot be related by way of saṁyoga or contact, since the subject is partless. The relation cannot be samavāya, or inseparable inherence, since the two are not related as cause and effect. Śaṁkara concludes, "that it must be of the nature of mutual adhyāsa, i.e. it consists in confounding them as well as their attributes with each other, owing to the absence of a discrimination between the nature of object and that of subject, like the union of mother-of-pearl and silver or of rope and snake when they are mistaken the one for the other owing to the absence of discrimination. The union of the two is itself apparent, mithyājñāna, and it vanishes when a man attains to right knowledge" [*The **Bhagavad-Gītā** with the Commentary of Sri Sankaracharya*]. This theory is not found in the ***Gītā,*** however much it may be implied by it.

The metaphysical idealism of the *Upaniṣads* is transformed in the ***Gītā*** into a theistic religion, providing room for love, faith, prayer and devotion. So long as we do not have the vision of the absolute, but are working from the side of the empirical world, we can account for it only on the theory of the supreme godhead of Puruṣottama. The impersonality of the absolute is not its whole significance for man. The ***Gītā,*** anxious to adapt the *Upaniṣad* idealism to the daily life of mankind, supports a divine activity and participation in nature. It tries to give us a God who satisfies the whole being of man, a real which exceeds the mere infinite and the mere finite. The supreme soul is the origin and cause of the world, the indivisible energy pervading all life. Moral attributes are combined with the metaphysical. The ***Gītā*** refuses to commit the fallacy of taking distinctions for divisions. It reconciles all abstract oppositions. Thought cannot act without *creating distinctions and reconciling them.* The moment we think the absolute, we have to translate the truth of intuition into terms of thought. Pure "being" is gone over into "nothing," and we have left in our hands a unity of being and nothing. This unity is as real as thought itself. Of course the ***Gītā*** does not tell us of the way in which the absolute as impersonal non-active spirit becomes the active personal Lord creating and sustaining the universe. The problem is considered to be intellectually insoluble. The mystery clears up only when we rise to the level of intuition. The transformation of the absolute into God is māyā or a mystery. It is also māyā in the sense that the transformed world is not so real as the absolute itself.

If through logic we try to understand the relation of the absolute to the world we assign to it a power or śakti. The inactive qualityless absolute, unrelated to any object, is converted by logic into the active personal Lord possessing power related to prakṛti or nature. We have "Nārāyaṇa brooding over the waters," the eternal "I" confronting the pseudo-eternal "not I." This latter is also called prakṛti or nature, since it generates the world. It is the source of delusion, since it hides the true nature of reality from mortal vision. The world is organically connected with the Puruṣottama. All things partake of the duality of being and non-being from Puruṣottama downwards. The element of negation is introduced into the absolute, and the unity is forced to unfold its inwardness in the process of becoming. The "ancient urge to action" is located in the heart of Puruṣottama. The original unity is pregnant with the whole course of the world, which contains the past, the present and the future in a supreme now. Kṛṣṇa shows to Arjuna the whole viśvarūpa (worldform) in one vast shape. In the radiance of eternity Arjuna sees nameless things, the form of Kṛṣṇa bursting the very bounds of existence, filling the whole sky and the universe, worlds coursing through him like cataracts. Contradiction constitutes the main spring of progress. Even God has the element of negativity or māyā, though He controls it. The supreme God puts forth His active nature or svāmprakṛtim and creates the jīvas, who work out their destinies along lines determined by their own nature. While all this is done by the supreme through his native power exercised in the perishable world, he has another aspect untouched by it all. He is the impersonal absolute as well as the immanent will. He is the causeless cause, the unmoved mover.

> He is within all beings—and without—
> Motionless, yet still moving; not discerned
> For subtlety of instant presence; close
> To all, to each; yet measurelessly far;

Not manifold, and yet subsisting still
In all which lives.
The light of lights, he is in the heart of the dark
Shining eternally.

The supreme is said to be possessed of two natures higher, parā, and lower, aparā, answering to the conscious and the unconscious aspects of the universe. The lower prakṛti produces effects and modifications in the world of nature or of causes; the higher prakṛti gives rise to the puruṣas, or the intelligent souls, in the world of ends or values. The two belong to one spiritual whole. Madhva cites a verse to this effect: "There are two prakṛtis for God, jaḍa, or unconscious, and ajaḍa, or conscious; the former is unmanifested prakṛti; the latter is Śrī or Lakṣmī, which upholds the former. She is the consort of Nārāyaṇa. With these two Hari creates the world." The ***Gītā*** accepts the Sāṁkhya theory of the evolution of the manifold from the homogeneous indeterminate matter, determined by the presence of spirit or puruṣa. Only the presence of puruṣa necessary to stimulate prakṛti to activity must be a real presence. It is therefore more correct to say that all activity is due to the combined effort of puruṣa and prakṛti, though the element of intelligence is more prominent in the subjective and that of matter in the objective world. Both of them form the nature of the one Supreme. They are the constitutive stuff of the world. That is why the Lord is said to be the support of the world as well as the all-illumining light of consciousness. The author of the ***Gītā*** does not describe the way in which the one nature of God manifests itself at one stage as unconscious matter, at another as conscious intelligence, and how these two products of one primal source appear to be antagonistic to each other during the course of the world progress.

While dwelling in man and nature the Supreme is greater than both. The boundless universe in an endless space and time rests in Him and not He in it. The expression of God may change, but in Him is an element which is self-identical, the permanently fixed background for the phenomenal alterations. The diversified existence does not affect His identity. "As the mighty air everywhere moving is rooted in space so all things are in Me." Yet space is space even without the "moving airs." The Lord is not tainted by the qualities of creation. The world as the expression of His nature does not detract from the self-sufficiency of God. Yet we cannot know the nature of God apart from the constitution of the world. If the identical principle is emptied of all content, of all that constitutes progress in knowledge and life, the God-in-Itself may become unknowable. It is also true that if we lose ourselves in the world, the reality may be hidden from our vision. It is necessary for us to know what God is independent of all relations to objects, and how He maintains Himself throughout all changes He brings about. Simply because relatedness to objects cannot be excluded, we need not think that the subject has no self-identity. If the expression is confused with the spirit, the ***Gītā*** theory will become one of cosmotheism. The author of the ***Gītā,*** however, explicitly repudiates such suggestions. The whole world is said to be sustained by one part of God, "ekāṁśena." In the tenth chapter Kṛṣṇa declares that He is manifesting only a portion of His endless glory. The immutability of the absolute and the activity of the Īśvara are both taken over in the conception of Puruṣottama.

[If] the hold which a work has on the mind of man is any clue to its importance, then the *Gītā* is the most influential work in Indian thought.

—S. Radhakrishnan

The personal Purusottama is from the religious point of view higher than the immutable self-existence untouched by the subjective and the objective appearances of the universe. He is looked upon as an impartial governor ever ready to help those in distress. Simply because He sometimes inflicts punishments we cannot call Him unjust or unkind. [In his *Commentary on the* ***Gītā***] Madhusūdana Sarasvati quotes a verse which reads: "Even as a mother is not unkind to her child whether she fondles or beats him, so also Īśvara, the determiner of good and evil, is not unkind." The impersonal absolute is envisaged as Puruṣottama for the purposes of religion. The idea of Puruṣottama is not a wilful self-deception accepted by the weak heart of man. While the dry light of reason gives us a featureless reality, spiritual intuition reveals to us a God who is both personal and impersonal. The principle of reconciliation is contained in the *Upaniṣads.* The Īśā *Upaniṣad* looks upon the real as both the mobile and the immobile. To dwell on either exclusively results in a darkness of knowledge or of ignorance. The ***Gītā*** tries to make a synthesis of the imperishable self and the changing experience. The supreme spiritual being with energy is Puruṣottama; the same in a state of eternal rest is Brahman. [In his *Commentary on the* ***Gītā***] Śaṁkarānanda quotes a verse which says: "There are two forms of Vāsudeva, the manifested and the unmanifested; the Parabrahman is the unmanifested, and the whole world of moving and unmoving things is the manifested." The Supreme has two aspects of the manifested and the unmanifested; the former is emphasised when prakṛti is assigned to its nature and Jīva is said to be a part of it. The stress is on the same side when Kṛṣṇa says: "Whatever is glorious, good, beautiful and mighty, understand that it all proceeds from a fragment of my splendour." When Kṛṣṇa calls upon us to become his devotees, when he shows the viśvarūpa, or the worldform, whenever he uses the first person, we have references to the manifested aspect of the Supreme. This side of divine nature is involved in the work of creation, where it loses itself in the succession of time and the waves of becoming. Beyond it all is another status, the silent and the immutable, than which there is nothing higher. The two together form the Puruṣottama. If we try to make out that the personal Lord is the highest metaphysical reality we get into trouble. "I will declare that in the object of knowledge, knowing which one reaches immortality, the highest Brahman, having no beginning or end, which cannot be said to be existent or non-existent."

The author of the ***Gītā*** frequently reminds us that the manifested aspect is a creation of his own mystic power, or yoga māyā. "The undiscerning ones, not knowing my transcendental and inexhaustible essence, than which there is nothing higher, think me, who am unperceived, to have become perceptible." On ultimate analysis the assumption of the form of Puruṣottama by the absolute becomes less than real. It is therefore wrong to argue that according to the ***Gītā*** the impersonal self is lower in reality than the personal Īśvara, though it is true that the ***Gītā*** considers the conception of a personal God to be more useful for religious purposes.

Before we pass on to the cosmology of the ***Gītā,*** we may note the relation between the conception of Puruṣottama and Kṛṣṇa, thus raising the question of the avatārs or incarnations.

Whether Kṛṣṇa is identical with Puruṣottama or only a limited manifestation of Him is a question on which there is difference of opinion. The theory of avatārs is mentioned in the ***Gītā.*** "Even though I am unborn and inexhaustible in my essence, even though I am Lord of all beings, still assuming control over my own prakṛti, I am born by means of my māyā." The avatārs are generally limited manifestations of the Supreme, though the Bhāgavata makes an exception in favour of Kṛṣṇa, and makes him a full manifestation, "Kṛṣṇas tu bhagavān svayam." The form given to him is indicative of his all-comprehensiveness. The peacock feathers of his head are the variegated colours which flood man's eyes. The colour of his complexion is that of the sky, the garland of wild flowers typifies the grandeur of the solar and the stellar systems. The flute he plays upon is that by which he gives forth his message. The yellow garment with which he decks his person is the halo of light which pervades space, the mark on his chest is the emblem of the devotion of the devotee which he proudly wears out of love to man. He stands in the devotee's heart, and so great is his grace to man that his feet, which symbolise it, are put one over the other so that they may have their full effect. Śaṁkara and Ānandagiri look upon Kṛṣṇa as only a partial manifestation of the supreme godhead. Kṛṣṇa, in the opinion of the author of the ***Gītā,*** is the Puruṣottama. "The foolish mistake me, clad in human form, ignorant of my supreme nature, the great Lord of all beings."

The theory of avatārs brings to mankind a new spiritual message. The avatārs are the militant gods struggling against sin and evil, death and destruction. "Whensoever righteousness languishes and unrighteousness is on the ascendant, I create myself. I am born age after age, for the protection of the good, for the destruction of the evildoers and the establishment of the law." It is an eloquent expression of the law of the spiritual world. If God is looked upon as the saviour of man, He must manifest Himself whenever the forces of evil threaten to destroy human values. According to Hindu mythology, whenever the forces of vice and wickedness, a Rāvaṇa or a Kaṁsa are in the ascendant, the representatives of the moral order, Indra, Brahmā, etc., along with Earth, which is said to suffer most, go to the court of Heaven and cry aloud for a world redeemer. The work of redemption, however, is a constant activity, though on occasions it becomes accentuated. The normal self-manifestation of God becomes emphatic when the world-order grows disproportionately evil. An avatār is a descent of God into man, and not an ascent of man into God. Though every conscious being is such a descent, it is only a veiled manifestation. There is a distinction between the self-conscious being of the divine and the same shrouded in ignorance. The human being is as good as an avatār, provided he crosses the māyā of the world and transcends his imperfection. The creator Puruṣottama is not separated from his creatures. The two do not exist apart. He is always fulfilling himself in the world. Man comes to full consciousness by actualising his potentiality. It becomes indifferent, then, whether we say God limits Himself in the form of man or man rises to God working through his nature. Yet an avatār generally means a God who limits Himself for some purpose on earth, and possesses even in His limited form the fullness of knowledge.

The philosophical intellect tries to relate the avatārs, or the ideals of perfection, to the great onward march of the world. The superior souls who focussed representative ages in their own selves became the embodiments of God in a special sense. These examples of men who established supremacy over their nature and made their outward substance reveal the God within are more effective for struggling individuals. From them can man take courage and try to grow into their stature. They are the moulds into which the seeking soul tries to cast itself, that it might grow towards God. What has been achieved by one man, a Christ or a Buddha, may be repeated in the lives of other men. The struggle towards the sanctifying of the earth or the revealing of the God-ideal has passed through several stages in the evolution on earth. The ten avatārs of Viṣṇu mark out the central steps. The growth in the sub-human or the animal level is emphasised in those of the fish, the tortoise and the boar. Next we have the transition between the animal and the human worlds in the man-lion. The development is not completely fulfilled when we come to the dwarf. The first stage of man is that of the brutish, violent, uncivilised Rāma with his axe, who devastates the rest of humanity; later we get the divine spiritual Rāma, who consecrates family life and affections, and Kṛṣṇa, who exhorts us to enter into the warfare of the world; and after him Buddha, who, full of compassion for all life, works for the redemption of mankind. Last of all we have the avatār yet to come, the militant God (Kalki) who fights evil and injustice with the sword in hand. Great crises in human progress are signalised by the appearance of avatārs.

THE WORLD OF CHANGE

To know the exact place of the māyā theory in the ***Gītā,*** it is necessary to distinguish the different senses in which the word is employed, and the exact bearings of the ***Gītā*** on them all. (1) If the supreme reality is unaffected by the events of the world, then the rise of these events becomes an inexplicable mystery. The author of the ***Gītā*** does not use the term māyā in this sense, however much it may be implied in his views. The conception of a beginningless, and at the same time unreal, avidyā causing the illusion of the world does not enter the mind of the author. (2) The personal Īśvara is said to combine within himself sat and asat, the immutability of Brahman as well as the mutation of becoming. Māyā is the power which enables him to produce mutable nature. It is śakti, or the energy of Īśvara, or ātmavibhūti, the power of self-becoming. Īśvara and māyā in this sense are mutually dependent and are both beginningless. This power of the supreme is called māyā in the ***Gītā.*** (3) Since the Lord is able to produce the universe by means of the two elements of His being, prakṛti and puruṣa, matter and consciousness, they are said to be māyā (higher and lower) of God. (4) Gradually māyā comes to mean the lower prakṛti, since puruṣa is said to be the seed which the Lord casts into the womb of prakṛti for the generation of the universe. (5) As the manifested world hides the real from the vision of the mortals, it is said to be delusive in its character. The world is not an illusion, though by regarding it as a mere mechanical determination of nature unrelated to God, we fail to perceive its divine essence. It becomes the source of delusion. The divine māyā becomes avidyāmāyā. It is so, however, only for us mortals, shut off from the truth; to God who knows it all and controls it, it is vidyāmāyā. Māyā to man is a source of trouble and misery, since it breeds a bewildering partial consciousness which loses hold of the full reality. God seems to be enveloped in the immense cloak of māyā. (6) Since the world is only an effect of God, who is the cause, and since everywhere the cause is more real than the effect, the world as effect is said to be less real than God the cause. This relative unreality of the world is confirmed by the self-contradictory nature of the process of becoming. There is a struggle of opposites in the world of experience, and the real is above all opposites.

There is, however, no indication that the changes of the world are only imaginary. Even Śaṁkara's non-dualism admits of real changes in the world; only the first change of Brahman into the world is regarded by him as an appearance, or vivarta. The world is a real emanation from the supreme Puruṣottama; only from the ultimate point of view it is not real, since it is ever at war with itself. The ***Gītā*** repudiates the view that "the world is untrue, without any fixed basis, devoid of any ruler, brought about by union caused by lust and nothing else." It follows that in the world we have a real development presided over by Īśvara. We cannot say that the ***Gītā*** looked upon the world as real only so long as we lived in it. There is no suggestion that the world is a troublous dream on the bosom of the infinite. While living in the world of becoming, it is possible, according to the ***Gītā,*** to possess the immortality of timeless self-existence. We have the supreme example of Puruṣottama, who makes use of the world undeluded by it. When we transcend māyā, time, space and cause do not fall away from us. The world does not disappear, but it only changes its meaning.

Puruṣottama is not a remote phenomenon in some supreme state beyond us all, but is in the body and heart of every man and thing. He maintains all existences in relation to one another. The world of souls and matter is the effect of his nature. God does not create the world out of a nothingness or a void, but from His own being. In the pralaya condition the whole world, including jīvas, exists in the divine in a subtle state. In the manifested state they are cut off from one another and forget their identity of source. All this is his sovereign yoga. The world is compared to a tree "with roof above and branches below." Prakṛti is a general feature of the world. The interminable antagonisms, the mutual devourings of the various forms of existence, the evolving, the differentiating, the organising and the vivifying of matter are all due to prakṛti. "Earth, water, fire, air, space, mind, buddhi or understanding, self-sense or ahaṁkāra are the eight-fold divisions of my prakṛti." This is God's lower nature. That which vitalises these and sustains the world is His higher. Rāmānuja writes: "The prakṛti, or the material nature of the universe, is an object of enjoyment; that which is other than this, which is insentient and object of enjoyment, is the life principle jīva, which is of a different order. It is the enjoyer of the lower one, and is in the form of intelligent souls." The ***Gītā*** supports Rāmānuja's view of reality, if we ignore its absolutist background and emphasise the idea of Puruṣottama with its dual nature of consciousness and matter. The metaphor of beads and string, according to Rāmānuja, points out how "the totality of intelligences and non-intelligent things, both in their state of cause and in the state of effect, which form my body, are like a number of gems on a string that hangs from me, who have my being in the Ātman."

The individual soul is said to be a portion of the lord, mamaivāṁśaḥ. Śaṁkara is not faithful to the intention of the author of the Gītā when he says that "aṁśa," or part, indicates an imaginary or apparent part only. It is a real form of Puruṣottama. Śaṁkara's position is correct if the reference is to the indivisible Brahman, who is partless, but then even Puruṣottama is imaginary, since there is in him an element of not-self. The actual individual is a kartṛ or doer; so he is not the pure immortal spirit, but the personal self, which is a limited manifestation of God. This portion is kept distinct on account of the form which it draws to itself, the senses and the mind. As the prakṛti has a definite magnitude, duration and vibration, even so does purusha acquire a definite extent and reach of consciousness. The universal is embodied in a limited context of a mental-vital-physical sheath. "Puruṣa joined with prakṛti enjoys the qualities born of nature and the cause of its birth, good or evil, is its connexion with the qualities."

THE INDIVIDUAL SELF

The individuals are subject to māyā, or delusion, being lost in outer appearances. Birth in the world of saṁsāra is the result of imperfection. Rotation in the circle of existence is inevitable so long as we are blind to the truth. We get rid of individuality when we transcend māyā and realise our true status. Any form the individual assumes is doomed to be superseded. The individual always tries to become something else. The infinite character cannot become fully explicit in any finite existence. It ever keeps on transcending its own finite self until the becoming reaches its end in being and the finite is taken over into the infinite. The finite world is an endless progress, an infinite perfectibility, an ever approximating approach to an ever-growing object of desire. It follows that all distinctions based on becoming and connexions with prakṛti are only transient. The eternality and plurality of puruṣas is assumed in the ***Gītā*** when its thought rests at the level of

Puruṣottama. The jīvas, then, are only distinct fragments of Puruṣottama individualised. From the standpoint of absolute truth, their individuality is dependent upon the object element. Even in this world those acts indicative of separate individuality are not due to the immortal actionless spirit, but are derived from the forces of prakṛti. "The qualities born of prakṛti constrain everybody to some action." If the puruṣas are eternal, it cannot be any delusion to think that they are the doers and are different from each other. The *Gītā* says: "He whose mind is deluded by egoism thinks himself the doer of actions which are wrought by the qualities of prakṛti." "Qualities move among qualities." It is a confusion with the object that is responsible for the false view of individuality. The basis of distinction is then not-self, while the self is the same in all, "dog or dog-eater." It is easy for Śaṁkara to press all these passages into the service of his non-dualism. He says: "Nor are there what are called ultimate particulars, or antyaviśeṣas, as the basis of individual distinctions in the self, since no evidence can be adduced to prove their existence in relation to the several bodies. Hence Brahman is homogeneous and one." We need not assume indefinable marks of individual identity to account for the distinctions of the world. Individuals are different because of their embodiments. As the *Mahābhārata* says: "A man bound up with guṇas is a jīvatma, or individual soul; when freed from them, he is paramātma, or supreme soul." Passages which proclaim the identity of the individual with the supreme are interpreted by Rāmānuja in a different way. For example, the declaration that "Brahman in each possesses hands and feet everywhere and envelops all" is taken by Rāmānuja to mean that "the purified nature of the Ātman, by virtue of its being devoid of the limitations of the body and such other objects, pervades all things." Again, when the *Gītā* says that the Puruṣa in each is "the witness, the permitter, the supporter, the enjoyer, the great lord and the supreme self," Rāmānuja is perplexed. "Such a puruṣa, by virtue of his connexion with guṇas, produced by the prakṛti, becomes the great ruler only with reference to this body, and the highest Ātman only with reference to this body."

From an occasional singular or plural usage we cannot draw any inference about the ultimate nature of the soul. When the stress is on the empirical side the plural number is used. "Never did I not exist, nor thou, nor these rulers of men; and no one of us will ever hereafter cease to exist." It is easy to infer from this a doctrine of the eternal plurality of souls. Rāmānuja observes: "the Lord Himself declares that the distinction of the self from the Lord as well as from other selves is the highest reality." Śaṁkara, on the other hand, urges "as the self, the Ātman, we are eternal in all the three periods of time (past, present and future)." He believes that the plural is used with reference to the bodies, which are different, as is clear from thc next verse relating to rebirth and not with reference to self. Metaphysically there is only one spirit.

The *Gītā* believes in rebirth until the ultimate state is reached. Birth following upon imperfection is bound to death, and vice versa. Birth and death occur as infancy, youth and age occur to a man's frame.

Nay, but as when one layeth
His wornout robes away
And taking new ones, sayeth
"These will I wear to-day."
So putteth by the spirit
Lightly its garb of flesh,
And passeth to inherit
A residence afresh.

Death only changes the scene. The instrument through which the player can express himself must be intact. The gradual failure of powers in old age, or their temporary failure in illness, though physical, reacts on the core of mind's being. When the body dies he is supplied with a new instrument. Our life does not die with us: when one body wears out it will take another. The kind of birth depends on the character we have developed. We are born in celestial regions, or as men on earth, or in the animal world, according as we develop character in which sattva, rajas or tamas predominates. Every step we gain is conserved for us. When Arjuna asks Kṛṣṇa about the fate of those who are not able to attain perfection, whether they go to ruin, Kṛṣṇa says that a man who does good never goes to ruin, but he obtains another birth "when he recovers the mental characteristics of his former life, and with them he again struggles onward for perfection." There is a conservation of all values. None can lose the way of the supreme if his heart is set on it. Rebirth continues till the goal is reached. The sūkṣma śarīra, or the subtle body, consisting of the senses and the mind, survives death and is the bearer of character. Rebirth is a discipline by which we can perfect ourselves. There is also a reference to the path of the gods through which the saṁsārins pass. The third path of the sinful is also mentioned.

ETHICS

The distinctness of particular persons, their finiteness and individuality, are only accidental, and do not represent the underlying truth. The individual will not gain the secret of peace, stable and secure, until he breaks down his apparent self-completeness and independence. True freedom means self-transcendence or union with the highest through logic, love or life. The end we seek is becoming Brahman or touching the eternal, *brahmasaṁsparśam.* This is the only absolute value.

It is in the power of all to destroy evil, to eliminate the corruption of the flesh, to redeem the lower nature and rescue the senses from bondage to passion. Each struggling individual will have to make a sustained endeavour to look into the truth with his own eyes, judge with his own reason, and love with his own heart. A half-truth won for ourselves is worth more than a whole truth learned from others.

Man is a complex of reason, will and emotion, and so seeks the true delight of his being through all these. He can reach the end by a knowledge of the supreme reality, or by love and adoration of the supreme person, or by the subjection of his will to the divine purpose. There is the impulse in him forcing him to get beyond his little self in these different directions. The end is the same whichever standpoint we adopt. It is the harmonious efficiency of the several sides of our life by which truth is attained, beauty created and conduct perfected. The ***Gītā*** is emphatic that no side of conscious life can be excluded. The several aspects reach their fulfilment in the integral divine life. God himself is sat, cit and ānanda, reality, truth and bliss. The absolute reveals itself to those seeking for knowledge as the Eternal Light, clear and radiant as the sun at noon-day in which is no darkness; to those struggling for virtue as the Eternal Righteousness, steadfast and impartial; and to those emotionally inclined as Eternal Love and Beauty of Holiness. Even as God combines in Himself wisdom, goodness and holiness, so should men aim at the integral life of spirit. The obstructions of the road are not operative when we reach the end. It is true that in the finite life of the individual there seems to be some kind of antagonism between contemplation and action. This is only a sign of our imperfection. When Kṛṣṇa is asked about the particular method to be adopted, he clearly says that we need not worry about this question, since the different pathways are not ultimately distinct, but lead to the same goal, and are found together in the end though they cross and recross one another on the road. Man does not function in fractions. Progress is correlated and not dissociated development. Knowledge, feeling and will are different aspects of the one movement of the soul.

The ***Gītā*** tries to harmonise the different ideals of life current at the time and correct their extravagances. Intellectual inquiry, strenuous self-sacrifice, fervent devotion, ceremonial observance and yogic exercises were looked upon as affording access to the divine. The ***Gītā*** synthesises them all and shows the exact place and value of each of them. It believes in the effectiveness of a combined attack. The harmonising ideal which all these different methods have in view is the increasing solidarity of the individual with the universe presided over by Puruṣottama.

Madhusūdana Sarasvatī considers that the ***Gītā*** adopts the three methods indicated in the *Upaniṣads,* karma or work, upāsana or worship, and jñāna or wisdom, and devotes six chapters to each in succession. Whatever be the truth of it, it emphasises the three great divisions of conscious life. The ***Gītā*** recognises that different men are led to the spiritual vision by different approaches, some by the perplexities of the moral life, some by the doubts of the intellect, and some by the emotional demands for perfection.

JNANA MARGA

The logical mind, unable to acquiesce in the partial, tries to grasp the totality of things, and finds no rest until it is anchored in the truth. It is buoyed up by the undying faith in its destiny to acquire supreme truth. The ***Gītā*** recognises two kinds of knowledge, that which seeks to understand the phenomena of existence externally through intellect, and that which by the force of intuition grasps the ultimate principle behind the apparent series. When subject to the logical intellect, the spirit of man tends to lose itself in nature and identify itself with its activities. To grasp the truth of existence in its source and reality within, it has to free itself from the snare of false identification. The intellectual apprehension of the details of existence is called vijñāna, as distinct from jñāna, or the integral knowledge of the common foundation of all existence. These two are only different sides of one pursuit. All knowledge is knowledge of God. Science and philosophy both try to realise the truth of the oneness of things in the eternal spirit. Scientific knowledge is said to be dominated by rajas, while spiritual knowledge is permeated by the quality of sattva. If we mistake the partial truths of science for the whole truth of spirit, we have the inferior knowledge, where the lowest quality of tamas predominates. The truth of the soul is a hypothesis so long as we are at the level of science. The endless becoming covers up the being. Science dispels the darkness oppressing the mind, shows up the incompleteness of its own world, and prepares the mind for something beyond it. It stimulates humility, since by its means we cannot know all. We are hemmed in between the forgetfulness of what was and the uncertainty of what shall be. To indulge in the imaginative desire to become acquainted with the first causes of things and the destiny of mankind, science admits, is a vain pursuit. If we want to get at the ultimate truth science has to be supplemented by another discipline. The ***Gītā*** holds that paripraśna, or investigation, is to be combined with service, or sevā. For the development of the intuitive power we require a turning of the mind in another direction, a conversion of the soul. Arjuna could not see the truth with his naked eyes, and so asked for the divine sight or spiritual vision. The viśvarūpa is a poetic exaggeration of the intuitional experience where the individual possessed by God sees all things in Him. The ***Gītā*** believes that for attaining this spiritual vision the individual should learn to live within and fix his mind on the highest reality. What hides the truth from our vision is not merely the fault of intellect, but also the passion of selfishness. Ajñāna is not intellectual error, but spiritual blindness. To remove it we must cleanse the soul of the defilement of the body and the senses, and kindle the spiritual vision which looks at things from a new angle. The fire of passion and the tumult of desire must be suppressed. The mind, inconstant and unstable, must be steadied into an unruffled lake, that it might mirror the wisdom from above. Buddhi, or the power of understanding and discrimination, needs to be trained. The way in which this power operates depends on our past habits. We should so train it as to bring it into agreement with the spiritual view of the universe.

It is as a means of mental training that the ***Gītā*** accepts the yoga system. The yoga discipline gives the directions by which we can lift ourselves from our mutable personality into a super-normal attitude, where we possess the key which is the secret of the whole play of relations. The essential steps of the yogic discipline are: (1) purification of mind, body and senses, that the divine may take possession of them; (2) concentration or withdrawal of the consciousness from the dispersed movement of thoughts running after the senses and fixing it on the Supreme; and (3) identification with the real when we reach it. The ***Gītā*** is not so very systematic as Patañjali's *Sūtras,* though the different sādhanas or instruments are referred to.

The ***Gītā*** offers us certain general principles acceptable to thinkers of all shades of opinion. We are asked to have faith or śraddhā, subdue the riotous impulses and hold fast in thought to God. An atmosphere of stillness and calm is necessary for the spiritual vision. In the silence following the firm control of the mind we can hear the voice of the soul. The true yoga is that which brings about spiritual impartiality, or samatvam. "Where the mind flickereth not like a lamp in a sheltered spot; where seeing the self by the self, one is satisfied in himself; where one experiences the absolute bliss known only to understanding, but ever beyond the senses, and standing where one swerves not from the truth; where no other gain is considered greater, and, where placed, one is not moved by the greatest pain—that state free from misery is yoga." It is not necessary for all to practise yoga in order that they may attain the spiritual insight. Madhusūdana Sarasvatī quotes a verse from *Vaśiṣtha:* "To suppress mind with its egoism, etc., yoga and jñāna are the two means. Yoga is the suppression of mental activity (vṛttinirodha), and jñāna is true comprehension (saṁyagavekṣaṇam). For some yoga is not possible, for others jñāna is not possible." The spiritual intuition may also be helped by work and worship.

While admitting the relevancy of the yoga discipline for spiritual training in some cases, the ***Gītā*** is not unconscious of its dangers. By mere fasting and such other methods we may only weaken the powers of the senses, while our relish for sense-objects may be intact. What is wanted is control of senses and indifference to the attractions of material objects. This is possible only with the rise of knowledge.

Spiritual intuition which is more perceptual in character is not uncritical conviction. It is supported by scientific judgment. It is a union of knowledge with austerity and passion, the most complete experience that we can possibly have, where we have no more confusion of mind, but enjoy true peace and rest of spirit.

When once the fullness of cognitive experience is reached, the other sides of consciousness, emotion and will, make themselves felt. The vision of God in the spiritual illumination is attained in an atmosphere of joy. The whole life-aspiration becomes one continuous adoration of the infinite. The knower is also a devotee and the best of them. "He who knows me worships me." To know the truth is to lift up our hearts to the Supreme, touch Him and adore Him. There is also a practical influence. The more profoundly we are conscious of our true nature, the deeper is our insight into the real needs of others. The good becomes "not merely the keystone of knowledge, but the polestar of conduct" in the famous phrase of Nettleship. We have the example of Buddha, the greatest jñāni or seer, whose love for humanity led to his ministry of mankind for forty years.

It is sometimes argued that knowledge or intelligence is indifferent to morality. Intelligence is not an essential part of character. Intellectually we make only mistakes or errors of judgment; morally we do wrong. The intellect is neither good nor bad, since it can be used to promote or destroy good life. All this may be true of our analytic understanding. Jñāna, or the wisdom of the ***Gītā,*** carries us beyond one-sided views and narrow standpoints to the comprehensive truth, where we feel that the differences between men are not ultimate, and that no conduct which is based on false distinctions can be good. We see that the lives of men have a common root, and that a self-existent eternal spirit is living and operating in all individual lives. When this truth is perceived, sense and self lose their power.

BHAKTI MARGA

The Bhakti mārga, or the path of devotion, indicates the law of the right activity of the emotional side of man. Bhakti is emotional attachment distinct from knowledge or action. Through it we offer our emotional possibilities to the divine. Emotion expresses a living relation between individuals, and becomes instinct with the force of religious feeling when it binds God and man. If we do not love and worship, we become shut within the prison of our own egoism. This way, when rightly regulated, leads us to the perception of the Supreme. It is open to all, the weak and the lowly, the illiterate and the ignorant, and is also the easiest. The sacrifice of love is not so difficult as the tuning of the will to the divine purpose or ascetic discipline, or the strenuous effort of thinking. It is quite as efficacious as any other method, and is sometimes said to be greater than others, since it is its own fruition, while others are means to some other end.

The origin of the Bhakti mārga is hidden in the mists of long ago. The upāsana theory of the *Upaniṣads* and the devotional way of the Bhāgavatas have influenced the author of the ***Gītā.*** He struggles to develop an order of ideas belonging to the religious level of the *Upaniṣads* to which they were not able to give free and unambiguous utterance. The absolute becomes in the ***Gītā*** "the understanding of them that understand, the splendour of the splendid," the first of gods and men, the chief of the ṛṣis, as well as death which ravishes all. Admitting that meditation of the unmanifested absolute leads to the goal, Kṛṣṇa urges that it is a hard process. It offers no foothold for the finite man from which he could approach it. The love which we feel for an object involves an element of separateness. However closely love may unite, the lover and the beloved remain distinct. We have to rest content with a dualism even as thought does; but it is not correct to describe the monism which transcends the dualism as a descent to a lower grade. Devotion to the Supreme is possible only with a personal God, a concrete individual full of bliss and beauty. We cannot love a shadow of our minds. Personality implies a capacity for fellowship, or communion, or a feeling together. There is the personal need for a personal helper. So God, into whose being the heart of love enters, is not the God who revels in bloodshed, not one who sleeps in serene abstraction while hearts heavy-laden cry out for help. He is love. He who gives up his whole to God and falls at His feet finds the gates of spirit lie open. The voice of God declares, "This is My word of promise, that he who loveth Me shall not perish."

It is not a rigid law of recompense that binds God to the world. The consequences of deeds may be averted by means of devotion to God. This is no supersession of the law of karma, since the law requires that even devotion should have its reward. Kṛṣṇa says: "Even if a man of evil conduct turns to me with a sole and entire love, he must be regarded as a saint," because he has turned to God with a settled will, and has therefore become a soul of righteousness. The Lord by Himself does not receive the sin or the merit of any. Yet He has so arranged the scheme of things, that nothing happens without producing its effect. In a sense it is true that "the Lord enjoys all sacrifices and penances." It is in this way that we have to reconcile apparently contradictory views expressed in passages like "none is hateful to Me and none dear," and "the devotees are dear to Me." Man is the object of God's constant care.

The nature of love towards God or bhakti is indescribable even "as the taste of the dumb person." The essential features of this emotional attachment may, however, be stated. There is the adoration of something looked upon as absolutely perfect. Since the object is perfection, nothing less than the highest conceivable will do. Nārada in his sūtras brings in the analogy of human love, where also the finite individual transcends himself and reaches out towards an ideal. Only the ideal very frequently reveals its actual nature. The object of devotion is the highest being, or Puruṣottama. He is the illuminator of souls as well as the vivifier of the world. God is not to be identified with the different elements which seem to be the ultimate realities at a lower level, nor is He the lord of sacrifices as the Mīmāṁsakas imagine. He is not to be confused with the several personal agencies which the mind of man attributes to the natural forces. He is not the puruṣa of the Sāṁkhyas. He is all these and more. The author of the ***Gītā*** emphasises how God lives in each individual. If the Supreme were quite foreign to the individual consciousness, He could not be an object of worship; if He were absolutely identical with the individual, even then worship is not possible. He is partly the same as and partly different from the individual. He is the divine Lord associated with prakṛti or Lakṣmī, in whose hands lies the treasure of desirable things. The prospect of union with Him is a vision of delight. "Fix thy mind in Me, into Me let thy understanding enter; thou shalt surely live with Me alone hereafter." All other love is only an imperfect manifestation of this supreme love. We love other things for the sake of the eternal in them. The devotee has a sense of utter humiliation. In the presence of the ideal he feels that he is nothing, and such an utter prostration of the self is the indispensable pre-requisite of true religious devotion. God loves meekness. The individual feels himself to be worthless apart from God. His devotion expresses itself as either love for God (prīti), or misery due to the absence of God (viraha). The self cannot but reject itself as worthless dross when it discovers the supreme value of the object to which it attaches itself. The devotee throws himself entirely on the mercy of God. Absolute dependence is the only way. "Merge thy mind in Me, be My devotee, prostrate thyself before Me, thou shalt come even unto Me. I pledge thee My troth, thou art dear to Me. Abandoning all dharmas, come unto Me alone for shelter; sorrow not, I will liberate thee from all sins." God insists on undivided devotion, and assures us that He will take up our knowledge and our error and cast away all forms of insufficiency and transform all into His infinite light and the purity of the universal good. Again, there is the continual desire to serve the ideal. The devotee "looks only on the object of his devotion, talks only about Him and thinks only of Him." Whatever he does he does for the glory of God. His work is absolutely unselfish, since it is indifferent to its fruits. It is an utter self-giving to the transcendent. When the devotee surrenders himself completely into the hands of the ideal, we do not have a blind intensity of feeling. It is an open-armed surrender in which feeling is displaced by life. God becomes the ruling passion of the mind. The devotee reaches his end, becomes immortal and satisfied in himself. He does not desire anything, sorrows not; he is filled with joy and peace—rapt in the spirit. Bhakti, or true devotion, according to the ***Gītā,*** is to believe in God, to love Him, to be devoted to Him and to enter into Him. It is its own reward.

For the true bhakti, we require first of all Śraddhā or faith. The highest reality has to be assumed or taken on faith till it reveals itself in the devotee's consciousness. Since faith is a vital element, the gods in whom the people have faith are tolerated. In view of the unlimited variety of the habits and minds of men, liberty of thought and worship is allowed to the individual. Some love is better than none, for if we do not love, we become shut up within ourselves. The infinite presents itself to the human soul in a variety of aspects. The lower gods are forms or aspects of the one Supreme. The ***Gītā*** ranks the avatārs of the divine as lower than Puruṣottama; Brahmā, Viṣṇu and Śiva, if they are not names for the Supreme acting as creator, preserver and destroyer, are also subordinated to Puruṣottama. The worship of *Vedic* gods is admitted. Out of a feeling of pity, the ***Gītā*** allows freedom to the multitudes worshipping kṣudra, devatas or petty divinities. So long as worship is done with devotion it purifies the heart and prepares the mind for the higher consciousness.

The philosophical justification of this tolerant attitude is suggested though not worked out. A man is what his thoughts are. Whatever he has faith in, that he will attain to. The world is a purposive moral order, where the individual obtains what he desires. "Those who make vows to the gods go to the gods; those who make vows to manes go to them." "Whichever form any worshipper wishes to worship with faith, to that form I render his faith steady. Possessed of that faith, he seeks to propitiate that deity, and obtains from it those beneficial things which are really given by Me." As Rāmānuja observes: "From Brahmā to a post, all things that live in the world are subject to birth and death caused by karma, therefore they cannot be helpful as objects of meditation." Only the true Lord Puruṣottama can serve as the object of devotion. The lower forms are stepping-stones to it. In chapter x we are called upon to fix our mind on particular objects and persons displaying power and grandeur to an extraordinary degree. This is called pratīka upāsana. In chapter xi the whole universe assumes the form of God. In chapter xii we dwell on the presiding God. Only the highest can give us freedom. Other devotees reach finite ends, while the devotees of the Supreme reach infinite bliss [Madhva's commentary on the ***Gita***].

The forms which bhakti takes are contemplation of God's power, wisdom and goodness, constant remembrance of Him with a devout heart, conversing about His qualities with other persons, singing His praises with fellow-men and doing all acts as His service. No fixed rules can be laid down. By these different movements the human soul draws near to the divine. Several symbols and disciplines are devised to train the mind to turn godward. Absolute devotion to God is not possible unless we give up our desires for sense-objects. So yoga is sometimes adopted. The impulse may take any form of adoration, from external worship to a periodical reminder to free us from the preoccupations of life. The ***Gītā*** asks us sometimes to think of God, excluding all other objects. This is a negative method. It also requires us to look upon the whole world as a supreme manifestation of God. We have to realise God in nature and self, and so regulate our conduct as to make it expressive of the divine in man. Supreme devotion and complete self-surrender, or bhakti and prapatti, are the different sides of the one fact. The ***Gītā*** recognises that the one infinite God can be approached and worshipped through any of His aspects. This tolerant spirit has made Hinduism a synthesis of different kinds of worship and experience, an atmosphere unifying many cults and creeds, a system of thought or a spiritual culture based on the fact that the one truth has many sides.

In the highest fulfilment of devotion, we possess a sense of certitude about the object. The experience is self-certifying in character. It is its own proof, svayam pramāṇam. Logical discussions are not of much avail. The true devotees do not worry about vain discussions concerning God. This is the highest kind of bhakti, from which there is no transition to anything else. It is devotion that is endless, *nirantara,* unmotived *nirhetuka.* Few there are who are willing to serve God for naught. The ***Gītā*** has not the weakness of emotional religions which deny knowledge and will for the sake of love. While all devotees are dear to the Lord, the possesser of wisdom is the dearest of all. The other three classes of devotees, the suffering, the seeker of knowledge and the selfish, may have petty aims and cease to love God when their desires are fulfilled, but the seer worships Him ever in purity of spirit. Bhakti, or intense love for God, becomes then a fire, scorching, burning and consuming all limits of individuality. The vision of truth is revealed. Without this restraint of the spiritual truth, the ***Gītā*** religion might lapse into emotionalism, and devotion itself might become a mere carnival of feeling.

What begins as quiet prayer, a longing for the sight of the beloved, ends in an irresistible rapture of love and delight. The worshipper becomes incorporate with God's being. He feels the force of the truth of the oneness of God in the universe. "Vāsudevaḥ sarvam iti." He escapes from the loneliness of life and the insignificance of a world where he was a mere particular to one where he becomes the instrument of the central Spirit. The largest human personality is only a partial expression of it. The genuine nature of each individual is the eternal spirit revealing itself in time and space. Knowledge and devotion become interdependent. True devotion issues in unselfish conduct. The devotee is consumed by an all-embracing beneficent love that seeks not its own or any return for its overflowing. It is like the divine love that brought the universe into being, maintains it and lifts it up to itself. Not the devotee but the power of spirit acts in him in a divine freedom. Absolute self-surrender and the dedication of all work to God mark the conduct of the true devotee. He has thus in him the content of the highest philosophy as well as the energy of the perfect man. Though here and there we come across passionate souls who do not worry about the affairs of the world, still the ideal devotee of the ***Gītā*** is one in whom love is lighted up by knowledge and bursts forth into a fierce desire to suffer for mankind. Tilak quotes a śloka from Viṣṇu Purāṇa, which says: "Those who give up their duties and sit down uttering the name Kṛṣṇa, Kṛṣṇa, are really the enemies of God and sinners. Even the Lord took birth in the world for the sake of righteousness."

It is obvious that for those who insist on devotion as the final nature of spiritual life, the end is not an immersion in the eternal impersonal, but a union with the Purushottama. The ***Gītā,*** however, recognises nirguṇa bhakti, or devotion to the qualityless, as superior to all else. Then the absolute becomes the most ultimate category. When devotion is perfected, then the individual and his God become suffused into one spiritual ecstasy, and reveal themselves as aspects of one life. Absolute monism is therefore the completion of the dualism with which the devotional consciousness starts.

KARMA MARGA

Through divine service or karma we can also reach the highest. Karma is act or deed, even that by which the impersonal becomes personal. Karma is said to be beginningless, and the exact manner by which the work of the world proceeds is hard to understand. At the end of creation the whole world is said to lie in the form of a subtle karma seed ready to sprout again at the next start. Since the world process is dependent upon the Lord, we can call Him the lord of karma. We are committed to some action or other. It is necessary to see to it that our conduct promotes the interests of righteousness, which at the same time results in spiritual rest and satisfaction. Karma mārga is the path of conduct by which the individual thirsting for service can reach the goal.

At the time of the ***Gītā*** many different views of right conduct prevailed, viz. the Vedic theory of the observance of rites and ceremonies, the Upaniṣad doctrine of a search after truth, the Buddhistic idea of the giving up of all actions and the theistic view of the worship of God. The ***Gītā*** tries to round them all into a consistent system.

The ***Gītā*** recognises that it is through work that we are brought into relation with the rest of the world. The problem of morality has significance only in the human world. The self of man alone of the objects of the world possesses a sense of responsibility. The individual aspires after spiritual happiness, but he cannot derive it from the material elements of the world. The pleasure which he strives after is of different kinds. What is derived from a deluded mind and false desires has more of tamas in it; what is derived from the senses has more of rajas, and the pleasure of self-knowledge has more of sattva in it. The highest satisfaction can come only when the individual ceases to look upon himself as an independent agent and feels that God in His infinite grace guides the world. The spirit in man is satisfied if it sees the spirit in the world. Good work is that which helps us to the liberation of the individual and the perfection of spirit.

Right conduct is whatever expresses our real unity with

God, man, and nature; wrong conduct is whatever does not bring out this essential structure of reality. The unity of the universe is the basic principle. Good is whatever advances towards completeness, and evil is whatever is inconsistent with it. This is the essential difference between Buddhism and the ***Gītā.*** Buddhism no doubt made morality central to the good life, but it did not sufficiently emphasise the relation of moral life to spiritual perfection or the purpose of the universe. In the ***Gītā*** we are assured that even though we may fail in our efforts, the central divine purpose can never be destroyed. It points out that the soul of the world is just, in spite of all appearances to the contrary. The individual fulfils his destiny when he becomes the instrument of the increasing purpose of God.

The finite centres should look upon themselves as members of an organism and work for the sake of the whole. The false claim to absoluteness and the wrong view that his independence is limited by that of others should be abandoned. The true ideal is lokasaṁgraha, or the solidarity of the world. The spirit of the whole works in the world. The good man should co-operate with it and aim at the welfare of the world. The ***Gītā*** repudiates the notion of individual claims. The best people have the largest burdens to bear. The venture of finite beings implies evil that has to be overcome. We cannot shrink from the task of fighting sin and injustice. The hesitating Arjuna was persuaded by Kṛṣṇa to fight, not for love of glory or lust of kingdom, but for the sake of the law of righteousness; but when we fight injustice we should do so, not in passion or ignorance which brings grief and disquiet, but in knowledge and with love for all.

Sense control becomes a characteristic of the good man. Passion imprisons our spiritual nature. It deadens discretion and fetters reason. To give full rein to the untamed impulses is to enslave the soul dwelling in the body. The ***Gītā*** requires us to develop a spirit of detachment and indifference to the results of action, the spirit of yoga, or impartiality. True renunciation consists in this. Giving up acts out of ignorance is tyāga mixed with tamas; giving up acts out of fear of consequences such as bodily suffering is tyāga with rajas in it; doing work in a spirit of detachment without fear of consequences is the best form, since it has more of sattva in it.

It is necessary to understand the exact bearing of the ***Gītā*** on the question of work. It does not support an ascetic ethics. The Buddhistic theory of inaction is interpreted in a more positive way. True inaction is action without any hope of reward. Analysing the nature of the act of karma, the ***Gītā*** distinguishes the mental antecedents from the outer deed, and calls upon us to control the former by suppressing all selfishness. Naiṣkarmya, or abstention from action, is not the true law of morality, but niṣkāma, or disinterestedness. Passion, anger and covetousness, the three ways to hell, are to be overcome. All desires are not bad. The desire after righteousness is divine. The ***Gītā,*** instead of demanding a rooting out of our passions, asks for a purifying of them. The physical-vital nature is to be cleansed, the mental-intellectual nature is to be purified, and then the spiritual nature finds its satisfaction. The ***Gītā*** is certain that inertia is not liberty. "Nor indeed can embodied beings completely relinquish action."

> The eye cannot choose but see,
> We cannot bid the ear be still,
> Our bodies feel where'er they be
> Against or with our will.
> [William Wordsworth]

Rest is not on earth; it is all life for ever. Work keeps up the circuit of the world, and each individual should try his best to keep it going. The whole setting of the ***Gītā*** points out that it is an exhortation to action. Work is inevitable till we attain freedom. We have to work for the sake of freedom, and when we attain it, we have to work as instruments of the divine. Then, of course, there is no more work necessary for preparing the mind or purifying the heart. The freed souls have no rules to obey, they do what they please, but the vital point is they do something.

The ***Gītā*** asks us to act in a way when action does not bind. The Lord Himself acts for the sake of humanity. Though from the absolute standpoint He is self-contained and desireless, He has always something to accomplish in the world. Even so is Arjuna asked to fight and do his work. The free souls have also the obligation to help others to discover the divine in themselves. Service of humanity is worship of God. To work desirelessly and impersonally for the sake of the world and God does not bind us. "Nor do these works bind Me, enthroned on high, unattached to actions." The ***Gītā*** draws a distinction between sannyāsa and tyāga: "Sannyāsa is renouncing all interested works; tyāga is giving up the fruit of all work." The latter is more comprehensive. The ***Gītā*** does not ask us to abhor the common business of life, but demands the suppression of all selfish desires. It is a combination of pravṛtti, or work, and nivṛtti, or withdrawal, that the ***Gītā*** upholds. Mere withdrawal is not true renunciation. The hands may be at rest, but the desires may be busy. What binds is not work, but the spirit in which it is done. "The giving up of karmas by the ignorant is really a positive act; the work of the wise is really inaction." The inner life of spirit is compatible with active life in the world. The ***Gītā*** reconciles the two in the spirit of the *Upaniṣads.* Action in the way indicated by the ***Gītā*** is skilled action. "Yogaḥ karmasu kauśalam," yoga is skill in works.

Whatever we do has to be done not in subjection to an external law, but in obedience to the inner determination of the soul's freedom. This is the highest kind of action. Aristotle says [in his *Ethics*]: "He is best who acts on his own convictions, while he is second best who acts in obedience to the counsel of others." To the unregenerate the scriptures are the authority. The injunctions of the *Vedas* are only external, and do not bind us when we reach the highest condition, where we act naturally in accordance with the law of spirit.

All work has to be done in purity of motive. We have to exclude from our minds subtle shades of selfishness, preferences for special forms of work, desire for sympathy and applause. Good karma, if it is to purify the mind and lead us to wisdom, should be performed in this spirit. The selfish egoist who looks upon himself as a god on earth and hunts after sense-pleasures is a demon adopting materialism in metaphysics and sensualism in ethics.

The theory of the guṇas or qualities plays an important part in the ***Gītā*** ethics. The bondage to guṇas causes the feeling of limitedness. The bonds belonging to mind are erroneously attributed to the self. Though action saturated with sattva is said to be the best kind of action, it is also urged that even sattva binds, since a nobler desire brings about a purer ego. For full freedom all egoism should cease. The ego, however pure it may be, is an obstructing veil and binds itself to knowledge and bliss. Getting beyond all qualities and occupying an impersonal cosmic outlook form the ideal state.

The ***Gītā*** transforms the Vedic theory of sacrifices and reconciles it with true spiritual knowledge. The outer gift is a symbol of the inner spirit. The sacrifices are attempts to develop self-restraint and self-surrender. The true sacrifice is the sacrifice of the sense delights. The god to whom we offer is the great Supreme, or the Yajña Puruṣa, the lord of sacrifices. We have to feel that all objects are divinely appointed means for the realisation of the highest ends and engage ourselves in work, resigning it all to God. Whether we eat or drink or whatsoever we do we should do all to the glory of God. A yogin always acts in God, and his conduct becomes a model for imitation by others.

The ***Gītā*** lays down several general principles for the regulation of human conduct. The golden mean is advised in some passages. The ***Gītā*** recognises the caste divisions as well as the theory of the stages of life. Men on a lower level of feeling and thought cannot all of a sudden be lifted up into a higher state. The humanising process takes a long time, sometimes several generations. The ***Gītā*** broadly distinguishes four fundamental types of individuals answering to the four stages of the upward ascent. Basing caste on qualities, the ***Gītā*** requires each individual to do the duties imposed by his caste. Svadharma is the work in agreement with the law of one's being. We worship God by doing our ordained duties. God intends every man for some work in connexion with society. The constitution of the social order is said to be divine. Plato supports an analogous doctrine [in his *Laws*]. "The ruler of the universe has ordered all things with a view to the excellence and preservation of the whole, and each part, as far as may be, has an action and passion appropriate to it . . . for every physician and every skilled artist does all things for the sake of the whole, directing this effort toward the common good, executing the part for the sake of the whole, and not the whole for the sake of the part." Though originally framed on the basis of qualities, caste very soon became a matter of birth. It is hard to know who has which qualities. The only available test is birth. The confusion of birth and qualities has led to an undermining of the spiritual foundation of caste. There is no necessity why men of a particular birth should always possess the character expected of them. Since the facts of life do not answer to the logical ideal, the whole institution of caste is breaking down. While it is easy to condemn the system from our present-day knowledge, we have to recognise in fairness to it that it attempted to build a society on a basis of mutual goodwill and co-operation and remedy the dangers of a competitive view of society. It recognised the supremacy not of wealth, but of wisdom, and its judgment of values is correct.

The last of the four stages is that of sannyāsa, where the individual is called upon to withdraw from life. This stage, it is sometimes said, is to be entered on when the body is shrinking and the subject feels unfit for work. True sannyāsa is the giving up of selfish desires, and this is possible even while we live as householders. It is not right to say that, in the view of the ***Gītā,*** we cannot attain mokṣa or freedom unless we resort to the last stage of sannyāsa.

Action performed in the spirit indicated by the ***Gītā*** finds its completion in wisdom. Egoism is eliminated and a sense of the divine is kindled. If we do the will we shall know of the doctrine. In that stage there is also a heartfelt devotion to the divine. Thus karma mārga leads us to a condition where emotion, knowledge and will are all present.

From our account it is clear that the path of service leads to mokṣa; only it is not karma in the sense of the Pūrva Mīmāṁsā. *Vedic* sacrifices do not lead us to freedom. They have only an instrumental use. They prepare the mind for higher wisdom. But karma performed as a sacrifice to God, and in a spirit of disinterestedness and impersonality, is quite as efficacious as any other method, and there is no need to subordinate it to the method of wisdom as Śaṁkara does, or that of devotion as Rāmānuja believes. In the interests of their own views, they make out that it was only to flatter Arjuna and coax him into action that Kṛṣṇa declares the path of karma to be superior. We cannot suppose that Arjuna was called upon to act with a lie in his soul. Nor is he an ajñānin who has to work for the sake of purifying his mind and heart. It is not possible for us to look upon Janaka, Kṛṣṇa and others as persons who indulge in works because they are men of imperfect wisdom. Nor is there need to think that after attaining wisdom there is no possibility for work. Janaka says that the true preaching was declared to him, which was to do karma, after killing selfish desires by wisdom. Even Śaṁkara allows that after the attainment of wisdom some karmas are necessary to sustain the body. If some acts are allowed, it is only a question of degree how much the freed soul does. If the individual is afraid of becoming once again subject to karma, it means that his sense-control is not perfect. Even if we believe that as Brahman is different from the world, so is Ātman from the body, there is nothing to prevent the body from performing acts. The ***Gītā,*** however, admits that men are of different temperaments, and some are inclined to withdrawal and others to service, and they will have to act according to the law of their own being.

Before we pass from this section it is necessary to note the views of the ***Gītā*** on the question of human freedom. The will of man seems to be determined by past nature, heredity, training and environment. The whole world seems to converge in the nature of the individual. Except indirectly, the determination by nature cannot be called an ordinance of God. "All existences follow their nature, and what shall coercing it avail?" Human effort seems to be vain, since God in the centre of things seems to whirl all individuals "as if mounted on a machine." If the will determined by nature were all, there is no human freedom. The Buddhists declare that there is no self, but only karma acts. The ***Gītā*** recognises a soul superior to the mechanically determined will. Whatever may be the truth of the ultimate state of the soul, when freed from bondage to nature, at the moral level it has a separate independent existence. The ***Gītā*** believes in human freedom. Kṛṣṇa, after describing the whole philosophy of life, asks Arjuna to "do as he chooses." There is no omnipotence of nature over the human soul. We are not obliged to follow the dictates of nature. We are actually warned against our likes and dislikes, which are "the besetters of the soul in its path." A distinction is made between what is inevitable in the make-up of nature which we cannot suppress and those wanderings and confusions which we can get rid of. Those beings whose souls have not struggled to the surface are driven by the current of nature. Human individuals in whom intelligence predominates check the process of nature. They refer all activities to the intelligent will. They do not lead unexamined animal lives, unless they are dominated by passion. "What propels a man to sin, often seemingly against his will, and as if constrained by some secret force?" The answer is given that "it is lust, which instigates him . . . it is the enemy of man on earth." It is possible for the individual to control his passion and regulate his conduct by reason. Śaṁkara writes: "As regards all sense-objects, such as sounds, there necessarily arises in each sense love for an agreeable object, and aversion to a disagreeable object. Now I shall tell you where lies the scope for personal exertion and for the teaching of the śāstras. He who would follow the teaching should at the very commencement rise above the sway of affection and aversion." Karma is only a condition and not a destiny. This follows even from the ***Gītā*** analysis of the act where fate is only one of five factors. For the accomplishment of any act, five elements are necessary. They are adhiṣṭhāna, or basis, some centre from which to work; kartṛ, or a doer; kāraṇa, or the instrumentation of nature; ceṣṭā, or effort; and daiva, or fate. This last is the power or powers other than human, the cosmic principle which stands behind modifying the work and disposing of its fruits in the shape of act and its reward.

MOKSA

Whatever be the method we pursue, wisdom, love or service, the end reached is the same, union of the soul with the highest. When the mind is purified and egoism is destroyed, the individual becomes one with the supreme. If we start with the service of man, we end by becoming one with the supreme, not merely in work and consciousness, but in life and being. Love culminates in the ecstasy of devotion, where soul and God become one. Whatever route we approach by, we end in seeing, experiencing and living the divine life. This is the highest form of religion or life of spirit, called jñāna in the wider sense of the term.

Jñāna as the method of attaining spiritual reality is distinct from jñāna as the spiritual intuition, which is the ideal. Śaṁkara correctly observes that mokṣa, or direct perception of God, is not an act of service or devotion, or for that matter cognition, however much it may be led up to by it. It is an experience or a direct insight into truth. It is to attain God that the different paths are tried. The ***Gītā*** is not wholly consistent in its evaluation of the different routes to reality. "Try to know Me. If you cannot contemplate Me, practise yoga. If you are not equal to this, try to serve Me by dedicating all your work to Me. If even this is found hard, do your duty regardless of consequences, giving up all desire for fruits." Again: "Better indeed is wisdom than constant practice; meditation is better than wisdom; renouncing the fruit of action is better than meditation; on renunciation follows peace." Each of the methods is preferred sometime or other. In the mind of the author any method will do, and what the method is is left to the individual's choice. "Some by meditation, others by reflection, others by action, others by worship . . . pass beyond death."

The supreme experience is freedom, and the word jñāna is employed to refer to both the goal of the adventure as well as the path leading to it. On account of this confusion some have been led to think that jñāna as a path is superior to the other methods of approach, and that cognition alone persists, while the other elements of emotion and will fall out in the supreme state of freedom. There does not seem to be any justification for such an opinion.

Freedom or mokśa is unity with the supreme self. It is called by different names: mukti, or release; brāhmī sthiti being in Brahman, ṇaiṣkarmya, or non-action; nistraiguṇya, or the absence of the three qualities; kaivalya, or solitary salvation; brahmabhāva, or the being of Brahman. In the absolute experience there is a feeling of the oneness of all. "The Ātman is in all beings, and all beings are in the Ātman." The state of perfection exceeds the fruits of righteousness, resulting from the observance of Vedic rites, performances of sacrifices and all other methods.

We have already said that different interpretations are given as to the place of work in the ultimate condition. The ***Gītā*** is not clear on the point whether there is any basis of individuality in the ultimate state. The final condition is called siddhi, or perfection; parā siddhi, or supreme perfection; parāṁ gatim, or the supreme goal; "padam anāmayam," or the blissful seat; śānti, or quietude; "śāśvatam padam avyayam," the eternal indestructible abode. These expressions are colourless, and do not tell us whether there is a continuance of individuality in the state of freedom. There are texts which assert that the released are not troubled about the concerns of the world. They have no individuality, and therefore no basis for action. Duality disappears and work becomes impossible. The freed man has no qualities. He becomes one with the eternal self. If prakṛti acts, and if the eternal is independent of the modes of prakṛti's workings, then in the state of mokṣa there is no ego, no will, no desire. It is a condition beyond all modes and qualities, impassive, free and at peace. It is not mere survival of death, but the attaining of the supreme state of being, where the spirit knows itself to be superior to birth and death, infinite, eternal, and unconditioned by manifestations. Śaṁkara takes his stand on these passages and interprets the freedom of the ***Gītā*** in the sense of the kaiyalya of the Sāṁkyhas. If we have a body clinging to us, nature will go on acting till the body is shaken off as a discarded shell. The impersonal spirit is detached from the workings of the body. Even Śaṁkara recognises that there will be life and action so long as there is the body. We cannot escape from the instrumentalism of nature. The Jīvanmukta, or the freed soul, possessing the body, reacts to the events of the outer world, though he does not get entangled in them. There is no suggestion of the transformation of the whole nature into the immortal dharma, the law of the infinite power of the divine. Spirit and body are an unreconciled duality, and the spirit can attain its perfection only when the sense of the reality of the body is shaken off. On this view we cannot think of the action of the highest Brahman, since the basis of all activity, the unstable formation in the bosom of the infinite, the temporary phenomenon is dissolved. A perfect relinquishment of our point of view seems to be the end of all progress. Śaṁkara is emphatic that our view of the infinite is not its true measure. The fullness of its life cannot be comprehended by us from our human standpoint. Adopting this view, he urges that those verses of the ***Gītā*** which imply the plurality of spirits do not refer to the ultimate state, but only to relative conditions.

We have other verses which suggest that action is possible even for the freed souls. The men of insight and wisdom imitate the supreme Lord and act in the world. The highest condition is not a laya or a disappearance in the supreme, but one of individuality. The freed spirit, though centred in impersonality, possesses its own individuality as a part of the divine soul. Even as Puruṣottama, who has the whole universe suffused through His being, acts, the liberated individuals should act. The highest state is one of dwelling in Puruṣottama. Those who have attained it are freed from rebirth and attain to the status of God. Release is not obliteration of individuality for all eternity, but a state of blissful freedom of the soul with a distinct existence in the presence of God. "My devotees come to me." The author of the ***Gītā*** seems to believe in a continuance of conscious individuality even in freedom. As a matter of fact, some passages suggest that the freed do not become God, but only attain sameness of essence with God. Freedom is not pure identity, but only qualitative sameness, an elevation of the soul to God-like existence, where petty desires have no power to move. To be immortal is to live in the eternal light. We do not cease to be selves, but deepen our selfhood, efface all stains of sin, cut asunder the knot of doubt, master ourselves, and are ever engaged in doing good to all creatures. We do not free ourselves from all qualities, but possess the sattva quality and suppress the rajas. Rāmānuja insists on this view, and makes out that the freed soul is in constant union (nityayukta) with God, and his whole life and being reveal it. Knowledge streams from the light in which he lives, and in his love for God he is practically lost. We seem to possess here a supreme existence attained not by a total exclusion of nature, but by a higher spiritual fulfilment of it. On this view we act and live in God; only the centre of activity shifts from the human self to the divine. The divine energy is felt to be pulsating through the whole world, taking different forms in different things. Each soul has its centre and circumference in God. The view of Rāmānuja holds to the truth of spiritual personality as a factor even in the highest experience.

There are then two conflicting views in the ***Gītā*** about the ultimate state, one which makes the freed soul lose itself in the impersonality of Brahman and attain a peace beyond the strife of the world, and the other where we possess and enjoy God, being lifted above all suffering and pain and the eagerness of petty desires, which are the badges of subjection. The ***Gītā*** being a religious work insists on the ultimateness of a personal God, and calls for a full flowering of the divine in man to its utmost capacity of wisdom and power, love and universality. From this we cannot, however, conclude that the ***Gītā*** view is opposed to that of the *Upaniṣads.* The controversy is only a particular application of the general problem whether the absolute Brahman or the personal Puruṣottama is the highest reality. In the discussion of ***Gītā*** metaphysics we have said that the ***Gītā*** does not repudiate the ultimate reality of the absolute Brahman, but it suggests that from our point of view this absolute reveals itself as the personal Lord. There is no other way for thought, human and limited as it is, to envisage the highest reality. Adopting the same standpoint, we may say that the two views of the ultimate state of freedom are the intuitional and the intellectual ways of representing the one condition. From our human standpoint the absolute seems to be a passive, relationless identity, making all action impossible while it is not really so. If we want to give positive descriptions of it, then Rāmānuja's account is the only available one. To make out that the two, the absolute and the personal God, are one, the ***Gītā*** says that in the highest reality impersonality and personality are combined in a manner that is incomprehensible to us. Even so the freed spirits may have no individuality, and yet have one by self-limitation. It is in this way that the ***Gītā*** harmonises the ever immobile quietism of the timeless self with the eternal play of the energy of nature.

Whatever the truth be regarding the state of the freed after death, so long as he continues to live in the world, he is committed to some action or other. Śaṁkara sees in his activity the modes of nature's working, and Rāmānuja the actions of the supreme. These are two different ways of expressing the impersonality of action. His work is done in a freedom of the soul and with an inner joy and peace which does not depend on externals for its source or continuance. The freed souls throw off the listlessness of scepticism. All darkness is dispelled from their countenances. They show in their animated looks and firm voice that they have the vitality of a spiritual persuasion which they do not and cannot distrust. They are not subject to the dominion of flesh or attraction of desire. They are not cast down in adversity or elated in prosperity. They are strangers to anxiety, fear and anger. They possess an easy mind and the unspoiled virgin outlook of a child.

The freed soul is beyond all good and evil. Virtue is transcended in perfection. The mukta rises above any mere ethical rule of living to the light, largeness and power of spiritual life. Even if he should have committed any evil acts which would under ordinary circumstances necessitate another birth on earth, no such thing is necessary. He is freed from ordinary rules and regulations. Absolute individualism is the view of the ***Gītā*** so far as the end is concerned. It would be a dangerous doctrine if these freed men should imitate Nietzsche's super-man, who has no patience with the weak and the unfit, the defective and the delinquent. Though they are freed from social obligations, the free spirits of the ***Gītā*** freely approve of them. The liberated do not suffer any vexation in themselves or cause vexation to others. It is their second nature to work for the welfare of the world. These noble souls regard with equal mind all things of the earth. They stand for a dynamic creative spiritual life, and see to it that the social regulations tend to the fuller spiritual unfolding or expression of human life. They do their appointed work, niyatam karma, ordained by the divine will which works in them.

While the ***Gītā*** insists much on social duties, it recognises a supra-social state. It believes in the infinite destiny of the individual apart from human society. The sannyāsin is above all rules, caste and society. This symbolises the infinite dignity of man, who can strip himself of all externals, even wife and children, and be self-sufficient in the solitude of the desert if he has his God with him. It is not an ascetic ideal that the sannyāsin adopts. He may be aloof from society, yet he has compassion for all. Mahādeva, the ideal ascetic, seated in the Himalayan snows, readily drinks poison for the saving of humanity. (pp. 532-80)

S. Radhakrishnan, "The Theism of the Bhagavadgītā," in his Indian Philosophy, Vol. I, *George Allen & Unwin Ltd., 1923, pp. 519-80.*

Sri Aurobindo (essay date 1926)

[*Aurobindo was a noted Indian poet, philosopher, essayist, and political activist whose writings include* Essays on the Gita, The Life Divine *(1940), and* The Human Cycle *(1949). In the following excerpt from the first-named work, he strives to decipher the ultimate spiritual message of the* Gītā, *suggesting that the poem's powerful cosmic spirituality offers a divinely inspired vision which transcends the dichotomy of spiritual and terrestrial life.*]

The world abounds with scriptures sacred and profane, with revelations and half-revelations, with religions and philosophies, sects and schools and systems. To these the many minds of a half-ripe knowledge or no knowledge at all attach themselves with exclusiveness and passion and will have it that this or the other book is alone the eternal Word of God and all others are either impostures or at best imperfectly inspired, that this or that philosophy is the last word of the reasoning intellect and other systems are either errors or saved only by such partial truth in them as links them to the one true philosophical cult. Even the discoveries of physical Science have been elevated into a creed and in its name religion and spirituality banned as ignorance and superstition, philosophy as frippery and moonshine. And to these bigoted exclusions and vain wranglings even the wise have often lent themselves, misled by some spirit of darkness that has mingled with their light and overshadowed it with some cloud of intellectual egoism or spiritual pride. Mankind seems now indeed inclined to grow a little modester and wiser; we no longer slay our fellows in the name of God's truth or because they have minds differently trained or differently constituted from ours; we are less ready to curse and revile our neighbour because he is wicked or presumptuous enough to differ from us in opinion; we are ready even to admit that Truth is everywhere and cannot be our sole monopoly; we are beginning to look at other religions and philosophies for the truth and help they contain and no longer merely in order to damn them as false or criticise what we conceive to be their errors. But we are still apt to declare that our truth gives us *the* supreme knowledge which other religions or philosophies have missed or only imperfectly grasped so that they deal either with subsidiary and inferior aspects of the truth of things or can merely prepare less evolved minds for the heights to which we have arrived. And we are still prone to force upon ourselves or others the whole sacred mass of the book or gospel we admire, insisting that all shall be accepted as eternally valid truth and no iota or underline or diaeresis denied its part of the plenary inspiration.

It may therefore be useful in approaching an ancient Scripture, such as the *Veda, Upanishads* or ***Gita,*** to indicate precisely the spirit in which we approach it and what exactly we think we may derive from it that is of value to humanity and its future. First of all, there is undoubtedly a Truth one and eternal which we are seeking, from which all other truth derives, by the light of which all other truth finds its right place, explanation and relation to the scheme of knowledge. But precisely for that reason it cannot be shut up in a single trenchant formula, it is not likely to be found in its entirety or in all its bearings in any single philosophy or scripture or uttered altogether and for ever by any one teacher, thinker, prophet or Avatar. Nor has it been wholly found by us if our view of it necessitates the intolerant exclusion of the truth underlying other systems; for when we reject passionately, we mean simply that we cannot appreciate and explain. Secondly, this Truth, though it is one and eternal, expresses itself in Time and through the mind of man; therefore every Scripture must necessarily contain two elements, one temporary, perishable, belonging to the ideas of the period and country in which it was produced, the other eternal and imperishable and applicable in all ages and countries. Moreover, in the statement of the Truth the actual form given to it, the system and arrangement, the metaphysical and intellectual mould, the precise expression used must be largely subject to the mutations of Time and cease to have the same force; for the human intellect modifies itself always; continually dividing and putting together it is obliged to shift its divisions continually and to rearrange its syntheses; it is always leaving old expression and symbol for new or, if it uses the old, it so changes its connotation or at least its exact content and association that we can never be quite sure of understanding an ancient book of this kind precisely in the sense and spirit it bore to its contemporaries. What is of entirely permanent value is that which besides being universal has been experienced, lived and seen with a higher than the intellectual vision.

I hold it therefore of small importance to extract from the ***Gita*** its exact metaphysical connotation as it was understood by the men of the time,—even if that were accurately possible. That it is not possible, is shown by the divergence of the original commentaries which have been and are still being written upon it; for they all agree in each disagreeing with all the others, each finds in the ***Gita*** its own system of metaphysics and trend of religious thought. Nor will even the most painstaking and disinterested scholarship and the most luminous theories of the historical development of Indian philosophy save us from inevitable error. But what we can do with profit is to seek in the ***Gita*** for the actual living truths it contains, apart from their metaphysical form, to extract from it what can help us or the world at large and to put it in the most natural and vital form and expression we can find that will be suitable to the mentality and helpful to the spiritual needs of our present-day humanity. No doubt in this attempt we may mix a good deal of error born of our own individuality and of the ideas in which we live, as did greater men before us, but if we steep ourselves in the spirit of this great Scripture and, above all, if we have tried to live in that spirit, we may be sure of finding in it as much real truth as we are capable of receiving as well as the spiritual influence and actual help that, personally, we were intended to derive from it. And that is after all what Scriptures were written to give; the rest is academical disputation or theological dogma. Only those Scriptures, religions, philosophies which can be thus constantly renewed, relived, their stuff of permanent truth constantly reshaped and developed in the inner thought and spiritual experience of a developing humanity, continue to be of living importance to mankind. The rest remain as monuments of the past, but have no actual force or vital impulse for the future.

In the ***Gita*** there is very little that is merely local or temporal and its spirit is so large, profound and universal that even this little can easily be universalised without the sense of the teaching suffering any diminution or violation; rather by giving an ampler scope to it than belonged to the country and epoch, the teaching gains in depth, truth and power. Often indeed the ***Gita*** itself suggests the wider scope that can in this way be given to an idea in itself local or limited. Thus it dwells on the ancient Indian system and idea of sacrifice as an interchange between gods and men,—a system and idea which have long been practically obsolete in India itself and are no longer real to the general human mind; but we find here a sense so entirely subtle, figurative and symbolic given to the word "sacrifice" and the conception of the gods is so little local or mythological, so entirely cosmic and philosophical that we can easily accept both as expressive of a practical fact of psychology and general law of Nature and so apply them to the modern conceptions of interchange between life and life and of ethical sacrifice and self-giving as to widen and deepen these and cast over them a more spiritual aspect and the light of a profounder and more far-reaching Truth. Equally the idea of action according to the Shastra, the fourfold order of society, the allusion to the relative position of the four orders or the comparative spiritual disabilities of Shudras and women seem at first sight local and temporal, and, if they are too much pressed in their literal sense, narrow so much at least of the teaching, deprive it of its universality and spiritual depth and limit its validity for mankind at large. But if we look behind to the spirit and sense and not at the local name and temporal institution, we see that here too the sense is deep and true and the spirit philosophical, spiritual and universal. By Shastra we perceive that the ***Gita*** means the law imposed on itself by humanity as a substitute for the purely egoistic action of the natural unregenerate man and a control on his tendency to seek in the satisfaction of his desire the standard and aim of his life. We see too that the fourfold order of society is merely the concrete form of a spiritual truth which is itself independent of the form; it rests on the conception of right works as a rightly ordered expression of the nature of the individual being through whom the work is done, that nature assigning him his line and scope in life according to his inborn quality and his self-expressive function. Since this is the spirit in which the ***Gita*** advances its most local and particular instances, we are justified in pursuing always the same principle and looking always for the deeper general truth which is sure to underlie whatever seems at first sight merely local and of the time. For we shall find always that the deeper truth and principle is implied in the grain of the thought even when it is not expressly stated in its language.

Nor [should] we deal in any other spirit with the element of philosophical dogma or religious creed which either enters into the ***Gita*** or hangs about it owing to its use of the philosophical terms and religious symbols current at the time. When the ***Gita*** speaks of Sankhya and Yoga, we [should] not discuss beyond the limits of what is just essential . . . , the relations of the Sankhya of the ***Gita*** with its one Purusha and strong Vedantic colouring to the nontheistic or "atheistic" Sankhya that has come down to us bringing with it its scheme of many Purushas and one Prakriti, nor of the Yoga of the ***Gita,*** many-sided, subtle, rich and flexible to the theistic doctrine and the fixed, scientific, rigorously defined and graded system of the Yoga of Patanjali. In the ***Gita*** the Sankhya and Yoga are evidently only two convergent parts of the same Vedantic truth or rather two concurrent ways of approaching its realisation, the one philosophical, intellectual, analytic, the other intuitional, devotional, practical, ethical, synthetic, reaching knowledge through experience. The ***Gita*** recognises no real difference in their teachings. Still less need we discuss the theories which regard the ***Gita*** as the fruit of some particular religious system or tradition. Its teaching is universal whatever may have been its origins.

The philosophical system of the ***Gita,*** its arrangement of truth, is not that part of its teaching which is the most vital, profound, eternally durable; but most of the material of which the system is composed, the principal ideas suggestive and penetrating which are woven into its complex harmony, are eternally valuable and valid; for they are not merely the luminous ideas or striking speculations of a philosophic intellect, but rather enduring truths of spiritual experience, verifiable facts of our highest psychological possibilities which no attempt to read deeply the mystery of existence can afford to neglect. Whatever the system may be, it is not, as the commentators strive to make it, framed or intended to support any exclusive school of philosophical thought or to put forward predominantly the claims of any one form of Yoga. The language of the ***Gita,*** the structure of thought, the combination and balancing of ideas belong neither to the temper of a sectarian teacher nor to the spirit of a rigorous analytical dialectics cutting off one angle of the truth to exclude all the others; but rather there is a wide, undulating, encircling movement of ideas which is the manifestation of a vast synthetic mind and a rich synthetic experience. This is one of those great syntheses in which Indian spirituality has been as rich as in its creation of the more intensive, exclusive movements of knowledge and religious realisation that follow out with an absolute concentration one clue, one path to its extreme issues. It does not cleave asunder, but reconciles and unifies.

The thought of the ***Gita*** is not pure Monism although it sees in one unchanging, pure, eternal Self the foundation of all cosmic existence, nor Mayavada although it speaks of the Maya of the three modes of Prakriti omnipresent in the created world; nor is it qualified Monism although it places in the One his eternal supreme Prakriti manifested in the form of the Jiva and lays most stress on dwelling in God rather than dissolution as the supreme state of spiritual consciousness; nor is it Sankhya although it explains the created world by the double principle of Purusha and Prakriti; nor is it Vaishnava Theism although it presents to us Krishna, who is the Avatar of Vishnu according to the Puranas, as the supreme Deity and allows no essential difference nor any actual superiority of the status of the indefinable relationless Brahman over that of this Lord of beings who is the Master of the universe and the Friend of all creatures. Like the earlier spiritual synthesis of the *Upanishads* this later synthesis at once spiritual and intellectual avoids naturally every such rigid determination as would injure its universal comprehensiveness. Its aim is precisely the opposite to that of the polemist commentators who found this Scripture established as one of the three highest Vedantic authorities and attempted to turn it into a weapon of offence and defence against other schools and systems. The ***Gita*** is not a weapon for dialectical warfare; it is a gate opening on the whole world of spiritual truth and experience and the view it gives us embraces all the provinces of that supreme region. It maps out, but it does not cut up or build walls or hedges to confine our vision.

[The *Gita*] is still received in India as one of the great bodies of doctrine that most authoritatively govern religious thinking and its teaching acknowledged as of the highest value if not wholly accepted by almost all shades of religious belief and opinion.

—Sri Aurobindo

There have been other syntheses in the long history of Indian thought. We start with the *Vedic* synthesis of the psychological being of man in its highest flights and widest rangings of divine knowledge, power, joy, life and glory with the cosmic existence of the gods, pursued behind the symbols of the material universe into those superior planes which are hidden from the physical sense and the material mentality. The crown of this synthesis was in the experience of the *Vedic* Rishis something divine, transcendent and blissful in whose unity the increasing soul of man and the eternal divine fullness of the cosmic godheads meet perfectly and fulfil themselves. The *Upanishads* take up this crowning experience of the earlier seers and make it their starting-point for a high and profound synthesis of spiritual knowledge; they draw together into a great harmony all that had been seen and experienced by the inspired and liberated knowers of the Eternal throughout a great and fruitful period of spiritual seeking. The ***Gita*** starts from this Vedantic synthesis and upon the basis of its essential ideas builds another harmony of the three great means and powers, Love, Knowledge and Works, through which the soul of man can directly approach and cast itself into the Eternal. There is yet another, the Tantric, which though less subtle and spiritually profound, is even more bold and forceful than the synthesis of the ***Gita,***—for it seizes even upon the obstacles to the spiritual life and compels them to become the means for a richer spiritual conquest and enables us to embrace the whole of Life in our divine scope as the Lila ["Cosmic Play"] of the Divine; and in some directions it is more immediately rich and fruitful, for it brings forward into the foreground along with divine knowledge, divine works and an enriched devotion of divine Love, the secrets also of the Hatha and Raja Yogas, the use of the body and of mental askesis for the opening up of the divine life on all its planes, to which the ***Gita*** gives only a passing and perfunctory attention. Moreover it grasps at that idea of the divine perfectibility of man, possessed by the Vedic Rishis but thrown into the background by the intermediate ages, which is destined to fill so large a place in any future synthesis of human thought, experience and aspiration.

We of the coming day stand at the head of a new age of development which must lead to such a new and larger synthesis. We are not called upon to be orthodox Vedantins of any of the three schools or Tantrics or to adhere to one of the theistic religions of the past or to entrench ourselves within the four corners of the teaching of the ***Gita.*** That would be to limit ourselves and to attempt to create our spiritual life out of the being, knowledge and nature of others, of the men of the past, instead of building it out of our own being and potentialities. We do not belong to the past dawns, but to the noons of the future. A mass of new material is flowing into us; we have not only to assimilate the influences of the great theistic religions of India and of the world and a recovered sense of the meaning of Buddhism, but to take full account of the potent though limited revelations of modern knowledge and seeking; and, beyond that, the remote and dateless past which seemed to be dead in returning upon us with an effulgence of many luminous secrets long lost to the consciousness of mankind but now breaking out again from behind the veil. All this points to a new, a very rich, a very vast synthesis; a fresh and widely embracing harmonisation of our gains is both an intellectual and a spiritual necessity of the future. But just as the past syntheses have taken those which preceded them for their starting-point, so also must that of the future, to be on firm ground, proceed from what the great bodies of realised spiritual thought and experience in the past have given. Among them the ***Gita*** takes a most important place. (pp. 3-10)

. . . . .

The essence of the teaching and the Yoga [of the ***Gita*** is] given to the disciple on the field of his work and battle and the divine Teacher . . . proceeds to apply it to his action, but in a way that makes it applicable to all action. Attached to a crucial example, spoken to the protagonist of Kurukshetra, the words bear a much wider significance and are a universal rule for all who are ready to ascend above the ordinary mentality and to live and act in the highest spiritual consciousness. To break out of ego and personal mind and see everything in the wideness of the self and spirit, to know God and adore him in his integral truth and in all his aspects, to surrender all oneself to the transcendent Soul of nature and existence, to possess and be possessed by the divine consciousness, to be one with the One in universality of love and delight and will and knowledge, one in him with all beings, to do works as an adoration and a sacrifice on the divine foundation of a world in which all is God and in the divine status of a liberated spirit, is the sense of the ***Gita***'s Yoga. It is a transition from the apparent to the supreme spiritual and real truth of our being, and one enters into it by putting off the many limitations of the separative consciousness and the mind's attachment to the passion and unrest and ignorance, the lesser light and knowledge, the sin and virtue, the dual law and standard of the lower nature. Therefore, says the Teacher,

> devoting all thyself to Me, giving up in thy conscious mind all thy actions into Me, resorting to Yoga of the will and intelligence be always one in heart and consciousness with Me. If thou art that at all times, then by my grace thou shalt pass safe through all difficult and perilous passages; but if from egoism thou hear not, thou shalt fall into perdition. Vain is this thy resolve, that in thy egoism thou thinkest, saying 'I will not fight'; thy nature shall appoint thee to thy work. What from delusion thou desirest not to do, that helplessly thou shalt do bound by thy own work born of thy swabhava. The Lord is stationed in the heart of all existences, O Arjuna, and turns them all round and round mounted on a machine by his Maya. In him take refuge in every way of thy being and by his grace thou shalt come to the supreme peace and the eternal status.

These are lines that carry in them the innermost heart of this Yoga and lead to its crowning experience and we must understand them in their innermost spirit and in the whole vastness of that high summit of experience. The words express the most complete, intimate and living relation possible between God and man; they are instinct with the concentrated force of religious feeling that springs from the human being's absolute adoration, his upward surrender of his whole existence, his unreserved and perfect self-giving to the transcendent and universal Divinity from whom he comes and in whom he lives. This stress of feeling is in entire consonance with the high and enduring place that the ***Gita*** assigns to bhakti, to the love of God, to the adoration of the Highest, as the inmost spirit and motive of the supreme action and the crown and core of the supreme knowledge. The phrases used and the spiritual emotion with which they vibrate seem to give the most intense prominence possible and an utmost importance to the personal truth and presence of the Godhead. It is no abstract Absolute of the philosopher, no indifferent impersonal Presence or ineffable Silence intolerant of all relations to whom this complete surrender of all our works can be made and this closeness and intimacy of oneness with him in all the parts of our conscious existence imposed as the condition and law of our perfection or of whom this divine intervention and protection and deliverance are the promise. It is a Master of our works, a Friend and Lover of our soul, an intimate Spirit of our life, an indwelling and overdwelling Lord of all our personal and impersonal self and nature who alone can utter to us this near and moving message. And yet this is not the common relation established by the religions between man living in his sattwic or other ego-mind and some personal form and aspect of the Deity, *iṣṭa-deva,* constructed by that mind or offered to it to satisfy its limited ideal, aspiration or desire. That is the ordinary sense and actual character of the normal mental being's religious devotion; but here there is something wider that passes beyond the mind and its limits and its dharmas. It is something deeper than the mind that offers and something greater than the Ishta-deva that receives the surrender.

That which surrenders here is the Jiva, the essential soul, the original central and spiritual being of man, the individual Purusha. It is the Jiva delivered from the limiting and ignorant ego-sense who knows himself not as a separate personality but as an eternal portion and power and soul-becoming of the Divine, *aṁśa sanātana,* the Jiva released and uplifted by the passing away of ignorance and established in the light and freedom of his own true and supreme nature which is one with that of the Eternal. It is this central spiritual being in us who thus enters into a perfect and closely real relation of delight and union with the origin and continent and governing Self and Power of our existence. And he who receives our surrender is no limited Deity but the Purushottama, the one eternal Godhead, the one supreme Soul of all that is and of all Nature, the original transcendent Spirit of existence. An immutable impersonal self-existence is his first obvious spiritual self-presentation to the experience of our liberated knowledge, the first sign of his presence, the first touch and impression of his substance. A universal and transcendent infinite Person or Purusha is the mysterious hidden secret of his very being, unthinkable in form of mind, *acintya-rūpa,* but very near and present to the powers of our consciousness, emotion, will and knowledge when they are lifted out of themselves, out of their blind and petty forms into a luminous spiritual, an immeasurable supramental Ananda and power and gnosis. It is He, ineffable Absolute but also Friend and Lord and Enlightener and Lover, who is the object of this most complete devotion and approach and this most intimate inner becoming and surrender. This union, this relation is a thing lifted beyond the forms and laws of the limiting mind, too high for all these inferior dharmas; it is a truth of our self and spirit. And yet or rather therefore, because it is the truth of our self and spirit, the truth of its oneness with that Spirit from which all comes and by it and as its derivations and suggestions all exists and travails, it is not a negation but a fulfilment of all that mind and life point to and bear in them as their secret and unaccomplished significance. Thus it is not by a nirvana, an exclusion and negating extinction of all that we are here, but by a nirvana, an exclusion and negating extinction of ignorance and ego and a consequent ineffable fulfilment of our knowledge and will and heart's aspiration, an uplifted and limitless living of them in the Divine, in the Eternal, *nivasisyasi mayyeva,* a transfigurement and transference of all our consciousness to a greater inner status that there comes this supreme perfection and release in the spirit.

The crux of the spiritual problem, the character of this transition of which it is so difficult for the normal mind of man to get a true apprehension, turns altogether upon the capital distinction between the ignorant life of the ego in the lower nature and the large and luminous existence of the liberated Jiva in his own true spiritual nature. The renunciation of the first must be complete, the transition to the second absolute. This is the distinction on which the ***Gita*** dwells here with all possible emphasis. On the one side is this poor trepidant braggart egoistic condition of consciousness, *ahaṁkṛta bhāva,* the crippling narrowness of this little helpless separative personality according to whose viewpoint we ordinarily think and act, feel and respond to the touches of existence. On the other are the vast spiritual reaches of immortal fullness, bliss and knowledge into which we are admitted through union with the divine Being, of whom we are then a manifestation and expression in the eternal light and no longer a disguise in the darkness of the ego-nature. It is the completeness of this union which is indicated by the ***Gita***'s *satatam maccittaḥ.* The life of the ego is founded on a construction of the apparent mental, vital and physical truth of existence, on a nexus of pragmatic relations between the individual soul and Nature, on an intellectual, emotional and sensational interpretation of things used by the little limited I in us to maintain and satisfy the ideas and desires of its bounded separate personality amid the vast action of the universe. All our dharmas, all the ordinary standards by which we determine our view of things and our knowledge and our action, proceed upon this narrow and limiting basis, and to follow them even in the widest wheelings round our ego centre does not carry us out of this petty circle. It is a circle in which the soul is a contented or struggling prisoner, for ever subject to the mixed compulsions of Nature.

For Purusha veils himself in this round, veils his divine and immortal being in ignorance and is subject to the law of an insistent limiting Prakriti. That law is the compelling rule of the three gunas. It is a triple stair that stumbles upward towards the divine light but cannot reach it. At its base is the law or dharma of inertia: the tamasic man inertly obeys in a customary mechanical action the suggestions and impulses, the round of will of his material and his half-intellectualised vital and sensational nature. In the middle intervenes the kinetic law or dharma; the rajasic man, vital, dynamic, active, attempts to impose himself on his world and environment, but only increases the wounding weight and tyrant yoke of his turbulent passions, desires and egoisms, the burden of his restless self-will, the yoke of his rajasic nature. At the top presses down upon life the harmonic regulative law or dharma; the sattwic man attempts to erect and follow his limited personal standards of reasoning knowledge, enlightened utility or mechanised virtue, his religions and philosophies and ethical formulas, mental systems and constructions, fixed channels of idea and conduct which do not agree with the totality of the meaning of life and are constantly being broken in the movement of the wider universal purpose. The dharma of the sattwic man is the highest in the circle of the gunas; but that too is a limited view and a dwarfed standard. Its imperfect indications lead to a petty and relative perfection; temporarily satisfying to the enlightened personal ego, it is not founded either on the whole truth of the self or on the whole truth of Nature.

And in fact the actual life of man is not at any time one of these things alone, neither a mechanical routine execution of first crude law of Nature, nor the struggle of a kinetic soul of action, nor a victorious emergence of conscious light and reason and good and knowledge. There is a mixture of all these dharmas out of which our will and intelligence make a more or less arbitrary construction to be realised as best it can, but never in fact realised except by compromise with other compelling things in the universal Prakriti. The sattwic ideals of our enlightened will and reason are either themselves compromises, at best progressive compromises, subject to a constant imperfection and flux of change, or, if absolute in their character, they can be followed only as a counsel of perfection ignored for the most part in practice or successful only as a partial influence. And if sometimes we imagine we have completely realised them, it is because we ignore in ourselves the subconscious or half-conscious mixture of other powers and motives that are usually as much or more than our ideals the real force in our action. That self-ignorance constitutes the whole vanity of human reason and self-righteousness; it is the dark secret lining behind the spotless white outsides of human sainthood and alone makes possible the specious egoisms of knowledge and virtue. The best human knowledge is a half knowledge and the highest human virtue a thing of mixed quality and, even when most sincerely absolute in standard, sufficiently relative in practice. As a general law of living the absolute sattwic ideals cannot prevail in conduct; indispensable as a power for the betterment and raising of personal aspiration and conduct, their insistence modifies life but cannot wholly change it, and their perfect fulfilment images itself only in a dream of the future or a world of heavenly nature free from the mixed strain of our terrestrial existence. It cannot be otherwise because neither the nature of this world nor the nature of man is or can be one single piece made of the pure stuff of sattwa.

The first door of escape we see out of this limitation of our possibilities, out of this confused mixture of dharmas is in a certain high trend towards impersonality, a movement inwards towards something large and universal and calm and free and right and pure, hidden now by the limiting mind of ego. The difficulty is that while we can feel a positive release into this impersonality in moments of the quiet and silence of our being, an impersonal activity is by no means so easy to realise. The pursuit of an impersonal truth or an impersonal will in our conduct is vitiated so long as we live at all in our normal mind by that which is natural and inevitable to that mind, the law of our personality, the subtle urge of our vital nature, the colour of ego. The pursuit of impersonal truth is turned by these influences into an unsuspected cloak for a system of intellectual preferences supported by our mind's limiting insistence; the pursuit of a disinterested impersonal action is converted into a greater authority and apparent high sanction for our personal will's interested selections and blind arbitrary persistences. On the other hand, an absolute impersonality would seem to impose an equally absolute quietism, and this would mean that all action is bound to the machinery of the ego and the three gunas and to recede from life and its works the only way out of the circle. This impersonal silence however is not the last word of wisdom in the matter, because it is not the only way and crown or not all the way and the last crown of self-realisation open to our endeavour. There is a mightier fuller more positive spiritual experience in which the circle of our egoistic personality and the round of the mind's limitations vanish in the unwalled infinity of a greatest self and spirit and yet life and its works not only remain still acceptable and possible but reach up and out to their widest spiritual completeness and assume a grand ascending significance.

There have been different gradations in this movement to bridge the gulf between an absolute impersonality and the dynamic possibilities of our nature. The thought and practice of the Mahayana approached this difficult reconciliation through the experience of a deep desirelessness and a large dissolving freedom from mental and vital attachment and sanskaras and on the positive side a universal altruism, a fathomless compassion for the world and its creatures which became, as it were, the flood and outpouring of the high Nirvanic state on life and action. That reconciliation was equally the sense of yet another spiritual experience, more conscious of a world significance, more profound, kindling, richly comprehensive on the side of action, a step nearer to the thought of the ***Gita:*** this experience we find or can at least read behind the utterances of the Taoist thinkers. There there seems to be an impersonal ineffable Eternal who is spirit and at the same time the one life of the universe: it supports and flows impartially in all things, *samam brahma;* it is a One that is nothing, Asat, because other than all that we perceive and yet the totality of all these existences. The blind personality that forms like foam on this Infinite, the mobile ego with its attachments and repulsions, its likings and dislikings, its fixed mental distinctions, is an effective image that veils and deforms to us the one reality, Tao, the supreme All and Nothing. That can be touched only by losing personality and its little structural forms in the unseizable universal and eternal Presence and, this once achieved, we live in that a real life and have another greater consciousness which makes us penetrate all things, ourselves penetrable to all eternal influences. Here, as in the ***Gita,*** the highest way would seem to be a complete openess and self-surrender to the Eternal. "Your body is not your own," says the Taoist thinker, "it is the delegated image of God: your life is not your own, it is the delegated harmony of God: your individuality is not your own, it is the delegated adaptability of God." And here too a vast perfection and liberated action are the dynamic result of the soul's surrender. The works of ego personality are a separative running counter to the bias of universal nature. This false movement must be replaced by a wise and still passivity in the hands of the universal and eternal Power, a passivity that makes us adaptable to the infinite action, in harmony with its truth, plastic to the shaping breath of the Spirit. The man who has this harmony may be motionless within and absorbed in silence, but his Self will appear free from disguises, the divine Influence will be at work in him and while he abides in tranquillity and an inward inaction, *naiṣkarmya,* yet he will act with an irresistible power and myriads of things and beings will move and gather under his influence. The impersonal force of the Self takes up his works, movements no longer deformed by ego, and sovereignly acts through him for the keeping together and control of the world and its peoples, *loka-saṁgrahārthāya.*

There is little difference between these experiences and the first impersonal activity inculcated by the ***Gita.*** The ***Gita*** also demands of us renunciation of desire, attachment and ego, transcendence of the lower nature and the breaking up of our personality and its little formations. The ***Gita*** also demands of us to live in the Self and Spirit, to see the Self and Spirit in all and all in the Self and Spirit and all as the Self and Spirit. It demands of us like the Taoist thinker to renounce our natural personality and its works into the Self, the Spirit, the Eternal, the Brahman, *ātmani sannyasya, brahmaṇi.* And there is this coincidence because that is always man's highest and freest possible experience of quietistic inner largeness and silence reconciled with an outer dynamic active living, the two coexistent or fused together in the impersonal infinite reality and illimitable action of the one immortal Power and sole eternal Existence. But the ***Gita*** adds a phrase of immense import that alters everything, *ātmani atho mayi.* The demand is to see all things in the self and then in "Me" the Ishwara, to renounce all action into the Self, Spirit, Brahman and thence into the supreme Person, the Purushottama. There is here a still greater and profounder complex of spiritual experience, a larger transmutation of the significance of human life, a more mystic and heart-felt sweep of the return of the stream to the ocean, the restoration of personal works and the cosmic action to the Eternal Worker. The stress on pure impersonality has this difficulty and incompleteness for us that it reduces the inner person, the spiritual individual, that persistent miracle of our inmost being, to a temporary, illusive and mutable formation in the Infinite. The Infinite alone exists and except in a passing play has no true regard on the soul of the living creature. There can be no real and permanent relation between the soul in man and the Eternal, if that soul is even as the always renewable body no more than a transient phenomenon in the Infinite.

It is true that the ego and its limited personality are even such a temporary and mutable formation of Nature and therefore it must be broken and we must feel ourselves one with all and infinite. But the ego is not the real person; when it has been dissolved there still remains the spiritual individual, there is still the eternal Jiva. The ego limitation disappears and the soul lives in a profound unity with the One and feels its universal unity with all things. And yet it is still our own soul that enjoys this expanse and oneness. The universal action, even when it is felt as the action of one and the same energy in all, even when it is experienced as the initiation and movement of the Ishwara, still takes different forms in different souls of men, *aṁśah sanātanah,* and a different turn in their nature. The light of spiritual knowledge, the manifold universal Shakti, the eternal delight of being stream into us and around us, concentrate in the soul and flow out on the surrounding world from each as from a centre of living spiritual consciousness whose circumference is lost in the infinite. More, the spiritual individual remains as a little universe of divine existence at once independent and inseparable from the whole infinite universe of the divine self-manifestation of which we see a petty portion around us. A portion of the Transcendent, creative, he creates his own world around him even while he retains this cosmic consciousness in which are all others. If it be objected that this is an illusion which must disappear when he retreats into the transcendent Absolute, there is after all no very certain certainty in that matter. For it is still the soul in man that is the enjoyer of this release, as it was the living spiritual centre of the divine action and manifestation; there is something more than the mere self-breaking of an illusory shell of individuality in the Infinite. This mystery of our existence signifies that what we are is not only a temporary name and form of the One, but as we may say, a soul and spirit of the Divine Oneness. Our spiritual individuality of which the ego is only a misleading shadow and projection in the ignorance has or is a truth that persists beyond the ignorance; there is something of us that dwells for ever in the supreme nature of the Purushottama, *nivasiṣyasi mayi.* This is the profound comprehensiveness of the teaching of the ***Gita*** that while it recognses the truth of the universalised impersonality into which we enter by the extinction of ego, *brahma-nirvāṇa,*—for indeed without it there can be no liberation or at least no absolute release,—it recognises too the persistent spiritual truth of our personality as a factor of the highest experience. Not this natural but that divine and central being in us is the eternal Jiva. It is the Ishwara, Vasudeva who is all things, that takes up our mind and life and body for the enjoyment of the lower Prakriti; it is the supreme Prakriti, the original spiritual nature of the supreme Purusha that holds together the universe and appears in it as the Jiva. This Jiva then is a portion of the Purushottama's original divine spiritual being, a living power of the living Eternal. He is not merely a temporary form of lower Nature, but an eternal portion of the Highest in his supreme Prakriti, an eternal conscious ray of the divine existence and as everlasting as that supernal Prakriti. One side of the highest perfection and status of our liberated consciousness must then be to assume the true place of the Jiva in a supreme spiritual Nature, there to dwell in the glory of the supreme Purusha and there to have the joy of eternal spiritual oneness.

This mystery of our being implies necessarily a similar supreme mystery of the being of the Purushottama, *rahasyam uttamam.* It is not an exclusive impersonality of the Absolute that is the highest secret. This highest secret is the miracle of a supreme Person and apparent vast Impersonal that are one, an immutable transcendent Self of all things and a Spirit that manifests itself here at the very foundation of cosmos as an infinite and multiple personality acting everywhere,—a Self and Spirit revealed to our last, closest, profoundest experience as an illimitable Being who accepts us and takes us to him, not into a blank of featureless existence, but most positively, deeply, wonderfully into all Himself and in all the ways of his and our conscious existence. This highest experience and this largest way of seeing open a profound, moving and endless significance to our parts of nature, our knowledge, will, heart's love and adoration, which is lost or diminished if we put an exclusive stress on the impersonal, because that stress suppresses or minimises or does not allow of the intensest fulfilment of movements and powers that are a portion of our deepest nature, intensities and luminosities that are attached to the closest essential fibres of our self-experience. It is not the austerity of knowledge alone that can help us; there is room and infinite room for the heart's love and aspiration illumined and uplifted by knowledge, a more mystically clear, a greater calmly passionate knowledge. It is by the perpetual unified closeness of our heart-consciousness, mind-consciousness, all-consciousness, *satatam maccittaḥ,* that we get the widest, the deepest, the most integral experience of our oneness with the Eternal. A nearest oneness in all the being, profoundly individual in a divine passion even in the midst of universality, even at the top of transcendence is here enjoined on the human soul as its way to reach the Highest and its way to possess the perfection and the divine consciousness to which it is called by its nature as a spirit. The intelligence and will have to turn the whole existence in all its parts to the Ishwara, to the divine Self and Master of that whole existence, *buddhi-yogam upāśritya.* The heart has to cast all other emotion into the delight of oneness with him and love him in all creatures. The sense spiritualised has to see and hear and feel him everywhere. The life has to be utterly his life in the Jiva. All the actions have to proceed from his sole power and sole initiation in the will, knowledge, organs of action, senses, vital parts, body. This way is deeply impersonal because the separateness of ego is abolished for the Soul universalised and restored to transcendence. And yet it is intimately personal because it soars to a transcendent passion and power of indwelling and oneness. A featureless extinction may be a rigorous demand of the mind's logic of self-annulment, it is not the last word of the supreme mystery, *rahasyam uttamam.*

The refusal of Arjuna to persevere in his divinely appointed work proceed from the ego sense in him, *ahaṁkāra.* Behind it was a mixture and confusion and tangled error of ideas and impulsions of the sattwic, rajasic, tamasic ego, the vital nature's fear of sin and its personal consequences, the heart's recoil from individual grief and suffering, the clouded reason's covering of egoistic impulses by self-deceptive specious pleas of right and virtue, our nature's ignorant shrinking from the ways of God because they seem other than the ways of man and impose things terrible and unpleasant on his nervous and emotional parts and his intelligence. The spiritual consequences will be infinitely worse now than before, now that a higher truth and a greater way and spirit of action have been revealed to him, if yet persisting in his egoism he perseveres in a vain and impossible refusal. For it is a vain resolution, a futile recoil, since it springs only from a temporary failure of strength, a strong but passing deviation from the principle of energy of his inmost character and is not the true will and way of his nature. If now he casts down his arms, he will yet be compelled by that nature to resume them when he sees the battle and slaughter go on without him, his abstention a defeat of all for which he has lived, the cause for whose service he was born weakened and bewildered by the absence or inactivity of its protagonist, vanquished and afflicted by the cynical and unscrupulous strength of the champions of a self-regarding unrighteousness and injustice. And in this return there will be no spiritual virtue. It was a confusion of the ideas and feelings of the ego mind that impelled his refusal; it will be his nature working through a restoration of the characteristic ideas and feelings of the ego mind that will compel him to annul his refusal. But whatever the direction, this continued subjection to the ego will mean a worse, a more fatal spiritual refusal, a perdition, *vinaṣṭi;* for it will be a definite falling away from a greater truth of his being than that which he has followed in the ignorance of the lower nature. He has been admitted to a higher consciousness, a new self-realisation, he has been shown the possibility of a divine instead of an egoistic action; the gates have been opened before him of a divine and spiritual in place of a merely intellectual, emotional, sensuous and vital life. He is called to be no longer a great blind instrument, but a conscious soul and an enlightened power and vessel of the Godhead.

For there is this possibility within us: there is open to us even at our human highest this consummation and transcendence. The ordinary mind and life of man is a half-enlightened and mostly an ignorant development and a partial uncompleted manifestation of something concealed within him. There is a godhead there concealed from himself, subliminal to his consciousness, immobilised behind the obscure veil of a working that is not wholly his own and the secret of which he has not yet mastered. He finds himself in the world thinking and willing and feeling and acting and he takes himself instinctively or intellectually conceives of himself or at least conducts his life as a separate self-existent being who has the freedom of his thought and will and feeling and action. He bears the burden of his sin and error and suffering and takes the responsibility and merit of his knowledge and virtue; he claims the right to satisfy his sattwic, rajasic or tamasic ego and arrogates the power to shape his own destiny and to turn the world to his own uses. It is this idea of himself through which Nature works in him, and she deals with him according to his own conception, but fulfils all the time the will of the greater Spirit within her. The error of this self-view of man is like most of his errors the distortion of a truth, a distortion that creates a whole system of erroneous and yet effective values. What is true of his spirit he attributes to his ego-personality and gives it a false application, a false form and a mass of ignorant consequences. The ignorance lies in this fundamental deficiency of his surface consciousness that he identifies himself only with the outward mechanical part of him which is a convenience of Nature and with so much only of the soul as reflects and is reflected in these workings. He issues the greater inner spirit within which gives to all his mind and life and creation and action an unfulfilled promise and a hidden significance. A universal Nature here obeys the power of the Spirit who is the master of the universe, shapes each creature and determines its action according to the law of its own nature, Swabhava, shapes man too and determines his action according to the general law of nature of his kind, the law of a mental being enmeshed and ignorant in the life and body, shapes too each man and determines his individual action according to the law of his own distinct type and the variations of his own original swabhava. It is this universal Nature that forms and directs the mechanical workings of the body and the instinctive operations of our vital and nervous parts; and there our subjection to her is very obvious. And she has formed and directs the action too, hardly less mechanical as things now are, of our sense-mind and will and intelligence. Only, while in the animal the mind workings are a wholly mechanical obedience to Prakriti, man has this distinction that he embodies a conscious development in which the soul more actively participates, and that gives to his outward mentality the sense, useful to him, indispensable, but very largely a misleading sense, of a certain freedom and increasing mastery of his instrumental nature. And it is especially misleading because it blinds him to the hard fact of his bondage and his false idea of freedom prevents him from finding a true liberty and lordship. For the freedom and mastery of man over his nature are hardly even real and cannot be complete until he becomes aware of the Divinity within him and is in possession of his own real self and spirit other than the ego, *ātmavān.* It is that which Nature is labouring to express in mind and life and body; it is that which imposes on her this or that law of being and working, Swabhava; it is that which shapes the outward destiny and the evolution of the soul within us. It is therefore only when he is in possession of his real self and spirit that his nature can become a conscious instrument and enlightened power of the godhead.

For then, when we enter into that inmost self of our existence, we come to know that in us and in all is the one Spirit and Godhead whom all Nature serves and manifests and we ourselves are soul of this soul, spirit of this spirit, our body his delegated image, our life a movement of the rhythm of his life, our mind a sheath of his consciousness, our senses his instruments, our emotions and sensations the seekings of his delight of being, our actions a means of his purpose, our freedom only a shadow, suggestion or glimpse while we are ignorant, but when we know him and ourselves a prolongation and effective channel of his immortal freedom. Our masteries are a reflection of his power at work, our best knowledge a partial light of his knowledge, the highest most potent will of our spirit a projection and delegation of the will of this Spirit in all things who is the Master and Soul of the universe. It is the Lord seated in the heart of every creature who has been turning us in all our inner and outer action during the ignorance as if mounted on a machine on the wheel of this Maya of the lower Nature. And whether obscure in the ignorance or luminous in the knowledge, it is for him in us and him in the world that we have our existence. To live consciously and integrally in this knowledge and this truth is to escape from ego and break out of Maya. All other highest dharmas are only a preparation for this Dharma, and all Yoga is only a means by which we can come first to some kind of union and finally, if we have the full light, to an integral union with the Master and supreme Soul and Self of our existence. The greatest Yoga is to take refuge from all the perplexities and difficulties of our nature with this indwelling Lord of all Nature, to turn to him with our whole being, with the life and body and sense and mind and heart and understanding, with our whole dedicated knowledge and will and action, *sarva-bhāvena,* in every way of our conscious self and our instrumental nature. And when we can at all times and entirely do this, then the divine Light and Love and Power takes hold of us, fills both self and instruments and leads us safe through all the doubts and difficulties and perplexities and perils that beset our soul and our life, leads us to a supreme peace and the spiritual freedom of our immortal and eternal status, *parām śāntim, sthānam śāsvatam.*

For after giving out all the laws, the dharmas, and the deepest essence of its Yoga, after saying that beyond all the first secrets revealed to the mind of man by the transforming light of spiritual knowledge, *gūhyāt,* this is a still deeper more secret truth, *gūhyataram,* the ***Gita,*** suddenly declares that there is yet a supreme word that it has to speak, *paraman vacaḥ,* and a most secret truth of all, *sarva-gūhyatamam.* This secret of secrets the Teacher will tell to Arjuna as his highest good because he is the chosen and beloved soul, *iṣṭa.* For evidently, as had already been declared by the Upanishad, it is only the rare soul chosen by the Spirit for the revelation of his very body, *tanum svām,* who can be admitted to this mystery, because he alone is near enough in heart and mind and life to the Godhead to respond truly to it in all his being and to make it a living practice. The last, the closing supreme word of the ***Gita*** expressing the highest mystery is spoken in two brief, direct and simple slokas and these are left without farther comment or enlargement to sink into the mind and reveal their own fullness of meaning in the soul's experience. For it is alone this inner incessantly extending experience that can make evident the infinite deal of meaning with which are for ever pregnant these words in themselves apparently so slight and simple. And we feel, as they are being uttered, that it was this for which the soul of the disciple was being prepared all the time and the rest was only an enlightening and enabling discipline and doctrine. Thus runs this secret of secrets, the highest most direct message of the Ishwara. "Become my-minded, my lover and adorer, a sacrificer to Me, bow thyself to Me, to Me thou shalt come, this is my pledge and promise to thee, for dear art thou to Me. Abandon all dharmas and take refuge in Me alone. I will deliver thee from all sin and evil, do not grieve."

The ***Gita*** throughout has been insisting on a great and well-built discipline of Yoga, a large and clearly traced philosophical system, on the Swabhava and the Swadharma, on the sattwic law of life as leading out of itself by a self-exceeding exaltation to a free spiritual dharma of immortal existence utterly wide in its spaces and high-lifted beyond the limitation of even this highest guna, on many rules and means and injunctions and conditions of perfection, and now suddenly it seems to break out of its own structure and says to the human soul, "Abandon all dharmas, give thyself to the Divine alone, to the supreme Godhead above and around and within thee: that is all that thou needest, that is the truest and greatest way, that is the real deliverance." The Master of the worlds in the form of the divine Charioteer and Teacher of Kurukshetra has revealed to man the magnificent realities of God and Self and Spirit and the nature of the complex world and the relation of man's mind and life and heart and senses to the Spirit and the victorious means by which through his own spiritual self-discipline and effort he can rise out of mortality into immortality and out of his limited mental into his infinite spiritual existence. And now speaking as the Spirit and Godhead in man and in all things he says to him,

> All this personal effort and self-discipline will not in the end be needed, all following and limitation of rule and dharma can at last be thrown away as hampering encumbrances if thou canst make a complete surrender to Me, depend alone on the Spirit and Godhead within thee and all things and trust to his sole guidance. Turn all thy mind to Me and fill it with the thought of Me and my presence. Turn all thy heart to Me, make thy every action, whatever it be, a sacrifice and offering to Me. That done, leave Me to do my will with thy life and soul and action; do not be grieved or perplexed by my dealings with thy mind and heart and life and works or troubled because they do not seem to follow the laws and dharmas man imposes on himself to guide his limited will and intelligence. My ways are the ways of a perfect and intelligence. My ways are the ways of a perfect wisdom and power and love that knows all things and combines all its movements in view of a perfect eventual result; for it is refining and weaving together the many threads of an integral perfection. I am here with thee in thy chariot of battle revealed as the Master of existence within and without thee and I repeat the absolute assurance, the infallible promise that I will lead thee to myself through and beyond all sorrow and evil. Whatever difficulties and perplexities arise, be sure of this that I am leading thee to a complete divine life in the universal and an immortal existence in the transcendent Spirit.

The secret thing, *gūhyam,* that all deep spiritual knowledge reveals to us, mirrored in various teachings and justified in the soul's experience, is for the ***Gita*** the secret of the spiritual self hidden within us of which mind and external Nature are only manifestations or figures. It is the secret of the constant relations between soul and Nature, Purusha and Prakriti, the secret of an indwelling Godhead who is the lord of all existence and veiled from us in its forms and movements. These are the truths taught in many ways by Vedanta and Sankhya and Yoga and synthetised in the earlier chapters of the ***Gita.*** And amidst all their apparent distinctions they are one truth and all the different ways of Yoga are various means of spiritual self-discipline by which our unquiet mind and blinded life are stilled and turned towards this many-aspected One and the secret truth of self and God made so real to us and intimate that we can either consciously live and dwell in it or lose our separate selves in the Eternal and no longer be compelled at all by the mental Ignorance.

The more secret thing, *gūhyatarm,* developed by the ***Gita*** is the profound reconciling truth of the divine Purushottama, at once self and Purusha, supreme Brahman and a sole, intimate, mysterious, ineffable Godhead. That gives to the thought a larger and more deeply understanding foundation for an ultimate knowledge and to the spiritual experience a greater and more fully comprehending and comprehensive Yoga. This deeper mystery is founded on the secret of the supreme spiritual Prakriti and of the Jiva, an eternal portion of the Divine in that eternal and this manifested Nature and of one spirit and essence with him in his immutable self-existence. This profounder knowledge escapes from the elementary distinction of spiritual experience between the Beyond and what is here. For the Transcendent beyond the worlds is at the same time Vasudeva who is all things in all worlds; he is the Lord standing in the heart of every creature and the self of all existences and the origin and supernal meaning of everything that he has put forth in his Prakriti. He is manifested in his Vibhutis and he is the Spirit in Time who compels the action of the world and the Sun of all knowledge and the Lover and Beloved of the soul and the Master of all works and sacrifice. The result of an inmost opening to this deeper, truer, more secret mystery is the ***Gita***'s Yoga of integral knowledge, integral works and integral bhakti. It is the simultaneous experience of spiritual universality and a free and perfected spiritual individuality, of an entire union with God and an entire dwelling in him as at once the frame of the soul's immortality and the support and power of our liberated action in the world and the body.

And now there comes the supreme word and most secret thing of all, *gūhyatamam,* that the Spirit and Godhead is an Infinite free from all dharmas and though he conducts the world according to fixed laws and leads man through his dharmas of ignorance and knowledge, sin and virtue, right and wrong, liking and disliking and indifference, pleasure and pain, joy and sorrow and the rejection of these opposites, through his physical and vital, intellectual, emotional, ethical and spiritual forms and rules and standards, yet the Spirit and Godhead transcends all these things, and if we too can cast away all dependence on dharmas, surrender ourselves to this free and eternal Spirit and, taking care only to keep ourselves absolutely and exclusively open to him, trust to the light and power and delight of the Divine in us and, unafraid and ungrieving, accept only his guidance, then that is the truest, the greatest release and that brings the absolute and inevitable perfection of our self and nature. This is the way offered to the chosen of the Spirit,—to those only in whom he takes the greatest delight because they are nearest to him and most capable of oneness and of being even as he, freely consenting and concordant with Nature in her highest power and movement, universal in soul consciousness, transcendent in the spirit.

For a time comes in spiritual development when we become aware that all our effort and action are only our mental and vital reactions to the silent and secret insistence of a greater Presence in and around us. It is borne in on us that all our Yoga, our aspiration and our endeavour are imperfect or narrow forms, because disfigured or at least limited by the mind's associations, demands, prejudgments, predilections, mistranslations or half-translations of a vaster truth. Our ideas and experiences and efforts are mental images only of greatest things which would be done more perfectly, directly, freely, largely, more in harmony with the universal and eternal will by that Power itself in us if we could only put ourselves passively as instruments in the hands of a supreme and absolute strength and wisdom. That Power is not separate from us; it is our own self one with the self of all others and at the same time a transcendent Being and an immanent Person. Our existence, our action taken up into this greatness Existence would be no longer, as it seems to us now, individually our own in a mental separation. It would be the vast movement of an Infinity and an intimate ineffable Presence; it would be the constant spontaneity of formation and expression in us of this deep universal self and this transcendent Spirit. The ***Gita*** indicates that in order that that may wholly be, the surrender must be without reservations; our Yoga, our life, our state of inner being must be determined freely by this living Infinite, not predetermined by our mind's insistence on this or that dharma or any dharma. The divine Master of the Yoga, *yogeśvaraḥ kṛṣṇaḥ,* will then himself take up our Yoga and raise us to our utmost possible perfection, not the perfection of any external or mental standard or limiting rule, but vast and comprehensive, to the mind incalculable. It will be a perfection developed by an all-seeing Wisdom according to the whole truth, first indeed of our human swabhava, but afterwards of a greater thing into which it will open, a spirit and power illimitable, immortal, free and all-transmuting, the light and splendour of a divine and infinite nature.

All must be given as material of that transmutation. An omniscient consciousness will take up our knowledge and our ignorance, our truth and our error, cast away their forms of insufficiency, *sarva-dharmān parityajya,* and transform all into its infinite light. An almighty Power will take up our virtue and sin, our right and wrong, our strength and our weakness, cast away their tangled figures, *sarva-dharmān parityajya,* and transform all into its transcendent purity and universal good and infallible force. An ineffable Ananda will take up our petty joy and sorrow, our struggling pleasure and pain, cast away their discordances and imperfect rhythms, *sarva-dharmān parityajya,* and transform all into its transcendent and universal unimaginable delight. All that all the Yogas can do will be done and more; but it will be done in a greater seeing way, with a greater wisdom and truth than any human teacher, saint or sage can give us. The inner spiritual state to which this supreme Yoga will take us, will be above all that is here and yet comprehensive of all things in this and other worlds, but with a spiritual transformation of all, without limitation, without bondage, *sarva-dharmān parityajya.* The infinite existence, consciousness and delight of the Godhead in its calm silence and bright boundless activity will be there, will be its essential, fundamental, universal stuff, mould and character. And in that mould of infinity, the Divine made manifest will overtly dwell, no longer concealed by his Yogamaya, and whenever and as he wills build in us whatever shapes of the Infinite, translucent forms of knowledge, thought, love, spiritual joy, power and action according to his self-fulfilling will and immortal pleasure. And there will be no binding effect on the free soul and the unaffected nature, no unescapable crystallising into this or that inferior formula. For all the action will be executed by the power of the Spirit in a divine freedom, *sarva-dharmān parityajya.* An unfallen abiding in the transcendent Spirit, *param dhāma,* will be the foundation and the assurance of this spiritual state. An intimate understanding oneness with universal being and all creatures, released from the evil and suffering of the separative mind but wisely regardful of true distinctions, will be the conditioning power. A constant delight, oneness and harmony of the eternal individual here with the Divine and all that he is will be the effect of this integral liberation. The baffling problems of our human existence of which Arjuna's difficulty stands as an acute example, are created by our separative personality in the ignorance. This Yoga because it puts the soul of man into its right relation with God and world-existence and makes our action God's, the knowledge and will shaping and moving it his and our life the harmony of a divine self-expression, is the way to their total disappearance.

The whole Yoga is revealed, the great word of the teaching is given, and Arjuna the chosen human soul is once more turned, no longer in his egoistic mind but in this greatest self-knowledge, to the divine action. The Vibhuti is ready for the divine life in the human, his conscious spirit for the works of the liberated soul, *muktasya karma.* Destroyed is the illusion of the mind; the soul's memory of its self and its truth concealed so long by the misleading shows and forms of our life has returned to it and become its normal consciousness: all doubt and perplexity gone, it can turn to the execution of the command and do faithfully whatever work for God and the world may be appointed and apportioned to it by the Master of our being, the Spirit and Godhead self-fulfilled in Time and universe. (pp. 481-500)

. . . . .

What then is the message of the ***Gita*** and what its working value, its spiritual utility to the human mind of the present day after the long ages that have elapsed since it was written and the great subsequent transformations of thought and experience? The human mind moves always forward, alters its viewpoint and enlarges its thought substance, and the effect of these changes is to render past systems of thinking obsolete or, when they are preserved, to extend, to modify and subtly or visibly to alter their value. The vitality of an ancient doctrine consists in the extent to which it naturally lends itself to such a treatment; for that means that whatever may have been the limitations or the obsolescences of the form of its thought, the truth of substance, the truth of living vision and experience on which its system was built is still sound and retains a permanent validity and significance. The ***Gita*** is a book that has worn extraordinarily well and it is almost as fresh and still in its real substance quite as new, because always renewable in experience, as when it first appeared in or was written into the frame of the *Mahabharata.* It is still received in India as one of the great bodies of doctrine that most authoritatively govern religious thinking and its teaching acknowledged as of the highest value if not wholly accepted by almost all shades of religious belief and opinion. Its influence is not merely philosophic or academic but immediate and living, in influence both for thought and action, and its ideas are actually at work as a powerful shaping factor in the revival and renewal of a nation and a culture. It has even been said recently by a great voice that all we need of spiritual truth for the spiritual life is to be found in the ***Gita.*** It would be to encourage the superstition of the book to take too literally that utterance. The truth of the spirit is infinite and cannot be circumscribed in that manner. Still it may be said that most of the main clues are there and that after all the later developments of spiritual experience and discovery we can still return to it for a large inspiration and guidance. Outside India too it is universally acknowledged as one of the world's great scriptures, although in Europe its thought is better understood than its secret of spiritual practice. What is it then that gives this vitality to the thought and the truth of the ***Gita***?

The central interest of the ***Gita***'s philosophy and Yoga is its attempt, the idea with which it sets out, continues and closes, to reconcile and even effect a kind of unity between the inner spiritual truth in its most absolute and integral realisation and the outer actualities of man's life and action. A compromise between the two is common enough, but that can never be a final and satisfactory solution. An ethical rendering of spirituality is also common and has its value as a law of conduct; but that is a mental solution which does not amount to a complete practical reconciliation of the whole truth of spirit with the whole truth of life and it raises as many problems as it solves. One of these is indeed the starting-point of the ***Gita***; it sets out with an ethical problem raised by a conflict in which we have on one side the dharma of the man of action, a prince and warrior and leader of men, the protagonist of a great crisis, of a struggle on the physical plane, the plane of actual life, between the powers of right and justice and the powers of wrong and injustice, the demand of the destiny of the race upon him that he shall resist and give battle and establish, even though through a terrible physical struggle and a giant slaughter, a new era and reign of truth and right and justice, and on the other side the ethical sense which condemns the means and the action as a sin, recoils from the price of individual suffering and social strife, unsettling and disturbance and regards abstention from violence and battle as the only way and the one right moral attitude. A spiritualised ethics insists on Ahinsa, on non-injuring and non-killing, as the highest law of spiritual conduct. The battle, if it is to be fought out at all, must be fought on the spiritual plane and by some kind of non-resistance or refusal of participation or only by soul resistance, and if this does not succeed on the external plane, if the force of injustice conquers, the individual will still have preserved his virtue and vindicated by his example the highest ideal. On the other hand, a more insistent extreme of the inner spiritual direction, passing beyond this struggle between social duty and an absolutist ethical ideal, is apt to take the ascetic turn and to point away from life and all its aims and standards of action towards another and celestial or supracosmic state in which alone beyond the perplexed vanity and illusion of man's birth and life and death there can be a pure spiritual existence. The ***Gita*** rejects none of these things in their place,—for it insists on the performance of the social duty, the following of the dharma for the man who has to take his share in the common action, accepts Ahinsa as part of the highest spiritual-ethical ideal and recognises the ascetic renunciation as a way of spiritual salvation. And yet it goes boldly beyond all these conflicting positions; greatly daring, it justifies all life to the spirit as a significant manifestation of the one Divine Being and asserts the compatibility of a complete human action and a complete spiritual life lived in union with the Infinite, consonant with the highest Self, expressive of the perfect Godhead.

All the problems of human life arise from the complexity of our existence, the obscurity of its essential principle and the secrecy of the inmost power that makes out its determinations and governs its purpose and its processes. If our existence were of one piece, solely material-vital or solely mental or solely spiritual, or even if the others were entirely or mainly involved in one of these or were quite latent in our subconscient or our superconscient parts, there would be nothing to perplex us; the material and vital law would be imperative or the mental would be clear to its own pure and unobstructed principle or the spiritual self-existent and self-sufficient to spirit. The animals are aware of no problems; a mental god in a world of pure mentality would admit none or would solve them all by the purity of a mental rule or the satisfaction of a rational harmony; a pure spirit would be above them and self-content in the infinite. But the existence of man is a triple web, a thing mysteriously physical-vital, mental and spiritual at once, and he knows not what are the true relations of these things, which the real reality of his life and his nature, whither the attraction of his destiny and where the sphere of his perfection.

Matter and life are his actual basis, the thing from which he starts and on which he stands and whose requirement and law he has to satisfy if he would exist at all on earth and in the body. The material and vital law is a rule of survival, of struggle, of desire and possession, of self-assertion and the satisfaction of the body, the life and the ego. All the intellectual reasoning in the world, all the ethical idealism and spiritual absolutism of which the higher faculties of man are capable, cannot abolish the reality and claim of our vital and material base or prevent the race from following under the imperative compulsion of Nature its aims and the satisfaction of its necessities or from making its important problems a great and legitimate part of human destiny and human interest and endeavour. And the intelligence of man even, failing to find any sustenance in spiritual or ideal solutions that solve everything else but the pressing problems of our actual human life, often turns away from them to an exclusive acceptance of the vital and material existence and the reasoned or instinctive pursuit of its utmost possible efficiency, well-being and organised satisfaction. A gospel of the will to live or the will to power of a rationalised vital and material perfection becomes the recognised dharma of the human race and all else is considered either a pretentious falsity or a quite subsidiary thing, a side issue of a minor and dependant consequence.

Matter and life, however, in spite of their insistence and great importance are not all that man is, nor can he wholly accept mind as nothing but a servant of the life and body admitted to certain pure enjoyments of its own as a sort of reward for its service or regard it as no more than an extension and flower of the vital urge, an ideal luxury contingent upon the satisfaction of the material life. The mind much more intimately than the body and the life is the man, and the mind as it develops insists more and more on making the body and the life an instrument—an indispensable instrument and yet a considerable obstacle, otherwise there would be no problem—for its own characteristic satisfactions and self-realisation. The mind of man is not only a vital and physical, but an intellectual, æsthetic, ethical, psychic, emotional and dynamic intelligence, and in the sphere of each of its tendencies its highest and strongest nature is to strain towards some absolute of them which the frame of life will not allow it to capture wholly and embody and make here entirely real. The mental absolute of our aspiration remains as a partly grasped shining or fiery ideal which the mind can make inwardly very present to itself, inwardly imperative on its effort, and can even effectuate partly, but not compel all the facts of life into its image. There is thus an absolute, a high imperative of intellectual truth and reason sought for by our intellectual being; there is an absolute, an imperative of right and conduct aimed at by the ethical conscience; there is an absolute, an imperative of love, sympathy, compassion, oneness yearned after by our emotional and psychic nature; there is an absolute, an imperative of delight and beauty quivered to by the æsthetic soul; there is an absolute, an imperative of inner self-mastery and control of life laboured after by the dynamic will; all these are there together and impinge upon the absolute, the imperative of possession and pleasure and safe embodied existence insisted on by the vital and physical mind. And the human intelligence, since it is not able to realise entirely any of these things, much less all of them together, erects in each sphere many standards and dharmas, standards of truth and reason, of right and conduct, of delight and beauty, of love, sympathy and oneness, of self-mastery and control, of self-preservation and possession and vital efficiency and pleasure, and tries to impose them on life. The absolute shining ideals stand far above and beyond our capacity and rare individuals approximate to them as best they can: the mass follow or profess to follow some less magnificent norm, some established possible and relative standard. Human life as a whole undergoes the attraction and yet rejects the ideal. Life resists in the strength of some obscure infinite of its own and wears down or breaks down any established mental and moral order. And this must be either because the two are quite different and disparate though meeting and interacting principles or because mind has not the clue to the whole reality of life. The clue must be sought in something greater, an unknown something above the mentality and morality of the human creature.

The mind itself has the vague sense of some surpassing factor of this kind and in the pursuit of its absolutes frequently strikes against it. It glimpses a state, a power, a presence that is near and within and inmost to it and yet immeasurably greater and singularly distant and above it; it has a vision of something more essential, more absolute than its own absolutes, intimate, infinite, one, and it is that which we call God, Self or Spirit. This then the mind attempts to know, enter, touch and seize wholly, to approach it or become it, to arrive at some kind of unity or lose itself in a complete identity with that mystery, *āścaryam.* The difficulty is that this spirit in its purity seems something yet farther than the mental absolutes from the actualities of life, something not translatable by mind into its own terms, much less into those of life and action. Therefore we have the intransigeant absolutists of the spirit who reject the mental and condemn the material being and yearn after a pure spiritual existence happily purchased by the dissolution of all that we are in life and mind, a Nirvana. The rest of spiritual effort is for these fanatics of the Absolute a mental preparation or a compromise, a spiritualising of life and mind as much as possible. And because the difficulty most constantly insistent on man's mentality in practice is that presented by the claims of his vital being, by life and conduct and action, the direction taken by this preparatory endeavor consists mainly in a spiritualising of the ethical supported by the psychical mind—or rather it brings in the spiritual power and purity to aid these in enforcing their absolute claim and to impart a greater authority than life allows to the ethical ideal of right and truth of conduct or the psychic ideal of love and sympathy and oneness. These things are helped to some highest expression, given their broadest luminous basis by an assent of the reason and will to the underlying truth of the absolute oneness of the spirit and therefore the essential oneness of all living creatures. This kind of spirituality linked on in some way to the demands of the normal mind of man, persuaded to the acceptance of useful social duty and current law of social conduct, popularised by cult and ceremony and image is the outward substance of the world's greater religions. These religions have their individual victories, call in some ray of a higher light, impose some shadow of a larger spiritual or semispiritual rule, but cannot effect a complete victory, end flatly in a compromise and in the act of compromise are defeated by life. Its problems remain and even recur in their fiercest forms—even such as this grim problem of Kurukshetra. The idealising intellect and ethical mind hope always to eliminate them, to discover some happy device born of their own aspiration and made effective by their own imperative insistence, which will annihilate this nether untoward aspect of life; but it endures and is not eliminated. The spiritualised intelligence on the other hand offers indeed by the voice of religion the promise of some victorious millennium hereafter, but meanwhile half convinced of terrestrial impotence, persuaded that the soul is a stranger and intruder upon earth, declares that after all not here in the life of the body or in the collective life of mortal man but in some immortal Beyond lies the heaven or the Nirvana where alone is to be found the true spiritual existence.

It is here that the ***Gita*** intervenes with a restatement of the truth of the Spirit, of the Self, of God and of the world and Nature. It extends and remoulds the truth evolved by a later thought from the ancient *Upanishads* and ventures with assured steps on an endeavour to apply its solving power to the problem of life and action. The solution offered by the ***Gita*** does not disentangle all the problem as it offers itself to modern mankind; as stated here to a more ancient mentality, it does not meet the insistent pressure of the present mind of man for a collective advance, does not respond to its cry for a collective life that will at last embody a greater rational and ethical and, if possible, even a dynamic spiritual ideal. Its call is to the individual who has become capable of a complete spiritual existence; but for the rest of the race it prescribes only a gradual advance, to be wisely effected by following out faithfully with more and more of intelligence and moral purpose and with a final turn to spirituality the law of their nature. Its message touches the other smaller solutions but, even when it accepts them partly, it is to point them beyond themselves to a higher and more integral secret into which is yet only the few individuals have shown themselves fit to enter.

The ***Gita***'s message to the mind that follows after the vital and material life is that all life is indeed a manifestation of the universal Power in the individual, a derivation from the Self, a ray from the Divine, but actually it figures the Self and the Divine veiled in a disguising Maya, and to pursue the lower life for its own sake is to persist in a stumbling path and to enthrone our nature's obscure ignorance and not at all to find the true truth and complete law of existence. A gospel of the will to live, the will to power, of the satisfaction of desire, of the glorification of mere force and strength, of the worship of the ego and its vehement acquisitive self-will and tireless self-regarding intellect is the gospel of the Asura and it can lead only to some gigantic ruin and perdition. The vital and material man must accept for his government a religious and social and ideal dharma by which, while satisfying desire and interest under right restrictions, he can train and subdue his lower personality and scrupulously attune it to a higher law both of the personal and the communal life.

The ***Gita***'s message to the mind occupied with the pursuit of intellectual, ethical and social standards, the mind that insists on salvation by the observance of established dharmas, the moral law, social duty and function or the solutions of the liberated intelligence, is that this is indeed a very necessary stage, the ḍharma has indeed to be observed and, rightly observed, can raise the stature of the spirit and prepare and serve the spiritual life, but still it is not the complete and last truth of existence. The soul of man has to go beyond to some more absolute dharma of man's spiritual and immortal nature. And this can only be done if we repress and get rid of the ignorant formulations of the lower mental elements and the falsehood of egoistic personality, impersonalise the action of the intelligence and will, live in the identity of the one self in all, break out of all ego-moulds into the impersonal spirit. The mind moves under the limiting compulsion of the triple lower nature, it erects its standards in obedience to the tamasic, rajasic or at highest the sattwic qualities; but the destiny of the soul is a divine perfection and liberation and that can only be based in the freedom of our highest self, can only be found by passing through its vast impersonality and universality beyond mind into the integral light of the immeasurable Godhead and supreme Infinite who is beyond all dharmas.

The ***Gita***'s message to those, absolutist seekers of the Infinite, who carry impersonality to an exclusive extreme, entertain an intolerant passion for the extinction of life and action and would have as the one ultimate aim and ideal an endeavour to cease from all individual being in the pure silence of the ineffable Spirit, is that this is indeed one path of journey and entry into the Infinite, but the most difficult, the ideal of inaction a dangerous thing to hold up by precept or example before the world, this way, though great, yet not the best way for man and this knowledge, though true, yet not the integral knowledge. The Supreme, the all-conscious Self, the Godhead, the Infinite is not solely a spiritual existence remote and ineffable; he is here in the universe at once hidden and expressed through man and the gods and through all beings and in all that is. And it is by finding him not only in some immutable silence but in the world and its beings and in all self and in all Nature, it is by raising to an integral as well as to a highest union with him all the activities of the intelligence, the heart, the will, the life that man can solve at once his inner riddle of Self and God and the outer problem of his active human existence. Made Godlike, God-becoming, he can enjoy the infinite breadth of a supreme spiritual consciousness that is reached through works no less than through love and knowledge. Immortal and free, he can continue his human action from that highest level and transmute it into a supreme and all-embracing divine activity,—that indeed is the ultimate crown and significance here of all works and living and sacrifice and the world's endeavour.

This highest message is first for those who have the strength to follow after it, the master men, the great spirits, the God-knowers, God-doers, God-lovers who can live in God and for God and do their work joyfully for him in the world, a divine work uplifted above the restless darkness of the human mind and the false limitations of the ego. At the same time, and here we get the gleam of a larger promise which we may even extend to the hope of a collective turn towards perfection,—for if there is hope for man, why should there not be hope for mankind?—the ***Gita*** declares that all can if they will, even to the lowest and sinfullest among men, enter into the path of this Yoga. And if there is a true self-surrender and an absolute unegoistic faith in the indwelling Divinity, success is certain in this path. The decisive turn is needed; there must be an abiding belief in the Spirit, a sincere and insistent will to live in the Divine, to be in self one with him and in Nature—where too we are an eternal portion of his being—one with his greater spiritual Nature, God-possessed in all our members and Godlike.

The ***Gita*** in the development of its idea raises many issues, such as the determinism of Nature, the significance of the universal manifestation and the ultimate status of the liberated soul, questions that have been the subject of unending and inconclusive debate. It is not necessary in . . . a scrutiny and positive affirmation of the substance of the ***Gita*** and a disengaging of its contribution to the abiding spiritual thought of humanity and its kernel of living practice, to enter far into these discussions or to consider where we may differ from its standpoint or conclusions, make any reserves in our assent or even, strong in later experience, go beyond its metaphysical teaching or its Yoga. It will be sufficient to close with a formulation of the living message it still brings for man the eternal seeker and discoverer to guide him through the present circuits and the possible steeper ascent of his life up to the luminous heights of his spirit. (pp. 501-09)

Sri Aurobindo, in his Essays on the Gita, *E. P. Dutton & Co., Inc., 1950, 580 p.*

Heinrich Zimmer (essay date 1943?)

[*Zimmer was a distinguished German Orientalist known for his seminal studies of Indian mythology, art, and philosophy. His posthumously published works, which were edited by Joseph Campbell, include* Myths and Symbols in Indian Art and Civilization *(1946),* The King and the Corpse: Tales of the Soul's Conquest of Evil *(1948),* Philosophies of India, *from which the following excerpt is taken, and* The Art of Indian Asia: Its Mythology and Transformations *(1955). Here, he describes the* Gītā *as a great synthesis of the austere pre-Aryan dualistic worldview and the monistic, life-oriented philosophies of the Vedic period. Since the exact date of the essay is unknown, the year of Zimmer's death has been used as the essay date.*]

It was in the great paradoxes of the epoch-making ***Bhagavad Gītā*** that the non-Brāhmanical, pre-Āryan thought of aboriginal India became fruitfully combined and har-

The gods looking at Krsna and Arjuna.

monized with the *Vedic* ideas of the Āryan invaders. In the eighteen brief chapters was displayed a kaleidoscopic interworking of the two traditions that for some ten centuries had been contending for the control and mastery of the Indian mind. (p. 378)

[The] non-Āryan systems (Jainism, Gosāla's teaching, Sāṅkhya, and Yoga) were characterized by a resolutely logical, theoretical dichotomy, which insisted on a strict distinction between two spheres, that of the life-monad (*jīva, puruṣa*) and that of matter (*a-jīva, prakṛti*), the pure and crystal-like, immaterial essence of the pristine individual and the polluting, darkening principle of the material world. The process of life was read as an effect of the interpenetration of these polar principles—an everlasting blending of two antagonistic forces, bringing to pass a perpetual procreating and disintegrating of compound, unsubstantial forms. The conjunction was compared to the mingling of fire with iron in a red-hot iron ball; it was a result of proximity and association, not proper to either principle *per se.* And the two could be understood in their distinct, mutually contrary, intrinsic natures only when separated and allowed to return to their simple, primary states—the corollary of all this in practice being a doctrine of asceticism (or rather, a number of varying doctrines of asceticism) aiming at the separation of the two incompatible principles. The process of life was to be halted. Purification, sterilization, was to be the great ideal of human virtue; and the goal, the attainment of absolute motionlessness in crystal purity—not the dynamism of the incessant processional of life. For the processes of nature (generation, digestion, assimilation, elimination, the dissolution of the dead body as it begets swarming tribes of worms and insects, metabolism, gestation) are all unclean. The will is to purge the whole thing away. Whether in the microcosmic alchemical retort of the individual, or in the macrocosm of the universal laboratory, the unclean process of elements forever uniting, forever sundering, is equally deplorable, a sort of general orgy of indecencies from which the self-recollecting spirit can only resign.

Contrast with this the vigorous, tumultuous, and joyous life-affirmative of the *Vedic Hymn of Food.* The new thing that the Brāhmans brought to India was a jubilant, monistic emphasis on the sanctity of life: a powerful and persistent assertion that the One Thing is always present as two. "I am both," asserts the Lord of Food; "I am the two: the life-force and the life-material—the two at once." The jejune disjunction of the world into matter and spirit derives from an abstraction of the intellect and should not be projected back upon reality; for it is of the nature of the mind to establish differences, to make definitions and discriminate. To declare, "There are distinctions," is only to state that there is an apprehending intellect at work. Perceived pairs-of-opposites reflect the nature not of things but of the perceiving mind. Hence thought, the intellect itself, must be transcended if true reality is to be attained. Logic is a help for preliminary clarification, but an imperfect, inadequate instrument for the final insight; its orderly notions, oppositions, and relationships must be overcome if the searching mind is to attain to any direct conception or realization of the transcendent truth. The One Thing that is the first, last, and only reality (this is the basic Brāhman thesis) comprises all the pairs-of-opposites (*dvandva*) that proceed from it, whether physically, in the course of life's evolution, or conceptually, as logical distinctions occurring to the intellect coincident with thought.

Founded in this realization of an all-unifying, transcendent principle, Brāhmanical thought of the period of the *Upaniṣads* was well fitted to absorb not only the divine personalities of the earlier *Vedic* pantheon but also the much more sophisticated philosophic and devotional formulae of the non-Āryan, aboriginal tradition. The ***Bhagavad Gītā*** is the classic document of the first stages of this adjustment. Its teaching is styled an esoteric doctrine, yet it has become the most popular, widely memorized authoritative statement of the basic guiding principles of Indian religious life. The text, an episode of eighteen brief chapters inserted in the *Mahābhārata* at the point of epic action where the two great armies are about to join in battle, is by no means all of a piece. Numerous contradictions have been pointed out by the Western critics, yet to the Indian mind these contradictions are precisely the value. For they represent the beginning of the great *rapprochement* and, besides, are readily resolved by a realization of the One in all.

The ranks of the warriors of the two rival armies of the *Mahābhārata* had been drawn up against each other, and all was prepared for the opening trumpet blast, when the leader of the Pāṇḍavas, Arjuna, desired to be driven by his charioteer into the field between, so that he might review, at a glance, both his own forces and those of his enemy cousins, the Kauravas. However, the moment he beheld, in both ranks, his friends and teachers, sons and grandfathers, nephews, uncles, and brothers, an emotion of the greatest pity and regret assailed him. His spirit was unmanned, and he doubted whether he should permit the battle to begin.

At this critical juncture his charioteer spoke and gave him heart. And the words uttered under these heroic circumstances, on the verge of the most tremendous battle of Indian epic history, are what have been termed the ***Bhagavad Gītā, The Song of the Blessed Lord;*** for the charioteer was none other than the god Kṛṣṇa, an Incarnation of the Creator, Preserver, and Destroyer of the world. The revelation was given by a friend to a friend, the young god to his companion, the prince Arjuna. It was an exclusive, an aristocratic, doctrine; for the god Kṛṣṇa, this divine particle of the holy supramundane essence who had descended to earth for the salvation of mankind, was himself a slayer of demons, himself an epic hero, while the noble youth to whom the words were addressed when he was in despair as to what to do (impotent, at the critical moment of his career, to determine what would be for him *dharma,* correct behavior) was the fairest flower of the epic period of Hindu chivalry. It had been because of his sympathy for this dispossessed young king that the beautiful, dark Kṛṣṇa had become his adviser in the somewhat allegorical role of charioteer, when he was about to enter battle for the recovery of his usurped throne and the winning of the sovereignty of the land of India. Kṛṣṇa wished not only to play the part of spiritual adviser to his friend, but also to utilize this vivid moment to proclaim to all mankind his doctrine of salvation *in* the world—which is known as the "Yoga of Selfless Action" (*karma-yoga*)—and all that it entails in the way of self-surrender and devotion (*bhakti*) to the Lord who is identical with the Self within all. The doctrine is "very difficult to grasp"; this is a fact emphasized again and again. For example: "The innermost principle of man's nature (the so-called 'Owner of the Organism': *dehin śarīrin*) is unmanifest, unthinkable, unchangeable. . . . One person beholds this Self as a marvel. Another speaks of It as a marvel. Still another hears-and-learns of It as a marvel (being instructed in the sacred esoteric tradition by a guru). Yet, though having heard and learned, no one has any real understanding of what It is."

The circumstances of the dialogue are described in vigorous, simple terms.

"Arjuna said: 'Place my chariot, O Changeless One, between the two armies, so that in this moment of impending battle I may behold those standing eager for war, with whom I have to fight. . . . '

"Thus addressed, Krsna drove the incomparable chariot between the two armies drawn up for battle, facing Bhīsma, Drona, and all the rulers of the earth. And he said: 'Behold, O son of Pṛthā, the Kauravas here assembled!'

"Then Arjuna gazed upon the two peoples: fathers, grandfathers, teachers, maternal uncles, brothers, sons, grandsons, companions, fathers-in-law, and friends. . . . " And he was overcome with horror at the thought of the dreadful fratricidal fury that was about to seize them all. On the one hand he was unwilling to precipitate the battle that should annihilate "those," as he said, "who are my own people," while on the other he was bound by the code of chivalry to avenge the injuries that he and his brothers had sustained from their cousins, and to assist his brethren in their just effort to recover their dominion. Not knowing what he should do, mind whirling, unable to distinguish the right from the wrong, Arjuna, in despair, turned to his friend and charioteer, Krsna; and as the divine words of God poured into his ears and heart, he was set at ease as to the mysteries of right and wrong.

Krsna's message culminates in the "supreme utterance," which commences in Chapter X.

> Now give ear to my supreme utterance. Because thou art dear to Me, I will proclaim it to thee for thy good. Neither the hosts of the gods nor the great seers know My source. Altogether more ancient than they am I. He who knows Me as the Unborn, the Beginningless, the Great Lord of the World, he among mortals, free from delusion, is released from all his sins. From Me alone arise the manifold states of mind of created beings: power of judgment, knowledge, purity of spirit, forbearance, true insight, discipline, serenity, pleasure and pain, well-being and distress, fear and reliance, compassion, equanimity, contentment, self-control, benevolence, glory and infamy. Likewise, the seven great Ṛṣis of old and the four Manus arose from Me alone, generated by My spirit; and from them descend these creatures in the world. He who knows in truth this manifestation of My might and My creative power is armed with unshakable constancy. I am the Source of all, from Me everything arises. Whosoever has insight, knows this. And with this insight the wise worship Me, overwhelmed by awe. . . .

"Time (*kāla*) am I, the Destroyer great and mighty, appearing here to sweep all men away. Even without thee [and thine act of leadership] none of these warriors here, in their ranks arrayed, shall remain alive. Therefore, do thou arise, win glory, smite the foe, enjoy in prosperity thy lordship. By Me, and Me alone, have they long since been routed. BE THOU NOUGHT BUT MY TOOL."

This is applied bhakti. The *bhakta,* the devotee, brings into realization in space and time, as the merely apparent cause, what for the time-and-space-transcending God is beyond the categories of the uneventuated and eventuated, the "not yet" and the "already done." The imperishable Self, the Owner of the perishable bodies, is the supreme director of the harrowing spectacle of Time.

> 'Having-an-end' are called these bodies of Him, the Eternal, who is the 'Owner of Bodies' (*śarīrin*), who is imperishable, boundless, and unfathomable. . . . Whoever thinks Him to be he who kills, and whoever thinks Him to be he who is killed—these two lack true insight; for He neither kills nor is killed. He is not born, nor does He die at any time; He did not become in the past nor will He spring into existence again at a future moment; He is unborn, eternal, everlasting—the 'Old One' (*purāṇa*); He is not killed when the body is killed. The man who knows Him to be indestructible, eternal, without birth, and immutable—how can he slay; or whom? Even as a man casts off old and worn-out clothes and puts on others which are new, so the 'Owner of the Body' (*dehin*) casts off worn-out bodies and enters into others which are new.

"As childhood, youth, and old age in this present body are to Him Who Owns the Body (*dehin*), so also is the attaining of another body. The Wise are not disturbed by this."

The Self is not affected when its mask is changed from that of childhood to that of youth, and then to that of age. The individual ego, the cherished personality, may feel disturbed, and may have difficulty adjusting itself to the changes and all the losses of life-opportunity that the changes imply, but the Self is unaffected. And it is equally unconcerned when the mask is put aside altogether at the time of death, and a new one assumed at the next birth. There is no death, no real change, for Him. Hence, whether the sequence be that of bodies or of the ages of the body, it weighs no more on Him than do the solstices of the seasons or the phases of the moon. There is no cause for grief. "Weapons do not cut Him, fire does not burn Him, water wet Him, or the wind dry Him away. He cannot be cut, He cannot be burnt, He cannot be wet, He cannot be dried away. He is changeless (*nitya*), all-pervading (*sarvagata*), stable (*sthānu*), unshakable (*acala*), and permanent (*sanātana*)."

The Owner of the Body is beyond event; and since it is He who is the true essence of the individual, one must not pity the perishable creatures for being such as they are. "Thou dost feel pity," says Kṛṣṇa to the confused warrior, "where pity has no place. Wise men feel no pity either for what dies or for what lives. There never was a time when I and thou were not in existence, and all these princes too. Nor will the day ever come, hereafter, when all of us shall cease to be." "There is no existence for nothingness; there is no destruction for that which is. Be assured that the very tissue of this universe is the Imperishable; it lies in no man's power to destroy it. Bodies come to an end, but 'He Who Is Clothed in the Body' (*śarīrin*) is eternal, indestructible, and infinite.—Fight then, O Bhārata!"

Karma Yoga, the great ethical principle incorporated in this metaphysically grounded realism of the Incarnate Divine Essence, requires that the individual should continue carrying on his usual duties and activities of life, but with a new attitude of detachment from their fruits, i.e., from the possible gains or losses that they will entail. The world and its way of actualization is not to be abandoned, but the will of the individual is to be united in action with the universal ground, not with the vicissitudes of the suffering body and nervous system. That is the teaching of the Incarnate Creator and Sustainer. That is the world-balancing crux of his supreme advice to man. "The practice of worship through offerings (*yajña*), the giving of alms (*dāna*), and austerity (*tapas*) should not be abandoned. Indeed, these works should be performed; for worship, charity, and austerity are purifying to the wise. And yet even such selfless works as these are to be performed with a resignation of all attachment to them and their fruits; that is My best and unwavering conviction." "Give thought to nothing but the act, never to its fruits, and let not thyself be seduced by inaction. For him who achieves inward detachment, neither good nor evil exists any longer here below." "Consider pleasure and pain, wealth and poverty, victory and defeat, as of equal worth. Prepare then for the combat. Acting in this way thou wilt not become stained by guilt."

The God himself acts—both as a macrocosm, through the events of the world, and as a microcosm, in the form of his Incarnation. That fact itself should serve as a salutary lesson. "There is naught in the Three Worlds," declares Krsna,

> that I have need to do, nor anything that I have not obtained and that I might gain, yet I participate in action. If I did not do so without relaxation, people would follow my example. These worlds would perish if I did not go on performing works. I should cause confusion [for men would relinquish the tasks and activities assigned to them by birth]; I should be the ruin of all these beings [for the gods, the celestial bodies, etc., would terminate their activities, following the example set by the Highest]. Just as ignorant people act, being attached to actions, even so should the wise man (*vidvān,* the comprehender) also act, though unattached—with a view to the maintenance of order in the world.

The unfatigued activity of the Divine Being controlling the universe is a matter of routine, a kind of ritual that does not deeply concern Him. In the same way, the perfect man should fulfill the duties of his life in a spirit of playful routine, so as not to break the whole course of the play in which the role (from which he has become deeply detached) involves him. "For it is impossible," says Kṛṣṇa, "for any being endowed with a body to give up activity-without-rest; but he who relinquishes the fruits (*phala:* rewards, results) of his acts is called a man of true renunciation (*tyāgin*)."

To suppose that, being endowed with a body, one can avoid involvement in the web of karma is a vain illusion. Nevertheless, it is possible to avoid increased involvement, and possible even to disengage the mind, by disregarding the consequences and apparent promises of one's unavoidable tasks and enterprises—that is to say, by an absolute self-sacrifice. One is to look for no reward in the fulfillment of one's duties as a son or father, as a Brāhman or as a warrior, in the performance of the orthodox rituals, in dispensing charity, or in whatever else the work of virtue may chance to be. "One should not give up the activity to which one is born (*sahajaṁ karma:* the duty incumbent on one through birth, caste, profession), even though this should be attended by evil; for all undertakings are enveloped by evil, as is fire by smoke."

The earthly plane is the sphere of imperfection, by definition as it were. Perfection, stainless purity, is to be reached only through disentanglement from the manifest sphere of the gunas—a spiritual progress that dissolves the individual, the mask of the personality and all the forms of action that pertain to it, in the undefiled, undifferentiated, anonymous, absolutely changeless realm of the Self. Meanwhile, however, the duties and obligations of the life into which one was born are those that are to be clung to. "Better one's own life-task and duty (*dharma*), though worthless and destitute of qualities (*vi-guṇa*), than the duty of another well-performed. He who performs the activities (*karma kurvan*) dictated by his inborn nature [which are identical with those of his place in society] incurs no stain."

Even a person born into an unclean caste (a sweeper, an undertaker, for example) should hold to the inherited career. By performing the work as well as possible, in the ordained way, he becomes a perfect, virtuous member of society; breaking loose and intruding upon other people's duties, on the other hand, he would become guilty of disturbing the sacred order. Even the harlot, as we have seen, though indeed within the hierarchy of society she is far below the state of the virtuous housewife, nevertheless, if she fulfills to perfection the moral code of her despicable profession, participates in the trans-individual, suprahuman Holy Power which is manifested in the cosmos—and she can work miracles to baffle kings and saints.

Kṛṣṇa, the divine proclaimer of the doctrine of the ***Bhagavad Gītā,*** offers himself not only as a teacher but also as a good example. He represents the willing participation of the Supreme Deity itself in the mysterious joy and agony of the forms of the manifested world—these being, finally, no less than Its Own reflection.

> Though I am unborn, though my Self is changeless, though I am the Divine Lord of all perishable beings, nevertheless, residing in my own material nature (*prakṛti*), I become a transitory being (*sambhavāmi*) through the magic divine

> power of playful illusive transformation which produces all phenomena and belongs to my own Self (*ātmamāyayā*). Whenever there occurs a relaxation or weakening of the principle of duty and a rise of unrighteousness, then I pour Myself forth. For the protection of the just and the destruction of the workers of evil, for the confirmation of virtue and the divine moral order of the universe, I become a transitory being among the perishable creatures in every age of the world.

According to the Hindu view, the entrance of God into the strife of the universe is not a unique, astounding entrance of the transcendental essence into the welter of mundane affairs (as in Christianity, where the Incarnation is regarded as a singular and supreme sacrifice, never to be repeated), but a rhythmical event, conforming to the beat of the world ages. The savior descends as a counterweight to the forces of evil during the course of every cyclic decline of mundane affairs, and his work is accomplished in a spirit of imperturbable indifference. The periodic incarnation of the Holy Power is a sort of solemn leitmotiv in the interminable opera of the cosmic process, resounding from time to time like a majestic flourish of celestial trumpets, to silence the disharmonies and to state again the triumphant themes of the moral order. These should predominate over, but not eradicate entirely, the numerous melodies and dissonant tones of the complex partition. The savior, the divine hero (the super-Lohengrin, Parsifal, or Siegfried), having set things aright by subduing the demon forces—both in their cosmic aspect and in their human garb of wicked tyrants and evil men—withdraws from the phenomenal sphere as calmly, solemnly, and willingly as he descended. He never becomes the seeming temporary victim of the demon powers (as did Christ nailed to the Cross) but is triumphant in his passage, from beginning to end. The Godhead, in its very aloofness, does not in the least mind assuming temporarily an active role on the phenomenal plane of ever-active Nature.

The descent is represented in Indian mythology as the sending forth of a minute particle (*aṁśa*) of the infinite supramundane essence of the Godhead—that essence itself suffering thereby no diminution; for the putting forth of a savior, the putting forth even of the mirage of the universe, no more diminishes the plenitude of the transcendent and finally unmanifested Brahman than the putting forth of a dream diminishes the substance of our own Unconscious. In fact, it may be said (and now that our Western psychology has begun to search these matters, this is becoming increasingly clear to us) that the Hindu view and symbolism of the macrocosmic universal māyā is based on millenniums of introspection, as a result of which experience the creative processes of the human psyche have been accepted as man's best clues to the powers, activities, and attitudes of the world-creative supramundane Being. In the process of evolving a dream world of dream scenery and dream people—supplying also a heroic dream double of our own ego, to endure and enjoy all sorts of strange adventures—we do not suffer the least diminution, but on the contrary realize an expansion of our personal substance. Unseen forces manifest themselves in all these images and by so doing enjoy themselves, realize themselves. It is likewise with God, when he pours forth his creative māyā-force. Nor is our psychic substance diminished by the sending forth of the sense forces through the gates of the sense organs to grasp the sense objects, swallow them, and present them to the mind; nor again is the mind diminished when it shapes itself to the patterns thus offered by the sense organs, copying them exactly in its own subtle substance—which is claylike, soft and malleable. Such activities, whether in dream or in waking, are expansive, self-delighting exercises of man's vital essence, which is ready for and easily capable of the facile self-transformations. Man's work therein is a microcosmic counterpart of the creative principle of the universe. God's māyā shapes the universe by taking shape itself, playing through all the transitory figures and bewildering events, and therein it is not the least diminished, but on the contrary only magnified and expanded.

The field of the micromacrocosmic manifestation was characterized in the Sāṅkhya in terms of an unceasing interplay of the three constituents or qualities of prakṛti, the so-called gunas. In the ***Bhagavad Gītā,*** this idea is taken over but completely assimilated into the Vedic Brāhmanical conception of the one and only Self.

> Whatever states there may be of the qualities of clarity (*sāttvika*), passion and violence (*rājasa*), and darkness-inertia (*tāmasa*), know verily that these proceed from Me; yet I am not in them—they are in Me. This whole universe of living beings is deluded by these states compounded of the three qualities; hence they do not know Me, Who am beyond them and immutable. For this divine illusion (*māyā*) of mine, which is constituted of [and operates through] the guṇas, is exceedingly difficult to traverse. Those who devote themselves exclusively to Me, however, traverse it.

The broad river of ignorance and passion is a dangerous torrent, yet the savior, the divine ferryman, can bring his devotees safely to the other shore. This is an image held in common by all Indian traditions. The Jaina saviors are termed Tīrthaṅkaras, "Crossing-Makers." The Buddha traverses a river by walking on its waves, and his Wisdom is known as the "Knowledge that has Gone to the Other Shore" (*prajñā-pāram-itā*). In the same spirit, the popular Mahāyāna savior Avalokiteśvara (Chinese: Kwan-yin; Japanese: Kwannon) is represented as a winged steed, named "Cloud" (*valāhaka*), who carries to the far-off bank of enlightened freedom-in-extinction all who wish to go.

An amusing allegorical tale, in the Buddhist sūtra known as the *Kāraṇḍavyūha,* represents Cloud as manifesting himself to a company of shipwrecked merchants who had set sail for the Jewel Isle. These had fallen in with certain alluring women on another enchanted island, who had seemed to receive them hospitably and freely allowed them to make love, but finally proved to be man-eating monsters only waiting to devour them. The seductresses had consumed many merchants before, who, like those of the present party, had been washed onto their beaches. At once alluring and devouring, they represent in the Buddhist allegory the enticing, destructive character of the sensual world. But over the island of these seductresses, the isle of the life of man's involvement in the world, the figure of "Cloud" (*valāhaka*), the savior, is wont to appear, from time to time, soaring through the sky. And he calls out: *Ko pāraga:* "Who is going to the other shore?" which is a familiar cry in India; for it is the cry of the ferryman when his boat puts in. The ferryman shouts it loudly, so that any travelers tarrying in the village may know that they must hurry; and the voice of Cloud rings loudly too. When the merchants hear it, those who can bring themselves to forsake the perilous pleasures of the island immediately mount the winged steed, and they are transported to the "other shore" of peace. But all who remain meet in time a terrible death. Moreover those, once mounted on the gigantic flying savior, who turn to look back for a last, fond view, inadvertently fall to a sorry death in the pitiless sea below.

The inhabitant of the perishable body—the indestructible life-monad (*puruṣa*), which according to the Sāṅkhya doctrine was to be regarded as the core and life-seed of each living individual—according to the composite system of the ***Bhagavad Gītā*** is but a particle of the one supreme Divine Being, with which it is in essence identical. Thus, with one bold stroke, the transcendental monism of the *Vedic* Brāhman doctrine of the Self is reconciled with the pluralistic life-monad doctrine of the dualistic, atheistic Sāṅkhya; and so the two teachings now are understood in India as descriptions from two points of view of the same reality. The nondual Ātmavāda presents the higher truth, whereas the Sāṅkhya is an empirical analysis of the logical principles of the lower, rational sphere of the pairs-of-opposites (*dvandva*). In the latter, antagonistic principles are in force, and these constitute the basis, or termini, of all normal human experience and rational thought. Nevertheless, it is a sign of nonknowing to suppose that because the dualistic argument is logical and accords with the facts of life, it is therefore consonant with the final truth. Dualism belongs to the sphere of manifestation, the sphere of bewildering differentiation through the interaction of the gunas, and is but a part of the great cosmic play of māyā.

The sole Well of Truth, speaking as Kṛṣṇa, declares:

> A part of My very Self, an eternal one, becomes a life-monad (*jīva-bhūta*) in the realm of the life-monads (*jīva-loka:* i.e., in the manifested sphere of creation, which is teeming with life-monads). This draws to itself mind and the five sense forces, which are rooted, and which abide, in the matter of the universe. When this Divine Lord (*īśvara*) thus obtains a body, and when again he steps out of it and departs, he carries these six forces or functions along with him from their abode or receptacle [the heart], and goes his way; just as the wind carries scents along with it from their abode. Ruling over the ear, the eye, touch, taste, and the sense of smell, as well as the mind, he experiences the objects of sense. People deluded by ignorance fail to behold Him whether He steps out of the body or remains within it united with the guṇas and experiencing the objects of sense; those do behold Him, however, who possess the eye of wisdom.

"The Lord (*īśvara*) dwells in the region of the heart of all perishable creatures and causes all beings to revolve (*bhrā-mayan*) by His divine deluding power (*māyā*) as if they were mounted on a machine (*yantrārūdha:* e.g. on a wheel provided with buckets for the irrigation of a rice-field)." "This Owner of the Body, inhabiting the bodies of all, is eternally indestructible: therefore thou shouldest not grieve for any creature."

As stated, the special doctrine of the ***Bhagavad Gītā*** is Karma Yoga, the selfless performance of the earthly task to be done; but this is not the only road to the freedom and sovereignty of the divine Self. Kṛṣṇa, the warrior-incarnation of the Supreme Being, recognizes many ways, corresponding to the various propensities and capacities of the differing human types.

> "Some," declares the God, "by concentration, bent on inner visualizations, behold, through their self, in their self, the Self Divine; others [behold or realize It] through the yoga-technique related to the Sāṅkhya system of Enumerative Knowledge; and still others through the yoga of selfless action. Others again, however, not knowing [these esoteric ways of introvert self-discipline and transformation], worship Me as they have been taught to in terms of the orthodox oral tradition; yet even these cross beyond death, though devoted exclusively to the revelation as communicated in the Vedas."

The ancient days of the Vedic, sacrificial, external routines had long passed at the time of the proclamation of the ***Bhagavad Gītā.*** The ceremonious priestly style of worshiping divine beings was no longer dominant. Nevertheless the value of such exercises for the reaching of the goal could still be acknowledged as a minor way. It long remained sanctified by tradition, but was rather cumbersome and old-fashioned. People not up to date in their philosophical ideas—the country cousins, the *pagani*—continued to practice these rather quaint routines, and of course experienced the usual, long-tested good effects; nevertheless the real adventurers and heroes of the supreme enterprise of the human spirit would follow the direct, much more intense, rapid and dependable, interior, psychological way of the new esoteric dispensation.

The Supreme Being, according to the Hindu view, is not avid to draw every human creature into his supramundane sphere immediately, through enlightenment, nor even to broadcast to everyone identical and correct notions concerning the nature and function of his divinity. He is not a jealous God. On the contrary, he permits and takes benign delight in all the differing illusions that beset the beclouded mind of *Homo sapiens.* He welcomes and comprehends every kind of faith and creed. Though he is himself perfect love, and inclined to all of his devotees, no matter what their plane of understanding, he is also, and at the same time, supremely indifferent, absolutely unconcerned; for he is himself possessed of no ego. He is not of the wrathful nature of the Yahweh of the *Old Testament.* He makes no totalitarian claim, like the Allah of Mohammed's coinage. Nor does he demand that sinful mankind should be reconciled to him through such an extreme payment as the supreme sacrifice of the Redeemer—the God's own son, his alter ego, Second Person of the Blessed Trinity, who, becoming incarnate as the sole adequate victim, the scapegoat branded as a criminal, the Lamb that takes upon itself the sins of the world, relieves unclean mankind of its merited death by shedding his own precious blood, hanging on the cross as history's most conspicuous victim of judicial murder.

"Whatsoever devotee seeks to worship whatsoever divine form (*rūpa*) with fervent faith, I, verily, make that faith of his unwavering. He, united to that form by that faith, keeps it worshipfully in mind and thereby gains his desires—which, in reality, are satisfied by Me alone. Finite, however, is the fruit of those of little understanding: the worshipers of the gods go to the gods, but My devotees come to Me."

Definite ideas, circumscribed notions and forms, the various personalities of the numerous pantheon of divinities, are all regarded as so many aspects, or reflections, of the shades of man's not-knowing-better. They all convey some truth—approximately and with varying shades of imperfection; yet they are themselves parts and effects of the cosmic play of māyā, representing its operation in the sphere of the intellectual and emotional organs. They share in the qualities of the guṇas. For example, mankind's purer, more spiritual conceptions of the divinities originate where there is a predominance of sattva guṇa (clarity, goodness, purity); wrathful, irascible, emotional views of God (where the deity displays an excess of activity) spring from the impulses of rajas guṇa; while semidivine beings of malevolent character—the gods of death, disease, and destruction—are born of the darkness of tamas guṇa. The aspects and personifications of the divine essence will seem to vary according to the prevalence of one or another of the guṇas in the nature of the devotee; and thus it is that the deities of the various races, culture periods, and levels of society conspicuously differ from each other. The Supreme Being itself, in its absolute aloofness from the interplay of the guṇas—though itself their source—is far from stooping to interfere with the particular propensities of the differing human types, but rather encourages and fortifies every pious inclination, of whatsoever kind, since of every human being it is itself the inner force.

"Whatsoever devotee seeks to worship whatsoever divine form (*rūpa*) with fervent faith. . . . " The "form" (*rūpa*) is the phenomenal manifestation of the transcendent divine essence in the garb of a divine personality, a godly individuality, and this is worshipful because accommodated exactly to the worshiping mind and heart. It may be a divinity of the most ancient orthodoxy (an Agni, Indra, Varuṇa), of the later Hindu piety (Śiva, Viṣṇu, Kālī), or of one of the still later, intrusive, missionizing systems (Allah and Christ). Casting the spell of delusion upon every creature, displaying through the acts of all his universal māyā, the Supreme Being is ever ready to allow each man to go along his own particular way of ignorance, more or less bedimmed, which he and his circle take for knowledge and wisdom. It is all perfectly all right so far as the Divine Being is concerned if the fish in the deep sea cling to their own two or three ideas about the world and life, if the birds in the lofty air cherish different ones, and if the denizens of the forests and of the cities of mankind have patterns of their own. The magnificent Tenth Chapter of the ***Bhagavad Gītā*** tells that the Divine Being Himself exists in all. "Whatsoever is the seed (*bīja*) of all creatures, that am I. There is no creature, whether moving or unmoving, that can exist without Me. I am the gambling of the fraudulent, I am the power of the powerful. I am victory; I am effort. I am the purity of the pure." Each is permitted and even encouraged to perpetrate his own particular delusion as long as he can go on believing it to be true. Once he realizes, however, that he is only trudging on a treadmill, keeping the world-as-he-sees-it in motion through his own activity, having to go on simply because he insists on going on yet remaining ever in the same place—just as he would remain if he were doing nothing at all—then the spell is broken; the desire, the need, for freedom comes; and the Divine Being is equally willing now to open the hidden way to the sphere beyond the round.

The Blessed Lord declared:

> 'Threefold is the vehement faith or desire (*śraddhā*) of the dwellers in bodies, according to their various natures: sāttvic, rājasic, or tāmasic. Hear thou the exposition of their kinds. The śraddhā of each is in accordance with his natural disposition, O Bhārata; indeed the man consists of his śraddhā, he is whatever his śraddhā is. Men in whom serene clarity or goodness (*sattva*) prevails, worship gods; men in whom violent activity and desire (*rajas*) prevail, worship yakṣas and rākṣasas; men in whom darkness and inertia (*tamas*) prevail serve evil spirits, ghosts, and specters; while those who store up vital energy or heat (*tapas*) by glowing, fierce austerities, according to procedures not prescribed by the sacred tradition, are possessed with a demonic determination: they are full of hypocrisy and selfishness; they are full of unconquered sensual longings, desires and passions and animalic strength (*kāma-rāga-bala*); they pull and tear by violence not only the living elements and beings that inhabit their bodies [in the guise of the functions and organs of the life-process], but even the divine Self, the godly principle [Kṛṣṇa says simply "Me"], which dwells in the interior of the body.'

The gods that men worship, however, are not the only symptoms of their guṇas. "The food also that is liked by each of them is threefold."

The guṇas, being the constituents of the world substance as it evolves out of its primeval state of perfectly balanced undifferentiation, are inherent in foods, as well as in everything else.

> Mild food, full of juice and taste, solid and pleasant, is beloved by men in whom sattva prevails. Acrid, bitter, pungent, sour, salty, sharp, harsh, and very hot food, burning (*vidāhin,* like hot curry) dishes, are preferred by people in whom rajas prevails. This diet gives pain, distress, and diseases [whereas the sāttvic food gives long life, strength, force, comfort, delight, and absence of disease]. Food that is stale, tasteless, and foul-smelling, being overdue, left over [from other meals], and ritually unclean, is liked by people of tāmasic disposition.

The attitude full of sattva asks for no reward (*phala*), and carries out rituals according to prescription, the devotee simply thinking "offerings must be made." When, however, the ceremonial is aimed at some reward or result, or carried out in a manner of sanctimonious arrogance (*dambha*) in order to pose as a perfect, saintly person, the attitude is that of rajas. Rajas produces egotism and ambition. Whereas ceremonials that do not conform to orthodox prescriptions (i.e., which are not included within the pale of the Brāhmanical tradition but are addressed either to malignant demons or to beings foreign to the accepted pantheon), or where the offered dishes are not distributed, later on, to worthy recipients (priests or Brāhmans, as a rule; in brief, any ritual that ignores the Brāhmans and their costly help), show an attitude, according to this priestly judgment, in which tamas prevails.

The balances of sattva, rajas, and tamas can be measured in every detail of human life and practice. Even in the rigorous ascetic austerities (*tapas*) of the traditional hermit groves the operations of all three can be readily discerned. For, as we read:

> Sattva prevails in tapas that is performed for its own sake, without an eye to any reward. Rajas prevails when tapas is performed out of reverence [for a deity] and regard for the purpose of worship, and out of sanctimonious arrogance (*dambha*). Austerity of this kind is fickle and unstable. But tamas dominates when the practices are undertaken for some foolish, mistaken idea, with great pain and suffering to oneself, or with a view to annihilating someone else (i.e., in the service of the destructive forces of death and darkness).

Similarly threefold are the attitudes toward charity (*dāna*), the giving of gifts. The giving is sāttvic when the gifts are bestowed upon worthy people who can make no return (poor people, orphans, widows, beggars, religious mendicants, saints, etc.), at the correct time and place and with the thought, simply, that one has to make gifts. The charity is rājasic when it is dispensed with an expectation of service in return, or for the sake of some reward from the gods or destiny according to the law of karma (*phalam:* fruit), or when the donation is made with reluctance, or when the gift is in bad condition, worn, or in disrepair. Tāmasic giving is that in which the gift is bestowed at an inappropriate place or time, from improper, wicked motives, or with contempt.

> Arjuna said:
>
> 'But under what coercion, O Kṛṣṇa, does a man, even against his will, commit sin, driven, as it were, by force?'
>
> The Blessed Lord replied:
>
> 'Desire (*kāma*), this furious, wrathful passion (*krodha*), which is born of the guṇa of violent action, is the great evil, the great hunger. Know that in this world this is the foul fiend.
>
> 'As fire is enveloped by smoke, a mirror by dust, and an unborn child in the womb by the integument that surrounds the embryo, so is understanding by desire. The higher intelligence (*jñāna*) of man—who is intrinsically endowed with perfect insight (*jñānin*)—is enveloped by this eternal fiend Desire, which assumes all possible forms at will and is an insatiable conflagration. The sense-forces (*indriyāṇi*), the mind (*manas*), and the faculty of intuitive awareness (*buddhi*), are all said to be its abode. Through these it bewilders and confuses the Owner of the Body, veiling his higher understanding. Therefore begin by curbing the sense organs and slay this Evil One, the destroyer of wisdom (*jñāna*) and realization (*vijñāna*). The sense-forces are superior [to the physical body]; the mind is superior to the senses; intuitive understanding again is superior to the mind; superior to intuitive understanding is He [*sa:* the Owner of the Body, the Self]. Therefore, having awakened to the fact that He is beyond and superior to the sphere of intuitive understanding, firmly stabilize the Self by the Self [or thyself through the Self], and slay the fiend who has the form of desire [or who takes whatever shapes he likes] and who is difficult to overcome.'
>
> Through contemplating sense-objects inwardly, visualizing and brooding over them, one brings into existence attachment to the objects; out of attachment comes desire; from desire, fury, violent passion; from violent passion, bewilderment, confusion; from bewilderment, loss of memory and of conscious self-control; from this perturbation or ruin of self-control comes the disappearance of intuitive understanding; and from this ruin of intuitive understanding comes the ruin of man himself.

The technique of detachment taught by the Blessed Kṛṣṇa through the ***Gītā*** is a sort of "middle path." On the one hand his devotee is to avoid the extreme of clinging to the sphere of action and its fruits (the selfish pursuit of life for personal aims, out of acquisitiveness and possessiveness), while on the other hand the negative extreme of barren abstinence from every kind and phase of action is to be shunned with equal care. The first mistake is that of the normal behavior of the naïve worldly being, prone to act and eager for the results. This only leads to a continuation of the hell of the round of rebirths—our usual headlong and unhelpful participation in the unavoidable sufferings that go with being an ego. Whereas the opposite mistake is that of neurotic abstention; the mistake of the absolute ascetics—such men as the monks of the Jainas and Ājīvikas—who indulge in the vain hope that one may rid oneself of karmic influxes simply by mortifying the flesh, stopping all mental and emotional processes, and starving to death the bodily frame. Against these the ***Bhagavad Gītā*** brings a more modern, more spiritual, more psychological point of view. Act: for actually you act no matter which way you turn—but achieve detachment from the fruits! Dissolve thus the self-concern of your ego, and with that you will discover the Self! The Self is unconcerned with either the individuality within (*jīva, puruṣa*) or the world without (*a-jīva, prakṛti*).

This formula of Karma Yoga, however, is not the only means; it can be supported and supplemented by the traditional devices of Bhakti Yoga—the way of fervent devotion to some incarnation, image, name, or personification of one's cherished god. Indeed, detachment from the fruits of unavoidable activities is rendered easier through such an attitude of self-surrender to the will of the Personal God—who, in turn, is but a reflex of the very Self that dwells within the heart of every being. "Whatever thou dost do, whatever thou dost eat, whatever thou dost offer in sacrificial oblation, whatever thou dost give away [in charity], whatever austerity thou dost practice, perform the work as an offering to Me [the Divine Being]"; i.e., resign it, hand it over, together with its fruits. Everything that is done is to be regarded as a willing offering to the Lord.

Thus it appears that there are two kinds of Karma Yoga, conducing to the same goal: 1. a primarily mental discipline, conducted on the pattern and basis of the Sāṅkhya, whereby the distinction between the guṇas and the Self is realized, and 2. an emotional, devotional discipline of surrender to the Lord (*īśvara*). The latter is an elementary, more popular, preliminary stage, to be continued until one has realized the phenomenal character of the Lord himself, as well as of the worshiping ego. These two (the Lord and ego) are, as two, annihilated in Brahman-Ātman, which is without form, name, personality, or the gentle movements of the heart.

"Resign mentally all of thine activities to Me. Taking Me as the highest goal, resort to the yoga-practice of inner awareness (*buddhi-yoga*), and keep the mind always fixed on Me."

"To all beings I am the same. To Me there is none either hateful or dear. Yet those who devote [and assign] themselves to Me with utter devotion (*bhakti*)—they are in Me, and I also am in them."

The consoling, enlightening wisdom of Kṛṣṇa is well summarized in the phrase *mattaḥ sarvaṁ pravartate,* "from Me everything arises." All of man's feelings, worries, joys, calamities, and successes come from God. Therefore, surrender them to him again in thy mind, through bhakti, and attain to peace! Compared with the enduring reality of the Divine Being, thy joys and calamities are but passing shadows. "In Him alone then take thy refuge with all thy being, and by His Grace shalt thou attain Supreme Peace and the Everlasting Abode."

Thus in the ***Bhagavad Gītā*** the old Brāhmanical way of the Vedic "path of sacrifice" (*karma-mārga*) is left far behind. The routines for gaining access to the Holy Power by virtue of the magic of elaborate sacrificial rites and offerings are definitely and explicitly discredited in favor of the purely mental and psychic ritualism of the "path of knowledge" (*jñāna-mārga*). And the redeeming strength of this knowledge is praised in the highest terms. "The ritual of sacrifice that consists in knowledge is superior to the sacrifice made of material offerings; for all activity [as displayed in the elaborate rituals of traditional sacrifice] attains its consummation in knowledge." "Even if thou art the most sinful of all sinners, yet by the raft of knowledge alone, thou shalt go across all wickedness. Just as a fire, come to full blaze, reduces the fuel to ashes, so does the fire of knowledge reduce all kinds of karma to ashes. For there exists here [in this world] nothing so purifying as knowledge. When, in good time, one attains to perfection in yoga, one discovers that knowledge oneself, in one's Self."

This comes very close to the formula of the *Yoga-sūtras* of Patañjali. The master stroke of the ***Bhagavad Gītā,*** as we have said, consists in its juxtaposition and coordination of *all* the basic disciplines of the complex religious inheritance of India. The Sāṅkhya, a Brāhmanized form of the old pre-Āryan dualism of life and matter, was, in essence, something very different from the all-affirming monism of the *Vedic* tradition, and yet the latter, as matured and introverted by the contemplative sages of the period of the *Upaniṣads,* was also a way of jñāna. Hence the two could be brought together; and in the ***Bhagavad Gītā*** the union is achieved—the Sāṅkhya idea of the pluralism of the life-monads being accepted as a preliminary view, representing the standpoint of the manifested world. But the theism of the *Vedas* also remains—as a convenient support for the mind during the earlier stages of its difficult progress toward detachment: the way of bhakti is taught, consequently, though no longer linked necessarily to the specific rituals of the earlier cult of exterior, material sacrifice. It is developed rather in its more personal and introverted, Tāntric form. . . . And finally, since the goal of all these disciplines is knowledge, the direct path of the absolutely introverted yogī is also accepted as an effective way.

> Having in a cleanly spot established his seat, firm, neither too high nor too low, made of a cloth, a skin, and kuśa-grass, arranged in the proper way, there seated on that seat, making the mind one-pointed and subduing the action of the imagining faculty and the senses, let him practice yoga for the purification of the heart. Let him hold his body firmly, head and neck erect and still, gazing at the tip of his nose and not looking around. With the heart serene and fearless, firm in the vow of continence, with the mind controlled and ever thinking of Me, let him sit, having Me as his supreme goal. Thus always keeping the mind steadfast, the yogī of subdued mind attains the peace residing in Me—the peace that culminates in Nirvāṇa."

And as for the state on earth of the one who has attained:

> He who is the same to friend and foe, alike in facing honor and dishonor, alike in heat and cold, in pleasure and pain, who is free from all attachment [to the sphere of conflicting experiences and pairs-of-opposites], to whom censure and praise are equal, and who remains silent and content with anything [good or evil, just as it comes], he who is homeless, steady-minded, and full of devout self-surrender—that man is dear to Me.
>
> He who sits as one unconcerned, and is not agitated by the guṇas; he who simply knows 'these guṇas are acting of themselves, they are whirling around,' and remains unmoved, not swerving—is said to have gone beyond the guṇas.
>
> 'Just as a lamp sheltered from the wind does not flicker. . . .' Such is the simile employed to describe the yogī who has subdued his mind, yok-

ing himself in the yoga exercise of concentration on the Self.

"He who resigns his activities to the Universal Self (*brahman*) by forsaking attachment to them and their results, remains unstained by evil—just as the lotus leaf remains unstained by water."—This also is a classic simile. Just as the leaves of the lotus, which because of their smooth oily surface are not affected by the water in which they grow and remain, so likewise the man established in the Self; the waves of the world in which he dwells do not destroy him.

"He who sees the Lord Supreme abiding equally in all transitory beings, the Imperishable in the things that perish—he truly sees. And when he beholds the manifold existences all centered in that One, expanding from that One, he then becomes that Brahman." (pp. 379-409)

Heinrich Zimmer, "The Philosophies of Eternity: Brahmanism," in Philosophies of India, *edited by Joseph Campbell, Bollingen Series XXVI, 1951. Reprint by Princeton University Press, 1969, pp. 333-463.*

Swami Prabhavananda and Christopher Isherwood (essay date 1944)

[*Prabhavananda was an eminent Indian religious leader, teacher, writer, and translator who is remembered in particular for his missionary work in the United States. His writings include* Yoga and Mysticism: Four Lectures *(1969). Isherwood was an English-born man of letters who is known for his largely autobiographical accounts of pre-Nazi Berlin. His* Berlin Stories *(1946), adapted by John Van Druten for his* I Am a Camera *(1952), was the basis for the musical and film* Cabaret. *In the following excerpt from the preface to their 1944 translation of the* Gītā, *Prabhavananda and Isherwood introduce the poem to Western readers, hailing it as one of the world's greatest religious documents.*]

Nowadays, it is becoming fashionable to translate the world's great books into some form of Basic English, or everyday speech. The ***Gita*** does not easily lend itself to such treatment. The Sanskrit in which it is written differs radically from modern English. It is compressed and telegraphic. It abounds in exact philosophical and religious terms. Its frame of reference is a system of cosmology unfamiliar to western thought. And indeed, it would be hard to evolve any uniform English style, modern or ancient, in which the ***Gita*** could be satisfactorily rendered. For the ***Gita,*** regarded simply as a piece of literature, is not a unity. It has several aspects, several distinct tones of voice. Let us consider each of them in turn.

First, the ***Gita*** may be regarded as part of an epic poem. It is all in verse. The first chapter is pure epic, continuing in the mood of the *Mahabharata* itself. The shouting of warriors, the neighing of horses and the outlandish names of chieftains are still sounding in our ears as the dialogue between Krishna and Arjuna begins. To translate this epic prologue as though it belonged to the philosophical discourse which follows would be to cut the ***Gita*** right out of its historical setting and deprive it of its vivid local colour.

Then, again, the ***Gita*** is an exposition of Vedanta philosophy, based upon a very definite picture of the universe. It is no use trying to disregard this fact for fear of alienating the western reader. The translator who uses 'reassuring' topical equivalents, and twists the meaning of the Sanskrit terms, may think he is building a bridge between two systems of thought, when actually he is reducing both of them to nonsense. (p. 9)

The ***Gita*** is also prophetic. Like the Vision of Isaiah and the *Psalms of David,* it contains ecstatic mystical utterances about the nature and attributes of God. These are poetry, and demand poetic expression. The diction must try to correspond to the inspiration. Ordinary prose will render them flat and boring.

Finally, the ***Gita*** is a gospel. Its essential message is timeless. In words which belong to no one language, race or epoch, incarnate God speaks to man, His friend. Here, the translator must forget all about Vedanta philosophy and Sanskrit terms; all about India and the West, Krishna and Arjuna, past and future. He must aim at the utmost simplicity. (p. 10)

Here is one of the greatest religious documents of the world: let us not approach it too pedantically, as an archaic text which must be jealously preserved by university professors. It has something to say, urgently, to every one of us. We have to extract that message from the terseness of the original Sanskrit, and here the great classical commentators can help us. (pp. 10-11)

Swami Prabhavananda and Christopher Isherwood, in a preface to The Song of God: Bhagavad-Gita, *translated by Swami Prabhavananda and Christopher Isherwood, New American Library, 1945, pp. 9-11.*

Aldous Huxley (essay date 1944)

[*Remembered primarily for his dystopian novel* Brave New World *(1932), Huxley was an eminent English man of letters. Considered a novelist of ideas, he was interested in many fields of knowledge, and daring conceptions of science, philosophy, and religion are interwoven throughout his fiction. In the following excerpt from an essay written in 1944, Huxley examines the* Gītā *in the context of enduring Oriental and Occidental spiritual traditions, lauding the poem as one of humankind's great universal religious documents.*]

More than twenty-five centuries have passed since that which has been called the Perennial Philosophy was first committed to writing; and in the course of those centuries it has found expression, now partial, now complete, now in this form, now in that, again and again. In Vedanta and Hebrew prophecy, in the *Tao Teh King* and the Platonic dialogues, in the *Gospel according to St John* and Mahayana theology, in Plotinus and the Areopagite, among the Persian Sufis and the Christian mystics of the Middle Ages and the Renaissance—the Perennial Philosophy has spoken almost all the languages of Asia and Europe and has made use of the terminology and traditions of every one of the higher religions. But under all this confusion of tongues and myths, of local histories and particularist doctrines, there remains a Highest Common Factor, which is the Perennial Philosophy in what may be called its chemically pure state. This final purity can never, of course, be expressed by any verbal statement of the philosophy, however undogmatic that statement may be, however deliberately syncretistic. The very fact that it is set down at a certain time by a certain writer, using this or that language, automatically imposes a certain sociological and personal bias on the doctrines so formulated. It is only in the act of contemplation, when words and even personality are transcended, that the pure state of the Perennial Philosophy can actually be known. The records left by those who have known it in this way make it abundantly clear that all of them, whether Hindu, Buddhist, Hebrew, Taoist, Christian or Mohammedan, were attempting to describe the same essentially indescribable Fact.

The original scriptures of most religions are poetical and unsystematic. Theology, which generally takes the form of a reasoned commentary on the parables and aphorisms of the scriptures, tends to make its appearance at a later stage of religious history. The ***Bhagavad-Gita*** occupies an intermediate position between scripture and theology; for it combines the poetical qualities of the first with the clear-cut methodicalness of the second. The book may be described, writes Ananda K. Coomaraswamy in his admirable *Hinduism and Buddhism,* 'as a compendium of the whole Vedic doctrine to be found in the earlier *Vedas, Brahmanas* and *Upanishads,* and being therefore the basis of all the later developments, it can be regarded as the focus of all Indian religion.' But this 'focus of Indian religion' is also one of the clearest and most comprehensive summaries of the Perennial Philosophy ever to have been made. Hence its enduring value, not only for Indians, but for all mankind.

At the core of the Perennial Philosophy we find four fundamental doctrines.

First: the phenomenal world of matter and of individualized consciousness—the world of things and animals and men and even gods—is the manifestation of a Divine Ground within which all partial realities have their being, and apart from which they would be nonexistent.

Second: human beings are capable not merely of knowing *about* the Divine Ground by inference; they can also realize its existence by a direct intuition, superior to discursive reasoning. This immediate knowledge unites the knower with that which is known.

Third: man possesses a double nature, a phenomenal ego and an eternal Self, which is the inner man, the spirit, the spark of divinity within the soul. It is possible for a man, if he so desires, to identify himself with the spirit and therefore with the Divine Ground, which is of the same or like nature with the spirit.

Fourth: man's life on earth has only one end and purpose: to identify himself with his eternal Self and so to come to unitive knowledge of the Divine Ground.

In Hinduism the first of these four doctrines is stated in the most categorical terms. The Divine Ground is Brahman, whose creative, sustaining and transforming aspects are manifested in the Hindu trinity. A hierarchy of manifestations connects inanimate matter with man, gods, High Gods and the undifferentiated Godhead beyond.

In Mahayana Buddhism the Divine Ground is called Mind or the Pure Light of the Void, the place of the High Gods is taken by the Dhyani-Buddhas.

Similar conceptions are perfectly compatible with Christianity and have in fact been entertained, explicitly or implicitly, by many Catholic and Protestant mystics, when formulating a philosophy to fit facts observed by super-rational intuition. Thus, for Eckhart and Ruysbroeck, there is an Abyss of Godhead underlying the Trinity, just as Brahman underlies Brahma, Vishnu and Shiva. Suso has even left a diagrammatic picture of the relations subsisting between Godhead, triune God and creatures. In this very curious and interesting drawing a chain of manifestation connects the mysterious symbol of the Divine Ground with the three Persons of the Trinity, and the Trinity in turn is connected in a descending scale with angels and human beings. These last, as the drawing vividly shows, may make one of two choices. They can either lead the life of the outer man, the life of separative selfhood; in which case they are lost (for, in the words of the *Theologia Germanica,* 'nothing burns in hell but the self'). Or else they can identify themselves with the inner man, in which case it becomes possible for them, as Suso shows, to ascend again, through unitive knowledge, to the Trinity and even, beyond the Trinity, to the ultimate Unity of the Divine Ground.

Within the Mohammedan tradition such a rationalization of the immediate mystical experience would have been dangerously unorthodox. Nevertheless, one has the impression, while reading certain Sufi texts, that their authors did in fact conceive of *al haqq,* the real, as being the Divine Ground or Unity of Allah, underlying the active and personal aspects of the Godhead.

The second doctrine of the Perennial Philosophy—that it is possible to know the Divine Ground by a direct intuition higher than discursive reasoning—is to be found in all the great religions of the world. A philosopher who is content merely to know about the ultimate Reality—theoretically and by hearsay—is compared by Buddha to a herdsman of other men's cows. Mohammed uses an even homelier barnyard metaphor. For him the philosopher who has not realized his metaphysics is just an ass bearing a load of books. Christian, Hindu and Taoist teachers wrote no less emphatically about the absurd pretensions of mere learning and analytical reasoning. In the words of the Anglican Prayer Book, our eternal life, now and hereafter, 'stands in the knowledge of God'; and this knowledge is not discursive but 'of the heart,' a super-rational intuition, direct, synthetic and timeless.

The third doctrine of the Perennial Philosophy, that which affirms the double nature of man, is fundamental in all the higher religions. The unitive knowledge of the Divine Ground has, as its necessary condition, self-abnegation and charity. Only by means of self-abnegation and charity can we clear away the evil, folly and ignorance which constitute the thing we call our personality and prevent us from becoming aware of the spark of divinity illuminating the inner man. But the spark within is akin to the Divine Ground. By identifying ourselves with the first we can come to unitive knowledge of the second. These empirical facts of the spiritual life have been variously rationalized in terms of the theologies of the various religions. The Hindus categorically affirm that thou art That—that the indwelling Atman is the same as Brahman. For orthodox Christianity there is not an identity between the spark and God. Union of the human spirit with God takes place—union so complete that the word 'deification' is applied to it; but it is not the union of identical substances. According to Christian theology, the saint is 'deified,' not because Atman *is* Brahman, but because God has assimilated the purified human spirit into the divine substance by an act of grace. Islamic theology seems to make a similar distinction. The Sufi, Mansur, was executed for giving to the words 'union' and 'deification' the literal meaning which they bear in the Hindu tradition. For our present purposes, however, the significant fact is that these words are actually used by Christians and Mohammedans to describe the empirical facts of metaphysical realization by means of direct, super-rational intuition.

In regard to man's final end, all the higher religions are in complete agreement. The purpose of human life is the discovery of Truth, the unitive knowledge of the Godhead. The degree to which this unitive knowledge is achieved here on earth determines the degree to which it will be enjoyed in the posthumous state. Contemplation of truth is the end, action the means. In India, in China, in ancient Greece, in Christian Europe, this was regarded as the most obvious and axiomatic piece of orthodoxy. The invention of the steam engine produced a revolution, not merely in industrial techniques, but also and much more significantly in philosophy. Because machines could be made progressively more and more efficient, western man came to believe that men and societies would automatically register a corresponding moral and spiritual improvement. Attention and allegiance came to be paid, not to Eternity, but to the Utopian future. External circumstances came to be regarded as more important than states of mind about external circumstances, and the end of human life was held to be action, with contemplation as a means to that end. These false and, historically, aberrant and heretical doctrines are now systematically taught in our schools and repeated, day in, day out, by those anonymous writers of advertising copy who, more than any other teachers, provide European and American adults with their current philosophy of life. And so effective has been the propaganda that even professing Christians accept the heresy unquestioningly and are quite unconscious of its complete incompatibility with their own or anybody else's religion.

These four doctrines constitute the Perennial Philosophy in its minimal and basic form. A man who can practise what the Indians call Jnana yoga (the metaphysical discipline of discrimination between the real and the apparent) asks for nothing more. This simple working hypothesis is enough for his purposes. But such discrimination is exceedingly difficult and can hardly be practised, at any rate in the preliminary stages of the spiritual life, except by persons endowed with a particular kind of mental constitution. That is why most statements of the Perennial Philosophy have included another doctrine, affirming the existence of one or more human Incarnations of the Divine Ground, by whose mediation and grace the worshipper is helped to achieve his goal—that unitive knowledge of the Godhead, which is man's eternal life and beatitude. The ***Bhagavad-Gita*** is one such statement. Here, Krishna is an Incarnation of the Divine Ground in human form. Similarly, in Christian and Buddhist theology, Jesus and Gotama are Incarnations of divinity. But whereas in Hinduism and Buddhism more than one Incarnation of the Godhead is possible (and is regarded as having in fact taken place), for Christians there has been and can be only one.

An Incarnation of the Godhead and, to a lesser degree, any theocentric saint, sage or prophet is a human being who knows Who he is and can therefore effectively remind other human beings of what they have allowed themselves to forget: namely, that if they choose to become what potentially they already are, they too can be eternally united with the Divine Ground.

Worship of the Incarnation and contemplation of his attributes are for most men and women the best preparation for unitive knowledge of the Godhead. But whether the actual knowledge itself can be achieved by this means is another question. Many Catholic mystics have affirmed that, at a certain stage of that contemplative prayer in which, according to the most authoritative theologians, the life of Christian perfection ultimately consists, it is necessary to put aside all thoughts of the Incarnation as distracting from the higher knowledge of that which has been incarnated. From this fact have arisen misunderstandings in plenty and a number of intellectual difficulties. Here, for example, is what Abbot John Chapman writes in one of his admirable *Spiritual Letters:*

> The problem of *reconciling* (not merely uniting) mysticism with Christianity is more difficult. The Abbot (Abbot Marmion) says that St John of the Cross is like a sponge full of Christianity. You can squeeze it all out, and the full mystical theory remains. Consequently, for fifteen years or so, I hated St John of the Cross and called him a Buddhist. I loved St Teresa, and read her over and over again. She is first a Christian, only secondarily a mystic. Then I found that I had wasted fifteen years, so far as prayer was concerned.

And yet, he concludes, in spite of its 'Buddhistic' character, the practice of mysticism (or, to put it in other terms, the realization of the Perennial Philosophy) makes good Christians. He might have added that it also makes good Hindus, good Buddhists, good Taoists, good Moslems and good Jews.

The solution to Abbot Chapman's problem must be sought in the domain, not of philosophy, but of psychology. Human beings are not born identical. There are many different temperaments and constitutions; and within each psycho-physical class one can find people at very different stages of spiritual development. Forms of worship and spiritual discipline which may be valuable for one individual may be useless or even positively harmful for another belonging to a different class and standing, within that class, at a lower or higher level of development. All this is clearly set forth in the ***Gita,*** where the psychological facts are linked up with general cosmology by means of the postulate of the *gunas.* Krishna, who is here the mouthpiece of Hinduism in all its manifestations, finds it perfectly natural that different men should have different methods and even apparently different objects of worship. All roads lead to Rome—provided, of course, that it is Rome and not some other city which the traveller really wishes to reach. A similar attitude of charitable inclusiveness, somewhat surprising in a Moslem, is beautifully expressed in the parable of Moses and the Shepherd, told by Jalaluddin Rumi in the second book of the Masnavi. And within the more exclusive Christian tradition these problems of temperament and degree of development have been searchingly discussed in their relation to the way of Mary and the way of Martha in general, and in particular to the vocation and private devotion of individuals.

We now have to consider the ethical corollaries of the Perennial Philosophy. 'Truth,' says St Thomas Aquinas, 'is the last end for the entire universe, and the contemplation of truth is the chief occupation of wisdom.' The moral virtues, he says in another place, belong to contemplation, not indeed essentially, but as a necessary predisposition. Virtue, in other words, is not the end, but the indispensable means to the knowledge of divine reality. Shankara, the greatest of the Indian commentators on the ***Gita,*** holds the same doctrine. Right action is the way to knowledge; for it purifies the mind, and it is only to a mind purified from egotism that the intuition of the Divine Ground can come.

Self-abnegation, according to the ***Gita,*** can be achieved by the practice of two all-inclusive virtues—love and non-attachment. The latter is the same thing as that 'holy indifference,' on which St François de Sales is never tired of insisting. 'He who refers every action to God,' writes Camus, summarizing his master's teaching, 'and has no aims save His Glory, will find rest everywhere, even amidst the most violent commotions.' So long as we practise this holy indifference to the fruits of action, 'no lawful occupation will separate us from God; on the contrary, it can be made a means of closer union.' Here the word 'lawful' supplies a necessary qualification to a teaching which, without it, is incomplete and even potentially dangerous. Some actions are intrinsically evil or inexpedient; and no good intentions, no conscious offering of them to God, no renunciation of the fruits can alter their essential character. Holy indifference requires to be taught in conjunction not merely with a set of commandments prohibiting crimes, but also with a clear conception of what in Buddha's Eightfold Path is called 'right livelihood.' Thus, for the Buddhist, right livelihood was incompatible with the making of deadly weapons and of intoxicants; for the mediæval Christian, with the taking of interest and with various monopolistic practices which have since come to be regarded as legitimate good business. John Woolman, the American Quaker, provides a most enlightening example of the way in which a man may live in the world, while practising perfect non-attachment and remaining acutely sensitive to the claims of right livelihood. Thus, while it would have been profitable and perfectly lawful for him to sell West Indian sugar and rum to the customers who came to his shop, Woolman refrained from doing so, because these things were the products of slave labour. Similarly, when he was in England, it would have been both lawful and convenient for him to travel by stage coach. Nevertheless, he preferred to make his journeys on foot. Why? Because the comforts of rapid travel could only be brought at the expense of great cruelty to the horses and the most atrocious working conditions for the post-boys. In Woolman's eyes, such a system of transportation was intrinsically undesirable, and no amount of personal non-attachment could make it anything but undesirable. So he shouldered his knapsack and walked. (pp. 11-21)

In the preceeding pages [I] have tried to show that the Perennial Philosophy and its ethical corollaries constitute a Highest Common Factor, present in all the major religions of the world. To affirm this truth has never been more imperatively necessary than at the present time. There will never be enduring peace unless and until human beings come to accept a philosophy of life more adequate to the cosmic and psychological facts than the insane idolatries of nationalism and the advertising man's apocalyptic faith in Progress towards a mechanized New Jerusalem. All the elements of this philosophy are present, as we have seen, in the traditional religions. But in existing circumstances there is not the slightest chance that any of the traditional religions will obtain universal acceptance. Europeans and Americans will see no reason for being converted to Hinduism, say, or Buddhism. And the people of Asia can hardly be expected to renounce their own traditions for the Christianity professed, often sincerely, by the imperialists who, for four hundred years and more, have been systematically attacking, exploiting and oppressing, and are now trying to finish off the work of destruction by 'educating' them. But happily there is the Highest Common Factor of all religions, the Perennial Philosophy which has always and everywhere been the metaphysical system of the prophets, saints and sages. It is perfectly possible for people to remain good Christians, Hindus, Buddhists or Moslems and yet to be united in full agreement on the basic doctrines of the Perennial Philosophy.

The ***Bhagavad-Gita*** is perhaps the most systematic scriptural statement of the Perennial Philosophy. To a world at war, a world that, because it lacks the intellectual and spiritual prerequisites to peace, can only hope to patch up some kind of precarious armed truce, it stands pointing, clearly and unmistakably, to the only road of escape from the self-imposed necessity of self-destruction. (pp. 21-2)

Aldous Huxley, in an introduction to The Song of God: Bhagavad-Gita, *translated by Swami Prabhavananda and Christopher Isherwood, New American Library, 1945, pp. 11-22.*

Juan Mascaró (essay date 1960)

[Mascaró is a Sanskritist whose translations include the Bhagavad Gītā *(1962), the* Upanishads *(1965), and* The Dhammapada *(1973). In the following excerpt from the introduction (written in 1960) to his translation*

of the Gītā, *Mascaró presents the main themes and ideas of the poem, praising it as a crowning achievement of Eastern thought and a spiritual document of universal value.*]

For over 3,000 years there has been an uninterrupted Sanskrit culture in India, if we include the Sanskrit of the *Vedas,* and Panini produced about 300 B.C. a perfect Sanskrit grammar, 'the shortest and fullest grammar in the world'.

Sanskrit literature is a great literature. We have the great songs of the *Vedas,* the splendour of the *Upanishads,* the glory of the ***Bhagavad Gita,*** the vastness of the *Mahabharata,* the tenderness and heroism found in the *Ramayana,* the wisdom of the fables and stories of India, the scientific philosophy of the Sankhya, the psychological philosophy of Yoga, the poetical philosophy of Vedanta, the laws of Manu, the grammar of Panini and other scientific writings, the lyrical poetry and drama culminating in the great poetry and dramas of Kalidasa.

There are, however, two great branches of literature not found in Sanskrit. There is no history and there is no tragedy: there is no Herodotus or Thucydides; and there is no Aeschylus or Sophocles or Euripides.

Sanskrit literature is, on the whole, a romantic literature interwoven with idealism and practical wisdom, and with a passionate longing for spiritual vision. There is a prayer in the *Vedas* which for over 3,000 years has been every morning on the mouth of millions of Indians. It is the famous GAYATRI:

TAT SAVITUR VARENIAM
BHARGO DEVASYA DHIMAHI
DHIYO YO NAH PRACODAYAT

'Let our meditation be on the glorious light of Savitri. May this light illumine our minds.' The poet of the *Vedas* who chanted these words saw into the future: the mind of India has never tired in the search for Light.

Greece and India give us complementary views of the world. In the Greek temple we find the clear perfection of beauty: in the Indian temple we find the sublime sense of Infinity. Greece gives us the joy of eternal beauty in the outer world; and India gives us the joy of the Infinite in the inner world.

In these verses of Keats on a Grecian urn we find Greece:

O Attic shape ! fair attitude ! with breed
Of marble men and maidens overwrought,
With forest branches and the trodden weed;
Thou, silent form, dost tease us out of thought
As doth eternity. Cold Pastoral!
When old age shall this generation waste,
Thou shalt remain, in midst of other woe
Than ours, a friend to man, to whom thou say'st,
'Beauty is truth, truth beauty,—that is all
Ye know on earth, and all ye need to know.'

And Wordsworth in 'Tintern Abbey' gives us the spirit of India:

And I have felt
A presence that disturbs me with the joy
Of elevated thoughts; a sense sublime
Of something far more deeply interfused,
Whose dwelling is the light of setting suns,
And the round ocean and the living air,
And the blue sky, and in the mind of man:
A motion and a spirit, that impels
All thinking things, all objects of all thought,
And rolls through all things.

In the *Vedas,* composed long before writing was introduced into India, and before grammarians could analyse language, we see man watching the outside world with joy and wonder. He feels life and he prays for victory in life. He watches the beauty of the dawn and the glory of the sun and he feels that fire and air, and the waters and the winds are living powers: he offers to them the fire of sacrifice. His life depends upon nature, and he knows that between nature and himself there is not an impassable gulf. Man loves this beautiful creation and he feels that his love cannot but be answered by a greater Love. And he sings to Varuna, the God who loves and forgives:

These words of glory to the God who is light shall be words supreme amongst things that are great. I glorify Varuna almighty, the God who is loving towards him who adores.

We praise thee with our thoughts, O God. We praise thee even as the sun praises thee in the morning: may we find joy in being thy servants.

Keep us under thy protection. Forgive our sins and give us thy love.

God made the rivers to flow. They feel no weariness, they cease not from flowing. They fly swiftly like birds in the air.

May the stream of my life flow into the river of righteousness. Loose the bonds of sin that bind me. Let not the thread of my song be cut while I sing; and let not my work end before its fulfillment.

Remove all fear from me, O Lord. Receive me graciously unto thee, O King. Cut off the bonds of afflictions that bind me: I cannot even open mine eyes without thy help.

Let the dread weapons that wound the sinner hurt us not. Let us not go from light into darkness.

We will sing thy praises, O God almighty. We will now and evermore sing thy praises, even as they were sung of old. For thy laws are immutable, O God: they are firm like the mountains.

Forgive the trespasses that I may have committed. Many mornings remain to dawn upon us: lead us through them all, O God.

Rig Veda II.28.I-9

Sometimes the seer of the *Vedas* has the consciousness of transgression of a spiritual law: there has been a sin of ignorance or weakness, or even a sin of ill-will. In repentance he asks for forgiveness and has faith that love forgives sins:

He placed apart the heaven and the earth. He set in motion the sun and the stars and spread our

> earth before them. His greatness gave wisdom to the children of men.
>
> And I speak with mine own heart and I ask: How shall I have communion with my God? What offerings of mine will he accept without anger? When shall I with a glad heart find his mercy?
>
> I ask others for I would fain know my sin: I seek the wise and I ask them. And one answer the sages give me: God, Varuna, is angry with thee.
>
> What hath been, O my God, my transgression? Why wouldst thou slay thy friend who sings praises to thee? Tell me, all-powerful God, that pure from sin may I hasten to thee in adoration.
>
> Loose from us the sins of our fathers. Forgive us our own sins, O Lord.
>
> It was not my will, it was an illusion. It was thoughtlessness or anger or wine. The stronger is near to lead astray the weaker: even sleep can lead men to sin.
>
> May I serve my God, the all-merciful. May I serve my jealous God free from sin. Our God gives wisdom to the simple; and leadeth the wise unto the path of good.
>
> May this song of praise come to thee, O Varuna: may this song of praise abide in thine heart. May it be well with our rest and our labour. May thy blessings be with us for evermore.
>
> *Rig Veda* VII.86

In the *Vedas* we have the dawn of spiritual vision and also the dawn of human thought. In their sublime 'Song of Creation' [*Rig Veda*] they consider the beginning of things:

> There was not then what is nor what is not. There was no sky, and no heaven beyond the sky. What power was there? Where? Who was that power? Was there an abyss of fathomless waters?
>
> There was neither death nor immortality then. No signs were there of night or day. The ONE was breathing by its own power, in deep peace. Only the ONE was: there was nothing beyond.
>
> Darkness was hidden in darkness. The all was fluid and formless. Therein, in the void, by the fire of fervour arose the ONE.
>
> And in the ONE arose love. Love the first seed of soul. The truth of this the sages found in their hearts: seeking in their hearts with wisdom, the sages found that bond of union between being and non-being.
>
> Who knows in truth? Who can tell us whence and how arose this universe? The gods are later than its beginning: who knows therefore whence comes this creation?
>
> Only that god who sees in highest heaven: he only knows whence comes this universe, and whether it was made or uncreated. He only knows, or perhaps he knows not.
>
> *Rig Veda* X. 129

In the last verse of this poem we have the beginning of philosophical inquiry: the poet of the *Vedas* saw that for the progress of the mind man requires doubt and faith.

In the *Vedas* we have the dawn of spiritual insight. In the *Upanishads* we have the full splendour of an inner vision.

About 112 *Upanishads* have been printed in Sanskrit, but the most important ones are about eighteen. The two longest, the *Brihad-Aranyaka* and the *Chandogya,* cover about 100 pages each. The length of most of the others ranges from about three to thirty pages, and a few are longer. The *Isa Upanishad,* one of the most important, has only eighteen verses. The earliest parts of the *Upanishads* are in prose and they may date from about 700 B.C. The verse *Upanishads* are generally much later. We know practically nothing of their authors: they seem to come from the Unknown.

From nature outside in the *Vedas,* man goes in the *Upanishads* into his own inner nature; and from the many he goes to the ONE. We find in the *Upanishads* the great questions of man, and their answer is summed up in two words: BRAHMAN and ATMAN. They are two names for one Truth, and the two are One and the same. The Truth of the Universe is BRAHMAN: our own inner Truth is ATMAN. The sacred OM is a name for both Brahman and Atman. This can be divided into three sounds, but the three roll in one: AUM. One of the meanings of OM is YES. Brahman, Atman, OM is the positive Truth, the Yes, of all.

Around this central idea we have all the questions and answers, the stories, the great thoughts and, above all, the wonderful poetry of the *Upanishads.*

At the beginning of the *Kena Upanishad* we have these questions and answers:

> Who sends the mind to wander afar? Who first drives life to start on its journey? Who impels us to utter these words?
>
> What cannot be spoken with words, but that whereby words are spoken. Know that alone to be Brahman, the Spirit; and not what people here adore.
>
> What cannot be thought with the mind, but that whereby the mind can think. Know that alone to be Brahman, the Spirit; and not what people here adore.

In the *Katha Upanishad* this question is asked by the boy Nachiketas when he meets the Spirit of Death:

> 'When a man dies, this doubt arises: some say "he is" and some say "he is not". Teach me the truth.'

The answer is the same as that of the ***Bhagavad Gita:*** 'The Atman, the Self, is never born and never dies.'

The spiritual experience of Atman is expressed in these words of the *Chandogya Upanishad:*

> There is a Spirit which is mind and life, light and truth and vast spaces. He contains all works and desires and all perfumes and all tastes. He enfolds the whole universe, and in silence is loving to all.

> This is the Spirit that is in my heart, smaller than a grain of rice, or a grain of barley, or a grain of mustard-seed, or a grain of canary-seed, or the kernel of a grain of canary-seed. This is the Spirit that is in my heart, greater than the earth, greater than the sky, greater than heaven itself, greater than all these worlds. This is the Spirit that is in my heart, this is Brahman.

If we ask where is Brahman, the Spirit of the Universe, the answer is given in the *Kena Upanishad:*

> He is seen in nature in the wonder of a flash of lightning. He comes to the soul in the wonder of a flash of vision.

If the thinking mind is not satisfied with answers in words of beauty, the *Upanishads* have something more definite to say. If we ask definitely 'What is Brahman?' the answer in modern terms would be:

> Brahman cannot be defined because it is Infinite. It is beyond thought and beyond imagination. It is nothing in the mind and nothing outside the mind, nothing past or present or future. These are only conceptions in time and space. But the nearest conception of Brahman we can have is to say that it is a state of consciousness beyond time when SAT, CIT, and ANANDA, Being and Consciousness and Joy are ONE.

We thus have the *Mandukya Upanishad* that explains the paradox that Brahman is all, and Brahman is nothing or no-thing:

> OM. The eternal Word is all: what was, what is, and what shall be, and what beyond is in eternity. All is OM.
>
> Brahman is all and Atman is Brahman. Atman, the Self, has four conditions.
>
> The first condition is the waking life of outward-moving consciousness, enjoying the seven outer gross elements.
>
> The second condition is the dreaming life of inner-moving consciousness, enjoying the seven subtle inner elements in its own light and solitude.
>
> The third condition is the sleeping life of silent consciousness when a person has no desires and beholds no dreams.
>
> The fourth condition is Atman in His own pure state: the awakened life of supreme consciousness. It is neither outer nor inner consciousness, neither semi-consciousness nor sleeping consciousness, neither mere consciousness nor unconsciousness. He is Atman, the Spirit Himself, that cannot be seen or touched, that is above all distinctions, beyond thought and ineffable. In the union with Him is the supreme proof of His reality. He is peace and love.

This short Upanishad goes on to say that Atman is OM. 'Its three sounds, A, U, and M, are the first three stages of consciousness. The word OM as one sound is the fourth state of supreme consciousness.' The *Kena Upanishad* says that 'He is known in the ecstasy of an awakening.'

As Atman, the Self in each one of us and in all, is Brahman, God, the Highest in us and in all, we might say that the problem of the moral law in the *Upanishads* is solved by fulfilling the words of Shakespeare in *Hamlet.* For 'self ', however, we should understand 'Self ':

> This above all,—to thine own self be true;
> And it must follow, as the night the day,
> Thou canst not then be false to any man.

At the same time, if we consider that the essence of our Being, our Self, is joy, ANANDA, we might think of the words of Spinoza about virtue: 'Blessedness is not the reward of virtue: it is virtue itself. We do not find joy in virtue because we control our lusts: but, contrariwise, because we find joy in virtue we are able to control our lusts.'

The essence of the *Upanishads* is summed up in the words 'TAT TVAM ASI', 'That thou art'. Salvation is communion with Truth: *Satyam jayate,* says the *Mundaka Upanishad,* 'Truth is victory', to find truth is to conquer. The joy of the Infinite is ever with us, but we do not know this truth. We are like the beggar in the story who had been begging all his life in the same place. He wanted to be rich, but he was poor. When he died they found a treasure of gold buried just under the place where he had been begging. If he had only known how easy it was to be rich! True knowledge of the Self does not lead to salvation: it is salvation. But this is not an intellectual knowledge or even a poetical vision: 'In the union with Him is the supreme proof of His reality.' We may read in the *Upanishads* that beyond our becoming there is our Being, that beyond suffering and sorrow there is Joy, that beyond the three stages of ordinary consciousness there is a fourth state of supreme Consciousness; but what we read are only words. We cannot know the taste of a fruit or of a wine by reading words about them: we must eat the fruit and drink the wine. The seers of the *Upanishads* did not establish a Church, or found a definite religion, but the seers of the Spirit in all religions agree that communion with the Highest is not a problem of words but of life.

It will be seen that the lofty doctrines of the *Upanishads* are doctrines for the few: the Himalayas of the Soul are not for all. Men want a simple concrete God, or even a graven image of a god. They want a rule of life, and above all they want love. The later seers of the *Upanishads* saw this and in the *Isa Upanishad* we have ideas that we also find in the ***Bhagavad Gita.*** Because of its importance it should be quoted in full:

> Behold the Universe in the glory of God: and all that lives and moves on earth. Leaving the transient, find joy in the Eternal: set not your heart on another's possession.
>
> Working thus, a man may wish for a life of a hundred years. Only actions done in God bind not the soul of man.
>
> There are demon-haunted worlds, regions of utter darkness. Whoever in life rejects the Spirit goes to that darkness after death.
>
> The Spirit, without moving, is swifter than the mind; the senses cannot reach Him: He is ever beyond them. Standing still, He overtakes those

> who run. To the ocean of His being the spirit of life leads the streams of action.
>
> He moves, and He moves not. He is far, and He is near. He is within all, and He is outside all.
>
> Who sees all beings in his own Self, and his own Self in all beings, loses all fear.
>
> When a sage sees this great Unity and his Self has become all beings, what delusion and what sorrow can ever be near him?
>
> The Spirit filled all with His radiance. He is incorporeal and invulnerable, pure and untouched by evil. He is the supreme seer and thinker, immanent and transcendent. He placed all things in the path of Eternity.
>
> Into deep darkness fall those who follow action. Into deeper darkness fall those who follow knowledge.
>
> One is the outcome of knowledge, and another is the outcome of action. Thus have we heard from the ancient sages who explained this truth to us.
>
> He who knows both knowledge and action, with action overcomes death and with knowledge reaches immortality.
>
> Into deep darkness fall those who follow the immanent. Into deeper darkness fall those who follow the transcendent.
>
> One is the outcome of the transcendent, and another is the outcome of the immanent. Thus have we heard from the ancient sages who explained this truth to us.
>
> He who knows both the transcendent and the immanent, with the immanent overcomes death and with the transcendent reaches immortality.
>
> The face of truth remains hidden behind a circle of gold. Unveil it, O god of light, that I who love the true may see!
>
> O life-giving sun, offspring of the Lord of creation, solitary seer of heaven! Spread thy light and withdraw thy blinding splendour that I may behold thy radiant form: that Spirit far away within thee is my own inmost Spirit.
>
> May life go to immortal life, and the body go to ashes. OM. O my soul, remember past strivings, remember! O my soul, remember past strivings, remember!
>
> By the path of good lead us to final bliss, O fire divine, thou god who knowest all ways. Deliver us from wandering evil. Prayers and adoration we offer unto thee.

The times of the *Vedas* were times of action, and of all human actions the sacrifice to the gods was the most important. This was a material sacrifice like the offerings to God in the *Old Testament;* but there is a tendency in man to go from the world of matter to the world of mind. Micah, the Hebrew prophet, about 720 B.C., was not satisfied with the external sacrifice. He wanted an inner offering, and he says:

> Wherewith shall I come before the Lord, and bow myself before the high God? shall I come before him with burnt offerings, with calves of a year old?
>
> Will the Lord be pleased with thousands of rams, or with ten thousands of rivers of oil? shall I give my first-born for my transgression, the fruit of my body for the sin of my soul?
>
> He hath shewed thee, O man, what is good; and what doth the Lord require of thee, but to do justly, and to love mercy, and to walk humbly with thy God?

Micah did not give us the metaphysics of an inner sacrifice as the *Upanishads* do. They give us our inner I AM who is ours and not ours, because it is the I AM of all, the I AM of the universe. According to Coleridge, the higher Imagination is 'the repetition in the finite mind of the eternal act of creation in the infinite I AM'. This idea might lead to the *Upanishads:* the Infinite is ever in us and the finite in us can have communion with the Infinite.

If we consider the great words of the *Upanishads* TAT TVAM ASI, 'That thou art', we find that from the world outside we are going into our inner world; but the words can be interpreted in different ways. 'I am Brahman' or 'I am Atman' or 'I am God' may sound strange unless we take it in the true meaning that only the I AM in me is: my little personality is practically nothing. On the other hand, TAT TVAM ASI can be interpreted in the sense that only God is, or 'Only Thou art'. In both cases our little personality disappears, as indeed it does disappear in the fourth state of consciousness described in the *Mundaka Upanishad.* But if we want to retain our personality and adore a personal God, then we can imagine Him as a Master and imagine ourselves as servants. Ramakrishna (1836-86), the Indian saint, describes it in these words:

> There are three different paths to reach the Highest: the path of I, the path of Thou, and the path of Thou and I.
>
> According to the first, all that is, was, or ever shall be is I, my higher Self. In other words, I am, I was, and I shall be for ever in Eternity.
>
> According to the second. Thou art, O Lord, and all is Thine.
>
> And according to the third. Thou art the Lord, and I am Thy servant, or Thy son.
>
> In the perfection of any of these three ways, a man will find God.
>
> Anonymous translation

The first way is the way of the *Upanishads* and of the *Vedanta;* the second way is the way of love, of Mary in the Gospels; the third way is the way of service, of Martha. The three ways have in common that what is important is something above our little self, whether we call this I AM, or 'Thou art', or whether we say, 'Thou art my Master.' In the three ways there is an absolute forgetfulness of our lower personality, and a recognition of a higher Personality. The Brahman of the *Upanishads* is, however, beyond all conception: it includes all, but it is beyond all. To become one with Brahman means a process of deep thought, before we can transcend thought. Love and work are easier ways.

The *Vedas* laid stress on the outer world, the world of action of the Immanent; and the *Upanishads* laid stress on the inner world, the world of knowledge of the Transcendent Spirit. In the *Isa Upanishad* we find the word Isa, God, and not the word Brahman, although the spirit of Brahman breathes through the *Upanishad.* We also find a harmony of action and knowledge, of the immanent and the transcendent. All action, including religious ritual, can be a means of reaching the inner meaning of things.

This vision of action with a consciousness of its meaning is interwoven in the ***Bhagavad Gita*** with the idea of love. If life or action is the finite and consciousness or knowledge is the Infinite, love is the means of turning life into Light, the bond of union between the finite and the Infinite. In all true love there is the love of the Infinite in the person or thing we love.

The ***Bhagavad Gita*** was included in the *Mahabharata.* This vast epic of over one hundred thousand slokas, or couplets, is the longest poem in the world: about thirty times as long as *Paradise Lost,* and about 140 times as long as the ***Bhagavad Gita!*** About four-fifths of the poem are stories, and these are centred around the main story which is the story of a war. The word Mahabharata, meaning the great Bharata, reminds us of Bharata, the son of Sakuntala, the founder of a dynasty of Indian kings. The story is told in the *Mahabharata,* and was used by Kalidasa in his great drama *Sakuntala,* the masterpiece of Indian poetry.

The main story of the *Mahabharata* centres around forces of good and evil represented, on the whole, as the Pandavas and the Kuravas. The father of Dhrita-rashtra and Pandu was the king of Hastinapura about fifty miles north-east of modern Delhi. At his death Pandu succeeded to the throne, as his eldest brother, Dhrita-rashtra, was blind. The sons of Pandu were Yudhishthira, Bhima, Arjuna, Nakula, and Sahadeva. We find their names in the first chapter of the ***Bhagavad Gita.*** Dhrita-rashtra had one hundred sons and the eldest was Duryodhana, the incarnation of evil. Pandu died and the blind king Dhrita-rashtra brought up in his place the five sons of his brother. The Pandavas became great warriors and Dhrita-rashtra appointed the eldest, Yudhishthira, as heir-apparent. This was the cause of the great rivalry and in the end of the great war.

The *Mahabharata* has eighteen books and the great battle where Duryodhana and all his armies were destroyed lasted eighteen days. The ***Bhagavad Gita*** has eighteen chapters. There is no doubt that the war described in the *Mahabharata* is not symbolic and that it may even be based on historical fact; but the problem is different when we find the dialogue between Krishna and Arjuna set in a background of war. The *Mahabharata* is the growth of centuries and to include a story in the *Mahabharata* was a way of securing its immortality. We find in the vast poem the story later on developed in the *Ramayana,* the stories of Nala and Damayanti, Savitri, Sakuntala and king Dushyanta, and many others. The ***Bhagavad Gita*** is like a little shrine in a vast temple, a temple that is both a theatre and a fair of this world; and whilst the war in the *Mahabharata* may be meant as a real war it is obvious that the war in the ***Bhagavad Gita*** has a symbolical meaning. The Arjuna and Krishna that we find in the rest of the *Mahabharata* are different beings from the Krishna and Arjuna of the ***Bhagavad Gita.*** We find in the ***Gita*** that there is going to be a great battle for the rule of a Kingdom; and how can we doubt that this is the Kingdom of Heaven, the kingdom of the soul? Are we going to allow the forces of light in us or the forces of darkness to win? And yet, how easy not to fight, and to find reasons to withdraw from the battle! In the ***Bhagavad Gita*** Arjuna becomes the soul of man and Krishna the charioteer of the soul.

When we think of the chariot of Arjuna we can remember the image of a chariot in the *Upanishads,* in Plato, in Buddha, in Blake, in Keats. Of these the most interesting for spiritual purposes is the chariot in Buddhism which is called 'He that runs in silence'; the wheels of the chariot are 'Right effort'; the driver is DHAMMA, or Truth. The chariot leads to Nirvana, the Kingdom of Heaven. The end of the journey is 'The land which is free from fear' . . .

The use of external images for spiritual purposes is quite common. The Song of Songs was incorporated in the *Bible* and a spiritual meaning given to it. St John of the Cross uses the imagery of marriage to describe the supreme communion of love. In the Sanskrit book of stories, the *Hitopadesa,* we find the following interpretation of Hindu ritual:

> The Spirit in thee is a river. Its sacred bathing place is contemplation; its waters are truth; its banks are holiness; its waves are love. Go to that river for purification: thy soul cannot be made pure by mere water.

Here we have the spiritual interpretation of the material bathing in the Ganges. We can also remember how parables have always been used for spiritual symbols. When Jesus spoke his parables he never meant them as 'true stories' but as stories of Truth, symbols leading to Truth.

If we want to understand the spiritual meaning of the ***Bhagavad Gita,*** we had better forget everything concerning the great battle of the *Mahabharata* or the story of Krishna and Arjuna in the vast epic. A spiritual reader of the ***Gita*** will find in it the great spiritual struggle of a human soul. The war imagery is even used by Krishna in the poem when at the end of Chapter 3 he says: 'Be a warrior and kill desire, the powerful enemy of the soul'; and again at the end of Chapter 4: 'Kill therefore with the sword of wisdom the doubt born of ignorance that lies in thy heart.' How could the treachery, robbery, and butchery of war be reconciled with the spiritual vision and love of the ***Bhagavad Gita***? How could we reconcile it with the Spirit of the ***Gita,*** and of all true spiritual seers, as expressed in those words of Krishna? 'When a man sees that the God in himself is the same God in all that is, he hurts not himself by hurting others: then he goes to the highest Path.' 13.28.

Scholars differ as to the date of the ***Bhagavad Gita;*** but as the roots of this great poem are in Eternity the date of its revelation in time is of little spiritual importance. As there are no references to Buddhism in the ***Gita*** and there are a few archaic words and expressions, some of the greatest scholars have considered it pre-Buddhistic, i.e. about 500 B.C. The Sanskrit of the ***Bhagavad Gita*** is, on the whole, simple and clear, like the oldest parts of the *Mahabharata.* This could be added as an argument for an early date; but the value of a spiritual scripture is its value to us here and now, and the real problem is how to translate its light into life.

The ***Bhagavad Gita*** is, above all, a spiritual poem and as such it must be judged; and it must be seen as a whole. An analytical approach will never reveal to us the full meaning of a poem.

If a Beethoven could give us in music the spirit of the ***Bhagavad Gita,*** what a wonderful symphony we should hear!

First of all come the stirring sounds of an impending battle, the great battle for an inner victory, and the despairing cry of the soul ready to give up the struggle. The soul is afraid of death: of the death of its passions and desires. It also fears the death of the body: is death the end of all? Then we hear the voice of the Eternal in man speaking to the soul that doubts and trembles: we hear about our immortality. After this come sounds infinitely serene and peaceful: the soul has peace from passions, and peace from fears and lower desires. The music becomes more urgent: it is the call to action, not action in time but action in Eternity: Karma Yoga. Those strains are followed by notes of eternal silence: it is vision, Jñana Yoga. Sweet human melodies are heard: it is the descent of Eternity into time, the incarnation of the divine. There is again a call to action, but this time the work is prayer, the deep prayer of silence which we find in Chapter 6. The music becomes more and more majestic: it is the revelation of God in all things in creation, but more evident in whatever is beautiful and good, in whatever has glory and power. Rising above the vast harmonies of this movement we hear a note of infinite tenderness. It is love. It is love that offers in adoration the whole of life to the God of Love, and God accepts the offering of a pure heart. The music rises again in tremendous crescendos that seem to overflow the limits of the universe: it is the vision of all things and of the whole universe in God. In this theme there is wonder and fear: the God of creation is also the God of destruction, the God of immortality is also the God of life and death.

After those ineffably sublime harmonies the music descends to softer melodies: it is the vision of God as man, as the friend of the struggling soul. Whatever we do for a human being we do it for Him.

> For I was a-hungered, and ye gave me meat: I was thirsty, and ye gave me drink: I was a stranger, and ye took me in: naked, and ye clothed me: I was sick, and ye visited me: I was in prison, and ye came unto me.
>
> Matt. 25:36

The vast symphony of the ***Bhagavad Gita*** goes on. After the tenderness of love for Krishna, the God of Love, we have the universal harmonies of Brahman in the Universe. From the ONE in the many attained by love, we reach the splendour of all in the transcendent ONE. The music now changes: it is made of melodies of light and fire and darkness, the three Gunas, the three forces of the universe. New harmonies now are heard because we have the Tree of transmigration, the Tree of life, and the music carries us on from earth to heaven and from heaven to earth. We hear now terrible sounds: it is the noise of evil in creation; but this is drowned in the sounds of the good in all. The music returns now to earthly melodies, and after them we hear the glory of the sacred sounds OM, TAT, SAT: the Infinite beyond the beginning, the middle and the end of all our work.

At the end of this great symphony the different themes of the previous chapters are interwoven into one. The melodies of vision, love, and work in Eternity become one simple final strain of unearthly tenderness and beauty, the simple call of God to man: 'Come to me for thy salvation.'

This is the symphony of the ***Bhagavad Gita.*** There are in it several themes which rise above the rest. There is Yoga. It is obvious that the spiritual Yoga of the ***Gita*** is love; but Yoga also means 'Samadhi', a state of inner communion with the object of contemplation. When this contemplation is turned upon any being or object in creation, we have poetry: when it is turned towards the Source of all creation we have Light, spiritual vision. Inner Yoga is said to be above the Scriptures, because the Scriptures may be contradictory: above all past and future Scriptures the ***Gita*** places spiritual experience.

> When thy mind leaves behind its dark forest of delusion, thou shalt go beyond the scriptures of times past and still to come.
>
> When thy mind, that may be wavering in the contradictions of many scriptures, shall rest unshaken in divine contemplation, then the goal of Yoga is thine.
>
> 2.52, 53

Spiritual experience is the only source of true spiritual faith, and this must never contradict reason, or as Sankara, c. 788-820 A.D., says in his commentary to the ***Bhagavad Gita:*** 'If a hundred scriptures should declare that fire is cold or that it is dark, we would suppose that they intend quite a different meaning from the apparent one!'

What is the indispensable condition for this spiritual experience? It is very simple, and it can be very difficult: it is the absence of desires. That is to say: if we want things as objects of possession we are in the lower region of 'having', but if we find in things objects of contemplation and inner communion we are in the higher region of 'being'. All true love is love of Eternity, and the inner Light of Being is revealed only when the clouds of becoming disappear. This is the meaning of the verse of the ***Gita*** that says: 'Even as all waters flow into the ocean, but the ocean never overflows, even so the sage feels desires, but he is ever one in his infinite peace' 2. 70. Man can only find peace in the Infinite, not in the finite. This is expressed very clearly by St John of the Cross when he says: *'Cuando reparas en algo, dejas de arrojarte al Todo',* 'When you set your heart on anything, you cease to throw yourself into the All.' If we desire anything for its finite pleasure, we shall miss its infinite joy. The final words of Krishna to Arjuna are: 'Leave all things behind.' St John of the Cross tells us how we are able to leave all things behind and how not to look back: it is not to leave a vacuum in the soul, but to desire the Highest in all with the fire of burning love.

Prayer is described in the ***Gita*** as a means to achieve inner union. It is interesting to compare Chapter 6 of the ***Gita*** with this passage from St Peter of Alcántara, the teacher of St Teresa:

> In meditation we consider carefully divine things, and we pass from one to another, so that the heart may feel love. It is as though we should strike a flint, and draw a spark of fire. But in contemplation the spark is struck: the love we were seeking is here. The soul enjoys silence and peace, not by many reasonings, but by simply contemplating the Truth.

When describing the state of the man who has found joy in God, the ***Bhagavad Gita*** says: 'When in recollection he withdraws all his senses from the attractions of the pleasures of sense, even as a tortoise withdraws all its limbs, then his is a serene wisdom'. 2. 58. St Teresa uses the same image when describing the prayer of recollection: 'I think I read somewhere that the soul is then like a tortoise or sea-urchin, which retreats into itself. Whoever said this no doubt understood what he was talking about.'

From the sense of harmony of the ***Gita*** comes its universal sympathy. This is suggested again and again through the whole poem, and it is definitely stated when Krishna says 'In any way that men love me, in that same way they find my love'. 4. II; and 'Even those who in faith worship other gods, because of their love they worship me'. 9. 23. This spirit of tolerance is expressed by St Teresa in her homely way when she advises her nuns against too much zeal: '*Ni hay para qué querer luego que todos vayan por nuestro camino*', 'There is no reason why we should want everyone else to follow our own path."

The importance given to reason in the ***Bhagavad Gita*** is very great. Arjuna is told that he must seek salvation in reason. 2. 49. And the first condition for a man to be worthy of God is that his reason should be pure—18. 51 and 18. 57. Reason is the faculty given to man to distinguish true emotion from false emotionalism, faith from fanaticism, imagination from fancy, a true vision from a visionary illusion.

Self-harmony, or self-control, is again and again praised in the ***Bhagavad Gita.*** All perfection in action is a form of self-control, and this sense of perfection is the essence of the Karma Yoga of the ***Gita.*** The artist must have self-control in the moment of creation, and all work well done requires self-control; but the ***Bhagavad Gita*** wants us to transform our whole life into an act of creation. Only self-control makes it possible for us to live in harmony with other people. Of course, as Kant clearly shows, self-control must be at the service of a good will; but a good will must have power, and all virtue depends on the power of self-control.

The great psychological problem of self-control can be solved in different ways, and some are much easier than others. The spiritual answer is 'Seek first the kingdom of God.' If the joy of the inner kingdom is found, then the words of Spinoza, previously quoted, have found their spiritual setting. As soon the joy of the higher comes, the pleasure of the lower disappears.

Many are the themes of the symphony of the ***Bhagavad Gita,*** but the central ones are three: JNANA, BHAKTI, and KARMA: Light, Love, and Life.

Jñana is the centre of the *Upanishads,* the means of reaching Brahman. The ***Gita*** also places the man of Jñana, the man of Light, above all men: he is in God. The three manifestations of Brahman revealed in Jñana are very present in the ***Gita:*** *Sat, Cit,* and *Ananda,* Being, Consciousness, and Joy.

Being can be felt in the silence of the soul. When an inner surrender of the self-conscious will takes place, there is great peace of mind and body, and gradually the movements of the mind seem to stop. There is no thinking, but there is a deep feeling of Being, of a deeper reality than the reality of ordinary consciousness. Faith in Being then becomes absolute: how could one doubt the deepest experience of one's life? Amiel describes glimpses of Being when he writes in his diary:

> 2nd January, 1880. Here there is a sense of rest and quietness. Silence in the house and outside. A tranquil fire gives a feeling of comfort. The portrait of my mother seems to smile upon me. This peaceful morning makes me happy. Whatever pleasure we may get from our emotions I do not think it can equal those moments of silent peace which are glimpses of the joys of Paradise. Desire and fear, grief and anxiety are no more. We live a moment of life in the supreme region of our own being: pure consciousness. One feels an inner harmony free from the slightest agitation or tension. In those moments the state of the soul is solemn, perhaps akin to its condition beyond the grave. It is happiness as the Orientals understand it, the happiness of the hermit who is free from desire and struggle, and who simply adores in fullness of joy. We cannot find words to express this experience, because our languages can only describe particular and definite conditions of life: they have no words to express this silent contemplation, this heavenly quietness, this ocean of peace which both reflects the heavens above and is master of its own vast depth. Things return to their first principle, while memories become dreams of memories. The soul is then pure being and no longer feels its separation from the whole. It is conscious of the universal life, and at that moment is a centre of communion with God. It has nothing and it lacks nothing. Perhaps only the Yogis and the Sufis have known in its depth this condition of simple happiness which combines the joys of being and non-being, which is neither reflection nor will, and which is beyond the moral and the intellectual life: a return to oneness, to the fullness of things, the πληρωμα, the vision of Plotinus and Proclus, the glad expectation of Nirvana.

This sense of Being is the sense of Brahman. From experiences similar to that described by Amiel, but of course infinitely greater, come the poems of St John of the Cross, the greatest spiritual poems of all time. In his aphorisms he says: 'In order to be All, do not desire to be anything. In order to know All, do not desire to know anything. In order to find the joy of All, do not desire to enjoy anything.' 'To be', 'to know', and 'to find joy' correspond to the SAT, CIT, ANANDA. 'Being, Consciousness, and Joy' of the *Upanishads.*

The great problem of the soul of man could then be expressed by the words of Hamlet which, as so often in Shakespeare, far transcend their context:

> 'To be, or not be—that is the question.'

Whilst Jñana, the Light of God, is the highest theme in the ***Bhagavad Gita***—'The man of vision and I are one' (7. 18), says Krishna—we find that it is Bhakti, love, which is the bond of union between man and God and therefore between man and man. We can read in the ***Gita*** words that sound like the words of Jesus: 'For this is my word of promise, that he who loves me shall not perish' 9. 31. 'He who in oneness of love, loves me in whatever he sees, wherever this man may live, in truth this man lives in me' 6. 31. The ***Bhagavad Gita*** does not emphasize that God is reached by Jñana, because Jñana *is* God; but it says again and again that love is the means to reach God in whom Light and Love are one: 'By love he knows me in truth, who I am and what I am' 18. 55 and 'Only by love can men see me, and know me, and come unto me' 11.54.

Socrates tells us that love is the messenger between the gods and man, and St John of the Cross says that 'It is love alone that unites the soul with God.' St Teresa in her homely way says 'What matters is not to think much, but to love much', *'No está la cosa en pensar mucho, sino en amar mucho'* although she adds that 'The love of God must not be built up in our imagination, but must be tried by works.' These ideas are in the spirit of the ***Bhagavad Gita.*** The vision of God is the grace of God; but the grace of God is the reward of the love of man.

We thus find in the ***Bhagavad Gita*** that love is interwoven with light.

Love is the power that moves the universe, the day of life, the night of death, and the new day after death. The radiance of this universe sends us a message of love and says that all creation came from love, that love impels evolution and that at the end of their time love returns all things to Eternity. Even as the rational mind can see that all matter is energy, the spirit can see that all energy is love, and everything in creation can be a mathematical equation for the mind and a song of love for the soul. Love leads to Light: Bhakti leads to Jñana, and Jñana is the joy of Brahman, the joy of the Infinite.

Our soul, like a bird in a cage, longs for the liberty of the vast air. We read the words of Pindar:

> Things of a day! What are we, and what are we not? A dream about a shadow is man: yet, when some god-given splendour falls, a glory of light comes over him and his life is sweet.

The finite longs for the Infinite and we feel the sorrow of things that pass away; but beyond the tears of mankind there is the rainbow of joy. We can love the Infinite in all, and thus we can find joy in all, as it was so beautifully expressed in the *Brihad-Aranyaka Upanishad:*

> It is not for the love of a husband that a husband is dear; but for the love of the Soul in the husband that a husband is dear.
>
> It is not for the love of a wife that a wife is dear; but for the love of the Soul in the wife that a wife is dear.
>
> It is not for the love of children that children are dear; but for the love of the Soul in children that children are dear.
>
> It is not for the love of all that all is dear; but for the love of the Soul in all that all is dear.

The ***Bhagavad Gita*** is a book of Light and Love, but it is above all a book of Life: after Jñana and Bhakti, we have Karma.

The word Karma is connected with the Sanskrit root *Kri* which we find in the English words 'create' and 'creation'. Karma is work, and work is life. The word Karma means also 'sacred work' and is connected with the sacrifice of the *Vedas:* the ritual of religion. This meaning has to be considered in reading the ***Gita.*** Karma, work or action, is often contrasted in the ***Bhagavad Gita*** with Jñana, or contemplation: external ritual is set in contrast with inner spiritual life. This was the great spiritual change that took place in the *Upanishads:* from external ritual they went into inner life. This contrast is also found in the ***Gita,*** but in the ***Gita*** the word Karma has acquired a far deeper meaning, and this leads to one of the most sublime conceptions of man. All life is action, but every little finite action should be a surrender to the Infinite, even as breathing in seems to be the receiving of the gift of life, and the breathing out a surrender into the infinite Life. Every little work in life, however humble, can become an act of creation and therefore a means of salvation, because in all true creation we reconcile the finite with the Infinite, hence the joy of creation. When vision is pure and when creation is pure there is always joy.

Perhaps an example from Homer can help us to realize the conception of Karma in the ***Bhagavad Gita.*** In Book VI of the *Odyssey,* whilst Odysseus is sleeping in the shelter of the olive tree Nausicaa, the lovely daughter of the good ruler Alcinous, is gone with her maidens to the river to wash laundry, and Homer says:

> In due course they reached the noble river with its never-failing pools, in which there was enough clear water always bubbling up and swirling by to clean the dirtiest clothes. Here they turned the mules loose from under the yoke and drove them along the eddying stream to graze on the sweet grass. Then they lifted the clothes by armfuls from the cart, dropped them into the dark water and trod them down briskly in the troughs, competing with each other in the work. When they had rinsed them till no dirt was left, they spread them out in a row along the sea-shore, just where the waves washed the shin-

> gle clean when they came tumbling up the beach. Next, after bathing and rubbing themselves with olive-oil, they took their meal at the riverside, waiting for the sunshine to dry the clothes. And presently, when mistress and maids had all enjoyed their food, they threw off their headgear and began playing with a ball, while Nausicaa of the white arms led them in their song.
>
> Translated by E. V. Rieu

Here we find the joy of vision and creation. The poet sees every action, however humble, under the radiance of eternal beauty, and we see the actors finding a pure joy in their work, as if they were working for Eternity. The poet sees things in an Eternity of beauty and joy, and the actors are doing their work beautifully, in the joy of Eternity. This is the spirit of Karma in the ***Bhagavad Gita.*** Nausicaa and her maidens were washing laundry for themselves and not for God; but they were in the joy of action, and therefore in the joy of God, the more so because they were unconscious of this greatness.

We find in Homer that work, even the most humble work, is beautiful. In the ***Bhagavad Gita*** we find that all work can be both beautiful and holy. We thus hear the words of Krishna: 'Offer to me all thy works and rest thy mind on the Supreme. Be free from vain hopes and selfish thoughts, and with inner peace fight thou thy fight' 3. 30. And with a variation of the same idea: 'Whatever you do, or eat, or give, or offer in adoration, let it be an offering to me; and whatever you suffer, suffer it for me.' This is the same voice of St Paul to the Corinthians: 'Whether therefore ye eat, or drink, or whatsoever ye do, do all to the glory of God' 1 *Cor.* 10:31. And this work must be unselfish: 'Let the wise man work unselfishly for the good of all the world' ***Gita*** 3. 25.

The praise of work as a means of salvation is later expressed in the poem and we hear that all men attain perfection when they find joy in their work, and they find joy in their work when their work is worship of God, because God is joy.

The greatness of the ***Bhagavad Gita*** is the greatness of the universe; but even as the wonder of the stars in heaven only reveals itself in the silence of the night, the wonder of this poem only reveals itself in the silence of the soul. We may begin when children to feel the mystery and wonder of this universe. One day, when very young, a few verses of the ***Gita*** may find their way into our hearts. We learn Sanskrit for the sake of the ***Bhagavad Gita.*** We read every translation we can find and compare different interpretations. We read the commentaries of Sankara and Ramanuja, histories of Indian philosophy and Sanskrit literature, and every publication on the ***Bhagavad Gita*** we can find. And far more than that: we may read the ***Bhagavad Gita*** in Sanskrit again and again, until we know the most important verses by heart, and chant them in Sanskrit, and the language of those verses becomes as familiar to us as our mother tongue. We may go to that poem in times of sorrow and joy and thus connect it with the deepest moments of our life; and write down the thoughts and emotions that the verses wake in us; and our reading may go on for years; and suddenly one day we may feel that we are reading the ***Bhagavad Gita*** for the first time. And why? Because new wonders have revealed themselves to us and we feel that the words of Arjuna are our own words: 'Speak to me again of thy power and thy glory, for I am never tired, never, of hearing thy words of life' 10.18.

What is the essence of this great poem, what is the meaning of it all? The essence of the ***Bhagavad Gita*** is the vision of God in all things and of all things in God. It is the vision of Dante when he says in his *Paradiso:*

> Nel suo profondo vidi che s'interna,
> legato con amore in un volume,
> ciò che per l'universo si squaderna.
>
> La forma universal di questo nodo
> creo ch'io vidi, perchè più di largo
> dicendo questo, mi sento ch'io godo.
>
> Within its deep infinity I saw ingathered, and bound by love in one volume, the scattered leaves of all the universe.
>
> The universal form of this complex whole I think that I saw, because as I say this I feel my joy increasing.

It is the vision of Arjuna in the ***Bhagavad Gita:***

> If the light of a thousand suns suddenly arose in the sky, that splendour might be compared to the radiance of the Supreme Spirit.
>
> And Arjuna saw in that radiance the whole universe in its variety, standing in a vast unity in the body of the God of gods.
>
> II.12-13

Love leads to Light, but the Light is not ours: it is given to us, it is given to us as a reward for our love and our good work. In the battle of the ***Bhagavad Gita*** there is a great symbol of hope: that he who has a good will and strives is never lost, and that in the battle for eternal life there can never be a defeat unless we run away from the battle.

The true progress of man on earth is the progress of an inner vision. We have a progress in science, but is it in harmony with a spiritual progress? We want a scientific progress, but do we want a moral progress? It is not enough to have more, or even to know more, but to live more, and if we want to live more we must love more. Love is 'the treasure hid in a field', and this field according to the ***Gita*** is our own soul. Here the treasure is found for which the wise merchant 'went and sold all he had'. And contrary to the law of matter where to give more means to have less, in the law of love the more one gives the more one has.

The spiritual visions of man confirm and illumine each other. We have the cosmic greatness of Hinduism, the moral issues of Zoroaster, the joy in Truth of Buddha, the spiritual victory of Jainism, the simple love of Tao, the wisdom of Confucius, the poetry of Shinto, the One God of Israel, the redeeming radiance of Christianity, the glory of God of Islam, the harmony of the Sikhs. Great poems in different languages have different values but they all are poetry, and the spiritual visions of man come all from One Light. In them we have Lamps of Fire that burn to the glory of God.

The finite in man longs for the Infinite. The love that moves the stars moves also the heart of man and a law of spiritual gravitation leads his soul to the Soul of the universe. Man sees the sun by the light of the sun, and he sees the Spirit by the light of his own inner spirit. The radiance of eternal beauty shines over this vast universe and in moments of contemplation we can see the Eternal in things that pass away. This is the message of the great spiritual seers; and all poetry and art and beauty is only an infinite variation of this message.

If we read the scriptures and books of wisdom of the world, if we consider the many spiritual experiences recorded in the writings of the past, we find one spiritual faith, and this faith is based on a vision of Truth. Not indeed the truth of the laws of nature gradually discovered by the human mind; but the Truth of our Being.

In the ***Bhagavad Gita*** we have faith, a faith based on spiritual vision. In this vision we have Light. Shall we see? This Song calls us to Love and Life. Shall we hear?

Every moment of our life can be the beginning of great things. (pp. 9-36)

Juan Mascaró, in an introduction to The Bhagavad Gita, *translated by Juan Mascaró, Penguin Books, 1962, pp. 9-36.*

Friedrich Schlegel on the *Bhagavad Gītā* (1815):

[The ***Bhagavad Gītā***] contains the modern system of Indian thought, connected by a common origin with the doctrines of the religious sect found in India by the Greeks, and called by them Samaneans, in contradistinction to the Brachmans. It is an episode of the Epic—*Mahabharata*—but philosophical throughout. It may almost be styled a manual of Indian mysticism; it is in great repute, and the best exponent of the actual Indian mind. There is a remarkable peculiarity about this book, as regards the unmeasured praise bestowed on leading deities, either not found at all in Menu's laws, or, at most, passed over without comment: whilst the old doctrines, the *Vedas,* and polytheism generally, are roughly handled. The essential creed expounded is that of an absolute divine unity, absorbing all distinction, and engulphing all things. Yet, in so far as it is connected with mythology, it may be termed poetic pantheism, not unlike the Neo-Platonic philosophy, which, it will be remembered, combined, under somewhat similar circumstances, with the then popular belief, in its last throes, expecting by these means to revive its drooping energies.

Friedrich Schlegel, in his Lectures on the History of Literature, Ancient and Modern, *George Bell, 1896.*

R. C. Zaehner (essay date 1962)

[*Zaehner was a noted Orientalist and religious scholar whose books include* Mysticism Sacred and Profane *(1957),* Hindu and Muslim Mysticism *(1960), and* Hinduism. *In the following excerpt from the 1962 edition of the latter work, he traces the development of theism in Indian thought, focusing on the conception of God in the* Gītā.]

In the *Upanishads* there are two trends of which the drift towards monism is one. The other is a trend towards a more or less clear-cut form of theism. We have no space to trace this tendency in detail here, but must be content to say that the Brahman-Ātman is spoken of not only as the imperishable, the All, and so on, but also as the Lord and king of all, the 'Inner Controller' who indwells the cosmos yet is other than it. The shift towards theism becomes more marked when we find the authors of the *Upanishads* using once again the term *deva* 'god', but not now in the sense of *a* god as in the *Rig-Veda,* but of 'God', the omnipotent, omniscient ruler of the universe. This tendency culminates in the *Śvetāśvatara Upanishad* where we once again meet with the *Vedic* god Rudra-Śiva, but this time not as the terrible archer of the forests who seeks whom he may devour, but as the Supreme Lord who is master over the perishable and imperishable alike (1.10)—a personal God, then, who transcends both the finite and infinite which together constitute the 'city of Brahman'. (pp. 80-1)

In the *Śvetāśvatara Upanishad* the Absolute is for the first time identified with a personal God, in this case, Rudra-Śiva. Though Śiva indwells the soul, he is not identical with it, he is the 'Person of the measure of a thumb, the innermost soul (*antarātman*) ever seated in the heart of creatures' (3.13); but since he is God worship is due to him as it is not due to an impersonal being (2.17), and it is therefore legitimate to invoke his protection and his grace (*prasāda*). The highroad to the knowledge of God which brings about *moksha,* however, is considered to be Yoga. The Yoga described in the *Śvetāśvatara Upanishad* is basically the same technique as that of the *Yoga-sūtras* and the ***Bhagavad-Gītā;*** it aims at mastering the senses and the mind, so that the mirror of the soul, unsullied by all temporal concerns, may perfectly reflect the God who is 'hidden in the heart'. The immanent God is thus to be known (*jñāna*) by Yoga, the transcendent God to be worshipped with loving devotion (*bhakti*).

Once, however, the Absolute—the supreme Brahman, Ātman, and Purusha—was identified with a particular god, it inevitably came to be associated with all the mythological accretions that in the course of time had converged to form the personality of that God. Śiva is no exception; and in him are combined the terrible Rudra of the *Rig-Veda* and the ithyphallic Yogin of the Harappā seals, and however much his worship may be spiritualized, these basic characteristics never leave him.

In the [*Mahābhārata*] it is not at all clear whether Śiva or Vishnu is to be regarded as the supreme Deity. Śiva's appearances are rare, but when he does appear, Krishna, the incarnation of Vishnu, invariably seems to take second place. Throughout there is tension and rivalry between the two gods, and this is never wholly dissipated even when they are fused into the single figure *Hari-hara, Hari* being one of the names of Vishnu and *Hara* of Śiva. (pp. 83-4)

Śiva is also *paśupati,* the 'Lord of animals', and there is scarcely an animal whose form he will not assume. Usually, however, it is as a bull that he is worshipped, and when in human form the white bull Nandin is his mount. Although the title *paśupati* is found in the *Atharva-Veda,* Śiva claims to have founded the religion of the *Pāśupatyas* which took no cognizance of the Vedic division of society into the four great classes or the four stages of life laid down by the Brāhmans [in the *Mahābhārata*]. This and other evidence suggests that there is much in the figure of Śiva that derives from non-Aryan sources. Brāhmanism, however, can absorb almost anything into itself, and so the rivalry between Śiva and Vishnu was resolved by the creation of a largely artificial *Trimūrti* or 'One God in three forms', Brahmā—Vishnu—Śiva, a trinity in which Brahmā is the creator, Vishnu the preserver, and Śiva the destroyer. This compromise was, however, without effect on popular religion, and Hindus are to this day predominantly worshippers of either Vishnu or Śiva or Śiva's [consort Śakti], each of which their devotees regard as the supreme Being.

There are too many threads that go to make up the disconcerting figure of Śiva for us to attempt to summarize his significance. Despite the fact that he was later to inspire the tenderest love among his devotees, he remains a *mysterium tremendum et fascinosum:* he terrifies and he fascinates. Unlike Vishnu and his incarnations there is little that is human about him; he transcends humanity, and the violence of the contradictions that he subsumes into himself gives him a sublimity and a mystery that no purely anthropomorphic figure could evoke. (p. 86)

From the sixth century onward the cult of Śiva was making increasing progress in the Tamil-speaking lands of south India where Jainism and to a lesser extent Buddhism were by now firmly entrenched. This movement, which was deeply devotional in character, reached its climax with Sambandhar who converted the local king from Jainism in the seventh century and in Mānikka Vāśagar who in the ninth century composed some of the loveliest hymns in praise of the love of God that have been written in any language. These and the other Tamil Śaivite saints together with their Vaishnavite counterparts started the great *bhakti* movement which was later to sweep across all India and which will engage us in a later chapter. The theology of the Tamil Śaivites, known as the *Śaiva Siddhānta,* was systematized by Maykandar Karulturai in the thirteenth century in his *Śiva-jñāna-bodham* which claims to be the quintessence of the *Āgamas,* as the sacred books of the Śaivites are called, and by Arulananti (Arunandi) Śivācārya, his pupil, in his *Śiva-jñāna-siddhiyār.* (p. 87)

The *Śaiva Siddhānta* presents perhaps the highest form of theism that India was ever to develop, for Śiva, even as a mythological figure, gives an overwhelming impression of 'otherness' and transcendence which the much milder and more superficially attractive figure of Vishnu rarely does. Vishnu is very much nearer to man and becomes incarnate as man.

The figure of Vishnu is even more complex than that of Śiva as he seems to have subsumed several other deities into his person. In the [*Mahābhārata*] we meet him in his incarnation as Krishna, the chieftain of the clan of the Yādavas, who allies himself with the Pāndavas in their fratricidal struggle with their cousins, the Kauravas. . . .

Vishnu is the god who from time to time becomes incarnate in order to rehabilitate the world. 'For the protection of the good and the destruction of evil-doers, and for the [re-]establishment of *dharma* I come into being in successive ages' [***Bhagavad-Gītā***]. The number of these incarnations or 'descents' (*avatār(a)s*) is not fixed, but those most commonly mentioned are his *avatārs* as a fish, a boar, a man-lion and a dwarf, as Paraśu-Rāma, who exterminated the Kshatriya class twenty-one times, as Rāma, the hero of the *Rāmāyana,* the shorter of the two Sanskrit epics, and as Krishna, one of the heroes of the *Mahābhārata,* the Greater Epic, and finally, and most surprisingly, as Buddha. At the end of this era he will reappear as Kalkin who will inaugurate a new and better age. (p. 91)

If the *Śvetāśvatara Upanishad* is the rock on which the fabric of Śaivite theism rests, this is doubly true of the ***Bhagavad-Gītā*** not only in its relation to the cult of Vishnu but also in its relation to the whole subsequent development of Hinduism. Though it does not rank as *śruti* as the *Śvetāśvatara* does, its influence has been far in excess not only of the *Śvetāśvatara* but probably of all the *Upanishads* put together; for though there are adumbrations of divine grace and divine love in the *Upanishads,* they are the faintest of adumbrations only: in the ***Gītā*** they became much more explicit. There are plenty of didactic passages in the *Mahābhārata,* but only on this one occasion does Krishna deign to reveal the full truth about himself, and this in great secrecy to Arjuna, his closest friend, at the most solemn hour of his life. True, he had been acclaimed as the Supreme Being by friend and foe alike time and again before, but nowhere else does he reveal himself as such or give instruction in the manner in which men should live their lives.

The ***Gītā*** can conveniently be divided into three parts: the first (Chapters I-VI) deals with the different ways in which the soul may win through to liberation, the second deals with the nature of God and ends up with the grand theophany in Chapter XI, while the last part, after going over much of the previous ground, ends up with what is a new gospel, not hitherto proclaimed in India, the gospel of the love of God for man. In the *Śvetāśvatara Upanishad* the transcendence of the personal God over and above the impersonal Brahman was affirmed, but God was seen rather as the exemplar of the soul than as the supreme object of loving devotion. Only with the advent of the *Śaiva Siddhānta* was the transcendent and rather aloof God of the *Śvetāśvatara* united to the highly personal God Śiva who claimed man's total devotion, service, and love. The ***Gītā*** was probably composed in the third or fourth century B.C., and it is thus our first literary source for *bhakti,* as devotional religion is called in India. The word *bhakti* derives from a root *bhaj-* the first meaning of which is 'to share or participate in' and this meaning is still present in the ***Gītā*** where Krishna is said to 'participate in' his devotees as much as they participate in him (4.11). The word is also very frequently used for sexual love and sexual union, and this aspect of it tends to be emphasized in the later *bhakti* sects: in the ***Gītā,*** however, there is no faintest suggestion of this.

The ***Gītā*** is not an easy text to interpret as it is not consistent with itself. The climax of the book is, however, the theophany in the eleventh chapter, in which Krishna, the incarnate God and inseparable friend of Arjuna, reveals himself to the latter in his 'supreme form as the Lord', and this revelation inspires the terrified Arjuna to confess Krishna as being 'more to be prized even than Brahman' (11.37). The theology of the ***Gītā,*** then, continues that of the *Śvetāśvatara Upanishad.* Brahman is both the timeless state of being which characterizes *moksha* and the source and origin of all that has its being in space and time. It is, then, both time and eternity. God, however, in the ***Gītā*** transcends both, and because he is personal you can never say that the liberated soul actually *becomes* God as you can say that it becomes Brahman; for the word *brahman* when used in this context means no more than 'eternal' as it normally does in the early Buddhist texts from which the term *brahmabhūta* 'become Brahman' seems to have been borrowed. *Moksha* means no more than to have been liberated from the bonds of *saṁsāra* into the freedom of immortal life; and because God is by definition beyond space and time, it also means that the soul participates in God's mode of existence without for that reason being identical with him, for though God, like Brahman, pervades all things both temporal and eternal, he transcends both as their overseer (9.10; 13.22). Though he is what is most inward in them and more characteristic of them than they are of themselves, he stands apart from them, contemplates them, and approves of them. He is the foundation of both eternal and temporal being. He is 'the foundation of Brahman, of the immortal and the imperishable, of the eternal *dharma,* and of absolute bliss' (14.27).

To understand the message of the ***Gītā*** properly one must see it in its setting. The great war between the Kauravas and the Pāndavas which King Yudhishthira, the eldest of the Pāndava brothers, had done everything in his power to prevent, is about to begin, and the two armies face each other for the fray. This time it is Arjuna, Yudhishthira's younger brother and Krishna's bosom friend, not Yudhishthira, whose heart sinks at the thought of the slaughter of many of those who are nearest and dearest to him and are yet ranged on the other side. Krishna's prime purpose in the ***Gītā*** is, then, to persuade Arjuna to go into battle with a clear conscience. He argues first that though you may kill the body you cannot kill the soul because it is eternal, and that since, according to orthodox teaching, the soul of a warrior slain in battle goes straight to heaven, he is really doing a service to his kinsmen in ridding them of their bodies. Secondly in refusing to fight he would be violating the *dharma* of his caste, the Kshatriyas or warriors, and thirdly that he would be accused by his enemies of having opted out of the war because he was afraid. If he goes through with the battle he cannot lose: either he will be killed, in which case he will go straight to heaven, or he will conquer, in which case he will inherit the earth. Arjuna, however, had already seen the heaven of Indra, who was his father among the gods, and had been but little impressed by what he had seen there, nor was he much more interested in inheriting the earth than was his otherworldly brother, Yudhishthira, who was not interested at all. Higher inducements had, then, to be offered. So Krishna proceeds to instruct him first on how final liberation can be won even by a warrior engaged in battle and secondly on how liberation need not necessarily conflict with and negate the deep attachment that bound Arjuna to himself. The first, he teaches, can be achieved by a total dissociation of one's 'self', which is eternal and not therefore responsible for acts committed in time, from acts performed by a temporal body at the behest of a temporal will, both of which are mere evolutes of matter (*prakrti* or *māyā*). In so doing he attains to the same separation of spirit from matter that is the reward of the most accomplished Yogin. In the heat of battle, then, he will be no different from the Yogin whose mind is stilled and to whom 'supreme bliss draws nigh, his passions stilled, for he has become Brahman and is free from strain. . . . Seeing himself in all things and all things in himself, he sees the same thing everywhere' (6.27,29). He will have passed beyond pleasure and pain, the sense of 'I' and 'mine' and all the opposites, for he will understand that since he has his true being outside time and space, he cannot die.

It is at this point that Krishna makes the transition from the teaching concerning the immortal soul and Brahman to the teaching concerning himself, that is, God. 'For him who sees all things in me and me in all things, I am not lost nor is he lost to me. The Yogin who participates in (*bhajati*—loves, is devoted to) me who am present in all contingent beings, who, grounded in unity, is yet engaged in all manner of occupations, abides in me.' The nature of God he can infer from the experience of liberation in which time and space are abolished, and he can thus feel himself present everywhere. His mind and thoughts intent on God he attains to the 'peace that culminates in Nirvāna and subsists in God' (6.14-15), for only when it is itself released from the bonds of *saṁsāra* can the soul draw nigh to God (9.28). Both the way of 'knowledge' (*jñāna*), that is, intensive Yogic concentration aimed at dissociating the eternal from the temporal in man himself, and the way of devotion (*bhakti*) are said to lead to the 'Nirvāna of Brahman' and so to God (6.14-15, 27-32), but *bhakti* is the easier way (12.5-7) and, unlike the ways of salvation prescribed by the *Vedas* and *Upanishads* which remained in the exclusive possession of the three 'twice-born' classes, it is open to all men including Śūdras and women.

Not only is the personal Lord higher than Brahman, he, like Varuna in the *Rig-Veda,* has also the power to bind and to loose—he can save his devotees from the effects of their own *karma,* or, in Christian terminology, he has the power to forgive sins and to remit the punishment due to sin. 'If even a man whose conduct is most evil devotes himself to me and none other, he should be considered good, for his intention is right. Very soon will he become righteous in soul (*dharmātmā*) and gain [thereby] eternal peace' (9.30-31). This does not mean that virtue goes unrewarded: on the contrary, it is its own reward, for 'all those whose evil deeds have come to an end and whose actions are good are released from the delusion of the opposites and participate in me, firm in their resolve' (7.28). The eternal *dharma,* then, is the one sure way to *moksha* within a world still bound. It is through God's grace alone, however, that the *karma* attaching to a soul can be cancelled out and that it can 'become Brahman' and through becoming Brahman be in a fit state to draw near to God.

Nor is God's grace limited to his devotees, for faith in *any* deity is God's own gift and will not fail of its reward (7.21), since all worship is really directed to the true God. This emphasis on grace is something new, for though divine grace is mentioned in the later *Upanishads* and becomes explicit in the *Śvetāśvatara,* it is made the main theme of the ***Gītā.*** Man 'who fears *saṁsāra* and desires *moksha'* [*Mahābhārata*], (14.35.12) need no longer grope alone in the darkness of matter towards the light of liberation, for he can now rely on the helping hand of a saviour God to lead him into the freedom of the elect. It would, however, be wrong to suppose that the Krishna of the ***Bhagavad-Gītā*** is primarily a God of love: his preference is not for the passionately devoted worshipper but for the wholly detached sage who yet acknowledges his overlordship.

> The man [he says] who has no hatred for any creature, is friendly and compassionate, unconscious of what he has or is, indifferent to pleasure or pain, patient, contented, ever disciplined (*yogin*), self-controlled, of firm resolve, his mind and intellect fixed on me, devoted to me—such a man is dear to me. The man from whom other people do not shrink and who does not shrink from other people, who is free from joy, impatience, fear, and excitement, liberated—such a man is dear to me. The man who is unconcerned, pure, capable, indifferent, unperturbable, and who gives up all active enterprises in his devotion to me—such a man is dear to me. The man who neither rejoices nor hates, who knows neither pain nor desire, and who abandons both what is pleasant and what is unpleasant, though full of devotion—such a man is dear to me. The man who makes no difference between friend and foe, who does not care whether he is commended or despised, whether it is hot or cold, or whether he experiences pleasure or pain, who is a stranger to attachment, indifferent to praise and blame, holding his peace, content with whatever comes his way, who has no home and whose mind is steadfast though full of devotion—such a man is dear to me. But those who reverence this immortal *dharma* as I have now declared it, who have faith in me, and for whom I am the highest end, such devoted men are exceeding dear to me (12.13-20).

Here there is only the slightest shift from the ideal of 'holy indifference' typical of the *Upanishads* to a somewhat warmer relationship between God and man. The doctrine of love which is called the 'most secret of all' is held in reserve for the last lines of the last chapter of the ***Gītā,*** yet even there there is the utmost restraint. The perfect man is the one who has dutifully performed the duties of his caste (in Arjuna's case the ruthless prosecution of a just but senseless war) yet knowing all the time that these actions are in no sense 'his'. Such a man's 'consciousness is wholly unattached, he has conquered self, desire has left him, and by renunciation he attains to that absolute perfection which consists in the disappearance of action (*karma*). And as he wins this perfection so does he win Brahman . . . which is the final goal of knowledge. Integrated, his intellect made clean, resolute in his self-control, putting behind him the senses and their objects, love (*rāga*) and hate, cultivating solitude, eating lightly, with body, speech, and mind controlled, constantly engaged in meditation, wholly dispassionate, abandoning all thought of self (*ahaṁkāra*), force, pride, desire, anger, and acquisitiveness, thinking nothing his own, at peace, [the perfected man] is conformed to becoming Brahman. Having become Brahman, his soul assuaged, he knows neither grief nor desire' (18.49-54).

To become Brahman or rather to realize that one always was and is Brahman had been the main purport of the teaching of the *Upanishads,* and no state higher than this could be conceived (6.22). But at the very end of the ***Gītā*** Krishna discloses the true nature of *bhakti;* for whereas in the early stages of the spiritual Odyssey *bhakti* may prove a short cut to *moksha,* it is only once that *moksha* has been achieved that the real life of *bhakti* which means participation in God's life can begin.

> Indifferent to all creatures he receives supreme devotion to me. Through devotion to me he comes to know me, who and how great I am in my very essence. Then knowing me in my essence he forthwith enters me. Though he be ever engaged in works (*karma*), relying on me, he reaches the eternal, undying state by my grace.

Even so, though to enter God may be a yet higher destiny than to 'become Brahman' there is as yet no suggestion that it means to love him and be loved by him. This is reserved for the very end, and it is Krishna's 'most secret doctrine of all' and his ultimate word.

> Hear again the most secret [doctrine] of all, my ultimate word. Because I greatly desire thee, therefore shall I tell thee thy salvation. Think on me, worship me, sacrifice to me, pay me homage, so shalt thou come to me. I promise thee truly, for I love thee well. Give up all the things of *dharma,* turn to me only as thy refuge. I will deliver thee from all evil. Have no care.

It is these last words that represent a decisive turning-point in the history of Hinduism, for the whole point of the teaching of the ***Gītā*** right up to the last had been that man's ideal course was to perform the duties imposed on him by the *dharma* of his caste while remaining all the time perfectly detached, with mind and soul fixed upon the eternal Brahman and on God. Now, however, at the very end, we are told that detachment and exalted indifference are only the first steps on the path that leads to union and loving communion with God: and it is this that is totally new.

The full significance of this aspect of the ***Gītā*** was first brought into relief by Rāmānuja, the great theistic philosopher of the eleventh century who did so much to make *bhakti* philosophically respectable. For Rāmānuja, as for the *Śaiva Siddhānta,* the phenomenal world is real and *māyā* is God's mode of operation in it. The soul, as in all Hindu thinking, is eternal and timeless, spiritual, unfractionable, pure consciousness (*cit*), and of the same substance as God. There are as many souls as there are bodies to house them, and souls, though like God and like each other in that they are eternal, are none the less distinct from each other and from God who is their origin. Only on achieving *moksha,* however, do souls enter into possession of their true, timeless nature. God is the Supreme Soul and all creation forms his 'body'—both the souls in eternity and the world in time. At the same time he is in a different category and wholly other than all that is not himself. In Scripture God as well as Brahman is repeatedly spoken of as being *nirguna* 'without qualities or attributes', but according to Rāmānuja he is wholly good, and *nirguna* can therefore mean no more than that he is devoid of bad attributes. Moreover, God is a person, and as a person he is possessed of all good qualities to a superlative degree.

> [God's] divine form is the depository of all radiance, loveliness, fragrance, delicacy, beauty, and youth—desirable, congruous, one in form, unthinkable, divine, marvellous, eternal, indefectible, perfect. His essence and nature are not to be limited by word or thought. He is an ocean of boundless compassion, moral excellence, tenderness, generosity, and sovereignty, the refuge of the whole world without distinction of persons. He, the one ocean of tenderness to all who resort to him, takes away the sorrows of his devotees. [By his incarnation] he can be seen by the eyes of all men, for without putting aside his [divine] nature, he came down to dwell in the house of Vasudeva, to give light to the whole world with his indefectible and perfect glory, and to fill out all things with his own loveliness.

As in the *Śaiva Siddhānta* so in the ***Gītā*** and Rāmānuja God imprisons souls in matter only to release them and unite them with himself. This constitutes his adorable 'game' (*krīdā, līlā*). Moreover, just as the devotee longs for God and loves him, so does God long for the soul. 'Whoever loves me beyond measure', God is represented as saying, 'him will I love beyond measure [in return]. Unable to bear separation from him, I cause him to possess me. This is my true promise: you will come to me'. God needs the soul as much as the soul needs God, and this means that the soul is neither annihilated nor absorbed in the liberated state, but experiences unending and ever-increasing love. The devotee, 'though he has come to possess me, is not himself destroyed, and though I give myself to one who worships me in this wise, it seems to me that I have done nothing for him'. In Rāmānuja God's love is unconditional.

Rāmānuja, like Śankara, called himself a Vedāntin; but his differences from Śankara are radical, and he knew it. Śankara saw in *bhakti* no more than a step on the ladder that leads to the realization that the One alone exists and that all human souls are this One, neither more nor less. Once this ineffable unity is realized, the soul is utterly at peace, beyond all the opposites and all experience: and since it is the One Reality itself, plainly, once this is realized, no further spiritual progress is possible. Worship of God or the gods is thus seen to be illusory, for it means no more than that you are worshipping yourself. Hence *bhakti* is a very inferior, because unreal, substitute for 'knowledge' (*jñāna*), that is, the realization of absolute unity. Rāmānuja will have none of this. For him liberation means no more than the transcendence of time and space—a transcendence that is the birthright of every human soul: it is no more than the 'isolation' spoken of in the Sāṁkhya-Yoga in which the soul becomes *like* God, but has no personal relationship with God. The love of God is a different and entirely new experience, and it takes place in eternity not in time. Liberation may be an excellent thing, but compared to the love of God it is as a mustard seed beside Mount Meru, and the selfish cultivation of one's own immortal soul is contemptuously dismissed as fit only for those who do not know how to love.

Rāmānuja called his system *viśishtādvaita* 'non-duality in difference', and he is only the first of Vaishnavite philosophers, of whom Madhva, Vallabha, Nimbārka, and the followers of Caitanya are the most important, who rejected Śankara's pure monism as being destructive of religion. Madhva, who lived in the thirteenth century, went much further than Rāmānuja and was not afraid to describe himself as a 'dualist' (*dvaita*). He makes a threefold distinction between God who alone is absolute and independent, human souls which are eternal, though subject to him, and matter. He differs from all other Indian thinkers in that he distinguishes three classes of soul—first those few elect spirits who are destined for liberation and for loving communion with Vishnu, his consort Lakshmī, and Vāyu (the Vedic wind-god, now transformed into the Holy Spirit), secondly the majority of souls which are of indifferent quality and can only look forward to an endless series of rebirths, and lastly souls of such hopeless depravity that they can only expect eternal punishment in hell. This extreme reaction against both Śankara and Rāmānuja with its emphasis on the activity of Vāyu as Holy Spirit and on the *eternal* pains of hell is generally thought to be due to Christian influence. It is certainly wholly untypical of Indian thought and never succeeded in capturing more than a fraction of the devotees of Vishnu. Rāmānuja's influence, however, bore fruit a thousandfold in the medieval flowering of the *bhakti* cults. (pp. 92-101)

R. C. Zaehner, "God," in his Hinduism, *second edition, Oxford University Press, Oxford, 1966, pp. 80-101.*

Owen Barfield (essay date 1967)

[*An eminent English man of letters known for his keen interest in spirituality, particularly Christianity and the teaching of Rudolf Steiner, Barfield is the author of respected works in many literary genres. His* Poetic Diction *(1929) is considered a seminal text on literary language, while his* Saving the Appearances *(1957) is deemed perhaps the pre-eminent work on the evolution of consciousness. In the following except from an essay first published in 1967, he maintains that the chief purpose of the* Gītā *is to raise the protagonist Arjuna's consciousness from the material realm to a higher, spiritual plane.*]

I want to [draw] your attention to something that stands at the very beginning of perhaps the greatest of all the doc-

The battle of Kurukshetra.

uments that have come down to us from the literature of the ancient East. I mean the ***Divine Song*** as it is called: the ***Bhagavad-Gita.*** You will all, I am sure, have read it, and you will recall how the scene is set at the opening. Two hostile armies are drawn up in battle array and the fighting is about to begin. But in the moment of extreme tension the warrior-prince Arjuna bids his charioteer drive him to a position between the two armies in order that they may talk for a little. It is done, and Arjuna, who is greatly troubled in his soul, reveals to the charioteer the source of his perplexity and his misery. It lies in the nature of civil war, where kinsman is ranged against kinsman and, for that and other reasons, Arjuna finds in himself no desire to fight. It is not because he is afraid. "I do not wish to kill," he says, "though they kill me." Looking ahead, he sees only evils of all kinds coming of the battle. Families will be disintegrated. All sorts of impiety will become rife. The enemy are criminals or tyrants, and yet if he kills them, he will incur sin. "I do not wish for victory, nor sovereignty, nor pleasures, nor even life." Having finished his long speech, Arjuna casts aside his bow and sits down in his chariot overcome by grief.

The charioteer is Krishna, an avatar of the Deity himself; and the song, as you know, consists of the dialogue that ensues between the man and the God. Krishna's immediate response to Arjuna amounts to an endeavor to transpose the thinking of Arjuna to another level or plane of consciousness altogether—to a fresh dimension, within which all the objections he has raised are irrelevant, because unreal or superseded. The wise grieve for neither the living nor the dead. "Never did I not exist, nor you, nor these princes; nor will any one of us ever hereafter cease to be. . . . There is no existence for that which is unreal; there is no nonexistence for that which is real." So Krishna argues, saying in effect that the true, the real self of Arjuna—as well as that of those he will be killing—is to be found only in an imperishable realm beyond action and beyond expression. "He who thinks one to be the killer and he who thinks one to be the killed, both know nothing. He kills not, is not killed. He is not born, nor does he ever die . . . " and so on. "*Therefore,*" says Krishna—and now there comes what is perhaps for most Western readers, on a first reading, a dramatic surprise, if not a rude shock. It shocked Thoreau, and later on it shocked Gandhi. Krishna has raised the discourse, one could say, to the level of the Absolute; he is endeavoring to make Arjuna see it from that perspective. It is a point of view from which the coming battle is irrelevant, because the whole of the world as we know it from the everyday point of view is an unreality, an illusion, a mere catenation of appearances. "*Therefore,*" he goes on—but he does not go on to say, as we rather expect: "Therefore withdraw from the battle and from the world and cultivate reality, cultivate the Absolute, cultivate the inexpressible." On the contrary, he utters the surprising conclusion: "*Therefore fight on!*"

There are three prominent features that I want to stress here. First, that the main purpose of the ***Gita*** is, clearly, to raise the thinking, or the consciousness of the protagonist, Arjuna, from the ordinary plane to a higher one, or into another dimension, to which quite different rules apply; secondly, the means by which this is accomplished is a communication and a revelation made by a spirit-being who already lives on that other plane, in this case a temporarily incarnate one: that is, the God Krishna himself; and thirdly, that we are told not to draw conclusions for the lower plane from the higher one, to which the ordinary logical categories do not apply. Whatever we, or others, do or leave undone is from that higher plane or point of view unreal or unimportant; but we are *not,* from this, to conclude, for instance, with the complacent Frenchman: "*Tout comprendre c'est tout pardonner,*" to endorse the papers "No action required" and file them away. On the contrary, we are to behave in exactly the opposite way. We are to follow the rules applicable to the lower plane, the ordinary dimension.

And note particularly . . . the change of atmosphere that immediately precedes, and then accompanies, that moment of vision or of direct experience that occurs later in the poem. In the *argument* Krishna has merely indicated the existence of this higher plane of consciousness. Later he raises Arjuna to an actual experience of it. He does this by revealing himself in his universal, divine nature:

> The great Lord then showed to the son of Pritha his supreme divine form, having many mouths and eyes. . . . If in the heavens, the lustre of a thousand suns burst forth all at once, that would be like the lustre of that mighty one. There the son of Pandu beheld in the body of the God of

Gods the whole universe all in one and divided into numerous divisions.

It is indeed another dimension of consciousness—a fundamentally inexpressible one (how inadequate, for instance, is that quantitative reference to "many mouths and eyes"!) and Arjuna shows his numinous awareness of the transition. We are told that his hair stood on end and "he bowed his head before the God, and spoke with joined hands."

There are then two different planes of consciousness with what I will call a "threshold" between them. The poem does not say that the threshold is one that can never be crossed. On the contrary, it is essentially the story of Arjuna's being led across it by Krishna. What the poem does inculcate is that, though it may be crossed, it does not cease for that reason to exist. It must not be forgotten; it must not be left out of account. The two opposite sides of the threshold must never be confused with one another. If they are, the result will be only a worse disorder. (pp. 111-13)

Owen Barfield, "Meaning, Language and Imagination: Imagination and Inspiration," in his The Rediscovery of Meaning, and Other Essays, *Wesleyan University Press, 1977, pp. 111-29.*

Kenneth Rexroth (essay date 1973)

[*Rexroth was an American poet, essayist, and translator whose writings encompass a wide variety of subjects, including religion, politics, and world literature. His books include* Classics Revisited *(1968),* The Elastic Retort: Essays in Literature and Ideas *(1973), and* The Morning Star *(1979), a volume of poetry. In the following excerpt, he briefly recapitulates the story and the philosophical message of the* Gīta.]

"Action shall be the sister of dream and thought and deed shall have the same splendor." So said Baudelaire. Sometime around the third century before the Christian era an unknown author inserted into the epic story of *The Mahabharata* a comparatively short religious document, not only small in comparison to the immense size of the epic itself—which was already becoming the gather-all for Hinduism—but shorter far than any of the scriptures of the other world religions. This is the ***Bhagavad-gita, The Lord's Song,*** one of the three or four most influential writings in the history of man. It is not only influential, it is more profound and more systematic than most religious texts. This statement may sound strange to those who are familiar with nineteenth century rationalist Western European critics who attempted to abstract a logically consistent philosophy from the ***Bhagavad-gita,*** and who ended up emphasizing its contradictions and ambiguities.

The ***Bhagavad-gita*** is not a philosophical work, but a religious one, and beside that, a song, a poem. It is not to be compared with Aristotle's *Metaphysics,* or the creed or catechism of the Council of Trent, but with the opening of the *Gospel According to St. John* or to the Magnificat in St. Luke. Its seeming contradictions are resolved in worship. In the words of the great Catholic Modernist, Father George Tyrrell, *Lex credendi, lex orandi,* "the law of faith is the law of prayer." What the unknown author of the ***Bhagavad-gita*** intended was precisely the resolution and sublimation of the contradictions of the religious life in the great unity of prayer.

The ***Bhagavad-gita*** is above all else a manual of personal devotion to a personal deity. But to establish this devotion and to give it the widest possible meaning the author subsumes all the major theological and philosophical tendencies of the Hinduism of his time. It is as though the *Summa Theologica* of St. Thomas Aquinas had been dissolved in his prayers and hymns for the feast of Corpus Christi. It so happens that as he lay dying St. Thomas said that that was what he had done. Unless the reader begins by understanding the devotional nature of the ***Gita,*** its many meanings will always elude him and its over-all meaning will be totally unapproachable.

There are two main strands of thought in the ***Gita*** which divide and sometimes interweave but which are nonetheless easy to distinguish and follow. First is an exposition of the nature of reality and of the Godhead and its self-unfolding, and second is a description, practically a manual, of the means of communion with the deity.

The poem starts out simply enough and scarcely seems to violate the context of the epic; in fact the first two chapters may largely be part of the original tale. At the major crisis of *The Mahabharata* the warring clans, and their allies numbering uncountable thousands, are marshalled for the crucial battle that will exterminate almost all of them. The Prince Arjuna is sickened by the vision of the coming slaughter and is about to turn away in disgust, and give up the battle. His charioteer Krishna advises him to fight. He tells him that no one really dies, that the myriad dead of the day on the morrow will move on in the wheel of life, and that anyway killer and killed are illusory, and that the warrior's duty is to fight without questioning, but with indifference to gain or glory, dedicating his military virtues to God as a work of prayer.

This advice horrifies modern commentators with their sophisticated ethical sensibility, although it is certainly common enough advice of army chaplains. We forget that the ***Bhagavad-gita*** begins in the epic context, as though the Sermon on the Mount were to appear in *The Iliad* evolving out of the last fatal conversation between Hector and Andromache. Even Radhakrishnan, India's leading philosopher of the last generation and spokesman on the highest level for Gandhi's *satyagraha,* spiritual non-violence, speaks of Arjuna's doubts before the battle as pusillanimous.

Krishna describes briefly the roads to salvation—work, ritual, learning, or rather, wisdom by learning, contemplation and devotion. He then describes the metaphysical structure of being which culminates in what nowadays we would call the inscrutable ground of being, Brahman, the source of the creative principle of reality. He then goes on to a most extraordinary concept. Behind Brahman, the ultimate reality in all Western theories of emanationist monism, lies Ishvara, the ultimate god behind all ultimates, who is a *person.* In answer to Arjuna's plea, Krishna reveals himself as the incarnation of the universal form, the embodiment of all the creative activity of all the universes. That itself is only a kind of mask, an incarnation, for he, Krishna, is the actual, direct embodiment of Ishvara, the Person who transcends the unknowable and who can be approached directly by the person Arjuna, as friend to Friend. The central meaning of ***The Lord's Song*** is that being is a conversation of lovers.

Nirvana, as Krishna defines it in the ***Gita,*** is the joy in the habitude of illumination, after the dying out of appetite. It is the medium in which the enlightened live, as in air. As we of air, they are conscious of it only by an effort of attention. Faith is Shraddha—bliss, the disposition to orient one's life around the abiding consciousness of spiritual reality. Bad karma, consequence, drains away in successive lives but good karma is saved up always, throughout all the thousands of necessary incarnations, to reach enlightenment. All men travel toward the eternal Brahman. When we reach the end of the road no space will have been travelled and no time spent. You are *sat, cit, ananda*—reality, truth and bliss—and always have been. Always becomes a meaningless word when *becomes* is transformed to *be.* The direct experience of God is not an act of service or devotion or even of cognition. It is an unqualifiable and unconditioned experience. Who illusions? You are the ultimate Self, but you dream. Work is contemplation. Rite is contemplation. Yoga is contemplation. Learning is contemplation. All are prayer. They are forms of dialogue between two subjects that can never be objects. Insofar as the noblest deed or the most glorified trance is not devotion, it is unreal.

The poem culminates in a hymn of praise to devotion itself—Krishna, speaking for his worshipers, himself to himself. The later sections are a long drawn-out cadence and diminuendo, of recapitulation, instruction and ethical advice. Then we are back, "marshalled for battle on the Field of Law," and Arjuna says, "My delusion is destroyed. Recognition has been obtained by me through Thy grace! I stand firm with my doubts dispelled. I shall act by Thy word."

Reading the ***Gita*** in a decent translation for the first time is a tremendously thrilling experience. No one who has ever heard it chanted, hour after hour in an Indian temple, before a statue of dark-skinned Krishna, dancing his strange shuffling dance, and playing on his flute, while a cluster of worshipers sat on the floor, silent and entranced, in their white robes, once in a great while someone uttering a short cry, like a Christian amen, is ever likely, no matter how long he lives, to forget it. More commonly of course one hears the chanting of the *Gita Govinda,* the song of Krishna's love adventures with Radha and the milkmaids—but, as any devout Hindu will tell you, the two songs are the same song. (pp. 21-4)

Kenneth Rexroth, "The 'Bhagavad-gita'," in his The Elastic Retort: Essays in Literature and Ideas, *The Seabury, 1973, pp. 21-5.*

Mircea Eliade (essay date 1978)

[*Eliade was a seminal Romanian historian of religion who also wrote acclaimed works of fiction and criticism. His many works include* Traité d'histoire des religions *(1948;* Patterns in Comparative Religion, *1958),* Le mythe de l'éternel retour: Archétypes et répétition *(1949;* The Myth of the Eternal Return; or, Cosmos and History, *1955), and* The Sacred and the Profane: The Nature of Religion *(1959). In the following excerpt from the second volume of his* Histoire des croyances et des idées religieuses *(1978;* A History of Religious Ideas, *1982), he interprets the* Gītā *as a brilliant synthesis of spiritual visions, a universal religious document, and the revelation of a God who is "at once personal and impersonal, creative and destructive, incarnate and transcendent."*]

With its 90,000 verses, the *Mahābhārata* is the longest epic in world literature. As it has come down to us, the text includes visions and numerous interpolations, the latter chiefly in the "encyclopedic" sections (books 12 and 13). However, it would be illusory to believe that we could reconstruct the "original form" of the poem. As to its date, "the idea makes no sense for the epic" (L. Renoü). It is assumed that the epic poem was already finished between the seventh and sixth centuries before our era and acquired its present form between the fourth century B.C. and the fourth century A.D. (Winternitz).

Its principal theme is the conflict between the two lines of Bhāratas: the descendants of the Kurus (the one hundred Kauravas) and the descendants of the Pāṇḍus (the five Pāṇḍavas). Duryodhana, the eldest of the Kauravas, son of the blind king Dhṛtarāṣṭra, is devoured by a demonic hate for his cousins; as a matter of fact, he is the incarnation of the demon Kali, that is, the demon of the most evil age of the world. The five Pāṇḍavas—Yudhiṣṭira, Arjuna, Bhīma, Nakula, and Sahadeva—are the sons of Pāṇḍu, younger brother of Dhṛtarāṣṭra. Actually, they are the sons of the gods Dharma, Vāyu, Indra, and the two Aśvins, and we shall later perceive the meaning of this divine parentage. On Pāṇḍu's death, Dhṛtarāṣṭra becomes king for the period before Yudhiṣṭhira grows old enough to take power. But Duryodhana does not resign himself. Among the traps that he set for his cousins, the most dangerous was the burning of a lacquer house in which he had persuaded them to live. The Pāṇḍavas escape by an underground passage and, with their mother, take refuge in the forest, incognito. A number of adventures follow. Disguised as a Brahman, Arjuna succeeds in obtaining the hand of Princess Draupadī, incarnation of the goddess Śrī, and takes her to the Pāṇḍavas' hermitage in the forest. Not seeing Draupadī, and believing that Arjuna is bringing only the food he had obtained as alms, his mother exclaims: "Enjoy this together." Thus the young woman becomes the common wife of the five brothers.

Learning that the Pāṇḍavas did not die in the fire, the blind king Dhṛtarāṣṭra decides to let them have half of the kingdom. They build a capital, Indraprastha, where their cousin Kṛṣṇa, head of the Yādava clan, joins them. Duryodhana challenges Yudhiṣṭhira to a game of dice. One of the dice being false, Yudhiṣṭhira successively loses his possessions, his kingdom, his brothers, and their wife. The king annuls the game and restores their possessions to the Pāṇḍavas. But soon afterward he permits a second game of dice; it is agreed that the losers shall live for twelve years in the forest and a thirteenth year incognito. Yudhiṣṭhira plays, loses again, and goes into exile with his brothers and Draupadī. The third book, *Vana-parvan* ("Book of the Forest"), which, with its 17,500 couplets, is the longest, is also the richest in literary episodes: the hermits tell the Pāṇḍavas the dramatic stories of Nala and Damayantī, Sāvitrī, Rāma, and Sītā. The following book describes the adventures of the thirteenth year, which the exiles succeed in spending without being recognized. In the fifth book ("Book of Preparations"), war seems inevitable. The Pāṇḍavas send Kṛṣṇa as ambassador; they demand the restoration of their kingdom, or at least of five villages, but Duryodhana refuses. Immense armies gather on either side, and war breaks out.

The sixth book contains the most famous episode in the epic—the ***Bhagavad Gītā,*** which we shall discuss further on. In the following books the various moments of the battle, which rages for eighteen days, are laboriously narrated. The ground is covered with the dead and wounded. The leaders of the Kurus fall one after the other, Duryodhana the last. Only three Kauravas escape, among them Aśvatthāman, into whom the god Śiva had just entered. With a horde of demons produced by Śiva, Aśvatthāman makes his way into the sleeping Pāṇḍavas' camp by night and butchers them, except the five brothers, who were away. Saddened by so much killing. Yudhiṣṭhira wants to renounce the throne and live as a hermit; but his brothers, helped by Kṛṣṇa and several sages, are able to make him abandon his decision, and he regally performs the horse sacrifice (the *aśvamedha*). After collaborating with his nephew for fifteen years, Dhṛtarāṣṭa retires to the forest with a few companions. Not long afterward, they are killed in a conflagration started by their own sacred fires. Thirty-six years after the great battle, Kṛṣṇa and his people perish in a strange way: they kill one another with reeds magically transformed into maces. The capital crumbles and disappears into the ocean. Feeling that he is growing old, Yudhiṣṭhira leaves power to his grandnephew Parikṣit (who, stillborn, was resuscitated by Kṛṣṇa), and, with his brothers, Draupadā, and a dog, sets out for the Himalayas. One after the other, his companions fall on the journey. Only Yudhiṣṭhira and the dog (which is really his own father, Dharma) hold out to the end. The epic concludes with a short description of Yudhiṣṭhira descending to the underworld and then ascending to heaven.

This monstrous war was decided on by Brahmā, in order to relieve the earth of a population that did not cease to multiply. Brahmā asked a certain number of gods and demons to become incarnate in order to provoke a terrifying war of extermination. The *Mahābhārata* describes the end of a world (*pralaya*), followed by the emergence of a new world under the reign of Yudhiṣṭhira or Parikṣit. The poem shows an eschatological structure: a gigantic battle between the forces of "good" and "evil" (analogous to the combats between *devas* and *asuras*); destruction on a cosmic scale by fire and water; resurgence of a new and pure world, symbolized by the miraculous resurrection of Parikṣit. In a certain sense we may speak of a grandiose revalorization of the old mythico-ritual scenario of the New Year. However, this time it is not a matter of the end of a year but of the conclusion of a cosmic age.

The cyclical theory becomes popular from the time of the Purāṇas. This does not mean that the eschatological myth is necessarily a creation of Hinduism. The conception of it is archaic and enjoys a considerable dissemination. What is more, similar myths are documented in Iran and Scandanavia. According to Zoroastrian tradition, at the end of history Ohrmazd will seize Ahriman, the six Ameśa Spentas will each lay hold of an archdemon, and these incarnations of evil will be definitively cast into darkness. As we [know], a similar eschatology is found among the ancient Germans: in the course of the final battle (the Ragnarök), each god will take on a demonic being or a monster, with the difference that the gods and their adversaries will kill one another down to the last of them and the earth will burn and finally be plunged into the sea; however, the earth will rise again from the aquatic mass, and a new humanity will enjoy a happy existence under the reign of the young god Baldr.

Stig Wikander and Georges Dumézil [in his *Mythe et épopée*] have brilliantly analyzed the structural analogies among these three eschatological wars. It may thus be concluded that the myth of the end of the world was known by the Indo-Europeans. The divergences are certainly marked, but they can be explained by the different orientations characteristic of the three Indo-European religions. It is true that the eschatological myth is not documented in the Vedic period, but this does not prove that it did not exist. As Dumézil expresses it (*Mythe et épopée*), the *Mahābhārata* is the "epic transposition of an eschatological crisis," of what Hindu mythology calls the end of a *yuga.* Now the *Mahābhārata* contains certain Vedic, or even pre-Vedic, elements. So it is permissible to put the myth of the end of an age among these archaic Āryan traditions, and the more so because it was known by the Iranians.

But we must immediately add that the poem represents a grandiose synthesis, decidedly richer than the Indo-European eschatological tradition that it continues. In describing the annihilation of the limitless human masses and the telluric catastrophes that follow, the *Mahābhārata* borrows the flamboyant language of the Purāṇas. More important are the theological developments and innovations. The "messianic" idea of the *avatāra* is set forth forcefully and rigorously. In the famous theophany of the ***Bhagavad Gītā*** (11. 12 ff.) Kṛṣṇa reveals himself to Arjuna as an incarnation of Viṣṇu. As has been observed [by M. Biardeau in his "Etudes de mythologie hindoue," 1971], this theophany also constitutes a *pralaya,* which in some way anticipates the "end of the world" described in the last books of the epic. Now the revelation of (Kṛṣṇa-)Viṣṇu as lord of the *pralaya* is pregnant with theological and metaphysical consequences. Indeed, behind the dramatic events that make up the plot of the *Mahābhārata,* it is possible to decipher the opposition and complementarity of Viṣṇu(-Kṛṣṇa) and Śiva. The latter's "destructive" function is counterbalanced by the "creative" role of Viṣṇu(-Kṛṣṇa). When one of these gods—or one of their representatives—is present in an action, the other is absent. But Viṣṇu(-Kṛṣṇa) is also the author of "destructions" and "resurrections." In addition, the epic and the Purāṇas emphasize this god's negative aspect.

This is as much as to say that Viṣṇu, as supreme being, is the ultimate reality; hence he governs both the creation and the destruction of worlds. He is beyond good and evil, like all the gods. For "virtue and sin exist, O King, only among men." Among yogins and contemplatives the idea had been familiar from the time of the *Upanishads,* but the *Mahābhārata*—particularly, the ***Bhagavad Gītā***—makes it accessible, and therefore popular, on all levels of Indian society. While glorifying Viṣṇu as the Supreme Being, the poem emphasizes the complementarity of Śiva and Viṣṇu. From this point of view, the *Mahābhārata* can be considered the cornerstone of Hinduism. Indeed, these two gods, together with the Great Goddess (Śakti, Kālī, Durgā), have dominated Hinduism from the first centuries of our era to the present.

The complementarity Śiva-Viṣṇu in a way corresponds to the complementarity of antagonistic functions that is characteristic of the great gods (creativity/destruction, etc.). Understanding this structure of divinity is equivalent to a revelation and also constitutes the model to follow in obtaining deliverance. Indeed, the *Mahābhārata* describes and glorifies, on the one hand, the struggle between good and evil, *dharma* and *adharma,* a struggle that acquires the weight of a universal norm, for it governs cosmic life, society, and personal existence; on the other hand, however, the poem is a reminder that the ultimate reality—the *brahman-ātman* of the *Upanishads*—is beyond the pair *dharma/adharma* and every other pair of contraries. In other words, deliverance involves comprehension of the relations between the two "modes" of the real: *immediate*—that is, historically conditioned—reality and *ultimate* reality. Upanishadic monism had denied the validity of immediate reality. The *Mahābhārata,* especially in its didactic sections, proposes a broader doctrine: on the one hand, Upanishadic monism, colored by theistic (Vaiṣṇava) experiences, is reaffirmed; on the other hand, there is acceptance of any soteriological solution that is not explicitly contrary to the scriptural tradition.

At first sight it may appear paradoxical that the literary work that depicts a frightful war of extermination and the end of a *yuga* is at the same time the exemplary model for every spiritual synthesis accomplished by Hinduism. The tendency to reconcile contraries is characteristic of Indian thought from the period of the Brāhmaṇas, but it is in the *Mahābhārata* that we see the importance of its results. Essentially, we can say that the poem (1) teaches the equivalence of Vedānta (i.e., the doctrine of the *Upanishads*), Sāṃkhya, and Yoga; (2) establishes the equality of the three "ways" (*mārgas*), represented by ritual activity, metaphysical knowledge, and Yoga practice; (3) makes every effort to justify a certain mode of existing in time, in other words, assumes and valorizes the historicity of the human condition; and (4) proclaims the superiority of a fourth soteriological "way": devotion to Viṣṇu(-Kṛṣṇa).

The poem presents Sāṃkhya and Yoga in their presystematic stages. The former means "true knowledge" (*tattva-jñāna*) or "knowledge of the Self" (*ātman-bodha*); in this respect, Sāṃkhya carries on Upanishadic speculation. Yoga designates any activity that leads the Self to *brahman* at the same time that it confers countless "powers." Most often, this activity is equivalent to asceticism. The term *yoga* sometimes means "method," sometimes "force" or "meditation." The two *darśanas* are regarded as equivalent. According to the ***Bhagavad Gītā,*** "only narrow minds oppose Sāṃkhya and Yoga, but not the wise (*paṇḍitas*). He who is truly master of the one is assured of the fruit of both. . . . Sāṃkhya and Yoga are but one" (5. 4-5).

It is also in the ***Bhagavad Gītā*** that the homology of the three soteriological "ways" is strictly demonstrated. This celebrated episode begins with Arjuna's "existential crisis" and ends with an exemplary revelation concerning the human condition and the "ways" of deliverance. Seeing him depressed by the war, in which he will have to kill friends and his own cousins, Kṛṣṇa reveals to Arjuna the means of doing his duty as a *kṣatriya* without letting himself be bound by *karma.* Generally speaking, Kṛṣṇa's revelations concern (1) the structure of the universe, (2) the modalities of Being, and (3) the ways to obtain final deliverance. But Kṛṣṇa takes care to add that the "ancient Yoga" (4. 3), which is the "supreme secret," is not an innovation; he had already taught it to Vivasvant, who revealed it to Manu, and Manu transmitted it to Ikṣvāku (4. 1). "It is by this tradition that the *ṛsi*-kings knew it; but, with time, this Yoga disappeared here below" (4. 2). Every time that order (*dharma*) is shaken, Kṛṣṇa manifests himself (4. 7), that is, he reveals, in a manner suited to the given "historical moment," this timeless wisdom. (This is the doctrine of the *avatāra.*) In other words, if the ***Bhagavad Gītā*** appears historically as a new spiritual synthesis, it seems "new" only to the eyes of beings who, like ourselves, are conditioned by time and history.

It could be said that the essence of the doctrine revealed by Kṛṣṇa lies in this brief admonition: Believe me and imitate me! For all that he reveals concerning his own being and concerning his "behavior" in the cosmos and in history is to serve as exemplary model for Arjuna: Arjuna finds the meaning of his historical life and, in conjunction with it, obtains deliverance by understanding what Kṛṣṇa *is* and what he *does.* Moreover, Kṛṣṇa himself insists on the exemplary and soteriological value of the divine model: "whatever the Chief does, other men imitate: the rule he follows, the world obeys" (3. 21). And he adds, referring to himself: "In the three worlds, there is nothing that I am obliged to do . . . yet I remain in action" (3. 23). Kṛṣṇa hastens to reveal the deep meaning of this activity: "If I were not always tirelessly in action, everywhere, men would follow my example. The worlds would cease to exist if I did not perform my work; I should be the cause of universal confusion and the end of creatures" (3. 23-24).

Consequently, Arjuna must imitate Kṛṣṇa's behavior: that is, in the first place, to continue acting, so that his passivity shall not contribute to "universal confusion." But in order for him to act "as Kṛṣṇa does," he must understand both the essence of divinity and its modes of manifestation. This is why Kṛṣṇa *reveals himself*: by knowing God, man at the same time knows the model to imitate. Now Kṛṣṇa begins by revealing that Being and nonbeing reside in him and that the whole of creation—from the gods to minerals—descends from him (7. 4-6; 9. 4-5; etc.). He continually creates the world by means of his *prakṛti,* but this ceaseless activity does not bind him: *he is only the spectator of his own creation* (9. 8-10). Now it is precisely this (seemingly paradoxical) valorization of activity (of *karman*) that is the chief lesson revealed by Kṛṣṇa: in imitation of God, who creates and sustains the world *without participating in it,* man will learn to do likewise. "It is not enough to abstrain from action in order to free oneself from the act; inaction alone does not lead to perfection," for "everyone is condemned to action" (3. 4-5). Even if he abstains from acting in the strict sense of the word, a whole unconscious activity, caused by the *guṇas* (3. 5), continues to chain him and integrate him into the karmic circuit. (The *guṇas* are the three modes of being which impregnate the whole universe and establish an organic sympathy between man and the cosmos.)

Condemned to action—for "action is superior to inaction" (3. 8)—man must perform the prescribed acts—in other words, the "duties," the acts that fall to him because of his particular situation. "It is better to perform, even if imperfectly, one's own duty (*svadharma*) than to perform, even perfectly, the duty of a different condition (*paradharma*)" (3. 35). These specific activities are conditioned by the *guṇas* (17. 8 ff.; 18. 23 ff.). Kṛṣṇa repeats on several occasions that the *guṇas* proceed from him but do not bind him: "not that I am in them; it is they that are in me" (7. 12). The lesson to be drawn from this is the following: while accepting the "historical situation" created by the *guṇas* (and one must accept it, for the *guṇas,* too, derive from Kṛṣṇa) and acting in accordance with the necessities of that "situation," man must refuse to *valorize* his acts and, in consequence, to attribute an *absolute value* to his own condition.

In this sense it can be said that the ***Bhagavad Gītā*** attempts to "save" all human acts, to "justify" every profane action; for, by the mere fact that he no longer enjoys their "fruits," *man transforms his acts into sacrifices,* that is, into transpersonal dynamisms that contribute to the maintenance of the cosmic order. Now, as Kṛṣṇa declares, only acts whose object is sacrifice do not bind (3. 9). Prajāpati created sacrifice so that the cosmos could manifest itself and human beings could live and propagate (3. 10 ff.). But Kṛṣṇa reveals that man, too, can collaborate in the perfection of the divine work, not only by sacrifices properly speaking (those that make up the Vedic cult) but by *all his acts,* whatever their nature. When the various ascetics and yogins "sacrifice" their psychophysiological activities, they detach themselves from these activities, they give them a transpersonal value (4. 25 ff.), and, in so doing, they "all have the true idea of sacrifice and, by sacrifice, wipe out their impurities" (4. 30).

This transmutation of profane activities into rituals is made possible by Yoga. Kṛṣṇa reveals to Arjuna that the "man of action" can save himself (in other words, escape the consequences of his taking part in the life of the world) *and yet continue to act.* The only thing that he must do is this: *he must detach himself from his acts and from their results,* in other words, "renounce the fruits of his acts" (*phalatṛṣṇavairāgya*); he must *act impersonally,* without passion, without desire, as if he were acting by proxy, in another's stead. If he strictly obeys this rule, his actions will not sow the seeds of new karmic potentialities or any longer enslave him to the karmic circuit. "Indifferent to the fruit of action, always satisfied, free from all ties, no matter how active he may be, in reality he does not act" (4. 20).

The great originality of the ***Bhagavad Gītā*** is its having insisted on this "Yoga of action," which one realizes by "renouncing the fruits of one's acts." This is also the principal reason for its unprecedented success in India. For henceforth every man is allowed to hope for deliverance, by virtue of *phalatṛṣṇavairāgya,* even when, for reasons of very different kinds, he is obliged to continue to take part in social life, to have a family, to be concerned, to hold a position, even to do "immoral" things (like Arjuna, who must kill his enemies in war). To act placidly, without being moved by "desire for the fruit," is to obtain a self-mastery and a serenity that, undoubtedly, Yoga alone is able to confer. As Kṛṣṇa teaches: "While acting without restriction, one remains faithful to Yoga." This interpretation of the Yoga technique is characteristic of the grandiose synthetic effort of the ***Bhagavad Gītā,*** which sought to reconcile all vocations: whether ascetic, mystic, or devoted to activity in the world.

In addition to the Yoga that is accessible to everyone and consists in renouncing the "fruits of one's acts," the ***Bhagavad Gītā*** briefly expounds a yogic technique properly speaking, which is restricted to contemplatives (6. 11 ff.). Kṛṣṇa decrees that "Yoga is superior to asceticism (*tapas*), even superior to knowledge (*jñāna*), superior to sacrifice" (6. 46). But yogic meditation does not attain its ultimate end unless the disciple concentrates on God: "With soul serene and fearless . . . , mind firm and ceaselessly thinking of Me, he must practice Yoga taking Me as his supreme end" (6. 14). "He who sees Me everywhere and sees all things in Me, him I never abandon, and he never abandons Me. He who, having established himself in unity, worships Me, who dwell in all beings, that yogin dwells in Me, *whatever be his way of life*" (6. 30-31; our italics).

This is at once the triumph of Yoga practices and the raising of mystical devotion (*bhakti*) to the rank of supreme "way." In addition, the ***Bhagavad Gītā*** marks the appearance of the concept of grace, foretelling the luxuriant development that it will attain in medieval Vaiṣnava literature. But the decisive part that the ***Bhagavad Gītā*** played in the expansion of theism does not exhaust its importance. That incomparable work, keystone of Indian spirituality, can be valorized in many and various contexts. By the fact that it puts the emphasis on the historicity of man, the solution that the ***Gītā*** offers is certainly the most comprehensive one and, it is important to add, the one best suited to modern India, already integrated into the "circuit of history." For, translated into terms familiar to Westerners, the problem faced in the ***Gītā*** is as follows: how is it possible to resolve the paradoxical situation created by the twofold fact that man, on the one hand, finds himself existing in time, *condemned to history,* and, on the other hand, knows that he will be "damned" if he allows himself to be exhausted by temporality and by his own historicity and that, consequently, he must at all costs find *in the world* a way that leads into a transhistorical and atemporal plane?

We have seen the solution offered by Kṛṣṇa: doing one's duty (*svadharma*) in the world but doing so without letting oneself be prompted by desire for the fruits of one's actions (*phalatṛṣṇavairāgya*). Since the whole universe is the creation, or even the ephiphany, of Kṛṣṇa(-Viṣṇu), to live in the world, to participate in its structures, does not constitute an "evil act." The "evil act" is to believe that the world and time and history possess an independent reality of their own, that is, to believe that *nothing else exists* outside of the world and temporality. The idea is certainly pan-Indian, but it is in the ***Bhagavad Gītā*** that it received its most consistent expression.

To realize the importance of the part played by the ***Bhagavad Gītā*** in the religious history of India, we must remember the solutions offered by Sāṃkhya, by Yoga, and by Buddhism. According to these schools, deliverance demanded, as a *sine qua non,* detachment from the world or even the negation of human life as a mode of existing in history. The discovery of "universal suffering" and the infinite cycle of reincarnations had oriented the search for salvation in a particular direction: deliverance *must* involve *refusal* to yield to the impulses of life and to the social norms. Withdrawal into solitude and ascetic practices constituted the indispensable preliminaries. On the other hand, salvation by gnosis was compared to an "awakening," a "freeing from bonds," the "removal of a blindfold that covered the eyes," etc. In short, salvation presupposed a break, a dislocation from the world, which was a place of suffering, a prison crowded with slaves.

The religious devalorization of the world was made easier by the disappearance of the creator god. For Sāṃkhya-Yoga, the universe came into being by virtue of the "teleological instinct" of the primordial substance (*prakṛti*). For the Buddha, the problem does not even arise; in any case, Buddha denies the existence of God. The religious devalorization of the world is accompanied by a glorification of the spirit or the Self (*ātman, puruṣa*). For Buddha himself, though he rejects the *ātman* as autonomous and irreducible monad, deliverance is obtained by virtue of an effort that is "spiritual" in nature.

The progressive hardening of the dualism spirit/matter is reminiscent of the development of religious dualism, ending in the Iranian formula of two contrary principles, representing good and evil. . . . [For] a long time the opposition good/evil was but one of many examples of dyads and polarities—cosmic, social, and religious—that insured the rhythmical alternation of life and the world. In short, what was isolated in the two antagonistic principles, good and evil, was in the beginning only *one* among the many formulas by means of which the antithetical but complementary aspects of reality were expressed: day/night, male/female, life/death, fecundity/sterility, health/sickness, etc. In other words, good and evil formed part of the same cosmic (and therefore human) rhythm that Chinese thought formulated in the alternation of the two principles *yang* and *yin.*

The devalorization of the cosmos and life, adumbrated in the *upanishads,* finds its most rigorous expressions in the "dualistic" ontologies and the methods of separation elaborated by Sāṃkhya-Yoga and Buddhism. The hardening process characteristic of these stages of Indian religious thought can be compared with the hardening of Iranian dualism from Zarathustra to Manichaeanism. Zarathustra likewise considered the world a mixture of the spiritual and material. The believer, by correctly performing the sacrifice, separated his celestial essence (*mēnōk*) from its material manifestation (*gētik*). For Zarathustra and for Mazdaism, however, the universe was the work of Ahura Mazdā; the world was corrupted only later, by Ahriman. But Manichaeanism and a number of Gnostic sects on the contrary attributed the Creation to the demonic powers. The world, life, and man himself are the product of a series of sinister or criminal dramatic activities. In the last analysis, this vain and monstrous creation is doomed to annihilation. Deliverance is the result of a long and difficult effort to separate spirit from matter, light from the darkening that holds it captive.

To be sure, the various Indian methods and techniques of seeking deliverance of the spirit by a series of more and more radical "separations" continued to have proselytes long after the appearance of the ***Bhagavad Gītā.*** For refusal of life—and especially of existence conditioned by sociopolitical structures and by history—had, after the *Upanishads,* become a highly regarded soteriological solution. Nevertheless, the ***Gītā*** had succeeded in integrating into a daring synthesis all the Indian religious orientations, hence also the ascetic practices involving abandoning the community and social obligations. But above all the ***Gītā*** had effected the resacralization of the cosmos, of universal life, and even of man's *historical existence.* As we have just seen, Viṣṇu-Kṛṣṇa is not only the creator and lord of the world, he resanctifies the whole of nature by his presence.

On the other hand, it is still Viṣṇu who periodically destroys the universe at the end of each cosmic cycle. In other words, *all* is created and governed by God. In consequence, the "negative aspects" of cosmic life, of individual existence, and of history receive a religious meaning. Man is no longer the hostage of a cosmos-prison that created itself, since the world is the work of a personal and omnipotent God. What is more: he is a God who did not abandon the world after its creation but continues to be present in it and active on all planes, from the material structures of the cosmos to the consciousness of man. Cosmic calamities and historical catastrophes, even the periodical destruction of the universe, are governed by Viṣṇu-Kṛṣṇa; *hence they are theophanies.* This brings the God of the ***Bhagavad Gītā*** close to Yahweh, creator of the world and lord of history, as the prophets understood him. In any case, it is not without interest to point out that, just as the revelation advocated by the ***Gītā*** took place during a horrible war of extermination, the prophets preached under the "terror of history," under the threat of the imminent disappearance of the Jewish people.

The tendency to totalization of the real that is characteristic of Indian thought finds in the ***Bhagavad Gītā*** one of its most convincing expressions. Accomplished under the sign of a personal God, this totalization confers a religious value even on undeniable manifestations of "evil" and "misfortune," such as war, treachery, and murder. But it is above all the resacralization of life and of human existence that had important consequences in the religious history of India. In the first centuries of our era, Tantrism will similarly attempt to transmute the organic functions (alimentation, sexuality, etc.) into sacraments. However, this type of sacralization of the body and life will be obtained by an extremely complex and difficult yogic technique; in fact, Tantric initiation will be restricted to an elite. But the message of the ***Bhagavad Gītā*** was addressed to all categories of men and encouraged all religious vocations. This was the privilege of devotion paid to a God who was at once personal and impersonal, creative and destructive, incarnate and transcendent. (pp. 232-46)

Mircea Eliade, "The Hindu Synthesis: The 'Mahābhārata and the 'Bhagavad Gītā'," in his A History of Religious Ideas: From Gautama Buddha to the Triumph of Christianity, Vol. 2, *translated by Williard R. Trask, The University of Chicago Press, 1982, pp. 232-46.*

Winthrop Sargeant (essay date 1979)

[*Sargeant was a distinguished American music critic and Sanskritist whose books include* Listening to Music *(1958) and* In Spite of Myself *(1970). In the following excerpt from the introduction to his 1979 interlinear translation of the* Gītā, *he provides a general overview of the poem, with particular emphasis on the work's philosophical and religious tenets. In Sargeant's view, the* Gītā *is a poetic affirmation of monotheism.*]

The ***Bhagavad Gītā*** is the most important single expression of Hindu religious thought. It is also one of the supreme mystical poems of all literature—a colloquy between God (Krishna, the *avatār,* or earthly incarnation, of Vishnu) and man, as represented by Arjuna, a young warrior who is faced with a moment of decision. It cannot be taken as the exposition of a consistent philosophy, for it contains too many contradictions. But the grandeur of its poetic canvas—involving infinite space and infinite time, the position of man in relation to the universe and God, the process of rebirth and the indestructibility of the human soul as conceived by the Hindus—gives it a purely literary, as well as religious, power that cannot escape the cultivated reader. Poetic figures of tremendous resonance are scattered through it: "The light of lights that is beyond darkness"; the statement of God—"On me all this universe is strung like pearls on a thread"; the Great Manifestation of Book XI where the God of the ***Gītā*** shows himself in his true form, pervading all the universe, including in his body all the gods, creating and consuming all that moves and does not move, existing from infinite time onward into infinite time, the beginning, middle and end of all things, "the imperishable, the existent, the non-existent and that which is beyond both;" or the famous lines, "If there should be in the sky a thousand suns risen all at once, such splendor would be of the splendor of that Great Being." Such images are powerful, and they take one into a cosmic realm that represents one of the furthest flights of the human imagination. A full philosophic description of this realm is beyond the capacities of a small essay like this one, and a history of the process by which the Hindu mind conceived it is elusive, mainly for the reason that, in India, time, "the mighty cause of world destruction," and with it, history, are foreign to ancient thought. Nobody knows even the date at which the ***Bhagavad Gītā*** assumed its definitive literary form. Speculations place its date somewhere between the time of Christ and 300 A.D. most of these speculations being based on the style of its text or on religious conceptions from which it has borrowed and which are known to be of prior date. Suffice it to say that the ***Bhagavad Gītā*** was conceived long after Buddhism had made its contribution to Hindu thought, and that it reflects, in its terminology and most of its concepts, the teachings of the *Upanishads,* the great post-Vedic compilations of religious lore that are generally conceded to date from between 700 and 400 B.C. The ***Gītā*** also reflects certain Hindu philosophical systems that were worked out later, using the *Upanishads* as their point of departure—notably the Sāṃkhya, Vedānta and Yoga philosophies, of which more will be said in due course.

All Hindu thought is derived, or purports to be derived, from the *Vedas,* the ecstatic poems, or hymns, brought to India, along with the Sanskrit language, by the Aryans who invaded the subcontinent somewhere in the neighborhood of 1600 B.C. It is obvious to any student of the subject, however, that these hymns represent a very different culture and outlook from that of the land of their adoption. They are, mostly, poems expressing awe and wonder at the marvels of nature, and prayers to, or celebrations of, the gods who created, or are embodied in, these marvels. Any metaphysics that they contain are of an elementary sort. In the tropical land of India, the Vedic Aryans intermarried with the native population, which may or may not have held more complex religious beliefs, and gradually the old Aryan religion, led by the god Indra, died out, to be followed by the lofty metaphysical speculation which may possibly have been a habit of thought of the peoples the Aryans conquered. There was undoubtedly a mixture of religious concepts in the ensuing canons of belief, and the *Vedas,* though they were radically departed from in the new, evolving religion, still maintained a certain prestige. The priesthood, while subjecting them to new interpretations and adding to them, not only in the *Upanishads* but also in the works known as *Brāhmaṇas* and *Araṇyakas,* still maintained the holy preëminence of the *Vedas,* though what they meant by the term *Veda* came increasingly to mean the thought of the *Brāhmaṇas,* the *Upanishads* and other later works. Thus, the ***Bhagavad Gītā*** often refers to the "*Veda*" and also uses the word "Aryan." By the former term it means this corpus of post-Vedic religious belief, and by the latter, a warrior group noted for honor, chivalry and beneficence—the group from which, theoretically at least, kings and princes arose.

The new cosmology of Hinduism—new, that is, in 500 B.C.—was a very complex affair, and it is this cosmology that is reflected in the ***Bhagavad Gītā.*** Here we find certain concepts developed in the *Upanishads.* The most lofty of them is the concept of *Brahman* (pronounced with the first syllable accented), a spirit which pervades the entire universe, and which is beginningless and endless, neither existent nor non-existent, devoid of attributes, "the eternal unmanifest," and the great and only reality, undifferentiated and imperishable. Elsewhere it is described as self-luminous, unknowable, devoid of any form or mode. And in the *Kaṭha Upanishad* it is described as "the offspring of austerity, created prior to the waters and dwelling with the elements in the cave of the heart, the soul of all deities, who was born in the form of the vital breath, who was created with the elements . . . whence the sun rises and whether it goes to set, in whom all the gods are contained, and whom none can ever pass beyond . . . by the mind alone is Brahman to be realized." *Brahman* is generally conceived in terms of negatives: what it is not, rather than what it is. It is also divided into the *Supreme Brahman* and the *Qualified,* or *Saguṇa, Brahman* (Brahman possessed of qualities), an active element which, in association with its own power of *māyā* (the power of illusion) becomes the creator and sustainer of the universe. *Brahman,* in Sanskrit, is neuter. Its masculine form, as the creator god Brahmā (pronounced with accent on the last syllable), represents a god who is more or less taken for granted, his duty having been performed long ago. The word *Brahman* is probably derived from the root *bṛh* which means "grow," "expand" or "evolve." In the *Vedas* it meant the power of sacrifice to bring a given result, or sacrifice itself. But the later Hindu metaphysicians made it into an absolute, the "pure consciousness" of the Vedānta.

Closely associated with *Brahman* in the ***Bhagavad Gītā*** is the Supreme Spirit, Supreme Self, Supreme Person or Supreme Soul, which is masculine, objectified in the ***Bhagavad Gītā*** in the character Krishna. This is the God of the ***Gītā,*** toward Whom all worthy human aspirations are directed. He is to be reached, according to the ***Gītā,*** by austerities, meditation and knowledge, but most easily of all by devotion or love (*bhakti*). This conception of the Supreme Spirit is not found in the Sāṁmkhya or Vedānta philosophies. It is the contribution of the Yoga school, and is adopted in the ***Gītā*** from that source. It gives the ***Gītā*** its monotheistic character. Actually, the ***Gītā*** is quite ambiguous about the relation of the Supreme Spirit to *Brahman.* At times it speaks of the two as being identical; at others it refers to *Brahman* as the female counterpart of the Supreme Spirit Who says at one point, "For me, great Brahman is the womb. In this I place the seed"; at still others it describes the Supreme Spirit as "the foundation of *Brahman.*" The nature of the Supreme Spirit is such that He is both transcendant and immanent.

Also closely associated with *Brahman* is the *ātman,* self or individual soul, known in the *Vedas* (where it was originally the name of the breath of life), but later acquiring a special status as the multiple essence of all animate things. It is both an individual self and something universal in all beings. It is, like *Brahman,* birthless and eternal. It is inviolable, "not slain when the body is slain," and it is that part of the human entity that passes from birth to rebirth in the process of reincarnation. The great Hindu philosopher Rāmānuja, following passages to that effect in the *Upanishads,* considered it to be identical with *Brahman,* a view that all Vedāntists had in common. The ***Gītā*** is at some pains to reconcile the idea of the individual *ātman* with the collective *ātman* or *Brahman,* and it often speaks of "seeing the same," i.e. seeing one's own *ātman* as being identical with all other *ātmans,* not only identical in type, but, by a mystical leap of the mind, identical in the sense of absolute identity. In one sense the *ātman* might be said to be the individual's portion of *Brahman,* but since both *Brahman* and the *ātman* are indivisible and identical, any distinction between the individual being and the cosmos represented by *Brahman* is meaningless. The *ātman* is, like *Brahman,* the supreme reality, pure infinite consciousness and the origin of the world. In the extremely subjective and idealistic Vedānta philosophy it is, in fact, the *only* reality, all else, including the visible universe, being illusion. The *ātman,* as it exists in the individual, however, is endowed with desire, ego, mind and senses, and is bound by these attributes until it can attain liberation and union with *Brahman.* The factors in its bondage are the *guṇas.*

The three guṇas—*sattva,* or illumination and truth, *rajas,* or passion and desire, and *tamas* or darkness, sloth and dullness—were originally thought, by the Sāṁkhya philosophers who first identified and named them, to be substances. Later they became attributes of the psyche. *Sattva* has been equated with essence, *rajas* with energy and *tamas* with mass. According to still another interpretation, *sattva* is intelligence, *rajas* is movement and *tamas* is obstruction. The word *guṇa* means "strand," "thread" or "rope," and *prakṛti,* or material nature is conceived as a cord woven from the three *guṇas.* They chain down the soul to thought and matter. They can exist in different proportions in a single being, determining his mental outlook and his actions. A man whose nature is dominated by *sattva* will be clear thinking, radiant and truthful. A man whose nature is dominated by *rajas* will be passionate, quick to anger and greedy. A man whose nature is dominated by *tamas* will be stupid, lazy and stubborn. But most men will be found to have elements of *guṇas* different from their dominating ones, i.e. to be motivated by a combination of *guṇas.* The aim of the upward reaching *ātman,* or self, is to transcend the *guṇas,* break free of their bondage, and attain liberation and union with *Brahman.* The *guṇas,* moreover, are constituents of that *māyā,* or power of illusion, possessed by Qualified (*Saguṇa*) *Brahman.* Through the *guṇas,* this *Saguṇa Brahman* creates and maintains the world (or the cosmic illusion) by its powers of projection and concealment. All the universe and all the things in it are the creations of *Saguṇa Brahman,* and all are subject to the influences of the *guṇas.* Only the sages are able to lift the veil of *māyā* and perceive the reality that is *Brahman* behind it. And only those who persevere in meditation, right action and the acquisition of knowledge through many lives are permitted to voyage beyond *māyā* and the *guṇas,* finally to reach *Brahmanirvāṇa* or the *nirvāṇa* of *Brahman.*

In this connection it is necessary to point out the essentially pessimistic view of life held by Hinduism, though the pessimism of this view is moderated by the conviction that the self is eternal, inviolable and essentially sorrowless, and by the possibility of ascending from life to life toward higher goals. All animate nature is involved in this process of ascent, unless by negative action it falls back toward lower planes of existence. It is interesting, here, to observe that all the great dramas in Sanskrit literature have happy endings. Death has no tragic implications. It leads to another life. A pig, by persevering effort, can become a man in a subsequent life; a man, by the same means, can become a great sage. In the contrary direction, a man whose life is one of debauchery can be reincarnated as a devil or as a pig, sometimes even as an insect. The goal of all persevering effort in meditation, devotion or the aquisition of knowledge is *nirvāṇa,* and *nirvāṇa,* a word derived from *nir vā,* "blow out" as a candle is blown out, constitutes divine non-existence. Thus, the object of all human effort is to reach extinction of the individual consciousness, and life, with its desires and sufferings, is presented as a tragic plight from which escape must be sought. The expression, "the acquisition of knowledge," as used above means not general education, but the specific knowledge of *Brahman* or God, who is held in the ***Gītā,*** and elsewhere in Upanishadic thought, to be "the supreme object of knowledge." The "wheel of rebirth" by which an individual passes through incarnation after incarnation is something to be left behind. And this brings us to the subject of transmigration.

Transmigration or reincarnation, or metempsychosis as it is sometimes called, is basic to the fabric of Hindu religious belief, as it is also to Theravāda, or Hīnayāna Buddhism. Conceptions of it differ however. What is it that passes on from life to life? The *ātman,* or self, of course, but the *ātman* has no personal traits, for personal traits are imposed upon it by the *guṇas,* though ***Bhagavad Gītā*** XV 8 says that the senses are also taken along. There are in India sages and yogins who claim to be able to remember all their former lives. The Dalai Lama of Tibet is discovered to be an incarnation of his predecessor through certain omens at some time after the former's death (this being, of course, a Buddhist practice). But perhaps the most convincing account of the reality of the process of reincarnation is to be found in the *Upanishads,* where, in at least one quotation, it appears, except for some fanciful elements, as a natural organic process not very much at odds with modern scientific thought. This quotation is from the *Bṛhadāraṇyaka Upanishad* (VI ii 16):

> Those who conquer the worlds through sacrifice, charity and austerity reach the deity of smoke, from smoke the deity of the night, from night the deity of the fortnight in which the moon wanes, from the decreasing half of the moon the deities of the six months during which the sun travels southward, from these months the world of the ancestors, and from the world of the ancestors the moon. Reaching the moon they become food. There the gods enjoy them just as here the priests drink the shining Soma juice—saying as it were 'Flourish, dwindle.' And when their past work (*karma*) is exhausted they reach this very *ākāśa* (ether), from the *ākāśa* they reach the air, from the air rain, from the rain the earth. Reaching the earth they become grain. Then they are again offered in the fire of man, and thence the fire of woman. Out of the fire of women they are born and perform rites with a view to going to other worlds. Thus do they rotate.

The "deity of smoke" is obviously reached through cremation. Some occult transformations follow including the temporary residence on the moon. But it is perfectly apparent that when the pilgrim becomes rain, waters the earth and becomes grain (a primitive scientific transformation), the grain is eaten by man, transferred by sexual intercourse to woman, who then gives birth to a new life. The ***Chāndogya Upanishad*** (V x 5-6) has a similar and perhaps more graphic account which ends: "They first reach the *ākāśa* (ether), and from the *ākāśa* air. Having become air, they become smoke; having become smoke, they become mist. Having become mist, they become cloud; having become cloud, they fall as rain water. Then they are born as rice and barley, herbs and trees, sesamum and beans. Thence the exit is most difficult; for whoever eats that food and injects semen, they become like unto him." A close, if primitive observation of natural processes is obviously at the bottom of all this, and very little of a supernatural element needs to be considered. Man, dying and being cremated, fertilizes the earth with rain, causes the plants to grow and uses them for his sustenance, then dies again and the process is repeated. Some quality, or minute quantity, is assumed to be constant throughout the cycle—and this is the *ātman.*

The Sāṁkhya philosophers also divided the universe into *prakṛti,* or material nature, and *puruṣa,* or spirit, its passive spectator or, according to another interpretation, the animating principle in men and other beings. The *puruṣa,* in the larger sense, is identified with the *paramātman* or Supreme Self. It is beginningless, has no cause beyond itself and is self-luminous and formless, existing both within and without, devoid of vital breath, devoid of mind, pure, and higher than the Supreme Imperishable (which is equated by Swami Nikhilananda with *Saguṇa,* or *Qualified Brahman*). The *Muṇḍaka Upanishad* goes on to say: "Of him (*puruṣa*) are born *prāṇa* (vital breath), mind, all the sense organs, *ākāśa* (ether), air, fire, water and earth, which supports all. The heavens are His head; the sun and moon His eyes; the quarters (of the compass) His ears; the revealed *Vedas* His speech; the wind is His breath; the universe His heart. From His feet is produced the earth," and so on. At the same time, the *puruṣa,* in the smaller sense, is the inner self of all beings, "not larger than a thumb and dwelling in the hearts of men," or "hidden in the cave of the heart" (*Muṇḍaka Upanishad*). There are many inspired descriptions of the *puruṣa* in the *Upanishads.* The *Īśa Upanishad* (16) says; "O Nourisher, lone Traveller in the sky! Controller! O Sun, offspring of Prajāpati! Gather your rays; withdraw your light. I would see, through Your grace, that form of Yours which is the fairest. I am indeed He, that *Puruṣa,* who dwells there." (All quotations from the *Upanishads* here are taken from the excellent translation by Swami Nikhilananda.) It is obvious from the Upanishadic texts that *puruṣa* is an attribute of both *Brahman* and *ātman.* In fact the term *puruṣottama*),(*puruṣa uttama*), or *Supreme Puruṣa,* is interchangeable with the term *Paramātman,* or Supreme Self. *Prakṛti,* or material nature, on the other hand, is divided into the unmanifest and the manifest *prakṛti.* The unmanifest, or unborn *prakṛti* is material nature in a potential or latent form, such as that which it assumes between cosmic dissolution and the creation that follows. As it emerges into creation, the intelligence, the ego of the individual and the five elements and five senses are produced. At the time of cosmic dissolution, all these elements return to the unmanifest *prakṛti* again. The manifest *prakṛti* is material nature more or less as we Westerners know it. It consists of the *guṇas,* those chains that bind down the self in one or another physical and mental condition. In order to attain release from the round of rebirths, and consequent union with *Brahman,* one must leave *prakṛti* behind.

And what are the creation and the cosmic dissolution? They are cyclical or periodic concepts referred to in the ***Gītā*** in those passages alluding to the Day and Night of Brahmā, and in the Great Manifestation of Book XI. Like the individual, the cosmos is dissolved and reborn at intervals—in the case of the cosmos, enormous ones. When Krishna says, "Supported by my own material nature, I send forth again and again this entire multitude of beings" (IX 8), or "All beings, Son of Kuntī, go into my own material nature at the end of a *kalpa* (i.e. a period of 4,320,000,000 years). At the beginning of a kalpa, I send them forth" (IX 7), he is speaking of the periodic creation and dissolution of all that exists. The length of the *kalpa* is one of those extravagant flights of the Hindu imagination that stand, in the ***Gītā*** and elsewhere, almost as figures of speech in an exalted kind of poetry. As the day of Brahmā breaks, the multitude of creatures is born, to go through its own cycles of rebirth, and perhaps by the liberating powers of Yoga to reach *Brahman* and rebirthlessness. A few billion years later, the universe is destroyed, or dissolved, and with it the multitude of creatures, who then return to the unmanifest *prakṛti* awaiting the creation of a new universe. Concepts like these explain why time, in the Hindu mind, is a relative and sometimes irrelevant thing.

Both the Sāṁkhya and the Yoga schools of philosophy accepted the division of the universe between *puruṣa* and *prakṛti.* The great difference between them was that Sāṁkhya, like Buddhism and Jainism, was a non-theistic philosophy, whereas Yoga taught the existence of a God or Supreme Spirit. The ***Bhagavad Gītā*** is greatly concerned with Yoga, but the Yoga that it sets forth is somewhat different from the strict school of Yoga taught by Patañjali, author of the *Yogasūtra,* which is thought by most authorities to date from somewhere between the second and fifth centuries A.D. It is the belief of some scholars that Yoga is a very ancient practice which existed among the Dravidian Indians long before the Aryan conquest. (The word "yoga" appears in the *Ṛg Veda* only as a general term meaning "yoke," as of horses and cattle. Its technical meaning was unknown to the Aryans.) And there is in existence a seal from Mohenjo Daro ante-dating the Aryan migration, which depicts a man seated in the "lotus" position associated with yogins as well as with the Buddha. But the earliest systematic record of Yoga practice is Patañjali's *Yoga-sūtra,* where he sets forth the rigorous practices of breath-control, meditational practices and physical exercises that have made the Hindu "yogī" able to perform astonishing feats such as surviving burial alive. There is not the slightest doubt about the genuineness of these feats. In 1838, a celebrated yogin was buried alive at Lahore in the presence of officials of the British army who were there to witness and record the event, and remained buried for a period of thirty days, after which he was exhumed. It took two hours to revive him completely from a trance in which his pulse had stopped and his temperature had fallen far below normal. But he survived and claimed that in the trance his thoughts and dreams had been of the most delightful sort. Some have pointed out that a small supply of oxygen may have filtered through the earth. But since then many other such tests have been performed. Quite recently in a documentary broadcast over Channel 13, New York, a yogin (Yogī Rāma) was confined in an air-tight box for a period of four hours, and came out of the box showing no ill effects whatever. Later on, Yogī Rāma was examined at the Menninger Clinic in Kansas, and some astonishment was reported over his remarkable control of his involuntary nervous system. Such demonstrations involve the breathing exercises of Haṭha (or physical) Yoga, in which the yogin can slow his breath indefinitely and slow his heartbeat and his metabolism and body temperature to a point resembling death, without actually dying. These breathing exercises are merely hinted at in the ***Bhagavad Gītā.*** Dasgupta, in his *History of Indian Philosophy,* says that the purpose of Yoga breathing exercises is to achieve absolute immobility, and he goes on to say that, in his opinion, the author of the ***Bhagavad Gītā*** was ignorant of Patañjali's *Yoga-sūtra.* The eminent mythologist and oriental scholar Mircea Eliade, however, is of the opinion that the ***Gītā,*** where Yoga is concerned, was a popularization, an effort to preach a kind of Yoga that could be practiced by ordinary people while they went about their daily tasks [*Yoga: Immortality and Freedom,* 1958].

At any rate the Yoga of the ***Bhagavad Gītā*** is of a gentler and much less taxing sort. Here Yoga is concerned with detaching the senses from the objects of sense, the elimination of desire, the carrying out of obligatory duties, the fixing of the mind on the self (*ātman*) or on God, the relinquishment of the fruits of action, the harmonization of attitudes toward the pairs of opposites (pleasure, pain; heat, cold etc.), the preservation of impartiality whether among friends or foes, the perception of one's own *ātman* as being identical with all other *ātmans,* and the subduing of greed and anger. The goal of all this is tranquility of mind and union with God. In one passage the ***Gītā*** shows what may be the influence of the Buddhist "middle way." The yogin should neither eat too much nor too little; he should neither sleep too much nor too little. These are commands not for the virtuoso Haṭha yogin who follows the extreme practices later reported in the *Haṭha Yoga Saṁhita,* a compendium of physical (Haṭha) yoga exercises, which seek destruction of mind, immobility of body and complete freedom from the necessity of food, drink and even breathing. They constitute a recipe for ordinary folk who wish to live a life of purity and religious devotion. In fact, the ***Gītā*** denounces those who practice the exaggerated austerities that are part and parcel of the Haṭha yoga system. All that is required on a physical level is for the yogin to seat himself in solitude on a seat of kuśa grass, antelope skin and cloth, meditate on a single object and perform what are presumably the most elementary of breathing exercises. The word "Yoga" derives from the root yuj, "yoke," in the sense of "control." It is used in several senses, however, in different places in the poem, sometimes as a general word for power, sometimes as meaning "belief" or "philosophy," once as meaning "acquisition," more usually as meaning discipline, steadfastness, duty, training or self-control. There are also in the ***Gītā*** different types of Yoga—the Yoga of action, the Yoga of knowledge, the Yoga of intelligence, the Yoga of devotion. Of these the Yoga of action is held to be the highest, perhaps partly because the hero of the poem, Arjuna, is a warrior and man of action, but also because the Yoga of action is the one necessary means of securing the *ātman* or self, an indispensable preliminary to all other types of Yoga. The Yoga of knowledge is something that cannot be attained without prior action. (One must remember that, in ***Gītā*** psychology the mind, as well as the body, acts.) There is a certain democratic aspect to the ***Bhagavad Gītā.*** Members of any caste can go to the highest goal of union with *Brahman,* and the greatest of evil doers, should he make an effort in the direction of Yoga, can also attain the same end.

[The *Gita* is] one of the supreme mystical poems of all literature—a colloquy between God (Krishna, the *avatār,* or earthly incarnation, of Vishnu) and man, as represented by Arjuna, a young warrior who is faced with a moment of decision.

—Winthrop Sargeant

Action (*karma*) in the ***Bhagavad Gītā*** is of several kinds. In its basic cosmological meaning it is the creative power of the individual which causes him to be reborn in this or that state. One accumulates good or bad *karma* according to one's deeds and thoughts. An accumulation of good *karma* entitles one to be born in a higher state of being, and, conversely, an accumulation of bad *karma* condemns one to be born in a lower state of being. Thus *karma* is the dynamic element in the universe, for all beings are busy accumulating it, and the gradual progression or retrogression of all animate life is dependent on it. Action is prompted by the *guṇas,* and is the result of desire. One of the main doctrines of the ***Gītā,*** repeated continually, is the elimination of desire for the fruits of action. Being human, one cannot exist without action. But one can avoid bad *karma* by acting without regard for the fruits of *karma.* Action from motives of self-interest, pleasure or gain is frowned upon. Thus, the ideal man always acts disinterestedly and without desire for the results of what he does, thinking to himself that it is the *guṇas* who are doing the action. This, in the ***Gītā,*** seems in Western eyes to be a moral paradox, since Krishna is urging the warrior Arjuna to enter the battle and kill his enemies. But, since Arjuna is a kṣatriya, or warrior, it is his duty (*dharma*) to fight. If Arjuna were to perform the duty of another caste, say, the duty of a brāhman, he would risk disaster. Caste duties are strict, and members of the warrior caste have theirs laid out for them. Moreover, the performance of caste duties leads to rebirth on a higher plane, and even, if the performer renounces all attachment to the fruits of his actions, to union with *Brahman*—or at the very least, in the case of a warrior, to heaven. The ***Gītā*** is somewhat ambiguous about good and evil in the Western sense. It presents a cosmos in which one's relation with the self and with *Brahman* transcends one's relation to one's fellow beings, though one perceives, if one is enlightened, that the selves of one's fellow beings are identical with one's own self. Action (*karma*) in the ***Gītā*** may be ritual action such as the performance of sacrifices, gifts or austerities, or it may be ordinary action such as carrying out one's duties in everyday life. All of it, of whatever type, goes into the accumulation of *karma* and determines one's birth in a future life, unless by disregarding its fruits, and rising above the influence of the *guṇas,* one reaches the *nirvāṇa* of *Brahman* instead of rebirth. Even God, though He has no need to, performs actions, according to the ***Gītā.*** His actions result in the maintenance of the universe.

Ahiṁsā, or non-violence is, paradoxically, one of the main tenets of the ***Gītā.*** It has probably been taken over from Jain and Buddhist philosophy where the idea originated, and it is today the basis of the vegetarianism of most devout Hindus (the *Upanishads* speak freely about the eating of meat, and meat was a staple diet of the Vedic Aryans). *Ahiṁsā,* however, is a basic tenet of Hinduism if only because, in the processes of rebirth, injury to an animal or even to an insect is injury to a fellow being who is on the path of transmigration. But the advocacy of *ahiṁsā,* or non-violence in the ***Gītā,*** a work which might in some ways be described as a call to battle, is one of its principal contradictions. The contradiction can only be explained away by maintaining that caste duty takes precedence over the injunction to *ahiṁsā,* and that a warrior who does his duty and kills his enemies is committing no evil as long as he acts with detachment and without regard for the fruits of his actions.

Gītā cosmology distinguishes between the imperishable and the changing—that which is unborn, permanent, and indestructible and that which is subject to birth, alteration and death. The *ātman* and *Brahman* are birthless, eternal and changeless. Both have existed from eternity and will exist into eternity. The body, on the other hand, along with all the other material objects in the universe, is subject to birth, change and death. Therefore one must transcend the body through Yoga action, Yoga meditation, knowledge or devotion, and reach the state of rebirthlessness which is the *nirvāṇa* of *Brahman,* or the extinction of the individual consciousness. In this state one is at one with *Brahman* and hence eternal and changeless—but one no longer exists as an individual. It is toward divine nonexistence that all enlightened beings strive.

God, in the ***Gītā,*** as has already been said, is the Supreme Self, the pervader of all the universe and its resting place. All beings exist in God and God exists, as the *ātman* or self, in all beings. Sometimes God is spoken of as *īśvara,* and in the ***Gītā*** He is referred to as *Yogeśvara* (*Yoga īśvara*) the Lord of Yoga. Krishna, who is mentioned by many nicknames, as is Arjuna, and is identified, when He speaks as "the Blessed Lord" or "The Blessed One," is an *avatār,* or "descent," of God. In Hinduism any god may descend to earth in one form or another, sometimes human, as in the case of Krishna. And such descents, or *avatāras,* are made by God, according to the ***Gītā,*** whenever unrighteousness prevails and humans are in need of a teacher who can lead them back to righteousness. Krishna is not merely God's representative. He is a human being in whom God has been incarnated, and thus God Himself, or the Supreme Spirit. India is full of lesser gods and godlings to whom sacrifices are made in order to gain this or that objective. The Hindu trinity, Brahmā, Vishnu and Shiva, is a powerful triad in modern, as well as historic India, though there have been few temples dedicated to Brahmā, the creator god, whose job was done long ago and who has very little interest in human concerns. Vishnu, in the ***Gītā,*** assumes the position of the Supreme Spirit, and Krishna is His particular *avatār.* At those points, as in Book XI where the Supreme Spirit appears as the destroyer and devourer of all things, He is identified with Shiva, god of destruction and renewal. But by themselves, unattached to the Supreme Spirit, Vishnu and Shiva occupy lesser positions and may be placated or invoked through sacrifices. Of the Vedic gods, Agni, the god of fire, has survived into modern Hinduism, and so have many others like Varuṇa, who, however, has been demoted from "sustainer of the universe" to a god of the waters. Vishnu, the "pervader" of the *Ṛg Veda,* has become one of the three most important gods of modern India, and Shiva, a minor figure in the *Ṛg Veda* has been promoted to rank with Vishnu and Brahmā, the creator god, helping form the trinity of present Hindu thought. Beneath such gods, popular Hinduism presents a tremendous array of minor gods and godlings, some of them dating from Vedic times—rudras (storm gods), ādityas (gods of sunlight), apsaras (water nymphs), vasus (beneficent gods connected with light), sādhyas (gods of exquisitely refined natures inhabiting the ether), maruts (storm gods), gandharvas (heavenly musicians), nāgas (fabulous serpents), demons, legendary sages and legendary warriors. There is the goddess, Kālī, or Durgā, wife of Shiva (and unknown in the *Veda*), a relative of the ancient Western mother goddess and a terrifying figure to Westerners, though she has a considerable cult devoted to her in India. There is Yama, the god of death, who has survived from Vedic times. There are also the two Aśvins, horsemen who draw the chariot of the dawn, and they also date from Vedic times. And so on and on. These gods, or spirits, lend a kind of mythological poetry to Hindu life. Most of them are mentioned in the ***Bhagavad Gītā.*** Besides all these, there are the *pitṛs,* or ancestors, sometimes referred to as the *manes.* These are souls who have departed life and exist in a limbo awaiting rebirth, and they are placated in the ***Gītā*** with offerings of balls of rice. One feature that distinguishes all these gods from *Brahman,* or the Supreme Spirit, is that they are subject to death at the dissolution of the universe, to the influence of the *guṇas,* and to rebirth at the creation of a new universe.

The ***Bhagavad Gītā*** also refers to the "three worlds," heaven, atmosphere and earth. Heaven is the abode of the gods, and a place of transitory residence where virtuous souls remain while awaiting rebirth. The atmosphere (*ākāśa*) is merely a place of transition between heaven and earth, though it contains its own inhabitants, notably the *sādhyas.* There is also a hell, which is the abode of demons and the temporary resting place of evildoers, but the ***Gītā*** is not very informative about it. Though the evildoers go there, they too await rebirth, so hell (*naraku*) is not a permanent place of residence either.

Among the actions that lead to divine union with *Brahman* are *tapas,* or austerity, *brahmacarya,* or sexual abstinence, and meditation. Austerity, in the ***Gītā*** at any rate, is merely the performance of right action, moderation in eating and sleeping and the elimination of desire for the fruits of action. The ***Gītā*** speaks out against exaggerated austerities in several places. *Brahmacarya* is the sexual abstinence of the young *Brahmacārin* (or student of *Brahman*) before he attains the status of householder, when it is perfectly correct for him to produce progeny by that desire "which is lawful in beings." But sexual abstinence is expected of all yogins who follow the path of Patañjali's Yoga. Meditation is not what the word connotes in the modern West, i.e. "thinking." It is, in fact, the opposite, the emptying of the mind of all thought, and the concentrating of it on a single object, the end of the nose, the space between the eyes—almost anything will do for the purpose of practice until the yogin is able to so control the focus of his mind so that its wayward and capricious nature is eliminated. Then he is able to concentrate (meditate) on the Supreme Spirit without danger of his mind being distracted. Meditation, as early as the *Upanishads,* became a substitute for Vedic sacrifice, probably, Dasgupta thinks, because of the influence of Buddhism, which abhorred the animal sacrifices that were common in Vedic times and even later. In some Vedic sacrifices thousands of animals were killed. Sacrifice is still practiced in India, and the sacrifices to the goddess Durgā or Kālī include animal and (clandestinely) even human sacrifice—a proceeding that was outlawed by the British Raj in the 1830's. But these are, after all, sacrifices practiced by a special cult. The majority of Hindus, and the worshippers of Vishnu in particular, are opposed to any sacrifice that takes life. The sacrifices mentioned in the ***Bhagavad Gītā*** are all of a subjective nature: performing action as a sacrifice, performing breathing exercises as a sacrifice, performing charity, meditation, austerity or Vedic recitation as sacrifices—even performing the "knowledge sacrifice" by acquiring wisdom concerning *Brahman,* the *ātman* and the Supreme Spirit.

Release or emancipation (*mokṣa* or *mukti*) is the aim of all right-thinking people, and it means release not only from the power of the *guṇas,* but also release from the cycle of rebirths and entrance into timeless *nirvāṇa.* Time (*kāla*) is, in fact, regarded as an enemy of man and a destroyer of all that exists. The greatest enemy of one who seeks salvation, however, is the binding power of the *guṇas* and their attendant senses, of which mind is the first. The inclusion of mind gives the Hindus six senses, and the attachment of these senses to the objects of sense leads to undesirable results. A debauched individual, ruled by *rajas* or *tamas,* is prone to desire, and there are frequent references in the ***Gītā*** to the effect that desire leads to anger, anger to madness and madness to destruction of the mind. Above the senses, including the mind (*manas*) is the faculty of *buddhi,* usually translated as "intelligence" or "insight." These translations are convenient but not wholly accurate. *Buddhi* is intuitive knowledge, and according to Sri Krishna Prem [*The Yoga of the* ***Bhagavat Gita,*** 1948], a sort of intuition that persists as a permanent attribute of consciousness, rather than coming in "flashes." In a few places *buddhi* and *buddhiyoga* appear (II, 39, 49, 50, 51) where it has an active quality, and there I have translated it as "intuitive determination."

Among the remaining technical terms to be discussed is the sacred syllable "Oṁ" which is said to comprise all the secrets of the universe. It is formed of three sounds "a," "u" and "ṁ" representing the three *Vedas* (*Ṛg Sāma* and *Yajur*), the three worlds (heaven, atmosphere and earth) the three chief dieties (Brahmā, Vishnu and Shiva), and the beginning, middle and end of all things. It is an auspicious *mantra* (or magical utterance) containing very sacred properties, and is used at the beginning and end of meditation, work, sacrifice and praise of the gods, as well as religious tracts like the *Upanishads.* In fact, the complicated colophon at the end of each book in some editions of the ***Bhagavad Gītā*** . . . reads "Oṁ, thus in the blessed ***Bhagavadgītā Upanishad,*** the knowledge of Brahman, the scripture on Yoga, the dialogue between Śrī Krishna and Arjuna, ends the (so numbered) book entitled the Yoga of (such and such)."

The gods of the Hindu religion are very much like the Greek gods. They live lives of their own, marry and beget progeny, and sometimes, according to the Purāṇas and the Epics, indulge in fairly scandalous activities. From time to time they descend to earth, assuming one form or another, and often the male gods impregnate human females who then give birth to great heroes. But, with the exception of Vishnu the "preserver" whose *avatār* Krishna is, the ***Bhagavad Gītā*** is not concerned with these gods, mentioning them only in passing. Far above them, pervading or containing them all, is the Supreme Self or Supreme Spirit represented by Krishna in his Vishnu *avatār* (in this case, Vishnu becomes identified with the Supreme Spirit). The universe revolves, and so do all the creatures within it, godlike, human, animal and vegetable. Pervading it all are *Brahman,* the *ātman* and the Supreme Spirit, all three of whom closely resemble each other if they are not, indeed, identical. Thus, the monotheism of the ***Gītā.*** (pp. 9-20)

Winthrop Sargeant, "Cosmology and Psychology," in The Bhagavad Gītā, *translated by Winthrop Sargeant, Doubleday & Company, Inc., 1979, pp. 9-46.*

Barbara Stoler Miller (essay date 1986)

[*Miller is an Orientalist who has written on and translated from Sanskrit literature. In the following excerpt from her* The Bhagavad Gita: Krishna's Counsel in Time of War, *she provides a concise introduction to the* Gītā, *focusing on the eighteen teachings that comprise it.*]

The ***Bhagavad-Gita*** has been the exemplary text of Hindu culture for centuries, both in India and in the West. The Sanskrit title ***Bhagavad-Gita*** has usually been interpreted to mean ***Song of the Lord,*** but this is misleading. It is not a lyric but a philosophical poem, composed in the form of a dialogue between the warrior Arjuna and his charioteer, the god Krishna.

As we read the ***Bhagavad-Gita*** today we can understand the paralyzing conflict Arjuna suffers knowing that the enemies it is his warrior duty to destroy are his own kinsmen and teachers. We can sympathize with his impulse to shrink from the violence he sees in the human condition, and we can learn from the ways Krishna teaches him to understand his own and others' mortality. Krishna's exposition of the relationship between death, sacrifice, and devotion dramatizes the Hindu idea that one must heroically confront death in order to transcend the limits of worldly existence. We may not share Arjuna's developing faith in Krishna's authority or be convinced by Krishna's insistence that one must perform one's sacred duty, even when it requires violence. But if we listen carefully to the compelling arguments and imagery of the discourse, we cannot but hear the voice of a larger reality.

The dramatic moral crisis that is central to the ***Bhagavad-Gita*** has inspired centuries of Indian philosophers and practical men of wisdom, as well as Western thinkers such as Thoreau, Emerson, and Eliot. Interpretations of the ***Gita,*** as it is commonly referred to in India, are as varied as the figures who have commented on it. From Shankara, the great Hindu philosopher of the eighth century, to Mahatma Gandhi, the leader of India's independence struggle in the twentieth century, each thinker has emphasized the path to spiritual liberation that was suited to his view of reality. These various interpretations reflect the intentionally multifaceted message of Krishna's teaching. The ***Gita***'s significance for Hindu life continues to be debated in India today.

Hinduism is not based on the teachings of a founder, such as Buddha, Christ, or Muhammad. It has evolved over centuries through the continual interplay of diverse religious beliefs and practices: popular local cults; orthodox traditions, including the ancient *Vedic* hymns, the ritual texts of the *Brahmanas,* and the mystical *Upanishads;* as well as heterodox challenges from Buddhist and Jain ideas and institutions. Even the word *Hindu* is a foreign idea, used by Arab invaders in the eighth century A.D. to refer to the customs and beliefs of people who worshipped sectarian gods such as Vishnu and Shiva.

Although the ***Gita*** exists as an independent sacred text, its placement within the sixth book of the great Indian war epic, the *Mahabharata,* gives it a concrete context. The religious and cultural life of the Indian subcontinent, and much of the rest of Asia, has been deeply influenced by the *Mahabharata,* as well as by the *Ramayana,* the other ancient Indian epic. Both poems have their roots in legendary events that took place in the period following the entry of nomadic Indo-Aryan-speaking tribes into northwestern

India around 1200 B.C. The composition of the epics began as these tribes settled in the river valleys of the Indus and the Ganges during the first millennium B.C., when their nomadic sacrificial cults began to develop into what are now the religious traditions of Hinduism.

The Hindu concept of religion is expressed by the Sanskrit term *dharma* ("sacred duty"), which refers to the moral order that sustains the cosmos, society, and the individual. The continual reinterpretation of *dharma* attests to its significance in Indian civilization. Derived from a Sanskrit form meaning "that which sustains," within Hindu culture it generally means religiously ordained duty, that is, the code of conduct appropriate to each group in the hierarchically ordered Hindu society. Theoretically, right and wrong are not absolute in this system; practically, right and wrong are decided according to the categories of social rank, kinship, and stage of life. For modern Westerners who have been raised on ideals of universality and egalitarianism, this relativity of values and obligations is the aspect of Hinduism most difficult to understand. However, without an attempt to understand it, the Hindu view of life remains opaque.

The epics are repositories of myths, ideals, and concepts that Hindu culture has always drawn upon to represent aspects of *dharma.* As befits their social position as warrior-kings, the figures of the epic heroes embody order and sacred duty (*dharma*); while their foes, whether human or demonic, embody chaos (*adharma*). The rituals of warrior life and the demands of sacred duty define the religious and moral meaning of heroism throughout the *Mahabharata.* Acts of heroism are characterized less by physical prowess than by the fulfillment of *dharma,* which often involves extraordinary forms of sacrifice, penance, devotion to a divine authority, and spiritual victory over evil. The distinctive martial religion of this epic emerges from a synthesis of values derived from the ritual traditions of the Vedic sacrificial cult combined with loyalty to a personal deity.

Most scholars agree that the *Mahabharata* was composed over the centuries between 400 B.C. and A.D. 400. Beyond its kernel story of internecine war, it is difficult to summarize. The work has its stylistic and mythological roots in the *Rig Veda;* its narrative sources are the oral tales of a tribal war fought in the Punjab early in the first millennium B.C. As the tradition was taken over by professional storytellers and intellectuals, many sorts of legend, myth, and speculative thought were absorbed, including the ***Bhagavad-Gita,*** which belongs to that layer of the epic which took form around the first century A.D. In its present form the *Mahabharata* is a rich encyclopedia of ancient Indian culture consisting of over one hundred thousand verses divided into eighteen books. The multiple layers of the text reflect its long history as well as attempts to reconcile conflicting religious and social values.

The epic's main narrative revolves around a feud over succession to the ancient kingdom of Kurukshetra in northern India. The rivals are two sets of cousins descended from the legendary king Bharata—the five sons of Pandu and the one hundred sons of Dhritarashtra. The feud itself is based on genealogical complications that are a result of a series of divine interventions. Pandu had become king because his elder brother, Dhritarashtra, was congenitally blind and thus ineligible for direct succession to the throne. But Pandu was unable to beget offspring because of a curse that forbade him intercourse with his two wives on penalty of death. After a long reign he renounces the throne and retires to the forest, where he fathers five sons (the Pandava brothers) with the help of five gods, and then dies.

The Pandava brothers are taken to be educated with their cousins at the court of Dhritarashtra, who has assumed the throne as regent in the absence of another adult heir. The princes' two teachers are their great-uncle Bhishma, who is revered for the spiritual power symbolized by his vow of celibacy, and the priest Drona, who is a master of archery and the teacher chosen by Bhishma to educate the princes in the martial arts. Arjuna becomes Drona's favored pupil when he vows to avenge his teacher's honor at the end of his training. The Pandavas excel their cousins in every warrior skill and virtue, which arouses the jealousy of Dhritarashtra's eldest son, Duryodhana.

Although Yudhishthira, Pandu's eldest son, has the legitimate right to be king, Duryodhana covets the throne, and in various episodes he attempts to assassinate his cousins or otherwise frustrate their rights. After thirteen years of exile imposed on them as the penalty for Yudhishthira's defeat in a crooked dice game played as part of a ritual, the Pandavas return to reclaim their kingdom. Duryodhana's refusal to step aside makes war inevitable. The description of the eighteen-day-long battle and concomitant philosophizing by various teachers takes up the bulk of the epic. The battle ends with the triumph of the Pandavas over their cousins—the triumph of order over chaos.

The setting of the ***Gita*** is the battlefield of Kurukshetra as the war is about to begin. It is not only a physical place but is representative of a state of mind. When the assembled troops are arrayed on the field awaiting battle, the sage Vyasa, the traditional author of the *Mahabharata,* appears to the blind Dhritarashtra and grants him a boon. He will be able to hear an account of the battle from Sanjaya, who is endowed with immediate vision of all things past, present, and future, thus enabling him to see every detail of the battle. Vyasa says to Dhritarashtra: "Sanjaya shall see all the events of the battle directly. He shall have a divine inner eye. . . . O King, Sanjaya has an inner eye. He will tell you everything about the battle. He will be all-knowing. Whenever he thinks with his mind, Sanjaya will see everything taking place during day or night, in public or in secret."

Sanjaya, the visionary narrator who serves as the personal bard and charioteer of Dhritarashtra, is thus the mediating voice through whom the audience of the ***Gita*** learns Krishna's secret teaching. Through Sanjaya's retelling, the mystery of life and death revealed to Arjuna enters into the bardic tradition that preserves it for all to hear. Sanjaya's role in the ***Gita*** begins with the opening verse, spoken by Dhritarashtra.

> Sanjaya, tell me what my sons
> and the sons of Pandu did when they met,
> wanting to battle on the field of Kuru,

on the field of sacred duty?

This question reverberates through the entire text, equating the field of internecine war with the field of sacred duty, where Arjuna's personal moral struggle is fought. In answer to Dhritarashtra's question, Sanjaya starts his recitation by recounting the dialogue about the war that he overhears between Duryodhana and Drona. This functions like a dramatic prologue, setting the scene of the ***Gita*** and preparing the audience to listen to Arjuna's dialogue with Krishna.

When Krishna and Arjuna enter Sanjaya's narrative, the focus shifts from action on the field of war to Arjuna's inner conflict. Arjuna's dejection is the spiritual abyss into which Krishna's teaching pours. In his misery Arjuna rejects the conventional rewards of battle and is filled with pity in face of the horrors of war. The dialogue that follows is aesthetically grounded in the tension between Arjuna's state of pity and his basic heroism. The representation of Arjuna's involuntary physical responses, such as his trembling body and bristling hair, dramatizes the pity he feels before the specter of disorder and impending slaughter. In Hindu aesthetic theory such responses are considered highly significant because they arise from inner feeling and cannot be simulated.

> Standing on their great chariot
> yoked with white stallions,
> Krishna and Arjuna, Pandu's son,
> sounded their divine conches. . . .
>
> Arjuna, his war flag a rampant monkey,
> saw Dhritarashtra's sons assembled
> as weapons were ready to clash,
> and he lifted his bow.
>
> He told his charioteer:
> "Krishna,
> halt my chariot
> between the armies!" . . .
>
> He surveyed his elders
> and companions in both armies,
> all his kinsmen
> assembled together.
>
> Dejected, filled with strange pity,
> he said this:
> "Krishna, I see my kinsmen
> gathered here, wanting war.
>
> My limbs sink,
> my mouth is parched,
> my body trembles,
> the hair bristles on my flesh.
>
> The magic bow slips
> from my hand, my skin burns,
> I cannot stand still,
> my mind reels.
>
> I see omens of chaos,
> Krishna; I see no good
> in killing my kinsmen
> in battle."

For Arjuna, and for the audience of the ***Gita,*** Krishna is a companion and teacher, as well as the god who commands devotion. Krishna's mythology suggests that he is a tribal hero transformed into cult divinity. In the ***Gita,*** Krishna is the incarnation of cosmic power, who periodically descends to earth to accomplish the restoration of order in times of chaos. The mundane and cosmic levels of his activity are interwoven to provide the background for his role as divine charioteer to Arjuna. The mightiest warrior in the epic, Arjuna is characterized not only by his physical prowess but by his spiritual prowess, which involves a mystical friendship with Krishna. From the start Arjuna knows that his charioteer is no ordinary mortal; he begs Krishna to dispel his uncertainty, and Krishna speaks with the authority of omniscience. As Arjuna's confidence and faith increase, the power of Krishna's divinity gradually unfolds before him in all its terrible glory, and Arjuna comes to see himself mirrored in the divine. Krishna's revelation of the cosmic spectacle forces Arjuna to accept the necessity of his own part in it.

Krishna directly addresses Arjuna's emotional attachments, uncertainty, and inability to act, and in the process, he enlarges Arjuna's awareness beyond the personal and social values that Arjuna holds sacred, compelling him to recognize why he must fight. Krishna insists that Arjuna's pity is really weakness and that the practice of true duty does not arise from personal passion but is part of a larger order that demands detachment. According to Krishna, Arjuna's objections to killing his relatives are based on the same subjective, worldly desire that blinds his foes to their folly. Krishna's solution lies on another level, one where oppositions coexist within his cosmic knowledge. Krishna, the omnipotent lord, teaches that the warrior's ordained duty (*dharma*) is grounded in the reciprocal relationship between cosmic and human action (*karma*), which is crucial to universal order.

In order to explore the paradoxical interconnectedness of disciplined action and freedom, Krishna develops his ideas in improvisational ways, not in linear arguments that lead to immediate resolution. The dialogue moves through a series of questions and answers that elucidate key words, concepts, and seeming contradictions in order to establish the crucial relationships among duty (*dharma*), discipline (*yoga*), action (*karma*), knowledge (*jñāna*), and devotion (*bhakti*). The concepts are drawn from many sources. Most important are several ancient systems of thought: Sankhya, the dualistic philosophy that analyzes the constituents of phenomenal existence; Yoga, the code of practical discipline based on dualism; Vedanta, the pantheistic doctrine of metaphysical knowledge; as well as Buddhism. Krishna teaches Arjuna the way to resolve the dilemma of renunciation and action. Freedom lies, not in the renunciation of the world, but in disciplined action (*karmayoga*). Put concretely, all action is to be both performed without attachment to the fruit of action (*karmaphalāsaṅga*) and dedicated with loving devotion to Krishna. Disciplined action within the context of devotion is essential to the religious life envisioned in the ***Gita.***

Each of the eighteen teachings that comprise the ***Gita*** highlights some aspect of Krishna's doctrine, but there is much repetition throughout them as the central themes are developed and subtly interpreted within the text. The text also has a broader triadic structure. In the first six teachings the dramatic narrative modulates into a series of theoretical and practical teachings on self-knowledge and the nature of action. The third and fourth teachings develop the crucial relation between sacrifice and action. The fifth and sixth teachings explore the tension between renunciation and action; Arjuna's query is resolved in the ideal of disciplined action. It is Arjuna's probing questions and his dissatisfaction with the apparent inconsistencies in Krishna's answers that expose Arjuna's state of mind and open him now to more advanced teachings. In the seventh teaching, focus shifts toward knowledge of Krishna. The language of paradox intensifies and hyperbole heightens, culminating in the dazzling theophany of the eleventh teaching. The theophany ends in a cadence on devotion, and the twelfth teaching develops this idea. Arjuna is transformed, not by a systematic argument, but by a mystical teaching in which Krishna becomes the object of Arjuna's intense devotion (*bhakti*). The representation of Arjuna's mystical experience of Krishna is poetically structured within the dialogue form to engage the participation of the audience in its drama.

In the final six teachings, the dialogue recedes as Krishna emphatically recapitulates the basic ideas he has already taught and integrates them into the doctrine of devotion. Devotion allows for a resolution of the conflict between the worldly life of allotted duties and the life of renunciation. By purging his mind of attachments and dedicating the fruits of his actions to Krishna, Arjuna can continue to act in a world of pain without suffering despair. The core of this devotion to Krishna is discipline (*yoga*), which enables the warrior to control his passions and become a man of discipline (*yogī*).

Arjuna can dedicate himself to Krishna only after his delusions about the nature of life and death have been dispelled and he has the power to see Krishna in his cosmic form. Once he has been instructed by Krishna in the most profound mysteries, Arjuna asks to see Krishna's immutable self. In the eleventh teaching, Krishna gives him a divine eye with which to see the majesty of his cosmic order. The aspect of himself that Krishna reveals to Arjuna on the battlefield embodies time's deadly destructiveness: a fearsome explosion of countless eyes, bellies, mouths, ornaments, and weapons—gleaming like the fiery sun that illumines the world.

At this juncture Sanjaya reenters the drama, interrupting the dialogue he is recounting and speaking in his own voice, as the bard who shares with the blind king and the audience what was revealed to Arjuna:

> If the light of a thousand suns
> were to rise in the sky at once,
> it would be like the light
> of that great spirit.
>
> Arjuna saw all the universe
> in its many ways and parts
> standing as one in the body
> of the god of gods.
>
> Then filled with amazement,
> his hair bristling on his flesh,
> Arjuna bowed his head to the god,
> joined his hands in homage, and spoke.

Sanjaya speaks twice again within this teaching, each time intensifying the theophany for his audience. Then the text continues in Arjuna's stammering voice of terror:

> Seeing the many mouths
> and eyes
> of your great form,
> its many arms,
> thighs, feet,
> bellies, and fangs,
> the worlds tremble
> and so do I.
>
> . . . .
>
> Seeing the fangs
> protruding
> from your mouths
> like the fires of time,
> I lose my bearings
> and I find no refuge;
> be gracious, Lord of Gods,
> Shelter of the Universe.

Arjuna begs, "Tell me—who are you in this terrible form?" Krishna responds:

> I am time grown old,
> creating world destruction
> set in motion
> to annihilate the worlds;
> even without you,
> all these warriors
> arrayed in hostile ranks
> will cease to exist.
>
> Therefore, arise
> and win glory!
> Conquer your foes
> and fulfill your kingship!
> They are already
> slain by me.
> Be just my instrument,
> the archer at my side!

Here the divine charioteer reveals his terrifying identity as creator and destroyer of everything in the universe. As destroyer, he has already destroyed both mighty armies. As creator, his cosmic purpose is to keep order in the universe, as well as in the human world. Although the sight of Krishna's horrific power is too much for Arjuna to bear and he begs to see him again in his calmer aspect, the experience brings Arjuna to the realization that his duty to fight is intimately linked to Krishna's divine activity. Overwhelmed by the vision of time's inexorable violence embodied in his charioteer, Arjuna sees the inevitability of his actions. He realizes that by performing his warrior duty with absolute devotion to Krishna, he can unite with Krishna's cosmic purpose and free himself from the crippling attachments that bind mortals to eternal suffering.

In the thirteenth teaching Krishna redefines the battlefield as the human body, the material realm in which one struggles to know oneself. It is less a physical place than a symbolic field of interior warfare, a place of clashing forces, all of which have their origin in Krishna's ultimate reality. In the teachings that follow, various aspects of Krishna's material nature (*prakṛti*) are analyzed in terms of the three fundamental qualities (*guṇa*) that constitute it—lucidity (*sattva*), passion (*rajas*), and dark inertia (*tamas*). The scheme of natural qualities, introduced in the third teaching, is now elaborated to amplify Krishna's relation to the world from the perspectives of metaphysics, morality, and religious tradition. In the long final teaching, in response to Arjuna's request to know the distinction between renunciation (*sannyāsa*) and relinquishment (*tyāga*) of action, Krishna returns to the central dilemma of action. He reiterates the crucial connection between action and devotion, and the dialogue closes with Arjuna's avowal that his delusion is destroyed and he is ready to act on Krishna's words.

At every stage of Arjuna's dramatic journey of self-discovery, the charioteer Krishna is aware of his pupil's spiritual conflict and guides him to the appropriate path for resolving it. Krishna urges him not to resign himself to killing but instead to renounce his selfish attachment to the fruits of his actions. By learning how to discipline his emotion and his action, Arjuna journeys far without ever leaving the battlefield. Krishna draws him into a universe beyond the world of everyday experience but keeps forcing him back to wage the battle of life. He advocates, on the one hand, the life of action and moral duty, and on the other, the transcendence of empirical experience in search of knowledge and liberation. Though much of Krishna's teaching seems remote from the moral chaos that Arjuna envisions will be a consequence of his killing his kinsmen, Krishna's doctrine of disciplined action is a way of bringing order to life's destructive aspect. When the puzzled Arjuna asks, "Why do you urge me to do this act of violence?" Krishna does not condone physical violence. Instead, he identifies the real enemy as desire, due to attachment, an enemy that can only be overcome by arming oneself with discipline and acting to transcend the narrow limits of individual desire.

The text of the ***Gita*** ends by commenting on itself through the witness of Sanjaya, who re-creates the dialogue in all its compelling power as he keeps remembering it. He recalls for the blind king Dhritarashtra, and for every other member of his audience, the correspondence between Krishna's wonderous form and the language of poetry that represents that form. Anyone who listens to his words gains consciousness of Krishna's presence. Sanjaya says:

> As I heard this wondrous dialogue
> between Krishna and Arjuna,
> the man of great soul,
> the hair bristled on my flesh.
>
> By grace of the epic poet Vyasa, I heard
> the secret of supreme discipline
> recounted by Krishna himself,
> lord of discipline incarnate.
>
> O King, when I keep remembering
> this wondrous and holy dialogue
> between Krishna and Arjuna,
> I rejoice again and again.
>
> In my memory I recall again
> and again Krishna's wondrous form—
> great is my amazement, King;
> I rejoice again and again.

(pp. 1-13)

Barbara Stoler Miller, "Introduction: The 'Bhagavad-Gita,' Context and Text," in The Bhagavad-Gita: Krishna's Counsel in Time of War, *translated by Barbara Stoler Miller, Columbia University Press, 1986, pp. 1-13.*

FURTHER READING

Bazemore, Duncan. "Life as a Battlefield: A *Gītā* Symbol as Interpreted by Sri Aurobindo." *International Philosophical Quarterly* XII, No. 2 (June 1972): 251-59.

Elucidates the eminent Indian thinker's view of the *Gītā* as a powerful symbolic affirmation of spirituality.

Bishop, Donald H. "The *Bhagavad Gītā.*" In *Indian Thought: An Introduction,* edited by Donald H. Bishop, pp. 62-80. New York: John Wiley & Sons, 1975.

An introduction to the *Gītā* as a seminal literary, philosophical, and theological document.

Dandekar, R. N. "Hinduism and the *Bhagavadgītā:* A Fresh Approach." *Journal of the Oriental Institute* XII, No. 3 (March 1963): 232-37.

Examines the *Gītā* in the context of the development of Hinduism.

Dasgupta, Surendranath. "The Philosophy of the *Bhagavad-Gītā.*" In his *A History of Indian Philosphy,* Vol. II, pp. 437-552. 1932. Reprint. Cambridge: Cambridge at the University Press, 1952.

An exhaustive and well-documented discussion of the *Gītā* against the background of Indian philosophy and theology. Also includes explanations of key Sanskrit terms.

Edgerton, Franklin. "The *Bhagavad Gītā,* or *Song of the Blessed One.*" *The Open Court* XXXVIII, No. 4 (April 1924): 235-46.

Comments on the nature of God according to the mystical vision presented in the *Gītā.*

Eliade, Mircea. "The Triumph of Yoga." In his *Yoga, Immortality, and Freedom,* pp. 143-61. New York: Random House, Pantheon, 1958.

Includes a detailed discussion of the *Gītā*'s view of yoga.

Fingarette, Herbert. "Action and Suffering in the *Bhagavad Gītā.*" *Philosophy East and West* XXXIV, No. 4 (October 1984): 357-69.

Posits that in the *Gītā* both "bondage and liberation are forms of suffering" and that the alternatives revealed in the spiritual crisis described in the poem "are two different ways of suffering."

Garbe, Richard. "Christian Elements in the *Bhagavad Gītā.*" *The Monist* 23 (October 1913): 494-516.

Explains that certain ideas in the *Gītā,* such as the notion of a loving God, should not be perceived as derived from Christianity, since the poem predates any possible Christian influence.

Hill, W. Douglas P. Introduction to his *The Bhagavad Gītā:*

An English Translation and Commentary, pp. 1-72. London: Oxford University Press, 1928.

Comments on the cult of Kṛṣṇa and offers a detailed review of the *Gītā,* with particular emphasis on the theological and philosophical doctrines presented in the poem.

Isherwood, Christopher. "The *Gītā* and War." In *Vedanta for the Western World,* edited by Christopher Isherwood, pp. 358-65. Hollywood, Calif.: Marcel Rodd, 1945.

Examines the *Gītā*'s teaching on war. According to Isherwood, the poem neither condemns nor condones war, as the *Gītā* regards "no action as of absolute value, either for good or evil."

Macnicol, Nicol. "War and Peace Aims in the *Bhagavad Gītā.*" *The Hibbert Journal* XXXVIII, No. 3 (1940): 329-41.

Identifies the doctrine of activism as fundamental to the *Gītā.*

Renou, Louis. *Religions of Ancient India.* London: Athlone Press, 1953, 139 p.

A lucid and concise discussion of Hinduism. Explains the key terms and ideas relevant to the *Gītā.*

Saroja, G. V. *Tilak and Śankara on the "Gita."* New Delhi: Sterling Publishers, 1985, 200 p.

Analyzes two important Indian interpretations of the *Gītā*: by the noted medieval philosopher Śankara; and by the political activist and journalist Balgangadhar Tilak (1856-1920).

Verma, C. D., ed. *The "Gītā" in World Literature.* New Delhi: Sterling Publishers Private, 1990, 252 p.

Collection of essays tracing the echoes of the *Gītā* in world literature.

White, David. "The Yoga of Knowledge of the *Gītā* according to Sri Aurobindo." *International Philosophical Quarterly* XII, No. 2 (June 1972): 243-50.

A concise analysis of the philosophical ideas presented in the *Gītā,* with particular attention to Aurobindo's thesis that, according to the poem, disciplined knowledge leads to intelligent action and ultimately to liberation.

———. "The *Bhagavad Gītā*'s Conception of Human Freedom." *Philosophy East and West* XXXIV, No. 3 (July 1984): 295-302.

Examines the *Gītā*'s view of freedom, concluding that the poem offers convincing and rational guidance for liberation through action.

Zaehner, R. C. "The Indian Contribution, II." In his *The Comparison of Religions,* pp. 69-133. Boston: Beacon Press, 1962.

Includes a commentary on the *Gītā* in the context of Indian and Western thought. This work was first published in 1958.

Additional coverage of the *Bhagavad Gītā* is contained in the following source published by Gale Research: *Classical and Medieval Literature Criticism,* Vol. 5 (*Mahābhārata* entry).

Ramon Llull

c. 1235-1316

Catalonian theologian, poet, and fiction writer.

INTRODUCTION

A missionary and mystic determined to resolve religious differences between Christians, Muslims, and Jews, Llull was devoted to the literary expression and rationalization of Christian doctrine. He created a system in which he attempted to demonstrate that all knowledge derives from a fundamental and divine truth. With this theory, which critics refer to as his "Art," he sought to explain all arts and sciences—from philosophy to medicine—in terms of analogical structures. Llull completed a vast number of treatises and other formal arguments, and also presented his Art through more easily accessible didactic stories; two works containing such exempla, *Evast and Blanquerna* and *Felix, or the Libre de meravelles,* were written in Catalan and are considered to be the first philosophical novels composed in a European vernacular. In addition, Llull was the first Christian philosopher to publish his principal works in a language other than Latin. Scholars value these writings not only for their mystical insights, but also for their influence on the course of Medieval and Renaissance European thought.

Llull was born to a land-owning family in Palma, on the Spanish island of Majorca. As a young man he lived a dissolute life in the court of King James I of Aragon, composing love poetry in the troubador style. He married in 1256, but continued his licentious lifestyle until 1263, when a series of mystical visions prompted him to leave his wife and dedicate himself to the Church. Fascinated by Christianity and its relation to Islam, the other major religion thriving in Majorca at that time, Llull embarked upon a nine-year period of study in 1265, learning theology, philosophy, Arabic, and Latin. During this time Llull began writing his lengthy *Book of Contemplation,* which he composed at least partially in Arabic, and later translated into Catalan. Scholars date the completion of the work to 1272, the same year in which Llull purportedly experienced a vision atop Majorca's Mount Randa that became the basis for his conception of the universe. All of Llull's subsequent writings address this vision, either in the form of an explicitly theological tract such as his *Ars inventiva veritatis,* written in about 1274, or somewhat implicitly, as in his prose romance *Blanquerna,* completed about 1285. For two years beginning in 1287 Llull taught his system at the University of Paris, opting thereafter to engage in missionary activity. He sailed to Tunisia during the 1290s—one of many expeditions he undertook to Asia and North Africa—to preach to the Muslims there, but was soon expelled. When not traveling he spent much of his time in Genoa and Paris, writing prolifically. He attended the Council of Vienne in 1311, where he presented a petition against the teachings of twelfth-century Arabic philosopher Averroës, attacking his idea of distinguishing between philosophical and theological truth. Llull journeyed again to North Africa in 1315, and was eventually stoned in the town of Bougie, Algeria, most likely as a consequence of his aggressive proselytizing. He died at sea shortly thereafter while returning to Majorca.

Over the course of his life Llull completed an enormous number of writings—by some counts over 300 works of theology, philosophy, science, and fiction. Subsumed under the synthetic concept of the Art, all of his works were designed to elucidate his vision of the divine origin of all knowledge. In his first important work, *The Book of Contemplation,* a penitent Llull relates personal reminiscences in which he criticizes courtly life. Although lacking the stylistic polish of his later works, Llull's writings in *The Book of Contemplation* are considered essential for an understanding of his Art. Llull also created stories featuring fictionalized versions of himself, contemplative individuals—often hermits—who expound his teachings. In *Blanquerna,* a work of utopian fiction, the eponymous hero is a monk who retreats to the forest, later emerging to teach his fellow monks the nature of his vision of the universe. Blanquerna then becomes a bishop, a Pope, and finally a hermit. This story also includes a widely praised section that has been published separately as *The Book of the Lover and the Beloved,* an allegorical romance in 366 passages—each a meditation for one day of the year—detailing Blanquerna's efforts to convert unbelievers to Christianity. A similar work, *Felix,* written in a more strident and satirical tone, centers on a young man plagued by religious doubt who is convinced by a hermit through a series of allegorical stories of the existence of God as He is revealed in the workings of the universe. The most famous tales in the work are those comprising *The Book of the Beasts.* A series of animal fables that has also been published separately, the book was intended, according to Llull, to be "brought to a king so that he might learn, from the things done by the beasts, how a king should reign, and how to keep himself from evil counsel and from treacherous men."

Among Llull's more strictly philosophical and theological works are a series of writings—including the *Ars brevis* and the *Ars magna,* and culminating with the *Ars generalis ultima* (1308)—that explain Llull's cosmology. The *Ars magna* and other expressions of his Art employ letters and symbols, illustrated in diagrams, that represent the Dignities—the Divine Attributes or perfections of God. Llull emphasized these abstractions in his description of the natural world and his organic ordering of human knowledge. For Llull, whom critics characterize as an essentialist who ascribes the reality of all beings and things to the presence of God within them, the Art attests to his belief in an absolute standard of truth—God—from which proceeds an analogical ordering of the cosmos. Truth of a theological nature, for example, leads to a consequent ethical or even scientific truth, the distance between the two spanned by Llull's liberal use of metaphor. Llull attempted to make this notion more accessible to a mass audience in his *Arbor scientiae,* in which sixteen trees, including trees of heaven, philosophy, minerals, and science symbolize the organic unity of knowledge.

The texts of Llull's works, which were originally written in Catalan, Arabic, and Latin, were disseminated throughout Europe and translated into dozens of languages. Prior to the twentieth century, however, only his *Libre de orde de cavalleria* was translated into English—a task undertaken by printmaker William Caxton, working from a French manuscript. Scholars note that Llull's ideals of courtly manners and knighthood, expressed in that work, became a standard on the subject in the fifteenth century. In the 1920s E. Allison Peers, a primary participant in what he called a "Llullian Renaissance," translated several of his works into English, but most still remain available for study only in Latin versions such as the eighteenth-century Mainz edition of his *Opera,* or collected works.

Although Llull was venerated in Majorca following his martyrdom, his reputation outside of Spain has fluctuated. During his own lifetime, in his poem *Desconort,* he expressed feelings of anguish at his failure to win widespread acceptance of his Art. After Llull's death Pope Gregory XI denounced his teachings as secular and unorthodox, as did the Dominican order. His thought regained currency, however, exerting an influence on, among others, Renaissance philosopher Giordano Bruno and Enlightenment philosopher and mathematician Wilhelm Gottfried Leibniz. In the nineteenth century Llull was beatified by the Roman Catholic Church, and his works became the focus of renewed critical attention during a rebirth of interest in Catalan literature. Peers' English translations of Llull's literary works piqued interest among English audiences, and in the 1950s Frances A. Yates inaugurated another wave of Llullian study, exploring and explicating his writings in the context of medieval mystical and esoteric traditions.

PRINCIPAL ENGLISH TRANSLATIONS

The Art of Contemplation (translated by E. A. Peers) 1925
Blanquerna (translated by E. A. Peers) 1926
The Book of the Lover and the Beloved (translated by E. A Peers) 1926
**The Book of the Ordre of Chyvalry* (translated by William Caxton; edited by A. T. P. Byles) 1926
The Tree of Love (translated by E. A. Peers) 1926
The Book of the Beasts (translated by E. A. Peers) 1927
Selected Works of Ramon Llull 2 vols. (translated and edited by Anthony Bonner) 1984

*Translated by Caxton in the 15th century from a French version of Llull's *Le libre del orde de cavalleria.*

CRITICISM

E. Allison Peers (essay date 1928)

[*In the following essay, Peers discusses what he believes are the enduring aspects of Llull's thought.*]

Few, if any, of the followers of St. Francis of Assisi have experienced more of the ups and downs which are proverbially associated with popular esteem than Ramon Lull, the Majorcan missionary and martyr. During the six centuries that have elapsed since his death, his reputation has been so high that he has more than once come within a short distance of canonization, and so low that his memory has had to endure, at one time general opprobrium, at another, all but complete neglect. For the last thirty years, in most of the Latin countries of Europe, a Lullian renaissance has been in progress; quite recently, it has extended farther north. During the present century, works of Ramon Lull's have been translated from their native Catalan into Castilian, French, Italian, German, and English. And this renaissance exhibits every characteristic of permanence; for Lull's new vogue has arisen, not (as in the past) from philosophical and theological ideals which have now become discredited, but from qualities in his character and writings which have ever appealed to the mind of man and must continue to do so for all time. To present this striking medieval figure as he appears to us today, to formulate, as it were, the articles of twentieth-century Lullism, is the object of this essay.

. . . . .

Ramon Lull was born in Palma, the capital of Majorca, in or about the year 1232. The story of his life is full of interest. Well descended, in high favor with the King of Aragon, who had recently wrested the island from the Moors, full of life, imbued with notions of chivalry, he was converted at about the age of thirty in circumstances as dramatic as any known to history. From that time until his death half a century later (he was martyred in Africa at about the age of 83) he had only one idea, that of spreading the knowledge of the Master in whose service he had enlisted. With such zeal he combined a temperament which was highly practical. He was no cloistered visionary, but a man who saw life whole, and it was as one of the earliest of the ever-growing band of Franciscan tertiaries that he found the best way of carrying his ideals into effect. All over Europe he traveled, and far beyond it, preaching, disputing, pleading, teaching: to Paris and Rome, to Malta, Cyprus, Armenia, to Egypt, Palestine, Ethiopia, Morocco. In the University of Paris he spent several long periods as a lecturer; from Rome, after many abortive efforts, he secured the establishment of a School of Oriental Studies. For chief among the means whereby he hoped to convert the world was the training of Franciscan missionaries in theology and in foreign languages, that they might be at least as well equipped to preach and teach as were prelates and university professors. One of the first fruits of this ideal was his beloved college of Miramar in Majorca, founded by the munificence of the younger son of James I, King of Aragon, in 1276.

Lull was a practical mystic, belonging to the rare natural type of contemplative-active. When one considers the strenuous life which he led and the amount of time which, by general consent and the internal evidence of his own works, he spent in the practice of contemplation, his activity as a writer is wonderful beyond belief. Credited by some authorities, and not without reason, with nearly five hundred books, he is generally recognized to be the author of over three hundred, the titles of most of which will be found in the bibliography compiled by the editors of the monumental *Histoire littéraire de la France* (Volume xxix) and in the more recent (1927) Lullian bibliography published by the Institut d'Estudis Catalans, of Barcelona. Most of these works are written in Catalan or Latin, a few also in Arabic. Their subjects are the most diverse imaginable: metaphysics, ethics, logic, theology, medicine, mathematics, chivalry, physics, alchemy—and, not least, didactic but eminently readable fiction. To the last-named class belongs Lull's literary masterpiece, one of the greatest works in Catalan literature, medieval and modern—the prose romance of ***Blanquerna,*** in which is contained the particularly beautiful little work entitled ***The Book of the Lover and the Beloved.***

Together with his project, which was only partly realized, of establishing missionary colleges all over the Christian world, Lull cherished another closely allied with it, the conversion of the heathen everywhere by means of a book which he had written, as he believed, by direct divine inspiration: the ***Ars Magna.*** This book was the source of the immense reputation which he made for himself during his lifetime and which persisted for centuries after his death. It is an "art," or "method," which claims, by means of the application of geometrical diagrams, to solve questions in theology, metaphysics, morals, and even natural science. Any handful of these questions and solutions, gathered at random, will show how Lull had absorbed the scholastic teaching of his day, and also how closely his method verged on rationalism. As we consider the magnitude of the book, and its author's orderliness, reasoning power, and use of the imagination, we are forced, in spite of our impatience with its puerilities, to admire it. And we can well understand what an appeal it would have made to Lull's own generation, when reinforced with his compelling personality.

. . . . .

After his death, which took place at about the end of 1315, there began to form about his head a double halo of sanctity and science. In Majorca, and, less markedly, in Aragon, the cult both of the martyr and of his work arose immediately, partly owing to the sympathy of the then Bishop of Majorca, who had approved and supported a school founded in the island before Lull's martyrdom to disseminate his teaching and could be relied upon to assure its progress. This Lullian School prospered long after the Miramar college came to an end, and for a time held the rank of a university.

In the late fourteenth century came a violent reaction against Lullism, due largely to the virulence of a notorious Dominican inquisitor, Nicholas Eymeric. In his fierce and fanatical attempts to prove that Lull's works contained heresies we see something more than a perverted enthusiasm and an individual enmity: we see a particular expression of the antagonism between two powerful religious orders. The well-known story of Dominic's girding of himself with Francis' cord to symbolize his desire for the unification of their two societies recurs almost tragically to the memory when one reads of the acrimony with which these societies fought over the man who in his lifetime knew both so well. From 1366 until his fall in 1394 Eymeric conducted a violent campaign against Lull's memory, denying both his inspiration and his personal sanctity, reviling his reputation, describing him as a heretic, an ignoramus, and a necromancer, appealing against him to Gregory XI, producing a condemnatory bull by that Pope now generally considered to have been a forgery, and extracting from Lull's genuine and his apocryphal works combined one hundred propositions which it was not difficult to brand as heretical.

Before the end of the century this persecution had worn itself out, and thenceforward, for many generations, Lull's teaching enjoyed a secure reinstatement in authority. In the ancient University of Cervera there was a Chair in Lullian Science ("the which is right holy and good," say its statutes) as early as 1403. Thirty years later, Lullian schools existed in Barcelona, Palma, and Randa; soon they spread southward to Valencia and westward to Castile, while no less a person than Cardinal Cisneros was responsible for the introduction of Lullian teaching into his newly-founded University of Alcalá, where he also founded a Lullian library and subsidized an edition of Lull's works. "I have a great affection," wrote Cisneros in 1513, "for all the works of the Doctor most illuminate, Ramon Lull, since they are of great importance and utility." The Council of Trent, fifty years later, maintained the same opinion; biographies of Lull began to appear in great numbers; and at length, at the beginning of the seventeenth century, Philip III of Spain championed the cause of his canonization.

But for this, it would appear, the psychological moment had already passed. Not only in Paris, where Lullism was so popular for two centuries, but also in Ramon's own Spain, the dawn of the Renaissance had quenched many feebler lights. The *causa pia* flickered lamentably: one type of Lullism was dead, and the other type, which lives today, had not been so much as thought of. A local and restricted beatification was all that the Majorcan martyr was awarded; and with the eighteenth century came a renewed persecution of his memory, led once more by the Dominican order, and followed by a neglect which spread well-nigh everywhere save only to Lull's native island.

The beginnings of the Lullian renaissance may be traced back as far as 1858, when Pius IX extended the use of the Office and Mass of Ramon Lull to the whole of the Franciscan order, as well as confirming the local use already referred to. About the same time, a little group of Catalonian scholars sprang up who did notable work in reediting Ramon's writings, publishing some of them for the first time, and clearing up many biographical difficulties which Pasqual, his great eighteenth-century biographer, had left unsolved. The chain of continuity between these scholars has never been broken. The successors of Quadrado, Rosselló, and Obrador will be remembered with no less gratitude than they: among clerics, Mn. Alcover and Mn. Galmés; among laymen, Jordi Rubió and Ramon d'Alòs. It would be tedious to recount all that these and many others have done in Catalonia to respond to the reawakened interest in Ramon Lull. It is sufficient to say here that it is they to whom is chiefly due the intelligent quality of that interest. For not only have they prepared editions, searched for manuscripts, studied sources, and compiled biographies: they have emphasized the complete reversal of values which makes Lull great today: they have guided the orientation of modern Lullism.

. . . . .

The world of today, it need not be said, makes no account of the encyclopaedism either of the ***Ars Magna*** or of its numerous and ineffective progeny. One-half of Ramon's dearly cherished projects are seen to have been fantastic visions; the other half have for so long been accomplished in all their essentials that it is difficult to imagine the time when they were considered daring reforms. Such upheavals of thought would have buried the work of a lesser man under their ruins. It is because Ramon Lull has survived them that he is everywhere receiving attention, not now as philosopher, theologian, mathematician, or alchemist (which last he probably was not) but for what he *was,* as distinguished from what he *did,* or has been popularly supposed to have done.

The Catalonian scholars of the mid-nineteenth century were inspired to study Ramon Lull by the Catalan renaissance: their principal desire was to exhibit him as one of the heroes of Catalonia and its language. It was an imposing gallery of portraits that diligent search in the neglected and well-nigh ruined ancestral castle brought to light: James the Conqueror, Ramón Muntaner, Arnau de Vilanova, Bernat Metge, are figures that will stand proudly anywhere. And Ramon de la Barba Florida (as Lull was named by the students of Paris) stood worthily among them. To his prose writings was largely due the fact that of modern European languages Catalan was the first to take a place beside Latin as the instrument of philosophy. He, and none other, was the herald of the glories of Catalan poetry, so pre-eminent, after so long an eclipse, to-day. He, again, was the greatest precursor, if not actually the first, of that noble company of Spanish religious writers, ascetics and mystics both, who flourished during Spain's Golden Age.

Having regarded Lull thus, and having set him upon a well-merited pinnacle, it was essential for these Catalan writers, not only to make accessible the works which justified their action, but also to make explicit their reasons. Then it was that Lull's claims to immortality, judged from the standpoint of pure literature, came to light. At its best, as critics of the English translation of ***Blanquerna*** have agreed, and as becomes still more manifest in the original, Lull's prose, so simple, naïve, and unaffected, is as beautiful as the Catalan language, and as direct in its appeal to the intellect as the thoughts which it expresses are to the heart. His verse, though unequal, has a similar charm, with the added distinction of being hardly influenced by Provençal in comparison with the verse of his contemporaries. As a poet he shines in both verse and prose: the vividness of his allegories, the beauty of his symbolism, the lofty flights of his imagination—all these and more mark him out both from his fellows and from his Catalan successors. It is curious that, in their wranglings over his theological terminology, his contemporaries could not see that he was a poet before he was a master of the schools, and, in this sense above all, a true "illuminate."

If Lull's position as patriarch of Catalan literature has made him a hero in Catalonia, how much more have his life and character endeared him to the entire Christian world. It may not be out of place here to say that the publication in English, five years ago, of the ***Book of the Lover and the Beloved*** has brought its translator letters from all over the world, from men and women of many different religions, races, and even colors, and that these correspondents have as a rule laid stress, not so much upon the book's content, as upon the personality which lies behind it. The fact is that the life of Ramon Lull, by virtue of its romance, picturesqueness, and poetry, as well as of its single-mindedness, makes an appeal to many whom the figure of the recluse, the philosopher, and the contemplative would never touch. To these—temperamentally actives and for the most part laymen—he has shown what is meant by conversion, renunciation, and love. He has shown them how a resolute spirit can triumph over weakness and temptation, find its nourishment in hardship, and win its satisfaction by sacrifice and martyrdom. He has shown them what, to a soul fired with love, is meant by a life devoted wholly to the service of God, that spends and is spent, toiling ceaselessly and joyfully with all its powers.

> "What meanest thou by love?" said the Beloved. And the Lover answered: "It is to bear on one's heart the sacred marks and the sweet words of the Beloved. It is to long for Him with desire and with tears. It is boldness. It is fervour. It is fear. It is the desire for the Beloved above all things. It is that which causes the Lover to grow faint when he hears the Beloved's praises. It is that wherein I die daily, and wherein is all my will."
>
> Pensively the Lover trod those paths which lead to the Beloved. Now he stumbled and fell among the thorns; but they were to him as flowers, and of a bed of love.
>
> Said the Lover: "O ye that love, if ye will have fire, come light your lanterns at my heart; if water, come to my eyes, whence flow the tears in streams; if thoughts of love, come gather them from my meditations."
>
> The Beloved clothed Himself in the garment of His Lover, that he might be His companion in glory forever. So the Lover desired to wear crimson garments daily, that his dress might be like that of his Beloved.

If it is as an active that Ramon appeals most widely to the world of today, he appeals most deeply as a contemplative. It is a shallow criticism that, by any criterion of mysticism, rejects him as a mystical writer: though he does not, as a rule, distinguish states, degrees, and steps of love, his books are full of references to the mystic way, and it is from their mystical quality that his writings derive most of their power. Nor can we deny Ramon Lull the personal title of mystic without completely disbelieving the records of his life. And because he transplanted a flower that is wont to grow in the cloister into the very center and heart of a troubled world, there are few that love flowers who will be in danger of passing it over.

What M. Sabatier finely says of St. Francis, we may say equally well of this Franciscan tertiary. He is of the race of mystics, for no intermediary comes between God and his soul; but, like Jesus Christ, he leads his disciples from the Tabor of contemplation down to the crowds and the plain. The comparison with St. Francis can be extended very widely. Ramon possessed in an unusual degree what the *Fioretti* speaks of as "that celestial virtue whereby all earthly things and transitory are trodden under foot and every barrier is removed which might hinder the soul from freely uniting itself to the eternal God." No more than St. Francis can he be imagined as identifying contemplation with inactivity. "His conclusion was that which was evidenced by his life; that the highest life which it is possible to lead is one in which the strength and the power to be effectively active in the outer world are gained in the mysteries of contemplation. Activity without contemplation may be both holy and effective, contemplation without activity may be equally holy and. . . . ever more effective, but it is the combination of both by which the effectiveness and the holiness are raised to their highest power" [D. H. S. Nicholson, *The Mysticism of St. Francis of Assisi*].

Any Franciscan who reads the ***Book of Contemplation, Blanquerna,*** or the finest of Lull's poems, will recognize in them the fashion of the master-hand. St. Francis desired that his followers should be the "jongleurs of the Lord": in Ramon Lull he had one who delighted in that name, or rather in the very similar names by which he preferred to call himself—the "jongleur" and the "fool" of love. St. Francis' writings were as scant as Lull's were voluminous, but there are striking similarities between them in style. All the apt phrases with which Fr. Paschal Robinson characterizes St. Francis can be applied to Lull as exactly as though they had been written of him: his combination, for example, of "great elevation of thought" with "picturesqueness of expression," and "his deep sense of the spiritual" clothed "with the spirit of romance." And two other phrases used by the same writer [in his *Writings of St. Francis of Assisi*] sum him up best of all:

> He was at once formidably mystic and exquisitely human. He had the soul of an ascetic and the heart of a poet.

. . . . .

Here, then, we have the Ramon Lull of the present and the future: a patriarch of literature, an apostle of religion, and a herald among the mystics. The part of his work which was never destined to be immortal is dead already, and of interest but as the mummy of a Pharaoh. The part which will live is, after six centuries have passed, taking on even now a new and a more extended existence. Even in another six centuries, though many more of his writings may have found oblivion, it is difficult to see how the name of Ramon Lull can be lost. Should the virile tongue of Catalonia be silenced, the apostle and the herald will outlive the patriarch. Reduce to ashes Lull's mass of writings by the flames of super-intensive production, and there will still remain, totally unharmed, ***Blanquerna*** and a collection of poetic fragments. For it is not conceivable that, while a spark of love for God remains in a human soul, Ramon's sublime hymns of love can be forgotten. (pp. 459-67)

E. Allison Peers, "Ramon Llull and the World of Today," in Hispania, *Vol. XI, No. 6, December, 1928, pp. 459-67.*

E. Allison Peers (essay date 1929)

[*In the following excerpt, Peers examines Llull's* Book of Contemplation, *describing the work as "an illuminating commentary alike upon his life and his temperament, upon his erudition and his literary art."*]

[The] great ***Book of Contemplation,*** was actually first written, wholly or partly, in Arabic. . . . Since it was afterwards translated into Catalan, and this task was completed in or about the year 1272, it evidently represents the first fruits of Lull's genius as an author. Indeed, his output was so great, and the reminiscences of his early life in the book are so frequent, that we may wonder if it does not perhaps incorporate parts of some spiritual journal or day-book which he kept from the time of his conversion. This, however, is but conjecture. The bare facts are that neither of the exact date of the work, nor of the place and circumstances in which it was written, have we any record; but the year 1272 fits best into our general biographical plan, and there are several signs that the book was begun, if not also ended, at an early stage in Lull's career.

First, there are many references in it to his court life which suggest that this had not yet receded into the background of his memory. Only one who had moved in court circles, or who at least was familiar with courtiers, would so frequently illustrate his reflections from the conduct of "kings and princes and noble barons of this world." Their disdain for gifts of small worth is described, their use of high-sounding titles, the crying aloud of their ordinances through their cities, their extravagant love of their possessions, their inaccessibility, the delight which men take in speaking with them, the greed of an evil prince for conquest and dominion without regard to justice, the intentions of an unworthy vassal in serving his lord and master, and the considerate treatment of a worthy vassal at the hands of a righteous prince, who will even die for his subjects. We see the king at his pleasures, with his falcons, horses and dogs, with troubadours, singers and musicians on the viol and lute, with *joglars* and "tellers of new things" to whom he gives money and garments "that they may spread abroad his fame over all the world." The courtiers' garments are described, the "spacious and painted halls" of their mansions, the knights with their richly caparisoned steeds, the ladies, painting their faces or embroidering their dresses and taking care that no spot or stain shall defile them. Rich banquets are set before us and "delicate wines" in goblets of gold. When these are despatched and men rise from table, there come *joglars* and flatterers (*lagoters*) with instruments of music, singing songs and speaking of vanities. These things are by no means to be despised and condemned, so the author says, unless indeed men think of nothing else, but "spend and squander upon them their time, their health, their youth and their riches."

Whole chapters discuss themes, to Ramon very obviously personal ones, such as the love between a prince and his people: the faithful and admiring vassal, it may further be noted, is a continually recurring figure. Most striking of all are the three chapters devoted respectively to princess, knights and *joglars* and their several vocations. In these we see less of the good side of the mediaeval court than of the evil. Princes who should guard their people from injustice appoint corruptible men as bailies, *veguers,* procurators and judges. Many princes are extravagant and wasteful, making war upon the slightest pretext rather than ensuring the safety of their subjects and improving conditions at home. The size of their retinues prevents them from getting into touch with their people; they hunt for their own amusement, while wolves, in the shape of conscienceless officials, devour their flock. So their lives pass in idleness, and they think complacently that God will honour them in the next world as He has honoured them in this, in which belief they are disastrously mistaken. Certainly it would appear that Ramon's travels have not shown him the better side of royalty:

> Many a time have I enquired of men who go about the world if they have seen a prince that is full of perfections, and never have I found any that could tell me of such a one.

The knights he presents to us are not much better than the princes, for they dishonour themselves and each other by frequent quarrels and the use of "proud and evil words." Created knights that they may root out evil men from the world, they appear rather to spend their time in slaying "the just men and those that love peace rather than war." More degraded still has become the office of *joglar;* for, while its earliest songs were in praise and honour of God, *joglars* sing now only of lusts and vanities, and their ballads and lays and music and dancing are held in the highest esteem.

Whether such criticisms were justified or no, it is clear that they must for the most part have been the outcome of personal reminiscence. Occasionally even, the vividness or the detail of a reference suggests a thinly disguised allusion to some recent event:

> I saw a stray dog enter the court of the king—old, lean, mangy, and very repulsive to look upon. And then I saw that the king and his knights cried out at it and all the dogs of the court attacked it and drove it from the palace.
>
> All the knights [of a court] know full well that the king loves a knight who approaches him gracefully, and they have knowledge thereof in the king's countenance and in the welcome which he gives to that knight every time that he appears before him.
>
> When an honoured king does honour to a vassal, and clothes him with royal vestments, and gives him a seat in his council, and makes him to share his secrets and admits him to his intimacy and love, then gives he him ever cause and occasion of joy and contentment and pleasure.

The marked strain of penitence which runs right through the ***Book of Contemplation*** is also suggestive of an early date, the more so because it is rather less marked in the later books than in the earlier. "Vile and poor am I," ends the prologue, "both by my nature and by my evil works, wherefore I am not worthy that my name be written in this book nor that the work be attributed to me." "How hast Thou suffered me to remain upon the earth," cries Lull in the fourth chapter, "who have been disobedient to Thee that art so great?" "Thou hast made me to remember," he says elsewhere, "the estate wherein I lived . . . companying with wild beasts and dead in my sins; for my solace and pleasure were with men who were beasts indeed." The greater part of one entire chapter is occupied with similar lamentations. "The more apt I found myself to sin, the more I allowed my nature to obey the dictates of my body." "A fool was I, to waste and squander everything that I have."

These definite and unmistakable allusions to Ramon's youth must be supplemented by scores of others, less personal if considered one by one, but as cumulative evidence of early date quite convincing. There is no other of Lull's works in which he refers to himself so often as "vile and mean," "full of sin and wholly sin," in which he marvels "that so small a body can contain so much evil," confesses that while his friends and relatives trusted him, he worked them nothing but harm, and laments that in time past he has served the flesh and the devil. His was not an unusually introspective nature and during the greater part of his long life he was able to forget the things that were behind in reaching forth to others that were before. If further proof were needed that the ***Book of Contemplation*** was begun soon after the return to Mallorca, it might be found in such passages as these which follow, all from the early chapters of the work, and telling of a mind still under the influence of a violent reaction from sin:

> Many a time have I loved this worldly life, so that I thought it to be life indeed. But now . . . I know that it is no life at all, and never shall I call it so again, but rather a lingering death.
>
> One of those am I who many a time through their faults have lost Thee. Wherefore I say now to my soul that it must never lose Thee more, lest . . . once Thou art lost Thou be never again found.
>
> But what of Thy servant, O Lord, whose life has been so unruly that he has placed his first intention in things vile and mean, and only his second intention in Thee?
>
> Since my beginnings and my youth have been spent in the ways of foolishness and have been given up to the works of sin, I beg Thy favour, O Lord, to grant me wisdom, that in my old age and at my end I may walk ever in wisdom's way.
>
> In the best time of my age, O Lord, I gave myself up wholly to sin . . . but now I would fain give up to Thee both myself and all things that are mine.
>
> Since the nature and property of this world is to torture all those that would find happiness in it, Thy subject and Thy slave, O Lord, renounces the world wholly and will have none of its glory or its happiness.

A few definitely autobiographical references, some of which are quoted elsewhere, confirm these suggestions of early date. The author describes how he has "endeavoured with all his might to learn the Arabic tongue, and to understand the words thereof," and begs God to grant him His grace and blessing, "to the end that soon, by the use of Arabic words, I may be able to . . . show forth the truth concerning Thy Sacred Passion and Holy Trinity." Clearly, when the first draft of this passage was written, Lull's studies had not progressed far, and that he eventually allowed it to stand when translating the book into Catalan probably means that he felt his Arabic still to be far from perfect. Another significant fact is that, fond as Lull always was, in his later works, of mentioning a number of others which he had already written, hardly a single citation or mention of his own works is made in the ***Book of Contemplation,*** which, on the other hand, is itself quoted freely in the ***Book of Doctrine for Boys*** (c. 1275), ***Blanquerna*** (c. 1283), the ***Art of finding truth*** (c. 1287), and elsewhere.

Turning now to consider the ***Book of Contemplation*** as a whole, we are struck at once by its length, which alone, whatever its merits may be, entitles it to a detailed consideration. In the modern Catalan edition, the text, without index, expository note or commentary, occupies seven volumes containing in all not far short of three thousand pages and well nigh a million words. The careful arrangement of the book, as well as the extent and the importance of its content, suggests that the composition was spread over a long period of time. It could surely not have been written in one year, as is asserted by the tradition which no doubt derives from the fact of its having three hundred and sixty-six chapters: indeed, it is much more likely to have occupied its author—between planning, execution and translation—for the greater part of his nine years in Palma. Lull himself is very conscious of its length, and the weightiness of its matter, for he describes himself picturesquely as an ant carrying on its back a burden larger than itself, which, for all its readiness to undertake it, it can hardly bear.

The divisions of the ***Book of Contemplation*** are marked by a typically mediaeval artificiality, not unlike that which disfigures the *Siete Partidas* of Alfonso the Wise. First, there is a chapter for reading on each day of the year, the last chapter (which, according to this system, will be read only in leap years) being divided into four parts, indictive of the nature of the three hundred and sixty-sixth day. The main division of the work is into five books, in remembrance of the five wounds of Jesus Christ on the Cross. A second division is into forty sections or distinctions, signifying the forty days which He spent in the wilderness. The three hundred and sixty-six chapters are divided each into ten paragraphs, in significance of the ten commandments given by God to Moses; each paragraph has three parts, in honour of the Holy Trinity; and the resulting thirty-fold division of every chapter serves to represent the thirty pieces of silver for which Christ was betrayed by Judas. Still farther is the symbolism pressed in the number of distinctions which each book contains: Book I, with nine, represents the nine heavens; Book II, with thirteen, Christ and the twelve Apostles; Book III, with ten, the five physical and the five spiritual senses; Book IV, with six, the six directions [of Christ on the Cross]; and Book V, which has only two, the two intentions [discussed below].

Artificial as these divisions seem to-day, it must be remembered that their symbolism illustrates the "two motives alone" with which the book was written, to praise God and have God's blessing, motives which are emphasized by the fact that in every division of every paragraph God is addressed by name, so that technically the work is one long address to the Deity. Its aim appears to have been to describe as much of God's nature and attributes as it is within the power of human mind to comprehend; to show Him, further, in His dealings with men; and, in a secondary and as it were a reflex sense, to describe man's relations and duties to God. In the fulfilment of this aim, as noble as it was ambitious, is implied the proof, by "necessary reasons" (*raons necessaries*) and incontrovertible argument, of the fourteen articles of the faith.

> He who will perceive (*apercebre*) the fourteen articles by necessary demonstrations, let him read in this ***Book of Contemplation;*** for in various places therein he will find and perceive that all these articles are indeed truth.

And likewise a more general appeal, both to the heart and to the intellect, is intended:

> As this ***Book of Contemplation*** is composed and made up of arguments both diverse and new, the which are set down and arranged so as to give fervour and devotion to men, as well as demonstration of the truth, to the end that they may learn to praise and love and serve Thee: therefore let him who desires his fervour and love and knowledge to grow and increase be a contemplator of this book to the glory and honour of his Lord God.
>
> He who has this book in his rememberance and understanding and love can be wise in things alike of the sense and of the intellect, and can confound and destroy all error in his soul and all evil thoughts and all temptations and all evil habits; and the same can he do in the souls of his neighbours.

A fair idea of the importance which Lull attributed to the ***Book of Contemplation*** may be gained from a study of its final chapter. Several pages are needed to describe its value (*bonea*). It will give joy and counsel and wisdom and consolation and hope. It will prove by "necessary reasons" the Unity and Trinity of God, and which "law" (*i.e.* religion) is the true one: for this reason Lull desires that it may be "given into the hands of faithful men" and "disseminated throughout the world." To those who conscientiously follow its teaching it will impart every virtue; it will develop all their faculties, both of body and mind; it will convert all who have strayed, bring sinners to repentance, and be "a rest from labour and a comfort and consolation to men and women who are orphans and poor." It teaches the distinction between greater good and lesser, between possible and impossible, between truth and falsehood. Nor do these assertions, each of which is developed at some length, exhaust the book's utility. "We have neither place nor time sufficient to recount all the ways wherein this book is good and great."

The ***Book of Contemplation*** is not only an exposition, but an "art" (by which word Lull always means "method"): indeed, it is several times described as "this Art of contemplation." It is meant for use—daily use, as we have seen—"by men learned and men simple, secular and religious, rich and poor." And full directions are given for that use by one who was a thorough believer, from the earliest days of his career until the latest, in the benefits which come from rule and order. To profit by it fully, he says, the reader should first gain from the chapter-headings a general idea of its contents; he may then study the whole book, devoting one day to each chapter for a year, and repeating the process for a second year if he so desire; after this he may study such paragraphs and arguments as appeal to him, seeking them out for the purpose. "Even as a man takes pleasure in finding one fair flower after another, even so may he have pleasure in the contemplation of one fair argument after another."

To give in a few words an idea of the content of this vast encyclopædia is not easy. The first book is of the Divine attributes, each distinction describing one attribute: infinity, eternity, unity, trinity, power, knowledge, goodness and truth. The opening chapter—"Of Joy"—is an arresting prologue to the theme of the treatise and gives an illuminating insight into the means by which the author rises to the height of his great argument. Three things should give us cause to rejoice: the existence of God, the existence of ourselves, and the existence of our neighbour. If a man has delight at the discovery of a precious stone, how much the more should he be glad to discover the Being of an infinite God! If we rejoice to see trees in leaf, flower and fruit, and have delight in river, wood and meadow, the beauties of which are without ourselves, how much the more should we take pleasure in our own being, and in the beauty and goodness which are within us! In giving thanks for life's exceptional and accidental blessings, we should not fail to remember those that are essential to—nay, inherent in—life itself.

These considerations lead naturally enough to the eight distinctions with the exposition of which the whole of the first book is occupied. The second book follows with equal suitability, considering the works of God in His creation of the world, His Providence and His Redemption of fallen man, and His attributes as illustrated by these works. The nature of creation is discussed in general terms before we pass to the creation of the world,—of the first matter of all, of the firmament, of the elements, of metals, of plants, of animals and of the angels. Next we come to the Divine ordinances in man. There is, first, the ordering of his body, with its five physical "powers": the *potencia vegetable,* by which he absorbs nourishment; the *potencia sensitiva,* which is served by the five senses; the imaginative power, corresponding to it in another sphere exactly; the power of reason, served by the "spiritual senses" to be described hereafter; and its complement, a *potencia mutiva,* which translates its mandates into action.

We pass to man's two intentions, the first of which is "to love, honour and serve God, and to know His goodness and nobility," and the second, "to possess those good things which come to him through the merits of the first intention." The principal importance of this division lies of course in the order in which the two intentions are placed. "As Thou hast created this world in regard of the next, and not the next in regard of this, even so hast Thou willed that the second intention in man should be in regard of the first, and not the first in regard of the second." Another chapter describes the position of man "between two motions (*moviments*) . . . , that which moves him to do good and that . . . which moves him to do evil," while still another sets him "between will and power." This leads up to a discussion of man's free will, and his power of choosing between truth and falsehood, good and evil, glory and punishment, a subject to which the author returns later. For the present he leaves it, stressing this point, that from God come all good things and nothing comes from Him that is evil.

Following his general scheme of progression, he next reaches the Incarnation and Passion of Christ,—subjects which, though of such transcendent importance, are treated here very briefly, and give place to the related themes of judgment, Paradise and the life to come. But a return is made almost immediately to the Redemption,—to its theology, that is to say, to the doctrine of original sin, the need for salvation and the sufficiency of the merits of Christ alone. Once again comes a very natural turn of thought. Lull is meditating upon the Person of Our Lord, in Whom is consummated our salvation:

> As the good knight in battle, through his ardour and his chivalry, receives many a blow and many a wound, even so, O Lord, was it needful that Thy Body should receive much torture and tribulation and trial, and be sorely wounded, since it had to bear so great a weight of sin as was Adam's and to set us free therefrom.

This consideration leads him to think of the Divine attributes which that work of redemption illustrates—of the Divine will, first, which brought it to pass, and afterwards of the dominion of God, and of His wisdom, justice, bounty, humility and mercy. Here and there, in the development of these themes, Lull repeats arguments used in his earlier chapters. In the main, however, considering the proportions of the book, we have little repetition to complain of.

The longest chapters in the latter part of Book II are on the Divine justice and humility, and both are distinguished by great variety of treatment, and by their application to the life of Lull's own day of the considerations set forward. In the two chapters which complete this book, the author returns to the future life of the righteous man and to the sources and the nature of his eternal happiness; and finally he sums up the two books of his treatise by a discourse upon the complete perfection (*acabament*) of God. Once more we may draw attention to the ease with which this supreme topic is introduced: the chief source of the eternal bliss of the righteous is the Divine Essence, and that Essence is the master-theme of their praises because it is perfection.

The third book, which is of greater length than the first two combined—and, according to Lull himself, of greater value than either—turns to the theme of man. It is, indeed, for the most part, a study of man, in his physical and spiritual natures, in his greatness and his littleness and in his various estates and callings. The plan which this third book follows is based upon the ten senses, and, at its beginning, for the space of many pages, it is interrupted while a long procession of characters, of every rank and occupation, files past the reader, who is invited to "take note of that which is done" by clerks, kings and princes, knights and pilgrims, judges, advocates and witnesses, physicians, merchants, and many persons besides. The chapters concerned with these characters, though in the nature of a lengthy digression, will, except perhaps to the philosopher and the theologian, be among the most interesting in the entire work.

We are shown a great company of clerics, seculars and religious alike, bishops, priests and deacons, hermits, monks and friars. The prelates are for the most part rich, but "give to the poor for the love of God in times of necessity." The inferior clergy spend much of their lives in study, and, having no family cares like laymen, are able to abstain from worldly trafficking and thoughts of money. Religious—"friars minor, friars preachers and others"—give themselves to prayer, abstinence and mortification; they are often despised by the world, even treated cruelly and unjustly, but, their affections being fixed on the world to come, they can bear such treatment with fortitude. This composite picture of the clergy is an idealistic one indeed, hardly qualified by more than the suggestion that not all clerks are "good clerks." Lull was still in the early years of his experiences of ecclesiastics. He was to write of them very differently as time went on.

There follow in the procession kings and princes, who have already been described; knights, "armed with wood and steel," fortifying castles, consulting omens, ever seeking an occasion to show their prowess; crusaders setting out for the Holy Land against the advice of those that have lost faith in the force of arms; pilgrims, on horseback or on foot, each with staff and scrip, bound for distant shrines and for churches where miracles are worked, some clad poorly and begging their way as they go, others "with sauces and barrels full of wine, with coin of gold and silver for their expenses." No chapter in the book is more vivid than this, which describes how the pilgrims are deceived by "false men whom they meet in hostelries and churches," how they gaze at the pictures, images and sculpture of the churches, find a welcome in monastery or hospice, and, on the "rough and perilous way" to and from their destinations, meet with "many a trial and misfortune by reason both of cold and of heat."

The strain of satire becomes more marked as we pass to the professions of medicine and of law. Judges and advocates alike are too often corrupt or corruptible: "for a small reward they will cause a man to lose many possessions and much money." "When I pass along streets and through public places," declares Lull, "I look for some upright judge or honest advocate. And I see none . . . for almost all are corrupt in their professions." They are flattered by princes and wealthy men, ride on well-fed mules and palfreys, partake of delicate meats, clothe themselves in sumptuous garments and sleep in soft, luxurious beds. The physician is tainted with a similar love of luxury, and is by no means always as cunning in his art as he should be; but for all the ignorance, greed and quarrelsomeness of the worst of his kind, Lull has a deep respect for the profession. In all its members he sees types of the Great Physician, and of the "healers of men's souls" who work at His bidding.

There follow still in the long procession merchants with cloth, hides, beasts, jewels and what not; money-changers in the city; sailors on the ocean; jesters and artists at court; and shepherds and labourers in the fields. We can only stay here to remark that Lull shows both interest in and knowledge of a sailor's life, and goes into it in more detail than into any other calling save that of the *joglar.* Next in the pageant come the *maestrals,* or workers with their hands—those skilled in wood and stone, silver and gold; then scriveners with parchment and ink, writing "letters of buying and selling"; shoemakers preparing, cutting and sewing their leather; tailors making *gramalles* [in a footnote the critic writes, "The *gramalla* was a long garment not unlike a cassock, reaching to the feet, and worn in Catalonia in the Middle Ages by city councillors"], together with coats and breeches, cloaks, capes and mantles; furriers, weavers, butchers, barbers, millers, glaziers, potters, bakers, gardeners, taverners, couriers, criers, waggoners, municipal officers, money-changers, gamesters, archers, calkers, porters, and a few more "offices" given only a passing mention: a notable assembly, both for its size and for the clearness with which, in a few bold strokes, each character is outlined.

The digression was worth making, not only for the information of an enquiring posterity, but also for those who, in studying the ***Book of Contemplation*** when it was written, would be led by it to ask themselves what is required of men in certain professions and what these professions symbolize. When the thread of the argument is taken up again, we find ourselves considering the sense of sight, and then, with a rapidity designed perhaps to atone for so many pages of portraits, the senses of hearing, smell and taste. At the fifth sense a halt is again made, and for many chapters we survey man's physical and moral sensibilities. Heat and cold, hunger and thirst, health and disease and like contraries come first, after which are considered shame, fear, vainglory, sensuality, and six of the seven deadly sins.

By far the longest part of the third book, however, is concerned with man's five faculties, or "spiritual senses," of cogitation, perception, conscience, subtlety and fervour. Under the first head comes a rather miscellaneous collection of subjects which are commonly included in man's cogitations: chief among these are the Divine Essence, the human nature of Jesus Christ, the works of angels and devils, the discordance between faith and reason, the problems of human frailty, the four last things, the nature of the three "virtues" or "faculties" (of memory, understanding and will) and the conflict between sense and intellect. The last topic leads Lull into a discussion of the functions of perception, and its application to natural and supernatural laws, before becoming theological once again, and applying the principles of perception to the attributes of God, to the Trinity, the Incarnation and the Deity of Jesus Christ. After a brief comparison . . . of the Christian, Jewish and Mohammedan faiths, he passes to the domain of ethics and discusses man's capacity for distinguishing between good and evil, truth and falsehood, wisdom and foolishness, perfection and imperfection. Yet even here he returns more than once to theology, discussing the origin of the universe, the resurrection of the dead, and the nature of prayer. The sections of the book which deal with conscience, subtlety (or subjection of sense to spirit) and fervour (*coratgia, frevor*) are very much shorter and more obvious in their argument than those which precede them.

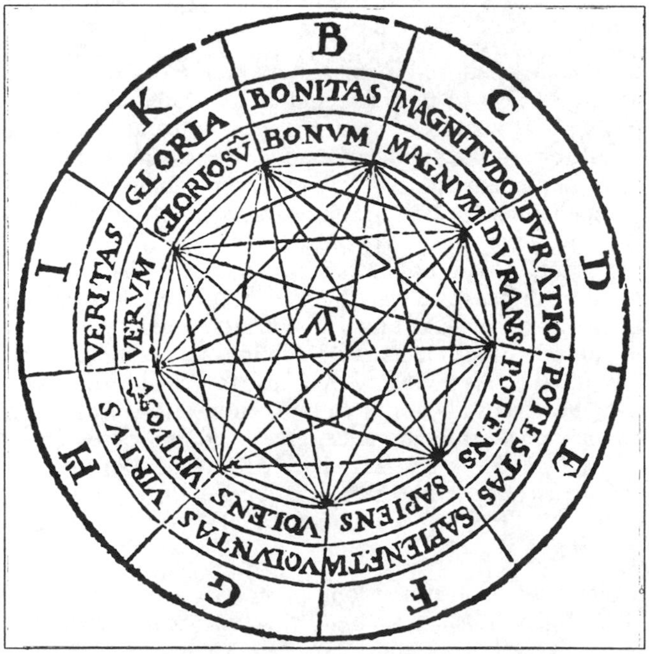

The first of four basic figures of the Art as contained in Llull's Ars brevis *(1617 edition).*

The fourth book is relatively short, and for most readers less easy to understand than the foregoing books, not only because it treats of philosophical and doctrinal subjects, but because it makes use of the device of the tree, which the author of the ***Book of Contemplation*** was to employ frequently. . . . The greatest space in this fourth book is devoted to "proving the articles of the faith," to an exposition of the ten commandments and to a homily on predestination.

Finally, we come to the summit of Lull's achievement in this gigantic work, the two distinctions on love and prayer, which between them make up more than one third of the whole. The forty-six chapters on love are a treatise on the subject in themselves, developed in the careful, logical fashion from which Ramon never for long departs, even though it leads him into hopeless artificialities. The progression of argument in the early chapters of the section illustrates this: the love of God to Himself, the love that is between the Divine and human natures of Christ, the love of Christ's human nature to itself, and the love that is between Christ and the angels. Only when he has speculated upon these lofty themes does the author descend to man, and here again, after considering the love for man of God the Father and God the Son, he pauses to consider the love of the angels for themselves and for man, before taking up the more profitable theme of the love which man must have to God.

Thereafter the plan of the distinction is straightforward and is interrupted very little: the love of man for God, for Jesus Christ, for the lovers of Jesus Christ, for Our Lady, for the virtues, for poverty and riches, for life and death. Some particular manifestations of love are next considered,—the love of prince and people, of parent and child, of oneself, of friends and of enemies—before the distinction ends, rather abruptly, with six chapters leading the reader to speculate upon love in its perfection and imperfection, in the hereafter and in its own consummation.

So beautifully, and with such manifest inspiration, was Ramon to write of love in later days, that the reader who already knows his subsequent works will turn with great expectancy to this fourth section of the ***Book of Contemplation.*** It is to be feared that he will suffer disappointment. There are few purple passages in it, few vivid images—certainly no more here than elsewhere in the book—few chapters which give any sign of eloquence. Lull could write in 1272 that "as the mule is brought to birth by the horse and the she-ass, so is the love of this world brought to birth by the body and the soul." He could find figures that were prosaic as well as apt, more readily than those composed of the stuff of the truest poetry. Here and there he uses the phraseology of *amic* and *amat,* by which he is probably destined to be remembered for more generations and in more countries than we can readily estimate. But he had not yet evolved that magic symbolism which makes the ***Book of the Lover and the Beloved*** so wonderful a collection of meditations. Indeed, the word *amat* in the ***Book of Contemplation*** is comparatively seldom used to indicate the Beloved, Christ. The finest passages of this fourth section of the work are probably those (to be described hereafter) on the theme of love for one's neighbour, as exemplified in the evangelization of the heathen.

The final section, of fifty-two chapters, on prayer, introduces so often the phrase "to adore and contemplate" that we may ask at this point the pertinent question: What meaning attaches, in this book, to the word "contemplation"? The comparison of any considerable number of passages in which it occurs will show that the meaning is a very wide one, and, while in most of these passages it will be synonymous with "meditation," or even with "consideration," "thought" or "study," there are a few in which it must perforce be applied to a more definitely mystical process, while in still more it bears its ancient technical meaning of the entire range of the life of mental prayer. So great is the field which the book covers that its title can be interpreted only in the very widest sense. In such frequent phrases as "prayer and contemplation," "to adore and contemplate," the meaning is wide and indeterminate, including probably both the higher and the lower processes of mental prayer, and, as the context often shows, being susceptible of more than one interpretation.

The section on prayer begins by dividing prayer into three parts or "figures":

> The first of these is prayer of the senses (*oració sensual*), wherein man calls upon Thee, O Lord, and speaks to Thee, adoring Thy virtues and honours, and begging of Thee grace, pardon and blessing. The second is prayer of the intellect (*oració entellectual*) wherein man has remembrance, understanding and love of Thee in his prayer, and contemplates Thee, having his remembrance, understanding and will directed towards Thy honours and Thy virtues. The third is that wherein man does good works, and uses justice and mercy and truth and the remaining virtues. . . . For whensoever he does this, then does he adore Thee and pray to Thee and call upon Thee (even if at such a time he have not remembrance and understanding of Thee) in remembering, understanding and willing some other thing after a righteous and virtuous manner.

Each of these "figures" (all of which, of course, are within the Catholic tradition) is applied in the chapters following, which present as matters for "adoration and contemplation" the Unity of God, the Blessed Trinity, God's Essence, infinity, eternity, power, wisdom, love and other attributes. A single chapter presents in a similar way Christ's human nature, after which are considered God's gifts to man. He aids him to do good and to fight against evil, gives him discernment between good and evil, grants him his soul's desires, promises him Paradise, aids him to bewail his shortcomings, forgives him his sins, inspires him to convert others, gives him the grace of continence and is ever his consolation. For all these gifts man must pray to God when he adores and contemplates Him. So far the distinction on prayer is easy enough to follow, apart from the free use of algebraical symbols to avoid repetition of words and phrases, a process both unfamiliar and disconcerting to the ordinary reader. The succeeding chapters return to artificiality, of a typically mediaeval kind, when they recommend the practice of "intellectual adoration and contemplation by means of etymology, allegory and anagogy"; it seems that this excursion into the fantastic is a result of Lull's reading in Arabic, his aim being to improve upon Oriental methods of devotion in the interests of Christianity. Unfortunately, he is very seldom happy in his attempts at adapting these methods.

In the concluding chapters of the book he is seen to better advantage. The chapter which shows "how good a thing is ordered contemplation and prayer" returns to first principles, if at a somewhat late stage in the treatise, and the remaining chapters, the number or length of which might—with advantage—have been increased at the expense of certain others, describe some of the fruits of prayer: they show, for example, how it gives man knowledge whether or no his soul is pure and clean, and whether the works which he performs are of truth or of falsehood. The three hundred and sixty-fifth chapter describes the more direct blessings which the contemplative soul receives, and the final (or complementary) chapter deals with the use of the book as a whole. (pp. 45-64)

Both with regard to style and to argument, the ***Book of Contemplation*** shows a maturity unusual in the first work of an unpractised writer. Lull has no *juvenilia:* indeed, he is rather disappointingly mature. In so far as his argument is concerned, this is not surprising. When a man of over thirty has been suddenly converted from a life of luxury and vice to one of self-denial and devotion, his ideas and habits are, not unnaturally, within ten years from his conversion, fixed and set. We find, in effect, precisely the same strictures in this book upon kings who refuse access to their subjects, *joglars* who sing lewd songs and women who paint their faces and dress extravagantly, as we find in books written ten, twenty and even thirty years later.

The very phrasing is in some places almost identical. It is more surprising to find how great a proportion of what is of permanent value in Ramon's thought is contained in the ***Book of Contemplation.*** The command of theology and philosophy, in one who had started, a few years before, from zero, and had, in that same period, mastered Arabic (to say nothing of other subjects) to the point of being able to write a book of a million words in it is as astonishing as the logical progression shown in a first work of that length, the rapid development of important these, the mastery of the author over his task—including the control of his digressions—from its beginning to its end. Ramon was to add to his knowledge,—principally in the natural sciences, and less markedly in comparative religion—and to incorporate his acquisitions in later books. But what he added in the course of forty or more years seems of small account in comparison with the broad and solid foundation that he laid in ten.

Most surprising of all in the ***Book of Contemplation*** is the maturity of Lull's style. This is for the most part clear and easy, seldom for long involved and never incomprehensible. Repetitions of phrase there are many: the worst fault of the book, indeed, is a frequent verbal heaviness, which might generally without much difficulty have been avoided. The use made of simile and metaphor, though it varies in extent, is, on the whole, considerable. Tracts of argument there are, indeed, unlighted by a single image, perhaps even by a single vivid phrase. But, on the other hand, many pages, especially in the distinction upon love, lend themselves readily to visualization. It is true that a number of the images most frequently called up are conventional (though not necessarily conventionally treated). A fair proportion come from the Gospels: the tree and its fruit, the shepherd and his flock, the winnowing of the wheat, the secret growth of a seed, and a number more. Others are familiar in all allegorical writing: the vessel filled with liquid, the river flowing into the sea, the relations between kings, knights and common people, the force of the sun's rays, the light of the sun compared with other lights. A few are ominously mathematical and deal with angles, triangles and circles. An interesting group of images, collected from various parts of the book, shows that Ramon was paying some attention to natural science. Such are the figures of the "stone seeking its centre," so finely used by St. Augustine, the testing of metals, the balance, the magnet, the mariner's compass, and—a simile queerly applied—the chemical composition of ink.

Most of these images occur too frequently for the places of their occurrence to be here specified, but there are two which are far more common than any others, and give the impression of being used as often as the rest put together. One of these, familiar to all readers of the mystics, is that of fire, under very many of its principal aspects, such as its qualities and appearance, its action on wood and other materials, and its comparison and reactions with water. The second is the image of the mirror, inspired in the first place, conceivably, by St. Paul and St. James, but also, in all probability, by Lull's own conception . . . of the crucifix as the mirror of his soul.

> Ah, Jesus Christ my Lord! Praised be Thou and blessed be all that is Thine; for Thou hast set before our bodily eyes the mirror of the holy Cross, that it may be a mirror to our souls, which shall be moved thereby to meditate upon the grievous trials and the painful death which were suffered and sustained by Thy righteous Human Nature.

In the main, Lull's use of figures is apt. He scarcely ever, as in his later books, relates "examples" or parables, and his similes are usually brief. Here and there, indeed, they are weak, as when God's knowledge and ours are compared to oil and the water on which it floats, or when Christ's persecution by the Jews between His trial and His death is likened to "the blowing of the leaves of a tree by the wind whithersoever it lists." But more commonly they are applied at least adequately, and not a few of them are easily recalled to the memory. That of the author, for example, comparing himself, in the prologue to his enormous work, with "a mariner who is lost in the ocean, and has hope, O Lord, in Thee that Thou wilt draw him therefrom with joy." The lightning, flashing in all directions, and searching vainly for an infinite God. The rays of the sun, lighting up a dark and muddy path, yet receiving no contamination from it. The child with his tame bird, which he loves so much that he squeezes it with his caresses almost to death. The man who goes to sleep and dreams that he is clothed in white or in crimson, only to awaken and find himself naked. These few examples are sufficient to show that Lull had already learned much that was to stand him in good stead as a writer.

If we compare this estimate of Lull's style with what is said . . . of the books of his late middle age and decline, we shall discover that there is little to find fault with in these that is not already present in the ***Book of Contemplation.*** Its *longueurs,* its heaviness, its repetitions never entirely disappear. Its good things, of course, become better, but not so much better as we might reasonably expect.

It is the magnitude and the variety of the ***Book of Contemplation,*** rather than its style, that have caused Catalan writers to surpass one another in eulogy of it, and even to lose themselves in hyperbole. To the old Lullists it was the "Contemplador major," and it is somewhat in this spirit that modern Lullists have regarded it also. It is the "obra màxima lulliana," for example, to En Mateu Obrador: "l'obra capdal, verament magna, de Ramón Lull." Dr. Torras i Bages, in a work too little known, describes it as "the masterpiece of the Beatus and the greatest work in the whole of Catalan literature,"—a bold claim indeed. Menéndez y Pelayo, the great Castilian scholar, is no less impressed by its magnitude, but realizes that magnitude does not always imply greatness. To him the work is an "enorme enciclopedia ascética."

For ourselves we incline for once to the Castilian point of view rather than to that of Ramon's own countrymen. Clearly, the ***Book of Contemplation*** is the eldest brother of all Lull's other works, and from the very beginning of his career sets a definitive seal upon his genius. Were twentieth-century methods, arguments and conceptions those of the Middle Ages, it is possible that we might think of it as the first Lullists did, or Joan Bonlabi in the sixteenth century, or even Obrador and his contemporaries,—as resembling, that is to say, in the firmament of Lull's many works, "the sun among the stars." As it is, much of it has been outgrown by modern thought, and even apart from this it contains too little of what is destined to be immortal in the writings of Ramon the Lover. Let us think of some of the elements that are absent from it. Excepting only the rigidly allegorical stories of the three damsels and the hermit, near the end of Book V, it is entirely lacking in that narrative element which diversified so many of Lull's later polemical books and gave Catalonia and Europe one masterpiece of early fiction. It is almost entirely without poetry: that lovely flower which in the later works can be plucked so freely has hardly begun to bud in this. It has little eloquence or passion—and we are to find much of both in Lull before long. It is quite devoid of humour—yet even that is not absent from Lull's temperament, though we could hardly expect it to reach its full flowering here. All these great gaps were soon to be filled, most of them very worthily: it seems unwise to heap excessive praise upon a work which is so shortly to be followed by others no less remarkable.

Yet Dr. Torras i Bages did well to focus his readers' attention upon it, reminding them, at the time when he first wrote, that it was preserved in no accessible Catalan edition. "He who knows not the ***Book of Contemplation*** knows not the Beat Ramon Lull" was his bold assertion, and, unlike some such claims, it is a true one. Though there are other of Ramon's works which throw upon their author a light more revealing, this book is undoubtedly an illuminating commentary alike upon his life and his temperament, upon his erudition and his literary art. Further, its sheer length, its extreme variety, its comparative equality, its mastery both of subject and expression combine to make it a wonderful achievement. It may not in literal truth "comprehend well-nigh all the knowledge of its epoch," but it is certainly "an immense canvas whereon is depicted the marvellous harmony of the relations between existence create and increate, of nature finite and infinite, of Divine attributes and human faculties, of the hierarchies of heaven and the estates of men in the world, of society civil and religious, of spirit and matter, . . . a brilliant panorama of the universe seen through the glass of luminous contemplation." Bold, indeed, is the comparison of it with the *Divine Comedy,* and, on the merits of the two works, unjustified, but at least there are analogies between the two upon different planes. Let us sum up the qualities of the ***Book of Contemplation*** in the words of another Catalan writer—a poet who can bring to the study of it much that the work itself lacks, and who is overawed less by its length than by its amazing diversity:

> It is a work as full of illumination as of effort, of loftiness and of humility, of ascent and descent alike. It is not a work that climbs upward by slow degrees, but rather a living staircase, with angels ascending and descending upon it. It is no spiritual ladder, like the work of St. John Climacus . . . but a succession of swift and powerful flights like those of the marine eagle that can so often be seen at Miramar, now soaring upward towards the dazzling sun, now, as it were, falling—so swift is its descent—into the ocean. . . . Even so, ever and anon, does Ramon mount up with wings to the ineffable heights, then downward sweeps to the depths of his own heart,—nay, to his own mind which has been dwelling in a vale of darkness.
>
> [Riber in his *Vida i actes*].

"A work of gladness and boldness" it is, in short, "a mingling of fervour and fear," a *gran contemplador,* as it was well named long ago after its author, for it is the work of a "great contemplator" indeed. (pp. 76-81)

E. Allison Peers, in his Ramon Lull: A Biography, *Society for Promoting Christian Knowledge, 1929, 454 p.*

Frances A. Yates (essay date 1954)

[*Yates was an English educator and critic best known for her studies of Renaissance literature and philosophy. In the following excerpt, originally published in 1954, she examines several of Llull's works, exploring the astrological and cosmological bases of his philosophy.*]

Lull was one of the most prolific authors who ever lived. Only a small proportion of his work is generally known, and much of it is still unpublished. The ***Tractatus de astronomia*** is only one of the unpublished works which have a bearing on his attitude to astrology, and on astrology in the Art. There are numerous others of equal, perhaps even greater, importance from this point of view. There are others again, of vital importance for this line of inquiry, which have been printed—but in editions now so rare that they might just as well be unpublished and are, in fact, more accessible in manuscript form. (p. 30)

The early Lullists were not so ignorant of these writings as we are, for they worked from manuscripts of which there are still vast numbers and there must have been still more in earlier times. Lull wished the knowledge of his Art to be disseminated as widely as possible and very numberous copies were made of the works connected with it.

Apart from all this buried treasure, there is the corpus of Lull's writings which is accessible in print but which has never been examined for traces of the interests and outlook now revealed to us by the ***Tractatus de astronomia.*** People have searched the printed works for Lull's views on alchemy; but not (so far as I know) for his elemental theory. In the following pages we shall glance at some of the printed works to see what we can find. The survey will be far from complete. I have not read all of Lull's printed works, and those which I use here, and from which I quote, could be made to yield far more than I have drawn from them.

The *Liber Contemplationis in Deum*

This stupendously long work was one of Lull's earliest productions, and was written about 1272. Said to have been first written in Arabic, it exists in both Latin and Catalan versions. It is an encyclopedia covering the whole craation—both macrocosm and microcosm, both the world of nature and the world of man—and expounding the ways of God in the Creation and Redemption of the world. Written throughout in a vein of extreme mystical fervour, it shows Lull moving towards the vision in which the Art was revealed. Salzinger [in his 'Revelatio'] says that he first understood the 'secret' of the Art in the long and very extraordinary allegories in the fifth book, which he interpreted (rightly or wrongly) in terms of the Art. We shall not attempt to follow Salzinger into those mysteries, but it is certainly true that the materials of the Art are present in this work.

The first book of the ***Liber contemplationis*** is on Divine Attributes, of which it discusses eight, namely Infinity, Eternity, Unity, Trinity, Power, Knowledge, Goodness, Truth. . . . (pp. 30-1)

The second book is on the created universe as divine revelation, ending with man. The third book continues on man, in all his aspects, including man in society, and on ethics. The fourth is philosophical and theological and aims at proving the articles of the faith. The fifth is on love and prayer, and contains the allegories which Salzinger thought so important.

The material for which we are looking is in the second book which, in going through the created world as the revelation of the attributes of God, deals with angels, with the heaven or firmament in which are the signs and planets, with the elements through which the influence of the heaven comes into all created things, with the animal and vegetable worlds, with metals (on which there is a long section), and with man—the last subject being continued in the next book. As will be seen, Lull is working through what will later be the 'subjects' of the Art, *Deus, Angelus, Coelum, Homo,* and so on.

It is repeatedly stated that the elements of which all terrestrial substances are composed depend on the heaven.

> Thine is the work of great artifice and order, that Thou willest that there should be in the firmament signs and planets through which the elemental bodies existing among us may be regulated and ordered.

And

> Thou willest, O God, that the bodies of the firmament should have dominion over and action on the *elementata.*

And the intense preoccupation with the movements and behaviour of the celestially ordered elements—the interest which was to be one of the mainsprings of his thought and Art—is already prominent in this early work in which he contemplates the ordered distribution and movements of the elements and the

> concatenation and ligature . . . through which fire is hot in itself and dry through earth; air is moist in itself and hot through fire; water is cold in itself and moist through air; earth is dry in itself and cold through water.

Here is the emphasis on the distinction between the 'proper' and 'appropriated' qualities in the elements which was to play such a part in his system of doing astrology.

Though the ***Liber contemplationis*** follows a mystical trend which is common to all religious tradition in its contemplation of the revelation of the divine in the patterns of the universe, we can see already present in it the peculiarities of Ramon Lull who was not only a mystic but a mystic who sought to demonstrate scientifically the object of his love. In the ***Liber contemplationis,*** the 'artista' is feeling after his Art.

The *Doctrina Pueril*

It is said to have been during Lull's retirement on Mount Randa in 1274 that the Art was fully revealed to him by God in a vision, and it was after this that the ***Ars generalis*** or ***Ars magna*** took shape. Not long after the vision, he visited Prince James of Mallorca at Montpellier and probably there composed two works, the ***Libre del orde de cavalleria*** and the ***Doctrina pueril.***

The ***Doctrina pueril*** belongs to the pedagogic class of Lull's works, and is a book of general knowledge for the young which he dedicated to his son. This compact little encyclopedia, written after the full revelation of the Art, should be read by all students of the Art.

A chapter in the work treats of the arts of geometry (which is introduced with a reference to the astrolabe), arithmetic, music and astronomy. Of astronomy, Lull says:

> Astronomy is a demonstrative science through which man has knowledge that the celestial bodies have dominion over and operate upon the terrestrial bodies, and it shows that the virtue which is in the celestial bodies comes from God who is sovereign over the heavens and over all that is.
>
> You must know, my son, that this is a science which belongs to the 12 signs and the 7 planets, according to whether these concord or contrast in heat, dryness, cold, and moisture; for it is according to this that they have operation on terrestrial bodies. . . .
>
> Gentle son, I counsel thee not to learn this art, for it is of great difficulty and one may err in it; and it is dangerous, for the men who understand it best use it ill, for the sake of the power of the celestial bodies ignoring and despising the power and the goodness of God.

We have here, digested into a few sentences, a simplified form of the doctrine of the ***Tractatus de astronomia,*** including the warning of its preface against erroneous astronomy. To do this science through the concords and contrasts of the elemental qualities would be to do astrology by the ABCD method [the critic has noted that "Lull lays down the 'alphabet' of his art by assigning A, B, C, or D to each planet according to its elemental 'complexio' "]. And we note too that *bonitas, potestas, virtus,* come into the discussion of the power of the stars.

There is a great deal more on Lull's elemental theory in the ***Doctrina pueril,*** in the chapter on medicine (which gives in a simplified form the theory of 'grading' expounded in the medical works), in the chapter on the 'science of nature', and in that on 'the four elements'. The importance which Lull attached to elemental theory is shown by the large amount of space given to it in this highly compressed pietistic and ethical handbook.

Felix or the *Libre De Meravelles*

About ten years later, Lull wrote an encyclopedia for adults, the ***Libre de meravelles,*** which imparts the Lullian world of knowledge, and the Lullian outlook, in the pleasing form of a story about the instructive adventures of a young man called Felix. More is revealed in this work than was suitable for the young readers of the ***Doctrina pueril*** to know.

The prologue to the work (which again can only be consulted in printed texts in Catalan) invokes the *bonitas, magnitudo, eternitas, potestas, sapientia,* and *voluntas* (to translate the Catalan words into terminology more familiar to us) of God and states that it will treat of God, Angels, the Heaven, the Elements, Plants, Metals, Beasts, Man, Paradise, and Hell. The work does in fact follow this plan, in which we may recognize variations on the *Deus, Angelus, Coelum,* etc., of the Art.

At the opening of the story, Felix is a prey to religious doubt owing to the sad fate of a fair shepherdess in whom he was interested. But a holy hermit proves to him the existence of God by various arguments, one of which involves taking a stick and drawing a circle round Felix which represents 'the firmament'. The Trinity is proved by arguments which seem to recall St Augustine's *De Trinitate* and which also use the 'dignitates' or divine attributes *bonitas, aeternitas* and so on (the concepts used are not quite the same as in the Art). And in the chapter on the Virgin Mary, it is stated as an analogy (or is it more than that?) to her immaculacy that 'in every body composed of the four elements, one element enters into another element without either of them corrupting the other'.

After the first book on *Deus,* comes a short book on *Angelus,* and with the third book we reach the subject *Coelum* ['the Heavens']. 'Bel ami,' inquires Felix of a shepherd, 'how is it that the stars which are in the firmament, and the planets, are influent on the four elements, and on that which is composed of the elements?' He is told, amongst other things, that 'by participation of the essence of the celestial bodies in the terrestrial comes the influence of which you ask.' Felix next asks whether in the twelve signs and the seven planets there are heat, moisture, cold and dryness. The shepherd replies that astronomers have appropriated the four qualities among the twelve signs and the seven planets because it is through their influence that these are stronger at one time than at another in terrestrial things.

In answer to the question as to whether fate or the stars are 'necessary', the shepherd says that God has power to alter the influences of the constellations according to whether he wishes to judge or to pardon men.

In short, the attitude to the stars here again seems to be that of the ***Tractatus,*** with its denial of necessity and its emphasis on the elements. When at the beginning of the next book on 'The Elements' we find a king having his elder son taught natural science because the knowledge of this is more useful for the art of government than that of arms we feel inclined to suppose that this 'natural science' may have included the improved method of doing astrology through the elements which the preface of the ***Tractatus*** advises for princes and magistrates.

The instruction on the elements in this book takes the form of a long lecture given by a philosopher to the king's son and his suite, which Felix attends. The king's son compares the elemental process with those by which justice engenders charity in a sinful man. And he further seems to compare correspondencies and contrasts amongst virtues and vices with those amongst the elements. And then he goes on to compare the engendering of the Son by the Father, with the giving by God of virtue to the elements that they may engender their like.

The transitions from elemental theory to law and ethics, and to theology—which seem to the king's son to arise so obviously from the philosopher's lecture on the elements—occur again and again in the books which follow on plants, metals, beasts, and man. In these books, Felix is being led to contemplate the *bonitas, magnitudo, virtus* and other attributes of God as revealed in different forms on the steps of the ladder of creation. In every book, pages and pages are devoted to elaborate expositions of elemental theory working in plants, metals, beasts, and man. And in every book, the elemental theory leads immediately to theological analogies, often accompanied by lamentations that these things are not demonstrated more clearly to the Saracens so that they may thereby be converted to the Catholic faith. Moreover we are told again and again that all this is fully worked out in the ***Ars demonstrativa.***

As one reads the pleasing tale of the adventures of Felix, which are set in a fascinating world in which Christian hermits, philosophers, abbots, knights and jongleurs, rub shoulders with Saracens, Jews, and other infidels, one realizes with increasing astonishment the utter precision of its plan. Felix is being conducted through the 'subjects' of the Art, and being taught to see on every step of the ladder of creation the *bonitas, magnitudo, virtus,* etc., of God as revealed in the working of the elements on all the steps. And this revelation demonstrates to him the truth of the Incarnation and the Trinity.

In the book on 'Plants', Felix wanders through a wood in which he meets a philosopher who is seated under the trees reading a book beside a beautiful fountain. This philosopher has retired into the wood in order that through plants and trees he may contemplate, understand, and love their Creator. The philosopher tells him of a hermit who lives in the wood, 'looking at what nature does in trees and herbs', so that through that work he may contemplate God 'according to the art of philosophy and theology', which art is ordered 'according to the order of the ***Ars demonstrativa'.***

Sitting under the tree, the philosopher contemplates in it

the *bonitas* and *magnitudo* of God (la granea e la bonesa de Deu). Felix asks how so great a tree can have come from a small seed. In reply he is told a story about a fire lighted by a peasant which grew great because the *virtus* of the fire was able to convert to itself things containing less *virtus.* Felix then asks a question about the *virtus* of Jesus Christ which was greater than that of men. The philosopher warmly compliments him on his intelligence in having asked this question (in relation to the problems of *virtus* in fire and in the tree) and tells him of a man who has an ***Ars demonstrativa*** for showing the truth to those in error, but to whom no one will listen.

The philosopher spoke long to Felix about 'the generation of plants and how they signify that there is generation in God through which God the Father engendered God the Son without corruption'. This subject develops later into a story which the philosopher tells to Felix about a 'wise Saracen' who was disputing with a 'wise Christian'. The Saracen asked the Christian a question about the generation of the Son from the Father. The Christian in his reply said that generation in God is 'nobler' than that in trees, and went on from that to demonstrate the infinity, eternity, and incorruptible perfection of the Trinity.

Leaving the wood, the philosopher and Felix come to a beautiful plain in which are growing many medicinal herbs having great *virtus,* given to them, so the philosopher explains, to signify the *virtus* of God. The philosopher imparts to Felix in this chapter information, interspersed with illustrative stories, about the precise virtues of medicinal herbs in accordance with their elemental *complexio.* For example, rhubarb is *calidus* and *siccus* (calt e sech) and the reason why it is good for fevers is because the hot and dry of fever has concordance with it and so adheres to it and so goes out of the patient's system with the rhubarb when the patient is purged. This leads on to an astonishing story about how a heretic became convinced of the superior *virtus* of the Christian faith, to the demonstration of *virtus* in the Three Persons of the Trinity, and to a discussion of the 'vegetative nature' in Christ in connexion with the homage paid to him by plants on Palm Sunday.

There is much more of the same kind of thing in the book on metals. This book, by the way, contains a chapter on alchemy in which Lull states his disbelief in the possibility of the transmutation of metals and seems to be 'against' alchemy. Together with the misreading of the preface to the ***Tractatus de astronomia*** as 'against' astrology, this passage has done much to throw people off the scent as to the true nature of the Lullian system. There is less direct reference to elemental theory in the book on beasts which consists mainly of a long and interesting allegory. The book on man is full of the elements in relation to man, leading off all the time into theological analogies.

A very large part of the book on man is taken up with virtues and vices—each virtue paired with an opposite vice, as in the 'Alphabet' of the Art, though more virtue-vice pairs are given here than in the ***Ars brevis*** alphabet. Many of the virtues and vices given in the extended list in the ***Libre de meravelles*** also appear in some of the diagrams of the Art to which such constant reference is made in the course of Felix's adventures—namely the ***Ars demonstrativa.*** (pp. 31-7)

The last two books of the ***Libre de meravelles*** are on Paradise and Hell. In the former we read of the divine *dignitates* of *bonitas, magnitudo* and so on in the angelic world, and in the latter the fiery torments of the damned are interpreted as a hellish reversal of the true elemental processes.

The adventures of Felix are highly instructive to the student of the Lullian Art, and there can be little doubt that the work was intended to popularize the Art and to present its principles in a simplified and pleasing form. It showed the fundamental importance of the influence of the heaven on the elements, and of the study of the elements in all terrestrial substances, in plants, in metals, in animals, in man. It showed how this study revealed the presence of the divine *bonitas, magnitudo, virtus* and so on present on all the steps of the ladder of creation. And it showed how by analogy from the divine-elemental workings one could perceive the workings of virtue and vice in ethics and law, and—most important of all—could demonstrate to the Saracens and all unbelievers in an infallible manner the divine workings in the Trinity and the Incarnation.

It shows to us the crucial role of the Lullian elemental theory for the whole of the Lullian Art. It was amongst the trees and the plants that the hermit was working out the ***Ars demonstrativa,*** the art of 'philosophy and theology' through which truth could be demonstrated. The workings of the medicinal herbs demonstrated the workings of Faith. Felix's adventures among the plants should send us back to look at the 'Tree of Medicine', where BCDEFGHIK are seen working together with ABCD to form an Art by which 'metaphorically' we may understand Law and Theology. And, as we know from the ***Tractatus de astronomia,*** the arts of medicine and of law were done by 'astronomy'.

Some of the diagrams in early manuscripts of the ***Ars demonstrativa*** make very clear the basis of that Art in elemental theory. . . . [A page of ***Ars demonstrativa*** diagrams from a manuscript in Paris which may be contemporary with Lull] shows the wheels of 'Theologia', 'Philosophia', and 'Ius' in close relation to the wheels of the 'Elementa'. The curious thought-transitions of the characters whom we meet in the ***Libre de meravelles*** are due to their thorough training in the Art.

Blanquerna

The story of Felix connects with the romance of ***Evast and Blanquerna*** (written at Montpellier between 1283 and 1285). Blanquerna retired into a forest to contemplate, emerged from thence as a great teacher, and eventually became Pope. In this book, as in the adventures of Felix, there are constant references to the Art.

Blanquerna's early education is significant. He learned grammar, logic, rhetoric, natural philosophy, medicine, and theology. And he learned medicine out of Lull's own **Book of the Principles and Grades of Medicine** (that is the ***Liber principiorum medicinae***), from which it follows that he must also have studied the ***Tractatus de astronomia,*** or the teaching contained in that book, without which the medical theory cannot be understood. After studying the book on medicine he proceeded with great facility to the study of theology.

On emerging from the forest, Blanquerna became instructor to the monks in a monastery, expounding to them 'by the natural arguments of philosophy how the creatures give knowledge of the Creator and his works', and through his teaching the monks increased greatly in virtue. Blanquerna promised them that they would be able to learn in a year the 'art' of the four general and most necessary sciences which are theology, natural philosophy, medicine, and law. It is clear that the monks were taught the Lullian Art of medicine with its 'metaphorical' connexions with law and ethics, with philosophy and theology.

When Blanquerna became Pope he did what Lull so often urged in vain on real Popes, he encouraged the teaching of the Lullian Art. At the request of an 'artista', the teaching of theology, natural philosophy, medicine and law was reformed and taught by the methods of the Art. The 'natural philosophy' which was thus reformed must have been, I would suggest, the science of 'elemental astrology' with its close connexions with medicine, and thence 'metaphorically' with law and with theology.

In ***Blanquerna*** there are long sections devoted—as in the story of Felix—to the pairing and contrasting of virtues and vices. When Blanquerna became Pope, a teacher was appointed whose office it was 'to show by means of nature (per natura) how man could mortify within himself the vices, and strengthen the virtues'. This teacher no doubt knew how to use the 'elemental' diagrams of the Art as analogous to the 'virtue-vice' diagrams.

The visions of the hermits of ***Felix*** and ***Blanquerna*** under the trees are all repetitions of Lull's own vision. [An] artist who depicts this shows Lull as a hermit under two trees, who develops, like the hermits of the romances, into the teacher of the Art.

The tree—as well as its other meanings [In a footnote the critic writes, "its primary meaning is, of course, that of the Cross"]—had, I believe, for Lull the meaning of representing the working of the elements in nature, particularly in the vegetable world so essential for the art of medicine; and this was the fundamental 'exemplum' upon which he based his Art. . . .

The *Libre Del Orde De Cavalleria*

In the ***Book of the Order of Chivalry,*** an old knight has retired from the world to become a hermit in a wood, meditating every day under a tree well covered with fruit near a clear fountain. Here a squire comes upon him, whom he instructs in the virtues and in the rules of chivalry, presenting him with a book on that subject.

This work contains the usual virtue-vice pairs, which we know from ***Felix*** and ***Blanquerna*** (though the ***Order of Chivalry*** is earlier than both those works, having been written at about the same time as the ***Doctrina pueril***). Its world is that same world of forests, knights, clerics, in which we have become accustomed to look for allusions to the Art. And there can be no doubt, I think, that the book of the rules of chivalry, based on the knight's duty to defeat (or 'devict') vices by virtues, is a branch of the Art for the use of knights.

From ***Blanquerna,*** it would appear that it was a part of Lull's missionary and crusading plans that the knights who went on the crusade should be instructed in the Art, so that they should be able to convince the infidels either by arms or by arguments, or both. Pope Blanquerna advises the 'Masters of the Temple and of the Hospital' (that is, of course, the leaders of the two great crusading orders) that they should arrange schools 'wherein their knights should learn certain brief arguments, by means of the ***Brief Art of finding Truth,*** that they might prove the articles of the Holy Faith' and so maintain it 'by feats of arms or by learning'. It is fitting therefore that the 'hermit under the trees' should appear in the ***Book of the Order of Chivalry*** as the instructor of knights. Like the other hermits, he no doubt taught how to deduce, not only ethics and law, but also philosophy and theology from the book of nature, or of the creatures, of which the tree was the example. One of the Karlsruhe miniatures illustrating the life and work of Lull shows the 'principles' of the Art attired as knights, and going forth to devict infidelity and error.

First written in Catalan, the ***Book of the Order of Chivalry*** became a standard text-book for the rules of chivalry. It was widely disseminated in beautiful French manuscripts and early printed in various languages. In the English translation by William Caxton, it was popular and may have been known to the poet Spenser. Its opening words state that as God rules over the seven planets which have power over terrestrial bodies, so ought kings and princes to have lordship over knights. Therefore

> To signify the seven planets, which are celestial bodies and govern and order terrestrial bodies, we divide this Book of Chivalry into seven parts.

The *Liber De Ascensu Et Descensu Intellectus*

The ***Book of the Ascent and Descent of the Mind*** was written about 1305. The first printed edition is illustrated by a helpful woodcut, which shows the ladder of ascent and descent—the steps of which are labelled Lapis, Flamma, Planta, Brutum, Homo, Coelum, Angelus, Deus. The plan of the book follows this scheme, which is roughly that of the 'subjects' of the Art; and the prologue states that the method followed will be that of the ***Ars generalis,*** which shows how to ascend from inferior to superior things, and vice versa.

We shall not begin, as the book does, at the bottom of the ladder, but take a flying leap to the step *coelum.*

Here we find, under the 'action of the heaven' the list of the twelve signs and the seven planets, with a short account of their characteristics, and in each case is noted the elemental affinity. It is like the list of the 'old principles' in the ***Tractatus de astronomia,*** though much less full on the characteristics of the signs and planets. And though the list seems meant primarily to draw attention to the elemental affiliation of each sign and planet, it does not assign to them the ABCD elemental notation, as in the ***Tractatus.***

Under the 'nature of the heaven' are listed the eighteen principles—*bonitas, magnitudo* and so on (i.e., the meanings of B to K as *absoluta* and *relata* in the alphabet of the Art) with the exception of *contrarietas* which, of course, is not substantially in the heaven but only *per accidens.* Also *sapientia* becomes *instinctus,* and *voluntas* becomes *appetitus* as in the ***Tractatus.*** In each case it is stated that these 'principles' are the true causes of things here below. For example, the *bonitas* of heaven causes the inferior *bonitates,* as the *bonitas* of a stone, a plant, a lion, or of the body of a man.

In short, what we have here is an abbreviation of the ***Tractatus de astronomia,*** with its list of the signs and planets as the 'old principles' of astronomy, followed by the 'principles' of *bonitas* and so on which are the true influence of the heaven.

We may now start at the bottom of the ladder and give some quotations from the various steps of the ascent to see how this works out.

In the discussion of 'stones' on the first step, Lull gives examples of the characteristics of various stones. For example, the stone jasper has the power of stanching the flow of blood from wounds. The intellect 'descends' to inquire into this operation of the stone jasper, and considers that 'the super-celestial bodies are naturally the first cause of this . . . as Saturn which is *siccus et frigidus* and causes the dry and cold of jasper through which it has the power of stanching blood.'

Then the intellect doubts, and inquires further what can be the medium between jasper and Saturn which is outside the *genus* of coldness and dryness. And then the intellect 'believes that the medium is the natural *bonitas* of jasper and Saturn, and their *magnitudo* and so on; and the reason why it believes this and does not know it is because it does not have experience of this through sense.'

We can easily recognize this as a rather more cautious form of the theory of the ***Tractatus*** through which *bonitas,* etc. influence their similitudes on things below and are the true medium of the influence of the heaven on the elements.

On the step *planta* of its ascent and descent, the *intellectus* inquires into the problems arising from mixing herbs in medicines, such as are discussed at length in Lull's medical works. It wants to know what will happen when lettuce, which is cold and moist, is mixed in an electuary with rose which is dry and cold. It 'descends' to learn this, and understands that since lettuce is cold *per se* and rose is cold *per accidens,* the former will be stronger than the latter. We recognize this as the principle of 'devictio'. There is much here, too, on the 'graduating' of medicines, and through studying these matters the intellect is able to move up and down the ladder from this step.

So through the elements and their relation to the true principles of heaven, the intellect moves up and down the ladder of being. Above the heaven, in the angelic world, the 'principles' *intellectus* and *appetitus* become *sapientia* and *voluntas;* and on the top of the ladder, with *Deus,* the principles emerge in their true glory. *Bonitas, magnitudo* and the rest are here the 'dignitates Dei'. The existence of God is proved, also the Trinity and the Incarnation, very briefly but to the satisfaction of the intellectus. This work shows very clearly the integration on the step *coelum* of the ladder of the down-flowing divine principles with astrological influences, whence the divine principles are manifested, through the workings of the star-controlled elements, at lower stages of the ladder. Hence the pattern of the elements is of prime importance to the intellect as it descends from, or rises to, God through his vestiges in creation, or the 'Book of Nature'.

The *Arbor Scientiae*

We have found an abbreviated version of the ***Tractatus de astronomia*** on the step *coelum* of the ladder of ascent and descent. In the forest of trees into which we are now about to force a way we shall find on the Tree of the Heaven practically the whole of the theory of the ***Tractatus*** given in a very illuminating form and related to all the other Trees in this forest of knowledge, the ***Arbor scientiae,*** which Lull states that he wrote for the purpose of explaining his Art.

The Forest Encyclopedia belongs to an earlier period of Lull's life than the Ladder Encyclopedia. It was written during the autumn and winter of the year 1295 when Lull was in Rome trying, without success, to interest Pope Boniface VIII in his missionary and crusading plans which included as their mainstay the propagation of the great Art. It was during this year that he wrote the poem entitled ***Desconort*** ('Disconsolateness') in which he pours out his profound depression at his failure and in which occurs the stanza which we quoted on an early page of this article where the Art is defined as 'an ***Ars generalis,*** newly given by the gift of the Holy Spirit through which one may know all natural things . . . valid for law, for medicine, and for all sciences, and for theology which I have most at heart. No other Art is of such value for resolving questions, and for destroying errors by natural reason.

The opening words of the prologue to the ***Arbor scientiae*** present Ramon Lull disconsolate and tearful, and 'singing his ***Desconort*** beneath a great tree, to alleviate somewhat the grief which he had when he could not accomplish in the court of Rome the sacred work of Jesus Christ and the public weal of all Christendom.' A monk heard Ramon singing and came to comfort him. When he learned the cause of his sorrow this monk advised him to compose an encyclopedia of the sciences which should be less subtle to the understanding than his great Art. That is, he advised Lull to present the principles of his Art in a more popular form which would make it more widely known and acceptable. Lull decides to take this advice, and, reflectively considering a beautiful tree covered with leaves and fruit, he resolves to present the simplified and popular form of the Art in the form of the ***Arbor scientiae.***

We are again strongly reminded of how the philosopher in the ***Libre de meravelles*** initiated Felix into all wisdom from the plants and trees. And we cannot doubt that if only Blanquerna, and not Boniface VIII, had been Pope, the ***Arbor scientiae*** would have been joyfully accepted at the court of Rome. The ***Arbor scientiae*** is a work of colossal length, though not quite as long as the ***Book of Contemplation.*** The Catalan version of it has been published in the Palma edition. The most modern Latin editions of it are two published at Lyons in 1635 and 1637, for it is not included in the Mainz edition—though Salzinger in his 'Revelatio' made use of its Tree of Heaven, in conjunction with his manuscript copy of the ***Tractatus de astronomia,*** as one of the main keys to the arcana of the Art.

The fifteenth-century manuscript of the Catalan version in the Biblioteca Ambrosiana contains an illustration which shows Ramon and the monk at the foot of the Tree from which all the sciences branch off. The illustrated printed editions also give an inclusive Tree-diagram, showing all the sciences as branches of it, with Ramon and the monk at its foot; they also give separate Tree-diagrams for each science.

There are sixteen Trees in the Lullian Forest. Each is divided into seven parts—roots, trunk, branches, twigs, leaves, flowers, and fruit. Most of them have eighteen roots, and these are the meanings of BCDEFGHIK as *absoluta* and *relata* in the 'Alphabet' of the Art. There are some variants of this eighteen-root system in the later Trees, but all of them connect with it. The Trees are, therefore, the Art in tree form. (pp. 37-44)

Frances A. Yates, "The Art of Ramon Lull: An Approach to It Through Lull's Theory of the Elements," in her Lull & Bruno: Collected Essays, Vol. 1, *Routledge & Kegan Paul, 1982, pp. 9-77.*

Paolo Rossi (essay date 1961)

[*In the following excerpt, Rossi explores metaphysical aspects of Llull's "Art," including its aspiration toward "a description of universal reality."*]

At the beginning of the sixteenth century, Henry Cornelius Agrippa traced a summary picture of the diffusion of Lullism in Europe in a dedicatory letter prefixed to his commentary on the ***Ars brevis*** of Ramon Lull: Pedro Daguì and his disciple Janer were well-known in Italy, the teaching of Fernando de Cordoba had far-reaching influence in the European schools, Lefèvre d'Etaples and Bovillus in Paris were profoundly indebted to Lull, and finally the brothers Canterio had shown the marvellous possibilities of the Art not only to French and German but

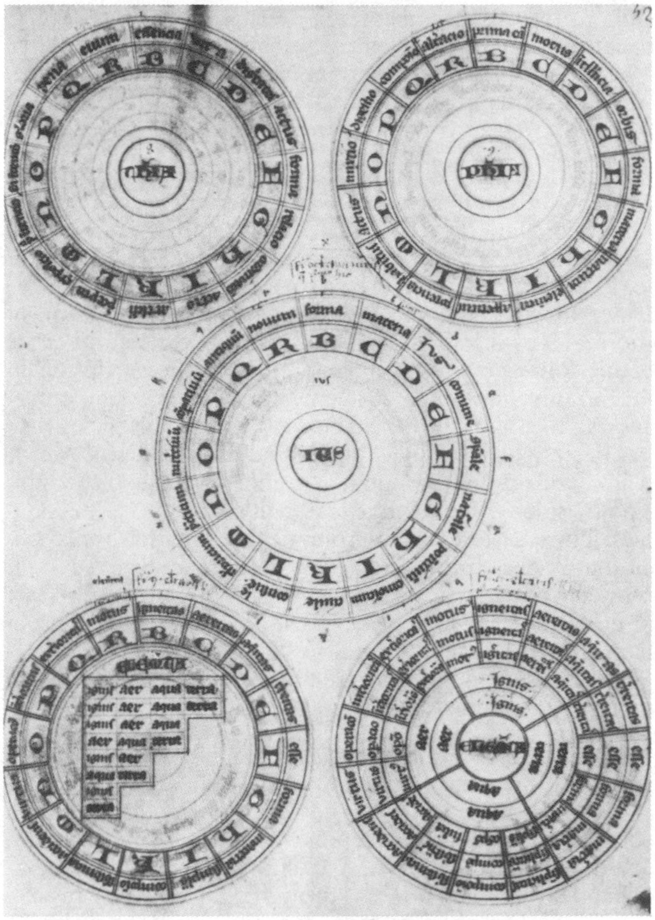

Wheels of theology, philosophy, law, and the elements, from Llull's Ars demonstrativa.

also to Italian readers. While referring to the great masters of Lullism, Agrippa also dealt briefly with Lull's *combinatoria,* clarifying its significance and explaining the reasons for its superior efficacy: the Art—so he affirmed—contains nothing trivial, it does not deal with specific objects; precisely for this reason it is to be regarded as the queen of all arts, an easy and sure guide to all sciences and all doctrines. The ***Ars inventiva*** is characterized by its universal applicability and certainty; aided only by this art men will be able, without being required to possess any other knowledge, to eliminate all possibility of error and to find "de omni re scibili veritatem et scientiam". The *arguments* of the Art are infallible and irrefutable; the principles and theorems of each particular science are illuminated by it and derive their validity from it ("omnium aliarum scientiarum principia et discursus tamquam particularia in suo universali luce elucescunt"); finally, because it embraces every science, the Art has the task of ordering every facet of human knowledge.

Agrippa who, many years later, fiercely attacked Lullian technique, thus emphasized in the preface to his commentary two of the fundamental characteristics of the Lullian art as it appeared to the Renaissance. Firstly, it is seen as a general and universal science which, dealing with absolutely certain principles and infallible proofs, makes it possible to establish an absolute criterion of truth; secondly, because it is conceived as the science of sciences, it offers a key to the exact and rational ordering of all knowledge, whose various aspects are all comprised in, and verified by, it.

In fact, the young Agrippa was only giving vivid and clear expression to widely accepted opinions. He was not the first to insist on the usefulness of the Art for invention, and on its encyclopaedic comprehensiveness. The subject of logic understood as the key to universal reality—i.e. as concerning not human discourse but the articulation of the real world itself—is in Lull's own texts and in those of his followers closely bound up with the aspiration to find a universal order of ideas and sciences which corresponds to the order of the cosmos itself. This endeavour has been rightly called a "logico-encyclopaedic tendency"; it is a central and dominant "motif" in Lullian thought, side by side with his "mystical" and "rationalist" tendencies. The mastering of the rules of the Art and the classification of ideas imply and presuppose, moreover, a system of memory-training which is presented as an integral part of encyclopaedic logic. But in order to clarify these problems, it will be useful to outline briefly some of the fundamental aspects of Lullism, referring to Lull's texts and to those of the Lullist tradition.

In Lull the Art is presented as a "logic" which is at one and the same time a "metaphysic" ("ista ars est et logica et metaphysica"); differing, however, from both "in modo considerandi suum subiectum" and "in modo principiorum". While metaphysics considers beings (*entia*) as independent of the mind, "prout conveniunt in ratione entis", and logic considers them according to the existence they have in the mind, the Art, being supreme among human sciences, considers them under both aspects. In contrast to logic, which is concerned with "second intentions", the Art is concerned with "first intentions"; while logic is "an unstable and fallible science", the Art is "enduring and stable"; it is capable of discovering the true laws inaccessible to logic. By practising the Art for a month it is possible not only to find the principles common to all sciences but also to achieve much better results than would be attained by studying logic for a whole year. However, knowledge of traditional logic and of natural sciences seems to be considered as useful for the acquisition of the Art:

> Homo habens optimum intellectum et fundatum in logica et in naturalibus et diligentiam poterit istam scientiam scire duobus mensibus, uno mense pro theorica et altero mense pro practica . . .

As it is shown to be closely connected with science, metaphysics, and ontology, the Art cannot be reduced to a mere formal knowledge and, on the other hand, it has connections with the kind of "exemplarist" metaphysics and universal symbolism which together constitute the basis and premiss of the Lullian doctrine. The reduction of complex concepts to simple and irreducible ideas, the use of letters and symbols to indicate basic ideas, the manipulation of the *combinatoria* by means of mobile figures, the conception of a perfect "artificial language" (superior to the common language and to the terminologies of the separate sciences) and finally the notion of a kind of conceptual manipulation which, once constructed, works by itself independently of man—these and other characteristics of the *Ars combinatoria* have led great historians, from Baeumker to Gilson, to compare the *combinatoria* with some justification to modern formal logic. In contrast to other less well-informed historians, however, Baeumker and Gilson have clearly indicated the strong influence exerted on Lull's thought by the exemplarism and symbolism mentioned above. For Lull, God and the divine hierarchy are the archetypes of reality while the entire universe is made up of a gigantic collection of symbols, referring, beyond their appearance, to the structure of the Divine Being ("Dei similitudines secundum possibilitatem receptionis creaturae sunt impressae in qualibet creatura . . . quaelibet creatura sui summi artificis portat signum" [***Compendium artis demonstrative***]).

In the same way, the "trees" in the ***Arbre de Sciencia*** do not represent a merely formal classification of knowledge: they are related, by means of a complicated symbolism, to the profound reality of things—the reality which the philosopher, in fact, tries to discover by analysing the meanings of the various parts of the trees. The eighteen roots of the first trees, which represent the world of creatures, correspond to the "principles" of the Art. Thus, as has been justly remarked, the "roots" or fundamental realities of things, the "principles" of Art, and the ranks of the divine hierarchy appear, in Lullian terminology, as interchangeable and equivalent terms.

The close connections between the Art and the theory of the Elements have been brought to light recently in a broad survey by Miss F. Yates ["The Art of Ramon Lull," *Journal of the Warburg and Courtauld Institutes,* 1954]. She has shown the traditional "logical approach" to Lullian doctrine (as for instance that in Prantl's *Geschichte der Logik*) to be partial and insufficient. An accurate study of the unpublished ***Tractatus novus de Astronomia*** of 1297 has not only thrown light on the application of the rules of the Art to astrology but has also demonstrated how in Lull's works the nine divine principles (whose "influences" had been identified in the ***Tractatus de Astronomia*** with those of the signs of the Zodiac and of the planets) constitute the basis of the application of the Art to the most diverse subjects: medicine, law, astrology, theology, and in the ***Liber de lumine*** to the study of light.

Starting from this Lullian exemplarism, it is possible to arrive at an identification of the Art with cosmology. This, among other things, is shown by one of the first Lullist texts to which Miss Yates has drawn our attention. Thomas Le Myésier, the author of the *Electorium Remundi* (Paris, Nat. lat. 15450) written at Arras in 1325, was a personal friend and enthusiastic disciple of Lull. In this ambitious compilation, he sets out to present the essential tenets of his master's doctrine: the Art has a definite function, viz. to defend the Christian faith against the Averroists by leading all men to an understanding of Truth and the divine mysteries. In the introductory part the connections between the Art and cosmology are clearly revealed; the circle of the universe, a graphic representation of which is described in detail by the author, includes the angelic sphere around which rotate the *primum mobile,* the empyrian, the crystalline sphere, the sphere of the fixed stars and the seven spheres of the planets. The earth, upon which an animal and a man are depicted, is surrounded by the spheres of air, fire and water. The circle of the universe is divided into nine segments each corresponding to one of the nine letters of the Lullian alphabet (BCDEFGHIK) in their double meaning of absolute and relative predicates and, following Lull's teaching, the significance of the letters changes according to the spheres.

The *Electorium* of Le Myésier is certainly not an isolated work; from the first half of the fifteenth century onwards, the interest in cosmology is evident in Lullian literature, which was spreading throughout Europe. Enthusiasm for Lullism—or, at least, a strong leaning towards it—is combined in many texts with the idea of an Art whose organization reflects that of the universe, i.e. a correspondence between a unified and hierarchic universe and an Art constructed in a way that is applicable to all branches of knowledge. Indeed, the first great European philosopher with Lullist affinities—Nicholas of Cusa—emphasizes the exemplarism and the theory of the divine hierarchy as the fundamental principles of Lullism: "Primum fundamentum artis est quod omnia, quae Deus creavit et fecit, creavit et fecit ad similitudinem suarum dignitatum" [quoted from P.E.W. Platzeck's *La Combinatoria Luliana*]. The principles of the combinatory art (*bonitas, magnitudo, aeternitas, potestas, sapientia, voluntas, virtus, veritas, gloria*), again make their appearance here as "principia essendi et cognoscendi"; they have not a mere formal significance but express the characteristics of the divine hierarchy and thus of all living beings. The exemplarist metaphysic guaranteed the absolute infallibility of this type of logic concerned with reality rather than with human discourse. Nicholas of Cusa, while proposing to reform the terminology of the Lullian Art and at the same time criticizing Gerson, expressed his agreement with Lullian doctrine in one of his notes to the ***Ars magna.*** He adheres even more closely to Lullian exemplarism in his doctrine of the ascent and descent of the intellect, according to which a knowledge of God can be attained by observing the quasi-divine qualities in living creatures, so that the intellect can ascend to a knowledge of God and His attributes by an acquaintance with nature, the mirror of His perfection.

This theory had been fully developed in the ***Liber de ascensu et descensu intellectus*** written by Lull at Montpellier in 1304. It was taken up again by Nicholas of Cusa, as a theory which, by way of analogies and symbols, proceeds to a reconstruction of the divine model of creation. By its description of a complicated ladder of beings (stones, plants, animals, man, God) this theory corresponds remarkably to another trend which concerned itself with an encyclopaedia of the complex hierarchy of the cosmos. We find the same cosmological framework in the *Liber creaturarum* of Raimond Sibiuda (Sabunde, Sebond) which influenced not only Nicholas of Cusa but also Lefèvre d'Etaples, Bovillus and Montaigne. It was written between 1434 and 1436; in fact, at the time when Nicholas of Cusa was enthusiastically reading and transcribing Lull's writings. Here we find not only the doctrine of intellectual ascent and descent and the affirmation of an Art conceived as "radix et origo et fundamentum omnium scientiarum", which can be very quickly assimilated and gives marvellous results ("quia plus sciet infra mensem per istam scientiam, quam per centum annos studendo Doctores"), but also the image of a natural ladder whose different steps are memorized and represented by means of "figures." The sequence of steps presents a unified image, both hierarchic and organic, of the universe. The first step corresponds to the things which are, but do not live, feel or understand (minerals and metals, the heavens and the celestial bodies, and artificial objects); the second belongs to those which are and live, but lack feeling and understanding (plants); the third to the animals, which are, live and feel; finally the fourth, which includes man, is characterized by life, feeling and understanding. Man, as a microcosm, sums up in himself the properties of the universe and is the living image of God.

On the other hand, the Lullian art was frequently combined with the cabala. In a famous passage, Pico [della Mirandola] significantly likens the *Ars combinatoria* to the most sublime type of natural magic which concerns itself with the superior beings in the superlunary world. And Pico saw the *alphabetaria revolutio* suggested by Lull as connected with the mystic significance of letters and names which forms an integral part of cabalistic thought. The mechanism of Lullism and the great cosmological constructions of the cabala thus meet on the common ground of symbolism, allegory and mystic exemplarism. Letters, images, figures and combinations of figures were seen in both cases as referring to the secret book of the universe, which the philosopher has to read and to interpret, penetrating beyond the appearance of symbols or, as Bruno later said, beyond the shadows of ideas.

. . . . .

It should be clear from what we have said so far that Lullian art aspires to a description of universal reality and that this description is organized, in its turn, as a real encyclopaedia. In the ***Arbre de Sciencia,*** written at Rome in 1295, the function of the "trees" is represented explicitly as a means of making the Art more "popular" and more easy to acquire. The encyclopaedia, moreover, is represented as an integral part of the great reform of knowledge planned by Lull. Articulated into seventeen trees, the encyclopaedia is based on a central idea: the fundamental unity of human knowledge corresponds to the unity of the cosmos. The eighteen roots of the tree of sciences are made up of nine "transcendent principles" and the nine "relative principles" of the Art (*differentia, concordantia, contrarietas; principium, medium, finis; majoritas, aequalitas, minoritas*). The tree is subdivided into sixteen branches, each corresponding to one tree in the forest of science: the *arbor vegetalis* (plants and their application to medicine), *sensualis* (sensible, sentient and animal beings), *imaginalis* (those beings conceived in the mind which are "similar" to those real beings belonging to the preceding trees), *humanalis, moralis* (ethics, doctrine of vices and virtues), *imperialis* (connected with the *arbor moralis,* referring to the *regimen principis* and politics), *apostolicalis* (ecclesiastical government and hierarchy of the Church), *coelestialis* (astronomy and astrology), *angelicalis* (Angels and the Angelic Powers), *eviternalis* (immortality, the extraterrestrial world, hell and paradise), *maternalis* (Mariology), *christianalis* (Christology), *divinalis* (theology, the divine hierarchy, the substance and person of God, divine perfection and creation). The *arbor exemplificalis* (where the subjects of the preceding trees are shown allegorically) and the *arbor quaestionalis* (enumerating four thousand *quaestiones* concerning the preceding trees), are both presented as "auxiliaries" as far as the *corpus* of the encyclopaedia is concerned.

The unity of the world of knowledge appears, therefore, based on the fact that the absolute and relative principles of the Art make up the common roots of the world of nature and the world of civilization. The Lullian image of the tree of sciences, significantly taken up by Bacon and Descartes, was to have a particularly successful career, but above all it was to keep alive for a long time in European thought the Lullian aspiration to create an organic and unified *corpus* of knowledge, and a systematic classification of the elements of reality. To be sure, there were many promptings in the same direction derived from other sources and other spheres of thought, but Lefèvre d'Etaples and Bovillus, Pedro Gregoire and Valerio de Valeriis, Alsted and Leibniz, when dealing with these problems, refer explicitly to Lull's own writings and those of his followers. The "pansophic ideal" which was to dominate the whole of seventeenth-century culture, implied the necessity, on the one hand, of being acquainted with all spheres of intellectual activity, on the other hand of possessing a law, a key or a language applicable to them all, vouchsafing an immediate insight into the alphabet imprinted on things by the Creator. The substantial unity and identity of structure, the profound harmony of the real cosmos and the world of knowledge, will thus become manifest. (pp. 183-92)

Paolo Rossi, "The Legacy of Ramon Llull in Sixteenth-Century Thought," in Mediaeval and Renaissance Studies, *Vol. V, 1961, pp. 182-213.*

J. N. Hillgarth (essay date 1971)

[*Hillgarth is an English historian specializing in the study of Medieval Europe. In the following excerpt, she presents an overview of Llull's art, thought, and character.*]

Ramon Lull wrote no formal autobiography. Despite what is often said, his novel ***Blanquerna*** is not an autobiography: its hero is at best an ideal projection of his personality. The contemporary Latin *Life* of Lull, although of great value since it was based on Lull's own reminiscences as an old man, is most incomplete and has apparently been 'touched up' by its monastic author. It would scarcely be an exaggeration to say, however, that Lull's philosophy is his autobiography. The whole of his thought, as will be seen, is intensely personal in inspiration and his writings are full of appeals to God and his readers and of lamentations at the lack of success of his Art. Lull's life, superficially extraordinarily picturesque, is intimately linked to his philosophy.

Lull was born, probably in 1232 or early 1233, in the capital of the island of Majorca, the Ciutat de Mallorques, not to be known as Palma until the sixteenth century. Only a few years before Lull's birth, in 1229, James I of Aragon, at the age of twenty-one, had led a Catalan army to the conquest of Majorca. The island thus recently recovered for Christendom had been held by Islam for over three centuries. Many of the Moslem population still remained living in Majorca, most of them now working the land for their new Christian masters, though a considerable number of Moslems who had taken sides with James during the conquest or who had obtained terms from him were able to preserve some of their property and live free under Christian rule. Lull's birthplace was still among 'the most nearly Moslem of Christian cities'. Communities of Jews also continued to exist in various towns of Majorca, the richest in the Ciutat. Lull was brought up against this background of mixed races and conflicting creeds. His father had been a rich citizen of Barcelona who had come over with King James, had acquired considerable property in Majorca, and had decided to settle there. Lull received the education of a knight of the period and became an accomplished troubadour. He was some ten years older than James I's second son, another James, destined to rule the independent kingdom of Majorca created for him by his father. Lull became the prince's seneschal and presumably travelled with him in the federation of Catalonia—Aragon, in the newly conquered territory of Valencia and, beyond, to France and Castille.

Lull's marriage to Blanca Picany took place before September 1257. But neither this marriage nor the birth of two children seems to have had much effect upon him. A legend declares that, while riding one day, he saw a lady he admired enter a church in the Ciutat de Mallorques and spurred in after her through the great west doorway. Another story, taken up and elaborated by Brantôme, describes how this lady, in order to be rid of Lull's attentions, invited him to her house and there, to his horror, displayed to him 'the breast he had so extolled in his verses, being slowly consumed by a malignant cancer'. I will return later to the question of the possible foundation for this legend. In Lull's own writings and in the contemporary biography one can read Lull's account of his conversion, which took place when he was thirty years old, probably in 1263. While he was trying one evening to compose a love poem (doubtless a 'lay' or 'virolay' in Provençal) to some Majorcan lady, there appeared, suspended in mid air before him, a vision of Christ crucified. This vision was repeated upon four more nights in all before his obstinate nature was convinced of its reality and that it must be obeyed.

Lull saw that his whole life must be changed. 'His conscience told him', the contemporary biography states, 'that these apparitions signified that he should speedily abandon the world and devote himself wholly to the service of Christ.' But how was he to serve God? How better could he serve Christ who had died for him than by enduring martyrdom for His sake? His mind naturally turned to the conversion of Islam, the hostile faith he saw all around him in his native island. Despite his lack of learning Lull then resolved to write 'the best book in the world against the errors of infidels'. He also saw that he could do little unaided and he decided to go to the pope and to Christian kings and princes to ask them to found monasteries where future missionaries could be trained in Arabic and other Eastern languages.

Although it is possible that the contemporary *Life* has somewhat anticipated Lull's plans and that they were not so clear in his mind at the time of his conversion as they later became, there is no doubt that the account of Lull's three main aims which is given here is basically correct. One may note the action of three very important elements in Lull's nature, the sudden and impetuous daring, which made him think immediately of offering his life for his new master, Christ; the emphasis on reason and the necessity for rational and informed argument, which appears clearly in his resolution to write a book to convert infidels and in the stress on the adequate training of missionaries; and, lastly, the realism which made Lull see the necessity of obtaining the support of the powers of Christendom. All these elements in Lull will become more evident as we proceed, and we shall return to them when we come to examine his character as revealed by his life and writings. The consistency of Lull's vision and the concentration of his spirit on the task which seemed paramount to him, the conversion of Moslems, are clear throughout his life.

If the contemporary *Life* somewhat anticipates Lull's plans, it also shows us the hesitation and delay between Lull's first clear resolutions and his carrying them into practice. Lull's hesitation is understandable. He had led until now an entirely worldly life and the *Life* tells us that he knew no Arabic and scarcely any Latin. The tasks he had set himself were immense and he was quite unprepared to undertake them. Three months passed after the visions had appeared to him before Lull attended a sermon at the Franciscan Church on the Feast of St. Francis. The bishop who was preaching spoke of the life of the Saint and of his abandonment of his worldly goods. It was moved by this account that Lull, in his turn, proceeded to sell most of his possessions, reserving a small portion for his wife and children. Lull then set out on a pilgrimage to a series of shrines, of which Rocamadour, in the Dordogne, and St. James of Compostella are mentioned by name in the *Life.* He went 'with the intention never to return' to Majorca.

It was after he had completed these pilgrimages that Lull met, probably in Barcelona, St. Ramon de Penyafort, former Master-General of the Dominican Order, then (in about 1265) aged about ninety but still very active. The influence of Ramon de Penyafort on Lull seems to have been decisive. Not only did he, in agreement with Lull's relations and friends, dissuade Lull from going to study at Paris before he was ready, but also, as the *Life* clearly implies, set him to work, once back in Majorca, to acquire the fundamental grounding he needed, both in Latin and also, even more important, in Arabic.

Here the practical side of Lull's nature is apparent. He was fully conscious of his own complete lack of training for the tasks he had undertaken. He was prepared to spend the necessary time (nine years of study)—and he was already over thirty and therefore far from young by medieval standards—in acquiring a profound knowledge of Arabic language and philosophy, and also in studying Christian philosophy and theology. There can be little doubt that Lull did well to follow the advice of Ramon de Penyafort: Majorca could give him something unavailable at Paris, a thorough training in Arabic, together with an intimate knowledge of Islam as a living faith. The two things combined gave him a unique advantage over almost all the great scholastics who were his contemporaries, Albert the Great, Thomas Aquinas, Bonaventure, Duns Scotus. On the other hand, Majorca could not provide Lull with Christian libraries or teachers to compare with those of the great universities. The somewhat 'old-fashioned' nature of Lull's philosophy, which belongs, in many ways, more to the twelfth century than to his own age, must in large part be ascribed simply to his lack of contact, during his years of study, with any leading centre of Christian thought.

It seems certain that Lull's insistence on two main weapons in the debate he was preparing with Islam comes from the Dominicans, and probably from Ramon de Penyafort: the founding of colleges to train missionaries in Oriental languages and the holding of learned disputations between properly prepared missionaries and the representatives of other religions. Already, under St. Ramon's leadership, the Dominicans were engaged in founding such colleges and had taken part in several public disputations, notably one at Barcelona in 1263 between the Jewish Rabbi Moses ben Nahman and the Dominican Father Pau Cristiá, which was presided over by King James I. St. Ramon persuaded Thomas Aquinas to write the *Summa contra gentiles* (begun in 1258), and it was probably he who encouraged the Catalan Dominican Ramon Martí to compose his *Explanatio symboli* in 1257 and his *Pugio fidei contra Iudaeos,* though the latter work was not finished until 1278, some years after Ramon de Penyafort's death. In both these books, as in Aquinas's *Summa,* an attempt is made to provide a rational apologetic for Christianity.

During the nine years of study (c. 1265-74) which Lull spent in Majorca he continued to live in his house in the Ciutat, surrounded by his family, and there he eventually began to write. It was during these years, when he was between thirty-two and forty-one, that there accumulated in Lull the latent force and energy that were to surge out dramatically in the extraordinary period which preceded and followed the illumination on Mount Randa.

The long years of preparation, study, and prayer were to bear fruit in the first of an almost endless series of works. The first three of these preceded the revelation of Randa: they were all written in Arabic, although they are only preserved today in Catalan and Latin versions made almost immediately, most probably by Lull himself. These works are the ***Compendium of the Logic of al-Ghazzāli,*** the ***Book of Contemplation,*** and the ***Book of the Gentile and the Three Wise Men,*** the first of Lull's controversial works. In all three works the influence of Lull's Arabic studies and of his preoccupation with Islam are evident.

Here I shall confine myself to the ***Compendium*** and the ***Book of Contemplation.***

The ***Compendium*** is a kind of notebook for Lull's early ideas. It deals with al-Ghazzāli's *Logic* but also includes some questions taken from his *Book of Philosophy.* It also includes theological questions, which do not appear at all in al-Ghazzāli, for instance an exposition of the Anselmian principle, 'Credo ut intelligam', stressing the necessity of faith for the understanding of dogma. Al-Ghazzāli's influence on Lull's philosophy will be referred to below. One should note here that the ***Compendium*** shows that the differences between the logic of Lull and that of the Western Schools derive in part from the fact that Lull first learned logic from al-Ghazzāli. For Lull, as for al-Ghazzāli, logic was purely an instrument, strictly subordinate to theology, not, as it came to be at Paris in the thirteenth century, an independent discipline.

The symbolic element in Lull, triangles and circles, appear in the text of the ***Compendium,*** although without the illustrations that are found in later works. So does the representation of philosophical terms by letters of the alphabet, a feature of Lull's own 'algebraic' logic. This was the beginning of the celebrated 'Combinatory Art' of Lull, 'with its complex semi-mechanical techniques, involving symbolic notation and combinatory diagrams', so much admired by many scholars from the Renaissance to our own day, so much abhorred by others [quotation from R.D.F. Pring-Mill].

In the ***Compendium of the Logic of al-Ghazzāli*** and in the great ***Book of Contemplation,*** a truly seminal work which, in a sense, anticipates all the major features of his subsequent writings, Lull was groping towards his ***Art of finding Truth.*** This ***Art*** was to unite all the particular arts sketched in the ***Book of Contemplation***—a logical art of disputation and conversation, an art of prayer and contemplation, an art of rhetoric and many others but, above all, an art of predestination, which would revise and correct the popular arts of divination. In the ***Book of Contemplation*** the theory of the Divine Attributes or 'Dignities', as Lull calls them, appears clearly for the first time, but it is only in the ***Art*** that the Dignities emerge as the principles by which truth can be discovered (principles of knowing as well as of being). It is only in the ***Art*** that the method by which they can be combined, the algebraic logic of the ***Compendium,*** is made clear.

The ***Art*** is, then, a clarification and fusion of Lull's earlier theories. In it, as will be seen, Lull attempts a synthesis of Arabic and Christian thought. There is no doubt that Lull saw this clarification and the synthesis that it made possible as given him by a divine revelation. The claim is often repeated in his writings and is found in his *Life* [a contemporary biography of Lull written by a monk of the Chertreuse de Vaurert]. The revelation enabled him to write the book on which he had long mediated against the errors of infidels. His illumination was, therefore, *intellectual* and seems to have consisted in a sudden insight which determined the philosophical basis of his system (pp. 1-9)

The *Life* says: 'Ramon ascended up into a certain mountain [Randa], not far from his home, in order to contemplate God there in greater tranquillity. When he had been there for not quite eight days it happened one day, while he was intently gazing up to heaven, that suddenly God enlightened his mind, giving him the form and manner of making the book [he had desired to write] against the errors of infidels.' In [a] miniature [of the scene] Lull is on the left, with the Hand of God raised above him in blessing. He is saying to God: 'You have willed to show me today the substantial and accidental principles of all things, and you have taught me to make of them two figures.' 'The two parts of that statement', it has been noted, 'refer to the two most striking features of [Lull's] ***Art of finding Truth:*** the doctrine of the Dignities, and the techniques of the *ars combinatoria.*' The 'substantial and accidental principles' are, respectively, the Divine Attributes (Dignities) and the relative predicates. . . . Lull distinguishes two series of principles. The first consists of the Dignities, absolute, transcendental principles. In the final form of the ***Art*** (the ***Ars generalis ultima*** of 1305-8) they are nine: Goodness, Greatness, Eternity, Power, Wisdom, Will (or Love), Virtue, Truth, and Glory. . . . The second series also consists (in the last ***Art***) of nine Principles: Difference (in God the distinction of Persons), Concordance (in God between the Three Divine Persons), Beginning, Middle, End, and Equality, together with Contrariety, Majority, and Minority (the last three only predicable of created things). This series of relative or 'accidental' predicates is used by Lull to discuss the relations of the first series between themselves, in relation to creation, and indeed it serves as the basic instrument of any inquiry.

God, in so far as He can be known to man, consists, for Lull, of a series of essential Attributes, which also form the absolute principles of the ***Art.*** The Lullian Dignities, which are broadly equivalent to the Platonic Ideas, play the central role in his system. They are the instruments of God's creative activity, the causes and archetypes of all created perfection. The Lullian world is one of analogy and symbols, a translucent universe in which the least thing is a living token of the presence of God. The essence of the ***Art*** does not, as is often thought, consist in demonstration but in the metaphysical reduction of all created things to the Dignities, transcendental aspects of reality, and in the comparison of particular things in the light of the Dignities. This comparison is effected through the third and fourth figures [diagrams found in the ***Art***]. Lull here uses the letters BCDEFGHIK, which already designate the nine absolute and relative principles. . . . Through the right combinations of letters the right solution to any problem can be found, for the principles which compose the Figures are the general principles of all sciences and whatever is can be reduced to them, implicitly or explicitly, by abstracting the essential Goodness, Greatness, etc., contained in angels, stars, plants, etc. 'Through the application of the transcendent Dignities through multiple analogies, the innumerable multitude of different objects of the mind can be reduced to one supreme mental unity and, metaphysically, to the Divine Unity' [quoted from E. W. Platzeck in Orbis Catholics, 1960].

The complex evolution of the Lullian Art from the primitive ***Art of finding Truth*** of c. 1274 to the final ***Ars generalis ultima*** of 1308 has been explained by two simultaneous ambitions—on the one hand a desire to apply the Art to each particular science, on the other the necessity Lull felt to simplify and perfect its logical structure, 'on account of the fragility of human intellect which he had experienced at Paris', so that it could be used by all, learned or unlearned. Lull's treatises on different sciences (cosmology, physics, law, medicine, astronomy, geometry, logic, psychology) are mainly interesting as applications of his general Art. . . . The ***Ars generalis ultima,*** as also the ***Tree of Science*** (***Arbre de ciència*** or ***Arbor scientiae***) of 1295-6, are more philosophical and less polemical in purpose than the original ***Art of finding Truth.*** A vast encyclopedia which found favour in the Renaissance, the ***Tree of Science*** is an attempt to classify all human knowledge under a unified plan. These later works of Lull, the ***Tree of Science*** and the ***Ars generalis ultima,*** were to be far better known to posterity than the original ***Art.*** The original purpose of the Art as a method of converting infidels was largely forgotten. Later centuries, down to Leibniz, were to see Lull's Art as a 'clavis universalis', a key to all knowledge.

For Lull himself, however, the Art was essentially a method of 'converting men', not of 'converting propositions', although the best way of converting men seemed to be precisely by converting propositions, i.e. by the use of syllogistic argument and algebraic logic. The reduction of all creation to the Divine Unity has been pointed out to be the ultimate ambition of the Art. The desire for the reunification of the Church (divided into hostile East and West) and for the complete unification of mankind through Christendom dominated Lull's life as well as his writings, 'that in the whole world there may not be more than one language, one belief, one faith'.

The greatest obstacle to the conversion of the world, as Lull often repeated, was the existence of Islam. Already in the twelfth century men like Peter the Venerable of Cluny had begun to realize the size of the problem, the fact that Christianity covered only a relatively small part of the world. In the thirteenth century, after the Mongol invasions, it was generally known that there were ten or possibly a hundred unbelievers for every Christian. And round Christianity, separating it from the supposedly more or less simple and convertible masses of Mongols and other pagans, was the Islamic barrier. But, although this general picture was fairly clear to most intelligent and educated Christians, only a very few Christian thinkers were prepared to put forward any practical proposals for meeting the situation, and indeed very few people were equipped to do so. Apart from Roger Bacon the greatest of these thinkers was Ramon Lull. Lull saw that if the Mongols were not converted to Christianity they would be converted to Islam (this in fact was what happened). Accordingly Lull, like Bacon, concentrated his attention on Islam and on its religious philosophy, the most formidable non-Christian creed known to Western Europeans at this time.

Lull's Art and his whole philosophy and theology are apologetic and Franciscan in inspiration, aimed at conversion by peaceful persuasion. Lull's advocacy of an armed crusade came late in his life: even then it was intended as a means, not an end. Yet although it was primarily a philosophy of conversion, of Christians to true Christianity, of the non-Christian world to the spiritual empire of Christ, Lull's philosophy was also in a very real sense a philosophy of combat. Lull's life, at least in its last thirty years (1287-1316), was a continual battle with Islam, not only in Spain and North Africa, but also in Paris. There, in opposition to the rationalist philosophers of the Faculty of Arts, whose master was Aristotle, as interpreted by Averroes, Lull sought to re-establish the organic unity of truth, of philosophy and theology.

In this great contest for the conversion of the world Lull's arms were those of intellect and love. His was one of those rare minds able to assimilate, in their search for a synthesis, the truths of different and opposing schools. His philosophy has the emphasis on the intellect characteristic of the Dominicans, the stress on the will typical of the Franciscans. But Lull's synthesis aimed at embracing not merely the schools of thought of medieval Christianity but the religious philosophies of Islam and of Judaism. It has been well described as a 'frontier philosophy', for some of its central doctrines and their development within his system were due to Lull's living contact with Jewish and, above all, Moslem scholars. From all the diverse elements on which he drew Lull succeeded in constructing a perfectly coherent system. It is unique in the Medieval West but it becomes intelligible if it is seen to draw its life ultimately from the Platonic tradition.

All Lull's contemporaries, Christians, Jews, and Moslems, shared a vision of the world based more or less directly on Neo-platonism. This included the common belief in a hierarchy or ladder of creation, stretching from God down through the spiritual world of the angels, through the celestial spheres and the spheres of the four elements (Fire, Air, Water, Earth), to man, and, below man, to animals and to inanimate creation. In 1274, when Lull gazed up at heaven from his mountain in Majorca, the stars above him moved with the music the spheres had played since Pythagoras' day. Lull saw there in his mind, as did all his contemporaries, the concentric spheres of the seven planets, then that of the fixed stars—the 'firmament'—and beyond it the Empyrean. This series of spheres ascending from earth to the Empyrean was identified for all the heirs of Neo-platonism with the celestial stage in the ladder of creation, between angels and men. Lull saw the influence of the Divine Dignities descending, coming down through the stars and planets and through the four elemental spheres. These last spheres were situated below the moon but above the earth, and through their combination, under the influence of the celestial bodies, the bodies of men and all inanimate things were constituted and governed, though the souls of men could free themselves from their control.

This vision of the world was, until the seventeenth century, that of most educated men. It provided, therefore, a common ground for discussion. These and other common beliefs, such as the organization of reality by numerical-geometrical symbolism and the idea of man as a microcosmos, were all incorporated by Lull into his system. The circular figures of his Art, it has been brilliantly suggested [by E. W. Platzeck], are an attempt to mirror the Neoplatonic spheres whose complex and irregular dance had sunk into Lull's mind on Mount Randa with the force of a divine revelation. Lull's Art, he could claim, was infallible because it was 'based on the actual structure of reality, it was a logic which followed the true patterns of the universe'. From a combination of the elements, admitted as 'scientifically' valid by men of all religions, Lull could climb the ladder of creation to the Dignities which acted on men through the elements. Equally well he could begin, as he often did, with the top of the ladder, the Dignities themselves.

[If] the spiritual Logic of Ramon Llull does not earn a place for him among the great Scholastic masters such as Aquinas or Scotus, it surely wins his position in the first rank of the great moral teachers, such as Saints Bernard or Francis, and sets his *Art* apart as one of the Middle Age's most ambitious and enthusiastic projects for exhorting the soul to righteousness.—*Mark D. Johnston, in his* Spiritual Logic of Ramon Llull, *1987.*

Although the deployment of the Dignities by means of algebraic logic, circular figures, etc., appears to have been invented by Lull, the emphasis on Divine Attributes as the basis for a philosophical system is not peculiar to him. Under many other names—that of the Dignities seems to be unknown elsewhere—and with varying clarity they appear in the systems of the ancients and of the three great Monotheist religions, Judaism, Christianity, and Islam, many centuries before Lull's time. Lull's emphasis on the Dignities comes to him from Christian sources. These sources are not mentioned either in his *Life* or in his own works but they can be deduced from internal evidence. One can find the Divine Attributes, or at least some of their names, in the *Psalms* and the *Book of Wisdom,* in Augustine and the medieval Augustinian tradition, for instance in St. Anselm and the Victorines in the twelfth century. One can find them in Pseudo-Dionysius; they ultimately derive from the Platonic Ideas, as interpreted by Plotinus. A very probable source of Lull's teaching on the Dignities is the *De divisione naturae* of John Scotus Erigena, the Irish philosopher of the ninth century and translator of Pseudo-Dionysius. The fact that Scotus explains in a manner similar to Lull the action of the Dignities through the elements is very significant and the comparison with Scotus is far closer than any brought out so far with Moslem or Jewish or other Christian sources.

Nevertheless, a doctrine of the Divine Attributes closely resembling that of Lull was held by both Moslems and Jews. Lull's knowledge of the works of al-Ghazzāli may have led him to select the Neoplatonic and Christian doctrine of the Attributes as the basis for his system. We have already seen that one of Lull's first works (c. 1272) was a ***Compendium*** in Arabic of the *Logic* of al-Ghazzāli. Lull's appreciation of this ***Compendium*** is shown by his translating it first into Latin and then into Catalan. Lull's ***Compendium*** reveals knowledge of al-Ghazzāli's *Book of Philosophy* or *Metaphysics,* as well as of his *Logic.* The *Metaphysics* contains a detailed study of some of the Divine Attributes which would have shown Lull the importance they possessed for a Moslem philosopher of the first rank. When Lull came to dispute with Moslem scholars he found that they might differ from him as to the number and names of the Divine Attributes (to which they gave the general name of *hadras*)—a Moslem spokesman points out these differences in one of Lull's later works—but in general they admitted their existence and their place in theology. A greater difference between Lull and Moslems is mentioned by him in the ***Ars generalis ultima*** of 1308. Moslems are here said to admit the Dignities but, in order to defend the Unity of God, they do so only with regard to God's extrinsic activity and in order to explain the diversity of created things. Lull, on the contrary, sustained the existence and activity of the Dignities on their own account, as it were, so as better to defend the 'plurality of God', that is the doctrine of the Trinity.

Lull's disputations with Moslems, which made him recognize important differences of this kind, appear to have led

Tree diagram illustrating Llull's Liber principiorum medicinæ, *from the Mainz (1721-42) edition of his works.*

him to explore even further the role of the Dignities within his own system. In his later works Lull developed a doctrine of correlative principles, in which, as in the basic theory of the Dignities, both Christian and Moslem influences can be traced. The doctrine of the correlatives in fact grows out of the original theory of the Dignities and [according to R.D.F. Pring-Mill in his *Microcosmos*] 'derives from the essentially active Nature of God' and of the Dignities as his Attributes. Each Divine Attribute 'necessarily unfolds into a triad of interconnected principles', agent, patient, and the action itself. This unfolding, seen as an image of the relations within the Trinity itself, impresses an 'ineradicably Trinitarian structure' on creation, 'in that the correlatives end by being the innate, original, true, and necessary principles of every subject. Their interaction serves to weave all three series of principles, absolute [the Dignities], relative, and correlative, into a single web of active relations.'

Lull states in his ***Compendium artis demonstrativae*** (c. 1276) that, in order to express this complex doctrine of the correlatives, he had been obliged to have recourse to an 'Arabic mode of speech, in order to reply to the objections of the infidels'. Lull could have found the idea of the correlatives in al-Ghazzāli's *Metaphysics,* together with the doctrine of the Dignities. He could also have found it, however, in Augustine, *De Trinitate,* which, in its turn, was drawing on Plotinus. It is probable that Lull had both al-Ghazzāli and Augustine in mind, though he expressly indicates his indebtedness to Arabic vocabulary. Lull was thus enabled to elaborate a theory of the universe which, of all medieval theories, came closest to a general hypothesis which should explain all observable phenomena. On the basis of the generally accepted Neoplatonism of his time Lull had reared a splendid Trinitarian vision of creation, man and nature alike. God is seen in all creation. The medieval desire for unification is here carried to its logical extreme.

It was not only with Islam that Lull could claim to have established the basis for rational discussion. Jewish scholars also agreed that the Divine Attributes (the sephiroth) were no mere logical principles but essences identifiable with God and serving as His instrumental causes. The sephiroth's nature and nine names, as understood by the Jewish cabalists, correspond even more closely than the Moslem *hadras* to Lull's Dignities. Lull is known to have been in direct relations with several eminent Rabbis in Barcelona, two of whom were disciples of one of the leading mystical cabalists. Cabalist ideas were held by large numbers of the Jewish middle classes in Spain and North Africa. They constituted a reaction against the rationalism of Maimonides. The cabalist doctrine (at least at this time) was one of concentration on the contemplation of God in Himself, through the sephiroth. It resembled the mystical contemplation of God through the Dignities that Lull's Art, as one of its principal objects, was intended to make possible. Lull's ***Liber praedicationis contra Iudaeos,*** written in Barcelona in 1305, makes use throughout not only of Biblical texts but of arguments based on the Dignities and their correlative principles.

It has been argued in the past that the figures of the Art and indeed much else in his works were taken by Lull from the Moslem philosopher, Muḥyi-al-Dīn ibn-'Arabi (1165-1240). Unfortunately the work supposed to be by Lull which was used for the purposes of comparison, the *De auditu cabbalistico,* is now universally considered apocryphal. There may well be resemblances between Muḥyi-al-Dīn ibn-'Arabi and Lull, but these appear to derive from similarities of temperament and from the fact that both moved in the same world of ideas, and not from direct borrowing on the part of Lull. It is far more probable that Lull was influenced as to his theory of the Dignities by the orthodox Moslem, al-Ghazzāli, one of whose works we know Lull translated, than by the pantheistic mystic ibn-'Arabi. As to the figures of the Art, if Lull was influenced by any external source here, it is most likely to have been by the tradition of schematic illustrations, notably of circles, found in manuscripts of Isidore, *De natura rerum,* and in similar widely disseminated works.

One of the many striking features of Lull's philosophy and theology which owe their prominence in his system to his polemical inspiration is his so-called rationalism. Yet again Moslem philosophy and theology, and in particular the thought of al-Ghazzāli, can be seen to have influenced him. It may seem a paradox to maintain that al-Ghazzāli, whose main work was intended to demonstrate the *insufficiency* of reason, should have influenced Lull in this direction. But Lull, in his ***Compendium,*** was not working on al-Ghazzāli's *Destructio philosophorum* but on his objective exposition of *The Tendencies* (or *Aims*) *of Philosophers* (known to the medieval West as his *Metaphysics* or *Book of Philosophy*). In the *Tendencies* al-Ghazzāli is content in the main with *setting out* the views of al-Farābi and Avicenna which he combats elsewhere. In the *Metaphysics,* for instance, are found all possible rational proofs of the existence of God, proofs rejected in the *Destructio philosophorum.* Both al-Ghazzāli (in the *Metaphysics*) and Lull saw in mathematical deduction the ideal method of reasoning. Lull was doubtless influenced here by his Christian predecessors, from Boethius to the School of Chartres. The idea that theology was itself a science is often found in the twelfth century. However, al-Ghazzāli's introduction of geometrical reasoning into the very science of theology must surely lie behind Lull's application of figures and algebraic logic to the actions of the Divine Attributes. For al-Ghazzāli also, as for Lull, theology, while a science, was above all other sciences, their crown and completion. The opening words of al-Ghazzāli's *Metaphysics* could have been written by Lull: 'It has been the custom of philosophers to begin with natural science. We have chosen, however, to put divine science first, since it is more necessary and of greater complexity (*diversitatis*) and because it is the goal of sciences and of their investigation.'

Lull must also have known the tradition of Moslem scholastic theology, the *kalām,* which was criticized by al-Ghazzāli but which continued to flourish in Islam. This tradition set out to provide a rational apologetic for dogma. Everything the Koran teaches about God was considered to be capable of grasp by human reason. The work of the *kalām* was not, therefore, as in Christian theology, essentially one of explanation and defence of the divine mysteries, but one of proof and demonstration. In the concrete problem of faith and reason the criterion of the *kalām* was not the faith in itself but a faith or law that is only fully credible when supported by supposedly certain arguments and demonstrations. Lull knew that Moslem scholars believed the Christian faith could not be proved and had often been told this by Christians. His desire to reply to the arguments of Moslem theology goes far, when taken together with the influence of al-Ghazzāli and of the Christian theology of the twelfth century with its methods of mathematical deduction, to explain Lull's misnamed rationalism.

In fact Lull is very far from being a rationalist, though he is himself partly responsible for this charge's being levelled against him, since he often promises to *prove* the Trinity or the Incarnation by 'necessary reasons' (*rationes necessariae*). This is certainly a misleading phrase which has led astray the theologians of the schools from Lull's day to our own. Lull's reasons are really reasons of congruence and analogy, sometimes ingenious, sometimes puerile, and his position is that of St. Anselm; 'I believe in order that I may understand.' Faith is not contrary to intellect but illuminates it.

In controversy with Moslems and Jews Lull could always begin by assuming a monotheist faith and general acceptance of the exemplarist position, together with belief in the Divine Attributes. Lull asserts that the Christian doctrine of the Trinity and the Incarnation is more *appropriate* to belief in the Unity and power of God than are the Islamic definitions. The Moslem belief implies the Christian creed. Lull therefore presents it as incomplete rather than false. Lull begins, like St. Thomas Aquinas and most apologists, by defending the Christian faith from the charge that it is contrary to reason. He then attempts to go further, however, and to show that Christianity alone fully honours God, asserts his Unity, and proves his existence. Lull argues that the Moslem or Jew of goodwill who already admits the existence of God and of His principal Attributes cannot rationally refuse to accept Christian doctrine, while, on the other hand, a Christian armed with the Lullian Art can resolve satisfactorily all objections against Christian dogma.

Lull was well aware that the usual line adopted by Christian apologists, that of disproving the Moslem faith but refusing to argue rationally about the Christian, was disastrous. He gives an example of this type of approach in a late work, where he apparently refers to the celebrated Dominican Ramon Martí—a direct disciple of St. Ramon de Penyafort, who had so much influenced Lull—whose *Pugio fidei* was used by Pascal. 'It is said', Lull recounts, 'that a certain Christian religious learned in Arabic was in Tunis disputing with the king. This religious proved by an attack on Moslem morality that the law of Mahomet was erroneous and false. The king, who knew something of logic and of natural philosophy, was convinced and said to the Christian, "From now on I refuse to be a Moslem; prove to me that your Faith is true and I will embrace it and see that it is adopted in my whole kingdom under pain of death." The religious replied: "The Christian faith cannot be proved, but here is the creed in Arabic, accept it." . . . The king replied: "I refuse simply to abandon one belief for another without proof and without understanding the new faith. You have done ill, for you have taken from me the belief I had and given me nothing in return." The king then had the religious and his companions banished from Tunis.' Lull concludes: 'I personally know this religious and his companions.'

Lull's *Life,* in its account of Lull's first mission to North Africa, to Tunis in 1293, contains an example of his method of disputation, very different from that of Ramon Martí. . . . According to the *Life* he began by placing himself on a terrain where the Moslems could not refuse battle. Lull told them that he had come to them since he was familiar with the arguments for Christianity and wished to hear those that could be advanced for Islam. If they could prove to him that their arguments were the stronger he was prepared to become a Moslem. After various days of debate Lull is supposed to have addressed the Moslems as follows: 'It behoves every wise man to maintain the faith that attributes to the Eternal God, in whom all the wise of the world believe, the greatest Goodness, Power, Glory, and Perfection, etc., and all these things in the greatest Equality and Concordance. . . . Now, as I understand, from the arguments that you have set before me, all of you Saracens, who are under the law of Mahomet, do not understand in the aforesaid and other Divine Dignities proper, intrinsic and eternal acts [in God], without which these Dignities would have been otiose from all eternity. The Acts of Goodness are to be able to cause good, to be able to become good, and to be able to do good. . . . And so on for the other Dignities. But, since you reserve these acts to two Divine Dignities alone, Wisdom and Will, it is clear that you consider the other Dignities, Goodness, Greatness, etc., otiose. In consequence you place an inequality and discordance between the [Dignities], and this is not admissible. By admitting that the essential acts of the Dignities, Reasons, or Attributes are, in equality and concordance, intrinsic and eternal, Christians demonstrate clearly that there exists a Trinity of Persons, Father, Son, and Holy Spirit, in one unique Divine Essence and Nature.' For Lull, as this passage shows, to deny the Trinity is blasphemously to postulate the otiosity of God. God by His very Nature must be eternally diffusive, the Father generating the Son and both breathing the Holy Spirit. In the *Life* Lull goes on to promise to prove the Incarnation from the Art.

Although he had such confidence in argument, Lull realized that no arguments were invincible. This is shown, for instance, when, at the end of the ***Book of the Gentile*** (c. 1272), the Gentile (or pagan), who has listened to the successive expositions of a Jew, a Christian, and a Moslem, leaves them, by their own wish, without stating which of the three rival faiths he intended to embrace. Lull implicitly recognizes here the necessary role of grace in Christian theology in perfecting the work begun by reason.

This recognition brought with it a tolerance and objectivity rare for the age and an emphasis on the necessity for free, not forced, conversion. Lull reacts against the objection based on the Omnipotence of God and a crude doctrine of Predestination with which he clearly had often to contend and which tended to underestimate the place of man's free will. Perhaps it is not absurd to see here, once again, the influence of al-Ghazzāli. It is known that he held that no Christian who had practised his religion and had not received sufficient information to enable him to see the superiority of Islam would be condemned to Hell. Lull seems to attempt to respond to this tolerant doctrine when he states that the Moslem who dies without sin and in good faith will suffer only bodily not spiritual pains in the next world. Throughout his life, but especially and almost exclusively in the early works and again in his last years, Lull advocates a return to the peaceful methods of the Apostles. He is the first theorist and publicist of missions and even after crusades had become (in 1291) an integral part of his plans they were still considered as subordinate to missions and as intended mainly to secure a free hearing for missionaries, the same sense in which crusades were allowed by St. Thomas Aquinas.

Conversion, in any case, was to be by persuasion and persuasion had to be based on knowledge, on a study of the manners and life, the philosophy and mode of reasoning of the different non-Christian peoples. Louis Massignon, one of the greatest of modern Islamic scholars, singles out Lull as exceptional for his knowledge of Islam among the Christian thinkers of the Middle Ages. He understood its psychology, he celebrated the beauty of its liturgical language, the depths of its religious spirit, and he recognized how close it was to Christianity. No doubt Lull was here over-optimistic, but without his optimism could he have persisted for more than forty years, against never-ending discouragement or indifference on the part of successive rulers of the Catholic Church and of the kingdoms of Western Europe?

Lull never speaks unkindly of Moslems, though he does at times (but only in texts written for Christians) speak harshly of Mahomet, since, he says, 'he is to blame that as many miserable souls go to Hell as rivers never cease to flow into the sea'. There is a most refreshing absence of prejudice and of any air of superiority in Lull's approach to Islam. He never has recourse to the common trick of Christian writers of explaining adherence to Moslem dogmas by the dissolute character of Arabs or of Moslems in general.

Lull is known to have discouraged Christians engaged in controversy with Moslems from any direct attack on Mahomet (and so, presumably, on the Law of Islam). On his first missionary journey, to Tunis in 1293, Lull confined himself to disputing peacefully and philosophically with a small number of Moslem scholars, some of whom were apparently converted and ready to be baptized at the time he was expelled from the city. On his second visit to North Africa, in 1307, his tactics, according to the *Life,* appear to have been intended to earn him immediate martyrdom; in this they were nearly successful. He is said to have begun by entering the main square of Bougie and crying out in a loud voice: 'The Law of Christians is true, holy, and acceptable to God; that of Moslems is false and erroneous, and this I am prepared to prove.' The somewhat natural consequence of his action was an immediate attack on him by the Moslem crowd. Lull was then led before the local Kādi, whom he calmly engaged in discussion and had little difficulty in reducing to a stupefied silence. As a result he spent six months in prison before being again banished. In view of Lull's earlier missionary doctrine it seems difficult to accept these dramatic scenes as entirely authentic. It is possible to see, however, a certain hardening of his attitude to Islam in his account of his ***Disputation*** with a Moslem scholar, 'Hamar', while he was imprisoned at Bougie. This account, drawn up in 1308, reveals a new impatience and bitterness, perhaps due in part to Lull's advancing years (he was now over seventy) and also to his recent maltreatment and imprisonment at Bougie.

The *Life* ends in 1311 and so it is not available for Lull's last mission to North Africa, in 1314-15, when he returned to Tunis. This mission is attested, however, not only by several letters of James II of Aragon of 1314 and 1315 but also by the colophons of a number of works of Lull, dated in Tunis from July to December 1315. Most, if not all, of these works appear to have been dedicated to the King of Tunis 'and his learned clerks'. They contain the arguments Lull had advanced in earlier years. It seems that at the end of his life Lull returned to the approach he had used in Tunis in 1293, if, indeed, he had ever really abandoned it.

. . . . .

Lull's character has been the object in recent years of several studies, which contain much of value. Some of the authors in question, however, have so emphasized one side of Lull's nature that, reading them, one might easily conclude that he was fundamentally unbalanced. Lull was apparently an only child, possibly (we do not know) born late in his parents' lives. He grew up into a spoilt young gallant. He was subject on one occasion at least and perhaps more often to a violent nervous depression, followed by a corresponding period of exaltation. Because of this some of his nervous states have been described as 'manic-depressive'. This analysis seems to be defective. It appears to be linked with the idea of Lull as a utopist. We have seen that Lull was appointed at an early age seneschal (i.e. head of the royal household) to the future James II of Majorca. It is evident that he possessed a careful organizing side to his nature. When his training in Arabic was completed and his first ***Art*** was written Lull lost no time in presenting it to the future James II and in securing from him the foundation of a College where it could be taught. Lull's projects seem always to have been prepared with much care, often over a period of years. When he had seen the College of Miramar begin to teach and had written, there and at Montpellier, his first cycle of works, explaining and elaborating on the *Art,* he was ready to move outwards from his own kingdom of Majorca on to the European stage. He knew the real centres of power, the papacy, the Courts of France and Aragon, and it was there that he went. It is quite unrealistic to say of him, as a recent biographer [Llinarès] does, that he was 'incapable de passer à la réalisation'.

All the blame for the relative failure of Lull's practical projects cannot be laid on his shoulders. The difficulties of international politics were mainly responsible for this failure. Lull's first patron, James II of Majorca, even when he was in possession of his kingdom, did not enjoy the power necessary to carry out Lull's projects, and, from 1285 to 1298, Majorca was in the hands of Aragon. The greater powers, France and Aragon, were not deeply interested in Lull's missionary projects. James II of Aragon was prepared to grant Lull permission to preach in the synagogues and mosques of his dominions. Philippe IV of France was prepared to recommend Lull to others and to obtain for him a recommendation of his writings from the university of Paris. Both James and Philippe were also prepared to listen to Lull's crusading plans and to give them some attention, but James was principally interested in the war against Granada and later in the acquisition of Sardinia, and Philippe was absorbed in his struggle against the papacy and against the Flemish. The papacy, in its turn, was so largely taken up, from 1282, with the war against the Sicilians and the House of Aragon, and, later, with the increasingly bitter conflict with France, that it was quite unable to assist Lull.

Lull's response to this situation was courageous and realistic. In the ***Desconort*** of 1305 (or perhaps of 1296) he records the failure of his Art, God-given as he believed it was, to win acceptance, and the failure of his projects. Even Miramar had collapsed. The imaginary hermit with whom Lull engages in dialogue in this poem (the pessimistic and questioning side of Lull's nature engaged in discussion with his optimistic side) says that after Lull's death 'a better time will come in which men, thanks to the study of the Art, will conquer the errors of this world and will achieve much good'. Lull persevered, despite discouragement; before he died he saw the Council of Vienne (1311-12) adopt one at least of his proposals in its establishment of chairs for the teaching of oriental languages to future missionaries.

Lull's realism is shown in many ways. Although he belonged to the traditional school of thought with regard to the papacy and his Platonist ideal of unity made him desire that an emperor should rule the world in co-operation with the pope, he was capable of appreciating in practice the rise of national states. For the Holy Roman Emperor, champion of the Church and Defender of the Faith, to whom St. Bernard had turned, Lull substituted in practice the kings who had supplanted the Emperor. Lull's realism led him through the intricate maze of European politics. His approach to the different kings of Europe, James II of Aragon, Philippe IV of France, Frederick of Sicily, might vary but his main aim, the conversion of infidels, never changed. In a somewhat similar way Lull clearly thought that all languages should be reduced to one and for this universal language he chose Latin. But that he saw the new importance of the romance languages, as he did that of the new national states, is shown by the fact that he was the first Christian writer of the Middle Ages to compose elaborate philosophical treatises in a language other than Latin.

While Lull's reason was certainly in control of his emotions, there is no doubt that his nature was intensely affectionate and that he possessed a great emotional force, as well as a great force of will. The force of his emotions appears in the extreme nervous depression he underwent in 1293 at Genoa, on which the interpretation of his character as that of a manic-depressive, to which I have already alluded, is mainly based. Lull's depression on this occasion seems, however, to be unparalleled in the rest of his life. It is completely intelligible in terms of a reaction caused, first, by his failure to obtain any support for his projects at Rome, secondly, by failure of his Art to win acceptance so far at Paris or elsewhere, and, thirdly, by his sudden realization, when he was on the point of embarking on his first missionary journey to Tunis, of the great personal danger involved. Lull's force of will enabled him to recover from this intense reaction and nervous depression and, later, to overcome further discouragements and rebuffs which would have vanquished most men. His emotions and his will gave him the driving force to persist with his projects for missions and crusades and with the endless revision and redrafting of his ***Art.***

If we wish to understand Lull's character our best source is his ***Book of Contemplation,*** the greatest work he wrote and one of the most extraordinary books of the Middle Ages. This was perhaps the first book Lull wrote. It suffers from the many defects of the beginner. It anticipates, as has been said, all Lull's subsequent writings and it is immensely rich in interest and fantasy, but it is very repetitive, it is badly organized, and, for modern readers at any rate, it is far too long. The ***Book of Contemplation*** contains the first draft of much of Lull's philosophy and the foundations of his mystical theology. It also contains very much of interest for the student of Lull's psychology. Lull was far from possessing the interest in and the talent for introspection of St. Augustine, but he does reveal much of himself in the course of the book.

While he was writing it (in 1270-2?) Lull had sold most of his possessions and, in a world where he had been known, until very recently, as a brilliant and elegant courtier, now appeared in the thick, coarse habit usually worn by hermits. But he was still living with his family, most of the year in the Ciutat de Mallorques, perhaps occasionally visiting his remaining country properties. There is a great tension in the ***Book of Contemplation,*** that of a man still partly attached to the world, living with his wife and children, 'subject to the order of matrimony', but wishing all the time to be alone to pray and to think. It is remarkable that though Lull was longing, as he says several times, to finish the book and to be free to set out for the Holy Land as a missionary, with the hope of martyrdom, he should yet have spent several years writing this enormous work in Arabic and then probably another year translating it into Catalan. It is true that his thought was maturing slowly and he was waiting for the insight he needed to write another book, the long-desired ***Art.*** But he also seems to have felt a compulsion to set down his views on every aspect of philosophy, theology, psychology, logic, contemplative prayer, and the evils of his age, all with the intention of praising God, not only for his own conversion but for the whole of His Creation and Revelation to men. While doing this Lull continually recalls his past life and compares it with his present existence.

If we read his works or study his life Lull appears as naturally sympathetic and attractive to others. Open to the world, curious and observant of men and things, he was able, in later years, while wandering from court to court, with few credentials and no possessions, to excite the interest and sympathy of kings and scholars. This general impression is confirmed by the ***Book of Contemplation.*** The dominant note of Lull's character, as revealed here, is that of joy. Lull, who accuses himself of so many sins in the ***Book of Contemplation,*** thanks God that his nature was free of rancour, and in this, if not in all his self-analysis, one may believe him. Although after his conversion Lull felt he had never experienced joy before this time, he expresses his wonder elsewhere that men can be 'joyful at times in good, at times in evil'. After his conversion joy filled his life. The ***Book of Contemplation*** begins with an explosion of joy. 'Honour and reverence to you, Lord God, who have given so much grace to your servant that his heart swims in happiness and joy as the fish in the sea . . . For you, Lord, have given me so much grace that wherever I go, I go joyfully, and wherever I am I rejoice, and wherever I turn my face I am glad. And this is so, Lord, because I am all in you and you are all joy and rejoicing. . . . If there are any men who wish to rejoice and be filled with joy, let them come to me, for they will find me as full of joy as a fountain spilling over with water.'

Together with the note of joy there is that of daring. Throughout his life Lull was prepared to dare anything for love, when he was a young man for the love of women, after his conversion for the love of God. For him love was almost identified with daring. As a young man he risked death for love. 'Men who are daring and adventurous', he writes, 'often find their life hanging on a point or a moment. This was so with me, for I, Lord, have so often been daring in the service of sin, that I cannot tell how often I have been at the point of death and of damnation to eternal fire.' He concludes an extraordinary address to Christ: 'If You have endured travail and pain and death for us sinners, I am he, who, in order to enjoy the pleasures of lust, have often put myself in peril of death and have sustained much travail and many troubles and many terrors.' The *Life* tells us that Lull, *immediately* after he had decided to serve Christ, resolved that he would give his life for His sake. This impetuosity is so characteristic of Lull that the story must be true. His desire for martyrdom is a constantly recurring theme in the ***Book of Contemplation,*** and one cannot doubt its sincerity, if it is sometimes oddly expressed. 'The first thing I tasted in the world was milk', he writes, 'the last thing I shall taste will be death. May it please you, Merciful Lord, that as my mouth's first taste was of milk which enlivened the body, even so the last thing I taste may be blood flowing from my body, dying for Your love.'

Lull leaves us in no doubt as to the passionate love for women that filled his life before his conversion. The metaphors of human love come naturally to him when he is beginning the vast task of writing the ***Book of Contemplation.*** His conversion did not enable him to forget the past. On the contrary he had to struggle against very powerful memories. The most natural things reminded him of his past loves. 'The scents of flowers and of applies have made me remember and imagine lust,' he was to write many years later, 'and the touch of soft beds and of flesh has often made me sin against my Beloved: I did not refrain my imagination but I let it grow in imagining the delights of this world.' It may be symptomatic that in 1299, over thirty-five years after his conversion, when Lull was asked what may seem a purely 'scientific' question, 'Whether the rays or light of the sun are bodies', he should have begun his reply: 'As the power of the imagination moves the senses to desire . . . '

But Lull's most moving memories of his old passion are to be found in the ***Book of Contemplation.*** 'As great drought and great cold are the pestilence of the fruits of the earth,' he writes, 'so, Lord, the beauty of women has been the plague and tribulation of my eyes', and again: 'I, Lord, have loved women many times, so much that neither night nor day was there anything in my heart but love of them. In my great folly, Lord, I took those things I loved as if they were gods, for I loved them as You should be loved.' It is almost in despair that he cries out to God, 'How is it that in my heart I find so many loves and so many memories and so many desires when there is only One God who should be loved?' The fatal power Lull saw in the love of women appears throughout his works. In the ***Doctrina pueril,*** written for his son, then about fourteen years old, Lull wrote, as if some distant memory of the tale of Troy was stirring in his mind: 'Beloved son, lust makes men go to war and kill and wound each other: women have been the causes of the destruction and burning of castles and cities.'

There are glimpses of the young Lull in the ***Book of Contemplation,*** clothed in fine garments, scented with musk and amber, his hands covered with precious stones, bearing garlands of flowers, on his way to one of the 'evil women' he describes, who has 'painted herself white and red and dyed her hair and eyebrows and coloured her mouth and eyes that she may be beautiful in the eyes of men'. For the amusement of the ladies he loved and no doubt also for that of the young Prince James, his master, and of the Court of Aragon, Lull took his place among the troubadours and jongleurs, who, 'by the instruments they sound and by the new songs they compose and sing, and by the new dances they make and by the words they say' caused 'the Goodness of God to be forgotten and the great glory and the great pain that are in the other world'.

There is a dualism in Lull when he writes of human love. It had its origins in the Neoplatonic tradition which saw the soul as imprisoned in the body. But this tradition, generally accepted in the Christian Middle Ages, was reinforced in Lull by an almost pathological insistence on the corruption and filth behind the beautiful exterior. The legend of the woman with a cankered breast may well not be devoid of some foundation in fact.

Lull was seeking in women something he could not find. 'Because of their great lust', he writes, 'men wish to have many women and are not content with one, and they seem to find more pleasure with those they do not possess than with those who are at their disposal, and because of this evil of sensuality they change from one woman to another . . . and for all their search they cannot find the fulfilment they are seeking.' The deception he experienced and probably also a revulsion from his absorption in the pleasures of love prepared Lull's mind, it would seem, for the dramatic conversion which has been recounted above. There is a story in the ***Book of Contemplation*** which gives one some insight into Lull's mind in the period shortly before the visions of Christ on the cross appeared to him. 'I saw a stray dog, old, thin, covered with scabs, an unpleasant sight, come into the royal Court, and I saw, Lord, the king and knights chase it away and the dogs of the Court bite it and expel it out of the palace. When I saw that, Lord, I thought of myself and that if I grew old in sin until death and died in sin and thought to enter into glory, I should be a stranger there, as this dog was in the royal Court and that I should be maltreated by the demons as he had been maltreated by the king's dogs.'

The change in Lull's life was not easy. 'The greatest strife I have ever felt was when I changed from sin to the work of penance. So hard and so heavy a thing is it to the sinner to leave sin that never, without Your aid, Lord, would contrition or repentance of my sins have entered my heart.' Whether the visions of Christ actually appeared to Lull's eyes or only to his imagination he always considered them an act of divine love, which responded to his burning need for love, the same need that had impelled him to his frenzied pursuit of women.

The critical phase of life for many men appears to be that between twenty-eight and thirty-five, the time when their personality attains its full maturity. Lull understood this fact clearly, though he did not express it in the language of modern psychology. Looking back a few years later on the event which had changed the direction of his life Lull wrote: 'I have been mad from the beginning of my days until I was over thirty, when there arose in me remembrance of Your wisdom and a desire to praise You and memory of Your passion. So, as the sun has greatest force at midday, I have been foolish and devoid of wisdom until the middle of my life.'

Lull's conversion changed the direction of his life but not his character, which was already formed. The joy and intrepid daring that were, as has been seen, the dominant notes of his character continued to express themselves in new ways. The troubadour of ladies, 'singer of vanities and lying satirist', as he described himself, 'from now on proposed to be a true troubadour of God', of Christ and his Mother. The courage and passion Lull had shown in love of women became passionate courage displayed for the love of God. The spirit who had delighted in the amusements of the Court of Aragon and in provincial love affairs now flew higher and further, 'through woods, over hills, across plains, by deserts and towns, to courts, castles, and cities, marvelling at the marvels of the world, questioning whatever he did not understand . . . '.

We have seen something of Lull as apostle to the Moslems and of his desire to bring the whole world to the knowledge of Christ. In the mysticism that inspired Lull's ceaseless activity, as in his lyrical poems, the ***Cant de Ramon*** and the ***Desconort,*** which leap up to heaven like flames kindled by the love of God, there is present the troubadour who had begun to write under a different inspiration. Lull's mysticism is very human, far removed from any attempt to reach the heights of Pseudo-Dionysian doctrine, where God dwelt, for so many mystics of the Middle Ages, far beyond all affirmation or negation. Lull's mysticism is based on the love of the Incarnate Christ and of the Virgin, 'the Queen of Heaven, of the earth, of the sea, and of all that is'. There is great emphasis on the use of reason in contemplation, but there is also great emphasis on the value of tears. Lull's tears had flowed, he tells us, for love of women. Unless they flowed now as he prayed, prayer seemed to him useless and in vain. Reason is at the service of love.

In Lull's mystical writings the influence of the courtly Art of Love of the troubadours, of contemporary 'romans', such as the *Roman de la Rose,* and of Franciscan mysticism is blended with very strong Eastern influences. Lull's mysticism, like his philosophy and his apologetic, combines East and West in an original synthesis. Eastern influence is evident in Lull's literary writings in general, in his multiplication of parables and in his collections of proverbs. It is expressly acknowledged in two of his mystical works. The prologue to the ***Hundred Names of God*** (***Cent Noms de Déu***) reveals that Lull had studied the manner in which Moslems meditated on the ninety-nine Names of God in the Koran and he sought, in this poem, to surpass the Koran by overthrowing a particular Moslem superstition. The manner of Lull's most famous mystical work, ***The Book of the Lover and the Beloved,*** with its 366 short verses, is taken from the Moslem mystics or 'sufis', who, Lull tells us, 'have words of love and short examples [on which they meditate and] which arouse great devotion'. But there is much in this book, too, of the poetry and language of the troubadours and much of Lull's own life.

The Lover of the book is the soul of man, the Beloved is the Christian God, but the language, as in Muḥyi-al-Dīn ibn-'Arabi's mystical writings, is often indistinguishable from that of human love. 'Indifference is death and love is life.' 'Nearness and distance are the same to the Lover and the Beloved, for as water and wine are mixed in one, so are the loves of the Lover and the Beloved, as heat and light are one so are their loves joined . . .' Or again: 'The Lover lay in the bed of love; the sheets were of joys and the covering was of sighs and the pillow was of tears. And whether the cloth of the pillow was of joys or of sighs lay in dispute.'

In another of Lull's mystical works, ***The Tree of the Philosophy of Love,*** the death and burial of the Lover (the Lover of ***The Book of the Lover and the Beloved***) are described in passages where the imagery reminds one of contemporary 'romans'. (In much the same way some scenes of Lull's novel ***Blanquerna*** betray memories of Parsifal and of the legend of the Graal. ***Blanquerna,*** indeed, was evidently meant to be diffused by jongleurs, as if it were a 'chanson de geste'.) In ***The Tree of the Philosophy of Love*** we read:

> When the Lover had died of love, the pages of love bathed him and washed him with the tears which he had let fall for love, tears that had been treasured by Memory of love; and they covered him with fine white samite, in token that the Lover was washed of his sins. On this white samite they placed another red, in token that the Lover had died a martyr for love, and on this red

> they laid a covering of gold, in token that the Lover was proven and had been loyal to his Beloved and to love. After this they laid the body of the Lover in a bed of patience and humility, and with candles of love lighted they bore him to the church of love.

But beautiful as this allegory is, it is to ***The Book of the Lover and the Beloved*** that one returns for the most perfect expression of Lull's love of God. In the extreme concentration of the verses of this book the philosophy of Lull's endlessly proliferating Arts and encyclopedias has been translated into pure verbal music. 'The Lover and the Beloved were met together and their voices were silent and the eyes with which they made signs of love wept tears and their loves spoke.' In another verse there is a distant reflection of the dawn so often invoked in Provençal poetry, when the song of the lark tells the lover he must leave his love. 'The birds sang the dawn and the Beloved awoke, who is dawn, and the birds finished their song and the Lover died for the Beloved at dawn.'

Lull's mind and heart were open to the world and to nature. 'His senses are always ready to seize on all the richness of this world and to rejoice in it.' He loved 'the brightness of dawn and of the morning star, fields, flowers, streams, and woods'. As his philosophy grew clearer in his mind he came to see the whole of nature as a reflection of the Dignities, the perfections of God. Blanquerna's habit, when a hermit, of rising at midnight and contemplating the heavens reminds one of Lull himself, who never forgot the illumination he had received when gazing upwards from the high table-mountain of Randa or indeed the monastery at Miramar, which he had persuaded James II of Majorca to found, set on a shelf in the mountainside, high above the Mediterranean.

But Lull was not by nature a solitary and, much as he loved to recall Randa and Miramar, he did not linger long in his beautiful island, after his first works were written and Miramar was founded. For him contemplation issued in action, in incessant effort, by voice and pen, to carry forward the mission with which he believed he had been entrusted. His preoccupation with Islam did not prevent him from seeing that much needed changing in Christendom. His gift for satire had not left him with his conversion. In the ***Book of Contemplation,*** and in the two first philosophical-social novels of Europe, ***Blanquerna*** and ***Felix,*** there is sharp and unsparing satire of almost all the classes and occupations of his day; kings, knights, judges, doctors, merchants, pilgrims, jongleurs all come under the whip of his censure. The only social groups which he praises in the ***Book of Contemplation*** are the clergy (whom he followed St. Francis in treating, at least at this time, with undeviating filial respect) and the workers of the fields, on whom, as he saw, the whole social pyramid rested, and who were robbed by kings and knights and forced to fight in their useless wars, in which their crops and vines were destroyed and their houses burnt. They were tricked and defrauded by thieves; even birds and beasts combined to spoil their harvests and kill their animals.

Lull was not content to satirize the world he lived in. He also put forward proposals for the reformation of Christendom of which some were of such daring and novelty that centuries were to pass before their realization drew near. Most notably, one passage in ***Blanquerna*** sketches a plan for a *Pax Christiana,* a society of nations presided over by the papacy.

Lull cannot be convincingly compared with any of the great scholastics of the thirteenth century, Aquinas, Albert the Great, Bonaventure. He lacked their rigorous philosophical training but he possessed, as has been seen, a great advantage over them. Unlike them he was not a man of only one world, that of Latin Christendom, for he was equally at home in the great civilization of Islam which disputed the Mediterranean world with Latin and Greek Christianity.

The only leading Christian philosopher and theologian of the thirteenth century with whom Lull can usefully be compared is Roger Bacon (c. 1220-92); comparisons have in fact been attempted between Bacon's *Opus maius* (1266) and Lull's ***Art*** and other writings, and it is possible that Lull used the work. Both Lull and Bacon were Franciscans, though Lull's Franciscanism was less formal than Bacon's—Lull's supposed entrance into the Franciscan Third Order late in his life, some thirty years after his conversion, is not completely certain, although attested by tradition. Both were concerned above all with the conversion of infidels by rational arguments to be employed by missionaries trained in Oriental languages, and also with the reform of Christendom. Bacon, like Lull, pursued the idea of the unity of knowledge and of the sciences, subordinated to theology. When Pope Clement IV asked Bacon to send him the books he had written, Bacon apparently thought that he had had a revelation. The perfect pope he had long dreamed of had at last arrived. The analogy with Lull's portrait of the desired ideal pope in ***Blanquerna*** is evident.

There are very great differences, however, between Bacon and Lull. It is not merely that in Lull, despite his many disappointments, one cannot find the bitterness of Bacon when his plans failed to win acceptance. It is also that Bacon refused to produce proofs of Christianity intelligible to the mass of the infidels, since he thought such proofs would necessarily be imperfect. Wisdom was not to be diffused but to remain the property of small and select circles. Lull, on the contrary, composed his philosophical works in Arabic or Catalan, and often in verse, and made continual efforts, as has been said, to simplify and popularize his philosophy and to make it generally accessible.

A greater difference still between Lull and Bacon was due to the very different settings of their lives. While Bacon's life gravitated between Paris and Oxford, Lull's journeys covered France, Italy, and the whole of the Mediterranean. While both Bacon and Lull were greatly attracted by Arabic culture, Lull's knowledge of Islam was gained at first hand and he knew far more of its religious philosophy than did Bacon.

The influence on Lull's philosophy of the great Moslem philosopher, theologian, and mystic, al-Ghazzāli (1033-c. 1111) has already been indicated. It has been said of al-Ghazzāli that 'he brought philosophy and philosophical theology within the range of the ordinary mind'. In this, as also in his struggle against the Moslem philosophers who laid undue stress on philosophy as independent of theology, al-Ghazzāli reminds one of Lull. There are, indeed, many undeniable ways in which Lull far more closely resembled, at least externally, a Moslem 'sufi' or ascetic teacher (which al-Ghazzāli was, among many other things) than he did any Doctor of Paris or Oxford. Lull's wandering life, dressed in a coarse cloth habit not unlike the thick woolen dress of the 'sufis', preaching in the streets or squares of Christian or Moslem cities or retiring for periods to hermitages, his popular approach to philosophy and attempt to combine it with mysticism, his enmity towards Averroists and free-thinkers who refused to admit a revelation, his radical zeal for reform and desire to return to times of primitive fervour, his visions, his emphasis on eschatology, the very suspicion he aroused, as did the 'sufis', in the official theologians, all these can be paralleled in the Islam of his time, in Spain and North Africa. Lull's mysticism owed much in its form, as we have seen, to that of the 'sufis'. The way the different cardinals in ***Blanquerna*** each receives a mission to propagate devotion to a different verse of the *Gloria in excelsis,* 'Laudamus te', 'Quoniam tu solus sanctus', etc., corresponds surprisingly closely to the way that different 'sufis', according to Muḥyi-al-Dīn ibn-'Arabi, each took a different verse of the Koran and went through the world preaching it, 'Praised be God', 'There is no God but Allah', etc. There is nothing strange in these parallels or in others that could be adduced. Lull, in preparing to combat Islam, had steeped himself for years in its literature and mysticism. He had taken many of his arms from his adversaries.

More than in Roger Bacon or in al-Ghazzāli or ibn-'Arabi the inspiration of Lull's life should be sought in the founder of Bacon's Order, in St. Francis, whose example Lull had followed when he abandoned his possessions. Both were brilliant and gay as young men, both, in later life, were capable of astonishing the world they had abandoned. The way St. Francis appeared before Innocent III in the guise of a troubadour prefigures the behaviour of Lull's wise fool, 'Ramon lo foll', in ***Blanquerna,*** and probably to some extent Lull's actual behaviour (though Lull also presented formal petitions to several popes). Again, the appearance of St. Francis before the Sultan of Egypt provided a model for Lull's appearance before different Moslem rulers in North Africa. The 'spiritual vision of marvellous clarity and penetration' [quoted from D. Knowles in his *Religious Orders in England*] which shines through the writings of St. Francis is stamped again on the writings of Ramon Lull, fresh and living as the Franciscan imitation of the Passion of Christ that seals the pages of Lull's own existence.

It has been said with reason that the touchstone by which all writers of the Middle Ages were tried and which few survived was the transition from the medieval world to that of humanism. It is not surprising that Lull should have attracted disciples in his lifetime. But Lull's fame did not die with those who had known him. It survived them, it survived the Middle Ages. He was of passionate interest to Nicholas of Cusa, to Giordano Bruno, to Leibniz. The reason, it may be suggested, why both his life and his philosophy continue today to appeal to the intellect as well as to the imagination is that, when once he had found in God the end of his desires, he was able to transmute the passionate love which inspired his nature into a frame of action as rational, as unitary, as the structure of his thought. The demonstration of the unity of truth, the peaceful union of all men were Lull's aims. To the pursuit of these aims his life and writings were dedicated. (pp. 9-45)

J. N. Hillgarth, in her Ramon Lull and Lullism in Fourteenth-Century France, *Oxford at the Clarendon Press, 1971, 504 p.*

Kenneth Leech (essay date 1978)

[*Leech is an English clergyman and critic who has written extensively on Christianity in contemporary society. In the following essay, he describes Llull as an essentially unoriginal thinker—a "conventional Augustinian"—and a Neoplatonic mystic primarily concerned with the synthesis of Arabic and Christian thought.*]

Ramon Lull was a native of Palma in Majorca, then part of a kingdom which had for a long period been in Muslim possession, and had only recently been reconquered by King James I of Catalonia-Aragon in 1229. Large numbers of Moors were still living there, as were many Jews, and the young Ramon was brought into contact at an early age with a variety of religious traditions and ethnic groups. This early experience was of decisive significance for the development of his thought and his theological concerns.

His early life was that of a page at the royal court, and during this period he composed many love lyrics after the pattern of the troubadours, which he sang to his mistresses. His marriage to Blanca Picany, some time before 1257, seems to have made little difference to his pattern of life. However, at the age of thirty, while composing a troubadour song, he received a vision of Christ crucified, which was repeated five times. From this moment, he says, his

The hermit and the squire, from a fifteenth-century French manuscript of Llull's Le libre del orde de cavalleria.

sole desire was to serve God and to preach the Gospel. So he became a 'Fool of Love', a holy troubadour singing of the Love of God.

Soon after this, he heard a sermon on St Francis Day, and he was strongly drawn to the Franciscan ideal of poverty and self-giving love. As a result he later became a Tertiary, a member of the Franciscan Third Order, indeed 'the most distinguished tertiary of the thirteenth or indeed of any other century' [according to J. R. H. Moorman in his *History of the Franciscan Order*]. Earlier, however, it was the Dominican influence of Ramon de Penyafort, the former Master-General of the Dominican Order, which had encouraged him to study at Majorca in order to acquire some basic knowledge of Arabic. For, soon after his accession in 1276, King James II had set up, at Ramon's inspiration, a missionary college at Miram in Majorca to train missionaries in Arabic and in the understanding of Islam. Here Ramon studied and taught, and in 1285 he persuaded Pope Honorius III to set up a school of Arabic in Rome. Ramon's future life was to be very largely dominated by the Arabic-speaking world of Islam, and his strong desire to preach the Gospel there and to seek a synthesis of Christian and Muslim theological thought.

In 1291 Acre fell, and Syria was evacuated. It meant the end of Christian work in vast areas of the east. The following year, at the age of sixty, Ramon Lull set out for North Africa. He landed at Tunis but, after a short attempt at preaching, he was arrested and deported. Fifteen years later, in 1307, he was back in North Africa. In the streets of Bugia he is alleged to have cried out, 'The law of the Christians is holy and true, and the sect of the Moors is false and wrong, and this I am prepared to prove.' So he was taken into custody, but he carried on his evangelistic activity in prison, and was later deported again.

In 1314, at the age of eighty-two, he again set out for Bugia, where he stayed for a little while, before moving to Tunis. There he was received by the Moors, and he debated in the villages. But at the end of 1315 he returned to Bugia where he was battered to death.

Lull was beatified by Pope Pius IX and a special Mass and Office was allowed in Majorca and throughout the Franciscan Order. His literary output was vast, amounting to nearly five hundred published works, and many others have been ascribed to him. Among his most important writings are ***The Book of the Gentile and the Three Wise Men,*** an allegory of a travelling Gentile who meets a Jew, a Christian, and a Saracen; ***The Book of Contemplation,*** a seven-volume work originally written in Arabic; ***The Hundred Names of God,*** and ***The Book of the Tartar and the Christian*** (on the Athanasian Creed), both written in Rome; ***Felix or The Book of Marvels,*** written in Paris; ***The Book of the Five Wise Men; The Tree of Science;*** and [***The Book of the Lover and the Beloved***].

Although a whole tradition of Lullism grew up after his death, Lull was in general not an original theological thinker, but a rather conventional Augustinian who held that the inquiring mind could acquire all truth. His teaching on the 'Great Art' was held to place too much emphasis on the place of reason, and it was doubts about his orthodoxy in this area which prevented his canonization in 1376. Throughout his writing there is very strong emphasis on reason. Memory and will, he tells us, join and ascend the mountain of the Beloved, so that reason too should rise. Lull seemed to have little or no place for darkness or the *via negativa* in his scheme except as a temporary phenomenon. His concern to refute the heresy of Averroism, with its doctrine of the total separation of God from the world and of the eternity of matter, led him to the opposite position of virtually identifying theological with philosophical truth. Hillgarth [in her *Ramon Lull and Lullism in Fourteenth Century France*] notes that 'the somewhat old-fashioned' nature of Lull's philosophy which belongs in many ways more to the twelfth century than to his own age must in large part be ascribed simply to his lack of contact, during his years of study, with any leading centre of Christian thought.' Yet there is also in Lull a Franciscan tenderness and a devotion to the Passion and to the love of God. He was deeply influenced by St Bonaventure, not only in his view that the creation of the world by God could be demonstrated by the light of reason, but also in his belief that all human wisdom, when compared with mystical illumination, was folly. Nevertheless, his view of illumination was intellectual. God, he held, consisted of a series of essential attributes. But the instruments of God's creative work in the world are the Dignities, absolute transcendental principles. In ***The Art of Contemplation,*** they are said to be nine in number: Goodness, Greatness, Eternity, Power, Wisdom, Will, Virtue, Truth, and Glory. Through these principles, closely similar to Plato's Ideas, all created perfection is brought about. Every element in creation is a symbol of the presence of God.

Lull's vision of the world was essentially that of Neo-Platonism. There was a hierarchy of creation, stretching from God, through the spiritual world and the celestial spheres, to the spheres of the four elements, to man, the animals, and matter. The Divine Dignities exercised their power throughout the created order. Although the actual word 'Dignities' seems to be peculiar to Lull, the idea of 'Divine Attributes' is extremely ancient, appearing in the Old Testament Wisdom literature, in Plotinus, Pseudo-Dionysius, and Augustine among others. The immediate source of Lull's use of it may have been John Scotus Erigena, the ninth-century Irish thinker. But a similar view of Divine Attributes was held by Muslims and Jews. Lull was acquainted with the works of al-Ghazzali, and this may be the reason for his selection of the Divine Dignities as the basis of his system.

For at the heart of Lull's thought and work is the concern for some kind of synthesis between Arabic and Christian thought, and this emerges in particular in ***The Art of Contemplation.*** Islam was seen as the greatest obstacle to the conversion of the world. Yet few Christians seemed able or willing to devote their energies to a serious Christian-Islamic dialogue. Apart from Roger Bacon, only Lull did so. Lull's central thesis was that the approach to Islam should be one of conversion by peaceful means, through gentle persuasion and dialogue. Yet linked with this was a militant ideology of combat and confrontation, and his later years (1287-1316) saw him involved in a continuous battle with Islam. But Lull went further than this. Through intellect and love, he believed that a synthesis between Christian theology and Islam was possible.

In his view, the Holy Trinity was mirrored in the created order. There was a Trinitarian structure of creation, God is seen throughout the created order, and his attributes are active through all the levels of created life. Lull's emphasis on intellectual and even mathematical reasoning makes him closely akin to al-Ghazzali who used geometrical ideas in his scientific theology. Also, deeply rooted in medieval Islam was the *kalām,* or Islamic scholastic theology, which set out a rational apologetic for dogma, based on proof and demonstration. Lull, in disputing with Muslims, sought to prove the truth of Christian dogma by the same necessary reasons (*rationes necessariae*). He insisted that the Trinity and the Incarnation were *more* appropriate to Islamic belief in the Unity and Power of God than Islamic theology itself was. So Lull saw Islam as incomplete rather than false. It is difficult to over-stress the degree to which this view represented an advance on the conventional thinking of his age. However, Lull did not believe that reason could replace grace in the work of conversion, and at the end of ***The Book of the Gentile,*** the Gentile traveller, having listened to the expositions of Jew, Christian, and Muslim, is still left undecided.

Lull's recognition of the essential place of Divine grace [according to Hillgarth] 'brought with it a tolerance and objectivity rare for the age, and an emphasis on the necessity for free, not forced, conversion.'

And, in spite of his exaltation of reason, Lull is remembered most of all as the 'Fool of Love'. The approach to Christ through folly is deeply embedded in the Franciscan tradition: it is here that we find 'the most developed form of western folly for Christ's sake' [according to John Saward in *Theology and Prayer*]. St Francis himself had claimed that 'the Lord told me that he wanted me to be a new fool in the world; and he did not want to lead us by any other way than by that learning'. So Lull, like Francis before him, saw himself as one of God's *joglars* who, unlike the earthly *joglars,* sang only of the love of God.

> I desire to be a fool
> that I may give honour and glory
> to God, and
> I will have no art nor device in my words
> by reason of the greatness of my love.

And so in the book ***Blanquerna,*** sometimes wrongly described as an autobiography, Lull appears before the Papal Court as a Fool. As a troubadour is intoxicated with the love of his lady, so Lull is intoxicated with the love of Christ his Beloved.

[***The Book of the Lover and the Beloved***] is a small part of the larger work ***Blanquerna,*** which may date from Lull's time at Miramar. It is a somewhat extravagant religious romance. A wealthy youth, Evast, marries the beautiful Aloma, and after years without a child, a boy, Blanquerna, is born to them. In due course, he leaves them to pursue the solitary life. He wanders into a wood, but later is chosen as the abbot of a monastery, then as bishop, and finally as Pope. But he ends his time as a hermit in the mountains. ***The Book of the Lover and the Beloved*** may have been written before ***Blanquerna,*** and was subsequently incorporated into it as Chapter 99. It was composed as a guide to contemplation, with a short passage for every day of the year. The language is that of human love, and it belongs to the long tradition of mystical writing in which the relationship of God and the soul is portrayed in the terms of sexual love. In his description of the origin of the work, Lull also explains its purpose.

> Blanquerna was in prayer and considered the manner wherein to contemplate God and his virtues; and when he had ended his prayer he wrote down the manner in which he had contemplated God. And he did this daily, and brought new arguments to his prayer, so that after many and varied manners he should compose ***The Book of the Lover and the Beloved,*** and that these manners should be brief, and that in a short space of time, the soul should learn to reflect in many ways. And with the blessing of God, Blanquerna began the book which he divided into as many verses as there are days in the year, and each verse suffices for the contemplation of God in one day, according to the art of the ***Book of Contemplation.***

(pp. 1-8)

Kenneth Leech, in an introduction to The Book of the Lover and the Beloved, *by Ramon Lull, edited by Kenneth Leech and translated by E. Allison Peers, revised edition, Sheldon Press, 1978, pp. 1-9.*

Willis Barnstone (essay date 1983)

[*Barnstone is an American educator, poet, translator, and critic. In the following essay, he elucidates Llull's philosophy of love and its relation to Islamic and Neoplatonic mystical traditions.*]

> Whether the friend and the beloved are near or far is all one and the same, for their love mingles as water mingles with wine. They are linked as heat with light; they agree and are united as essence and being
>
> Ramon Llull

Ramon Llull, the Illuminated Doctor and Fool of Love, was born in the Ciutat de Mallorques about 1232, only a few years after Jaume I of Aragon led a Catalan army to the *reconquista* of Mallorca (1229). The island was still largely inhabited by infidels. The very presence of the infidels—Arabs and Jews—was a prime source of Llull's knowledge and obsessions: his absorption of Islamic and Jewish thought and, at the same time, his zeal to alter such doom-inviting thought through his own writing and proselytizing.

In that unique mingling in Spain of three religious and philosophic traditions, the Catalan philosopher had access to the Arabic language, to which he devoted nine years of study and in which he wrote his first major work, the ***Book of Contemplation of God*** (1271-1276); also from Arabic he translated the ***Logic of al-Ghazali*** (1275-1287); from

Averroes, who gave Latin Europe its first medieval Aristotle and commentary, he derived knowledge and venom for his attacks on the Parisian Averroists; and from the Sufi poets, as he states in the introduction to the ***Book of the Friend and the Beloved*** (1282-1287), he learned that the Saracens have books with "words of love" whose manner he would imitate. Llull also knew the Kabbalistic tradition of the *Book of Splendor (Zohar)* and the work of Maimonides, who wrote in Judeo-Arabic; from the Kabbalah, with all its trees of life, alphabets, and logical diagrams, he probably took, according to Jocelyn Hillgarth [in her *Ramon Lull and Lullism in Fourteenth-Century France*] and Miguel Cruz Hernández, [in his *El pensamiento de Ramon Lull*] his notions for his own marvelous thinking machines; his theological computers with their sets of tables and movable disks, those concrete poems that instructed Giordano Bruno and Leibnitz and that led Jonathan Swift to satire in the fourth part of *Gulliver.* Above all, the presence of the infidels impelled Ramon Llull to his life mission of conversion and his hope for martyrdom. Although his legendary success in achieving a bloody death in Barbary is now thought to be false, it is certain that from the heathen he learned reason and mystery. As Gerald Brenan [in his *Literature of the Spanish People*] has pointed out, only a Spanish Catalan, that is, a European, had the "plasticity of mind" and "the adventurousness of spirit to absorb the mysticism of the East" and "combine it with a reckless rationalism."

The Christians of Mallorca spoke Catalan as their native language. Catalan was then riding the cultural wave of the expanding empire of Catalonia-Aragon, which included the provinces of Aragon, Catalonia, Valencia, and the Balearic islands, and extended to Athens (where even today the word Catalan signifies a Frankish pirate). The kindred language of Provençal had fallen into literary decline after the Albigensian Crusade of 1209, but the Catalans continued writing courtly poems in the Provençal troubadour manner, as did the Portuguese-Gallicians at the western edge of the peninsula. The lexicon, manner, and attitudes of the troubadours provided the last contemporary source for Llull's work. Yet for all the biblical, Neoplatonic, Sufi, Kabbalistic, and Christian impact on his work, in his poetry and poetic prose, Llull never ceased to be a troubadour *a lo divino.*

As a young man Llull is said to have lived the life of the young knight and courtier. Privileged, a seneschal to Prince Jaume—the future King of Mallorca—he apparently had many women and wrote conventional love poems. He married, had two children, and continued his pursuit of women with those courtly passions that are, as Denis de Rougement writes, always adulterous and vaguely impossible. Whatever Llull did he did with twice the energy of others, and so his involvement with women was intensely sensual, and the legends of his encounters are confirmed at least in principle, if not in fact, by his own confessions in the ***Book of Contemplation.*** One day when the young gallant was riding through the city of Mallorques, he saw a lady he desired enter a church; he spurred his horse and galloped in after her through the great west door, right up to where she was kneeling. Another story, taken up by biographers, has Llull entering the chamber of the same lady. To get rid of him the lady uncovered herself and, to his horror, displayed to him "the breast he had so extolled in his verses, being slowly consumed by a malignant cancer." Soon after, while trying to compose a love poem to a lady, there appeared to him, suspended in midair, a vision of Christ on the cross. The vision was repeated four nights in a row, and now, as Llull himself writes, his life was changed. Thereupon he decided to dedicate his life to study, writing, conversion of the heathen, and martyrdom. He turned his back on worldly possessions, dressed in a coarse habit, and, like the Gautama, abandoned his wife and children for his new god.

Llull's passion for women henceforth was directed toward the male figure of God. He wrote of himself "As great drought and great cold are the pestilence of the fruits of the earth, . . . so, Lord, the beauty of women has been the plague and tribulation of my eyes." And "I, Lord, have loved women many times, so much that neither night nor day was there anything in my heart but love of them. In my great folly, Lord, I took those things I loved as if they were gods, for I loved them as You should be loved." His obsession with women had been more than courtly fancy in the Neoplatonic tradition of adoration for earthly beauty as a reflection of a virtuous soul. As Hillgarth writes, his human love was accompanied by "an almost pathological insistence on the corruption and filth behind the beautiful exterior," and, again quoting Hillgarth, "Some passages where Llull dwells on certain physiological processes are too revolting to be translated." After his conversion he proposed to be "a true troubadour of God: "Sènyer, que sia vertader juglar, en donar laor vertadera de son Senyor Déu." In his advice to his son to seek God, we see an equation of violence, desire for women, and desire for God: "Beloved son, lust makes men go to war and kill and wound each other; women have been the causes of the destruction and burning of castles and cities." A further example of the transfer of passions for the body to a sensual apprehension of death and of God is in the revealing lines: "The first thing I tasted in the world was milk, the last thing I shall taste will be death. May it please you, Merciful Lord, that as my mouth's first taste was of milk which enlivened the body, even so the last thing I taste may be blood flowing from my body, dying for Your love."

To prepare for his new life of writing, conversion, and martyrdom, Llull set out on a mission of self-education. He began an intense, nine-year study of Arabic, the prestigious peninsula language for theology and philosophy. His intimate knowledge of Arabic and Islam gave him a unique advantage over all the great scholastics who were his contemporaries: Albertus Magnus, Thomas Aquinas, St. Bonaventura, Duns Scotus. During this same period he wrote in Arabic the vast ***Book of Contemplation,*** a work of some one million words, which he then translated into Catalan. As such it was the first philosophical work in Europe written in a vernacular language.

After Llull's first efforts in Arabic and Catalan, his prodigious energy never lapsed and he wrote at least 243 books, including many works in Latin. He also traveled to Italy and France to seek support for his educational missions and his later religious crusades. He did found five centers of learning, but failed to convince popes and patrons to help him in his larger scheme of founding colleges to train missionaries in Oriental languages. (Llull had in mind the struggle between Islam and Christianity.) In Paris he taught and spoke against the Averroists, and while he was largely unsuccessful in Paris and Montpellier in imposing his views, his ideas were taken up by Thomas Le Myesier of Arras, a secular clerk at the University of Paris; studies by Le Myesier were the basis of later Llullism in Paris and Western Europe. As a lay Franciscan monk, Llull traveled to Cyprus in 1301, again unsuccessful in obtaining aid for his projects, then to Lesser Armenia, and perhaps to Jerusalem. He also began a series of three trips to Tunis and Algeria—missions of conversion. In 1307 on his second North African mission he was imprisoned for six months and expelled, and before reaching Italy he was shipwrecked off Pisa, losing all his books and manuscripts. Finally in September 1315 he was again in Tunis. Pursued, as in earlier missions, by hostile street mobs, he is popularly said to have achieved his much desired martyrdom. Apparently, however, he died in Mallorca some time in 1316 in his eighty-third year.

Ramon Llull combines the character of a man of action with that of a philosopher, theologian, and mystic. As a proselytizing missionary he sought the death of the body in the service of God. As a mystic he sought a second death, through love for God, so that the soul, released from the body and earthly time, could achieve union with God.

The ***Book of Contemplation*** contains Llull's basic notions of language, philosophy, and mystical theology, which persist through his work and which are distilled in the late ***Ars generalis ultima*** of 1308. In the ***Book of Contemplation*** Llull introduces his theory of the Divine Attributes or Dignities, which are further elaborated in his ***Art of Finding Truth*** (1274). Also from this period Llull compiled the ***Compendium of the Logic of al-Ghazali,*** in which we first find his celebrated *ars combinatoria,* combinatory art, in which philosophical terms are designated by specific letters of the alphabet. By combining these letters according to his own algebraic logic and with the aid of combinatory diagrams—the early computers—he could solve any problem in all the sciences of the world.

The basis for Llull's combinatory art was the letters assigned to the nine Dignities, which are Goodness, Greatness, Eternity, Power, Wisdom, Will (or Love), Virtue, Truth, and Glory. Since the entire structure of knowledge is held together in one Divine Unity, an analogical manipulation of its parts, that is, of its Dignities, affords a specific knowledge of plants, people, angels, and stars.

To understand Llull's Divine Attributes or Dignities we should recall that these notions appear in Muslim philosophy under the general name of *hadras,* and in the Kabbalah under the name of *sephiroth.* Jewish scholars also assigned nine names to the *sephiroth,* which were the essences identifiable with God. As in Llull, contemplation of God was achieved through concentration on his divine attributes, that is, on the *sephiroth.*

But the doctrine of the Dignities is also found in Augustine and Anselm and of course it ultimately derives from the notion of Platonic Ideas, which was spread to the Sufi East and the Christian West through Plotinus. As we know, throughout much of the latter Middle Ages, Christians, Jews, and Muslims shared, in one form or another, a Neo-platonic view of the world, which included a common belief in a hierarchy or ladder of creation, "Stretching from God down through the spiritual world of the angels, through the celestial spheres and the spheres of the four elements (fire, air, water, earth)," of which man and woman were composed, "to animals and inanimate creation." The idea of man and woman as a microcosm, in which the universe was contained and through which it could be understood, stands at the heart of the Neoplatonic tradition, which was thoroughly accepted by thirteenth-century minds. As early as the ninth century, John Scotus Erigena, the Irish philosopher and translator of Pseudo-Dionysius, could write: "There is no creature which cannot be understood to be *in* man. Man is composed of the same four elements, distributed in much the same manner as in the universe. . . . Only in man can the two created worlds of the universe meet, the spiritual world of angels and intelligences, and the corporal world or nature. . . . Man is the center of the whole universe." So the key to the investigation of the universe is the study of human beings.

Ramon Llull combines the character of a man of action with that of a philosopher, theologian, and mystic. As a proselytizing missionary he sought the death of the body in the service of God. As a mystic he sought a second death, through love for God, so that the soul, released from the body and earthly time, could achieve union with God.

—Willis Barnstone

Now humans are divided into soul and body. The soul is divided into three powers—will, intellect, and memory—while the body has four qualities—imagination, sensation, vegetation, and the elemental plane. In a primitive way, if we understand God's Nine Divine Attributes or Dignities, man's three powers, and the four constituents of his or her body, we are equipped to engage in the combinatory art of Llull's philosophy. The allegorical figures in the ***Book of the Friend and the Beloved*** are explicitly defined theologically according to God's Dignities, the soul's powers, and the body's four constituents.

Llull's essential mystical ideas are contained in the short volume, the ***Book of the Friend and the Beloved*** (***Libre d'amic e Amat***), the most poetic writing in the Llull canon. Unlike his other endlessly proliferating, encyclopedic volumes, the ***Book of the Friend and the Beloved*** is brief and often beautiful. I should say from the outset, however, that this concise volume shares with his longer works a double obsession: a mania for apparent order (exactly 366 verses—Pythagoras is always lurking in Llull) and at the same time a rambling disorder. While the ***Book of the Friend and the Beloved*** contains the essence of Llull's mystical notions, the ideas never follow in any discernible sequence. Clusters of ideas can be detected only by linking verses from disparate sections of the work. Indeed, the ***Book of Chaos,*** the title of one of Llull's cosmogonical books, would be an appropriate title for this work which glitters as if 366 stars were thrown at random into the heavens.

The ***Book of the Friend and the Beloved*** was composed some time between 1282 and 1287 in Mallorca. It is included, along with the ***Art of Contemplation,*** in Llull's ***Blanquerna,*** an allegorical romance of a hermit, much like Llull himself, who roams through forest and cities, seeking to persuade strangers to convert to his Christian god. Each of the 366 passages, in poetic prose, stands for one day's contemplation of God. Among the models for the book is the writing of Sufis, as Blanquerna states in the prologue:

> While Blanquerna considered after this manner, he remembered how that once when he was Pope a Saracen related to him that the Saracens have certain religious men, and that among others are certain men called Sufis . . . , and these men have words of love and brief examples which give to men great devotion; . . . When Blanquerna had considered after this wise, he purposed to make the book according to the manner aforementioned.

Unlike the *Song of Songs,* its original cause, or Saint John of the Cross's "Spiritual Canticle," its ultimate flower, the ***Book of the Friend and the Beloved*** is of uneven quality. Some passages are pristinely beautiful, medieval garden scenes of musical birds and mystical lovers:

> The birds sang at dawn, and the friend awoke: he is the dawn. And the birds stopped their singing, and the friend died in the dawn for his beloved.

But more verses are tediously repetitious and heavy with scholastic argument as Llull rearranges personified ideas. At his best the allegorical scene is magical. He attempts to go beyond words to the ineffable. Love takes him where speech fails, for, as in John of the Cross, earthly love is the allegory for mystical union:

> A bird sang in the grove of the beloved. The friend came and said to the bird: if we cannot understand each other through language, let us understand each other through love, for in your song my beloved is revealed to my eyes.

Llull's lexical resources are minimal. He uses few words and repeats them. Since the thought is carried through an allegorical personification of Platonic Ideas, his depiction of character and things has very little conviction on the first level of experience. A tree of love or a lion of virtue is scarcely a live tree or a fearful lion, for they owe their existence to their allegorical rather than to their mimetic meaning, which of course weakens the impact of their earthly reality. When Llull's alchemy is right, however, he turns ideas into conceptual objects, fully as sensual as Emily Dickinson's " 'Hope' is the thing with feathers."

The perception of the two lovers is crucial to our reading of the text. To the extent that the troubadour suitor of his beloved lacks human reality, the book ceases to be literature, ceases to relate to an event, and becomes simply a code for theological argument. But of course the lovers do take on reality of a kind, however symbolic their actions, however consistent the author's wish to disincarnate his creations. Words communicate information and no words have been invented that can evoke corporeal presences and at the same time rid them of their corporality. Religious commentators have normally maltreated texts from Sappho to John of the Cross by not acknowledging a hint of literalness, by not permitting Sappho or the lovers in the "Spiritual Canticle" to embrace. For our purposes we will read the text both for its literal and its secondary meanings, which contextual information helps to clarify.

The friend and the beloved are both male. Despite allegorical intent, insofar as the lovers are human and real, we witness an erotic union between two kissing and embracing men. Their union on earth is a metaphor for the mystical union of man and God. The ultimate literary source of the lovers is the biblical *Song of Songs.* The allegorical meaning of the lovers' union derives from later traditional interpretations of the *Song of Songs.* In order to see the ***Book of the Friend and the Beloved*** in its literary-historical context, we will look at the role of the lovers in biblical and Arabic precursors, and in John of the Cross.

The resemblance between the ***Book of the Friend and the Beloved*** and the *Song of Songs* lies in the situation of the two lovers, the solitude, the search, the sickness of the lover because of love, the encounter in the garden, the trees, the fruits, the Edenic atmosphere. Llull uses specific phrases and words derived from the biblical idyll: "Your love is a seal," or "The friend saw himself taken and bound, wounded and killed, for the love of his beloved." In passage 88 we have "The friend was sick with love," which echoes "Say I am sick with love." And again in 51: "Where is your beloved?" is, but for the personal pronoun, the biblical "Where is my beloved?" The search for the beloved is the persistent theme of both books.

The *Song of Songs* love lyrics are secular in origin. Their religious allegorization was a religious afterthought to secure their inclusion into the holy canon of the Bible. So Jewish theology saw the Shulamite as representing the love of the people for their church or for God, and Christian theology, even more imaginative, saw the Shulamite as the people expressing love for Christ, an anachronistic feat of Christianization which even Dante, despite his affection for Virgil, did not offer his favorite. The mystical interpretations by Saint John of the Cross and Luis de León have the Shulamite as the *soul* seeking union with God. Although Llull, along with Saint Bonaventura, Bernard de Clairvaux, Saint John of the Cross, and others, goes back to the actual text for phrases and episodes (albeit in Latin translation), for the meaning they invest in their versions and commentaries they rely on the tradition of allegorical interpretation. An exception to the Latin allegorists is Fray Luis de León. León translated and explicated the *Song of Songs* directly from the Masoretic Hebrew text (that is, from its "corrupt, uncommented, primitive, and original" form), and for this imprudence he spent nearly five years in the Inquisitional prison at Valladolid.

The *Song of Songs* is a short idyll or play for voices, a fragmentary love story, unsurpassed in images, language, and dramatic passion. It is the love of a woman for a man and a man for a woman. It is explicitly erotic:

While the king lay on his couch
the spikenard aroma of my body filled the air.
My love is a bouquet of myrrh
as he lies at night between my breasts.

Although the atmosphere is lyrical and idealized, the lovers are real. Their existence as religious metaphors comes later, after the fact. Unlike Llull's lovers they never fade into conceptualization or blur into theological syllogisms.

In the *Song of Songs* the lover is a woman, the beloved a man. These roles are followed by Saint John of the Cross in his three central poems, which use the diction of the *Songs of Songs,* "Dark Night" (Noche oscura), "O Living Flame of Love" (Llama de amor viva), and "The Spiritual Canticle" (El cantico espiritual). So in each poem John of the Cross speaks androgynously as a woman, "Salí sin ser notada" (I [*fem.*] left unseen), for the soul, the *anima,* is feminine and seeks its masculine counterpart, the *animus,* that is, God. "The Spiritual Canticle" is remarkably faithful to the biblical original, both in phrase and meaning, and although the Doctor of Nothingness writes a full book to explain its allegory, the poem itself, like the *Song of Songs,* introduces no theological language into the text; and, in further contrast to Llull, the personages are dramatically real and alive.

As for the lovers' roles in other versions of the quest for divine union through love, we find very interesting variations in the sex of the lovers. Normally the poet (who is usually male) speaks through the lover. In the *Song of Songs* and John of the Cross, the lover is a woman seeking a male God. In the tradition of Mary Magdalene and Christ, the lover may be a prostitute seeking God. The Spanish Arabic poet Shuhtair, born in Gaudix (c. 1212-1269), describes in full detail his intercourse as a female whore with God. The lover may also be a man seeking God the woman. These roles are common in Gnostic texts. An outstanding example of a male lover seeking union with a female spirit is in the work of Ibn al-Farid (1181-1235), the Egyptian mystic who lived fifty years before Llull. Finally, there is the homosexual tradition of the greatest of the Sufi poets, Rumi (1207-1273), who, like Llull, abandoned wife and children to follow his divine beloved. In Rumi's ecstatic poems the beloved was a stranger named Shams al-Din, who was of course at the same time God.

To understand these traditional love metaphors of the mystical experience, we may glance briefly at the sexual roles of Llull's immediate Islamic precursors, Ibn al-Farid and Rumi, remembering that Llull states that he learned the words of love from the Sufis.

Many Arabists consider Ibn al-Farid the major mystical poet in Arabic literature. A follower of the Neoplatonic tradition, which is climaxed in the work of his fellow Egyptian Plotinus, al-Farid's central poem is *The Poem of the Way,* also called *Tai'iya* (meaning an ode rhyming on the letter *t*), for each of its 760 couplets ends on *t.*

Like Plotinus and later Christian mystics, the speaker seeks union with divinity. To reach the divine female principle in himself he must divest himself of all ties with the phenomenal world and become that woman with whom he identifies. Saint John of the Cross's gloss "I die because I do not die" (*muero porque no muero*) is anticipated in Ibn al-Farid's

My death in passion's ecstasy forher
Is sweetest life, and if I do not die
In love, I live for ever in death's throes.

The Egyptian's path to the woman is by way of an inward journey. Ultimately he cries, "I am she!" With all his senses he becomes one with her. She penetrates his eyes, his tongue; he draws her in like perfume and she touches every nerve. He holds her in a kiss and their bodies dissolve. To find her he must forget himself and wake to her within himself. This leads him, astonishingly, to embrace himself. Physical and spiritual union with the woman ultimately means union with the spirit of Mohammed, with God, and entry into light. In beautiful lines he writes of coming into light which is a lightning flash:

my dawn shone forth
In splendour; all my darkness fled away.
Here I attained a height the intellect
Recoils before, and she was my junction
And my union with myself.
I beamed with joy (for I had reached myself).

In the last lines he has become so intermingled with God that he speaks with the voice of God Himself or Herself. He has undergone monistic theosis; he is divinized in blissful and ecstatic union with the godhead. In this state, like an astronaut with supremely divine powers, he commands galaxies and angels:

By me was guided all the shining stars
Upon their courses; all the planets swim
About my heavens as my will controls
All things I own; my angels prostrate fall
Before my sovereignty.

Ibn al-Farid's inward flight to God, through love for the woman, is one of many mystico-erotic doctrines which, as Miguel Cruz Hernández writes, was an immediate Neoplatonic Sufi model for Ramon Llull. Hernández also mentions the psycho-physical elements of love in others who developed kindred systems of the science of love: Muhammed Ibn Dawud of Bagdad (869-910), author of *Book of the Flower (Kitab al-Zahra),* Ibn Hazm of Córdoba, author of *The Necklace of the Dove* (*Tawq al-Hamama*), and above all Ibn Arabi of Murcia (1165-1240), the pantheistic mystic, whose Dignities have often been compared to those elaborated by Llull. For our purpose of showing an identity of methods and purpose, if not influence, I wish to deal with Rumi, the greatest of the Persian mystical poets, whose ideas and poetic expression of love have an extraordinary affinity with those of our Catalan poet.

Jalal al-Din Rumi was born in 1207 at Balk near the Afghan frontier and died at Konya in 1273 in Turkey. In 1244, when Rumi was thirty-seven, he met a wandering dervish named Shams al-Din, and, as R. A. Nicholson wrote, he "found in the stranger that perfect image of the Divine Beloved which he had long been seeking." Rumi left his wife and children, and the two men remained inseparable until, toward the end of his life, he found another beloved in Salah al-Din Zarkub. The mystical poems addressed to Shams al-Din are placed largely in the pastoral, Edenic garden setting we find in the *Song of Songs* and in Llull's ***Book of the Friend and the Beloved.***

In Rumi's garden are allegorical beasts, flowers, and trees; and the tree is a basic metaphor for the mystical ascension to God. Ramon Llull wrote his ***The Tree of the Philosophy of Love*** (*El arbre de filosofia d'amor*) in 1298 in which he creates a hierarchical system from roots, trunk, branches, foliage, leaves, flowers to its ultimate fruit, which yields only one fruit: God. Rumi, for his part, in speaking of the tree of love, writes "know that the branch of Love is in pre-eternity and its roots in post-eternity." For each writer the tree provides an escape from ordinary time to eternity. In Llull the branches spread wide till they give shelter to the whole world, and force their way upward in quest of love's heaven on earth.

To ascend the tree of love one must depart from the prison of the body, from the world. Rumi wrote, "In the body's prison I am drowned in blood," and "Do not despair, my soul, in the darkness of this prison, for that king who redeemed Joseph from prison has come." The king is God. In the very last verse of the ***Book of the Friend and the Beloved,*** Llull speaks of the same prison of the senses and worldly time: " 'Say, O Fool! What is this world?' He answered: 'It is the prison-house of them that love and serve my beloved.' " Once in the garden, the bird is there to communicate spiritual messages. Rumi has the nightingale sing of the Beloved: "henceforward the nightingale in the garden will tell of us, it will tell of the beauty of that heart-ravishing Beloved." For Llull the bird sings what cannot be said in speech, that is, it gives song to the ineffable, to that mystical "dying in life" that goes beyond speech and that is only understood through love. In those exquisite passages we have examined, Llull writes:

> The birds sang at dawn, and the friend awoke: he is the dawn. And the birds stopped their singing, and the friend died in the dawn for his beloved.

and:

> A bird sang in the grove of the beloved. The friend came and said to the bird: if we cannot understand each other through language, let us understand each other through love, for in your song my beloved is revealed to my eyes.

The meeting in the garden is between a lover and his beloved. The encounter is fulfilled through kisses, embraces, and physical union. Physical love in most mystical tracts is a metaphor for spiritual union. Although words are inadequate, as John of the Cross writes, similes may be useful. In Rumi and Llull the friend is the slave of the beloved, and his life and death are dedicated to the beloved's service. The scholarly argument of whether the recurrent troubadour notions of courtly love have a precedent in Islamic poetry should disappear upon looking at the poetry not only of Rumi but of a host of secular and divine lovers who precede the Provençal period.

In Rumi the lover is drawn to the protective bosom of the Beloved. He is drawn to his lips and his embrace: "Today your beauty has another lineament, today your delectable lip has another sweetmeat." And then, "In this snow let us kiss his lips, for snow and sugar refresh the heart." While the sexual encounter in Llull is also between two male lovers, at one moment the friend is the active participant, at another he is passive and the beloved takes the initiative, as we see in this passage:

> The beloved revealed himself to his friend, clothed in new and scarlet robes. He stretched out his arms to embrace him. He inclined his head to kiss him; and he remained on high that his friend might ever seek him.

The new and scarlet robes probably refer to Christ, and it is fitting that Christ—who, apart from the fierce Pantokrator representation in Byzantine mosaics, is traditionally depicted as a sensitive, curving, androgynous figure on the cross—should be the object of the friend's passion. In another passage of embraces, kisses, and union, the beloved is again the active lover, and when he speaks the friend is speechless, which is also appropriate to a love which is divinely ineffable:

> The friend and the beloved met together, and their caresses, embraces and kisses, their weeping and tears, bore witness to their meeting. Then the beloved asked the friend concerning his state, and the friend was speechless before his beloved.

The garden, the bird, the lovers, the embraces lead to that instant, perhaps that eternity, unmeasured by the clock, to that ocean without port. Both Rumi and Llull, in their ascension, leave the garden and fly upward through the seven heavens to the place of the Beloved. Their imagery is cosmic, as they pass the moon and the sun.

Now we should speak mainly of Ramon Llull's expression of the mystical experience, although here, as in other aspects of his philosophy of love, the monistic and theistic elements of divine union go beyond the lexicon of Catholic theology. Indeed, the nature of Llull's mystical experience cannot be described adequately unless we make reference to Islamic and Kabbalistic traditions.

Much of Ramon Llull's philosophy is given to the elaboration of a logical system by which one perfects the essences and powers of one's soul in order to reach the Divine Attributes or Dignities of God, in order to reach God's embrace. But only in the ***Book of the Friend and the Beloved*** are we given an extended metaphor of the actual experience. In other words, the philosophy explains externally; the ***Book of the Friend and the Beloved*** is the act itself, if only in words.

Llull passes through the traditional states of painful, purgatorial darkness before reaching the steps of illumination and union. At the beginning of the volume, he asks: "How long shall it be till the darkness of the world is past?" When, past the dark night, will the ascension begin? "When will the time come when water, which by its nature flows downward, will change its nature and mount upward?" When that instant comes, space and time will fade. He writes of the unbounded experience: "Love is an ocean; its waves are untroubled by the winds; it has no port or shore."

What can be said for the lovers at the moment of union? Is the lover distinct or one with God? In Kabbalistic mysticism, as Gershom Scholem points out, the lover may achieve union but never *theosis.* The notion of divinization is an unacceptable arrogance. One joins God but one is not God. This is the essence of theistic mysticism, clearly evidenced in Fray Luis de León. But in Islamic mysticism, one often becomes God, as we have seen in Ibn al-Farid. The history of Islam contains numerous figures who claim—even one from the cross—to be God speaking. This is the essence of monistic mysticism. In the course of ecstatic contemplation of God, the union (*enosis*) is such that there is an identity of subject and object.

Llull aspires to the oblivion of union, to the loss of personality, yet just as clearly he is committed theologically to an ultimate separation of human and divine essences, even at the moment of their commingling. Speaking of that oblivion, he writes: "The friend perished in this ocean, and with him perished his torments, and the work of his fulfillment began." Then he makes clear that while the human and divine lovers are "one actuality in essence," their actual entities are distinct, as distinct as water from wine, heat from light, essence from being:

> Love, loving, the friend and the beloved are so directly united in the beloved that they are in essence one presence, and the friend and the beloved are, at the same time, distinct, concordant, with no contradiction or diversity of essence.

So while qualitatively the same, they are nevertheless distinct and separate equalities in agreement. Indeed, they must be two entities in order to agree, in order to be concordant. Thus logically and by poetic metaphor Llull depicts a mystical union of distinct lovers in which, though joined, the lovers ultimately do not lose their separate identities. We see this confirmed in the beautiful passage where differences are emphasized:

> Whether the friend and the beloved are near or far is all one and the same, for their love mingles as water mingles with wine. They are linked as heat with light; they agree and are united as essence and being.

The Book of the Friend and the Beloved is the quintessential medieval love tale *a lo divino.* The courtly efforts of the humble and generous suitor serve the beloved, who is a male figure—man, Christ, the Father. Unlike the profane courtly story, however, the suitor is not left pining. His love is consummated sexually in the garden through union with the beloved. And the union is also mystical.

Ramon Llull elaborates the philosophy of love for God in his long studies: in the ***Compendium of the Logic of al-Ghazali,*** in the ***Book of Contemplation,*** in the ***Ars magna,*** and ***Ars inventiva,*** in the ***Philosophy of the Tree of Love*** in which sixteen trees, from mineral trees to angelic trees, take us to God. His argument is ingenious and his combinatory art and charts of movable letters have given him the curious reputation of having invented the first computers—although the source for his letter computers is clearly in the Kabbalah and in Islamic philosophers. While his philosophy and theology represent a culmination of scholastic obsessions which to a modern reader may border on the divinely ridiculous, the essence of his mystical doctrines resides far more convincingly and accessibly in the actual experience of mysticism expressed through the metaphors in the ***Book of the Friend and the Beloved.*** The work is marred by lack of purpose and order in the sequence of days; moreover, most of the stanzas are tedious because of the relentless, scholastic manipulation of Platonic ideas in which Memory, Will, and Intellect debate and vie for predominance among the soul's powers, and in which corporeal essences and divine Dignities are repetitiously catalogued. Yet among the 366 days of meditation are magical hours in the garden. A whole year of ecstasy would, after all, be painful tedium—which is perhaps the defect of Jorge Guillén's supremely beautiful *Cántico.* But in those moments on "The Summit of Delight," the "Cima de la delicia," we hear the nightingale's unheard song and, to use a phrase from Rumi, our ears have eyes and our eyes have ears. Llull is then a visionary poet. The Illuminated Doctor and Fool of Love shows us how the ordinary cloud which circles and confines each

Fourteenth-century depiction of Llull's voyage to Tunis and his debate with the doctors of Islam.

of us to our solitude will, through love, become a cosmic illuminated cloud through which lovers converse:

> Love shone through the cloud which had come between the friend and the beloved, and made it to be as bright and resplendent as the moon by night, as the daystar at dawn, as the sun at midday . . . ; and through that bright cloud the friend and the beloved held converse.

The ***Book of the Friend and the Beloved*** is a culminating moment of mystical ecstasy which takes us from those Pythagorean numbers and Plato's allegorical cave, through the Plotinian ladders of creation and the Dionysian negative way to the Augustinian garden, from the Kabbalistic chariots and trees of life to the logical Islamic ascension to paradise. Llull's lovers, who first appear in the secular lyrics of the *Song of Songs,* show us that the experience of love, whether secular or divinely mystical, however illuminated or distorted through interpretation, appears again and again as the insuperable experience of literature. (pp. 111-26)

Willis Barnstone, "Ramon Llull: The Illuminated Doctor's Mystical Lovers," in his The Poetics of Ecstasy: Varieties of Ekstasis from Sappho to Borges, *Holmes & Meier, 1983, pp. 111-28.*

Anthony Bonner (essay date 1985)

[*In the following excerpt, Bonner characterizes Llull's* Felix *as a novel of social criticism.*]

For the past hundred years or so Llull has been known primarily as a literary figure and a mystic. This has meant that his reputation has been based chiefly on his two novels, ***Blanquerna*** and ***Felix,*** parts of which have achieved even greater independent fame: the ***Book of the Lover and the Beloved*** (part of ***Blanquerna***) as Llull's greatest mystical work, and the ***Book of the Beasts*** (part of ***Felix***) as Llull's best-known narrative work. This reputation, although presenting a limited vision of Llull's total endeavor, has had a very real justification in that these novels are among the first monuments of Catalan literature, and they may well constitute the first prose novels on contemporary themes in European literature. And since they are the only two such works Llull wrote, it is instructive to compare them.

They have, to be sure, many things in common. Both are, like Bunyan's *Pilgrim's Progress,* didactic and moral in purpose; plot, character, and so on, are present, if at all, merely as an outer decoration to make the inner message more appealing and more comprehensible. Both are directed, not to the Moslems and Jews for the purpose of conversion, but rather towards the Christian world itself; they are therefore not apologetic, but reforming works. The reform propounded in both, moreover, although spiritually grounded, is very strongly social. They also have a curious formal resemblance, in that they both contain works, as mentioned above, that seem extraneous to the main development of the novels, and which many critics believe to have been written separately—perhaps previously—and then inserted somewhat arbitrarily into the larger works. Moreover, they were written fairly close to each other in time, both in what we have called the quaternary phase of Llull's development: ***Blanquerna*** in about 1283, and ***Felix*** some five years later. Lastly, there is the curious linking detail of a hermit named Blanquerna, who plays an important role in ***Felix.***

The differences between the two works, however, are notable. ***Blanquerna*** is a utopian novel, in which the main characters lead exemplary lives, create ideal institutions, or run them in ideal fashion. ***Felix*** is a novel of social criticism aimed at existing institutions, people in positions of responsibility, and contemporary attitudes. As a result, ***Blanquerna*** breathes an air of sweetness and light, while ***Felix*** breathes a somewhat harsher, countercultural air. There is also a structural difference: Blanquerna is a real protagonist, acting and being acted upon; Felix, going about "wondering at the wonders of the world" and seeking instruction, merely provides the thread on which a series of exemplary tales are strung.

Although both are works of instruction, the things taught in each are very different. The instruction of ***Blanquerna*** is institutional in the religious and ecclesiastical sense of the word, as one can see from the titles of its main sections: Matrimony, Monastic Life, Prelacy, Papacy and the Hermit's Life. The instruction of ***Felix*** is encyclopedic and includes the entire medieval universe, as is also clear from the titles of its inner divisions: God, Angels, the Heavens, the Elements, Plants, Minerals, Animals, Man, Paradise, and Hell.

To concentrate now on ***Felix,*** one is immediately struck how the aforementioned succession of topics does not constitute a straightforward journey up or down the ladder of being, as we find for instance in the Nine Subjects of the ***Ars brevis.*** It is rather the order of creation: God, after creating the angels, created the elemental principles from which all the rest is derived, up to the end of the chain, which is man. And since man is at the apex of creation, it is only right that Book VIII, on Man, should occupy almost three-fifths of the entire novel.

As opposed to Llull's other encyclopedic works, and as one would expect in a work of fiction, the treatment is not expository or demonstrative. Instead it is almost purely exemplarist. Indeed, the *exempla,* or *exemplis* as Llull calls them in Catalan, the little allegorical tales or explanations, are the very stuff out of which ***Felix*** is woven and by which the ladder of being is made intelligible. They are the narrative equivalents of the metaphors of the artistic and scientific works. It is not only through them that the instruction of ***Felix*** is imparted, and that Felix resolves his own inner struggle with doubt and achieves spiritual understanding, but they themselves constitute part of the double message of the novel. For they are held up as models for instruction. In the Epilogue, these very *exempla* are treated as an open-ended body of lore that Felix can then use to go forth into the world to teach others what he has learned.

If this part of the message is methodological, or concerned with second intentions as Llull would have put it, the goal of that method, or the first intention of the book, is stated clearly in the opening paragraph of the Prologue: that God may "be known, loved, and served." This is consistent with the creationist structure of the work, in that this theme, which runs like a litany throughout the novel, is given by Llull as the ultimate purpose of the Creation—that God in fact created man that He might be known and loved. Since the basic purpose of ***Felix*** is the salvation of souls, it seeks to teach the reader to know and love God either directly (hence Book I) or through His works (hence the encyclopedic nature of the rest of the novel).

The reverse of the coin, man's failure to love and know God, is given as the cause of the world's being in the pitiable condition it is. This theme, which also runs through the entire novel, is the doorway through which Llull can introduce his social criticism. And this social criticism has two aspects worth observing: who is doing it and to whom it is directed.

To take the latter aspect first, it is soon evident that Llull repeatedly singles out those in power—princes, prelates, and wealthy burghers—as the ones who, by their example and position of leadership, bear the greatest weight of responsibility for the sorry state of the world, and who should most try to set it right. So in a sense one could call ***Felix*** a moral and spiritual manual for leaders.

As to who is doing this teaching, one begins to notice after a while that it is hardly ever a member of the ecclesiastical, feudal, or mercantile establishment, but rather a succession of holy men or philosophers who mostly live apart from society as hermits or shepherds. These teachers are consistently critical of the society they have left, of its misuse of power, of its opulence and wealth, of its self-indulgence, of its subversion of proper Christian values and spirituality. ***Felix*** represents a very Franciscan form of *contemptus mundi,* mixed with a typically medieval admiration for solitary meditation. The novel is also a plea for a return to the purity of the pre-establishment Church, with the Apostles and Martyrs as models. The Prologue also stresses this theme of the work: "One no longer finds the fervor and devotion there was in the time of the Apostles and Martyrs, who were willing to languish and die for the sake of knowing and loving God."

Another model, one not unconnected with that of the Apostles, is that of the *joculator Dei* or minstrel of God, a kind of pilgrim that Llull would have going from court to court entertaining his hosts with morally and spiritually instructive stories, rather than with the worldly vanities propagated by the troubadours. In fact, one could say that the work consists of Felix's preparation for the task entrusted first to him and then to his successor of becoming a *joculator Dei,* a kind of latter-day Apostle going through the world recounting the *exempla* that constitute the wonders of the ***Book of Wonders.***

To these general considerations, I must add a word about Book VII, the ***Book of the Beasts,*** which, in modern times at least, has become better known than the rest of ***Felix.*** First of all, its place within the general structure of ***Felix*** could hardly be more anomalous. Instead of the treatise on animals we might have expected after those on Elements, Plants, and Minerals, the ***Book of the Beasts*** consists of a series of animal fables, with no narrator or teacher as in the other books, and in which Felix himself disappears from view. Moreover, it is the only work in which Llull used identifiable preexisting material to any notable degree. And the nature of this material is interesting: with the exception of the name and character of the main protagonist, taken from the French *Roman de Renart,* it is all of oriental origin. There is one story from the *Seven Wise Masters* (also called the *Book of Sindbad* or *Sendebar*), one from the *Thousand and One Nights,* and no fewer than ten from the Arabic *Kalila and Dimna* which stems ultimately from the Indian *Panchatantra.* Even the one autobiographical bit seems to refer to Llull's unfortunate relations with the Moslem slave who taught him Arabic.

Most extraordinary, perhaps, is the psychological and narrative unity Llull imposes on this material. The reader, accustomed to the loosely connected string of *exempla* of the first six books of ***Felix,*** begins the chain of animal fables of the ***Book of the Beasts*** in the same frame of mind. His surprise comes when he begins to see more and more pieces of the narrative fitting into place and realizes that he is experiencing a different literary world, one with a plot that builds and sweeps the reader along to a truly dramatic ending.

The modern reader's tendency to think of animal fables as a branch of children's literature or as elegant court *amusettes* leads to another surprise. As Dame Reynard's machinations become more and more appalling and her power greater and greater, the reader sees how penetrating and realistic are Llull's observations of the nastier side of palace politics; the surprise comes from confronting a kind of medieval predecessor to George Orwell's *Animal Farm.* The realization that this is indeed a political tract is confirmed by the Epilogue: "Here ends the ***Book of the Beasts,*** which Felix brought to a king so that he might learn, from the things done by the beasts, how a king should reign, and how to keep himself from evil counsel and from treacherous men."

All scholars have agreed, chiefly because of the place and date of composition of ***Felix,*** that the king in question must be Philip IV the Fair of France, who at that time was young (around twenty), still inexperienced (some three years of reign), and whom Llull perhaps felt he had a certain freedom to advise (since Philip was the nephew of Llull's patron, James II of Majorca). But no adequate historical counterpart to Dame Reynard has been suggested. All the more notorious "evil councilors" of Philip's reign, such as Pierre Flote, Guillaume de Nogaret, and Enguerran de Marigni, came into prominence some ten years later.

There is surprising agreement among scholars as to the place and date of composition of ***Felix.*** The opening sentence of the Prologue, "In a foreign land there was once a man who was sad and melancholy," coupled with the account in Book VIII, Chapter 89, of a man coming to Paris to ask King and University to support his missionary work based on the ***Ars demonstrativa,*** has led most scholars to agree that the work was written in Paris during Llull's first stay there in 1288-9. (pp. 649-55)

Anthony Bonner, "'Felix,' or the Book of Wonders: Introduction, in Selected Works of Ramon Llull (1232-1316), Vol. II, *edited and translated by Anthony Bonner, Princeton University Press, 1985, pp. 649-58.*

FURTHER READING

Johnston, Mark D. *The Spiritual Logic of Ramon Llull.* Oxford: Clarendon Press, 1987, 336 p.

Examines "the manifold and various ways in which Ramon Llull strives to adapt Scholastic Logic to his own theological and metaphysical values."

Peers, E. Allison. Introduction to *The Art of Contemplation,* by Ramon Lull, edited and translated by E. Allison Peers, pp. 1-15. New York: Macmillan, 1925.

Highlights seminal aspects of Llull's art and thought as expressed in his *Art of Contemplation.*

Pring-Mill, R. D. F. "The Analogical Structure of the Lullian Art." In *Islamic Philosophy and the Classical Tradition,* edited by S. M. Stern, et al., pp. 315-26. Columbia: University of South Carolina Press, 1972.

Applies the ideas of "elemental theory" suggested by Frances A. Yates to the *Ars demonstrativa,* an early version of Llull's "Art."

Selmer, Carl. "Ramon Lull and the Problem of Persuasion." *Thought* XXIII, No. 89 (June 1948): 215-22.

Biographical study of Llull's missionary activities in the Middle East.

Das Nibelungenlied

c. 1200-10

(Also known as *Der Nibelunge Nôt* and *Lay of the Nibelungen*) German poem.

INTRODUCTION

Considered the most important epic of Germany's medieval period, the *Nibelungenlied* has been lauded by critics for its skillful mingling of fiction and history into a lyrical and structurally unified whole. The poem was first translated from Middle High German to German in 1757, and it encompasses Germany's ancient heroic songs, the fall of the Burgundian Empire in the year 437, and the courtly romance tradition of twelfth- and thirteenth-century Europe. Scholars have long been fascinated by the ambiguity of the themes and characters in the *Nibelungenlied* and they note that, although the poem's subject matter is primarily historical, its tone is distinctly modern. According to Frank G. Ryder, the *Nibelungenlied* "is a true work of world literature, faithful to its time but not bound by it, comprehensible and of significance to an audience centuries removed."

Almost nothing is known of the *Nibelungenlied*'s author other than the fact that he was an Austrian of the Danube region and may have stood in some relationship to Bishop Wolfger of Passau. Historians speculate that the poet was either a minnesinger (poet or musician), a knight, or a cleric due to his familiarity with the court and court life. Furthermore, critics generally believe that the *Nibelungenlied* was written by a single author because the entire poem is unified in action, thought, and diction. Structurally, the *Nibelungenlied* consists of two parts which are further divided into thirty-nine adventures, each varying in length. In total, the poem contains more than 2,300 quatrains, or rhyming four-lined stanzas with the first three lines equal in length and the concluding line longer for emphasis. The fact that the epic was written in quatrains rather than stanzas suggests that it was originally meant to be sung. References to historical people and events within the *Nibelungenlied,* in addition to its prominent employment of chivalric conventions, have enabled scholars to date its composition between 1200 and 1210.

The first part of the *Nibelungenlied* focuses on the mythic hero Siegfried and his murder, while the second portion, which is largely historical in content, concerns the fall of the Burgundians, a tribe residing in the southern part of Germany. The poem opens in Worms, at the Burgundian court of three royal brothers—Gunther, Gernôt, and Gîselher—and their sister Kriemhild. Siegfried, a prince from the Netherlands, travels to Worms with the intention of marrying Kriemhild but must wait a year before seeing her. In the meantime, he distinguishes himself in numerous battles, partly through his own strength and partly

Siegfried and the dragon, in an 1841 illustration by Julius Hübner.

through magic: according to legend, Siegfried once killed a dragon and bathed in its blood, making his skin invulnerable, with the exception of a small spot between his shoulders; afterwards, he conquered the Nibelungs, a name meaning "inhabitants of the mist," winning their treasure, a sword, and a cloak which makes its wearer invisible. Gunther wishes to marry Brunhild—an Icelandic queen of fantastic strength—and he persuades Siegfried to wear the magic cloak on his behalf and win Brunhild through a series of duplicitous physical contests, in return for Kriemhild's hand in marriage. The ruse is successful, culminating in the double wedding of Gunther with Brunhild and Siegfried with Kriemhild. Eventually, Brunhild discovers that she has been duped into marrying Gunther and she employs Hagen, Gunther's vassal, to murder Siegfried. After tricking Kriemhild into revealing Siegfried's vulnerable spot, Hagen invites Siegfried on a hunting trip, during which Hagen treacherously stabs him in the back. Once Siegfried is dead, Hagen sinks the treasure of the Nibelungs in the Rhine, significantly decreasing Kriemhild's power and influence.

In the second half of the *Nibelungenlied,* ten years have passed and Kriemhild marries Etzel (Attila the Hun) on the promise of his vassal Rüdiger that he will defend her from her enemies. Still more years pass before Kriemhild invites her brothers and their party to Etzel's court with the intention of avenging Siegfried's death. Although Etzel receives the Burgundians courteously, Kriemhild persuades some of Etzel's lords to attack the Burgundians; a bloody battle ensues and, eventually, all of the Burgundians are slain except for Gunther and Hagen, who are captured by Dietrich of Bern and brought to the queen. When Hagen refuses to tell Kriemhild where he has sunk the Nibelung treasure, she has Gunther beheaded. Hagen again refuses to reveal where the treasure is hidden, and Kriemhild furiously cuts off his head with Siegfried's sword. Kriemhild, in turn, is killed by Hildebrand, Dietrich's vassal, who is outraged by her ruthlessness.

Because the *Nibelungenlied* existed for centuries in oral form, historians have found it impossible to document its sources with any degree of certainty. The mythological figures of Siegfried and Brunhild may be traced to a number of earlier songs, specifically in the Norse *Eddas,* where Siegfried battles a dragon and breaks through a circle of flames to awaken the sleeping Brunhild from a trance. They fall in love, but ultimately Siegfried must leave her, and, after drinking a magical potion which causes him to forget Brunhild, he marries Kriemhild. Many events in the *Nibelungenlied* are also derived from history. Scholars maintain that the Burgundians were attacked and slain by the Huns around the year 437, and it is believed that Attila was murdered by his second wife, a German princess seeking revenge for the death of her brothers. Other historical figures from the *Nibelungenlied* include Gunther (Gundicarus), who was the King of Burgundy, and Dietrich (Theodoric the Great), who was King of Italy in 493. Scholars believe that although the *Nibelungenlied* closely resembles a number of its sources, its poet greatly altered historical events and modernized some of the early characters to comply with his artistic vision and to meet the expectations of his thirteenth-century audience.

Over thirty manuscripts of the poem dating from the thirteenth through the sixteenth centuries have been found, testifying to the *Nibelungenlied*'s widespread popularity during the Middle Ages. Of these, the most important are three thirteenth-century manuscripts known as the A, B, and C. While none of these documents is considered the original poem, scholars contend that manuscript B, or the St. Gall manuscript, is nearest to the original, so B is the source for most modern translations. J. J. Bodmer made the first modern German translation of the *Nibelungenlied* from the B and C manuscripts in 1757. Entitled *Chriemhilden Rache, und die Klage* (*Chriemhilde's Revenge, and the Lament*), it contains only the second portion of the original poem and did not attract much attention. Fifteen years later, Christopher Müller reedited Bodmer's version of the poem and prefixed the first part to it, publishing the piece as *Nibelungen Lied* (1772; *Lay of the Nibelungen*). Numerous German translations followed, but an English translation did not appear until 1814, when several strophes—supposedly translated by Sir Walter Scott—were included in *Illustrations of Northern Antiquities.* The first complete English prose translation was made by Jonathan Birch in 1848. Based on Karl Lachmann's 1816 German edition, it was poorly received. Notable later English translations include Margaret Armour's 1897 translation, *The Fall of the Nibelungs,* and A. T. Hatto's 1969 version entitled *The Nibelungenlied.*

Scholars have lauded the *Nibelungenlied*'s simple and concise lyricism as well as its structural unity, apparent through several instances of parallelism. For example, vengeance by a wronged woman is an important motif in both sections of the poem; Brunhild has Siegfried killed for deceiving her and Kriemhild murders Hagen and her brothers for their part in Siegfried's death. Commentators are also unanimous in their praise of the poem's characterization, maintaining that the *Nibelungenlied* features fully developed and psychologically interesting individuals who provide a sharp contrast to the stock character types most often represented in medieval literature. From a thematic standpoint, the *Nibelungenlied* is highly complex, and scholars tend to disagree on the poem's overall message. The most obvious theme is provided by Kriemhild in the opening strophes of the poem when she asserts that "all joy must end in sorrow." Some critics have accepted this statement as the *Nibelungenlied*'s central motif, but others have asserted that the poem's overall message is more complex. Another significant theme is the code of chivalry to which Siegfried adheres. Like other knights errant, he must travel a great distance, wait for a long period of time, and prove his loyalty through various adventures before he can marry Kriemhild. The fact that he is murdered is a highly irregular occurrence in medieval poetry, and many critics have interpreted his death as the *Nibelungenlied* poet's denunciation of the courtly romance tradition. Elements of Christianity are also visible in the *Nibelungenlied,* and several scholars have gone to great lengths to prove its significance to the poem. These major themes notwithstanding, commentators generally agree that the *Nibelungenlied*'s values ultimately reflect those of the heroic epic, drawing from Germany's ancient Teutonic heritage and its emphasis on loyalty, courage, and fatalism. Critics assert that this feature explains the predominance and importance to the epic of Hagen and Kriemhild, whose unquestioning loyalty—Hagen to his lord and Kriemhild to her husband—brings about the poem's tragic conclusion.

Bodmer published his translation of the *Nibelungenlied* at a time when German scholars were preoccupied with classical learning; since it did not fit the classical epic mode, thc *Nibelungenlied* was soon rejected as a second-rate medieval poem. August Wilhelm Schlegel initiated literary analysis of the work in 1802 when he examined it with genuine appreciation during a series of lectures in Berlin. Shortly thereafter, the German Romantics embraced the poem as part of their national legacy and often compared it with Homer's *Iliad.* Eventually, the *Nibelungenlied*'s fame spread to England, where, in 1831, Thomas Carlyle wrote the first piece of English criticism on the epic, purporting that it "takes undisputed place among the sacred books of German literature." Later critical discussion of the epic was more tempered; in reaction to the Romantics, commentators again compared the *Nibelungenlied* to the *Iliad* and concluded that their differences were greater than their similarities. Finding the *Nibelungenlied* generally inferior to the *Iliad,* they cited as the poem's major weaknesses its dependence upon a narrative rather than a dramatic format and its many thematic inconsistencies. Twentieth-century scholarship on the *Nibelungenlied* has typically followed two major trends, one towards source study and the other towards literary analysis. Critics who have examined the poem's sources generally explore the extent to which the author blended historical fact, myth, and poetic invention. Commentators who have studied the aesthetic merits of the *Nibelungenlied* focus on such aspects of the work as the relationship between artistic form and its complex characters, and the poet's ambiguous treatment of heroism and the courtly romance tradition. Many modern scholars have scrutinized the structure of the *Nibelungenlied,* noting how its various disparate sequences contribute to a unified whole. According to D. R. McLintock, "what we admire in the epic is not its moral, social, or psychological insights, but its literary qualities—the power of its individual scenes and the grandeur of the total architecture to which they contribute."

While critics continue to debate the message of the *Nibelungenlied,* they agree that the epic was a significant influence on the development of European literature. The poem has inspired numerous translations and adaptations, including Richard Wagner's renowned three-part opera *Der Ring des Nibelungen* (1853) and Friedrich Hebbel's classical drama *Die Nibelungen* (1862). As Daniel Bussier Shumway has written, "there are perhaps greater poems in literature than the *Nibelungenlied,* but few so majestic in conception, so sublime in their tragedy, so simple in their execution, and so national in their character, as this great popular epic of German literature."

PRINCIPAL ENGLISH TRANSLATIONS

Das Nibelungen Lied; or, the Lay of the Last Nibelungers (translated by Jonathan Birch) 1848

The Fall of the Nibelungers, otherwise the Book of Kriemhild (translated by William Nanson Lettsom) 1850

The Fall of the Nibelungs (translated by Margaret Armour) 1897

The Nibelungenlied (translated by George Henry Needler) 1904

The Nibelungenlied (translated by Daniel Bussier Shumway) 1909

The Lay of the Nibelung Men (translated by Arthur S. Way) 1911

The Song of the Nibelungs: A Verse Translation from the Middle High German Nibelungenlied (translated by Frank G. Ryder) 1962

The Nibelungenlied (translated by A. T. Hatto) 1969

CRITICISM

Thomas Carlyle (essay date 1831)

[*A noted nineteenth-century essayist, historian, critic, and social commentator, Carlyle was a central figure of the Victorian age in England. In his writings Carlyle advocated a Christian work ethic and stressed the importance of order, piety, and spiritual fulfillment. Known to his contemporaries as the "Sage of Chelsea," Carlyle exerted a powerful moral influence in an era of rapidly shifting values. Below, Carlyle discusses character, plot, and structure in the* Nibelungenlied, *noting the poem's impact on European literature.*]

In the year 1757, the Swiss Professor Bodmer printed an ancient poetical manuscript, under the title of *Chriemhilden Rache und die Klage* (Chriemhilde's Revenge, and the Lament); which may be considered as the first of a series, or stream of publications and speculations still rolling on, with increased current, to the present day. Not, indeed, that all these had their source or determining cause in so insignificant a circumstance; their source, or rather thousand sources, lay far elsewhere. As has often been remarked, a certain antiquarian tendency in literature, a fonder, more earnest looking back into the Past began about that time to manifest itself in all nations (witness our own *Percy's Reliques*): this was among the first distinct symptoms of it in Germany; where, as with ourselves, its manifold effects are still visible enough.

Some fifteen years after Bodmer's publication, which, for the rest, is not celebrated as an editorial feat, one C. H. Müller undertook a *Collection of German Poems from the Twelfth, Thirteenth, and Fourteenth Centuries;* wherein, among other articles, he reprinted Bodmer's *Chriemhilde* and *Klage,* with a highly remarkable addition prefixed to the former, essential indeed to the right understanding of it; and the whole now stood before the world as one Poem, under the name of the ***Nibelungen Lied,*** or ***Lay of the Nibelungen.*** It has since been ascertained that the *Klage* is a foreign inferior appendage; at best, related only as epilogue to the main work: meanwhile out of this ***Nibelungen,*** such as it was, there soon proceeded new inquiries, and kindred enterprises. For much as the Poem, in the shape it here bore, was defaced and marred, it failed not to attract observation: to all open-minded lovers of poetry, especially where a strong patriotic feeling existed, this singular, antique ***Nibelungen*** was an interesting appearance. Johannes Müller, in his famous *Swiss History,* spoke of it in warm terms: subsequently August Wilhelm Schlegel, through the medium of *Das Deutsche Museum,* succeeded in awakening something like a universal popular feeling on the subject; and, as a natural consequence, a whole host of Editors and Critics, of deep and of shallow endeavour, whose labours we yet see in progress. The ***Nibelungen*** has now been investigated, translated, collated, commented upon, with more or less result, to almost boundless lengths: besides the Work named at the head of this Paper, and which stands there simply as one of the latest, we have Versions into the modern tongue by Von der Hagen, by Hinsberg, Lachmann, Büsching, Zeune, the last in Prose, and said to be worthless; Criticisms, Introductions, Keys, and so forth, by innumerable others, of whom we mention only Docen and the Brothers Grimm.

By which means, not only has the Poem itself been elucidated with all manner of researches, but its whole environment has come forth in new light: the scene and personages it relates to, the other fictions and traditions connected with it, have attained a new importance and coherence. Manuscripts, that for ages had lain dormant, have issued from their archives into public view; books that had circulated only in mean guise for the amusement of the people, have become important, not to one or two *virtuosos,* but to the general body of the learned: and now a whole System of antique Teutonic Fiction and Mythology unfolds itself, shedding here and there a real though feeble and uncertain glimmer over what was once the total darkness of the old Time. No fewer than Fourteen ancient Traditionary Poems, all strangely intertwisted, and growing out of and into one another, have come to light among the Germans; who now, in looking back, find that they too, as well as the Greeks, have their Heroic Age, and round the old Valhalla, as their Northern Pantheon, a world of demigods and wonders.

Such a phenomenon, unexpected till of late, cannot but interest a deep-thinking, enthusiastic people. For the ***Nibelungen*** especially, which lies as the centre and distinct key-stone of the whole too chaotic System—let us say rather, blooms as a firm sunny island in the middle of these cloud-covered, ever-shifting, sand-whirlpools—they cannot sufficiently testify their love and veneration. Learned professors lecture on the ***Nibelungen,*** in public schools, with a praiseworthy view to initiate the German youth in love of their fatherland; from many zealous and no wise ignorant critics we hear talk of a 'great Northern Epos,' of a 'German *Iliad;*' the more saturnine are shamed into silence, or hollow mouth-homage; thus from all quarters comes a sound of joyful acclamation; the ***Nibelungen*** is welcomed as a precious national possession, recovered after six centuries of neglect, and takes undisputed place among the sacred books of German literature.

Of these curious transactions, some rumour has not failed to reach us in England, where our minds, from their own antiquarian disposition, were willing enough to receive it. Abstracts and extracts of the ***Nibelungen*** have been printed in our language; there have been disquisitions on it in our Reviews: hitherto, however, such as nowise to exhaust the subject. On the contrary, where so much was to be told at once, the speaker might be somewhat puzzled where to begin: it was a much readier method to begin with the end, or with any part of the middle, than like Rabelais' Ram (whose example is too little followed in literary narrative) to begin with the beginning. Thus has our stock of intelligence come rushing out on us quite promiscuously and pellmell; whereby the whole matter could not but acquire a tortuous, confused, altogether inexplicable, and even dreary aspect; and the class of 'well-informed persons' now find themselves in that uncomfortable position, where they are obliged to profess admiration, and at the same time feel that, except by name, they know not what the thing admired is. Such a position towards the venerable ***Nibelungen,*** which is no less bright and graceful than historically significant, cannot be the right one. Moreover, as appears to us, it might be somewhat mended by very simple means. Let any one that had honestly read the ***Nibelungen,*** which in these days is no surprising achievement, only tell us what he found there, and nothing that he did not find: we should then know something, and, what were still better, be ready for knowing more. To search out the secret roots of such a production, ramified through successive layers of centuries, and drawing nourishment from each, may be work, and too hard work, for the deepest philosopher and critic; but to look with natural eyes on what part of it stands visibly above ground, and record his own experiences thereof, is what any reasonable mortal, if he will take heed, can do.

Some such slight service, we here intend proferring to our readers: let them glance with us a little into that mighty maze of Northern Archæology; where, it may be, some pleasant prospects will open. If the ***Nibelungen*** is what we have called it, a firm sunny island amid the weltering chaos of antique tradition, it must be worth visiting on general grounds; nay, if the primæval rudiments of it have the antiquity assigned them, it belongs specially to us English *Teutones* as well as to the German. (pp. 1-4)

Apart from its antiquarian value, and not only as by far the finest monument of old German art; but intrinsically, and as a mere detached composition, this ***Nibelungen*** has an excellence that cannot but surprise us. With little preparation, any reader of poetry, even in these days, might find it interesting. It is not without a certain Unity of interest and purport, an internal coherence and completeness; it is a Whole, and some spirit of Music informs it: these are the highest characteristics of a true Poem. Considering farther what intellectual environment we now find it in, it is doubly to be prized and wondered at; for it differs from [the] *Hero-Books* [or *Heldenbuch*], as molten or carved metal does from rude agglomerated ore; almost as some Shakspeare from his fellow Dramatists, whose *Tamburlaines* and *Island Princesses,* themselves not destitute of merit, first show us clearly in what pure loftiness and loneliness the *Hamlets* and *Tempests* reign.

The unknown Singer of the ***Nibelungen,*** though no Shakspeare, must have had a deep, poetic soul; wherein things discontinuous and inanimate shaped themselves together into life, and the Universe with its wondrous purport stood significantly imaged; overarching, as with heavenly firmaments and eternal harmonies, the little scene where men strut and fret their hour. His Poem, unlike so many old and new pretenders to that name, has a basis and organic structure, a beginning, middle, and end; there is one great principle and idea set forth in it, round which all its multifarious parts combine in living union. Remarkable it is, moreover, how along with this essence and primary condition of all poetic virtue, the minor external virtues of what we call Taste, and so forth, are, as it were, presupposed; and the living soul of Poetry being there, its body of incidents, its garment of language, come of their own accord. So, too, in the case of Shakspeare: his feeling of propriety, as compared with that of the Marlowes and Fletchers, his quick sure sense of what is fit and unfit, either in act or word, might astonish us, had he no other superiority. But true Inspiration, as it may well do, includes that same Taste, or rather a far higher and heartfelt Taste, of which that other 'elegant' species is but an ineffectual, irrational apery: let us see the herald Mercury actually descend from his Heaven, and the bright wings, and the graceful movement of these, will not be wanting.

With an instinctive art, far different from acquired artifice, this Poet of the ***Nibelungen,*** working in the same province with his contemporaries of the *Heldenbuch,* on the same material of tradition, has, in a wonderful degree, possessed himself of what these could only strive after; and with his 'clear feeling of fictitious truth,' avoided as false the errors and monstrous perplexities in which they vainly struggled. He is of another species than they; in language, in purity and depth of feeling, in fineness of invention, stands quite apart from them.

The language of the *Heldenbuch* . . . was a feeble half-articulate child's-speech, the metre nothing better than a miserable doggrel; whereas here in the old Frankish (*Oberdeutsch*) dialect of the ***Nibelungen,*** we have a clear decisive utterance, and in a real system of verse, not without essential regularity, great liveliness, and now and then even harmony of rhythm. Doubtless we must often call it a diffuse diluted utterance; at the same time it is genuine, with a certain antique garrulous heartiness, and has a rhythm in the thoughts as well as the words. The simplicity is never silly, even in that perpetual recurrence of epithets, sometimes of rhymes, as where two words, for instance *lip* (body, life, *leib*) and *wip* (woman wife, *weib*) are indissolubly wedded together, and the one never shows itself without the other following,—there is something which reminds us not so much of poverty, as of trustfulness and childlike innocence. Indeed a strange charm lies in those old tones, where, in gay dancing melodies, the sternest tidings are sung to us; and deep floods of Sadness and Strife play lightly in little curling billows, like seas in summer. It is as a meek smile, in whose still, thoughtful depths a whole infinitude of patience, and love, and heroic strength lie revealed. But in other cases, too, we have seen this outward sport and inward earnestness offer grateful contrast, and cunning excitement; for example, in Tasso; of whom, though otherwise different enough, this old Northern Singer has more than once reminded us. There, too, as here, we have a dark solemn meaning in light guise; deeds of high temper, harsh self-denial, daring and death, stand embodied in that soft, quick-flowing, joyfully-modulated verse. Nay farther, as if the implement, much more than we might fancy, had influenced the work done, these two Poems, could we trust our individual feeling, have in one respect the same poetical result for us: in the ***Nibelungen*** as in the *Gerusalemme,* the persons and their story are indeed brought vividly before us, yet not near and palpably present; it is rather as if we looked on that scene through an inverted telescope, whereby the whole was carried far away into the distance, the life-large figures compressed into brilliant miniatures, so clear, so real, yet tiny, elf-like, and beautified as well as lessened, their colours being now closer and brighter, the shadows and trivial features no longer visible. This, as we partly apprehend, comes of *singing* Epic Poems; most part of which only pretend to be sung. Tasso's rich melody still lives among the Italian people; the ***Nibelungen*** also is what it professes to be, a *Song.*

No less striking than the verse and language, is the quality of the invention manifested here. Of the Fable, or narrative material of the ***Nibelungen,*** we should say that it had high, almost the highest merit; so daintily, yet firmly, is it put together; with such felicitous selection of the beautiful, the essential, and no less felicitous rejection of whatever was unbeautiful or even extraneous. The reader is no longer afflicted with that chaotic brood of Fire-drakes, Giants, and malicious turbaned Turks, so fatally rife in the *Heldenbuch:* all this is swept away, or only hovers in faint shadows afar off; and free field is opened for legitimate perennial interests. Yet neither is the ***Nibelungen*** without its wonders; for it is poetry and not prose; here too, a supernatural world encompasses the natural, and, though at rare intervals and in calm manner, reveals itself there. It is truly wonderful with what skill our simple, untaught Poet deals with the marvellous; admitting it without reluctance or criticism, yet precisely in the degree and shape that will best avail him. Here, if in no other respect, we should say that he has a decided superiority to Homer himself. The whole story of the ***Nibelungen*** is fateful, mysterious, guided on by unseen influences; yet the actual marvels are few, and done in the far distance: those Dwarfs, and Cloaks of Darkness, and charmed Treasure-caves, are heard of rather than beheld, the tidings of them seem to issue from unknown space. Vain were it to inquire where that Nibelungen-land specially is: its very name is *Nebel-land,* or *Nifl-land,* the land of Darkness, of Invisibility. The 'Nibelungen Heroes' that muster in thousands and tens of thousands, though they march to the Rhine or Danube, and we see their strong limbs and shining armour, we could almost fancy to be children of the air. Far beyond the firm horizon, that wonder-bearing region swims on the infinite waters; unseen by bodily eye, or at most discerned as a faint streak, hanging in the blue depths, uncertain whether island or cloud. And thus the ***Nibelungen Song,*** though based on the bottomless foundations of Spirit, and not unvisited of skyey messengers, is a real, rounded, habitable Earth, where we find firm footing, and the wondrous and the common live amicably together. Perhaps it would be difficult to find any Poet of ancient or modern times, who in this trying problem has steered his way with greater delicacy and success.

To any of our readers who may have personally studied the ***Nibelungen,*** these high praises of ours will not seem exaggerated: the rest, who are the vast majority, must endeavour to accept them with some degree of faith, at least of curiosity; to vindicate, and judicially substantiate them would far exceed our present opportunities. Nay, in any case, the criticism, the alleged Characteristics of a Poem are so many Theorems, which are indeed enunciated, truly or falsely, but the Demonstration of which must be sought for in the reader's own study and experience. Nearly all that can be attempted here, is some hasty epitome of the mere Narrative; no substantial image of the work, but a feeble outline and shadow. To which task . . . we can now proceed without obstacle.

The ***Nibelungen*** has been called the Northern Epos; yet it has, in great part, a Dramatic character: those thirty-nine *Aventiuren* (Adventures), which it consists of, might be so many scenes in a Tragedy. The catastrophe is dimly prophecied from the beginning; and, at every fresh step, rises more and more clearly into view. A shadow of coming Fate, as it were, a low inarticulate voice of Doom falls, from the first, out of that charmed Nibelungen-land: the discord of two women, is as a little spark of evil passion, that ere long enlarges itself into a crime; foul murder is done; and now the Sin rolls on like a devouring fire, till the guilty and the innocent are alike encircled with it, and a whole land is ashes, and a whole race is swept away.

Uns ist in alten mœren Wunders vil geseit,
Von helden lobebœren Von grozer chuonheit,
Von vronden und' hoch-geziten Von weinen und von chlagen
Von chuner rechen striten Muget ir nu wunder hören sagen.

We find in ancient story, Wonders many told,
Of heroes in great glory With spirit free and bold,
Of joyances, and high-tides Of weeping and of woe,
Of noble Recken striving, Mote ye now wonders know.

This is the brief artless Proem; and the promise contained in it proceeds directly towards fulfilment. In the very second stanza, we learn:—

Es wühs in Burgonden Ein vil edel magedin,
Das in allen landen Niht schoners mohte sin
Chriemhilt was si geheien Si wart ein schöne wip
Darumbe müsen degene Vil verliesen den lip.

A right noble maiden Did grow in Burgundy,
That in all lands of earth Nought fairer mote there be;
Chriemhild of Worms she hight She was a fairest *wife:*
For the which must warriors A many lose their life.

Chriemhild, this world's-wonder, a king's daughter and king's sister, and no less coy and proud than fair, dreams one night that "she had petted a falcon, strong beautiful and wild; which two eagles snatched away from her: this she was forced to see; greater sorrow felt she never in the world." Her mother, Ute, to whom she relates the vision, soon redes it for her; the falcon is a noble husband, whom, God keep him, she must suddenly lose. Chriemhild declares warmly for the single state; as indeed, living there at the Court of Worms, with her brothers, Gunther, Gernot, Geiselher, "three kings noble and rich," in such pomp and renown, the pride of Burgunden-land and Earth, she might readily enough have changed for the worse. However, dame Ute bids her not be too emphatical; for "if ever she have heartfelt joy in life, it will be from man's love, and she shall be a fair wife (*wip*), when God sends her a right worthy Ritter's *lip.*" Chriemhild is more in earnest than maidens usually are when they talk thus; it appears, she guarded against love "for many a life-long day," nevertheless, she too must yield to the destiny. "Honourably she was to become a most noble Ritter's wife." "This," adds the old Singer, "was that same falcon she dreamed of: how sorely she since revenged him on her nearest kindred! For that one death died full many a mother's son."

It may be observed that the Poet, here, and at all times, shows a marked partiality for Chriemhild; ever striving, unlike his fellow singers, to magnify her worth, her faithfulness, and loveliness; and softening as much as may be, whatever makes against her. No less a favourite with him is Siegfried, the prompt, gay, peaceably fearless hero: to whom, in the Second *Aventiure,* we are here suddenly introduced, at Santen (Xanten) the Court of Netherland; whither, to his glad parents, after achievements (to us partially known) "of which one might sing and tell for ever," that noble prince has returned. Much as he has done and conquered, he is but just arrived at man's years: it is on occasion of this joyful event, that a high-tide (*hochgezit*) is now held there, with infinite joustings, minstrelsy, largesses, and other chivalrous doings, all which is sung with utmost heartiness. The old King Siegemund offers to resign his crown to him; but Siegfried has other game a-field: the unparalleled beauty of Chriemhild has reached his ear and his fancy; and now he will to Worms, and woo her, at least "see how it stands with her." Fruitless is it for Siegemund and the mother Siegelinde to represent the perils of that enterprise, the pride of those Burgundian Gunthers and Gernots, the fierce temper of their uncle Hagen; Siegfried is as obstinate as young men are in these cases, and can hear no counsel. Nay, he will not accept the much more liberal proposition, to take an army with him, and conquer the country, if it must be so; he will ride forth, like himself, with twelve champions only, and so defy the future. Whereupon, the old people finding that there is no other course, proceed to make him clothes;—at least, the good queen with "her fair women sitting night and day," and sewing, does so, the father furnishing noblest battle and riding gear;—and so dismiss him with many blessings and lamentations. "For him wept sore the king and his *wife,* but he comforted both their bodies (*lip*); he said, 'ye must not weep, for my body ever shall ye be without care'."

Sad was it to the Recken, Stood weeping many a maid,
I ween, their heart had them The tidings true foresaid
That of their friends so many Death thereby should find;
Cause had they of lamenting Such boding in their mind.

Nevertheless, on the seventh morning, that adventurous company, "ride up the sand" (on the Rhine beach to Worms), in high temper, in dress and trappings, aspect and bearing, more than kingly.

Siegfried's reception at King Gunther's court, and his brave sayings and doings there for some time, we must omit. One fine trait of his chivalrous delicacy it is that, for a whole year, he never hints at his errand; never once sees or speaks of Chriemhild, whom, nevertheless, he is longing day and night to meet. She, on her side, has often through her lattices, noticed the gallant stranger, victorious in all tiltings and knightly exercises; whereby it would seem, in spite of her rigorous predeterminations, some kindness for him is already gliding in. Meanwhile, mighty wars and threats of invasion arise, and Siegfried does the state good service. Returning victorious, both as general and soldier, from Hessen (Hessia), where, by help of his own courage and the sword Balmung, he has captured a Danish king, and utterly discomfited a Saxon one; he can now show himself before Chriemhild without other blushes than those of timid love. Nay, the maiden has herself inquired pointedly of the messengers, touching his exploits; and "her fair face grew rose-red when she heard them." A gay High-tide, by way of triumph, is appointed; several kings, and two-and-thirty princes, and knights enough with "gold-red saddles," come to joust; and better than whole infinities of kings and princes with their saddles, the fair Chriemhild herself, under guidance of her mother, chiefly too in honour of the victor, is to grace that sport. "Ute the full rich" fails not to set her needle-women to work, and "clothes of price are taken from their presses," for the love of her child, "wherewith to deck many women and maids." And now, "on the Whitsun-morning," all is ready, and glorious as heart could desire it: brave Ritters, "five thousand or more," all glancing in the lists; but grander still, Chriemhild herself is advancing beside her mother, with a hundred body-guards, all sword-in-hand, and many a noble maid "wearing rich raiment," in her train!

> Now issued forth the lovely one (*minnechliche*), as the red morning doth from troubled clouds; much care fled away from him, who bore her in his heart, and long had done; he saw the lovely one stand in her beauty.
>
> There glanced from her garments full many precious stones, her rose-red colour shone full lovely: try what he might, each man must confess that in this world he had not seen aught so fair.
>
> Like as the light moon stands before the stars, and its sheen so clear goes over the clouds, even so stood she now before many fair women; whereat cheered was the mind of the hero.
>
> The rich chamberlains you saw go before her, the high spirited Recken would not forbear, but pressed on where they saw the lovely maiden. Siegfried the lord was both glad and sad.
>
> He thought in his mind, how could this be that I should woo thee? That was a foolish dream; yet must I for ever be a stranger, I were rather (*sanfter,* softer) dead. He became, from these thoughts, in quick changes, pale and red.
>
> Thus stood so lovely the child of Siegelinde, as if he were limned on parchment by a master's art; for all granted that hero so beautiful they had never seen.

In this passage, which we have rendered, from the Fifth *Aventiure,* into the closest prose, it is to be remarked, among other singularities, that there are two similes; in which figure of speech our old Singer deals very sparingly. The first, that comparison of Chriemhild to the moon among stars with its sheen going over the clouds, has now for many centuries had little novelty or merit; but the second, that of Siegfried to a Figure in some illuminated Manuscript, is graceful in itself; and unspeakably so to antiquaries, seldom honoured, in their Black-letter stubbing and grubbing, with such a poetic windfall.

A prince and a princess of this quality are clearly made for one another. Nay, on the motion of young Herr Gernot, fair Chriemhild is bid specially to salute Siegfried, she who had never before saluted man; which unparalleled grace the lovely one, in all courtliness, openly does him. "Be welcome," said she, "Her Siegfried, a noble Ritter good;" from which salute, for this seems to have been all, "much raised was his mind." He bowed with graceful reverence, as his manner was with women; she took him by the hand, and with fond stolen glances, they looked at each other. Whether in that ceremonial joining of hands there might not be some soft, slight pressure, of far deeper import, is what our Singer will not take upon him to say; however, he thinks the affirmative more probable. Henceforth, in that bright May weather, the two were seen constantly together: nothing but felicity around and before them.—In these days, truly, it must have been that the famous Prize-fight, with Dietrich of Bern and his Eleven Lombardy champions, took place, little to the profit of the two Lovers; were it not rather that the whole of that Rose-garden transaction, as given in the *Heldenbuch,* might be falsified and even imaginary; for no mention or hint of it occurs here. War or battle is not heard of; Siegfried the peerless walks wooingly by the side of Chriemhild the peerless: matters, it is evident, are in the best possible course.

But now comes a new side-wind, which, however, in the long run also forwards the voyage. Tidings, namely, reached over the Rhine, not so surprising we might hope, "that there was many a fair maiden;" whereupon Gunther the King "thought with himself to win one of them." It was an honest purpose in King Gunther, only his choice was not the discreetest. For no fair maiden will content him but Queen Brunhild, a lady who rules in *Isenland,* far over sea, famed indeed for her beauty, yet no less so for her caprices. Fables we have met with of this Brunhild being properly a *Valkyr,* or Scandinavian Houri, such as were wont to lead old northern warriors from their last battle field, into Valhalla; and that her Castle of *Isenstein* stood amidst a lake of fire; but this, as we said, is fable and groundless calumny, of which there is not so much as notice taken here. Brunhild, it is plain enough, was a flesh-and-blood maiden, glorious in look and faculty, only with some preternatural talents given her, and the strangest, wayward habits. It appears, for example, that any suitor proposing for her has this brief condition to proceed upon: he must try the adorable in the three several games of hurling the Spear (at one another), Leaping, and throwing the Stone; if victorious, he gains her hand, if vanquished he loses his own head; which latter issue, such is the fair Amazon's strength, frequent fatal experiment has shown to be the only probable one.

Siegfried, who knows something of Brunhild and her

ways, votes clearly against the whole enterprise; however, Gunther has once for all got the whim in him, and must see it out. The prudent Hagen von Troneg, uncle to love-sick Gunther, and ever true to him, then advises that Siegfried be requested to take part in the adventure; to which request Siegfried readily accedes on one condition: that should they prove fortunate he himself is to have Chriemhild to wife, when they return. This readily settled, he now takes charge of the business, and throws a little light on it for the others. They must lead no army thither; only two, Hagen and Dankwart, besides the king and himself, shall go. The grand subject of *waete* (clothes) is next hinted at, and in general terms elucidated; whereupon a solemn consultation with Chriemhild ensues; and a great cutting out, on her part, of white silk from Araby, of green silk from Zazemang, of strange fish-skins covered with morocco silk; a great sewing thereof for seven weeks, on the part of her maids; lastly a fitting-on of the three suits by each hero, for each had three; and heartiest thanks in return, seeing all fitted perfectly, and was of grace and price unutterable. What is still more to the point, Siegfried takes his Cloak of Darkness with him, fancying he may need it there. The good old Singer, who has hitherto alluded only in the faintest way, to Siegfried's prior adventures and miraculous possessions, introduces this of the *Tarnkappe* with great frankness and simplicity. "Of wild dwarfs (*getwergen*)," says he, "I have heard tell, they are in hollow mountains, and for defence wear somewhat called *Tarnkappe,* of wondrous sort;" the qualities of which garment, that it renders invisible, and gives twelve men's strength, are already known to us.

The voyage to Isenstein, Siegfried steering the ship thither, is happily accomplished in twenty days. Gunther admires to a high degree the fine masonry of the place; as indeed he well might, there being some eighty-six towers, three immense palaces, and one immense hall, the whole built of "marble green as grass;" farther he sees many fair women looking from the windows down on the bark, and thinks the loveliest is she in the snow-white dress; which, Siegfried informs him, is a worthy choice; the snow-white maiden being no other than Brunhild. It is also to be kept in mind that Siegfried, for reasons known best to himself, had previously stipulated that, though a free king, they should all treat him as vassal of Gunther; for whom accordingly he holds the stirrup, as they mount on the beach; thereby giving rise to a misconception, which in the end led to saddest consequences.

Queen Brunhild, who had called back her maidens from the windows, being a strict disciplinarian; and retired into the interior of her green marble Isenstein, to dress still better, now inquires of some attendant, Who these strangers of such lordly aspect are, and what brings them. The attendant professes himself at a loss to say; one of them looks like Siegfried, the other is evidently by his port a noble king. His notice of Von Troneg Hagen is peculiarly vivid.

> The third of those companions He is of aspect stern,
> And yet with lovely body, Rich queen, as ye might discern;
> From those *his rapid glances,* For the eyes nought rest in him,
> Meseems this foreign Recke Is of temper fierce and grim.

This is one of those little graphic touches, scattered all over our Poem, which do more for picturing out an object, especially a man, than whole pages of enumeration and mensuration. Never after do we hear of this stout, indomitable Hagen, in all the wild deeds and sufferings he passes through, but those *swinden blicken* of his come before us, with the restless, deep, dauntless spirit that looks through them.

Brunhild's reception of Siegfried is not without tartness; which, however, he, with polished courtesy, and the nimblest address, ever at his command, softens down, or hurries over: he is here, without will of his own, and so forth, only as attendant on his master, the renowned king Gunther, who comes to sue for her hand, as the summit and keystone of all earthly blessings. Brunhild, who had determined on fighting Siegfried himself, if he so willed it, makes small account of this king Gunther, or his prowess; and instantly clears the ground, and equips her for battle. The royal wooer must have looked a little blank when he saw a shield brought in for his fair one's handling, 'three spans thick with gold and iron,' which four chamberlains could hardly bear, and a spear or javelin she meant to shoot or hurl, which was a burthen for three. Hagen, in angry apprehension for his king and nephew, exclaims that they shall all lose their life (*lip*), and that she is the *tiuvels wip,* or Devil's wife. Nevertheless Siegfried is already there in his Cloak of Darkness, twelve men strong, and privily whispers in the ear of royalty to be of comfort; takes the shield to himself, Gunther only affecting to hold it, and so fronts the edge of battle. Brunhild performs prodigies of spear-hurling, of leaping, and stone-pitching; but Gunther, or rather Siegfried, 'who does the work, he only acting the gestures,' nay who even snatches him up into the air and leaps carrying him,—gains a decided victory, and the lovely Amazon must own with surprise and shame, that she is fairly won. Siegfried presently appears without *Tarnkappe,* and asks with a grave face, When the games then are to begin?

So far well; yet somewhat still remains to be done. Brunhild will not sail for Worms, to be wedded, till she have assembled a fit train of warriors; wherein the Burgundians, being here without retinue, see symptoms or possibilities of mischief. The deft Siegfried, ablest of men, again knows a resource. In his *Tarnkappe* he steps on board the bark, which seen from the shore, appears to drift off of its own accord; and therein, stoutly steering towards *Nibelungen-land,* he reaches that mysterious country and the mountain where his Hoard lies, before the second morning; finds Dwarf Alberich and all his giant sentinels at their post, and faithful almost to the death; these soon rouse him thirty thousand Nibelungen Recken, from whom he has only to choose one thousand of the best; equip them splendidly enough; and therewith return to Gunther, simply as if they were that sovereign's own body-guard, that had been delayed a little by stress of weather.

The final arrival at Worms; the bridal feasts, for there are two, Siegfried also receiving his reward; and the joyance and splendour of man and maid, at this lordliest of high-tides; and the joustings, greater than those at Aspramont or Montauban—every reader can fancy for himself. Remarkable only is the evil eye with which queen Brunhild still continues to regard the noble Siegfried. She cannot understand how Gunther, the Landlord of the Rhine, should have bestowed his sister on a vassal: the assurance that Siegfried also is a prince and heir-apparent, the prince namely of Netherland, and little inferior to Burgundian majesty itself, yields no complete satisfaction; and Brunhild hints plainly that, unless the truth be told her, unpleasant consequences may follow. Thus is there ever a ravelled thread in the web of life! But for this little cloud of spleen, these bridal feasts had been all bright and balmy as the month of June. Unluckily, too, the cloud is an electric one; spreads itself in time into a general earthquake; nay that very night becomes a thunder-storm, or tornado, unparalleled we may hope in the annals of connubial happiness.

The Singer of the ***Nibelungen,*** unlike the Author of *Roderick Random,* cares little for intermeddling with 'the chaste mysteries of hymen.' Could we, in the corrupt, ambiguous, modern tongue, hope to exhibit any shadow of the old, simple, truehearted, merely historical spirit, with which in perfect purity of soul, he describes things unattempted yet in prose or rhyme,—we could a tale unfold! Suffice it to say, king Gunther, Landlord of the Rhine, falling sheer down from the third heaven of hope, finds his spouse the most athletic and intractable of women; and himself, at the close of the adventure, nowise encircled in her arms, but tied hard and fast, hand and foot, in her girdle, and hung thereby, at considerable elevation, on a nail in the wall. Let any reader of sensibility figure the emotions of the royal breast, there as he vibrates suspended on his peg, and his inexorable bride sleeping sound in her bed below! Towards morning he capitulates; engaging to observe the prescribed line of conduct with utmost strictness, so he may but avoid becoming a laughing-stock to all men.

No wonder the dread king looked rather grave next morning, and received the congratulations of mankind in a cold manner. He confesses to Siegfried, who partly suspects how it may be, that he has brought the 'evil devil' home to his house in the shape of wife, whereby he is wretched enough. However, there are remedies for all things but death. The ever-serviceable Siegfried undertakes even here to make the crooked straight. What may not an honest friend with Tarnkappe and twelve men's strength perform? Proud Brunhild, next night, after a fierce contest, owns herself again vanquished; Gunther is there to reap the fruits of another's victory; the noble Siegfried withdraws, taking nothing with him but the luxury of doing good, and the proud queen's Ring and Girdle gained from her in that struggle; which small trophies he, with the last infirmity of a noble mind, presents to his own fond wife, little dreaming that they would one day cost him and her, and all of them, so dear. Such readers as take any interest in poor Gunther will be gratified to learn, that from this hour Brunhild's preternatural faculties quite left her, being all dependent on her maidhood; so that any more spear-hurling, or other the like extraordinary work, is not to be apprehended from her.

If we add that Siegfried formally made over to his dear Chriemhild the Nibelungen Hoard, by way of *Morgengabe* (or, as we may say, Jointure); and the high-tide, though not the honey-moon being past, returned to Netherland with his spouse, to be welcomed there with infinite rejoicings,—we have gone through as it were the First Act of this Tragedy; and may here pause to look round us for a moment. The main characters are now introduced on the scene, the relations that bind them together are dimly sketched out: there is the prompt, cheerfully heroic, invulnerable and invincible Siegfried, now happiest of men; the high Chriemhild, fitly-mated, and if a moon, revolving glorious round her sun, or *Friedel* (joy and darling); not without pride and female aspirings, yet not prouder than one so gifted and placed is pardonable for being. On the other hand, we have king Gunther, or rather let us say king's-mantle Gunther, for never except in that one enterprise of courting Brunhild, in which too, without help, he would have cut so poor a figure, does the worthy sovereign show will of his own, or character other than that of good potter's clay; farther, the suspicious, forecasting, yet stout and reckless Hagen, him with the *rapid glances,* and these turned not too kindly on Siegfried, whose prowess he has used yet dreads, whose Nibelungen Hoard he perhaps already covets; lastly, the rigorous and vigorous Brunhild, of whom also more is to be feared than hoped. Considering the fierce nature of these now mingled ingredients, and how, except perhaps in the case of Gunther, there is no menstruum of placid stupidity to soften them, except in Siegfried, no element of heroic truth to master them and bind them together,—unquiet fermentation may readily be apprehended.

Meanwhile, for a season all is peace and sunshine. Siegfried reigns in Netherland, of which his father has surrendered him the crown; Chriemhild brings him a son, whom in honour of the uncle he christens Gunther, which courtesy the uncle and Brunhild repay in kind. The Nibelungen Hoard is still open and inexhaustible; Dwarf Alberich and all the Recken there still loyal; outward relations friendly, internal supremely prosperous: these are halcyon days. But, alas, they cannot last. Queen Brunhild, retaining with true female tenacity her first notion, right or wrong, reflects one day that Siegfried, who is and shall be nothing but her husband's vassal, has for a long while paid him no service; and, determined on a remedy, manages that Siegfried and his queen shall be invited to a high-tide at Worms, where opportunity may chance for enforcing that claim. Thither accordingly, after ten years absence, we find these illustrious guests returning; Siegfried escorted by a thousand Nibelungen Ritters, and farther by his father Siegemund who leads a train of Netherlanders. Here for eleven days, amid infinite joustings, there is a true heaven on earth: but the apple of Discord is already lying in the knightly ring, and two Women, the proudest and keenest-tempered of the world, simultaneously stoop to lift it. *Aventiure* Fourteenth is entitled 'How the two queens rated one another.' Never was courtlier Billingsgate uttered, or which came more directly home to the business and bosoms of women. The subject is that old story of Precedence, which indeed from the time of Cain and Abel downwards, has wrought such effusion of blood and bile both among men and women; lying at the bottom of all armaments and battle-fields, whether Blenheims and Waterloos, or only plate-displays, and tongue-and-eye skirmishes, in the circle of domestic Tea: nay the very animals have it; and horses, were they but the miserablest Shelties and Welsh ponies, will not graze together till it has been ascertained, by clear fight, who is master of whom, and a proper drawing-room etiquette established.

Brunhild and Chriemhild take to arguing about the merits of their husbands: the latter fondly expatiating on the preeminence of her *Friedel,* how he walks 'like the moon among stars' before all other men, is reminded by her sister that one man at least must be excepted, the mighty king Gunther of Worms, to whom by his own confession long ago at Isenstein, he is vassal and servant. Chriemhild will sooner admit that clay is above sunbeams, than any such proposition; which therefore she, in all politeness, requests of her sister never more to touch upon while she lives. The result may be foreseen: rejoinder follows reply, statement grows assertion; flint-sparks have fallen on the dry flax, which from smoke bursts into conflagration. The two queens part in hottest, though still clear-flaming anger. Not, however, to let their anger burn out, but only to feed it with more solid fuel. Chriemhild dresses her forty maids in finer than royal apparel; orders out all her husband's Recken; and so attended, walks foremost to the Minster, where mass is to be said; thus practically asserting that she is not only a true queen, but the worthier of the two. Brunhild, quite outdone in splendour, and enraged beyond all patience, overtakes her at the door of the Minster, with peremptory order to stop: 'before king's wife shall vassal's never go.'

> "Then said the fair Chriemhilde, Right angry was her mood:
> Couldest thou but hold thy peace, It were surely for thy good,
> Thyself hast all polluted With shame thy fair bodye;
> How can a Concubine By right a King's wife be?"
>
> "Whom has thou Concubined?" The King's wife quickly spake;
> "That do I thee," said Chriemhilde; For thy pride and vaunting's sake;
> Who first had thy fair body Was Siegfried my beloved Man;
> My Brother was it not That thy maidhood from thee wan.

In proof of which outrageous saying, she produces that Ring and Girdle; the innocent conquest of which, as we well know, had a far other origin. Brunhild bursts into tears; 'sadder day she never saw.' Nay, perhaps a new light now rose on her over much that had been dark in her late history; 'she rued full sore that ever she was born.'

Here, then, is the black injury, which only blood will wash away. The evil fiend has begun his work; and the issue of it lies beyond man's control. Siegfried may protest his innocence of that calumny, and chastise his indiscreet spouse for uttering it even in the heat of anger: the female heart is wounded beyond healing; the old springs of bitterness against this hero unite into a fell flood of hate; while he sees the sunlight, she cannot know a joyful hour. Vengeance is soon offered her: Hagen, who lives only for his prince, undertakes this bad service; by treacherous professions of attachment, and anxiety to guard Siegfried's life, he gains from Chriemhild the secret of his vulnerability; Siegfried is carried out to hunt; and in the hour of frankest gaiety, is stabbed through the fatal spot; and, felling the murderer to the ground, dies upbraiding his false kindred, yet, with a touching simplicity, recommending his child and wife to their protection. 'Let her feel that she is your sister; was there ever virtue in princes, be true to her: for me my Father and my men shall long wait.' 'The flowers all round were wetted with blood, then he struggled with death; not long did he this, the weapon cut him too keen; so he could speak nought more, the Recke bold and noble.'

At this point, we might say, ends the Third Act of our Tragedy; the whole story henceforth takes a darker character; it is as if a tone of sorrow and fateful boding became more and more audible in its free, light music. Evil has produced new evil in fatal augmentation: injury is abolished; but in its stead there is guilt and despair. Chriemhild, an hour ago so rich, is now robbed of all: her grief is boundless as her love has been. No glad thought can ever more dwell in her; darkness, utter night, has come over her, as she looked into the red of morning. The spoiler too walks abroad unpunished; the bleeding corpse witnesses against Hagen, nay he himself cares not to hide the deed. But who is there to avenge the friendless? Siegfried's Father has returned in haste to his own land; Chriemhild is now alone on the earth, her husband's grave is all that remains to her; there only can she sit, as if waiting at the threshold of her own dark home; and in prayers and tears, pour out the sorrow and love that have no end. Still farther injuries are heaped on her: by advice of the crafty Hagen, Gunther, who had not planned the murder, yet permitted and witnessed it, now comes with whining professions of repentance and goodwill; persuades her to send for the Nibelungen Hoard to Worms; where no sooner is it arrived, than Hagen and the rest forcibly take it from her; and her last trust in affection or truth from mortal is rudely cut away. Bent to the earth, she weeps only for her lost Siegfried, knows no comfort, but will weep for ever.

One lurid gleam of hope, after long years of darkness, breaks in on her, in the prospect of revenge. King Etzel sends from his far country to solicit her hand: the embassy she hears at first, as a woman of ice might do; the good Rudiger, Etzel's spokesman, pleads in vain that his king is the richest of all earthly kings; that he is so lonely 'since Frau Helke died;' that though a Heathen he has Christians about him, and may one day be converted: till, at length, when he hints distantly at the power of Etzel to avenge her injuries, she on a sudden becomes all attention. Hagen, foreseeing such possibilities, protests against the match; but is overruled: Chriemhild departs with Rudiger for the land of the Huns; taking cold leave of her relations; only two of whom, her brothers Gernot and Giselher, innocent of that murder, does she admit near her as convoy to the Donau.

The Nibelungen Hoard has hitherto been fatal to all its possessors; to the two sons of Nibelung; to Siegfried its conqueror: neither does the Burgundian Royal House fare better with it. Already, discords threatening to arise, Hagen sees prudent to sink it in the Rhine; first taking oath of Gunther and his brothers, that none of them shall reveal the hiding-place, while any of the rest is alive. But the curse that clave to it could not be sunk there. The Nibelungen-land is now theirs: they themselves are henceforth called Nibelungen; and this history of their fate is the ***Nibelungen Song,*** or ***Nibelungen Noth*** (***Nibelungen's Need,*** extreme need, or final wreck and abolition).

The Fifth Act of our strange eventful history now draws on. Chriemhild has a kind husband, of hospitable disposition, who troubles himself little about her secret feelings and intents. With his permission, she sends two minstrels, inviting the Burgundian Court to a high-tide at Etzel's: she has charged the messengers to say that she is happy, and to bring all Gunther's champions with them. Her eye was on Hagen, but she could not single him from the rest. After seven days' deliberation, Gunther answers that he will come. Hagen has loudly dissuaded the journey, but again been overruled. 'It is his fate,' says a commentator, 'like Cassandra's ever to foresee the evil, and ever to be disregarded. He himself shut his ear against the inward voice; and now his warnings are uttered to the deaf.' He argues long, but in vain: nay, young Gernot hints at last that this aversion originates in personal fear:

> Then spake von Troneg Hagen: "Nowise is it through fear;
> So you command it, Heroes, Then up, gird on your gear;
> I ride with you the foremost Into King Etzel's land."
> Since then full many a helm Was shivered by his hand.

Frau Ute's dreams and omens are now unavailing with him; 'whoso heedeth dreams,' said Hagen, 'of the right story wotteth not:' he has computed the worst issue, and defied it.

Many a little touch of pathos, and even solemn beauty lies carelessly scattered in these rhymes, had we space to exhibit such here. As specimen of a strange, winding, diffuse, yet innocently graceful style of narrative, we had translated some considerable portion of this Twenty-fifth *Aventiure,* 'How the Nibelungen marched (fared) to the Huns,' into verses as literal as might be; which now, alas, look mournfully different from the original; almost like Scriblerus's shield when the barbarian housemaid had scoured it. Nevertheless, to do for the reader what we can, let somewhat of that modernized ware, such as it is, be set before him. The brave Nibelungen are on the eve of departure; and about ferrying over the Rhine; and here it may be noted that Worms, with our old Singer, lies not in its true position, but at some distance from the river; a proof at least that he was never there, and probably sang and lived in some very distant region: . . .

> There rode von Troneg Hagen, The foremost of that host,
> He was to the Nibelungen The guide they lov'd the most:
> The Ritter keen dismounted, Set foot on the sandy ground,
> His steed to a tree he tied, Look'd wistful all around.
>
> "Much scaith," von Troneg said, "May lightly chance to thee,
> King Gunther by this tide, As thou with eyes mayst see:
> The river is overflowing, Full strong runs here its stream,
> For crossing of this Donau Some counsel might well beseem."
>
> "What counsel hast thou, brave Hagen," King Gunther then did say,
> "Of thy own wit and cunning? Dishearten me not, I pray:
> Thyself the ford wilt find us, If knightly skill it can,
> That safe to yonder shore We may pass both horse and man."
>
> "To me, I trow," spake Hagen, "Life hath not grown so cheap,
> To go with will and drown me In riding these waters deep;
> But first, of men some few By this hand of mine shall die,
> In great King Etzel's country, As best good will have I.
>
> But bide ye here by the River, Ye Ritters brisk and sound,
> Myself will seek some boatman, If boatman here be found,
> To row us at his ferry, Across to Gelfrat's land:"
> The Troneger grasped his buckler, Fared forth along the strand.
>
> He was full bravely harness'd, Himself he knightly bore,
> With buckler and with helmet, Which bright enough he wore:
> And, bound above his hauberk, A weapon broad was seen,
> That cut with both its edges, Was never sword so keen.
>
> Then hither he and thither Search'd for the Ferryman,
> He heard a splashing of waters, To watch the same he 'gan,
> It was the white Mer-women, That in a Fountain clear,
> To cool their fair bodyes, Were merrily bathing here.

From these Mer-women, who 'skimmed aloof like white cygnets,' at sight of him, Hagen snatches up 'their wondrous raiment;' on condition of returning which, they rede him his fortune; how this expedition is to speed. At first favourably:

> She said: "To Etzel's country, Of a truth, ye well may hie,
> For here I pledge my hand, Now kill me if I lie;
> That heroes seeking honour Did never arrive thereat

So richly as ye shall do, Believe thou surely that."

But no sooner is the wondrous raiment restored them, than they change their tale; for in spite of that matchless honour, it appears, every one of the adventurous Recken is to perish.

Outspake the wild Mer-woman: "I tell thee it will arrive,
Of all your gallant host No man shall be left alive,
Except king Gunther's chaplain, As we full well do know;
He only, home returning, To the Rhine-land back shall go."

Then spake Von Troneg Hagen, His wrath did fiercely swell:
"Such tidings to my master I were right loth to tell,
That in king Etzel's country We all must lose our life:
Yet show me over the water, Thou wise all-knowing *wife.*"

Thereupon, seeing him bent on ruin, she gives directions how to find the ferry, but withal counsels him to deal warily: the ferry-house stands on the other side of the river; the boatman, too, is not only the hottest-tempered of men, but rich and indolent; nevertheless, if nothing else will serve, let Hagen call himself Amelrich, and that name will bring him. All happens as predicted: the boatman, heedless of all shouting and offers of gold clasps, bestirs him lustily at the name of Amelrich; but the more indignant is he, on taking in his fare, to find it a counterfeit. He orders Hagen, if he loves his life, to leap out.

"Now say not that," spake Hagen: "Right hard am I bested,
Take from me for good friendship This clasp of gold so red;
And row our thousand heroes And steeds across this river:"
Then spake the wrathful boatman, "That will I surely never."

Then one of his oars he lifted, Right broad it was and long,
He struck it down on Hagen, Did the hero mickle wrong,
That in the boat he staggered, And alighted on his knee;
Other such wrathful boatman Did never the Troneger see.

His proud unbidden guest He would now provoke still more,
He struck his head so stoutly That it broke in twain the oar,
With strokes on head of Hagen; He was a sturdy wight;
Nathless had Gelfrat's boatman Small profit of that fight.

With fiercely raging spirit, The Troneger turn'd him round,
Clutch'd quick enough his scabbard, And a weapon there he found;
He smote his head from off him, And cast it on the sand,
Thus had that wrathful boatman His death from Hagen's hand.

Even as Von Troneg Hagen The wrathful boatman slew,
The boat whirl'd round to the river, He had work enough to do;
Or ever he turn'd it shorewards, To weary he began,
But kept full stoutly rowing, The bold king Gunther's man.

He wheel'd it back, brave Hagen, With many a lusty stroke,
The strong oar, with such rowing, In his hand asunder broke;
He fain would reach the Recken, All waiting on the shore,
No tackle now he had; Hei, how deftly he spliced the oar.

With thong from off his buckler! It was a slender band;
Right over against a forest He drove the boat to land;
Where Gunther's Recken waited, In crowds along the beach;
Full many a goodly hero Moved down his boat to reach.

Hagen ferries them over himself "into the unknown land," like a right yare steersman; yet ever brooding fiercely on that prediction of the wild Mer-woman, which had outdone even his own dark forebodings. Seeing the Chaplain, who alone of them all was to return, standing in the boat beside his *chappelsoume* (pyxes and other sacred furniture), he determines to belie at least this part of the prophecy, and on a sudden hurls the chaplain overboard. Nay, as the poor priest swims after the boat, he pushes him down, regardless of all remonstrance, resolved that he shall die. Nevertheless it proved not so: the chaplain made for the other side; when his strength failed, 'then God's hand helped him,' and at length he reached the shore. Thus does the stern truth stand revealed to Hagen, by the very means he took for eluding it: 'he thought with himself these Recken must all lose their lives.' From this time, a grim reckless spirit takes possession of him; a courage, an audacity, waxing more and more into the fixed strength of desperation. The passage once finished, he dashes the boat in pieces, and casts it in the stream, greatly as the others wonder at him.

"Why do ye this, good brother?" Said the Ritter Dankwart then,
How shall we cross this river, When the road we come again?
Returning home from Hunland, Here must we lingering stay?"—
Not then did Hagen tell him That return no more could they.

In this shipment 'into the unknown land' there lies, for the more penetrating sort of commentators, some hidden meaning and allusion. The destruction of the unreturning Ship, as of the Ship Argo, of Æneas' Ships, and the like, is a constant feature of such traditions: it is thought, this ferrying of the Nibelungen has a reference to old Scandinavian Mythuses; nay to the oldest, most universal emblems shaped out by man's Imagination; Hagen the ferryman being, in some sort, a type of Death, who ferries over his thousands and tens of thousands into a Land still more Unknown.

But leaving these considerations, let us remark the deep fearful interest, which, in gathering strength, rises to a really tragical height in the close of this Poem. Strangely has the old Singer, in these his loose melodies, modulated the wild narrative into a poetic whole, with what we might call true art, were it not rather an instinct of genius still more unerring. A fateful gloom now hangs over the fortunes of the Nibelungen, which deepens and deepens as they march onwards to the judgment-bar, till all are engulphed in utter night.

Hagen himself rises in tragic greatness; so helpful, so prompt and strong is he, and true to the death, though without hope. If sin can ever be pardoned, then that one act of his is pardonable; by loyal faith, by free daring, and heroic constancy, he has made amends for it. Well does he know what is coming; yet he goes forth to meet it, offers to Ruin his sullen welcome. Warnings thicken on him, which he treats lightly, as things now superfluous. Spite of our love for Siegfried, we must pity and almost respect the lost Hagen, now in his extreme need, and fronting it so nobly. 'Mixed was his hair with a grey colour, his limbs strong, and threatening his look.' Nay, his sterner qualities are beautifully tempered by another feeling, of which till now we understood not that he was capable,—the feeling of friendship. There is a certain Volker of Alsace here introduced, not for the first time, yet first in decided energy, who is more to Hagen than a brother. This Volker, a courtier and noble, is also a *Spielmann* (minstrel), a *Fidelere gut* (fiddler good); and surely the prince of all *Fideleres;* in truth a very phœnix, melodious as the soft nightingale, yet strong as the royal eagle: for also in the brunt of battle he can play tunes; and with a *Steel Fiddlebow,* beats strange music from the cleft helmets of his enemies. There is, in this continual allusion to Volker's *Schwertfidelbogen* (Sword-fiddlebow), as rude as it sounds to us, a barbaric greatness and depth; the light minstrel of kingly and queenly halls is gay also in the storm of Fate, its dire rushing pipes and whistles to him: is he not the image of every brave man fighting with Necessity, be that duel when and where it may; smiting the fiend with giant strokes, yet every stroke *musical?*—This Volker and Hagen are united inseparably, and defy death together. 'Whatever Volker said pleased Hagen; whatever Hagen did pleased Volker.'

But into these last Ten *Aventiures,* almost like the image of a Doomsday, we must hardly glance at present. Seldom, perhaps, in the poetry of that or any other age, has a grander scene of pity and terror been exhibited than here, could we look into it clearly. At every new step new shapes of fear arise. Dietrich of Bern meets the Nibelungen on their way, with ominous warnings: but warnings, as we said, are now superfluous, when the evil itself is apparent and inevitable. Chriemhild, wasted and exasperated here into a frightful Medea, openly threatens Hagen, but is openly defied by him; he and Volker retire to a seat before her palace, and sit there, while she advances in angry tears, with a crowd of armed Huns to destroy them. But Hagen has Siegfried's Balmung lying naked on his knee, the Minstrel also has drawn his keen Fiddlebow, and the Huns dare not provoke the battle. Chriemhild would fain single out Hagen for vengeance; but Hagen, like other men, stands not alone; and sin is an infection which will not rest with one victim. Partakers or not of his crime, the others also must share his punishment. Singularly touching, in the meanwhile, is king Etzel's ignorance of what every one else understands too well; and how, in peaceful hospitable spirit, he exerts himself to testify his joy over these royal guests of his, who are bidden hither for far other ends. That night the wayworn Nibelungen are sumptuously lodged; yet Hagen and Volker see good to keep watch: Volker plays them to sleep: 'under the door of the house he sat on the stone; bolder fiddler was there never any; when the tones flowed so sweetly they all gave him thanks. Then sounded his strings till all the house rang; his strength and the art were great, sweeter and sweeter he began to play, till flitted forth from him into sleep full many a care-worn soul.' It was their last lullaby; they were to sleep no more. Armed men appear, but suddenly vanish, in the night; assassins sent by Chriemhild, expecting no sentinel: it is plain that the last hour draws nigh.

In the morning the Nibelungen are for the Minster to hear mass; they are putting on gay raiment; but Hagen tells them a different tale: "ye must take other garments, Recken;" "instead of silk shirts hauberks, for rich mantles your good shields;" "and, beloved masters, moreover squires and men, ye shall full earnestly go to the church, and plain to God the powerful (*Got dem richen*) of your sorrow and utmost need; and know of a surety that death for us is nigh." In Etzel's Hall, where the Nibelungen appear at the royal feast in complete armour, the Strife, incited by Chriemhild, begins; the first answer to her provocation is from Hagen, who hews off the head of her own and Etzel's son, making it bound into the mother's bosom: "then began among the Recken a murder grim and great." Dietrich, with a voice of preternatural power, commands pause; retires with Etzel and Chriemhild; and now the bloody work has free course. We have heard of battles, and massacres, and deadly struggles in siege and storm; but seldom has even the poet's imagination pictured anything so fierce and terrible as this. Host after host, as they enter that huge vaulted Hall, perish in conflict with the doomed Nibelungen; and ever after the terrific uproar, ensues a still more terrific silence. All night, and through morning it lasts. They throw the dead from the windows; blood runs like water; the Hall is set fire to, they quench it with blood, their own burning thirst they slake with blood. It is a tumult like the Crack of Doom, a thousand-voiced, wild stunning hubbub; and, frightful like a Trump of Doom, the *Sword-fiddlebow* of Volker, who guards the door, makes music to that death-dance. Nor are traits of heroism wanting, and thrilling tones of pity and love; as in that act of Rudiger, Etzel's and Chriemhild's champion, who, bound by oath, "lays his soul in God's hand," and enters that Golgotha to die fighting against his friends; yet first changes shields with Hagen, whose own, also given him by Rudiger in a far other hour, had been shattered in the fight. "When he so lovingly bade give him the shield, there were eyes enough red with hot tears; it was the last gift which Rudiger of Bechelaren gave to any Recke. As grim as Hagen was, and as hard of mind, he wept at this gift which the hero good, so near his last times, had given him; full many a noble Ritter began to weep."

At last Volker is slain; they are all slain, save only Hagen and Gunther, faint and wounded, yet still unconquered among the bodies of the dead. Dietrich the wary, though strong and invincible, whose Recken too, except old Hildebrand he now finds are all killed, though he had charged them strictly not to mix in the quarrel, at last arms himself to finish it. He subdues the two wearied Nibelungen, binds them, delivers them to Chriemhild; 'and Herr Dietrich went away with weeping eyes, worthily from the heroes.' These never saw each other more. Chriemhild demands of Hagen, Where the Nibelungen Hoard is? But he answers her that he has sworn never to disclose it, while any of her brothers live. "I bring it to an end," said the enfuriated woman; orders her brother's head to be struck off, and holds it up to Hagen. "Thou hast it now according to thy will," said Hagen; "of the Hoard knoweth none but God and I; from thee, she-devil (*valendinne*), shall it for ever be hid." She kills him with his own sword, once her husband's; and is herself struck dead by Hildebrand, indignant at the woe she has wrought; king Etzel, there present, not opposing the deed. Whereupon the curtain drops over that wild scene, "the full highly honoured were lying dead; the people, all had sorrow and lamentation, in grief had the king's feast ended, as all love is want to do:

Ine chan iu nicht bescheiden Waz sider da geschach,
Wan ritter unde wrovven Weinen man do sach,
Dar-zuo die edeln chnechte Ir lieben vriunde tot:
Da hat das mœre ein ende; Diz ist der Nibelunge not.

I cannot say you now What hath befallen since,
The women all were weeping, And the Ritters and the prince,
Also the noble squires, Their dear friends lying dead:
Here hath the story ending; This is the ***Nibelungen's Need.***

We have now finished our slight analysis of this Poem; and hope that readers, who are curious in this matter, and ask themselves, What is the ***Nibelungen***? may have here found some outlines of an answer, some help towards farther researches of their own. (pp. 14-39)

It has been called a Northern *Iliad;* but except in the fact that both poems have a narrative character, and both sing "the destructive rage" of men, the two have scarcely any similarity. The Singer of the ***Nibelungen*** is a far different person from Homer; far inferior both in culture, and in genius. Nothing of the glowing imagery, of the fierce bursting energy, of the mingled fire and gloom, that dwell in the old Greek, makes its appearance here. The German Singer is comparatively a simple nature; has never penetrated deep into life; never "questioned Fate," or struggled with fearful mysteries; of all which we find traces in Homer, still more in Shakspeare; but with meek believing submission, has taken the Universe as he found it represented to him; and rejoices with a fine childlike gladness in the mere outward shows of things. He has little power of delineating character; perhaps he had no decisive vision thereof. His persons are superficially distinguished, and not altogether without generic difference; but the portraiture is imperfectly brought out; there lay no true living original within him. He has little Fancy; we find scarcely one or two similitudes in his whole Poem; and these one or two, which, moreover, are repeated, betoken no special faculty that way. He speaks of the "moon among stars;" says often, of sparks struck from steel armour in battle, and so forth, that they were *wie es wehte der wind,* "as if the wind were blowing them." We have mentioned Tasso along with him; yet neither in this case is there any close resemblance; the light playful grace, still more, the Italian pomp, and sunny luxuriance of Tasso are wanting in the other. His are humble, wood-notes wild; and no nightingale's, but yet a sweet sky-hidden lark's. In all the rhetorical gifts, to say nothing of rhetorical attainments, we should pronounce him even poor.

Nevertheless, a noble soul he must have been, and furnished with far more essential requisities for Poetry, than these are; namely, with the heart and feeling of a Poet. He has a clear eye for the Beautiful and True; all unites itself gracefully and compactly in his imagination: it is strange with what careless felicity he winds his way in that complex narrative, and be the subject what it will, comes through it unsullied, and with a smile. His great strength is an unconscious instinctive strength; wherein truly lies its highest merit. The whole spirit of Chivalry, of Love and heroic Valour, must have lived in him, and inspired him. Everywhere he shows a noble Sensibility; the sad accents of parting friends, the lamentings of women, the high daring of men, all that is worthy and lovely prolongs itself in melodious echoes through his heart. A true old Singer, and taught of Nature herself! Neither let us call him an inglorious Milton, since now he is no longer a mute one. What good were it that the four of five Letters composing his Name could be printed, and pronounced, with absolute certainty? All that was mortal in him is gone utterly; of his life, and its environment, as of the bodily tabernacle he dwelt in, the very ashes remain not: like a fair heavenly Apparition, which indeed he was, he has melted into air, and only the Voice he uttered, in virtue of its inspired gift, yet lives and will live.

To the Germans this ***Nibelungen Song*** is naturally an object of no common love; neither if they sometimes overvalue it, and vague antiquarian wonder is more common than just criticism, should the fault be too heavily visited. After long ages of concealment, they have found it in the remote wilderness, still standing like the trunk of some almost antediluvian oak; nay with boughs on it still green, after all the wind and weather of twelve hundred years. To many a patriotic feeling, which lingers fondly in solitary places of the Past, it may well be a rallying-point, and "Lovers' *Trysting-tree.*"

For us also it has its worth. A creation from the old ages,

still bright and balmy, if we visit it; and opening into the first History of Europe, of Mankind. Thus all is not oblivion, but on the edge of the abyss, that separates the Old world from the New, there hangs a fair rainbow-land; which also in (three) curious repetitions, as it were, in a secondary, and even a ternary reflex, sheds some feeble twilight far into the deeps of the primeval Time. (pp. 44-5)

Thomas Carlyle, "The Nibelungen Lied," in The Westminster Review, *Vol. XV, July, 1831, pp. 1-45.*

The Eclectic Review (essay date 1848)

[*In the following excerpt, the reviewer examines the* Nibelungenlied *from an aesthetic viewpoint, favorably comparing the epic poem to the* Iliad.]

If we . . . carefully examine [the ***Nibelungenlied***] in an aesthetical point of view, we shall discover—leaving age and form out of the question—so much internal beauty, as to justify its being termed the *German Iliad.* The internal similarity of the characters brought forward in both poems, is great and surprising. The womanly beauties, *Helen* and *Chriemhild,* are the source of all the stirring events, and in consequence, both poems display an equal share of mighty heroism. King *Etzel* forcibly reminds the reader of Priam, whilst Siegfried forms a side-piece to Achilles. Odysseus and Ajax are united in the person of Hagen, the stout, crafty, and haughty Recke. The greatest similarity exists in the description of the heroic life of both nations. Gunther may be compared with Agamemnon, Gernot with Menelaus, and Dietrich of Bern with Æneas. The mode of living and manners are similarly described, as, for example, the secluded state of the women, their skill in weaving and the sewing of garments; the high value which the heroes place upon the garments woven by the hand of women, the dwellings and presses filled with costly articles and store, the liberality with which they are given away, love of pomp, an eager desire for combat, etc.

With regard to the construction of the whole, it may be said to be so simple, the harmony and unity pervading it so rigidly correct and unaffected, and the keeping of the most varied figures so perfect, that the painter has only to copy the poet, in order to produce the most finished and most glorious work of art. Throughout the poem the main personalities, Chriemhild and Siegfried, Hagen, Gunther, Brunhild, and others, placed as they are in the foreground, shine above all the rest. It cannot certainly be denied, that the historical and traditional background might have been brought out into more light and with more force, in order to impart to the whole a more finished aspect and character. The tragical interest would have gained greatly, if, for example, the curse which rested on the Nibelungen treasure had been pronounced with more distinctness. Nor do we miss with less difficulty, if not inconvenience, more finish and execution in some single figures and images, as for example, in Volker, the little Ortlieb, and others. The manner too, is, perhaps, now and then stiff, as if cast in inflexible iron; yet it is by no means affected and clumsy; nay, in point of grace and sprightliness, it carries the palm over the mass of heroic poems of more recent periods.

We find in the ***Nibelungenlied*** almost all the qualifications which pertain to a first-rate work of art. How animated and consummate are the various natures we here behold in a state of action! The whole is, in this respect, a faithful portrait of the German nation, so excellently described by Tacitus, and other ancient writers. The rudeness which now and then prevails, is an expression of the period in which the poem was composed, and, is depicted in such a manner as to lead us to suppose that the whole originated with the superabundance of natural untutored powers, and impulses, rather than with the great irritability of a sickly and corrupt race. Again; how finished is the description of individual character; as, for example, *Siegfried's* innocent and harmless integrity, coupled with so much Titanic valor, exercised, too, almost without consciousness or pride, so as to render him amiable even in his most daring defiance. And *Chriemhild,* how chaste and virgin-like! and with features, too, that remind the reader of Grecian loveliness and grace. Even the very act of betraying the secret confided to her by *Siegfried,* is only a natural outbreak of offended consciousness and self-regard, provoked by the over-bearing and fiend-like character of Brunhild. And so is, indeed, her second blunder, which is based on her intense love of her husband. The very revenge she takes on her ungrateful brother, and the fierce and crafty Hagen, is palliated by so many acts of the most revolting injustice, that we need hardly have recourse to the character of the age to find an excuse for it. Less finished, perhaps, although full of poetical truth, and equally attractive, is the description of Queen Brunhild. Indeed, her secret passion for *Siegfried,* is handled with so much delicacy and true *savoir faire,* as to suffer no abhorrence to spring up against this personage.

The most finished character, in our opinion, is Hagen; and we may safely say, that throughout the whole range of poetry there are very few sketches equal to it. It is in the second part of the poem where he appears to the greatest advantage,—where Hagen, evidently seized by the foreboding and prediction of his impending fate, accelerates his own ruin and that of his companions. Here the poet endeavours to represent his hero as colossal as possible, making him preserve to the last, and in the midst of the most prodigious acts of wrath, a truly chivalrous degree of honour. By his side we find the minstrel *Volker,* the 'fidelere gut,' whose fiddle-bow is more than a match for iron or steel, and cannot be resisted by the helmet, the shield, or coat of mail, the moment it descends on either. This *Volker* is an exceedingly interesting character, which, little as it is carried out, represents, with the rest of his warlike companions, all that is heroic, and truly noble.

How this Epos, calm as was the poet's mode of creation, progresses rapidly and smoothly,—how the interest is maintained and increased throughout, and especially towards the end, where the destruction of the most valiant, and the terrible massacre of the Nibelungen is described with wonderful force and skill,—this, and more, may be inferred from what has been briefly pointed out, and from the few specimens with which we have illustrated our opinions. (pp. 48-50)

A review of "The Lay of the Nibelungen," in

The Eclectic Review, *Vol. 88, July, 1848, pp. 26-50.*

Richey contrasts the *Nibelungenlied* with the *Iliad:*

If we contrast the ***Lay of the Nibelungs*** with the *Iliad*—although, it has been truly said, it is but a comparing of beer to wine—we cannot fail to be struck by the absence of the dramatic element; there are many passages of the poem in which debate and conflict of opinions could easily have been elaborated into effective dramatic scenes without injury to the narrative; such as the 24th adventure, in which the Burgundians deliberate whether they should accept the invitation to the Court of Etzel; on all such occasions, however, the several characters speak as little as possible; they converse after a very practical fashion, and only enough to explain the resolution which they ultimately carry into execution. It is evident that the weariness which everyone who reads the ***Lay of the Nibelungs*** straight through cannot fail to experience, arises from the failure of the author to give that distinct individuality to his several characters which can only be gained by enabling them sometimes to express their conflicting opinions in full and free debate.

A. G. Richey, in Fraser's Magazine, *March 1874.*

The Spectator (essay date 1888)

[In the excerpt below, the anonymous reviewer asserts that the Nibelungenlied *"does not fulfil the primary conditions of a truly national epic," but praises the poem's aesthetic qualities, claiming that it "ranks with the finest productions of poetical genius."]*

It is the boast of the Germans that they alone possess, besides the Indians, the Persians, and the ancient Greeks, a national epic. The boast is a pardonable, and, on the whole, also a legitimate one; but a close comparison of the ***Nibelungenlied*** with all the other epic poems in existence will not hold water. We do not allude to the relative poetical merit of the *Mahâbhârata, Shah Nameh,* or the great Homeric Epopee, but to their importance and bearing from a national point of view. An epic poem can only be said to be truly national if it is intimately interwoven with the history of the people—whether mythical or authentic—if it pervades all the classes of the nation as a living remembrance, and, finally, if it exercises a deep and lasting influence on the mode of thought of the people. We need not specially point out that all these conditions are completely fulfilled by the Homeric epic, for instance. But can this be said of the ***Nibelungenlied***? Besides the mythological element, chiefly represented by the "Siegfried-Saga," there are two historical elements to be met with in the German poem. The principal one of these two elements refers to the destruction of the Burgundian Empire by the Huns—but not by Attila—in 437. From allusions dating from a much later period, we may safely infer that songs regarding the Burgundian catastrophe were composed soon after the event, when the recollection of it was still fresh in the memory of the people. These national songs were, however, soon forgotten in Germany, amidst the great commotion and dislocation of the nations in those days. There was, therefore, no continuity of tradition as regards the principal historical element of the ***Nibelungenlied.*** The second historical element in the poem—relating to the "Thidreks-Saga"—is based on an anachronism, connecting, as it does, three Kings, the Burgundian Gunther, the Hunnish Attila, and the Ostrogoth Theodoric the Great, or Dietrich von Bern, who died respectively in 437, 454, and 526. The last-named King was, indeed, the favourite hero of German folk-lore, and his memory was long cherished by the people; but his name was connected with the Burgundian legend and the Siegfried myth as late as the seventh century only, when the latter was transformed from a purely mythical fable into a hero-legend. All these facts show that there was no continuity of either the historical or the mythical elements in connection with the ***Nibelungenlied,*** which cannot, therefore, have exercised in its primitive form that influence on the German people which Homer's poem did on the Greeks. When the great German epic assumed towards the end of the twelfth century the form in which it is known to us, the poem was considerably modernised. It was divested of its gross mythological ingredients, the fabulous creatures were humanised, and Christian elements were, in general, substituted for the heathenish ones. Thus refined and modified, the poem seems to have become a great favourite with the then select and cultured circles of society; but it never became, so to say, the common property of the people.

We do not wish to imply by the foregoing remarks that the ***Nibelungenlied*** was not—to use a modern expression—popular at all in its time. A poem of which there are about twenty-nine more or less complete manuscripts extant, must have enjoyed a certain popularity, at least at the beginning of the thirteenth century, and it was, above all, the text known as the "Vulgata" which seems to have been in great favour. Gradually the popularity of the poem waned, and after the death of Maximilian I.—the so-called *letzte Ritter*—in 1519, the ***Nibelungenlied,*** together with the other relics of mediæval German poetry, was forgotten for a considerable space of time. The Swiss poet, Bodmer, who possessed more of the instinct than the genius of poetry, and whose attention was called to a manuscript of the poem, was the first to rescue it from perpetual oblivion by publishing a fragment of it in 1757. This publication passed, however, unnoticed, and so did Professor C. H. Müller's complete edition of the ***Nibelungenlied*** in 1782, although it was dedicated to Frederick the Great. The latter had himself a very poor idea of the poem, of which he wrote in 1789 that it was *nicht einen Schuss Pulver werth;* which harsh judgment was quite explicable in a King whose literary tastes were thoroughly French, and who, in his political aspirations for Germany, did not look backwards to the mythical days of "horned Siegfried," but rather forward to the dawn of the nineteenth century. Single efforts to raise the poem in public estimation proved unavailing, until the romantic school hit upon the ingenious idea of making it the medium of patriotic enthusiasm. The spirit of Teutonism had, according to their opinion, to be aroused in the young of Germany in order to enable them to fight the French successfully. Wilhelm Schlegel struck the key-note by his lectures on the ***Nibelungenlied*** at Berlin in 1803. The philologists followed in the wake of the "Romantic Patriots," and here it was, above all, Jacob Grimm who showed that the clue to the German epic was to be found in the Northern version of it, in the *Eddas*, without which the ***Nibelungenlied*** is, in fact, quite unintelligible.

If we have dwelt so fully on the history of the composition of German epic, and on its vicissitudes, it was simply to show that it does *not* fulfil the primary conditions of a truly national epic, and that the enthusiasm entertained for it by the Germans of latter days was not the result of any continuous growth, but the outcome of an artificial propaganda. Considered from a purely æsthetical point of view, however, the ***Nibelungenlied*** ranks with the finest productions of poetical genius. All the characters are sketched with marked outlines, and the whole poem is distinguished by a grandeur of conception which justified Heine in declaring that a Frenchman can hardly form a just notion of the majestic vigour of the ***Nibelungenlied.*** It took some time before the Germans themselves fully realised the poetical beauty of their national epic, partly because it was used, as we said above, by the romanticists as a purely politico-sentimental vehicle, and by the philologists as an abundant source for linguistic disquisitions. These two schools, which have done so much to obscure the poetical charm of the epic, are still more numerously represented in the constantly increasing and alarmingly vast *Nibelungen* literature than the æsthetic school which sees in the poem nothing but the poem.

In England, the German epic first became known partially at least, through extracts in prose, interspersed with metrical translations, which appeared in 1814, in the *Illustrations of Northern Antiquities.* These metrical renderings were attributed by Lockhart to Walter Scott, who, we need not add, would have been better qualified than any other English poet, perhaps, to produce a translation which might worthily have been placed by the side of the original. This first attempt at acclimatising the ***Nibelungenlied*** in this country seems to have passed unnoticed, and it was reserved to Carlyle to call special attention to it. In 1831 there appeared in the *Westminster Review* his well-known essay, "The ***Nibelungenlied***," for which Simrock's modern High-German translation was used as a mere peg on which to hang a general survey of the epic, as far as its literature was known in those days, together with some metrical renderings. In 1846, Mr. J. Gostick gave some extracts from the poem in his *Spirit of German Poetry;* and two years later, Mr. J. Birch published at Berlin a translation of the ***Nibelungenlied*** which purported to be complete, but only reproduced the poem in its curtailed form as edited by Lachmann, who merely recognised twenty songs as genuine. Mr. Birch was not successful with his versification, and his translation was superseded, in 1850, by that of Mr. W. N. Lettsom, who followed the edition of Braunfels, containing the original middle High-German text and a modern High-German version. Lettsom seems to have possessed a thorough knowledge of modern High-German, and he was in so far able to handle English verse that he could assimilate the English metre to the German one, at least as regards the cæsura at the end of each half-line; but he was not a poet, and he failed to produce a version truthfully reflecting the spirit of the original.

Our readers will see that there was ample room for a new English translation of the ***Nibelungenlied,*** and we looked hopefully forward to the publication of the volume before us, when it was first announced. Unfortunately, our expectations have not been realised. In the first instance, a translation of a poem like the ***Nibelungenlied*** should not be issued without a full historical and literary introduction. Mr. Lettsom has one which is fairly in keeping with the state of the *Nibelungen* criticism of 1850; whilst Mr. Foster-Barham's sketchy preface of about three pages not only gives the reader no information whatever about the great poem, but actually betrays the translator's historical and literary ignorance regarding the subject of the poem. The translation itself is, as a whole, an unsatisfactory performance. Not only are a number of verses quite unscannable, but the cæsura at the end of the half-lines has frequently been neglected. Nor has the original metre been scrupulously followed in the last half-line of each stanza. As a specimen of the translator's versification, we will quote, out of many similar stanzas, the following only:—

> Then spake the monarch Gunther: 'Let me an answer hear;
> Tell me now, I pray you, how they both do fare,
> Etzel and Dame Helke in the far Hunland?'
> To whom replied the Margrave: 'That shall you understand.'

That Mr. Foster-Barham is capable of producing more melodious verse, he has shown in several instances. We take at random the following stanza from the "Adventure," in which the first meeting between Siegfried and Chriemhilda is described:—

> Then came the lovely one, as does the rosy morn
> Through sombre clouds advancing. From Siegfried's heart love-lorn
> Fled all the care that bound him, and which he long had known;
> Before him now the maiden in queenly beauty shone.

This is a far happier rendering than the one given by Mr. Lettsom, and we cannot but exclaim: *O! si sic omnia!*

The translator seems to have followed, like Mr. Lettsom, the above-mentioned edition of Braunfels, in which the following last stanza is wanting, now given in all complete editions of the poem, and in accordance with which it is universally called ***Das Nibelungenlied,*** instead of, as was done formerly, ***Der Nibelungen Noth:***—

> Ich sag' euch nicht weiter von der grossen Noth:
> Die da erschlagen waren, die lasst liegen todt.
> Wie es auch im Heunland hernach dem Volk gerieth,
> Hier hat die Mär ein Ende: das ist *das Niebelungenlied.*

SIMROCK.

Mr. Foster-Barham says on the title-page, "Translated from the German," which almost sounds like an admission that his version was *not* made from the original middle High-German; nor can we imagine that any scholar acquainted with the original work would have issued an English translation without prefixing an appropriate disquisition on the poem, which in its present English garb will be quite unintelligible to the generality of readers. We might point out several other defects in connection with the volume before us, but we will content ourselves with saying that an English version of the ***Nibelungenlied,*** fully worthy of the original, would be a most valuable contribution to our literature; but let no one rashly undertake the gigantic task. Only an English poet, fully conversant with both middle and modern High-German, and thoroughly acquainted with the extensive *Nibelungen* literature of the present day, could successfully perform the great achievement. To all those who do not combine those qualities, we should address the warning, "Hands off!" (pp. 22-3)

A review of "The 'Nibelungenlied'," in The Spectator, *Vol. 61, No. 3106, January 7, 1888, pp. 22-3.*

George Henry Needler (essay date 1904)

[*In the following excerpt from Needler's introduction to his translation of the* Nibelungenlied, *he provides an historical, cultural, and textual overview of the work.*]

ORIGIN OF THE SAGA

All the Aryan peoples have had their heroic age, the achievements of which form the basis of later saga. For the Germans this was the period of the Migrations, as it is called, in round numbers the two hundred years from 400 to 600, at the close of which we find them settled in those regions which they have, generally speaking, occupied ever since. During these two centuries kaleidoscopic changes had been taking place in the position of the various Germanic tribes. Impelled partly by a native love of wandering, partly by the pressure of hostile peoples of other race, they moved with astonishing rapidity hither and thither over the face of Europe, generally in conflict with one another or buffeted by the Romans in the west and south, and by the Huns in the east. In this stern struggle for existence and search for a permanent place of settlement some of them even perished utterly; amid the changing fortunes of all of them, deeds were performed that fixed themselves in the memory of the whole people, great victories or great disasters became the subject of story and song. We need only to recall such names as those of Ermanric and Theodoric to remind ourselves what an important part was played by the Germanic peoples of that Migration Period in the history of Europe. During it a national consciousness was engendered, and in it we have the faint beginnings of a national literature. Germanic saga rests almost entirely upon the events of these two centuries, the fifth and sixth. Although we get glimpses of the Germans during the four or five preceding centuries, none of the historic characters of those earlier times have been preserved in the national sagas.

With these sagas based on history, however, have been mingled in most cases primeval Germanic myths, possessions of the people from prehistoric times. A most conspicuous example of this union of mythical and originally historical elements is the Nibelungen saga, out of which grew in course of time the great national epic, the ***Nibelungenlied.***

The Nibelungen saga is made up of two parts, on the one hand the mythical story of Siegfried and on the other the story, founded on historic fact, of the Burgundians. When and how the Siegfried myth arose it is impossible to say; its origin takes us back into the impenetrable mists of the unrecorded life of our Germanic forefathers, and its form was moulded by the popular poetic spirit. The other part of the saga is based upon the historic incident of the overthrow of the Burgundian kingdom by the Huns in the year 437. This annihilation of a whole tribe naturally impressed itself vividly upon the imagination of contemporaries. Then the fact of history soon began to pass over into the realm of legend, and, from causes which can no longer be determined, this tradition of the vanished Burgundians became united with the mythical story of Siegfried. This composite Siegfried-Burgundian saga then became a common possession of the Germanic peoples, was borne with many of them to lands far distant from the place of its origin, and was further moulded by each according to its peculiar genius and surroundings. In the Icelandic Eddas, the oldest of which we have as they were written down in the latter part of the ninth century, are preserved the earliest records of the form it had taken among the northern Germanic peoples. Our ***Nibelungenlied,*** which is the chief source of our knowledge of the story as it developed in Germany, dates from about the year 1200. These two versions, the Northern and the German, though originating in this common source, had diverged very widely in the centuries that elapsed between their beginning and the time when the manuscripts were written in which they are preserved. Each curtailed, re-arranged, or enlarged the incidents of the story in its own way. The character of the chief actors and the motives underlying what we may call the dramatic development assumed widely dissimilar forms. The German ***Nibelungenlied*** may be read and appreciated as one of the world's great epic poems without an acquaintance on the part of the reader with the Northern version of the saga. In order, however, to furnish the setting for a few episodes that would in that case remain either obscure or colorless, and with a view to placing the readers of [the ***Nibelungenlied***] in a position to judge better the deeper significance of the epic as the eloquent narrative of a thousand years of the life of the people among whom it grew, the broad outlines of the saga in its Northern form will be given here.

THE NORTHERN FORM OF THE SAGA

Starting at the middle of the fifth century from the territory about Worms on the Rhine where the Burgundians were overthrown, the saga soon spread from the Franks to the other Germanic peoples. We have evidence of its presence in northern Germany and Denmark. Allusions to it in the Anglo-Saxon poem, the *Wanderer,* of the seventh century and in the great Anglo-Saxon epic *Beowulf* of a short time later, show us that it had early become part of the national saga stock in England. Among the people of Norway and Iceland it took root and grew with particular vigor. Here, farthest away from its original home and least exposed to outward influences, it preserved on the whole most fully its heathen Germanic character, especially in its mythical part. By a fortunate turn of events, too, the written record of it here is of considerably earlier date than that which we have from Germany. The Eddas, as the extensive collection of early Icelandic poems is called, are the fullest record of Germanic mythology and saga that has been handed down to us, and in them the saga of Siegfried and the Nibelungen looms up prominently. The earliest of these poems date from about the year 850, and the most important of them were probably written down within a couple of centuries of that time. They are thus in part some three centuries older than the German ***Nibelungenlied,*** and on the whole, too, they preserve more of the original outlines of the saga. By bringing together the various episodes of the saga from the Eddas and the Volsung saga, a prose account of the mythical race of the Volsungs, we arrive at the following narrative.

On their wanderings through the world the three gods Odin, Hönir, and Loki come to a waterfall where an otter is devouring a fish that it has caught. Loki kills the otter with a stone, and they take off its skin. In the evening they seek a lodging at the house of Hreidmar, to whom they show the skin. Hreidmar recognizes it as that of his son, whom Loki has killed when he had taken on the form of an otter. Assisted by his sons Fafnir and Regin, Hreidmar seizes the three gods, and spares their lives only on the promise that they will fill the skin, and also cover it outwardly, with gold. Loki is sent to procure the ransom. With a net borrowed from the sea-goddess Ran he catches at the waterfall the dwarf Andvari in form of a fish and compels him to supply the required gold. Andvari tries to keep back a ring, but this also Loki takes from him, whereupon the dwarf utters a curse upon the gold and whosoever may possess it. The ransom is now paid to Hreidmar; even the ring must, on Hreidmar's demand, be given in order to complete the covering of the otter's skin. Loki tells him of the curse connected with the ownership of the gold. When Hreidmar refuses Fafnir and Regin a share in the treasure, he is killed by Fafnir, who takes possession of the hoard to the exclusion of Regin. In the form of a dragon Fafnir dwells on Gnita Heath guarding the hoard, while Regin broods revenge.

From Odin is descended King Volsung, who has a family of ten sons and one daughter. The eldest son is Sigmund, twin-born with his sister Signy. King Siggeir of Gautland sues for the hand of Signy, whom her father gives to Siggeir against her will. In the midst of King Volsung's hall stood a mighty oaktree. As the wedding-feast is being held there enters a stranger, an old man with one eye, his hat drawn down over his face and bearing in his hand a sword. This sword he thrusts to the hilt into the tree, saying that it shall belong to him who can draw it out again; after which he disappears as he had come. All the guests try their strength in vain upon the sword, but Sigmund alone is able to draw it forth. He refuses to sell it to Siggeir for all his proffered gold. Siggeir plans vengeance. He invites Volsung and his sons to Gautland, and returns home thither with his bride Signy, who before going warns her father to be upon his guard.

At the appointed time King Volsung and his sons go as invited to Gautland. In spite of Signy's repeated warning he will not flee from danger, and falls in combat with Siggeir; his ten sons are taken prisoners, and placed in stocks in the forest. For nine successive nights a she-wolf comes and devours each night one of them, till only Sigmund remains. By the aid of Signy he escapes. The she-wolf, it was said, was the mother of Siggeir.

To Sigmund, who has hidden in a wood, Signy sends her eldest boy of ten years that Sigmund may test his courage and see if he is fit to be a helper in seeking revenge. Neither he, however, nor his younger brother stands the test. Signy sees that only a scion of the race of Volsung will suffice, and accordingly disguises herself and lives three days with Sigmund in the wood. From their union a son Sinfiotli is born, whom also, after ten years, she sends out to Sigmund. He stands every test of courage, and is trained by Sigmund, who thinks he is Siggeir's son.

Bent on revenge, Sigmund repairs with Sinfiotli to Siggeir's castle. After Sinfiotli has slain the king's two sons, he and Sigmund are overpowered and condemned to be buried alive. With Sigmund's sword, however, which Signy has managed to place in their hands, they cut their way out, then set fire to Siggeir's hall. Signy comes forth and reveals to Sigmund that Sinfiotli is their own son; and then, saying that her work of revenge is complete and that she can live no longer, she returns into the burning hall and perishes with Siggeir and all his race.

Sigmund now returns home and rules as a mighty king. He marries Borghild, who later kills Sinfiotli with a poisoned drink, and is cast away by Sigmund. He then marries Hjordis. Lyngvi, the son of King Hunding, was also a suitor and now invades Sigmund's land. The latter hews down many of his enemies, until an old man with one eye, in hat and dark cloak, interposes his spear, against which Sigmund's sword breaks in two. Sigmund falls severely wounded.

In the night Hjordis seeks the scene of the combat and finds Sigmund still alive. He refuses to allow her to heal his wounds, saying that Odin no longer wills that he swing the sword. He tells Hjordis to preserve carefully the pieces of the broken sword; the son she bears in her womb shall yet swing the sword when welded anew, and win thereby a glorious name. At dawn Sigmund dies. Hjordis is borne off by Vikings and, after the birth of her son, she becomes the wife of the Danish prince Alf.

The son of Hjordis was called Sigurd. He grew up a boy of wondrous strength and beauty, with eyes that sparkled brightly, and lived at the court of King Hjalprek, the father of Alf. Regin, the dwarfish brother of Fafnir, was his tutor. Regin welds together the pieces of the broken sword Gram, so sharp and strong that with it Sigurd cleaves Regin's anvil in twain. With men and ships that he has received from King Hjalprek Sigurd goes against the sons of Hunding, whom he slays, thereby avenging the death of his father. Regin has urged him to kill Fafnir and take possession of the hoard. On the Gnita Heath he digs a ditch from which, as the dragon Fafnir passes over it, he plunges the sword into his heart. The dying Fafnir warns him of the curse attached to the possession of the gold; also that Regin is to be guarded against. The latter bids him roast the heart of Fafnir. While doing so he burns his finger by dipping it in the blood to see if the heart is done, and to cool his finger puts it into his mouth. Suddenly he is able to understand the language of the birds in the wood. They warn him to beware of Regin, whom he straightway slays. The birds tell him further of the beautiful valkyrie Brynhild, who sleeps on the fire-encircled mountain awaiting her deliverer. Then Sigurd places Fafnir's hoard upon his steed Grani, takes with him also Fafnir's helm, and rides away to Frankenland. He sees a mountain encircled by a zone of fire, makes his way into it and beholds there, as he deems it, a man in full armor asleep. When he takes off the helmet he finds that it is a woman. With his sword he cuts loose the armor. The woman wakes and asks if it be the hero Sigurd who has awakened her. In joy that it is so, Brynhild relates to him how Odin had punished her by this magic sleep for disobedience, and how that she had yet obtained from him the promise that she should be wakened only by a hero who knew no fear. She now teaches Sigurd many wise runes, and tells him of harm to fear through love of her. In spite of all, however, Sigurd does not waver, and they swear an oath of mutual faithful love.

Next Sigurd comes to King Gjuki at the Rhine, and joins in friendship with him and his sons Gunnar and Hogni. Queen Grimhild gives Sigurd a potion which causes him to forget Brynhild and be filled with love for her own daughter Gudrun, whom he marries. Gunnar now seeks Brynhild for wife, and Sigurd goes with him on his wooing-journey. They come to the castle encircled by fire, where Brynhild lives. She will be wooed only by him who will ride to her through the flames. Gunnar tries in vain to do this, even when mounted on Sigurd's steed Grani. Sigurd and Gunnar then exchange shapes and the former spurs Grani through the flames. He calls himself Gunnar the son of Gjuki, and finally Brynhild consents to become his wife. Three nights he shares her couch, but always his sharp sword lies between them. He takes the ring from her finger and places in its stead one from Fafnir's treasure. Then he exchanges form again with Gunnar, who is soon after wedded to Brynhild. Only now does Sigurd recollect the oath that he once swore to Brynhild himself.

One day Brynhild and Gudrun are bathing in the Rhine. A quarrel arises between them when Brynhild takes precedence of Gudrun by going into the water above her in the stream, saying that her husband is a braver and mightier man than Gudrun's. Gudrun retorts by revealing the secret that it was Sigurd in Gunnar's form, and not Gunnar himself, who rode through the flame, and in proof thereof shows her the ring taken by Sigurd from Brynhild's finger. Pale as death, Brynhild goes quietly home: Gunnar must die, she says in wrath. Sigurd tries to pacify her, even offering to desert Gudrun. Now she will have neither him nor another, and when Gunnar appears she demands of him Sigurd's death. In spite of Hogni's protest Gunnar's stepbrother Gutthorm, who has not sworn blood-friendship with Sigurd, is got to do the deed. He is given the flesh of wolf and serpent to eat in order to make him savage. Twice Gutthorm goes to kill Sigurd, but cowers before the piercing glance of his eyes; at last he steals upon Sigurd asleep and thrusts his sword through him. The dying Sigurd hurls the sword after the fleeing murderer and cuts him in two. To Gudrun, who wakes from sleep by his side, he points to Brynhild as the instigator of the crime, and dies. Brynhild rejoices at the sound of Gudrun's wailing. Gudrun cannot find relief for her grief, the tears will not flow. Men and women seek to console her by tales of greater woes befallen them. But still Gudrun cannot weep as she sits by Sigurd's corpse. At last one of the women lifts the cloth from Sigurd's face and lays his head upon Gudrun's lap. Then Gudrun gazes on his blood-besmirched hair, his dimmed eyes, and breast pierced by the sword: she sinks down upon the couch and a flood of tears bursts at length from her eyes.

Brynhild now tells Gunnar that Sigurd had really kept faith with him on the wooing-journey; but she will live with him no longer and pierces herself with a sword, after foretelling to Gunnar his future fate and that of Gudrun. In accord with her own request she is burned on one funeral-pyre with Sigurd, the sword between them as once before.

Atli, king of the Huns, now seeks Gudrun for wife. She refuses, but Grimhild gives her a potion which causes her to forget Sigurd and the past, and then she becomes the wife of Atli. After Sigurd's death Gunnar had taken possession of the Niflungen hoard, and this Atli now covets. He treacherously invites Gunnar and the others to visit him, which they do in spite of Gudrun's warnings, first of all, however, sinking the hoard in the Rhine. On their arrival Atli demands of them the hoard, which, he says, belongs of right to Gudrun. On their refusal he attacks them. Hosts of fighters on both sides fall and in the end Gunnar and Hogni, the only two of their number remaining, are bound in fetters. Gunnar refuses Atli's command to reveal the hiding-place of the hoard, bidding them bring to him the heart of Hogni. They kill a servant and bring his heart to Gunnar; but Gunnar sees how it still quivers with fear, and knows it is not the heart of the fearless Hogni. Then the latter is really killed, and his heart is brought to Gunnar, who cries exultingly that now only the Rhine knows where the hoard lies hidden. In spite of Gudrun Atli orders that Gunnar be thrown into a den of serpents. With a harp communicated to him by Gudrun he pacifies them all but one, which stings him to the heart, and thus Gunnar dies. Gudrun is nominally reconciled with Atli, but in secret plans revenge for the death of her brothers. She kills Atli's two sons, gives him at a banquet their blood to drink and their hearts to eat. In the night she plunges a sword into his own heart, confesses herself to him as his murderer, and sets fire to the castle, in which Atli and all his remaining men are consumed.

The Saga as preserved in the Nibelungenlied

The saga as we find it in the German ***Nibelungenlied*** differs very widely in form and substance from the Northern version which has just been outlined, though the two have still enough points of similarity to indicate clearly a common origin. Each bears the stamp of the poetic genius of the people among whom it grew. Of all the sagas of the Germanic peoples none holds so prominent a place as the Nibelungen saga, and it may safely be said that the epic literature of the world, though offering poems of more refined literary worth, has none that are at the same time such valuable records of the growth of the poetic genius of two kindred peoples through many centuries of their early civilization as the Edda poems of this saga and the ***Nibelungenlied.*** It is impossible here to undertake a comparison of the two and point out in detail their parallelism and their respective significance as monuments of civilization; suffice it to indicate briefly the chief points of difference in the two stories, and note particularly those parts of the ***Nibelungenlied*** that have, as it were, suffered atrophy, and that point to earlier stages of the saga in which, as in the Northern version, they played a more important rôle.

First, as to the hoard. The ***Nibelungenlied*** knows nothing of its being taken by Loki from Andvari, of the latter's curse upon it, and how it came finally into the possession of Fafnir, the giant-dragon. Here it belongs, as we learn from Hagen's account (strophes 86-99), to Siegfried (Sigurd), who has slain the previous owners of it, Schilbung and Nibelung, and wrested it from its guardian the dwarf Alberich (Andvari). From this point onward its history runs nearly parallel in the two versions. After Siegfried's death it remains for a time with Kriemhild (Gudrun), is treacherously taken from her by Gunther (Gunnar) and Hagen (Hogni), and finally, before their journey to Etzel (Atli), sunk in the Rhine.

The protracted narrative of Sigurd's ancestry and his descent from Odin has no counterpart in the ***Nibelungenlied.*** Here we learn merely that Siegfried is the son of Siegmund. His father plays an entirely different part; and his mother's name is not Hjordis, as in the Edda, but Siegelind.

Of Siegfried's youth the ***Nibelungenlied*** knows very little. No mention is made of his tutelage to the dwarf smith Regin and preparation for the slaying of the dragon Fafnir. The account of him placed in the mouth of Hagen (strophes 86-501), how he won the hoard, the *tarnkappe,* and the sword Balmung, and slew the dragon, is evidently a faint echo of an earlier version of this episode, which sounds out of place in the more modern German form of the story. From the latter the mythical element has almost entirely vanished. It is worthy of note, moreover, that the very brief account of Siegfried's slaying of the dragon is given in the ***Nibelungenlied*** as separate from his acquisition of the hoard, and differs in detail from that of the Edda. Of Sigurd's steed Grani, his ride to Frankenland, and his awakening of Brynhild the ***Nibelungenlied*** has nothing to tell us. Through the account of Siegfried's assistance to Gunther in the latter's wooing of Brunhild (Adventures 6 and 7) shimmers faintly, however, the earlier tradition of the mythical Siegfried's awakening of the fire-encircled valkyrie. Only by our knowledge of a more original version can we explain, for example, Siegfried's previous acquaintance with Brunhild which the ***Nibelungenlied*** takes for granted but says nothing of. On this point of the relation between Sigurd and Brynhild it is difficult to form a clear account owing to the confusion and even contradictions that exist when the various Northern versions themselves are placed side by side. The name of the valkyrie whom Sigurd awakens from her magic sleep is not directly mentioned. Some of the accounts are based on the presupposition that she is one with the Brynhild whom Sigurd later wooes for Gunnar, while others either know nothing of the sleeping valkyrie or treat the two as separate personages. The situation in the ***Nibelungenlied*** is more satisfactorily explained by the theory that they were originally identical. But we see at once that the figure of Brunhild has here lost much of its original significance. It is her quarrel with Kriemhild (Gudrun) that leads to Siegfried's death, though the motives are not just the same in the two cases; and after the death of Siegfried she passes unaccountably from the scene.

But it is in the concluding part of the story—the part which, as we shall see, has its basis in actual history—that the two accounts diverge most widely. So strange, indeed, has been the evolution of the saga that the central character of it, Kriemhild (Gudrun) holds a diametrically opposite relation to her husband Etzel (Atli) at the final catastrophe in the two versions. In the Nibelungenlied as in the Edda the widowed Kriemhild (Gudrun) marries King Etzel (Atli), her consent in the former resulting from a desire for revenge upon the murderers of Siegfried, in the latter from the drinking of a potion which takes away her memory of him; in the ***Nibelungenlied*** it is Kriemhild who treacherously lures Gunther and his men to their destruction unknown to Etzel, in the Edda the invitation comes from Atli, while Gudrun tries to warn them to stay at home; in the former Kriemhild is the author of the attack on the guests, in the latter Atli; in the former Kriemhild is the frenzied avenger of her former husband Siegfried's death upon her brother Gunther, in the latter Gudrun is the avenger of her brothers' death upon her husband Atli.

Mythical Element and Historical Element

A sifting of the *Nibelungen* saga reveals a mythical element (the story of Siegfried) and a historical element (the story of the Burgundians and Etzel). How, when, and where these two elements were blended together must remain largely a matter of conjecture. This united central body received then from time to time accessions of other elements, some of them originally historical in character, some of them pure inventions of the poetic imagination.

The Siegfried myth is the oldest portion of the *Nibelungen* saga, and had already passed through a long period of development before its union with the story of the Burgundian kings. Like so many others of its kind, it is part of the spiritual equipment of our Germanic ancestors at the dawn of their recorded history. It grew gradually with the people themselves and has its counterpart among other peoples. Such myths are a record of the impressions made upon the mind of man by the mighty manifestations of the world of nature in which he lives; their formation may be likened to the unconscious impressions of its surroundings on the mind of the child. And just as the grown man is unable to trace back the formation of his own individuality to its very beginnings in infancy, so is it impossible for the later nation in its advanced stage to peer back beyond the dawn of its history. It is in the gloom beyond the dawn that such myths as this of Siegfried have their origin.

Though modern authorities differ greatly in their conjectures, it is generally agreed that the Siegfried story was in its original form a nature-myth. The young day slays the mist-dragon and awakens the sun-maiden that sleeps on the mountain; at evening he falls a prey to the powers of gloom that draw the sun down again beneath the earth. With this day-myth was probably combined the parallel myth of the changing seasons: the light returns in spring, slays the cloud-dragon, and frees the budding earth from the bonds of winter.

In the course of time this nature-myth became transformed into a hero-saga; the liberating power of light was humanized into the person of the light-hero Siegfried. This stage of development had already been reached at the time of our earliest records, and the evidences point to the Rhine Franks, a West Germanic tribe settled in the fifth century in the country about Cologne, as the people among whom the transformation from nature-myth to hero-saga took place, for it is among them that the saga in its earliest form is localized. By the Rhine Siegfried is born, there he wins the Nibelungen hoard, and in Frankenland he finds the sleeping valkyrie. By the Rhine, too, he enters into service with the Nibelungen kings and weds their sister.

The Franks had as neighbors up-stream in the first half of the fifth century the Burgundians, an East Germanic tribe. These Burgundians, who were closely allied to the Goths, had originally dwelt in the Baltic region between the Vistula and the Oder, whence they had made their way southwestward across Germany and settled in the year 413 in *Germania prima* on the west bank of the Rhine about Worms. Here a tragic fate was soon to overtake them. In the year 435 they had already suffered a reverse in a conflict with the Romans under Aëtius, and two years later, in 437, they were practically annihilated by the Huns. Twenty thousand of them, we are told, fell in battle, the remainder were scattered southward. Beyond the brief record by a contemporary, Prosper, we know but little of this event. It has been conjectured that the Huns were on this occasion acting as auxiliaries of Aëtius. At any rate it is fairly certain that Attila was not personally on the scene.

We can easily imagine what a profound impression this extinction of the Burgundians would produce upon the minds of their neighbors the Rhine Franks. Fact, too, would soon become mingled with fiction. This new feat was ascribed to Attila himself, already too well known as the scourge of Europe and the subduer of so many German tribes. A very few years later, however, fate was to subdue the mighty conqueror himself. With the great battle of Châlons in 451 the tide turned against him, and two years afterwards he died a mysterious death. The historian Jordanes of the sixth century relates that on the morning after Attila's wedding with a German princess named Ildico (Hildikô) he was found lying in bed in a pool of blood, having died of a hemorrhage. The mysteriousness of Attila's ending inspired his contemporaries with awe, and the popular fancy was not slow to clothe this event also in a dress of fiction. The attendant circumstances peculiarly favored such a process. Historians soon recorded the belief that Attila had perished at the hands of his wife, and it was only a step further for the imagination to find the motive for the deed in the desire of Hildikô to avenge the death of her German kinsmen who had perished through Attila. The saga of Attila's death is before long connected with the growing Burgundian saga, Hildikô becomes the sister of the Burgundian kings Gundahari, Godomar, and Gislahari, and her deed is vengeance taken upon Attila for his destruction of her brothers. (pp. vii-xx)

It is unnecessary here to record the speculations—for beyond speculations we cannot go—as to how the union of this historical saga of the Burgundians and Attila with the Siegfried saga took place. In the course of time, and naturally with greatest probability among the Rhine Franks who followed the Burgundians as occupants of *Germania prima,* the two were brought together, and the three Burgundian kings and their sister were identified with the three Nibelungen kings and their sister of the already localized Siegfried saga. It is also beyond the scope of this introduction to follow the course of the saga northward or to note its further evolution during its wanderings and in its new home until it was finally recorded in poetic form in the Edda. We have now to consider briefly the transformation it passed through in Germany between this date (about 500) and the time (about 1200) when it emerges in written record as the ***Nibelungenlied.***

An account has already been given of the chief features in which the ***Nibelungenlied*** differs from the Northern form. As we saw there, the mythical element of the Siegfried saga has almost entirely evaporated and the historical saga of the Burgundian kings and Attila has undergone a complete transformation. That the originally mythical and heathen Siegfried saga should dwindle away with the progress of civilization and under the influence of Christianity was but natural. The character of the valkyrie Brynhild who avenges upon Sigurd his infidelity to her, yet voluntarily unites herself with him in death, as heathen custom demanded, is no longer intelligible. She recedes into the background, and after Siegfried's death, though she is still living, she plays no further part. The ***Nibelungenlied*** found its final form on Upper German, doubtless Austrian, territory. Here alone was it possible that that greatest of all transformations could take place, namely, in the character of Attila. The Franks of the Rhine knew him only as the awe-inspiring conqueror who had annihilated their neighbors the Burgundians. In Austrian lands it was quite otherwise. Many Germanic tribes, particularly the East Goths, had fought under the banner of Attila, and in the tradition handed down from them he lived as the embodiment of wisdom and generosity. Here it was impossible that epic story should picture him as slaying the Burgundian kings through a covetous desire for their gold. The annihilation of the Burgundians is thus left without a motive. To supply this, Kriemhild's character is placed upon an entirely different basis. Instead of avenging upon Attila the death of her brothers the Burgundian kings, Kriemhild now avenges upon her brothers the slaying of her first husband Siegfried. This fundamental change in the character of Kriemhild has a deep ethical reason. To the ancient heathen Germans the tie of blood-relationship was stronger than that of wedlock, and thus in the original version of the story Attila's wife avenges upon him the death of her *brothers;* to the Christianized Germans of later times the marriage bond was the stronger, and accordingly from the altered motive Kriemhild avenges upon her brothers the slaying of her *husband.* In accordance, too, with this ethical transformation the scene of the catastrophe is transferred from Worms to Attila's court. Kriemhild now looms up as the central figure of the second half of the drama, while Etzel remains to the last ignorant of her designs for revenge.

This transformation of the fundamental parts of the saga was accompanied by another process, namely, the addition of new characters. Some of these are the product of the poetic faculty of the people or individuals who preserved and remoulded the story in the course of centuries, others are based upon history. To the former class belong the Margrave Ruediger, the ideal of gentle chivalry, and Volker the Fiddler-knight, doubtless a creation of the *spielleute.* To the second class belong Dietrich of Bern, in whom we see the mighty East Gothic king, Theodoric of Verona; also Bishop Pilgrim of Passau, a very late importation, besides several others in whom are perpetuated in more or less faint outline actual persons of history. This introduction of fresh characters from time to time as the saga grew has led to some strange anachronisms, which however are a disturbing element only to us readers of a modern day, who with sacrilegious hand lift the veil through which they were seen in a uniform haze of romance by the eye of the knights and ladies of seven centuries ago. *They* neither knew nor cared to know, for instance, that Attila was dead before Theodoric was born, and that Bishop Pilgrim flourished at Passau the trifling space of five hundred years later still.

The Manuscripts

Among the German epic poems of the Middle Ages the ***Nibelungenlied*** enjoyed an exceptional popularity, as is evident from the large number of manuscripts—some thirty, either complete or fragmentary—that have been preserved from the centuries immediately following its appearance. Three are of prime importance as texts, namely, those preserved now in Munich, St. Gall, and Donaueschingen, and cited as A, B, and C respectively. Since the time when Lachmann, about a century ago, made the first scientific study of the poem, a whole flood of writings has been poured forth discussing the relative merits of these texts. Each in turn has had its claims advocated with warmth and even acrimony. None of these three principal manuscripts, however, offers the poem in its earliest form; they all point to a still earlier version. It is now generally admitted that the St. Gall manuscript (B), . . . contains the best and most nearly original text.

Stages in the Evolution of the Poem

Hand in hand with the discussion of the relative authenticity of the manuscripts went the consideration of another more important literary question,—the evolution of the poem itself. Even if we knew nothing of the history of the Nibelungen saga as revealed in the Edda and through other literary and historic sources, a reading of the poem would give us unmistakable hints that it is not, in its present form, a perfect literary unit. We detect inconsistencies in matter and inequalities of style that prove it to be a remodelling of material already existing in some earlier form. What, then, has been the history of its evolution? How did this primeval Siegfried myth, this historical saga of the Burgundians and Attila, first come to be part of the poetic stock of the German people? What was its earliest poetic form, and what series of transformations did it pass through during seven centuries of growth? These and many kindred questions present themselves, and the search for answers to them takes us through many winding labyrinths of the nation's contemporary history. Few products of German literature have so exercised and tantalized critics as the ***Nibelungenlied.***

In this connection we have to remind ourselves that comparatively little of what must have been the large body of native poetry in Germany previous to the eleventh century has come down to us. Barely enough has been preserved to show the path of the nation's literary progress. Some of the important monuments have been saved by chance, while others of equal or perhaps greater value have been irrecoverably lost. The interest in the various incidents of the Nibelungen story was sufficient to keep it alive among the people and hand it down orally through many generations. If we could observe it as it passed from age to age we should doubtless see it undergoing continuous change according to the time and the class of the people that were the preservers of the native literature in its many ups and downs. Lachmann in the year 1816 was the first to bring scientific criticism to bear on the question of the ***Nibelungenlied*** and its origin. Applying to it the same methods as had recently been used by Wolf in his criticism of the Homeric poems, he thought he was able to discover as the basis of the complete epic a cycle of twenty separate *lieder,* ballads or shorter episodic poems, on the strength of which belief he went so far as to publish an edition of the poem in which he made the division into the twenty separate lays and eliminated those strophes (more than one third of the whole number) that he deemed not genuine. It is now generally admitted, however, that the pioneer of Nibelungen investigation fell here into over-positive refinements of literary criticism. Separate shorter poems there doubtless existed narrating separate episodes of the story, but these are no longer to be arrived at by a process of critical disintegration and pruning of the epic as we have it. An examination of the twenty *lieder* according to Lachmann's division convinces us that they are not separate units in the sense he conceived them to be. Though these twenty *lieder* may be based upon a number of earlier episodic poems, yet the latter already constituted a connected series. They were already like so many scenes of a gradually developing drama. Events were foreshadowed in one that were only fulfilled in another, and the incidents of later ones are often only intelligible on the supposition of an acquaintance with motives that originated in preceding ones. It is in this sense only, not according to Lachmann's overwrought theory, that we are justified in speaking of a *liedercyclus,* or cycle of separate episodic poems, as the stage of the epic antecedent to the complete form in which we now have it. But beyond this cycle we cannot trace it back. How the mythical saga of Siegfried and the Nibelungen, and the story of the Burgundians and Attila, were first sung in alliterative lays in the Migration Period, how as heathen song they were pushed aside or slowly influenced by the spirit of Christianity, how with changing time they changed also their outward poetical garb from alliteration to rhyme and altered verse-form, till at last in the twelfth century they have become the cycle of poems from which the great epic of the ***Nibelungenlied*** could be constructed—of all this we may form a faint picture from the development of the literature in general, but direct written record of it is almost completely wanting.

Character of the Poem

The twelfth and thirteenth centuries witnessed far-reaching changes in the social and intellectual life of the German lands, the leading feature of which is the high development of all that is included under the name of chivalry. It is marked, too, by a revival of the native literature such as had not been known before, a revival which is due almost entirely to its cultivation by the nobility. From emperor down to the simple knight they were patrons of poetry and, what is most striking, nearly all the poets themselves belong to the knightly class. The drama has not yet begun, but in the field of epic and lyric there appear about the year 1200 poets who are among the greatest that German literature even down to the present time has to show. The epic poetry of that period, though written almost entirely by the knights, is of two distinct kinds according to its subject: on the one hand what is called the Court Epic, on the other hand the National, or Popular, Epic. The Court Epic follows for the most part French models and deals chiefly with the life of chivalry, whose ideals were embodied in king Arthur and his circle of knights; the National Epic drew its subjects from the national German saga, its two great products being the ***Nibelungenlied*** and the poem of Gudrun. Court Epic and National Epic are further distinct in form, the Court Epic being written in the rhymed couplets popularized in modern times in English by Sir Walter Scott, while the National Epic is composed in four-lined strophes.

Though we know the name and more or less of the life of the authors of the many court epics of the period, the name of the poet who gave the ***Nibelungenlied*** its final form has not been recorded. As we have seen, the poem is at bottom of a truly popular, national character, having its beginnings in mythology and early national history. For centuries the subject had been national property and connected with the name of no one individual. We have it now in the form in which it was remodelled to suit the taste of the court and the nobility, and like the court epic to be read aloud in castle hall. That it is written in four-lined strophes and not in the usual rhymed couplets of the court epics is doubtless due to the fact that the former verse-form had already been used in the earlier ballads upon which it is based, and was simply taken over by the final moulder of the poem. This latter was probably a member of the nobility like the great majority of the epic poets of the time; he must at least have been well acquainted with the manners, tastes, sentiments, and general life of the nobility. Through him the poem was brought outwardly more into line with the literary ideals of the court circles. This shows itself chiefly in a negative way, namely, in the almost complete avoidance of the coarse language and farcical situations so common with the popular poet, the *spielmann.* Beyond this no violence is done to the simple form of the original. The style is still inornate and direct, facts still speak rather than words, and there is nothing approaching the refined psychological dissection of characters and motives such as we find in Wolfram von Eschenbach and the other court writers.

When we look to the inner substance we see that the ground ideals are still those of the original Germanic heroic age. The chief characters are still those of the first stages of the story—Siegfried, Brunhild, Gunther, Kriemhild, Hagen. The fundamental theme is the ancient theme of *triuwe,* unswerving personal loyalty and devotion, which manifests itself above all in the characters of Kriemhild and Hagen. Kriemhild's husband Siegfried is treacherously slain: her sorrow and revenge are the motives of the drama. Hagen's mistress has, though with no evil intent on Siegfried's part, received an insult to her honor: to avenge that insult is Hagen's absorbing duty, which he fulfils with an utter disregard of consequences. Over this their fundamental character the various persons of the story have received a gloss of outward conduct in keeping with the close of the twelfth century. The poet is at pains to picture them as models of courtly bearing, excelling in *höfscheit, zuht, tugent.* Great attention is paid to dress, and the preparation of fitting apparel for court festivities is described and re-described with wearisome prolixity. A cardinal virtue is *milte,* liberality in the bestowal of gifts. Courtesy toward women is observed with the careful formality of the age of the minnesingers. It was above all Siegfried, the light-hero of the original myth, whose character lent itself to an idealization of knighthood. Ruediger holds a like place in the latter part of the poem. In the evident pleasure with which the minstrel-knight Volker of the sword-fiddlebow is depicted, as well doubtless as in occasional gleams of broader humor, the hand of the minstrels who wrought on the story in its earlier ballad stages may be seen. And the whole poem, in keeping with its form in an age strongly under church influence, has been tinged with the ideals of Christianity. Not only does the ordinary conversation of all the characters, including even the heathen Etzel, contain a great number of formal imprecations of God, but Christian institutions and Christian ethics come frequently into play. Mass is sung in the minster, baptism, marriage, burial are celebrated in Christian fashion, the devil is mentioned according to the Christian conception, we hear of priest, chaplain, and bishop, Christians are contrasted with heathen, and Kriemhild, in marrying Etzel, has a hope of turning him to Christianity. In Hagen's attempt to drown the chaplain whom the Burgundians have with them as they set out for the land of the Huns we have perhaps an expression of the conflict between the heathen and the Christian elements, possibly also a reflection of the traditional animosity of the *spielmann* to his clerical rival.

The ***Nibelungenlied*** and the *Iliad* of Homer have often been compared, but after all to no great purpose. The two epics are alike in having their roots deep in national origins, but beyond this we have contrasts rather than resemblances. The *Iliad* is a more varied and complete picture of the whole Greek world than the ***Nibelungenlied*** is of the German, its religious atmosphere has not been disturbed in the same way as that of the saga of early Germanic times projected several centuries into a later Christian age, and it possesses in every way a greater unity of sentiment. In the varied beauty of its language, its wealth of imagery, its depth of feeling and copiousness of incident the *Iliad* is superior to the ***Nibelungenlied*** with its language of simple directness, its few lyrical passages, its expression of feeling by deeds rather than by words. Homer, too, is in general buoyant, the ***Nibelungenlied*** is sombre and stern. And in one last respect the two epics differ most of all: the *Iliad* is essentially narrative and descriptive, a series of episodes; the ***Nibelungenlied*** is essentially dramatic, scene following scene of dramatic necessity and pointing steadily to a final and inevitable catastrophe. (pp. xx-xxviii)

George Henry Needler, in his The Nibelungenlied, *Henry Holt and Company, 1904, 349 p.*

Shumway on the poem's Teutonic heritage:

[The central theme of the ***Nibelungenlied***] is the ancient Teutonic ideal of *Treue* (faithfulness or fidelity), which has found here its most magnificent portrayal; faithfulness unto death, the loyalty of the vassal for his lord, as depicted in Hagen, the fidelity of the wife for her husband, as shown by Kriemhild, carried out with unhesitating consistency to the bitter end. This is not the gallantry of medieval chivalry, which colors so largely the opening scenes of the poem, but the heroic valor, the death-despising stoicism of the ancient Germans, before which the masters of the world, the all-conquering Romans, were compelled to bow.

Daniel Bussier Shumway, in his The Nibelungenlied, *Houghton Mifflin Company, 1909.*

Calvin Thomas (essay date 1909)

[*Thomas was an American educator who wrote and edited several works on Germanic languages and literature. Here, he briefly assesses the* Nibelungenlied*'s textual history to determine how much of the poem is derived from early legends and how much of the text may be attributed to poetic invention.*]

The [***Nibelungen Lay***] is, on the whole, the most important poetic production of mediæval Germany. When it was exhumed in the eighteenth century, after ages of neglect, during which its very existence had been forgotten, and the sense for things mediæval had well-nigh vanished, the great Frédéric, Roi de Prusse, declared that it was not worth a charge of powder. A little later, in the ardour of the romantic revival, it was extolled by enthusiasts as the peer of the *Iliad.* The point of sanity will be found between these two opinions, but rather nearer to the latter. When the poem is put on trial, the devil's advocate may justly urge that it is not a national epic at all in the sense of picturing great deeds performed by representatives of the nation, or of mirroring truly the national life at any period, or of embodying highly important elements of culture for the people at large. The core of it is a tale of foul murder and fiendish vengeance. It portrays an ethical code which is essentially revolting and was already happily obsolete when the poem was written. As a tale of the brave days of old it is no polychrome Homeric canvas, picturing a whole epoch and dominated by that admirable Greek temperance which would have nothing in excess—μηδεν αγαν; it is rather a black-and-white cartoon in which excess is the rule, and truth and proportion are subordinated to an intense setting forth of strong passion and ruthless conduct ending in a mighty disaster.

But with all its limitations the ***Nibelungen Lay*** is a powerful poem and a human document of many-sided interest. It is really incommensurable—a thing of its own kind which it boots little to compare with anything else in literature. It is national in the sense of being thoroughly German. Its greatest merit is its strong delineation of certain characters, especially Hagen, Siegfried, and Kriemhild. These take the imagination captive and haunt it afterward as do only the creations of a great poet.

The theme is the murder of Siegfried and the vengeance wreaked therefore by his wife Kriemhild, who is the pivot of the whole story from first to last. The actual murderer is Hagen, but his deed is thought of as virtually that of the Burgundian royal house, whose total destruction is accordingly involved in Kriemhild's revenge. In an earlier phase of the saga Hagen was an independent king and his motive for the murder greed of wealth. But in the poem he and his motive are translated, so to speak, into the terms of mediæval chivalry. He appears as the vassal of the Burgundian king Gunter, and his motive is a desire to avenge the wrong done, as he thinks, to his liege mistress Brunhild. As Gunter's wife, Brunhild learns how she has been tricked by Siegfried in Gunter's interest on two critical occasions of her life—in the bride-winning games at Isenstein, her former home in the far North, and on her wedding-night at Worms. She must have the life of the overweening Netherlander, and Hagen makes himself the tool of her spiteful rage. After the cowardly assassination is done, Kriemhild continues for some time to live at Worms, giving generously to the poor. To prevent her from thus gaining a dangerous ascendency the ruthless Hagen robs her of the treasure she has from Siegfried, and thus increases her dormant hatred. In due time she marries Etzel the Hun, invites her kin to visit her, and brings on a fierce conflict in which they are all slain. In the end Kriemhild herself is put to death by the angry Hildebrand on account of the carnage she has caused, and Etzel is left to mourn with his court over the calamity.

As a first step toward a just appreciation of the poem one would like to know in what shape the author found his material. How far was he a true maker, how far merely a compiler or redactor? Did he follow a manuscript or an unwritten tradition? In either case, had his predecessors already combined the heterogeneous elements of the story into a semblance of artistic unity, or did he first make the combination himself? These questions cannot be answered in a manner to leave no room for doubt, and they are mixed up in the literature of scholarship with a manuscript question. Of the ten complete manuscripts of the poem which exist, there are three which are certainly nearer than the others to the lost original. They differ considerably in length and other respects, and each has had its eminent partisans. Basing his studies on the shortest of the three rival manuscripts, the distinguished scholar Lachmann concluded that the poem was an agglomeration of twenty old ballads—neither more nor less—pieced together with newer matter. On internal evidence of various kinds—incongruities, contradictions, confused chronology, strange lapses of memory, and so forth—he attempted a rigorous separation of the old matter from the new. For a long time after Lachmann's views were first fully set forth, in 1841, they held a prominent place in critical discussion, dividing scholarship into contending schools. Even now there is nothing like agreement over matters of detail, but two things have become tolerably clear. The first is that we really have to do, as Lachmann thought, with disparate elements of very different age, which were handed down for centuries by oral tradition in some sort of poetic form. The second is that the evidence relied on by Lachmann and his school is not sufficient to warrant his very rigorous and definite conclusions as to the number, character, and boundaries of these more ancient poetic elements. A keen and cautious Dutch scholar, R. C. Boer, sums up the results of a long investigation thus: "Neither episodic single songs nor a variform prose tradition formed the source, nor yet song-books in which certain groups of single songs were combined to represent a part of the tradition; but briefer versions of the entire story." This means that the nameless poet of the twelfth century simply retold and expanded in his own way, under the influence of chivalry and a veneer of Christianity, a story which was already old as a connected narrative.

The probable genesis of the the saga, or concatenation of sagas . . . [began with] a *Märchen* telling of Siegfried, the slayer of a dragon, the winner of a fabulous treasure, the unfaithful lover of a bewitched maid, whom he had found in an enchanted place, surrounded by flames or ice or difficult waters. By tasting the blood or anointing himself with the fat of the dragon, he had acquired some superhuman quality, such as an invulnerable horny skin or the power to understand the voices of birds. But Hagen and a slayer of Hagen were already a part of the story before the Burgundians and the historical Attila ever came into it. In the ***Nibelungen Lay*** Siegfried has become a Lowland prince, whose home is at Xanten, which was once on the Rhine, though not so now. In the main he is a knight of the twelfth century, fitted out richly with the swiftness of foot, bravery, strength, and beauty which mediæval minstrelsy everywhere delighted to exalt. But on his way to becoming a pink of chivalry the character of the ancient *Märchen hero* had passed, in the hands of the gleeman, through an intermediate stage, that of the *Recke,* or fighting adventurer, who likes combat above all things, and is not overcompunctious in his dealings with womankind. Traces of this character cling to him in the poem. Thus he goes to Worms to woo the famously fair Kriemhild, attracted by the supposed danger of the enterprise. But on arriving at the Burgundian court, instead of saying anything about his errand he challenges Gunter to fight for his kingdom. Further on when he is vexed with Kriemhild for betraying a secret that he has unwisely confided to her, he beats her black and blue. His whole relation to Brunhild is not that of a chivalrous knight, but that of a gleeman's *Recke,* who enjoys putting forth his strength for the conquest of a shedevil. Not much is made of his supernatural attributes, though these, too, still cling to him. The only one of them that really counts in the story is the hiding-cloak which he uses for tricking Brunhild—an unchivalrous fraud such as the gleemen delighted in. The idea of the treasure-guarding dwarfs is translated into the terms of feudalism. Alberich, the dwarf-king, is Siegfried's vassal, having been conquered by him in single combat and put in charge of his Burg, which seems to be located somewhere on the coast of the North Sea. When Siegfried comes and demands men in order to make a show before Brunhild, Alberich quickly furnishes a thousand richly caparisoned knights.

The character of Brunhild was worked out very unfortunately by the German gleemen. In the *Edda* and the Volsung saga she is a prophetic valkyr whom Odin has pricked with the sleep-thorn for disobedience. There is great poetry in her short-lived passion for Sigurd. But it is not at all certain that she was from the first a valkyr. She belonged rather, one may guess, to the general type of *Märchen* heroine, the princess-hard-to-woo. She was a maid bewitched by some superior power and left in a lonely, forbidding place, approachable only by the one predestined lover who, in addition to being fearless, should have just the right equipment and know just what to say and do. The gleemen were fond of providing the maiden-hard-to-woo with a savage father who hung all suitors to a tree or shut them up in prison. The more perilous and difficult the game, the greater the successful hero's glory. In the case of Brunhild some dim reminiscence of a former semi-divine character may have survived to the age of chivalry, when games of strength and skill were only less important than fighting. So Brunhild became an athletic maid, living in a remote isle of the sea, mistress of her own fate, and resolved not to wed unless it were some suitor who should first vanquish her in certain games. Unsuccessful competitors were put to death. She had the strength of many men combined, but it depended on her virginity. In this conception there was fun enough for the jolly gleemen and their none too dainty audiences, but little of poetry for the afterworld. The Scandinavian Brynhild is majestic and terrible, the athletic vixen of the ***Nibelung Lay*** not much better than horrible.

When did the Burgundians come into the story? As Theoderic the Great died in 525, and as sometime must have passed before the facts of his life were so far forgotten as to make it possible to think of him as the guest-friend of Attila, who died in 452, we may perhaps date the incipient crystallisation back to about the year 600. And then there are later historical incrustations. Thus in the poem we find the Saxons and Danes invading Burgundian territory, where they are met and badly beaten by Siegfried, fighting for King Gunter. So, too, in the Latin *Waltharius,* the Burgundians are identified with the Franks. A curious fact is the appearance of Bishop Pilgrim of Passau, a historical personage of the tenth century, in the *Lay* as Kriemhild's uncle. She is hospitably received by him on her way from Worms to the land of the Huns. It is as if a Tennysonian idyl should represent Queen Guinevere as visiting her uncle, Bishop Butler, of the *Analogy!*

In its fundamental character as an accretion of the ages,

rough-hewn little by little into a sort of artistic whole, lies at once the strength and the weakness of the ***Nibelung Lay.*** If one tries to regard it as an epic for the reader and applies to it the criteria proper to that species of composition, one can draw up a rather formidable list of shortcomings. In the first place, it is terribly prolix. A poet inventing outright and unhampered by tradition, if endowed with only a fair measure of architectonic talent, could have told the story in half the number of stanzas that the poem contains. It is full of irrelevancies and tedious repetitions, especially descriptions of clothes, equipage, and festal functions. The bard never tires of coming back to the splendours of court life, the costly trappings of his princely personages, the brilliance of their retinues, their wonderful hospitality, their lavish generosity toward their vassals, their studious observance of all the elegant formalities. And then the metrical form itself is responsible for much ineptitude. Very often the thought of a stanza is really complete at the end of the third line, and the fourth is quite vacuous—mere padding. Add to this the lavish use of stereotyped formulas and stock rhymes. The author, if one insists on literary criteria, was but a mediocre craftsman and did not really command the resources of the language.

From our modern point of view these are rather serious defects, and they are not exactly done away with by accounting for them historically. The maxim *tout comprendre c'est tout pardonner* has its limitations in the æsthetic as well as in the moral sphere. The critical reader will never get from the ***Nibelung Lay*** the degree of pleasure that epic poetry at its best is capable of affording. At the same time it is well enough to remember that our modern literary standards, which have evolved slowly through centuries of reading, were non-existent for the author of the ***Lay*** and his public. It is true that he wrote, in a sense, for the reader; but in so doing it was only natural that he should lean heavily on the tried and tested methods of the gleeman. And then he wrote for reading aloud; for even after the ability to read had become comparitively common among the aristocratic laity, the costliness of large manuscripts put them beyond the reach of the many. So the great majority of knights and dames continued to get their poetry by way of the ear. But he who listens is in a different position from him who reads. The listener has no time to reflect and compare and theorise, even if we suppose him capable thereof. What counts for him is the immediate thrill. If an episode is entertaining and he knows the story in a general way, he is satisfied and does not bother his head with any subtleties of literary criticism.

So it was with the mediæval gentry who listened to the ***Nibelung Lay.*** The groundwork of the story, with its exciting interplay of love, jealousy, hate, and vengeance, was familiar to them and sanctified, so to speak, by a long poetic tradition. We think of the poem as a product of their time, but they thought of it as a tale of long ago. And they were not troubled by anachronisms, for they knew no such thing as historical perspective. The scene was laid in a vague past in which strange things had happened and towering personalities had been swayed by towering passions. At the same time they looked into a mirror of present realities; for the dominant idea of the poem is loyalty, and that is precisely the idea that held the feudal system together. Hagen's crime, the cardinal fact of the whole story, and all his later insolence towards Kriemhild, grow out of a perverted *Treue* towards his liege mistress. It is his unswerving fidelity to her that saves him from being loathsome and makes him a hero. One can imagine the knights and ladies of the twelfth century following with an interest much more personal than it has for us that ancient tragic tale of a liegeman's *Treue.* Nor were they bored, we may be very sure, by the ever-recurring descriptions of raiment, equipage, and ceremony. These things bulked very large in their own lives, and to make much of them was a poet's surest passport to their favour. (pp. 48-57)

Calvin Thomas, "The Indigenous Epic of the Middle Ages," in his A History of German Literature, *1909. Reprint by Kennikat Press, 1970, pp. 43-64.*

Arthur E. Hutson and Patricia McCoy (essay date 1954)

[*In the excerpt below, Hutson and McCoy study the original sources of the* Nibelungenlied, *noting its skillful blending of historical fact and myth, and conclude that the poem was written by a single author.*]

The ***Nibelungenlied,*** like the *Beowulf,* is a poem embodying materials drawn from Germanic history, mythology, and legend, a story of "old, unhappy, far-off things, and battles long ago." . . . It contains the story of Siegfried,

An 1883 illustration of Siegfried battling the dragon, by Wilhelm von Kaulbach.

dragon-slayer and winner of the treasure of the Nibelungs; his courtship of Kriemhild, sister of Gunther, King of the Burgundians, and their marriage; his winning of Brunhild, by a trick, for Gunther; the feud between Brunhild and Kriemhild; the murder of Siegfried by Gunther's vassal, Hagen; the marriage of Kriemhild to Etzel, King of the Huns, and Etzel's invitation to the Burgundians; the death of Gunther and Hagen in Etzel's hall; and finally, the death of Kriemhild.

We recognize parts of this story from our knowledge of its most recent version, that found in Wagner's operas called the *Ring of the Nibelungs.* We notice, also, that Wagner's version is in many respects quite different from that of the ***Nibelungenlied.*** Wagner saw the story as one in which the most important personages were Siegfried and Brunhild, and, like many Germans of his time, he thought of them as figures drawn from the Germanic pantheon: a culture-hero, almost a demi-god, and a Valkyr, a battle-maiden, the chooser of the slain destined for Valhalla. In order to attain his artistic objective, he wrote two operas, *Das Rheingold* and *Die Walküre,* which tell of the events preceding the story of Siegfried and the rival queens found in the ***Nibelungenlied.*** In the central opera, *Siegfried,* he tells the story of the dragon-slaying and the winning of the hoard, and includes an event scarcely glanced at in the ***Nibelungenlied,*** the betrothal of Siegfried and Brunhild. And in the final opera of the cycle *Die Götterdämmerung* (*The Twilight of the Gods*), he tells of the murder of Siegfried and the self-immolation of Brunhild on his funeral pyre, this last incident also not found in the ***Nibelungenlied.***

Wagner's version, also, makes much more use of Germanic mythology than does the ***Nibelungenlied.*** The Middle High German poem, written in a thoroughly Christian atmosphere, could not well bring in Wotan, the principal deity of the Germanic pantheon; but Wagner's presentation of the story demanded the presence of these gods. For such materials he went to the versions of the story current in medieval Scandinavia, preserved in the Eddas, and, most completely, in the thirteenth-century Icelandic *Volsungasaga.*

The *Volsungasaga* tells a story very like that found in the ***Nibelungenlied,*** but it contains also other elements not found in the Germanic poem, especially the story of the birth of Siegfried (called Sigurd in the Norse), and the events which took place after the death of Gunther (Gunnar) and Hagen (Hogni). Although it was written down some two hundred years after the ***Nibelungenlied,*** it was not in the least influenced by that poem; rather, it is another version of the same story, drawn from the same source.

And here we must repeat what we said earlier, that the ***Nibelungenlied*** is a poem embodying elements drawn from Germanic mythology, legend, and history. In the ***Nibelungenlied,*** it is true, the mythological elements are of the slightest, if indeed, strictly speaking, they exist at all. Folklore material is there in plenty: the slaying of the dragon, for instance, and the *Tarnkappe,* the hood of invisibility, are matters met with in many fairy tales. Basically, however, the story is legend founded on history.

The historical fact underlying the legends, found widely throughout the Germanic-speaking areas, is the destruction of the Burgundian capital at Worms, in 437, by the Huns, whose king was Attila. We recognize that this must be the same name as Etzel, found in the ***Nibelungenlied,*** and Atli, in the *Volsungasaga.* The Burgundian princes, was we know from an early document called the "Law of the Burgundians," were named Gibica, Gundahari, and Gislahari: and these must be the same names as Gibich, father of Gunther, Gernot and Giselher. The treacherous invitation of Etzel at his wife's prompting, and his killing of Gunther and Hagen, must be a legendary reflection of the defeat of the Burgundians, for people do not celebrate their defeats in their stories; rather, they adapt history to legend in order to explain their defeats. Modern examples of this phenomenon are not lacking.

The adaptation of history to legend is the prerogative of the epic poet, who need have no concern with fact as such. Theodoric of Verona, or Dietrich von Bern, another famous German legendary and historical figure, died in 526; yet the ***Nibelungenlied***-poet has him present at the death of Kriemhild, which must have been nearly a century earlier. Probably the poet was not in the least aware that he was mixing up his centuries, for he was a poet, not a historian, and, just as Wagner was to do many centuries later, he used whatever material he had as his artistic necessities demanded.

The Germanic values of the ***Nibelungenlied*** still prevail, beneath the courtly façade. Gunther is a medieval prince, adept in political intrigue; but it is not difficult to see in him, as in King Siegfried, the earlier "bestower-of-rings" and "shield-of-knights." This courtliness, however, owes something to the expanding influences of French models. None of the earlier Germanic stories takes any great interest in romantic love; and love between man and woman is one of the primary forces of the ***Nibelungenlied.*** In this the epic is the product of its time, the late Middle Ages; for romantic love was not earlier a source of the question of loyalties.

Its simplicity and uniformity of diction, its classical richness, so well disciplined, seem ample testimony, combined with the usual linguistic and literary tests, of [the *Nibelungenlied*'s] single authorship.

—Arthur E. Hutson and Patricia McCoy

The ***Nibelungenlied***-poet could have found easy scope for lyricism in the magical background of the poem. The ring and girdle of Brunhild, the winning of the Hoard, the awakening of Brunhild within the circle of fire—these episodes, and many more, could have carried him from his artistic purpose. Fortunately, these temptations were not victorious; perhaps, if they had prevailed, the ***Nibelungenlied*** would be only another interesting lay of medieval

Germany. As in other poetry of epic stature, however, the mythological tradition behind the creation of the work is either told in episodic, narrative fashion, or implied. In the ***Nibelungenlied,*** most of this material is implied. It is very difficult to trace the mechanical techniques by which the effect is accomplished. Why does Brunhild tower over Kriemhild, in spite of their mutual ownership of the magical objects of power, and the greater number of lines which are given to Kriemhild and her revenge? Why, without a single explicit line of proof, does Hagen tower above Gunther, worthy to be the nemesis of Siegfried and the last of the men of Nibelung to die in battle? Even without any knowledge of the Eddas or the *Volsungasaga,* any perceptive reader can feel their stature.

Keeping the mystic elements in the background, the poet of the ***Nibelungenlied*** saves his lyric power for more human and personal topics, as does Dante in the episode of Paolo and Francesca in the *Divine Comedy.* The German poet's description of Siegfried's first meeting with Kriemhild is scarcely to be rivaled:

> Even as the full moon stands before the stars, so pure in her radiance that all clouds must run away before her, so did she stand in beauty among her ladies.

For Dante's Francesca, "the greatest pain of all is remembrance of past happiness in present woe"; for Kriemhild, "all pleasure, no matter how sweet, must at last turn to pain." But, whether the emphasis be upon fate or upon the Christian eternity, the sweetest passages in both epics are those of human love.

Scholarly search for the author of the ***Nibelungenlied*** has, to date, been inconclusive. A bishop of the late tenth century—Pilgrim of Passau—had created most of the main incidents of the story, as his own version of popular legend; he is accepted as a main source for the poem. A Minnesinger known as *"Der Kurenberger"* is known to have written at least fifteen detached stanzas in the same metre. Yet, although the "folk-epic" theory of the nineteenth century has long been in disrepute, no valid scholarship has established the identity of the poet. The uniformity of style, as well as the method of incorporating myth, points to a single author. Karl Lachmann, the Germanic scholar, has found at least twenty lays of ancient origin which seem to form a part of the poem; his research, although of the "folk-epic" school, has indicated to many modern critics the probability of individual authorship; it is unlikely, they argue, that these vastly rich background sources could have been coordinated in such a manner by a "folk-author." Furthermore, his nineteen "twelfth-century additions" would appear to indicate a uniformity too great for a "folk epic." It is, in fact, unlikely that any poem of epic stature could have been other than individual in authorship. An epic cannot have "the quality of growth, rather than of authorship," although centuries of growth may lie behind it.

Some critics believe that the ***Nibelungenlied*** was, in its earliest form, meant to be sung rather than read. Its verse-form, a four-line strophe, instead of the couplet-form of the later romantic epics, seems to corroborate this theory. There can be little doubt that the early lays of which it is formed were sung in courtly circles. But the music of the German epic is not the music of the Minnesinger; there is now little question that it was meant to be read. There were, as we have seen, many versions of the story available, but this does not mean that it grew by itself from the songs of minstrels. The story of the fall of the Burgundian kingdom must have inspired many poets, even as the absorption of the Geats led to the creation of the semi-mythological Beowulf. But, as the *Beowulf* is now accepted as the creation of an individual, so must the ***Nibelungenlied*** have been a unification of many poetic tales by one author. Its simplicity and uniformity of diction, its classical richness, so well disciplined, seem ample testimony, combined with the usual linguistic and literary tests, of its single authorship. But it is very pleasant to think of the poem as recited to the sound of harps. Its meter, with the marked caesura, the measured half-line of three feet, with the last half-line of each strophe extended to four feet, seems admirably suited to such presentation. However, the careful artistic variation of accent indicates that it was meant to be read. (pp. 297-302)

Arthur E. Hutson and Patricia McCoy, "Nibelungenlied," in their Epics of the Western World, *J. B. Lippincott Company, 1954, pp. 297-336.*

Arnold H. Price (essay date 1959)

[Price is a German-born American critic and editor. Below, he explores how the Nibelungenlied *poet used characterization to enhance the narrative technique of the work, suggesting that "the author's attempt to provide the major figures of the epic with an entirely new characterization not only supplies a coherent and realistic motivation, but also a theme for the epic."]*

The new and profound insights into human behavior which have been developed by modern psychology might, if properly applied, lead us both to understand and appreciate better than before the art of characterization in early literature. A reappraisal following this approach would assume that the human mind during the historical period has undergone few if any changes and that many authors possess intuitive insights into human behavior comparable to modern scientific discoveries in this field. Conversely, an investigation based on these precepts requires that we shed any preconceived ideas concerning a past era and that we consider the characters found in earlier fiction as though they were contemporaries.

The medieval period is a case in point. It has frequently been either denounced as the Dark Ages, the epitome of superstition and ignorance, or it has been glorified as the prototype of the Romantic age, filled with dashing knights, innocent princesses, pious monks, and honest burghers. Modern scholarship has gone a long way in providing us with a realistic understanding of this era and in making it meaningful for us. Yet there are aspects of medieval literature that so far have eluded our full comprehension.

The efforts of generations of German philologists to develop a workable interpretive approach for their best known medieval epic, the ***Nibelungenlied,*** may serve as the example. Here we have a literary theme that apparently received its main stimuli from two originally separate settings, the defeat of the Burgundians by the Huns in 437, and the intrigues and feuds in the Franconian royal family resulting in the assassination of King Sigibert in 575 and the execution of Queen Brunichild in 613. The stories of these events merged into one fable, which in the course of several centuries absorbed additional historical elements as well as a few supernatural features. This theme forms the basis for the ***Nibelungenlied,*** written by an unidentified Austrian or Bavarian author and eventually forgotten.

The ***Nibelungenlied*** itself was not rediscovered until the middle of the eighteenth century, when scholars found several manuscript versions. For several decades it received scant notice, and it was not until the German Romantic movement that it became generally known again. At the same time, German philologists, influenced by Romantic concepts about folk literature, in particular by the belief that epic works could only grow naturally or "create themselves" (*sich selbst zu dichten*), began to atomize the ***Nibelungenlied*** into what they believed to be its original component parts. Although subsequent scholarship established that the epic was the work of one author, the original tendencies to idealize its characters and to glorify its setting continued to influence German readers and philologists, and the ***Nibelungenlied*** retained the elevated status of a national epic, expounding what were considered to be typical German heroic virtues.

The problem before us is to understand the peculiar role of this epic, which was designed to be neither history nor fiction. The ***Nibelungenlied*** appears at a point in the literary development of a people when, having little capacity for accepting a fictitious plot of this magnitude, they still insist that the fable should appear real. This age did not look upon epic as a figment of the imagination, but as an account of actual events, and it accepted the magic aspects of the plot with no more hesitation than its modern counterpart will overlook unrealistic elements in contemporary fiction. Since the epic is first of all a good story with human appeal, the supernatural features in the fable provide it with a special charm and force.

It is assumed therefore that the epic writer in developing his plot is bound by a certain factual framework which his audience expects him to observe. Apparently there is little opportunity for him to make an original contribution: however while being restricted to minor changes in the plot the author may provide a deeper understanding of the characters and their motivation. It seems that primitive audiences tolerate major changes in the characterization quite readily. A writer grafting his set of new characterizations on the old plot of an epic must however, proceed with caution, as he cannot usually render a running commentary of his own on how he conceives the motivation of the characters. He must rely mostly on recasting major dialogues and on adding incidental conversations and monologues. To the writer of the ***Nibelungenlied,*** who used this technique with great skill, characterization was not a device to add more color to his presentation; it was his only way of giving meaning to a fable whose mythological and historical setting he was neither able nor willing to accept as real.

. . . . .

The writer of the ***Nibelungenlied*** places a woman, the Burgundian Princess Kriemhild, at the center of the plot, recounting the development of her personality from early womanhood to her death through a portrayal of passion, intrigue, and violence. He skillfully employs the opening scene to indicate this theme, and in particular to lay the foundations for the characterization of Kriemhild by giving the reader a glimpse of the emotional potentialities of the heroine. The epic begins with Kriemhild relating to her widowed mother Ute a violent dream about two eagles killing a falcon she had raised. And when her mother tells her that the falcon of her dream stands for a man, the young princess bursts out saying, "Why talk to me about man, dear mother mine? I want to be forever without the love of a knight. I want to stay beautiful like this until my death, so that man's love shall never bring me trouble."

A modern reader encountering such an opening scene in a contemporary play or novel would readily accept it as an initial characterization of the heroine's violent streak. Scholars have established this falcon scene as an original contribution of the unknown author of the ***Nibelungenlied.*** Proceeding, however, from the assumption that the Kriemhild of the first part of the epic is a heroic character, in this instance over-idealized good, and from the misdirected criticism that dreams cannot foretell the future, they have denied this scene any place in the fable, looking upon it primarily as a poetic device to forewarn the reader of the ultimate tragic ending. If critics concede to the author any attempt at characterization through this scene, they cite it as additional evidence for their preconceived notions of Kriemhild's "innocence." What could be more innocent than a girl abhorring marriage?

This opening scene not only serves as the cornerstone for the characterization of the heroine, but also as an essential part of the plot, since it is Kriemhild's hostile attitude towards marriage that brings Siegfried into the story. The scene shifts from Worms, Kriemhild's home, to Xanten, some 200 miles down the Rhine, where young Prince Siegfried has just been knighted. Immediately, he announces that he wants no other than Kriemhild for his wife, the princess who has turned down so many suitors, and that to this end he would use force, if necessary. Two traits of Siegfried's stand out from this scene: first the strong attraction he feels for the girl who he knows abhors marriage, and secondly his willingness to use force for personal rather than political purposes. The poet underscores the negative nature of these traits by having his parents vigorously attempt to dissuade him.

Siegfried takes no heed of his parents' advice and on his arrival in Worms proceeds, without indicating his real motive, to challenge the Burgundians to combat. They easily dissuade him from this folly and receive him as a guest. The poet uses this scene to characterize the leading personalities at the Burgundian court. Gunther, the ruling king, relying on others for advice, appears to be weak. Thus his brother Gernot does most of the dissuading of

Siegfried. Hagen, a Burgundian vassal and their best mind, shows his knowledge of the world by correctly identifying Siegfried—without ever having seen him—and by advising the court of Siegfried's three sources of exceptional power, his control of the *Nibelungen* treasure, the magic cape that may render him invisible, and his personal invulnerability, gained through his bath in the dragon's blood. It is on the basis of this advance information, that the Burgundians decide to be conciliatory to Siegfried.

Siegfried accepts the Burgundian invitation, suddenly shedding his threatening attitude, and endeavors to conceal his real motive for his trip. The plot does not appear to move on, as Siegfried spends a year as a guest of the Burgundians without even seeing Kriemhild. He then almost singlehanded defeats the invading Saxons and on his return reports to Kriemhild. Yet the lengthy fable serves to introduce gradually the complex nature of Siegfried's character. His bravery in combat, his generosity towards the defeated enemy, and his willingness to help his hosts are apparent; less noticeable is his ignorance of the ways of the world, in particular his inability to hide his motives and his shyness towards Kriemhild.

The plot moves on when Gunther hears about Brunhild, the virgin queen endowed with magic strength, who is willing to marry only that man who can defeat her in a contest of force. Siegfried counsels against the project, but when Gunther asks for help, agrees to go along and in return obtains Gunther's promise of Kriemhild's hand. Siegfried leads Gunther to Brunhild's castle, explains his presence to Brunhild by posing as one of Gunther's vassals, and uses both stealth and force to subdue Brunhild for Gunther.

Siegfried's first deception leads to another. On their return, a double wedding, Gunther-Brunhild and Siegfried-Kriemhild, is celebrated in Worms. But Brunhild, who will lose her magic strength upon consummation of her marriage, asks her husband why he permits his sister to be married to one of the vassals, and when Gunther lies clumsily, she denies him consummation. Gunther calls again on Siegfried's help, who during the following night protected by his magic cape forces Brunhild to submit to Gunther. Siegfried does not touch her himself, but with the same thoughtlessness that characterizes his role in this episode he secretly takes Brunhild's belt and ring and later gives them to Kriemhild. This scene has been difficult to interpret, since it apparently falls outside the heroic theme of the epic. A recent and competent commentator (Panzer, *Das Nibelungenlied*) rightly rejects any attempt to style this episode a comic interlude, but offers as the only explanation the theory that it represents a relatively unsuccessful adaptation of a fairytale motif. While undoubtedly the magic elements predominate in these Brunhild scenes, the problem is not one of literary precedent but of their role in what the author conceives to be the major theme of the epic. For this we have to shed any *a priori* schematic characterizations of an "innocent" Kriemhild, a "heroic" Siegfried, or a "proud" Brunhild and only consider the author's consistent effort to develop his major characters. Then Brunhild emerges as a woman with a highly developed social sensitivity, while Siegfried's character exhibits streaks of brutality and folly. And when the author refers to him during his bedroom exploits as a brave man (*kuene man*), such characterization is probably best understood as irony.

Shortly after the double wedding, Siegfried and Kriemhild leave for their home in Xanten. They are described as very much in love with each other, and this the author does not consider inconsistent with Kriemhild's previous dislike of marriage. However, before she leaves Worms, Kriemhild insists on her share of the Burgundian kingdom, but being opposed in this by her two older brothers and her husband, settles for 32 maidens and 500 men, who follow her to Xanten. This scene is of hardly any significance to the plot, but it brings out for the first time Kriemhild's rather tenacious attitude toward property, particularly her inheritance. The author passes quickly over the next ten years. Siegfried takes over the government of his father's kingdom, and both couples settle down to family life. After those many years, the plot is slowly revived by Brunhild, who is still wondering why Siegfried never performs the services of a vassal.

Perhaps the motivation by which the thread of the story is picked up again is somewhat tenuous but at this point Kriemhild emerges as the chief character of the epic. It is also the first time that one can discern two versions in describing the main characters. The B text, as it is called, reflecting apparently the original version, maintains the complexity of the leading personalities that has been noted so far, while the C text is the work of a subsequent editor of the original version. C is stylistically much smoother, more factual in approach, and in particular simplifies the chief characters, primarily by adding or changing a few key passages. Wherever the original author had achieved characterization through indirect means, as for instance dreams or revealing incidents, the editor responsible for C did not recognize their full meaning and therefore retained them, although they contradicted this simplified approach. The reason for this editorial policy lies in his inability to understand fully the subtle technique employed by the first author. The tendency of C to divide the cast into "good" and "bad" characters serves as an interesting contrast to the complex concepts of the original author.

Brunhild manages to persuade Gunther to invite Siegfried and Kriemhild to Worms, and according to the B version Brunhild, while concerned about Siegfried's status, was not consciously hostile to him. C, however, describes Brunhild in two added lines as being driven by the devil to wait for an opportunity to show Kriemhild's inferior status. C thus tries to establish a patent cause for the subsequent quarrel of the two queens, an incident that triggers the tragic turn of the plot. Any interpretation of this scene and any assessment of the responsibility for the fight will vary, depending on whether one derives it from a preconceived characterization of the two queens, i.e. Kriemhild's innocence and Brunhild's pride, or whether one tries to understand the author's effort to develop the devious depths of Kriemhild's personality. The author depicts the queens sitting together, and has Kriemhild think of her husband and tactlessly remark that he should rule all these lands. The ensuing argument gives Brunhild the opportunity to make the point—which had been bothering her for so long—that Siegfried had been passed off to her as Gunther's vassal. The queens part unreconciled after agreeing that their status should be decided by which one gained precedence in entering the church. Kriemhild returns with the ring and belt that Siegfried had taken from Brunhild, gaining precedence by dumbfounding Brunhild through accusing her of having been Siegfried's concubine. After the service, she finishes Brunhild off by showing her ring and belt to substantiate her accusation.

The scene brings out the worst in the two women. In particular Kriemhild was far from the truth in asserting that Siegfried should rule Gunther and that he had been intimate with Brunhild. On the other hand, Brunhild's rejoinder that Siegfried had claimed to owe Gunther service was only erroneous to the extent that she had been elaborately deceived. Moreover, she exposes the absurdity of Kriemhild's claim by her simple counterquery: Why did you let him love me, if he was yours? Finally, the reactions of the men should serve as an additional clue as to how the author wants this scene assessed: The Burgundians rally around their queen, while Siegfried beats his wife for her part in the quarrel.

From this point on the action moves swiftly, with each character falling into place. Immediately, Brunhild, deeply hurt, complains to Gunther, who calls Siegfried to account. Siegfried in turn offers to swear that he never claimed to have had intimacies with Brunhild, and the Burgundians accept this explanation for the time being. Then Hagen, who had had his eye on Siegfried's gold (i.e. power) for some time, injects himself and begins to plot and to urge Siegfried's death. Gunther, weakly keeping the details of Brunhild's wedding to himself, is ineffective in making a case for Siegfried. Moreover, when Kriemhild continues to provoke the Burgundians by playing the first lady at court, Gunther can only argue how dangerous it is to attack Siegfried. Then, Hagen steps in with a ready-made plot to murder Siegfried, and Gunther gives in and permits him to proceed.

Hagen's plot relies on Siegfried's well-known helpfulness. Gunther pretends to be depressed, is asked by Siegfried what the trouble is, and in reply makes up a story about a threatening attack by the Saxons. Siegfried, of course, offers to help, and they prepare for war. Hagen takes the opportunity to call Kriemhild to take leave and finds her distraught over her quarrel with Brunhild. He pretends that reconciliation can be effected and offers to be of service. Kriemhild thereupon asks him to protect Siegfried in battle, revealing the secret of his vulnerability. She tells him about the spot on her husband's back that was not covered by the dragon's blood with its magic protective powers and on Hagen's request sews a mark on Siegfried's clothes to indicate the place. After that, Hagen has little trouble in having the alleged war changed to a hunt and tricking Siegfried into a position where he can kill him.

The characterization of Kriemhild that emerges from this scene is similar to that in the quarrel incident with Brunhild. Kriemhild's inability to perceive Hagen's intentions is closely related to her tactlessness towards Brunhild. Moreover, in both instances, she panics, by flying into wild accusations in the quarrel scene and then later by revealing to Hagen Siegfried's secret. But both scenes have a deeper meaning, which the author skillfully reveals by having Kriemhild gradually become aware of the implications of her actions. As she had been distraught over her quarrel with Brunhild, she shows an increasing uneasiness about her deal with Hagen. Thus when Siegfried leaves for the last time she tries to keep him from going by telling him of two dreams she had about his being killed by two bears and two mountains. Her tensions move rapidly to a climax: Siegfried's body is placed in front of her door. A chamberlain tells her merely that the corpse of a knight has been found there. Kriemhild, not having been informed of her husband's death, realizes the truth in a flash, crying out that it is Siegfried, and that Hagen has killed him on Brunhild's advice. Thus Kriemhild, having no other information about Hagen's intentions than what he had told her and having received no news about Siegfried's fate, suddenly becomes aware of the murder plot and by necessity of her participation in it.

The seeds of Siegfried's destruction must therefore in part be sought in Kriemhild's character. It was she who had the violent dream as a young girl, who believed that marriage would ruin her, and who more recently had maneuvered her husband into an impossible position by accusing her hostess and sister-in-law of having been his mistress. And it was she who ultimately made Siegfried's death possible by betraying his vulnerable spot. Kriemhild's participation in the murder plot makes it impossible to describe her role in the second half of the epic (where she manages to have her three brothers, Hagen, and a host of Burgundians killed) as primarily motivated by revenge for Siegfried's death. The difficulty with the revenge theme was first recognized by the editor of C: In the earlier B version neither Gernot nor Giselher, her youngest brother, is a party to the murder plot, and both stay home from the hunt, but yet Kriemhild has them killed in the end. C harmonizes this apparent contradiction by adding a verse stating that they had known of the plot.

The author of B, having excluded the revenge motive, proceeds to supply his own rationale for Kriemhild's role in the destruction of her brothers. Again, as in the first half of the epic, the author develops slowly and by indirect means the deeper motivations in Kriemhild's character, until during the final scenes he lets the true violence of her personality burst forth in full force. Moreover, he provides additional depth in his literary treatment by contrasting her character with that of her brother Giselher, who had always loyally supported her and whom she also has killed.

The author begins the second part of the epic by making Kriemhild evade revenge. Thus by saying that the occasion is not opportune she prevents her father-in-law from avenging his son's death. She refuses to go home with her son and father-in-law and stays at Worms, thus separating herself voluntarily from her husband's kinfolk on whom she normally would have relied for revenge. And when at Hagen's instigation Gernot and Giselher mediate between her and her oldest brother, she even forgives Gunther his role in Siegfried's death. The editor of C, however, in accordance with the revenge theme, has Kriemhild do so under duress.

Hagen kills Siegfried not for personal reasons, but because he considers his death necessary for reasons of state, one of which is the acquisition of Siegfried's gold. It is with this in mind that he promotes the reconciliation, as a first step towards persuading Kriemhild to bring the gold to Worms. Once the gold has arrived, Hagen has no difficulty in finding a pretext to take it away from her over the ineffective protests of her three brothers. He then sinks it in the Rhine. With this grievance, the author supplies Kriemhild with an overriding motive to take revenge on Hagen.

Kriemhild has stayed for some thirteen years with the Burgundians when Etzel, king of the Huns, asks her in marriage. Her brothers are for the match, while Hagen opposes it and Kriemhild, the devout Christian, decides to accept the offer of a pagan, although not without misgivings. She wants the money and the power of her new position and on the other hand is afraid her reputation would suffer through her marriage to a pagan; however, she feels that this disadvantage perhaps might be made up if she could avenge Siegfried's murder. In the end, however, the thought that Etzel could replace the gold that Hagen had taken from her seems to turn the scales in favor of accepting the offer.

The author proceeds then to enlarge on the conflicting pressures bearing upon the heroine after her arrival at Etzel's court. Thus during the wedding she thinks constantly of Siegfried; then after she has strengthened her position at court, she compares it favorably with that she had as a widow with the Burgundians; her mood changes again, and she thinks of Hagen and wants revenge; again her thoughts wander back to Worms, and she dreams of holding hands with her brother Giselher and kissing him at all hours; all the time, however, she is unhappy, blaming Hagen and Gunther for having made her marry a heathen; but she is also quite clear that with the power at her disposal she can destroy Hagen, and thus cries for her friends at home, while at the same time she cannot wait for her day of revenge. In the end, she persuades Etzel to invite the Burgundians for a visit.

The remainder of the epic describes the annihilation of the Burgundians at Etzel's court through Kriemhild's instigation. There is no question that the issue lies between her and Hagen; but the author goes beyond simply narrating the plot and he describes her motivation in depth. He depicts Kriemhild as being driven by a desire to recover the gold that Hagen had taken from her; this is what she asks him for upon his arrival at Etzel's court; it is for this that she kills her brother Gunther; and she finally kills Hagen when she realizes that he will not reveal where the gold is hidden in the Rhine. The editor responsible for C attempts at various places to weaken this motivation by adding lines which introduce revenge for Siegfried's death as an additional motive.

Not only does the author of B describe various attempts of Kriemhild to start the fight with the Burgundians, but he has her make sacrifices that go beyond human limits. Thus Kriemhild, in addition to risking the life of her young son (who is killed in the initial stages of the combat), also pays for Hagen's life with the lives of many of Etzel's followers. And here again the author responsible for C feels that he has to diminish the heroine's ferocity and adds a verse indicating that Kriemhild had not expected such losses.

But the author of B employs another subtle device to bring out her fierceness. He makes Kriemhild also responsible for the death of her brother Giselher, whose recent betrothal he tenderly describes. It was Giselher who had stood by her after her husband's death and of whom she dreamt so fondly. Upon the arrival of the Burgundians, Kriemhild greets her brothers, but kisses only Giselher. Hagen, the realist, reacts by tightening his helmet in disgust, because he must have known that she was capable of sacrificing even her favorite brother.

In the final scene, the events surrounding Kriemhild's death should leave little doubt as to how the author wants her character to be understood. Hagen, in telling her that he had tricked her into having Gunther killed, calls her a she-devil (*vâlandinne*) to her face. Kriemhild thereupon kills Hagen with her own hands, and when Etzel denounces her for this murder, the renowned Hildebrant kills her, saying that he is avenging Hagen.

. . . . .

The author's attemt to provide the major figures of the epic with an entirely new characterization not only supplies a coherent and realistic motivation, but also a theme for the epic, i.e. that man carries the seed of his destruction in his character. Only one person is immune to this rule, and that is Rumolt, a minor figure among the Burgundians, who does not join the last fatal trip because he sees no reason why he should not enjoy life in Worms while he can. This theme of man's eventual self-destruction is heightened by several contrasts, such as the virility ascribed to Siegfried, the tenderness surrounding Giselher's engagement, and the elaborate descriptions of courtly state and glamour. Perhaps even the magic powers enjoyed by Siegfried tend to enhance his weaknesses of character. Intermingled with these and contrasting with other scenes is a melancholy mood of resignation. If strength cannot save Siegfried, nor true love and faith prevent Giselher's fate, then neither education nor a religious life seems to be effective against one's own folly. Thus the author brings out that Kriemhild is a regular churchgoer and attached to Christian principles. Similarly, he relates that Siegfried received a careful education. One may even detect an undertone of irony in some of these scenes, an irony that blends into the pessimistic tenor of the epic.

What remains, is to assess the degree of the author's success in his attempt at characterization. His problem was that he was essentially bound by a combination of plots whose motivations were no longer valid in terms of twelfth-century society. While the ***Nibelungenlied*** is not a historical source and while only some of its characters and scenes are, indirectly, related to historical events, the core of its plot and in particular the motivations of the earlier fable clearly reflect the milieu of Merovingian dynastic strife. The lax marital customs of this Franconian royal family engendered a fierce struggle among women competing for the same king. Thus King Chilperich I (561-584) had a succession of wives, one of whom, Queen Fredegunde (died 597), caused a rival to be murdered. History also relates that a foreign princess put up a strong resistance to being married to Chilperich because she wanted no part of this sorry mess. The conflicts between various branches of the Merovingian dynasty abound in murder, assassination, intrigue, and treachery. Thus Fredegunde had King Sigibert (561-575) assassinated during a hunt. It was also customary for the Franconian kings to keep a treasure of gold as a means for maintaining their political influence. The author could not fall back on these original motivations which were no longer understood in his day, but instead he developed the characterization in depth and supplied a new rationale for the plot. The author's degree of success should not so much be measured in terms of the few loose ends that his new approach left (such as Siegfried's unexplained prior acquaintance with Brunhild and her country), but by the fact that his interpretation has been accepted as consistent with the traditions of this epic.

However, the brilliant insight which the author shows in respect to characterization strikes us at points as distinctly modern or perhaps universal in application. We have no means of knowing whether this knowledge was pragmatic, reflecting only observation, or whether it extended into the realm of theory. The general assumption that the author was a cleric and the pessimistic outlook of the epic seem to indicate that the direction of his thought was rather eschatological than scientific. It would therefore be premature to label the devices he employs with psychological labels, such as dream analysis, ambivalence, subconscious, and the like. It is, however, clear, that this knowledge was not general at that time, as the changes introduced by the editor responsible for C indicate.

In reappraising the ***Nibelungenlied,*** we should keep in mind that we are dealing with fiction. The epic is not designed to provide a scientific discourse or to record a case history. It should be primarily judged as a piece of art, but to the extent that it reflects life the realism and depth relate directly to its literary qualities. A better understanding of the technique employed by the author in this respect should result in a higher estimation of this epic, even though (or perhaps because) this approach dulls the glamour of a primarily "heroic" interpretation. (pp. 341-50)

Arnold H. Price, "Characterization in the Nibelungenlied," in Monatshefte, *Vol. LI, No. 6, November, 1959, pp. 341-50.*

Franz Schoenberner (essay date 1961)

[Schoenberner was a German author and journalist who edited the anti-Nazi magazine Simplicissimus *prior to World War II. In the following excerpt from his introduction to Margaret Armour's translation of the* Nibelungenlied, *Schoenberner traces elements of Romanticism in the poem, asserting that it is "as full of nostalgic admiration for an ancient and primitive heroic past as were the German romantics toward the end of the eighteenth century."]*

The original saga of the Nibelungs was conceived in the mythological twilight of an era when pagan Germanic tribes populated the impenetrable wilderness between the Rhine and the Elbe. Clad in woolly bear fells and drinking their beery mead out of aurochs' horns, they worshiped Wotan and Freya and Baldur and other deities of nature created in the image and out of the imagination of wild warriors and hunters.

Their somber primordial myths, their dark legends of invincible heroes, of giants and dwarfs and dragons hiding in the forest, lived on for hundreds of years only by oral tradition, committed to the often failing or falsifying memory of one generation after the other; or they were sometimes partly lost and forgotten before they could be preserved in writing, as happened to the original German saga of the Nibelungs. Its oldest trace is to be found in the two Eddas and in the Volsunga Saga, documents not of Germanic, but of Icelandic literature. It was this Scandinavian source which inspired Richard Wagner to make the Nibelungs famous throughout the world by his musical genius and the rather dubious poetry of his librettos, whose assonant verses are a weak pastiche of the alliterative verse used by the Nordic epic.

But this is not of special importance in our context because the old Icelandic saga itself, not only its Wagnerian version, differs completely, except for names, from the epos presented here in English. The ***Nibelungenlied*** is not an ancient folk saga, but a work of art, a great poem written only around 1200 A.D. in a rather complicated rhymed strophe, the so-called 'Nibelungenstrophe,' by a poet still unknown but certainly of extraordinary powers. As Carlyle said of him more than 125 years ago: 'Like a fair heavenly Apparition, which indeed he *was,* he has melted into air, and only the Voice he uttered, in virtue of his inspired gift, yet lives and will live.'

Though perhaps discounting something of Carlyle's emphatic praise, the modern American reader, too, will find that the intrinsic poetic force of this long poem is still alive, not only in the Middle High German original (which even in Germany only learned men are able to read), but also in the English [translations]. . . . (pp. xi-xii)

But we should not forget that the ***Nibelungenlied*** is a lied, a poem, intended to be sung by bards who, as in Homer's time, wandered from one castle or princely court to the other, delighting their audiences with their epic or lyric verses and usually well rewarded by their patrons. They were not simple folk singers but professional artists, as were the minnesingers, those knights-errant of poetry to whom the author of the ***Nibelungenlied*** may have belonged, though he was less interested in the great theme of *Minne,* of love, than in the lore of old German myths.

The late twelfth and early thirteenth centuries produced a high flowering of culture in Germany with its masterworks of Gothic architecture and sculpture and its painting. It was the time of the minnesinger Walther von der Vogelweide and the poet Wolfram von Eschenbach, the time of the illustrious emperor Frederick II, a Renaissance man born two hundred years too early, whom Dante puts into hell as an atheist.

But the poet of the ***Nibelungenlied*** was evidently a romantic, as full of nostalgic admiration for an ancient and primitive heroic past as were the German romantics toward the end of the eighteenth century, who so enthusiastically rediscovered the Middle Ages and in the process also the old manuscripts of the ***Nibelungenlied,*** hidden and forgotten for hundreds of years. (The first fragmentary translation was published in 1765 by Johann Jakob Bodmer, a Swiss professor and minor poet.)

This explains the strange and fascinating dualism of the ***Nibelungenlied***: the author had the audacity or naïveté to revive dim ancestral memories and to transpose the old, thoroughly pagan, heroes of ancient German myths and barbaric sagas into a much more civilized atmosphere. It is not really the atmosphere of his own time but at least that of a more recent past, when the concepts of Christianity and the codes of knightly honor have superseded the primitive laws of the virgin forest, and the heroes dwell in royal splendor, clad not in bear fells but precious silks and brocades described time and again, in every detail, with almost feminine delight.

Sometimes one could almost suspect that the poet, far from naïve, consciously chose to tell his great story with a kind of artful artlessness in a simple and unemotional style, somewhat archaic even for the ears of his contemporaries.

This could be an artistic device which makes it easier to disregard the sometimes incongruous mixture of two worlds. So, for example, to quote only two of many similar instances, the cynical arch villain and expert killer Hagen has at the crossing of the Danube vainly tried to drown the chaplain in order to disprove the prophecy of a mermaid that the cleric will be the only man to return. But Hagen later admonishes the threatened Burgundians to go to mass, in full armor of course, shortly before embarking on the most savage massacre ever pictured by a poem, with Christian knights quenching their thirst by drinking, like cannibals, the blood of slain enemies.

This is, of course, only the bloodthirsty climax of the tragedy which the poet builds up from one dramatic step to the next with the unfailing instinct and skill of an accomplished artist. The whole is so well constructed that we feel sure it must be the work of a single master capable of balancing and contrasting gentleness against ferocity in alternating scenes and sometimes even in the same character. Hagen as well as Kriemhild, for example, distinguishes himself by the extremes of utmost fidelity and blackest treachery, the latter originating in the former. Had there been only a compilation of various old songs, as may be true in the case of Homer, or the combined effort of several poets, such daring strokes of psychological insight into the dark contradictions of the human soul would hardly have been possible, or at least could not have been followed up with such consistency.

Strangely enough the name of the Nibelungs, evidently derived from the word *Nebel* (mist), is transferred in the second part of the epic without explanation to the Burgundians, perhaps because it goes with the treasure they have made their own by devious means. Or the whole misty confusion may go back to mistakes in older folk songs later carelessly incorporated into the ***Nibelungenlied.*** Besides, there are certainly faded and twisted remembrances of ages past involved, combining both mythical and historical elements.

The shining hero Siegfried, murdered by the somber 'Nibelung' Hagen, seems akin to Baldur, the god of light and daytime, killed by the treacherous, nebulous powers of darkness and night. And the ill-fated expedition of the Burgundians or Nibelungs to the court of Etzel (Attila), king of the Huns in Hungary, recalls the migration of the nations and the great battle in which a Burgundian army under a king Gundicarius (or Gunther) was destroyed by the Huns in 437 A.D. Actually the historians know of Attila's second wife, a German girl Hildico, who in the Gudrun saga, called by that name, murders her husband in order to avenge the killing of her brothers—just the reverse of the ***Nibelungenlied,*** where, by the way, Etzel's deceased first wife is named Helca. Kriemhild, Gudrun, Hildico, Helca are evidently all more or less identical. Dietrich of Bern has nothing to do with Bern in Switzerland: he is Theodoric, King of the Ostrogoths, who in fact reigned fifty years after Attila and resided in Ravenna. Evidently the old bards had a bad memory for names, frequently jumbled quite different sagas together, and thus often created a thorough confusion. Good poets rarely excel in a logical orderliness of mind, to the eternal despair of philologists, who in their turn are of course almost never good poets. At any rate this extended marginal note may suffice to give the scholars their due. (pp. xii-xiv)

Being a good poet and therefore highly sensitive, he is evidently carried away by the typically romantic, rather morbid admiration for the exactly opposite type, the primitively violent warrior, the bestially cruel but somehow noble savage, or the fascinating great criminal. (This trend is one of the oldest and most constant characteristics of romantic literature, from Tacitus through Rousseau and Nietzsche to Faulkner, Hemingway, Robinson Jeffers, and many others.) That is why the poet of the ***Nibelungenlied*** makes his colleague, the minstrel Folker, such a horrifying swordsman, as fierce as Hagen, and why the rather weak joke of Folker's murderous fiddling with his mighty bow is repeated so often with such smiling satisfaction.

There is another little weakness in this great poet: his almost obsessive interest in treasures, in gold and jewels and precious apparel of all kinds given away at every possible occasion in fantastic quantities with rather monotonous regularity. Modern American readers, perhaps slightly shocked by such crass materialism in a medieval epic, should be reminded that in those good old days lavish hospitality and prodigal giving were among the most indispensable virtues of kings and nobles proud and ambitious enough to value a good reputation. Minstrels and bards, even then usually impecunious, had to rely completely upon the largess of their patrons, whose riches naturally attracted and inspired the poetic imagination. By praising so highly and so insistently the fabulous generosity of legendary heroes, the poet probably intended to exercise upon his audience a certain educational influence by the power of good examples. Very human, indeed! (pp. xx-xxi)

Franz Schoenberner, in an introduction to The Nibelungenlied, *translated by Margaret Armour, The Heritage Press, 1961, pp. xi-xxiii.*

M. O'C. Walshe (essay date 1962)

[*Walshe edited* Medieval German Studies *(1965) with A. T. Hatto and is the author of* Medieval German Literature: A Survey. *In the following excerpt from the latter work, he provides an overview of the poem in which he praises its artistic form and complex characters.*]

Beside the court epic, though not always sharply distinguishable from it, we find a second epic *genre* in Middle High German, to which the designation Heroic Epic is given today. The older term *Volksepos* formerly applied to this type of poetry has now been abandoned; it was based on the romantic conception of the difference between *Volksepos* and *Kunstepos,* which is no longer accepted. The tales of the Nibelungen, of Kudrun and of Dietrich von Bern are, after all, just as much individually fashioned products of the poetic art as are *Parzival* and *Tristan.* The essential difference between, e.g., *Parzival* on the one hand and the ***Nibelungenlied*** on the other is one of subject-matter and, to some extent, the audience for which it was intended. In general the Franco-Celtic romances of King Arthur appealed more to the taste of the courtly world than the traditional Germanic story-material preserved from earlier times, which was felt to be old-fashioned and was not so easily brought into line with the new courtly ideals. Only in the case of the ***Nibelungenlied*** was the gap more or less successfully bridged—and yet even this great work was passed over in silence by courtly writers other than the unconventional and irrepressible Wolfram.

Germanic heroic poetry had its origins in the period of the Great Migrations (ca. 375-500). The great events of those stirring times made a profound impression on the minds of the Germanic peoples, and stimulated their poetic imagination. But the vision of the early Germanic poet, though it might be stirred by the fate of nations, confined itself to the deeds and enterprises of individuals: it was not political, but personal, and the mainsprings of action were seen as motives of personal ambition, greed, vengeance, loyalty and the like. A favourite historical character from the period of the Migrations makes a frequent appearance in the heroic epics, the Ostrogoth Theoderic (*Dietrich von Bern*), who ruled in Italy from 493-526; others were Attila, king of the Huns (MHG *Etzel,* Old Norse *Atli*), who died in 453, and Ermanaric, the Gothic king who committed suicide when his Black Sea kingdom was destroyed by the Hunnish incursion in 375. In fact Ermanaric soon came to replace the figure of Theoderic's historical opponent Odovacar, whom he murdered in 493. Odovacar still appears in the *Hildebrandslied* in the role of the tyrant which his murderer's apologists had assigned to him, but in later versions Ermanaric has taken his place. Thus not only is everything reduced to the personal level, but personalities are arbitrarily juggled with no regard to either chronological sequence or historical accuracy—indeed, one and the same character can be looked upon in a different light by different Germanic nations. The Burgundians, and hence later the Franks who came to occupy their territory on the Rhine, regarded Attila as the ruthless tyrant and conqueror who had destroyed their kingdom, while the Goths, who had been his allies, preserved a favourable picture of him. There were therefore two distinct and contrasting traditional views of Attila, both of which played their part in the early history and development of the Nibelungen story.

But neither in this case nor in any other can we trace a continuous German tradition through surviving texts. It is precisely in the field of the heroic epic that the biggest gap in our knowledge of medieval literature exists. The early stages of the tales which go to make up the Middle High German heroic epics are either not preserved at all, or at least not in German. The Church was partly responsible for this state of affairs, since although we are told that Charles the Great made a collection of such heroic material, his son Louis the Pious destroyed it, and numerous testimonies show clerical disapproval for such pagan tales. From the Old High German period the *Hildebrandslied* alone is preserved, almost miraculously in the circumstances, in German, while the Latin poem of *Waltharius* seems to preserve another early lay in a disguised form. For the rest we have traces of such material in Latin form in the Gothic history of Jordanes and the Langobard history of Paulus Diaconus, and apart from this we have the heroic lays of Scandinavia and England, where the clerics were less intolerant.

Yet though it vanished from the surface, the heroic tradition did not perish in Germany. The ancient court poets disappeared with the courts to which they had been attached, but the matter of which they sang was preserved, even if often much altered, in oral tradition. As late as the 12th century we find clerical writers complaining of the 'lying tales', the competition of which they evidently feared. The precise conditions under which this material was transmitted are not entirely clear: presumably nobles and peasants alike retained their fondness for the old stories and handed down versions of them in unwritten form, versified or otherwise. By the mid-12th century written versions of some stories existed, though these are lost, doubtless because they quickly became old-fashioned in the eyes of the public of the period. It is only in the 13th century that texts emerge which are fated to achieve preservation; the very first such text to appear is at the same time the greatest work of the whole *genre,* the ***Nibelungenlied*** or, as its original title was, ***Der Nibelunge Nôt.*** (pp. 220-22)

The ***Nibelungenlied,*** unlike the vast majority of the epics [in medieval German literature], is in strophic form. The *Nibelungen* stanza consists of four long lines, each divided into two by a cæsura, and with the rhyme-scheme *aabb.* Each half-line before the cæsura has a feminine ending. Each half-line has three full beats except the last, which has four. The somewhat monotonous rhythm which this would yield if treated with too great regularity is diversified by the great freedom of handling: intermediate dips are frequently omitted at different points, so that a good deal of rhythmic variety is achieved.

The name of the author of the ***Nibelungenlied*** is unknown. He was presumably in the service of Wolfger, Bishop of Passau from 1191-1204, and later Patriarch of Aquileia. It is also possible that he was in the service of the Duke of Austria—the two possibilities do not conflict, as it appears that chancery officials were sometimes lent by the bishop to the Austrian Duke. There has been some rather fruitless speculation regarding his social status. In earlier times the overworked term 'Spielmann' was applied to him as a matter of course, and it has recently been fashionable to declare that he was a knight. The probability would in fact seem to be that he was a clerk in minor orders in the bishop's service. His anonymity was doubtless deliberate, but had he been a person of standing the chances are that his name would have been recorded in some source.

Whatever may be the solution of this question, the poem itself poses for us a number of more important problems somewhat different in kind from those presented by the other epics. The first question is: what is the precise extent, in the strictly literal sense, of our author's work? In the case of *Parzival,* for example, no one doubts that Wolfram himself composed the 24,000 lines of the poem, whatever views may be held about his sources. But in the case of the author of the ***Nibelungenlied,*** there are two reasons why we cannot be equally sure that he did likewise. In the first place, we do not possess an absolutely authentic text of the poem as it left his hands about 1204, since the main manuscripts diverge considerably among themselves; and secondly, since his sources were German, we do not know exactly how much matter he took over unchanged from them. Those who worked from French sources had at least the trouble of translating those sources, however literally, but the author of the ***Nibelungenlied*** may well have incorporated bodily whole sections of an earlier version. The question might therefore be put whether we should not rather speak of the *Nibelungen* poets in the plural, were it not that the work itself, despite all admitted weaknesses and inconsistencies, clearly reveals the one master-mind behind it. Nevertheless, before we can attempt an assessment of the poem as it stands, this situation makes it imperative to pass in review some of the facts regarding the development of the tradition.

Research into the origins of Germanic heroic poetry in general and the ***Nibelungenlied*** in particular has by now quite a long history, and in the course of time many different theories have been put forward. We may first of all note a view which once enjoyed wide popularity, but which is no longer held by serious scholars: the nature-myth theory. Modern scholars do not believe, for instance, that the story of Siegfried's death is a symbolic representation of night and day or summer and winter, of some ancient fertility-sacrifice, and the like. The origins of Germanic heroic poetry are today sought in history, not in mythology. (pp. 223-25)

Modern research has succeeded in throwing considerable light on the history of the Nibelungen theme. Many scholars have played their part in this, but perhaps the most significant contribution has been that of Andreas Heusler, although since his death in 1940 some of his theories have come in for severe criticism. We have seen that the story can be divided into two main parts, which we can call *Siegfried's Death* and *The Fall of the Nibelungs* (beginning with stanza 1143, canto XX) respectively. It will be convenient to begin with the history of Part II. This part has undoubtedly a historical core dating from the period of the Great Migrations. The Burgundians were an East Germanic tribe from the island of Bornholm in the Baltic, who settled on the Rhine in the 4th century A.D. In 437 they were overrun by the Huns (Attila was not present), their king Gundahari and many nobles were slain, and their kingdom was destroyed. We know nothing else about Gundahari, but the memory of his death remained fresh in the minds of the survivors, who settled in Savoy. In 453 Attila died of a hæmorrhage by the side of a Germanic maiden named Hildico. The chroniclers connected these facts and soon the story is that Hildico killed Attila to avenge her father. This may be taken as the beginning of the romantic transformation of history into fable. The land of the Burgundians was later occupied by the Franks, and it was presumably a Frank who composed the first poem on this subject, doubtless a short lay like the *Hildebrandslied.* We can more or less reconstruct its contents from Northern sources. As always, the theme is seen in terms of purely personal relationships. The name of Hildico (i.e. 'Hildchen') was apparently turned into Grimhild to fit into the alliterative scheme with the names of her brothers. These were slain by Attila, but not in battle: they were treacherously murdered for a treasure they possessed. This form of the story found its way to Scandinavia and we find it, with some variations, in the Eddic *Atlakvida,* dating probably from the 9th century.

But this original core of the story of the Fall of the Burgundians (or Nibelungs, as they came to be called for some slightly obscure reason) was soon drastically remodelled, presumably by a Bavarian. The Bavarians were in contact with the Ostrogoths of Italy, directly or through the Langobards, and the Gothic-Langobard view of Attila was a favourable one. He had to be exonerated. In the new version, therefore, it was no longer Attila who slew the brothers, but Grimhild herself, who took vengeance on them for the murder of her first husband, Siegfried. The figure of Attila was thus made secondary to that of the avenging sister. This form of the story remained current in the Bavarian region for some four or five centuries, till about 1160. It was then, in Heusler's view, converted under the influence of the new epics translated from the French into a long strophic poem, called by him *Die ältere Not.* This work is not preserved, but there are good grounds for believing that it once existed, and it furnished the model and basis for Part II of the ***Nibelungenlied.*** Its author must have known in some form the story included in Part I, since he presumably used it to motivate his own version.

The basis of Part I is more problematical. Here there are two separate strands which seem to have been secondarily linked: the story of Siegfried's murder (the essential feature of Part I), and the mythical tales of Siegfried's youth, which the ***Nibelungenlied*** passes over briefly.

The story of Siegfried's murder may or may not reflect an

actual historical event, but it does depict only too clearly the atmosphere of the Merovingian court, at which crimes of all sorts, and especially the murder of relatives, were of frequent occurrence. The tale probably went somewhat as follows:

> King Gunther of Worms woos the maiden Brünhild, who can only be won by some deed of superhuman strength and daring. Gunther is unable to fulfil the conditions, and so the maiden is won for him by Siegfried. As a reward Siegfried receives Gunther's sister Kriemhild. But Siegfried either deceives Gunther with Brünhild, or is accused of doing so. He is therefore slain by Hagen, who is apparently a half-brother of Gunther's.

This was the approximate content of a lay which a Frankish poet composed in the 6th century, and which also found its way northwards. But we also find less distinct traces of further lays dealing with the hero's youth. Here, however, we are no longer in the sphere of pseudo-history but of myth and fairy-tale. What the ***Nibelungenlied*** tells us of this is little enough and is not free from contradictions:

> In Av. II we hear that Siegfried is the son of Sigemunt and Sigelint of Xanten. His strength and skill are stressed, but overlaid by the account of his courtly upbringing, in marked contrast to the usual conception of the wild, untamed youth. Only the name of his father is traditional here. But in Av. III Hagen gives a brief account of Siegfried's youthful deeds. Once young Siegfried rode out alone, and before a hollow mountain he found Schilbung and Nibelung, who sought his aid in sharing out an immense hoard, giving him the sword Balmung as a reward. But when they quarrelled he slew them and thus became lord of the treasure and of Nibelung Land. The dwarf Alberich at first sought to avenge them, but was conquered and had to give Siegfried the *Tarnkappe.* In a single stanza Hagen gives the contents of a second lay: Siegfried slew a dragon and bathed in its blood, thus acquiring a horny skin which no weapon could pierce. In Avv. VII and X we find obscure traces of a third motive, of the former betrothal of Siegfried and Brünhild, about which Northern sources have more to tell. In Av. VII, when Siegfried accompanies Gunther to Iceland, Brünhild seems to know him. Later, at the double wedding, she weeps on seeing Siegfried with Kriemhild. She explains that she is sorrowful at seeing Gunther's sister wedded to a serf.

We conclude with Heusler that the ***Nibelungenlied*** as we know it had two main sources, a lay and an epic. The lay, corresponding to Part I, was presumably composed in the Rhineland about the mid-12th century and is referred to as the German Lay of Brünhild. Its nature is admittedly somewhat problematic. We are on firmer ground when we come to consider the *ältere Not,* for if Heusler is right, chapters 356-92 of the Norwegian *Thidrekssaga* are directly based on this. In any case we can assume that this work was an epic poem of some length, the first German Nibelungen epic. The author was an Austrian, familiar with the Danube landscape. He chose the well-known strophic form of four lines, which we also know from the love-songs of Der von Kürenberg. Bartsch and others have even suggested that this poet was the author of the old version, and the suggestion is not unreasonable, especially as Kürenberg's style has a distinctly epic-dramatic quality; but of course there is absolutely no proof.

After these somewhat lengthy preliminaries, we are now perhaps in some position to assess the actual achievement of the Nibelungen author. Basically what he seems to have done is this: he took the *ältere Not* as his model, and created a counterpart to it from the Lay of Brünhild and other sources. This formed Part I of his epic. He expanded and altered the *ältere Not* itself, perhaps doubling its original length, to form Part II. Each of these main parts consisted then of about 1000 stanzas, and he further composed a transitional section of about 400 stanzas. The expansion of lays to form Part I was not done without considerable difficulty, and involved serious contradictions. The main peaks of action here were expanded into full-length scenes, and epic breadth was achieved, sometimes rather desperately, by very full descriptions of courtly festivities and the like, as well as of battles and hunting incidents. The middle section (Avv. XVII-XXIII) seems to have been our poet's independent invention, but Part II also underwent much modification, perhaps not always for the better. But there is no doubt that as the story progresses the poet's skill becomes the greater. We must, however, bear in mind that we do not possess the original text in absolutely authentic form. (pp. 225-28)

It is certain that the later parts of the [*Nibelungenlied*] are better than the earlier ones, that the poet only achieved complete mastery of his theme and material with practice—a not uncommon observation in medieval writings.

—M. O'C. Walshe

It remains to attempt an artistic assessment of the ***Nibelungenlied.*** There is no doubt that the unknown poet was an artist of the first rank, who moulded the traditional material in masterly fashion. He converted the loosely-connected strands into a single, unified, dramatic whole. And the central figure of this drama is a woman. The principal character is not Siegfried, nor is it his murderer Hagen—though he remains very much in the foreground—but it is Kriemhilt who dominates the tale from first to last and gives it unity. It is the history, as Heusler has it, of Kriemhilt's two marriages, of her development from the tender maiden at the court of Worms to the she-devil of the final scenes in the land of the Huns. The poet undertook to make this development credible, and in this he succeeded, whatever other faults we may find with his work.

From the very beginning Kriemhilt is consistently placed in the very centre of the stage. She is introduced in stanza 2 (which indeed was originally the first stanza):

> Ez wuohs in Burgonden cin vil edel magedîn,
> daz in allen landen niht schœners mohte sîn,
> Kriemhilt geheizen: si wart ein schœne wîp.
> dar umbe muosen degene vil verliesen den lîp.

> There grew up in Burgundy a noble maiden, such that in all the
> world none might be more fair; she was called Kriemhilt: she
> became a beautiful woman. For that many warriors had to die.

Right from the start we are given a hint of the tragic outcome which is associated with the person of Kriemhilt. We hear of her dream that she had a fair falcon, which was torn in pieces by two eagles. Her mother interprets this to mean that she will gain a handsome husband and lose him again, whereupon she is ready to renounce all love: *daz ich von mannes minne sol gewinnen nimmer nôt.* In Av. II we meet Siegfried. He comes to Worms but has to wait a whole year before he is permitted to see her. This honour is only accorded him after his victory over the Saxons. When he does see her, her appearance is described in the courtliest terms:

> Sam der liehte mâne vor den sternen stât,
> des schin sô lûterlîche ab den wolken gât,
> dem stuont si nû gelîche vor manger frouwen guot.
> des wart dâ vil gehœhet den zieren heleden der muot.

> As the bright moon stands out before the stars, whose light is so
> clear reflected from the clouds, so she stood out before many a
> fair lady. Thus the hearts of the handsome heroes were raised on high.

The poet shows here that he is fully capable of creating a lyrical atmosphere when he wishes. The later contrast is all the more effective. In her marriage to Siegfried the girl matures into a woman. The scene which precipitates the catastrophe is masterly. Kriemhilt's naïve pride in her fine husband arouses the anger of Prünhilt, who as queen demands precedence at the church door. Kriemhilt flares up and lets fall the unforgivable words *'Wie möhte mannes kebse immer werden küneges wîp?'* ('How might a vassal's concubine ever become a king's wife?'). Siegfried's death can no longer be averted. Unwittingly Kriemhilt even aids his murderer Hagen by pointing out her husband's vulnerable spot. With his death her world is in ruins: *von ir wart allen freuden mit sîme tôde widerseit* (she renounced all joy at his death). The first unpleasant trait which makes its appearance in Kriemhilt is covetousness. But even this appears only gradually, and is very skilfully hinted at and half excused by the poet. For when she begins to give away Siegfried's treasure, Hagen fears that she may thereby gain supporters. On his advice the treasure is taken from her and sunk in the Rhine. To her grief at Siegfried's death is thus added resentment at the loss of the treasure. Thirteen years pass before an opportunity of revenge presents itself. Etzel, the mighty king of the Huns, woos her. At first she will not hear of a second husband, but finally it occurs to her that she can be avenged and at the same time regain the treasure. Yet she remains another thirteen years in Hunland before she makes any attempt to put this plan into operation. In a psychologically fine passage in Av. XXIII, she at last makes up her mind. She persuades Etzel to invite her brothers and Hagen to a festival in Hunland. In the final portion of the poem the point of view is shifted. Till now we have seen everything through Kriemhilt's eyes. From now on the action is seen through the eyes of the Nibelungs, and especially of Hagen. This emerges clearly in Kriemhilt's next appearance, when the guests arrive at Etzel's castle:

> Kriemhilt diu küneginne mit ir gesinde gie
> dâ si die Nibelunge mit valschem muote enpfie.
> si kuste Gîselhêren und nam in bî der hant.
> daz sach von Tronege Hagene: den helm er vester gebant.

> Kriemhilt the queen and her retinue went to receive the Nibelungs
> with false intent. She kissed Giselher and took him by the hand.
> Hagen of Tronege saw that, and bound on his helmet the faster.

Giselher, the youngest brother, had not been involved in the conspiracy against Siegfried. At once she asks where the treasure is; Hagen replies that it lies sunk in the Rhine. This angers her, and when she learns that her brothers have been warned of their peril, her fury knows no bounds. Dietrich von Bern rebukes her with the word *vâlandinne* ('she-devil'), an expression which recurs later at the highest point of tension. Henceforth she does all in her power to encompass the destruction of Hagen and her brothers—she knows no further restraint. Beside her thirst for vengeance her covetousness appears more and more openly. At last there comes the famous scene: Gunther and Hagen are captives. Kriemhilt demands the treasure from Hagen. He says that as long as Gunther lives he has sworn never to reveal its hiding-place. She has Gunther beheaded, and then Hagen declares in age-old words:

> Nû ist von Burgonden der edel künec tôt,
> Gîselhêr der junge, und ouch hêr Gêrnôt.
> den schaz den weiz nu niemen wan got unde mîn:
> der sol dich, vâlandinne, immer wol verholen sîn!

> Now the noble king of the Burgundians is dead, Giselher the
> young, my lord Gernot too. Now none knows of the treasure but
> God and I: from thee, she-devil, it shall for ever be hid.

Kriemhilt strikes off his head with Siegfried's sword. Hildebrand, Dietrich's chief retainer, can no longer bear the spectacle, and with a mighty blow he slays Kriemhilt. As the tale had begun with the young maiden Kriemhilt, so now it ends with the death of the *vâlandinne,* who was responsible for the final grandiose catastrophe:

diu vil michel êre was dâ gelegen tôt.
die liute heten alle jâmer unde nôt.
mit leide was verendet des küneges hôchgezît,
als ie diu liebe leide ze aller jungest gît.

Ine kan iu niht bescheiden waz sider dâ geschach,
wan ritter unde frouwen weinen man dâ sach,
dar zuo die edelen knehte ir lieben friunde tôt.
hie hât daz mære ein ende: daz ist der Nibelunge nôt.

All the pride of chivalry there lay dead. Folk were all filled with sorrow and distress. The king's festival had ended in woe, as joy ever brings sorrow in its train. I cannot tell you what happened after that, but that knights and ladies were seen weeping, and the noble squires, for their dear friends' death. Here the tale is ended—that is the Distress of the Nibelungs.

The figure of Siegfried is dwelt on with especial affection by the poet. . . . Siegfried's character, or at least his career as narrated, is not without some contradictions. The wild, uncontrollable hero of tradition was ill-fitted for a fashionable knight on the classical model. The attempt to transform him produced a curious figure who combines, or rather fails to combine, features of Tristan and the young Parzival side by side. First of all we learn—quite in the style of the courtly romances—of his youth and the careful education he received at the hands of his father Siegmund. Incidentally this shows that the poet was ignorant of tradition here, since in other versions Siegmund was killed in battle before his son's birth, whereas in the ***Nibelungenlied*** he actually survives him. Siegfried's investiture is described with all the pageantry of the court epics, and we then hear of how he first leaves home to go to Worms. In complete contradiction to this comes Hagen's immediately following narrative of Siegfried's youthful deeds, the winning of the treasure and the fight with the dragon—an account based on genuine tradition. Siegfried's behaviour on his arrival at Worms, too, accords better with the picture of a wild youth, good-natured but fond of fighting, than of a polished knight and prince. This wildness is emphasised repeatedly. Besides this all the traits in his character are pleasant ones: candour, liberality, readiness to help, generosity towards defeated foes. The effect of love on this untamed son of nature is depicted with skill and not without humour: the mighty hero's colour changes and he does not dare to hope that he can ever win the love of the fair Kriemhilt:

er dâhte in sînem muote 'wie künde daz ergân,
daz ich dich minnen solde? daz ist ein tumber wân.
sol aber ich dich fremeden, sô wære ich sanfter tôt.'
er wart von den gedanken vil dicke bleich unde rôt.

He thought in his mind 'How could that ever be, that I should be thy true-love? That is a foolish hope. But if I must avoid thee, then I'd sooner be dead'. At the thought he often became pale and then red.

On his journey to woo Prünhilt some contradictory traits again appear which are due to tradition. Siegfried knows the way to Iceland—how, we are not told—and also the fact that Prünhilt seems to know him is unmotivated in the poem as it stands. It is hard to say how much or how little our poet knew of other versions—but in any event he would have had difficulty in using the motif of a previous betrothal. Av. VIII ('How Siegfried went to Nibelungenland') provides an opportunity for describing all sorts of mad pranks which again fit better the picture of the traditional than of the courtly Siegfried. But his brilliant, joyous, natural character is displayed to the full especially in the description of the hunt which ends in his murder. Here too he shows off his strength for the last time by killing a bear with which he has first jovially terrified the cooks. Then comes the catastrophe. Hagen has deliberately 'forgotten' to arrange for any wine to be brought. Accordingly a race to the spring is proposed. Siegfried wins the race, but waits till Gunther has drunk. As he then bends over the water, Hagen thrusts a spear into his back. Mortally wounded, he hurls his shield with his last strength at Hagen, who falls stunned: *het er swert enhende sô wære ez Hagenen tôt* ('Had he had his sword in his hand, it had been Hagen's death'). Siegfried's last words are addressed to Gunther, requesting him to take care of Kriemhilt:

Die bluomen allenthalben von bluote wurden naz.
dô rang er mit dem tôde: unlange tet er daz,
wan des tôdes wâfen ie ze sêre sneit.
dô mohte reden niht mêre der recke küene und gemeit.

The flowers round about became wet with blood. Then he wrestled with Death, but not long, for Death's blade ever cut too sharply. Then the bold blithe hero could speak no more.

The figure of Hagen is less prepossessing but more important for the story as a whole. Next to Kriemhilt, he is the chief character, and next to her, he dominates the greatest number of scenes. Originally, it seems, a half-brother of Gunther's with perhaps an elfin father, he is here Gunther's chief retainer, standing to him in somewhat the relation of Hildebrand to Dietrich. Just as there is something demonic about Kriemhilt in Part II, so there is about Hagen from the very beginning. For a moment one might be tempted to compare his role with that of Mephistopheles. Such a comparison, however, would be unfair: he is not devilish by intent, however ruthless his actions may appear, for they spring in the main from unconditional, blind loyalty to his lord. This loyalty is really the basic trait of Hagen's character—a fatal, catastrophic loyalty. But he does not remain static. He too develops, in a direction contrary to Kriemhilt. As her character deteriorates, so Hagen's becomes notably more attractive. If in Part I the demonic element is in the foreground, in Part II Hagen makes a more human appeal to us. An essential element in his nature is a certain unshakeable inner strength which knows no fear, but which also shrinks from no means to achieve what he regards as legitimate ends. If in Part II he is a foil to Kriemhilt, in the first part he is placed over against Siegfried, with whom he is sharply contrasted. He is the bold, experienced, and also cunning warrior, not wild and reckless like Siegfried. Where Siegfried is frank and unsuspecting, Hagen suspects everybody. As a warrior he is overshadowed by Siegfried, as appears most clearly in the war with the Saxons, and this is intolerable to him. This alone suffices to make him Siegfried's secret foe. After the scene before the church, when Kriemhilt has uttered the words *'mannes kebse'*, it is at first he alone who urges Gunther to slay Siegfried, nor does he desist until Gunther agrees. His motives are not unmixed: to loyalty is added personal envy. But his own special quality of suspicion also plays a part: he cannot bring himself to credit that the nocturnal scene between Siegfried and Prünhilt was entirely innocent. After the murder Hagen behaves with utter ruthlessness toward Siegfried's widow. He throws the corpse before her door—though this is a refinement on the earlier version in which it was cast into her bed. He also deprives her of the treasure. Yet this is not done out of mere spite, but to rob her of all possibility of revenge. For the same reason he seeks to prevent her marriage to Etzel. The whole of Part II is dominated by the hostility of Hagen and Kriemhilt. And here comes the master-stroke: the author changes sides, turns against his erstwhile heroine and makes Hagen his new hero. The switch was implicit in the sources, but its execution reveals the genius of the poet. When Etzel's messengers bring the invitation to Hunland, Hagen, suspecting the worst, warns against acceptance, and only the reproach of cowardice induces him to agree. But then he takes charge of the expedition, and by his care, skill and courage ensures the safety of the Nibelungs on the journey from which he knows full well they will never return. And in the battles which come Hagen takes a leading part. His comradeship-in-arms with the knightly minstrel Volker shows him in a warmer human light than before; and finally, in opposition to earlier tradition, he is assigned the final speech of defiance when Kriemhilt for the last time demands to know the whereabouts of the treasure—and it is his death which finally decides Hildebrand to slay Kriemhilt.

Of the other characters, Prünhilt, despite the not inconsiderable role she plays in the story, remains somewhat shadowy, partly because her whole nature must have made it difficult for the poet to fit her into the courtly atmosphere he was so anxious to create, and to which she was even less well adapted than Siegfried, and partly because he clearly did not want her to overshadow Kriemhilt. So she appears where required in the story, goes through the prescribed motions, and when her part is finished after Siegfried's death, she disappears without a trace. Gunther is a typical king to outward seeming, but inwardly a weakling, entirely dependent on the advice of his entourage. He lacks the moral strength to oppose Siegfried's killing, and plays an altogether shameful role in the whole affair. Only in the final battles, in which he fights with becoming bravery, does he attain to a previously unwonted dignity. Nothing in his life becomes him like the leaving of it.

The figure of Etzel is almost as shadowy as that of Prünhilt in Part I, though as the involuntary tool of Kriemhilt's revenge he constitutes a certain counterpart to Gunther. There is one figure, however, whose role is not large in the economy of the poem, but on whom the poet dwells with much affection. This is the genuinely tragic figure of Margrave Rüedeger, who has sworn to avenge Kriemhilt's wrongs. When the Nibelungs come to Bechelaren he receives them with great honour, and Giselher is betrothed to his daughter. Yet at the last he too is drawn by his oath into the battle against the Burgundians to whom he is bound by the closest ties, trapped in a conflict of loyalties from which there is no escape. He is, too, the only figure in the whole poem who seems definitely inspired by Christian thinking, and who is concerned not only with honour but with his own salvation:

> 'Daz ist âne lougen, ich swuor iu, edel wîp,
> daz ich durch iuch wâgte êre und ouch den lîp,
> daz ich die sêle vliese, des enhân ich niht gesworn.
> zuo dirre hôchgezite brâht ich die fürsten wol geborn.'

> 'That I do not deny, I swore to you, noble lady,
> that I for you would risk my honour and my life,
> but that I should lose my soul, that I did not swear. I it was who brought the noble princes to this festival.'

But all is unavailing, and Rüedeger falls by the very sword he had given to Gernot. In some respects the role of Dietrich von Bern is not unlike that of Rüedeger, though he survives the tragedy—but only at the price of losing all his warriors save Hildebrand.

The dramatic quality of the ***Nibelungenlied*** has frequently been stressed. In fact its structure has been compared with that of Schiller's *Wallenstein.* It is perhaps above all this dramatic structure, coupled with its subtle yet penetrating psychology, on which the greatness of the poem rests. Nor must we overlook the author's extreme skill in handling a strophic form which could only too easily have become intolerably monotonous. The style shows various elements which betray its complex origin. If we approach it from a reading of *Iwein* we are struck by its simplicity and the archaic flavour of its vocabulary and phraseology. Many words and syntactic turns belonging to the traditional heroic stock, but banned by Hartmann from the court epic of 1200, are still to be found here: words such as *recke, degen, wîgant* for 'hero', expressions like *hort der Nibelunges* ('the Nibelung's treasure'), strike an unexpected note against the heavily-stressed courtly background. On the other hand the courtly influence extends beyond mere descriptive passages to include a number of significant concessions to the more refined taste and outlook of 1200, and at several points the asperities of the traditional narrative have been toned down. Thus in the scene where Siegfried has to come to Gunther's assistance on his wedding-night, despite an element of grotesque comedy which remains, Siegfried surrenders the conquered Prünhilt unravished to her rightful husband in contrast to the older, cruder version. Likewise the corpse of Siegfried is no longer cast into Kriemhilt's bed but placed before her door; and in the concluding scene Dietrich is too noble a character to be entrusted with the slaying of Kriemhilt, so this task is transferred to Hildebrand. Some scenes are based on models from the court epic: thus the bleeding of Siegfried's wounds in the presence of his murderer is taken from *Iwein,* and it is just conceivable that the figure of young Siegfried owes something to Parzival, while Siegfried's murder in the forest has analogues in French.

But for modern tastes the ***Nibelungenlied*** seems to have one marked failing. The long descriptions of courtly festivals and splendid costumes which occur so frequently seem positively disturbing against the background of the age-old story. They seem to hang round it like a splendid but ill-fitting garment, and the question arises whether this unsatisfactory impression is due to a weakness of the poem, or to a failure in comprehension on the part of the modern reader. The theme of the poem, as has been truly said, is that joy and sorrow—*liebe unde leit*—are inextricably intermingled, and that joy turns to sorrow in the end. It is therefore argued that the scenes of splendour and courtly 'joy' are deliberately introduced at important places in the story in order to point this moral with tragic irony. It has been urged too that the courtly *milieu* was so much a matter of course in 1200 that the poet was unable to conceive his heroes, even Siegfried and Hagen, except in terms of the splendid chivalry of his day. There is doubtless an element of contradiction between these points of view, yet there is some force in both contentions. Naturally any medieval author took for granted the background of his own period with a degree of naïve assurance which our own more historically-minded age finds hard to accept, and naturally too the author of the ***Nibelungenlied*** was intensely alive to the effects of contrast and dramatic irony. But also he was a poet who was visibly learning his craft as he proceeded, and he was concerned too, at a lower level of creation, with a purely formal, technical problem. The highly-coloured, 'courtly' descriptive passages occur almost entirely in the first half of the poem. In at least one case, the account of the upbringing and knighting of young Siegfried, a serious contradiction is involved. It is perhaps legitimate to assume that the poet's enthusiasm for things courtly ran away with him here. Further, he was concerned in Part I to expand a short lay into a long narrative, and the introduction of such matter provided a useful method of doing this. It is certain that the later parts of the poem are better than the earlier ones, that the poet only achieved complete mastery of his theme and material with practice—a not uncommon observation in medieval writings.

Labels such as 'Court Epic' and 'Heroic Epic' are a mere device of literary historians who need some method of classifying their material, and should not be regarded as having more than a relative validity. Nevertheless, the attempt to transfer the ***Nibelungenlied*** from the category of the heroic to that of the court epic is not entirely justified. If we cannot strip off the 'courtly layer' without doing violence to the poem, we must still recognise that its fundamental spirit and ethic belong to an earlier age and that the process of adaptation was not complete—indeed the very attempt was largely abandoned by the poet as the work progressed and he freed himself from some of his earlier enthusiasms. Towards the end, the courtly overlay is scarcely deeper than the Christian veneer, and this is borne out by the fact that the poem was obviously not acceptable to all fashionable literary circles of its day. Nevertheless the ***Nibelungenlied*** did set a fashion. It made it possible for traditional heroic themes to be treated in 'serious' literature and provided a model for them to follow—at a respectful distance. The ***Nibelungenlied*** is not, as has been urged, the peak and dominating centre of medieval German poetry, for here *Parzival* stands supreme. But it is undoubtedly that epic work of the German Middle Ages most easily appreciated by the modern reader, doubtless just because it is not so rigidly bound up with the attitudes and views of the early 13th century. Its fundamentally simple yet profound human appeal makes it more accessible today than the greater, but more complex and difficult *Parzival* could ever become.

It only remains to tell how before long a poet appeared who decided that the text of the ***Nibelungenlied*** as it stood was in need of improvement. His adaptation is found in manuscript C. The C editor added strophes to increase the 'courtly' atmosphere; he also disapproved of the author's treatment of Kriemhilt, whose character he sought to redeem by blackening still further that of Hagen. We may regret his intervention, but yet he showed some tact and skill in his self-imposed task. But this was not enough. All complete manuscripts contain as an appendix a poem in couplets called *Die Klage,* which tells in great detail how the dead were buried, how Etzel's messengers brought the news of the tragedy to Bechelaren, to Passau and to Worms, and how Bishop Pilgrim of Passau ordered one Meister Kuonrat to write down the story in Latin. This poem was written about 1220 in Bavaria, and suffers from intolerable diffuseness and a sentimentality far removed from the old heroic spirit, but typical of some 13th-century writing. It is of some interest for the history of the Nibelungen story, but its literary value is of the slightest, and as an appendix to the great work to which it is attached, it is nothing short of a monstrosity. (pp. 229-38)

M. O'C. Walshe, "The Classical Age: The 'Nibelungenlied'," in his Medieval German Literature: A Survey, *Cambridge, Mass.: Harvard University Press, 1962, pp. 220-38.*

D. G. Mowatt (essay date 1962)

[*In the excerpt below, Mowatt discusses the* Nibelungenlied *in the context of its literary merit and its credibility as a national epic.*]

The ***Nibelungenlied*** has on occasion been compared to the *Iliad.* The fact that Germans have been impelled to make, and foreigners disposed to deride, such a comparison, is revealing in itself, for it shows the veneration both works have suffered. Assessment of their literary merit has been geographically conditioned, with Homer belonging to western civilization as a whole, and the ***Nibelungenlied*** for the most part only to Germany. But in both cases scholars have painstakingly erected a barrier between heritage and inheritors. The occasional whiff of vanished glory that came over has been made to serve the literary and political establishment. The interesting circumstance that both works deal with events and customs that must have appeared exotic, if not bizarre, to their authors, is not emphasized. The suggestion that the virtues of our Achaean or Germanic ancestors could have been held up to bardic ridicule is discouraged. And yet they obviously are. Agamemnon, as Robert Graves points out in the introduction to his recent translation, *The Anger of Achilles* (1959), is completely out of his depth throughout most of the *Iliad.*

What poet, after all, would wish to identify himself with a bloodthirsty, conceited and obstinate king, who is not successful even by his own standards, and eventually comes to a sticky end? And the career of King Gunther in the ***Nibelungenlied*** is no more exemplary. Like Agamemnon, he is killed in ignominious circumstances, by a woman. Admittedly she is only his sister. But his wife shows little respect for his kingly person either: she removes him from their conjugal bed on the first night, and hangs him on a convenient nail till morning. It seems that the whole concept of royal infallibility was at least questionable in the eyes of these two poets.

The ***Nibelungenlied*** goes further in this direction than Homer, and the efforts of its scholarly guardians not to notice the fact have been correspondingly stronger. Unfortunately, the increase in narrative detachment seems to have involved a deterioration in traditional clichés, so that the recitals of bloody deeds and barbaric splendours are even more perfunctory in the ***Nibelungenlied*** than in the *Iliad.* Stripped of its irony, the ***Nibelungenlied*** is tedious in the extreme, and can only be taken seriously by someone in desperate need of a heroic past. The blond Germanic beast marching bravely towards his fate is not to everyone's taste. Nor, for that matter, is the hidebound medieval court, obsessed with power and protocol. As long as these two elements were kept isolated, and regarded with bovine earnestness, the ***Nibelungenlied*** was guaranteed a cool reception by most people, and in most ages. It was offered, and rejected, as a work extolling two self-contradictory orthodoxies, neither of which is very interesting in itself. Luckily, however, orthodoxies are seldom sacred in literature and the ***Nibelungenlied*** is no exception to this rule. Positions are certainly taken up in the work, but they clash, sometimes comically, sometimes tragically, and very little is left of any of them at the end. The particular pretensions chosen for undermining were historically conditioned. Instead of Trafalgar, the sanctity of the home and the royal family, for instance, they had their heroic past, the sanctity of woman and an ideal of courtly behaviour. Instead of the hydrogen bomb, or sex, they had mythical figures like Sifrid and Brünnhilde on which to focus their hopes and fears.

Much work has been devoted to finding out something about the author, and the literary tradition in which he worked. . . . The yield is meagre: he was an unknown poet, probably of knightly (i.e. unexceptionable) status, writing at the turn of the twelfth and thirteenth centuries. He was probably Austrian, and may have worked for a certain Bishop of Passau. He must have known earlier versions of parts (perhaps the whole) of the material he was using, because variations on the same characters and situations are found scattered throughout Scandinavian and German literature. Any attempt to achieve greater precision on this score must be speculative. All the Scandinavian sources are later than the ***Nibelungenlied,*** although parts of them must be based on much earlier material. . . . In Germany there is the *Hildebrandslied* (written down at Fulda in the nineth century), which treats the story of Dietrich, Hildebrand and his son in archaic and highly idiosyncratic language. It is possible that the ***Nibelungenlied*** poet was familiar with a version of this poem, but if so he made no use of it. The Walther story referred to by Hildebrand in stanza 2344 is similarly unexploited, apart from this one mention.

The truth is there are no immediate sources; and those who need something to compare with the finished product have been reduced to reconstructing earlier versions for themselves. The process is circular, and the result unverifiable. . . . It seems reasonably certain that there were in existence a number of short episodic lays clustering round such figures as Sifrid, Brünnhilde, Dietrich, Hagen and Kriemhilde; and perhaps an extended narrative treating the downfall of the Burgundians. Nothing is established for these works beyond the bare probability of their existence.

The ultimate sources of the ***Nibelungenlied*** are much easier to discern. They are: legend (from a heroic past in the fourth to sixth centuries), chivalry (an orthodoxy from the twelfth and thirteenth centuries) and myth. The wars and great migrations following the advent of the Huns in eastern Europe threw up legendary heroes like Theoderic (Dietrich) of Verona, Hildebrand, Hagen and Gundaharius (Gunther), King of the Burgundians. Some of these men actually existed, as Theoderic, who ruled over Italy from 493 to 526, and Gundaharius, whose kingdom by the Rhine was in fact destroyed by the Huns (though not under Attila) in 435. Others, like Hildebrand, are just prototypes of the Germanic fighting hero. These figures carry their legendary past with them, and their social unit is the family or tribe, As might be expected from their origins, there is often something of the landless knight or exile about them, especially when heroic exploits are involved. But the details of their dress, speech, eating and courting habits, public rituals and, in the case of Rüdeger at least, of their moral preoccupations, are taken from medieval courtly society. These details constitute the second, or chivalric, element. The third, or mythological, element is embodied in figures like Sifrid, Brünnhilde and Alberich the dwarf, who stand out as belonging to no society at all, as being in some way subhuman or superhuman.

So much for the ingredients. The mixture seems to have gone down well, to judge from the number of manuscripts which have survived, and it is not difficult to see why. Past greatness, present pretensions and the possibility of rejuvenation (or destruction) from outside—this is a combination which must exercise a perpetual fascination for all self-conscious societies. It is true that an expansive community may believe for short periods that sophistication is an irreversible process; but recent history has shown how easily the most complex network of relationships can be reduced to primitive posturing, given the right circumstances. And this is exactly what happens in the ***Nibelungenlied,*** where a highly developed society reverts under strain.

We are shown, first of all, the court at Worms. It is presided over by the brothers Gunther, Gernot and Giselher, and actually run by Hagen. Everyone knows his place, and there are set procedures for every situation. They are, on the whole, a tedious and complacent company. Their sister Kriemhilde is outwardly an exemplary Burgundian lady, but she shows signs of being self-willed about her emotional life (stanza 17), and has an ominous future foretold for her (stanza 14).

The court at Santen is much the same. As at Worms, the homogeneity extends to the names Sigebert and Sigelinde, but their son Sifrid is even more of a misfit than Gunther's sister. Not only is his name wrong (just as Kriemhilde refuses to alliterate with her brothers), but he has a rather unorthodox past. As we later learn from Hagen, he is invulnerable, has slain a dragon and owns a magic treasure.

The court at Isenstein, by contrast, is dominated by a single remarkable woman, determined to rely on her own strength until the right man arrives. Her demands are quite simple: he must be the best (i.e. the strongest and bravest) man available. This is not perhaps so very different from the standard applied at Worms, where the king is by definition endowed with both these qualities. But the really anti-social thing about Brünnhilde is that she insists on putting royal pretensions to the test, and killing all the mighty monarchs who fail. She is a challenge to people like Gunther to justify their title. Of course Gunther himself is no fool, and would never dream of exposing himself to such a blast of reality; but the arrival of Sifrid opens up new possibilities. Here, suddenly, is a man who equates kingship with conquest (stanzas 108 ff.), just like Brünnhilde, and who is eminently capable of meeting the challenge. Moreover he wants to marry Gunther's sister, and is prepared to go to any lengths to do so. Presented with this happy circumstance, it is an easy matter for the practised diplomat to manipulate Sifrid into satisfying all Brünnhilde's demands incognito, leaving all the credit, and the tangible prize, to Gunther. There is the rather intimate question of the bed, but after that has been solved and hushed up the glory of Burgundy seems assured.

The thing which destroys the foundations, if not at first the complacency of Worms, is the tension between inflated appearance and mean reality. The qualities in Sifrid and Brünnhilde that eventually uncover this tension are precisely those which the Burgundians have tried to use for their own aggrandizement. Brünnhilde is too honest and uncompromising to accept the official version of Sifrid's status, and once again she insists on putting appearances to the test. The quarrel between the two queens and the ritual murder of Sifrid are the result. Sifrid's own crime is simply to behave in character. He is quite willing to let the Burgundians use his strength, but he makes no attempt to disguise his superiority. He is quite blandly indifferent to all the jealousies, rules and compromises which hold the society together. He is not interested in money (stanzas 558, 694-5), status (stanza 386), face-saving ceremony (stanzas 748-9) or political etiquette (stanzas 314-15). And, worst of all, he seems to have forgotten all about the sanctity of women as soon as he married Kriemhilde (stanzas 858, 894). Such innocence is in itself provocative. His one vulnerable spot is known only to Kriemhilde, and she, like a good Burgundian, betrays it to Hagen.

With Sifrid dead, and his treasure hastily dumped in the Rhine, it is left to Kriemhilde and Hagen to fight it out. In the process, the whole way of life at Burgundy is inexorably deflated and destroyed. The last magnificent tournament ends in a brutal killing; the elaborate political speeches are reduced to childish defiance; the subtly interlocking loyalties and prohibitions to blind tribal solidarity; the splendid feasting and drinking to the final macabre meal of blood, with corpses for benches. The mighty king is trussed up, and slaughtered by his sister. The crown of courtly womanhood is carved up by Dietrich's retainer.

Loyalty and good faith, made for security, are turned to destruction, so that allegiance to either side is the equivalent of a death sentence. Neutrality, on the other hand, is impossible, as even Dietrich discovers. He does, it is true, survive, but stripped of all the relationships which he and Hildebrand had built up round themselves (stanza 2319). Rüdeger, a much weaker and more dependent character, is pathetically caught in a dilemma of his own making. His hospitality and his readiness to oblige a lady, both excellent social qualities, have tied him equally to the Burgundians and to Kriemhilde. Obsessive generosity, designed to win lifelong friends, provides the instrument of his death. The bonds that once held society together now destroy it. At Etzel's court everyone is an exile. (pp. v-x)

D. G. Mowatt, in an introduction to The Nibelungenlied, *translated by D. G. Mowatt, Dent, 1962, pp. v-x.*

Dickerson on Hagen's significance:

[It] would not be farfetched to say that the disaster at Gran is Hagen's own creation. To be sure, there were many causes leading up to it; Siegfried's theft of the ring and the belt, Brunhild's jealousy of Kriemhild, Rüdeger's oath, Kriemhild's madness, to name the most important. But these are only isolated links in a long chain of events. It is Hagen who fuses these links together, thus bestowing upon the poem the unity and logic of its action; namely, the gradual and progressive destruction of an entire people.

Harold D. Dickerson, Jr., in Semasia: Beitrage zur Germanisch-Romanischen Sprachforschung *(1975).*

Werner A. Mueller (essay date 1962)

[*In the following excerpt, Mueller critiques the characters of the* Nibelungenlied, *arguing that, despite their heroic efforts, they are incapable of achieving tragic greatness.*]

The Nibelungen story fails to represent a dominant idea that can be clearly grasped. As a work of art embracing the reflections of infinity rather than of material limitations, although its subject matter is stark reality, the song defies a verbal statement as to its special message, a schoolbook explanation of its intent that can be catalogued as factual truth, yet in reality prevents the reader from experiencing its full, spiritual validity. The story takes the reader from the court of Worms to Xanten, Isenstein, through Austria and Hungary, covering scores of years characterized by actions and events that cause the death of countless men, the boldest and the noblest under drastic circumstances, while whole tribes are virtually annihilated. Although distant historical events have given substance to the story, passed on as legends or as myths, it is not history we read about. In the absence of the idea of a nation or a country as a moral force and romantically extolled, the work can also not be labeled a national epic, as Virgil's *Aeneid* constituted for the Romans, and as which it is occasionally proclaimed by modern patriots. Regardless of their nationality or their Teutonic heritage, the people of the song appeal to us chiefly as they are human beings of flesh and blood, of greatness and of folly, psychologically convincing both in their strength and in their failings. Now tasting earthly pleasures and delights, now suffering the opposites, they find themselves involved in struggle and intrigues concerning dubious precepts like honor and prestige, in the pursuit of which they reach grandeur as well as infamy. The greatness of their will and tragic end, their struggle for assertion of their personalities and for self-preservation in a world of human conflicts arising from within and from without, arouse a definite response in us who are beset by similar complexities. Kindness, refinement, lofty thoughts, developing to dubious ideologies or crushed by violence and primitive brutality, have left a greater stain upon our age than witnessed by the Nibelungen. Although the tragic story of their greatness and their failure is narrated with epic objectivity and as the literary theme *per se,* causing the reader to reflect as he is moved by its inherent truth, the search for tangible ideas imbedded in the song has occupied the critics up to our time.

Stirred by the collective doom of friend and foe, of guilty and of innocent, the author of the "*Klage*" was the first to add elaborate comments to the ***Nibelungenlied*** soon after it was circulated [Karl Bartsch, *Die Klage,* 1875]. Praising the faithfulness of Kriemhild, who revenged her murdered husband, the author cleanses her from any guilt of which the reader might accuse her, replying in particular to those who claim that she is suffering well deserved torments of hell. As Hagen is declared the villain who caused it all, "*der vâlant der ez allez riet*" (1250), Kriemhild is said to be in heaven, living in the love of God. The *Klage*-author is convinced that God's eternal order is upheld and that justice prevails in the end, according to his personal concepts of right and wrong, of guilt and punishment, and in accordance to his knowledge of God's will. This moralistic attitude of judging and ascribing guilt and innocence, contrasting Siegfried as the man of light with Hagen as a character of darkness, the former good, the latter evil, has found its followers up to our time. While Josef Weinheber reflects: "*Immer entsteht dem lichten / Siegfried ein Tronje im Nu . . . ,*" Wilhelm Dilthey speaks of the demonic quality of Hagen, symbolizing the powers of darkness that destroy the one who walks in the light [*Von Deutscher Dichtung und Musik,* 1933]. Also Gustav Ehrismann considers guilt and punishment leading ideas of the epic; experienced by the heroes as their fate, both categories are particularly applicable to Brunhild and to Kriemhild, each of whom contracts a guilt for which she finds her proper punishment [Ehrismann, *Geschichte der Deutschen Literatur bis zum Ausgang des Mittelalters, 2. Teil, Mittelhochdeutsche Literatur, Schulussband,* 1935]. As outcome of such thinking in terms of right and wrong, of black and white, and in accordance to the dubious quality of justice as proclaimed by man, Hagen is now condemned as a ruthless murderer by one, now extolled or considered expiated by another commentator; similarly, Kriemhild is declared guilty and a true *vâlandinne* or praised as revenger "immaculate" [Friedrich Ranke, *Deutsche Literaturgeschichete in Grundzügen,* 1946]. Werner Fechter even sees in Hagen both, the envious intriguer who sows evil and finds pleasure in destroying and the very tool of God, assassinating Siegfried, the truly guilty one [*Siegfrieds Schuld und das Weltbild des Nibelungenliedes,* 1948]. As Siegfried's guilt or innocence is likewise subject to controversial appraisals, Katharina Bollinger finds him implicated not merely by a moral and objective guilt as Fechter states, but also by a *"Seins-Schuld",* a kind of existential guilt [Bollinger, *Das Tragische im höfischen Epos,* 1939]. Andreas Heusler, on the other hand, speaks of Siegfried's "*Kindesunchuld,*" a naive and childlike innocence whose victim he becomes [*Germanistische Abhandlungen, Festschrift für Hermann Paul,* 1902], while Dietrich von Kralik considers him the innocent victim of Brunhild, who is the really guilty person of the song [*Das Nibelungenlied,* trans. Karl Simrock, 1954]. These contradictory interpretations of moral guilt in modern days present interesting parallels to man's confusion and dilemma not unlike those which are reflected in the work itself. In the absence of moral absolutes, however, and in consideration of man's ambiguous views on glory, honesty, or honor, on right and wrong, subject to personal evaluation at any age, this moralistic attitude of judging the heroes of our song fails to exert persuasive force and to do justice to the total implications of the work.

Some of the very critics who think in terms of light and dark, of glorious and inglorious deeds, of strong and weak, seem also influenced by patriotic or national concern, seeing in the song an idealization of their German ancestors. For some of them the faithfulness of Kriemhild, a Germanic heroine of exemplary traits, is the essential theme; others dwell upon the heroic attitude that is extolled in the song as its primary merit. The bold acceptance of a higher fate, now with defiance, now with enthusiasm; the unflinching resistance to unconquerable circumstances as man's greatest achievement; the blind obedience to the commands of loyalty and leadership; the readiness to die heroically in the pursuit and in the name of honor—all these are stressed as the leading ideas of the Germanic epic, which were particularly suited to endorse nationalistic ideologies in vogue when these interpretations were popular. These commentators do not write about the great futility of which the story tells; they praise the spirit of the men who rise above their fate by either bravely killing others or by dying in heroic battle without tears, and they presume man's greatness has been proved, his victory affirmed, a catharsis achieved.

Another group of modern interpreters is guided by psychological theories, enabling them to crystalize a variety of themes that seem embedded in the story. Thus Arnold H. Price declares the modern idea that man carries the seed of his destruction as psychological necessity within himself, the possible theme of the epic [Price, "Characterization in the Nibelungenlied," *Monatshefte* LI (December 1959)]. Without assuming that the poet himself was aware of such a theory, Price describes the brilliant insight of the author in respect to his characterizations. Thus the poet deliberately stresses Kriemhild's "violent streak" early in our epic when she voices her intent to stay beautiful and happy and never to suffer man's love. Kriemhild's very horror of marriage significantly exerts a special attraction to Siegfried, indicating a negative tendency in his nature, too. Eventually both are married and very much in love with each other, which "the author does not consider inconsistent with Kriemhild's previous dislike of marriage," as Price states. But due to the devious depth of Kriemhild's personality she subconsciously maneuvers her husband into an impossible situation when she announces that Brunhild has been his mistress; as further indication of the true violence and fierceness inherent in her character, Kriemhild makes Siegfried's death possible by revealing his vulnerable spot to his enemy. As Price concludes: "The author's attempt to provide the major figures of the epic with an entirely new characterization not only supplies a coherent and realistic motivation, but also the theme for the epic, i.e. that man carries the seed of his destruction in his character." Acceptance of the logic and the power of such psychic drives in man as a dominating force, taking the place of moral principles, as Price seems to imply, would reduce man to the world of instincts, appetites and hidden urges, precluding moral choice; this world is further complicated by man's ability to rationalize and to idealize his destructive drives to which he submits. Not unlike the vague idea of fate, this view fails to give due credit to man's spiritual potentialities, to his moral strength, to his sense of truth, and to his free will. As the creative process of man's artistic inspiration and expression has escaped scientific explanation, also man's spiritual experiences of God and of infinity as well as of himself as free-willed participant in the great stream of life, the basis for his moral consciousness, reflect far greater forces than psychological approaches can identify.

An outgrowth of this modern probing and explaining of human behavior are the speculative theories imposed upon the song that try to state some natural laws involved, upheld or violated, which are declared the causes for its tragic course. Thus Werner Fechter advances the thought that the *Nibelungenlied* describes the guilt of Siegfried who stepped out of his order when he, the *"Sonnenheros mit dem strahlenden Blick,"* failed to take Brunhild for his wife, *"die ihm Bestimmte, Gleichartige."* Failing to fulfill his superhuman possibilities, Siegfried was faithless to himself, that means to his own character, by marrying *"ein blosses Menschenweib,"* while he helped Gunther to wed with impudence a superhuman being to whom he had no claim. These violations are Siegfried's guilt; everything else develops in consequence of it, as Fechter concludes, and Siegfried's murder as well as the outcome of the struggle confirm the existence of a higher justice. Also Bert Nagel considers Siegfried and Brunhild predestined to be mates and sees in their failure to find the way to each other the cause for the ensuing catastrophe that makes the tragedy complete [Nagel, "Die Künstlerische Eigenleisturg des Nibelungendichters," *Wolfram Jahrbuch,* 1953]. The guilt, however, is less Siegfried's than Gunther's, with whose wooing the tragic complexities begin. The contradictions of Siegfried's and Brunhild's relationship constitute the important psychological background of the story, maintaining a constant condition of tension which is increased by the paradoxical state of life as found in the personality of Siegfried, *"des starken Schwachen,"* strong in his heroic qualities, yet weak in his desire for Kriemhild's love. Nagel calls the song a tragedy of guilt, ending with catharsis as symbolized by tears rather than by expressions of despair.

Next to this motive of Brunhild's love and jealousy of Siegfried, which mostly seems inferred by the critics from the existing or re-constructed, literary sources of the ***Nibelungenlied,*** but which appear neglected, if not entirely unused by the poet himself, the theme of power likewise has found a number of new supporters recently. Thus Siegfried Beyschlag analyzes the idea of a realistic struggle for power as the essential topic of the song ["Das Motiv der Macht bei Siegfrieds Tod," *German.-Roman. Monatsschrift* XXXIII (1952)]; since political realities are the foremost concern of the ruling kings, rating higher than personal relationships and loyalties, Siegfried's assassination is necessary due to the threat to the security of the court of Worms which he poses. As even Ruediger is guided by political necessities (!), Gunther and his brothers, too, must decide in favor of the regal power against their kin and friends. Also Kriemhild's revenge is conceived not merely as a retribution for the murder of her husband, but for the restoration of the power which Siegfried represented for her. As political considerations are the dominating forces effective in the story, as Beyschlag maintains, its tragedy is really Siegfried's murder since it constitutes a gross political blunder, whose consequences are pitilessly described. Also W. J. Schroeder sees in the struggle of the Nibelungen chiefly a fight for power that finds its logical conclusion in the murderous battle at the end [*Das Nibelungenlied,* 1954]. Declaring the possession of the treasure a symbol of power, which the Nibelungen had to take, as also Friedrich Neuman does, Schroeder characterizes Kriemhild's actions in the second part of the story as chiefly directed to regain the treasure. There is no antithesis of good and evil in the song, but merely of strength and weakness in the sense of Nietzsche. The law of nature that the best, i.e. the strongest, must be the first also prevails in human society. Worldly power not supported by strength must decline. Kriemhild and Gunther do not act from strength, but from fear of lacking power; thus they fight for mere survival and no longer strive to enlarge their power. Weakness, however, is guilt, and death is the price for weakness, for the hybrid claim of power, and for arrogance. Hagen realizes his master's weakness and tries to keep an outside appearance of Gunther's strength alive. The Nibelungen are driven by natural necessities as compelling as Homer's *αναγκη*; man's acceptance of nature's will as his fate constitutes his wisdom and heroic greatness.

Dated or absurd as some of these interpretations may seem today, they constitute a serious effort to verbalize the implications, the message, and the idea of this great work of art that exerts such stirring impact upon the reader. Although the moralistic, the patriotic, the psychological, and the philosophic-speculative approaches may illuminate some special aspects of the epic, they fail to realize its complex totality or to reflect its wider scope. Some analytical investigations of the text, however, stand out for sober observations which seem beyond dispute. After his life-long occupation with the ***Nibelungenlied,*** Friedrich Panzer comes to the conclusion that its deepest concern have never been events of our material world, but *"die geistigen-sittlichen Vorgänge im Innenleben des Menschen"* and his *"Bewährung in den Konflikten"*, man's spiritual and moral sense and his behavior in adversities, a statement which we like [Panzer, *Das Nibelungenlied,* 1955]. Friedrich Neumann sees in the story of the Nibelungen a conglomerate of literary sources as it is *"echtes Schicksal in eine . . . schwer deutbare Handlung des Leides hinüberentwickelt"* [Neuman, "Nibelungenlied und Klage," *Die Deutsche Literatur des Mittelalters,* 1940]; what once was accepted as genuine fate has changed for the poet of ***Der Nibelunge Not*** to experiences of suffering and sorrow which he, not in affinity with the Germanic concept of blind fate, found difficult to assimilate. *"Leid"* as the primary theme of the work is also stressed by Friedrich Maurer, who defines it as the very opposite of honor, namely as the consciousness of insults and dishonor suffered, as *"Beleidigung"* rather than grief, as which Neumann sees it [Maurer, *Lied,* 1951]. For Maurer *leid* and honor are the motivating forces in Kriemhild, Hagen, Ruediger, and Hildebrand. Kriemhild's revenge is not inspired by her faithfulness, but signifies her quest for restoration of her injured honor; Hagen is driven by concern about the honor of his masters, of Brunhild, of the Burgundian realm, and of himself. The treasure thus becomes the symbol of honor rather than of power; who has the treasure also has the honor. Although Maurer considers *"das furchtbare Leid, . . . das schicksalshaft über den Menschen in der Welt kommt,"* the essential subject of the song, it does not signify to him its deepest meaning, which, as he likewise realizes, has not been clearly formulated by the artist. The silence of the poet as to his intent can be interpreted in several ways, as Maurer believes: it can imply a silent condemnation of man's way who, without reference to God, yields to his human passions and to the ideas of honor and revenge; it also might suggest the poet's *"stumme Frage nach dem Sinn solchen Geschehens,"* the question of the meaning of the tragic events which he could not truly comprehend, as Neumann suggests, or to which he did not know the answer, as Maurer states.

What constitutes the essence of this elusive work that has no definite idea advanced to which its various critics could agree? What is its central topic with which the poet seems chiefly concerned? The song is not the story of Siegfried and of Brunhild, of Kriemhild and of Hagen, of Ruediger or Giselher, of Ihring, Wolfhart, Gunther, or Dietrich and of Etzel. They all take merely a part in it, they move and act, they are involved in a very complex interrelationship as they are poised partly against each other and partly with each other; all are eventually the victims of events which they themselves collectively were active to beget. Thousands of brave men additionally, good vassals all, share in the fortunes and misfortunes of the leading principals, while thousands more, bereft of husbands, kin and friends, stand mute around the scene, silent and unidentified. Greater than the sum of singular events, of tales of individuals, of groups, or relatives and foes, the epic of the Nibelungen relates man's greatest, universal theme, the story of himself; as it specifically depicts the Nibelungen's "Not," it stresses man in his dilemma, without the comfort of his pondering the precarious state in which he finds himself, soliciting our sympathy and leading us to contemplation in regard to ourselves.

Volker and Hagen in Etzel's court, in an illustration by Alois Kolb, 1925.

At the very beginning of the song a tragic chord is struck, alluring, ominous, of sad grandeur as it develops further on. Yet in dramatic contrast to its notes, foreboding woe and sadness, melodious happy chords abound, enthralling by their beauty. These lusty melodies reflect man's joy of life, as we have seen, his sensitivities and his refinement, his lofty spirit and his honorable bearing; the tragic chords remind us of man's basic vanity and weakness, of his dangerous potentialities that make him stumble in the end, destroying prematurely his happiness, his very joys, his earthly life. Without a special message, the epic gains its greatest actuality from its valid reflection of man's realities as the poet experienced them and passed them on to us in the symbolic story of the Nibelungen, symbolic for the ways of man, both for his strength and for his failures. Two obstacles that man encounters in his life determine his dilemma, his futility, and his tragic end: the one is the duality within himself, a part of his existence; the other is the paradox that he encounters chiefly as experience from without. With both he has to cope, yet both defy his reason and his command, preventing him from finding or maintaining completion, lasting harmony, and final peace. In everything he wills, he values, and pursues, there are the possibilities of either harming or advancing him, with parallel effects, sometimes reversed, upon his fellowmen. There is potential good and evil inherent in his values, in his convictions and emotions which he upholds with various strength at different times. Not any of these forces are ever fully realized or are pursued with singlemindedness, but each concept is colored by some other one and fused to a conglomerate of contradictory ingredients; each might now dominate, now yield, now be abandoned, now again prevail.

Even the Nibelungen's very joy of life, a basic and essential trait for a happy existence, embraces the potentials of happiness and failure. Characterized by noble, generous behavior, by loftiness of aims and fearlessness, it sometimes ends in disregard of ethics. It is the *hohe muot,* the joyous, spirited acceptance of life, so characteristic of the heroes of our story, which leads to carefreeness, to arrogance and recklessness, even to violence. The *"hohe muot"* (680) of Siegfried entices him to boisterous deeds such as the stripping of the ring from Brunhild's finger and as the taking of her belt as souvenir and an eventual gift to his own bride, actions that some consider a part of Siegfried's guilt, which means his doom. Kriemhild clearly realizes the danger for her spouse to be carried away by his " *'übermuot'* " (896, 3), which she describes to Hagen, this "charming carefreeness," as K. Bollinger calls it, which is so typical of Siegfried's disposition and of which he is the victim. Yet this high, excessive spirit can also collapse with equal speed as it arises. Setting out to Worms with unquestioned assurance of winning Kriemhild for his wife, exhibiting to Gunther and his men nothing but " *'starkez ubermüeten'* " (117, 4), as Ortwin correctly states, he succumbs to doubt and diffidence when he eventually meets the maiden of his choice. He is ready even to give up his heart's desire, to admit defeat, and to return to Xanten before Giselher persuades him to stay on. The decision to journey to Isenstein is another example of a high-spirited, courageous disposition that inspires the four men who partake in it. But soon this *hohe muot* leads to deception, which is morally not objectionable on the level of the fairy tale to which this episode belongs, but to which the keen participants agree in their *"übermüete"* (387, 2); in the spirit of great self-assurance they are unconcerned about the danger of the fraud to which they agree and are completely unaware of the tragic complications which it is to have for them. A similarly reckless disposition characterizes the Burgundians at their arrival at Etzel's court when none of them deigns it advisable to inform the guileless king of Kriemhild's threatening designs:

> *Swie grimme und wie starke si in vîent wære,*
> *het iemen gesaget Etzeln diu rehten mære,*
> *er het' wol understanden daz doch sît dâ geschach.*
> *durch ir vil starken übermuot ir deheiner ims verjach* (1865).

The following disaster might well have been stalled by Etzel if arrogance and pride would not have prevented the Nibelungen from speaking to the king, as the poet states. But Hagen's short and untrue answer: " *'uns hât niemen niht getân'* " (1863, 1), with which he brushes Etzel's worried question aside, sets the tone for all the Nibelungen. Since Kriemhild is present when Hagen lies to Etzel, stating that the Burgundians were accustomed to go around in arms during the first three days of any festivities, which the queen knows not to be true, this statement underscores his reckless spirit as it indicates his obvious unconcern about her hostile disposition, but at the same time conveys to her that the Nibelungen are ready to fight.

Perhaps this tendency of man to be carried from a wholesome disposition of joy and self-assurance to the extremes of pride and recklessness, of arrogance and violence, can be described as lack of self-restraint, i.e. a lack of *mâze* and self-discipline. The question then would be how far this lack is due to ignorance, to education, to unwillingness, or due to emotions, to folly, to beliefs, or even to ideals of strength and other precepts of behavior which man proclaims as values. The fact remains that man is just one step away from turning what seems sound and great to a provocative, ignoble thing, as the Nibelungen well exemplify. Volker stains the record of his courageous fighting spirit by deliberately killing his opponent in a tournament; in his eagerness to fight he also advocates disobedience to one's leader as he lures Wolfhart into battle against the strict orders of the latter's master:

> *Dô sprach der videlære: "der vorhte ist gar ze vil,*
> *swaz man im verbiutet, derz allez lâzen wil.*
> *daz kan ich niht geheizen rehten heldes muot"* (2268, 1-3).

Hagen approves of Volker's bold suggestion not to obey one's master in everything: *"diu rede dûhte Hagenen von sînem hergesellen guot"* (2268, 4). Wolfhart is ready to attack, heeding Volker's challenge, but he is held back by Hildebrand, who correctly calls his nephew's rashness a mad and foolish anger: " *'ich wæne du woldeste wüeten durch dînen tumben zorn'* " (2271, 3). Upon Volker's further taunts, however, the hot-headed, youthful Wolfhart leaps against the *videlære,* tearing the older Hildebrand and all the Amelungians into the wanton fight that was useless and unpremeditated and brought death to all, Hagen, Gunther and Hildebrand being the sole survivors.

The coexistence of kindness and brutality, of gentleness and violence in man is a further aspect of his duality. Even the kindest and most generous of all, the marcgrave Ruediger, can strike a fellowman to death merely because he casts suspicion on the other's integrity. Ruediger's deed is done in anger, aggravated by his inner disquietude, yet it is not followed by regret as if kindness had never touched his heart. Reversely, a most brutal man like Hagen can be filled with sudden kindness and extend his sympathy and lasting friendship to a man like Ruediger who comes to fight with him. None of the heroes of the song fails to reveal inherent kindness at some time and violence, if not outright brutality, at another time. Volker, whose gentler traits are echoed by his music, by his refined behavior at Bechelaren, and by his warmth of friendship with Hagen, does not only substitute his fiddler's bow, with which he lulls his wearied comrades to their last sleep, by a sword of violent intent and force, used in a noble fight; he also kills quite brutally an unnamed marcgrave who tries to aid a wounded comrade, still living on the pile of seven thousand dead, during a lull in the battle. Incidentally, it is at the advice of Giselher, a hero *"getriuwe unde guot"* (1099, 4) and *"sô rehte tugenlîch gemuot"* (2161, 4) that these dead and wounded are tossed from the landing of the stairs into the court before the hall.

As the poet narrates how his heroes now pray to God or ask for His advice, now fall victim to the devil's promptings, he reminds us drastically of another, perhaps most fundamental conflict in man's nature. It is the contrast of his knowledge and awareness of God, of man's possibility of pleasing Him and finding peace in his direction toward Him, and of his vain, if not devilish pursuits in life which are in disregard of God. The sorry end of Ruediger, a man bemoaned by all, appears of special sad significance not just because he is so generous and kind, the father of all virtues, but because he is a man, torn and impelled by inner contrasts, victim of his duality. Troubled by both, the inner voice of God and outside appeals in conflict with his conscience, he choses to heed the call of man and to fulfill what one expects of him. Thus he sacrifices a state of harmony with God, trying to preserve his state of worldly honor in the eyes of men.

The tragedy of Kriemhild likewise is her complete surrender of peace and grace in God while yielding to the forces of human passions and desires that lead to her devilish revenge. At the beginning of the song Kriemhild is pictured as a truly gentle woman, restrained, refined, modest in all her *"magtlîchen zühten"* (615, 1). Her beautiful renown, the beauty of her bearing, of her composure and appearance are corresponding to the beauty of her soul, a soul that knows itself in harmony with God. The happy years as Siegfried's wife have altered her but little; they have added more self-assurance to her personality, some worldliness and vanity. The sudden death of Siegfried brings forth passionate grief as well as furious thoughts in her, intensified perhaps by the awareness that she herself has been a factor in the betrayal of her husband, though unsuspecting and unknowing. After four days of frantic grief she enters an existence of seclusion in complete retreat from the realities of life; she takes her lonely residence next to the church where she can pray to God to have mercy on Siegfried's soul, whose grave she visits daily; *"si alle zît dar gie"* (1103, 2). She has abandoned the common joys of life, even the vanities of special dress, as she has lost all interest in further happiness on earth. But her life of mourning, praying, and remembering in seclusion does not prevail for many years; eventually the world intrudes both from without and from within. She is urged and persuaded to agree to a reconciliation with her brother, the ruling king and secret partner in her husband's murder. Then she is forced to a decision in regard to her wealth, once Siegfried's gold, of which she has been totally oblivious ever since his death more than three years ago. The treasure is taken from the custody of Alberich and brought to Worms, where Kriemhild now begins to use it freely, making new friends by means of it. Hagen, however, soon insists that it is taken away from her in hostile violation of her rights, which not only renews old wounds but also adds to her awareness of the dishonor and the wrongs that she has suffered for so long without any defense. After a further period of sadness and of passive mourning, extending over many years, a second marriage is proposed to her which she is urged by friends and kin to accept although it is entirely against the inclinations of her heart. The promise of new happiness has no appeal to her. Had she not known that love must end in grief and happiness in sorrow? Did she not taste the greatest happiness that can be found as long as she was Siegfried's wife? Now the grief is hers which once she had foreseen would follow married happiness. Also the possibilities of new prestige and wealth have lost their lure for her. The consciousness, however, of being the victim of brutal violence and fraud, of hateful and dishonoring actions, and the latent wish to right and revenge the wrongs which she and Siegfried had to suffer from Hagen's hand especially, have never been entirely extinguished in her troubled mind since that very moment when she first called to God in her despair, asking that He might assist her friends in punishing the murderers of her husband. Thus she agrees to a new marriage merely as it renews the latent hope for possible revenge, a thought that gradually increases to such compelling urge that her entire personality seems totally reversed as it is saturated by that single wish; the mourning, passive widow leaves her solitude of praying to grow into a scheming woman, dishonest, heartless, cruel, eventually a *vâlandinne.* This latter term suggests no longer a human, God-inspired person, but a fiendish subject of the devil, devoid of love and pity, a creature without a soul, a mockery of God. No greater contrast in one person seems imaginable, dramatically revealing his dual nature and conflicting potentialities, than Kriemhild represents. First the gentle maiden, modest, refined, withdrawn, watching Siegfried from a distance and keeping her love virtuously in her heart; eventually a blushing, tender bride and a devoted wife; later a lonely widow, a recluse in her residence, going to church devoutly to pray for Siegfried's soul, scorning all joys of life. Then Kriemhild, the revenger, kneeling before one of her vassals or pleading for assistance in spite of stern rebukes from those who are obliged to serve her; offering vessels filled with gold to buy and bribe her men for treachery, for murder and for arson; and finally wielding a sword against her hated enemy, defenseless yet relentless as he is, beheading him with her own hands. Kriemhild, the leading person of the song, emerges as the greatest example of man's conflicting potentialities; of either seeking and preserving a state of peace in God, of which man can experience an acute awareness as part of his existence at moments of grace and quiet surrender; or of upholding concepts of vain and dubious substance without contact with God, in the pursuit of which he yields to his anxieties and easily neglects his soul. While Ruediger is briefly conscious of his contrary directions and his predicament in consequence of man's duality, at least for one enlightened moment, Kriemhild fails to realize the tragic contrasts of her being as she slowly descends to be the tool of crude emotions and ambitions that prompt her vile designs, the victim of her dual nature.

Even to Kriemhild's great opponent, wanton and ruthless

Hagen, a final state of harmony with God has been attributed. Bodo Mergell [in "Nibelungenlied und höfischer Roman," *Euphorion* 45 (1950)] . . . declares him acting in regard to Ruediger in God's behalf, thus rising from the level of trachery and guilt to fulfillment *"im Angesicht Gottes,"* in a pronounced contrast to Kriemhild's path that ends in darkness and despair. Although this interpretation of Hagen's kindness toward Ruediger goes too far when it suggests redemption in the eyes of God, the sudden rise of true humanity even in a man like him can serve as a further example of man's contrasting inclinations in terms of his direction, toward his spiritual potentialities or toward the appeals of his earthly existence, worsened by atavistic instincts. In Hagen's case, however, the latter influences clearly predominate, exemplified particularly by his un-Christian, unforgiving, and provoking actions toward Kriemhild, for whose sufferings he showed not only complete disconcern, but true delight up to the last. Where man seems determined in his actions by one of his divers potentials, he does not necessarily accomplish the extremes. When Ruediger turns deaf to the appeal of God, he does not change into a devilish person; or when Hagen shows kindness instead of grim intent, he still does not attain the status of a pious man. Only the central figure of the song, Kriemhild, embraces the extremes most drastically, winning our affection as child of God, gaining our sympathy in her distress and conflict of emotions, arousing pity and compassion as she descends, distorted in her fall, bereft of any soul, as she appears.

One might add to the list of man's conflicting possibilities his potentials of love and hate as were described above, or of reason and emotion as they appear in conflict with each other. There are also contrasting wishes and beliefs, upheld with various strength at different times, and there are ideologies and values which now appear important, now of no consequence, now even fully contradictory. By whatever terms man's double and unsteady nature is characterized, the Nibelungen dramatically exemplify how man is harboring the opposites within his dual nature, how he is oscillating between his potentialities, how he is likely to succumb, to stumble, and even to destroy himself.

Though mostly unaware of their duality, the Nibelungen experience the paradox as a reality which they clearly perceive, accepting it as part of their existence, dumbfounded, yet without reflection or demur. When man in his contrasting drives has concentrated his intent upon a certain aim which he pursues, he frequently accomplishes the very opposite of what he planned. Kriemhild merely hastens Siegfried's death while she is anxious to protect him, giving away the secret of his vulnerable spot and even marking it for the betrayer whose help she anxiously solicits. Ruediger's oath to Kriemhild, rendered without suspicion of any future complications, obliges him eventually to partake in an ignoble deed that is in conflict with his conscience and utterly contrary to the spirit with which the oath was offered. His welcome guests and friends whom Ruediger accompanies as loyal guide to days of joy as he believes, he really leads into a trap to grief and death; he even is compelled to help in their destruction. While Giselher avoids an open clash with Ruediger, whose enemy he paradoxically has become, Gernot accepts the grim reality and slays the marcgrave without further hesitation, using the very sword that Ruediger had given him as a token of good will. The sword that Gernot lifts for honor's sake against the man who merely fights to save his honor; the sword that once belonged to Ruediger's own son; the gift of which the widow of the giver had heartily approved while he was still alive; and most dramatically, the gift that kills the giver—all these round up the paradoxes that mark the final moments of troubled Ruediger. Staying away from the hostilities that turned the planned festivities of Etzel into an ugly farce, he might have pondered his own eagerness with which he once persuaded Kriemhild to accept his master's hand; what he had hoped would bring new happiness to both, also enhancing Etzel's glory, has turned to grief and shame, disgracing the reputation of his noble king.

Also Hagen's endeavors to perpetuate the power and the honor of his masters beget the very opposite of what he intends, involving his king in great dishonesty that causes Gunther's death and the annihilation of his brothers and his loyal subjects. The treasure of Siegfried, too, brought to Worms upon Hagen's initiative, is of no advantage to the Burgundians but merely detrimental. When Kriemhild gains new friends by means of this gold, it is sunk into the Rhine where nobody benefits from it. This stealing of the treasure, however, arouses new resentment in Kriemhild and strengthens her hate and her desire for eventual revenge, whose victims all the Nibelungen eventually become. But Kriemhild, too, accomplishes merely the opposite of what she desperately wants; she neither stills her grief, nor does she restore her honor or prestige by her disgraceful plots, but she only increases her dishonor, her humiliation, and her frustration on earth which are at their highest when she finally kills Hagen who still can sneer at her. Unable even to enjoy the briefest momentary satisfaction, her grief and hate slightly relieved by her impetuous act of killing the cause of all her turmoil, she herself becomes the screaming victim of Hildebrand's violent blows with which he slays her instantly. The fact that Kriemhild is killed by one of her own subjects while her husband king stands idly by, presents perhaps another paradox, unless one is inclined to judge Hildebrand's spontaneous deed an act of mercy rather than of angry retribution, of which he himself, however, is scarcely aware.

While most of these reversals defy man's purpose from without, resulting from realities beyond the individual's perception or control, man also must experience the paradox within himself. Thus Kriemhild's final hate engulfs her favorite brother for whom she longs and whom she loves, making her pitiless to his requests for mercy and causing his death. Also Gunther betrays his sister against his emotional inclinations and brotherly affections when he allows the stealing of the gold; " '*si ist diu swester mîn*' " (1131, 3), he weakly argues before he agrees to Hagen's plan. Etzel, too, must have encountered a painful change of heart when he condoned the slaying of his wife whose wishes and desires he called his greatest joy only shortly ago. Hagen's faithfulness to Brunhild and to his masters' court makes him faithless to Kriemhild and to Siegfried regardless of his previous feelings toward them and in spite of the fact that the one is his master's sister, the other his master's best and most faithful friend. Gernot feels compelled to challenge Ruediger, seeing him slay so many of the Nibelungen: " *'daz müet mich âne mâze: ich'n kans niht an gesehen mêr'* " (2216, 4), killing his friend and former host as he is killed in turn by him.

The poem underscores the paradox which man encounters in his will and actions as it dramatically describes the vicissitudes that grace or cloud his daily life. These are the alternating happy chords accompanying his realities, as Volker's gentle melodies insert an element of beauty and of peace into the grimness of the hour; his weary comrades put their premonitions aside and go to sleep although danger is imminent. The luxury with which the visitors are housed, their beds covered with foreign silk and fur as rarely have been offered to kings before, is contradictory to both the melancholy mood that haunts the weary guests, and the hostess' devious designs to have them murdered in their sleep. Siegfried rides through the woods in his most carefree mood, the lustiest of the hunters, a radiant child of nature and a very prince of men, shortly before he is mortally pierced, the greatest quarry of the hunt. The peaceful place where he is slain, the forest with its mysteries, the spring that gives cool water, the grass, the tender flowers now stained by his warm blood, all these present a gripping contrast to the act of murder, a foul, ignoble deed pursued with ruthlessness. The imminence and power of the paradox, shaping the Nibelungen's realities and defying their intent, are thus persuasively intensified as feast and *hôchgezît* are carefully described as background to the struggles that ensue, and as man's hopes and pleasures are vividly narrated before disaster strikes.

Oblivious or aware of those threatening reversals that foil their will, the Nibelungen accept the resulting reality as part of their existence that cannot be disputed or averted. There are almost no accusations or complaints against a higher power, nor are there any elevating thoughts expressed, praising divine authority when man has been frustrated or dies forlorn. While to the modern reader the adversities encountered present inducement to religious speculations in regard to providence or justice, the Nibelungen fail to engage in such reflections of their realities. Dietrich and Ruediger alone appear spiritually disturbed as they briefly ponder their conflicting situations. They feel forsaken by God rather than victims of reality as they experience their dilemmas; they sadly realize their paradoxical position that they engage in doing what is against their moral conscience, fighting against their friends, upholding worldly concepts that are in contrast to the promptings of their Christian souls. Dietrich enters the fight against the last surviving Nibelungen, with whom he sympathizes, in conflict with his inclinations and his spiritual convictions, adhering to the manners that are expected from a warrior of his reputation, not unlike Ruediger who threw himself into the final battle against his very friends, both of them vaguely haunted by a sense of moral despair.

Endowed with the potentials of opposites, foiled in their efforts by the paradox, the Nibelungen fail to achieve a victory that is commensurate with their struggle and their will. Now in compliance with their moral values and traditions, vague and conflicting as they often are, now following expediency or simply driven by emotions, they rarely satisfy more than one momentary urge by their spontaneous decisions in their reactions to reality. Neglecting their spiritual potentialities, they also fail to reach a state of inner peace and harmony that could endure or carry them above adversities. Their aims and values are ambiguous, confused, and contradictory as they initiate aggressive actions or engage in violent hostilities; their course becomes erratic and their intent subject to frequent change as they experience the paradox which distorts their will. Eventually they die as victims of their earthly values and realities not less than of themselves, suffering total defeat.

Being without a reconciliatory turn, the story ends in sadness and in failure as its last major characters are slain. Thousands have lost their lives before, dying in consequence of various aspects of their ethics, their emotions, and their will. Fighters of great renown, Gunther and Hagen do not lose their lives in wild and lusty battle, but are infamously beheaded as prisoners; they are not victims merely of Kriemhild's hatred and frustration, but also of their own convictions, errors, and anxieties; beginning with the murder of Siegfried, for which they were unwilling to make amends or show regret, they pursue a course of action detrimental to themselves. Having initiated the inglorious death of Gunther, first by involving him in Siegfried's death, then by referring to the oath of silence as long as his last king was still alive, Hagen dies as an utter failure. When all his kings are dead and nothing is left for which he still might fight, he dies with unforgiving hatred of his greatest enemy, clinging in proud defiance to the spectre of heroic poise while unconvincingly evoking God:

> *"Nu ist von Burgonden der edel künec tôt,*
> *Gîselher der junge, und ouch her Gêrnôt.*
> *den schaz den weiz nu niemen wan got unde mîn:*
> *der sol dich, vâlandinne, immer wol verholn sîn"* (2371).

Kriemhild's *leid* unstilled and her revenge short of its goal, unless atonement for the death of Siegfried was her chief aim and moral purpose, she herself is slain partly in consequence of honor which she has violated by her last, desperate deed, partly in revenge of Hagen, who was " *'der aller beste degen, / der ie kom ze sturme oder ie schilt getruoc'* " (2374, 2-3), as Etzel says of him. Bemoaning the fact that such a hero had to die from the hand of a woman, and regardless of the mockery, contempt and violence which he suffered from him, the king allows his own wife to be miserably slain by the impetuous old Hildebrand. As all the active members of the strife lie dead, the house of the Burgundians virtually destroyed, no victory gained by anyone, Dietrich and Etzel weep in mourning for the thousands who have died. Countless others far and near join in their tears as sadness spreads. Thus ends the song, the final chapter of the Nibelungen, without offering consoling thoughts, without affirming justice, mercy, grace, a gripping story of man's ways.

As joy has given way to sorrow and only tears remain, as all in which man gloried has found a gloomy end, the reader is aware of man's forlorn and tragic state. The Nibelungen, however, do not consider themselves partakers in a tragedy. Stunned by Siegfried's death as Kriemhild is, steeped in moral conflict or God-forsaken, as Ruediger and Dietrich briefly feel, the Nibelungen experience only a temporary consciousness of tragic circumstances that mark their lives; they neither reflect upon the nature or significance of these, nor do they share a tragic view of life as such. Thus in the absence of pronounced spiritual doubt, of moral qualms, or of a lingering sense of failure, they do not gain the stature of tragic characters, regardless of the greatness of their struggle and of their final fall. (pp. 59-75)

Werner A. Mueller, in his The Nibelungenlied Today: Its Substance, Essence, and Significance, *The University of North Carolina Press, 1962, 97 p.*

Frank G. Ryder (essay date 1962)

[Ryder is an American scholar of Germanic languages, an editor, and a translator. In the following excerpt from the introduction to his translation of the Nibelungenlied, *Ryder studies the major themes, characters, and ideology of the poem to demonstrate its overall unity.]*

Around the year 1200 an unknown Middle High German poet, probably an Austrian knight-cleric, composed an epic poem which ranks as the most impressive single work of medieval German literature and stands in the small company of great national epics, with the *Iliad,* the *Aeneid,* the *Roland,* and the *Cid.* In mastery of poetic form and in certain aspects of structure the author was no rival for Homer or Vergil. His parity with his French and Spanish counterparts may even be debated. In every other way—in the pure art of story, in the creation of epic figures, in vigor and directness of characterization, in monumental scope and power—his work can bear comparison with any of the great epics. Like them, it is a true work of world literature, faithful to its time but not bound by it, comprehensible and of significance to an audience centuries removed. (p. 1)

In the largest view the work is bipartite. Two great complexes of epic action are joined together: in the first part the life and death of Sigfrid, his glory, fault, and betrayal; in the second the massive destruction of those who betrayed him, engineered by Kriemhild his wife and in the end engulfing her.

The great human emotion which dominates the entire action is the drive for retribution—"overweening pride . . . and awful vengeance" (strophe 1003). The mood is that of fated tragedy, but the pathos of inevitable loss is countered by the valor, excellence, and "loyal commitment" (*triuwe*) of chivalry. The theme, struck so often in the lines of the poem, is the inexorable connection of *liebe* and *leide,* of happiness, that is, and what it must end in: suffering and grief: *als ie diu liebe leide z'aller jungeste gît* (strophe 2378)—the almost literal counterpart of Chaucer's *For evere the latter ende of joye is wo.* (pp. 1-2)

THE UNITY OF THE POEM

Since, in the most common view, the two stories which serve as the principal bases for Part I and Part II come from two different traditions of the Germanic epic, and since, approximated in their "original" form they would offer one major and several minor points of contradiction, it has long been the fashion to emphasize the points of internal inconsistency in the ***Nibelungenlied*** and to dwell at length on the separateness of its sections. This has been doubly true because of the tendency, only recently being reversed, to regard the genesis of the poem as rather more interesting and worthy of critical study than its finished state.

If we look at the ***Nibelungenlied*** as a complete work we certainly find it to be bipartite, but we also find that elements of repetition, explicit harmony, and correspondence are a major feature of the structural design of the poem. It is written, as it were, in two books or parts, but this is accepted and by and large turned to artistic advantage, not fumbled with or glossed over. The roster of evidence is extensive, and it ranges from structural features to details of seemingly coincidental mirroring. We can only allude to them here.

On the broadest thematic level, of course, we have already noted that vengeance is at the heart of both I and II. In each part there is also vengeance from a lady-liege wronged (Brunhild in I, Kriemhild in II), and in each part Hagen is, for the lady-liege in I, for the victims of the lady in II, the towering agent of revenge.

The complex of consultation, courtship, and marriage occupies a patently important position in both parts of the poem. Structurally—quite aside from *Kulturgeschichte*—the two aspects of the complex are closely related. The initial impulse for the bringing together of the two geographically removed participants is in each part a scene of "marriage counseling"—Sigfrid and his parents discussing the courting of Kriemhild, Attila being advised to marry the widow of Sigfrid. (With the quadripartite diagram of I, the theme is repeated in Gunther's plan to seek the hand of Brunhild—and the debate which follows. In II there is a similar subplot of different structure in Giselher's betrothal to Ruedeger's daughter.) In each of the major instances and one of the subthemes, the journey of courtship caps the initial impulse of the action, completing the conjunction of the two great forces involved. In I, Sigfrid goes to Burgundy himself—and the whole process is more extended and encrusted with "atmosphere." In II, Ruedeger comes to court Kriemhild in Attila's stead. Remember however that the "John Alden" motif is present prominently though in a singular way in I also. Sigfrid performs an indispensable part in the wooing of Brunhild!

Of extreme importance in the development of both plots and of parallel ironic effect on a grand scale—the proper forms of courtly life in distorted service of base intent—is the motif of the dissembling invitation. The degree of intensity differs but the centrality is undeniable. The renewal of the tragic action in I hinges on the invitation of the Nibelungs to Worms by the affronted and suspicious Brunhild who maneuvers her vacillating husband into doing what is chivalrically right but pragmatically disastrous. The downfall of the Burgundians is engineered out of their invitation to Attila's court, secured by the disingenuous Kriemhild in the delusion of her courteous husband. Gunther also repeats his pattern of taking the wrong step for the right reasons.

We have already alluded to the importance of another motif; initiative seized by a vassal precipitates involvement, reluctant or otherwise, of master and man alike (Hagen and the treasure, Hagen and Folker starting the fight in the hall, Wolfhart drawing Hildebrand into the battle against the Burgundians, the latter both in II).

Among the many lesser parallels which serve to bind the two parts together are: the importance of omens (dreams and mermaids); the identification of strangers by Hagen (Sigfrid in I, Ruedeger in II); Hagen's awful gifts of death to Kriemhild (the corpse of her husband, the head of her son), the tears of an injured liege-lady as incitement to action (Brunhild's before Hagen, Kriemhild's before the Huns); the manifestation of highest nobility just before death (Sigfrid and Ruedeger).

Certain correspondences are doubtless of less significance because they stem from the paraphernalia of the court poet (e.g., the pressing of the white hand of the beloved) or the inevitable etiquette of the courts (the surrender of armor, acceded to in I at Brunhild's, refused in II at Attila's court).

The cohesive impact of all such motifs is only strengthened by the similar use *within* one part or the other of equally striking parallels. One has already been noted. The device thus becomes a central unifying aspect of the poem. To mention only one more: The two instances, ironic in their contrast, of Kriemhild entrusting a loved-one to the care of another knight, her brother Gunther to Sigfrid in Adventure 6, Sigfrid to Hagen in 15.

True, if Homer nods, this poet occasionally falls asleep. Dankwart's protestation of innocence in the whole business of the plot against Sigfrid—"I was merely / A youth . . . when Sigfrid lost his life" (1924)—is either duplicity in dire straits, which is highly unlikely and out of character, or evidence of the writer's forgetfulness. Those who emphasize sources see it as an oversight in combining two epic traditions or models. There are other inconsistencies which should not, granted, elude the critic but which should also not be blown up beyond their due. By no means all the contradictions and structural flaws represent defective bridges between Parts I and II. Does Kriemhild know who killed her husband or not? (1008, 1010, 1012, 1024, 1033; also 1093 after 1046!) Whatever became of Brunhild?

In sympathetic defense of Homeric lapses it was long ago pointed out that Vergil seems to forget from one part of his poem to the other just what wood the Trojan horse was made of, and that Cervantes in the space of a few pages has Sancho riding on a donkey he had just lost. And these oversights are not urged as demonstration that *Don Quixote* was written by two or more hands or that the *Aeneid* is an obvious composite.

CHARACTERS

The rare power of the ***Nibelungenlied*** stems not only from the relentless sweep of its action, but also—perhaps more—from its extraordinary *dramatis personae.* In range and in intense individuality they entirely transcend the courtly epic in the narrower sense (Hartmann von Aue, Heinrich von Veldeke) and are fully the equals of Wolfram's Parzival and Gottfried's Tristan and Isolde. They are, I think, far superior as characters in literature and in "life" to Roland and Olivier. The poet exhibits his mastery and range of portrayal, his transcending of stereotype (a disease endemic to medieval literature) in two principal ways. He does it in the creation of individual characters of fascinating variety and complexity, like Kriemhild, Gunther, and Hagen, and he does it in his displaying of that ideal figure to which any great narrative artist of this time must inevitably turn: the perfect knight. The recent and laudable trend toward more internal criticism of the ***Nibelungenlied*** has led to a wise emphasis upon the courtly background of the poem and the identification of Sigfrid as an exemplar of knighthood. It is important to realize however that by the explicit testimony of the poet there are two perfect knights in this poem (along with many who receive *de rigueur* praise, and Hagen whose final encomium is from Attila: "The finest thane / Who ever carried shield or went to war"; (2374). Sigfrid receives superlative praise in life. His death is an apotheosis. Yet it can hardly be denied that the ultimate tribute is rendered to Ruedeger, by those he fought against as well as by his other friends—Ruedeger had no foes except in battle. Fierce Hagen praises only Ruedeger in all the poem: "There'll never be one like you anywhere. . . . May the good Lord grant your virtues live forever" (2199). Every other person who speaks of him speaks in similar terms. The poet has his own summation: "The model of chivalry" (2202).

How different are these men, and how different the ideals they represent. The pattern of values by which medieval courtly life was ultimately guided and illuminated, during the brief span of its flourishing, is a strangely monolithic structure, a vertical scale of merit and prerogatives. By virtue of birth and accomplishment every man had his place on it. The value words of Middle High German are like points on this scale, unlike their modern cognates which imply moral judgments. Thus *êre* (modern *Ehre* "honor") was a complex of ideas in which "superiority" and "excellence" were the central notions, with a peripheral area of what we should perhaps call "honors," the tribute one got for high position and merit. (The difficulties for the translator are apparent.) The historical and sociological genesis of this value system, in the age of the Crusades, is well and succinctly described in one of the few recent treatments in English of the German aspect of this pattern, Martin Joos and F. R. Whitesell's *Middle High German Courtly Reader* (1951), an excellent general introduction to the narrative literature of the period.

Recent revaluation of the ***Nibelungenlied*** has, as we have noted, led to closer identification of the poem with the courtly tradition, and perhaps inevitably to the consideration of Sigfrid and other figures as typically courtly personages. This involves a certain reaction against the earlier dichotomy of courtly epic and heroic or popular epic. In the terms of the latter, the ***Nibelungenlied*** and its actors are on the old Germanic level of warrior ethics where valor and strength are utterly paramount, fierce loyalty in combat is the prime virtue, pride and good name transcend even the bond between father and son, strife is normal and an early death virtually guaranteed, where women function largely as a source of feuding and men carry on their shoulders a chip of mythic proportions.

Germanic heroism, being part of its ancestry, is not incompatible with the chivalric ideal. Both can serve as references in our examination of the figures of Sigfrid and Ruedeger. But Sigfrid and Ruedeger do not exist as abstractions, and further, the greater a work of literature, the more its characters are apt to resist classification by cultural and historical clichés. Our recourse is to the text.

It is amply clear that Sigfrid *is* set up as a chivalric paragon, and his personality and his actions accord reasonably well with the courtly pattern. He is brave, strong, handsome (in that order of frequency in adjectival modifiers, by the way). His "courtesy" is a source of praise, and he is represented as a master in paying court to noble ladies. His initial gentleness and modesty vis-à-vis Kriemhild are noteworthy. Equally essential: In his proud assumption of the rights accruing to sheer strength and prowess, in his acknowledged surpassing of other men in all arts of war, actual or feigned, indeed in all his conscious and unconscious hauteur he is a medieval knight on the grand scale. He acts unthinkingly, and this is right because it proceeds from both inborn and cultivated excellence. All this is true and valid, but not exclusively so. Germanic heroes were brave and strong, and they were certainly full of pride. If they reflected about anything it was about fate. There are also limits to the courtly interpretation itself.

Comparison of Sigfrid with any good Arthurian hero in Chrétien or Hartmann will show that there is in Sigfrid a strong element of the fated Germanic hero, perhaps even of the doomed demigod (here largely humanized). He is also a character from the world of Achilles, with whom he shares not only valor and strength and magic invulnerability, but also headstrong will, pride, lack of foresight, stubbornness, and childlike naïveté. (Unlike Achilles he does not *choose* glory and a short life over a long undistinguished one—nor of course does he sulk.) In these terms his death is the inevitable working of that same law which in the *Iliad* determines the finite limit of human greatness—a sort of positive correlation between transcending excellence and early tragedy.

The one-line standard of chivalric merit is not entirely valid in its own terms. The handiest fault of a true courtly hero is temporary failure to live up to the code, or some misapprehension of what the code is, a tendency for example to take things too easily and not go out on the required adventures (Hartmann's Erec). Sigfrid certainly does all the required things, yet he gets into definitive trouble. It is clear that his initial fault is not a failure to live up to the monolithic standard. Rather it is to some degree a flaw of a sort that is familiar in the traditional analysis of tragedy from Aristotle on. His overbearing self-confidence is recognized and stated by his own wife when she unwittingly reveals his secret vulnerability to his foe Hagen: "I should never fear . . . Had he not this rash and headstrong will" (896). It is the same characteristic that worries his parents when he announces he will conquer what he wants with his own hands. This trait leads him to his original and seminal misstep, his agreement to do Gunther's courting for him—with the chain of misfortunes to which that casual agreement led. His proud confidence—a right and natural thing for the true courtly hero—starts him on the road to his downfall.

It is only fair to say that this character trait is activated, so to speak, by a clear and overriding purpose: "Not so much for love of you I take / This step, as for your lovely sister's sake, . . . that she should be my wife" (388).

Similarly, it is his very sense of propriety and courtesy which, in the decision to go on the hunt and in his waiting to drink at the spring, guarantees the success of the base plot against him. The picture is obviously a subtle and perhaps in part an ambiguous one. On the one hand he is a paragon of merit, and his death is at the hands of evil men. There are many passages which make this explicit. On the other hand his downfall is in some degree "his own fault" and thus not the reduction of a wholly good man to utter misfortune which Aristotle warned us is not right for tragedy. A certain tension between these two views of Sigfrid cannot, in my opinion, be erased from the lines of the ***Nibelungenlied.*** It is right to say that his very heroic excellence leads to his downfall but not to deny absolutely the presence of guilt. . . . It is not right to call him entirely a courtly hero or entirely a fated Germanic warrior, nor even a sum of these and no more. He is rather a character of independent psychological interest and some complexity, viewed by a writer with reliable insight and a mixed ethical viewpoint.

There is another kind of tension in the poet's view of all this, and it lifts him well above the "Arthurians." For him the world and life are not totally subsumed under the courtly ethos. That ethos and the world can be in mortal conflict. The way of the Arthurian knight is beset by magicians and dragons, Sigfrid's by human beings and human destiny.

A further indication that the author of the ***Nibelungenlied*** did not subscribe entirely to nor create his figures in the light of the chivalric code lies in the figure of Ruedeger. Critics and readers have viewed Ruedeger in a variety of lights but to all of them he remains one of the magnificent figures of the medieval epic—of the whole breadth of epic narration—not simply for his moving nobility, but for the artistic perfection with which his role is created and executed. He is the "best" character in the poem—his standing adjective is *guot* "good, noble, excellent, kind"—and his suffering is, among all the woes of this somber tale, the most acute, the most inevitable, and the least deserved.

The central variance at which critics find themselves concerns the nature of the decision forced on Ruedeger during the battle at the court of the Huns. G. F. Jones, in "Rüdiger's Dilemma" (*Studies in Philology,* LVII, No. I [1960]) makes eminently clear the danger of interpreting his dilemma in terms of modern equivalents of old value words. We have already seen that *êre,* which is explicitly at issue in Ruedeger's mind, is not the moral term which it has become in modern *Ehre,* that it means "honors," "honored fame" (and is so translated here), that is, what Falstaff and Norfolk mean by "honor." Jones feels that Ruedeger has, essentially, his good name at stake, not any inner moral principle (a post-Kantian notion) that he "decides in favor of his worldly reputation," identifying "God" at most with his obligation of safe-conduct, though even here his good name was at stake as well. He therefore is disposed to question any reading based on "grave spiritual conflict" (Panzer, de Boor) or "conflict of two duties" (Ehrismann). In Jones' own words Ruedeger is "other-directed," and his dilemma (not conflict) is not a precisely even balance of equally compelling obligations. (Jones does agree that "Rüdiger's abstract words already had strong moral overtones" but he feels they must be kept in their Germanic context.)

I prefer the essentially different, more internally oriented interpretation. The reader must decide for himself how he feels, always remembering to accord full weight to the historical considerations which buttress the opposite stand. The modern reader will after all tend to ignore the "medieval" view in proportion as he is unfamiliar with it. It is my feeling that the author of the ***Nibelungenlied*** transcended the medieval view himself and was thus quite capable of creating a modern—or timeless—internal conflict.

Ruedeger is both a high noble and a vassal. His allegiance to Attila is a given quantity. His commitment to Kriemhild takes on the force and weight of that allegiance in the very process of her marriage to Attila. But that marriage would not have come about except for the additional personal pledge of loyalty which he gives her, not just to persuade her, though it does so, but to give expression to the full but still conventional extent of a great vassal's loyalty to his lady-liege. From Kriemhild's point of view the stages of Ruedeger's commitment can be and are viewed in an ulterior light. For Ruedeger it is only the unfolding in words of the same loyalty which we (not Ruedeger) must remember as the driving force and justification behind the revenge of Hagen for the wrong done to Brunhild. When Ruedeger says "If you had among the Huns no one but me, / . . .A man would pay for any harm he did to you" (1256), he means it in one way, and Kriemhild takes it in another. What Ruedeger did, he did in complete good faith and innocence, and the structure and geography of the ***Nibelungenlied*** is such that no accusation of "contrivance" can be leveled. One obligation, sacred in the structure of feudalism but perfectly familiar in some form to any Western society, is now established. The other will be set up with equal care and logic.

Each visit at Ruedeger's court cements further the bond between him and the Burgundians, and the culmination of them is the whole complex of the last sojourn of the Burgundians at Pöchlarn; hospitality, exchange of gifts, pledge of loyalty, betrothal of Giselher to his daughter . . . In terms equally sacred, with all the formal sanction of tradition and custom that supported the other bond, Ruedeger is now friend and kinsman of the Burgundian lords. In absolutely equal degree he is bound to the two poles of a mortal conflict. It is one of those perfect situations of inner conflict which are among the highest manifestations of tragedy in Western literature—the one great level to which the Greeks gave little consideration, for where but in the figure of Neoptolemus in Sophocles' *Philoctetes* is such a carefully balanced internal conflict presented? And that play, perhaps significantly, ends not as a "regular" tragedy but in resolution and reconciliation.

With the beginning of hostilities at Attila's court a terrible chasm opens between the two allegiances on which Ruedeger's existence is concentrated. The revelation of Ruedeger's reaction is accomplished with fine psychological realism. He tries to effect a reconciliation, but disintegration has proceeded too far. He knows what the end must be: "Alas that no one has the power to turn / This evil aside" (2136). His grief and immobilization misinterpreted as cowardice, Ruedeger turns in the fury of frustration and anger upon the man who voiced the accusation and fells him with one blow—adding as the poet says "one more grave misfortune" to the woes of his king, Attila. When Kriemhild recalls his pledge and in her anguish and desperation demands his loyalty, when even Attila falls to his knees before him, Ruedeger states his dilemma with utter clarity. It is one of the great situations of spiritual crisis in literature:

> "Unhappy man, that I should live to see
> My honors forfeit, my inner loyalty
> And the decent breeding God enjoins—surrendered!
> This, oh Lord in Heaven, I wish my death had hindered!
>
> Whichever course before me I reject,
> To do the other, I've done a cursed act.
> If I do neither, I face the people's wrath
> And their reproach. Counsel me now, who gave me breath!"
>
> (2153-2154)

He first attempts to gain release from the obligation to Attila and Kriemhild by surrendering the symbols of that obligation. With this he might have purchased the right to abstain from fighting. (Jones' treatment here is detailed and excellent.) This is fruitless. Attila turns the offer back with promise of outright gift. The issue is settled and Ruedeger makes his decision to fight for Kriemhild and Attila—perhaps only because it is the more ancient loyalty. "Today the cost is paid with Ruedeger's life. / The kindness you and my lord have done to me— / I now must die for that" (2163).

One critic has said that Ruedeger obeys the queen even though he knows it will mean his death. He could equally well have said "because he knew it." Ruedeger is cognizant of the necessity of tragic choice but no less so of the atonement in the light of which alone it can be made. What remains is the full development by the poet of all the pathos latent in the tragic situation, and it is done with perfection.

To my mind the only place where the purely medieval, chivalric (or Germanic) ethos plays a role is in the words "If I do neither . . . " Even this however is not essential.

I take it that if the basic question of interpretation is ever to be decided it must be decided on the grounds of the text. Not only Ruedeger's reputation is at stake, as might be the case in a purely Germanic *or* "courtly" reading, but explicitly his eternal soul. "I swore to risk for you both honors and life, / But not to lose my soul" (2150). I consider it of great significance that he is willing to risk *êre*—the very concept we were talking about, but not another and higher thing, his soul. It is in this light that I prefer to view the two strophes above, a tragic choice, either path ending in soul-damaging guilt, not a dilemma, either horn entailing loss of good name (*êre*). His ascription of his "decent breeding" to God, his cry for divine counsel, seem also to comport better with a mind divided by two equal inner loyalties. The most striking image in which his dilemma is couched reinforces the notion of equal allegiances. "He placed upon the balance soul and life" (2166). (This could perhaps be read merely as a stereotyped expression for "risk.")

It is also my understanding of Ogier, the possible source or parallel of Ruedeger, that he and other heroes of *Les quatre fils Aymon* are not (cf. Jones) "motivated largely by concern for their good names," rather that the poem implies a very strong inner, ideal sense of right action. Probably Ogier and almost certainly Ruedeger should be seen as men who transcend the strict system of externally oriented standards.

One more moot point and we are through. The reader will have to decide what he thinks of Panzer's suggestion (*Das Nibelungenlied,* 1955) that the secrecy and the extent of Ruedeger's promise to Kriemhild constitute a degree of tragic error. The relation of this to the conflict is obvious.

The figures of Sigfrid and Ruedeger are each restricted to one section of the poem. They serve to unite the poem only on the ideological level, as it were, each constituting an exemplar of knighthood. Yet the ideal pictures of which they are the realized prototypes are themselves highly divergent. If anything, Sigfrid and Ruedeger function to emphasize the division of the epic into two great actions.

The creation of the few characters treated here—and of so many others, major and minor—is a literary achievement of high order, particularly in a period which tends more to types than to individuals, to Byzantine profiles rather than to portraits.

—Frank G. Ryder

The uniting characters, the ones who by their presence in both actions give continuity to the poem are Kriemhild, Hagen, and Gunther. The greatest of these is Kriemhild. Out of the terrible injury done her in the first part grows the fury of vengeance which dominates the second. She is, in a way, a one-dimensional figure, any subtleties of inner tension must remain hypothetical. Even the playing of the terrible trump card in the quarrel with Brunhild cannot be proved to be ironic. On the other hand—partly because of her nature and partly through the structure of her role and the architecture of the poem—she is the clear reference or triangulation point for even the physically most remote segments of the plot. Sigfrid goes to court Brunhild in order to gain Kriemhild's hand, just as he fought in the Saxon War in order to establish his merit in her eyes and her brothers'. She is the point at issue in the debate over the visit to Attila, and it is her invitation which draws the whole Burgundian nation from Worms to Vienna.

In the course of developing action, seen across the whole content of the epic, it is necessary for Kriemhild to move from a person only wronged to one who carries a just cause to punishable excess, and finally to a raging Medea who must be destroyed. (Similarly the Burgundians and Hagen must evolve from conniving murderers to proud defiers of a just fate, and then to heroic victims of unwarranted evil.) It is easy to view the changes as if they were made within Part II or in the interval before it. Actually, if Panzer and others are right, there is a very early doubt cast upon the unmitigated priaseworthiness of Kriemhild's character. Not only does she seem unusually eager to secure her full share of wealth and vassals before she leaves for Xanten as Sigfrid's wife, she also displeases Sigfrid by urging such demands and, further, makes the extraordinary, almost insulting selection of Hagen and Ortwin as the chief vassals to accompany her. The first two might be subsumed under the normal exchanges of courtly form, though even here there is legitimate doubt. The last is a clear affront and is so regarded by Hagen. In her attack on Brunhild she is certainly not blameless. Sigfrid takes her to task—we find out later how vigorously and crudely—for her irresponsible tongue. Whatever weight be given to these reservations, the overwhelming fact of the first part is that vastly more than condign revenge is taken upon Sigfrid and Kriemhild and that she is the rightful object of pity.

The figure of Kriemhild becomes more problematical in the period after the cruel return of Sigfrid's corpse. That she feels a wild desire for vengeance is scarcely out of character with the Germanic heroic tradition which, here as elsewhere, breaks through the courtly. Mixed with her blind grief, however, is cautious foresight. She keeps Sigmund from starting a battle because she knows his forces are too few. But she also says "Wait until some better time, / My lord, and you and I shall avenge this crime / Against my husband" (1033). The central objects of her hate are Hagen and Brunhild (1010), Gunther and Hagen (1046).

The poet takes advantage of this limited association to motivate in part one of the most difficult of all his scenes: Kriemhild's decision to remain at Worms. A great deal has been written in theoretical justification of this decision (the ancient Germanic priority of family over marriage, etc.), yet the fact remains that her first reaction is horror, that she stays with murderers, that she must leave her son to the care of his grandfather. When her mother and her innocent brothers rightly urge her to stay, when she removes herself from all contact with Hagen and Gunther, the situation regains some of its psychological validity.

Out of her decision to remain, and out of her second cruel deluding proceeds the new element in the motivation of revenge, the treasure. First its loss functions as a further motivation for—or reawakening of—the plan of revenge. In the second part it helps, by the growing emphasis placed on it, to cast a harsher and more sinister light on the queen. There is really no other new external factor to be taken into account. Why then is her vengeance not just? Why must she too be destroyed?

Quite apart from what the author may be trying to tell us about the logical conclusion of the philosophy of "an eye for an eye," there are several reasons. Her revenge, originally directed against Hagen (plus, at most, Gunther and Brunhild), extends like an awful malignancy to the whole race of Burgundians. To reply that this was necessary because the original on which Part II is based has as its theme the destruction of the Burgundians is to strip the poet of every vestige of skill and his plot of verisimilitude. Further, as Hagen notes more than once, her thoughts of vengeance are abnormally long. For well over a dozen years she has cherished them. Her very scheming is inordinate: not only her deception of guileless Attila, nor her seeking of mercenary help, but such devices as the malicious separation of pages and squires from knights. (The treatment of strophe 1912 leaves us of course in a quandary about the most horrifying addendum of Kriemhild's guilt: Did she or did she not voluntarily sacrifice her own son in order to start the fight?) Her extension of revenge (and refusal of mercy) even to Giselher, who was loyal to her, is a crucial point. And the poet gets the fullest effect from the frantic and calumnious suspicion with which she greets the silence that ensues upon the death of good Ruedeger. Her final enormities in the treatment of Gunther and Hagen raise the crescendo to its final, deafening intensity, and she becomes what Hagen calls her, a fiend of hell.

Hagen stands in fascinating contrast to Sigfrid (and Ruedeger) on the one hand, to Gunther on the other. The reader may do his own analysis of this monumental epic figure (the only one in all the poem, by the way, whose physical appearance is described: 1734). His is the most terrifyingly consistent personality in the whole epic. In this he is the antithesis of Gunther, whose character, Panzer said, is that he has no character. (Perhaps better balanced is the assessment of Gunther as the man of pathetic indecisiveness and troubled but ineffective conscience—still psychological worlds apart from Hagen.)

Hagen shares with Sigfrid and Ruedeger the attributes of bravery, strength, loyalty, and courtesy, but also an astonishing considerateness (summed in 1526: "a help and solace"), in seeming contrast to his savage temper but manifesting itself time and again, in every solicitude a good officer shows for his men.

He also shares Sigfrid's wide knowledge of lands, routes, and people, but in all other ways is his opposite. He exhibits in every possible context a total and often savage awareness. His own motives and duties are clear to him and he scorns concealment, once the deed is done. Before the deed he will use every resource of cunning and deception to secure his goal. He lives in the conviction that the end—it is either loyalty (so violent and absolute as to be Germanic rather than chivalric in flavor) or vengeance or both—justifies all means. Even the poet is appalled at his own creation: "thc false and faithless man" (911), "I doubt if ever knight will do such deed / Of treachery . . . " (906).

The poet's fine sense of ironic fate makes this man the very one through whom Sigfrid is brought closer to the Burgundians—in the Saxon War, in the journey to "Iceland," and in getting Kriemhild to prepare the fine clothes for that journey.

The creation of the few characters treated here—and of so many others, major and minor—is a literary achievement of high order, particularly in a period which tends more to types than to individuals, to Byzantine profiles rather than to portraits. It reminds us again that this is a work centered on character, not merely event. The emphasis is achieved not by psychological analysis (no medieval specialty) but, as Bert Nagel (*Zeitschrift für deutsche Philologie,* LXXVI [1956]) has well said, by the marshaling of actions and words to reveal inner states.

THE IDEOLOGICAL WORLD OF THE POEM

The reliability and superiority of the ***Nibelungenlied*** as a source book for courtly life has already been alluded to. The reader will scarcely have any trouble finding and, if he wishes, categorizing the passages. Remarkably enough, this job was not completely done—and the logical conclusions drawn therefrom—until 1945, when Nelly Dürrenmatt's book *Das Nibelungenlied im Kreis der höfischen Dichtung* appeared. The author's thesis is well sustained and balanced. The ***Nibelungenlied*** is closer to the courtly epics than scholars have thought. The author is courtly where he can be. He treats generously the major aspects of the knight's career, from his chivalric upbringing to his funeral rites. External qualities and gestures mirror inner worth and bearing, and so on.

The relationship of the personalities in the poem to the value system of chivalry has been considered in the treatment of Sigfrid and Ruedeger.

There are substantial exceptions to this harmony of epic and ethos (or custom). The ideal of loyal allegiance (*triuwe*), so central to the poem, is not merely courtly. It is also a cardinal virtue of the early Germanic tribal code, and the closest tie between that ethos and the feudal. And it is also in part the personal construct of the author.

In many features, large and small, the work is noncourtly (even anticourtly). Brunhild in "Iceland" is certainly no lady. Wolfhart and Hagen are something more than Arthurian knights when it comes to combat or the antecedent exchange of insults. Chivalric moderation and control (*mâze*) is about as prominent in this poem as "nothing in excess" is in the *Iliad.* Passions in general are wilder, more "Germanic." And above all Dame Fortune does not stand as presiding genius over this work, rather Moira and Nemesis, as Dürrenmatt says.

One is tempted to add another basic distinction, made especially clear by Joos and Whitesell:

"[The] epic hero [courtly variety] is essentially a social climber. . . . " Words describing behavior and attitudes are not used "for differentiating and individualizing . . . characters" but "for praising or for dispraising, in various degrees, persons who were all theoretically of the same stamp." In our poem we deal with a "society of island personalities," somewhat like sovereign nations, "where each party is only partly known to or understandable by each other; where compromise is the only basis for stability, and stability may at any moment explode into catastrophe." Here "the diversity of persons" is the "source of its motivations (that is to say, . . . dramatic conflict and psychologically autonomous drives rather than decorum and convention . . . motivate social acts)."

The Germanic heroic tradition and chivalric culture were not the only transcendent systems of thought available to a poet in the year 1200. What of the relation of the ***Nibelungenlied*** to the ordering of reality and life represented by medieval Christianity?

The question is not easily answered. The vocabulary of Karl Bartsch's edition has over 100 entries under *got,* but this means little enough, since an equal list might be compiled, for example, from a highly profane modern. The world in which the characters move is one at least externally and formally Christian. Yet there is really only one genuine prayer in the whole epic: Ruedeger's at the time of his spiritual crisis.

The poem abounds in the *realia* of religion: churches, sacred precincts, the mass, the duties of religion, priests and monks, baptisms, funerals. The issue of religion is specifically raised in the contemplated marriage of Kriemhild to Attila—both by Attila (1145) who worries lest Kriemhild object because he is a pagan, and by Kriemhild, who does object—though not without such thorny inconsistencies in the presentation that one is strongly tempted to regard the whole business as an afterthought.

Ruedeger, of course, meets her objection with the encouraging idea that Attila, who has already a number of Christian courtiers, might be converted. Nothing comes of this.

Significantly, there is an almost total absence of heaven as the basis of immortality. The body seems *in toto* doomed to finality, good name and fame are what is undying. This is voiced by Hagen, in a striking phrase: "May the good Lord grant your virtues live forever" (2199). God is not asked to grant personal immortality, and there is no speculation in the poem about the rewards of the afterlife.

Attila's court is a monument of tolerant coexistence, specifically and it would seem nostalgically praised: "Under his rule (but scarcely any more) / Men lived by Christian faith or pagan lore, / As they might choose" (1335). (If the poet was indeed associated with the cathedral chapter of Passau, he lived in a society not entirely unlike this, where in addition to bishop, priests, and monks there were—not pagans perhaps—but secular nobility of several ranks and members of the middle and lower classes.)

The Christian elements in the ***Nibelungenlied*** are thus usually taken as superficial or *pro forma.* The work has been called a "purely secular poem." The one substantial area of doubt centers in the figure of Ruedeger, but his kindness to all men is usually interpreted as an extension of a chivalric virtue and hence religiously ambiguous. There are at least two passages which are, for this view, somewhat disquieting. Ruedeger, as we know, clearly regards his decency and good breeding as enjoined by God (2153), and it is not only his life and good name he risks but, of explicitly greater import, his soul (2150, 2166). (He is the only character in the poem who seems to be aware of having one. Without exception, all other substantial references to "soul" occur in connection with the ministrations of Kriemhild and the priests to the spirit of the slain Sigfrid, and they could all be *pro forma.* But Ruedeger's soul is important to him—and to us.)

The epilogue added to Part I by the writer of manuscript C—in which Kriemhild uses much of her treasure to found a cloister—cannot be urged in support of a strong religious direction in the poem. At most it indicates either that this writer found in the material as it came to him nothing incompatible with his religious sense—or, in substantial contrast, that he felt the action needed to be capped and balanced by a more churchly conclusion—a sort of implied moral, as it were.

Nagel, who sees a substantial Christian element in the poem, rests his case not only on Ruedeger but also on the incontestable reduction, compared to known sources, in the importance of magic and mythic features. He also considers the saving of the chaplain through God's hand to be a piece of positive evidence.

Considerations of this nature make one uneasy about the labels "religiously superficial," "purely secular." It may be quite impossible to prove, hence perhaps useless to speculate, that the poet not only introduced Christian motifs and reduced non-Christian ones, but in general told a story by whose characters and events he was fascinated and moved but also in a quiet way profoundly appalled. Both old Germanic valor and the pride of chivalry come to the same violent end. That tragic end was traditional for the ancient hero, but *not* for the knight, in his typical literary manifestation. The poet thus writes counter to the tradition of his own contemporaries. Did he intend that his readers look upon the story, shake their heads, and perhaps take warning? The same question, with the same difficulties, has been raised about Homer's attitude toward war.

If we do not feel this, we may be subtly forced to another reading: that the first part shows us how it is the will of fate and the nature of man for greatness to be brought low, and that this is triumphant and somehow right. For the second part a reading of this sort has more drastic implications, for then we may be faced with more than a glimpse of that most harrowing of combinations, a mystique of violence, the raising of force, terror, suffering and destruction into a splendid *Götterdämmerung,* a submerged desire not only to do rightful vengeance or to counter fatedness with defiance, but to move as it were one step ahead of fate and plunge into the maelstrom in a glorious act of annihilation.

Another area of medieval culture whose prominence in

the ***Nibelungenlied*** has recently received greater attention is courtly love, the service of *minne,* which we know largely from the troubadours. . . . [A] substantial part of [Sigfrid and Kriemhild's] story is in the true *minne* spirit: the eager longing for the remote beloved, the refining influence of her sweet gentleness, the long wait and the proof of loyalty—all the "apprenticeship in love." But the dual nature of the poem is apparent here, too; there is no lack of frank sensual pleasure and the culmination of love is not neglected. (pp. 11-33)

Frank G. Ryder, in his The Song of the Nibelungs: A Verse Translation from the Middle High German "Nibelungenlied," *Wayne State University Press, 1962, 421 p.*

A. T. Hatto (essay date 1964)

[*An English educator, translator, and editor, Hatto is a recognized authority in German studies who has written several works on medieval poetry. In the following excerpt from the introduction to his translation of the* Nibelungenlied, *originally published in 1964, Hatto investigates numerous inconsistencies involving the poem's characters and plot but adds that, despite its imperfections, the* Nibelungenlied *"is the world's best heroic epic bar one."*]

THE POEM AS AN ENTITY

Criticism of the ***Nibelungenlied*** has sometimes been unbalanced in the lands that lay claim to it, while elsewhere, with some notable exceptions, critics have tended to lean too heavily on what has been written in German. Modernizations of the ***Nibelungenlied*** and learned studies during the nineteenth century all speak of affection for the poem and of an awareness of a great heritage: but either the work was misinterpreted romantically or it was used for theoretical reconstructions which implied its fragmentation. The reaction was long in coming, but when it came it was just as painful. The extreme modern position is the super-aesthetic one of regarding the ***Nibelungenlied*** as a perfect and self-sufficient entity without a past. Faced with self-contradictions, lapses, or incongruities in the use of epithets, one declares them to be merely apparent, and bangs one's head on one's desk till illumination should come. This reaction against neglect of poetry in the interest of learned theorizing is healthy, and the pan-aesthetic approach is no doubt the best for countless literary masterpieces. The method can be profitable when applied to our poem within reason—but reason draws a very firm line. . . . [Although] the poet wrote on parchment, he was not composing in a vacuum, whether social or aesthetic, but, instead, he was writing and then reciting under the pressure of live and far from unanimous audiences who somehow had to be appeased. This is a situation well known to students of traditional poetry.

The ***Nibelungenlied*** is not 'a perfect work of art' and of its nature could never have become one, yet it is none the less a powerful poem. In order totally to exclude the application of a critical approach suited to another age I shall enumerate its most alarming blemishes, assuring the reader that this is not undertaken in the spirit of a pedant who lists, say, the self-contradictions of a Jane Austen, but because the nature of these faults reveals the poem as belonging to a type of literature peculiarly its own. It is one thing when we are told that a character in an Edgar Wallace thriller, last heard of in Cape Town, suddenly reappears in Tierra del Fuego because the novelist's charwoman has knocked a flag from his wall-map, and southern capes are all one to her. It is quite another thing when we find that a poet of Homer's genius 'nods', as it must be conceded he does. That even Homer nods is a warning that we are dealing with a type of poetry different from our own, poetry with its own laws that bear mightily on the poet, whoever he may be.

INCONSISTENCIES, OBSCURITIES, PREVARICATIONS

With some strain on our gallantry, though helped by memories of Penelope, we may suppose Kriemhild to have kept her radiant looks at thirty-eight, when she married King Etzel, and we may concede her a son seven years later. Nevertheless we feel that time—even epic time, the most elastic—has been stretched to its limits. But when we turn to her contemporaries Giselher and Dancwart we find that time has snapped. For Giselher retains the description of 'boy' or 'youth' for thirty-six years, and Dancwart, who went to Iceland to woo Brunhild as one of four tough men, claims shortly before his death in the second part to have been a 'tiny child' when Siegfried was killed. Of all names in the ***Nibelungenlied,*** the plural 'Nibelungs' is used in two senses. Up to the end of Chapter 18, when Siegfried's father returns home after burying him, it is applied either to members of King Nibelung's dynasty or (more frequently) to the latters' vassals and men, whereas from Chapter 25 onwards till the end it is applied to the Burgundian warriors, except in the phrase 'the land of the Nibelungs'. Here it might seem possible to argue that the Burgundians have taken the name together with the Nibelung treasure; but this will not do, since there is no intimate symbolic link between the Burgundians and the treasure, either in the form of a curse or in any other way than by tenacious possession. (The acquisition of the Nibelung treasure was in no wise a turning-point in the lives of the Burgundians, even though Kriemhild, in our author's ambiguous fashion, seems to make it a matter of Hagen's life or death at the end.) Moreover there are still Nibelungs in Nibelungland who are the deadly enemies of the Burgundians, the murderers of their lord Siegfried. It is therefore not surprising that the poet succeeded in confusing himself in his use of the name of 'Nibelung' on one occasion.

The common measure of all these faults is lack of harmony between the two halves of the epic, and it is only a step farther in thought to suppose that this lack of harmony was due to imperfect harmonization by a poet who was welding two not entirely congruous plots together, a supposition which has been triumphantly vindicated by comparison with parallel versions.

A strange *non sequitur* occurs just before the fighting breaks out in Etzel's hall. We are told:

> Kriemhild's old grief was embedded deep in her heart. Since there was no beginning the fighting in any other way, she had Etzel's son carried to

> the board. (How could a woman ever do a more dreadful thing in pursuance of her revenge?)

The boy is fetched, but nothing happens. Hagen allows himself the offensive remark that the young prince has 'an ill-fated look', and that is all. The slaughter begins only when Dancwart, sole Burgundian survivor of a bloody battle in the squires' quarters, appears at the door, blood-stained and sword in hand. At his news, Hagen starts the fighting by beheading the young prince.

> Next he dealt the tutor who had charge of the boy a vehement two-handed blow so that in an instant his head lay on the floor by the table—such pitiful wages did he mete out to that pedagogue.

The poet quite fails to tell us how Kriemhild's decision to fetch her son caused the fighting to break out, or why his tutor should be punished so ruthlessly. Actually, he has made the fighting in the hall inevitable with the slaughter of the Burgundian squires, and it would not matter whether Kriemhild's son were there or not. The words 'since there was no beginning the fighting in any other way' are meaningless in this situation and are beyond rescue by any purely aesthetic or logical method of interpretation. Recourse to the parallel version of the *Thiðrekssaga,* however, furnishes a complete explanation, though it leaves us wondering how our poet could be so clumsy. In this Norse compilation, Grimhild says to her son, who is appreciably older here:

> . . . if you have the courage go up to Hogni (Hagen) . . . clench your fist and buffet him on the cheek with all your might . . .

This the boy does, and Hogni strikes off his head for his pains. Now the meaningless phrase 'since there was no beginning the fighting in any other way' takes on a pregnant meaning, now we understand the words 'how could a woman ever do a more dreadful thing in pursuit of her revenge', and now we understand why the boy's tutor must be punished. As with the defloration of Brunhild, so with Kriemhild's sacrifice of her child to her revenge; when dealing with this passage in his source, the poet judged that the younger generation would not tolerate it as it stood; indeed, his notable elaboration of the massacre of the pages was largely in order to free Kriemhild from the need to sacrifice her offspring. Yet whilst removing the child's provocation he retained all that led up to it, even an expression of indignation at a deed no longer done. When the reader has read this epic, he will be in no doubt that the author was a great poet: nevertheless, he is capable of such shoddy, even stupid work as this! We have found him compromising again, attempting to please the moderns and yet giving the ancients as much of the old version as he dared.

When Gunther wins Brunhild by fraud at the games, she duly makes him sovereign of Iceland there and then; but at the end of this episode and of the next, she can take no decisions until her kinsmen have assembled from far and wide. If we look below the surface we find that the reason for this assembly is to provide a motive for Siegfried to sail to Nibelungland to fetch his Nibelungs, some of whom he afterwards took to Worms on two occasions, first to the wedding, and then on his fatal visit to Gunther and Brunhild. In this way the poet not only provided a chapter which showed Siegfried's Nibelungs at home but he also caused them and the Burgundian Nibelungs to mingle, suggesting (however implausibly) some sort of continuity.

In the scenes in which Hagen tricks Kriemhild into revealing the position of Siegfried's vulnerable spot, the poet is again very careless. Playing on Kriemhild's inordinate love for her husband, which indeed is her own vulnerable spot, Hagen pretends that war is at hand and prevails upon her to mark the place on Siegfried's battle gear with a cross so that he may 'guard' it in the fray. He then calls off the war and calls on a hunt, for which Siegfried expressly takes magnificent hunting-clothes. Now, while Siegfried had his battle dress on, the poet had said: ' . . . when Hagen had observed the *mark* . . . '. It would have been easy for him later at the stream, over which Siegfried was bending, to have made Hagen 'aim at his mark', that is, at the remembered position. Instead he writes: ' . . . Hagen hurled the spear at the *cross* . . . '—which was not there. When we recall *why* the poet has introduced this motif we are astonished at the contradictions of his art; for he contrived this scene in order to involve Kriemhild in her darling's death as a victim of her deadly enemy Hagen. There is nothing to contradict the notion that this fine conception was all our poet's own: and yet (if it really be he) he can be so slipshod. The moral surely is that—true to his dramatic genius—he was far more interested in confrontations of character than in the machinery by which he achieved them, or, as has been well observed by another writer, the poet is less concerned with 'why' than with 'how'. Chapter 29, in which he confronts Hagen and Kriemhild immediately on the Burgundians' arrival in Hungary, well illustrates this moral. The scene is an afterthought of the poet's, and a very fine one, which he obtains at the expense of leaving the Burgundian kings engulfed in a crowd in the courtyard, waiting to be received by Etzel, politest of monarchs. Only when Hagen returns from his tense scene with Kriemhild can the royal guests detach themselves and move on into the palace!

It would be futile to attempt an exhaustive treatment of the poet's more venial shortcomings in logical development and in the attribution of motives, whether he be too abrupt, obscure, ambiguous, or disingenuous; for this is no place in which to celebrate the triumph of the card index over a poet who little dreamt of us. Yet a bare selection must be given both for what it will tell us about him and his art and in order to alert the reader. It may perhaps encourage the latter, if he knows that others long familiar with the text can be as puzzled and irritated as he by the surprises that are sprung on us. The criterion of these shortcomings is in any case not given by the mass of scholarship that has accumulated about the poem, but by the poet's own great gifts, which challenge us to come to terms with both his lapses and his taciturnities. These can sometimes be questioned with profit, and our first example might be a case in point.

Before the wooing party leaves for Iceland and on its arrival there, it appears that Siegfried and Brunhild have prior knowledge or acquaintance of each other; but nothing is ever divulged. Are we meant to feel that something is going wrong, that this semi-mythic pair were perhaps destined for each other? The poet leaves us with our questions, and we remember that such is the pattern of life. In harmony with this effect there is Brunhild's obsession with Siegfried's status—was he a sovereign, or vassal to Gunther? In Worms she has ample occasion to satisfy herself of the truth, both during the wedding festivities and Siegfried's visit ten years later. Such things were known at great courts and were fittingly enshrined in ceremonial. Brunhild, however, clings to her memory of how Siegfried took second place to Gunther in Iceland, and she surely notes Gunther's evasiveness when he is taxed with it. She had harboured some expectation of Siegfried; but what it was we are never clearly told. She assumed that Siegfried had come to woo her, but was confident of her power to frustrate him. Here, then, the poet's silences, though disturbing, have some positive features.

The next two examples are of a sort met with elsewhere in heroic epic. Ancient elements of the story are preserved unchanged, though preceded and followed by modern elements, thus making an incongruous effect.

On their voyage to Iceland, Gunther, Siegfried, Hagen, and Dancwart, four men all told, and two of them kings, set sail and man the oars. If the smallness of the party was intended to underline their heroism, the effect is marred later by Siegfried's sailing for his Nibelungs. Similarly, on the way to Hungary, Hagen ferries an army of more than ten thousand men across the Danube. Again the change in texture is gross, and we know that a contemporary objected. Since the former example occurs in the first, and the latter in the second half of the work, it would be idle to declare that the poet had yet to learn his trade. Rather did he bow too low to tradition, judging that the diehards would insist on their version, the second of which has its humorous aspects.

If Brunhild appears to remain morbidly uncertain whether Kriemhild is wife to a liegeman, Kriemhild (as the story is told) does not *know* whether Brunhild had been possessed by Siegfried. Each takes her stand by the symbolic act that she has witnessed. Brunhild has seen Siegfried hold Gunther's horse for him to mount; Kriemhild has been given the tokens of Brunhild's virginity. The issue whether the symbols lie is never raised, fatal insults are exchanged on the strength of them, events march past the truth, the blind rush to their destruction. It is permissible for a poet to leave his characters in the dark, should he choose to do so; but it is unusual, whether in epic or in drama, to leave the audience in the dark too. We know that Siegfried was not Gunther's vassal, and we know that Siegfried did not deflower Brunhild: but we are unable to assess how far the queens believe the charges which they hurl at one another. This brings us very near to life; but the question whether the poet was consciously striving after dramatic realism must be deferred.

If the poet is sometimes thrifty in his use of motive, on other occasions he moves fitfully among several. Hagen alleges two grounds for murdering Siegfried, and Kriemhild has two for killing Hagen. Hagen swears that Siegfried must die for having boasted he was Brunhild's lover, for with him, too, the symbol reigns supreme. Making little headway with this argument, Hagen puts the proposition to Gunther that if Siegfried were dead, Gunther would be lord of many lands. The idea that Siegfried's power is a threat to Gunther receives no support from the poem; for on the contrary, Siegfried saved Gunther from invasion. When Hagen has murdered Siegfried he exults at having ended his dominion. Thus, if we are to believe Hagen, he made away with Siegfried both in order to redeem his queen's honour and to increase the power of his king, though this motive, as we saw, is hollow. Kriemhild pursues Hagen over the years with unrelenting thoughts of revenge, but when she at last has him at her mercy she makes the immediate point at issue the loss of Siegfried's treasure, with a prospect (feigned or otherwise) of Hagen's being spared if he returns it. This is a scene, be it noted, in which Hagen wins a great moral victory over Kriemhild even though the gold which he refuses to yield was ill-gotten, and it is only when the much-wronged woman draws Siegfried's sword from Hagen's side to make an end of him that the motive of revenge for ruined love returns. This vacillation between two motives is not due to deep calculation. The welding together of the two halves of the poem was based on Kriemhild's passion to avenge the murder of her husband: yet no requirement either of logic or of sentiment could dislodge the magnificent scene in which, since early times, Gunther and Hagen were faced with the alternatives of giving up the treasure or dying. Our poet thus has to shift from one motive to the other, as the plot requires him to do.

Here it would be wrong to speak of contradictions, since neither Hagen's nor Kriemhild's double motives are incompatible. Despite the plausible 'mock-ups' which barristers, psychologists, and novelists offer us, it is never possible in life to disentangle the motives for people's actions, be they saintly or devilish or merely human, and rarely will a deed have been prompted by one unalloyed impulse. As a matter of literary history, however, it is possible to account for Hagen's and Kriemhild's shifting motives in terms of corresponding elements of plot which the poet decided to adopt, together with all that follows from them. This is no isolated phenomenon in the history of heroic poetry. The story of Patroclus requires a 'blind' Achilles who sends his friend to his death and thus brings on his own: but the story of Achilles himself requires a clear-sighted hero who makes a conscious choice between fame with early death and long life with obscurity. These two Achilles come and go in the *Iliad,* but the fact that they are combined into a figure of absorbing interest does not deceive us as to their origins. There is no lack of other examples, either in the *Iliad* or the ***Nibelungenlied.*** The existence of divergent motives and characteristics attendant on additions or modifications of plot offered a challenge to the poets concerned. According to their skill and insight they made more or less of their chances. Here it must be admitted that, although he offers no contradiction, the Nibelung poet visibly shifts his ground.

As last examples of the poet's unconcern for clarity I will cite the two scenes in which the Burgundian leaders first plot the death of Siegfried and then sink his Nibelung treasure.

In the former case, Hagen (who was absent from the queens' quarrel) obtains the story from Brunhild and swears to take vengeance on Siegfried. Next, some warriors, whom we can only *infer* to be Hagen and Gunther, plot the death of Siegfried and are joined by Ortwin and Gernot, and then by Giselher, who, true to his role, objects. Hagen now utters his colourful 'Are we to rear cuckoos?' which, whatever its precise meaning, must refer to the theme of adultery. To this, Gunther replies that Siegfried has always treated them well. Hagen then attacks from another quarter with the argument that if Siegfried were out of the way many kingdoms would subserve Gunther, a thought that saddens that feckless monarch. There is an interval during which Siegfried's knights appear to celebrate their queen's victory over Brunhild with jousting, while Gunther's are downcast. And then, without transition—the effect is like that of a nagging dream—Gunther and Hagen are in counsel again. This time Gunther takes our breath away by asking how the thing can be done, and, reassured by the technical excellence of Hagen's plan, he assents to it. Gernot and Giselher had presumably blown out from the conspiracy as airily as they had blown in, for they assert their complete innocence later. They act as though they had an alibi; yet the poet has taken no pains to establish it. But, after all, they knew that something was afoot and quite failed to warn their 'dear sister'. To thinking men they are revealed as hypocrites—but did the poet intend it? We are even more in the dark about Gunther. We could argue—but argument will not get us far with this poet—that Gunther declined to have Siegfried killed in revenge for adultery not because he knew of Siegfried's innocence but because such revenge would have implied the truth of the charge; so that his reminder of Siegfried's loyalty will have proceeded from cunning rather than from the better side of his weak nature. His quickening interest in the means by which Siegfried could be safely removed is compatible with either interpretation, and so we are left guessing once more.

In the episode of the sinking of the treasure this impression of murky complicity among the privy council at Worms is heightened. It is Hagen who first suggests a reconciliation between Kriemhild and her brothers as a means of gaining possession of her treasure. The plan succeeds outwardly, though naturally Hagen was not received back into favour. (Whether Kriemhild was sincere on her part is yet another question which, for lack of assistance from the poet, we cannot answer.) The poet now hurries us past the point at which the Burgundians prevail upon Kriemhild to send for the treasure without telling us what was said. Whether or not Kriemhild foresaw the possibility from the outset, she now employs her treasure to enlist warriors, whereupon Hagen decides to deny her the use of it. Gunther reminds him either weakly or cunningly but in any case fulsomely of the reconciliation, and at Hagen's shrewd offer to take the blame he allows his sister to be deprived of the hoard. Falling into his role, Giselher protests that were Hagen not his kinsman he would die, and Gernot then offers the compromise which brings the poet to his objective, namely the sinking of the treasure in the Rhine. Kriemhild goes piteously to Giselher, who promises to protect her—*when* they came back from abroad! All three brothers quit Worms, leaving Hagen to do the deed. On their return, they blame Hagen severely: but that this is all make-believe invented for the purpose of an alibi emerges from our poet's statement that before Hagen sank the treasure they had sworn to keep it secret as long as one remained alive. The reason why the poet 'blows' the alibi this time is that he has no choice: without the oath of secrecy there can be no final scene in which Hagen defies Kriemhild over the treasure. All three brothers, but Giselher most of all because of his show of tender feeling towards his sister—one of his stock roles—are revealed as nauseating hypocrites beside whom Machiavelli is a man of charm. Did the poet intend this? If he did, how long did he wish us to retain this impression? Upwards of twelve years later Kriemhild will dream that she is kissing 'Young' Giselher. And not long after that she will be sacrificing him, with many another, to her revenge.

The poet's treatment of time is unusual. On the one hand, he punctuates the various actions with intervals of such size that if we accept them at their face value they threaten to tear the characters apart; though, if we take our stand by the characters, these intervals tend to become nominal, suggesting 'a long time', in keeping with the poet's weak sense of numbers. On the other hand, the poet's thoughts are always flying to the final catastrophe towards which events are inevitably leading, thus bracing his sprawling tracts of time; but here the time in which he deals is a moral rather than chronological medium, time that knows a fulness, time that brings dark deeds to payment. These two different aspects of time merge in Kriemhild who is *lancrœche*—'tenacious in the pursuit of revenge long harboured'. She is the blind and also conscious instrument of retribution on the Burgundians, whether of Fate or of Divine Justice, a conception that will have had much to do in deciding the poet to adopt an elongated time scheme when combining the two sources of his epic, rather than bringing them together as closely in time as possible. The longest interval in the unified epic need have been no longer than it took to dry the widow's tears: and the poet rightly judged that it must be a 'long' time, if ever. But the other long intervals, Kriemhild's wedded bliss with Siegfried (some ten or eleven years), and her quiescent years in Hungary (twelve years), wantonly long as they are, lessen the effect of her protracted widowhood. Had the poet told us just enough to imagine Kriemhild as an old woman (he tells us nothing at all) he might have bought all these years at some profit and have added to the intensity of her revenge. As it is, Kriemhild's imperishable beauty, and the quarter of a century during which she nurses revenge, war against each other, with a 'Young' Giselher of fifty further to confuse the poet's meaning, and a Dancwart who was both a child and a man in the first part, or an awful liar in the second. It was, therefore, a characteristic of this poet's art not to worry too much about time, in the belief that time would surely come into its own—'in the end'.

As a result of the cross-relations in time which the poet gives us—they are mostly of a forward-looking nature—our interest is never quite absorbed in present actions: rather does he teach us to view them in the shadow of future events. And, from the opening scene, he has spanned these minor arches of anticipation with a lovely vault reaching out far beyond the loss of Siegfried into Kriemhild's great sorrow, in which she nurses her plans for revenge—the maiden dream in which she is shown all that matters of her future life in condensed symbolic language:

> In disen hohen eren troumte Kriemhilde,
> wie si züge einen valken, starc, scœne und wilde,
> den ir zwene arn erkrummen. daz si daz muoste sehen:
> ir enkunde in dirre werlde leider nimmer gescehen.
>
> (In the midst of such magnificence Kriemhild dreamt she reared a falcon, strong, handsome, and wild, but that two eagles rent it while she perforce looked on, the most grievous thing that could ever befall her).

She takes her dream to her mother, who tells her that the falcon is a noble man and that unless God preserves him he will soon be taken from her. Certainty as to who the two eagles will be grows as the first part unfolds. The poet's contemporaries of course knew from the beginning.

The poet never tires of directing our attention to the signs of calamity to come. Yet his hints of what will happen remain dark. Never is the future made so precise as to detract from the immediacy of the present. Only in dreams and in a fairy prophecy does the future break in upon us more clearly, and this is just as it should be. Although his characters are touched lightly by time, the poet himself does not make light of time. He is as far from playing with time as from weaving entrancing patterns with it, as in the *Odyssey.* He respects its logical order, abandoning it only on few occasions. His flight from the present is as brilliant and admirable in one instance as it is shifty and disturbing in another. Various poems about Siegfried's younger and wilder days must have been circulating in Germany at the end of the twelfth century, but they could not be encompassed in a poem that was to be held together by the love and hate of Kriemhild. Yet the plot of the ***Nibelungenlied*** turns on several attributes of Siegfried that were acquired in his wilder days. It turns on his owning a cloak of invisibility, on his skin hardened in dragon's blood, and to a lesser degree on his Nibelung treasure. The poet gives us this essential information in a vignette. We are invited to peep through a casement opening on the hero's mythic past. For when Siegfried arrives at Worms, Hagen, most knowledgeable of Burgundians, looks out on the stranger through a window, concludes that it can only be he, and gives the court a thumbnail sketch of him. A second flight from the present is one with which we are familiar. After overpowering Brunhild, Siegfried took her ring and girdle. 'Later he gave them to his wife . . . '. The poet says that Siegfried handed over the tokens 'later' so as to avoid the necessity of narrating the scene in full in its due position in time; for in such a scene Siegfried would have to say something, and why should he say anything but the truth? And if he told the truth, could Kriemhild still humiliate Brunhild? And, if not, could there be a murder and revenge?

The poet's lack of concern with surprise does not mean that he does not build up tension. All knew that Kriemhild must humble Brunhild by flaunting her ring and girdle; that bloody fighting must break out in Etzel's hall; that, like a fury, Kriemhild must kill Hagen with her own hands. The question was *how*?

The poet breaks up the clash between the queens into three stages of rising intensity: at the tournament, and at the cathedral door, first before, then after mass. Confrontations, taunts, half-hearted attacks, demonstrations of force, pushing and shoving and threatening, and other provocations and counter-provocations mount and mount, with the blissful unawareness of Etzel as background—unawareness on the part of the one man who could have halted the downward march of events—till the dramatic appearance of Dancwart prompts Hagen to his fatalistic atrocity and so unleashes the battle. At the end, Kriemhild questions her captive Hagen on the subject of the treasure and is defeated in the traditional way, when her eye falls on his sword and she remembers the young lover Hagen took from her.

We have come very near to discussing the dramatic aspects of the poem. But this theme is best approached through the characters.

THE ART OF CHARACTERIZATION

[In] *Tristan,* there is a tendency even in so 'literary' a poet as Gottfried to make the episode the unit of characterization thanks to the contradictory demands of the foreign plot, which he respected. How much more must this be the case with the less independent poet of the ***Nibelungenlied,*** who was not only concerned with strong native traditions but also committed to harmonizing for the first time two distinct plots which, despite incongruities in their behaviour, shared some leading characters. What, for instance was the poet going to do with a king who dishonestly married a queen beyond his own wooing and who then connived at the murder of his brother-in-law, but who afterwards fought and died as a hero? What would he do with a murderer who (in spite of his bad case) rises to the heights of fortitude in adversity? Or with a young woman of more than usual spirit who reappears as an implacable she-devil? We have already learned enough to know that the poet will say as little as possible about his characters' motives and keep explicit contradiction to a minimum. 'Character' will be commensurate with the deed in hand. The human psyche is in any case still largely inscrutable (as honest analysts have readily admitted), and the souls of kings are even more so—why say more than one knows? Crude though some aspects of our poet's art may be in the eyes of the modern reader, this aspect of his art is virile and mature, especially if one remembers how certain of our contemporaries go grubbing for motives in the dustbin of the mind.

The key to the problem is contained in the aphorism 'die Rolle prägt den Kopf' ["The role decides the soul"], and it has been wittily said that the central figures—the oldest in the Nibelung tradition—'must not be weighed down by too much *soul*'; whereas Rüdiger, one of the more recent figures, himself lays claim to having one. Because the poet has narrated so many deeds, and such stark ones, he has surrendered some of his freedom to reveal his characters' motives or to place them in their best light. To understand his position one need only ask how much of the nobler Greeks' characters Homer could have left unchanged had he gone on to relate the pillage, atrocity, sacrilege, and rape that attended the fall of Troy.

It is therefore true as a general rule that the later a figure was introduced into the Nibelung tradition the more harmoniously are its actions motivated—which is far from saying 'the greater is its impact on the imagination'. Knowledge of the genesis of the poem helps to account for fluctuations in character as the figures rise from or sink back into the older strata of the story. Thus it is hazardous, if not futile, to try to bridge the 'faults' by psychologizing the characters. Despite their fluctuations, the characters were no doubt continuous in the poet's imagination, but he did not expound this to the reader. He did not reduce his figures to a mechanism, however refined. To him his characters were *the people who did those deeds.* He has greater insight into human nature than he puts explicitly into words, and to find it we must read between the lines, adding nothing of our own. His characters' actions are mostly so incisive that although we cannot always show their continuity we sense it and accept it. Are Kriemhild the fulfilled young wife and Kriemhild the widow who forsook her child one and the same person? Why did she not return to the Netherlands to mother the pledge of Siegfried's love? One shudders to think what deep motives could be found by relating her failure to do so with other of her acts. What 'complex' or perversity does it argue when a woman dotes on her husband but abandons their offspring? Was this warped emotion also responsible for her carelessness with her second son at Etzel's banquet? Should we remember here that she once dreamt that she was kissing her brother? Or (worst of all) ought we to take note that she was tenacious of her gold? This is *not* the way to approach the problem. The truth is that by giving Siegfried such a definite background as the Netherlands, Norway, and Nibelungland, by making him ruler there and by giving him a son in concern for whose good name the hero finds moving words as he lies dying, the poet has created for Kriemhild a centre of interest away from Worms, whereas the continuation of the story demands that she remain there. By keeping her in Worms he inevitably casts a shadow on her motherhood. Either he has invented her son or he has retained him from an unknown source, and, being unprepared to sacrifice him and his father's fine words, he decides to debit Kriemhild's character with the consequences, in view of her future ruthlessness. If he means us to understand that every human feeling died in Kriemhild when she buried Siegfried, he does not say so. The way he tells it is this. Kriemhild's kinsmen, and more particularly Giselher, entreat her to remain in Worms, but she answers that she cannot, for how could she bear the sight of her enemies? And now her mother Uote and her brother Gernot add their entreaties, pleading that she has few blood-relations in the Netherlands—a very powerful argument in itself but in shocking bad taste in the circumstances. Siegmund, for his part, thinks it necessary to reassure her that she would not be made to 'pay' for the loss of Siegfried if she returned, an ambiguous expression which might mean anything from loss of status to death by blood-feud. But she has allowed herself to be persuaded by her relations, and when Siegmund begs her not to leave her son an orphan she at first overlooks this in her answer. Only when her refusal to go back with them is plain does she commend her 'dear little son' to the care of the Netherlandish warriors when they should arrive back home. Characteristically, this is the last we hear of the matter. If pressed, the poet would have admitted that it was very damaging to Kriemhild, for he hints as much through Siegmund's amazement. But, as so often, his rule is 'least said, soonest mended'. We note Kriemhild's failure as a mother and feel that after this she may perhaps be capable of anything.

It has been argued that in causing Kriemhild to remain at Worms, the poet made it possible to show her in the utter desolation of her widowhood, humiliated without an effective friend by Hagen's distrainment of her treasure, and despairing of revenge and then only recalled to action by Etzel's suit through Rüdiger. The poet does achieve all this: but it would be wrong to regard it otherwise than as a virtue born of necessity. In staying behind in Worms, Kriemhild sacrificed her child and Siegfried's, and prospects of immediate revenge by forces perhaps as strong and brave as Etzel's and infinitely more willing to fight for her.

When the plot demands it, the leading characters follow old ways. Otherwise they follow the new. In historical terms this means that, in our poem, acts rooted in the Heroic Age alternate with others more typical of the poet's own chivalric period. This does not necessarily imply a contrast, since the latter grew out of the former and the knight inherited some of the qualities of the Germanic warrior, and similarly with their women. Thus natural links between the two outlooks exist and it is not to be thought that because *we* must not build bridges there are gaping rifts within the characters. In raising the question of Kriemhild's motherhood I have already drawn attention to the most challenging problem.

Our Hohenstauffen poet was understanding to an astonishing degree of the archaic mentality of his main characters, but there are times when he gives up, as for example with Siegfried and Brunhild, who become figures of fun when showing their strength. Another aspect of his attitude towards character is seen in his treatment of Hagen. Although Hagens shows himself indifferent to the Church and Christian morality, his solicitude for his comrades is such that he urges them to be confessed before battle. Why? The scholar who claimed that Hagen had matured to a state of sublime selflessness showed himself not unmarked by the time and place in which he lived. A less bewildered and more consciously cynical interpretation would be that Hagen as an experienced commander knew that men fight better confessed than unconfessed. But the answer that begs fewest questions is 'good commanders do just this on such occasions'. Following the plot on the one hand and avoiding indefensible inconsistencies on the other, the characterization of Hagen is, as another has said, strictly *ad hoc.* This leaves us an area in which to look for development within the characters, with the warning that such development is not the supreme law of their being.

THE CHARACTERS

It has been truly said that the conception of Kriemhild holding the two halves of the epic together for the first time would not have been possible before courtly authors like Thomas of Britain and Chrétien de Troyes had achieved the form of the biographical romance. But although Kriemhild—a mere woman—is the first character to be named, and only weeping and then silence follow her death, it would be wrong to read the ***Nibelungenlied*** as her biography. If the wealth of deeds, to which she contributes so mightily, is held together by her personality they are not capable of being absorbed by it. The fine moments of Siegfried's death-scene are swiftly engulfed in her agony and mourning. But in the second half there grows inexorably something that defies treatment only in relation to her, something that defeats her in the moment of her triumph: the clear-sighted and fatalistic heroism of Hagen, heroism as darkly splendid as Siegfried's was bright, and achieved at far greater cost.

Kriemhild begins as a charming young princess and ends as a *vâlandinne* or 'she-devil', a woman who has sacrificed her nature to revenge, the business of men. I will follow this clue through the maze of the action.

In the opening scene, in which her mother reads her dream of a falcon, Kriemhild divines what a tragic love could do to her, and she resolves to avoid the joy of love forever and so avoid its pain. When her falcon comes, however, she accepts him gladly, and when on the second night of her wedding he returns from a strange absence, unlike the fretful Brunhild she allows him to silence the question on her lips. We are never told whether she knows the truth about his taming of Brunhild; but it is with pride, not jealousy, that she allows the court to think that he enjoyed King Gunther's Queen. She is very much in love with her young husband. When he and she make their preparations to leave Worms a delicate symmetrical arrangement in the fourth lines of the first two strophes of Chapter Eleven informs us that Siegfried will be master; for when she hears that he is soon to take her home, *she* is *glad* to learn it, but when he hears that she first intends to secure her share of the Burgundian patrimony, *he* is *loath* to learn it—and nothing comes of her intention. But then she shows much spirit and some lack of tact in asking Hagen, of all men, to follow her north as her liegeman. Nothing comes of this, either, for as Hagen angrily explains, the place of those of Troneck had always been at the court of Burgundy. And so they depart. The next significant moment comes ten years later when the pair have returned to Worms. Although Brunhild has planned the confrontation, it is Kriemhild who tactlessly provokes the quarrel by praising Siegfried in superlative terms, reviving imperial claims which he has long since abandoned on being tamed by her love. Although she withdraws so far as to offer Brunhild parity in husbands, the damage has been done. Brunhild means to establish her own precedence and this brings out the worst in Kriemhild. Nothing less than the manifest utter defeat of Brunhild will content her now. Some of Kriemhild's concern for her status may have been inspired by pride in her husband, but it is shot through with self-love. In the scene in which Hagen tricks her into divulging the whereabouts of Siegfried's vulnerable spot she relates without resentment how her husband had beaten her for her loose talk. 'How perfectly matched this couple must have been!' we are bound to exclaim, 'if this imperious woman could so sweetly accept a thrashing from her husband.' It is on her love for Siegfried that Hagen plays, and we may well think it excessive, because blind, since in the very words with which she owns her fault towards Brunhild she begs Hagen not to let Siegfried pay for it. Her unconscious fears at what she has done express themselves in warning dreams. And when her chamberlain announces a corpse on the threshold she knows everything in one revealing flash. She resolutely insists on the public proof of Hagen's guilt by the ordeal beside the bier. For those with eyes to see (and only Hagen appears to have them) the future can be read at the graveside. Until now we have suspected that Kriemhild was inordinately attached to her spouse. When, weeping tears of blood, she has his magnificent coffin raised for a last look at his face, we know it. Her love was Siegfried's and her own undoing, and it will prove the undoing of them all. Now comes the most tenuous part of the clue, Kriemhild's resignation from motherhood, with which I have dealt above. After residing at Worms for some time she goes through a reconciliation with Gunther, but not with Hagen, whereupon her brothers betray her anew over Siegfried's treasure, with Hagen as the driving force; for Hagen clearly sees that she is winning allies with her bounty. When Etzel sends to woo her she is persuaded to surrender her person to him and to overcome her scruples against re-marriage and a pagan husband, only when Rüdiger, by his oath of alliance, has placed the instruments of vengeance in her hands. Her invitation to her brothers seems inspired by both revenge and homesickness. In the series of confrontations with Hagen in Hungary, of which she gets the worst only because she is a woman, her passion for revenge is goaded to frenzy. She was certainly careless about her son Ortlieb, but since the poet behaves so irresponsibly here, it is futile to discuss her reactions. Now comes a whole list of warriors, from both sides, whom she sacrifices to her revenge: Bloedelin, Iring, Rüdiger (why does she weep when Rüdiger at last resolves to fight? The poet leaves us with yet another enigma, which has not failed to draw the unwary), then Gernot and Giselher, who refuse to buy their lives with Hagen's, and finally, in cold blood, Gunther. Strangely enough, it is overlooked by the commentators . . . that these sacrifices are due equally to Hagen. After all, he did murder Siegfried and he now glories in it; and the only thing that is needed to avoid the destruction of the house whose faithful guardian he claims to be is for him to walk out of the hall and die fighting. But Hagen does not see this. He drags them all down with him, and such is the poet's sympathy that Hagen wins most of the kudos. This is not without its bearing on our assessment of Kriemhild's situation. The poet's gift of glory to Hagen, though Hagen only partly deserves it (it is all at Kriemhild's expense), is inspired by male prejudice. Our poet's pride of sex makes him as mean towards Kriemhild here as Homer's pride of race made him momentarily ungenerous towards Hector, when he would not suffer Hector to slay Patroclus until first Apollo had shattered him and then a nobody, Euphorbus, had struck him between the shoulders, thus cheating the Trojan leader of his glory. For just as Brunhild as a woman was expected to behave with docility on the nuptial couch, however, much she may have been deceived, so Kriemhild, whatever her wrongs, as a woman was forbidden to pursue revenge to the destruction of good warriors. . . . Women must not take up the sword to slay. Their womanhood should prevent them. Isolde's feelings acknowledge, Kriemhild's violate this rule. The events of the last chapter confirm this. Dietrich, the one figure who rises above the conflict, sets aside his own good grounds for vengeance and delivers Gunther and Hagen to Kriemhild, bound, with a recommendation to mercy, thus contradicting his premature verdict that she was a she-devil. She is given her chance to find her woman's nature; but this she cannot achieve. The grim years of widowhood and exile have robbed her of the power to do so. Though outwardly she may have warmed to Rüdiger's daughter and proved a worthy successor to Queen Helche, her heart is frozen over. Yet, as we have seen, the hot fount of her revenge was her love for her young husband, thwarted and turned to hatred for his slayer, a love that we may well call vast when we measure it by its obverse. Impelled by this fury that possesses her, she now kills Hagen, the finest warrior of them all, and, masculine pride thus having been outraged, she at once pays the price for so far overstepping her bounds. A woman whose will was as strong as a man's risked being branded as a monster. Such women were far less rare in the heroic Age of Migrations, when warriors had need of them. But men of the high Middle Ages thought them either comic or objectionable. Indeed, it has been well said that Kriemhild could never have been invented in our poet's generation. The marvel is that he could re-create her.

Kriemhild's antagonist Hagen is not easy to assess because the very events that elicit his good qualities spring from his darker nature. This blend of the heroic and the sinister has appealed mightily to German writers in the past. One critic saw in Hagen's bearing the self-assertion of the ethical personality against odds, overlooking (or brushing aside) the fact that Hagen was a murderer. Another, as we saw, viewed him in a Christian or near-Christian light as a man who had attained to selfless care for his dear ones. It would of course be unprofitable to try to measure so magnificent a figure with a conventional moral tape. But we shall get nowhere with this enigmatic personage until the nature of his guilt has been established.

Hagen was not present at the quarrel of the queens, no doubt in order that the impact of Brunhild's grief upon him might be the greater. Shortly afterwards, he came and found Brunhild in tears. He asked her what was the matter and she 'told' him, and he then swore that Siegfried should pay for it. Although he had time and opportunity to amplify and if necessary correct Brunhild's account, which (whatever its content) must have been one-sided, he never wavered in his intention to kill Siegfried. What counted more with him than the truth was the fact that the language of the ring and girdle had appeared to be confirmed by the tears of his queen, witnessed by all. He therefore went to work on Kriemhild craftily, though Kriemhild was the sister of his lord and also his own kinswoman. Other motives than revenge for tarnished honour lurk below the surface. We gain some insight into Hagen's self-control and political acumen during the first clash with Siegfried when, in his youthful arrogance, Siegfried challenged Gunther to fight for their two kingdoms: for on this occasion Hagen permitted himself no more than the reproach: 'He ought to have refrained. My lords would never have wronged him so . . . ', leaving threats and bluster to his nephew Ortwin. Kriemhild's invitation to Hagen to follow her to the Netherlands as her (and therefore Siegfried's) vassal must have galled him, and his angry refusal is no doubt aimed against her husband as much as against herself. Siegfried's pre-eminence irked Hagen. He could not suffer his king to be outshone. Failing to persuade Gunther on the point of his marital honour, he suggests to him that if Siegfried were dead, Gunther would be lord of many lands, and this Hagen may well have believed, since, as Siegfried lies dying, Hagen exults at having ended his dominion, and he asserts that there will now be few to oppose the Burgundians. To this must be added Hagen's first expression of a wish that Siegfried's treasure should come to Burgundy, long before the queens have quarrelled, when Siegfried and Kriemhild's visit was being mooted. Here the poet is said to have 'sown the seed' of Hagen's intention to acquire the hoard.

The trait which explains most of Hagen's deeds is his political clearsightedness followed by ruthless action. It has been well said of him that he 'represents the type of responsible statesman who has to do what he sees is necessary, even against public opinion and against a weak sovereign'. The quarrel of the queens convinced him that the time had come for Siegfried to go, leaving him to choose but the means. Hagen foresees so clearly that his house must perish if his lords go to Hungary that he scarcely needs confirmation either from the fairies' prophecy or from his experiment with the Chaplain—so that the incidents in which they occur are to be interpreted as a demonstration in epic terms of his superior insight. The dullest member of the audience now knows that Hagen knows. All that can follow for Hagen is resignation, which in so active a man means dedication. It is this same clearsightedness which explains his brutal slaughter of the innocent Ortlieb. The appearance of Dancwart at the door tells him that the moment for the inevitable battle has come, and so he summons fate punctually himself. His words and deeds are governed by supreme economy. Only once does he reverse a decision, when his foolish lord makes the invitation to Hungary an issue not of policy but of courage. Stung by Giselher's taunt, Hagen accepts the challenge, with the outcome he so clearly surveys, and withdraws his opposition. In this scene Hagen had reminded Gunther of their fell deed. Accused by the blood at Siegfried's bier, he had been too proud to deny his guilt. And later, face to face with Kriemhild, he had again owned it. And when at last she had him at her mercy, he truthfully observed that things had turned out just as he thought they would.

Hagen's motive for murdering Siegfried was therefore political rather than personal in a petty sense. So long as Siegfried could be used to further the Burgundian interest, as in the war against the Saxons or the wooing of Brunhild, Hagen used him without prejudice. But when he sensed a threat in Siegfried, he made away with him, and his action was as impersonal as it was efficient.

With the one exception of the fateful visit to Hungary, it is always Hagen who forces the pace when important decisions have to be made. He is the power behind the throne. Thus the degree of Hagen's guilt is great, and when he is about to incur it, the poet admits it and even tends to harp on it. Nevertheless, in the second half of the poem, increasingly, when the plot requires grim resistance from Hagen the poet seems to overlook Hagen's guilt and gains sympathy for him in his reversal of fortune as for one betrayed.

Hagen, we are told, was a tall man of impressive appearance and gait, with eyes that struck terror in the beholder. For all his splendid presence, his was no face that a girl would wish to kiss. He was nevertheless capable of kindness, as well as of stern loyalty towards kinsmen whom he cannot always have esteemed. He approves of the proposed marriage between Giselher and Rüdiger's daughter with benignity as well as policy. Towards Eckewart, and even more towards Rüdiger, he shows perfect chivalry and tact: for in returning Eckewart's sword on the frontier he restores his honour, and in asking for Rüdiger's shield in battle he makes it possible for him to rise above his tragic dilemma and give proof of his affection for the Burgundians and also to reassert himself as the Bestower of Gifts. To do this, it has been argued, Hagen asserts the claims of friendship against those of his fealty to Gunther, for to accept Rüdiger's gift is to bind himself to Rüdiger, thus bringing about his neutrality. Such warm regard for the reputations of others as Hagen shows, and such readiness to redress them, if tarnished, are rare qualities, and this may help to explain why Hagen felt bound to restore Brunhild's esteem at any cost, after Kriemhild had shattered it. Honour was what he understood best. Hagen's high moral qualities in the second half are underlined by the poet's presentation of Volker and Dancwart as his physical superiors, and his greater depth also appears at once if we compare him with another vassal-in-chief, Hildebrand, who fails to deal with young hotheads, or with the amiable young berserk Wolfhart, who dies happy to have been slain by a King. And again, Hagen's great stature is seen when we confront him with the shifty kings of Burgundy. For, having judged a situation and taken action, Hagen abides by the deed, he is not assailed by vain regrets. Hagen remains unbroken to the end, active, and yet resigned to the fate which (unlike Siegfried) he has long foreseen.

True to his style, the poet offers no direct hint whether Hagen in any way purges his guilt. Kriemhild indeed subjects him and his companions to a purgatory of steel and fire from which they emerge with enhanced loyalty towards each other. But Hagen's brutal killing of Ortlieb is an unpromising entry into any purgatory, and the notion had better be dismissed. Our poet fell short of Homer morally as well as artistically: he failed to relate Hagen in his greatness to Hagen at his depths. We understand and accept Hagen with gratitude as an ancient heroic figure in a medieval setting. But we feel no need to glorify either him or his 'Nibelung spirit', as they have been glorified anachronistically in these days of industrial civilization. Marvel at Hagen we surely must. But with their perverse 'will to death', Hagen and his friends are best viewed from a distance.

Kriemhild and Hagen are evenly matched in their grim magnificence, and the poet pits them against each other with great skill. The ruined love of a passionate woman and the 'honour' of a masterful man are terrible forces to be reckoned with. The poet makes it wholly credible that they should hold each other in check for so long.

The three Burgundian kings form the centre of a highly dangerous court. Although nothing of importance can be undertaken without Gunther's at least tacit consent, whether it be a murder or a grand theft of treasure, his younger brothers Gernot and Giselher are always free to speak their minds. Gernot's role is that of a middle term between his elder and younger brother: sometimes he is Cox to Gunther, at other times he is Box to Giselher. Giselher's part is that of 'junior lead'. The hypocrisy and treachery of all three towards their sister are differentiated broadly in descending degrees. Yet a word of caution is necessary here. It may well be that the poet would not have approved of this additive approach to his characters, and that when he makes them protest their honesty and innocence he means both them and us to believe it—for the moment.

Gunther is a king in name but in little else. In the last scenes, in which all show themselves as doughty fighting men, he, too, hardens into a hero and so may be thought to atone somewhat for his past. He is also a very courteous man—so courteous and smooth that it is difficult to catch his drift. Before the poem begins he has already learnt to rely on Hagen. Confronted with the imponderable threat of young Siegfried, and with Ortwin calling for swords, he is sorry that Hagen stays silent so long, and it is significant that when Hagen does speak up he is 'Hagen the strong'. On such strong men can weak kings lean. But Gunther had to be weak in the first half of the poem because the plot required it. Only a weak man would have left the winning and taming of his wife to another. Gunther, however, is not only weak but also vain and deceitful. He finds it possible to aspire to the love of a woman beyond his own power to woo, and as her publicly acknowledged conqueror to make her his wife. But his reward for aspiring so far above himself is farcical humiliation. When Siegfried, at his own suggestion, so far demeans himself as to hold Gunther's stirrup as his 'vassal' while Brunhild and her ladies look on, Gunther feels exalted. On their return from Iceland, Siegfried had to remind Gunther that Kriemhild's hand was to be his reward. But perhaps this may be excused, on the grounds that no man should seem in a hurry to give away his sister. Gunther's yellow streak is skilfully hinted at as early as the fourth chapter. An attack by Liudegast and Liudeger has been announced, and Siegfried sees Gunther anxious and silent. Frankly asked by Siegfried why he has so much changed from his former happy ways, Gunther replies with an unwarrantable insinuation:

I cannot tell everyone about the vexation I have

> to bear, locked away in my heart . . . One should complain of one's wrongs to proven friends.

It is an answer that would pain the heart of any honest man. No wonder Siegfried changes colour violently. When counter-measures are agreed on, Siegfried goodnaturedly asks Gunther to stay at home with the ladies—and Gunther does so, although Siegfried himself is a king, and there is a king in the field against them.

In the last analysis Gunther's weakness can be made to bear the whole responsibility for the tragedy. Faced on the nuptial couch with the choice between the physical enjoyment of Brunhild and the truth, he might have chosen the latter: but in fact he chose the former.

Although Gunther denies it later, he connived at Siegfried's murder. He at first resisted Hagen's suggestion. Then the argument that, were Siegfried dead, Gunther would rule many kingdoms made him 'sad'. And when Hagen proposed a secret murder, Gunther showed alert interest in the means, and, satisfied on this score, he did not withhold his consent. On this we have the poet's observation:

> The king followed his vassal Hagen's advice to evil effect, and those rare knights began to set afoot the great betrayal.

When the deed is done, however, Gunther breaks out into laments, only to be checked by murderer and victim alike, in words that leave us in doubt which of the two despised him the more. In view of his share in the murder of Kriemhild's husband, Gunther's facile protest 'after all, she is my sister', twice uttered, sickens us: when Hagen suggests taking her Nibelung treasure (for which Gunther then fabricates an alibi), and when Hagen advises against her marriage with Etzel. A strange thing, plausibly grounded in the character of a weak and perfidious man, is that when the Burgundians set out for Hungary, Gunther places his reliance in the dubious reconciliation between Kriemhild and himself, which he has in any case already dishonoured. On the way there, Gunther even fails to stand up for his own Chaplain when Hagen throws him into the Danube. And in Etzel's hall he trusts to his glibness to justify Hagen's slaughter of Ortlieb to the outraged father. It is long after the fighting has begun, when he refuses to buy his life at the expense of Hagen's, that he moves into a more favourable light, which holds him till the end. It is widely thought that the two heroic lays from which the ***Nibelungenlied*** descended were of Burgundo-Frankish origin, and it must be admitted that in Gunther's character there is enshrined a blend of perfidy, cowardice, cunning, finesse, and physical courage that strikes one as peculiarly Merovingian.

Apart from the doubling role already referred to, Gernot is almost without function in the poem. Yet several times he steps forward from the background to test the situation before it is safe for Gunther to commit himself, or to supplement an official act of Gunther's. It is Gernot who bids Siegfried welcome when he is still thirsting for a fight—whereupon they pour out Gunther's wine, which, once drunk, will be binding on all. Gernot acquits himself well at the Saxon wars, but he is of course overshadowed by Siegfried. It is Gernot who produces the compromise which results in the sinking of Kriemhild's treasure. Like his elder and his younger brother, he is very courteous. After Gunther, for reasons that escape us, has overlooked the death of Helche when welcoming Rüdiger, Gernot offers their condolences. And when Volker, publicly and apparently without prior discussion, has brought the question of a royal marriage with Rüdiger's daughter to the highest pitch of embarrassment, Gernot eases the situation with a gallant and tactful statement, only to have Hagen intervene and make a match not with him as the bridegroom but the other 'young king', Giselher. Gernot receives some prominence in the battle in Etzel's hall, from having inherited Giselher's traditional role as the recipient of a sword from Rüdiger, a gift with which he will slay the donor. His high-sounding exchange with Rüdiger merges into another between Giselher and Rüdiger by means of the ambiguous line: 'Then said the son of fair Uote of Burgundy'. The context shows that Giselher is meant.

The role of Giselher as a youth of tender years persists throughout the poem, as we have seen. And we have also seen how the poet sends Giselher into action with reckless disregard for his 'character' when gentle speech is needed. For he scarcely intended us to think of Giselher as a nauseating old hypocrite, which is what Giselher amounts to if we simply add him up. Giselher is clearly intended to present a foil of youth, innocence, and loyal affection to the dark figures of Gunther and Hagen. But, as the poet unfolds his story, all three attributes are dissipated. Giselher's youth vanishes in a whirl of years, his innocence and loyalty (at least towards his sister) in the storm of events. The word '*triuwe*'—loyal affection'—is always on his lips, yet he never once takes effective action against treachery. It was in his knowledge and power to have warned Kriemhild and Siegfried. After a protest which proves as ineffectual as Gunther's, no sooner is he back with his brothers from the planned alibi which enables Hagen to sink the treasure, than we are told: 'Giselher especially would have liked to give proof of his affection'. But this does not prevent him from acting his part in the feigned dismissal of Hagen from royal favour. This conceded, the counterclaim that Giselher is unmatched in the poem for the certainty and clarity of his feeling for what is true, just, and noble may, for what it is worth, also be conceded. It is only Giselher's will and ability to practise what he preaches that are in question. His latent worth comes out in battle. When Dietrich tells the Burgundian leaders in confidence how matters stand with Kriemhild and they see how things must end, Giselher is notably absent. Only gradually does it dawn on the 'young' man that they are doomed. But as their fate becomes clearer and clearer to him, he matures visibly, so that he can at last look death steadily in the face. When he advises that the corpses be thrown from the hall he gains the commendation of no less a man than Hagen. Next, his childish faith in his sister's mercy breaks down. On Rüdiger's arrival on the scene of battle, his hope flares up again, only to be dampened once more when this bond, also breaks. He now finally accepts his fate and grows to royal and heroic stature, fully deserving the tribute in death of his gallant victor and victim, Wolf-

Kriemhild discovers Siegfried's body, in a 1923 drawing by Josef Hegenbarth.

hart. Giselher seems to have retained his sister's affection through all the crooked course of their lives, for, homesick in Hungary, she dreams that she is kissing him. Nor does Giselher show bad conscience towards her. It is quite conceivable that life at a medieval court as in other places where politics are paramount, bred up schizophrenic attitudes. Only when one's own position was secure could one give way to natural affection. Such may have been the very air that our poet breathed. Nevertheless, it is when trying to assess Giselher, of all the characters in this poem, that we sense the risks we take in dealing with the figures of medieval epic in terms of modern characterization. In the background there is always the knowledge that the truly 'young' Giselher of an earlier epic on the destruction of the Burgundians, in which his role is readily understood, has been stretched back over the years into the very different separate plot that ended in the death of Siegfried.

All the foregoing characters lived together serenely in high estate at Worms, so we are told in the first chapter, and long might they have continued to do so but for their becoming involved with two people of very different calibre.

Siegfried and Brunhild go together. Each has a quasi-mythical aura. Each is of a different order from that of normal men and women, both in their superhuman strength and in the nature of its limitations. Their excess of strength breeds fear and respect for each. Yet at times it also invests each with an air of burlesque. Each is broken and done with before the first part of the poem is over, and from the same fundamental cause: entanglement in ordinary human affairs through love. There is a hint of prior acquaintance between Siegfried and Brunhild, and there is an indefinable suggestion that something has gone wrong between them. For the conditions set for Brunhild's wooers are such as to exclude all but Siegfried, and it is in fact Siegfried who fulfils them, though on behalf of another man and to win another woman. Nevertheless, beyond the lurking suspicion that Siegfried in some way meant much to Brunhild, all remains wrapped in mystery, and must forever remain so.

When we first meet Siegfried, he has still to emerge from a wildness which we divine from his dragon-slaying past in Hagen's description but which surprises us in a prince of the Netherlands so tenderly nurtured as he is said to be. The violence and impetuosity with which he challenges Gunther to fight for their two kingdoms come as a great shock to the urbane court of Burgundy. It is only by a desperate exercise of tact that the cooler heads at Worms manage to avoid a battle with the stranger and stave off a nameless threat to their society. Despite young Siegfried's courtly trappings, the scene partakes of the timeless confrontation of civilized men with barbarians. Siegfried's love for Kriemhild, however, soon tames him and even induces him to demean himself as Gunther's 'vassal' after they have met, an act which at the same time automatically excludes him as a possible suitor for Queen Brunhild. When Kriemhild and Siegfried are married this slight imbalance is redressed. The second part of the poem may show Kriemhild as a woman with all the makings of a virago, but the first makes it clear that Siegfried's mastery was never in doubt and that his tenderness and superabundant virility made him a perfect match for his spirited young wife. Having crowned his high endeavours in war, adventure, and love, Siegfried matures rapidly into a charming man with an open nature, who is ever ready to help a friend. Also, in appropriate contexts, he can still give expression to his huge vitality through roughest horseplay, as when he captures a bear and looses it among his companions. At such times he is of course a figure of fun. But Siegfried is not one of those boring heroes who suffer from too much bone in the head, as might be inferred from this incident with the bear. He owes his treasure to knowing how to play *tertius gaudens,* no easy gambit. Whatever we think of its ethics, his handling of Gunther's wooing expedition is masterly. After his frank and friendly nature and his courtesy have exposed him to his murderer, and the poet has bedded him so fittingly upon the flowers, his dying words reveal a character as sensitive and intelligent as it is loving and considerate for the wife and child he will be leaving. This is no ox that falls beneath the axe but a human being possessed of all the qualities that make a man truly noble.

How far can such a character be responsible for his own tragic end, conceding that Siegfried has been elevated appreciably by the last poet in the interests of the new fashions of chivalry and love-service, and in order to make his murder more detestable? It has been said that Siegfried died because he talked. This is true so far as he need not have divulged the whereabouts of his vulnerable spot to his wife any more than Samson with Delilah. But if we were to think that he had told Kriemhild in words of his taming of Brunhild, there is no evidence to support it—the poet has seen to that. Rather is it to be thought that in handing over Brunhild's ring and girdle to Kriemhild he said nothing. For had he said anything he would have told the truth, and Kriemhild would then have had to lie to call Brunhild his paramour. Siegfried's fault will have been his surrender to his wife of the tokens of Brunhild's virginity, leaving their silent accusation uncorrected. Whether he had already incurred guilt through planning and carrying out the deception of Brunhild in Iceland is another question. As in ancient Greece, Germanic and then medieval German heroes were permitted to be resourceful on occasion if abnormal circumstances seemed to call for it. Nevertheless, despite this caveat, it is undeniable that Siegfried twice violated the will of a woman whose only fault (if fault it be) was to have taken extreme precautions to find a suitable mate, and this, he must have known, was dangerous, if not immoral. Siegfried took this risk upon himself in pursuit of his own love, and he paid for it with his life.

Both Siegfried and Achilles were mighty heroes with a vulnerable spot, and therefore both died young, though Siegfried (as our poet tells the tale) enjoyed ten or eleven years of married life. The great difference between them is that Achilles consciously chose fame and early death with all the insight and apartness which this knowledge brought him, whereas Siegfried lived without care and had to learn the bitter lesson in the last few moments that remained to him after he had been treacherously struck down.

The figure of Brunhild has suffered a great decline in the ***Nibelungenlied,*** compared with what it must have been in the original lay, in which, so it seems, she was a woman whose sense of outraged honour at having been wooed by one warrior for another made her press ruthlessly for the elimination of her 'first man', so that it has been claimed in respect of our Brunhild that the poet failed in his task. For this decline, two interconnected reasons are urged. First, that as feelings grew to be more refined, the starkness of the old plot was toned down, as when Siegfried was no longer permitted to deflower Brunhild. Second, that a 'heroic' woman of ancient Germanic stamp, to whom honour was all, could not maintain her place in the poetry of the chivalric age, which was dominated by the great lady of the court. Brunhild's display of physical strength both in the arena and on her nuptial couch furnished opportunities for burlesque of which a minstrel poet might safely avail himself—and tragedy and burlesque do not accord well within one character.

Just as in Worms Siegfried admits to knowledge of Brunhild's ways and of the ocean paths to her distant court, and on his arrival there recognizes her land and her person, so he in turn is recognized by one of her attendants. And Brunhild herself knows of 'mighty Siegfried', assumes that he has come to woo her, does not fear him so far as to accept him, unless he defeat her in her contests, and when the visitors present themselves, addresses Siegfried by name before Gunther, although it is clear from protocol that Siegfried must be Gunther's 'vassal'. Corrected by Siegfried on this score, Brunhild then addresses herself to Gunther without any show of emotion. When Siegfried returns from his expedition to Nibelungland, Brunhild offers him a greeting that marks him out from his followers. Until Brunhild takes her seat at the wedding feast, there has been no sign of distressed feelings. Custom would have sanctioned consummatino of her marriage in Iceland, with her kinsmen and warriors within call, and had she harboured suspicions then, this would have been the best place in which to clear them up. But it is only when she sees Kriemhild sitting at Siegfried's side that her feelings get the better of her and she bursts into tears. According to the text (and what else have we to go by?) Brunhild's reason for weeping is that it troubles her to see her sister-in-law sitting as bride to a vassal, and she threatens not to consummate the marriage unless she learns why this is so. Gunther's reply adds nothing to the eloquent fact that Kriemhild and Siegfried are sitting opposite, in the seat of honour: he says that Siegfried is a king as mighty as himself and thus a fitting mate for his sister. Gunther's evasiveness, surely is an insult to a young bride with whom he is due to spend the remainder of his life. His answer ought to have provoked her to ask why Siegfried acted in Iceland as though he were Gunther's vassal. But no such question is asked. It takes the knotty form, reiterated at the bed-side, that Brunhild demands to know why Kriemhild has been married to Siegfried. Outwardly at least, for the next ten years Brunhild will cling to the idea that Siegfried was Gunther's vassal, until her quarrel with Kriemhild brings matters to a head, though now she will refuse Gunther her favours unless he answers her question. Gunther of course cannot do so and he resorts to force, with lamentable results. Outward forms of etiquette and protocol in the Middle Ages could have left no queen in doubt as to the sovereign status of a king in Siegfried's position: yet for ten years Brunhild is at grips with the problem how Kriemhild can hold her head so high despite Siegfried's imagined servile status. Finally, when her insistence provokes Kriemhild to call her a paramour, her thought is that if Siegfried has boasted of enjoying her he must die. She is not mollified by Gunther's superficial solution of the crisis, whereby Siegfried clears himself by his readiness to swear an oath, nor does she, on the other hand, explicitly demand Siegfried's death. Her tears and her account of what happened during the quarrel are enough to seal Siegfried's fate. Hagen takes over, and Brunhild all but disappears from the story. At the end of the first part of the poem, after the murder of Siegfried, Brunhild sits indifferent in her pride while Kriemhild weeps. Later, she is shown to be inaccessible to Etzel's envoys. And during the last night that she will ever spend with Gunther, as 'the Queen', unnamed, she pleasures him as a dutiful wife.

The poet gives us very little guidance during all these events. After her tears at the banquet, and just before the two queens are escorted to their nuptials, the poet assures us that 'As yet there was no enmity between them'. And when, after ten years, Siegfried and Kriemhild revisit Worms, and Siegfried sits as before in the seat of honour, Brunhild's feelings are said, in an ironical double-entendre, to be 'still friendly enough towards him to let him be (live)'. It is surely better to take the poet at his word here, rather than impute, without evidence, feelings of sexual jealousy to Brunhild. The poet's hints also have the function of pointing forward to the time when Brunhild will quarrel with Kriemhild and then wish to have Siegfried killed.

I have several times drawn attention to the dangers of 'explaining' the characters beyond what the poem gives us, and the danger is nowhere greater than in elaborating on Brunhild's silences. It is not permissible to resort to Northern versions of the story in order to show that Brunhild loved Siegfried, nor can we prove that such versions of the story were known to Austro-Bavarian audiences for them to fill in the background themselves. We must abide by the version before us. Here the salient fact seems to me to be Brunhild's fixed idea that Siegfried was Gunther's liegeman, to which she adheres tenaciously despite all too tangible evidence to the contrary. Surely this is either her last legal hold on a situation that is growing beyond her, or, if she really believes it, a vital illusion? For if she accepts it as true that mighty Siegfried is a sovereign king, she must admit that she has been most shamefully deceived, and cheated of the one eligible mate in the story. The decisive moments of her life were those in which Siegfried and Gunther came to Iceland and she was wooed and won, and it is to this time of decision that she reverts when she insists that Siegfried is a vassal, because then she witnessed all the outward signs of it. By implication she reverts to that time also during her wedding night when she demands to know the truth, else Gunther shall not lie with her. For Brunhild must divine that only the man who vanquished her at the game of war can vanquish her at the game of love. Although a second deception settles this issue superficially, doubt still lurks in her mind. She had taken it for granted that, if any, Siegfried was to be her mate, so that now when she has been won by another, she is forced to believe (or at least to act as though she believes) Siegfried to be Gunther's vassal. Her tragedy is that pride and suspicion force her in the end to destroy her own defences and learn with certainty of her deception.

Great has been Brunhild's fall since the proud days in Iceland. Whereas she had once commanded and if need be fought to express her will, in the new state to which her womanhood has reduced her she has to live by her wits like any other lady in medieval society. When she sets to work to persuade Gunther to invite Siegfried and Kriemhild, she speaks 'subtly'.

> 'Whatever heights of power a royal vassal might have reached [she says], he should not fail to do his sovereign's bidding.' Gunther smiled at her words, since whenever he saw Siegfried, he did not reckon it as homage.

The man who had no right to possess Brunhild, smiles in a superior way at the perplexity his deceit has occasioned. But what was Brunhild thinking? *Did* she intuitively feel cheated of her rightful mate? A situation of this sort offers a poet of the Heroic and Modern Ages great opportunities, and they were and have been taken. But, for the reasons given, the odds were against it in Austria at the beginning of the thirteenth century, and all that we are offered are tears, riddles, and silence.

Of the remaining figures, that of Rüdiger is by far the most interesting. In his association with the Burgundians he probably does not go back beyond the immediate, epic, source of the second half of our poem. He is thus not deeply involved in primary events, and this makes it possible for him to be shown as possessing more recent 'medieval' as well as 'heroic' qualities. As ambassador and suitor by proxy for Kriemhild's hand he shows some skill, only failing, in his honest enthusiasm for his mission, to divine Kriemhild's ulterior motives for consenting, so that he binds himself to her personally for the future beyond his oath of allegiance to his queen. In this, however, his hand was forced: Rüdiger had to succeed on his lord's behalf, and such were Kriemhild's terms. As host at Pöchlarn, his warmth and generosity are above praise (Chapter 27). His testing time comes when the fighting has begun in Hungary and his sovereigns demand that he fight for them. It is torment for Rüdiger to have to make up his mind. On the one hand he is bound by his feudal oath to Etzel and his personal oath to Kriemhild: on the other, he feels in honour bound to the Burgundians, and very strongly bound indeed, both because he had been their host and escort and because of the marriage tie between his daughter and Giselher (which, however, remained unconsummated). The terrible dilemma in Rüdiger's heart is that he is gripped by conflicting obligations, on the one hand of law and ethics, on the other of custom and sentiment, obligations the common meeting-ground of which was 'honour' or reputation in the eyes of the world, the best part of a medieval warrior, so that whatever choice Rüdiger makes, whether to fight on the one side or on the other, or to abstain, he is disgraced. This anguish causes him to speak of his 'soul'.

> There is no denying it, noble lady, [he says to Kriemhild] that I swore to risk my life and position for you: but that I would lose my soul I never swore. Remember, it was I who brought those highborn kings to the festival here.

Fine as the words sound, Rüdiger is overstating his case. No man can lose his soul for an offence against custom, rather than against Christian teaching. Socially and humanly lamentable though it was to have to fight men with whom he had such close ties of friendship, no confessor would have detected sin in it. Rather would he have found sin in a breach of the sacred oaths that bound a liegeman to his lord, or in the scanting of a private oath, such as that of Rüdiger to Kriemhild. Rüdiger knows this in his heart, and it is a magnificent tribute to friendship within the harsh code of feudal society that he does not consent to do the one possible thing until Etzel and Kriemhild have demeaned themselves by kneeling to him (reversing the normal roles of lords and vassals) and until he himself has offered to return his fief, preferring poverty and exile; after which his king and queen have no recourse but to beg him to have pity on them! (Here is a feast of high sentiment, and there is more to come.) Thus shamed into accepting an obligation from which he has technically freed himself—the feudal oath of the period in any case had a clause exempting the vassal from the duty to fight to his own dishonour—Rüdiger prepares to enter the fray, now a loyal vassal who sacrifices everything to his lord, but also a broken-hearted man. To him in this state Hagen's request for his shield comes as a marvellous deliverance. It at once conveys that Hagen fully understands Rüdiger's position as a vassal and it gives Rüdiger a chance to show himself for the last time as the generous man that he is and so grow again to full stature. Rüdiger is now fit to die. He need fear no longer for his 'soul', by which we understand his 'worldly honour'. Posthumously, too, his honour is redeemed, for although he sought death as the solution of his dilemma, he slew his slayer, and slaying him, slew a king.

The scene that ends in Rüdiger's death has been rightly recognized as one of the great beauties of the poem. Momentarily, a bridge of magnanimous understanding is flung across the chasm of hostility. The earlier poet planned it that Rüdiger and his son-in-law Giselher should slay each other, with Giselher using Rüdiger's gift-sword; but our poet judged this no longer tolerable, and transferred Giselher's role to Gernot. He wrested the last bit of high-flown sentiment out of a situation in which a beloved host stands committed to fight his guests, friends, and relations, and one notes that there is rather too much talking, with some smack of heroics, as in the exchange between Rüdiger and Volker or when Gernot tells Rüdiger that he will try to deserve his gift sword dearly—if need be by killing the donor. The question of Rüdiger's 'soul' is not logically pursued, for when he decides to fight we are told he will hazard both body and soul. But perhaps this is bitter irony. Hearing Giselher place the bonds of the kindred above those of marriage, Rüdiger begs God to have mercy on them. And when at last he fights he enters the fray in a berserk fury and dies without a further thought of his salvation. To assert, as has been claimed, that Rüdiger suffers a Germanic fate with a Christian character, is to deny to pagans the sentiment of friendship. But it must be admitted that the exploitation in poetry of a conflict between duty and friendship was not possible much before this time, when the ferment of Christian civilization was loosening the tongues of poets.

The remaining characters call for little discussion, since they are for the most part types.

The Austro-Bavarians inherited a favourable image of Attila ultimately from his allies, the Ostrogoths, so that the Etzel of the ***Nibelungenlied*** is far from being a Scourge of God. Rather does he remind us of other great kings of medieval literature, of King Arthur and Charlemagne, in his role of an amiable *roi fainéant.* For example, when in his courage he is about to enter the fray in person he is pulled back with decisive result by his shield-strap! But for his blissful unawareness of what was brewing under his very nose there would have been no catastrophe. The arrogance of others is blamed, however, for his having been kept in the dark. We see him smiling benignly on one and all until Hagen makes his brutal remark on Ortlieb's ill-fated look, and even then Etzel shows gentlemanly restraint. It is hard not to visualize him anachronistically as blinking good-humouredly over his spectacles. Nevertheless, where he perceives action to be necessary his response is swift and decisive. When Volker, his guest, is in danger of being killed by the indignant Huns whom Volker has so wantonly bereaved, King Etzel races out on to the scene from a window at breakneck speed, despite his years, and quells the disturbance.

Dietrich, a king in exile, alone succeeds in preserving his neutrality nearly to the end. Although much beholden to Etzel, he is evidently not so closely bound to him as Margrave Rüdiger, nor has he sworn an oath to Kriemhild. As a comrade-in-arms of Hagen's from the days when Hagen was hostage to Etzel, he warns the Burgundians on their arrival and takes the field against the two survivors only when he learns the terrible news from Hildebrand that his hot-headed war-band, all that remains to him in the world, has been drawn into battle against orders and slain to a man, bar Hildebrand. The stunning impact of this news all but unmans him, yet he recovers himself and goes to Gunther and Hagen. His reproaches to them, and the self-conquest which his generous terms imply, reveal lofty greatness of soul. With Dietrich there is least risk in speaking of a Christian character.

Dietrich's Master-at-Arms, old Hildebrand, shows a great

descent from the magnificent figure of the ancient Lay of Hildebrand. In our poem he is an old campaigner with a somewhat professional air, despite his noble birth. His failure to restrain his nephew Wolfhart even with a high tackle suggests a devoted sergeant-major attempting to deal with a rash young officer, and it is amusing and revealing that when Wolfhart breaks loose Hildebrand races him to be first in the battle. On his return as sole survivor, part-architect of his lord's ruin, he adopts a hangdog air. His tendency to bandy insults with his betters, perhaps inherited from misunderstood memories of his tragic altercation with the son he had to slay, is sharply curbed by Dietrich. His running away from Hagen is a slur on the name of Hildebrand, and we do not mind that Dietrich's former role of executing Kriemhild has fallen to him.

Volker the 'Fiddler' or 'Minstrel' is a typical figure of heroic epic in whom accretion through successive stages of growth is evident. Although important minstrels might belong to a lord's household and even own a fief, their status was normally plebeian. Nevertheless, we are expressly told that Volker was a noble lord with many good warriors of Burgundy as his vassals, but that he was called 'Minstrel' because of his skill with the fiddle. In our poem he is, then, a gentleman amateur. His public tribute to Gotelind in Pöchlarn of a song to his own accompaniment, for which she rewards him richly with bracelets, does not quite tally with what we know of the cult of Minnesang. We do not know the words of Volker's song. But we do know that no plebeian at this time would have been permitted to address a lady directly on the subject of love, a fact which accords with Volker's noble status. During a pause in the carnage in Etzel's hall, Gunther turns to Hagen to comment on Volker's prowess in 'fiddling' on Hunnish helmets, and Hagen voices his regret that he sat higher in the hall than Volker, whom he had chosen as his comrade-in-arms. Here we have a reference to Volker's humbler status, and we can safely assume that this German Taillefer had been a minstrel of plebeian status in the epic source of our poem and a favourite figure with its poet, who was himself a minstrel, and that the 'last' poet (that is, our poet) went the whole way in ennobling in rank a figure who was already felt by admiring audiences to be noble at heart. Volker's fortunes were assured, once he had been picked as Hagen's battle-companion, yet in our poem he still bears the traces of a self-made man. In the opening chapter, he is introduced as a man of flawless courage, and when he is presented to Rüdiger's daughter in recognition of his great courage he is honoured by a kiss normally reserved for social equals. It was said above that Volker's superior physical prowess serves to underline Hagen's greater depth of character, and it is also true that Volker's light-hearted, musical temperament provides a foil to the grim and sceptical side of Hagen. Although Volker is at one with Hagen in his foreknowledge of the doom that awaits them, he does not let it weigh on him at Pöchlarn, where, in his vivacious manner, he is the life and soul of the party and even paves the way to a marriage.

It was no doubt owing to the ambiguity of this 'noble fiddler' that the last poet and his continuators between them introduced Volker thrice. And it is a strange coincidence, if coincidence it be, that documentary evidence is to hand, from Flanders in the earlier part of the twelfth century, of an enfeoffed minstrel of the same name, *Folkirus joculator.*

AFFINITIES WITH DRAMA

Two ideas have been confirmed as true by this review of the leading figures. First, characters tend to lose their consistency if one goes beyond an episode or related group of episodes, and consistency may be jeopardized if one leaps from one half of the poem to the other. And second, even in vital passages, the poet often prefers to let actions speak for themselves. This latter feature, which is perhaps favoured by the compact shape of the strophe, is suggestive of drama, and we may well inquire whether other features of the poet's art point in this direction.

The ancient Germanic heroic lay was a short epic-dramatic poem in which tense dialogue furnished the crises, and it is undeniable that over the centuries our poem has inherited much of the spirit of the lay, despite the different aims of epic. The various clashes between Kriemhild and Hagen, and the exchanges between Rüdiger, Wolfhart, Hildebrand, and Dietrich on the one side and the Burgundian heroes on the other, speak for themselves. Beyond this, two contrasting 'dramatic' styles have been discerned, one the general style of our poet's predecessors, the other his own contemporary style of presentation. The former culminates in powerful symbolic gestures: Kriemhild flaunting Brunhild's ring in triumph (to which our poet has added her girdle); the flinging of Siegfried's corpse on to Kriemhild's bed (which our poet has toned down to depositing it on her threshold); Kriemhild's reading of Siegfried's unscarred shield to the effect that he has been murdered; Hagen's killing of the ferryman on the way to Hungary; his breaking the oar and smashing the ferry; and his lacing on of his helmet more tightly on arriving at Etzel's court. The second style has aptly been called 'scenic'. The last poet can 'produce' a whole episode within the bounds of a single scene like a true dramatic artist, as in Chapter 29 when he makes Hagen and Volker leave Gunther standing in Etzel's forecourt, walk over the broad space, seat themselves against the palace wall on a bench, and sustain the curiosity of the Huns who stare at them as though they were strange beasts—whereupon Kriemhild espies them through a window, prostrates herself before her warriors in order to move them to avenge her, descends the Stair—the scene of so many fights and flytings to come—and draws close to the two heroes, who grimly keep their seats while Hagen displays Siegfried's sword Balmung on his knees. . . . Or there is the dramatic appearance of Dancwart at the top of that same Stair, viewed from within the hall, with drawn sword, and all bespattered with gore. Or to revert to an outstanding example from the first part, the quarrel of the queens in Chapter 14 in three stages: at the tournament, and then, with the prima donnas magnificently gowned and with supporting ladies on either side, at the cathedral door on the steps, before and after mass.

The last poet tried to retain all the pictorial gestures of his sources, although (as we have seen with the ring and girdle) he was not above tampering with them if need be. But he also signally added to them in the scene in which Hagen requests and receives the shield of Rüdiger. As to the poet's own scenic effects, he tended to reserve them for the high points of his narrative. In one instance in which he stints us of all indication of time and place, his very bareness contributes to the close atmosphere of the transaction, namely where courtiers plot the death of Siegfried.

The total visual effect of the ***Nibelungenlied,*** however, is gaunt and dim compared with that of the *Iliad,* which even distinguishes an upper and lower air and glories in the accurate evocation of movement. With regard to this latter quality, of all those writing in Germany at the beginning of the thirteenth century, Wolfram von Eschenbach alone could challenge Homer.

Considerations of dramatic effect often swamp those of epic in our poem. Since the days of the heroic lay there had been the well-used stylistic device, also known to our poets, of indirect speech changing to direct without transition. The splendid set speeches in which Homer abounds have no parallel in the ***Nibelungenlied.*** Instead we find naturalistic dialogue, dramatically presented, which Homer on the other hand avoids. Similarly also, the stately repetitions of set utterances in Homer (halving a beginner's work with his lexicon) have no counterpart in the German poem.

The dramatic features of the ***Nibelungenlied*** are innate. Whereas there was no secular drama in German at this time there was of course the liturgical drama of the Church as well as agrarian ritual in the village, both of which may have contributed towards forming the 'symbolic' style of our poet's sources. On the other hand, there was as yet little book reading in private among the laity. Instead, however, poems like *Parzival* and *Willehalm* (to name works that were eminently suited to such treatment) were publicly recited, and one does not need to be endowed with much feeling to know that they must have been recited with every resource of voice and gesture, though documentary evidence is lacking. Certain genres of contemporary love-song (like that of the *Tagelied* or *alba*) were also surely performed with mime, and, no doubt, so were those racy ditties that dealt with peasant frolics. The setting in which we imagine the ***Nibelungenlied*** to have been performed—we do not know whether it was sung, chanted, or intoned—may thus have been not too remote from that of cabaret, though naturally on a far more serious plane. Yet all evidence is lacking, so that it is not possible to contradict those who argue that the poem was chanted in a liturgical style with a 'deadpan' demeanour.

THE ETHOS OF THE POEM

Has the ***Nibelungenlied*** a 'meaning'? That is, can its action, together with the poet's *obiter dicta* and hints between the lines, be shown to serve a dominant group of ideas and sentiments, whether they amount to 'a message', a 'philosophy', or a more or less consistent attitude towards life? In the case of the *Aeneid* or *Paradise Lost* one would think that this question could be answered in the affirmative, for all their rich diversity. But from what has already been said about the ***Nibelungenlied*** it will come as no surprise that, in its case, the question is not easy to answer.

In his penultimate strophe the last poet offers the comment that Etzel's high festivity has ended in sorrow, for joy must always turn to sorrow in the end. In the first strophe (whose internal rhymes declare it to be the work of a later hand), by pairing fame and toil, joy and lamentation, with the negative element always in the second place, a redactor suggests from the outset that joy will turn to sorrow. Thus the poem is set in the framework of a simple yet effective pessimism. Throughout the poem we are told sententiously of the dire consequences of this or that deed, and, as the story unfolds, we must admit that joy does give way to sorrow in the end, since almost every festivity in the ***Nibelungenlied*** is clouded by untoward events. The victory-feast at which Siegfried meets Kriemhild for the first time is gay enough (but we know that Siegfried is being pulled irrevocably from his orbit by the power of love). The wedding-feast at Worms is marred by Brunhild's tears and all the dark things they stand for. Siegfried and Kriemhild's visit to Worms ends in the murder of the former. Etzel's festivity, the one that gave rise to the poet's final comment on the nature of joy and sorrow, ends in carnage and destruction. No resolution of the conflict of joy and sorrow is offered. Sorrow is left to reign supreme.

When we consider that the ***Nibelungenlied*** was recited to Christian courts of the high Middle Ages, we are rather taken aback. Christians, believing the Crucifixion to have been not a tragedy but a triumph, are nothing if not optimists, and their optimism duly left its marks on the tragic themes inherited from the heathen past by medieval men in Germany. In thirteenth-century poetry, fathers no longer kill their sons at the dictates of honour, sons-in-law no longer kill the fathers who pursue eloping daughters. The Arthurian romances—the narrative literature par excellence of the courts—are singularly lacking in stark themes of any kind and always end on a note of harmony restored, and thus of hope. If anything very drastic happens in a tale of this period, as when Helmbrecht the farmer's son turns robber and is first mutilated by the sheriff and then lynched by the outraged villagers, it is sure to be a cautionary tale. There was great hope that by noting young Helmbrecht's terrible end one would be able to muster sufficient self-control to escape his fate. Was the ***Nibelungenlied,*** which had the only plot whose ancient, tragic outlook defied all essential change through the centuries, perhaps a cautionary tale or a great penitentiary sermon in verse on pride, with the Pride and Fall of the Burgundians as example?

There is something to be said for this idea as long as it is duly subordinated to the other, dominant qualities of the epic. It would be an exaggeration to claim that hundreds of years of Christian teaching had eradicated the sentiments of the blood-feud among the German nobility of the period, yet these nobles knew where they stood before the Church in matters of revenge. Thus any great story of revenge which, like the ***Nibelungenlied,*** dwelt sententiously though not pontifically on the inevitable consequences of high-handed deeds, could not fail to impress the listeners in a moral and cathartic sense. The fall of the Burgundians must have amounted to more in their eyes than an admirable feat of vengeance by Kriemhild or an abominable misfortune to the Burgundians, according to which side they took, if they paid attention to how the story is told. Like most heroic poets, our poet leaves the moral to his listeners. But he furnishes us with a hint or two in his use of words meaning 'pride', 'haughtiness', 'arrogance', or 'high spirits' at significant points. Such hints, hedged about with his usual taciturnities as they are, sometimes raise more problems than they solve, yet never do they take on a priestly or theological tone. Just as not one of the heroes, not even Rüdiger, gives a thought to his heavenly salvation as he dies, so not one of these references to 'pride' is linked with anything but death and destruction, and not always explicitly with them. So far as the good of his characters' souls is concerned, our poet offers no comment. Thus, although we must assume that the ***Nibelungenlied*** was written by a Christian poet for Christian audiences, and that he leaves loose ends for thoughtful Christians to take up if they so please, the mood which the theme induced was not a Christian mood, and the result is not a Christian poem.

From a loftier ethical point of view, the ***Nibelungenlied*** is a poem of dire retribution for proud and arrogant deeds, with physical courage and group loyalty offering some purgation. The tragic events of which it tells are a web woven to a greater or lesser degree, in their blind arrogance, by all its leading characters. But whereas Homer lets it be known that the forces which punish *hybris* are divine, it is quite astonishing that our poet, writing in a priest-ridden age, offers not a word of guidance whether the sanction behind his retribution be impersonal Fate or the Providence of the Holy Trinity. We may well suspect the latter, for what else are we to think? But it is significant for the whole art of this singular and reticent person that he never once implies it.

The poet yielded his imagination to his un-Christian subject-matter to an extent that baffles us in a Christian of the high Middle Ages. Was his heart breaking with all the wicked ruin of his story? If it was, he kept his feelings to himself. He did not attempt to put them into words.

THE TWO-FOLD TEXTURE OF THE POEM

Those who come to the ***Nibelungenlied*** from other traditions of heroic poetry are struck and even troubled by its contrasting textures. Some passages, like the exchanges between Siegfried and Kriemhild, they find unbelievably gentle or 'soft'; others almost incredibly savage. These contrasts, they say, go far beyond modulations from the major to the minor key, from warlike to peaceful pursuits, such as may be considered normal in heroic epics. And these critics note quite rightly that the double texture of the ***Nibelungenlied*** must be due to the poet's endeavour to accommodate his grim heritage to the new Romance fashions. For the chivalric ideal and the cult of courtly song were penetrating the sterner and more conservative south-eastern marches of the Empire from the West during the very generation in which our poet was at work, and in attempting to bridge the two divergent cultures he was accepting his greatest compromise, a compromise which, like the others, was forced upon him from without. It would not have been possible for the poet, had he so wished, to resist such modern influences at this time at any leading court of Austria. We may, despite obvious influences from courtly narrative, disregard the assertion that the ***Nibelungenlied*** was intended as a Kriemhild biography roughly to be classed with *Iwein* and the like; while, on the other hand, to claim that the stylized love scenes, ceremonies, tournaments, and displays of finery are the price which the poet paid for having a ***Nibelungenlied*** at all, might be to underrate his creative interest in what is of lesser interest to us. To acquire the full sense of how this poet stood at the hinge of old and new, we need only compare the *Song of Roland.* Writing about A.D. 1100, the last poet of the *Roland* needs to make few concessions to the arts of peace. As to the love of woman, there is very little of it—notoriously little in the eyes of our love-sick age, whose ideas on the subject go back in unbroken succession to the twelfth century but no farther. Chiding Roland for his rashness in failing to summon the Emperor betimes with his horn, Oliver tells him that he will never lie in the arms of Oliver's sister Aude. And when Charles returns without Roland, Aude dutifully dies of grief. This is all. When young warriors of archaic stamp love each other as Roland and Oliver do, their sisters may be thrown in to seal the bond. So it was with Siegfried and Gunther, and so it remained, until new and imperious conceptions of love forced their way into Austria.

Great epics are said to arise from an awareness on the part of a new and more literate age that an old order is passing away even in memory. If this is so, the ***Nibelungenlied*** came at the latest possible moment, at a time when modern notions threatened altogether to engulf the ancient subject-matter. That they did not do so entirely—and this may be accounted a marvel—can be set down to two factors. First, an earlier epic on the Fall of the Nibelungs, dated '*c.* 1160', came at the *right* time, before Romance fashions were making themselves felt. There is some danger of inviting ridicule by indulging in laments for lost poems whose beauties can only be surmised, but of this we may be sure: *Diu Nôt* was a very powerful, concentrated epic of unified texture, to which the poet of the ***Nibelungenlied*** owed an incalculable debt. The second factor that contributed to the rise of a great heroic epic as late as *c.* 1200 was the unique imagination of the last poet, who, building on *Diu Nôt,* found it possible to recapture and elaborate richly upon the temper of a past age, and at the same time work creatively in terms of the new, giving each of two fundamentally opposed generations what it wanted, though at an unavoidable cost in consistency.

But our poet, in the main, does not confront new and old haphazardly. He subdues the ancient spirit to contemporary notions of form. The putting of old wine into new skins, too, has its dangers, but the poet manages it without much damage to the vintage and even laces his beverage on occasion. As his story unfolds, its tone grows ever sterner. The modern and courtly veneer is progressively stripped off to reveal harsh political realities. A state of affairs that can be recognized as an ideal present begins to recede into the past, at first gently, then more swiftly till it reaches breakneck speed, yet not before the graces of contemporary society have been dwelt on lovingly for the last time at Pöchlarn. Already at the beginning there is a sharp reminder of the conflict between seemly order and uncurbed violence when Siegfried challenges Gunther at Worms, but with the roles reversed. For it is Siegfried (who will be so reliable when Kriemhild's love has tamed him) that offers a threat to society, while the Burgundians, as yet unmasked, appear as its upholders. And at the end, the noble figure of Dietrich survives, after Rüdiger has gone down, to give us hope for the modern generation.

THE POET'S ACHIEVEMENT

After this lengthy discussion it is time baldly to set forth the positive achievement of the last poet.

Taking two sources for the first half of his poem, and the older epic *Diu Nôt* for the second, and placing in Hagen's mouth only what his audience needed to know from various lays on Siegfried's youth, the last poet fashioned a great epic of revenge with two crises. He succeeded largely in harmonizing two plots with conflicting elements, and he braced them together not only by the motive of revenge, which had long exerted an influence on them, but also through the unity of some of the characters and even through their mutual relations, above all in the case of Kriemhild and Hagen. He created new episodes (Chapter 8, Chapter 15, Chapter 29), one of them of outstanding quality, 'How Kriemhild upbraided Hagen and he did not rise to greet her' (Chapter 29). He created new characters, preeminent among them Dancwart and Wolfhart. He sometimes showed considerable independence in his treatment of existing characters. For instance, he reshaped Siegfried in the role of a charming and well-bred prince, retaining some of his rougher characteristics for comic and dramatic effect. He also enriched the characters of Rüdiger and Hagen above all in their exchanges over Rüdiger's shield. In fusing the Kriemhild of the first and second parts, he revealed to us the soul of a woman frustrated in love, and altogether he gave Kriemhild a new prominence. He added much social and psychological refinement to what he found in his sources. Thanks to the patient work of scholars, who have never ceased to feel the challenge of this epic, it is now possible to make these statements on the work of the last poet with some assurance. There is much that we should still like to know. But we know that we could only know this if we had the poet's lost sources before us, those sources which the very success of his great epic was soon to condemn to oblivion.

CONCLUSION

The ***Nibelungenlied*** is inferior to the *Iliad,* which far surpasses it in the beauty of its structure, the maturity of its ethos, the magificence of its language, its astonishing power of conjuring up line, mass, colour, and movement, and indeed in most other respects. Our poem is bare of the grand and weighty diction that we find in *Beowulf,* nor has it any natural setting so charged with 'atmosphere', elegiac or otherwise, as the scene at Grendelsmere. The only notice taken of the beauties of nature is when Siegfried falls to die upon the flowers, a masterly touch, though nature here serves as a backcloth. Our poem knows no supreme moment of the heroic imagination, like that of the *Roland* when the hero at last blows his horn, and blows so loud that his temples burst while Charles catches its echoes in far-off France. The zest, colour, and robust good sense of the *Cid* are absent from the tense and ruthless ***Nibelungenlied,*** whose moments of high chivalry are a little overdone. It lacks the naïve charm of the *Cattle Raid of Cooley,* that prose epic with a perfect plot, in which the bulls of Ulster and Connaught settle what heroes have left unsettled. Yet, when all these loose comparisons have been made, such are the strength, vitality, and tension of the ***Nibelungenlied*** that it could be claimed with great force, as I myself would claim, that it is the world's best heroic epic bar one. (pp. 300-47)

A. T. Hatto, "An Introduction to a Second Reading," in The Nibelungenlied, *translated by A. T. Hatto, Penguin Books, 1965, pp. 293-347.*

McLintock on the *Nibelungenlied's* aesthetic merits:

Recent years have seen numerous interpretations of the ***Nibelungenlied.*** Scholars have sought to elicit its 'meaning' or 'message' and imagined they could divine the author's 'intention': he was contrasting 'pagan' and 'Christian' values, deploring revenge, finding fault with old-style 'demonic' heroism, or demonstrating the baleful effects of lay arrogance. Some of these readings, one suspects, would have been incomprehensible to the poet and his audience; others perhaps capture attitudes that they would have shared. Most tend to reduce the work to an exemplum; the epic, however, refuses to be compassed by neat interpretative schemes. The poet was an artist, not a thinker, and if we wish to appreciate his poem we must approach it aesthetically. . . .

What we admire in the epic is not its moral, social, or psychological insights, but its literary qualities—the power of its individual scenes and the grandeur of the total architecture to which they contribute.

D. R. McLintock, in German Life and Letters, *January 1977.*

Carl S. Singer (essay date 1967)

[In the essay below, Singer evaluates the Nibelungenlied *poet's depiction of Siegfried, particularly focusing on the death scene in the sixteenth adventure and how it influences the poem as a whole.]*

Against the background of all but the most recent ***Nibelungenlied*** research a certain incongruity attaches to a study which for the most part abandons the excavation operations into *Urgestein* in favor of an assay of the top ground: the shape and sense assumed by a particular event within the design of the poem itself. That it has been customary to break open the surface of the ***Nibelungenlied***—despite occasional avowals of respect for its workmanship—and to hunt beneath it for the relics of earlier ages, buried in such challenging disorder, is, of course, quite understandable. For the poem is an undeniably "open" work of art. With its imperfect, uneasy assimilation of heroic sagas and attitudes into a social setting that has many courtly trappings, the ***Nibelungenlied*** as a whole not only affords but actually demands exegesis by reference to the sources and traditions which seem so often to have forced the poet's hand to overtly contradictory gestures.

Here the scholar is confronted by a problem, in particularly acute form, that usually frustrates a purely literary approach to medieval writing and enforces instead at least a partial detour into literary and cultural history. Given the medieval writer's reverence for his sources, his frequently unreflecting acceptance of the traditions of his people, it is impossible to determine, simply on the basis of an examination of his work itself, where and to what extent he has performed as an artist, where in fact his performance is conscious and intentional; discussion of the meaning and merits of execution of any particular episode in his work predicates knowledge of what his contemporaries and earlier authors with whom he might have been familiar made of the same or similar material. And it is, as I say, not surprising that in the case of the ***Nibelungenlied*** this necessary detour has been pursued with greater zeal than all paths leading back to an appreciation of the poem as it stands. For, while the information it, in conjunction with its accessible preforms, offers about the cultural past of the Germanic peoples is of unquestionable value, the poem itself—with its inconsistencies, numerous lame and colorless sequences, and general lack of linguistic polish—would not seem to repay an earnest consideration of its aesthetic qualities.

Of late, nonetheless, the experiment of talking at length about the ***Nibelungenlied*** as literature has been made—and with a fair degree of success. I am referring to Gottfried Weber's *Das Nibelungenlied, Problem und Idee* [1963], which has demonstrated that it is both possible and profitable to deal with questions of characterization and thought in the poem as we have it. The medieval work will, despite the fresh perspective opened by Weber's book, no doubt continue to suffer in comparison with such masterpieces as those of Wolfram and Gottfried. But I am sufficiently encouraged by the results of Weber's investigation to attempt to come to terms with the ***Nibelungenlied*** poet's art as it is exhibited in an episode acknowledged by all but the most intent pursuants of *Urgestein* to be of distinctly effective craftsmanship: the account of Siegfried's death given in the sixteenth Aventiure. With the minimum number of citations from the findings of the excavating parties required to establish roughly the traditions and materials our poet had to work with (I again give warning that no new shafts will be dug here), I shall present an analysis of the principles involved in the construction of the fatal hunting contest and consider the implications of its course and outcome for the poem as a whole.

Andreas Heusler, whose work remains the starting point for all discussions of the sources and earlier forms of the ***Nibelungenlied***'s narrative content, states, with something less than his usual certainty, that the configuration of Siegfried's death as having occurred on a mock hunting expedition is very old, perhaps indeed a part of the earliest version of the Siegfried story we can hope to reconstruct. "Die groβe Aventiure mit der Jagd und Siegfrieds Tode geht, wie wir glauben, in ihrem Kern und manchen Einzelheiten auf die Urstufe zurück" [Heusler, *Nibelungensage und Nibelungenlied,* 1955]. He is joined in this judgment by Stout, Schröder and Panzer, who point out that even in the *Edda* version, where Siegfried is killed while sleeping in bed, there are indications that the death was originally associated with a hunt [J. Stout, *und ouch hagene,* 1963; Franz Rolf Schröder, "Sigfrids Tod" *GRM* XLI (1960); Friedrich Panzer, *Das Nibelungenlied, Entstehung und Gestalt,* 1955]. And the *Thidrekssaga* does actually narrate a hunt-death, so that, as long as we accept prevailing critical opinion that the *Thidrekssaga* and the ***Nibelungenlied*** do make use of a common source, it seems clear that, no matter how far back the hunt motif extends, the ***Nibelungenlied*** poet cannot at any rate have been the first to have employed it in conjunction with the murder.

There is, again, general agreement that, while the hunt itself is not new, the length and detail of its depiction in the sixteenth Aventiure are in large measure the products of the poet's own creative effort. In the *Thidrekssaga* the description of Siegfried's death is given in some eighty lines, the sixteenth Aventiure contains eighty-six strophes. All that the two versions have in common—and thus all that we must assume our poet to have derived from their common source—are Hagen's ruse itself of having a hunt announced, Siegfried's subsequent ignoble death at Hagen's hands while quenching the thirst raised in the process of the hunt, and elements of Siegfried's final speeches together with Hagen's triumphant boasts. The rest would, at first glance, appear to be our poet's own invention. Many scholars are inclined, however, to whittle away at the originality of this *amplificatio,* to credit the poet not with inventiveness but rather a peculiar facility for importing into the body of the episode numerous suitable motifs culled from a far ranging array of sources. The most plausible of these conjectured derivations seems to me the link, suggested by Singer [as cited in Heusler], Heusler, Panzer and others, between the farewell scene of Siegfried and Kriemhild (Str. 918-25), where the hero fails to heed his wife's premonitions and anxious warnings, and similar scenes found in the medieval French epic *Daurel e Beton* and its probable sources in twelfth-century French literature, most notably *Boeve de Hanton.* From this complex of stories, which Heusler refers to as the "welsche Erzählung," may also derive Siegfried's charge to his assassins to maintain their loyalty to, and protection of, Kriemhild (Str. 996-7)—a plea having no counterpart in the *Thidrekssaga's* version of his death speech. On the other hand, Panzer's attempt to adduce one or another "source" for virtually every detail of the Aventiure—Siegfried's bearing and splendid hunting habit fashioned in accordance with descriptions set forth in the *Ruodlieb,* the profusion of dogs and hunters a possibly conscious reminiscence of the fourth book of the *Aeneid,* the fatal race to the spring suggested by no less than three French epics, Siegfried's capture, unleashing and eventual slaying of the bear a surviving motif of a primitive Young-Siegfried saga (the Starkhans fairytale complex), etc.—strike me as being obsessive and predicated on the bizarre surmise that the poet was so extraordinarily well read as to be in no need (or perhaps simply incapable) of any invention whatsoever. After this cursory look at the materials likely to have been utilized in the composition of the sixteenth Aventiure (we shall have further occasion to touch upon the question of sources), what presents itself as most properly and securely the ***Nibelungenlied*** poet's own contribution is the hunt itself (Str. 926-77); as Heusler puts it: "Neuschöpfung ist . . . diese breite Ausmalung der Jagd, bis zur Ankunft am Wasser."

We have, consequently, in this sequence a relatively pure example of our poet's art. As such the hunt may serve as the point of departure for a discussion of the sixteenth Aventiure and its significance within the body of the poem: here we may legitimately begin an assessment of the weight and function of detail and incident. But before we proceed it should be mentioned that there has long existed something like a standard interpretation of the sense of the hunt-*amplificatio,* one which, perhaps because of its simplicity, has been felt to clear up all the questions which arise in the face of the poet's apparent effort to make something new out of the story of Siegfried's death. It has been a convention of ***Nibelungenlied*** scholarship to concentrate on the fact of Siegfried's predominance during the progress of the hunt and to see in these fifty-odd strophes the conscious realization of the poet's intention to give Siegfried a last and most vivid moment of glory directly before he dies: to evoke, in its full power, the splendor of his life and juxtapose it against the darkness of Hagen's murderous attack. Panzer's statement: "Ihre besondere Wirksamkeit erreicht sie [die Aventiure] vor allem durch Kontrastbildung, auf die der Dichter hier mit höchster Meisterschaft bedacht war. Unmittelbar vor seinem frühen Untergang zeigt sich uns der Held noch einmal im hellsten Glanz seines einzigartigen Seins, in der Fülle von Reichtum, Jugend, Kühnheit und Kraft . . . "; and Weber's: "seine ganze Kunst hat der Dichter aufgeboten, Sivrits Ausgang in lichten Glanz zu tauchen—die gesamte Jagdaventiure ist ja darauf hin angelegt—und die Kontraste scharf gegeneinander abzuheben" may be taken as typical. This view pays tribute to a somewhat coarse, if successfully staged effect; it does not, in my opinion, discover the essential configuration of event informing the poet's treatment of the episode: a configuration which makes of the hunt and its calamitous sequel not simply an arresting *tour de force* but rather an achieved exhibition and advancement of the thought of the poem as a whole. In the course of the analysis of the setting of Siegfried's last triumph, its manner, and the conditions under which it proceeds, it will become clear that the poet here completes a process—carried on from the outset of the work—of qualifying the splendor to which a Siegfried character may attain, of dismissing, albeit sorrowfully, as folly Siegfried's very disposition to "shine" in a world at the mercy of the powers of darkness.

The question of when the hunt motif became a part of the *Nibelungen* tradition is not, as we have seen, crucial to our inquiry. What is important is the fact that the poet found the motif so well suited to his purposes that he decided to dwell upon it, to transform the incident of a hunt such as that found in the *Thidrekssaga* into a lengthy and colorful spectacle. We must, accordingly, ask what the poet calculated a hunting pageant could offer as a background for the final deeds of Siegfried, how he intended it to affect our impressions of the murder. That "pageant" suggests itself as a description of the episode provides, it seems to me, the answer. In our poet's construction, and doubtless for the first time, the hunt becomes an emphatically courtly affair, and Siegfried, by his surpassing performance within it, is associated—rather more successfully than in such touches as the fact of his education or his highly formalized *Minne* experience—with an existence animated by courtly concerns and habits.

> Geladen vil der rosse kom vor in über Rin,
> di den jagetgesellen truogen brot unde win,
> daz vleisch mit den vischen und andern manigen rat,
> den ein künic so riche vil harte billichen hat.
> (Str. 927)

—so the hunt begins, an activity of a piece with the receptions, banquets and festivals so numerous in the first part of the poem; the hunt, like all these scenes, is characterized by pomp and ceremony and a representative overflow of wealth and comfort, in short, by all those qualities usually subsumed under the courtly concept of *hoher muot.* And this, the poet means us to see, is precisely Siegfried's element: throughout these fifty strophes he is presented as devoting all his energies—and not without grace—to a deliberate enjoyment of the festival he is capable of making out of his life in his steady certainty of good form and prowess. But, of course, as de Boor notes: " . . . anders als im Artusroman klingt hinter jedem dieser freudig lärmenden Feste ein dunkler Schicksalston . . . das Fest erhält einen neuen Sinn: es wird zum Erweis des Leitsatzes, daß alle Freude zuletzt Leid gebiert" [Helmut de Boor, *Geschichte der deutschen Literatur von den Anfängen bis zur Gegenwart,* 1962]. The poet is in fact constantly at work to undermine the sense of security, the joy of life implicit in courtly forms, to reduce with his gloomy pronouncements of approaching doom the brilliance of the courtly festival to a pale, unsteady flicker. And this then is the nature of the affinity the poet so obviously felt to exist between a pageant and Siegfried's death: the hunting contest, which Siegfried only apparently wins—wins only so long as Hagen is content to preserve the illusion of a contest, yields a test of the courtly style of existence, a demonstration of its ephemeral beauty and, at the same time, its insubstantiality.

The devices employed by the poet to identify Siegfried's manner and bearing during the course of the hunt as "courtly" (I shall discuss the courtly aspects of Siegfried's behavior in the death scene itself later on) are, for the most part, fairly straightforward. The most obvious perhaps is the six-strophe (Str. 951-56) description of Siegfried's weapons and hunting apparel: " . . . der herliche jägere der was hohe gemuot" (Str. 955, 1. 4)—such *Schneiderstrophen,* dedicated to a meticulous enumeration of articles of gold, fur, etc., give expression here as elsewhere in the poem to high spirits coupled with a consciousness of extreme social elevation and refinement. But Siegfried's distinction, his seemingly unique right to such accoutrements as the tokens of perfectly realized strength and *zuht,* comes clear above all in his conduct of the hunt itself.

> Do sprach der herre Sifrit: "ich han der hunde rat,

niwan einen bracken, der so genozzen hat
daz er die verte erkenne der tiere durch den tan.
wir komen wol ze jegede," sprach der Kriemhilde man.

(Str. 932)

There is an unmistakable feeling for elegance here—doubtless, as has been noted, not as fully developed as that exhibited by Tristan in his protracted discourse on the skinning and dismemberment of game, but something nonetheless quite opposed to the seizures of brutish frenzy which frequently prevail in the poet's descriptions of physical activity. Founded on such ingrained control and expertise, Siegfried's sport with his prey becomes yet another show of effortlessness, a vivid reinforcement to our impressions of the ease that has invariably accompanied his movements throughout the work. For nine strophes (Str. 934-42) the poet parades a fine array of beasts before his eager hunter, importing even a lion into the *Waskenwald* to heighten his exuberance—"des begonde smielen der degen küene unde balt" (Str. 940, 1. 4).

We should, however, pause here with the recognition that this rapid multiplication of fallen animals—clearly one of the high-points of Siegfried's final hours—seems a rather lame approach to an apotheosis. It is plausible, I suppose, to see in the disappointingly mechanical progress of Siegfried's hunting triumph simply evidence of the poet's limitations as an artist. And yet, do not the limitations lie rather in the character of Siegfried himself, his character as it is conceived and depicted by the poet? The sportsman, happy in the exercise of his consummate power and skill, may be fascinating to watch but he is not likely to enlist even the poet's contemporaries' sympathies as profoundly as those who have no time for sport in their preoccupation with that ultimate reality in the ***Nibelungenlied***—the fated certainty of death. But this preoccupation and the heroic dimensions of behavior we find associated with it in the second part of the poem are utterly alien to Siegfried, for, again, specifically to the extent that he is motivated by a complex of courtly principles and aspirations, he must be solely concerned with the realization of his potential for human nobility—in *life,* in a constant festival of vitality. That Siegfried has no thought for death would not in an Arthurian romance in any way detract from his stature; in the ***Nibelungenlied,*** however, the exploits of the star of a courtly life-festival cannot be possessed of ultimate human dignity, for the pageant is constantly subject to abrupt termination: Hagen has merely to lay hands on a spear.

"Das jagt was ergangen und doch niht gar" (Str. 943, 1. 1)—Siegfried, whose seemingly boundless desire for self-display the poet gladly indulges, is made to provide yet another care-free show of energy with his remaining oversize deeds, deeds which effect a crucial distortion: the courtly festival takes on the aspect of a mindless, burlesque frolic. I refer, of course, to his two-round bout with the bear (Str. 946-50; 957-62). Siegfried spies a bear, catches it single-handed, brings it back alive to the camp site, sets it free, and, after the bear has knocked over a few pans and scared a few cooks in its race to the woods, Siegfried is again alone able to catch it, kills it and lets it again be carried back to the camp. As mentioned above, Panzer considers this incident to be derived from a Young-Siegfried saga, which in turn supposedly owes many details to the Starkhans fairy-tale. This source citation, like some others in Panzer's work, does not strike me as particularly compelling; but whether or not the poet was guided at this point by a reminiscence of an episode from the story of Siegfried's youth is a question not apt to facilitate insight into the poet's intention. What is the sense of this construction in the context of the sixteenth Aventiure, the account of Siegfried's death? Heusler's approach to an explanation, though it does not go far enough, certainly does more justice to the work as we have it: "Helleres Licht fällt auf eine ganz neu eingeführte Krafttat des Helden . . . Dieses farbensatte Zwischenspiel [der Bärenfang] lenkt den ersten, grauen Lauf der Quelle zu spielmännischer Lustigkeit und Daseinsfreude herum. Auf den Ton von Lebensgenuß ist auch das übrige gestimmt. . . . " Doubtless the poet is here once again occupied in conjuring up a species of "Daseinsfreude," but not really for the sake of spattering patches of color on his grey story; he means to reveal the more clearly with this exceptionally bright sequence the boundaries of his hero's character, the invalid simplicity of his scheme of life.

"Do sprach der degen hinder sich / 'Ich wil uns hergesellen guoter kurzewile wern' " (Str. 946, 1. 4, 947, 1. 1); "er braht iz an die fiwerstat durch sinen hohen muot / zeiner kurzewile der recke küene unde guot" (Str. 950, 1. 3-4); "und waer' iz wol verendet, si heten vroelichen tac" (Str. 960, 1. 4). Siegfried's quarry is, in short, *kurzewile;* he is impelled by the desire to create for himself, and for those around him inclined to watch, diversion, better still, a permanent entertainment. And like all pure entertainment, Siegfried's sport does not involve the will, does not drive towards any practical goal: the release from the pressures of the heroic existence—the constant considerations of self-assertion and defense—implicit in the very notion of a hunt is amplified and made an autonomous value in the charmingly senseless repetition of the bear game. But at the same time that the activity is devoid of purpose, it is so masterfully performed as to dazzle one and all; Siegfried, as the star of the pageant, does in fact come to resemble the rather common type of circus performer who refuses to undertake his impossible feats until he has handicapped himself to an extent which would ensure in his less talented spectators total incapacitation. (It will be recalled that on both occasions when Siegfried undertakes to catch the bear he has little use for a horse—finding it quite natural that he should run down his prey on foot.) Such *kurzewile* is then for the poet the very form of an existence animated by courtly *hoher muot;* and in its pursuit Siegfried effectively accomplishes the poet's delineation of his character. It should be realized, moreover, that what we would unhesitatingly identify in the works of Hartmann and Wolfram as a morally and spiritually indifferent adventure is here presented as an expression of Siegfried's *habitual* mode of being; the artistic sense informing the hunt lies, to a considerable extent, in the ability of the various incidents to sum up Siegfried, to provide an integrated, continuously developed image for what his actions have revealed—piecemeal—throughout the poem. For Siegfried, as the poet depicts him, is constantly playing, seemingly unable to make a move without setting up an interesting game, organizing an elaborate frolic.

The search for evidence of this trait will not prove very taxing: Siegfried's knack for provoking the sort of challenge to his manhood and strength in which he revels throughout the hunt fairly dominate our perceptions of him from the very moment of his arrival in Worms. We need not assume with Heusler and Neumann ["Schichten der Ethik im Nibelungenlied," *Fetschrift für Eugen Mogk,* 1924] that his bizarre overtures to Gunther and his court reflect one of the poet's more conspicuous failures to convincingly transform the older bellicose *Recke* Siegfried into a love-sick *Ritter;* the fact is that in our poem Siegfried's menacing gestures (though conceivably a reaction against his father's very warnings) are mere antics, suited at best to call forth a no doubt invigorating but quite irrelevant struggle—our Siegfried is in need of Kriemhild and not her brother's land. And no matter how disadvantageous to his real goal this mock declaration of war by champion might possibly prove to be, it is plain that Siegfried finds the tension it has occasioned highly exhilarating:

> Des antwurte Sivrit, der kreftige man:
> "müet iuch daz, her Hagene, das ich gesprochen han,
> so sol ich lazen kiesen daz die hende min
> wellent vil gewaltec hie zen Burgonden sin."
> (Str. 122)

> "War umbe bitet Hagene und ouch Ortwin,
> daz er niht gahet striten mit den friwenden sin,
> der er hie so manegen zen Burgonden hat?"
> (Str. 125, 1. 1-3).

Again in the "Sachsenkrieg" (the fourth Aventiure), where Siegfried's performance appears at first glance dictated exclusively by the prosaic, practical consideration of defending his hoped-for future brother-in-law's domain and honor, we nonetheless find the hero attempting to make things a bit more interesting, willfully imposing on himself and his troops the handicap of extreme numerical inferiority—that the danger, the thrill of battle may increase.

> "Swenne iwer starken viende zir helfe möhten han
> drizec tusent degene, so wold' ich si bestan,
> und het ich niwan tusent: des lat iuch an mich."
> (Str. 160, 1. 1-3)

> Do sah er her daz groze daz uf dem velde lac,
> daz wider siner helfe mit unfuoge wac:
> des was wol vierzec tusent oder dannoch baz.
> Sivrit in hohem muote sach vil vroelichen daz.
> (Str. 181)

And, although Siegfried seems strangely hesitant and—even in his cunning—uneasy at the outset of the Brünhild expedition (cf. Str. 330, 385-6; doubtless the poet here sees his design obstructed by an older tradition of Siegfried's past relations with Brünhild and cannot smooth over the discrepancies), he soon reverts to form: his efforts on Gunther's behalf are deliberately portrayed as an outrageous game—"von sinen schoenen listen er hete kraft genuoc / daz er mit dem sprunge den künic Gunther doch truoc" (Str. 464, 1, 3-4)—within Brünhild's own "geteiltiu spil." But Siegfried's innate playfulness, his impulsion towards a continuous vitality festival, receives within this sequence its most intriguing expression in the eighth Aventiure, which is the account of Siegfried's doings amongst the Nibelungen: doings whose overt senselessness has embarrassed—unnecessarily as we shall see—quite a few of the poem's scholars.

The eighth Aventiure is generally accredited to be the poet's own "invention," and here the usual slightly pejorative connotation of this word in ***Nibelungenlied*** research seems, on the face of it, quite justified. Clearly, the episode brings little that is new—in great part it simply recapitulates the account Hagen gave in the third Aventiure of how Siegfried came to have the Nibelungen treasure. Moreover, the episode is unmotivated, or rather detonates its motivation, for Siegfried has ostensibly set out to gain a support force of Nibelungen who would hold Brünhild to her bargain, and it would seem that time is of the essence (cf. Str. 481): why then does Siegfried conceal his identity and waste so much time in a match with his own giant-gatekeeper—in a *rematch* with the dwarf Alberich? Of late Joachim Bumke has essayed the customary path around such puzzles: in what strikes me as a highly fanciful extension of some work done by de Boor, he has come up with a theoretical source so distant in detail and overall shape from the incident in our poem that even the poet's own audience would probably have remained unconvinced of the connection [Joachim Bumke, "Sigfrids Fahrt ins Nibelungenland. Zur achten Aventiure des Nibelungenliedes," *BGDSL,* LXXX (1958)]. In any case the problem remains: what did the poet expect to achieve with the incident—why did he bother with it at all? Heusler offers a relatively plausible explanation: "Auf diesen überraschenden Einfall [the construction of the eighth Aventiure] führte der Wunsch des Erzählers, das zauberische Land der Nibelungen mit seinen Riesen und Zwergen auf die Bühne zu bringen zu heiter-spiel-männischer Wirkung . . . zu [der] Jung-Sigfridsage von der Hortgewinnung bildet unsere Einlage ein Nachspiel." This is, as I say, plausible; but it neglects the fact that, no matter how merry it may have made the audience, the journey to the land of the Nibelungen is primarily Siegfried's lark. And this is important, for Siegfried's conduct here is congruent—so clearly so as to argue conscious intention on the part of the poet—with his exploits in the hunt, the rematch with the dwarf specifically, it might be said, a rehearsal of the bear game. Here as there a pointlessly repeated triumph, indulged in for its own sake—for sport. We note that Siegfried actually does have a bit more trouble with his dwarf than he will later with his bear—"des libes kom in sorge do der waetliche gast" (Str. 495, 1, 4), but that the fight takes place at all reveals, precisely, that such "sorge" is not for Siegfried a present reality. And this I take to be the function of the eighth Aventiure: to reinforce the poet's studied construction of a Siegfried figure in whom a total absorption with life, with his own vitality, excludes all thought of death. With this exclusion, all physical confrontations with danger become for Siegfried—as for the Gawan figure of courtly romance [*Iwein*]—entertaining, if purposeless, adventures: invariably won contests of skill and strength. For Siegfried, in effect, there is never any question of how he and those who depend upon him may most easily survive, the constant question is for him instead: how he may most pleasurably and impressively *win.*

"Der ber begonde vliehen vor den hunden dan; / im kunde niht gevolgen *wan Kriemhilde man.* / der erlief in mit dem swerte . . . " (Str. 962, 1. 1-3) (my italics)—with the recognition that this must always be the manner of Siegfried's triumph, not only here but from the outset of the poem on, we come face to face with what I have spoken of earlier as the essential configuration of events in the sixteenth Aventiure. It is not enough to say with de Boor, Panzer, Weber, et al. that the hunt is designed to show off Siegfried to good advantage; the design, it should now be clear, arises as an exact test of Siegfried's type of superiority and is closely calculated to demonstrate the habitual course of his actions. The course and the boundary set to it as well. From strophe 930 to strophe 977 the hunt proceeds as a *contest,* proceeds, that is, on a surface that is a representative extension of Siegfried's way of life. And we must pause here to recall whom the poet has entrusted with this so felicitous design of the hunting party, whom he has appointed master of Siegfried's final ceremony.

"Welle wir uns scheiden," sprach do Hagene,
"e daz wir beginnen hie zu jagene?
da bi wir mügen bekennen, ich und die herren min,
wen die besten jegere an dirre waltreise sin.

Liute und gehünde suln wir teilen gar.
so ker' ietslicher swar er gerne var.
swer danne jage das beste, des sol er haben danc."

(Strs. 930 and 931, 1. 1-3)

That it is Hagen who, directly before he kills Siegfried, organizes one last game for him to win: here, it seems to me, lies the center of the poet's construction upon the traditional account of Siegfried's death. He has superimposed upon the older, brutal metaphor-irony still quite apparent in the *Thidrekssaga*—Siegfried regards himself a hunter and is in reality the hunted—an additional ironic scheme, one that is much less straightforward and yet superbly suited to his purposes. Now Siegfried is led to regard himself, as so often before, the victor—at the very moment he is to suffer his first but definitive defeat.

Curiously enough, this basic element in the poet's contribution to the story of the hunt has been, as far as I am able to tell, decidedly neglected by scholars of the ***Nibelungenlied.*** Heusler does note: "Sigfrids Überlegenheit bringt der jüngste Dichter mit andern, weniger einfachen Mitteln zur Anschauung. Er trennt die Fürsten gleich zu Anfang, begleitet Sigfrid auf seiner Jagd, läßt ihn . . . 'der pris von dem gejägede' gewinnen" (Heusler's point of comparison here is the *Thidrekssaga* version of the hunt); and, of course, note has been made of the second offer of contest which initiates the race to the spring (Str. 972); but I have not found any specific comment on Hagen's role in setting up this new frame to the action of the hunt. Conceivably, however, the frame itself has been tacitly considered something of an embarrassment, for it is quite obviously askew to the advancement of the murder plot. Hagen is not setting a trap here, he gains nothing by dispersing the members of the party since he has no intention of covertly falling upon Siegfried on some lonely hunting trail, indeed Gunther, who must be considered Hagen's accomplice in this sequence, deliberately has the party reassembled at the camp site before the process of the murder begins in good earnest (Str. 944). It is tempting, therefore, to accept Heusler's line of argument as a way of making sense out of the matter and to see in the proposal of contest with which the hunt commences nothing more than an artificial device with which the poet means to accord the "superiority" of his hero yet another prize. But, again, why have Hagen be the one to announce that there is a prize to be competed for?—Hagen who, to judge by even his first speeches in the poem which establish once and for all the fact of Siegfried's unparalleled abilities, knows better than anyone that Siegfried must certainly be the winner. In short, why should Hagen arrange for a demonstration to his fellow warriors that the man he is about to kill is possessed of unique superiority? There is no answer to be found on the surface of the poem's action: Siegfried's shining performance must be injurious to Hagen's black cause and can only serve to aggravate the indignation of those who witness his dastardly attack. And yet, after this contest has run its inevitable course—"Do sprachen sine jegere: 'müg' ez mit fuoge wesen, / so lat uns, her Sifrit, der tier ein teil genesen. / ir tuot uns hiute laere den berc und ouch den walt.' " (Str. 940, 1. 1-3), directly after Siegfried's triumph becomes exponential in his bear-game finesse—"Do sprachen die daz sahen, er waere ein kreftec man" (Str. 963, 1. 1), Hagen incites Siegfried to—yet another contest.

Do si wolden dannen zuo der linden breit,
do sprach von Tronege Hagene: 'mir ist des vil geseit
daz niht gevolgen künne dem Kriemhilde man,
swenne er wolde gahen. hey wolde er uns daz sehen lan!'

(Str. 972)

Especially with the last half-line of this strophe (whose extraordinary effectiveness leaves little doubt that we may treat the ***Nibelungenlied*** as art) we are in fact provided with an answer, the symbolic sense of the contest design comes clear. The poet empowers his grim Hagen to mimic the exuberant rhythm so palpable in Siegfried's ever-confident movements; Hagen will once again strike up the gay, lively beat—to demonstrate that he may stop it at will, that Siegfried, for all his innate grace, must dance to Hagen's tune.

But this is, we recall, precisely the summation of Siegfried's character achieved in the sixteenth Aventiure: as we and Hagen know him, dance Siegfried must.

Do sprach von Niderlande der küene Sifrit:
"daz muget ir wol versuochen, welt ir mir loufen mit
ze wette zuo dem brunnen. so daz ist getan,
dem sol man jehen danne, den man sihet gewunnen han."

(Str. 973)

Patently insatiable of victory, Siegfried must take up the challenge—must "win" again; and like the true star performer that he is, he not only grants his opponents a head start (Str. 974) but also takes on an extreme weight handicap (Str. 975). "Do sach man bi dem brunnen den küenen Sifriden e. / Den pris an allen dingen truoc er vor manigem man." (Str. 976, 1. 4, Str. 977, 1. 1)—here, as always, the poet movingly reports the happy manifestations of Siegfried's vitality; consequently, Heusler does not hesitate to comment: "Dieser Wettlauf der drei Helden gibt Sigfrid eine allerletzte Gelegenheit, sich als vordersten zu bewähren," but with this he again neglects the fact that Siegfried does not propose the contest on his own; Weber's remark here is much more to the point: "Dann schreitet Hagen zur Tat, sich mit seinem Wettlaufvorschlag geschickt an Sivrits Mentalität anpassend." Siegfried's performance is indeed first-rate, but it is all part of Hagen's show, he has simply allowed Siegfried to win a race to his own death.

The hunt is not, incidentally, the first occasion in the poem where Hagen manages to direct the fun and games of his superior opponent. As Maurer, Beyschlag and Weber have noted [Friedrich Maurer, "Das Lied im *Nibelungenlied,*" *Angebinde: Jahn Meier zum 85. Geburtstag,* 1949; Siegfried Beyschlag, "Das Motiv der Macht bei Siegfrieds Tod," *Zur Germanisch-Deutschen Heldensage,* 1961], Hagen does in fact continually suggest ways of occupying Siegfried's time from the moment the latter puts aside his bellicose airs. Thus at the outset of the "Sachsenkrieg" he counsels Gunther to mention their problem to Siegfried (Str. 151); and when Siegfried attempts to restrain Gunther from courting Brünhild, Hagen promptly declares that Siegfried should himself be given a leading part in the expedition (Str. 331); and again, when Gunther asks Hagen to be the messenger of the courting mission's happy outcome, Hagen insists that Siegfried be the one to go—no doubt with a view of reinforcing Siegfried's lie to Brünhild that he is Gunther's "eigenman" (Str. 532). And, of course, Hagen's entire plan of finding out, and taking advantage of, Siegfried's weak spot is founded on the certainty that he can move Siegfried about at will: one has only to announce a war, or a hunt (anything that promises excitement), and Siegfried is sure to take part (cf. Str. 874-75 and the fifteenth Aventiure). But in all these cases Hagen is guided by immediately practical considerations, he employs his knowledge of Siegfried's strength and disposition to ensure himself and his king the greatest possible benefit of the hero, to place him at their disposal. What goes on in the hunt, however, is of quite a different nature. There are, as we have seen, no such practical considerations involved in Hagen's contest proposals. Here he has nothing to gain from Siegfried's triumph—except a symbolic triumph of his own. Or perhaps we had better say at this point that it is the poet who wishes to exhibit the inevitable triumph of a Hagen over a Siegfried, who records, doubtless in sadness, the inevitable obliteration of Siegfried's frothy happiness through the grim fundament of Hagen's existence. For the subtlety of thought inherent in the design of the hunting contest seems to me rather beyond a Hagen: it arises directly from the poet's own grand conception of his work.

Why does Hagen murder Siegfried and how does the death of the contest winner, that is, the murder as it is depicted in the sixteenth Aventiure, function within the ***Nibelungenlied*** as a whole? While the second part of our question has not often been dealt with, scholars have offered a bewildering variety of answers to the first. Franz Rolf Schröder sees the confrontation of Siegfried and Hagen as the reflection of a myth pattern: in his view the Siegfried figure was at one time conceived of as a god of fertility and growth who, like Adonis, had *per force* to suffer a violent death—inflicted upon him by a demonic and bestial enemy. There is, possibly, a mythological dimension still to be observed in the poet's description of Siegfried's death agony—"Die bluomen allenthalben von bluote wurden naz. / do rang er mit dem tode . . . " (Str. 998, 1. 1-2)—the hero's ebbing life force coloring the flowers does fit the pattern Schröder has indicated. But for the rest of the poem, and specifically for the hunt itself, Siegfried, despite his extraordinary attributes, is presented as a highly developed form of *human* being, as a courtly knight, and Hagen, Gunther's vassal, has very little about him of the hog (Schröder hears in the name "Hagen" an echo of words meaning "wild boar"). At any rate, Schröder's theory discloses nothing of the poet's *conscious* construction of both the hunt and of the antagonism that finds its culmination within it. Other scholars concerned with an explanation of the events of the ***Nibelungenlied*** itself have found numerous ways of dealing with the murder as an essentially rational, or at least humanly understandable occurrence. Thus Beyschlag finds in Hagen's actions, as well as those of virtually everyone else in the poem with the significant exception of Siegfried himself, an illustration of the dictates of *Machtpolitik;* he points to Hagen's uneasy acknowledgement of Siegfried's incredible strength and his strained silence during the latter's challenge in the third Aventiure, his wish that the Burgundians had control of Siegfried's treasure (Str. 774), his declaration to Gunther that the Burgundians would acquire new lands and power through Siegfried's death (Str. 870); and he feels that Kriemhild's boasts and insults to Brünhild are in fact the effective cause of Hagen's murderous fury, precisely because the vassal sees in them the potential danger represented by Siegfried to Gunther's honor and dominion. Weber, on the other hand, while admitting that questions of power do play a certain role, posits an antagonism of type between Siegfried and his murderer, and advances a Hagen who acts primarily out of personal motives, and not as a result of the indirect insult to his king given in Kriemhild's quarrel with Brünhild. "[Unmittelbar nach dem Frauenzank] blitzartig packt er zu, macht sich—eine reine Zweckmaßnahme—augenblicks zum Anwalt seiner Herrin . . . Er ist zur Meintat entschlossen—Neid, leidenschaftlicher Haß, gekränktes Ehrgefühl, Machtwille und Machtgier bestimmen ihn—, und er hat Gunther eisern dahin gebracht wohin er ihn—offenbar seit längster Zeit (vgl. 870)—haben wollte." Maurer, however, attempts to exonerate Hagen of such base feelings, nor does he feel that a power struggle should be made accountable for Siegfried's death; for him the murder reveals above all a deep commitment on Hagen's part to the honor of his rulers, to both Gunther and Brünhild: "Nun verstehen wir auch Hagen, der ohne persönlichen Ehrgeiz oder Neid auf Siegfried und der nicht aus gekränktem Geltungsbedürfnis handelt; sondern zunächst als Fürsorger für seine Herren, dann als Rächer der beleidigten Ehre Brünhilds und des Burgundenhauses, schließlich als Wahrer der Ehre der Burgundenkönige und seiner eigenen Ehre."

Some sort of case can be made for each of these explanations, but their very profusion indicates that the motivation of Hagen's deed is far from clear-cut. Accordingly, Beyschlag's approach, which is the most direct (and does in fact work out quite well in the *Thidrekssaga*) proves to be the least tenable. For Neumann, extending one of Heusler's lines of argument, effects with a few references to the ***Nibelungenlied*** as we have it what to my mind is an entirely persuasive rebuttal of the power struggle theory. "Die Vorstufen des Nibelungenlieds hatten . . . einen Siegfried, der in Worms seßhaft geworden war . . . An einigen Stellen . . . finden wir also einen Hagen, der Siegfrieds Machtmittel als lockendes Ziel sieht, den starken Siegfried als Last empfindet. Aber dieser Hagen setzt einen Siegfried voraus, der in Worms den Burgunden Raum wegnimmt . . . Er paßt nicht zu jenem hoch-höfischen Siegfried, der als ein König in Xanten wohnt und nur als höfischer Gast zu den Burgunden kommt." And it should be recalled that Siegfried has been no mere neutral, if courtly, guest; he is, on the contrary, up to his death an unfailing source of support to the Burgundians—a defender of the realm whose very death-trap Hagen is able to set by having Gunther pretend to be in need of his services. By his happy, energetically helpful disposition, Siegfried wants nothing of, and could never be a threat to, the Burgundians, and Hagen, who has had full use of his strength, knows this quite well. The same objection may be raised, though perhaps with somewhat less force, to the interpretations of Weber and Maurer. Surely both Hagen and Gunther are reduced in stature by the very fact of Siegfried's totally successful existence, and in the vassal this could well lead to envy, in the king a feeling of diminished honor: whenever Siegfried appears on the stage, all other actors must be regulated to the background; but Hagen has secured (and probably could continue to do so) compensation for himself and his king. He controls Siegfried from the background—and he who controls may, after all, well consider himself superior. Again, it is true that Hagen, in the midst of the general lamentations over Siegfried's demise, does indulge in a primitive, malicious outburst of the sort that would confirm Weber's explanation of his deed—

> Do sprach der grimme Hagene: "jane weiz ich waz ir kleit.
> ez hat nu allez ende unser sorge unt unser leit.
> wir finden ir vil wenic, die türren uns bestan.
> wol mich deich siner herschaft han ze rate getan."
>
> (Str. 993)

but only the violent flow of Hagen's words, and not, as Heusler and Neumann emphasize, their denotation, correlates with the situation as presented in the ***Nibelungenlied*** itself. And Hagen's last comment in the sixteenth Aventiure, with which he justifies his indifference to Kriemhild's certain sorrow and wrath—" 'diu so hat betrüebet den Prünhilde muot. / ez ahtet mich vil ringe, swaz si weinens getuot.' " (Str. 1001, 1. 3-4)—while clearly in line with Maurer's interpretation, seems to me to be in reality something of a listless rationalization. It isn't that Hagen doesn't care about Kriemhild: he simply doesn't care.

Thus, although the poem does, as we have seen, contain lines confirming each of these views, they are isolated and do not come together in a convincing pattern of cause and effect; the conflict which leads to Hagen's attack seems blurred. Neumann again stresses that in the earlier versions of the story—where, as we can still see in the *Völsungasaga* and the *Thidrekssaga,* Brünhild is more closely involved with Siegfried and quite adamant in her demands that he be killed, where Gunther himself is no passive onlooker but rather actively concerned with his honor, where, finally, Siegfried's presence does actually constitute a concrete threat—the murder was the very opposite of a puzzlement. Neumann also has, however, what I regard as a very valuable suggestion as to how we may yet make sense of the proceedings. "Die Tat Hagens war der Ritterwelt grade dann verständlich, wenn ein argloser Ritter, ein Muster der Treue durch die fast unbegründete Treulosigkeit eines heimtückischen Gegners fiel." Not only the murderous assault but also, as we have seen, the prelude to it which the poet allows Hagen to compose in the hunting contest, are in fact virtually lacking in motivation. But this lack, arising as it does primarily in the poet's conscious transformation of the *Recke* Siegfried into a harmless, courtly knight with dominions of his own, seems to me something which the poet consciously exploits, something which contributes a great deal to the realization of his new design upon the Nibelungen tradition. If I may avail myself of an anachronous comparison: there is a Iago-like quality to the villainy Hagen practices during the course of the hunt; like Iago, Hagen gets whatever he wishes out of his victim and plays upon him even as he is engineering his destruction—for his own, inscrutable reasons; and in so doing, Hagen becomes, for the space of the hunt, like Iago an incarnation of destructive force, a demon. Hagen's game with the invariable winner of games is inhuman: so removed from human concerns and reason as to indicate the agency of a non-human power. But for the thought of the poem as a whole such *must* be the nature of the enemy to which Siegfried succumbs. The poet grants him boundless success in life, but only so that his fall may illustrate that such success is at the mercy of a force above, and in control of, human life—that it is, consequently, frivolous to let such success go to one's head. The force which shapes human destiny in the ***Nibelungenlied*** is not, of course, God; it is a sinister fate whose inexorable enmity to man the poet habitually cites in the midst of the Burgundians' gay and festive moments, in the midst of Siegfried's triumphs—whether of vitality or love. Our poet deliberately employs a Hagen with little reason to kill Siegfried and less to play with him beforehand. This Hagen becomes an instrument, helping fate to a triumph which abyssmally undermines those of which a courtly Siegfried is capable.

And the poet would show us that it is, to a large extent, that aspect of Siegfried's courtliness that comes clear in his predilection for games, it is his perpetual *hoher muot* that makes him such an easy prey of a Hagen. He cannot, as the Burgundians in their death struggle, master fate by a grim acceptance of its dictates; on the contrary, in his high enjoyment of life he so repeatedly ignores the omens of approaching death that when he is finally felled his reactions can only be those of childish surprise and angry bewilderment. Nonetheless, from the very beginning the omens are clear. Early in the third Aventiure, Siegmund, hearing of his son's plan to court Kriemhild, counsels Siegfried to be wary of Hagen (Str. 54); yet, we recall, Siegfried singles out Hagen for special, taunting attention in his show of battle readiness on his arrival at Worms (see above). Again, although Siegfried—for reasons not firmly established in the poem—seems initially alarmed at Gunther's own courting plans, he gladly works out the tactics of deception by which Brünhild is ensnared; when yet another, more intimate deception is called for, he not only freely offers his services, but also—in the innocence of his sport (cf. Str. 665)—takes tokens of tribute from the subdued Brünhild, tokens which he thoughtlessly passes on to Kriemhild, thus creating the immediate pretext for Hagen's attack. The poet comments: "ine weiz ob er daz taete durh sinen hohen muot. / er gab iz sinem wibe; daz wart im sider leit" (Str. 680, 1. 2-3) and "swaz er ir geben solde, wie lützel erz beliben lie!" (Str. 684, 1. 4). Just as in the hunt, we find Siegfried here playfully seconding fate in its game with him: always, in distinction to the heroes of the second part of the poem, with blissful ignorance of what he is doing. And it is this—precisely—constitutional blindness to danger which the poet again stresses in Siegfried's farewell to Kriemhild at the outset of the sixteenth Aventiure. Kriemhild, whose disclosure of Siegfried's secret to Hagen is itself so devoid of necessity as to point towards the direct, malevolent intervention of fate, gives her husband a quite compelling warning; but Siegfried is too avid a sportsman to remain home: " ' . . . mit holden magen din / soltu kurzewilen; ine mac hie heime niht gesin' " (Str. 919, 1. 3-4); he disregards all threats because he does not believe that his glorious life *can* in fact be threatened. But the poet sharpens in us awareness that this is a grievous error—"Da mit reit ouch Sifrit in herlichem site. / zeinem kalten brunnen verlos er sit den lip." (Str. 917, 1. 1 and 3)—with what is perhaps the most explicit anticipation to be found in the poem, we have been informed in the second strophe of the sixteenth Aventiure that Siegfried, totally possessed of "herlichem site," will indeed meet his fate on the hunt. The irony would be tragic, except for the fact that Siegfried is not merely unwary but in fact incapable of recognition.—I am in complete agreement with Weber's assessment:

> Es ist eine wenig differenzierte Seelenhaltung, es ist Verblendung, die selbst angesichts der tiefen traumgewarnten Verstörtheit Kriemhildens so sprechen kann . . . [das] gehört wesensmäßig zu Sivrit: das Unvermögen der tieferen Wahrnehmung und Erkenntnis! Es ist Klugheit der höheren Art, ist im tiefsten der Geist, woran es ihm gebricht. Er ist immer nur der strahlende Kämpfer und Kampfbegierige, der nach Tätigkeit drängt . . . eine sehr einseitige, unvollkommene, am Äußeren haftenbleibende Art von Ritterweise, untermischt mit Reckenart—so jedenfalls ganz und gar nicht haltbar, wie der Dichter in tiefster Seele erfahren hat.

"Schicksalsgebundenheit bedeutet *in concreto* Untergangsbestimmtheit . . . ": in Siegfried *hoher muot* arises in an inability to perceive, and thus come to terms with, reality—the reality of human existence as it is presented in the ***Nibelungenlied.*** There is, however, a variety of spiritual fundament to Siegfried's courtly exuberance, one upon which all delight in contests must ultimately rest. Complementary to his absolute disinclination to think of death, there animates Siegfried the knightly conviction that there are certain rules to the game of life, rules which will always be observed by his fellows as faithfully as by himself. Thus we read several times in the poem of his concern for justice (Str. 43, 714); we witness his counseling of charity to a vanquished foe (Str. 315); above all, we come to see that he fully expects the goodness of his proper conduct to impress those around him and to be repaid in kind—" 'ine weiz hie niht der liute, die mir iht hazzes tragen. / alle dine mage sint mir gemeine holt, / ouch han ich an den degenen hie niht anders versolt.' " (Str. 923, 1. 2-4). So in the farewell scene of the sixteenth Aventiure Siegfried replies to Kriemhilds anxious observation that there are quite possibly people at Gunther's court whom they have offended, who would wish them harm (Str. 922); Siegfried finds this inconceivable—directly after his deception of Brünhild has become a public scandal. But, after all, he undertook the deception only for Gunther's sake, and he has publicly reprimanded his wife for her insult and he has privately given her a good beating to teach her to hold her tongue: things are indeed quite simple for Siegfried. His blindness then stems not only from a disbelief that his life can be threatened but also from a certainty that his actions are so distinctly as they should be that no one would want to threaten him.

In the course of the hunt, predominantly in the death scene, the poet dwells on Siegfried's faith in the conventions of polite society—a faith which, as a constituent element of his *hoher muot,* is to be implicated in his fall. We have noted above Siegfried's feeling for elegant hunting practice; this feeling is matched by his insistence, after hearing that there is no wine, on what is the hunter's *due:* " 'man enpflege baz der jegere, ich enwil niht jagetgeselle sin. / Ich hete wol gedienet daz man min baz naeme war' " (Str. 965, 1. 4 and 966, 1. 1). "Gedient" and "versolt" (see above): the words and the concept of human behavior they express—so apparent in Siegfried's courtly gesture of deference to Gunther's thirst after he has won the race to the well (Str. 978)—are all that occurs to Siegfried in the very moment of his death, all that he can hold up against the fate that has finally hunted him down.

> Do sprach der verchwunde: "ja ir vil boesen zagen
> waz helfent miniu dienest, daz ir mich habet erslagen?
> ich was iu ie getriuwe: des ich engolten han.
> ir habt an iuwern magen leider übele getan"
> (Str. 989)

And, as Hagen congratulates himself on having accomplished the murder (Str. 993), Siegfried must protest:

"Ir muget iuch lihte rüemen," sprach do Sifrit.
"het ich an iu erkennet den mortlichen sit,
ich hete wol behalten vor iu minen lip" . . .
(Str. 994, 1. 1-3)

Clearly, it is impossible for a Siegfried to come to terms with what has happened: aside from his pleas for Kriemhild's safety, his words amount to a complaint (to a non-existent contest director) that there has been a grave infraction of the rules. But Hagen and fate have finished with Siegfried's contests, this assault was in earnest. The distinction, in power and depth of recognition, between the anguished lamentations of a Rüdeger or Dietrich and Siegfried's complaint might perhaps be given in the contrast: "how wretched is man's state" and "this is unfair." Siegfried, because he is so used to, and fond of, winning, conspicuously fails of heroism in suffering his only loss. But heroism is for the ***Nibelungenlied*** poet *the* form of human dignity. Weber rightly concludes: "Sivrit ist ganz und gar unvollendeter . . . Zur Freiheit der heldischen Entscheidung gelangt er nicht mehr; seine überdimensionalen Kampfleistungen allein machen ihn noch nicht vollauf zum Helden."

From the relatively safe distance of a spear shot, Hagen directs his lethal blow, as he must, to the one point where his victim is vulnerable—to the spot between his shoulders. Accordingly, Siegfried's protest is well founded; the manner of Hagen's assault is in the highest degree dishonorable: a manner which Siegfried reserves for his encounters with animals. And yet the dishonor is determined in large measure by Siegfried's nature itself, for in death, still absorbed with his glorious strength, he does not attain to insight but instead suffers only an exhaustion of his animal-like vitality.

Den ger im gein dem herzen stecken er do lie.
also grimmelichen ze flühten Hagen nie
gelief noch in der werlde vor deheinem man . . .
(Str. 982, 1. 1-3)

—the image presented in this strophe, whose alliteration effectively captures the still enormous power of Siegfried's heart beat, initates the ultimate reversal of Siegfried's contest victories: Siegfried is still fast enough to catch up with Hagen (Str. 984), but this race leaves him spent. Before he was able to outrun his bear and slay it, now his breath fails him and he falls to the ground. That man, and not just beasts, may be hunted; that fate, which observes no rules, does not indefinitely allow man to make of his life so many games: these are things which must remain beyond Siegfried's comprehension. "So groze missewende ein helt nu nimmer mer begat" (Str. 981, 1. 4)—the poet does consider Hagen's deed ugly in its darkness and he mourns the brilliance it obliterates. He would, however, have us see throughout the spectacle of the sixteenth Aventiure that Hagen must be the victor, that there can indeed be no contest between Siegfried, who knows and thinks only of life, and Hagen, who is sworn to, and possessed by, the powers that control life. For the work as a whole, Siegfried's death marks the forms and principles of courtly existence as being devoid of value to man in his inevitable confrontation with these powers. It is hoped that in the above analysis of the sixteenth Aventiure the art involved in the construction of this disillusioning spectacle has come clear. (pp. 163-83)

Carl S. Singer, "The Hunting Contest: An Interpretation of the Sixteenth Aventiure of the 'Nibelungenlied'," in The Germanic Review, *Vol. XLII, No. 3, May, 1967, pp. 163-83.*

D. G. Mowatt and Hugh Sacker (essay date 1967)

[In the excerpt below, Mowatt and Sacker point out the strengths and weaknesses of the Nibelungenlied, *asserting that it has achieved universal appeal despite "an intriguing combination of incompetence and contrivance."]*

The ***Nibelungenlied*** is an intriguing story, and one difficult to pin down as to its essential nature. Although several attempts have been made in the last half-century to represent it as a sort of novel about Kriemhilde, this is patently unsatisfactory: she hardly appears at all in the first third of the poem, and even if her will for revenge counts for a lot in the last third, the attention centers on the Burgundians at bay. Indeed, just as much as Kriemhilde's story, it could be considered Hagen's, for, displaced from his central advisory position for a time by Sifrid, Hagen later does away with the usurper, and then leads the Burgundians to glory and death. But if the ***Nibelungenlied*** is anyone's story, it is surely the Burgundians' as a whole—the story of their involvement with Sifrid, of Gunther's misplaced marital ambitions, of the consequences for them all of Sifrid's murder; the story of the relationship between Hagen and Sifrid, Hagen and the three kings, all of them and Kriemhilde; the story of the Burgundian encounters with other peoples and finally with the Huns, whom they use for their own destruction.

The minimal descriptive framework might perhaps be that the work shows how a society—the Burgundian court—which begins as unified, static and inflated, becomes fragmented by the effort to absorb alien elements, and only manages to reunite in the simplicity of self-destruction. But to understand this process, one has to give full weight to the alien elements, to the elemental values which link Sifrid with Brünnhilde and Nibelungland, and one has to realize how sharply these contrast with the values of the Burgundians. One also has to accept that Kriemhilde remains throughout a Burgundian, choosing to stay with her own people even when they have killed her husband, working in a sense together with Hagen in the last third of the tale for the annihilation of all. What the ***Nibelungenlied*** presents is two contrasting ideals—of social control and of instinctual action—hankering for one another; and it shows with what disastrous effects for both they can combine.

Not that this disaster appears internally inevitable from the beginning, in spite of the narrator's frequent references to the end that does in fact come about; the pauses, the human trivialities, the interventions from outside counteract the impression of any single-minded master plan. Several times the story nearly peters out, although always there is a lingering dissatisfaction, an unresolved complication, which either leads to or is receptive of further development. One of the attractions of the ***Nibelungenlied*** is the way in which the plot thickens and then thins out again—and nevertheless leads to total resolution at the end. Disaster on the scale which is finally achieved is explicable from the nature of the initial encounter, but there is nothing inexorable about the way it is worked out—chance and triviality are given their due.

The unravelling of the plot is narrated impersonally, with detachment, in repetitive phrases, expansively, and with a commentary which lacks all except the most elementary discrimination. Were the story simple and rational, the banality of it all would be extreme. As it is, there is conveyed a feeling that no master-mind was responsible, that this is how things happened—and it is up to the audience to make sense of it or not. According to the narrator, all his tale shows is that happiness always ends in sorrow—an unpretentious cliché which is certainly more appropriate to the story than some that modern critics have supplied, but which remains so detached as to be totally unintrusive. So too, when Hagen murders Sifrid, his treachery is deplored by the narrator, but no attempt is made to explain to the audience how we should reconcile our moral disapproval with the admiration we are made to feel (even to some extent at the time) for his reckless courage and bravado. Such a narrator cannot be regarded as offering an adequate interpretation of the events he records; rather, we are left to treat his comments lightly and supply quite different ones of our own.

The off-hand, repetitive phrases in which the story is told have a similar effect. Deriving almost certainly from a tradition of spontaneous oral poetry, in which the story-teller makes up a more-or-less different version of a traditional tale each time he tells it and is able to keep going only by repetitiveness of phrase and metre, this style too conveys the impression, not of a high-powered intelligence generating at each successive moment the uniquely appropriate phrase for the situation—the ideal of most modern poetry—but of an entertainer who is himself impressed by these stories of long ago and yet keeps his distance, allowing them a good deal of latitude, since he himself only half knows what matters and what does not.

There are, indeed, many signs in the work of a rather threadbare, minimal competence. The poem rambles on repetitiously, lines and stanzas are filled out with padding, new starts occur for no apparent reason, characters are introduced two or three times over, unmistakable changes in style or metre appear to serve no purpose, internal inconsistencies are not uncommon, the sequence of events is often muddled, the passage of time operates in some respects but not in others, the forms *du* and *ir* are sometimes interchanged at random, the pairs or groups in which the characters confer or dispute are broken up and reformed more in the fashion of dreams than of reality, characters behave now in one way, now in a seemingly incompatible way, without anyone remarking on the change—there is simply no attempt to make everything fit. This frequent unconcern with the logic of detail is, however, not all that disturbing. Partly it is counteracted by our perception of a deliberate and largely successful effort on the part of the author (or authors) to impose some sort of order on recalcitrant material, but more essentially, in our view, by the fact that it is on this basis of casual disorder that many of the most successful effects of the work are founded.

Let us first of all indicate some results of conscious control on the part of the poet, all elementary, but nonetheless satisfying. There is, for instance, the general balance of the work: the fact that it divides into two approximately equal halves before and after Etzel's appearance on the scene—or again, into three more or less equal parts, dividing first after Sifrid's murder and then before Kriemhilde invites her kinsmen to Hunland. There is the Bechelaren interlude, where an idyllic pause is strategically placed just before the grim finality of the last battles. There is the way in which Volker—a Burgundian minstrel who plays no part in the first two thirds of the story, but who emerges as Hagen's most unconditional support in the last third—is yet mentioned a few times early on to prepare us for his later importance. So too, if the Saxon war is a muddle, there is the carefully controlled progression of the battles at Etzel's court.

Again, if idealising adjectives are in general rather indiscriminately applied to everyone, nevertheless Sifrid is more often described as "strong" than anyone else, and Hagen alone frequently appears as "grim." The anticipations of disaster which are scattered throughout the epic and which are apparently used simply to fill out certain stanzas, nevertheless seem to be grouped in a more or less sensible manner; for instance, in the very first âventiure we find three separate ones (2,4; 6,4; 19,4), of which each anticipates a different event in the future and which together span the whole work, while in the following three âventiuren there are hardly any at all. Also, if the murder of the Danube ferryman is rather puzzling, and Hagen's feat of rowing the whole army of 10,000 across the river single-handed a bit improbable, yet it is clear that the crossing as a whole is a well utilized symbol: before it the Burgundians still hope for a way back, after it they increasingly brace themselves to face certain death. Lastly, if it is an insoluble problem just why the name Nibelungs, which in the first two-thirds of the poem is reserved for the inhabitants of the land where Sifrid's treasure came from, from the time of the Danube crossing is frequently applied to the Burgundians, there is something rather touching in the way the text apparently tries to ease the transition for us by mentioning at this very point that some of Sifrid's original Nibelungs accompany the Burgundians on their last journey. All of these features, and many more, bear witness to a conscious control applied to recalcitrant material by some ordering mind—and depend for their appeal precisely on their only partial effectiveness. A systematically and efficiently controlled work would make a very different impression.

There are two rather more general features which, like those just listed, are commonly admired today, and which were probably also largely intended by the author or authors. One is the dramatic tension and density of a number of scenes, such as those presenting the first arrival of Sifrid at Worms, the quarrel between the two queens, or the confrontation of Hagen and Kriemhilde shortly after the Burgundians arrive at Etzel's court. The effect of such scenes depends partly on the tensely charged dialogue, but perhaps even more on their general role in the work; in them conflicts which are latent suddenly explode, exposing dramatically before our eyes hidden tensions more intense than we knew, and by the explosion providing further impetus for the future. Many of these scenes were first composed centuries earlier for the short lays that were the forerunners of our ***Nibelungenlied,*** but they were retained, adapted and even initiated by whoever composed this latter, and it is difficult to believe that they have not always been appreciated.

Also generally admired, if sometimes reluctantly, with some degree of bafflement, is the overall structure of the plot: the way the courtship of Sifrid leads over to his murder and the widowhood of Kriemhilde, and this in turn to her second marriage and revenge on her kinsmen. There can be little doubt that this structure was more or less consciously contrived, and that, whatever the problems it throws up, its contriving was a remarkable achievement. Without it, the work would fail on an elementary level and lose much of its appeal, at least for the general reader.

Most of what has been said so far is generally agreed: the ***Nibelungenlied*** appears to many as an intriguing combination of incompetence and contrivance. But does this mixture, together with the plot, account for the remarkable hold it exercises on its readers? Has enough now been said about the work itself, and do we now need to turn to its sources and to the background of mediaeval culture in order to appreciate it further? Certainly these extraneous factors partially account for the rather patronizing admiration of the ***Nibelungenlied*** shown by some readers, but we suggest that much of its hold on the imagination derives from an interplay of elements which was probably not consciously intended by the mediaeval author (or authors) and which has not to any appreciable extent been analyzed by modern critics. This interplay depends for its success on the relationships between the consciously controlled overall structure and the material itself, the individual elements which appear to some extent out of control. These two levels of phenomena, conscious design and seemingly random detail, are linked together in elusive and unpredictable, but nonetheless extremely revealing and significant ways.

It is, for instance, only from this point of view that the various characters become really interesting. Consider Kriemhilde. The work reveals a consciousness that as a girl she was demure, as a wife proud, when newly widowed grief-stricken, at the end a she-devil murdering tens of thousands for a personal vendetta. But no comment is passed on the relationship of these stages to one another. Thus while some modern readers have maintained that the stages are not integrally connected—Kriemhilde just playing the particular role required by each situation in turn—others believe equally firmly that they constitute the main point of the poem and present a straightforward characterological sequence. Each of these verdicts can be supported by reference to the mediaeval background, to other works in which the development of the main characters is minimal or maximal, but neither of them is adequate to the situation. The simple fact is surely that this sort of presentation provides a challenge, a provocation to wonder about human nature as portrayed in this poem. Progress cannot be made by denying the problem, but only by abstracting this and other patterns until common features become apparent.

The results, if not simple, can be illuminating. For instance, if Kriemhilde appears initially as shy and retiring, later as demonically possessed, she is nowhere shown as enjoying easy, yet actively reciprocal relationships with others, nowhere as behaving in a positively creative and outgoing manner. And if the likelihood of such behaviour is regarded as small in the largely male world that is portrayed, yet it will be seen that Kriemhilde reacts to the limitations imposed on women in a man's world differently from any other character. When told by her mother that she can only be fulfilled by a man's love, she says in that case she will remain beautiful as she is. Brought up by her brothers in unusual seclusion, she goes out of her way to encourage the eldest of them to domineer over her, at least nominally, and to dispose of her as he likes. Sought out by and married to the only truly outgoing and spontaneous man in the poem, who is also (not surprisingly) the strongest individual, as well as somewhat brash, she at once lays claim on his behalf to a share in her brothers' possessions, or, failing that, to their chief retainer, Hagen, and later provokes the fatal quarrel with Brünnhilde by the superbly ingenuous remark that all the Burgundian lands should be Sifrid's. (Of course, by the simple standards to which Sifrid tends to revert and which she is now invoking as she looks at him in all his manly splendour, this is true; for if the disposal of Burgundy, and of herself, had been settled by recourse to arms, as Sifrid first suggested, he would doubtless have taken the lot.) Thus Kriemhilde may be considered to show signs even in the first third of the ***Nibelungenlied*** of both a preoccupation with domination and power, and a (typically Burgundian) inability to act openly and directly.

Under these circumstances, Sifrid may well represent Kriemhilde's one chance of getting away from herself, of becoming part of a simpler and more straightforward nature. Once he is married, however, Sifrid shows the same casual disregard for her personality and needs that he shows for those of all others—a characteristic largely responsible for his death—and gives her tokens of his manly exploits without apparently bothering to explain much about them or to think what she might use them for. And in fact, when she uses them as support in her quarrel with Brünnhilde (over which of their husbands is preeminent—no trivial issue for either of them), all Sifrid does is to treat it as silly women's talk and give her a thrashing.

On this level there is not all that much difference between Kriemhilde's relationship with Sifrid and that of the other Burgundians. She, like them, is preoccupied with the protocol of power and is not naturally outgoing. For her, as for them, Sifrid appears to represent a liberation, a new range of activity which only he can offer. But for her, as for them, he brings with him an insouciance which is irreconcilable with their deepest worries. And so it is not surprising that it is in the name of Burgundian kinship that

Kriemhilde, remembering even as she does so that there could be reasons for not trusting any of her relatives, betrays Sifrid to Hagen. Moreover, she opens the scene by expressing her pleasure that she has a husband so able to help her kinsmen, and then, after revealing that the noble man thrashed her for her trouble-making, proceeds to confess that her one worry for him is that his *übermuot* might lead him into danger—although it is only through her intervention at this precise moment that this danger could prove real. It is largely because of the correlation on some unconscious but perfectly convincing level between the precise phrasing of such a scene and the generalities of the overall structure of the triangle Burgundians-Kriemhilde-Sifrid that, in our opinion, the ***Nibelungenlied*** makes the deep appeal it does make.

The particular aspect considered here can be extended (with appropriate modification and development) in every direction. The treasure, something which only a Sifrid can acquire but in which a Sifrid has no interest, becomes in the hands of the Burgundians an inert lump which fascinates Hagen and Kriemhilde, even though neither of them understands its nature. Also, once it has been seen how Kriemhilde and Hagen join to destroy Sifrid, it can be better understood that they join to destroy their society and themselves in his name. Certainly they fight, but they are fighting from a common standpoint to a common goal—and it is only on this level that Kriemhilde's refusal to leave Burgundy after the murder and Hagen's subsequent unremitting provocation of her can be understood. (pp. 8-16)

In [the ***Nibelungenlied***] disregard for logic and consistency at a commonsense level is more marked than in most other works, even of its own time. This disregard is tempered by a degree of rational control which provides some sort of commonsense framework, but which is not itself adequate to explain the appeal of the poem. This appeal is, however, explicable to a large extent in terms of the correlation between apparently random detail and overall structure at a fairly high degree of abstraction—a correlation which very probably exists in all great works of art, but which, in the case of the ***Nibelungenlied,*** is intimately related to the apparent carelessness of composition. (p. 16)

D. G. Mowatt and Hugh Sacker, in their The Nibelungenlied: An Interpretative Commentary, *University of Toronto Press, 1967, 144 p.*

Kriemhild slays Hagen in Etzel's court, in an 1867 illustration by Julius Schnorr von Carolsfeld.

Charles Moorman (essay date 1971)

[*Moorman is an American educator who specializes in medieval literature. In the following excerpt, he comments on the poet's treatment of heroism in the* Nibelungenlied, *concluding that the poem is "without a single hero."*]

The hero (or at least one of the heroes) of the ***Nibelungenlied*** . . . retains his origin in Germanic mythology even after the nearly eight hundred years that separate historical from dramatic time in the poem. Siegfried, despite his rather prosaic parentage and his twelfth-century courtliness and refinement, is in the ***Nibelungenlied*** still much the same godlike figure who in the early myths slew the dragon and pierced the wall of flame surrounding Brunhild's castle. There is, to be sure, some slight evidence for the existence of a historical Siegfried and Brunhild, based for the most part on onomastics and rough similarities to incidents in Gothic history, but their story from its very beginnings smacks strongly of mythic origins—particularly the incident of Brunhild's awakening, which seems to have its ultimate origin in myths of the sun god and the sleeping beauty.

Strangely enough, however, the important sources for the Siegfried story are Scandinavian rather than German, although the legend itself is probably of Low German origin. The story probably originated among the Franks and was carried by traders or raiders to Scandinavia, perhaps as early as the sixth century. It first appeared in written form in a number of lays contained in the so-called *Elder Edda,* a collection of verses put together in the thirteenth century; and because most of these poems date from the earlier period of Viking conquests they preserve early Germanic myths and themes. Luckily, the songs of the *Elder Edda,* which deal with scattered events in the life of Siegfried, can be supplemented by the account of the hero in the prose *Volsunga saga,* essentially a paraphrase of the

Elder Edda, which contains enough detail to place the earlier lays in a narrative context. The *Thidreks saga,* a thirteenth-century Norwegian saga dealing with the life of Dietrich of Berne, the historical Theodoric the Great, contains a lengthy retelling of the Siegfried story and is chiefly important because it derives not only from the earlier Scandinavian versions of the legend but also, as the author himself tells us, from the stories of North German merchants.

These three documents, along with some abbreviated forms of the tale in the *Prose Edda* of Snorri Sturluson and in the *Nornagests saga* (which despite their brevity add a number of details to the longer accounts) and some scattered allusions to it in various late medieval songs and poems (including *Beowulf*), constitute our main sources for the Siegfried legend. Without attempting to recount these early forms of the legend in all their conflicting detail or to reduce them to an Ur-Siegfried, let us summarize them briefly. They deal with a hero of divine origin, being descended from Odin, who early in life with the help of a miraculous sword kills a dragon, wins an enormous treasure, and is rendered invulnerable, save for a small spot between the shoulder blades, by the dragon's blood. He goes on to rescue the sleeping Brunhild from a magic circle of fire and gives her a ring of bethrothal, only to leave her after a short time to pursue his adventures. He arrives at the court of Guiki where under the influence of a potion he marries the king's daughter, Kriemhild. Siegfried assists Gunther, one of Kriemhild's brothers, in wooing Brunhild by riding through the fire circle and, later, by deceitfully subduing her on Gunther's behalf by spending a night at her side during which he replaces her bethrothal ring with one taken from the treasure.

In time Kriemhild and Brunhild become involved in a deadly wrangle concerning the relative nobility of their husbands, and Brunhild learns of Siegfried's deception. When Kriemhild shows her the fatal ring, Brunhild prevails upon Gunther's and Kriemhild's brother Hagen to arrange the death of Siegfried, using as a pretext an opportunity for Hagen to acquire the treasure. Siegfried is killed; Brunhild commits suicide; and Kriemhild after a period of several years marries Etzel, who murders her brothers to possess Siegfried's treasure and is in turn killed by her.

It should be clear from even so brief a summary that Siegfried and Brunhild are creatures of myth. . . . Siegfried is descended from the gods; . . . he, like Achilles, is invulnerable from attack, save in one spot; and . . . he is able, having tasted the dragon's blood, to communicate with the birds. Brunhild in the older legends likewise shows mythic ancestry. There are various tests, passing through a ring of fire or taming a horse, which the hero must pass to marry her, and the *Thidreks saga* states that her great strength is dependent upon her virginity.

Both Siegfried and Brunhild, moreover, carry vestiges of their origins into the courtly world of the ***Nibelungenlied*** and so seem strangely ill at ease in the elegant court of Gunther and Kriemhild. Like Achilles, Siegfried is essentially an isolated figure, and though he assists Gunther to woo Brunhild, he does so for purely selfish reasons. And like Achilles, he is proud and arrogant beyond any requirement of the heroic code. Although he assures his father that he will conduct his courtship first by "friendly requests," and by force only if these fail, he in fact answers Gunther's courteous welcoming speech with the haughty demand that Gunther turn over to him all his land, castles, and people. (He does not, interestingly enough, even mention to Gunther at this meeting his desire to wed Kriemhild.) It takes all the diplomacy that Gunther and his advisers can muster to pacify the arrogant young lad.

Furthermore, the poet is careful to mention Siegfried's supernatural accomplishments when he is introduced into the action. When Siegfried approaches Gunther's castle, Hagen recognizes him and tells Gunther at some length of the hero's acquiring of the treasure (in this version, from two mighty princes, Schilbung and Nibelung, and an accompanying force of twelve giants and seven hundred warriors), his winning of the *Tarnkappe* which renders its wearer invisible, and his battle with the dragon.

In the days that follow, Siegfried is indeed somewhat tamed by the Burgundian court, "for he aspired to a noble love"; yet when the opportunity arises to prove his valor in Gunther's war against the Saxons, his old arrogance returns, and having instructed Gunther to remain at home, he leads a force of one thousand Burgundians to victory against forty thousand Saxons.

Returning to Burgundy, he becomes again very much the courtier, but when he agrees to undertake Gunther's courtship of Brunhild, he spurns Gunther's offer of thirty thousand troops and will allow only Gunther, Hagen, and Dancwart to accompany him on the dangerous mission. In winning Brunhild for Gunther, he makes use not only of his almost supernatural strength but also of the *Tarnkappe;* he uses the magic cloak a second time in subduing Gunther's reluctant bride.

The tone [of the *Nibelungenlied*] is courtly and elegant save for an occasional outburst by Siegfried, and the formalities of court life are described in detail; were it not for the foreshadowings of the dark days to come, one would be deceived into expecting a happy issue from the events.

—Charles Moorman

Siegfried's essential character is perhaps best revealed in his theft of Brunhild's ring and girdle. His motive must be sheer pride (as indeed the poet all but states directly), the kind of adolescent irresponsibility that underlies Achilles' sending Patroclus into battle and Roland's refusing to blow the olifant. In taking the ring and girdle and turning them over to Kriemhild, he obviously thinks himself immune to any sort of tragic consequences, and this attitude demonstrates clearly the arrogance that marks all his actions but those involved in his courtship of Kriemhild.

Even his last actions, save one, are marked by heroic arrogance. Upon being told that the Saxons are again threatening the Burgundians, he flies into an almost egomaniacal rage:

> I, Siegfried, shall prevent it with all energy, as befits your honour, and I will deal with them now as I dealt with them before. I shall lay waste their lands and castles before I have finished with them, let my head be your pledge for it! You and your warriors must stay at home and let me ride against them with the men that I have here. I shall show you how glad I am to help you. Believe me, I shall make your enemies suffer.

And on his final hunt, having terrified the hunting party by loosing a captured bear in camp, he indulges in a fit of pique because no wine is brought to him: "Unless we hunters are better looked after," he says, "I'll not be a companion to the hunt. I thought I had deserved better attention."

Strangely enough, however, in describing Siegfried's murder the poet suggests that the hero's assumed courtliness rather than his inherent *hubris* is directly responsible for his death: on reaching the spring, Siegfried courteously stands aside to allow Hagen time to dispose of Siegfried's bow and sword; the poet then comments significantly that Siegfried "paid for his good manners."

Brunhild, though her role in the ***Nibelungenlied*** is much reduced from the early versions of the story, asserts her mythic origins in much the same way. She is clearly related to the fairytale figure of the sleeping beauty. She rules alone in splendid isolation in Isenland, there imposing a series of well-nigh impossible tasks on her suitors, failure in which carries a penalty of death. As in the older legends, she greets the initial wedding-night advances of Gunther with scorn and violence. She is perpetually concerned over Siegfried's apparent failure to pay his feudal obligations, and not only is she quick to challenge Kriemhild's suggestion that Gunther is not Siegfried's overlord but also, "enthroned in her pride," she refuses to mourn the death of Siegfried.

As with Siegfried, however, the poet apparently has taken pains to subdue the barbarian spirit of the mythical Brunhild. There is no indication, for example, that she suggests to either Gunther or Hagen that Siegfried be murdered; and the poet has omitted, perhaps deliberately, her exultant laugh upon hearing of Siegfried's death. Most important is the fact that Brunhild does not commit suicide but simply disappears from the action of the poem.

But both Siegfried and Brunhild, though softened considerably by time and by the courtly interests of the poet, retain something of their mythic origins. To be sure, Siegfried is no longer the "youthful day who is destined to rouse the sun [Brunhild] from her slumber," nor is he the "bright summer" who has overthrown the dragon of winter and the dwarfs of darkness, but the poet does retain enough of the hero's original character and exploits to separate him rather sharply from those "new men" with whom he has come to dwell, particularly Gunther and Hagen.

Gunther, and presumably the members of his court as well, are, like Agamemnon and Hygelac, ultimately descendants from history rather than from myth and, as in the Homeric epics and *Beowulf,* their origins have considerable bearing upon their roles in the poem. The *Lex Burgundionum,* a sixth-century chronicle, mentions among a list of earlier rulers of Burgundy one Gundaharius, almost certainly the Gunther of the poem, who established the Burgundian nation along the Rhine in the first years of the fifth century. In 435 the Burgundians revolted against their Roman overlords and were defeated by the Roman general Aetius. They rebelled again, however, the following year and this time were almost annihilated by a combination of Roman and Hunnish forces. Attila apparently did not himself take part in this engagement—most certainly he did not die in it—in which some twenty thousand Burgundians were killed, but it is quite natural that he, the archetype of the voracious Hun, later became associated with the slaughter.

The tenth-century Latin epic *Waltharius,* devoted to the exploits of Walter of Aquitaine, mentions a few of the ***Nibelungenlied*** characters, though it does not relate them to the slaughter of the Burgundians. Two of the lays of the *Elder Edda* deal with Etzel's marriage to Gunther's sister and his consequent destruction of the Burgundians in an attempt to gain the Nibelung treasure: the *Atla Kvidha,* dating back to the ninth century, and the *Brot,* a fragment of an Eddic lay on the death of Siegfried. There is no hint in either lay, however, of the role of avenger later assumed by Kriemhild; in the *Elder Edda* Etzel is the sole villain and his motive is the theft of the treasure.

Thidreks saga not only connects the Siegfried story with that of the Burgundians' destruction through the motif of Kriemhild's revenge but also introduces into the action Dietrich of Berne. Dietrich is the historical Theodoric the Great who, although he is in the poem living in exile at Etzel's court, actually died in 526, almost a hundred years after the dramatic period of the action. Significantly, in the *Thidreks saga* Etzel is no longer the instigator of the slaughter but has become Kriemhild's tool in her revenge.

While it is impossible here to untangle the complex web of sources, a few generalizations are possible. First, there is no clear source for the ***Nibelungenlied,*** although scholars have freely manufactured hypothetical ancestors, particularly the so-called *Diu Nôt* of 1160. Second, the poem has its ultimate origin in two kinds of material: a myth involving a dragon-killer and the maiden whom he rescues, and the historical destruction of the Burgundians by the Huns. Third, while the exact cause and circumstances of the union of myth and history are of course unknown, a statement of Saxo Grammaticus in 1131 referring to "Kriemhild's famous betrayal of her brothers" demonstrates that the change necessary to that union—Kriemhild's revenge—had been accomplished at least by that date.

The poem as we have it thus stands at the end of a long period of development for which we have very few documents. Nor do we have any evidence of the existence of an oral tradition, though it seems to me safe to assume that one existed since, despite this paucity of sources, the development of the complex story of the fall of the Nibelungs can be seen to be marked by the same sort of changes we have noted elsewhere. There is the same combination of mythical and historical elements and the same distortion of history. And I think it demonstrable also that the poem exhibits the blending of past and present standards of conduct and the fusion of heroic and corporate values that so mark the heroic as a type.

But with a startling difference. Unlike the Homeric epics, *Beowulf,* and the *Song of Roland,* the ***Nibelungenlied*** was not written at a time in which a new, highly organized, nationalistic civilization was beginning to emerge from a long period of political chaos and confusion. Quite the opposite, in fact. Germany had suffered less than any other western kingdom from the collapse of the post-Carolingian kingdoms in the late ninth century and thus was able not only to preserve some semblance of order in the centuries that followed but also, through its almost universal military conscription, to beat off the Viking attacks which were paralyzing the rest of western Europe. Moreover, the strong rule of Otto I in the late ninth century prevented, or at least delayed, the rise of feudalism in Germany. In fact, had it not been for the continuing quarrels between the German emperors and the eleventh- and twelfth-century popes, Germany might have avoided completely the feudal disunity that plagued the emerging nations of medieval Europe.

But by the mid-twelfth century the German emperors had largely lost control of their empire. They might still jockey for power in the never-ending game of playing baron against bishop, but they had little or no authority of their own. Even the greatest of the Hohenstaufens, Frederick Barbarossa, was unable to bring together in his forty-one-year reign the remnants of the Ottonian Empire, Germany and northern Italy; despite his astute political maneuvering, he was forced to overextend what were at best limited powers and so succeeded neither in uniting a Germany torn by the feud of Guelphs and Ghibellines nor in annexing an Italy united under papal auspices against him. And with the death of Frederick's heir, Henry VI, in 1197, Frederick's advances toward unity quickly disintegrated in a maelstrom of renewed civil wars. From the time of the writing of the ***Nibelungenlied*** until the end of the Middle Ages, there was no effective central government in the Ottonian Empire: in Italy each city-state governed its own affairs; in Germany the individual principalities remained autonomous.

Despite the barbarism of the times, however, the Viennese court, which the poet, whatever his status, doubtless knew well, considered itself a haven of culture and refinement. Declared a *civitas* in 1137, Vienna under the Babenbergs had become a provincial center of both commerce and art. Yet this culture, largely imported from France, had no real relation to its setting, existing as it did in the midst of political turmoil which might at any minute destroy it and upon which it had no visible influence. The reign of the Ghibelline Philip of Swabia, during which the ***Nibelungenlied*** was written, was as precarious as it was brief. His election as emperor was immediately challenged by the Guelphs, who with the support of the pope placed against him Otto of Brunswick. The renewed feud over the imperial crown between the princes of Church and State raged in such fury that Philip could not be crowned until 1205 and was assassinated in 1208. The new ideals of chivalry might well exist in the courtly romances imported from France and imitated by German poets; Emperor Philip and the margraves of Babenberg might even try to create for themselves an atmosphere of sophisticated courtliness. But the realities of German politics demanded that the nation's great lords adopt ruthless and calculated policies far removed from the chivalric values of the more settled French courts of the period.

It has often been remarked that the ***Nibelungenlied*** presents a startling contrast of courtly and barbaric conduct, and it is hardly surprising that this should be true. The poet certainly had occasion to observe the gulf between the imported, largely artificial standards of chivalry and the harsh, practical laws of political survival. *Gentilesse,* whatever its virtues and graces, perished or was at best simply pushed aside in the apparently never-ending struggle for power between Guelph and Ghibelline. A Siegfried softened by the amenities of court life became the easy prey of an unscrupulous Hagen, and a naive Etzel the tool of an unprincipled Kriemhild.

The legend of Siegfried and the fall of the Nibelungs emerged, as we have said, as the ***Nibelungenlied*** after a very long period of germination. In its seeds doubtless lay all sorts of possibilities for development and interpretation. But the form it finally took in the one finished poem that has survived is almost certainly attributable to the perception and genius of the man who composed it. Unlike Homer, he could not look back from a newly emerged and already settled commercial state across the gulf of a dark age to a more individualistic, albeit more barbarous, age of heroes. Had he known Greek history, he might well have imagined himself instead to be still inhabiting the dark chaos of post-Mycenaean times, looking back through the confused tales of heroic legend to an even less settled, though ostensibly more heroic, time but forward only to the uncertain conflict of warlords. Still the legend itself, even if it did not offer a solution, might at least provide the poet with a means of defining the times. For it might be shaped into an image of the debilitation of the heroic Ottonian code into ineffectual *luxuria* on the one hand and unprincipled barbarism on the other.

The ***Nibelungenlied*** is thus a poem without a single hero. To a degree far greater than had Homer, the poet makes of the old legend a contemporary poem, and he finds no real heroes in his own time. Without ever descending to the level of political allegory, the reshaped legend defines the central issues of early thirteenth-century Germany: the barbarous, self-destructive warfare between states, the ineffectual leadership of the rulers, the seizure of power by the ruthless and the treacherous, the lack of concern for national welfare, the failure of the Church to maintain order, and the more universal failure of the nobility to live by the chivalric code which it professed or indeed by any standard of decent behavior.

And these themes are everywhere supported by the poem's tone of despair, by its sense of futility, and by its sure knowledge that joy must end in sorrow—not, as in *Beowulf* and the Norse sagas, because the gods themselves cannot prevent it but because man in his perversity so wills it. From beginning to end, from Kriemhild's dream to Dietrich's and Etzel's laments, the poet foretells the dreadful consequences of unprincipled action. He is careful to frame the story with a clear statement of its theme: the young Kriemhild tries to avoid marriage because "there are many examples of women who have paid for happiness with sorrow in the end," and after the final slaughter we are again reminded that "joy must ever turn to sorrow in the end."

But the structure of the poem provides the most convenient point of departure for a discussion of its general intent and its relation to the heroic tradition. The bipartite form of the legend—the crude joining of the stories of Siegfried's death and the Burgundians' destruction by the single strand of Kriemhild's revenge—was at once the poet's greatest problem and the means by which he could best present his theme. There can be no doubt that the coupling of myth and history presented enormous difficulties of structure. The extended chronology and complex relations of the major characters made the *in medias res* technique of the *Odyssey* impossible; one simply could not summarize by retrospective narrative the complicated events of Adventures 1–9, nor was there a single character who could be made to report them with any degree of objectivity. The "natural" way of treating the story, on the other hand, straight chronological narration, could easily, because of its premature first climax (the death of Siegfried) and its tendency to degenerate into a series of personal combats, blunt or even completely obscure the theme which the poet wished at all costs to express.

His answer to this technical problem was to adopt a chronology which, though linear and straightforward, varies in tempo and intensity according to his needs, moving from a deceptively leisurely beginning to a swiftly moving climax and conclusion. The exposition is handled slowly and carefully, allowing the reader to fix in mind clearly the essential qualities of the characters, particularly Kriemhild's pride and Siegfried's rash haughtiness. With the arrival of Siegfried at Worms, Kriemhild is temporarily put aside in order to introduce Gunther and Hagen and to develop, through the apparently digressive Saxon war, Siegfried's prowess. Only then does the pet permit Siegfried to see Kriemhild and introduce the first stirrings of romance. Next he introduces Brunhild through Gunther's journey to Isenland, and the contrast between Siegfried and Gunther is reinforced through Siegfried's conduct in the games and his journey to the hall of the Nibelungs. With Siegfried's return the poet turns to the romance of Siegfried and Kriemhild and relates Siegfried's subduing of the prideful Brunhild.

Up to this point he has proceeded in leisurely fashion, relating the principal events, the journeys and trials, in the unhurried spirit of the French romance. And indeed, were it not for the absence of the endless psychologizing of Chrétien's heroes and heroines, the reader would almost imagine himself to be reading an *Yvain* or an *Erec and Enide.* The tone is courtly and elegant save for an occasional outburst by Siegfried, and the formalities of court life are described in detail; were it not for the foreshadowings of the dark days to come, one would be deceived into expecting a happy issue from the events. Yet the apparently discursive nature of the narrative is not without its effect, for it plants securely in incident after incident the seeds of later action: the fierce Siegfried is lulled into a false security by the sophisticated manners of an alien court; Kriemhild's youthful independence is overmatched by her growing love for Siegfried; Hagen's devotion to his lord, Gunther, is everywhere apparent. The gay atmosphere of the Burgundian court is, like the courtly tone of the poem, a willful deception.

This tone is broken sharply at Adventure 14, "How the Queens Railed at Each Other," and the suspense of the narrative is increased, event following event more swiftly now and almost without elaboration. With the argument of Kriemhild and Brunhild the niceties of court life are abandoned, and the participants begin to reveal their essential characters. Siegfried treats the affair with cavalier self-confidence; Gunther avoids the issue by hedging; Kriemhild, though dutifully submitting to her husband's judgment and a beating, is apprehensive and fears for his life; and Hagen, inflamed at the insult to Gunther's wife, weaves a complex web of deceit to redress the wrong. The courtly tone returns briefly in the elaborate hunt which follows, but it serves only to increase suspense and to set the stage for Hagen's brutal murder of Siegfried.

From the death of Siegfried until the arrival of the Burgundians in Hungary the tempo of action slows down again, though the prevailing tone is sorrow rather than the festival joy of the early books. Kriemhild's alternating grief and rage, even in the midst of her marriage festivities, are dwelt upon by the poet in preparation for her new role in the days to come, and indeed all the characters reveal themselves more and more during this interval: Gunther becomes more irresolute, Hagen firmer and grimmer. The journey to Hungary itself is enormously expanded by the poet. As the Burgundians pass milestone after milestone—the warnings by Hagen, the incidents of the rude ferryman and the fated chaplain, the attack by Gelpfrat, even the idyllic stay at Pöchlarn—they are met by portents of the terror to come. Every incident, even Rudiger's innocent gift of a sword to Gernot, is wreathed round by ironies indicating that the Burgundians will never retrace their steps to their homeland.

With the arrival of Gunther's army at Etzel's court in Hungary, the poet abandons the joyful courtliness of the first books, the mounting suspense of the days preceding Siegfried's murder, and the steadily darkening mood of the middle books to break forth into a strident narrative that fairly leaps from crisis to crisis and battle to battle. The great tableaux follow each other in breathless succession: Hagen refusing to arise at Kriemhild's approach, Kriemhild begging Dietrich for escort through the slaughter of the banquet hall, Volker fiddling the battle-weary Burgundians to sleep, Hagen restoring Rudiger's honor by begging from him his shield. No room now for courtliness or suspense or sorrow; everything is subordinated to the swift pace of the action, and when at last the climax comes and Kriemhild at the height of her savagery executes Hagen with Siegfried's sword, the tale is done. No funeral games or denouement as in Homer, no funeral lament as in *Beowulf,* no commission to continue the struggle as in the *Song of Roland* remain to be recounted. The poem ends upon a shrieking discord of destruction, its final note, like its first, a grim reminder that "joy must ever turn to sorrow in the end."

The poet thus solves the chronological problem of his highly discursive material by alternating both tone and tempo according to his immediate needs, principally those of characterization and mood. But even more important than the problem of chronology was the difficulty of producing the necessary change in the character of Kriemhild, who must be transformed from a sympathetic heroine and widow to a vicious monster whose death we welcome. In the hands of the ***Nibelungenlied***-poet this apparent obstacle to a unified structure becomes itself a means of unification; whatever its sources may have been, the ***Nibelungenlied*** as we have it is Kriemhild's poem. She is the first character to appear and her death is the last event. There is hardly an action in the entire poem which she does not in some way motivate or in which she is not directly involved. Hagen, grim and terrible as he is, and Gunther, the only other major characters who bridge the gap between the two halves of the poem, seldom take upon themselves the responsibiity of action; whatever greatness they finally achieve lies in their resistance to the overwhelming force of her character.

The poet's greatest accomplishment in characterization, and through characterization, in unity, is that he is able to develop the character of Kriemhild from obstinate maiden to charming bride to grief-stricken widow to revengeful devil convincingly and meaningfully. And this is no mean accomplishment for the medieval poet, who tended either to think of characters simply as "the people who did those deeds" or to envisage them as acting, as do Roland and the Norse heroes, from fixed traits of character. The notion that a character can be "round," to use E. M. Forster's happy term, and hence apparently contradictory is a late development in fiction. And though certainly Kriemhild is no round character, yet her development in the poem is as carefully planned as that of a Jamesian heroine.

We first see her as a charming, though willful, girl, yet the poet assures us that she is fated to cause the deaths of many knights. This ominous foreshadowing, one of the poet's most notable traits, not only immediately prefigures the dark days to come but also places the blame for the tragedy upon Kriemhild—specifically upon the "enmity of two noble ladies" and the "terrible vengeance she took on her nearest kinsman." There can be little doubt that the poet is fully aware of the changes that future events are to make in the character of Kriemhild and that he is here preparing us for these changes.

Kriemhild's own reaction to her dream of the ill-fated falcon destroyed by two eagles clearly establishes the strain of fierce pride and independence that is later to dominate her whole character. She vows to her mother that she will never marry since she intends to keep her beauty until death and "never be made wretched by the love of any man." She knows of many women who "have paid for happiness with sorrow in the end," and by not marrying she hopes to "avoid both." But she has not yet met Siegfried.

Though Kriemhild disappears from the action during Siegfried's arrival at the Burgundian court, his war with the Saxons, and his courtship of Brunhild on behalf of Gunther, her presence is constantly felt. It is to win her that Siegfried performs his great deeds, and we are gradually made aware of her growing affection for him. We are told how she watches him from her window as he takes part in the games and how she regrets his absence when he rides on circuit with the other knights. She blushes with relief when he returns from the Saxon campaign, and at their first meeting she takes his hand and the two exchange tender looks in secret. When the time finally comes for her bethrothal, she has fallen so in love with Siegfried, that, her statements to her mother forgotten, she grants without demur her brother's request that she marry the young lord.

Her pride having been conquered by love, she becomes in every way the devoted, dutiful wife. Yet we are not allowed by the poet to forget the strength of her character. At Siegfried's announcement that they are to go to his home in the Netherlands, she states that she must first receive from her brothers her proper share of her family's lands. Siegfried pridefully overrules her and rejects Gunther's offer of the property. However, while accepting without comment Siegfried's renunciation of her inheritance, she nevertheless insists that proper honor and allegiance be shown to her, demanding that one-third of the household knights form her retinue. Her interest here in preserving her own property and the allegiance due her does much to explain her later indignation over Hagen's theft of Siegfried's treasure.

It has often been remarked that Kriemhild is responsible for the quarrel between the two queens that precipitates the murder of Siegfried. Yet such is not strictly the case. True, Kriemhild's remark upon watching Siegfried in the games that she has "a husband of such merit that he might rule over all the kingdoms of this region" actually invokes the argument, but it is from her point of view a simple expression of joy in her husband's prowess. Brunhild, however, has brooded for over ten years on the apparent failure of Siegfried to render his proper feudal obligations to Gunther and so willfully interprets Kriemhild's casual remark as a slight to her own and, she believes, higher-born husband. But Kriemhild in all innocence goes on praising Siegfried until Brunhild's blunt statement that Siegfried is Gunther's vassal brings her up short. Immediately, her fierce pride aroused, she retaliates by daring to enter the church before Brunhild, who as reigning queen could rightfully assume the privilege of entering first. Furthermore, her anger now having completely usurped her judgment, she reveals the dreaded secret of Brunhild's wedding night and produces the ring and girdle which Siegfried in his boyish pride had taken. Siegfried and Gunther are able to calm the waters, even to the extent of punishing their wives, but Kriemhild's pride has sealed both their fates.

Yet Kriemhild has not yet become the terrifying character who will murder Hagen. Her revelation of Siegfried's vulnerability is, like her statements of pride in his prowess, an act of innocence, this time motivated by a genuine concern for her husband's welfare; weeping, she begs him not to attend the fatal hunt. Upon receiving the news of his death, she faints, but upon awakening, in one shriek she commits her whole life to revenge. "If I knew who had done this," she cries, "I should never cease to plot his death."

There is little need to describe in detail Kriemhild's actions in the final section of the poem except perhaps at a few critical points. For no matter how strange and contradictory her individual acts may seem, they are actually all of a piece; they all come from her pride, transformed by the death of Siegfried, who alone could subdue it, into a passion for revenge which never for an instant leaves her mind. First, she refuses to return to the Netherlands with Siegmund. This is, on the surface at least, a strange decision, for she not only remains in the midst of her husband's murderers but also renounces her rightful role as queen and, more important, as mother. She then suddenly becomes concerned with the disposition of Siegfried's treasure, her nuptial dowry, and is furious when Hagen steals it. Next she marries Etzel, a stranger and a pagan. Finally, she apparently sacrifices Ortlieb, her son by Etzel, in what seems to be a meaningless act of brutality.

Yet all these actions, contradictory and motiveless if taken one by one, are parts of a carefully wrought pattern of character development. The vow of revenge which Kriemhild takes upon Siegfried's death underlies her every subsequent action, and the two apparently irreconcilable strands of her character so carefully established in the first part of the poem, her fierce natural pride and her adoration of her husband, are in one awful moment turned into a single unbreakable cord of anger and passion. For revenge she will forsake throne and child and so, like Lady Macbeth, deliberately unsex herself; she will fight for her treasure, not for itself but only for its power to support her in her cause. For revenge she will marry a heathen; for revenge she will sacrifice her child to enlist the aid of Etzel. One by one the great heroes and allies of the Hungarians yield to her passion. No means, no device, no trick is beneath her; every decent impulse, every scruple must be suppressed. Bribery, cajolery, threats are her weapons; that Dietrich must sacrifice his men and Rudiger his soul in order that she accomplish her ends is of no consequence to her. It is altogether fitting, and consistent, that at the end she should execute Hagen with Siegfried's sword. The charming maiden who once blushed at the name of Siegfried must personally even the score.

I have dwelt at some length on the role of Kriemhild to demonstrate that the poet has used the startling change in her character which he inherited from the Nibelung tradition as a means of unifying the poem. But this analysis should also show that Kriemhild in becoming the structural center of the poem becomes also its thematic center: whatever values and attitudes the poet professes are expressed in her character and actions. And the key to her character and actions can be plainly seen in the utterly unscrupulous barbarism of her campaign for revenge. Her willful and prideful nature is conquered briefly by love, but, roused by the murder of her husband, reasserts itself with such force that it destroys two powerful nations. In accomplishing her revenge, moreover, Kriemhild steps completely outside the normal bounds of decent human conduct; she conducts herself according to no acknowledged standards of civilized behavior. Loyalty, truthfulness, understanding, consideration for others, mercy—these mean nothing to her.

Integrity, if the word be interpreted to mean a single-minded devotion to one's cause, however self-centered, she may be said to have; and it is her undoubtable integrity that has led some critics to see in her something of the indomitable, individualistic spirit of the epic hero. But hers is an integrity and an individualism run wild. Like Achilles sulking in his tent, Beowulf attacking the firedrake single-handed, and Roland refusing to summon help, Kriemhild is obsessed by a *hubris* that blinds her to the consequences of her actions. But unlike Achilles, Beowulf, and Roland, she never for a moment perceives her folly. Achilles is at last brought to reality by Priam and Roland by the sight of his slaughtered army, but Kriemhild dies unshaken by the devastation she has caused. She thus represents the furthest extension of one facet of the heroic temper: obsessed and proud, the hero becomes a monster.

Kriemhild's counterpart among the Burgundians is, of course, Hagen, and he is in every way her equal, though his heroic barbarism stems from a motive different from hers. If Kriemhild's *hubris* results from an exaggerated sense of integrity, then Hagen's character emerges from the opposing chivalric virtue, loyalty to one's master and concern for his welfare. Just as Kriemhild is willing to sacrifice her brothers, her husband, her child, and her nation to avenge a personal wrong, so Hagen is willing to plot, murder, and sacrifice his nation to protect Gunther. Siegfried is warned by his father of Hagen before he sets forth to woo Kriemhild, and it is only at Gernot's command that Hagen refrains from answering Siegfried's peremptory challenge when the young hero arrives at Worms. It is Hagen who suggests that Siegfried fight the Saxons since Gunther cannot assemble his forces in time and Hagen who proposes that Siegfried assist Gunther in the courtship of Brunhild. During their stay in Isenland Hagen time and again expresses his fear that Gunther will fail in the brutal games which Brunhild proposes. At Kriemhild's suggestion that he become her vassal, Hagen becomes furious and vows that he will follow no master but Gunther.

His loyalty to Gunther is his only motive in murdering Siegfried, but for Hagen it is motive enough. Coming upon Brunhild in tears, he immediately vows that Siegfried will suffer for having offended Gunther's queen. Gunther, true to his placid nature, is inclined to overlook the quarrel, but Hagen—like Kriemhild, dedicated forever to a vow taken in an instant—plies his master's feeble, though greedy, will with hopes of acquiring Siegfried's lands. Nor will he leave off his urging until master yields to vassal and he is permitted to arrange the complex deception by which he is able to elicit from Kriemhild the secret of Siegfried's vulnerable spot and so treacherously destroy the young hero.

But like integrity in Kriemhild, fidelity in Hagen breeds barbarity rather than heroic valor. Just as there is no real need for Kriemhild to sacrifice her child, so there is no excuse for Hagen's placing Siegfried's body outside Kriemhild's door. Yet again, as in Kriemhild, *hubris* in Hagen does not obscure intelligence or political cunning, both of which he devotes singlemindedly to the fulfillment of his vow. He gains control of Siegfried's treasure and later destroys it, not from greed but because he realizes that Kriemhild would buy supporters with it. He urges Gunther against the ill-fated journey to Hungary, not from cowardice but because he alone realizes the depth of Kriemhild's hatred. On arriving in Hungary he advises Gunther to heed Dietrich's warnings. However, once taunted by Gernot's assaults on his loyalty and honor, once assured by his failure to kill the chaplain (prophesied to be the only survivor of the expedition) that destruction is inevitable, Hagen becomes in effect the leader of the Burgundians—indomitable, fearless, and, like Kriemhild, utterly committed to his vow to protect Gunther.

If in his last days of stubborn resistance he reaches a kind of grandeur, it is a grandeur born of desperation, and, like Satan's in the early books of *Paradise Lost,* it is the grandeur of the prideful damned. Loyalty has bred guile, guile murder, and murder a cold, haughty cruelty. Yet Hagen is given one great moment, as Kriemhild is not. Recognizing the plight of the innocent, haunted, noble Rudiger, Hagen allows him to save face, to become again the patron rather than the victim of the Burgundians by begging from him his shield and repaying him with immunity from his own dread blows, an exchange which "good Rudiger acknowledged . . . with a polite bow." Even so, the incident seems to have been included to complete the poet's treatment of Rudiger rather than to soften our judgment of Hagen. It is fitting that in his last breath Hagen refuses to yield to Kriemhild the secret of Siegfried's treasure even though she promises his life in return (a promise she doubtless had no intention of keeping).

If Kriemhild and Hagen represent the ideals of chivalry, integrity, and loyalty reduced to barbarous cruelty, Gunther represents another possibility of failure in the chivalric code—its lapse into courtly vanity and ineffectualness. He relies on Hagen for every decision and can be maneuvered even into participating in murder at Hagen's urging. He is completely shaken and confused by Siegfried's first challenge and is all too willing, again at Hagen's urging, to allow the young stranger to fight his wars and even to do his courting. His habitual deceit and treachery are shown clearly in his allowing Siegfried to subdue his bride and later in publicly glossing over Siegfried's part in the affair. Although he plainly connives in the murder of Siegfried, and for the basest possible motive, he washes his hands of the matter by denying his complicity. Here he is plainly contrasted with Hagen, who comes to glory in his murder of Siegfried, treacherous as it is, as a symbol of his supreme loyalty to his master. True, at the end Gunther gains in stature by his conduct in battle, but only after he has tried and failed to lay the entire blame for the first battle on the Hungarians' massacre of the squires and has exhausted the possibilities of reconciliation.

Gunther, then, represents a chivalry gone to seed. He is at home only in the peaceful dalliance of his own court, contentedly enjoying the mock battles and petty intrigues of princely life. The difficult tasks of warfare and courtship he is willing to leave to others, and when a time finally comes in which glibness and deceit will no longer serve, he placidly allows Hagen to lead him into destruction.

The minor figures exhibit in much the same way the failure of thirteenth-century German chivalry to provide a fully operative standard of behavior. Etzel is naive and ineffectual to the point of foolishness, and Gernot and Giselher seem the pawns of their elder brother. Only Rudiger stands out, and it may well be that the poet is using him as an index of the fate of good men in troubled times. Indeed, had he survived, Rudiger might well have emerged as the hero of the poem. Kind, generous, brave, loyal, he is a paragon of chivalric virtue. His court is happy and free from the intrigues that plague Gunther's palace. Yet he is destroyed by the times, and the instrument of his destruction is his own good conscience. In making every possible effort to fulfill Etzel's commission to court Kriemhild on the king's behalf—and he is the best possible choice for the mission—Rudiger swears a personal oath of loyalty to Kriemhild, an oath closely related to his feudal oath to Etzel. Surely no harm could come from such a well-meaning gesture. Later he entertains the Burgundians lavishly on their way to Hungary and, again in good faith, acts as their escort. He even pledges his daughter's hand to the young Giselher. When the conflict comes he is thus caught between two sets of values, his feudal oaths and his natural duties to his guests and family. Although critics have maintained that he overstates his case, he nevertheless believes that he has perjured his soul, that either choice will be disastrous both on earth and in Heaven. Significantly, he expresses here the only Christian doctrine contained in the poem.

Nor will Kriemhild release Rudiger from his terrible dilemma even though he offers to return his fiefs. Both she and Etzel beg and plead and wheedle until Rudiger, at last exhausted by their entreaties, relents and goes brokenhearted into battle. It is, as we have said, Hagen who releases him by allowing him to assert his chivalric manhood and to display in a single greathearted gesture his essential nobility. In the end Rudiger dies, ironically the victim of the very sword he had given Gernot during the happy days at Pöchlarn.

In the death of Rudiger one senses the fate of all good Christian men and the ultimate failure of chivalry in the war-torn Germany of the poet's age. In a world ruled by the weak and the treacherous and dominated by the ruthless, true lordship, true integrity, true loyalty (and surely Rudiger represents all three) are caught up in a whirlpool of conflicting values and are destroyed by their own perversions.

The ***Nibelungenlied*** is, in the end, a testament of despair.

The poet may indeed have been able to look back to the myths and events of the distant past, to the very origins of the traditions he inherited—the springtime, magical world of a matchless Siegfried and a shining Brunhild, the heroic figure of a Kriemhild defending her brothers against the treachery of her barbarian husband, and the organized empire of Otto I—but the poem shows no evidence of such a vista. For in the course of time and history Siegfried had become merely boyish, Brunhild merely jealous, and the loyal sister a harridan. It remained for the poet to record forever the degeneration of the bright dream of heroism. (pp. 109-31)

Charles Moorman, "The Nibelungenlied," in his Kings & Captains: Variations on a Heroic Theme, *The University Press of Kentucky, 1971, pp. 109-31.*

Stephen L. Wailes (essay date 1978)

[*In the following excerpt, Wailes examines the concept of heroism in the* Nibelungenlied *from three perspectives: as a feudal epic, as a heroic epic, and in terms of archaic form.*]

Discussion of the ***Nibelungenlied*** as heroic epic must begin with a concept of heroism and with the admission that the composition of the poem is far removed in time and cultural context from the "Heroic Age" of the Germanic peoples. This discussion is organized around a definition of heroism which we believe accurately describes the behavior of the principal characters in Germanic heroic literature, and which permits us to evaluate the action of the poem that is particular to the feudal and chivalric culture for which it was created. The same definition is valid for the archaic patterns of story which underlie the epic. Heroism is defined as the exemplary behavior of prominent persons. It is important to understand that this is not limited to consideration of admirable or laudable actions, those viewed by the audience with favor, which are associated with the general usage of terms such as "hero" and "heroism." This definition lacks an ethical orientation, remaining true in this regard to the legends of the Germanic Heroic Age which are filled with characters who are not admirable. Indeed, one of the most familiar and memorable types in these legends is the great tyrant—for instance, Atli or Jormunrekk—and we meet as well great villains (Hagen, murderer of Siegfried), calumniators (Unferth), hotheads (Hadubrand, Wolfhart), and, to be sure, heroes admirable in all respects (Walther). The subject of Germanic heroic poetry is character; the vision of the poetry includes character of all qualities. Unless we wish to limit the term "heroism" to particular moments of the poetry when nice people do good things, we shall find the proposed definition true to the breadth and realism of the depiction of character in the poems, which deal with many varieties of human motives and experiences, provided these are not trivial. The poems set forth examples of human types and human behavior, but not of trifling character traits or prosy experiences. For the medieval audience, Siegfried and Hagen exemplified contrasting human types, but the fact that they contrast does not lessen the reality or importance of either. Both are deeply rooted in man's experience.

Another question is the distance in time of the ***Nibelungenlied*** from the "Heroic Age"—a term we use to designate the Period of Migrations (*Völkerwanderung*), roughly from the second through the eighth centuries of the Christian era, when the Germanic tribes were moving south and west through Europe from their earlier homes in Scandinavia and along the southern coasts of the Baltic Sea. We apply the term "Heroic Age" to this epoch by analogy to the Heroic Age of Greece, because the historic and quasi-historic events and personalities of Germanic heroic poetry belong to that period of Germanic history. It is broadly true that the Germanic Heroic Age was tribal and pagan. But the development of feudal medieval society virtually eliminated the tribal nature of Germanic civilization, and the dominance of Christianity in western Europe left few vestiges of pagan religion in the time when the ***Nibelungenlied*** was composed. This poem is filled with the culture of chivalric courts, including at least the forms of Christianity. Its socio-political foundation is feudal monarchy. The author and his audience knew far less of the Germanic Heroic Age than we know, nor can we assume that they had much greater exposure to stories and tales reflecting this age than do diligent scholars of the present day. Thus the poem we read is not a direct emanation from the pagan and tribal culture of the fifth century; its connection to Germanic culture is more tenuous than that of *Beowulf*, composed nearly five hundred years earlier. It must be read first as it was understood by the feudal and chivalric audience for whom it was written.

We will proceed by examining the heroism of three levels of story in the ***Nibelungenlied:*** that of A.D. 1200, that of the Heroic Age, and that of the archaic period of Germanic culture, by which is meant simply the period before the Heroic Age, extending back thousands of years to the quite uncertain origins of the Germanic peoples. This approach is indeed similar to the tradition of ***Nibelungenlied*** scholarship one might call archeological, which has regarded the poem as a kind of literary midden to be probed and sifted for traces of earlier life, but the excesses of that approach will hopefully be avoided here. We shall not stop at particular lines and stanzas to suggest that they, like little diamonds, have withstood the abrasion of time and reveal to us an earlier poem on the subject. (The distinguished scholar Helmut de Boor, in his edition of the poem, suggests that the first line of stanza 1717 may be "an archaic word of Kriemhild from the primal song.") Instead, the essential heroism of the story for each of the three cultures will be examined.

Nibelungenlied *as Feudal Epic*

Let us begin with the ***Nibelungenlied*** as a feudal epic and focus attention immediately on those episodes and that embroidery of the story which seem inconsistent with the heroic character of the tale, however it might be defined. The reference is to the sartorial stanzas, the long passages of pomp and ceremony, the long and digressive story of the Saxon War, Siegfried's pointless journey to the land of the Nibelungs, the extravagant hunting contest, and the rather "slow" chapters following the double wedding. Although there might seem to be a similarity between these retarding episodes and the frequent interpolated tales in heroic poems like the *Iliad* and *Beowulf,* the phenomena are quite different. *Beowulf* is particularly famous as a repository of legends not directly connected to the plot line of the story, and, although on the first reading these legends can irritate one by seeming to distract from the matter at hand, their thematic and tonal unity with the story of Beowulf soon becomes apparent. The theme of *Beowulf* is German heroism, refracted into the text in differing shades and intensities from sources more or less remote in Germanic culture. This is not the case in the ***Nibelungenlied,*** where the plot is unitary and remarkably controlled, where we have only one significant digression into legends not integral to the plot (Hagen's summary of Siegfried's youthful exploits) and where a few allusions to other stories (references to Hagen's residence with Etzel, to Nuodung and Witege) exist. In the ***Nibelungenlied,*** episodes in the life of Siegfried himself seem to retard the movement of the story: why are the Saxon war and Siegfried's trip to the land of the Nibelungs for a host of warriors who are never needed described at such length? The story of Siegfried's love and death is little advanced by these chapters. And why does the author linger over banquets, journeys, and the glories of wardrobe? Must the critic apologize for these episodes and descriptions when presenting the poem as heroic epic?

One must realize the tremendous importance of externals for the estimation of internal worth in chivalric culture. Though the sartorial stanzas are too frequent, a compositional defect, they express an understanding of human dignity gained through the estimation of worldly stature which is basic in the epistemology of feudalism. For the poet and audience of the feudal epic, the great man could not be separated from the insignia of greatness, including the magnificence of dress. This way of seeing things is very foreign to the modern reader, but in the period of the ***Nibelungenlied*** there was no conception of honor and distinction based on the individual's own self-respect apart from the respect accorded him by members of society. This was rooted in wealth and class. By reminding the audience continually of the wealth and class of his principals—seen in dress, jewels, generosity, banquets, jousts, ceremonious journeys, and receptions—the poet emphasizes that these are prominent persons whose behavior is exemplary. One may object that the passages under discussion are too long or too frequent, but this is a criticism of the literary craft of the author, not a rejection of the character of the passages as inappropriate to heroic story.

The apparently digressive adventures of Siegfried require justification on different grounds. The only explanation of the Saxon war that is obvious is that it shows Siegfried ingratiating himself with the Burgundians in order to bring closer to reality his dream of marrying Kriemhild. This is an unsatisfactory explanation, because in terms of his marriage quest the Saxon war does him little good, and the bargain he presently strikes with Gunther, through which he obtains Kriemhild's hand, has nothing at all to do with the Saxons. A more interesting interpretive possibility is this: by leading the Burgundian forces against the Saxons and Danes, Siegfried redresses exactly the error of his own behavior when he first came to Burgundy. On that occasion he belied his careful education and training in princely conduct by challenging the king, Gunther, to single combat for possession of lands and wealth. This unprovoked aggression amazed the royal court, which responded by rejecting violence as a means of territorial expansion: "We do not aspire to gain any land by force at the price of the slaying of one warrior by another. . . . " In the next chapter the Danes and Saxons announce an attack on Burgundy quite as unprovoked as Siegfried's, and at Hagen's suggestion Siegfried is made leader of the defensive forces. Thus there is balance and symmetry between the chapters. The Saxon war may depict a positive social example, a powerful man acting responsibly in defence of legitimate authority.

Another possibility, and one which complements without excluding the foregoing, is to understand the Saxon war as a way of studying the character of Siegfried in relation to the characters of Hagen and Gunther, both of whom shrewdly exploit Siegfried's capacity as a fighting man. Hagen even diminishes his own luster as first asset of the King by proposing that Siegfried be given the job of defeating the Saxons. The episode also reveals the calculating nature of Gunther, who can mask his face in sorrow to elicit Siegfried's inquiry, then pretend to doubt Siegfried's good faith ("One should complain of one's wrongs to proven friends"), and finally seem to act graciously by accepting an offer of help which he had counted on from the start. The episode suggests contrasting characters: Siegfried the natural and spontaneous warrior, Hagen the chancellor and dynastic statesman, Gunther the subtle king. One thinks of Othello among the Venetians.

Following this interpretation, Siegfried's trip to the land of the Nibelungs may be understood as a further study of character. Once again it is Hagen who pushes Siegfried into action. Quite emphatically he expresses concern that Brunhild may go back on the agreement once she is surrounded by her kinsmen and vassals, whereupon Siegfried volunteers to sail off alone and fetch a thousand men. This is a curious moment, for surely Brunhild—still possessed of her fabulous strength, backed "by over seven hundred bold fighting-men that were seen there under arms," as well as by the kinsmen and vassals who had been arriving "day by day, morning and evening . . . by companies" before Hagen commented on the possibility of danger—had power enough to overwhelm the three Burgundians and Siegfried. One may suspect Hagen of voicing a pretended fear (Brunhild never, in fact, threatens violence after the contest), knowing that Siegfried in his headstrong way will rush off to distant lands for help. Brunhild being won, perhaps Hagen is trying to get rid of a man whom the Burgundians no longer need.

Whatever Hagen's motive, Siegfried does rush off. Arriving in Nibelungenland, he does not go about raising forces in a direct and efficient manner, as the alleged urgency of his mission would demand, but makes a game of it instead. Disguising his voice and keeping his identity secret, he picks a fight with his own gatekeeper and then with his vassal Alberich. Both fights are so violent that Siegfried fears for his life. Here, as in his appearance before the Burgundians, Siegfried seems to be an enormously vital but immature young man, unable to restrain his craving for physical adventures, insensitive to the psychologies and interests of persons around him. It is as though the poet were studying naive and robust masculine character through the person of his hero.

The three episodes leading immediately to Siegfried's death—the pretended second Saxon war, the hunt, and the footrace to the spring—demonstrate again the manipulative control of Hagen over Siegfried and the enthusiasm with which Siegfried enters into any kind of physical contest. His behavior in the hunt lacks all temperance and moderation (cardinal virtues in chivalric society), and by accepting the handicap of a single dog rather than a pack, he seems to flaunt his prowess. Although Siegfried dominates the story here with his raw strength and vitality, the audience never forgets that the whole episode is part of Hagen's plot to kill him. Accepting Hagen's challenge to a footrace, Siegfried insists on the handicap of lying in the grass at the start and of carrying all his gear and weapons as he runs. Thus he literally carries the instrument of his murder to the place where he may be safely killed. He acts like an exhibitionist of strength, and his strength is harnessed for his own destruction. Hagen, who has harnessed it, strikes the final blow.

It seems possible that the story of Siegfried sketched out in the episodes considered above was intended by the author and viewed by his audience as a representation of a human type and a testing of that type under political circumstances around the year 1200. Siegfried's behavior is heroism in the sense defined earlier. His life exemplifies a particular aspect of human nature, a particular kind of masculine character; Siegfried is a standard of this potentiality in human life. His career is glorious and unsuccessful. This does not mean that the poet viewed him with distaste or meant him to seem stupid or fatuous; it means that the poet and his audience recognized the limits of exuberant masculine character in the real world, where the forces of pride, ambition, jealousy, greed, and political expedience manipulate and even destroy such personalities.

If portions of the feudal epic permit the audience to regard Siegfried as heroic, what of his killer? Hagen has already been referred to as a great villain, and in the sense that this term is generally applied to a doer of evil deeds, it is justified. But if a moral posture is discarded, Hagen becomes the great example of a blood-and-iron chancellor, a Bismarck to his king, whose behavior is governed by the political interests of the house of Burgundy as he understands them.

One can trace in the ***Nibelungenlied*** the ominously powerful and assertive figure of Siegfried as it impinges upon Burgundy, and thus upon Hagen, from the early days when "Fired by his courage, he tried the mettle of many kingdoms and rode through many lands to put his strength to the test," through his assault on Gunther (barely averted by statesmanship) and the remarks of Kriemhild to Brunhild, which no doubt reached Hagen's ears and seemed to show a threatening ambition in the Netherlandic king ("I have a husband of such merit that he might rule over all the kingdoms of this region. . . . He ranks above my noble brother Gunther . . . "). Finally, Hagen urges that Gunther extend his power by elimination of his rival ("Hagen kept putting it to Gunther that if Siegfried were no more, Gunther would be lord of many kingdoms . . . "). Hagen's reaction to Siegfried seems always to favor putting him in responsible—and dangerous—situations. That he should finally propose and contrive his murder is merely the last expression of the interests and attitudes that motivate Hagen throughout the epic. Conduct such as Hagen's, governed by the single-minded pursuit of power, is a familiar theme in literature, as in life; yet even as the murderer of Siegfried, Hagen lives in a pattern of heroism. He exemplifies with grandeur a fundamental part of human nature. For the feudal author and audience, Hagen was proof of the proposition made many years later in the *Leviathan* by the political philosopher Thomas Hobbes: "So that in the first place, I put for a general inclination of all mankind, a perpetual and restless desire of power after power, that ceaseth only in death."

The scholar Johann Jacob Bodmer, who in 1757 first published part of the ***Nibelungenlied,*** gave it the title "Kriemhild's Revenge." He saw clearly that the figure of Kriemhild dominates the latter part of the poem through her ineluctable drive for vengeance, and one may say that the two main parts of the poem, the story of Siegfried and the story of the Burgundians' visit to Etzel, are united by Kriemhild. She motivates every critical event of the Siegfried story, and her power of will drives the poem on after Siegfried's death. But were her deeds heroic in the vision of the courtly audience of the year 1200? A version of the poem that considerably softens the portrait of Kriemhild (version C) and seems to have been made shortly after the version on which Hatto's translation is based (version B) suggests that the maniacal and bloody Kriemhild was too strong a concept for the general taste. It surely is no kin to the lovely and gentle conventional heroine of chivalric narrative, whom Kriemhild is made to resemble in the period of her courtship with Siegfried.

Yet the audiences of 1200 recognized in Kriemhild, no less than in Hagen, the heroic trait of will, that utter tenacity of purpose which will not be deflected from its object. Such power of will, which need not be exerted for a good cause, is the essence of heroic literature. Germanic poetry is concerned more with the deed than with the immediate cause, more with the character than with the deed; we need not admire the ends to which their wills are bent in order to stand in awe of Kriemhild and Hagen, who are locked in a struggle which death must resolve. One of the most exalted moments in the poem is Hagen's remark when he sees the head of Gunther carried in by the hair, just before he defies Kriemhild for the last time: "You have made an end as you desire, and things have run their course as I imagined." One laconic phrase ("as you desire") summarizes the terrible power of will possessed by this woman who has brought thousands of knights and her three brothers to their deaths. Another phrase ("as I imagined") epitomizes the marvelous strength of will possessed by the man who has hastened events toward his own foreseen destruction. Such will is a quality of human character which European civilization has always held to be heroic.

The final aspect of heroism in the feudal epic is of quite a different stamp; it is found in the story of Rüdiger. Introduced at the beginning of the second part of the epic, Rüdiger, who is entrusted by Etzel with a most responsible and sensitive mission, is distinguished from the other warriors around Etzel by his gentility and grace. He shows a keen sense of the debt he owes Etzel, his liege lord, when he refuses to travel to Burgundy except at his own cost. Received in friendship by the Burgundians, he persuades Kriemhild to marry Etzel merely by taking oaths to act as her advocate and champion should her honor be threatened in the future. Thus, Rüdiger is bound to his king and queen by the sacred ties that bound vassal to lord in feudal society, as well as by the personal vows exacted by Kriemhild.

The ties which soon bind him to the Burgundians are no less earnest. He offers them hospitality while they are on their way to Etzel, thus incurring the traditional obligation of a host to his guests; his daughter is betrothed to Giselher, and as part of her dowry, Rüdiger makes his pledge to Giselher and his brothers: "I shall be your sincere and devoted friend always." He and his wife bestow gifts upon their guests, an act which binds the givers no less than the recipients. In addition, Rüdiger personally escorts the Burgundians to Etzel, thus tacitly vouching for the safety of their journey.

Readers have long appreciated the artistry with which the poet achieves such a division of loyalties in Rüdiger. When called upon by Etzel and Kriemhild to enter battle against the Burgundians, Rüdiger tries to escape from the agonizing dilemma—"Whichever course I leave in order to follow the other, I shall have acted basely and infamously." Ultimately, he cannot deny the justice of the claims pressed upon him by the King and Queen. It is the institutional obligations that Rüdiger respects when forced to make a choice, not those arising from customs or human feeling. Although the decision brings him to despair, he honors the claims of liege upon vassal, which he holds superior to those of friend upon friend. As Volker puts it when he sees Rüdiger advancing toward them, "Rüdiger means to earn his lands and castles from us." This is a positive standard of behavior in feudal society, for Rüdiger represents the sacrifice of personal inclination for the sake of social laws, the subordination of individual feeling to the order of the whole. To the audience of A.D. 1200, this was exemplary.

But the story of Rüdiger has a further aspect in Hagen's request that Rüdiger surrender his shield to him. In this incident, the values of friendship and social role are juxtaposed once again, for Hagen gives Rüdiger the opportunity to affirm his love for the Burgundians at the very moment when his actions might seem to deny it. Hagen's request allows Rüdiger to make a gesture of affection, and to the medieval audience for whom gestures and symbolic actions spoke far more eloquently than words, Hagen's act bespeaks a deep humanity. Of course, Rüdiger is admired for agreeing to the gift, thus affirming the friendship and concern he expressed when first giving gifts to the Burgundians (and specifically a shield to Hagen), but many will find Hagen's request more remarkable. All will agree that Hagen's behavior after the gift is exceptional: the first vassal of the Burgundians steps aside from the assault of Rüdiger and says he will not fight him, even if he should kill the kings. Here we seem to have a preference for affection rather than institutional obligation, just the opposite of the situation in which Rüdiger acknowledged Etzel's claims. For the poet of the ***Nibelungenlied,*** fidelity seems to have been a virtue above all. The story of Rüdiger may be read as a study of fidelity, in which one man exemplifies loyalty to the high laws of society, and another man exemplifies loyalty to the heart's ties. As a whole, the story does not seem to be directed toward a judgment on the primacy of one kind of fidelity over the other on occasions when they conflict, though Rüdiger's decision conforms to the general values of the day.

Lay of Atli

We will now turn to the stories that comprise the ***Nibelungenlied*** as they were known during the Germanic Heroic Age. This is in large part a speculative enterprise, for the textual evidence of such stories is slender. The Old Norse "Lay of Atli," which is preserved in the *Edda* and may date from the ninth century, is the earliest literature on the story of the Burgundians, but the historical connections of the legends suggest that some form of heroic song preserved them during the Heroic Age. It will be useful at this point to review the historic content of the epic, for, like *Beowulf,* it reflects historical figures and events.

We know that the Burgundians, a Germanic tribe, crossed to the left bank of the Rhine and established themselves there in the first years of the fifth century. Around A.D. 435 they attempted to move further west, which led to fighting with troops under the command of the Roman soldier Aetius. Then in A.D. 437, the Burgundians suffered an annihilating defeat at the hands of "Huns," probably Hun troops under Roman leadership. In this battle, King Gundaharius was killed "along with his people and family." Clearly the name Gundaharius is the name we know as Gunther, and other members of the family mentioned by the sixth-century "Burgundian Law" (in Latin)—Gislaharius, Gundomaris, and Gibica—evidently correspond to the characters Giselher, Guthorm (in Old Norse sources), and Gibech. (In the main manuscript tradition of the ***Nibelungenlied,*** Gibech is reduced to a minor character, but in one fifteenth-century manuscript, "Gibich" is the name of the father of Gunther and his siblings.) Thus the second part of the ***Nibelungenlied*** deals with historic personalities, the Burgundian kings, and may reflect the decisive defeat inflicted upon them by Hun armies. These, however, were not commanded by Attila.

Of course, the character Etzel corresponds in some respects to the Attila of history. Phonetic differences between the names are easily explained by laws in the evolution of the Germanic languages. Both Etzel's geographic seat of power and the vast array of peoples and princes under his sway agree with history, and it is possible that his actual marriage in A.D. 453 to a Germanic princess whom the chronicles name "Ildico" is mirrored by his fictional marriage to Kriemhild, the element *-ild* or *-hild* being common to the names. The Gothic historian Jordanes tells us that Attila died during his wedding night with Ildico, apparently from a severe hemorrhage. By the early sixth century there were two versions of Attila's death current in Europe, as recorded by the chronicler Marcellinus Comes [in *Chronica minora saec. IV. V. VI. VII,* 1894]: "Attila was slain at night by a knife and the hand of a woman. Some maintain that he was killed by a hemorrhage." The more sensational version is reflected in the work of the ninth-century Poeta Saxo, who declares that Attila was killed by his queen and goes on to supply a motive—revenge, specifically revenge for her father. (We are not told what happened to her father.) Thus the historic and quasi-historic accounts center on two events: the destruction of the Burgundians and the death of Attila. Of these events, the former is the base for the second part of the ***Nibelungenlied,*** but the latter plays no role in the epic. Some believe that Kriemhild's revenge on Hagen and the others is derived from the early accounts of the queen's revenge on her husband, and some early Old Norse poems, such as the "Lay of Atli," show Atli (= Attila) killed by Gudrun (= Kriemhild) in revenge for his destruction of her brothers. But the fact remains that continental European tradition as documented in the ***Nibelungenlied*** tells of the fall of the Burgundians, but not of the death of Attila.

A good way to appreciate the heroic content of the fall of the Burgundians in the Heroic Age is to analyze the "Lay of Atli" and note the correspondences between this early poem and the ***Nibelungenlied.*** The poem begins with the arrival of a messenger from Atli at the court of Gunnar (= Gunther). The invitation to visit Atli which he delivers is received with mistrust and foreboding. Gunnar says that none of the material inducements promised by Atli are of any interest to him. Hogni (= Hagen) speaks of the warning sent by their sister, Atli's wife. The people are silent; no one advises Gunnar to go. And then, in a passage difficult to understand in detail but eloquent in spirit, Gunnar accepts the fatal challenge and announces that he will travel to Atli. Here heroic character is in evidence: men embrace danger gladly because they can not seek to avoid it. Gunnar and Hogni, despite virtual foreknowledge of death, accept Atli's invitation because no brave man would do otherwise. For the cultures of the Heroic Age, discretion and prudence were not heroic qualities; the leader who weighed every hazard in a delicate balance did not enjoy the respect of his followers. This moment in the "Lay of Atli" is comparable to Hagen's role in the second part of the epic, for Hagen understands the sinister implications of the invitation, and once the decision to accept is made, he embraces his fate with a reckless courage like that of Hogni and Gunnar.

The fighting in the "Lay of Atli" is compressed into a few lines. With Gunnar and Hogni captive, Atli demands the treasure. Gunnar demands that the heart of Hogni be cut out and brought to him, but he does not say why. They first cut out the heart of a cowardly thrall, which Gunnar recognizes and scorns because of its unmanly quivering; only then do they kill Hogni and bring his heart. "Hogni laughed when they cut out his heart"—and in this instance one finds a heroic apotheosis. The man who walks bravely toward death is the man who laughs as they take his life, laughs because he is fearless and because the pain is nothing, laughs because the only defeat to be dreaded is the defeat of spirit and the spirit that exults in the final instant is unbroken. Perhaps Hogni understands the device Gunnar has invented to make sure Atli never obtains the treasure. Seeing Hogni's heart, Gunnar pays tribute to him and then defies Atli: now that only Gunnar knows of the treasure, it will be forever hidden. He meets his horrible death with high dignity, playing the harp as the vipers slither around him in the snake pit. Here again is the exemplary indifference that seems to have been dearly valued in Germanic culture of the Heroic Age, an age of turmoil and relentless warfare in which the warrior who could laugh at death must have been a model to his society. Readers of the ***Nibelungenlied*** will see how well the epic follows the "Lay of Atli" in the spirit of these final events, although the details of the action are rather different and the roles have been changed.

It will be interesting to digress briefly and to consider the correspondences in tone and attitude between the Germanic heroism of the "Lay of Atli" and the Germanic mythology of the life and death of the gods. Heroism is grace in death, for the certainty of death is always present, and in the last analysis the hero is the man who meets the inevitable with style. The Germanic universe presented by the poems in the *Edda* and by Snorri Sturluson in his *Prose Edda* is a precarious equilibrium of opposed forces, with the sense of imminent destruction hanging over the whole. The rule of Thor, Odin, and other gods known collectively as the Aesir is achieved by constraining great monsters: the wolf Fenrir, bound but certain to slip his bonds in the future; the hound Garm, tethered but sure to break the tether; the enormous World Serpent, thrown into the seas by Thor but alive and ominous; the diabolical giant Loki, bound and tormented by dripping poison but certain to get free. The entire universe tends toward the last days, the cosmic confrontation of powers of life and order with powers of death and chaos: Ragnarök. All the slain heroes in Valhalla train daily for it; their life after death is a continuing preparation for the final battle. In that battle the gods will be destroyed as they destroy the monsters; cosmic fire will envelope the world, and the waters will rise; the universe will revert to its primal elements; and then life will begin again, a new generation of gods will take power. In this cyclical conception of the universe we see the inevitability of death, the tendency of all things and all orders to move toward dissolution. The heroism of the gods—and this term is used advisedly, referring to the exemplary behavior which all gods exhibit to their believers—consists in their struggle against chaos despite the knowledge that chaos will prevail. Their victories are all the more poignant because they are doomed. No wonder the Heroic Age valued the man who acted with courage, gladly accepting the battles that would lead eventually to his death. It makes no difference whether the ethos exists prior to the cosmology or the cosmology is a pattern influential on the ethos; the simple agreement between them is eloquent.

The "Lay of Atli" concludes with the murder of Atli by Gudrun, a story which, as noted earlier, does not appear in the ***Nibelungenlied.*** This tale of a woman's revenge well illustrates the importance of blood feud in Germanic tradition and also the prominent role which the Heroic Age gave to women. It is comparable to a well-known story told by the eighth-century historian Paul the Deacon in his *History of the Langobards.* Rosemund was carried off by Alboin after a battle in which he killed her father. He married her and had the skull of her father made into a wine goblet. At a banquet, having had too much to drink, Alboin passed the goblet made of her father's skull to Rosemund "and . . . invited her to drink merrily with her father." Rosemund was deeply aggrieved, "and straightway she burned to revenge the death of her father by the murder of her husband." She did so very efficiently. Women of heroic will and uncompromising devotion to a principle of honor are frequent figures in Germanic literature. In the ***Nibelungenlied,*** this theme underlies both the story of Kriemhild and that of Brunhild.

Brunhild has hardly any active role in the epic once she has married Gunther. Although it is her complaint to Gunther that leads directly to the murder of Siegfried, the instigator of the murder remains Hagen. (The poet's remark, "the hero was to lose his life at the instigation of Brunhild . . . ," is hard to reconcile with the story he tells.) However, if the poems which survive in the *Edda* offer any evidence, Brunhild's role was far more important in the Heroic Age. A fragmentary poem about the death of Sigurd (= Siegfried) is a good source for studying the role of Brunhild, and the *Thidreks saga,* a thirteenth-century Norwegian prose saga based on continental traditions, is another. These and many other poems of varying age indicate that for the Heroic Age the betrayal of Brunhild by Siegfried, which always involves his refusal to take her as his wife, created an instance of a woman who has been dishonored and burns for vengeance. The "Fragment of a Sigurd Lay" in the *Edda* tells that Brunhild instigates the murder of Sigurd, greeting the news of his death with an awful laugh, then revealing that the accusations she made in order to have him killed were false. She is a character of the Rosemund and Kriemhild pattern: the strong, tormented, vengeful woman who drives events forward to the bloody righting of wrong. By comparisons with other tales that more directly express the ethos of the time, the ***Nibelungenlied*** can also be understood as illustrative of the Heroic Age and its ethos of conflict and violence. We recognize heroism, i.e., exemplary behavior of prominent persons, in the uncompromising correction of injury to family or person (Kriemhild and Brunhild) and in the splendid fatalism with which fighting men go to their death (Hagen). During the Heroic Age, stories were told about historic personalities, though the lack of agreement on historic backgrounds for Siegfried and Brunhild suggests that heroic poetry was not limited to inspiration from history, and the episodes of the ***Nibelungenlied*** apparently were autonomous tales which were linked together on some occasions.

The Enigma of the ***Nibelungenlied***

The discussion of the epic thus far represents ideas familiar to most students of the poem and espoused by many. When the question of archaic patterns of story underlying the poem arises, the sense of movement in an accepted frame of reference is lost. Indeed, the very existence of such patterns is a matter of debate. It is one aspect of the important problem of history and myth as foundations of heroic epic.

For the better part of a century, this problem was argued by scholars of the ***Nibelungenlied.*** One group held that the stories of Siegfried were nature myths of the kind found among all primitive peoples. Another group believed that it was possible to identify the hero and his adventures with particular gods and divine acts of Germanic religion: Odin, Baldr, and Freyr were advanced as the model of the hero; Siegfried's death by a woman's betrayal was likened to Baldr's, and his fight with a dragon recalled the battle of Thor and the World Serpent. On the other side of the issue were those who saw not only the evident connections to history—the empire of the Huns, the destruction of the Burgundian dynasty—but also a host of other connections. Siegfried and Brunhild were derived from actors in Merovingian politics, Rüdiger was thought to represent a twelfth-century Spanish hero, the entire ***Nibelungenlied*** was taken as a satire on figures and events of the reign of the German emperor Henry V. The excesses of both points of view are obvious today, and they were a matter of concern long ago. In 1909 the German scholar Andreas Heusler, whose famous book on Nibelung saga and the ***Nibelungenlied*** ["Geschichtliches und Mythisches in der germanischen Heldensage," *Sitzungsberichte der Königl. Preussischen Akademie der Wissenschaften* 23 (1909)] was to appear twelve years later, reminded scholars that the historical and mythological approaches to heroic story stood like Scylla and Charybdis, wrecking many efforts to reach the truth.

Heusler acknowledged four sources drawn upon by the *Heldendichter* responsible for heroic poetry: history, private life, personal invention, and narrative matter at hand (in which he included myth and folktale). Of these sources he regarded personal invention as by far the most important, stressing that heroic poetry was *poetry* and that history and myth, whatever contribution they might make to the tale, were fundamentally changed by the process of artistic creation. Thus Heusler saw no need to search for archaic foundations of the Nibelungen story: elements and details might be archaic, but the foundations were the work of Frankish poets of the fifth and sixth centuries. In his classical analysis, he passed over in silence the question of historic or mythic bases for the tales of Siegfried and Brunhild, presenting instead the content of the first poems [*Nibelungensage und Nibelungenlied,* 1965]. When discussing the earliest version of the fall of the Burgundians he acknowledged the role of historical event—"the subject matter may be understood as freely formed history"—but the trend of his discussion was to show that art, not history, accounted for the character of the tales:

> One sees that this saga is something quite different than distorted history garbled by the mouth of the people. What is bruited from house to house may finally have precious little resemblance to the real event, but all this does not produce a work which one must only cast in verse in order to have a Lay of the Burgundians. This Lay is, in structure and thought, a child of art, the creation of an anonymous poet.

The position of the Chadwicks with regard to Germanic heroic poetry is comparable to, though not identical with, that of Heusler. In their monumental study of early literatures they represent the view that heroic poetry is inspired by real persons and events, although it admits a good deal of "fiction"—that kind of imaginative story attributed by Heusler to "personal invention"—and also draws frequently on the superhuman or supernatural. Rejecting the theory that Siegfried and Brunhild have their origins in mythic conceptions, the Chadwicks also regard as unlikely the view that they spring from the personal invention of a poet. The Chadwicks' knowledge of heroic literature suggests an origin in history: "Our belief is that primary heroic stories are contemporary, i.e., that the first stories which celebrate a hero's exploits are composed within living memory of the events. . . . We do not know any examples of heroic poetry or saga relating to recent events, in which the leading characters are fictitious" [H. Munro Chadwick and N. Kershaw Chadwick, *The Growth of Literature,* Vol. 1, 1932-40]. The supernatural elements so abundant in the Siegfried stories are to be explained as "poetic conventions, which are themselves based upon real beliefs of the time or of former times. . . . The superhuman prowess attributed to heroes is another convention, but due to other causes—hero-worship, in the modern sense, and the tendency to exaggeration stimulated thereby."

Both Heusler and the Chadwicks would deny that there are underlying, archaic patterns of story which are vital to the understanding of the tales in the ***Nibelungenlied*** as they were known in Germanic culture. Following their approach to heroic poems, we would seek to go back no further in time than the fifth century, when the first poems were composed. There would be no justification in considering mythical models for the two main stories in the epic: the life and death of Siegfried and the fall of the Burgundians. But if it is true that Heusler and the Chadwicks speak for a majority of recent scholars on this problem, important objections to their views have been made. These concern the first part of the ***Nibelungenlied,*** the story of Siegfried and Brunhild.

Early in this century, Friedrich Panzer brought to light surprisingly close agreements between this story and several folktales. Of particular importance was his juxtaposition of the wooing of Brunhild with a Russian folktale of bridal quest, which led him to the conclusion that the heroic tale was derived from the folktale. Although many criticisms of his theory have been made, and the folktale in question has been shown to be international rather than strictly Russian, Panzer's thesis that this tale underlies the wooing of Brunhild by Siegfried has by no means been disproved, and the relation of epic to broadly distributed popular stories remains puzzling. In recent years the idea that Siegfried is derived from a mythical archetype has been advocated by Franz Rolf Schröder and Otto Höfler, though with differing emphases [Franz Schröder, "Mythos und Heldensage," *Germanisch-romanische Monatsschrift* 36 (1955)]. Schröder connects Siegfried to the mythological pattern of the conquest of chaos by divine sons who themselves die, but are resurrected. Höfler breaks new ground by proposing that historical events were understood in Germanic culture as re-enactments of myth, and that the figure of Siegfried derives from the historical Arminius, leader of Germanic warriors in a successful battle against Roman troops in the first century. Arminius' exploit was then understood as the re-enactment of a cosmic victory, expressed in the story of Siegfried by his slaying of a dragon. Höfler's reasoning is bold and rests on a number of hypotheses; it remains to be seen whether his thesis will be accepted.

Thus it is clear that no unanimity exists regarding the origins of the tales told in the first part of the ***Nibelungenlied.*** The influence of history and myth is esteemed differently in different quarters, and the prudent scholar will probably admit a complex pluralism of sources and many unanswered questions. It is also clear that the second part of the ***Nibelungenlied*** is thought to be based on history. Even Schröder, an advocate of mythic patterns behind heroic saga, holds the fall of the Burgundians to be completely non-mythical [*Zur germanisch-deutschen Heldensage,* 1961]. As our own contribution to the problem of myth and history in the ***Nibelungenlied,*** we would like to challenge this received opinion. A few preliminary remarks are necessary.

Mythologization of History

One must assume that the Germanic peoples had traditional stories long before any record of these stories was made, and that the foundation of their traditional lore was mythic in nature, serving to explain the universe and human existence. One assumes that this tradition did not come to an abrupt end with the Period of Migrations, nor did it end abruptly with the nominal Christianization of Germanic tribes, but continued to exist at least until the thirteenth century, when mythological poems were recorded in the *Edda* with the "Lay of Atli" and the "Fragment of a Sigurd Lay." No doubt there was a gradual attenuation of the religious content of the traditional stories, so that the tales of Thor which seem ludicrous to us may have seemed ludicrous to the educated Icelanders who caused them to be preserved in writing, although the narrative patterns of the stories, the sequence of incidents and clusters of motifs, remained visible if not fully intact.

Making these assumptions, one still requires a theory of the relationship of traditional narrative, mythic in origin, to the unique facts of history. Only such a theory can be a guide in an analysis of the fall of the Burgundians, a tale long in tradition but with historic detail so near the surface. This guiding theory is essentially that of Otto Höfler, who speaks of "the mythological transposition of historical events." These are the formulations of the eminent scholar of comparative religion, Mircea Eliade:

> . . . the historical character of the persons celebrated in epic poetry is not in question. But their historicity does not long resist the corrosive action of mythicization. The historical event in itself, however important, does not remain in the popular memory, nor does its recollection kindle the poetic imagination save insofar as the particular historic event closely approaches a mythical model.

> . . . the recollection of a historical event or a

> real personage survives in popular memory for two or three centuries at the utmost. This is because popular memory finds difficulty in retaining individual events and real figures. The structures by means of which it functions are different: categories instead of events, archetypes instead of historical personages. The historical personage is assimilated to his mythical model (hero, etc.), while the event is identified with the category of mythical actions (fight with a monster, enemy brothers, etc.) [Mircea Eliade, *Cosmos and History: The Myth of the Eternal Return,* 1954].

The task at hand, then, is to examine the account of the Burgundians' fall in the ***Nibelungenlied*** for evidence of the assimilation of history to mythical models.

Let us begin by noting the major differences between the account in the ***Nibelungenlied*** and what we understand to be historic fact. Attila had nothing to do with the destruction of Gundaharius and his people, but Etzel presides over the death of Gunther and the others. The destruction of Gundaharius took place in west-central Europe, on the left bank of the Rhine, as the Burgundians tried to move further westward, but in all sources the Germanic heroes must undertake a long journey to their enemy's kingdom to the east, where they meet battle and death. In the poetic accounts, a legendary treasure plays a vital role: Attila craves it and the Germanic heroes take the secret of its whereabouts to their death. They die, and the treasure is lost. Historic records give no indication that the Burgundians had a vast treasure, much less that it had anything to do with the destruction of the tribe. These discrepancies are at least as striking and important as the agreements between poetry and history. They easily permit the theory that history provides no more than coloration and incidental detail to a traditional pattern of story.

The thesis is this: in the fall of the Burgundians we are dealing with the Journey to the Other World. Attila has been assimilated to the giant, ogre, or fiend who rules that world; the Burgundians have been assimilated to the god who makes the journey.

Many Germanic myths exist in which a god travels to a world of chaos or death, usually on the quest for some precious object necessary for the maintenance of order and continuation of life. The god Freyr sends his servant (or, perhaps, his alter-ego) to the frost ogres to woo for him a woman without whom he languishes miserably. Thor travels to the realm of the giant Hymir to obtain a huge cauldron in which ale for the banquet of the gods may be brewed. Odin travels to the old giant Vafthrudnir, ostensibly for a riddling contest, but in effect to destroy a rival for his position as master of arcane lore; Thor travels to the land of the giants to regain his hammer, the weapon on which the security of the Aesir rests, from the giant-king Thrym. All these journeys result in conflict, and most end with the god's destruction of his enemy: Thor smashes Hymir and Thrym with his hammer and kills them, Odin's triumph costs the life of Vafthrudnir, and Skirner, armed with Freyr's magic sword, compels the giantess to meet the god. One might also mention the journey of Thor and three others to Utgard, where his divine power seems ineffective until the deceptions involved are understood.

These myths, preserved in the *Edda* or in Snorri's *Prose Edda* in late and adulterated forms, tell of gods who travel to a hostile Other World where they triumph in replicated conflict with monsters, obtaining something precious—a bride, a cauldron (symbolizing the plenty of life), a divine weapon, unrivaled mastery of wisdom—something that could be considered great treasure. The contours of similarity with the story in the ***Nibelungenlied*** are clear, and if space permitted, it would be worthwhile to discuss similarities of detail such as the extraordinary journey which signals the transition from this world to the other, represented in myths by the passing of mountains and a ring of fire (the story of Skirnir) or by a river, a bridge, and a sentinel (Hermod's journey to Hel), or other devices, and continued in the poems about the Burgundians with a crossing of the fabulous forest Myrkwood ("Lay of Atli") or the Danube crossing in the ***Nibelungenlied.*** The Danube crossing is rich in motifs suggesting a transit to the Other World: the river is raging and nearly impassable, mermaids with knowledge of the future are present, a single ferryman guards the crossing and must be slain by Hagen. The Danube functions here like the River of Death's Domain in Finnish tradition, the river bordering the kingdom of Gorre in Celtic tradition (see Chrétien's *Lancelot*), and the river Styx in Greco-Roman myth. Hatto's sarcastic comparison of the Danube and the Styx [The *Nibelungenlied,* 1965] holds more truth than he realizes.

But if the contours are clear, there are still some big differences. The fate of the heroes is not that of the gods, and the role of the treasure seems exactly the reverse—it is sought by the power of death, and lost.

In his influential book *The Singer of Tales,* Albert Lord suggests that patterns of story told about gods are eventually told about demigods and then about mortals. His point is very nearly that of Eliade's. However, he states the important point that patterns with heroes assimilated to gods must make adjustment for the mortality of men: "When gods became demigods, the possibility of a dying god who is not resurrected came into being . . . when a mortal took over the story of the dying god, it was inevitable that eventually in tradition his death without resurrection would have to be recorded." With respect to this problem, though gods might travel to the kingdom of death and return from it victorious with a boon symbolizing life, human heroes traveling to that kingdom must succumb, for it is not given to men to carry away the victory from death. Thus the victory of the enemy in that distant kingdom to the east was an inevitable part of the pattern of story once this pattern accepted men in the archetypal role of the gods. The fall of the Burgundians has a meaning far older and far deeper than the destruction of a Germanic tribe in A.D. 437. It means no less than that all men must die.

Let us turn to the motif of the great treasure. The gods of Germanic myth characteristically possess treasures coveted by the powers of death. These treasures are often the goddesses themselves, especially Freyja, who we know was linked to love and fertility, but also the enigmatic goddess Idun, who guarded the apples of youth. Idun was once abducted by a giant, and the Aesir aged rapidly. The attempts of giants and dwarves to gain control of goddesses are symbols of the continuing threat to life itself. In two stories told of Freyja, the gods are placed in the impossible position of having to buy their own security by surrendering her to the giants: Thrym will return Thor's hammer only if given Freyja in exchange, and a clever giant bargains to build a fine defensive wall around Asgard provided that he be given Freyja, the sun, and the moon if he completes his work in one season. The gods face a choice in these situations, but no alternative. The loss of Freyja means the loss of fertility, or the triumph of death, a meaning made more clear by the associated loss of the sun and moon in the second story. But the gods, being gods, can solve these dilemmas, and in each case the divine power of Thor brings the final solution by destroying the enemy.

By the craft and power of death, the Burgundians are placed in the same predicament as the Aesir—they must surrender their treasure to save their lives. Understanding the symbolism of the treasure in Germanic tradition, we see that this is no choice at all, for the symbol of life cannot be abandoned and life itself retained. While gods might solve the dilemma with their own craft and power, men cannot. Men must die and their treasure must be lost. If one were to question the events of the Nibelung legend rationally, one might ask why the Germanic heroes always refuse to buy their lives at the cost of their gold. In fact, ransoms for political leaders were a common phenomenon. To explain their decision as heroic defiance is certainly true to one level of the story, but at a deeper level, that of the archaic pattern, there is simply no possibility of ransom. At the time when the old pattern was told of men, the treasure could not be retained by the heroes, as it had been obtained and retained by the gods.

It is interesting to consider the mythic history of the Nibelung treasure in this connection. It originated as the ransom paid by a group of gods for their very lives. Odin and two other gods travel to a weird place—possibly the Other World—where they kill an otter, which turns out to be the son of a powerful dwarf. That night the dwarf seizes the gods "and set(s) this as their ransom: they must fill the otterskin, and cover it outside too, with gold." One god obtains this gold from another dwarf who, in the shape of a fish, lives in a pool of water; with it he purchases the gods' freedom. Thus in the story of the treasure's origin we see just the situation in the story of the treasure's end: it must be produced by and surrendered to a malevolent power, or the heroes of the story will die. Because it did not belong to the gods, its loss to the dwarf does not symbolize the gods' death, but from this point on in its history there is an essential connection between its possession or surrender and the life or death of the owner. The dwarf's son, Fafnir, kills him to obtain it, Sigurd kills Fafnir and obtains it, the Burgundians kill Siegfried to obtain it. The treasure thus passes from a purely mythic level of story, through the history of a demigod (Sigurd), to final possession by men. (The alternate account sketched in the ***Nibelungenlied,*** whereby Siegfried's slaying of the dragon has nothing to do with his obtaining the treasure, runs counter to dominant tradition.) When the men die, the treasure passes into oblivion in the depths of the great river. Brought forth by the gods from obscure, watery-subterranean origins to ransom their lives, it is consigned by men to watery obscurity when demanded as ransom for their lives. The tradition is symmetrical and beautiful, the symbolism consistent.

It may seem that this discussion has wandered rather far from the notion of heroism which was to provide its theme. In fact, it has not. In archaic societies, where historical personages were assimilated to archetypes and historic events to categories, tales told of these persons and events could not but be exemplary because they expressed again the universal examples which myths embody. The archaic patterns of story which underlie the fall of the Burgundians show the exemplary behavior of prominent persons, that is, their heroism. (pp. 123-41)

Stephen L. Wailes, "The 'Niebelungenlied' as Heroic Epic," in Heroic Epic and Saga: An Introduction to the World's Great Folk Epics, *edited by Felix J. Oinas, Indiana University Press, 1978, pp. 120-43.*

Holger Homann (essay date 1982)

[*In the following excerpt, Homann asserts that Hagen undergoes a metamorphosis between the first and second parts of the* Nibelungenlied, *after which he emerges as a heroic figure.*]

It has always been realized that the poet's delineation of

Kriemhild holds Gunther's head before Hagen, in an 1805 illustration by Johann Heinrich Füssli.

the Hagen figure in the ***Nibelungenlied*** is far from unambiguous. The earlier parts of the work tell of Hagen's scheming and plotting that lead to Siegfried's murder and the taking of the Nibelungen treasure from Kriemhild. These are told in such a way that the reader cannot help but loathe and despise this man. In the later part of the epic, however, Hagen's strength, forcefulness, and courage in the face of certain doom bespeak a greatness of character worthy of our admiration. Our impressions of Hagen are shared by the poet: The murder of Siegfried fills him with abhorrence, and nowhere in the epic does he take back his early censure *sô grôze missewende ein helt nu nimmer mêr begât.* On the other hand he cannot suppress his admiration of Hagen's conduct at Etzelnburc and eulogizes him as *den küenesten recken der ie swert getruoc.* The modern critic confronted with these sharply contrasting sides of the protagonist as well as the poet's changing attitudes can do one of two things. He can accept the poet's view, acknowledge that the Hagen of the first part of the ***Nibelungenlied*** differs from that of part II as night from day, and then try to explain how these differences came about and how they bear on the interpretation of the epic as a whole. Or he can attempt to prove that these contrasts are only apparent and that careful study can discern an underlying element that is present in all of Hagen's deeds, guides all his actions, and allows us to perceive Hagen as a unified character after all.

Earlier scholarship, concerned mostly with the genesis of the epic, the origin and the gradual amalgamation of the plot elements, tends to stress discrepancies because they help identify the various strata. The inconsistencies in the character of Hagen thus are ascribed to the heterogeneity of the material the poet incorporated into his epic and are used to buttress the contention that the *personae* enter the epic as preformed characters and do not undergo any psychological development. De Boor's statement about Kriemhild [in *Die höfische Literatur,* 1957], which can be thought of as the prevailing opinion, can also be applied to Hagen:

> Unvoreingenommene Betrachtung wird es unterlassen, in der Kriemhild des ersten und des zweiten Teiles eine folgerichtige psychologische Entwicklung zu suchen, . . . Die eine Kriemhild ist so menschlich wahr und ergreifend wie die andere. Jedoch einen psychologischen Entwicklungsroman zu suchen, hieße . . . die Fragestellung unerlaubt modernisieren. Dem Dichter ist Kriemhild jeweils die Gestalt, die sie aus den Voraussetzungen des Stoffes und seines Ethos sein mußte; sie ist hier wie dort exemplarisch. Aber sie *ist* es; der Dichter fragt nicht danach, wie sie es wurde.

However, Gottfried Weber [in *Das Nibelungenlied,* 1963] did look for a psychological constant in both the "bad" and the "good" Hagen. He finds it in Hagen's affinity to that dark and sinister force Weber calls *dämonisch-untergründig:*

> Es ist entscheidend für die Wesenserkenntnis Hagens . . . , daß er, der durchaus auch 'gute', ethisch positive Züge in sich birgt, durch die schicksalhaften Ereignisse, die ihm begegnen und in die er hineingezogen wird [i.e., especially Gernot's and Giselher's attack on his courage (1462 f.) and the encounter with the *merwîp*], vom Dämon, der in ihm bereit liegt, überwältigt wird—ein Bild, dessen großartige dunkle Gewalt den Dichter erschauern läßt, dessen heroische Größe im Dämonischen er fraglos bewundert, freilich schaudernd bewundert.

Thus Weber, while presenting an element that might conceivably underlie all of Hagen's actions, still maintains the dichotomy of the character. Not so some more recent attempts to harmonize the two Hagens. Efforts in this direction will always be greatly influenced by whichever of the two parts of the ***Nibelungenlied*** most impressed the critic. If he attaches greater weight to the events in Worms and lets this influence his understanding of the later *âventiuren,* then Hagen will emerge a much more sinister and evil person than if the critic's perception of the character proceeds from the events narrated in the second part of the epic. Neither approach, however, can avoid distorting the story. Let me cite three examples to support this statement.

In an attempt to exonerate Hagen and show him as "a politically oriented vassal of great human intelligence" who uses "all means at [his] disposal [for] success or even mere survival in the political order," Ursula R. Mahlendorf and Frank Tobin present—*inter alia*—Hagen's perhaps vilest deed, namely tricking the unsuspecting Kriemhild into revealing Siegfried's sole vulnerable spot and thus involving her in her husband's death, as nothing more than proof of his "ability to predict people's reactions" ["Hagen: A Reappraisal," *Monatshefte* 63 (1971)]. At the other end of the spectrum we have critics such as J. Stout and Harold D. Dickerson, Jr. Stout decries Hagen's noblest gesture, namely his request for Rüdeger's shield, a gesture that allows this most troubled man to show once more and for all to see his unchanged feelings of friendship towards the Burgundians, as the act of a vulture (*Aasgeier*), scoundrel (*Bösewicht*), and hypocrite (*heuchelt*) trying to exact one more present from the man *von des milte verre wart geseit* [*und ouch Hagene,* 1963]. And Dickerson, attempting to portray Hagen as a "destroyer of values, a creator of voids," must strip him of any and all qualities that might be perceived with favor: his "much vaunted courage is nothing less than perverted urge to destroy," and Hagen's well known statement to Kriemhild that he came to Etzelnburc because his lords were going there and he was their *man* (1788) is for Dickerson "only empty talk, the utterance of a supremely cynical mind" ["Hagen: A Negative View," *Semasia* 2 (1975)]. Clearly, bias colors these interpretations just as it did in those nationalistic commentaries of a bygone era.

Proceeding from the premises that the ***Nibelungenlied*** is the work of one author and should be considered (until proven otherwise) to be consistent within its own framework and that the author should be taken literally both in his condemnation and his admiration of Hagen, I shall in this essay advance and attempt to support the thesis that the murderous Hagen of the first part has experienced a metamorphosis, that this metamorphosis can be demonstrated from textual elements, and that acceptance of this idea of change allows a more precise understanding of the text. The starting point for this endeavor is neither Hagen's murder of Siegfried nor his heroism at Etzelnburc, but rather the events surrounding the crossing of the Danube, i.e., the events at the seam of the two parts of the epic. The arguments will concentrate on four relatively short scenes, of which three have not yet found their commentators and one still raises unanswered questions.

When on the morning of their twelfth day out the Burgundians reach the Danube river, they discover that it has swollen above its banks and is—in the absence of boats—extremely hazardous to ford. Hagen, sent by Gunther to find some means of safe crossing, comes across two bathing nixies and extorts from them not only information about the sole available ferryman but also knowledge of the future for him and his party. Following the advice of the *merwîp,* Hagen finds and kills the ferryman, takes his boat to where the others are waiting, singlehandedly transports the whole company across the river, and after having unsuccessfully attempted to drown the chaplain destroys the boat.

This synopsis of the events connected with the river crossing omits one very short scene of less than three stanzas which is seemingly of no import for the future course of events, but just might provide a starting point for an interpretation of the Hagen figure. When Hagen returns with the boat the Burgundians notice the bloodstains on it and bombard him with questions. It is especially Gunther who recognizes their significance and wants to know what befell the ferryman. Hagen replies that he has not seen any ferryman and that no one has suffered any harm from him:

> Dô sprach er lougenlîche: "da ich daz schif dâ vant,
> bi einer wîlden wîden, dâ lôstez mîn hant.
> ich hân deheinen vergen hiute hie gesehen;
> ez ist ouch niemen leide von minen schulden hie geschehen."
>
> (1568)

This is so blatant that the poet's comment that Hagen spoke *lougenlîche* seems quite superfluous; by making it, however, he does draw special attention to the lie and encourages the question: why does Hagen lie? Since the text does not provide an explicit answer we must deduce the probable reason. To do so convincingly, we must also consider Hagen's other lies. Honesty and straightforward behavior are not values per se for Hagen since he makes frequent use of untruths and of his knack for manipulating, making people believe things that are not so and leading them to act deceitfully themselves.

When Gunther unwisely but also quite intractably has made up his mind that only Brünhild will serve as his bride, it is Hagen who advises enlisting Siegfried's assistance. To be sure, he does not mention Siegfried's *Tarnkappe,* the cloak that makes its wearer invisible and that will be the very means by which Brünhild is to be deceived and overcome, and his actual words are, at least on the surface, innocuous enough: *ir bittet Sîvrîde mit iu ze tragene die vil starken swaere* (331.2-3). But they have their suggestive effect: in the narrative summary of the consultation, interposed between dialogue scenes, we read the simple statement: *Sîvrît der muose füeren die kappen mit im dan* (336.1).

When Brünhild inquires of Siegfried why he was not present at the competition, it is Hagen who saves the situation with the ready lie that the thought of [Gunther's competing with] her had depressed them all so much that Siegfried had withdrawn to the ship (472-473).

After Kriemhild has publicly humiliated Brünhild, Hagen convinces the kings with rather dubious and inflammatory arguments that the scandal can only be rectified by killing Siegfried and immediately presents the treacherous plan of a fictitious declaration of war (874-875).

Before leaving for the not-to-be war, Hagen visits Kriemhild, ostensibly to take his leave, in reality to induce her to reveal Siegfried's vulnerable spot. Note how double-edged his response is to her worry that Siegfried may be made to pay for her indiscretion towards Brünhild: *ir* [=Kriemhild and Brünhild] *wert versüenet wol nâch disen tagen,* which Kriemhild must take as reassurance, not knowing that the already established price for this reconciliation is to be Siegfried's life (891.3-905).

When the ferryman does not pay any attention to Hagen's shouts and promises of gold, he remembers the nixies' advice and claims to be Amelrich, a vassal of the ferryman's own overlord Else. The discovery of this deceit leads to the fight in which Hagen kills the ferryman (1552-1562).

And later when the Burgundians, now in Etzelnburc, set out for church fully armed and Etzel voices his surprise at this untoward behavior, Hagen prevents any further discussion with the quickly invented explanation that it is the custom of his lords *daz si gewâfent gân z'allen hôhgezîten ze vollen drîen tagen* (1863).

All these instances of lying occur at crucial points of the plot either where the action takes a new turn or when events threaten to stop a course of action already embarked upon. Without recourse to deceit Gunther would never have overcome and wed Brünhild; had Kriemhild not been made afraid for Siegfried's life through the false declaration of war, she would never have divulged Siegfried's weak point; only the impersonation of Amelrich brought the ferryman across the Danube river and allowed the continuation of a journey that might have come to its end right then and there; and finally, had Etzel been told the true state of affairs he might have tried and succeeded in preventing the blood bath. A pattern becomes visible. The kings, especially Gunther, set their minds on some difficult undertaking, then find that they are incapable of carrying it out themselves and expect their chief advisor to make it possible for them. When Gunther in his hubris decides to woo Brünhild and cannot be deterred from this by any warnings, then a good vassal cannot but assist to the best of his ability his lord in this undertaking. And if the royal wish can be brought to fruition only through deceit, then deceit is the way to go. This is true for the expedition to Isenstein, for the murder plot, and for the river crossing. And Hagen, whose stated goal in life is to be the best of vassals, applies his considerable intelligence and cunning and accomplishes what seemed impossible. When necessary, he does not hesitate to lie, deceive, and dissemble in the service of his king, and his loyalty justifies his actions.

Does this rationale also apply to his assertion that he has seen no ferryman and done harm to no one? To be sure, the deed itself was done while carrying out his king's command, but at this point Hagen has already obtained the boat and his lie does not contribute to his success in this task. Also, Hagen does not lie *for* his lords (as in the previous instances) but rather *to* them. For whom and to what purpose then the lie? For himself perhaps, because he wants to avoid the responsibility for the killing and the sure-to-follow troubles with the Bavarian counts Else and Gelphrat, who are bent on avenging their man's death? Hardly, for Hagen has never been the sort to deny his deeds, and he will admit this one once the Burgundians are safely on the other side of the river. And this is the key: Hagen's lie serves one purpose and one purpose only, namely to ensure that the journey be continued. To this end he keeps from his kings entirely what he learned from the nixies, hides behind a highly ambiguous statement the reason for destroying the boat, and lies in the matter of the ferryman's death. Knowledge of any of these events may have induced the Burgundian kings to return to Worms, taken all together almost certainly so. By withholding the truth Hagen deprives his lords of the opportunity to reconsider; he decides for them—manipulates them. When he finally tells the whole truth in order to forewarn them—and tell he must as it is his duty as a vassal—he confronts them with a *fait accompli:* there is no way back.

Hagen manipulating his lords is, at this point of the story, nothing really new. He has always done it, e.g., when he indirectly furthered the Kriemhild-Siegfried match (331, 346, 532), when he convinced the kings of the necessity of Siegfried's death (867-876), and when he plotted to deprive Kriemhild of the Nibelung treasure (1128-1134). But all these previous instances differ from the present one in that the final decision lay then with Gunther and his brothers, since they had the choice at least either to follow Hagen's advice or to reject it (as they to their misfortune did when they welcomed Etzel's suit for Kriemhild or when they accepted his later invitation). As Mahlendorf/Tobin have shown, in all his scheming and manipulating, Hagen is always looking out for his lords' advantage, security, and position in the world. But not here. Here he holds from them their last chance to determine their fate themselves and destines them to doom in the land of the Huns. Why does he do it? Weber traces the change in Hagen's behavior back to the council scene where Etzel's invitation to Etzelnburc was discussed. Hagen's forceful advice against this venture (he calls Kriemhild *lancraeche* and predicts *ir muget dâ wol verliesen die êre und ouch den lîp* [1461.3-4]) is silenced by Giselher's sally (1463.2-3):

> sît ir iuch schuldec wizzet, friunt Hagene,
> sô sult ir hie belîben unt iuch wol bewarn,
> und lâzet, die getürren, zuo mîner swester mit
> uns varn.

The implication that fear for his life may be the biased reason for his advice is not lost on Hagen; angrily he asserts that there is no better man to accompany them on this journey and that he shall prove it. It is quite conceivable that Gernot's and Giselher's words still rankle Hagen in this later episode and that he is resolved to avoid doing anything that might be construed as a renewed attempt at saving himself. Although deeply hurt, he has remained the loyal vassal who will employ all his resources of knowledge and cunning *so mag* [sie] *niht gewerren der argen Kriemhilde muot* (1472.4): he induces Gunther to proclaim a general mobilization (1472), selects personally the thousand best men from the more than 3000 that followed Gunther's call to arms, delays repeatedly the departure of Etzel's messengers to allow Kriemhild as little time as possible to plan her revenge, and finally assumes himself the role of leader and guide (*dar leite si dô Hagene, dem waz* [the countryside] *wol bekant* [1524.3], and *Dô reit von Tronege Hagen z'aller vorderôst* [1526.1]). All his actions bespeak Hagen's foremost concern: the safety and well-being of his lords. And this is not affected in the slightest way by Gernot's and Giselher's insulting remarks.

The key scene for the changes in Hagen's motivation must be his encounter with the nixies. G. Weber has made a good case for Hagen's affinity to the demonic world, from his *rabenswarzer varwe* (402.3) to his almost superhuman knowledge of men and the world. But only when the nixies share with him their knowledge of the future—knowledge not meant for men—does he become a part, however small, of the demonic realm. This, his first personal encounter with forces beyond human capabilities, expands Hagen's existence. Henceforth, Hagen will live and act on two levels, with twofold responsibilities and loyalties. He will continue to protect his lords against all dangers (by informing them of the nixies' prophecy, by personally leading the rear guard action against the Bavarian counts, and by foiling Kriemhild's moves). But this loyalty is no longer absolute, for it is now subordinate to a greater purpose; namely to see the predicted future come about. He has accepted the nixies' prediction and feels himself to be an agent of destiny.

Hagen's twofold responsibilities to the future and his lords, the former being the more important, can be shown in a number of scenes.

He informs his lords of the true events surrounding the crossing of the Danube after, and only after, he has made sure that the journey can no longer be broken off.

Immediately after the successful river crossing Hagen loses his position as guide and leader, a position for which he is eminently qualified and which was accorded to him as a matter of course, see stanzas 1419.4 and 1756.

> Dô si nu wâren alle komen ûf den sant,
> der künec begonde vrâgen: "wer sol uns durch
> daz lant
> die rehten wege wîsen, daz wir niht irre varn?"
> Dô sprach der starke Volkêr: "daz sol ich eine
> bewarn."
>
> (1586)

This is quite an extraordinary event, so important apparently that the poet reports it twice (the second time in 1594). Hagen accepts this development without demur. We may assume that he approves of it, that he willingly surrenders his responsibility as the company's guide to his successor Volker. He is freed of an obligation, without losing any of his influence. He no longer leads the way to a local destination, but rather to a destiny of death and destruction.

Scholars have variously noted how slowly the events in Etzelnburc gain momentum, how Kriemhild and Hagen must again and again provide new impetus to move the action forward until finally, together, they bring about the inevitable tragedy. On the side of the Huns, it is only Kriemhild who desires the confrontation with the visitors. Her prospects for success would be small indeed were it not for Hagen, who alone of the Burgundians also seeks conflict; the Burgundian kings do not believe almost to the end that Kriemhild intends to do them harm. Why should I beware? is Gunther's response to Dietrich's warning (1727.1). On the other side, Etzel is determined to be the perfect host and seems to be prepared to accept the most outrageous behavior from his guests. When Volker wantonly kills the Hunnish dandy and in doing so almost precipitates general battle, Etzel intervenes and declares the death to have been accidental, not intentional (1896). No doubt, should Etzel learn of his queen's evil intentions he would find a way to put paid to her plans. And here fits the brief scene in which Hagen lies to Etzel.

After Hagen and Volker thwart the attempted night attack of the Huns, the Burgundians the next morning go to church fully armed. When Etzel inquires after the reason for this they are given the perfect opportunity to explain to him what really is going on. But Hagen, who recommended the full armor and thus fulfilled his responsibility to the kings, again forestalls any chance to avoid the catastrophe with his easy lie that it is the custom of the Burgundians to go armed for three full days at all high festivities (1863). Kriemhild, who is present and knows better, must keep her silence lest her plans be upset. For once the archenemies cooperate in the macabre game of treachery and deceit: his life and her silence will bring about what Kriemhild would call revenge, Hagen the fulfillment of destiny.

The last scene I want to discuss in this context does not involve a lie by Hagen; however, it is important for my argument that Hagen has become the agent of a superhuman, otherworldly force. Upon Kriemhild's instigation, the Burgundian squires are slain in their quarters while the nobles are at the banquet in the royal hall. Only Dancwart, Hagen's brother, survives the battle. Covered with blood he storms into the banquet hall and announces the news of the slaughter.

> Dô sluoc daz kint Ortlieben Hagen der helt guot,
> daz im gegen der hende ame swerte vlôz daz bluot
> und daz der küneginne daz houbet spranc in die schôz.
>
> (1961)

The motivation is apparent: Hagen slays Ortlieb in revenge for the deaths of the squires. At the same time this is the one deed Etzel can not let go unavenged; now he can no longer retain his detachment, just as the attack on the squires has involved the Burgundians. The fight has become unavoidable. But there seems to be something more to the scene.

The poet tells us that at the banquet Kriemhild cannot forget what has been done to her. When the strife cannot be provoked in any other way, Kriemhild has Etzel's son Ortlieb brought into the hall (1912.1-3). We do not know exactly what is in Kriemhild's mind, but the introductory when-clause and the poet's comment *wie kunde ein wîp durch râche immer vreislîcher tuon* lend Kriemhild's order, so normal in other circumstances, an ominous air. Four of Etzel's men go straight away and carry Ortlieb to the royal table. Four men serving as a personal guard for a prince we can understand. But why do they carry him? We know from earlier references that Ortlieb must be six or seven years old, old enough to walk by himself. Nor are we told of any physical handicap he may have. On the contrary, Etzel is extremely proud of him and has high hopes for him (1914-1917). Then again, why is he carried into the hall? Perhaps we may see this as a ceremonial entrance, an entrance which the person does not actively perform but rather has to endure passively. And then there are Hagen's words with which he accompanies his sword blow that severs Ortlieb's head so that it falls into Kriemhild's lap:

> nu trinken wir die minne und gelten's kuneges win.
> der junge vogt der Hiunen, der muoz der aller erste sîn.
>
> (1960.3-4)

De Boor comments on these lines that they are reminiscent of "ursprünglich germanische[m] Brauch" and ascribes to them "feierlich-sakrale[n] Klang"; Weber echoes when he speaks of "Worte uralten germanisch-sakralen Brauchtums." Both are alluding to the ritualistic "Minnetrunk", the ceremonial conclusion of a sacred meal in honor of and a sacrifice to the gods and the dead. If we see this together with Hagen's reply to Etzel's expression of fatherly pride, namely that to him the boy looks *veiclîch getân* 'destined for death' (1918.3, before Dancwart brings the news of the squires' death), then Ortlieb's death takes on aspects of a ceremonial sacrifice: the young innocent prince, chosen by fate, must be sacrificed so that the battle may begin, just as Agamemnon had to sacrifice his daughter Iphigenia so that the Greeks could carry war into the land of the Trojans. And Hagen is the one who speaks the ritual words and delivers the death blow, who assumes the role of the priest and makes the horror possible.—Is this to make a mountain out of a molehill? Perhaps, but the fact remains that by eliminating the motif of Ortlieb slapping Hagen (if indeed it ever was part of the story) the poet also did away with a pat, superficial motivation and created a much starker scene with a decidedly atavistic quality.

Taking my clues from Hagen's lies and the changes in their motivation, I have tried to demonstrate that there is no need to bend the textual evidence in an effort to show us an "all good" or "all bad" Hagen. The frequently noted dichotomy of the character does indeed exist, but it is a dichotomy brought about by the events narrated in the epic. After the encounter with the *merwîp,* where Hagen learns what the future holds for him and his party if they should continue the journey, he functions on two levels: on one he remains the vassal obligated to protect and further the interests of his lords; on the other, and this takes precedence, he perceives himself as an agent of fate and leads the Burgundians to their destined end. It is on this second level that the Hagen figure acquires an almost demonic dimension that transcends concerns for reputation, influence, and power and inspires his uncompromising heroism. (pp. 759-69)

Holger Homann, "The Hagen Figure in the 'Nibelungen lied': Know Him by His Lies," in MLN, *Vol. 97, No. 3, April, 1982, pp. 759-69.*

Mueller on the modern significance of the *Nibelungenlied:*

The ***Nibelungenlied*** as an epic record of collective human tragedy appears to be more pertinent today than it has been perhaps to previous generations—if such assertion is permissible in retrospect to 750 years since its appearance in its present form, or to twice 750 years since the downfall of the Burgundians to which the song refers. Man of today is filled with a new consciousness of human limitations and of man's paradox, of his forlornness in a disenchanted world; he is aware of the necessity for self-inspection and for a re-appraisal of his values, and he is also conscious of his need of faith. Stunned by the immensity of recent wars, collectively involved in violent destruction, now killing without hate, now slaying with a vengeance, man has emerged less arrogant and less secure, less righteous and assured than he has been before. Yet the significant events of recent history are still too close to be transmuted from mere records of reported or experienced actuality into the form of art, a symbol of man's yearning to embrace the truth as well as of his contacts with infinity, affirming his spiritual potentialities with which alone he might endure his guilt. The greater the events that mark human experiences, the greater is the distance needed to view them from a disengaged perspective to obtain validity. The story of ***Der Nibelunge Not*** as an authentic symbol of human actions and emotions, of values cherished and of errors made, obtains a new immediacy today by its valid reflection of complexities which as a basic part of man lead him into distress, as the tragic events of recent years again have proved.

Werner A. Mueller, in his The Nibelungenlied Today: Its Substance, Essence, and Significance, *The University of North Carolina Press, 1962.*

Edward R. Haymes (essay date 1986)

[*In the excerpt below, Haymes asserts that Siegfried's destruction by the Burgundians was intended by the* Nibelungenlied *poet as an argument against the courtly romance tradition.*]

Es wuohs in Burgonden ein vil edel magedîn,
daz in allen landen niht schoeners mohte sîn,
Kriemhilt geheizen; si wart ein scoene wîp.
dar umbe muosen degene vil verliesen den lîp.

[There grew up in Burgundenland a girl of noble rank,
so that there was nowhere anyone more beautiful.
Kriemhild was her name. She became a beautiful woman.
For that reason many knights had to lose their lives.]

This strophe—the first in the so-called B-Version—forges a thematic link between the motif of feminine beauty, derived from chivalric literature, and the carnage that closes the epic. The death motif is stressed by being placed in the rhythmically anomalous fourth descending half line of the strophe. Throughout the poem this position will be used to draw attention to the overall catastrophe-bound direction of events. Three of the first four strophes of the B-Version conclude with a reference to the fall of the Burgundians. Much attention has been paid to these epic prefigurations and they have often been held to be mere strophe-fillers, devices to provide the poet with a method of ending his strophe when he had run out of "real" narrative material. It has also been noted that they leave little suspense about the outcome of the story. We must, however, bear in mind that the events of the story were well-known to every hearer long before the singer began his performance. Suspense in the sense of the modern murder mystery is both unknown and impossible in a traditional plot such as that of the ***Nibelungenlied.***

In spite of our knowing from the beginning "how things turn out," I would argue that the prefigurations actually play a role in heightening suspense. [German scholar] Siegfried Beyschlag has correctly observed that the prefigurations shift the attention of the audience from the "what" to the "how". It is just this focus of attention on the "how" of the narration that makes the individual performance of a traditional story interesting. The epic prefigurations remind the hearer that specific events are to come and draw attention to the way in which they are presented. In place of the mystery, the enigma that often enshrouds the outcome of a modern story, our attention is drawn to the telling of the tale, to the ability of the singer to make his story move along. The prefigurations of the ***Nibelungenlied*** allow the poet to draw out the catastrophe to great lengths while keeping the hearer's attention on specific motifs or events that contribute to it. The strophe cited above is a prime example. The motifs of courtly beauty worship and carnage are sounded together in a fashion designed to link them in the hearer's mind and to make him sensitive to their appearance as the narrative continues.

After the briefest introduction of the Burgundian *dramatis personae,* this pair of motifs is reinforced through the narration and interpretation of Kriemhild's falcon dream. Like the general warning of the opening, this scene allows the narrator to remind the audience of the fact that Kriemhild will lose Siegfried. The tension created by the dream is only resolved when Siegfried is actually killed. (The oracle of the mermaids in strophes 1533-1549 performs the same function for the second half). The motif of love, *minne,* is introduced here for the first time although it was implicit in the reference to Kriemhild's beauty at the opening. The noun *minne* appears three times and the verb *minnen* once in the short space of four strophes. The final strophe of this opening *aventiure* (as the chapters of the ***Nibelungenlied*** are traditionally called) reiterates the baleful prefiguration of the opening strophe, but in greater detail:

> Der was der selbe valke, den si in ir troume sach,
> den ir besciet ir muoter. wie sêre si daz rach
> an ir naehsten mâgen, die in sluogen sint!
> durch sîn eines sterben starb vil maneger muoter kint. (19)
>
> [He was the same falcon, the one she saw in her dream,
> which her mother interpreted. How dreadfully she avenged it
> on her closest kin, who had killed him!
> Because of his one death, many a mother's son died.]

By the end of this opening *aventiure* there will have been little doubt in the minds of the poem's hearers that there is a close connection between *minne* and the catastrophe awaiting the Burgundians.

During the two decades preceding the composition of the written ***Nibelungenlied,*** the literary horizon of German aristocratic society had been dominated by chivalric literature, by romance and *Minnesang.* These forms were in turn derived from French and Provençal models. Central to both genres was the concept of *amor, amour,* or—in German—*minne.* The word *minne* had had a wide range of meanings prior to the arrival of chivalric literature in Germany. It could refer to love between the sexes, but it could equally appropriately be used to designate the love of man for God or even the friendly feelings that were supposed to prevail between relatives or between a host and his guests. Within the framework of chivalric literature, *minne* generally came to mean that which we call "courtly love," the special love situation that exists between a knight and his lady. Within chivalric literature in Germany we can distinguish three different species of courtly *minne.* The first of these (let us call it Reinmar-*minne* in honor of its most famous lyric celebrant, Reinmar von Hagenau) concerns the unrequited love of a knight for an unapproachable lady. The second type (Tristan-*minne*) involves lovers from the first type in an illicit sexual relationship. In the lyric this type of *minne* is present largely in the *Tagelied* or *alba,* the dawn song of lovers as they are parted by the sunrise and its threat of exposure. The third type of *minne* exists in our period mainly in the romances. This type involves the love of a knight for the woman who becomes his wife. The first two types are rare in the romances (except for the special cases of Lancelot and Tristan) and the last type (with at least one exception, discussed above in the chapter on genre) is totally unknown in the lyric. The reason for this distribution lies in the nature of the two literary forms. While the lyric thrives on the tension generated by the impossibility of the love affair or by the danger surrounding its consummation, the romance moves toward a total resolution of the lacks and tensions existing at its outset. The romance hero moves toward a situation characterized by harmony and this situation includes the resolution of any *minne* problems that arise in the course of the story.

Connoisseurs of the Siegfried tradition will have been astounded at the opening strophes of the second *aventiure.* Siegfried grows up here in a courtly atmosphere, protected by parents and tutors from the shocks of the natural world. The poet seems to go far beyond any narrative necessity to emphasize the protected nature of Siegfried's upbringing: "vil selten âne huote man rîten lie das kint". (25,1) ("they very seldom allowed the young man to ride out alone"). In the understated language of the poem "very seldom" here means "never". There could be no greater contrast to the traditional story of Siegfried's youth. The simplest assumption we could make here would be that the poet simply did not know the traditional story and fashioned a youth narrative from the normal usage of the nobility in the late twelfth century. We are disabused of this notion, however, in the following *aventiure.* In strophes 86-99 Hagen tells the well-known story of Siegfried's wild youth, his battles with dwarves and dragons and his gaining of the Nibelungen hoard. We can only assume after hearing this that—like the introduction of the *minne*-motif in the first *aventiure*—this new version of Siegfried's youth was intended to draw attention to itself.

If this is the case, then we must ask what the purpose of this striking variation from tradition was, what the contemporary audience would have derived from it. The variations all point in one direction: the establishment of Siegfried as a powerful king, as a man who would be the social equal of Gunther. The wild youth in the forests of the traditional Siegfried story would not have made Siegfried's place as a king in organized feudal society at all clear. The nontraditional emphasis on aristocratic upbringing, the lavish ceremony surrounding Siegfried's knighting, and the repeated reference to the power of Sigmund over his broad realm leave no doubt that we are dealing with a well-established king, an appropriate husband for Kriemhild.

In the light of the thematic importance given *minne* in the first *aventiure* we should not be surprised at the emphasis given here to Siegfried's ability to awaken love in the hearts of the women and girls at his own court. Consequently his first interest after being dubbed a knight is *minne:* "Do gedâht ûf hôhe minne das Siglinde kint". (47,1) ("Siglinde's son then turned his thoughts to courtly love"). I have rendered the words "hôhe minne" as "courtly love" here, but I doubt seriously that the original audience of the ***Nibelungenlied*** felt the same shock of recognition on hearing the words as that felt by the modern Germanist schooled in the tradition of such scholars as Friedrich Neumann. In modern scholarship the term has come to mean the rarified, unfulfilled love we have labeled "Reinmar-*minne.*" Siegfried does play the Reinmar role later, but it is doubtful that the term here means anything more than "love for a person of high station". Siegfried's initial preparations for a wooing expedition certainly do not point in the direction of a passive Reinmar-type lover.

Siegfried sets out for Worms with a small contingent in order to win the beautiful Kriemhild. His arrival in

Worms is one of the most surprising scenes in the poem for the modern reader and it may well have been equally surprising for the medieval hearer. Although the arrival scene itself is traditionally patterned, Siegfried's aggressive demand that Gunther meet him in single combat with nothing less than the realms of the two kings at stake does not fit into the expectations aroused by the narrative up to this point. One would at least expect some mention of the main purpose of his visit. There may well be some echoes of the romances in this strange behavior. Iwein, for example, arrives in the land of the king Askalon, challenges him to combat and finally gains (albeit without demanding or expecting it) his land and his wife by killing him. (Such conquests may well have been a reflection of political reality in this period of rampant territorialization). Siegfried's power play is countered by Gunther's insistence on his hereditary right to the lands and castles of Worms. This exchange sets up a dichotomy between the established power represented by Gunther's hereditary claims and Siegfried's apparent readiness to call the traditional order into question. In this readiness Siegfried is clearly allied with the heroes of the romances, whose political fortunes are based on the possibility of finding the opportunity to win a castle, a wife and a realm by a successful passage through various tests of their knightly prowess. On the other hand, Gunther's claim—far from representing "courtly" values as most critics have maintained—is based on traditional values, on values that would have been associated with the world of the past and therefore with the traditional epic.

The traditional interpretation of Siegfried's arrival at Worms has held the field for so long that it may be difficult to give up the idea that he represents an earlier stratum of ethical behavior than does Gunther. There may be traces of pre-courtly behavior in Siegfried's unexpected challenge, but within the framework of the value systems represented in the ***Nibelungenlied*** it is apparent that more contemporary questions of behavior and of political reality are playing the dominant role. If we recall the political activities of the Staufen dynasty leading up to 1200, we can see that a major concern of imperial politics had been the establishment of a hereditary kingdom, an "Erbreich" to secure both the certain succession of the Staufen rulers and the stability of the empire.

Opposed to the hereditary succession espoused by both the Staufen emperors and by Gunther were two models of kingship. The older one was that of election, which prevailed in Germany far beyond the Staufen attempts to eliminate it. The election model, however, plays no discernible role in any of the literary treatments of kingship from the period. Although hereditary succession never became political reality for the would-be imperial dynasties, it is the only model that we find in the quasi-traditional heroic poetry of the thirteenth century.

The new concept of kingship presented in the romances, however, stands in sharp contrast to the stable hereditary power sought by the Staufen monarchs (and enjoyed by the dynastic princes of the empire). Almost without exception the heroes of the romances have to earn their kingship through deeds of prowess and service. We have already mentioned Iwein, who is probably the most striking example, since he gains a kingship for which he was not predestined by heredity through force of arms in single combat. Erec, moreover, must demonstrate his fitness to assume his own hereditary throne through the arduous series of adventures following his recognition of his inadequacy. Parzival fails his initial test and must earn his right to be king as well. There is considerable evidence that this model was intended for persons lower on the social scale than the king, that it may have been intended to offer *ministeriales* a model for social advancement. The documented popularity of *Iwein* among *ministeriales* may indicate that the model was very attractive. The notion that one could gain political and feudal power through one's own valor and force of arms was certainly attractive to social groups that were always seeking ways of expanding their power. The model provided by Iwein's defeat of Askalon would seem to provide legitimacy to the use of force under certain circumstances. At least two powerful *ministeriales* chose this motif for pictorial representation in their castles.

There can be little doubt that the model of knight-errant offered by the romances was threatening to those who already held power. The knight-errant represented social chaos, a return to the law of the jungle that had been partially limited by the ideas of stability through established power and hereditary succession. The notion that one's kingship was always on the line was not conducive to stability and order. Siegfried himself is the beneficiary of the established law in his own land, but he refuses to use the mechanisms for bride-winning offered by his position and follows instead the model of the chaotic forces of knight-errantry. Any doubt we might have that Siegfried is a representative of the new-fangled literary chivalry is quickly dispersed by his subsequent adoption of the role of courtly lover, of *Minneritter*. The two models had been introduced to Germany from France and were enjoying great popularity at aristocratic courts. It would perhaps be useful if we could identify the literary movement with specific courts and thus with specific political interests, but it is obvious from what follows that the ethical models provided by the chivalric literature of the type represented by Hartmann and the *Minnesänger* did not meet with the approval of the poet of our ***Nibelungenlied.***

Siegfried's boisterous attack on the complacent peace of the court at Worms is followed by his equally shocking assumption of the role of the (almost) hopeless lover. The knight-warrior is replaced by the knight-lover. The concluding strophes of the third *aventiure* clearly establish Siegfried in the role of a practitioner of what we have called Reinmar-*minne:*

> Er gedâht' ouch manege zîte: "wie sol daz gescehen,
> daz ich die maget edele mit ougen müge sehen?
> die ich von herzen minne und lange hân getân,
> diu ist mir noch vil vremde: des muoz ich trûric gestân".
>
> . . . . .
>
> er leit ouch von ir minne dicke michel arbeit. (136;137,4)

[He often thought: "How can that take place

that I may see the noble maid with my own eyes?
whom I love in my heart and long have done so.
She is unknown to me. For that I must be sorrowful.

. . . . .

he suffered because of love for her often much pain"]

Such explicit description of the lover's suffering is unthinkable without the literary model of *Minnesang.* The poet cannot let the opportunity slip by to sound once again the motif of *minne* and suffering, perhaps in ironic extension of the lyric motif of the lover's suffering quoted above:

Sus wont' er bî den herren, daz ist alwâr,
in Guntheres lande volleclîch ein jâr,
Daz er die minneclîchen die zîte niene gesach,
dâ von im sît vil liebe und ouch vil leide gescach. (138)

[After that he lived with the lords, that is quite true,
in Gunther's country an entire year,
during which he never saw the lovely maiden
from whom later much joy and much suffering was to come.]

The suffering lover caught up in Reinmar-*minne* has but one outlet for his love: *minnedienst,* the service of the lady. Service and love are inextricably intertwined in the symbolic language of both the lyric and the romance. From the earliest *Minnesang* on we find language denoting feudal service and vassalage used to describe the relationship between the lover and his lady. The lover is "untertan", "subject" to his lady, she his "vrouwe", "lady" (in the sense of feudal superiority) and so on.

Siegfried needs an opportunity to render service to Kriemhild and this opportunity presents itself in the form of the Saxon war. Siegfried offers his service and it is gratefully accepted. We find a very strong statement of a service relationship between Siegfried and Gunther in the concluding lines of the war council. Siegfried says "iu sol mit triuwen dienen immer Sîfrides hant". ("Siegfried's hand shall ever serve you faithfully"). (161,4) The formality of the pledge clearly places Siegfried in a position of obligation if not of subordination to Gunther.

As the chapter on the historical horizon of the period has shown, *dienst, ministerium,* was a major political issue of the day. Feudal obligations were being clarified in new relationships such as those between the emperor and the newly created duke of Austria in the *privilegium minus.* In that document, the service owed the emperor by the duke was strictly limited. At the same time the ministeriales of many lords were seeking to turn their service into social advantage. Many had become very rich and powerful, lacking only the legal recognition of their *nobilis* status to make them the equals of any lords in the empire. The literary insistence on the virtue of service found in the romances makes it clear that service was an important issue for the intended audience of those works, namely for the aristocratic courts of Germany.

A further enrichment of the service idea in the thought of the period came about with the propagation of the concept of *militia dei,* the service of God, which had taken on new strength through the Crusades and their very concrete version of military service for God. In an early work of Crusade propaganda in German, the translation of the *Chanson de Roland* by the Priest Konrad, written some decades before the ***Nibelungenlied*** (the dating is disputed), we find Charlemagne referred to as "gotes dinist man," an expression that might be translated as "God's *ministerialis*". The combination of clerical and secular service ideologies forms an important part of the horizon of expectations that greeted the appearance of the written ***Nibelungenlied.*** Keeping in mind that service was depicted in the chivalric romance as a positive value, as an important part of knightly virtue, we can now look more closely at the service motif in the ***Nibelungenlied.*** Although it does not have the thematic weight of the linking of *minne* and carnage found in the second strophe of the epic, we do find a very early instance of the word *dienen* (to serve) in the sixth strophe. Here it is used, interestingly enough, to denote the subjugation of many knights to Gunther's power: "in diente von ir landen vil stolziu ritterscaft". ("many proud knights served them from their lands"). The same sense of the word is repeated when Siegfried challenges Gunther to a duel for his kingdom:

Dîn erbe und ouch daz mîne sulen gelîche ligen.
sweder unser einer am andern mac gesigen,
dem sol ez allez dienen, diu liute und ouch diu lant (114).

[Your heritage and mine shall be counted as equal.
Which ever of us shall defeat the other,
it will all serve him, both lands and people.]

The sense of "dienen" meaning feudal subservience is thus well established before Siegfried makes his first offer of service in response to the challenge of the Saxon and Danish kings. It is obvious to the connoisseur of chivalric romance and lyric that a form of *minnedienst,* love service, is taking place here. The successful conclusion of this service leads directly to the goal of *minnedienst: lôn,* reward. Siegfried is allowed to see Kriemhild for the first time. With this *minne-dienst-lôn* sequence a pattern is established that will recur around the wooing of Brünhild.

Since the concept of reward for a lover's service is derived from *Minnesang,* it is no surprise to find the scene full of *Minnesang* motifs. We need only turn to Walther von der Vogelweide to find a close parallel to the Nibelung depiction. After describing the wonders of a May morning, Walther says that he knows something that would please him even more and he describes the appearance of a lady at court:

Swâ ein edeliu schoene frowe reine,
wol gekleidet unde wol gebunden,
dur kurzewîle zuo vil liuten gât,
hovelîchen hôhgemuot, niht eine,
umbe sehende ein wênic under stunden,
alsam der sunne gegen den sternen stât,—
(46,10-15).

[Wherever a noble beautiful lady pure
well dressed and well coiffed,
goes out into company for her own amusement,

in courtly pride, not alone,
now and then glancing around,
just as the sun stands before the stars—]

We find almost all of these motifs—the grand entrance, the finery, and the image of sun opposed to the night—again in Kriemhild's appearance before the Burgundian court. There is no reason to believe that Walther's poem was the source of the ***Nibelungenlied*** depiction, since the elements brought together were common in the *Minnesang* of the period. Walther's poem merely demonstrates conveniently their currency as *Minnesang* topoi.

One could, however, almost believe that Walther and the Nibelungen poet were describing the same scene when we turn to Kriemhild's great entrance:

Nu gie diu minneclîche, alsô der morgenrôt
tuot ûz den trüeben wolken (281,1-2a).

[Now the lovely lady entered like the morning
breaking through the dark clouds.]

The image is varied a few lines later:

Sam der liehte mâne vor den sternen stât,
des scîn sô lûterlîche ab den wolken gât.
dem stuont si nu gelîche vor maneger frouwen guot (283,1-3).

[Just as the bright moon stands before the stars
as its light so purely comes down from the clouds,
so she stood in the same way before many fine ladies.]

The effect of her appearance is to drive away the "nôt", the distress felt by the frustrated lover. The key words of "gruoz" and "kus" (greeting and kiss) are used here in a situation quite foreign to *Minnesang.* Throughout the remainder of the scene there are echoes of the lyric language too numerous to cite here.

It is characteristic for the narrative technique of the Nibelungen poet that he manages to touch lightly on the thematic connection between *minne* and carnage, even though it is not the future catastrophe that is referred to, but only the Saxon war just concluded. One of the captured kings remarks:

Der künec von Tenemarke der sprach sâ zestunt:
"diss vil hôhen gruozes lît maneger ungesunt
(des ich vil wol enpfinde) von Sîvrides hant".
(298,1-3)

[The king of Denmark spoke at that time:
"because of this high greeting many men lie wounded
(which I also can feel) from Siegfried's hand".]

After a leisurely conclusion to the festival and an easily dissuaded attempt on Siegfried's part to return home, the poet concludes the *aventiure* with a final clear statement of the theme of love and suffering:

Durch ir unmâzen scoene der herre dâ beleip.
mit maneger kurzewîle man nu die zît vertreip,
wan daz in twang ir minne: diu gab im dicke nôt.
dar umbe sît der küene lac vil jaemerlîche tôt
(324).

[Because of her matchless beauty the lord remained there.
With many entertainments they passed the time.
He was a prisoner of her love, it gave him much distress.
For this love the bold one would one day lie dead.]

The combination of the *minne* topos of suffering and the real pain of death in the last two lines borders on the grotesque. The poet apparently wished to show the literary conventions of courtly love in a particularly ironic light.

As we turn to the wooing of Brünhild, we leave the conventions of *Minnesang* completely behind. The emphasis here lies once again on the developing service relationship between Siegfried and Gunther. In the council scene preceding the journey to Isenstein, we find Siegfried firmly ensconced in the position of chief advisor to Gunther, a subordinate position. He renders the feudal obligation of *consilium* and, although his advice is overruled, he is ready to render *auxilium* if his "lord" is willing to provide the appropriate payment. The payment for Siegfried's service is, of course, Kriemhild's hand in marriage.

The entire Isenstein episode seems to have been put together to demonstrate Siegfried's new subordinate status. Upon their arrival in Isenstein, Siegfried performs the highly symbolic act of holding Gunther's stirrup for him to mount. In the year 1077 Emperor Henry IV had demonstrated his subjugation to Pope Gregory VII in Canossa with just this symbolic gesture. In spite of the fact that Henry, like Siegfried, had ulterior motives, the scene has remained through the centuries and up to the present day a symbol of humiliation. Siegfried feels that he is merely playing a role to gain a much-desired goal, but Gunther cannot resist feeling pride:

daz sâhen durch diu venster diu waetlîchen wîp.
des dûhte sich getiuret des künec Guntheres lîp (396,3-4).

[The beautiful ladies saw it all through the windows.
Gunther felt himself made worthier by all of this.]

Gunther's feeling is especially justified by the presence of the ladies, the ultimate judges of one's chivalric worth. In the following strophe the stirrup service is described in some detail and the narrator makes the telling observation in the last line: "alsô diente in Sîfrit, des er doch sît vil gar vergaz" (397,4) (In this way Siegfried served him, which he completely forgot later). Gunther's failure to realize the importance of Siegfried's pretended social role will be of central importance to the development of the plot.

The following scene in Brünhild's court is the crux of the entire deception and it is constructed with the utmost care. The men enter according to rank with Gunther in front. Brünhild ignores his position along with all the other indications he and Siegfried have given of their claimed ranks. She welcomes Siegfried alone:

"sît willekomen, Sîfrit, her in diz lant.
was meinet iuwer reise? gern het ich daz bekant."(419,3-4)

["Welcome, Siegfried, here in this country.
What is the purpose of your trip? I would like to know that".]

Siegfried immediately, but politely sets her straight:

"Vil michel iuwer genâde, mîn vrou Prünhilt,
daz ir mich ruochet grüezen, fürsten tohter milt,
vor disem edelen recken, der hier vor mir stât,
wand'er ist mîn herre: der êren het ich gerne rât.
Er ist geborn von Rîne, was sol ich dir sagen mêr?
durch die dîne liebe sîn wir gevarn her.
der wil dich gerne minnen, swaz im dâ von geschiht.
nu bedenke dichs bezîte: mîn herre erlâzet dich es nicht. (420-21)

["You give me too much honor, Lady Brünhild,
that you deign to greet me, generous prince's daughter,
ahead of this noble knight, who stands here before me,
for he is my lord—I would gladly forgo the honor.
He was born on the Rhine, what should I say more?
for your sake we have traveled here.
He wishes to gain your love, whatever may befall him.
Now think on it a little; my lord will not relent.]

Siegfried tactfully draws Brünhild's attention to the position of Gunther in the procession. He also states clearly that he is Gunther's man, his vassal. This is all done in public, before Brünhild's entire court. As if all this were not enough, he again refers to Gunther as "ein künic hêr"' ("a noble king") and insists that he was forced (presumably be feudal obligation) to undertake the voyage against his will:

ja gebôt mir her zu varne der recke wolgetân:
môht' ich es in geweigert han, ich het iz gerne verlân.
(422,3-4)

[The handsome knight commanded me to make the journey:
if I had been able to refuse him, I would gladly have done so.]

Brünhild answers, repeating the unexpected claims of feudal subordination, but placing them in a conditional frame: "ist er dîn herre unt bistu sîn man," (423,1) "if he is your lord and if you are his vassal". Gunther will have to undergo the games. If he wins, Brünhild will become his wife, if she wins, he loses his life.

Siegfried's aid in the games is not a part of the public deception, since only Gunther and Siegfried know about it, but the following untraditional episode continues the pattern of feudal service. After the games have been won, Siegfried fears that Brünhild may gather her vassals and still refuse to accompany Gunther back to Worms. In order to be prepared for such a move, Siegfried secretly sets out to collect a small army of his own men from Nibelung Land. This is such a clear case of feudal *auxilium* that Brünhild is in doubt as to whether she is obligated to greet Siegfried personally when he arrives: "her künec, ir sult mir sagen, sol ich die geste enpfâhen oder sol ich grüezen si verdagen?" (510,3-4) "My king, should I greet the guests, or should I not?"

The two major episodes of the Siegfried story that have no parallel anywhere else in the numerous versions of the Nibelung story—the Saxon war and the journey to Nibelungen Land—both constitute feudal *auxilium* on Siegfried's part. In the Saxon war, Siegfried himself leads the battle and plays the role of chief vassal to Gunther, who remains at home. In the Isenstein episode, Siegfried travels to his own lands and assembles an army to support Gunther in a situation that never turns to war. Clearly there is more involved here than a simple deception of Brünhild. From the standpoint of the traditional story, there was no need for a deception in this form. If Siegfried and Gunther were equals, then Gunther would have the right to woo on his own. The entire vassal "fiction" refers more to the world into which the story was brought than to the world from which it came.

During the return voyage to Worms, Siegfried performs one more public act of service, an act that is more demeaning than any he had undertaken before. Gunther wishes to send word back to Worms that the expedition has been a success and that they are all on their way back for a great marriage celebration. Hagen is asked to carry out this service, but he refuses, saying: "ich bin niht bote guot," (531,1) ("I'm no good at being a messenger"). The unusual word order of this statement may also suggest that Hagen does not feel that it is his proper place in the social order of Gunther's court. He has another suggestion: "Nu bitet Sîfride füeren die boteschaft". (532,1) ("Now ask Siegfried to carry the message"). Performance of messenger service is too much even for Siegfried, who has voluntarily rendered every kind of feudal service up to this point. Gunther speaks:

"Des ger ich an iuch Sîfrit: nu leistet mînen muot,
daz ich ez immer diene," sprach der degen guot.
dô widerredete iz Sîfrit, der vil küene man,
unz daz in Gunther sêre vlêgen began. (534)

["I desire that of you Siegfried now carry out my will,
so that I will always repay you through service," spoke the good knight.
Siegfried refused, the very bold man,
until Gunther began to implore him to go.]

Gunther's language reveals that he has become used to having Siegfried carry out his will. In this case, however, Siegfried resists and is only convinced to carry the message by a reference to the ultimate goal of his service, to Kriemhild.

Upon his arrival in Worms, Siegfried appears before Kriemhild in a scene in which the discrepancies between his actual status and the role he is playing are emphasized.

Siegfried's first words to Kriemhild and Uote are: "nu gebt mir botenbrôt!" (553,1) ("Now give me a messenger's reward!"). Even the seemingly objective level of the narration reflects the social impossibility of the scene: "Si bat den boten sitzen: des was er vil bereit". (556,1) ("She bade the messenger sit; he was very ready to do this"). A messenger of the appropriate social level would never sit in the presence of a royal princess. There follows a charming discussion of the problem of rewarding such a high-born messenger:

dô sprach diu minneclîche: "mir waere niht ze leit,
ob ich ze botenmiete iu solde geben mîn golt.
dar zuo sît ir ze rîche: ich wil iu immer wesen holt". (556,2-4)

[Then spoke the lovely one: "It would be no pain for me
if I were to give you gold as a messenger's reward.
But you are too rich for that: I will always be grateful".]

The giving of gifts always expressed the position of the persons involved in the feudal hierarchy. The acceptance of a gift meant that one accepted one's inferior status as well. Kriemhild does not wish to demean Siegfried by offering him gold. "Rîch" in this context also means powerful and high in social status. Kriemhild's last words may contain something of a social pun. They are generally read to mean that Kriemhild wishes to reward Siegfried through her gratitude, something that would be in keeping with Siegfried's and her independent and equal status. The word "holt," however, is closely related to the word "holde" which means servant as well as beloved or lover. Kriemhild may be subtly suggesting that she is also willing to serve Siegfried in love. Siegfried insists on receiving a gift. Even if he had thirty lands in his power, he would still be happy to receive a gift from her, in other words, he would still be her servant. He reinforces the symbolic meaning of giving and receiving by passing the rich gifts on to Kriemhild's servants immediately. The scene concludes with a final reference to the "messenger":

Ez enwart nie bote enpfangen deheines fürsten baz.
getorste si in küssen, die vrouwe taete daz. (562,1-2)

[There was never any prince's messenger better received.
If she had dared, the lady would have kissed him.]

Siegfried then goes about giving orders to the Burgundians in regard to the upcoming arrival and the attendant festival. By doing this he once again assumes the role of Gunther's chief vassal.

Upon Gunther's and Brünhild's arrival the festival Siegfried has prepared unrolls in all its pageantry and moves toward its high point, the marriage of Gunther and Brünhild. Gunther is so involved in his own triumph that he forgets to grant Siegfried his reward. Siegfried reminds him of his side of the bargain, remarking that he has gone through a lot of trouble ("michel arebeit") for Gunther. Kriemhild is brought in and is married to Siegfried as part of the overall festivities.

The banquet scene that follows has been the subject of much critical speculation in spite of the fact that it has been thoroughly prepared by the poet. Brünhild weeps at the sight of the new couple across the table from her. Under the influence of Norse versions of the Nibelungen story, scholars have been tempted to see an expression of jealousy and disappointment in Brünhild's outburst. In the Norse versions Siegfried and Brünhild had actually been betrothed before Siegfried came to Worms. There may well be an echo of such a version in this scene and in the scene in which Brünhild recognizes Siegfried upon his arrival with Gunther in Isenstein, but the poet of our Middle High German Nibelungen epic has completely changed the meaning of the episode, since Siegfried's betrayal of Brünhild is as much political as personal here. Brünhild weeps for just the reason she states:

"Ich mac wol balde weinen", sprach diu schoene meit.
"umbe dîne swester ist mir von herzen leit.
die sihe ich sitzen nâhen dem eigenholden dîn.
daz muoz ich immer weinen, sol si alsô verderbet sîn". (620)

["I have reason to weep," spoke the beautiful maiden.
"I sorrow in my heart for your sister.
I see her sitting here so near to your base vassal.
I must forever weep if she is to be thus ruined."]

Brünhild carries the social degradation of Siegfried a step further by replacing "man" (usually "vassal") with "eigenholt", which usually means servant, or at best *ministerialis* and emphasizes the ownership of the person by his overlord. At first Gunther tries to mollify her by promising to explain everything later, but Brünhild knows that "later" will be too late. She must know what is going on now:

"daz ich iu nimmer wolde geligen nâhen bî,
ir'n saget mir, wâ von Kriemhilt diu wine Sîvrides sî".
(622,3-4)

["that I would never lie near beside you
unless you tell me why Kriemhild is Siegfried's beloved".]

Gunther's insistence that Siegfried has just as many castles and wide lands as he does and that he is a powerful king only serves to deepen the mystery and to further convince Brünhild that she has been tricked in some way. Brünhild's suspicion is, of course, also the reason that she humiliates Gunther during their wedding night. She must know the true state of affairs before she gives up her virginity, and thus her power, to any man.

Siegfried's renewed aid for Gunther in the second bridal night changes all that and Brünhild is physically forced to accept Gunther and to believe that he is truly the man she intended to marry. She remains unsatisfied with the explanations that have been offered concerning Siegfried's status—because they are no explanations at all.

Although no longer able to avenge herself, Brünhild continues to be haunted by the inconsistency between the Siegfried who introduced himself at her court as Gunther's man and the apparently independent king who pays no tribute to his supposed feudal lord. Brünhild is still brooding about the situation ten years after Siegfried and Kriemhild have left for their own kingdom:

> Nu gadâht ouch alle zîte daz Guntheres wîp:
> "wie treit et alsô hôhe vrou Kriemhilt den lîp?
> nu ist douch user eigen Sîfrit ir man:
> er hât uns nu vil lange lützel dienste getân".
> (724)

> [Now Gunther's wife thought all this time:
> "How is it that Lady Kriemhild carries herself so proudly?
> Since her husband Siegfried is our *ministerialis:*
> he has rendered us no service for a very long time".]

At this important point in the poem the poet spends several stanzas on Brünhild's brooding and on her insistence on having Gunther invite Siegfried and Kriemhild to Worms. The narration of a character's thoughts is very rare in the epic, so rare that we cannot afford to dismiss the matter of Brünhild's thoughts as most critics have done in the past. Just as in the case of the passage concerning Brünhild's weeping at the wedding banquet cited above, critics have generally tended to see Brünhild's concern as a front for jealousy. The disjuncture between Siegfried's claimed and demonstrated status and his behavior, however, is just too great a dissonance within the feudal order on which her claim to royal status and power rests.

Gunther at first resists, pointing out the great distances they would have to travel. Brünhild then returns to Gunther's claimed lordship over Siegfried and asks with "listigen sitten" (cunning):

> "Swie hôhe rîche waere deheines küniges man,
> swaz im gebüte sîn herre, daz sold'er doch nicht lân".
> (728,1-2)

> ["However rich and powerful any king's vassal may be,
> whatever his lord commands, he must carry it out."]

Gunther betrays his failure to grasp the importance of the question for Brünhild and the potential social dynamite involved in the apparently harmless deception on Isenstein:

> des ersmielte Gunther, dô si daz gesprach.
> er'n jahes im niht ze dienste, swie dicke er Sîfriden sach.
> (728,3-4)

> [Gunther smiled to himself when she said this.
> he never considered it service as often as he had seen Siegfried.]

Gunther finally agrees to invite Siegfried and Kriemhild for a court festival.

Brünhild makes one more attempt to discover something about the mysterious social structure when she asks Gere, the messenger to Siegfried and Kriemhild indirectly whether the years of living as a vassal's wife have had a deleterious effect on Kriemhild's courtliness and beauty:

> "nu sagt mir, kumet tuns Kriemhilt? hât noch ir schoener lîp
> behalten iht der zühte, der si wol kunde pflegen?" (771,2-3)

> ["Now tell me, is Kriemhild coming? Has her beauty
> retained any of its courtly grace, of the kind she once displayed?]

Gere wisely answers only the first of the questions.

The opening days of the court festival are apparently untroubled and Brünhild does not return to the question until Kriemhild begins to boast of her husband's virtues and power on the occasion of a tournament. It is interesting that Kriemhild expresses her boast in political terms: "ich hân einen man, das elliu disiu rîche ze sînen handen solden stân". (815,3-4) ("I have a husband who deserves to have all these lands in his power"). Before turning to the following word-battle between Kriemhild and Brünhild, it might be well to recall in this connection a scene we have not yet discussed.

As Siegfried and Kriemhild prepare for their departure from Worms following their marriage, there is a discussion of the disposition of the Burgundian heritage. Kriemhild expects to have her part of the heritage placed under Siegfried's control and to have power over a considerable part (presumably a fourth) of the Burgundian kingdom. Siegfried good-naturedly refuses the Burgundian holdings, saying that his own holdings are more than sufficient. Kriemhild does insist on taking Hagen—Gunther's most illustrious vassal—to lead her guard, but she is dissuaded when Hagen refuses to even consider leaving Gunther and the court at Worms. Kriemhild's demands at this point establish clearly that she is very concerned about political power, that it is not simply Brünhild's political interests that precipitate the conflict. With the political and personal interests of the two queens, it is no wonder that the battle takes on such proportions.

Kriemhild's claim at the tournament is at first met with a simple reference to the fact that the Burgundian lands could not be ruled over by Siegfried as long as Gunther is alive. Kriemhild reiterates her general claim to the superiority of her husband and only then does Brünhild make the first—albeit rather tentative—claim that Siegfried is Gunther's vassal. After a mollifying introduction "Jane solt du mirz, Kriemhilt ze arge niht verstân". (820,1) ("You shouldn't take this too hard, Kriemhild"), Brünhild refers to the simple fact that Siegfried himself had claimed to be Gunther's vassal:

> dô jach des selbe Sîfrit, er waere 'sküneges man.
> des hân ich in für eigen, sît ichs in hôrte jehen". (821,2-3)

> [Siegfried himself maintained that he was the king's vassal.
> For this reason I have held him to be unfree, since I heard him state it".]

Kriemhild's reply is based on the assumption that Brünhild is at least mistaken. She says that she would have been badly treated to have been married to a vassal. She demands that Brünhild cease such talk. For her part, Brünhild says that she cannot cease, since that would mean giving up her claim to the service of many knights who were, along with Siegfried, subject to her. Kriemhild insists that she must give up such claims, since Siegfried has never performed service for anyone. She also ironically repeats Brünhild's own question about the payment of tribute:

> Unde nimet mich immer wunder, sît er dîn eigen ist,
> unt daz du über uns beide so gewaltec bist,
> daz er dir sô lange den zins versezzen hât.
> (825,1-3)

> [I really must wonder, since he is your *ministerialis*,
> and since you are so powerful over us both,
> that he has so long failed to pay any tribute.]

The political tensions of the entire first half of the ***Nibelungenlied*** are here clearly expressed, but they are as close to being resolved as they will ever be. Since neither Kriemhild nor Brünhild knows enough of the situation to place the blame for their problem where it belongs, they decide to test their claims before a public forum.

In the largely illiterate society of the twelfth century such public demonstrations could create legal and social facts where none had existed before. We have already observed the use of public demonstration in connection with the deception at Brünhild's court. In the present scene each queen sets out to demonstrate through the richness of her clothing and of her attendants that she is the preeminent queen and that her husband is the more powerful lord. The public is alerted to the unusual nature and therefore to the possible importance of this particular visit to the cathedral by the fact that the two queens appear separately rather than together as had been their practice. Upon arriving at the church portal, the queens reopen their verbal warfare in their respective attempts to gain precedence. Brünhild is now the aggressor as she orders Kriemhild aside: "Jâ sol vor küniges wîbe nimmer eigen diu gegân". (838,4) ("Never should a servile woman go before a king's wife"). Kriemhild replies with the insult she had previously kept back. She says that Brünhild had dishonoured her own body: "wie möhte mannes kebse werden immer küniges wîp?"(839,4) ("How could a vassal's paramour ever become a king's wife?") Brünhild reacts sharply:

> "Wen hâstu hie verkebset?" sprach dô des küniges wîp.
> "daz tuon ich dich", sprach Kriemhilt. "den dînen schoenen lîp
> den minnet' erste Sîfrit, der mîn vil lieber man.
> jane was ez niht mîn bruoder, der dir den magetuom an gewan.
> War kômen dîne sinne? ez was ein arger list.
> zwiu lieze du in minnen, sît er dîn eigen ist?
> (840;841,1-2)

> ["Whom are you calling paramour?" said the king's wife.
> "I am calling you one," said Kriemhild. "Your lovely body
> was loved first by Siegfried, my own dear husband.
> It wasn't my brother who took your virginity.
> Where was your mind? It was beneath you.
> Why did you let him make love to you if he was your servant?"]

The effect of this charge of adultery is so powerful that Kriemhild can enter the cathedral ahead of Brünhild. After the mass, Brünhild demands proof of Kriemhild, who promptly displays the ring and belt taken from Brünhild during Gunther's second wedding night. Once again the public demonstration speaks a more powerful language to the assembled public than any verbal claim made by the participants.

The ensuing scene involving Gunther and Siegfried does nothing to clear up the situation since neither of them has any desire to have it cleared up. Siegfried offers to swear an oath that he never claimed to have made love to Brünhild, but Gunther somehow allows his readiness to stand for the oath. Gunther and Siegfried manage to keep the secrets surrounding the wooing and winning of Brünhild from coming out in the open, but they have also failed to remove the tensions that had led to the conflict. Brünhild now knows that something very wrong has taken place, that she had been won and wed under false pretences. The poem does not dwell on this situation, but simply allows the initiative to pass from Brünhild to Hagen.

Although the motivation for Siegfried's murder has been a central object of research for decades, scholars have generally overlooked the fact that there is no clear overriding reason for the act. Critical speculation on this point is rife. Hagen may see Siegfried as a rival for his position or for the power of his king, but we must remember that it was Hagen who maneuvered him into this position. Gunther may have been sufficiently frightened by the threat of exposure to be willing to support the murder. Siegfried is, after all, the only person who knows the real secret of his winning of Brünhild. Brünhild certainly has reason to be troubled. The reasons that are cited in the text are curiously disjointed and certainly insufficient to justify the crime. Hagen bases his first argument on the insult to Brünhild. When this argument fails to win over Gunther and his brothers, he suggests that the Burgundians will gain immense power and wealth through Siegfried's death. The multiplicity of reasons leaves the entire question of motivation in a curious limbo. Other versions of the Nibelungen story base Siegfried's murder on Brünhild's jealousy and this may well have been the prime mover in the German tradition known to our Nibelungen poet. In shaping the Middle High German poem, however, he has eliminated the jealousy motif in favor of a political motivation and the emphasis in our text has consistently been on the deception of Brünhild rather than on any relation she may have had to Siegfried before the beginning of the narrated story. The central point in our highly political version is that Siegfried denies his true social position in order to help Gunther win Brünhild. In so doing he has denied his true being as defined by the thought of the Middle Ages. His continual rendering of service confirms his social abasement in Brünhild's eyes and makes the discrepancy between what she is told by Siegfried before and what she is told by Gunther after the wedding even more problematic. We are not given much insight into her thoughts and feelings, but we are allowed to see again and again that the status question is the most important question in regard to Siegfried.

Hugo Bekker has suggested [in *The Nibelungenlied: A Literary Analysis,* 1971] that Siegfried's failure in Brünhild's eyes was his violation of the law of kingship. True kingship would have brought Siegfried to her as suitor and he would have won her on his own. By helping Gunther and denying his own kingship, Siegfried has "sinned" against the one code that gave shape to Brünhild's existence, the code that had made the games necessary in the first place. As long as Brünhild could believe that she had married the greatest king, she could be satisfied with her lot. When she discovers that Siegfried is actually the greater king, that he could have had her and refused, then she must seek Siegfried's death. Siegfried has insulted the two things that mean the most to her: the ideal of kingship and her own person.

Bekker's thesis takes on a new dimension when seen in the light of the political and social struggles of the Staufen period. Siegfried not only places his kingship in question, he publicly becomes a *dienstman,* a *ministerialis,* and in so doing places the entire fabric of society in question. Brünhild represents the judgment of a society that is dependent on stable mores and on a respect for the congruence of being and appearance. Brünhild passes on her role of social arbiter to Hagen, who carries out the murder.

Our poet reinforces his emphasis on service in a striking piece of narrative symmetry. Siegfried is called upon to repeat his first performance of service to Gunther as a part of the murder plot. Gunther and Hagen pretend to have been challenged anew by the Danish and Saxon kings and Siegfried falls right into their trap with an offer to serve: "daz ich iu gerne diene," ("that I gladly serve you") (886,3a). Thus Siegfried's penchant for service leads him into this last trap.

Hagen immediately makes use of this readiness. He goes to Kriemhild with an offer to protect Siegfried at the spot where he was vulnerable. After killing the dragon, Siegfried had bathed in the monster's blood and had become invulnerable everywhere the blood had touched his skin. A leaf had fallen from a tree onto his back, however, and had prevented the blood from completing its task. Knowing this, Hagen asks Kriemhild for the secret of the vulnerable spot so that he can protect him there during battle. Kriemhild agrees to sew a tiny cross onto Siegfried's cape so that Hagen can protect the spot. This mark later becomes, of course, the target for Hagen's spear.

A final indication of the literary reason behind Siegfried's death is inserted just before the treacherous blow is struck. Siegfried and Hagen run a foot race to a spring in the forest, but the thirsty hero steps back to let Gunther drink first. This echoes Siegfried's continual acts of service and deference and we are told "Do engalt er sîner züchte." "There he paid for his good manners (or good upbringing)." (980,1a) Stephen Jaeger suggests that this line might be understood within a pattern of criticism of courtly manners. His interpretation is good as far as it goes, but the use of the expression strongly suggests that the specific chivalric elements of service we have pointed out in this chapter are what is being referred to here as "züchte". This last act of courtly deference is being paid for with Siegfried's life.

Service is not only an important question of social and political life in twelfth-century Germany, it is also an important motif of literature. As we have remarked elsewhere, the chivalric romances—those of Hartmann von Aue in particular—stress service as the cornerstone of a knightly ethic. Let us recapitulate here the role of the two most important literary conventions derived from chivalric poetry: *minne* and service. The poet lays great stress on the connection between *minne* and the coming catastrophe. Siegfried is motivated entirely by *minne* to seek Kriemhild. As a result of his entering into a Reinmar-*minne* situation Siegfried is forced to seek opportunities for *minnedienst,* for love service, leading first to his heroic performance in the Saxon war—rewarded by his first meeting with Kriemhild—and then to his fateful agreement to help Gunther win Brünhild. In the episode of the journey to Isenstein we find two elements emphasized. The first is Siegfried's public and repeated insistence that he is Gunther's vassal. The second is the assumption on Brünhild's part that Siegfried is the candidate and not Gunther. The fact that Siegfried is the only man who can fulfill the requirements set by Brünhild makes it doubly clear that a natural affinity is being violated, that Siegfried is violating his natural calling to be Brünhild's husband for the sake of *minne.* As a final confirmation of the vassal motiv, we find Siegfried performing military *auxilium* by bringing a thousand men from his own lands. Siegfried then caps everything by performing messenger service. The narrator's emphasis on Siegfried's performance of servile duties is out of all proportion to their importance for the traditional plot. We must assume that the poet wished to place this emphasis where he did and that Siegfried's service is of central thematic importance for the poem.

Siegfried's entry into a *de facto* servile relationship to Gunther and its resultant catastrophe call the entire service ethic into question. Does the Nibelungen poet wish to condemn service *per se?* Such a radical rejection seems unlikely in a society in which practically every member (except the king) was involved in some sort of *ministerium.* The question involved here is the pattern of service presented by the chivalric literary genres current just prior to the ***Nibelungenlied***'s composition. This pattern is linked at once to the motif of *minne* and to the pattern of destabilizing behavior associated with knight-errantry. Siegfried reaches his goal, a goal dictated by courtly love conventions, by calling his own social status into question. This crucial point is at the center of Brünhild's attack on Siegfried. It is also at the center of the possible motivations for Siegfried's murder. Siegfried loses his life because he is willing to place his very feudal being in question in order to gain the wrong woman. The alliance between the inherently conservative oral tradition of the heroic legend of the Nibelungs and the highly critical inclusion of elements from chivalric literature in this epic makes a powerful argument for the preservation of established lines of order, for the respecting of hereditary aristocracy, and against the blurring of real differences through an implied chivalric egalitarianism. (pp. 45-66)

Edward R. Haymes, in his The "Nibelungenlied": History and Interpretation, *University of Illinois Press, 1986, 145 p.*

FURTHER READING

Andersson, Theodore M. *The Legend of Brynhild.* Ithaca, N.Y.: Cornell University Press, 1980, 270 p.

Examines the multiple accounts of Brunhild throughout Norse and German legends to assess the evolution of her character.

Bäuml, Franz H. "Transformations of the Heroine: From Epic Heard to Epic Read." In *The Role of Woman in the Middle Ages,* edited by Rosmarie Thee Morewedge, pp. 23-40. Albany: State University of New York Press, 1975.

Contends that Kriemhild's many inconsistencies may be attributed to the transformations her character underwent while the *Nibelungenlied* advanced from oral to written form.

Bekker, Hugo. *"The Nibelungenlied": A Literary Analysis.* Toronto: University of Toronto Press, 1971, 178 p.

Critical discussion of unity and meaning in the *Nibelungenlied.*

Bohning, Elizabeth Edrop. *The Concept of 'Sage' in "Nibelungen" Criticism: The History of the Conception of 'Sage' in the "Nibelungen" Criticism from Lachmann to Heusler.* Bethlehem, Pa.: Times Publishing Company, 1944, 254 p.

Investigates criticism regarding the historical, mythical, and poetic origins of the *Nibelungenlied.*

Bostock, J. K. "The Message of the *Nibelungenlied.*" *Modern Language Review* LV, No. 2 (April 1960): 200-12.

Controversial study that endeavors to show the *Nibelungenlied* poet's intentions based on a reading of the B manuscript.

Curschmann, Michael. "The Concept of the Oral Formula as an Impediment to Our Understanding of Medieval Oral Poetry." In *Medievalia et Humanistica: Studies in Medieval and Renaissance Culture.* Transformation and Continuity, edited by Paul Maurice Clogan, n.s. 8, pp. 63-76. Cambridge: Cambridge University Press, 1977.

Traces the development of the *Nibelungenlied* from its oral tradition to its written form in manuscripts A, B, and C and explains the variations in the three manuscripts.

Dickerson, Harold D., Jr. "Hagen: A Negative View." *Semasia: Beitrage Zur Germanisch-Romanischen Sprachforschung* 2 (1975): 43-59.

Considers Hagen a malevolent figure responsible for the destruction of the Burgundians.

Gentry, Francis G. "Hagen and the Problem of Individuality in the *Nibelungenlied.*" *Monatshefte* LXVIII, No. 1 (Spring 1976): 5-12.

Discusses the role of the individual in society in the *Nibelungenlied* and the Arthurian romances; the critic finds that contrary to the romances, the individual in the *Nibelungenlied* is an integral part of society and is therefore charged with moral responsibility in decision-making.

Haymes, Edward R. "Hagen the Hero." *Southern Folklore Quarterly* 43, Nos. 1, 2 (1979): 149-55.

Suggests that Hagen was fashioned after the German mythical hero and that his importance in the *Nibelungenlied* decreased as the manuscript version of the work shifted from heroic epic to romance poem.

———. *The Nibelungenlied: History and Interpretation.* Urbana and Chicago: University of Illinois Press, 1986, 145 p.

Collection of essays surveying the historical background and significant thematic elements of the poem.

Jones, George Fenwick. "Rüdiger's Dilemma." *Studies in Philology* LVII, No. 1 (January 1960): 7-21.

Studies the extent of Rüdiger's moral struggle in the thirty-seventh adventure of the *Nibelungenlied* from an historical perspective.

Kirchberger, Lida. "The Crown in the *Nibelungenlied.*" *Monatshefte* XLVIII, No. 5 (October 1956): 261-72.

Analyzes the significance of the crown in the *Nibelungenlied,* concluding that its emphasis in the poem is on political and historical—rather than courtly—themes.

Lösel-Wieland-Engelmann, Berta. "Feminist Repercussions of a Literary Research Project." *Atlantis: A Women's Studies Journal* 6, No. 1 (Fall 1980): 84-90.

Asserts that the *Nibelungenlied* may have been written by a woman.

McConnell, Winder. "Marriage in the *Nibelungenlied* and *Kudrun.*" In *Spectrum Medii Aevi: Essays in Early German Literature in Honor of George Fenwick Jones,* edited by William C. McDonald, pp. 299-320. Stuttgart, Germany: Kümmerle Verlag, 1983.

Analyzes the contrasting treatments of marriage in the two works, asserting that the catastrophic conclusion of the *Nibelungenlied* was caused by marriages founded on "false premises."

McLintock, D. R. "The Reconciliation in the *Nibelungenlied.*" *German Life and Letters* XXX, No. 2 (January 1977): 138-49.

Investigates the reconciliation between Kriemhild and Gunther in the nineteenth adventure of the *Nibelungenlied* to determine if Kriemhild's final destruction of the Burgundians is justified.

Mowatt, D. G. "Studies towards an Interpretation of the *Nibelungenlied.*" *German Life and Letters* XIV (1960-61): 257-70.

Identifies popular critical methods for interpreting the *Nibelungenlied.*

Mueller, Werner A. *The "Nibelungenlied" Today: Its Substance, Essence, and Significance.* Chapel Hill: The University of North Carolina Press, 1962, 97 p.

Overview of the *Nibelungenlied* in which Mueller outlines the poem's moral content and significance to European literature.

Salmon, Paul. "The German-ness of the *Nibelungenlied.*" *New German Studies* IV, No. 1 (Spring 1976): 1-26.

Documents German traits in the B and C manuscripts of the *Nibelungenlied,* concluding that the C text is both the oldest and the most German of the two.

Shumway, Daniel Bussier. Introduction to *The Nibelungenlied,* pp. xi-xlvi. Boston: Houghton Mifflin Company, 1909.

Introductory essay in which Shumway details the sources of the *Nibelungenlied.*

Thorp, Mary. "The Unity of the *Nibelungenlied.*" *The Journal of English and Germanic Philology* XXXVI, No. 4 (October 1937): 415-80.

Observes unity of thought and action throughout the *Nibelungenlied* but considers the poem's characterization inconsistent.

Wailes, Stephen L. "Bedroom Comedy in the *Nibelungenlied.*" *Modern Language Quarterly* 32, No. 4 (December 1971): 365-76.

Interprets the bedroom scene between Brunhild and Gunther as courtly humor, adding that it does not detract from the serious nature of the poem.

Wilson, H. B. "Blood and Wounds in the *Nibelungenlied.*" *Modern Language Review* 60, No. 1 (January 1960): 40-50.

Postulates that the recurrent appearances of blood and wounds in the *Nibelungenlied* are symbolic of Christ and Christianity.

Pindar

518 B.C. - c.446 B.C.

Greek poet.

INTRODUCTION

Since ancient times, Pindar has been been considered the supreme lyric poet of archaic Greece. His surviving works, primarily odes celebrating the victors of athletic contests, display bold imagery and dazzling verbal virtuosity within the conventions of choral lyric poetry. Until the 1960s, the epinician (victory ode) genre was imperfectly understood by scholars; classicists now recognize that Pindar's poetic treatment of mythological and ethical themes follows an established tradition that must be viewed against the backdrop of the culture and religion of his times. As the most eloquent and original representative of the Greek archaic age, Pindar has been for centuries a subject of critical comment and a wellspring of poetic inspiration.

Little is known with certainty of Pindar's life. He was born in the city of Thebes, in the province of Boeotia, and is thought to have been a member of the nobility. Biographical sources state that as a young man, Pindar received training in music and song in Athens. His earliest poem, *Pythian 10,* was written in 498 B.C., when he was twenty years old. During his fifty-year career as a professional poet, Pindar traveled throughout the Greek world, witnessing the Persian threats to Greek independence in the early decades of the fifth century B.C. and the subsequent rise of Athenian democracy and power. Pindar's odes were typically written in honor of Greek monarchs and aristocrats; among his most influential patrons were members of Sicily's ruling family. Pindar additionally enjoyed a close relationship with the noble families of the island of Aegina, for whom he wrote several odes, notably *Nemean 5* and *Pythian 8.* Despite his Theban origins, Pindar became a pan-Hellenic poet, owing partly to his reputation for tact, and partly to the nature of the social occasions for which his odes were composed. Pindar wrote poems honoring victors in the Olympic, Nemean, Pythian, and Isthmian games, athletic competitions which were also religious festivals during which citizens from all Greek states competed under a sacred truce. Internecine political conflicts were disregarded and emphasis was placed rather on the common culture shared by Greeks and the individual's striving for excellence. Thus, Pindar was hired to celebrate victors from both Athens and Thebes, mutual enemies for much of the fifth century B.C. In *Olympian 13* Pindar described the public nature of his poetic vocation as "one man at a people's bidding." He was widely esteemed in his own lifetime, and shortly after his death, writers such as Herodotus and Plato referred to him as an acknowledged authority. His last surviving work is *Pythian 8,* written to celebrate the victory of a wrestler from Aegina in 446 B.C. Pindar died some time before the outbreak of the Peloponnesian War in 431 B. C.

Pindar's corpus of lyric poetry is among the best-preserved of ancient Greece. Scholars believe that his poems were originally saved by the individuals or communities for whom they were written. Thus *Olympian 7,* an ode commemorating the victory of a boxer from Rhodes and glorifying the mythical history of that island, was reported to have been inscribed in gold in the temple of Athena in the Rhodian city of Lindos. Such odes were originally performed to musical accompaniment by a trained chorus who sang and danced in front of an audience, often following the instructions of the poet himself. In the latter part of the fifth century B.C., changes in Greek music, in conjunction with the development of Athenian tragedy, rendered the non-dramatic choral lyric unfashionable. As a result, by the fourth century B.C. Pindar's odes were read rather than performed. In the Hellenistic period the scholars of Alexandria's great library, especially Aristophanes of Byzantium (fl. c. 194 B. C.), preserved, catalogued, and rearranged Pindar's surviving works. These were divided into three basic categories: religious poems, poems of indeterminate character, and secular poems written for individuals. In the following centuries all but a portion of the secular poems (the victory odes) perished. Pindar's extant poems survive in 142 manuscripts, all of which derive from an anonymous second-century A.D. edition. The seventeenth-century English poet Abraham Cowley was the first to translate some of Pindar's odes into English (1656).

Pindar's choral odes are a branch of melic poetry, a type of verse designed to be sung, and as such, belong to an ancient and continuous tradition of Indo-European poetry. Choral lyric had close associations with the Dorian Greek tribes of the Peloponnesus: the earliest extant sample of this poetry is a fragment of a maiden's song by Alcman, a poet active in Sparta in the seventh century B.C. Scholars believe that the first composer of victory odes for choral presentation was Pindar's older contemporary, Simonides of Keos (556 B.C. - 468 B.C.), who had won fame in the Greek world as a professional poet commemorating military and athletic victories. The choral lyrics of Pindar employed intricate metrical and syntactical structures, called Aeolic and dactylo-epitritic rhythms, and were arranged in stanzas entitled strophe ("turn"), antistrophe ("counterturn"), and epode ("stand")—names reflecting the choreographed nature of choral performance. Pindar is particularly renowned for his dextrous handling of verse forms, constantly inventing novel metrical patterns in every one of his lyrics.

In the latter part of the twentieth century, commentators have emphasized the importance of understanding Pindar's poetry in the context of archaic-age religion and society. The religious outlook of archaic-age Greeks reflected their conception of the gods as omnipotent, whimsical, and inscrutable: in Pindar's victory odes human life is treated as an ephemeral phenomenon, subject to the wishes of the immortal gods. Such transitory joy as mortals experience derives solely from the grace of the gods who might send catastrophe at any moment. In such a precarious universe, Pindar asserts the importance of the aristocratic ordering of human societies. Noble families are descended from the unions of mortals and gods that took place in the mythical heroic age; aristocrats are therefore the citizens best suited to victory in the games as well as to rule their communities with wisdom, strength, and justice. Since both the gods and other men are prone to envy, however, in praising any man the poet must proceed with tact and circumspection. Scholars have demonstrated that, in addition to commending the victor, Pindar seeks in certain odes to guide the behavior of the nobles by making aristocrats aware of the evils resulting from an immoderate use of their power. As Frank J. Nisetich has written, Pindar does not simply celebrate worldly success in his odes, he *evaluates* it, placing it "against the background of failure and death."

Consistent with the epic poetry of Homer and the lyric poetry of other archaic-age writers, Pindar's thought and style are dominated by such elements as the relevance of myth to contemporary human affairs, the contrasting of one value with its opposite, the general principles underlying particular human actions, and the fragility of human life in the face of divine intervention. These themes are represented with particular force in *Pythian 3,* an ode written c. 474 B.C. to celebrate a victory in the single-horse race achieved by Hieron, tyrant of Syracuse in Sicily. The poem narrates the double myth of the woman Koronis and her son by the god Apollo, Asklepios. In relating how Asklepios, an accomplished healer, was destroyed by Zeus for daring to raise a man from the dead, Pindar contrasts the human transgression of natural limits with the purity and wisdom of the gods. Since this ode additionally discusses Hieron's illness, scholars believe that it was intended both as consolation for the Sicilian ruler and as a reminder of his mortality. Pindar compares Hieron with the mythical heroes Peleus and Kadmos, men who, despite achieving the summit of human happiness, were beset with sorrows from Zeus.

Pindar has exercised a profound influence on European poets in both ancient and modern times. His status as the preeminent lyric poet of Greece was echoed by the Roman poet Horace (65 B.C. - 8 B.C.), who wrote in his *Odes* "Whoever strives . . . to rival Pindar, relies on wings fastened with wax by Daedalean craft, and is doomed to give his name to some crystal sea." In this very work, Horace nevertheless attempted to imitate Pindar's *Olympian 2;* similarly, Vergil in his *Aeneid* imitated *Pythian 1.* In the Middle Ages Pindar's works were unknown in western Europe, but were studied in Byzantium. In 1513 the Venetian publisher Aldus Manutius published the first modern edition of the poet's works. Italian imitations of Pindar appeared later in the sixteenth century, although his most eminent Renaissance imitator was the French poet Pierre de Ronsard. Ronsard's synthesis of French and Greco-Roman poetry inaugurated a school of elevated lyric verse in continental Europe analogous to the development of the Pindaric ode in English poetry by such seventeenth-century writers as John Milton, Ben Jonson, Abraham Cowley, and John Dryden. In the eighteenth and nineteenth centuries numerous writers read and were influenced by Pindar's odes, notably Thomas Gray, Percy Bysshe Shelley, William Wordsworth, Johann Wolfgang von Goethe, Friedrich Holderlin, Friedrich Schiller, and Victor Hugo. Modern scholars frequently remark, however, that much of this Pindaric poetry unsuccessfully attempts to imitate Pindar's poetic style and structure. In the nineteenth century German scholars elucidated many of the historical and philological complexities of Pindar's works, while simultaneously attempting to discover thematic unity in individual victory odes. The conventions of choral lyric poetry, however, were misunderstood until the latter part of the twentieth century, when American and English scholars clarified the nature of Pindar's religious outlook, his handling of mythological material, and the social context of the victors for whom his odes were composed and performed. By analyzing individual choral lyrics with reference to their social and religious underpinning, current Pindar scholars have fostered a new appreciation of Pindar's worldview and imaginative power. As Hugh Lloyd-Jones has stated, "Pindar was a human being writing for other human beings, and those who wish to understand him will neglect the historical dimension only at their peril. He does honour to the victor by placing the moment of felicity which his triumph gives him in the context of his historical situation against the background of the permanent situation of the world as the gods govern it."

PRINCIPAL ENGLISH TRANSLATIONS

Pindaric Odes (translated by Abraham Cowley) 1656
Pindar in English Verse (translated by Henry Francis Cary) 1823
The Extant Odes of Pindar Translated into English, with an Introduction and Short Notes (translated by Ernest Myers) 1874
The Odes of Pindar (translated by John Sandys) 1915
The Odes of Pindar (translated by Richmond Lattimore) 1947
The Odes of Pindar (translated by C. M. Bowra) 1969
Pindar's Victory Songs (translated by Frank J. Nisetich) 1980

CRITICISM

Abraham Cowley (essay date 1656)

[*An English poet, dramatist, essayist, and scholar, Cowley began his writing career at a markedly early age, producing the verse romance "Pyramaus and Thisbe" (published 1633) when he was ten years old. His varied output includes comedies and satires; the three-volume* The Civil War *(1679); and* Poems *(1656). This last-named book is a collection of various works, including "Davideis," an epic concerning the biblical king, and "Pindarique Odes," in which Cowley employs a verse form later used by John Dryden and other poets. The following excerpt is drawn from the preface to the "Pindarique Odes" in which Cowley states the difficulties of translating Pindar's poetry.*]

If a Man should undertake to translate *Pindar* Word for Word, it would be thought that one *Mad-man* had translated *another;* as may appear, when he that understands not the *Original,* reads the verbal Traduction of him into *Latin Prose,* than which nothing seems more *Raving.* And sure, *Rhyme* without the Addition of *Wit,* and the *Spirit* of *Poetry (quod nequeo monstrare & sentio tantum)* would but make it ten times more *distracted* than it is in *Prose.* We must consider in *Pindar* the great Difference of Time betwixt his Age and ours, which changes, as in *Pictures,* at least the *Colours* of *Poetry;* the no less Difference betwixt the *Religions* and *Customs* of our Countries, and a thousand Particularities of Places, Persons, and Manners, which do but confusedly appear to our Eyes at so great a Distance. And lastly (which were enough alone for my purpose) we must consider that our Ears are Strangers to the Musick of his *Numbers,* which sometimes (especially in *Songs* and *Odes*) almost without any thing else, makes an excellent *Poet.* For though the *Grammarians* and *Criticks* have labour'd to reduce his Verses into regular Feet and Measures (as they have also those of the *Greek* and *Latin Comedies*) yet in effect they are little better than *Prose* to our Ears. And I would gladly know what Applause our best Pieces of *English Poesie* could expect from a *Frenchman* or *Italian,* if converted faithfully, and Word for Word, into *French* or *Italian Prose.* And when we have considered all this, we must needs confess, that after all these Losses sustained by *Pindar,* all we can add to him by our Wit or Invention (not deserting still his Subject) is not like to make him a *Richer Man* than he was in his *own Country.*

Abraham Cowley, in a preface to his The Complete Works in Verse and Prose of Abraham Cowley, Vol. II, *edited by Rev. Alexander B. Grosart, AMS Press, 1967, p. 11.*

John Dryden (essay date 1685)

[*Regarded by many as the father of modern English poetry and criticism, Dryden dominated literary life in England during the last four decades of the seventeenth century. A prolific and accomplished dramatist, Dryden also wrote a number of satiric poems and critical works, some of which are acknowledged as his greatest literary achievements. In* Absalom and Achitophel *(1681),* Religio Laici *(1682), and* The Hind and the Panther *(1687), he displayed an irrepressible wit and forceful line of argument which later satirists adopted as their model. In his critical works, particularly* Of Dramatic Poesie *(1668), Dryden effectively originated the extended form of objective, practical analysis that has come to characterize most modern criticism. In the following excerpt from an essay written in 1685, Dryden compares the Roman poet Horace to Pindar and suggests which meters should be employed in imitating Pindaric verse.*]

As difficult as [Horace] makes it, and as indeed it is, to imitate Pindar, yet, in his most elevated flights, and in the sudden changes of his subject with almost imperceptible connexions, that Theban poet is his master. But Horace is of the more bounded fancy, and confines himself strictly to one sort of verse, or stanza, in every Ode. (p. 266)

Since Pindar was the prince of lyric poets, let me have leave to say, that, in imitating him, our numbers should, for the most part, be lyrical: for variety, or rather where the majesty of thought requires it, they may be stretched to the English heroic of five feet, and to the French Alexandrine of six. But the ear must preside, and direct the judgment to the choice of numbers: without the nicety of this, the harmony of Pindaric verse can never be complete; the cadency of one line must be a rule to that of the next; and the sound of the former must slide gently into that which follows, without leaping from one extreme into another. It must be done like the shadowings of a picture, which fall by degrees into a darker colour. (p. 268)

John Dryden, "Preface to Sylvae (The Second Miscellany) (1685)," in his Essays of John Dryden, Vol. I, *edited by W. P. Ker, Oxford at the Clarendon Press, 1900, pp. 251-69.*

William Congreve (essay date 1706)

[*Congreve was an English poet and playwright who is considered one of the masters of Restoration drama. Many scholars regard his last play,* The Way of the World *(1700), as a masterpiece of the comedy of manners. In the following essay, originally written as a preface to his* A Pindaric Ode, Humbly Offered to the Queen, on the Victorious Progress of Her Majesty's Arms, under the Conduct of the Duke of Marlborough *(1706), Congreve attempts to rectify misconceptions concerning the irregular structure of the Pindaric ode. This preface helped create a vogue for the Pindaric ode in eighteenth-century English poetry.*]

The following ode is an attempt towards restoring the regularity of the ancient lyric poetry, which seems to be altogether forgotten or unknown by our English writers.

There is nothing more frequent among us than a sort of poems entitled "Pindaric odes," pretending to be written in imitation of the manner and style of Pindar, and yet I do not know that there is to this day extant in our language one ode contrived after his model. What idea can an English reader have of Pindar (to whose mouth, when a child, the bees brought their honey in omen of the future sweetness and melody of his songs), when he shall see such rumbling and grating papers of verses pretending to be copies of his works?

The character of these late Pindarics is a bundle of rambling incoherent thoughts, expressed in a like parcel of irregular stanzas, which also consist of such another complication of disproportioned, uncertain, and perplexed verses and rimes. And I appeal to any reader if this is not the condition in which these titular odes appear.

On the contrary, there is nothing more regular than the odes of Pindar, both as to the exact observation of the measures and numbers of his stanzas and verses, and the perpetual coherence of his thoughts. For though his digressions are frequent, and his transitions sudden, yet is there ever some secret connection, which though not always appearing to the eye, never fails to communicate itself to the understanding of the reader.

The liberty which he took in his numbers, and which has been so misunderstood and misapplied by his pretended imitators, was only in varying the stanzas in different odes; but in each particular ode they are ever correspondent one to another in their turns, and according to the order of the ode.

All the odes of Pindar which remain to us are songs of triumph, victory, or success in the Grecian Games. They were sung by a chorus and adapted to the lyre, and sometimes to the lyre and pipe; they consisted oftenest of three stanzas. The first was called the strophe, from the version or circular motion of the singers in that stanza from the right hand to the left. The second stanza was called the antistrophe, from the contraversion of the chorus, the singers in performing that turning from the left hand to the right, contrary always to their motion in the strophe. The third stanza was called the epode (it may be as being the after-song), which they sung in the middle, neither turning to one hand or the other.

What the origin was of these different motions and stations in singing their odes is not our present business to inquire. Some have thought that by the contrariety of the strophe and the antistrophe they intended to represent the contrarotation of the *primum mobile* in respect of the *secunda mobilia,* and that by their standing still at the epode they meant to signify the stability of the earth. Others ascribe the institution to Theseus, who thereby expressed the windings and turnings of the Labyrinth in celebrating his return from thence.

The method observed in the composition of these odes was therefore as follows. The poet, having made choice of a certain number of verses to constitute his strophe or first stanza, was obliged to observe the same in his antistrophe, or second stanza, and which accordingly perpetually agreed, whenever repeated, both in number of verses and quantity of feet. He was then again at liberty to make a new choice for his third stanza, or epode, where accordingly he diversified his numbers as his ear or fancy led him, composing that stanza of more or fewer verses than the former, and those verses of different measures and quantities, for the greater variety of harmony and entertainment of the ear.

But then this epode being thus formed, he was strictly obliged to the same measure as often as he should repeat it in the order of his ode, so that every epode in the same ode is eternally the same in measure and quantity in respect to itself, as is also every strophe and antistrophe in respect to each other.

The lyric poet Stesichorus (whom Longinus reckons amongst the ablest imitators of Homer, and of whom Quintilian says that if he could have kept within bounds, he would have been nearest of anybody, in merit, to Homer) was, if not the inventor of this order in the ode, yet so strict an observer of it in his compositions that the "three stanzas of Stesichorus" became a common proverb to express a thing universally known—*ne tria quidem Stesichori nosti*—so that when anyone had a mind to reproach another with excessive ignorance, he could not do it more effectually than by telling him, "he did not so much as know the three stanzas of Stesichorus"; that is, did not know that an ode ought to consist of a strophe, an antistrophe, and an epode. If this was such a mark of ignorance among them, I am sure we have been pretty long liable to the same reproof; I mean in respect of our imitations of the odes of Pindar.

My intention is not to make a long preface to a short ode, nor to enter upon a dissertation of lyric poetry in general. But thus much I thought proper to say for the information of those readers whose course of study has not led them into such inquiries.

I hope I shall not be so misunderstood as to have it thought that I pretend to give an exact copy of Pindar in this ensuing ode, or that I look upon it as a pattern for his imitators for the future. Far from such thoughts, I have only given an instance of what is practicable, and am sensible that I am as distant from the force and elevation of Pindar as others have hitherto been from the harmony and regularity of his numbers.

Again, we having no chorus to sing our odes, the titles as well as use of *strophe, antistrophe,* and *epode* are obsolete and impertinent, and certainly there may be very good English odes without the distinction of Greek appellations to their stanzas. That I have mentioned them here and observed the order of them in the ensuing ode is therefore only the more intelligibly to explain the extraordinary regularity of the composition of those odes which have been represented to us hitherto as the most confused structures in nature.

However, though there be no necessity that our triumphal odes should consist of the three aforementioned stanzas, yet if the reader can observe that the great variation of the numbers in the third stanza (call it epode or what you please) has a pleasing effect in the ode and makes him return to the first and second stanzas with more appetite than he could do if always cloyed with the same quantities and measures, I cannot see why some use may not be made of Pindar's example, to the great improvement of the English ode. There is certainly a pleasure in beholding anything that has art and difficulty in the contrivance, especially if it appears so carefully executed that the difficulty does not show itself till it is sought for, and that the seeming easiness of the work first sets us upon the inquiry. Nothing can be called beautiful without proportion. When symmetry and harmony are wanting, neither the eye nor the ear can be pleased. Therefore certainly poetry, which includes painting and music, should not be destitute of them—and, of all poetry, especially the ode, whose end and essence is harmony.

Mr. Cowley, in his Preface to his Pindaric odes, speaking of the music of numbers, says, "which sometimes (especially in songs and odes) almost without anything else makes an excellent poet."

Having mentioned Mr. Cowley, it may very well be expected that something should be said of him at a time when the imitation of Pindar is the theme of our discourse. But there is that great deference due to the memory, great parts, and learning of that gentleman that I think nothing should be objected to the latitude he has taken in his Pindaric odes. The beauty of his verses [is] an atonement for the irregularity of his stanzas, and though he did not imitate Pindar in the strictness of his numbers, he has very often happily copied him in the force of his figures and sublimity of his style and sentiments.

Yet I must beg leave to add that I believe those irregular odes of Mr. Cowley may have been the principal, though innocent, occasion of so many deformed poems since, which instead of being true pictures of Pindar have (to use the Italian Painters' term) been only *caricaturas* of him, resemblances that for the most part have been either horrid or ridiculous.

For my own part I frankly own my error in having heretofore miscalled a few irregular stanzas a Pindaric ode, and possibly if others who have been under the same mistake would ingenuously confess the truth, they might own that never having consulted Pindar himself, they took all his irregularity upon trust and, finding their account in the great ease with which they could produce odes without being obliged either to measure or design, remained satisfied, and it may be were not altogether unwilling to neglect being undeceived.

Though there be little (if anything) left of Orpheus but his name, yet if Pausanius was well informed, we may be assured that brevity was a beauty which he most industriously labored to preserve in his hymns, notwithstanding, as the same author reports, that they were but few in number.

The shortness of the following ode will, I hope, atone for the length of the Preface, and in some measure for the defects which may be found in it. It consists of the same number of stanzas with that beautiful ode of Pindar which is the first of his ***Pythics;*** and though I was unable to imitate him in any other beauty, I resolved to endeavor to copy his brevity and take the advantage of a remark he has made in the last strophe of the same ode, which take in the paraphrase of Sudorius.

> Qui multa paucis stringere commode
> novere morsus hi facile invidos
> spernunt, et auris mensque; pura
> omne supervacuum rejectat.

(pp. 143-47)

William Congreve, "A Discourse on the Pindaric Ode," in Eighteenth-Century Critical Essays, Vol. I, *edited by Scott Elledge, Cornell University Press, 1961, pp. 143-47.*

Pausanias (fl. fifth century B.C.) relates some anecdotes concerning Pindar's life:

Crossing over the right side of the course [at Thebes] you come to a race-course for horses, in which is the tomb of Pindar. When Pindar was a young man he was once on his way to Thespiae in the hot season. At about noon he was seized with fatigue and the drowsiness that follows it, so just as he was, he lay down a little way above the road. As he slept bees alighted on him and plastered his lips with their wax. Such was the beginning of Pindar's career as a lyric poet. When his reputation had already spread throughout Greece he was raised to a greater height of fame by an order of the Pythian priestess, who bade the Delphians give to Pindar one half of all the first-fruits they offered to Apollo. It is also said that on reaching old age a vision came to him in a dream. As he slept, Persephone stood by him and declared that she alone of the deities had not been honored by Pindar with a hymn, but that Pindar would compose an ode to her also when he had come to her. Pindar died at once, before ten days had passed since the dream.

Pausanias, quoted in Ancilla to Classical Reading, *by Moses Hadas, 1954.*

Samuel Taylor Coleridge (essay date 1815)

[*Coleridge was the intellectual center of the English Romantic movement and is one of the greatest poets and critics in the English language. He was also the first prominent spokesman of German idealistic philosophy in England and the forerunner of modern psychological criticism, specifically in his conception of the organic nature of literary form—a theory in which Coleridge contends that a work of literature is determined by inspiration rather than by external rules. In the following excerpt from his* Biographia Literaria, *written in 1815, Coleridge criticizes Abraham Cowley's ideas about rendering Pindar's poetry in English.*]

It is not to be denied that men of undoubted talents, and even poets of true, though not of first-rate, genius, have from a mistaken theory deluded both themselves and others in the opposite extreme. I once read to a company of sensible and well-educated women the introductory period of Cowley's preface to his *Pindaric Odes, written in imitation of the style and manner of the odes of Pindar.* "If (says Cowley) a man should undertake to translate Pindar, word for word, it would be thought that one madman had translated another; as may appear, when he, that understands not the original, reads the verbal traduction of him into Latin prose, than which nothing seems more raving." I then proceeded with his own free version of the second Olympic composed for the charitable purpose of *rationalizing* the Theban Eagle.

> Queen of all harmonious things,
> Dancing words and speaking strings,
> What God, what hero, wilt thou sing?
> What happy man to equal glories bring?
> Begin, begin thy noble choice,
> And let the hills around reflect the image of thy voice.
> Pisa does to Jove belong,
> Jove and Pisa claim thy song.
> The fair first-fruits of war, th' Olympic games,
> Alcides offer'd up to Jove;
> Alcides too thy strings may move!
> But oh! what man to join with these can worthy prove?
> Join Theron boldly to their sacred names;
> Theron the next honor claims;
> Theron to no man gives place;
> Is first in Pisa's and in Virtue's race;
> Theron there, and he alone,
> Ev'n his own swift forefathers has outgone.

One of the company exclaimed, with the full assent of the rest, that if the original were madder than this, it must be incurably mad. I then translated the ode from the Greek, and as nearly as possible, word for word; and the impression was, that in the general movement of the periods, in the form of the connections and transitions, and in the sober majesty of lofty sense, it appeared to them to approach more nearly, than any other poetry they had heard, to the style of our bible in the prophetic books. The first strophe will suffice as a specimen:

> Ye harp-controuling hymns! (or) ye hymns the sovereigns of harps!
> What God? what Hero?
> What Man shall we celebrate?
> Truly Pisa indeed is of Jove,
> But the Olympiad (or the Olympic games) did Hercules establish,
> The first-fruits of the spoils of war.
> But Theron for the four-horsed car,
> That bore victory to him,
> It behoves us now to voice aloud:
> The Just, the Hospitable,
> The Bulwark of Agrigentum,
> Of renowned fathers
> The Flower, even him
> Who preserves his native city erect and safe.

(pp. 86-7)

Samuel Taylor Coleridge, "Language of Metrical Composition," in his The Collected Works of Samuel Taylor Coleridge: Biographia Literaria; or, Biographical Sketches of My Literary Life and Opinions, *edited by James Engell and W. Jackson Bate, Princeton University Press, 1983, pp. 58-88.*

John Addington Symonds (essay date 1877-79)

[*Symonds was an English poet, historian, and critic who wrote extensively on Greek and Italian history and culture; he also made several highly praised translations of the literature of the Italian Renaissance, as well as some of Sappho's poetry. In the following excerpt from the first edition of his* Studies of the Greek Poets, *Symonds examines Pindar's style, imagery, ethical beliefs, and religious notions, maintaining that the poet's treatment of mythological themes reflects trends in early Greek philosophy.*]

At the time of Pindar's youth, lyrical poetry in Greece was sinking into mannerism. He, by the force of his originality, gave it a wholly new direction, and, coming last of the great Dorian lyrists, taught posterity what sort of thing an ode should be. The grand preeminence of Pindar as an artist was due in a great measure to his personality. Frigid, austere, and splendid; not genial like that of Simonides, not passionate like that of Sappho, not acrid like that of Archilochus; hard as adamant, rigid in moral firmness, glittering with the strong keen light of snow; haughty, aristocratic, magnificent—the unique personality of the man Pindar, so irresistible in its influence, so hard to characterize, is felt in every strophe of his odes. In his isolation and elevation Pindar stands like some fabled heaven-aspiring peak, conspicuous from afar, girdled at the base with ice and snow, beaten by winds, wreathed round with steam and vapor, jutting a sharp and dazzling outline into cold blue ether. Few things that have life dare to visit him at his grand altitude. Glorious with sunlight and with stars, touched by rise and set of day with splendor, he shines when other lesser heights are dulled. Pindar among his peers is solitary. He had no communion with the poets of his day. He is the eagle; Simonides and Bacchylides are jackdaws. He soars to the empyrean; they haunt the valley mists. Noticing this rocky, barren, severe, glittering solitude of Pindar's soul, critics have not unfrequently complained that his poems are devoid of individual interest. Possibly they have failed to comprehend and appreciate the nature of this sublime and distant genius, whose character, in truth, is just as marked as that of Dante or of Michael Angelo.

Since I have indulged in one metaphor in the vain attempt to enter into some *rapport* with Pindar, let me proceed to illustrate the Pindaric influence—the impression produced by a sympathetic study of his odes upon the imagination saturated with all that is peculiar in his gorgeous style—by the deliberate expansion of some similes, which are by no means mere ornaments of rhetoric, but illustrations carefully selected from the multitude of images forced upon the mind during a detailed perusal of his poetry. One of the common names for Pindar is the Theban Eagle. . . .

This simile describes the rapidity and fierceness of Pindar's spirit, the atmosphere of empyreal splendor into which he bears us with strong wings and clinging talons. Another image may be borrowed from Horace, who says,

> Fervet immensusque ruit profundo Pindarus
> ore;

likening the poet to a torrent, unrestrained, roaring to the woods and precipices with a thunderous voice. This image does not, like the other, fix our attention upon the quality peculiar to Pindar among all the poets of the world—splendor, fire, the blaze of pure effulgence. But it does suggest another characteristic, which is the stormy violence of his song, that chafes within its limits and seems unable to advance quickly enough in spite of its speed. This violence of Pindar's style, as of some snow-swollen Alpine stream, the hungry Arve or death-cold Lutschine, leaping and raging among granite boulders, has misled Horace into the notion that Pindar's odes are without metrical structure:

> numerisque fertur
> Lege solutis:

whereas we know that, while pursuing his eagle-flight to the sun, or thundering along his torrent-path, Pindar steadily observed the laws of strophe, antistrophe, and epode with consummate art. A third figure may be chosen from Pindar himself.

> As when a man takes from his wealthy hand a goblet foaming with the dew of the grape, and gives it with healths and pledges to his youthful son-in-law to bear from one home to the other home, golden, the crown of his possessions, gracing the feast and glorifying his kinsman, and makes him in the eyes of the assembled friends to be admired for his harmonious wedlock: so I, sending outpoured nectar, the Muse's gift, to conquering heroes, the sweet fruit of the soul, greet them like gods, victors at Olympia and Pytho.

Then, too, he adds: "With the lyre and with the various voices of flutes I have come with Diagoras across the sea, chanting the wave-born daughter of the Cyprian goddess and the bride of Helios, island Rhodes." In this passage we get a lively impression of some of the marked qualities of Pindar. Reading his poetry is like quaffing wine that bubbles in a bowl of gold. Then, too, there is the picture of the poet, gorgeously attired, with his singing-robes about him, erect upon the prow of a gilded galley, floating through dazzling summer-waves towards the island of his love, Rhodes or Sicily or ægina. The lyre and the flute send their clear sounds across the sea. We pass temple and citadel on shore and promontory. The banks of oars sweep the flashing brine. Meanwhile the mighty poet stretches forth his golden cup of song to greet the princes and illustrious athletes who await him on the marble quays. Reading Pindar is a progress of this pompous kind. Pindar, as one of his critics remarks, was born and reared in splendor; splendor became his vital atmosphere. The epithet φιλαγλαοσ, which he gives to Girgenti, suits himself. The splendor-loving Pindar is his name and title for all time. If we search the vocabulary of Pindar to find what phrases are most frequently upon his lips, we shall be struck with the great preponderance of all words that indicate radiance, magnificence, lustre. To Pindar's soul splendor was as elemental as harmony to Milton's. Of the graces, Aglaia must have been his favorite. Nor, love as he did the gorgeousness of wealth, was it mere transitory pomp, the gauds and trappings of the world, which he admired. There must be something to stir the depths of his soul—beauty of person, or perfection of art, or moral radiance, or ideal grandeur. The blaze of real magnificence draws him as the sun attracts the eagle; he does not flit moth-like about the glimmer of mere ephemeral lights.

After these three figures, which illustrate the fiery flight, the torrent-fulness, the intoxicating charm of Pindar, one remains by which the magnetic force and tumult of his poetry may be faintly adumbrated. He who has watched a sunset attended by the passing of a thunderstorm in the outskirts of the Alps; who has seen the distant ranges of the mountains alternately obscured by cloud and blazing with the concentrated brightness of the sinking sun, while drifting scuds of hail and rain, tawny with sunlight, glistening with broken rainbows, clothe peak and precipice and forest in the golden veil of flame-irradiated vapor; who has heard the thunder bellow in the thwarting folds of hills, and watched the lightning, like a snake's tongue, flicker at intervals amid gloom and glory—knows in Nature's language what Pindar teaches with the voice of Art. It is only by a strained metaphor like this that any attempt to realize the *Sturm und Drang* of Pindar's style can be communicated. In plainer language, Pindar, as an artist, combines the strong flight of the eagle, the irresistible force of the torrent, the richness of Greek wine, the majestic pageantry of Nature in one of her sublimer moods.

Like all the great lyrists of the Dorian school, Pindar composed odes of various species—hymns, prosodia, parthenia, threnoi, scolia, dithyrambs, as well as epinikia. Of all but the epinikian odes we have only inconsiderable fragments left; yet these are sublime and beautiful enough to justify us in believing that Pindar surpassed his rivals in the threnos and the scolion as far as in the epinikian ode. Forty-four of his poems we possess entire—fourteen Olympians, twelve Pythians, eleven Nemeans, seven Isthmians. Of the occasions which led to the composition of these odes something must be said. The Olympian games were held in Elis once in five years, during the summer: their prize was a wreath of wild olive. The Pythian games were held in spring, on the CrissÆan plain, once in five years: their prizes were a wreath of laurel and a palm. The Nemean games were held in the groves of Nemea, near Cleonæ, in Argolis, once in three years: their prize was a wreath of parsley. The Isthmian games were held at Corinth, once in three years: their prize was a wreath of pine, native to the spot. The Olympian festival honored Zeus;

that of Pytho, Phœbus; that of Nemea, Zeus; that of the Isthmus, Poseidon. Originally they were all of the nature of a πανηγυρισ or national assembly at the shrine of some deity local to the spot, or honored there with more than ordinary reverence. The Isthmian games in particular retained a special character. Instituted for an Ionian deity, whose rites the men of Elis refused to acknowledge, they failed to unite the whole Greek race. The Greek games, like the Schwing-feste and shooting-matches of Switzerland, served as recurring occasions of reunion and fellowship. Their influence in preserving a Panhellenic feeling was very marked. During the time of the feast, and before and after, for a sufficient number of days to allow of travellers journeying to and from Olympia and Delphi, hostilities were suspended throughout Nellas; safe-conduct was given through all states to pilgrims. One common feeling animated all the Greeks at these seasons: they met in rivalry, not of arms on the battle-field, but of personal prowess in the lists. And though the various families of the Hellenic stock were never united, yet their games gave them a common object, and tended to the diffusion of national ideas. (pp. 345-51)

[We] must not suppose that Pindar sang slavishly the praise of every bidder. He was never fulsome in his panegyric. He knew how to mingle eulogy with admonition. If his theme be the wealth of a tyrant like Hiero, he reminds him of the dangers of ambition and the crime of avarice. Arcesilaus of Cyrene is warned to remit his sentence of banishment in favor of a powerful exile. Victors, puffed up with the pride of their achievements, hear from him how variable is the life of man, how all men are mere creatures of a day. Handsome youths are admonished to beware of lawlessness and shun incontinence. Thus Pindar, while suiting his praises to the persons celebrated, always interweaves an appropriate precept of morality. There was nothing that he hated more than flattery and avarice, and grasping after higher honors than became his station. In him more than in any other poet were apparent the Greek virtues of ευκοσυια, σωφροσυνη, and all the moral and artistic qualities which were summed up in the motto μηδεν αγαν. Those who are curious to learn Pindar's opinions on these points may consult the following passages: ***Nem. viii.*** 32; id. vii. 65; ***Pyth. xi.*** 50; ***Isthm. vii.*** 40; id. v. 14; and, lastly, ***Pyth. x.*** 22, which contains this truly beautiful description of a thoroughly successful life, as imagined by a Greek:

> That man is happy and songworthy by the skilled, who, victorious by might of hand or vigor of foot, achieves the greatest prizes with daring and with strength; and who in his lifetime sees his son, while yet a boy, crowned happily with Pythian wreaths. The brazen heaven, it is true, is inaccessible to him; but whatsoever joys we race of mortals touch, he reaches to the farthest voyage.

With this we may compare the story of happy lives told by Crœsus to Solon, and the celebrated four lines of Simonides: "Health is best for a mortal man; next, beauty; thirdly, well-gotten wealth; fourthly, the pleasure of youth among friends."

Closely connected with Pindar's ethical beliefs were his religious notions, which were both peculiar and profound. Two things with regard to his theology deserve especial notice—its conscious criticism of existing legends, and its strong Pythagorean bias, both combined with true Hellenic orthodoxy in all essentials. One of the greatest difficulties in forming an exact estimate of the creed of a philosophical Greek intellect is to know how to value the admixture of scientific scepticism on the one hand, and of purer theism on the other. About Pindar's time the body of Hellenic mythology was being invaded by a double process of destructive and constructive criticism. Xenophanes, for example, very plainly denounced as absurd the anthropomorphic Pantheon made in the image of man, while he endeavored to substitute a cult of the One God, indivisible and incognizable. Plato still further developed the elements suggested by Xenophanes. But there was some inherent incapacity in the Greek intellect for arriving at monotheism by a process of rarefaction and purification. The destructive criticism which in Xenophanes, Pindar, and Plato had assailed the grosser myths, dwindled into unfruitful scepticism. The attempts at constructing a rational theosophy ended in metaphysics. Morality was studied as a separate branch of investigation, independent of destructive criticism and religious construction. Meanwhile the popular polytheism continued to flourish, though enfeebled, degenerate, and disconnected from the nobler impulses of poetry and art. In Pindar the process of decadence had not begun. He stood at the very highest point which it was possible for a religious Greek to reach—combining the æsthetically ennobling enthusiasm for the old Greek deities with so much critical activity as enabled him to reject the grosser myths, and with that moderate amount of theological mysticism which the unassisted intellect of the Greeks seemed capable of receiving without degeneracy into puerile superstition. The ***First Olympian*** ode contains the most decided passages in illustration of his critical independence of judgment:

> Impossible is it for me to call one of the blessed ones a glutton: I stand aloof: loss hath often overtaken evil speakers.

Again:

> Truly many things are wonderful; and it may be that in some cases fables dressed up with cunning fictions beyond the true account falsify the traditions of men. But beauty, which is the author of all delicious things for mortals, by giving to these myths acceptance, ofttimes makes even what is incredible to be credible: but succeeding time gives the most certain evidence of truth; and for a man to speak nobly of the gods is seemly; for so the blame is less.

These two passages suffice to prove how freely Pindar handled the myths, not indeed exposing them to the corrosive action of mere scepticism, but testing them by the higher standard of the healthy human conscience. When he refuses to believe that the immortals were cannibals and ate the limbs of Pelops, he is like a rationalist avowing his disbelief in the savage doctrine of eternal damnation. His doubt does not proceed from irreligion, but from faith in the immutable holiness of the gods, who set the ideal standard of human morality. What seems to him false in the myths he attributes to the accretions of ignorant opinion and vain fancy round the truth.

The mystical element of Pindar's creed, whether we call it Orphic or Pythagorean, is remarkable for a definite belief in the future life, including a system of rewards and punishments; for the assertion of the supreme tribunal of conscience, and, finally, for a reliance on rites of purification. The most splendid passage in which these opinions are expressed by Pindar is that portion of the ***Second Olympian*** in which he describes the torments of the wicked and the blessings of the just beyond the grave:

> Among the dead, sinful souls at once pay penalty, and the crimes done in this realm of Zeus are judged beneath the earth by one who gives sentence under dire necessity.
>
> But the good, enjoying perpetual sunlight equally by night and day, receive a life more free from woes than this of ours; they trouble not the earth with strength of hand, nor the water of the sea for scanty sustenance; but with the honored of the gods, all they who delighted in the keeping of their oath pass a tearless age: the others suffer woe on which no eye can bear to look. Those who have thrice endured on either side the grave to keep their spirits wholly free from crime, journey on the road of Zeus to the tower of Kronos: where round the islands blow breezes ocean-borne; and flowers of gold burn some on the land from radiant trees, and others the wave feeds; with necklaces whereof they twine their hands and brows, in the just decrees of Rhadamanthus, whom father Kronos has for a perpetual colleague, he who is spouse of Rhea throned above all gods.
>
> Peleus and Cadmus are numbered among these: and thither was Achilles brought by his mother when she swayed the heart of Zeus with prayer: he who slew Hector, the invincible firm pillar of Troy, and gave Cyenus to death and Eo's Æthiopian son.
> (pp. 355-60)

Passing to the consideration of Pindar purely as an artist, we may first examine the structure of his odes, and then illustrate the qualities of his poetry by reference to some of the more splendid proemia and descriptions. The task which lay before him when he undertook to celebrate a victory at one of the Greek games was this: Some rich man had won a race with his chariot and horses, or some strong man had conquered his competitors by activity or force of limb. Pindar had to praise the rich man for his wealth and liberality, the strong man for his endurance of training and personal courage or dexterity. In both cases the victor might be felicitated on his good-fortune—on the piece of luck which had befallen him; and if he were of comely person or illustrious blood, these also offered topics for congratulation. The three chief commonplaces of Pindar, therefore, are ολβοσ, αρετη, ευτυχια, wealth or prosperity, manliness or spirit, and blessings independent of both, god-given, not acquired. But it could not be that a great poet should ring the changes only on these three subjects, or content himself with describing the actual contest, which, probably, he had not witnessed. Consequently Pindar illustrates his odes with myths or stories bearing more or less closely on the circumstances of his hero. Sometimes he celebrates the victor's ancestry, as in the famous ***Sixth Olympian,*** in which the history of the Iamidæ is given; sometimes his city, as in the ***Seventh Olympian,*** where he describes the birthplace of Diagoras, the island Rhodes; sometimes he dwells upon an incident in the hero's life, as when in the ***Third Pythian*** the illness of Hiero suggests the legend of Asclepius and Cheiron; sometimes a recent event, like the eruption of Etna, alluded to in the first Pythian, gives color to his ode; sometimes, as in the case of the last Pythian, where the story of Medusa is narrated, the legendary matter is introduced to specialize the nature of the contest. The victory itself is hardly touched upon: the allusions to ολβοσ, αρετη, ευτυχια, though frequent and interwoven with the texture of the ode, are brief: the whole poetic fabric is so designed as to be appropriate to the occasion and yet independent of it. Therefore Pindar's odes have not perished with the memory of the events to which they owed their composition. (pp. 362-63)

The originality and splendor of Pindar are most noticeable in the openings of his odes—the proemia, as they are technically called. It would appear that he possessed an inexhaustible storehouse of radiant imagery, from which to draw new thoughts for the commencement of his poems. In this region, which most poets find but barren, he displayed the fullest vigor and fertility of fancy. Sometimes, but rarely, the opening is simple, as in the ***Second Olympian***: "Hymns that rule the lyre! what god, what hero, what man shall we make famous?" Or the ***Ninth Pythian***: "I wish to proclaim, by help of the deep-girdled Graces, brazen-shielded Telesicrates, Pythian victor," etc. Rather more complex are the following: ***Nem. iv.,*** "The joy of the feast is the best physician after toil; but songs, the wise daughters of the Muses, soothe the victor with their touch: warm water does not so refresh and supple weary limbs as praise attended by the lyre;" or again: ***Ol. xi.,*** "There is a time when men have greatest need of winds; there is when heaven's showers of rain, children of the cloud, are sorest sought for. But if a man achieves a victory with toil, then sweet-voiced hymns arise as the beginning of future fame," etc., etc. But soon we pass into a more gorgeous region. "As when with golden columns reared beneath the well-walled palace-porch we build a splendid hall, so will I build my song. At the beginning of the work we must make the portal radiant." Or again: "No carver of statues am I, to fashion figures stationary on their pedestal; but come, sweet song! on every argosy and skiff set forth from Ægina to proclaim that Pytheas, Lampon's son, by strength of might is victor in Nemean games, upon whose chin and cheek you see not yet the tender mother of the vine-flower, summer's bloom." Or again: "Hallowed bloom of youth, herald of Aphrodite's ambrosial pleasures, who, resting on the eyelids of maidens and of boys, bearest one aloft with gentle hands of violence, but another rudely!" (pp. 365-66)

Pindar compares his odes to arrows, to sun-soaring eagles, to flowers of the Muses, to wine in golden goblets, to water, to a shrine which no years will fret away. Another strange figure may be quoted from the ***Third Nemean*** (line 76): "I send to thee this honey mingled with white milk;

the dew of their mingling hangs around the bowl, a draught of song, flowing through the Æolian breath of flutes." It will be perceived that to what is called confusion of metaphors Pindar shows a lordly indifference. Swift and sudden lustre, the luminousness of a meteor, marks this monarch of lyric song. He grasps an image, gives it a form of bronze, irradiates it with the fire of flame or down-poured sunlight. (pp. 366-67)

After so much praise of Pindar's style, it must be confessed that he has faults. One of these is notoriously tumidity—an overblown exaggeration of phrase. For example, when he wants to express that he cannot enlarge on the fame of Ægina, but will relate as quickly as he can the achievements of Aristomenes which he has undertaken, he says: "But I am not at leisure to consecrate the whole long tale to the lyre and delicate voice, lest satiety should come and cause annoy; but that which is before my feet shall go at running speed—thy affair, my boy—the latest of the noble deeds made winged by means of my art." The imaginative force which enabled him to create epithets like Φιλαγλαοσ, παμπορφυροσ, and to put them exactly in their proper places, like blocks of gleaming alabaster or of glowing porphyry—for the architectural power over language is eminent in Pindar; the Titanic faculty of language which produced such phrases as ϵξ αδαμαντο κϵχαλκϵυται μϵλαιναν καρδιαν ψυχρα φλογι, did also betray him into expressions as pompous and frigid as these: ποικιλοφορμιγγοσ αοιζασ . . . σχοινοτϵνϵια τ αοιδα διθυραμβων. These, poured forth by Pindar in the insolence of prodigality, when imitated by inferior poets, produced that inflated manner of lyrical diction which Aristophanes ridicules in Kinesias. (pp. 368-69)

Pindar uses images like precious stones, setting them together in a mass, without caring to sort them, so long as they produce a gorgeous show. Apparent incoherences, involving difficulty to the reader, and producing a superficial effect of obscurity, constitute another class of his alleged faults—due partly to his allusive and elliptical style, partly to his sudden transitions, partly to the mixture of his images. Incapable of what is commonplace, too fiery to trudge, like Simonides, along the path of rhetorical development, infinitely more anxious to realize by audacity the thought that seizes him than to make it easy to his hearer, Pindar is obscure to all who are unwilling to assimilate their fancy to his own. La Harpe called the *Divine Comedy une amplification stupidement barbare:* what, if he had found occasion to speak the truth of his French mind, would he have said about the Odes of Pindar? Another difficulty, apart from these of verbal style and imagination, is derived from the fact that the mechanism of Pindar's poetry, carefully as it is planned, is no less carefully concealed. He seems to take delight in trying to solve the problem of how slight a suggestion can be made to introduce a lengthy narrative. The student is obliged to maintain his attention at the straining-point if an ode of Pindar's, even after patient analysis, is to present more than a mass of confused thoughts and images to his mind. But when he has caught the poet's drift, how delicate is the machinery, how beautiful is the art, which governs this most sensitive fabric of linked melodies! What the hearers made of these odes—the athletes for whom they were written, the handsome youths praised in them, the rich men at whose tables they were chanted—remains an impenetrable mystery. Had the Greek race perceptions infinitely finer than ours? Or did the classic harmonies of Pindar sweep over their souls, ruffling the surface merely, but leaving the deeps untouched, as the soliloquies of *Hamlet* or the profound philosophy of *Troilus and Cressida* must have been lost upon the groundlings of Elizabeth's days, who caught with eagerness at the queen's poisoned goblet or the by-play of Sir Pandarus? That is a problem we cannot solve. All we know for certain is, that even allowing for the currency of Pindar's language and for the familiarity of his audience with the circumstances under which his odes were composed, as well as with their mythological allusions, these poems must at all times have been more difficult to follow than Bach's fugue in G minor to a man who cannot play the organ. (pp. 369-71)

John Addington Symonds, "Pindar," in his Studies of the Greek Poets, Vol. I, *Harper & Brothers, Publishers, 1880, pp. 340-71.*

T. S. Eliot (essay date 1938)

[Perhaps the most influential poet and critic to write in the English language during the first half of the twentieth century, Eliot is closely identified with many tenets of the Modernist movement: experimentation, formal complexity, and artistic and intellectual eclecticism. He introduced a number of terms and concepts that strongly affected critical thought in his lifetime, upholding traditionalism, discipline, and the idea that poets must be conscious of the living tradition of literature in order to create works of artistic and spiritual validity. Following Eliot's midlife conversion to Anglicanism, much of his criticism evaluates literature on the basis of Christian values and standards. In the following excerpt, originally published in 1938, Eliot maintains that the Pindaric ode has not yet been "practised successfully in English."]

Poseidon riding a dolphin, with Triton, in a drawing by Adam Elsheimer (1578-1610).

Whether the Pindaric ode is in itself a form of verse unsuited to the English language is an idle speculation, because everything is impossible until some one has done it. We can only say that this is a form which no one has yet practised successfully in English. To have made something of it would have strained the powers of a Milton. No one with less mastery could succeed with it, and only poets of less mastery have attempted it. But of those who did attempt it, I claim that it was Cowley who practised it most successfully. To have practised an alien and unassimilated form of verse better than any one else may seem a negligible distinction; yet to assert that Cowley's odes are more interesting than those of Dryden, and much better than those of Gray and Collins, gives that distinction greater interest.

My familiarity with the Greek language has never been adequate to the appreciation of Pindar's odes in the original; and in translation they are very dull reading. I am therefore not in a position to affirm that those who profess to enjoy these odes are in reality mistaking their enjoyment of their own proficiency in Greek verse for enjoyment of poetry. But of English imitations, one may say that only a poet to whom sublimity came naturally, such as Milton, is qualified for such a task; and that to aim at sublimity and fail is one of the worst sins that a poet can commit. (p. 579)

T. S. Eliot, "A Note on Two Odes of Cowley," in Ben Jonson and the Cavalier Poets, *edited by Hugh Maclean, W. W. Norton & Company, Inc., 1974, pp. 578-84.*

Quintilian (96?) on Pindar's artistic stature:

Of the nine lyric poets Pindar is by far the greatest, in virtue of his inspired magnificence, the beauty of his thoughts and figures, the rich exuberance of his language and matter, and his rolling flood of eloquence—characteristics which, as Horace rightly held, make him inimitable.

Quintilian, quoted in Ancilla to Classical Reading, *by Moses Hadas, 1954.*

Gilbert Norwood (lecture date 1943-44)

[*Norwood was an American classical scholar whose books include* Greek Comedy *(1932) and* Pindar *(1945). In the following excerpt from a lecture collected in the latter work and originally delivered in 1943-44, he treats Pindar's views on the human condition, asserting that the poet's ideas "defy systematization."*]

All who are fascinated by the history of human thought and civilization examine with natural eagerness the doctrines expounded or implied by Greek poets, philosophers, orators, and historians; but Pindar, though a mighty poet, has here little importance. My aim is to prove this at least, in order to save others unneeded pains.

An adequate yet lucid abstract of Pindar's expressed views concerning the divine nature and government, human life, happiness, and death is not merely difficult to make, but impossible. The cause of this must be sought in the civilization, and in the particular phase of culture, wherein he grew and worked. The Athenian Age of Enlightenment had not yet dawned. Even the Ionian spirit of his own day was foreign to him: his great rival Simonides, for instance, showed much greater intellectual power and clarity of ethical expression. From the scientific thought of his own day he turned with dislike and contempt. Stobaeus reports that his phrase "they pluck wisdom's fruit while yet unripe" was directed against the students of nature. Pindar was as much behind the times in science as in politics: one can hardly believe that he lived and wrote a whole century later than both Solon and Thales. Yet one editor could write: "In every department of intellectual and aesthetic culture, mighty waves of progress kept rolling over Hellas in the first half of the fifth century B.C., communicating irresistible impulses to a man of Pindar's genius and temperament." That monstrously misleading sentence exemplifies our modern passion to "trace influences" and arrange genealogical trees of poetry. The ***Ninth Paean*** shows that Pindar knew no more than a savage about solar eclipses, though Thales had explained them. In another fragment he avers that the Nile-flood is caused by a statue six hundred feet high, moving its feet. He is so sure [in ***Olympian 3***] that the Pillars of Heracles—what we call the Straits of Gibraltar—mark the limit of western navigation that he uses them to typify the bounds impassable to human enterprise; yet his younger contemporary Herodotus knew of many who had sailed through them. We shall never appreciate Pindar if we think of him as of Goethe, who in his study at Weimar read everything, heard everything, that was passing in Europe and corresponded with, or was visited by, countless significant and attractive people, from Napoleon the First down to the latest budding poet or diplomatist. But even more momentous than ignorance about mere facts, or even about scientific method, was the lack of mental training, of conscious and definite intellectual discipline, which hampered all Greeks born before the Sophistic Age. He was unable to do what became easy enough two generations later: namely, to form concerning religion, sociology, ethics, and politics a body of ideas which, however mistaken or insufficient, was yet coherent and defensible. His mental state was such that we can hardly describe it, still less enter into it: we contemplate a man of poetic genius, glorious yet steadily controlled imagination, perfectly trained for his profession, who nevertheless did not know how to think, in the full sense of apprehending, marshalling, coördinating facts and beliefs about them.

To discuss Pindar's views in our own day is, then, to employ a language, ruled by logic and destined to the systematization of facts, concerning a man who was logical only by fits and starts; whose power to correlate truths or views was rudimentary and rarely applied; who, being destitute of the scientific temper, overlooked crude inconsistencies in the doctrines that he from time to time propounded. Homer, his predecessor, we never regard as a thinker at all; Euripides, forty years later than Pindar, was clearly a conscious and adroit philosopher; but here stands a poet in whose work constructive thought stirs indeed, yet only in embryo. Into the world of radiant myth a breath of intelligence has stolen: he feels dimly the eternal truth that man must understand life or perish, and seeks half instinctively to transform emotions into ideas. What are we to do with him, we who could not write a line of these odes but whom twenty-four centuries of mental experience have endowed with a skill, which he would have looked on as superhuman, in the manipulation of facts, fancies, theories, and their conglomerations?

The usual method has been somewhat ludicrous, recalling those agile Lilliputians who swarmed over the bound and recumbent body of Gulliver. We advance upon Pindar with brains full of logic, ethics, anthropology, and Heaven knows what, saying: "Let us draw up a report on the system of doctrine inherent in the productions of this remarkable stranger!" We work over him until we evolve an intelligible and coherent conspectus, which, however, the poems as they stand, if read with an open mind, invariably refute in whole or in part. Here we have to face the authority of Professor Werner Jaeger, the most recent scholar to offer a systematization, who in *Paideia* deals with whatever alleged aspects of Pindar seem relevant to his own subject: namely, Pindar as an educator, a description of him which I at least cannot accept. Jaeger discovers "a whole system of philosophy" in his remarks concerning ancestry and the changes of merit and fortune in the succeeding generations of noble families. What system? Pindar's remarks (apart from his poetic magnificence, which, though beyond praise, is quite another affair) are the baldest truisms, such as that in the ***Sixth Nemean*** (vv. 8–11), where Alcidamas brings glory to his family after a generation without fame, "like the fruitful ploughlands, which by turns now grant men copious livelihood from the plains, now again rest from bearing and gather strength." Jaeger's eloquent and striking discussion of the myths is no more convincing. Here is one typical passage. "His heroes are contemporary living and struggling men. He sets them in the mythical world . . . a world of ideal patterns, whose lustre beams over them and whose renown will as they strive exalt them to similar heights and arouse their best powers. That is what gives the use of myth in Pindar its special purport and value." Wilhelm Schmid also affirms this view that the myth is often presented so as to give Pindar's friends a pattern of conduct—"You have heard what Heracles did: imitate him." That is mere assumption without evidence, easy for even such admirable scholars to make, because we moderns know how we should set to work if (for instance) we wrote a lyric eulogizing some young clergyman and saw fit to adorn our poem with the story of St. Paul and the snake at Malta. We should say "Imitate St. Paul"; certainly not "St. Paul reminds me of you." But this latter corresponds to Pindar's normal intention, though (to be sure) he expresses it less crudely. For we must remember not only his usual attitude towards success in the Games, but also the fact that, save in one passage alone, he drops not a hint of this notion about patterns found in the heroic age; and—perhaps even more notably—the ***Sixth Pythian*** says, in so many words, that the hero of myth, Antilochus, resembles the athlete whom Pindar is now extolling. In any case, ethical system there is none to see, nor indeed does Jaeger here claim to find any, only a reason for a single element in Pindar's work. He is far more cautious and balanced than a good number of earlier scholars whose tortured arguments, wanton assumptions, and astounding results compose a dismal museum of sterile and repellent monsters. We are told that such absurdities as the following are Pindar's views. "Man is to conquer his fate." If he does, it cannot be fate: in any case, Pindar says nothing even faintly like this. "It is a god who bestows virtue, and a god *who takes it away.*" This assertion of something more diabolical than any diabolism otherwise known to me is made by its inventor the basis of his doctrine that Pindar has kinship with—of all people on earth—Plato! "Power is identical with justice." That Pindar held no such frantic view is proved by I know not how many passages. "Apollo teaches the philosophy of the One and the Many." Pindar, of course, knew no more about this doctrine than he knew about the binomial theorem; and Apollo, I conceive, was in like case.

These conclusions, and others only less surprising, would of themselves raise suspicion that Pindar's ideas defy systematization; and unprejudiced scrutiny of his writings will prove its impossibility. No specific attack upon any one doctrine or statement of Pindar's is here intended. Some, to be sure, will be dismayed by his worship of success, still more by his gibes at those who fail—though here I must interpolate that, whatever he writes concerning the Games, he bestows majestic and poignant eulogies upon men who went down to heroic defeat in battle. The epinician odes, despite notable exceptions, undoubtedly leave us, on the whole, with a superficial and selfish conception of the good life. But, again, such a tone may be partly excused by the very nature of an epinician ode and by a wish to delight the patron. In any case, my intention is not to display the superiority of your principles or mine to Pindar's, not to dwell on his omission to define elementary moral ideas such as justice, or the extreme paucity of his specific rules; but to show that he had no system at all.

Let us drive straight at the heart of this, and point to his most fatal irrationality—an ambiguous use of the word *areta.* There are, perhaps in all languages, words that sum up root-ideas of the race which uses them, and are accordingly the translator's despair; *areta* is one of these. It can best be translated "excellence," if we insist on one word. In philosophers it usually means "virtue"; in non-philosophic writers it may be moral excellence or any other, normally with an implication of beneficent potency. But we may spare ourselves travail over this elusive word, which in Pindar has only by fits any moral content. The point is that he uses it both of excellence and of the success won thereby. Here are two examples on each side. In ***Pythian I*** 94 "the kindly *areta* of Croesus meets not death"; in ***Olympian VI*** 9 ff., "*aretae* untried by peril receive honour neither among men nor in hollow ships"—there is the "excellence" meaning. In ***Olympian VII*** 89, "a man who has won *areta* by boxing"; in ***Nemean V*** 52: "to win a double *areta* by victory in boxing and in the *pancration*"—there is the "success" meaning. A writer who uses the same word for merit and for success puts himself hopelessly out of court as an exponent of ethics.

And how, according to Pindar, does a man succeed? Here we stand at the very centre of Pindar's . . . the only word

I can find is "brooding"—not thought or emotion or faith, but consciousness that man lives amid forces greater than he. Nothing could be more familiar than that sense: Homer has it, centuries before Pindar, and so has everyone else who can be called human. But Pindar uses language suggesting that he holds some definite answer to our question, language that apparently deceives the poet himself and has certainly deceived many students. In truth, his brooding (as I called it) and his statements are sadly muddled; let me offer the clearest description of this tangle which I have been able to produce.

He often names three factors as needed for success, though he never mentions all three as combined. One is *phua,* literally "nature"; in Pindar it means "good innate quality," and embraces both what we call "virtue" and what we call "talent" or "natural aptitude," whether of mind or of body. Another factor of success is personal effort. Another is Heaven's grace—God causes us to win. What relation exists between these three? The connexion between *phua* and effort seems plain enough: they are the material and the use thereof, like the stones and the mason's labour which together produce a wall. What of Heaven's favour? We never hear in so many words that if it is added to the other two factors we must succeed, only that if it is not added we cannot succeed. Nevertheless we are compelled to assume the former proposition; for, if a man having all three elements does not necessarily succeed, it is impossible to tell what agency can thwart Heaven and make him fail, impossible to understand how anyone ever succeeds. Now: suppose two men, both possessing *phua,* both using effort, wrestle for a prize. A wins; and this, by the rule just stated, proves that A has God's grace (otherwise he would have lost), and that B has not God's grace (otherwise he would have won). Thus we behold two men, equal in other respects, on one of whom grace is bestowed, to the other of whom grace is denied. For the grant or refusal of this blessing no reason is, on the premises, conceivable: that is, we know nothing about the divine favour except that it shows itself in the result. Therefore "divine favour" is merely a lofty periphrasis for "success": the man does in fact win and we therefore assume that he must have God's grace. And what we have said about the wrestling-match is true of more important and lengthier enterprises—of what we call success in life. His frequent phrase τυχα θεων—significantly hard to translate: "divine fortune" seems best—is then merely a pious flourish resulting not from theology or any other species of thought. It says nothing whatever about either God or man, being an empty phrase, useless except to prevent boastfulness in those who do not see through it.

Next, what of *phua?* We can know nothing about its quality, its quantity, even its existence, until it reveals itself in action. For instance, we must not infer it from ancestry, for the poet reminds us more than once that a man with no particular *phua* may spring from heroic stock; though, it is important to remark, if on the other hand he does possess *phua,* he derives it from noble ancestors. So we observe a person succeeding after effort and for that reason only we assume his *phua,* which thus appears as the moral analogue of "divine fortune," and is brought in because of Pindar's preoccupation with ancestry, just as Heaven's grace was brought in by his instinctive piety. Once more, the whole position crumbles to this, that some succeed while others fail! Still at a loss to understand whereon success according to Pindar is based, we turn to the third factor, effort; and learn that one may put forth vigorous effort all to no purpose, because *phua* or divine grace, or both, are lacking. In the ***Third Nemean*** (40 ff.) he thus delivers himself: "Through inborn glory a man hath mighty weight; but whoso hath acquired only instruction, dim light is his: now to this, now to that, his spirit turneth, never doth he come forth with decisive step, but to no purpose his heart tasteth of enterprises without number." There is effort, and there its outcome, if inherited excellence of spirit does not aid.

In the fascinating and varied legends of Greece Pindar found one example of failure which profoundly impressed his heart and imagination. Ajax was not only conspicuous among the heroes who fought at Troy, but also a member of that family which Pindar delighted to eulogize beyond all others. Yet his end was dreadful: nay, ignominious. After the death of Achilles, he and Odysseus both laid claim to the weapons of their comrade, as being next to him in desert. The Greek army adjudged them to Odysseus, and Ajax in bitter disappointment slew himself. Why this collapse of so great glory? Ajax had *phua,* his efforts were long-continued and heroic. Does Pindar, then, allege that he lacked the favour of Heaven? No—if only because such an explanation would have been resented by the poet's friends and patrons. In this particular case, forgetting all the fancies which we have sought in vain to organize, he suddenly remembers a solution which would apply in endless other instances of failure: the power wielded by a dishonest opponent; for Odysseus, he writes, gained the award by his cajoling eloquence. So the base after all do often prosper—only for a time, it is true; but it cannot be said that the good have any advantage over them here, for he repeatedly asserts that no mortal enjoys lasting good fortune.

At the outset we noted that in studying Pindar, perhaps even more than in studying any other Greek of the great ages, it is misleading to mark off separate departments such as religion or politics. True; but you and I are modern people, for whom clearness of head is, if not an achievement, at least an aim. Therefore I cannot avoid saying at this point: "Let us next consider the gods—their nature, conduct, and place in the Universe, their dealings with man now and hereafter." In Pindar's mind these topics are interwoven; and I shall be forced to repeat some matters already discussed. Moreover, his statements on religion and the future of the soul, though more intelligible than those on ethics, contradict one another even more sharply.

Nevertheless, we may open with a fact simple as well as interesting. However we judge Pindar's doctrinal pronouncements, we can all see that he was a man of strong and genuine religious *mood,* of piety. It has been admirably said that "What matters is the quality of his concern with religion and behaviour. If his disapproval seems capricious or his remedies inadequate, it is because he was scarcely concerned with a system of life, whether in theory or in practice." His devotion to Delphi and its god was one of the two profoundest and most enduring passions of his life. Beside his own house he built a chapel dedicated to the Mother of the Gods and to Pan. Croiset [A. Croiset in his *La Poesie de Pindare,* 1880] has noted that many details told of the gods by Homer are quite alien to Pindar in spirit: we cannot (for example) imagine his writing of Hephaestus' limp. Aeschylus himself, though endowed with immensely more spiritual depth, was no readier to revise current myths in the name of edification. The difference between them here is that, whereas Aeschylus was a moral and intellectual reformer of theology, Pindar's imagination was fired by the divine or heroic figures that blazed in the verse of Homer, Hesiod, and Stesichorus; and he alters legend for the sake of το καλον, the noble and lovely, to keep the adored radiance undimmed. In the ***First Olympian*** he proclaims his rejection of a traditional story as a slander upon the gods, offering a new version; and that is only the most celebrated instance. Theoretically inconsistent with this, but in temper appropriate, is the rebuke: "What hopest thou of wisdom, wherein but little, surely, one man availeth beyond another? Thou shalt find no way to search out the purposes of Heaven by human mind, that was born of a mortal mother." Nevertheless, gods and men are akin, as we learn in the opening lines of the ***Sixth Nemean.*** "One is the race of men, one the race of gods, and from one mother we both draw breath. Yet an utter diversity of power sundereth us, so that one race is naught, while for the other Heaven's bronze abode endureth unshaken everlastingly. But none the less we draw near in some measure to the immortals by greatness of mind or form, although we know not the course that fate hath ordained we should run, whether in the day or in the hours of night." Not only has he much to say concerning piety and worship: he thrills also to the gaiety and excitement attending upon religious celebrations. Dionysius of Halicarnassus has preserved for us the opening of a dithyramb which summons the gods to holy revels. Here is Rhys Roberts' translation of the first lines:

> Shed o'er our choir, Olympian Dominations,
> The glory of your grace,
> O ye who hallow with your visitations
> The curious-carven place,
> The heart of Athens, steaming with oblations,
> Wide-thronged with many a face.
> Come, take your due of garlands violet-woven,
> Of songs that burst forth when the buds are cloven.

Possibly the most extraordinary of Pindar's works is another dithyramb, or rather, a tattered portion thereof, which after a vigorous remark on an early and, as he says, "spurious" pronunciation of the letter S, leaps at once to a wild and (to tell the truth) incredible picture of a carnival in Heaven itself. Everyone seems to be there, even the Naiads and Artemis, all celebrating a Dionysiac festival! Another scene in Heaven we know, unfortunately, by report alone. Aristides the rhetorician writes that, according to Pindar, when Zeus, at his own wedding, asked the gods if they had any boon to ask, they begged him to create certain gods who should glorify in word and music his mighty achievements and all the frame of his creation. That reads like a prophecy of the archangels' song wherewith Goethe opens his *Faust.*

What is the relation between these heavenly powers and the Universe? Let us first speak of the "present world," discussing later the soul's destiny. Pindar asserts that man's life depends on divine government; but this doctrine is so familiar to us that we must here be especially on our guard against hasty assumptions and note precisely what it is that he says.

Dominion lies in the hands of a personal authority, entitled "God" (θεοσ), or "gods" (θεοι), or, by the traditional name, Zeus, King of Heaven. A passage (vv. 49 ff.) in the ***Second Pythian*** proclaims his majesty and unchallengeable power, in language that recalls the Old Testament. "The Lord accomplisheth every purpose according to his desire. He overtaketh even the eagle upon the wing and passeth by the dolphin amid the waters. He hath bowed down the man of high stomach and upon another he bestoweth glory that waxeth not old." But we seldom read of the material Universe in this connexion, never of any jurisdiction over individual deities. We hear, in fact, three things only about the divine rule of our present life. First, as we noted earlier, success and happiness depend upon God's favour; and this (we saw), as presented by Pindar, means nothing. Second, our life is a system, not a chaos; but the evidence justifying attribution of this doctrine to Pindar is meagre and disputable. A passage (vv. 25 ff.) in the ***Eighth Olympian*** implies, perhaps, that Aegina's justice reflects Heaven's justice; and the close of the ***Second Pythian*** points, in my view, to a *régime* that embraces mankind. Third, one sole passage declares plainly that in this life God rewards righteousness as such, purely as a matter of principle and with no reference at all to the personal comfort or interests of an individual deity. That memorable pronouncement occurs in the ***Fifth Nemean*** (vv. 32 ff.), where Peleus rejected Hippolyta because (we are told) he dreaded the anger of Zeus if he violated the laws of hospitality, and the god, "noting it well," granted him the divine Thetis as his bride. Elsewhere, the reason given for kindnesses conferred by individual gods upon men—such reason, however, being seldom offered—is never righteousness. The man or woman has kinship with the god, or has granted him some boon: hospitality is mentioned, and what may be termed love.

Pindar thus stands far below his Athenian contemporary Aeschylus in theological profundity, power, and clearness. Nevertheless, a passage in his latest-written ode shows him groping towards the concept of a universe morally governed. The first three stanzas of the ***Eighth Pythian*** set us in presence of a religious apprehension that begins to feel its way past the traditional names and figures of the Greek pantheon.

> Daughter of Justice, gracious Tranquillity, whereby cities come to greatness, thou that holdest the master-keys of war, accept the glory that Aristomenes hath won by victory at Pytho. For thou knowest how, at the due moment, to perform or to receive acts of gentleness. But whenever one thrusts merciless rancour upon his heart, thou sternly confrontest the might of thine enemies, and their insolence falleth into

> the deep. And he, even Porphyrion, knew not that it was thou whom he unrighteously assailed; but that profit is best which a man taketh from the house of one who consenteth thereto. Even the proud their own violence throweth down at the last. Typhos, the hundred-headed Cilician, escaped it not, nor the king of Giants: they were quelled by the thunderbolt and by the arrows of Apollo.

Pindar, here touched by the belief, vivid throughout Aeschylus' tragedies, that the Universe is governed, and governed by a moral Power, conceives this Power as some kind of person, as possessing (that is) emotions and will in addition to a rule or standard of government: hence the personification of Tranquillity and the surprising description of her nature. The history of Greek religion offers few more exciting moments than this, if we observe precisely how far Pindar moved towards creating, like Aeschylus, a new theology. Zeus and Apollo here, and here only, in his works, are subsidiary to this new goddess Hesychia, or Tranquillity—to this extent, that, whereas she is said to overthrow *hubris* or Insolence, in general, they overthrow its exponents, the giants Porphyrion and Typhos. She is, quite exactly, a "spirit," whereof Zeus and Apollo are representative. But the poet never says so much: only if we study his language and state with modern precision what he suggests, do we arrive at so striking a dogma; and we are especially to mark that he refuses, almost in so many words, to accept that dogma firmly, for though he mentions Apollo by name, he will not mention Zeus, but only his weapon—"they were quelled by the thunderbolt and by Apollo's shafts." This passage, then, permits us an exact conception of the difference between Pindar and Aeschylus in theological boldness and mental clarity.

But all this, the momentous and engaging outcome of an instinctive piety and a sense of righteousness irrational (however strong), meets repeated contradiction when the poet deals with legends or popular doctrine which irrational instinct, again, induces him to accept. Gods as individuals perform, without censure from him, actions which he condemns in men. Whereas murder is deplored even when committed by his favourite Aeginetans, Apollo causes the death of Coronis' innocent neighbours without evoking a censorious word; but the god suddenly becomes very tender of the guiltless when his own unborn child is threatened in the course of the same affair (***Pyth. III*** 36 ff.). Zeus intervenes in the ***Tenth Nemean*** with what we should call shameless injustice. What does Pindar call it? He first broadly hints that Castor and Polydeuces (whom Zeus aided) were in the wrong, but after the god has thrown omnipotence into the scale we find only this comment: "whoso striveth with his betters will regret the meeting." In the ***First Nemean,*** Hera seeks to destroy the baby Heracles, and comment there is none. As for sexual morality, it cannot in fact be said that the standard set for mankind is higher than the standard applied to gods, because the latter does not exist. Hippolyta receives censure for her conduct toward Peleus (***Nem. V*** 52 ff.), Coronis for her amour with Ischys (***Pyth. III*** 11 ff.), Clytaemnestra for the murder of her husband which sprang from adultery (***Pyth. XI*** 17 ff.); but gods indulge themselves without stint or blame, the chief instance being Zeus' amour with Alcmena, a uniquely atrocious affair (as we should say) on which Pindar thrice dwells fondly, in one place citing it among the glories of Theban history. Gods, as individuals, never right any wrongs that are not directed against themselves: they stand for nothing at all except their own comfort, rank, and privileges, exactly like the Dorian nobles eulogized by Pindar, who were not leaders in any spiritual or moral sense. Here I cannot refrain from pausing to remark once more how woefully scholars have been led astray by their insistence on reading into him moral or theological ideas familiar elsewhere. Coppola [G. Coppola in his *Introduzione a Pindaro,* 1931] describes Ixion, Coronis, Asclepius, and Tantalus as examples not only "of the truth" (whatever that may mean) but also "of God's awful justice," although not a syllable of this can be found in Pindar, who on the contrary tells us at each incident, save perhaps in the case of Asclepius, that the wrongdoer had annoyed the particular deity by encroaching on his privileges.

By one legend Pindar is confessedly disconcerted: for a moment he realizes the mental and moral chaos which we are studying. One of Heracles' labours was to steal the herd of Geryon, a giant dwelling in Spain, and drive it back, undiminished, to his taskmaster in Greece. Two fragments deal with this story. One is quoted in a passage of Plato's *Gorgias,* where Callicles uses it to prove the right of the strong over the weak: the first phrase was quoted more often in antiquity than any other that Pindar wrote. To this we should join another fragment, which (as the metre shows) belongs to another poem; but that for our purpose matters nothing. The whole compound, then, goes something like this. "Custom, the king of all mortals and immortals, leadeth on the extreme of violence with a high hand, justifying it. This I gather from the deeds of Heracles; for to the giant-built portal of Eurystheus he drove the kine of Geryon, taking them without prayer or price. . . . Thee, O Geryon, I praise compared with him; howbeit, let me keep utter silence concerning what Zeus doth not prefer." Here theological and moral bankruptcy finds plain avowal. Heracles being a son of Zeus, whatever he does must be called just though we know it is unjust.

In that age there was a strong belief in the spite, the φθονοσ, of Heaven. This should be distinguished from the personal annoyance felt, and revenge exacted, by a specific deity for a specific offence, as when Athena, vexed by the sauciness of Arachne, who claimed to spin better than the goddess, transformed the girl into a spider. No: the *phthonos* doctrine was even more discouraging: divine power, "Heaven" as we say, "the god" as Greeks often said, punishes and destroys notable eminence or success among mankind, not because of any sin or foolishness, but automatically. This view is trenchantly set forth by the Persian Artabanus in Heodotus. "Do you observe that God blasts exalted creatures and does not suffer them to be shown forth, but what is petty does not gall him? And that it is always upon the largest buildings and the tallest trees that he hurls his thunderbolts? God is wont to curtail all eminence . . . for he suffers no other save himself to be proud." Now, Pindar twice endorses this belief, once in his earliest poem, the ***Tenth Pythian*** (vv. 20 f.), written when he was twenty years old, the other in the ***Seventh***

Isthmian (vv. 30 ff.), when he had passed sixty. But we must not overemphasize these two widely sundered utterances. Each is merely a brief prayer: "These people have high fortune: may Heaven's spite not pounce upon them." Pindar is but quoting, unwisely as we may think, a popular belief.

Concerning the forces that govern human life, only one further remark seems needed. Again and again he says or implies that whatever happens to man is due to an impersonal State of Things named *moira* or *potmos* or *tyche,* regarded sometimes as a definite agency (whether identified or not with Heaven's will), sometimes as a brief rendering of the fact that the future is hidden. The first idea we may call Fate, the second the Inscrutable. Let us see examples. First, the definite agency identified with Heaven's will: "they came, not without the gods, but some *moira* led them" (***Pyth. V*** 76). Second, the definite agency not identified with Heaven's will: "Whatever excellence Lord *potmos* has granted me, the course of time will bring to fruition" (***Nem. IV*** 42). Third, the inscrutable: in the ***Eighth Isthmian*** (v. 36) destiny, το πεπρωμενον, actually defeats the wishes of gods—Zeus and Poseidon; in the ***Sixth Paean*** we read that Troy was bound to fall, and that "Zeus dared not cancel fate." Pindar, in fact, imbibed from popular superstition and talk the virus of that most dangerous and common error, to sum up a collection of facts under a proper name and then suppose that mention of the name accounts for the facts thus summarized. The most familiar example is Fortune, whose immense vogue stands high among the achievements of stupidity. Though nothing more than a convenient name for the fact that we do not know what is to happen, it has been elevated by countless writers into an authentic Person *with a power over human life.* Many, including Pindar, though they have not always definitely personified the unknown future, have yet accepted the error for which the personification stands, namely, that Fortune, Destiny, Doom, Chance are separate from events and have power over them. Again and again in the odes we come upon this night of the intelligence. The ***Second Olympian*** proclaims (vv. 35 ff.) that Moira *brings* joy blent with sorrow: the absurd distinction, between what befalls us and the quasi-deification of what befalls us, is complete and emphatic. Apart from certain virtues of language, the sentence has less than no value: it conveys nothing beyond the familiar tidings that prosperity, is not permanent, that sooner or later things change; and its verbal elaboration sets up a pernicious semblance of knowledge. The ***First Isthmian,*** after telling us that Asopodorus was wrecked on the boundless main, proceeds: "but now again his natal star hath set his feet in the way of his old prosperity." A moment's thought about this "natal star" will dissolve it like vapour. We are simply not told *how* Asopodorus regained his original prosperity: Pindar infers that the man was "born lucky." In ***Pythian XII*** 30, "the fateful is beyond shunning" must be thought inferior even to *che sarà sarà,* because the pretentious wording may persuade the unwary that something has been said.

Concerning the soul and its destiny Pindar has left us passages that are among the most beautiful and impressive that he, or indeed any other pagan, ever wrote. A little while ago we heard verses from the ***Sixth Nemean*** where to men is attributed kinship with the gods. That idea receives more vigorous expression in this fragment of a dirge: "The body of all men is subject unto o'ermastering death; but the wraith of him that lived endureth yet alive, for that alone cometh from the gods. It sleepeth while the limbs are active; but while we sleep it showeth in many dreams the oncoming judgment of bliss and woe." The soul's immortality had long been a familiar doctrine, but Pindar was the first to explain it by a divine origin. Of the judgment after death which those last words foreshadow, an august picture is given by the ***Second Olympian,*** where for the first time in European literature we hear the tremendous doctrine that reward and punishment for the deeds of earthly life are meted out in another, on a principle moral and moral only.

> Wicked spirits of the dead forthwith pay here the penalty, and one below the earth judgeth sins done in this realm of Zeus, delivering the account with hostile rigour. But the righteous, alike in the night-watches and by day, possess the sun for ever, receiving a life that hath less trouble. They vex not earth with the strength of their hands, or the sea-waters, for an empty livelihood: nay, those who rejoiced in keeping their oath pass a tearless life beside honoured gods; the others bear a load of suffering whereon the eye dwelleth not. All who have endured, for three sojourns on either side, to keep their souls utterly from injustice, traverse the highway of Zeus to Cronos' tower. There ocean-breezes are wafted round the island of the blessèd; and golden flowers blaze, some on land from shining trees, and others the water nourisheth, with garlands whereof they entwine hands and brows amid the just counsels of Rhadamanthys, whom the mighty Father keepeth as a ready helper seated beside his throne.

Another fragment from the dirges also depicts the blessed.

> Upon them below the earth shineth the sun's power, while with us is night. In meadows of scarlet roses lie their city's outskirts, shaded by frankincense, heavy with golden fruits. Some take their pleasure in horses and bodily feats, some in chess-play, some in the harp, and among them perfect bliss gloweth ever in flower. Fragrance is spread over that delightful region everlastingly as they mingle all kinds of incense upon the altars of the gods amid flame that shineth afar.

Into the details of Pindar's eschatology this is not the place to enter, especially as in a later lecture we shall return to the ***Second Olympian*** and the cycle of lives. These and other passages are based upon doctrines taught by the religion, or religions, of "mystery," as it was called—a revealed religion, a personal way of life, distinct from the state-cults which appear far more frequently in Greek literature. It is from a Father of the Church, Clement of Alexandria, that we know Pindar's words concerning the blessedness of initiation into the mysteries: "Happy is he who hath seen them before he goeth below the earth! He knoweth the end of life; he knoweth its god-sent beginning."

But, whether the reason for these visions of eternity is or is not a momentary assumption of doctrines favoured by the patron for whom he writes, we must recognize that elsewhere he strangely forgets this awful radiance which beams upon his page from the confines of the Universe. In another mood he proclaims that the only reward after death for righteousness is fame. The ***Tenth Olympian*** asserts that, if a man has wrought fair deeds but dies without the glory conferred by song, his effort is empty and the joy that he has gained lasts but a fleeting moment. Our condition beyond the grave is shadowy and negative: nothing happens to us except that our "dim mind" receives news of honour won by our descendants, as he says concerning Cyrene's buried kings. We remember those poignant words in the ***Eighth Pythian***: "Creatures of a day, what are we? What are we not? The dream of a shadow, such is Man. But when God bestoweth radiance, then a glory resteth upon us, and days of pleasantness." All we may hope is a splendid hour. The ***Eleventh Nemean*** (13 ff.) gives yet gloomier warning: "If a man hath prosperity and surpasseth another in beauty and showeth forth his might by gaining the prize of contests, let him remember that he arrayeth himself in mortal limbs and shall at the end of all assume a garment of earth."

My ungrateful and invidious task, of exhibiting a great poet's incoherence and irrationality in theological and moral doctrine, can now be closed, by citation of two notable passages. They show his thought just as it unfolds and allow us to surprise him (as it were) in the act of failing to disentangle ideas. We have already noted the story of Peleus in the ***Fifth Nemean.*** There Pindar is beyond reproach: with no fumbling he tells us that Peleus avoided adultery because he feared God's anger, and that God because of this rewarded him. But examine the story as told in the ***Eighth Isthmian.*** Peleus belongs to the Aeacids, splendid warriors who are also "chaste and discreet of heart" (v. 28). "These things the blessèd gods also remembered in their council" . . . and so Thetis was given to Peleus as "most pious" (v. 44). Thus far, the Isthmian agrees with the Nemean; but here the whole matter springs from personal desires of Zeus and Poseidon, each wishing to marry Thetis. Had there been no domestic trouble in Heaven, Peleus and his virtue would never have been thought of. Here, then, is to be discerned a blend of the moral-government idea with a conception of deities no less absorbed than men in their personal concerns.

Another instance of such imperfect development can be found in the ***Fourth Pythian*** (90 ff.), where, indeed, suspicion may arise that the language is purposely ambiguous. "The speedy arrow of Artemis hunted down Tityos, so that one should set his desire on embracing love which lieth within his power." That is hard to translate fairly, because it contains a rather pleasant but also rather baffling manipulation—shall we say juggling?—of idiom. It can be, and on the face of it surely is, one more report of divine action prompted only by personal reasons, not by a zeal for morals in general. Most of Pindar's audience would find nothing more than the sense: "Artemis slew him to thwart and punish his lustful attempt." Such use of a purpose-clause attached to mention of punishment can be paralleled easily: they correspond to our colloquial threat: "I'll teach you to"—do something already done, which we threaten to punish. Nevertheless, Pindar does say "one," which, though in Greek often used with allusion only to the particular person concerned, admits the possibility of taking the clause in a non-rhetorical sense; that is, as a real purpose-clause, meaning that the goddess slew Tityos so as to provide a moral lesson for all mankind. We must not dogmatically assert that Pindar meant only one of these two things: here again is confusion of two ideas, a deity's private revenge and a deity's championship of righteousness.

Quo semel est imbuta recens . . . The most alert and original thinker never frees himself from all the unreason, all the inconsistencies, cherished in early years: some dogmas remain unchallenged because unconscious; and Pindar combined with poetic genius a capacity to retain prepossessions, despite all shocks and all evidence, which would have made even Samuel Johnson shake his head. We are not to wish him otherwise, for such things add pungency to his work.

Of sociology and politics it is even truer than of religion and ethics that Pindar's views—vigorous though not profound—cannot be discussed under the two heads separately without a frigid and misleading schematization. The two subjects must, of course, merge in any case; for him, they so merge as to form practically one. You will recall the ***Fourth Pythian,*** an ode written to persuade King Arcesilas of Cyrene that he should permit an exiled noble to return home. In the final stanzas, social and political ideas are inextricably mingled: a state shaken by discord, good-fellowship, slander, last-ditch politicians, opportunism, drinking-parties, music, political quietism. That is but the strongest evidence of a spirit which appears repeatedly: we must, then, follow Pindar's cast of mind. Fortunately we shall meet here rarely or never the self-contradiction that baffles us in our study of his religion and ethics.

He shared without misgiving the interests and standards of those kings, despots, and land-owning nobles for whom almost exclusively his odes were composed, whereas the democratic city of Athens claims but two brief and undistinguished items in this collection. Pindar's loyalty, both instinctive and conscious, clung to an order that was losing ground in the life of Greece: he loved the old pieties and traditions of quiet rural folk, oligarchical in their government, who found in military and athletic distinction enough to gratify ambition or pride. Here certain misunderstandings may easily arise, which it is important to dissipate. First, it may be objected that, since we possess little save his epinicians, we cannot expect to gain a full view of his interests: taking in hand to celebrate a boxer's or a wrestler's or a charioteer's success, he extols prize-winning more loudly than he might in his paeans, dirges, or dithyrambs; when his patron commands great wealth and influence, it need mean little if he dilates on those advantages with frequency and rapture. Second, it may with even greater cogency be remarked that his other works, fragmentary as they now are, present another picture. In addition to the religious fragments already noted, and the tender play of emotion, more frequent in these half-lost poems than in the epinician odes, who can forget the noble praise of that democracy which led Greece in its battles for liberty? At Artemisium, he says, "the sons of the Athenians laid the glorious foundation-stone of freedom"; and the most celebrated fragment of all salutes her thus: "O glistening city, violet-crowned, dear to song, bulwark of Hellas, famous Athens, haunted by divine presences!" The conclusion from all this lies near to hand, that he not only did his best (as was inevitable and proper) to sympathize with those for whom he wrote, but also deliberately feigned unquestioning enthusiasm for their prejudices. A good deal was said about this in the first lecture; and no sincere critic can fail to set beside the fragment about Geryon and convention the notably outspoken advice to a youth, that he must imitate—as we should put it—the chameleon: "My son, with whatever city thou consortest, let thy mind resemble the skin of the sea-beast on its rock: cheerfully accepting circumstance, let thy thought alter as occasion bids." All this has truth and importance; nevertheless we shall find it easy to learn whereon Pindar's heart is really set if we read him with an open mind, allowing his spirit to work upon us, and above all if we note advice or comment which, being on the face of it irrelevant, must reveal his true mind, as in the great passage of the ***First Pythian*** where he urges Hiero to grant his newly founded city a Dorian constitution; and the enthusiasm of his earliest ode for "worthy governments wielded by the high-born, generation after generation." It cannot be gainsaid that far the most pervasive and important of his social and political interests is devotion to the ideals and method of life followed by that old nobility to which he himself belonged. He proclaims the divine right of aristocracy.

Pindar's beliefs are based, here as elsewhere, not upon coördinated principles, but upon what is in fact done, or traditionally stated to have been done, by people whom, because of his temperament, upbringing, and personal concerns, he happens to admire. Though ever insistent that his friends' wealth and power be rightly used, he shows no inclination to discuss the methods by which they were acquired; though Herodotus reports that the great Aeginetan fortunes were made by swindling the helots who pilfered and sold what they could of the immense loot gained by the victory over Persia at Plataea. He is prone to judge the fruit by the tree. Between the gods and the nobles of his own day he observes differences great, indeed, but less than they have ever been in the view of any other civilized man. That grave and stately ode, the ***Sixth Nemean,*** where Achilles and Memnon move closer to us than the sturdy athletes not long dead, begins (you will remember) in austere grandeur with a proclamation that gods and men are one race, drawing the breath of life from the same mother. Despite the vast superiority of the gods in power, despite their immortality, Pindar discerns an unbroken, though steeply descending, line of existence and glory that stretches from Zeus or Poseidon to the Aeginetan victor of yesterday: "as if (says Pater) the actual roads on which men walk, went up and on, into a visible wonderland." Why not, if his friends are literally god-descended? To grasp this unfamiliar thought, we need but try to imagine Aeschylus relating, as Pindar relates, that Heracles faced three confederate deities in combat. Assuredly he thought a youth, beautiful, well-born, and bathed in glory won at the Games, comparable with Hector or Heracles and so (at however great a distance) with Apollo. That may explain why he consistently omits the, to us, obvious admonition that the youth should take Heracles as his model: he belongs by right of birth to that shining brotherhood. Had we all kept these ideas in mind, less surprise would have been aroused by the ***Sixth Pythian,*** where a lad who showed loyalty to his father in some matter of charioteering is compared to Antilochus, who before Troy laid down his life in defence of his father Nestor.

How wide a gulf yawns here between Pindar and Homer, the men of whose day are utterly outshone by the heroes that besieged windy Troy! When Hector advances to burst open the gates of the Greek camp, he snatches up a boulder "which not two men, the best in the village, could easily have heaved up onto their waggon from the ground—such men as live now: but he tossed it lightly single-handed." Pindar portrays the unity of glorious present with glorious past—equally glorious, he would fain believe, despite King Pausanias' vengeance upon the poet's native Thebes, despite the Athenian subjugation of his beloved Aegina, because the salvation of Greece at Salamis and the wrestling-prize at Pytho are alike illumined by the one joy worth supreme effort: by αιγλα (that is his great word), "radiance"—almost what we mean by "halo." An astounding failure in perspective, true; but shared by many. An Olympian festival was celebrated during the very days when Xerxes was marching into Central Greece and the allied fleet falling back from Artemisium. There are phrases in the ***Fifth Isthmian*** which can be understood only if we believe that Pindar, at any rate for the moment, sets athletic success on a level with the victory at Salamis; and Marathon, which he mentions thrice, was for him nothing but a centre of athletic contests. Who shall discern limits to the lethal stupidity of a long-dominant class whose education has been moulded to suit, not to correct, their prejudices? In the struggle against Persia, Thebes had covered herself with infamy, siding with the invader and actually fighting against Greece at Plataea. Small wonder that her poet speaks faintly and ambiguously! But in the ***Eighth Isthmian*** (vv. 6 ff.), to our relief, he utters nobler language, though still in sorrow and doubt: "We are freed from mighty griefs . . . some god hath averted from us the stone of Tantalus that hung over our heads." Then he turns back to his never-failing joy, the praise of gymnastic prowess.

In this devotion to his own class and their chosen forms of achievement he is haughtily serene and free from misgiving. Euripides sneered at athletes as "ornaments of the piazza," and Pindar would have thought that excellent, if too curt. Xenophanes complained that such pursuits "do not fatten the public treasury." "Why should they?" Pindar would ask. These men exist beautifully: it is they who make the city splendid; without them, whether the treasury was empty or crammed, it would be a scene of brisk squalour. He feels no temptation to conciliate the ordinary citizen by spurious *addenda* like the English journalist's praise of a duke as "democratic" because he resembles the artisan in his excitement about pugilism or horse-racing. (It would be just as sensible to call the artisan "aristocratic.") He loves the nobleman for his lineage and his instincts, with no pretence that he has once in his life done anything for his lowly fellow-citizens save permit them to bask in the radiance of his achievement. It is a curious fact, proceeding from the poet's own austere avoidance of material detail no less than the spareness of Greek life as compared with the modern, that, for all his admiration and loyalty, Pindar nowhere develops a picturesque background for these beautiful triumphant figures corresponding to that painted by modern writers, particularly the English. Here are no stately homes with echoing corridors, panelled dining-rooms, gracious lawns and sunken rose-gardens, no rich and powerful public-school tradition: and nothing which, however different, could evoke similar emotions.

Vast changes were coming in Pindar's day, and coming fast: he was the prophet of ideals that vanished as he sang, and lived to see the Athenian *demos* attain the height of glory, wealth, dominion, and self-confidence. In Athens, "patriotism" had taken on a meaning which he could barely understand, certainly not accept. He thought himself a patriot; and some might hold that he was justified therein, since, no less than Aristides himself, he was all for the *polis,* the city-state, which had given him birth, education, ideals, and a religion. But the vital difference lay here, that his affection for oligarchy enabled him to identify his country (as we should call it) with his own class. As Coppola remarks: "for him a free state is one where the power is in the hands of the nobles." That is why the multitude never comes to life in his poems as an assemblage of real persons. Despite his unforgettable praise of Athens as freedom's bulwark against Persia, he had no love for democratic principles. Nor, despite his friendship with the princes of Sicily, did he love monarchy. His most notable comment on political life occurs in the ***Eleventh Pythian,*** where (be it observed) sociology and ethics are as much in view as politics. Let me for once offer a paraphrase in our modern terms. "Of all classes in the state, I find that the *bourgeoisie* enjoys the greatest prosperity. The life of monarchs offends me. My heart is set on the communal virtues, which keep envy at arm's length. If a man avoids arrogance by quietly seeking eminence in those virtues, and those only, he will end his life in happiness and leave his children the best legacy, a good reputation."

So much, then, for Pindar's views, or prejudices, about God and man. His maxims deserve serious attention only when considered each for the moment in its special context: quite apart from their truth or falsity, they cannot be organized into a body of doctrine or even into coherence of prejudice, save where they show his affection for land-owning aristocracy. But even if we appraise them in isolation, we must not attribute to them remarkable potency. There is less than nothing in the notion that they are "keys" to the myths wherein they occur. Occasionally, no doubt, we understand a particular passage better if we observe the aphorism and if we also possess the contemporary facts that caused the poet to moralize. But to grasp a mass of writing intellectually differs altogether from appreciating a poem; and in Pindar the latter has a thousand times more value. Anyone who followed Dissen would be prepared to use Canterbury Cathedral as a storehouse of obsolete passports; for these maxims are uniformly trite and obvious. But they were not trite to Pindar's contemporaries, or to Pindar himself? That may be; and granting for the sake of argument that the poet supposed the value of his myth to lie in exposition of the aphorism which introduces or closes it, that possibility affects nothing except his status as a critic. Morality does not make great poetry, or poetry at all. Greatness resides in his rendering of glories won today or long ago, to which the aphorism is no more a key than the stairway by which we enter a picture-gallery is the key to Botticelli's "Birth of Venus" or Turner's "Crossing the Brook." Greatness may reside too in the language, not the matter, of the aphorism itself: Perrotta writes concerning that noble passage in the ***Second Pythian*** where the might of God is said to outstrip the eagle and the dolphin: "So vigorous an assertion is no longer a maxim: it is a sentiment." Precisely! Pindar's genius works by imagination and feeling.

That is to say, he is a poet. Does any poet think at all while actually making poetry, not discussion in verse? What intellectual quality inheres in his work results from his training and experience—his verse is grammatical, because he has been to school; it declares the Alps more majestic than the Laurentian Mountains, because he has travelled. But his poetry, the quality in which the work differs from prose, is not intellectual and cannot be intellectual, for it springs from emotion caused by spiritual insight and governed by imagination. His relation to the world within and without him resembles not the relation of an astronomer to the stars, but the relation of a saint to God. It is possible to prove the astronomer mistaken by the use of mathematics: it is impossible to prove the saint wrong by the use of theology. Pindar, in some ways unparalleled, is here at one with all the genuine poets that ever sang. Some things which he wrote are utterly obsolete and were never of great value. His poetry endures; because, like all poetry, it outsoars the region where obsolescence has its reasons and its meaning.

It is right, then, that we should at once remind ourselves of a poem where, passing far beyond Dorian political notions, he has produced the noblest example of Dorian poetry ever written, the myth of the ***Tenth Nemean.*** No doubt, as we remarked a few moments ago, the intervention of Zeus in the combat should be condemned as unrighteous. But we are now to contemplate the whole story in another mood, the emotion evoked by grave beauty of language and by the sublimity of Polydeuces' choice, which raised up his dying brother to share his immortality. Even Pindar has nowhere else attained this perfection of austere beauty, the counterpart in verse of those Aeginetan marbles which hold for ever the exquisite brief moment when rigour passes into plain yet heroic dignity. With the simplest language and a strong majestic rhythm he creates an awful loveliness; the straigthforward tale by miracle takes on sublimity. Could human language be more frugal than that which describes the epiphany of Zeus? . . . "Thus he spake; and Zeus came unto him face to face and uttered this word: 'Thou art my son . . . ' " When the smoking thunderbolt crashes down, and Idas with his brother dies, we find an unsurpassed example of that rare achievement, grandeur evoked by the plainest phrase: . . . "together in the wilderness they were consumed by fire." *E solo in parte vidi il Saladino.* Though their antagonists were thus destroyed, one of the Twin Brethren fell mortally wounded, and the climax of the story is Polydeuces' loyalty to his dying brother—loyalty in a situation even stranger and more distracting than some have realized. For Polydeuces believes that he himself (like Castor) is mortal, prays that in this hour he may find the death which one day must overtake him, and laments his plight as a mortal bereft of a faithful friend. Then comes the revelation "thou art my son," and the strange secret of his own and his brother's begetting, which on a sudden reveal to Polydeuces that Heaven is his for the asking, while Castor, gasping at his feet, will soon depart for ever below the earth—unless the choice is taken of one day's death and one day's life for both in everlasting alternation. At this moment of confused heartbreak and dazzling wonder the hero takes his decision without a pause.

Greater love was not known in Greek legend, or greater loyalty. (pp. 44-71)

Gilbert Norwood, in his Pindar, *University of California Press, 1945, 302 p.*

Bruno Snell (essay date 1947)

[*Snell was an influential German classicist, best known for his study of the evolution of Greek thought,* Die Entdeckung des Geistes *(1948;* The Discovery of the Mind: The Greek Origins of European Thought, *1953). In the following excerpt, originally published in* Antike und Abendland *in 1947, Snell focuses on Pindar's* Hymn to Zeus, *placing his art and thought in the context of the archaic age, and paying particular attention to black-figured vase painting, the philosophy of Heraclitus, and the poetry of Hesiod.*]

The city of Thebes where Pindar was born boasted a richer store of myths and tales than any other place in Greece. Here Semele had given birth to Dionysus the dispenser of wine, and Alcmene had nurtured Heracles who cleansed the world of its monsters. The citadel had been ruled by Cadmus who brought with him from Phoenicia the art of writing, the source and foundation of all civilized life. He had sown the dragon's teeth from which the Spartoi, the ancestors of the Thebans, were sprung, and he led Harmonia in marriage. The unfortunate Labdacids had sojourned in this little town: Laius, Iocaste, her son Oedipus, and his children Eteocles, Polynices, Antigone and Ismene. The narrow lanes of Thebes produced the seer Tiresias; Niobe lived there, the wife of king Amphion versed in song; it was from here that Trophonius and Agamedes set out for Delphi to build the temple of Apollo—these are just a few of the mythical personages who dwelt in the city of Thebes, some of greater, some of lesser renown such as Ismenus son of Apollo, and the ash nymph Melia.

In Greece heroic tales are attached to the places which had been important centres of Mycenean times. Over Mycenae and Tiryns which, during that earlier age, had been the most powerful bastions in the land, Thebes had this advantage that her position remained strong long after other citadels had fallen. Some cities, like Athens, may have outstripped her in the end, but they were at first of so little significance that the stories associated with them had no chance of winning a large and loyal audience. Even a figure like Theseus in the last analysis remained an exclusively Athenian hero.

To the lyric poet of the archaic age the ancient stories afforded an easily accessible source upon which to draw for the embellishment of a festival, and if these stories were those of his own land he was able to weave them into poems which his listeners might relish for their old associations as well as his new interpretation. Already as a boy Pindar felt that this unimposing home town of his, the walls along which he walked day after day, the springs from which he drank, a street here and a square there,

Perseus, accompanied by Athena, carrying off the head of Medusa - a myth retold in Pythian 12.

were profoundly linked with the past, with the age of the gods and demi-gods. From childhood on he lived close to memories fondly cherished, not only by Thebans, but by all the Greeks. By force of circumstances, therefore, he grew up in an atmosphere of spiritual riches, and this to a poet is probably far more valuable than the quality we call genius or talent. Later in his life he exploits his great treasure with a sense of pride; fully conscious of the wealth of this heritage he steps before his countrymen and asks: which sample from the multitude of our myths shall I give you? A hymn to Zeus, preserved only in fragments, begins (fr. 29):

> Shall we sing of Ismenus, or of Melia of the golden distaff,
> Or of Cadmus, or the strong race of the Spartoi,
> Or Thebe with the dark-blue headband,
> Or of the daring strength of Heracles,
> Or the joyful majesty of Dionysus
> Or the wedding of white-armed Harmonia?

This poem stood at a conspicuous place in the edition of Pindar brought out by the Alexandrian grammarians; it introduced the first book of his works. The extant pieces had been divided into 17 books, with the poems about the gods—such as the pæans addressed to Apollo, and the dithyrambs to Dionysus—preceding the songs in praise of mortals. But the leading position was taken by the hymns, and among them the place of honour was granted to the ***Hymn to Zeus,*** a composition of great fame. Later, in the middle ages, the religious works of Pindar were lost one and all; only a few fragments were preserved in the writings of other ancient authors. (pp. 71-2)

Descriptions of nature are rare in Pindar's work, as generally in the classical poetry of the fifth century, but this one surely stands among the boldest and grandest of all literature. His nature is not, as we to-day would expect it, invested with a soul. He does not empower it to experience sensations. It is viewed with the greatest objectivity, but from a very particular vantage point. Nature has become the stuff of a mythical image; in characteristically Pindaric fashion, reciprocity and correspondence have become the key factors in his vision, so that we are confronted with a truly Heraclitean proportion: those in the sky regard the earth as those on earth regard the sky. This is not the only place where Pindar betrays a kinship with Heraclitus' doctrine of energetic tensions, of the pregnant correlations by which all living things are at once separated and united. In the final analysis even the idea that the great deeds and the beauty of the world require song to praise them is founded on the knowledge that the individual thing is limited, imperfect, in need of completion, and that even greatness perishes, while song is indestructible, and beauty depends on the 'wise' for its manifestation. And evidently it is up to the wise man to show that the world discloses its greatest beauty in the wealth of its correlations, through its correspondences and contrasts: nay, that the essence of this beauty resides in the agreement and balance of its parts.

One picture which Pindar draws fits his own technique admirably (***Nem.*** 7.77): 'The Muse is joining together gold and white ivory and the lily-flower which she has taken from the dew of the sea.' Piece after piece he moulds his song from precious materials, continually changing his design, until he has fashioned a mosaic rich with gold, ivory, and white coral—the 'lily-flower taken from the dew of the sea'. More than once he calls his writing a weaving of chaplets. The strands of a garland disappear and emerge again into view, tracing a complex pattern of parallels and contrasts; just so the fibres of Pindar's poem, though far apart and distributed over its length, require to be perceived together. A rather superficial example will perhaps help to make this clear. In a triumphal song we expect certain data about the victor, such as his name, the name of his father, and his home. Pindar is fond of introducing these details in such a way that the victor may first be referred to by the name of his father, later in the poem he is called by his own, and in the end he is merely identified by the name of his country. In this fashion Pindar is able to provide the necessary information unobtrusively and without repeating himself. He has very much the same approach towards other factors which form the stock-in-trade of a victory ode: staples such as myth, maxim, and so forth. They emerge, they vanish to make room for another motif, they rise to the surface once more, as if by chance and without immediate provocation: and all the time they are the strands without which the whole design would not be harmonious. Pindar elects to create this ornate tapestry because he wants to represent reality and nothing else; it is no concern of his to trace an orderly process pedantically from beginning to end, nor does he mean to 'get somewhere', to develop an idea or a programme. The very structure of his poetic designs confirms the message of his senses that all things are inextricably woven into a whole; the literary form he uses is a faithful mirror of the world which he sees. For all that, the individual parts are not subordinated to the whole so as to play an inferior role. They are not like the scenes, or even the sentences, of a tragedy which are each determined by the plot of the whole, no matter whether they quicken or retard the action (that, incidentally, is the reason why it is so much easier to assign a tragic fragment its place in a lost drama). We recognize in this an archaic element for which there are many analogies in the plastic art of the pre-classical age. The makers of black-figured vase paintings, for example, show a tendency to weave the figures into the composition without leaving any space unused. Their interest in creating an ornamental, a heraldic pattern is stronger than their desire to construct an organic group, autonomous in its relation to the background. This holds good even for the nude human body; each organ is stressed in its individual perfection, beautifully shaped and strongly marked off against its neighbour. They are vigorous limbs which radiate an intense vitality, but they are anything but properly integrated into the balanced ensemble of a body. Their shape is in no way affected by the pressure or pull of other limbs, or by a burden or resistance exerting its weight from without.

Pindar remained loyal to this archaic manner although his creative activity lasts down to the middle of the fifth century. Throughout the fifty years of his life which are open to our view there is no trace of a stylistic development, such as was the achievement of his contemporary Aeschylus in Athens. It is a logical consequence of Pindar's mode of thinking that his poems are crowded with geometric figures, such as ring composition, figure-eight-loops, parallelisms and mirror images. The decorated character of his art is most fully revealed in its metrical form. Never again has the world seen poetry which equals that of Pindar in keeping its far-flung variations under the strictest control by means of measure and number. Therefore the demands which it makes on the metrical skill of the author are beyond compare. Without the Greek text we cannot, unfortunately, discuss Pindar's verse, for it rests on conditions which are foreign to our own sense of rhythm. In our tongue a verse is based on the regular alternation of stressed and unstressed syllables. In Greek, on the other hand, a verse is formed by the orderly succession of long and short syllables, to which our ears are not attuned. The most we can do is to arrange the long and short syllables in a metrical scheme, and then to point out certain variations. But the rhythmic cadence which filled these skeletons with life must remain a mystery to us. It is as if we spotted correspondences and variations in the notation of a Bach fugue without subjecting them to the test of our hearing for which they are after all meant.

Pindar's metrical art is his own creation. Some of his contemporaries tried, without fully succeeding, to imitate his verse, but in the end it died with him. He refines the play of responses and variations which had been introduced by the earlier choral lyrists; at the same time he boldly magnifies its scope until he accomplishes a towering edifice. Large strophic formations are multiplied according to rigid rules; each subdivision begins with lines similar to those which the older poets had already used, but in the sequel they undergo kaleidoscopic changes through extension, shortening and rearrangement. Pindar did not turn off into the Attic route: that led to a totally different destination. The choral odes of early tragedy begin to use the variation of a particular type of line to pass on to other types, to release themselves from the tight fetters of a rigid metrical scheme, and thus to achieve an organic strophic structure while allowing themselves a freer development of themes. In later tragedy and in the new dithyramb this ultimately led to the creation of extended compositions in free metrical form. In all Greek lyric poetry, and particularly in choral poetry, the metric design was carried by music which—at least as far as the older period is concerned—has disappeared to the last note. Thus we shall never have more than a vague idea of the special quality of Pindaric metres. Only this much we may know, that like his thinking they recalled the texture of tapestries, and that therefore they were magnificently appropriate to the vision and thought of the poet.

But we have not yet said our last word about the art of Pindar. His is not a disinterested toying with forms; he does not unveil the correlations which exist in the world merely because he is delighted with the intricate pattern of reality, but because he has discovered in them a higher meaning. As the Muses at the wedding of Cadmus sing of the wedding of Zeus [in the ***Hymn to Zeus***], they magnify the festival of the mythical king of Thebes. As in the sky the final marriage of Zeus led to the perfection of order among the gods and in the world, the same order found its place on earth through the union of Harmonia with Cadmus. And the Pindaric chorus, by singing of this in the presence of the Thebans, reinforces the greatness and the sanctity of their city, and puts them under an obligation to obey this noble tradition, and to maintain the hallowed order. The wise poet espies the element of divine splendour which, coming from Zeus, illumines the mythical Cadmus and casts its lustre even upon the Thebes of his own time. He points to it, and that is his praise. The transitory world participates in the divine, and it is the task of the poet to make this known.

Pindar describes Delos as a star in the sky of the gods, not to create a mood, or simply to voice a private aesthetic response, but in order to celebrate the island. On other occasions when Pindar calls an island a 'radiant star' that is praise enough; how much greater is the glory of Delos whose radiance exists for the gods! When Heraclitus stresses such mutual correlations between gods and men, we witness a disinterested intelligence at work; in Pindar, everything is geared to the practical demands of life, to the active concern of praising. The two men differ also in another respect. Pindar retains an immediate intuition of the divine; he is able to reproduce its brilliance, and to grasp it, directly and spontaneously, as a mythical fact. In the thought of Heraclitus the deity shows a tendency to become abstract, to detach itself from the world of the senses. An 'invisible' harmony ranks higher in his scale than the agreements which meet his eyes. Pindar and Heraclitus, however, have this in common that the divine, the One, forms their objective; Heraclitus ponders over it and seeks to understand it, while Pindar approaches it with pious contemplation, and is content to praise it. One is a philosopher, the other a poet.

In these days a Christian poet who intones his *Te deum laudamus* is unable to regard the works of God with the same candour and simplicity which were Pindar's privilege. Hoelderlin imitates Pindar in giving praise a central role to play in his hymns—there are, of course, also echoes of the Christian Praise of the Lord in his work—and Rilke, following in the steps of Hoelderlin but once more under the influence of new Christian impulses, thinks of the poet as one 'elect to acclaim'. But the object of their praises does not stand clearly revealed before their eyes; in fact both of them declare that the poet ought to make a concerted effort to seek out this object. It is obvious, therefore, that we cannot expect them to sound the simple and unbroken strains which we hear in the panegyrics of the archaic age of Greece. Pindar owes it to the transitory conditions of his hour that his praise is as pure and as perfect as that of no other poet of Europe. The effulgence of the divine, he feels, is reflected in the appearances of the world; his sensuous delight in the multiplicity of things is not yet obscured by the knowledge that the essence which really matters is located beyond the visible world, and that it can be known only by reason. As a result his intuition is strong and lucid, his expression lively and straight. To be sure, he has his problems; he no longer takes it for granted that the divine is readily discerned in the phenomena about him. Wisdom is required to point it out and to establish its value; only a soaring flight of the mind will contrive to place the divine within our grasp. This conviction is the source of the stately eloquence which distinguishes Pindar's style above that of all the other poets of his time, and which gives his eulogies their peculiar greatness. Though the voice of this genre of poetry is about to be stilled, its flame burns brighter than ever before.

Not all things participate in the divine to an equal degree. But the wise man descries it in the outstanding examples of each kind all around him: among treasures it resides in gold, among the fish it is found in the dolphin, in the eagle among the birds, in the king and the victor among human beings. The **Fifth *Isthmian*** begins: 'Mother of Helios, Theia the many-named: for your sake men have made the great strength of gold to be a thing prized above other possessions', and, so he continues, 'by the honour which you bestow men win respect and glory in all sorts of contests'. Here he endeavours to seek the divine in the principle which is responsible for the value of precious things: a mythology which is Pindar's very own, although we might again refer to Hesiod. This principle he calls Theia, which simply means the divine. We seem to have reached the borderline where intellectual abstraction begins, but Pindar's Theia is 'Mother of the Sun'; the sun, it appears, diffuses his radiant warmth because of her, and the divine finds its purest expression in the sun. At the same time Theia has 'many names'; she reveals herself in many ways, and we need a variety of designations to praise and invoke her.

Sappho, in a poem of her old age, had confessed that her joy in the beauty of this world drew its strength from her love of the sun. In the course of the more than one hundred years which separate Pindar from Sappho this archaic type of piety, the willingness to identify the divine with brightness and light, had fallen into decay in the rest of Greece. Pindar and his ancient faith make a rather isolated stand in a world that had largely changed. At times, therefore, he feels the urge to defend himself, to indulge in demonstration. Occasionally he is moved by an impulse not unlike the zeal of an apologist to enter into theological and mythological speculations of the sort which his compatriot Hesiod had brought into currency at the beginning of the archaic age. Austerity and a sense of purpose provide the link between the two Boeotians, one the forerunner, the other the accomplisher of pre-classical poetry, that rich and colourful art.

Hesiod stands on the threshold between the era of the epic and the age of the lyric. A new awareness of reality is the chief factor which separates him from the epic. Under the impact of his hard life as a peasant and herdsman the world of the heroic tales, the songs of his rhapsodic profession, came to be shrouded in a cloud of questions and doubts, and he turned his eyes towards the more concrete forms of his immediate surroundings. He ceased to look for the divine in the restricted aristocratic society of the Olympians who interfere in the actions of kings and heroes as they see fit. Instead he sought to obtain a more exact and systematic knowledge of the divine as a power affecting all. The result of this shift is his theogonic scheme. But he continues to subscribe to the epic tradition in one important respect: he describes his system as one that has come into being, not as one that exists in the present.

His Muses sing of the present, the past, and the future, of the birth of the gods, and the coming into being of a living and meaningful world. In Pindar also the Muses sing of this epic event, how the world gradually came to be put in order; but their real function is one which accords with the lyric rather than the epic: to praise the beauty of Zeus's works.

In the course of the years between Hesiod and Pindar the archaic lyrists became conscious of the tensions of the soul, of the intricate interrelations in matters of the mind, and of the limits restricting the old values. Pindar does not, unlike most writers of archaic lyrics, speak of his private sensations, or of the intellectual links between him and other men, nor does he enlarge upon the values which he rejects. All he does is to state objectively what he considers most precious, what he associates with the divine, how that which is limited partakes of that which is universal and lasting, how man has a share in what is higher than man. Thus although there are no direct ties between his speech and that of his predecessors, the world which he pictures is fully instinct with the new dimension discovered by them. The seeds sown by the lyrists before him are brought to fruition in the festival poetry which stems from the cult hymn: and that is his particular achievement. His deity has the very same qualities which Archilochus and Sappho predicated of the soul to distinguish it from the body: tension, intensity, and the capacity to merge separate objects under its force. This means that Pindar's deity is no longer a power of, so to speak, historical efficacy, a power which at any one moment activates one particular event. Instead he visualizes it in the form of pervasive splendour and eternal meaning, 'going through all things' as we might say with Heraclitus, and manifesting itself in a counterplay of opposites. The suitable mould in which to express this new concept is no longer the epic but the lyric ode, as is notably proved by Pindar's ***Hymn to Zeus.***

While Pindar was at work in Thebes, Attica produced a view of the world which differed appreciably from his. Tragedy makes the claim that there should be justice on earth; consequently the tragedians demand more of men, and also of the gods, than is usually fulfilled. In their world praise could not but lapse into silence. Pindar deliberately keeps away from such thoughts which he considers presumptuous. On occasion he may comment that some trait of the tradition which he reports appears to dim the glory of the divine, but he never permits himself to question the beauty and order of life, whatever the weaknesses and vanities of our earthly existence. Never does he feel called upon to play the reformer. With noble insouciance he takes the world as he finds it; its celestial threads of gold cannot be completely blacked out by its shadows. All that matters is to 'turn the brightness outward' (***Pyth. 3***.83), to insist on the beauty which has enveloped him so generously from childhood on. This is the way for a poet to prove his worth; and few of the poets who came after Pindar could vie with his genius for doing just this. (pp. 81-9)

Bruno Snell, "Pindar's Hymn to Zeus," in his The Discovery of the Mind: The Greek Origins of European Thought, *translated by T. G. Rosenmeyer, Cambridge, Mass.: Harvard University Press, 1953, pp. 71-89.*

Gilbert Highet (essay date 1949)

[*A Scottish-born writer and critic, Highet was a classical scholar and distinguished educator best known for his* The Classical Tradition *(1949). In the following excerpt from that work, Highet examines the Pindaric tradition in European lyric poetry from Horace to Thomas Gray.*]

The chief classical models for the modern formal lyric were Pindar and Horace; and then, far behind them, Anacreon (with his imitators), the poets of the Greek Anthology, and Catullus.

Pindar was born about 522 B.C., was trained at Athens in music and poetry, wrote hymns, songs of triumph, and festal lyrics all his life with the greatest success, and died about 442. Coming from the territory of Thebes, which lay a little apart from the full current of Greek life and thought, he seems to belong to an age earlier than the busy, revolutionary, thought-searching fifth century. He is more, not less, intense. But his intensity is emotional and aesthetic; in his poems we see few of the struggles and triumphs of the intellect. His spiritual energy, however, is compellingly strong, his power to see visions and to make them intensely and permanently alive in a few speedy words is unsurpassed in any poetry, and the inexhaustible wealth of his vocabulary and sentence-structure makes readers (unless they prefer prose to poetry) as excited as though his subjects equalled his eloquence in greatness.

His surviving poems (apart from some fragments discovered very recently) are four books of choral songs intended to celebrate the victories of athletes at the national sports festivals held every year at the great shrines of Greece. They pay little or no attention to the actual contests, and not much more to the personality of the winner, unless he is a great ruler; but they glorify his family—both for its past achievements (in which the victory is a unit) and for the grand legends with which it is linked. Above all they exalt *nobility* of every kind, social, physical, aesthetic, spiritual. These poems were not recited, but sung by a large choir, with Pindar's own music and a beautiful intricate dance to intensify the effect of the superb words.

The two chief difficulties in understanding Pindar are not the results of our own ignorance, or of our distance from him. They have always existed. They troubled his readers in classical times. Horace, himself a skilful and sensitive poet, felt them too.

The first difficulty is the actual structure of his poems—their metre and their pattern. They are of every kind of length, from a trifle twenty-four lines long to a titan of just under 300. Being dance-songs, they must be built up of repeated and varied rhythmical units. But what are the units? How are they repeated and how are they varied?

The odes are all divided into sections—groups of verses which we might call stanzas.

In a few poems the stanzas are all exactly the same. Evidently the dance here was a single complex evolution, repeated again and again.

Most of the odes are in a form like *A-Z-P:* where *A* and *Z* are two stanzas almost exactly equal, and *P* is a briefer, quieter stanza, differently arranged but on a similar rhythmical basis. The same *A-Z-P* pattern is then repeated throughout the poem. Here the dancers apparently performed one figure (*A*), then retraced it (*Z*), and then performed a closing movement (*P*) to complete that section of the poem. Or else, after dancing *A* and *Z,* they may have stood still singing the closing group of verses (*P*). These units are called, in Greek, strophe (*A*), antistrophe (*Z*), and epode (*P*). Poems built on a single stanza-pattern are called monostrophic; the *A-Z-P* poems triadic.

So far, good. But can these stanzas be broken down further—into verses or lines—as a ballet can be dissected, not only into movements, but into separate elements and subordinate figures? At this point scholars usually stopped, until the nineteenth century. They saw the single or triple stanza-division (which they knew from Greek tragedy, where the choruses sang and danced in similar patterns), but they could not be sure of the component units of each stanza. In the first editions of Pindar the stanzas were chopped up into series of short lines, more or less by guesswork, and their readers assumed that he wrote 'irregularly', varying the length and pattern of his lines by caprice, and balancing only stanza against stanza.

Scholars now know, however, that Pindar divided his stanzas by breathing-spaces into verses, rhythmical units of varying length and pattern—not so much like the regular lines of a modern poem as like the varying musical phrases that make up a 'romantic' symphonic poem. The verses in each stanza correspond to each other almost exactly. In the *A-Z-P* pattern, the units composing the *A* and *Z* stanzas correspond all through the poem; and the units of the *P* stanzas correspond all through the poem.

The result is more complex than most of our poetry, and much more like our music. For instance, a sonnet is made up of fourteen iambic lines, all of the same length within a syllable and all on exactly the same rhythmical basis. The variety is produced by the rhyme-scheme, which makes the lines interweave on a pattern like this:

--------------*a*
--------------*b*
--------------*a*
--------------*b*

--------------*c*
--------------*d*
--------------*c*
--------------*d*

--------------*e*
--------------*f*
--------------*g*
--------------*e*
--------------*f*
--------------*g*

The stanzas of Pindar's odes, on the other hand, have no rhymes, and they hardly ever have more than two lines the same in shape, so that one stanza may look like this

-------*a*
-------*a*

----*b*
---*c*
----*b*

-----------*d*
--------*d'* (shortened)

------*e*
-----*f*
------*e*
-----*f*

And then the same pattern will be echoed in the next stanza; and there will be a rhythmical kinship running through *a, b, c, d, e,* and *f,* so that a few basic dance-movements can be felt pulsing through them all despite their differences. If you read aloud one of Pindar's odes with a strong but fluent rhythmical beat, you will sense behind it the intricately interweaving rhythm and music of choir and ballet. The odes could even be set to music and sung and danced, now that these patterns have been worked out by devoted scholars; but until the nineteenth century nothing of them was known, except the broad stanza-grouping *A-Z-P* (with an occasional *A-A-A-A*), built up out of metrical units irregular and apparently haphazard in length and rhythm.

The second difficulty in Pindar has not yet been solved. This is that no one can follow his train of thought. Horace, the calm, restrained, elegant, enlightened Epicurean, said Pindar's poetry was like a torrent rushing down rain-swollen from the mountains, overrunning its banks, boiling and roaring. We feel its tremendous power, we are excited and exalted and overwhelmed by its speed and energy, it is useless to argue and analyse, we are swept away as soon as we begin to read. True; but does it make sense?

In eras when reason was stronger than emotion or imagination, people thought Pindar wrote like an inspired lunatic. He was a madman like Blake, who saw fine visions and rammed them together without sequence or even coherence, or filled in the intervals with meaningless spouting. Malherbe called his poems balderdash, *galimatias.* Boileau saw them as 'beautiful disorder'. Horace felt them to be imaginative energy uncontrolled, and he had read more of Pindar than any modern man. Contemporary scholars have constructed various schemes to make Pindar's thought seem continuous. An admirable recent book by Dr. Gilbert Norwood of Toronto [*Pindar,* 1945] suggests that each poem is dominated by a single visual image—a harp, a wheel, a ship at sea—symbolizing the victor and his family and circumstances. Others have tried to link stanza to stanza by finding repetitions of key-words and key-phrases at key-points. I believe myself that it is not possible for us to find either a continuous train of thought or a central imaginative symbol or a series of allusive links in every one of Pindar's odes. The unity of each poem was created by the single, unique moment of the festival for which it was written. The nation-wide contest, the long training and aspiration, the myth of city or family that inspired the victory, the glories of the earlier winners in the same city or family, the crises of contemporary Greek history, the shrine itself and its god—all these excitements fused into one burning glow which darted out a shower of brilliant images, leapt in a white-hot spark across gaps unbridgeable by thought, passed through a commonplace leaving it luminous and transparent, melted a group of heterogeneous ideas into a shortlived unity, and, as suddenly as a flame, died. It is difficult to recapture the full significance even of Greek tragedy or early comedy, without the acting, the scenic effects, the chorus, the dancing, the great theatre, and the intense concentration of the Athenian audience. In reading Pindar's triumphal odes it is almost impossible to understand them unless, simultaneously, we revive in our own minds the high and unifying excitement created by the poetry and the music and the dancing and the rejoicing city and the glorious victor and the proud family and the ennobling legend. We have nothing left but the words and a ghost of the dance. The thoughts and images of Pindar's poems do not always succeed each other in logical sequence. They are chosen for their beauty and their intensity and their boldness. They are often grouped by a process like free association, and linked simply by contrast, by the poet's wish *not* to be logical, but to be nobly inconsequent, divinely astonishing, as unique as the triumphal moment.

The greatest Roman lyricist, Horace (65-8 B.C.), said it was too dangerous to try to rival Pindar. He wrote at a time when the Greco-Roman world, still trembling with the fury and exhaustion of generations of war and civil war, needed no excitement, no audacity, no excess, but calm, moderation, thought, repose. His odes were not composed for a single unique moment, but for Rome and its long future. They are all in precisely arranged four-line stanzas, or (less often) couplets. Unlike Pindar's lyrics, they fall into a comparatively small range of variations on traditional line- and stanza-forms. The patterns which Horace prefers are based on models created by the Greek lyric poets Alcaeus and Sappho, who worked in the seventh and sixth centuries, several generations earlier than Pindar. From them, too, he adopted a number of themes—although we cannot certainly tell how many, since nearly all they wrote has vanished. He could not copy Sappho's deep intensity of emotion, nor the songs of fierce hatred and riotous revelry which Alcaeus sometimes sang; but he reproduced and deepened Alcaeus' political sensibility, the keen love of nature felt by both Alcaeus and Sappho, something of their bold independent individualism, and much of their delicate grace, which produces effects as surprising in their subtlety as Pindar's in their power.

After describing the dangers of emulating the dashing energy of Pindar, Horace compares Pindar to a swan. For the Italians this did not mean the mute placid beautiful creature which floats somnolent on the lake, but the strong-winged loud-voiced bird which in flight soars high above everything but the eagle. Why not the eagle itself, the bird of Jove? Probably because, although a conqueror, the eagle is not a singer; it symoblizes power to be feared more than beauty to be admired. Still, one of his followers preferred to think of Pindar as the Theban eagle. Eagle or swan, he flies too high (says Horace) for us to attempt to follow him on man-made wings, without falling, like Icarus, into the sea.

I, Horace goes on, am like a bee, hard-working, flying near the ground on short flights, gathering sweetness from myriads of different flowers. Certainly the swan is stronger, more distinguished, more beautiful; but the bee makes honey, the substance which is unique in the world, fragrant of innumerable blossoms, and not only a food but a symbol of immortality. Rarely has one poet contrasted his work and character so emphatically with that of a great predecessor. The contrast is important, because it images the division between the two most vital ideals of formal lyric poetry in modern literature. Among the lyricists who follow classical inspiration, consciously or unconsciously, some are descendants of Pindar, some of Horace. The Pindarics admire passion, daring, and extravagance. Horace's followers prefer reflection, moderation, economy. Pindaric odes follow no pre-established routine, but soar and dive and veer as the wind catches their wing. Horatian lyrics work on quiet, short, well-balanced systems. Pindar represents the ideals of aristocracy, careless courage and the generous heart. Horace is a *bourgeois,* prizing thrift, care, caution, the virtue of self-control. Even the music we can hear through the odes of the two poets and their successors is different. Pindar loves the choir, the festival, and the many-footed dance. Horace is a solo singer, sitting in a pleasant room or quiet garden with his lyre.

Characteristically, Horace often undervalued his own poems. Brief, orderly, tranquil, meditative, they are less intense and rhapsodical but deeper and more memorable than those of Pindar. Cool but moving, sensitive but controlled, elusive but profound, they contain more phrases of unforgettable eloquence and wisdom than any other group of lyrics in European literature.

Inspiration and reflection; passion and planning; excitement and tranquillity; heaven-aspiring flight and a calm cruise near the ground. These are not only differences between two individuals or two schools of lyric poetry. They are the distinguishing marks of two aesthetic attitudes which have characterized (and sometimes overemphasized) two different ways of making poetry, music, painting, oratory, prose fiction, sculpture, and architecture. Detach Pindar and Horace from their background, and read them as poets in their own right. Pindar, the bold victor who sang with the same conquering energy that possessed his own heroes, who made his own medium, who dominated the past and future by the comet-like intensity of his moment, is he not 'romantic'? Horace, the man who ran away in the civil war, the ex-slave's son who worked his way up to become the friend of an emperor, the poet who built his monument syllable by syllable as carefully as bees build their honeycomb, the apostle of thought, care, self-control, is he not 'classical'?

The distinction has often been misapplied. All Greco-Roman literature and all its imitations and adaptations in modern languages have been called 'classical'. Modern literature which shuns regular forms, which is conceived as a revolt against tradition, which gives full and free expression to the personality of the writer, which values imagination more than reason and passionate emotion more than self-restraint, has been called 'romantic' and very often 'anti-classical'. The distinction between the two attitudes to art is useful enough, although it tends to make us forget that there are many others. But it is a dangerous mistake to call one 'classical' and the other 'anti-classical', and to assume that *all* Greco-Roman literature with its modern descendants is 'classical' in this sense. It is painful to hear such a poet as Shelley described as 'romantic', when 'romantic' is taken to mean 'turning away from Greek and Latin literary tradition': for very few great English poets have loved Greco-Roman literature more deeply or understood it better. And it ruins our appreciation of Greco-Roman literature, of which a large and important part is tensely emotional and boldly imaginative. The word *classical* simply means 'first-class', 'good enough to be used as a standard'; and by derivation it came in the Renaissance to be a general description for all Greek and Latin literature. It is still employed in that sense at those universities which have a Chair of Classics or profess Études Classiques; and in this book it has been used to mean that, and nothing more.

Pindar and Horace, then, are both classical poets—in the sense that they belong to the same literary tradition, the tradition which sprang from Greece and grew through Rome. But in many of their aims and methods they are quite different; and much of the greatest modern lyric poetry can be best understood as following the practice of one or the other. There are bold exuberant free-patterned odes, which derive from Pindar. There are brief, delicately moulded lyrics, seriously meditative or ironically gay, which derive from Horace. And in the work of some poets we meet both styles. Milton produced both Pindaric odes and Horatian sonnets. Ronsard began by soaring up with Pindar, and then, with Horace, relaxed. This is possible because the two attitudes are not polar antitheses. After all, both Pindar and Horace were lyric poets; Pindar, for all his excitement, kept a firm control of his language and thought; Horace, though usually restrained, sometimes breaks into plangent grief or daring imagery. Therefore the two schools, Pindaric and Horatian, are not opponents, but complements and sometimes allies.

Other Greek poets, and one other Roman, were admired by modern lyricists, but much less than Pindar and Horace. The most famous of these Greeks was Anacreon, who sang of love, wine, and gaiety in the sixth century B.C. Nearly all his poems have been lost; but a certain number of lyrics on the same range of subjects, written by later imitators, survived and for some time passed under his name. To them we owe many pleasant little images of the lighter aspects of life, frail pleasure or fleeting melancholy: youth as a flower which should be plucked before it withers, love not an overmastering daemon but a naughty Cupid. In form, the Anacreontics (as the imitators are called) were simple and easy and singable. (*The Star-Spangled Banner* was written to the tune of a modern Anacreontic song called *Anacreon in Heaven*). They are slight things, but charming. For instance

> In the middle of the night-time,
> when the Bear was turning slowly
> round the hand of the bright Keeper,

came a knocking, came a tapping; and when the poet opened his door, there entered, not a raven, but a little boy with a bow. The poet warmed and sheltered him; in return, after he had dried his bowstring, he fitted a sharp arrow to it, and . . .

There was also the Greek Anthology, an enormous collection of epigrams and short lyrics on every conceivable subject, from almost every period of Greek literature. It contains a vast quantity of trash, some skilful journeyman work, and a surprising number of real gems: small, but diamonds. Some of our poets have been indebted to it in developing the modern epigram, and many of its themes were taken up, partly through the Renaissance Latin poets and in part directly, into the sonnets and lesser lyrics of France, Italy, England, and other countries.

Catullus, who belonged to the generation before Horace and lived a life as short and passionate as his own poems, left a handful of love-lyrics which have never been surpassed for intensity of feeling and directness of expression. Every lover should know the greatest:

I hate and love. You ask how that can be?
I know not, but I feel the agony.

Some, like the poems on Lesbia's pet sparrow, are gay, easy, and colloquial. Others are epigrams and lyrics forged out of white-hot pain and passion, yet with perfect craftsmanship. Most of them are too great to copy, but modern poets have adapted some of the themes, and sometimes disciplined themselves by emulating Catullus' rapidity and his truth.

Long before the Renaissance began, lyric poetry already existed in Europe. Provençal, French, Italian, English, German, Spanish poets had made song-patterns of much beauty and intricacy. Perhaps in the very beginning the songs of the vernacular languages had grown out of the Latin hymns of the church; but they soon left behind any link with the parent language. Therefore, when Pindar and Horace and the other classical lyric poets were rediscovered, the discovery did not create modern lyric poetry. It was not like the theatre, where the emergence of Greek and Latin comedy and tragedy was a complete revelation of hitherto undreamed-of forms and creative possibilities. Poets who already commanded the rhyme royal, the sonnet in its various shapes, ottava rima, and many more complex stanza-forms scarcely needed to borrow many patterns from the classics.

What they did borrow was, first of all, thematic material. Not the broad subjects—love and youth and the fear of death and the joy of life—but a number of clear and memorable attitudes to the subjects of lyric poetry, images or turns of thought that made them more vivid; and, of course, the whole range of imagery supplied by Greco-Roman myth. More important, they enriched their language on the model of Pindar's and Horace's odes, taking it farther away from plain prose and from conventional folk-song phraseology. And in their eagerness to rival the classics, they made their own lyrics more dignified, less colloquial and song-like (with a tra-la-la and a hey nonino), more ceremonial and hymnlike. This was the most important change that classical influence brought into modern lyric: a graver, nobler spirit. To mark these debts and their general kinship with the classics, the Renaissance lyric poets frequently copied or adapted the verse forms of Pindar, Horace, and the others; and, for more ambitious and serious lyrics, they chose the name *ode.*

It is a Greek word, meaning *song,* brought into modern speech through its Latin form *oda.* Neither Pindar nor Horace used it as a name for their poems, but it is so firmly linked with them now, and so clearly indicates their qualities of loftiness and formality, that it can scarcely be abandoned. Many modern lyrics are songs, written for the moment. An ode is a song in the classical manner, written for eternity.

Horace was known throughout the Middle Ages, although seldom imitated in the vernacular languages. Pindar was unknown; and his poetry was stranger, more brilliant and violent. Therefore, when he was rediscovered, he made a deeper impact on the Renaissance poets. The modern formal lyric became, and remained, more Pindaric than Horatian. The first edition of Pindar's odes was printed at Venice by the great publisher Aldus in 1513. Educated men already knew Horace's admiring reference to Pindar's unapproachable loftiness. This was a challenge, and the Renaissance poets were not men to refuse it.

The earliest vernacular imitations of Pindar were in Italian. Probably the hymns of Luigi Alamanni (published at Lyons in 1532-3) have priority. But the loudest and boldest answer to the challenge of Pindar's style and reputation came from France a few years later, and made the name of Pierre de Ronsard,

the first who in all France
had ever Pindarized.

Ronsard was born in the Loire country in 1524. Like Chaucer and Ercilla, he was a royal page, and in his early manhood travelled abroad in the king's service. One of his young companions infected him with enthusiasm for Vergil and Horace, and while still in his teens he began to write love-poems on themes drawn from the classics. But a serious illness, which made him partly deaf, debarred him from continuing a diplomatic and courtly career. Aged twenty-one, he determined to turn to poetry and classical learning—for the two were then, in the expanding Renaissance, almost indissolubly allied. He had already had the good fortune to find an excellent teacher, Jean Dorat, and followed him to the Collège de Coqueret, a small unit of the university of Paris. Dorat (*c.* 1502-88) was one of the many superb teachers, with a strong but winning personality, learning both wide and deep, a mind constantly in pursuit of new beauties, and a sensitive literary taste, who helped to create the Renaissance and its literature. He was the formative influence, while Ronsard and his young friends were the energy and the material, of the group of poets who rebelled against the traditional standards of French poetry and proclaimed revolution in ideals and techniques. They called themselves the Pléiade, after the group of seven stars which join their light into a single glow.

The revolution preached by the Pléiade was neither so violent as they believed nor so successful as they hoped. It was, nevertheless, important enough. In a sentence, it amounted to a closer synthesis between French poetry and Greco-Latin literature, the two meeting on an *equal* basis. Its three chief landmarks were:

the publication of *The Defence and Ennoble-*

ment of the French Language by Ronsard's friend Joachim Du Bellay in 1549;
the appearance of Ronsard's *The First Four Books of the Odes* in 1550;
the staging of Jodelle's *Captive Cleopatra* and *Eugène* in 1552.

As young men do, the Pléiade issued extravagant claims to originality, heaped contempt on their predecessors, and made daring experiments from which they later recoiled. But in the main they were right, and successful.

Du Bellay's thesis was this. It is unpatriotic for a Frenchman to write in Latin. It is an admission of inferiority for a Frenchman to write in French without trying to equal the grandest achievements of Greek and Latin literature. Therefore French poetry should 'loot the Roman city and the Delphic temple', raising the literature of France to a higher power by importing into it themes, myths, stylistic devices, all the beauty of Greece and Rome. Abandon the old medieval mystery-plays and morality-plays. But also abandon the idea of writing plays in Latin. Write tragedies and comedies as fine as those of the classical dramatists, but in French. Abandon the old-style French lyrics, leave them to provincial festivals and folk-gatherings: they are 'vulgar'. But also abandon the idea of writing lyrics in Latin or Greek. Write 'odes still unknown to the French muse' containing all that makes Pindar great, but in French.

Du Bellay was right. Nationalism narrows culture; extreme classicism desiccates it. To enrich a national literature by bringing into it the strength of the continent-wide and centuries-ripe culture to which it belongs is the best way to make it eternally great. This can be proved both positively and negatively in the Renaissance. It was this synthesis of national and classical elements that produced, in England, Shakespeare's tragedies and the epics of Spenser and Milton. It was the same synthesis in France that, after a period of experiment, produced the lyrics of Ronsard, the satires of Boileau, the dramas not only of Racine and Corneille but of Molière. It was the failure to complete such a synthesis that kept the Germans and certain other nations from producing any great works of literature during the sixteenth century, and made them spend their efforts either on imitating other nations, writing folk-songs and folk-tales, or composing faded elegances in faded Latin.

Ronsard and his friends claimed that he was the first Frenchman to write odes, and even to use the word *ode.* The brilliant investigations of M. Laumonier [in his *Ronsard poète lyrique,* 1923] and others have made it quite clear that, as his opponents pointed out at the time, he invented neither the word nor the thing. The word *ode* had been used in both French and current Latin years before Ronsard started writing; and the actual invention of the French ode is due to Clément Marot quite as much as to Ronsard. It is not even clear whether, as he declared, Ronsard was the first of his group to write odes in the manner of Pindar.

What is absolutely certain is that Ronsard was the founder of elevated lyric poetry on classical models, not only for France, but for all modern Europe. He achieved this by the bold step of publishing a huge single collection of ninety-four odes all at once, *The First Four Books of the Odes.* This act he conceived as rivalry with Pindar (who left four books of triumphal odes containing forty-four poems) and Horace (who left four books of odes, 103 poems in all, but on the average much shorter than Ronsard's), and as the annunciation of a new trend in French poetry. Although he drew subjects and models for these poems not only from Pindar but from Horace, and Anacreon, and many other sources both within and without classical lyric, the most striking and ambitious of his odes were written in rivalry with Pindar, and with them we can begin a survey of Pindaric odes in modern literature.

Horace said that following Pindar's flight was like soaring on artificial wings, and was apt to end in a spectacular failure. Did Ronsard succeed?

Pindar's odes deal with victories at the Olympic and other national games. Ronsard tried to find subjects even nobler. The first one in book 1, for instance, praises King Henri II for concluding a successful peace with England, and the sixth glorifies François de Bourbon on the victory of Cérisoles. But most of them were written for a friend or a patron with no particular occasion to celebrate, and are merely encomia. Therefore the sense of exultation and immediate triumph which swept through Pindar's victory odes is often absent from Ronsard's, and is replaced by an elaborate but sometimes frigid courtesy.

In power of imagination and richness of style, Ronsard falls far below Pindar. His sentences are straightforward, often coming very close to rhyming prose. Often enough their meaning is obscure, because he felt that, to be a poet like Pindar, he must cultivate the dark profundity of an oracle. He usually achieved this, however, not by writing sentences in which every word is charged with deep significance, their order too is meaningful, and whole phrases contain many different layers of thought, through which the reader must slowly penetrate; but by using lofty periphrases and alluding to strange myths, all of which become quite clear as soon as one recognizes the reference. The sentences themselves are far simpler and less various than those of Pindar. His vocabulary is neat and pretty (with an unfortunate passion for diminutives, which he owed to Marullus), but, apart from proper names, seldom has anything comparable with the blazing new-forged compounds and the white-hot poetical words of Pindar. The myths he introduces are far from being flat and conventional. Some are deliberately abstruse. Some are as rich as a Renaissance tapestry. *Odes,* 1. 10 contains a fine, and largely original, description of the birth of the Muses, their presentation to their father 'Jupin', their song of the battle between the Gods and the Titans, and the power with which Jupiter rewarded them. Such myths are not pedantic. But they are not heroic. They have not Pindar's burning intensity. They contain no pictures like Pindar's lightning-flash vision of the maiden Cyrene straining motionless in combat with a lion [in ***Pythian 9***], and we feel that Ronsard could not see such things, because his eyes were not opened.

Ronsard's Pindaric odes are divided into strophes, antistrophes, and epodes. In itself this is uselessly artificial, since they were not meant to be sung by a choir and danced. The stanzas are made up of blocks of short lines, mostly varying between six and nine syllables from poem to poem. Each stanza is practically uniform; there is none of Pindar's ebb and flow. The rhymes are usually arranged in couplets interspersed among quatrains. What is most important is this: nearly every stanza is hermetically sealed off, to form one group of sentences without carry-over; and within each stanza the sense nearly always stops at the line-ending, and seldom elsewhere. This is far more limited and hampered than the style of Pindar, whose thought flows on from line to line, stanza to stanza, triad to triad, without necessarily pausing at any point not dictated by the sense, until the end of the poem. Evidently Ronsard still has the little two-forward-and-two-back rhythms of the folk-dance running in his head. That epitomizes the differences between his odes and those of Pindar. Ronsard's are a simpler, more naïve, thinner, less melodious imitation of a rich, polyphonic, warmly orchestrated lyrical work.

In 1551 Ronsard gave up the attempt to rival Pindar. In fact he had neither the character nor the environment which would enable him to become a second Pindar; he was too soft, and his public too shallow. In the odes he often refers to his attempt to copy Homer and Vergil in a plaster cast of the *Aeneid,* called *The Franciad;* but his soul was not deep enough and strong enough to enable him to complete such a task, and he abandoned it after four books. In the same way, he gradually dropped the manner and matter of Pindar, and returned to the poet whom he had once boasted of surpassing. He abandoned the *A-Z-P* arrangement in strophe, antistrophe, and epode, and took to writing in couplets and little four-line and six-line stanzas. His tone became quieter, melancholy instead of heroic, frivolous instead of triumphant. He boasted less often of playing a Theban string, and turned towards the softer, more congenial music of Horace, Anacreon, and the Greek Anthology.

Still, his attempt, and the supporting work of the Pléiade, were not useless. He set French lyric poetry free from the elaborate stanza-forms in which a very few rhymes, difficultly interwoven, confined the poet's thought. He shook off much of the heritage of folk-song, which had originally been natural and had become conventional and jejune. He and his brother-stars in the Pléiade added many valuable words and stylistic devices to the French language, from their study of Greek and Latin poetry. He showed that French lyric could be noble, and thoughtful, and equal in majesty to the greatest events it might choose to celebrate.

The Italian Ronsard—or, as he hoped, the Italian Pindar—was Gabriello Chiabrera (1552-1638), whose epitaph, written by Pope Urban VIII, boasted that he was the 'first to fit Theban rhythms to Tuscan strings, following the Swan of Dirce (Pindar) on bold wings which did not fail', and that, like his great fellow-townsman Columbus, he 'found new worlds of poetry'. In his youth Chiabrera was made enthusiastic for the study and emulation of classical literature by association with Paulus Manutius, son of the publisher Aldus, and by hearing the lectures of Marc-Antoine Muret, the brilliant friend and commentator of Ronsard. His Pindaric poems are partly independent creations, but partly modelled on those of Ronsard and the poetry of the Pléiade. They are only a small proportion of his large output, which includes several epics, dramas, pastorals, and 'musical dramas' (opera libretti written in an attempt to re-create the true effect of the combination of music and words in Greek tragedy). His *Heroic Poems* (*Canzoni eroiche*) contain about a hundred odes, of which twelve are divided like Pindar's into strophes, antistrophes, and epodes. They are all composed in stanzas of six, eight, ten, and sometimes more than ten lines. The lines are uneven in length, sometimes having three beats, or four, or five. The rhymes are unevenly distributed: a typical pattern being *abab cddc efef.* So both rhythm and rhyme are irregularly balanced; but the pattern struck out in the first stanza is carefully preserved in all the others. The general effect is therefore quite like that of Pindar's odes, except that the turning triadic movement of the dance is lost. The few triadic poems run in shorter, simple stanzas.

Chiabrera had genuine victories to celebrate. He wrote a number of these poems after naval battles in which the galleys of Florence played a successful part against the Turks, enslaving Turkish prisoners and liberating Christian slaves. However, neither in them nor in his numerous poems glorifying various Italian dignitaries of state and church did he achieve anything like Pindar's volcanic blaze: only a mild and pleasing warmth. The besetting sin of baroque poetry is already traceable in his poems—the habit of introducing a classical allusion not to support and add beauty to the poet's own invention, but as a substitute for imagination. The odes are crowded with Greco-Roman deities and myths, Apollo and the Muses, the tears of Aurora for Memnon, the beams of bright Phoebus, and the roars of the Titans; yet Chiabrera puts them in, not because they excite him, but because they are expected. The melody of his odes is very charming, for he is skilful at interweaving rhyme and rhythm, but they do not sound so much like Pindar's triumphal odes as like gracefully elaborated Italian canzoni. Like Ronsard, whom he admired and strove to emulate, Chiabrera was really a songster.

The word *ode* was introduced into English in Shakespeare's time. For Shakespeare it meant a love-poem. He used it to describe one in *Love's Labour's Lost,* and in *As You Like It* Rosalind complains that her lover (true to one of the conventions of pastoral) is carving ROSALIND on the tree-trunks, hanging odes upon hawthorns and elegies upon brambles. Spenser's exquisite *Epithalamion* is not a Pindaric ode, despite its metrical complexity: apparently it is a blend of the Italian canzone with Catullus' wedding-poems. The earliest extant English poem actually called an ode is an address to the Muses printed in the introduction of Thomas Watson's εκατομπαΘια, or *Passionate Century of Love,* and signed by one C. Downhalus (1582): it is a pleasant little piece in six-line stanzas, but very far from the Pindaric pattern.

The first actual imitations of Pindar in English came two years later. They were in *Pandora,* published in 1584 by John Southern. The book contains three odes and three 'odellets'. The first ode, addressed to the earl of Oxford, promises to capture 'the spoyle of Thebes' and cries:

> Vaunt us that never man before,
> Now in England, knewe Pindars string.

However, Southern does not really know Pindar's string; he is roughly and ignorantly copying Ronsard. His odes are merely poems in a regular four-beat rhythm, arranged in couplets and quatrains and divided into stanzas called strophes, antistrophes, and epodes—but not even keeping the *A-Z-P* Pindaric pattern which Ronsard understood and followed. Southern's sole importance is historical. Even at that it is not very great, for his 'imitation of Pindar' was only an ignorant copy of the work of another imitator.

The first truly Pindaric poem in English is one of the greatest. This is Milton's prelude and hymn *On the Morning of Christ's Nativity,* which he began on Christmas morning, 1629. Not long before, he had bought a copy of Pindar: it is now in Harvard University Library, and shows by its annotations how carefully he read it. After a short prelude—in which he calls on the Heavenly Muse to give the poem as a Christmas present to Jesus—Milton breaks into a rich, powerful, and beautiful descriptive hymn in a regular succession of eight-line stanzas. The lines are of irregular length, rhyming *aabccbdd* and rising to a final alexandrine. The hymn is therefore not written in triads like most of Pindar's odes. What enables us to call it Pindaric is the dancing metre with its controlled asymmetry, the vivid imagery, and, most of all, the splendid strength and vividness of the myths, both the dying deities of Greece and Rome:

> In consecrated earth,
> And on the holy hearth,
> The Lars and Lemures moan with midnight plaint

and the glorious new spirits of Christianity, visiting the earth to celebrate the incarnation of God:

> The helmèd cherubim
> And sworded seraphim
> Are seen in glittering ranks with wings displayed.

At last, a modern pupil of Pindar, meditating on the greatest theme in Christian thought, and using all the eloquence and imagination with which both classical antiquity and biblical learning had endowed him, had achieved an even stronger and loftier flight than the eagle of Thebes.

Ben Jonson also attempted the Pindaric vein, with interesting and original results. In the same year as Milton wrote his Pindaric hymn on Christmas, Jonson completed his *Ode on the Death of Sir H. Morison.* This is actually built in the triadic form *A-Z-P;* and, although the rhymes are arranged in couplets in the 'turn' and 'counter-turn', and not much more elaborately in the 'stand', the lines are so widely varied in length and so skilfully married to the meaning that the effect is broader, more Pindaric, than the rather operatic stanzas of Chiabrera, and more thoughtful than the lilting odes of Ronsard. And yet, the thoughtfulness, the slow pace, the frequent epigrams (more spacious than Pindar's brief aphorisms), are really derived from Jonson's favourite poet Horace. One famous stanza will show the free form and the meditative tone:

> It is not growing like a tree
> In bulk, doth make man better be;
> Or standing long an oak, three hundred year,
> To fall a log at last, dry, bald, and sere:
> A lily of a day
> Is fairer far in May,
> Although it fall and die that night;
> It was the plant and flower of light.
> In small proportions we just beauties see;
> And in short measures, life may perfect be.

This, then, is the first of many great modern odes in which the styles of the two great classical lyricists, Pindar and Horace, interpenetrate to form a new beauty.

The modern ode was created very slowly, after many failures. In these two poems of Milton and Jonson it was newly born. We can now attempt to define it. In modern literature an ode is a poem combining personal emotion with deep meditation on a subject of wide scope or broad public interest. It is short enough to express one emotion in a single movement, but long enough to develop a number of different aspects of that emotion. It is either addressed to one person (human or superhuman) or evoked by one occasion of particular significance. Its moving force is emotion more than intellect; but the emotional excitement is tempered, and its expression arranged, by intellectual reflection. The emotion of the ode is stirred and sustained by one or more of the nobler and less transient events of human life, particularly those in which temporary and physical facts are transfigured by the spiritual and eternal. The interplay of the emotions and reflections which make its material is reflected in the controlled irregularity of its verse-form.

> 'Who now reads Cowley?' asked Pope, adding
>
> 'Forgot his epic, nay Pindaric art.'

Abraham Cowley (1618-67) was a precocious and talented poet who claimed to be the inventor of the English Pindaric ode, and for a long time imposed this claim upon the public. His rhapsodic odes (published in 1656) were indeed directly suggested by his study of Pindar; and he said in his preface that he tried to write, not exactly as Pindar wrote, but as he would have written if he had been writing in English (and, by implication, in the seventeenth century). He was rightly determined not to make a plaster cast, but to re-create and rival. Therefore he abandoned Pindar's triadic form and replaced it by irregular verse, without even the stanzaic regularity of Milton's and Jonson's odes. If it had not been rhymed and had not possessed a certain basic pulse, we should now call it free verse. This, however, was not Cowley's invention. Madrigals in free asymmetrical patterns, bound together only by vague rhyme-schemes, were common before his day; Milton himself, Vaughan, and Crashaw had already published more serious poems in equally free forms. If Cowley made any innovation, it was in using a free form, not to follow the ebb and flow of song, but to represent the gush and lapse and swell of emotional excitement. The real effect of his work was to make the concept of a Pindaric ode, in which the poet's emotion masters him and is imaged in the irregular metre, familiar to English poets and their readers. His poems themselves are negligible.

Ode means 'song'. Poets knew this, in the Renaissance and the baroque age: they endeavoured to enhance the beauty of their odes by having them set to a musical accompaniment, or by making them reproduce, in words, the movement and harmony of music. Those who wrote Horatian lyrics, if they thought of music, usually designed their work for one singer, or at most a small group. But with its broad sweep and surging emotion, the Pindaric ode was fully able to reproduce or to evoke the music of a choir and an orchestra.

In a very early ode of this kind Milton emphasizes the juncture of poetry and music:

> Blest pair of sirens, pledges of heaven's joy,
> Sphere-born harmonious sisters, Voice and Verse,
> Wed your divine sounds, and mixed power employ.

And he goes on to describe the eternal music of heaven, where the bright seraphim and cherubim are the orchestra, and the blessed souls sing everlastingly to their music. He does not, however, attempt to echo musical sounds in his own beautiful lines.

The first English opera (*The Siege of Rhodes*) was performed in 1656, and, after the Restoration, English musical taste turned eagerly towards the new Italian music—highly emotional yet extremely dignified, gorgeously decorative and often quite unreal. In 1683 the London Musical Society inaugurated annual performances of musical odes in honour of the patron of music, St. Cecilia. Purcell himself set the first. In 1687 John Dryden produced a technical masterpiece, his *Song for St. Cecilia's Day,* to be set by the Italian composer Draghi. Beginning with a reminiscence of Ovid, proceeding to a combination of biblical and pagan musicology, then evoking the sound of trumpets, drums, flutes, violins, and the organ, it ends with a Grand Chorus on the Last Judgement.

This was little more than a skilful trick; but ten years later Dryden changed skill into art, and wrote, for the same occasion, *Alexander's Feast.* It was a great success. Dryden thought it the best poem he had ever writ; and long afterwards it was splendidly reset by Handel.

This was only one, although the greatest, of the many musical Pindaric odes written in the baroque period. They are Pindaric in the studied irregularity which reflects their connexion with music (and of course in much else beside—in their use of myths, their loftiness of language, &.); but where Pindar designed his poems for the dance, these odes are written for orchestra and stationary singers. (I have sometimes thought that the Horatian odes with their musical settings find their best parallel in the fugue, the Pindaric odes like *Alexander's Feast* in the grand toccatas and chaconnes which Bach wrote to test the fullest powers of his own art, and the odes of the revolutionary period in the symphony.) A recent writer has distinguished four classes of these works—sacred odes, cantata odes, 'occasional' or laureate odes, and odes for St. Cecilia's Day—and has worked out from contemporary criticisms and parodies (such as Swift's *Cantata*) the qualities which were considered necessary to make a good musical ode. Clearly it was a difficult art, but—like opera and oratorio—an art in which success was much hoped for and highly rewarded. Contemporary poets have made few attempts to marry their poems to music in this way, and the most moving recent works have been made by blending new music with literature already accepted: Copland's *Lincoln Portrait* and Vaughan William's *Serenade for Music.*

The greatest lyricist of the eighteenth century did not write a Pindaric ode for music. Instead, he wrote a Pindaric ode which contained music, the music not only of the orchestra but of nature:

> The rocks and nodding groves rebellow to the roar—

the light dance of spirits and the floating grace of Venus herself. Gray's *Progress of Poesy* begins and ends with an allusion to Pindar, and, with true Pindaric dignity, sets Gray himself in the direct line of mighty poets with Shakespeare, Milton, and Dryden. Perhaps, as a Bard, he could foresee his successors, Keats and Wordsworth and Shelley.

Most of the Pindaric odes written in the baroque period were not musical but ceremonial. With the aid of Pindar, poets celebrated the births, marriages, and deaths of the nobility and gentry; the accessions, coronations, birthdays, jubilees, and victories of monarchs; the founding of a society, the announcement of an invention, the construction of a public building, any public event that expressed the pomp and circumstance of the age. The result was exactly as Horace had predicted—a series of spectacular, bombastic failures. More bad poems have been written in the intention of rivalling Pindar than in any other sphere of classical imitation. True poets are literally inspired by their subjects: energy and eloquence are breathed into them, they are excited, mastered, dominated, they *must* write. Their problem is to control their emotions, and to direct them to the point of maximum expressiveness. But mediocre poets are not overwhelmed by their subjects, not even excited by them. They try, therefore, to borrow the themes and expressions of true poetic excitement from some other poet who was deeply moved and memorably eloquent. With the best available wax, and selected high-grade feathers, they construct artificial wings, launch themselves off into the azure air in pursuit of Pindar, the Theban eagle, and fall into the deep, deep bog of bathos with a resounding flop.

It was particularly difficult to be truly Pindaric in the seventeenth and eighteenth centuries. Pindar lived in an age abounding in great poets, where prose, and the type of thought best expressed in prose, were not yet fully developed. The baroque period was an era of orderly thought, measured prose, and cool, symmetrical verse. Even the lyrics of such an age usually chime with all the regularity and less than the harmony of church bells. The distinction between ordinary common sense and emotional excitement, whatever its cause, was then marked by a broad, almost impassable frontier. Therefore the poets who announced that they felt themselves transported by Pindaric excitement convinced neither themselves nor their audience nor posterity.

'What wise and sacred drunkenness
This day overmasters me?'

—cries Boileau; but he knows perfectly well that he is stone sober, and determined to write a Pindaric ode.

Even if the baroque poets had been capable of feeling and expressing genuine enthusiasm, the subjects of their Pindaric odes were seldom such as to generate it. That is the fatal defect of 'occasional' poetry. Pindar loved the great games, the handsome youths striving against one another, the horses and the chariots and the shouting crowds. Countless baroque poets were personally quite indifferent to the marriage of His Serene Highness or the erection of a new Belvedere in his lordship's grounds, but made odes on such subjects as a matter of duty. Boileau, who detested war, wrote an ode on the capture of Namur. The results of the spurious excitement produced by poets labouring their wits on tasks like these are painful to the lover of literature, unless he has a hypertrophied sense of humour. If he has, he may even collect some of the finer examples, such as Edward (*Night Thoughts*) Young's panegyric on international trade:

Is 'merchant' an inglorious name?
No; fit for Pindar such a theme;
Too great for me; I pant beneath the weight.
If loud as Ocean were my voice,
If words and thoughts to court my choice
Outnumbered sands, I could not reach its height.

Kings, merchants are in league and love,
Earth's odours pay soft airs above,
That o'er the teeming field prolific range.
Planets are merchants; take, return,
Lustre and heat; by traffic burn;
The whole creation is one vast Exchange.

When Shadwell was made Poet Laureate in 1688, and began the practice of producing annual birthday odes for the king, he initiated a long, heavy tradition of laureate poetry in which inspiration was replaced by perspiration.

Truly great Pindaric odes unite strong and rapid eloquence with genuine and deep emotion. It is a rare combination. The baroque era, for all its talk about the poetic sublime and the need of rivalling Pindar, seldom achieved it. Even although the themes of death and virtue and young womanhood were, and are, profoundly significant, Dryden failed to make anything really moving out of them in his ode *To the Pious Memory of the Accomplished Young lady, Mrs. Anne Killigrew.* It has been called 'the finest biographical ode in the language'; but it contains so much verbal cleverness that Dryden clearly either did not feel deeply about the girl's death, or was unwilling to give his emotions free expression. It was nearly a century later that Thomas Gray, with his sensitive spirit and his love of wonder, found subjects to excite both himself and the readers of his Pindaric odes, and, not only in the passion of the words and rhythms, but in the gloomy forebodings and defiant challenges of the Bard, announced the age of revolution. (pp. 230-44)

Gilbert Highet, "The Renaissance and Afterwards: Lyric Poetry," in his The Classical Tradition: Greek and Roman Influences on Western Literature, *Oxford University Press, 1949, pp. 219-54.*

Favorinus (fl. c. second century) on Vergil's imitation of Pindar:

Now among the passages (of the *Aeneid*) which particularly seem to have needed revision and correction is the one which was composed about Mount Aetna. For wishing to rival the poem which the earlier poet Pindar composed about the nature and eruption of that mountain [***Pythian 1***], he has heaped up such words and expressions that in this passage at least he is more extravagant and bombastic even than Pindar himself, who was thought to have too rich and luxuriant a style.

Now in the first place, Pindar has more closely followed the truth and has given a realistic description of what actually happened there, and what he saw with his own eyes; namely, that Aetna in the daytime sends forth smoke and at night fire; but Vergil, laboring to find grand and sonorous words, confuses the two periods of time and makes no distinction between them. Then the Greek has vividly pictured the streams of fire belched from the depths and the flowing rivers of smoke, and the rushing of lurid and spiral volumes of flame into the waters of the sea, like so many fiery serpents; but our poet, attempting to render "a lurid stream of smoke," has clumsily and diffusely piled up the words atram nubem turbine piceo et favilla fumantem, "a dusky cloud smoking with eddies black and glowing ash," and what Pindar called "founts," he has harshly and inaccurately rendered "balls of flame." . . .

Favorinus, quoted in Ancilla to Classical Reading, *by Moses Hadas, 1954.*

John H. Finley, Jr. (lecture date 1952)

[In the following excerpt from a lecture originally delivered at Oberlin College in 1952, Finley discusses Pindar's use of symbolism, comparing his understanding of how images convey meaning to those of Homer and Aeschylus. The critic further discusses the theme of harmony in several of Pindar's odes.]

Pindar and Aeschylus were born within a few years of each other in or about the late twenties of the sixth century. Both saw at close range the massive events that led in the great age of Greece, and both intensely felt the breath and movement of the times. Having gone in youth from Thebes to Athens for his musical training, Pindar could have known almost as well as Aeschylus the temper of the recently and painfully founded democracy. He seems even to have had ties with the family of Cleisthenes, the founder. The two young men presumably knew each other in these years, though there is no information that they did. Pindar felt continuing admiration for Athens during her period of glory in the Persian wars and for a time thereafter, but the paths of the two men already diverged with the wars, Thebes having submitted to Persia with resultant loss, shame, and lingering need of self-justification. Both visited Sicily during the 470's for performances of their works at the invitation of the Syracusan dynast, Hieron. Aeschylus, who seems otherwise to have passed his life and produced his some ninety plays in Athens, died on a second visit to Sicily in 456 / 5. Pindar must have traveled throughout Greece and the islands, possibly to Cyrene in Africa, as performances of his choruses dictated. Besides our four books of odes for athletic victors, he left thirteen books, chiefly of works for religious festivals, such as paeans, dithyrambs, and hymns, and to a less extent, of poems for individuals, such as threnoi and enkomia, of all of which only fragments remain. He survived Aeschylus by at least a decade, during which time the military expansion of Athens evoked by her success in the Persian wars and begun during Aeschylus' lifetime reached its height. The Athenians overran Pindar's native Boeotia during the decade from 457 to 447, and a year earlier invested the island city of Aegina, where Pindar was much at home and for which more of his extant poems were composed than for any other state. The divergence, somewhat masked at the start, between the innovating temper of Athens and the conservative spirit of Thebes and the other Greek oligarchies grew starker with each year after Salamis. If much in theme and cast of mind and style unites the two men, the currents of their times served equally to divide them.

Ancient commentators more commonly ally them on grounds of style than, with their sharper historical sense, do modern scholars. Eduard Meyer [in *Geschichte des Altertums,* 1939] confronts them in a fine passage as spokesmen respectively of a dying and of a growing culture, and this judgment expresses the usual view. The two emerge almost Hector and Achilles. "Strong was the man who fled but still stronger he who pursued him behind." On historical grounds the appraisal is just. The future was on the side of the progressive spirit of reason and independent inquiry which Athens embodied and Aeschylus deeply felt, and tragedy, the vehicle which he created, was the vehicle of the future, in the sense that it presents characters in their inner independence and responsibility, trying to grasp and deal with their fates. His lonely and innovating Prometheus has no counterpart in Pindar. If it is held a chief achievement of the Greeks to have reached a view of man as obedient to reason and through reason molding nature and society, Aeschylus is by far the more creative and prophetic figure.

Yet this historical judgment is one-sided. It weighs too little those elements of response to life which show less openly in history. It is true that of all the well-known Greek writers Pindar has been the least understood in modern centuries. Only Milton, Marvell, and Gray greatly reflect him; even Pound, who might have been expected to respond to him, mysteriously fails, perhaps because at first glance Pindar seems chiefly an apologist for the established order. The surface reasons for this neglect are clear enough; the latent reasons are harder to catch. The athletic setting of his poems can seem alien and even trivial. His language can be imperious, steep, and on occasion private, but not more so than Aeschylus' language, which is more understood. A more essential difficulty is that he speaks, and evidently thinks, through an elaborate set of symbols, partly figures from the heroic tradition such as Achilles or Ajax, partly divine figures or, so to speak, momentarily divine figures, such as Hesychia, Quietude, at the opening of ***P.* [*Pythian*] *8*** or Theia, The Bright One, in ***I.* [*Isthmian*] *5.*** His gods and heroes are of course well known, and most of these divinized abstractions appear in Hesiod's *Theogony* and in other writers. The difficulty is really not in these figures themselves but in the train of thought that they carry. Pindar is beyond compare the symbolist among Greek poets, not in conscious rejection, like the French symbolists, of common logic or in any ascetic effort to reach a more absolute plane of being, but because these heroic or religious figures are his natural way of stating the relationships and meanings of life. This is what is meant by those who speak of his prelogical way of thinking. A state of being evokes to him another plane of completer being on which the gods or heroes move, and in speaking of the one he soon passes to the other. But legends are naturally imprecise and inclusive. The Ajax of one poem, for example, is not quite the Ajax of another. Even in the same poem, he can include several meanings. "The greater mass of men is blind of heart," Pindar writes in ***N.* [*Nemean*] *7.*** "Could it see the truth, brave Ajax furious from the armor had not driven the smooth sword through his chest." (vv.24-27). The scene is Ajax's suicide after the dead Achilles' arms had been awarded Odysseus rather than himself. But what does the crowd's blindness precisely mean? Is Pindar defending himself against specific recent criticism, or making a more general claim that in the confusions of life the poet discerns true grounds of excellence as the crowd does not? Or does the figure of the suffering Ajax include, as it does in two other poems (***I.4,N.8***), the Dorian ideal of the man of honor and endurance, and thus look in part to the victor, not to the poet? It is often impossible to define Pindar's exact implication. This is so because of the inclusiveness of symbols, notably his. They cover several facets of a state of being which to him is the essential meaning of an occasion and the true ground of his poem. The difficulty of understanding him is not in his boldness of language or use of myth or cult, but in the weight of meaning which his mythic figures carry.

This is one difficulty; a second may go deeper. Aeschylus reflects the rational and innovating temper of Athens in his characteristic use of the sequence of three plays, the trilogy, by which he expresses time and development. Even the darkest of the extant plays, the *Seven Against Thebes,* concludes its trilogy, if not with progress, at least with emergence from error and violence. The other plays, except the unique *Persians,* have to do with evolutions, which, to be sure, transcend analytical reason in the sense that they involve suffering and experience, yet culminate in reason since suffering and experience bring a higher order. Aeschylus has enormous hope in the world. He believes in the possibility of progress, though it is not an easy progress and must be won by something like Aristotle's cleansing of the heart as applied to a whole society. His thought expresses itself so to speak in a line; Pindar's in a point. Through his conservative Theban background, but in large part certainly through his visionary temperament, Pindar is not interested in social change. His concern is for absolute being, a state which he feels men rise to in great moments and which alone sheds meaning on life. To follow him is chiefly to penetrate the various meanings which he attaches to this absoluteness and to see its relationship to ordinary life. Such a vision causes him to reject certain gross or violent myths about the gods; "leave war and every strife remote from the immortals." (***O.*** ***[Olympian]*** ***9.*** 40-41) In this sense he can be said to share Aeschylus' innovating outlook. But the impulse is different. His world is basically static, whereas Aeschylus' is evolutionary; hence the previous comparison to the point and the line. To compare them with their contemporaries, Pindar verges toward Parmenides, Aeschylus toward Heraclitus; the one toward unity and rest, the other toward change and movement. It is of course true that movement implies goal, and though Heraclitus sees the upward and downward balance of the world, he approves the soul's ascent to the final fire. Similarly the movement of Aeschylus' trilogies culminates in rest and order finally achieved. This vision of a final order beyond change is the bond between the four men, not least between Aeschylus and Pindar. It is astonishing that so violent an age as theirs could have produced this striving for ultimate harmony. Or perhaps highest energy has an affinity for rest and one should find parallels in Michelangelo's neo-Platonism or the sense of transcendence in Shakespeare's late comedies. But however that may be, Pindar and Aeschylus rise to this sense of order at very different stages, Pindar from the immediate events of common life, Aeschylus through an historical vision of the painful ascent of society as a whole.

Pindar is difficult, then, through both the method and the object of his thought. His method is the symbolism whereby he evokes a kind of ideal counterpart of known reality, static and timeless, inhabiting a lucent region like Olympus in the *Odyssey,* "which is not shaken by winds nor ever wet with rain nor does snow draw near it, but the clear air spreads cloudless, and light courses flashing." His object is to lay hold on the repose of this ideal realm, since he feels that self-transcendence, the flash of the gods in this world, is the only thing that gives it value. It could be said that this difference between the two is simply the difference between lyric poetry, the poetry of mood, and dramatic poetry, that of movement and conflict. This is of course true but does not alter the fact that each found or partly created a form appropriate to himself. The two forms, as suggested, also reflect two societies, the static regimen of the oligarchies and the evolving order of Athens. This is an important fact which bears even on the character and growth of these forms, and we shall return to it. But it is not, as an historical judgment suggests, the fact of final importance in our understanding of the two men. In every human life, even the most energetic and progressive, there must exist feeling for static form. If it were lacking, there could be no sense of the identifying essences of things: spring as contrasted to winter, youth as contrasted to age, all the apprehensible orders of existence through which at any given moment the world takes shape and repose. The fact of final importance about Pindar is not his oligarchic origins, though these may have inclined him to this way of thought, but the way of thought itself. If Aeschylus has been more relevant to Western political history since the Renaissance, and if his processes of mind have been easier for modern centuries, the fact does not diminish Pindar's relevance. It stands essentially outside of history and intellectual change, in the sense that response to the reposed shapes of life and feeling for a momentary or lasting harmony in things are themselves apperceptions which defy change.

Since a chief problem in understanding Pindar is his symbolic cast of thought and, despite some differences, a similar outlook shows in the great Aeschylean figures, it may be well to start with this outlook. The word symbol is ambiguous. In one sense every word, every sound, signifies something beyond itself. Certainly the attempt to express sensory impressions through words ends by conveying something quite different from the object originally perceived; and this something different is both less and more, less because it cannot convey the original object in its own completeness, more because it also conveys feelings about the object. Since feelings are thus involved even in sensory images, it follows that the most seemingly casual image in speech or writing tells something about the observer's attitude as well as about the observed. Homer's "Hector of the glancing helmet" or "wine-dark sea" evoke not only a man or the sea, but convey a certain nobility in Hector as warrior and a certain expanse and dark majesty in the sea. But if it is thus impossible to distinguish exactly between an image and a symbol, symbols seem to bear a heavier weight of meaning and to exist proportionately less for purposes of objective description. Their main burden, if one may put it so, is of categorization. They lift the thing or act which they describe largely out of its own existence into something significant of a larger setting. Symbols have especially to do with the observer's feelings. Granted that images carry such feelings also, their main function is toward the object. The emphasis of symbols is more intellectual. Though they do not break the sensory bond with life but express the mind's categories through the involvement of the senses, they yet chiefly convey meaning and significance. At the start of the *Agamemnon* are two passages about eagles. In the first they shriek vengeance for the young which have been stolen from their nests. In the second Artemis is angry because they kill a pregnant hare. Malraux sees in the age-old motif of beak and talon expression of the world as will and violence. This feeling is here. The first eagles are the Atreidae's just violence against the adulterer Paris; the second eagles are the evil involved in this just violence, which destroys peace and interrupts order and fertility. In killing Iphigeneia in order to calm the winds and let the army embark, Agamemnon acts with the second as well as with the first eagles. When Orestes describes himself in the *Choephoroe* as the eagle's son (v.247), he falls heir to this fearful involvement of just with unjust violence, which is the subject of the trilogy. The word symbol as used here will mean such a description of something only in part for itself, but chiefly for its overtone of judgment or categorization.

This method of expressing meaning, not by open statement and analysis, but through the refraction of the senses, is of course native to the arts in all periods. But it has a special quality in the verse which comes into existence before the development of prose as an opposite and competing form. Prose forces poetry to mark off its own ground. The French symbolists consciously rejected processes of thought suitable to logical inquiry and reasoned choice, in favor of a more intuitive and direct apperception of being. A cardinal point of John Dewey's was that reason exists to solve problems, and though it would be untrue of much philosophic and speculative prose, not to mention the prose of fiction, to say that it has no concern with the sphere of being but only with that of Dewey's problem-solving, the sphere of action, yet the growth of prose has tended to relegate verse to the former sphere. These distinctions are elusive. Verse in trying to catch the nature of things of course looks to action also, since awareness of reality is the premise for action. What is involved seems something like the distinction between pure and applied science. Each has its characteristic emphasis, but it is hard to say where the one begins and the other ends or whether they are ever quite distinct. Similarly, awareness of life simply in itself precedes and surrounds any specific plans for life. Prose being incomparably the vehicle for the latter, verse in realizing itself has tended toward the former, increasingly in the last century. The point now being made is that in the early Greek centuries, as in the first stages of other literatures, this was not the case. Prose did not exist as a literary medium, evidently because the rational and empirical outlook which is at the heart of prose had not yet developed. One may therefore be justified in speaking, with Vico, of an age of feeling which expresses itself in particulars (the mythic figure) as contrasted to an age of reason which expresses itself in generalization (philosophic or scientific law) or in adopting the terms of Brooks Adams, age of faith and economic age. There need be no implication that feeling withers as reason grows. The continual redefinition of the arts asserts feeling's perpetual youth. But the opposite is what concerns us here—in Vico's terms, the undisputed reign of feeling before the rise of reason. Part of the charm of Greek literature is that it traversed these phases and their complex subdivisions with pristine response to each.

It is accordingly possible to speak of two main periods of Greek literature, which may be called the periods of symbolic and of conceptual thought. The point of division between the two, earlier in Ionia, is in Athens about the middle of the fifth century. This is the age of Anaxagoras and Protagoras, of Socrates' early manhood and Thucydides' youth, of the first enthusiasm for physical and historical inquiry, of nascent logic and political theory, and of the beginnings of serious interest in prose style. This is the turning point that leads to Aristotle and to the conceptual analysis of the arts and sciences which is the groundwork of Western thought. What is meant by the term conceptual thought is clear enough. It is the search for categories behind the sensuous play of image, for rational simplification underlying apparent variety. The term symbolic thought is less clear. It too seeks order and simplification, but not by evading the play of image which instead of being a source of confusion and hindrance is the very language by which it speaks and even sees.

What is implied in the term symbolic thought may be clarified by the example of the *Odyssey*. Odysseus in his travels goes through three main kinds of experience. The first is inward and moral. The lotus-eaters are languor and drowning of the will; Circe's arts are evidently the sensual pleasures; the Sirens' song is the intellectual pleasures. (The Sirens offer a Faustian vision; they explain history and nature. "We know all that the Argives and Trojans suffered by the gods' will in broad Troy; we know whatever comes into existence on the all-nourishing earth" [12.189-191]). Odysseus' visit to the underworld and speech with the dead, though akin to the Sirens' song as satisfying the mind, are more intimate and emotional as related to private memories and fears. Calypso at first glance resembles Circe, but her essential meaning is different: the Olympian possibility of life clear of death and age, though at the price of family, home, and the bonds of common humanity. These adventures comprise a kind of inward travel. A second category has to do with kinds of society. The Cyclopes live in primitive loneliness without ships or agriculture, dependent on their flocks. ("They have neither counselling assemblies nor established laws, but inhabit lonely caves on peaks of the high mountains. Each rules over his children and wives, and they have no regard for each other." [9.112-115]). They are as far below the social and inventive Greeks as the almost godlike Phaeacians are beyond them. In the latters' country it is perpetual spring. Their magic ships cross the seas without the work of helmsman or oarsmen. They live at ease in wealth and grace, and the very gods at times dine with them. They are slightly soft. ("We are not good boxers or wrestlers, but fast runners and unrivaled oarsmen. We love banquets, the lyre and the dance, changes of clothing, warm baths, and the bed." [8.246-249]) The Cyclopes and the Phaeacians are evidently primitive and Utopian extremes. A third class of adventures is geographical. Odysseus sees the island from which the winds come, the land where the sun pastures his cattle (clouds in the early form of the myth, whether or not consciously so to Homer), the famous strait with whirlpool and reefs, essence of the sea's danger, and the country "where a sleepless man might earn two wages, as herdsman and as shepherd of the white-fleeced flocks; so close are the paths of day and night." (10.84-86) It may be added that Odysseus himself is a not less representative figure, dominated as he is by the opposite desires for knowledge and for home, placelessness and place, uncommitment and commitment, life as idea and life as choice.

The query is, how conceive the cast of thought behind this story. Are the adventures allegorical? The answer is certainly no, if by allegory is meant the conscious dressing of a concept in sensuous form, for example, Bunyan's Vanity Fair for Temptation, Dante's Virgil for Reason, or Prodicus' two goddesses for the virtuous and the profane life. Not only is the story too translucent for such a purpose and the adventures too clearly on one plane, but Homeric Greek lacks words for such abstractions as sloth, the sensual pleasures, the intellectual pleasures. The generation of the sophists first fully elaborated these and similar terms, and Socrates' famous difficulties in the Dialogues had a double cause: not only that abstractions are elusive but that the very words for them had to be coined or recast. Prodicus' story of the two goddesses, just mentioned, seems the first clear example of allegory in Greek. To repeat, this definition of allegory assumes that the intellectual abstraction is already in the narrator's mind and that he invents the sensuous terminology to give the abstraction color. But if Homer lacks such abstractions, is his narrative simply an adventure story like a thousand others? The answer is again no, since otherwise posterity would hardly have found in Odysseus' travels the obvious meaning that they contain, nor would Odysseus have kept for later ages his character as the adventurer in experience. He is not a random adventurer like Sinbad but one whose voyage is felt to be analytical of experience generally, or at least of masculine experience.

How then conceive a process of thought which seems to have no need of concepts, yet deals with what is later recognized as their substance? The answer is no longer simple. It apparently calls for two assumptions: first, of sensuous feeling for experience so strong and so fresh as to suffuse whatever judgments the mind makes, with the result that the judgment and the experience become intertwined, each invoking and expressing the other; and second, of some confinement and limitation not so much of experience as of the accepted means of expressing it, through ritual or dance or cycles of stories about known characters. This latter assumption may be slightly retrospective, positing such traditions because they are seen to have existed. Yet it is not in fact hard to imagine stories getting started in a simpler and more comprehensible society and then accreting other stories, so that cycles would come to be formed which would perpetuate themselves because they remained relevant. These would comprise, so to speak, a common denominator of the varied experience of individuals, but would be capable of change as new talent and fresh conditions prompted. Parry's analysis of the methods of oral poetry [Milman Parry in his *The Making of Homeric verse,* 1971], though not directed to this question of the way in which an unlettered poet sees reality, is nevertheless relevant in describing a tradition which keeps familiar forms of expression because they are both functional to the singer and known to his hearers, yet which is continually hospitable to changes that a new singer brings and other singers, as well as audiences, learn from him and make their own. As said, it is not hard to understand the growth of such stories about known characters in accepted situations, or to see how they could comprise a kind of chart of common experience, on a more exalted and wider plane, to be sure, but basically proportionate to experience because it was their function to interpret it. This was our second assumption, of a vocabulary of character and situation so familiar that the poet phrases all his major insights and judgments through its sensuous medium, indeed himself thinks through its medium.

This thinking through a sensuous medium was our first assumption and remains the harder. Yet exactly this assumption is necessary if, until the age of Socrates and the sophists, or a little earlier outside the mainland, the Greeks did not begin to rely on conceptual analysis for those central interpretations of the world, the state, moral standards, and the relationships of social life which reason was later to furnish through its medium of prose. As suggested, poetry still supremely expresses our existential awareness of all these relationships, though in rivalry now with a conceptual prose which is not always and only directed toward problem-solving, but rises to visions of reality also. Even prospective poets today go to school to Aristotle's reason, not to Homer's symbol, and learn habits of conceptuality which they must later unlearn. The present passionate rejection by poetry of anything but directest feeling partly signifies intuition's struggle against our universal schooling in concept. Yet all societies depend on some widespread common view of reality. Intuition grasps the fuller meanings and the imperfections of these accepted schemes, and the emergent symbols of the arts portend revisions which will later be rationally grasped and incorporated. But all this is easier to understand in societies in which analytical reason already partly clarifies the reigning view. The progress from the rank jungle of primitive folk tale to Homer's lucid poems was mysteriously won not by conscious reason but by the intuitive refinement of myths. Recent writers are helpful who reject the Thomistic and Kantian breach between sense-impression and reason, holding that, even in early childhood, we do not perceive the world as an undifferentiated flow of impressions, but already sort out one tree as like another and a second dog as like a first. This is to say that analytical reason does not alone divide experience into categories but that the senses from the first play their part. Or it is at least to say that we should not recognize as categories only those which reason finally sorts out, but that we achieve these categories also by the joint play of mind and sense. Admitted that, in this intense region where mind and sense jointly grasp the world, emotion enters also and a child can feel a tone of joy or sorrow as well as almost a personality in a plaything or piece of furniture. Yet to define truth as only that which reason isolates comes near assuming a life free of emotion and the senses, as if these were liabilities and not part of our equipment for apprehending the world. All these are ours simultaneously and if we do not understand how they operate indissolubly in the symbols of art, yet these symbols remain statements of inclusive truths because truths most fully representative of our consciousness. The poet always works with them, the early poet more easily and naturally because he does not have to unlearn reliance on reason only. Circe is simultaneously a person, a category of experience, and a quality of emotion. She has this inclusive meaning, because to Homer ways of seeing reality, separate to us, are not yet separate.

So much for the working of symbolic thought, little though these explanations may have lightened its mystery. The early poet's sense of not knowing how his insights came to him seems what is expressed in his appeal to the Muses and in the character of Apollo as an unpredictable god whose presence or absence cannot be foreseen. Such statements are particularly characteristic of Pindar and seem to imply a kind of intent waiting, not for any rational scheme, but for images and stories to form in his mind which would illuminate the present and contain its special meaning. The clear fact in any case remains that, before Socrates, the Greeks received from the poets alone their central interpretations of reality. This period of symbolic thought begins with Homer, notably includes Aeschylus and Pindar, and extends to Sophocles as its last complete spokesman. It came to an end only when the philosophers succeeded the poets as classifiers of experience and purveyors to society of the main relationships of things.

Homer's symbolic world is less complicated than those of Pindar and Aeschylus. Odysseus sees among the dead exemplars of social and family life, and if the great moments of the *Iliad* and *Odyssey* transcend such common categories, these experiences of Odysseus in the underworld remain characteristic of the poems. Achilles asks of his son; Agamemnon talks of his wife; Odysseus sees his mother; Ajax is a former friend, now an enemy. The heroines with whom Odysseus speaks are those who had union with the gods and became the means whereby something godlike brightened their mortal offspring. Tantalus, Ixion, and Sisyphus, by contrast, were too confident of their mortal powers and ended in futile pain because these powers were in fact less than godlike. Here is a clear world of orderly categories, with suggestion of its wonder and hints of its limits. Add to these the further categories of the travels, inward or of the world (though both, as we have seen, are on the same plane in Homer), and something like an outline of life emerges. The world of the *Iliad* is similar, if less simply presented. On a first stage are natural objects, each possessing its own characteristic color and enjoying almost a life of its own: the wine-dark sea, the shadowy mountains, the stars, roaring waves, stubborn cliffs, the seasons, animals (each in its character, so that in the similes lions are comparable to attackers, wolves to a fierce, wasps to an angry, sheep to a broken company), also man-made things, the swift ship, the sharp bronze. All these describe a stable world of clear recurrent forms. At another stage are the kinds and conditions of men or, since a human being is inseparable from the role in which life casts him, the kinds and conditions of fates: Thetis as a mother, Briseis as a disappointed girl, ignoble Thersites, laboring and somewhat limited Ajax, managerial Odysseus, the three old men, Nestor still intensely immersed in life, Phoenix now beyond it (almost Aristotle's distinction between practical understanding, *phronesis,* and wisdom, *sophia*), and Priam, the essential figure of age, as once fortunate, now close to submergence. These and the many other characters comprise a gallery of recurrent attitudes representative of sex, age, endowment, and fortune. The greatest figures rise beyond these commoner categories, and Achilles in his intense and visionary loneliness merges with the fearful brilliance of war itself, as contrasted to Hector, whose life is the peaceful ties of city, family, and settled duty. The fire of war attends the one as a motif, the water of peace attends the other. If Achilles is the greater, it is because he will not solace and distract himself with social bonds, however benign, but rises through intensity of spirit to awareness of the spirit's limits, beyond which are the timeless gods, each in his due realm. Achilles thus resembles the Odysseus of the *Odyssey,* except that the actual world is good enough in the latter's eyes to draw him home from Calypso's offer of escape from common life, whereas Achilles returns to his mortal limits with sorrow and resignation, if with new mercy also.

The purpose of the foregoing was not to discuss the *Iliad* or *Odyssey,* a world in themselves, but to suggest their cast of symbolism. As compared with, say, Polynesian folk tale, Homer's poems are intensely intellectual. External nature, even human beings and inward states of mind have their identifiable and recurrent forms. There is order in the world which the mind can grasp. Aristotle's rational analysis of experience is potentially already present. In that sense, the lucidity of the Greek vision of life begins with Homer. But as compared with Pindar, he seems less aware of what he is doing, less conscious that what he tells of Troy or Odysseus is essentially analytical. He of course makes clear that the great events of his poems happened in a remote past, when men were handsomer, richer, stronger, and closer to the gods. Hector lifted a stone, "which two men, strongest of the people, could not easily pry from the ground onto a cart, such as mortals now are." (12.447-449) The tradition of Homer's blindness (which may reflect the fact and was at least common in singers, as Demodocus in the *Odyssey* and the reference in the *Hymn to Apollo* show) is memorable because it catches his attitude of peering with the eyes of the mind into a vanished past. Yet this sense of their pastness does not make his heroes the less real to him or prevent his describing their every action in detail. Here we are back at the point made earlier about a fixed set of characters and situations. So thoroughly do these possess Homer's imagination that, though he is in fact describing nature and experience, he does so entirely through the traditional medium of his heroic theme. Pindar stands more consciously at some remove from the heroes. He too expounds reality through the legendary figures, and partly also through his divinized abstractions, but he is more fully aware than Homer that these comprise an ideal world. He does not think, as the sophists and philosophers were to do, through abstractions, but familiar shapes of gods and heroes preside for him over existence giving it meaning and order. His intelligible world too is a world of symbols. Yet he realizes, as Homer seems not to, that something more than years separates these figures from ordinary reality. They are the theme of Muses and poets, the means by which the gods inspire knowledge; they are the substance of his *sophia,* wisdom, which is what he calls his poetry. The mystery of Homer's symbolic clarification of the world is greater, because he seems unaware that he is telling anything beyond the acts of his heroes, whereas in fact they embody a lucid and intelligible order. Pindar is more nearly at the threshold of conscious reason, and his figures, who to Homer fought on the dusty plain of a real Troy or before an actual Thebes, have now partly risen out of history, like cloud-shapes standing clear of the horizon. This is not to say that they have ceased to be historical to Pindar, but that they have somehow become existential also.

Aeschylus differs in these same ways from Homer and also in his sense of time. The echo of the great events in Athens during his life and his intense awareness of social change endow Aeschylus' personages with the quality of belonging to a series in time. This evolution may take place within one figure, as evidently in Prometheus in the lost later plays of the trilogy, but even in our one play Prometheus carries innovation and struggle with him. Most Aeschylean figures exist in this way on two planes, as themselves and as stages in a process. Agamemnon's decision for the army and against Iphigeneia looks to his death; his death to vengeance by his son; the latter's punishment by the Furies to the establishment of a new order by Athene through the Areopagus. This sense of time and process is at the core of Aeschylus' thought and, as a revolutionary idea, may surpass even his creation of tragedy. Certainly it is the motive force behind it. His sense of time is prefigured in Hesiod's *Theogony* in the account of the painful ascent from primal chaos to the Olympians' bright sway, but the *Works and Days,* if it is in fact by the same author, knows nothing of this ascent as applied to men. On the contrary, we have fallen from the gold to the iron age, and for all human purposes, the stern round of the seasons and the laws of labor and morality are fixed and changeless. This is Homer's tacit assumption also, though he looks to far more than the farmer's round. As we have seen, his shapes are the static forms of sea and land, animal and artifact, man and woman, youth and age, wisdom and folly, repose and violence—a thousand attitudes of life, recognizable, recurrent, suffused with a kind of six-o'clock-in-the-morning light, the reflection of their beauty and vitality. Homer's world could be serenely orderly, were it not for the at once shattering and irradiating entrance into it of passion, heroism, and death. With these, a further, uncertain dimension is given the world, which opens now upon the gods and something akin to them in the heroes. Pindar shows this feeling both for static forms and for something still brighter but disturbing beyond them. His difference from Homer, we have also seen, is that he is more fully conscious that the heroes represent a higher kind of meaning. Aeschylus differs from both in that no forms are static to him, unless it be the final vision of order that he catches, for example, in the rule of justice begun with the Areopagus. And since his personages are thus involved in time and change, they come nearer expressing ideas. The conflicts of characters on the stage obviously take meaning from more general conflicts, and it was his sense of these that inspired Aeschylus' great creative act. In both his sense of time and new vehicle of the stage, he moves away toward conscious concept and action based on reason. Yet, needless to say, he too sees the world through his personages. Why otherwise present the figures of gods and heroes on the stage? It was Plato who devised, though Euripides in moments foresaw, the drama of ideas. In their reliance on symbol rather than on concept, Pindar and Aeschylus remain true contemporaries, though the one saw life as participation in changeless being, the other as involvement in changing process.

Two lines of thought have been pursued so far. The first, concerned with poetic symbolism, saw in Pindar and Aeschylus, as well as in Homer, minds for whom reality was chiefly comprehensible through heroic figures and situations, not through ideas. Though artists continue to see life in this way (and all people in so far as reality comes to us in the senses' clothing), the early age of Greece, when prose did not yet exist, gained its main clarifications by this means. The fact chiefly explains the classic, if by classic is understood the lifting of the specific to the representative and the assumption of order and meaning in these representative forms. The second point had to do, not with the means, but with the temper of Pindar's and Aeschylus' thought. As Aeschylus' trilogies treat evolutions, so they show a new absorption with process and a mind morally concerned with change. Are morality and social change the roots of reason and science? The definition of reason as problem-solving would seem to say so, and in fifth-century Athens the social revolution bred and accompanied the intellectual revolution. The old myths no longer sufficed to explain a greatly enlarged and quickly changing world, and sophists and philosophers leapt to supply by reason the clarifications once given by myth. Aeschylus comes far nearer than Pindar toward taking this portentous step. Needless to say, he does not take it. He is too deeply immersed in his characters and in the complex meanings which they carry. But his temper is partly moral, whereas Pindar's is religious. Aeschylus is so absorbed with change that he risks losing that final sense of rest and participation that alone gives value to any moment of life. He struggles toward a receding future; Pindar accepts a perpetual present. But this is only to repeat what was said at the start, that if Aeschylus has been more comprehensible to modern times, Pindar's response to pure being is outside history. (pp. 3-22)

. . . . .

"What god, what hero, what man shall we proclaim?" Pindar asks at the beginning of ***O. 2.*** This chain of participation whereby heroes in their great moments share something of gods, and men something of heroes runs through the odes and is the most characteristic thing about them. It was described earlier as a metaphor, a way of seeing things together. It was also called a set of symbols, figures spanning the interval between time and timelessness. The victors are fully involved in time and place; the heroes are partly thus involved through their ties with certain cities and the fact that they were once men; the gods stand clear above all and could be quite beyond events if they did not look to the world almost as much as the world looks to them. The whole system, if anything so fluid and iridescent may be called a system, is strangely complete. It includes not only the exterior sphere of time, place, and history, but the inner sphere of character and state of mind also. This symbolic and mythological cast of thought characteristically looks both outward and inward at the same time, or rather, so objectifies the inward that it appears side by side with the outward. Strictly speaking, a myth means a divine happening, for example, the birth of Athene from Zeus's head or the fact that the sun has cattle—which is to say, the judgment that the purest emanation of Zeus is intelligence or the natural fact of clouds in the sky. Legend relates historical happenings, foreign war at Troy or domestic war at Thebes. Folk tale has to do with representative attitudes of life: in the earlier example, Circe's enchantments, which are sensual, as contrasted to the Sirens', which are intellectual, or the motif in the *Iliad* that Achilles must choose either a long and inglorious or a short and glorious life, a choice expressing the brevity of anything intense. Folk tale thus has largely to do with inner states, legend with outward events, myth with both. But though one may mark off these spheres, they in fact coalesce, and Peleus, for example, as Pindar conceives him, is a figure from all three. The presence of the gods at his marriage to Thetis is mythological, as catching one phase of connection between men and gods; his ties with Aegina and Magnesia are legendary; his resistance to the blandishments of the queen of the Magnesians is from folk tale. But to note this mixture is simply to restate the simultaneously external and internal character of such symbolic thought. The stories told of the heroes were an immense projection of possible motives, states of mind, and responses to the world, all tied to known scenes and places but also transcending scene and place because, being connected also with the gods, they verged on the changeless. It is because any victory starts such a train of connection in Pindar's mind that the victory itself ceases to be the main subject of an ode, but is only the first step in a series of relationships, which is in fact the subject. (pp. 57-8)

If to Pindar the specific facts surrounding any victory tend to drop away (as they do not for Bacchylides) and in their place imagination lifts the transitory event to a plane of absoluteness, it is because he can feel that victory implies poetry and poetry vision. This assumption betrays the communal origins of Greek choral verse; more than that, it reveals the need of a society, as yet largely untouched by rationalism, for mythological statement of its standards. The time was coming when philosophers would assume this interpretative social task, with gains but at the cost of fraying the fine tie between act and import, the thing done and the thing implied. The poetry of an age of faith like Pindar's does not so much 'give to airy nothings a local habitation and a name' as, contrarywise, transport local habitations and names to the ideal range of airy nothings. The odes have a formal likeness to such a painting as El Greco's "Burial of Count Orgaz," which by showing in the lower part the Count's miraculous burial in the presence of his contemporaries and, in the upper part, his reception in paradise, places him in the setting of his society and the society in that of its faith. Yet if inherited social practice underlies the odes, Pindar's intensity drew this inheritance toward his private vision. At no point is the fact clearer than in the odes about to be discussed, those loosely connected by what we have called the theme of harmony. They fall into two main classes: those which in the serene moment of celebration catch sound of a higher order, partly moral, partly of music and poetry, partly religious, and those troubled odes which miss this order. In the latter Pindar's loneliness is quite clear, and one sees to what privacy of symbolism he had come, however communal in origin his poetic role was and however passionately he wished to see himself in this role. The parallel to El Greco, different as he is from Pindar, suggests how productive of a strongly individual style this complex union of private vision with accepted forms can be.

Olympian 14. The short poem ***O. 14,*** for a young victor of the near-by Boeotian town of Orchomenus, has a quality of limpid effortlessness unmatched in the odes. Though the early date usually ascribed to it has lately been questioned, it carries the tone of at-homeness in the familiar which has seemed characteristic of the years before the war and the journey to Sicily. The fact that the Charites, Graces, whom it addresses are at once cult figures in Orchomenus and inward figures of Pindar's imagination, closely associated with his view of poetry, may help explain the intimacy of the poem.

> "Guardians of the fair-horsed seat which shares the streams of the Cephissus, O royal and storied Charites of bright Orchomenus, watchers of the Minyae bred of old, hear me since I pray. Through you all joyous things and sweet are won for mortals, if a man be wise, if a man be fair, if a man be glorious. Even the gods hold neither dance nor feast without the holy Charites, but keepers of every act in heaven, enthroned by Pythian Apollo of the golden bow, they hymn the quenchless glory of the Olympian sire.—O lady Aglaia and Euphrosyne who take delight in song, children of the mightiest god, attend now, and Thalia, lover of melody, seeing this festal band at fortune's moment stepping light. In Lydian strain and meditated verse I come singing Asopichus, because through thee the Minyan land is called Olympic victor. To Persephone's black-walled house go, Echo, now bringing the sounding message to his father, that seeing Cleodamus you may tell how among Pisa's famous dells his son crowned his young hair with the wings of brilliant triumph."

In the first strophe, the three Charites are joint presiding presences; in the second, they descend to touch the particular occasion and moment and, in so doing, take on separate identities. They are reposed at first, then, so to speak, join the festal dance. Their presence is harmonious order, and Pindar first feels this order in the pleasant setting of the ancient city by the meadows of the Cephissus. The harmony then passes inward and is felt in the long Minyan past, but in the present also as shown in wisdom (poetry), personal beauty or the beauty of act ('if a man be wise, if a man be fair, if a man be glorious'). At last it is fully seen as a divine principle, forever present in the beauty of the gods' pure being. When the Charites are called 'guardians of all acts in heaven,' the words suggest Aristotle's definition of pleasure, as a tone of happiness accompanying right function. But these goddesses are more than an attendant tone; they are the completion and actuality itself of right and happy things, and come nearer being principles of achieved and expressed form. Thus they accompany Apollo's singing as the fact of its perfection, are present in the gods' entirely beautiful life, and their celebration of Zeus's power is the actuality of his lucid order.

This idea of harmony as the special trait and possession of the Olympians is of course not unique to Pindar. No idea is more classic in its emphasis on repose as opposed to striving, attainment as opposed to search, rest through vision of the intelligible as opposed to excitement through sense of the unknown, preference of the limited (in Plato's terminology) to the chaotic and unlimited. Needless to say, these latter states are not foreign to Greek; they notably underlie the Promethean mood of struggle from which tragedy sprang. Nor, despite the present poem, does Pindar keep the vision of repose much more steadily than does Aeschylus. Just as the vitality of late archaic sculpture strains against a sense of limit, so, as argued earlier, does the intense vigor of both men's styles. The ordering synoptic mind is always being disturbed in them by the assaults of impressions. Yet the vision of repose, impossible though it was for them to keep, is their strongest common bond. If we had the lost plays of the Promethean trilogy, in which Prometheus and Zeus, striving and limit, were brought into final harmony, the fact would be clearer, but the merging of the dark possessive Furies in the Olympian light of freedom and mercy at the close of the *Eumenides* shows sufficiently how Aeschylus' mind, however involved in process, sought finally to transcend it. Pindar comes nearer doing so. The moments of transcendence which we have just considered in the poems on vicissitude are a way of expressing order and harmony. The difference of the present poem and those now to be considered is that they are more fully given to the festal moment of celebration. Xenophanes' poem on the banquet, in which he seeks a grace of speech and act consonant with reason, shares Pindar's desire for a time of pause when former urgency is at rest and the imagination's higher shapes rise clear. This is the moment when music crowns athletics, and since to him athletics includes war and, more widely, testing action of any kind, music in turn embraces all goals of action, almost in the sense of Aristotle's final cause. It is, in effect, contemplation. The Charites of the present poem are close to Apollo and hence to poets, but they are in the natural beauty of Orchomenus also, as well as in its past and in all present grace of person or act. When he says of the Grace, Thalia, in the second strophe, "through thee the Minyan land is called Olympic victor" (vv. 19-20), he feels that everything best in natural surroundings, tradition, and training has brought the boy to his victory, and it is the beneficent harmony of all these that he wishes to catch. Being akin to such influences, poetry can draw them into itself and see them for a moment as part of the greater Olympian peace. It can even in the exquisite last lines send beyond the grave its apperception of this timeless order.

Pythian 1. If this limpid poem, like the Theban odes ***I. 3*** and ***4,*** shows Pindar in the world which he knew and loved best, it is otherwise with the famous opening of ***P. 1,*** the coruscating ode in honor of Hieron's chariot victory at Delphi in 470, some years after the poet's return from Sicily. Victory again rouses associations of music and these again a vision of the celestial order, but a virtuosity second to none in the odes now replaces the earlier mood of gay and tender grace. He starts with the lyre, which leads to thoughts of music's enchantment, which in turn puts wrath to sleep (the eagle, sign of Zeus as power) and rouses song (sign of Zeus as harmony) on Olympus.

> "Golden lyre, Apollo's and the violet-tressed Muses' joint possession, whom the step heeds, joy's overture, and whose commands singers obey when throbbing you create the rising chords of preludes that invite the dance. And the warrior bolt of the eternal fire you quench. Sleeps then on Zeus's staff the eagle, sheathing on either side his pinions swift, the king of birds. Upon his beaked head you strew dark-visaged cloud, his eyelids' sweet confinement, and slumbering he lifts his liquid back, by your tides bound. And even savage Ares leaving far his spear's harsh edge softens his heart a-dozing, and your shafts enchant the souls of deities through the art of Leto's son and the deep-bosomed Muses." (vv. 1-12)

It is interesting that Pindar cannot dispel images of violence when he thinks of Hieron. As the story of the cannibal banquet rises to his mind to be rejected in ***O. 1,*** so here, though the fires of the thunderbolt are quenched by music, and the eagle and Ares sleep, their violence seems at first only hypnotized, not dead, as if music held no sure ascendency. This lurking doubt about the security of order in everything having to do with the tyrant runs through the poem. Pindar prays that Hieron may remember his military triumphs with joy and calm of soul, but knows that he is ill and likens him to the suffering Philoctetes. Again, he prays that Hieron's newly-founded city of Aetna may keep peace and Doric order, yet he both implies disorder and fears war with the Carthaginians and Etruscans whom Hieron had defeated at Cymae in 474. "I beseech thee grant, son of Kronos, that tame at home the Phoenician and Tyrrhenian war cry stay, that saw with groans its pomp of sail at Cymae; so did they suffer shattered by the lord of Syracuse, who struck their youth into the sea from their swift-faring ships, and drew Greece up from heavy slavery." (vv. 71-75) What Salamis is to Athens and Plataea to Sparta, he says, Gelon's and Hieron's victory over the Carthaginians at Himera is to Syracuse. Yet even this splendid praise does not still a sense of unrest. As in the ode to Theron, Pindar stops short because, he says, people murmur at the great; nevertheless he bids Hieron persist in glory and not give up such celebrations as this.

> "What citizens hear of others' happiness burdens their secret soul. Yet—since envy passes pity—spurn not magnificence. Steer the people with a tiller just. On an unequivocating block beat out your speech. If never so slight a flashing spark fly up, it is held great because it comes from you. You are the treasurer of men's destinies, and witnesses exact attest your either course." (vv. 84-88)

The danger of suppressed violence lurks behind this cryptic advice, and the impression remains of a tense equipoise between serenity and harshness, both in the forces that beat on the king and in the king himself. The poem closes with a contrast between Croesus' benign reputation and the dark name of the tyrant Phalaris. Pindar's nominal point is how differently they were commemorated in history, but this difference of reputation only states outwardly the inner and spiritual difference between harmony and violence which is the theme of the poem.

To return then to the lyre and eagle of the start, the lyre was at first simply the music of the choral dance. But presently it became the universal and divine music which is the beauty of the world and the repose of the soul. Yet he is not so sure at the beginning as he was in ***O. 14*** that the gods represent only this harmony. The savage eagle that watches on Zeus's sceptre is, when awake, the living power of his thunderbolt. In the marvelous lines on the eagle's sleep a vision of the world as possible harmony rises, and strife drops away from the gods. Here, perhaps at its clearest, is Aeschylus' and Pindar's great common theme. Hesiod's *Theogony* had prefigured the rise of Zeus's serene sway out of the conflict and disorder of the generation of the Titans, and the *Prometheia* and *Oresteia* trace the winning of a similar peace out of suffering. Pindar is less directly interested in suffering, though the allusion to Philoctetes here and statements in other poems about endurance of pain and danger show that to him too harmony emerges out of struggle. He is characteristically more concerned with the state of peace itself than with its acquisition. In the odes the contest is over, and celebration brings the moment of vision which is the goal and reward of effort. In the present poem, as we have seen, this vision is at first not quite secure. Yet after the opening lines he rises to a great affirmation that harmony is in fact the mark of the gods, reflected in all orderly and beautiful things and menaced only by the brutal residue of the Titanic past. Zeus then becomes wholly identified with harmony, and the fires sent up from Aetna by Typhos, the imprisoned enemy of the gods, become the violence that cannot yield to calm.

> "But all things that Zeus detests flee over land and the restless sea at the sound of the Pierides' singing, he too who lies in Tartarus harsh, the gods' foe, Typhos the hundred-headed. A many-named cave in Cilicia nurtured him long ago; now Sicily and Cymae's sea-fenced banks oppress his shaggy chest, and a heavenly pillar holds him, icy Aetna, the keen snow's yearlong nurse. From whose recesses pour pure fonts of unapproachable fire, as rivers coil by day ablaze their stream of smoke, and nightly the red flame carries and rolls cliffs with a crash to the sea's flat. That ancient serpent spouts Hephaestus' terrible springs, portent awesome to see, awesome for dwellers near to hear. Such is the creature bound beneath the dark-leaved peaks and plain of Aetna, and the raking bed he lies on stabs his back. O Zeus, who keepest this mountain, brow of the fertile land, may it be ours to please thee." (vv. 13-29)

The fear and reverence of the last lines express Pindar's disturbed contemplation of violence. But if Zeus had once used force to restrain the unruly harshness of nature, it is now buried alongside this harshness and no longer a part of him. The soul can and must put away its agitation; this is the plea to Hieron. Civilization is capacity to hear the intelligible order in the world, and the music of the lyre reflects a harmony in Zeus himself.

Nemean 9. In a number of odes the idea of harmony extends more generally from music to life and conduct. It has of course these associations in the poem to Hieron but they are clearer elsewhere. In ***N. 9,*** one of two poems to Chromius, the Syracusan viceroy in the newly founded town of Aetna and long a lieutenant of both Gelon and Hieron, the man's tried fidelity in war and council is conceived as flowering at last in quietude, *hesychia.* To Thucydides the word means a settled and conservative outlook characteristic of the Spartans and opposite to the restless Attic temper, and Pindar's use is similar, if less political, more suggestive of settled personal habits and tastes. In the background of the ode is the dark sense of an impending last struggle with Carthage, and this darkness imparts itself to the account of the deaths of the noble Amphiaraus at Thebes and of Hector at Troy. But Chromius, whose honor and courage have resembled theirs, has been luckier than they. "If with his many goods a man gain honorable fame, no farther promontory may the foot of mortal touch. Quietude loves the banquet, and the green of triumph grows fresh and new with the calm of song." (vv. 46-49) Chromius has come more whole-heartedly and gracefully than Hieron to this state of peace, and though war and danger may still await him, they do not touch his spirit.

Pythian 4. The two odes to Arkesilas, tyrant of Cyrene, ***P. 4*** and ***5,*** products of Pindar's summer mood in the 460's, are similar. His feeling for Apollo, always clear, is especially present in these poems, the god having not only directed Battus, the founder of Cyrene, to Africa eight generations ago and repeated his favor in the present victory, but being the god of music and of all measure and repose. The lines from ***P. 5*** to Apollo were quoted earlier, "he who from heavy sickness offers men and women cure, who brought the lyre, and gives the Muse to whom he wills, inducing warless harmony in their hearts, and holds his secret mantic seat." (vv. 63-69) These ideas of prophecy, music, and healing flow together in ***P. 4*** to give this longest and most elaborate of the odes its special character. Medea's prophecy of a return to Africa by descendants of the Argonauts is mystically fulfilled many generations after when Apollo welcomes the stammering Battus at Delphi and directs him abroad. Jason as leader of the Argonauts has an identifying gentleness and even chivalry of spirit which mark him as the healer. Pindar connected his name with *ἰάομαι,* to heal, and he tells Arkesilas, for whom Jason is a prototype, "you are time's opportune physician, and Paean honors in you a saving light. A gentle hand must touch and tend the wound's affliction. Even the weak can easily shake a state, but to set it in place again is bitter struggle, unless of a sudden a god become the leaders' guide." (vv. 270-274) But if healing is in both Jason and Arkesilas, its manifestation is a spirit molded by music. When Jason first appears in Magnesia to reclaim his birthright from the insulting Pelias, he refuses to answer insult in like terms. "I claim to keep Chiron's instruction. From his cave I come, from Charicles and Philyra, where these holy centaur women brought me up. And through my twenty years no evil act or word spoke I to them." (vv. 102-105) The *Precepts of Chiron* was a work attributed to Hesiod which enjoined respect for Zeus and parents (commands reflected in ***P. 6***), but which was taught by the lyre and carried associations of music. The name Philyra surely evoked this meaning to Pindar. When then Jason meets his old father and kinsman, "he received them with gentle words and entertainment shared, while in hospitality fit he drew out bliss entire through five whole days and nights plucking joy's holy flower." (vv. 127-131) Here again, if on a somewhat massive scale, is the festal moment of pure being almost like the gods', such as he felt in the boy Asophichus' festival at Orchomenus or the old Chromius' banquet at Aetna. But it has more express overtones here of a harmony not only of music but of conduct and word. This emphasis (characteristically in this poem of the 460's, close in date to the Rhodian ode, ***O. 7***) is more of the world, less visionary and lyric, and has the golden mood of a placid landscape. The ode was ordered for Arkesilas by an exile from Cyrene, one Damophilus, and if Jason's quality as a healer looks to the king, his balance and restraint apply to the petitioner also. Pindar expresses the latter's wish to find happiness with music and quiet of mind near Apollo's spring at home, and in urging mercy toward him, reverts to the language of ***P. 1*** by saying that Zeus with time released the Titans. The accents both of the poem to Hieron and of that to Chromius return: the higher order which is Zeus's benign triumph, and the quietude which is the soul's similar release from struggle. The prominence of Apollo in this poem and in its companion, ***P. 5,*** matches the mellower vision which feels less sharply now the struggle of Zeus against his enemies, harmony against discord, but sees, perhaps too placidly, the happy working of healing and order through good men.

Pythian 8. This summer mood of confidence in the world was broken by the Athenian conquest of Boeotia and Aegina in the last years of his life. The apocalyptic close of ***P. 8*** of 446, the latest dated poem, was quoted earlier to show his change of outlook, and we shall return to it. Here the opening of the poem may serve as a final statement of the theme of harmony and of its attendant motif of repose. In these abrupt, allusive, and deeply felt lines, Quietude, Hesychia, has become an animate presence, herself embodying the inner character of harmony.

> "Loving-hearted Quietude, o child of Justice and strengthener of cities, you who hold the final keys of councils and of wars, receive for Aristomenes this rite of honor for his Pythic crown. You understand with perfect tact alike the gift and the acceptance of gentle things. But when a man lays in his heart cold rancor, you harshly face the enemy's assault and scuttle his insolence. Porphyrion did not know you when he taunted you unprovoked. The gain alone is glad that comes from the house of a willing giver. Violence trips the vaunter in the end. Cilician Typhos, the hundred-headed, escaped this not, nor the monarch of the giants, but they fell before the thunderbolt and Apollo's shafts, who welcomed with kindly heart from Cirrha home Xenarchus' son crowned with Parnassian green and with the Dorian song." (vv. 1-20)

It was said earlier that such symbolic and mythological thought as Pindar's moves simultaneously in the inner realm of state of mind and the outer realm of act, and the statement is well illustrated by this brilliant and moving passage. The kindliness of Quietude is a natural inheritance from her mother Justice, and it is through equity grown into graceful and generous habit that she makes cities great. The keys of councils and wars that she holds are her evenness of mind and freedom from obsessive and assertive moods. Her civic judgments are right because she can value such moments of private happiness as this festival for Aristomenes. "You understand with perfect tact alike the gift and the acceptance of gentle things." (vv. 6-7) In this statement Pindar is thinking not so much of the goddess as of a state of mind that can give with joy and receive with grace because it is at ease with itself and with the minds of friends. Her wrath, if ignorant of a final charity, comes near righteous anger. Her enemies are the violent and self-assertive, men who cannot feel a cheerful mutuality of giving and hence destroy the idea of community. Pindar presently reverts to the language of the poems to Hieron and Arkesilas, and Typhos and the giant Porphyrion are destroyers of an order which they cannot understand. At the date of this poem they obviously signify Athens, not by a simple equation but by exemplifying the will to conquest by which Athens had been led to destroy what he feels the benign older regimen of Greece. He no longer recognizes the city which he knew as a young man and of whose performance at Salamis he wrote the famous dithyramb. "That gain alone is glad that comes from the house of a willing giver" (v. 14) expresses perhaps naively an ideal of international action identical with private courtesy, and the breach between national and personal morality which Thucydides was to feel does not occur to him. When at the end it is Apollo who, with Zeus, destroys Porphyrion and the same god welcomes the victor home, it is clear that music and poetry continue for Pindar the sign of a more general harmony of act and impulse. This last poem lends weight to the early vision of the Charites as divine principles which he had had in the almost Arcadian ***O. 14.*** The feeling is graver now and much more aware of the possible dangers to harmony, but more conscious also of the range of spirit which harmony can include.

But his confidence in harmony sometimes failed. The word is being used in a slightly different sense to mean harmony between Pindar and his audience, though to him the meanings coalesced. He could not feel an order in the world which showed itself in the beauty of act and became fully manifest in music as an ordering and divine principle, yet at the same time feel no such bond between himself and his patrons. His discomfort at such moments is partly only his chagrin at not being appreciated as he expected to be, but it reflects also a sense that the very assumptions of his art are challenged. Outlooks were changing, and with time a victorious athlete would no longer be regarded with Pindar's eyes as the flower and ideal of a community, but simply as a practitioner of one, and not a very high, specialism. Similarly, a poet would come to be looked on as a practitioner in words, like the Pindarist in the *Birds* (905-959) who wants to supply an ode for the cloud-city. Beneath both changes would be an individualism which separated men from their communities or at least told them that knowledge of one's unique and separate self was the prerequisite to entering a higher and less tangible community of the mind. Tragedy was obviously a step in this new direction since it showed a disorder in the world and a loneliness in aspiration. Even though most of Aeschylus' heroes rediscover a community and Sophocles' early and late plays (all, that is, except the *Trachiniae* and *Oedipus King*) bring a similar repatriation of some kind, the old, half Eden-like rightness of the world had vanished and men were more aware of being alone. It is this rightness in the world that Pindar wants to see: hence it is this loneliness that disturbs him. Yet . . . the sixth century had already opened the path toward individualism, in monodic poetry, for example, or the signed vases of potters, and Pindar's very epinikion applied to notable men the choral forms once used toward gods alone. His heightened imagination and imperious style carried, whether he wished it or not, the marks of visionary inwardness. Thus the chagrin of the odes about to be discussed seems at bottom directed less against his patrons than against himself, as if he were being forced, like Oedipus, to see what he both wanted and did not want to see, namely, the loneliness of his imagination. The late poems that accompany the defeat of Boeotia and Aegina draw part of their power from his final realization that strength springs from within men rather than from a fixed social order, and by compensation these same poems find sources of renewal for the community. Conversely, the tendency to bland expansiveness in the Rhodian ***O. 7*** and the long ***P. 4*** to Arkesilas suggest the painful fact that lyric vision of the beauty of life and the unity of things does not easily survive years and success, at least in its pristine freshness.

Pythian 3. Two final poems to Hieron, ***P. 3*** and ***2,*** illustrate this breach of Pindar with his world, though the former less in itself than by anticipation of the latter. The cannibal banquet in ***O. 1*** and the resistance of Typhos to the celestial music in ***P. 1*** make clear that he from the first felt something acrid in the tyranny at Syracuse, and the coruscation of these odes partly reflects his nerving of himself against the unfamiliar. Certainly he could not easily apply to the tyrant's court those ancient communal associations of myth and rite which victory roused in him at home. ***P. 3*** does not commemorate a specific victory but is a poem of consolation to Hieron on his illness mentioned in ***P. 1*** and a reminder to him of both the peace and the glory which poetry gives. It is the gentlest of the poems to Hieron, and its tender hope that he may share and take comfort from Pindar's view of poetry prepares the way for the disappointment of ***P. 2.*** Its date is unclear, evidently after Pindar's return from Sicily and probably but not surely before ***P. 1*** of 470. It has to do with the possible and the impossible. Hence it recalls, though more softly, the theme of ***O. 1,*** Pelops' position as a courageous man between his father Tantalus' one-time felicity on Olympus and later entire exclusion. Pindar would be a healer like Asclepius or the centaur Chiron who reared him, but his healing would be the courage which poetry gives. In keeping with this wish is the opening mood of green and fresh remoteness with which he describes the girl Coronis, who was wed by Apollo long ago in Thessaly. "But she yearned for things impossible, sickness which many have. There is an idle-witted breed of mortals which scorns the thing at hand and searches the remote, hunting the wind with incompleted hopes." (vv. 19-23) She yielded vacuously to a stranger though she had already had union with Apollo, and like her was her son Asclepius, whom the god saved when she and her whole village were destroyed in punishment. He had the Apolline gift of healing but, like his mother, lacked the Apolline sense of limit, and Zeus destroyed him in turn for accepting money to bring back a man from the dead. "We must ask from the gods with mortal hearts what fits us, knowing the near path, of what destiny we are. Dear heart, crave not immortal life, but drain the practicable device." (vv. 59-62) The device is courage, like Pelops' in ***O. 1*** but of a quieter and more defensive kind as fits the sick king. Pindar holds up to him a bleaker truth than that with which Achilles consoled Priam in the fable of the jars of Zeus, that the gods give us two evils for every good, "which fools cannot decently bear, but the brave can, turning the fair side out." (vv. 82-83) But this good, thus outweighed in quantity by evil, outweighs it in worth and permanence, and Pindar sees again the vision of Peleus and Cadmus, happiest of mortals, who, though tried, yet had the supreme joy of marrying goddesses and seeing the calm Olympians on golden chairs at their weddings. What is this happiness which Peleus and Cadmus won, and with something like which Hieron may triumph over illness? It is in part the god-given fact of fame but in part also consciousness of an inner light matching the outward luster. "I will be small in small things and great in great, and I will tend in my heart my guiding god, serving him with the means at my command." (vv. 107-109) Pindar exhorts to the healing which he can give, the medicine of fame, but the tender and personal tone promises chiefly an inner healing. Asclepius and his mother Coronis, though touched by the god, betrayed their fortune through desire for an unattainable perfection of power or happiness, but Peleus and Cadmus were wiser in cherishing through later troubles the inner knowledge of their once-perfect joy. They are the true models, not so much in their glory as in their luminous and persistent gratitude for high fortune, and it is this tenacious joy that Pindar wishes the king.

Pythian 2. P. 3 seeks more transparently than any other ode to draw reality into Pindar's imaginative net. He would throw the skein of his verse around the king's life as if by so doing he could hold it. The complexity of his disappointment in ***P. 2*** is the measure of his hope. To the degree that he is made to realize that he cannot in fact transform the king and yet would not break with the real world as the subject of his verse, he feels that he alone is to blame for his self-deception, hence that he must remain loyal and grateful to Hieron. But as he also reflects that Hieron had not valued his generosity of feeling or had been influenced against him by jealous men, he is angry at him or at them rather than at himself. Mixed with both moods is a religious awareness that the gods deal unpredictably with men, but even this comfort is clouded by the sense of his enemies' indecent satisfaction. The occasion of this flood of emotion, C. M. Bowra brilliantly saw [in his *Problems in Greek Poetry,* 1953], was probably Hieron's choice of Bacchylides over himself to celebrate his last and greatest victory, with a chariot at Olympia in 468. Bacchylides' odes 5 and 4 had been composed for the same victories respectively as ***O. 1*** and ***P. 1,*** but, despite the extreme beauty of *Ba. 4,* evidently as minor and secondary commissions. Bowra argued that Pindar's disappointment was now the greater both because he had himself in ***O. 1*** expressed the hope of celebrating some day such a final success by Hieron and because Bacchylides' actual poem for the occasion, the weak *Ba.* 3, notably borrows from Pindar. If the two crows in ***O. 2*** which chatter futilely against Zeus's sovereign bird are in fact the uncle and nephew, Simonides and Bacchylides, Pindar's animosity is of eight years' standing. In Bacchylides' lucid and gentle style, with its clear succession of narrative and aphorism, any such symbolic complexity as Pindar's is quite lacking, and it is clear that he had felt, as Pindar had not, the force of the rational Ionic spirit which reduced poetry from its earlier interpretative pretensions to a largely decorative role. The heavy weight of meaning which Pindar's mythic figures carry reveals a mind which speaks and feels through such figures, whereas to Bacchylides narrative is simply narrative and carries no such symbolic burden. Accordingly beneath all overt reasons for chagrin there exists in Pindar's disappointment the sense that what is involved is his way of seeing reality through myth. If Hieron had failed to grasp or value what he had said of men's relationship to the gods through the figure of Pelops, or of harmony through the lyre and the rebellious Typhos, or of the impossible and the possible through the contrast of Coronis and Asclepius to Peleus and Cadmus, Pindar could well question all the social assumptions of his art. At least, his disturbance here and in ***N. 7*** and ***4,*** the two odes that show similar distress, touches his art because he is forced to recognize that visions which he thought social and communicable were in part private and lonely.

He begins by praising the formidable military strength of Syracuse, calling the city, as he had Athens, "god-inspired," *daimonios.* Through the familiar train of thought that prowess commands praise, he then reaches the ideas of poetry and of gratitude, and it is with this last that he wrestles. Citizens and allies have cause for gratitude to the great king. "As he whirls on his winged wheel, they say, Ixion by edict of heaven thus warns mankind: O return again and again to require benefactors with payment glad." (vv. 21-24) In ***O. 1*** Tantalus had been ungrateful to the gods, but Pindar had rather seen in him a certain mortal vagrancy and shallowness of mood which could not endure the bright Olympian calm. Ixion's story begins like his with acceptance on Olympus but ends much more violently with his attempt to seduce Hera.

> "Once in many-recessed chambers he attempted Zeus's wife. But in measure of himself must a man find limit in things. The errant union threw him into ruin complete when he came to bed; for he lay with a cloud, the madman, intent on his sweet delusion. In look she resembled the highest of goddesses, Kronos' daughter, but Zeus's hands set her, this pretty bane, as the man's trap. So he made his own four-spoked knot as his destruction, and falling in ineluctable fetters, got his message for all mankind." (vv. 33-41)

Ixion's traditional punishment was to be stretched on a rolling wheel, and Pindar sees in him a fearful copy of the love-charm, the iunx, which was a bird similarly bound and whirled. But Ixion's love was not in fact love, since Hera was beyond him, and in seeing her he saw only his own intense ambition, hence lay with a cloud. He is for Pindar a terrifying self-hypnotism which has lost its grip on reality and constitutes a love-charm directed toward itself. It is part of the power of this passage that the cloud-woman proves not to be a dissolving wraith but a creature as alone as her lover. The next lines describe the offspring of the union, which was the unnatural and inhuman Kentauros, who by further union with the mares on Pelion begot the centaurs. This misshapen progeny is not less descriptive of Ixion's mood. Pindar is not thinking of such a centaur as Chiron, whose half-animal form conveys a bond with earth and hence ancient kindliness and wisdom of the sort that made him a primal Socrates, fit teacher of Jason and Achilles. The centaurs here are the wild creatures that appear in the metopes of the Parthenon, and their violence is the offspring of Ixion's state of mind.

Pindar is even more shocked by this vision than by that of Typhos in ***P. 1,*** and as there, his mind goes to Zeus.

> "God completes for himself each end as he desires, god, who catches the winged eagle and passes the dolphin in the sea and bends the lofty-minded man and proffers others ageless celebrity. As for me, I must shun the crackling tooth of slander. From far off I have watched railing Archilochus defenseless for the most as he battened on his harsh-tongued enmities. Riches in wisdom with a happy lot is best." (vv. 49-56)

The mood of revulsion is almost Dante's. God alone gives fame and greatness, and to snatch at them is to end in angry and futile overreaching. Pindar is talking to himself when he draws back from the satirist Archilochus' state of mind. He contemplates him with the horrid fascination with which Dante looks at the furious souls in the bubbling swamp, or in Euripides' spirit when at the end of the *Hecuba* he has the queen transformed into a howling dog. To Archilochus the world had become a place which a man could only rail at, and he had wallowed in hatred. In ***P. 3*** Pindar had told Hieron that brave men can endure the evils that outnumber the good of life by turning the fair side out, and now he needs this advice himself. His alarm is both that he sees his code of honor in danger (the code which is implied in the idea of harmony and which in ***P. 4*** makes Jason refuse to answer Pelias with insult) and that by his own standards he knows that he must cling to the world and to worldly success. He had seen the hand of divinity in Hieron's life, and his whole poetry rested on the belief that triumph is not meaningless. It is with these thoughts that he turns from Archilochus to reassert that wisdom and happy fortune are in fact the best things in life: which is to say, that there is meaning in the social order, that he must accordingly remain loyal and grateful to Hieron, and that he must not drift with the mood of Ixion that he had evoked.

Yet he had been deeply hurt. One has the impression that he intended to end with the farewell to which he now rallies, praising Hieron for courage and wisdom and for a name second to none in Greek history. But just as what looks like the final epode draws to a close, he spins off in a strange and cryptic epilogue

> "Learn what kind of man you are and become it. A monkey is pretty to boys, endlessly pretty. But blessed was Rhadamanthus because he gained wisdom's untarnished fruit. No inward pleasure takes his soul in deceptions, such as always haunt mankind from the whisperer's arts." (vv. 72-75)

Hieron, he feels, has betrayed his own nature. The command that he learn and try to become the kind of man that he inherently is has a Delphic force. It tells much also of Pindar's view of his poems to the king, which were not to his own mind mere praise but revelations of Hieron's position toward himself, history, and the gods. If he had been fighting his own ingratitude, he now feels that the temptation is behind him and that he can at last address the king with a clear conscience. The monkey of folk tale, Bowra further argued, is incomparably the mimic; hence the boys who like the monkey are people who cannot distinguish authentic from borrowed and misused insight. This interpretation points the passage against Bacchylides and his supporters. But beyond any such reference is the more general meaning that these merely childish people and, much more, those others who take pleasure in intrigue and evil-speaking miss the sense of the permanent which Rhadamanthus had and which it is the task of poetry to convey. Though he is describing men around Hieron, some of their fault obviously infects the king.

He goes on,

> "A curse to both that none can fight are slander's covert spokesmen, intensely like foxes' hearts. And yet how gets the vixen profit in the end? I, as it were, while the other gear has its salt labor in the deep, remain the cork above the seine, unsunken by the brine. The slippery man can speak no solid sentence among the noble; yet he fawns and weaves his curving way toward all. I do not share his confidence. Let me love my friend. As an enemy I'll fly at my enemy like a wolf, in divers seasons treading devious paths. In every rule the straight-tongued man advances: by tyrants, or when the passionate crowd or when the wise survey the state." (vv. 76-88)

Some have seen a dialogue in these hard lines, but they seem reasonably clear as they stand. Pindar's slanderers are the foxes and also the net, while he is successively the cork and the wolf. The foxes' devious efforts get them nowhere; the cork neither shares the net's dark work in the depths of the sea nor is submerged. While the fox becomes almost a fawning dog in his attentions to people, the wolf straightforwardly loves his friends and hates his enemies. To be sure, he is a law unto himself and will walk in crooked paths when he sees fit. The line recalls Quietude's anger against her enemies in ***P. 8;*** she too can be relentless. Pindar's unconcern for politics as compared with a man's personal standards speaks in the last lines on tyranny, democracy, and aristocracy. Though he favors the last, he is interested in the honest mind for itself. The poem ends in this inward tone. He reverts to previous thoughts on the gods' unpredictability, who elevate now one man, now another. "But even this softens not the minds of the envious." (vv. 89-90) They believe as Ixion had that they, not the gods, create their own advantage, but fail through this delusion. He is at last at rest; he will bear his yoke lightly and not kick at the goad. "Be it mine to live acceptably with the just." (v. 96) He has returned by a complex road to the harmony which in happier moments he had assumed could unite character with music. Though he has again found meaning in the social order, he has done so only after a struggle with himself and with it which has yielded a more interior meaning.

Finally, two poems, ***N. 7*** and ***4,*** of uncertain date but evidently of much this same period of the late 470's and early 460's, show him in like straits nearer home. Both odes are for Aeginetans, and his distress is the greater because he might have expected fuller understanding than Hieron's from men of upbringing like his own. He himself largely created his troubles, and it was observed earlier that nothing in the odes throws a sharper light than this incident on the complicated blend of piety and nationalism which was Greek hero cult.

Paean 6. The most nearly complete of the papyrus fragments, ***Paean 6,*** was composed, he says, as a gift for the festival of the Theoxenia at Delphi, a ceremony intended to avert famine in Greece and lacking this year an appropriate song. "At the water by the bronze gate I heard the voice of Castalia lorn of men's dancing; therefore I came to redeem your brethren's plight and for my honor. I obeyed my heart as a child its mother sage as I drew near Apollo's grove, the nurse of crowns and feasts." (fg. 40. 7-15) The fact that the poem ends with praise of Aegina casts some obscurity on these lines. Was the chorus Aeginetan and did Pindar simply furnish the paean, and perhaps not as a gift, or did Aegina occur to him because Aeacus legendarily first averted famine by the cult of Zeus Hellanios, or, an unlikely proposal, did he add the final passage when the paean proved offensive? The fragmentary state of the ending prevents an answer. But what is quite clear, and the most interesting and impressive thing about the poem, is his intensity of religious illumination. He asks a question about the gods, which is likewise unclear because of the imperfect papyrus, and answers, "This the gods can impart to poets, but that men discover it is impossible. Yet since you know all, you maiden Muses, and through the father clothed in black cloud and through Mnemosyne have this right, then hear me now." (vv. 51-57) These more than conventional prayers for inspiration are in keeping with the visionary account of the fall of Troy that follows. His motive is praise of Apollo, whom he describes as violently opposing Athene and Hera in an effort to save his beloved city. "But resting on Olympus' golden clouds and peaks Zeus, the watcher of the gods, dared not dissolve the fated. Must then for hightressed Helen the blaze of shining fire obliterate broad Pergamon." (vv. 92-98) Yet as Apollo had brought Achilles to his death, so he dealt with Achilles' son Neoptolemus, though he could not prevent his sacking Troy. "But he never afterward saw his mother sage nor the horses of the Myrmidons in his father's fields." (vv. 105-107) Apollo had him killed in Delphi in a quarrel over the division of meats. This was the legend, but hardly with the emphasis which Pindar gives it. He is so carried away by his vision of Apollo that he both imputes violence to an Aeginetan hero, one of those to whom except for Heracles he usually feels closest, and forgets his own precept, "leave war and every strife remote from the immortals." (***O. 9.*** 40-41) The paean well illustrates the privacy of his imagination. His call to the Muses for knowledge that mortals alone cannot gain brings a revelation of the power of the angry god that blinds him to all else. Despite his concluding praise of Aegina as the "bright star of Zeus Hellanios" (apt praise for a city that had dedicated golden stars as a thank-offering for Salamis) and despite the marvelous line about Zeus's union with the island nymph, "then hid the golden tresses of the air your native mountain shadowed" (vv. 137-139), Aeginetans felt the slight.

Nemean 7. N. 7 is his attempt to explain himself. Even the obscure last poem to Hieron has no such complexity of allusion and undertone as this, the most errant of the odes. The reason for the obscurity has been repeatedly groped at: the natural imprecision of symbols, or perhaps not so much their imprecision at any one moment as their Protean way of gliding into new meanings. They are like vine branches that rerooting take on new life. He begins meditatively with the mysterious coming into existence of beauty and achievement, a theme to which we shall return in the last section.

> "Eleithyia, enthroned beside the deep-thoughted Moirai, child of mighty Hera, you who bring children to birth, o hear me. Without you, seeing

> neither light nor the black kindly-time, do we gain your sister Hebe of the bright limbs. Yet we draw our breath not all to equal ends. Difference divides each yoked to his own fate. Through you in his turn Theagenes' son, elect for prowess, Sogenes is sung in glory among pentathletes." (vv. 1-8)

Pindar feels the hidden forces that from the dark of birth and through the light and dark of childhood have brought the boy to his present brightness, and Eleithyia, the goddess of birth, acts in unseen accord with the Fates, with Hera, goddess of marriage, and with Hebe, goddess of youth. But the sunlight of achievement thus benignly and mysteriously brought is hedged by the second darkness of death; "even great fortitude falls in shadow deep for want of song." (vv. 12-13) Presently death becomes the storm that will come the day after tomorrow, which the wise man foresees. The meaning is slightly obscure because the wise man, the *sophos,* can also mean the poet, and some take it in this sense from the first. But Pindar seems to glide from one meaning to the other as he goes on. "Rich and poor voyage past death together. Odysseus' tale, I think, grew greater than his plight through sweet-voiced Homer, since on his fancies false and winged devices a glory sits, and art deceives beguiling us with words." (vv. 19-23) So far Pindar has traveled a familiar route, though with singular freshness and serenity: that the golden moment arises, to vanish except for poetry, which holds its timelessness. But having evoked Homer as the prototype of poets and through him Odysseus, he comes to the latter's enemy Ajax, the exemplar of mistreated and misunderstood men. The myth which had begun as illustration of the poet's power to commemorate now illustrates misunderstanding, and Ajax's position includes Pindar's.

> "The greater mass of men is blind of heart. Could it see the truth, brave Ajax furious from the armor had not driven the smooth sword through his chest; whom best in war save only for Achilles the escorts of blowing Zephyrus bore in vessels swift to Ilus' town to gain blond Menelaus' wife. But common comes the wave of Hades and falls unforeseen even on him who foresees. Yet honor lasts for them whose flowering fame god nurtures when they are dead." (vv. 24-32)

The sequence of thought recalls the words to Hieron in ***O. 1*** on the deceptive charm of poetry which finds credence through the blindness and rancor of man, and as there, the two elements of false charm and human short-sightedness serve to elicit the true character of the poet as visionary. He sees what escapes the crowd, clarifying the true fame that the gods give. Pindar is now in a position to explain his seeming slight to Neoptolemus in the paean, which he does more handsomely than persuasively by saying that the hero had come to Delphi with the pious intention of dedicating spoils of Troy but died there through the god's wish that an Aeacid forever lie near the temple as guardian of heroic processions and sacrifices. "No witness false attests the deeds, Aegina, of your and Zeus's offspring. This is my confidence as I state the sovereign road of song that from their home leads radiant virtue out." (vv. 49-52) The witness has been variously understood as Neoptolemus, Apollo, and Pindar, and though it seems to be Pindar, the point is minor, because he remains in any case the seer and spokesman of the god's purpose.

The poem is only half over, and he returns twice again to his honorable intentions toward Neoptolemus. He even compliments the victor's father on his 'courage for fair things,' which must mean courage to engage Pindar, and asserts his own high reputation among the Epirotes, Neoptolemus' people, and at home.

> "If there was burden, happiness follows greater. O give me place. If being lifted up I cried beyond the measure, I am not gruff to pay the victor grace. Light is it to weave crowns. Strike up. The Muse sets gold together and ivory pale and the lily flower which she draws from the wash of the sea." (vv. 75-79)

Having asserted his role as poet and the harmony of life which should accompany it, he can at last admit a possibility of damage from his exalted state at the time of the paean. The crown which he weaves in amends is, like the images at the start of ***O. 1,*** one of those perfect and no doubt unconscious statements of his purpose. The gold has its now-familiar glint of heroic achievement; the ivory, like white things elsewhere, is shining fame; and after the wave of death which sounded through the opening of the poem, the lily flower of coral which the Muse harvests from the sea is poetry's triumph over death. Intuition can hardly be purer. The poem ends with that tone of regained ease in a familiar world which we have seen in ***O. 14*** for the young victor of Orchomenus and in the Theban ***I. 4.*** The legendary bonds between Aeacus and Heracles, both sons of Zeus, express the living bonds between their cities, Aegina and Thebes. Hence Pindar feels special meaning in the fact that the victor's house lay between two shrines of Heracles, as in a yoke.

> "If man make test of man in anything, we'll call a loving and firm-hearted neighbor a happiness to neighbor worthy all. If even a god confirm this, then through you, o queller of the giants, Sogenes prays to keep in fortune and with fond heart toward his father the rich and holy street of his ancestors. For by your sacred groves as in a chariot's four-horsed yoke, his house lies as he leaves on either hand." (vv. 86-94)

The boy's and the family's future lies with Heracles. Pindar as a Theban votary of the hero expresses in the prayer both his allegiance to the standards which Heracles embodies and his sense of him as the prototype of victors. The injured Ajax of the beginning has become the triumphant Heracles of the end, and the change is more relevant to Pindar himself than to the boy. He concludes with a smile, "My heart will never admit to have torn Neoptolemus with rancorous words. But to rehearse the same thing three and four times is penury, like the senseless chant of children, 'Corinth, the son of Zeus.' "

At first glance the cause of Pindar's difficulty was simply his injudicious account of Neoptolemus in the paean. But that account showed in turn the privacy of his inner vision, and his attempt at self-exoneration was wayward and cryptic. He spoke intimately only in this mythological language; hence was in the position of trying to correct misunderstanding while leaving its true cause untouched. This is the characteristic poetic dilemma, that a man cannot know how clear to others those images will be which to him carry brightest meaning, but to Pindar, as we have seen, the difficulty was greater, because social tradition and the setting of the epinikion as well as all personal attachments to community and cult told him that his role was communal.

Nemean 4. A final poem, ***N. 4,*** shows him facing this dilemma, and his victorious solution of it seems to carry a new stage of self-awareness. This is one of three Aeginetan poems, including ***O. 8*** of 460 and ***N. 6,*** which mention the Athenian trainer Melesias, and the lighter tone of the reference to him here and in ***N. 6*** has been used to date these poems ahead of ***O. 8;*** which is to say, farther from the outbreak of hostilities between Athens and Aegina.

> "Joy is the best physician of finished toils, and songs, wise daughters of the Muses, touch and exorcise them. Even hot water wets not the limbs so soft as praises married with the lyre. The word lives longer than the deed which from the profound mind the tongue draws through the Graces' chance." (vv. 1-8)

The opening lines were quoted earlier to illustrate his association of praise with water; the final lines are of more concern here. Words that rise with mysterious grace from the depths of consciousness live their own life, outlasting their occasion. He says more serenely and without sense of a contrasting falseness and deception in poetry what is said in the previous poem and to Hieron in ***O. 1.*** The young victor's family, like the family in ***N. 6,*** had known many victories and many songs, and were his father living, he would have bent to his lyre playing this ode. Pindar remembers the boy's happy reception at the games for Iolaus in Thebes, and the memory again evokes the legendary comradeship of Heracles and the Aeacid Telamon, at Troy and against the rock-throwing giant Alcyoneus. "Unproven of war would he be shown who fails to grasp my words. For the doer is likeliest to suffer also." (vv. 30-32) The words suffice for the background of pain, which Pindar understands but passes over in favor of the moment of triumph. The contrast to Aeschylus is very clear, as is the fact that victory has again been caught up for him into his other world of heroic reality.

At this characteristic moment of transvaluation, he strangely pauses. The gesture has something in common with the many devices by which he marks new stages of poems, but goes well beyond those.

> "Rule and the pressing hours check me from length of story. Yet by a love-charm my soul is drawn to touch this new-moon rite. Then, though the deep sea's surges hold between, resist conspiracy. We shall be deemed to have come in light superior to our foes. Another man with jealous eyes revolves in the dark a hollow wit that falls to earth. What virtue Fate, the lord, has given me, I know well, creeping time will complete destined. O straightway then, sweet lyre, in Lydian tones weave this song too, beloved of Oenone and Cyprus, where Teucer distantly rules, the son of Telamon. Ajax holds his native Salamis and Achilles his radiant isle in the Euxine sea. Thetis rules in Phthia, and Neoptolemus in the reaches of Epirus, where high aloft the pastured headlands sloping fall from far Dodona to the Ionian sea. And Peleus visited with an enemy's hand Iolcus by the foot of Pelion and gave it to Haemonians in subjection." (vv. 35-56)

The steps of his thought are worth following carefully. The victory, as said, has carried him to his ideal world, but he knows that the canons of the epinikion forbid his drifting indefinitely into this world and away from the occasion at hand. Yet the love-charm that draws him 'to touch this new-moon rite' (namely, the present festival which is being held at the new of the moon) is precisely that he sees it as a time when the present is lifted up into the past and the meaning of both becomes bright. It is clear that criticism rather than any rule of art is the true cause of his hesitation. He may not be in Aegina; at least the line about the sea holding him says so if taken literally. If it is metaphorical like the cork and net in ***P. 2,*** he is caught in and must resist a sea of misunderstanding. His rival or critic is a man who ventures on no such symbolic flights as his but keeps to the shadow and the ground. What was said in connection with ***P. 2*** about Bacchylides' lucid, gnomic, and unsymbolic style could apply to this rival, though there is no reason to connect him with Bacchylides. Quite evidently what is objected to in Pindar is the more than earthly light in which he sees victory; for it is on passing into this light of ideality that he hesitates. Here more than before his whole way of thinking seems challenged, and he stands face to face with a kind of thought which does not, like his, see reality through myth. If the Athenian conquest of Boeotia and Aegina foreshadows the end of an older way of life, these lines equally foreshadow the end of an older way of thinking. His critic was far nearer the rational world of the sophists than ever Pindar could be. But he rallies, and in his restored confidence is a self-knowledge which leads to the greatest late poems. Milton remembers these lines when in the sonnet on his twenty-third year he states his faith that he will come, "to that same lot, however mean or high, Toward which time leads me and the will of Heaven." The two men's feeling for their task is not unlike. That Pindar in fact now feels new assurance is clear from the next lines. When he bids his lyre weave this song too (namely, as he had composed other songs) in honor of Aegina and Cyprus and all those distant lands where legend placed the Aeacids, he reënters the heroic world which was to him the only true commentary on the present world. He goes on to tell again the story of Peleus' attainment of the sea nymph. "He married one of the high-throned Nereids and saw about him seated in majesty the kings of sky and sea, who wove him gifts of strength to his after-race." (vv. 65-68) This is the ultimate Cadiz of Pindar's song. Peleus had clung to Thetis when she changed into a lioness and into fire, and something of his persistence and his reward remains both to the victor and to Pindar. Triumph over vicissitude is here, as well as the harmony which unites the poet with his community, and both with the divine order embodied in the heroes. (pp. 77-106)

John H. Finley, Jr., "Symbolic Thought," and "The Odes," in his Pindar and Aeschylus: Martin Classical Lectures, Vol. XIV, *Cambridge, Mass.: Harvard University Press, 1955, pp. 3-22, 57-178.*

Gilbert Murray (essay date 1956)

[*An English educator, humanitarian, translator, author, and classical scholar, Murray has written extensively on Greek literature and history and is considered one of the most influential twentieth-century interpreters of Greek drama. In the following excerpt from his* The Literature of Ancient Greece *(1897; rev. 1956), he provides an overview of Pindar's life and work, maintaining that aristocratic values and traditional religion are at the root of the poet's view of life.*]

Pindar, "by far the chief of all the lyrists," as Quintilian calls him, was born thirty-four years after Simônides, and survived him about twenty (522-448 B.C.). He is the first Greek writer for whose biography we have real documents. Not only are a great many of his extant poems datable, but tradition, which loved him for his grammatical difficulties as well as for his genius, has preserved a pretty good account of his outer circumstances. He was born at the village of Kynoskephalæ, in Bœotia; he was descended from the Ægidæ, a clan of conquering invaders, probably 'Cadmean,' since the name 'Pindar' is found in Ephesus and Thêra. The country-bred Bœotian boy showed early a genius for music. The lyre, doubtless, he learned as a child: there was one Skopelînus at home, an uncle of the poet, or perhaps his step-father, who could teach him flute-playing. To learn choir-training and systematic music he had to go to Athens, to 'Athênoclês and Apollodôrus.' Tradition insisted on knowing something about his relation to the celebrities of the time. He was taught by Lasus of Hermionê; beaten in competition by his countrywoman Corinna, though some extant lines of that poetess make against the story: *"I praise not the gracious Myrtis, not I, for coming to contest with Pindar, a woman born!"* And another anecdote only makes Corinna give him good advice—*"to sow with the hand, not with the whole sack,"* when he was too profuse in his mythological ornaments.

Head of a statue of Zeus, 525-500 B.C.

The earliest poem we possess (***Pyth. 10.***), written when Pindar was twenty—or possibly twenty-four—was a commission from the Aleuadæ, the princes of Pharsâlus, in Thessaly. This looks as if his reputation was made with astonishing rapidity. Soon afterwards we find him writing for the great nobles of Ægîna, patrons after his own heart, merchant princes of the highest Dorian ancestry. Then begins a career of pan-Hellenic celebrity: he is the guest of the great families of Rhodes, Tenedos, Corinth, Athens; of the great kings, Alexander of Macedon, Arkesilâus of Cyrene, Thêro of Acragas, and Hiero of Syracuse. It is as distinguished as that of Simônides. though perhaps less sincerely international. Pindar in his heart liked to write for 'the real nobility,' the descendants of Æacus and Heracles; his Sicilian kings are exceptions, but who could criticise a friendly king's claim to gentility? This ancient Dorian blood is evidently at the root of Pindar's view of life; even the way he asserts his equality with his patrons shows it. Simônides posed as the great man of letters. Pindar sometimes boasts of his genius, but leaves the impression of thinking more of his ancestry. In another thing he is unlike Simônides. Pindar was the chosen vessel of the priesthood in general, a votary of Rhea and Pan, and, above all, of the Dorian Apollo. He expounded the rehabilitation of traditional religion, which radiated from Delphi. He himself had special privileges at Delphi during his life, and his ghost afterwards was invited yearly to feast with the god. The priests of Zeus Ammon in the desert had a poem of his written in golden letters on their shrine.

These facts explain, as far as it needs explanation, the great flaw in Pindar's life. He lived through the Persian War; he saw the beginning of the great period of Greek enlightenment and progress. In both crises he stood, the unreasoning servant of sacerdotal tradition and racial prejudice, on the side of Bœotia and Delphi. One might have hoped that when Thebes joined the Persian, this poet, the friend of statesmen and kings in many countries, the student from Athens, would have protested. On the contrary, though afterwards when the war was won he could write ***Nemean 4.*** and the Dithyramb for Athens, in the crisis itself he made what Polybius calls (iv. 31) "a most shameful and injurious refusal": he wrote a poem of which two large dreamy lines are preserved, talking of peace and neutrality! It is typical of the man. Often in thinking over the best pieces of Pindar—the majestic organ-playing, the grave strong magic of language, the lightning-flashes of half-revealed mystery—one wonders why this man is not counted the greatest poet that ever lived, why he has not done more, mattered more. The answer perhaps is that he was a poet and nothing else. He thought in music; he loved to live among great and beautiful images—Heracles, Achilles, Perseus, Iâson, the daughters of Cadmus. When any part of his beloved saga repelled his moral sensitiveness, he glided away from it, careful not to express scepticism, careful also not to speak evil of a god. He loved poetry and music, especially his own. As a matter of fact, there was no poetry in the world like his, and when other people sang they jarred on him, he confesses, *'like crows.'*

He loved religion, and is on the emotional side a great religious poet. The opening of ***Nemean 6.*** is characteristic; so is the end of his last dated work (***Pyth. 8.***): *"Things of a day! what are we and what not? A dream about a shadow is man; yet when some god-given splendour falls, a glory of light comes over him and his life is sweet. Oh, Blessed Mother Ægîna, guard thou this city in the ways of freedom, with Zeus and Prince Æacus and Peleus and good Telamon and Achilles!"*—a rich depth of emotion, and then a childlike litany of traditional saints. His religious speculations are sometimes far from fortunate, as in ***Olympian 1.;*** sometimes they lead to slight improvements. For instance, the old myth said that the nymph Corônis, loved by Phœbus, was secretly false to him; but a raven saw her, and told the god. Pindar corrects this: *"the god's all-seeing mind"* did not need the help of the raven. It is quite in the spirit of the Delphic movement in religion, the defensive reformation from the inside. Pindar is a moralist: parenthetical preaching is his favourite form of ornament; it comes in perfunctorily, like the verbal quibbles and assonances in Shakespeare. But the essence of his morality has not advanced much beyond Hesiod; save that where Hesiod tells his peasant to work and save, Pindar exhorts his nobleman to seek for honour and be generous. His ideal is derived straight from the Dorian aristocratic tradition. You must start by being well-born and brave and strong. You must then do two things, *work* and *spend:* work with body and soul; spend time and money and force, in pursuit of αρετα, 'goodness.' And what is 'goodness'? The sum of the qualities of the true Dorian man, descended from the god-born, labouring, fearless, unwearied fighter against the enemies of gods and men, Heracles. It is not absolutely necessary to be rich—there were poor Spartans; nor good-looking—some of his prize boxers were probably the reverse. But honour and renown you must have. Eccentric commentators have even translated αρετα as 'success in games'—which it implied, much as the ideal of a mediæval knight implied success in the tourney.

Pindar is not false to this ideal. The strange air of abject worldliness which he sometimes wears, comes not because his idealism forsakes him, but because he has no sense of fact. The thing he loved was real heroism. But he could not see it out of its traditional setting; and when the setting was there, his own imagination sufficed to create the heroism. He was moved by the holy splendour of Delphi and Olympia; he liked the sense of distinction and remoteness from the vulgar which hung about the court of a great prince, and he idealised the merely powerful Hiero as easily as the really gallant Chromios. Not that he is ever conscious of identifying success with merit; quite the reverse. He is deeply impressed with the power of envy and dishonest arts—the victory of the subtle Ionian Odysseus over the true Æacid Aias. It was this principle perhaps which helped him to comprehend why Simônides had such a reputation, and why a mob of Athenian sailors, with no physique and no landed property, should make such a stir in the world.

It is a curious freak of history that has preserved us only his 'Epinîkoi'—songs for winners in the sacred games at Olympia, Pytho, Nemea, and the Isthmus. Of all his seventeen books—"Hymns; Pæans; Dithyrambs, 2; Prosodia, 2; Parthenia, 3; Dance-songs, 2; Encômia; Dirges; Epinîkoi, 4"—the four we possess are certainly not the four we should have chosen. Yet there is in the kind of song something that suits Pindar's genius. For one thing, it does not really matter what he writes about. Two of his sublimest poems are on mule-races. If we are little interested by the fact that Xenophon of Corinth won the Stadium and the Five Bouts at Olympia in the fifth century B.C., neither are we much affected by the drowning of young Edward King in the seventeenth A.D. Poems like *Lycidas* and ***Olympian 13.*** are independent of the facts that gave rise to them. And, besides, one cannot help feeling in Pindar a genuine fondness for horses and grooms and trainers. If a horse from Kynoskephalæ ever won a local race, the boy Pindar and his fellow-villagers must have talked over the points of that horse and the proceedings of his trainer with real affection. And whether or no the poet was paid extra for the references to Melêsias the 'professional,' and to the various uncles and grandfathers of his victors, he introduces them with a great semblance of spontaneous interest. It looks as if he was one of those un-self-conscious natures who do not much differentiate their emotions: he feels a thrill at the sight of Hiero's full-dress banquet board, of a wrestling bout, or of a horse-race, just as he does at the thought of the labour and glory of Heracles; and every thrill makes him sing.

Pindar was really three years younger than Æschylus; yet he seems a generation older than Simônides. His character and habits of thought are all archaic; so is his style. Like most other divisions of Greek literature, the lyric had been working from obscure force to lucidity. It had reached it in Simônides and Bacchylides. Pindar throws us back to Alcman, almost. He is hard even to read; can any one have understood him, sung? He tells us how his sweet song will *"sail off from Ægina in the big ships and the little fishing-boats"* as they separate homewards after the festival (***Nem. 5.***). Yet one can scarcely believe that the Dorian fishermen could catch at one hearing much of so difficult a song. Perhaps it was only the tune they took, and the news of the victory. He was proud of his music; and Aristoxenus, the best judge we have, cannot praise it too highly. Even now, though every wreck of the music is lost—the Messina musical fragment (of ***Pyth. 1.***) being spurious—one feels that the words need singing to make them intelligible. The mere meaning and emotion of ***Pythian 4.*** or ***Olympian 2.***—to take two opposite types—compel the words into a chant, varying between slow and fast, loud and low. The clause-endings ring like music: παλιγκοτον δαμσθεν (***Olymp. 2.***) is much more than *"angry and overborne."* The king of the Epeans, when *"into the deep channel running deathwards, he watched—ιζοισαν εαν πολιν—his own city sink"* (***Olymp. 10.*** 38), remains in one's mind by the echoing *"my own"* of the last words; so Pelops praying *"by the grey sea-surge—οιοσ εν ορφνα, alone in the darkness"*—in ***Olymp. 1;*** so that marvellous trumpet-crash in ***Pyth. 4.*** (*ant.* 5) on the last great word τιμαν. Many lovers of Pindar agree that the things that stay in one's mind, stay not as thoughts, but as music.

But his worthy lovers are few. He is hard in the original—dialect, connection, state of mind, all are difficult to enter into; ordinary readers are bewildered by the mixture of mules and the new moon and trainers and the Æacidæ. In translations—despite the great skill of some of them—he is perhaps more grotesquely naked than any poet; and that, as we saw above, for the usual reason, that he is nothing but a poet. There is little rhetoric, no philosophy, little human interest; only that fine bloom—what he calls αωτοσ—which comes when the most sensitive language meets the most exquisite thought, and which "not even a god though he worked hard" could keep unhurt in another tongue.

Pindar was little influenced either by the movements of his own time or by previous writers. Stêsichorus and Homer have of course affected him. There are just a few notes that seem echoed from Æschylus: the eruption of Ætna is treated by both; but Pindar seems quite by himself in his splendid description (***Pyth. 1.***). It is possible that his great line λυσε δε Ζευσ αφθιτοσ Τιτανασ is suggested by the *Prometheus* trilogy, of which it is the great lesson—*"Everlasting Zeus set free the Titans."* (pp. 109-16)

Gilbert Murray, "The Song," in his The Literature of Ancient Greece, *third edition, The University of Chicago Press, 1956, pp. 90-116.*

Hermann Fränkel (essay date 1962)

[*Fränkel was a noted German scholar whose* Dichtung und Philosophie des fruhen Griechentums *(1951;* Early Greek Poetry and Philosophy, *1962) is considered a landmark in the study of Greek literature and thought. In the following excerpt from that work, Fränkel examines the archaic-age values and modes of thought present in Pindar's poetry, also commenting on its unity and general style.*]

SOME PINDARIC WAYS OF THOUGHT

Pindar's poetry has character and substance because it is animated by a definite will and gives voice to definite ways of thought. In order to understand the spirit of his poetry better, we will look at some striking excerpts from the texts.

'Best of all things is water,' is the opening of the poem that stands first in our collection; but what this means is not apparent until one reads the whole context of the strophe (***Olymp. I,*** I):

> Best of all things is water; gold gleams like blazing fire in the night as the shimmering crown of nobility and wealth; and if you desire, my soul, to sing of contests, look not over or beyond the sun for another hotter star of light in the solitary aether, nor let us celebrate any games higher than the Olympian.

The 'priamel' figure [a stylistic device consisting of a chain linking great values] is obvious: to lead up to the Olympian games, in which Hiero had won the victory here celebrated, a sequence of things is named, each being the best in its kind: water, gold, fire at night (stars), the sun in the solitary heavens, the Olympic games. What this implies in more precise terms can be understood from the ideas of that time; and in fact, as often in Pindar, Heraclitean notions are just below the surface. According to Heraclitus water is the element of vegetative life in opposition to the lifeless and passive earth, while fire is the element of higher life in opposition to earth and water. Heraclitus also, as Pindar does here, compares gold as the ideal of material value with fire as a metaphysical yardstick of value. Thirdly, another characteristic saying of Heraclitus' provided the model for another pair of contrasts occurring in Pindar. A 'fire in the night' represents light set in opposition to darkness; but the sun by day 'in the solitary aether' is the one light, set over against all the lesser lights of heaven; no star can even be seen when the sun shines. In the same way an Olympic victory outshines all victories in other games. The opening of the poem then is intended to inculcate the notion of a supreme value by examples from different fields, in order to elevate the victory now being celebrated into the class of supreme values. Pindar's thought is consistently directed towards values, and this attitude dictates his choice of subject matter, both in what he admits and what he excludes.

The values of Pindar's world are personified in the figure of the gods in heaven, while in men value and non-value, heavenly and earthly, are curiously mingled. The theme of 'god and man' is touched on by Pindar in the opening of a victory ode for Alcimidas of Aegina (***Nem. 6,*** 1):

> One and the same is the origin of men and of gods; from one selfsame mother we breathe, of both kinds, but divided by great difference of power; for what is here is nothing, but the brazen heaven has eternal duration as an unshaken place of abiding. And yet in many things we come near to the great mind or nature of the immortals, although we know not where, according to what the day or the nights bring to us, fate has appointed the end towards which we hasten.
>
> Witness of this truth is now again Alcimidas, in whom it is shown that the inborn nature is like to crop-bearing fields, which in alternation bring now the nourishment of life in abundance for men from the ground and now, suspending their strength, repose in tranquility.

Here is the archaic swing of the pendulum from opposite to opposite as men and gods are understood according to their affinities and differences. The purposes of high-principled men are like those of the gods; but for the gods life and fulfilment of purposes are certain, secure and free, while among men they are uncertain and dependent on chance happenings that can be brought about by a single day or night. The antistrophe names the Nemean victor to whom the ode is dedicated. Alcimidas' family had a remarkable number of athletic victories to its credit; but from the list that Pindar gives it is obvious that not every generation had had its share. The family talent skipped some members, passing from grandfather to grandson, or from uncle to nephew. Pindar often speaks of heredity as the decisive factor in producing men of noble qualities; here, however, he sees a further indication of human frailty in that noble qualities often remain latent even in members of a gifted family. Just as previously the unshakable security of the gods was symbolized by the 'brazen' heavens, so here a comparison with the irregular productiveness of the earth serves to characterize the changing and unreliable nature of man. That which is always completely and abundantly present among the gods is to us earthly creatures often granted, but often withheld. In another passage Pindar says: 'Our life changes and alters all things in the whirlwind of the day; yet the children of the gods are free from all hurt (***Isthm, 3,*** 17). The gods have at their command that certainty of achievement which is denied to us: 'God achieves everypurpose according to his wish' (***Pyth. 2,*** 49).

In comparison with the gods, man is a mere nothing, according to the opening of Pindar's ode to Alcimidas; but Pindar is very far from the Christian notion of self-denial and contrition. For him the gods are our cousins, as it were, from the reigning family, since we all come ultimately from the same mother. Noble men are impelled by the divine inheritance in their blood to try to be like the Olympians. Their earnest will towards greatness and noble achievement is often disappointed, but Pindar does not on this account condemn lofty ambitions as improper; he takes them as a token of noble qualities of mind. But one should not set one's heart on too remote a goal: thus the poet prays (***Pyth. II,*** 5of.): 'God grant that I strive towards what is noble, aiming at that which is accessible according to my age.' This is in accord with the teaching which defines manly worth (*aretê*) as a union of two things: of striving towards lofty ends and of the ability to encompass them.

Thus Pindar is no advocate of pusillanimous prudence or of the golden mean of bourgeois contentment, nor does he applaud happiness in obscurity. This is certainly not the implication of the passage where he says: 'I will look for those pleasures which the day affords, and fare on tranquilly to old age.' This sentence has to be read in its context. We will cast back some distance, and begin where the poet is speaking of a kinsman of the victor's who had been slain in battle (***Isthm. 7,*** 25):

> . . . he for whom a fate was appointed by Ares of the brazen shield, but for brave men honour is compensation. For each man should know, who has undertaken in such darkness to keep off the bloody hail from his beloved homeland.
>
> . . . [corrupt passage] . . . that he wins for himself the greatest fame among his people whether he now lives or dies. Son of Diodotus [Pindar is now addressing the dead kinsman], following the example of the warrior Meleager, of Hector and of Amphiaraus, you have given up the blood of your young life,
>
> fighting amongst the foremost, where the bravest went into the fiercest fighting with the least hope. Beyond words was the sorrow that struck me at your death. But now [now that an Isthmian victory has been won] Poseidon [the god of the Isthmian games] has granted me peace after the storm. I will sing and adorn my hair with garlands. May no ill-will of the immortals do me harm!
>
> Such joy as the day brings I will pursue, and journey on in tranquillity to old age and the life appointed for me. We are all mortal, the one as much as the other; yet the daemon (the destiny of our life) is unequal. But he who directs his eyes to the far distance, he does not attain to treading the brazen floor of the dwelling of the gods. The winged horse threw off
>
> his rider Bellerophon, when he would fain have flown to the company of Zeus, to the heavenly mark of his journeying. A most grievous end awaits forbidden enjoyments. But to me, Loxias, proud in your locks of gold, in your contest at Pytho, grant the flower-rich coronet.

Here, at the end of the archaic age, we hear the same notes that were struck in an ode of Alcman's at the very beginning: 'Never shall a man fly to heaven,' 'There is a resentment of the gods: fortunate is he who lives one day in happiness without tears.' If Pindar here does what Alcman did in his day, in pointing out the limitations of our human condition, at the same time he sets the limits wide enough at least to come near to full divinity. He does not bid our wishes come to a halt until they dream of treading the 'brazen floor' of heaven and forcing an entry into 'the company of Zeus,' as Bellerophon in the legend sought to do. On another occasion he advises the victor: 'Seek not to become Zeus' (***Isthm. 5,*** 14). In great and noble men he expects to find a titanic drive to storm the heights of heaven, since it is part of our half-divine nature to strive ever upwards. Even if there is a warning of the bitter end that awaits measureless ambition, the tragic tension between ideal and accomplishment remains, and there is no attempt at a reconciliation. Thus we must not see a Stoic detachment from the individual's life or an Epicurean resignation of worldly ambition in Pindar's declaration that he intends, knowing what our human lot is, to meet with tranquillity whatever may be attached to his destiny; nor must we do so in the advice that he gives elsewhere (***Pyth. 3,*** 107), that one should adapt oneself to the moment, 'be great in great fortunes, and lowly in lowly.' He does not enjoin indifference, but understanding of the uncertainty of our existence, together with a noble courage in adversity (fr. 42):

> Let not strangers see what misfortunes are approaching us. This counsel will I give you: all that befalls us of happiness and success we should openly show to all men; but when there falls upon a man, by the gods' devising, insufferable calamity, this it is right for us to hide in darkness.

To the suffering Hiero he has this to say (***Pyth. 3,*** 80):

> You know the saying from ancient times: 'For one joy the gods send upon man two sorrows.' The fool cannot endure this becomingly, but the noble soul can, turning that which is good outwards.

The continuation of the poem (103–106) lays further stress on the basic instability of human fortune. The 'resentment' of the gods, i.e. the jealousy with which they guard their superiority over men, is ready at any moment to fall on him whose rash self-confidence provokes it; and then by the sternness of their chastisement they remind us of our limitations and of their power. Hence every cry of rejoicing must be accompanied by some such pious prayer as we heard before (***Isthm. 7,*** 39): 'May no ill-will of the immortals do me harm!' Perhaps the finest expression of this pious humility is in the ode to Theia. . . . Pindar is singing the praises of Aegina, with its great naval power; he has just referred to the great feats of arms formerly accomplished by the sons of Aegina. Now he turns to the most recent deed of valour, the naval victory of the Greeks at Salamis, in which the Aeginetan vessels played a distinguished part (***Isthm. 5,*** 46):

> Many a shaft is ready for my singing tongue to glorify the men of Aegina. Thus might even now the home of Ajax, Salamis, bear witness on their behalf as a monument raised up to the sea-people in battle, in the deadly storm of Zeus, that hailed death upon countless men. But let your boasting be drowned in silence. Zeus granted this as all else, Zeus the lord of all.

We men should not pride ourselves too much upon our advantages, since our existence is governed by the day ('ephemeral,' fr. 157), and the lord of all, Zeus, sends us days of very different kinds. All reality comes from above: 'To all things should thou assign Zeus as the cause' (***Pyth. 5,*** 25), and reality is basically of changeable nature (***Pyth. 2,*** 88):

> A man shall not strive against god, who often advances now this one, and then to another grants great honour. But not even this soothes the feelings of the envious.

The resentment of the gods takes care that our tree shall not grow up to heaven, and in this way it takes away any ground for envy on the part of our fellow men.

But how and why particular pieces of good and bad fortune come to us, is a question that Pindar does not answer, and does not even ask. He has no thought of attributing precise and detailed justice to the divine rule; what falls to the human lot is not reward and punishment, but change and reversal, and the law of reversal seems to the poet a kind of substitute for the principle of divine justice, as it formerly did to Solon. But this doctrine permits only an overall justification of the rather wilful divine government; in particular cases any lively moral feeling must be tempted to 'strive against the gods.' In one passage Pindar is telling the story of Heracles and Geryon. Heracles, the son of Zeus himself, had been commanded by his taskmaster to bring him the cattle of Geryon; he simply took them, without paying or asking leave; Geryon took up arms against this theft, and was slain by Heracles. At this point in his narrative Pindar makes it clear that he sympathizes with Geryon—with the man whose death was decided by Zeus; but in the same breath he beats a retreat, saying: 'Yet will I never say anything that is unpleasing to Zeus.' But again he says that a just man will not sit idly by while his property is stolen. Obviously the legend of Geryon had troubled Pindar; he was grappling with the same contradiction that Hesiod also had tried to resolve: divine rule and amoral force can neither be separated nor united. In another passage where he refers to Geryon again (fr. 169), he tries to sidestep the difficulty by speaking of the supreme power of *nomos,* which controls even the gods, and which can legalize even the worst act of violence (cf. also ***Nem. 9,*** 14f.). *Nomos* in Greek is anything that is current and accepted: usage, custom, norm, rule, constitution, law. Exactly what it means here is not clear, but in any case *nomos* is an ordering power. Pindar believes in order and rules, and he shrinks from radical questioning of any rule that he finds current.

Pindar is no critic and no theologian. Towards the Olympian gods he carefully keeps a measured distance. He does not try to work out how the gods exist in themselves or in relation to one another. His world of gods has no system, no articulation, no spatial depth. Everything is on one surface that is directed towards man and his world.

With reference to the doctrines held and the myths related of the gods, as also in reference to the legends of heroes, Pindar's belief is receptive, adaptable and free from speculation. He takes these things as they come, accepting any of them that he can turn to his uses. If he comes up against some story of dubious morality such as the despoiling and slaying of Geryon, he first protests against it, and then prudently declares that he has nothing to say. This pointed silence is one of his characteristic features. In an ode for the Aeginetans he speaks of the great heroes of Aegina; the narrative leads up to a point where he would have to tell of a fratricide whose perpetrators had to seek refuge in exile. Here Pindar, with a very obvious omission, tells us that he is ashamed to relate the abominable action which drove the Aeacidae from their native island, and he breaks off with a declaration that he prefers to ignore what is ugly and devote himself wholly to what is beautiful. These are his words (***Nem. 5,*** 16):

> Here I stop; not every truth may with advantage show its face, and silence is often the best path that a man can tread. Yet when the purpose is to praise the blessings of the gods or the might of arms or iron war, a long leap may be marked out for me; spring and strength are then in my knees; eagles wing their way over the sea to the other shore.

Pindar was not able entirely to escape the tendency towards criticism of the old legends, as we see it practised by his contemporary Hecataeus. In one instance we see him correcting before our eyes a legend which did not satisfy him in its current shape (***Olymp. 1,*** 24ff.). According to legend Tantalus had once bidden the gods to dinner and served up to them the body of his son Pelops (it was probably meant as a pious offering); all the other gods perceived the abomination and withdrew from the accursed banquet, but Demeter, whose anxiety for her lost daughter made her oblivious of everything else, helped herself to a little of the shoulder. The gods brought the boy back to life, and gave him a shoulder of ivory instead; in consequence a white birthmark was hereditary in the family. It is instructive to see how Pindar sets about his improvement. First he tells us that Clotho (the power of fate) took the resuscitated child, with his bright shining shoulder, out of the cooking-pot. Then he comes to a stop, full of doubt at the gross and crude miracle of bringing a cut-up body back to life; his final decision comes from the thought that it is not good to say that the gods sat down at a table where human flesh was served. Accordingly Pindar gives the story a new form, and tells it, 'contrary to tradition,' in a shape that leaves out the human sacrifice; he found it quite impossible to credit the gods with a cannibal gluttony. The reason that he gives is not that the story is impossible, but that 'it is fitting for men to speak good things of the gods, for thus one avoids offence' (35), and that 'speaking evil has often brought misfortune upon its authors' (53).

If Pindar is not given to theorizing about the gods, he is at least equally far removed from speculation concerning the mechanical ordering of the universe. He speaks of the natural philosophers as 'breaking off the withered fruits of wisdom' (fr. 209). So far as he concerns himself at all with physical phenomena in his poems, he interprets them in a moral or religous sense. A striking natural occurrence which exercised the scientists of his time was the yearly inundation of the Nile. They asked how it was possible that the river flowed in greater volume during the dry north African summer and autumn than at any other time. Pindar gave the native answer that a *daimon,* a figure in human shape a hundred fathoms tall, ruled over the river and regulated it according to the seasons (fr. 282). What he must have meant was that a divine power released the water and provided the fertile flood-plains when it was needed in order for the Egyptians to survive. To a solar eclipse of the year 463 Pindar could only react with undisguised consternation: he wholly ignores the theories which had already been advanced to account for the phenomenon. The catastrophe set his thought moving along purely religious lines. At the request of his native city he addressed a prayer to Apollo and his son Teneros, who jointly possessed a shrine and oracle in the Ismenion in Thebes; and the purpose of the ode seems to have been to ask the oracle for an explanation of the prodigy—how the eclipse was to be interpreted, and what should be done to avoid the disasters that it seemed to portend. The opening of the poem (***Paean 9***) was as follows:

> Lamp of the sun, what purpose do you have as you gaze, mother of the eyes? Noblest of stars, snatched away in the daytime you have made helpless the strength of men and the path of wisdom; treading a road of darkness you wander on new and unwonted ways. As a suppliant I come, swift guider of the car, to implore you: turn to some scatheless blessing for Thebes, commanding one, this terror to all mankind.
>
> [*Two lines missing*]
> Do you bear the sign of a coming war, or withering of the harvest? or depth of snow beyond measure, or the abomination of civil war? or . . . of the sea? or frost in our soil, or a summer season of rain, streaming with angry waters? Or will you overwhelm the earth in floods and make the race of men begin anew?

The Greek chorus does not approach its god with fantastic rites of purification or magical formulae; it voices its anxiety and its desires in human and natural terms. It even permits itself the liberty of ignoring, at least at the outset, Apollo and Teneros, the dwellers in the very temple in which the ode was performed. Instead of addressing them, he addresses in his opening words the power actually concerned, the 'lamp of the sun' (ακτισ αελιου fem. = 'sunbeam,' 'sunlight'). The 'lamp of the sun' had no temple and no place in the Greek pantheon, since in myth and cult Helius was a male divinity. Pindar, however, is speaking not of a person, but of the power of sunlight working in our lives; and in consequence he directs his prayer not to the god Helius, but to the 'mother of the eyes' who illuminates the universe for us. How differently a prayer like this moves us by its warmth and intimate tone, compared with Pindar's celebration in an ode for a Rhodian victor, of the principal deity of the island, Helius, as 'the father, the begetter of sharp rays (ακτινεσ) of light, the lord of fire-breathing steeds' (***Olymp. 7,*** 70)!

THE 'POWERS' IN PINDAR

The transformation that Pindar essayed in the ***Ninth Paean*** is a remarkable one. To the poet and his public the image of Helius as a shining male figure driving a car of fire was familiar from a thousand representations in poetry, painting and sculpture; yet in his prayer Pindar diverges from the ruling tradition in a cardinal point. The image of the horses was indeed retained in allusions to the 'path' or 'way' of the sun; but for a male figure he substitutes a female, or rather he substitutes a certain something that has scarcely anything personal about it. He straightforwardly and naturally approaches and addresses the sunlight, conceiving it without any external trappings as that which it really means to men, as 'the mother of the eyes.' Here we come upon a feature that is very important in Pindar's thought. (pp. 471-81)

[In archaic Greek thought there is] a distinction between the anthropomorphic divinities, conceived as persons, and the powers which were identical with natural phenomena and forces. Such a power, for example, is *Eris,* the love of conflicts and battle: a violent force which brings its victims so under its spell that they are set at variance with their normal nature and take on instead her spirit and perform her work; another is the compelling power of chance (*Tyche*), which suddenly alters the whole course of our life. Others are self-blinding which draws calamitous consequences after it (*Atê*); the charm and attraction (*Charis*) that can proceed from men or things or actions; the winning power of persuasion and conviction (*Peithô*); the power of art (*Mousa*), and many others as we find them named and described especially in the *Theogony* of Hesiod. Their names in Greek are mostly feminine. We might call them simply 'beings,' since they all have a clearly marked being or nature which is easy enough to grasp, though less easy to describe. 'Powers,' however, has become the technical term. The 'powers' are in truth no fictions or creations of art, but realities of timeless validity; each man may perceive them repeatedly when once his eyes have been opened to them.

Among the Greeks of the archaic period the reverence

which they felt towards such powers clothed itself in religious forms. These realities, as super-personal powers in life, belong alike to heaven and to earth. They are so natural that we can grasp them entire, yet they have a depth that goes beyond the mechanical universe. Pindar likes to interpret human life on the basis of 'powers' which work themselves out in it. In regard to these 'powers' his god-fearing ways of thought display an active originality which strikingly contrasts with his adherence to tradition in other respects. He has constantly something new to say of them; not a little of what he says is surprising: all is meaningful and convincing.

A boy whose thoughts are yet at play with the dreams of childhood has been victorious in the pentathlon; scarcely yet at home in the world, he has won great reputation in it, thanks to his inborn qualities (cf. ***Nem. 5,*** 40). Hence the poet at the opening of his ode addresses in terms of gratitude and honour the power who presides over birth (Elithyia), who at first moment of life imparts to each human child its peculiar qualities and thus helps to determine its destiny in life (***Nem. 7,*** 1):

> Elithyia, enthroned with the deep-minded Fates, daughter of mighty Hera (the goddess of marriage), hear me, bearer of children! Without you we do not behold the light or the darkness of night, we do not receive your sister Hebe (the prime of life between childhood and old age) with her shining limbs. Yet we do not all strive to the same ends: Different qualities divide us, binding each to his destiny. Thanks to you greatness (*aretê*) is ordained for Thearion's son Sogenes, and he is glorified in song among the pentathletes.

The powers will not be isolated, for they have their meaning only in the framework of the great whole that we call 'life.' Thus Birth is here enthroned together with Fates, is the daughter of Wedlock and the sister of Hebe: the coming into existence of the individual and the fulfilment of the qualities born in him are understood as sister powers. The end of the poem (99f.) completes the expression of the wish that a prosperous *hêbê* and a blessed old age may be in store for the boy.

In the actions and reactions of life the Pindaric powers sometimes become dynamic to a startling degree. The archaic law of polar ambivalence and the Heraclitean notion of the identity of opposites bring it about that the most mild and friendly of powers have a gloomy and insidious counterpart. The music of Apollo, which softens and tranquillizes all the forces of good, arouses the imprisoned prince of darkness to flaming and earth-shaking rage (***Pyth. 1,*** 1-16). Peaceful 'Tranquillity' can fight savagely when it is necessary to restrain a violator of peace (***Pyth. 8,*** 1-13). 'Comeliness, who grants to mortals all that is graceful, lends dignity' even to malicious falsehood, when she dresses it in the garb of pleasing legends (***Olymp. I,*** 30-51). *Hôra,* the season of youthful strength and vigour in men who have just matured, with the gay courage that she imparts and the winning charm that she sheds over them, is thus apostrophized in the opening strophe of an ode (***Nem. 8,*** 1):

> Sublime Hora, you bring the ambrosial joys of Aphrodite, dwelling in the eyes of youths and maidens, many a man you touch with mild hands of compulsion, yet others you touch otherwise.

The *hôra* which beams from the eyes of beautiful girls and boys brings with it a power and compulsion of two kinds, leading to beatitude or martyrdom.

The Pindaric powers are no bloodless allegories, dragging their weary feet across a puppet's stage; nor are they figures conjured up by the violent postulates of metaphysics from an unapproachable other-world, to stand shapeless and scarcely comprehensible before the eyes of the initiate. They are always in our midst, they work directly upon us and through us. In one of his dithyrambs (fr. 78) Pindar addresses the war-cry 'alala,' shouted by Greek armies before joining battle, in the following terms:

> Hear me, Alala, daughter of Ares, prelude of the spears, you to whom men fall as offerings for their homeland in death's holy sacrifice.

As 'prelude' to the holy self-sacrifice of brave men, and as the first beginning of a decisive event whose outcome only god knows, the battle-cry is a power of high rank; but it is from our own throats that it comes, by our own will that it is uttered.

The 'powers' thus become intermediaries between men and the great personal deities; intermediaries to whom no altars smoke, no worship is paid, but which in our souls we honour with pious reverence. Pindar is ready to see the powers as 'daughters' of the Olympians. He calls *Alala* a daughter of Ares; on the occasion of the eclipse he prays not to Helius, the father and begetter of the rays (***Olymp. 7,*** 70), but to the radiance itself and to the god's daughter 'lamp of the sun' (***Paean 9***), he prays to *Tychê,* the idea of fortuity in life, as a daughter of Zeus (***Olymp. 12***) who is lord of all reality; Truth also he addresses as 'daughter of Zeus' (***Olymp. 10,*** 13).

A power is by its very nature specific; it has its own laws and is master of a particular domain. The more clearly each of these figures is developed, the more powerful and realistic is the perspective afforded of the field in question. But clarification of details leads to confusion of the whole. The more 'powers' are discovered, and the more intensively one works out their characteristic properties, the more fragmented does our picture of life in general become. Music, a war-cry, tranquillity, fortuity, birth, truth, the charms of *Hôra*—all these have little in common, and a great deal of systematic work would be necessary if one wished to arrange all these disparate entities in their proper places in a general scheme. Pindar is no constructor of systems. He does indeed separate out the individual powers, but in setting them into an ordered arrangement he takes scarcely more than the first step. He is as far from having a systematic world-picture on this level as on the level of the gods or of physical nature.

Yet his work as a whole has a kind of uniformity which the reader perceives at once. However, to say that it lies in the style or the technique would obviously be unsatisfactory. There must be behind it a way of looking at things which makes a uniform style possible.

This attitude is not hard to find. Pindar's poetry is directed towards what is noble, great, beautiful, good and godly—in a word, towards values; and this attitude is so rigidly maintained that he excludes everything which does not have a positive or negative correlation with values. Just as Plato later directed the whole power of his philosophical thought towards the idea of 'the good,' so Pindar's poetry has the one aim of helping to realize all that is of value in life. It is from the uniform golden glow of values, shed equally over all his poems, that his creations derive their unity, both overall and in detail.

From a poet as innocent of abstract theorizing as Pindar, we should not expect a didactic verbal formulation of the notion that all values were essentially one. Yet on one occasion he does give such a formulation, so important did he reckon the conception to be. In the small portion that we possess of his entire output we find the opening of one ode pushing metaphysical speculation as far as a 'mother' of all values (***Isthm. 5,*** 1):

> Mother of the sun, Theia of the many names, thanks to you men have learned to value gold as great and mighty beyond all other things; hence are the competing ships in the sea and the horses straining at the chariot in the circling contest objects of admiration, because of your worthiness;
>
> hence (because of your worthiness) he on whose head many crowns are laid lays claim to the coveted glory in contest, having conquered by strength of arm or by fleetness of foot. But the contention of men is decided by their daemons (inborn fates).
>
> Two things are there that bestow the fairest flower of life with the bloom of happiness: that a man should prosper and that he should receive praise and reputation. Seek not to become Zeus; you possess all if of these two splendours a part falls to your lot. Mortal fortunes become a mortal.

The idea at the end of this extract is one with which we are familiar from the end of the first Pythian. Everything that a man may wish for himself is comprised in the double achievement of the victor: He has 'prospered' in the success and the favour of the gods which has befallen him in the shape of his victory; and he has 'praise and reputation' now bestowed by Pindar's poem in his honour. The opening of the poem is managed in 'priamel' form to lead up to the notion of the glory justly claimed by a victory in the games. But who is Theia?

Hesiod in his epic of gods and cosmic forces, of their origin and their kinship one with another, includes among the numerous names that make up his genealogies the Titans who were parents of the sun, the moon and the dawn. Old tradition gave him a name for the father, Hyperion: but no firm tradition prescribed the mother's name, and so Hesiod gave her the colourless general appellation of Theia, 'divine one' (*Theog.* 371). Pindar took up Hesiod's 'mother of the sun' and elevated her to a 'power.' While he saw in the other powers the daughters of the great personal gods, and in his prayer for Thebes addressed the daughters of Helius, he now took an opposite direction and raised his eyes towards the 'mother of the sun'.

For what Pindar intended to express by this personage it was convenient that Hesiod had given her a name meaning only 'divine one' without defining her any further. Since there are many individual values based upon her, the 'power' of value is in Pindar's eyes truly 'rich in names,' as there was no all-embracing expression in Greek for value in general. The closest approach is the word *timê,* which can mean 'honour,' 'dignity,' 'reward,' 'value' in a variety of shades of meaning. Pindar accords a key position to the word *timê* in the important opening verses of this Isthmian ode, which we must now examine more closely.

The sun is Theia's child: thus in the last resort all light in this world comes from her; but not only light, as Pindar now declares. This power of imparting and bestowing worth and merit is very clearly brought out by the way in which Pindar has arranged his words. 'Gold,' he says, is indebted to you for the fact that men have adjudged to it . . . unique force (that is, the highest material value); (you are the value of values) for it equally . . . comes about through your *timê* that the splendour of swift-moving ships and chariots provide a spectacle to arouse our admiration; (it is through your *timê*) that a victor in the games gains glorious fame as his becoming tribute. . . .' The examples chosen are representative of all other things to which a value attaches; thus Theia, in Platonic terms, is proclaimed as the very idea of value, that is, as the power which in every field creates and establishes value as something valid and binding. In the realm of material values she is the basis of the great purchasing power of imperishable gold and of the pride and power of those who possess it; her power is equally felt in everything through which a claim to praise and reputation . . . can be put forward, or by which our sense of admiration is aroused. . . . Now at last we are fully able to appreciate what it means that the verses which begin our collection of Pindar's odes should parade such a rapid and exuberant series of values before our eyes: water, the best of all; fire in darkness; gold as the crown of wealth; the one sun in the empty aether; the Olympian games. Thus the priamel figure can be understood at a deeper level: by enumerating the best things in a variety of fields the poet points towards that which is common to them all, the supreme value.

Nowhere else has Pindar advanced so far towards a Platonic conception of ideas as in this address to Theia. It can hardly be accidental that Plato himself speaks [in his *Republic* 7, 517 B.C.] of the idea of the Good, the summit of all ideas, as the mother of the sun (Helius): 'In the world of higher perception the last and scarcely able to be perceived is the idea of the Good; he who has beheld it knows that it is the basis of all virtue and beauty; in the sensible world it gave birth to light and to him who is the ruler of light (Helius). . . . '

If all values by their very essence are of one and the same nature, in which each individual value participates (to use Plato's expression) in the same way human value (*aretê,* manly worth, virtue) is a unitary whole. Of course, Pindar nowhere says this expressly, but this is probably because to him it was self-evident; many of his trains of thought rest on the presupposition that individual virtues cannot be severed one from another. It is only in this way that we can understand the high value that Pindar and his world set upon victories in the games. They thought not in terms of a specialized technical ability, but in terms of the demonstration, in this particular way, of the worth of an individual. If a man throws all that he has to give into pursuing a wholly ideal end; if he gives up his time and money, if he takes the risk of defeat and disgrace, if he undergoes the long and severe discipline of training with all its pains and privations and efforts, and puts out every ounce of his strength in the event itself; and if then the grace of the gods, without which no achievement is possible, chooses him as victor from all his competitors, then in Pindar's eyes he has given convincing proof of his *aretê.* And proofs of this kind were necessary, for the values in which Pindar believed were no other-worldly abstractions; they had to be fulfilled and realized in life.

THE ART OF PINDAR

From the point which we have reached in gaining this understanding of Pindar, it is but a short step to the end of our long quest for the unity of his various poems.

As we saw earlier, the material content of the longer poems differs enormously from one to another; there is, as it were, no vanishing-point towards which the various lines converge. If there is any general perspective which can confer unity on the poems, it must be one which transcends the individual poems. This applies not only to the victory odes, but to other varieties of choral lyric as well, since the same problem of unity presents itself in all.

It has been shown that the society for which Pindar worked believed in the unity of all values and that they were realized as examples in individual fields. In dealing with any such example it was tacitly assumed that the particular proof of worth, whatever it might be, represented the unity of all, as in the corn-market a single handful may represent the quality of a whole cargo. In each of his great choral odes Pindar sets forth the whole world of values—not in a theoretical outline of its basic features, but in concrete examples from its most important areas; and the proofs of worth may be adduced either at random or according to the accidental context of events. Any myth, represents the legendary past which contained all the models of all that could happen. Every pious reference to the gods contained, in principle, all religious feeling. Timeless truths of a general nature are incorporated in the various maxims. The words of the poet serve to typify all skills and abilities, all thought and language. The particular occasion of the poem is of course alluded to; it provides the nearest illustration of the ability of values to realize themselves in any present set of circumstances. It is in order to achieve this kind of completeness that we find in the typical Pindaric ode those five standard elements of subject matter which feature in it together. The victory ode, then, has also the particular purpose of taking up the recent achievement into the realm of values and of bringing the victorious athlete to his due place among the noble company of famous men, heroes and gods.

Pindar's art is thus an act of homage to values, and to human values in particular. Through this fact function also is more precisely determined. Values live in and upon the estimation that they enjoy; they have to be recognized and understood in theory, and realized and encouraged in practice; without this they would be as dead as a law that scarcely anyone knew or respected. It is the function of the poet, as the voice and conscience of the community, to make sure that the good is honoured, and with correct judgment to allot praise or blame to men and things. In the ode addressed to Hora Pindar declares (***Nem. 8,*** 32):

> . . . Hateful deception was practised from the earliest times, companion of crafty speech, hypocrisy, injurious slander, she who destroys that which shines brightly and raises to a hollow eminence that which lies in darkness.
>
> Father Zeus, let not such a nature be mine! Let me cleave to the simple path of life, so that in death I may not leave to my children an evil reputation. Others strive for gold or for possession of land insatiably; but I make my ambition that I may be pleasing to my fellow-citizens until my body is robed in earth, praising what is praiseworthy, and strewing blame on the impious.
>
> Virtue (*aretê*) grows upwards as a tree grows up watered by the lifegiving dew, rising up with the help of the wise (i.e. poets) and righteous among men to the fresh blue of heaven.

On behalf of the community the singer rewards the good that men do with sounding acclaim and undying glory, and thus animates those whom he addressed to ever continuing achievements. It is his hand that bestows the fairest of crowns—not a quickly fading garland like that which physically adorns the head of the victor, but an imperishable diadem (***Nem. 7,*** 77):

> It is easy to twine garlands—let it be; the Muse is forging for you gold together with white ivory and with the lily-flower from the dew of the sea (coral).

The special view that Pindar takes of goodness and greatness assigns a central position to his art in another sense also. To maintain a splendid appearance is also for him part of the noble character. Choral lyric, of which he is master, with its words and music and dancing of noble and richly attired performers, was for him and his circle itself something of value and reality, comparable with the proud pomp of the national games. Just as Heraclitus in his awakened consciousness experienced in his own existence the meaning of the cosmos, in Pindar's choral odes the idea of the good and great achieves self-awareness and triumphantly displays its own significance. Promise and performance here become one. It is for this reason that Pindar's art can so often and so explicitly speak about itself.

Pindar's poetry is a piece of life; it serves life and is nourished by life present and past. But it has no thought of taking reality as it is and representing it in its actual size and shape. Its subject matter is selected by a rigorously critical method and set out by a highly specialized art.

We virtually never hear in Pindar of men working hard

for their daily bread or of working for a living at all. Pindar often celebrates the great merchant families of Aegina, and speaks of their trading vessels sailing to every port (***Nem. 5,*** 1ff.); but he never mentions their cargoes or the bargains that were struck for them. Pindar knew his way about the markets: in one passage he enumerates the most famed products of the various regions of Greece—one produces the best hunting dogs, another the best milch goats, others the finest weapons or chariots, or the most exquisitely made mule-carts (fr. 106); but he is not thinking of the commercial value of these things, only of their unsurpassable quality. His poetry never stoops to the level of everyday life. It remains always on the lofty peaks of life, and even when it has to speak of the jovial atmosphere of a five-day banquet celebrated by the princes and nobles of the Argo's expedition, it speaks in religious accents of their 'culling the hallowed flower of goodly living' (***Pyth. 4,*** 131).

Among progressive circles of that day the notion of *historiê,* that is, an empirical stocktaking of all accessible reality was finding enthusiastic acceptance. The exclusive art of Pindar had no sympathy for such curiosity, and in contrast with Aeschylus, he was quite uninfluenced by the lively interest in geography then current. Here again it was not ignorance that was the cause: the much-travelled poet was no stranger to geography. His many passages in praise of cities and countries are true to nature, and he attributes to them the features that they actually possessed; but their spatial location receives no attention from him—the points of the compass are never mentioned. He never gives a continuous account of any land or people and its peculiarities; we almost never find in him (here also he differs sharply from Aeschylus) any mention of the strange and unusual things to be found in the wide world, of exotic costumes, manners or religion.

The one exception is of so peculiar a kind that it proves the rule. In his earliest datable poem (written in 498) Pindar comes to speak of the Hyperboreans, the chosen people of Apollo, and he gives a detailed picture of them (***Pyth. 10,*** 27):

> (Happy is he who has won in the great games and lives to see his son victorious in the Pythian contests.) The brazen heaven will he never scale, but in the realm of those gains which become our mortal estate he has sailed the longest voyage. Yet wandering by ship or by land you could not find the wondrous way to the folk of the Hyperboreans,
>
> among whom once Perseus dined, the leader of the people, bidden into their dwellings. When he came, he found them offering hecatombs of asses, a lordly sacrifice. In their feasts and songs of praise Apollo constantly takes most delight, and laughs to behold the braying wantonness of the creatures.
>
> The Muse is never absent from the life that the Hyperboreans lead; everywhere sound the choruses of maidens and the call of the lyre and the echo of the flute. They bind their hair with golden laurel for their glad-hearted festival. Neither sickness nor wasting old age is found among that sacred race. Far from pain and warfare do they dwell, freed from the anger that overtakes men on behalf of righteousness.

The people 'beyond the north wind' (for that is what *Hyperborean* means) do not dwell in our world but beyond it; the advantages which their 'sacred race' enjoys embody those joys which mortals long for in vain. Thus Pindar's description of their life and habits has nothing to do with ethnography, any more than the route to their country is a concern of geographers. The poet in fact says that one cannot get there by sea or by land; only Perseus, with his miraculous winged sandals, found the 'wondrous way' thither. This flight is for Pindar a parallel to an ascent to the 'brazen sky.' From the empirical point of view this represents a step backwards from the earlier notions of Aristeas, who made personal researches into the far North and on that basis assigned to the Hyperboreans a local habitation and a name. Pindar is not concerned with physical location, only with a symbol and its meaning. In the same way the 'pillars of Hercules,' the mountains which guard the straits of Gibraltar at the Western end of the known world, become for him a symbol of the farthest attainable good fortune (***Olymp. 3,*** 44; ***Isthm. 4,*** 12). As in one instance the imaginary Hyperboreans, so in another the real facts of geography serve merely as a help towards expressing the concept of values. In another passage Pindar makes similar metaphorical use of the names of two rivers. In the cold North-East, where one would gladly take refuge in the heat of summer, the Phasis was the *ne plus ultra* of navigation, as the Nile was in the warm South for which one longed in winter. With a delicate humour Pindar praises a prince in these terms (***Isthm. 2,*** 39):

> At his hospitable board the blustering wind never compelled him to reef his sail; he continued none the less, sailing in summer as far as to the Phasis and in winter to the Nile.

The image of the 'wind' of popularity which one attracts into one's sails by noble liberality is one with which we are already familiar. Here it is given a new turn. The wind of popularity began to blow too strongly, and the number of guests increased alarmingly, but Xenocrates did not consider reefing the sails of his generosity.

Just as Pindar neglected geography and spatial orientation in general (unless it had some further significance, such as neighbourhood), so he ignored chronology whenever he chose. His manner of presentation springs instantaneously from one point in time to another, and in dealing with a coherent sequence of events he is as likely to go backwards as forwards, and to make constant changes of course. Our sense of time is cruelly abused, but it is the price paid for the emergence of other and more important cross-relations.

The empiricist finds his satisfaction in the particular and the non-recurring: for Pindar on the other hand the individual instance is no more than an example, a test case. He treats the athletic contests with reference only to their significance; very seldom does he give details of a particular event. The victors whom he celebrates remain equally without individuality.

The graphic detail of description which Bacchylides indulges in for its own sake is used only sparingly by Pindar. Shape, colour, movement, light and dark, sounds and smells, scenes and physical objects—all such elements are brought in only occasionally, but for that very reason with the more telling effect. Two examples may be given from one poem. In an ode for a Rhodian victor Pindar happens to speak of the legend of Tlepolemus. Tlepolemus had incurred the misfortune of banishment for a homicide; but in the end his act turned into a blessing for him, since he became the founder of a flourishing settlement beyond the sea, in Rhodes in fact. The idea of bad luck changing to good is conveyed by Pindar in maxims (***Olymp. 7,*** 24):

> Around the spirit of man drift endless errors; he has no art to find out
>
> what now or at the last will be the best for him. Thus formerly the founder of this land with a staff of hard olivewood struck and slew in Tiryns in his anger Alcmene's bastard brother Licymnius coming from Midea. Bewilderment of the soul has often led the wisest astray. And he went to the god and asked of the oracle.

Pindar here talks partly in generalities and vague symbols, while the remaining part, the narrative, is in a dry chronicler's style: in its barren expanse only one detail stands out with terrible sharpness—the murder-weapon. Now to the continuation of the story. Apollo's management brings about the happy ending. He commands Tlepolemus to go to Rhodes. The oracle does not specify the island by name, but describes it as the place where (according to an old legend) the war-goddess Athene had been born from her father's head; the blacksmith-god Hephaestus contributed to the delivery by splitting Zeus' skull. Here is a second blow, but this time life, not death, results. In Pindar's text (***Olymp. 7,*** 33) Tlepolemus is sent off

> to the sea-washed land where once the king of the gods covered over the city with golden snowflakes, at that hour when, thanks to Hepaestus' art and the brazen stroke of his axe, Athene issuing from her father's head raised the battle-cry in ringing tones, and fear of her came upon heaven and mother earth.

Here the scene is depicted as factually and graphically as can be, but only because the greatness of the event justifies this lavishness.

In general Pindar appeals not to sensuous fancy but to spiritual understanding and appraisal. For this very reason the natural dimensions of space and time are neglected, as in general things that have no dignity and importance are ignored. Phenomena are as it were denatured, and empirical data serve only as the raw material from which his operations will extract the value-content. Instead of calling things simply by their names, Pindar likes to speak of their 'flower,' 'peak,' 'bloom' . . . , or however else we choose to render laudatory expressions.

A further peculiarity of Pindar's language deserves attention in this context. In his way of thinking, as in Plato's, which was very similar, an important part was played by the fact that someone should receive or possess or acquire a quality, that he should be distinguished by some value or disfigured by the lack of it. The indefiniteness of the Platonic 'participation' as an intermediary between the quality as an idea and the bearer of it found its primitive counterpart in Pindar in the deliberate vagueness of a great many terms expressing contact or association: a family 'mingles itself' . . . with eight victory-garlands (***Nem. 2,*** 22), and a victor is worthy 'to be mingled' with the praise of his fellow-citizens (***Isthm. 3,*** 3); sweet-voiced songs 'are familiar' with Hiero (***Olymp. 6,*** 97), a house is 'not unfamiliar' with festal pageantry and song (***Isthm. 2,*** 30), and Libya is 'not unacquainted' with beasts of the wild (***Pyth. 9,*** 58); sick men are called 'partners of self-generated pains' (***Pyth. 3,*** 47); and there are many other expressions of this sort in Pindar.

The doctrine of values imports a certain systematic element into Pindar's ideas of the world and of life. In this way his ethic makes at least some approach to a system; but his dogma of the gulf between man and god, with all the conclusions that he draws from it, tends to set a counter-system going: the man who strives towards the heights of heaven is again and again hurled down into earthly abasement. In addition there are further and more special truths which are valid in their own spheres. Despite all this, Pindar sees all essential reality as being quite coherent. The general connections, in his view, come about through an immense number of individual connections of all kinds and all directions; and to demonstrate such relationships is a major concern of his art, which helps us to understand many of its peculiarities.

The poet brings out the connections both between values (or their opposites) and their manifestations in life, and between the 'powers' and their working out in particular instances. A web of inter-relations is spun between the lively present and the venerable past, between an event (whether present or past) and a general rule which the event serves to illustrate. Religion, very appropriately, is brought into everything, and poetry, as the universal medium, concerns itself with all other things. Cross-relations connect one value with another and one piece of reality with another; a network of interactions connects the powers both with the gods and with values; the list could be greatly extended. To do justice to this multitude of inter-relations, 'the flower of songs of praise flits like a bee to ever new subjects' (***Pyth. 10,*** 53). The erratic flights with which Pindar's poetry darts from theme to theme illustrates by its example how, within the world of values, even those things remotest from each other possess a true connection. This fine but strong web of relations weaves the disparate elements of the odes together into that unity over which the one light of 'Theia' sheds its lustre. This then is the complete answer to our question concerning the inner bond of unity of Pindar's poetry, which we posed at the beginning of this section. (pp. 471-96)

When Pindar wrote the ode to Theia he was about forty years old. His career as a poet lasted another thirty years and more. By the end of his life his powers as an artist, far from declining, had risen to greater heights.

Pindar's last dated epinician was written in 446 for a boy from Aegina who had won the prize for wrestling at the Pythian games. It was to men and boys of this Dorian island that Pindar had dedicated many of his finest poems and his deepest reflections. What did he now in his old age have to say to Aegina and to the world, when for the last time he had to sing the praises of a victor and to set his fame in the universal context of values? (***Pyth. 8,*** 1):

> Kindly-hearted Peace, daughter of Justice, fairest ornament of cities, you who hold the master-keys both in counsel and in war, receive Aristomenes' honour for his Pythian victory. For you know how to do what is gentle and receive it with unfailing sureness of choice (*kairos*),
>
> just as on the other hand, when a man fills his heart with pitiless rage, sternly you confront those of hostile heart and with overmastering strength crush their arrogance to the dust. Porphyrio learned this lesson when he roused you beyond measure to anger. The most welcome gain is that which one receives from the possession of one who gives it willingly;
>
> but violence brings in time even the haughty to a fall. The hundred-headed Cilician Typhus did not escape you, nor did the king of the Giants; they were laid low by the thunderbolt and by the arrows of Apollo, who with friendly kindness received the son of Xenarces (Aristomenes), who is come crowned from Delphi with leaves from Parnassus and Dorian songs of joy.

This is the first triad of the ode. Its first and last words tell the world and posterity that Aristomenes the son of Xenarces has been favourably received by the Delphic god at the Pythian games (i.e. that he has been blessed with victory), and that he is now holding his festal procession into his native city of Aegina to the Dorian strains of Pindar's poetry. The opening calls on the community to give a friendly welcome to Aristomenes and the honour that he brings with him.

The city of Aegina is not, however, addressed under its own name and character, but Pindar addresses himself to the spirit that rules the citizens, the spirit of 'kindly-hearted Peace,' and the triad celebrates Peace as a 'power.' By peace he means conciliation and harmony in contrast to hatred and party strife. Harmony is the 'ornament' of cities, i.e. makes them prosper and have a fair appearance; she carries the 'master-keys' because only a régime at unity with itself possesses real authority. Harmony's authority is based not on strength but on justice, for she herself is a 'daughter of Justice.' Further more, mild Harmony is able 'with unfailing *kairos,*' i.e. with subtle tact and a sure feeling for what is proper to any given case, to strike her finger upon that which is equally acceptable to all interested parties. But her judgment is equally sure when it becomes necessary to put down a determined rebel by main force. Thus the inner nature of peace develops its own antithesis and complement in a Heraclitean manner. Mild by nature, she can also harden her heart if she is unable otherwise to prevail; peace brings about peace through war. As examples from mythology Porphyrio and Typhus are brought forward, two monsters who in earliest antiquity rose up against the gods. The thought of Porphyrio's arrogant challenge draws in its train, according to archaic rules, its own antithesis: friendship and harmony. The pendulum then swings back to force, which lays the evildoer low with his own weapon—force. This is illustrated by the fall of Typhus, who was defeated in battle by Zeus with his thunderbolt and Apollo with his arrows. At the end the punishing Apollo changes into the benevolent god who makes the Aeginetan Aristomenes win the prize at the Pythian games.

We pass over the following three triads. The fifth and last comes back to the victory gained by the boy Aristomenes as a wrestler, the event which motivated the poem (v. 81):

> On four bodies did you throw yourself from above to do them hurt. For them the decision in the Pythian games fell out not in favour of a happy home-coming; no happy laughter about them awakened joy when they came home to their mothers; through the lanes, avoiding their enemies they stole homeward, wounded by the bite of misfortune.
>
> He to whom recently great good luck has fallen soars up to the greatest bliss in high self-confidence on the wings of his distinctions (*aretai*); his mind dwells on things better than riches. For a little time our mortal joys blossom. Even so they are cast down and shattered by a turning aside of purpose.
>
> Creatures of the day: what is man? What is he not? Man is a shadow in a dream. But when glory comes, sent by the gods, then a bright radiance and a happy existence is granted to men. Beloved mother Aegina, protect this city in its free course, with the help of Zeus, of mighty Aeacus, of Peleus, stout-hearted Telamon and Achilles.

The last triad also goes in opposites, this time with a dynamic heightened into grandeur. The strophe casts a harsh light on the pride displayed by the procession in honour of the returning victor, by the powerful contrast of the shame and humility with which the defeated contestants go sneaking home. Nowhere else does Pindar so cruelly celebrate a victory; we can detect the hard and bitter feeling of old age.

The antistrophe brings in some general reflections. With a sharpness reminiscent of Archilochus Pindar gives opposing pictures of joy and sorrow, whose swift interchange is the lot of every passionate and ambitious man—and with other men Pindar is not concerned. A recent victory fills him with joy and self-satisfaction swelling into a chimerical optimism; then his habits of thought swing back to their opposite, and they sink into a faint-hearted despondency. It was a fundamental tenet of the archaic period that a change of outward circumstances brought about a radically new quality in man. At the beginning of the period a late epic writer and Archilochus (fr. 68) put it in the form that our thoughts and feelings make themselves like the day which Zeus sends us.

The epode begins abruptly with the word which contains the essence of that view of human nature: 'creatures of the day'. As the day changes, so do we change; we are not really anything, since there is nothing into which we cannot at some time be changed: 'What is man, and what is he not?' Since we have no firm and enduring substance, we are dreaming shadows in a dreamer's mind. This is expressed by Pindar in a verse which for weight and brevity has no rival even in his poetry. He then comforts his hearers again by swinging back to the brilliant fortune and delightful existence which a favourable day sent by the gods can bring to us—such a day as that which has now dawned for the young Aristomenes and the people of Aegina. To conclude the poem, after the expression of joy comes the regular expression of fear lest evil befall, here a pious prayer for the country's continued prosperity: 'May our mother Aegina, animated by the spirit of quiet and harmony in the community, may Zeus himself, her husband, together with the heroic sons and grandsons of them both, maintain the island in its freedom!' Pindar's prayer was not granted, for fifteen years later the Aeginetan community lost not only the last remains of its freedom, but its very existence, to the neighbouring great power, Athens. Pindar did not live to see it.

In this late poem there is no trace of calm and gentle exposition; the thought and emotion are brought out with elemental force, and the contrast between light and shade is sharper than ever. We find a like bitterness in a shorter ode from the same period, which was written to be performed at an official function in a provincial community. On the little island of Tenedos the new government was entering into office, which it was to hold for one year. At its head as *prytanis* was Aristagoras, a man still young and belonging to one of the patrician families. The solemnity which opened the governmental year was performed with sacrifice, prayer, a choral ode, and a festal libation in the *prytaneion* or town hall, which housed the 'hearth' (Greek *hestia*) of the community. In the home of the community, as in every private house, the hearth-goddess Hestia by immemorial usage received the first offering. It is with an invocation of Hestia that Pindar begins (***Nem. 11***):

> Daughter of Rhea, Hestia, you under whose care are the halls of cities, sister of Zeus most high and of Hera enthroned by his side, welcome with a blessing Aristagoras to your dwelling-place, blessing too his brothers in office about his radiant sceptre, them who, attending to your honour, concern themselves with Tenedos' welfare,
>
> honouring you with libations before all other deities, with the smoke of incense, while song and the lyre resound, and the commands of hospitable Zeus are discharged at the never-failing table. Let him carry through with acclaim his twelve months labours with uncorrupted heart!
>
> Among men I praise the good fortune of his father Hagesilas and the wondrous beauty and native fearlessness of Aristagoras. Yet he who enjoys blessings and surpasses others in beauty and has shown his might as the best in contests must remember that he is clothed in perishable members and that at the last he will be wrapped in earth.
>
> [*Second triad*] It is becoming for the citizens to praise him with good words and to adorn him in the honied tones of skilful songs. Sixteen shining victories in neighbouring games have crowned Aristagoras and his land with a glorious name, in the wrestling contest and the pancration proud of its fame.
>
> Yet the hopes too hesitant of his parents forbade the boy's powers to be proven in the contests at Pytho and Olympia. Surely, by oath, I say, he would have returned from the Castalian spring (i.e. from Pytho) and from the wooded hills of Cronus (from Olympia) with greater honour than his rivals in the fight.
>
> He would have celebrated in festal attire the four-yearly festival founded by Heracles (the Olympics), his hair bound with purple sprays of flowers. But many men are cast down from the possession of fortune by their hollow boasting, and many likewise, too greatly diffident of their powers, are made to stumble past the glory that is properly theirs by a spirit lacking in boldness, that drags them back by the arm.
>
> [*Third triad*] It would have been easy to trace the old Spartan blood in him, derived from Pisander who came with Orestes from Amyclae, bringing with him an Aeolian host with weapons of bronze, and to see his inheritance from his mother's Theban ancestor Melanippus. But excellences (*aretai*) that are handed down
>
> bring powers to light alternately among the generations of men. Even so the dark soil of the firm earth does not bring forth its fruits in every turning year, and the trees do not bear fragrant blossoms in constant abundance, but changing with the occasion. According to a like rule destiny behaves
>
> towards the human race, and Zeus has not placed in the hands of mortals any sure distinguishing mark. Nevertheless we indulge a lofty spirit and plan many deeds; for insolent hope holds our body in its yoke, and the spring of thoughtful foresight is beyond our reach. Moderate should be the gain that we pursue; insatiable desire breeds madness all the more violent.

The form given to the poem is unique. The language is simpler than elsewhere, the sentence-construction is uncommonly direct and regular for Pindar, and each of the three triads ends in the same way, on a dark and grave note. No other poem is so accurately and consistently constructed; it is as if Pindar on this one occasion had let himself be influenced by the new classical spirit. But this is true only of the form, not of the thought.

The first strophe and antistrophe are addressed to a goddess; the epode finds the objects of its praise among men. A congratulatory address to Aristagoras' father and the *prytanis* himself leads to an admonition beginning with a subordinate clause to this effect: 'When to anyone are granted such blessings as to him. . . . ' As the main clause we expect (judging from parallel passages) something like: 'then he must wish for no more, having reached the heights of human felicity; all beyond that is set apart for the gods.' We are not prepared for such a cruel twist and such a cutting contrast as the close of the triad brings.

The new triad begins afresh with a note of rejoicing. The assembled citizens are called upon to join in the praises of

Aristagoras as sung by Pindar. The poet is able to specify a considerable number of victories, but they have all been in insignificant local contests. Aristagoras' parents did not venture to enter him for the pan-Hellenic games, since they had no confidence in his being successful. Pindar avers on his oath that they misjudged the matter; it is as common for human beings to make mistakes of this as of the opposite kind. From this point on the poem is dominated by the ideas of excessive diffidence and overbold self-confidence of wonderful possibilities and the uncertainty of their achievement, of the lure of the unattainable, of longings that cannot be laid to rest.

At the opening of the third triad Pindar hails Aristagoras as being descended from great heroic figures and as the inheritor of noble qualities. But (he then tells us) one can never know for sure in which generation or in which individual the noble ancestry will manifest itself; for it is the law governing all earthly things that the finest qualities often remain dormant. Thus no prediction is possible, as indeed the power to judge and plan correctly in advance has been denied to mortals in general. Yet we still indulge ourselves in grandiose hopes and projects. Our desires and ambitions are like those of the gods, although divine knowledge and understanding are not ours. Such notions as these had been expressed by Pindar before, and so early a poet as Semonides of Amorgos had expressed them in his pedestrian way. . . . What is novel and surprising is the tragic intensification at the end of Pindar's poem: 'We ought to control ourselves, yet no desire burns so fiercely as the senseless longing for the unattainable.' The aged poet ends his sombre ode with a reference to consuming burning passion.

Although couched in general terms, the concluding words sound like an outburst of personal feeling. In praising the beauty of the young *prytanis,* Pindar may have had in mind Aristoxenus' brother, the boy Theoxenus. Like Ibycus, Pindar remained to the last susceptible to the charms of handsome and noble young men. The closing thought of the ***Eleventh Nemean*** is picked up again by the opening of a poem (fr. 123) to Theoxenus of Tenedos:

> Only in due season and measure (according to *kairos*) should one pluck the bloom of passionate longings, o my soul, in accordance with one's age; but if a man has seen the love-light darting from Theoxenus' eyes and is not consumed with passion, his dark heart has been forged of steel or iron
>
> in a slow fire. Despised by Aphrodite of the ensnaring eyes, he either toils for the sake of gold, or is a slave to female haughtiness. But I, thanks to the goddess, melt like the wax of the holy bee
>
> under the bite of warmth, when I look upon the fresh beauty of boys' bodies. So it seems that Peitho (persuasion) has taken up her abode also in Tenedos together with Charis (attractiveness), blessing the son of Hagesilas (Theoxenus).

We are told that it was at Argos, in the gymnasium, amidst the youths exercising themselves, that Pindar peacefully breathed his last, with his head on the knees of this very Theoxenus of Tenedos. The thought which legend has cast into this mould is thus put into words by Greek tradition: 'He was not only a poet of genius, but a man beloved of the gods.' (pp. 497-504)

Pindar died about 445, after producing poetry for at least fifty-two years. In the art that he had practised with incomparable mastery he found no successor of a like stature; the day of choral lyric as the leading poetical form was over. But it was more than a literary genre that died with Pindar: a whole age became dumb when his lips closed. The archaic period of Greek literature found in him its last great exponent and its consummation.

In Pindar's poetry archaic art reached its pinnacle. The subtlety and complexity of the form are late archaic; so is the luxurious ostentation of artistry in works of art. The pomp of language is a mature archaic feature: the thoughts are, as it were, draped in the folds of a costly robe, hung with finely-wrought adornments. Essentially archaic too is the animated course of his poems. The opening is abrupt and striking; then come constant changes of pace; he walks slowly in contemplation; then rushes furiously on; strides out with vigour, each step opening a new perspective; takes a zig-zag course between the attraction and repulsion of opposites; circles slowly round, to find himself at the end where he first began; or in one swift leap attains his distant goal. The basic principle of these choral songs is not the classical one of architectonic strength and visible construction, but the archaic one of fluid movement and development of numerous figures, following after and out of one another. In Pindar this play of form is made the vehicle of an important content; its changeable course reflects the active progress and completion of the ideas, makes them develop out of each other according to the sense, connect with one another or turn back upon themselves. But what is greatest and most personal in Pindar's poetry is of a spiritual nature: its dignity, now serious, now serene; its wilful abruptness, and then, on occasion, its heavy sweetness; and lastly, often restrained but always detectable, its titanic power.

Thus at its end the archaic epoch brought forth a literary phenomenon which displayed that period, already marked for extinction, in its most powerful and brilliant development, self-assured, clear and entirely pure. Unlike his Athenian contemporary Aeschylus, Pindar was and remained entirely an archaic Greek. In those tendencies which during his lifetime powerfully contributed to the advance of the human spirit he took no part at all. For the teachings of speculative cosmologists he had no sympathy, as he had no interest in enlightenment, in any empirical rationalizing of the world-picture. His was not a soul that could poke and peer and find fault: he was interested only in what he could admire. A pious and respectful adherent of tradition, he felt himself the chosen voice of the Greek race when he bore witness to the beliefs and purposes of the age that was to die with him.

It is not unique in history that a movement in its final development should in some respects have become the opposite of what it was at the beginning. Archilochus helped to introduce the archaic manner of thought and paved the way for lyric poetry by a revolutionary turn to the solid reality of primary and immediate data. The *I,* the *here* and *now,* were upheld with brutal rigour as the whole content of existence. Pindar replaced the first person by the impersonal 'one' of society; the transitory and the unique were to him no more than illustrations of the universal and eternal. He selects, interprets, re-arranges, praises and glorifies: the hatred and carping of Archilochus is repugnant to him (***Pyth. 2,*** 55). While at the beginning reality, starting with physical objects, was on principle accepted in all its earthiness, now, starting from physical appearance, it was equally on principle denatured and spiritualized. Parallel with this movement was the swing from deliberately naive directness and simplicity in expression to a challenging indirectness and complication. By now the epoch had run the gamut in this respect from one extreme to the other. The end had been reached, and from here no road leads farther.

From the regions to which Pindar had soared, from the thin air and burning light which the value of values cast over these dizzy heights, no path led to a further resting-place. The age that followed did not set out from this point, but from a station much nearer to earth. This position was established by a greater sobriety of thought, such as had been long represented by such men as Xenophanes and Simonides. Empirical enquiry widened the intellectual horizon and corrected many errors. Men took their bearings again in a richer and more variegated world; they became more versatile and practical. Instead of thinking in terms of mutually exclusive polar opposites, they preferred to quantify the one or the other, or looked for the golden mean. Thus the notion of the two social classes, the 'good' and the 'bad' became an anachronism; ambition and display of wealth came to be regarded as arrogance, and the democratic ideals of the middle-class virtues and proprieties were put into practice; dress became simple. Criticism and discussion replaced the unquestioning acceptance of the norms represented by the class which set the tone of society; intellectual ability came to be respected. Men learned to distinguish and analyse what they had formerly viewed only as a whole. Probably the most consequential of all the innovations was the definitive division of man into body and soul. Out of these and many other elements came gradually the classical ways of living and thinking. (pp. 505-07)

Hermann Fränkel, "The Last of Archaic Lyric" and "Retrospect and Prospect," in his Early Greek Poetry and Philosophy: A History of Greek Epic, Lyric, and Prose to the Middle of the Fifth Century, *translated by Moses Hadas and James Willis, Basil Blackwell, 1975, pp. 399-504, 505-08.*

Albin Lesky (essay date 1963)

[An Austrian classicist and educator, Lesky was the author of numerous publications on topics related to ancient Greece. His Geschichte der Griechischen Literatur *(1957-58;* A History of Greek Literature, *1966) is considered an authoritative text. In the following excerpt from the second edition (1963) of that work, he provides an overview of Pindar's life, times, and poetic achievement, describing the poet as "essentially a great individualist."]*

Pindar is the second of Boeotia's great poets. As a literary artist he represents a different tradition from Hesiod's, and he comes from a very different social level. Nevertheless, in those passages where his native qualities come out most strongly, we can see his affinity with the author of the *Theogony.* Both have the same religious attitude towards all phenomena, the same uncompromising severity in their assertions.

He was born at Cynoscephalae, a settlement belonging to Thebes, during the Pythian festival, as [Hesiod] the great venerator of the Delphic god tells us himself (fr. 193). The festival must have been that of 522 or of 518, since his floruit, i.e. his fortieth year, was reckoned in antiquity as coinciding with Xerxes' attack on Greece.

We possess four manuscript *Lives,* in addition to the article in Suidas. These are all either late antique or Byzantine, but they continue a teaching tradition that goes back to the earliest attested biographies of Pindar, compiled by the Peripatetic Chamaeleon and by Callimachus's pupil Ister. As so often, we find here a little that is useful wrapped up in a mass of fable, including such a pretty anecdote as that of the bees which prophetically deposited their honey on the lips of the slumbering child.

The difficulties of interpreting Pindar are exemplified in the question of his birthplace. In ***Pyth. 5,*** 76 he speaks of the Aegeids, a clan associated in mythology with Thebes and with Sparta and Therae: 'my fathers', he calls them. This raises the problem of the use of the first person in choral lyric: sometimes in Pindar it means the poet, sometimes the chorus, sometimes the generalized 'one'. In this passage the most distinguished exponents of Pindar have embraced directly opposed views. To take it as meaning the chorus seems the most likely, but it is quite conceivable that Pindar as a Theban might have named the Aegeids as his ancestors. The passage certainly cannot be taken as proving his aristocratic connections, and the various names given for Pindar's father in the ancient biographies make the whole question very obscure.

We can certainly believe that he came of a good family, and if he was sent to Athens as a boy, in addition to education in the arts he would have made contact with the old Attic nobility. Their position had been threatened for some time by the rise of new classes, but power was still largely in their hands, and aristocratic values were still in possession of the field. Even in the classical period these values remained largely current: indeed they never wholly faded from Greek consciousness. A stay in Athens in his youth would explain Pindar's close connection with the Alcmeonids, a family whose political activities were important rather than uniformly beneficial in Athenian history. The only epinicion which Pindar wrote for an Athenian (***Pyth. 7*** in 486) was for the Alcmeonid Megacles, who had been ostracized a little before. According to a scholium on v. 18 he composed a threnos for Megacles' father Hippocrates, a brother of Cleisthenes. Four years after Marathon the poet praised Athens, not for the defeat of the Persians, but for the magnificence with which the

Helios, god of the sun, rising from the sea at dawn.

temple of Apollo at Delphi, burnt down in 548, had been rebuilt by the Alcmeonids.

The biographies speak of Apollodorus and Agathocles as instructors of the young Pindar. Only the second of these names has much meaning for us, since Agathocles also trained the musical theorist Damon. A more important fact is that the men's choruses in Athens had a new and vigorous development after 508 as an officially recognized part of the Great Dionysia. It was thanks to the reformation of the dithyramb by Lasus of Hermione that it was able to maintain its place beside the rapidly maturing tragedy. Now since we can hardly suppose that Lasus was in Athens after the fall of the Pisistratids, the tradition that he was Pindar's teacher cannot be true in an immediate sense. The same holds good of Simonides, who despite the deep differences between the two men cannot have been without influence on the young Pindar.

Pindar's poetry brought him into contact with many of the political and cultural centres of his day, and in the course of his work he travelled widely. But unlike so many wandering poets of the archaic period, he remained always true to his native land. In his ***Paean for Ceos*** (32) he speaks of the value to a man of his homeland and kinsfolk, and the words apply to his own life also.

The earliest of the surviving epinicia, ***Pyth. 10,*** shows Pindar associated with Thessaly, whose noble families had enjoyed the services of many of the older poets. In the Pythia of 498 the double foot-race for boys was won by Hippocleas of Pelinna, and Thorax, the oldest of the great family of the Aleuads, commissioned Pindar to write an ode in celebration. The young poet, who was a guest-friend of Thorax and probably came in person to the performance, might have built great hopes for the future on this commission. We know nothing, however, of any continuance of their relations. In general Pindar does not seem to have had any sudden success. It was not until he went to Sicily that he made his name.

In his early period Pindar seems to have written mostly songs for religious usage, and since these have perished except for a few fagments, we know very little about his work at that time. Some papyri, however, have acquainted us with bits of his ***Paeans,*** in particular of the one which he had performed at the Theoxenia in Delphi (probably in 490), no other chorus being at his disposal. It is only a surmise that the singers were Aeginetans, but certainly Pindar here sings the praises of that island, which meant so much to him all through his life. Aegina, which like Boeotia had a mixed Dorian and Aeolic population, was at this time a dangerous rival to Athens and politically connected with Thebes. Power lay in the hands of an aristocratic upper-crust made up of wealthy and sport-loving families. This was the true world of the Pindaric epinicia. In this paean, despite all his flattery of the Aeginetans, Pindar wounded their feelings. Of Neoptolemus, a descendant of their national hero Aeacus, he related how for his cruel killing of the aged Priam he was punished by Apollo, who made him die a miserable death at Delphi. A few years later, in the ***Seventh Nemean,*** celebrating the victory of Sogenes of Aegina in the boys' pentathlon, Pindar included a retraction, and dwelt at length on the honour enjoyed by Neoptolemus in the Delphic sanctuary. But his relations with Aegina, which became so close later, seem not to be much in evidence before the Persian wars. There is, however, another connection, later to be very important, which is attested in 490: Xenocrates, brother of the tyrant Theron of Acragas, had won a chariot-race at Delphi, and the ***Sixth Pythian*** celebrates his son Thrasybulus, who had come from Sicily to compete. At this time Pindar had won some recognition as a poet, but he could not afford to be too particular, and so in the ***Twelfth Pythian,*** the only ode on a victory in music, he celebrated the flute-player Midas of Acragas, who had probably come with Thrasybulus to Delphi.

Pindar and his city played a rather special part in the time of mortal danger when Xerxes attacked Greece. The Thebans had 'Medized', and were threatened with annihilation by the victorious Greeks. The danger was averted by delivering up the most prominent pro-Persians: a god graciously moved aside the stone of Tantalus which had been poised above the city. This image is used by Pindar in the ***Eighth Isthmian:*** it is relevant that the ode celebrated the victory of an Aeginetan in the pancration. We can hardly doubt Pindar's connections with the pro-Persian nobility in Thebes. Even at the very height of his fame he repeatedly wrote in praise of members of the families who had been associated with the Persians (***Isthm. I.*** 3. 4). But in the years following the Greek victory his political mistakes were a heavy burden on him, and from Aegina's special position we can understand why it was there that Pindar looked for support and encouragement. He found it particularly in Lampon, whose son he had celebrated in the ***Sixth Isthmian,*** shortly before the great war.

It was his success in Sicily that determined Pindar's pan-Hellenic reputation. There in the west, after the successful repulse of the Carthaginian threat, the Greek world had developed under the leadership of capable tyrants into a political structure far beyond the small dimensions of the old city-states. The first place was taken by Hiero, who in 478, as regent of the twin state of Gela-Syracuse, had stepped into the inheritance of Gelo. In Acragas was his kinsman Theron, with whom his political relations were not always friendly. We have heard of the reception of Simonides: Pindar formed a close association with both courts. Despite the absence of immediate testimony, we can fairly certainly infer that he arrived in Sicily between 476 and 474, and lived a long time at the courts of Hiero and Theron. The multitude of new impressions that he received from the power and brilliance of this west Greek world is reflected in verses like those of the ***First Olympian*** celebrating Hiero's victory in 476. This was a victory in the horse-race: the more coveted victory in the chariot-race had fallen to Theron. For him also Pindar wrote an epinicion which was sung in Acragas at a great religious feast (***Ol. 3***). The same victory is alluded to in the ***Second Olympian*** in a very different, intimate and personal tone. The ode is not so much concerned with the event itself as it is to console Theron in sickness and cares. Apparently Theron was a follower of Orphic and Pythagorean doctrines, which provide Pindar with themes of consolation. We can easily understand that the mystical teachings concerning the destiny of the soul made a great impression on the poet: his strong Delphic background makes it unlikely that he was himself an initiate.

The two Ceans, Simonides and Bacchylides, must have crossed Pindar's path in Sicily. Many passages have been taken as polemic against them: thus the ancients interpreted the attack in ***Ol. 2.*** 86 upon the 'journeymen' who are like ravens croaking at an eagle. Other examples are the warning against flatterers and calumniators (***Pyth. 2.*** 74) and the attack on those who serve the muses with an eye to profit (***Isth. 2.*** 6). The view may be true of individual passages, but it is impossible to be sure of them all. Simonides and Bacchylides were certainly not the only ones who courted the Sicilian despots.

At the time of his return from Sicily Pindar could claim the first place among the choral lyrists of his day, and he had no doubt profited as much in pocket as in reputation from his stay in the west. Thence came the resource which enabled him to build near his house that temple of Rhea and Pan which was still there in Pausanias' time (9, 25, 3). We still possess remains of a song for a chorus of girls in honour of Pan, who was associated with the Great Mother as a companion and doorkeeper (fr. 95 ff.).

There followed a particularly creative period, in which the poet's services were sought from all quarters of Greece. His connection with the Sicilian courts was kept up for some time. The two odes already mentioned (***Pyth. 2*** and ***Isthm. 2***) show the poet's fear that enemies were at work against him in Sicily and in fact he was not able to celebrate either Hiero's second victory in the horse-race in 472 or the coveted victory in the Olympic chariot-race in 468. The latter commission was given to Bacchylides. The ode on the victory in the Pythian chariot-race of 470 was Pindar's last poem for Hiero (***Pyth. 1.***) The tyrant had had himself proclaimed at Delphi as the founder of Aetna, and thus had shown how much importance he attached to the new settlement under the rule of his son Dinomenes. Aeschylus wrote a play to celebrate the founding, and Pindar's ode is full of prayers for its success.

Now at the height of his career, Pindar could not close his eyes to the greatness of Athens in her confident development following the victory over the Persians. In the late 460's he published the dithyramb whose opening is so well known (fr. 76): 'Shining, violet-garlanded, song-renowned, glorious Athens, bulwark of Hellas, city of the gods!' Another passage (fr. 77) declares that the Athenians have laid the foundations of freedom. Ancient tradition relates that the Thebans fined the poet a thousand drachmae for thus praising the enemy city, while the Athenians made him a *proxenos* and gave him a large honorarium. There may be an element of truth in this, but the statue of Pindar in the Athenian agora (Pseudo-Aeschines *ep.* 4; Paus. I, 8, 4) was not brought into the story until later.

Pindar was now constantly making new friends. Among the victorious athletes who wanted to secure a monument of their achievement in his poetry were Rhodians (***Ol. 7***) and Corinthians. The Xenophon who won the foot-race and pentathlon in 464, a member of a rich and distinguished Corinthian family was not content with an epinicion (***Ol. 13***), and wanted a poem to glorify his ostentatious gift to Aphrodite. The temple of the goddess in Corinth was associated with ritual prostitution—itself a very unusual feature in Greek life—and for this purpose Xenophon gave fifty female slaves. Pindar can never have had a more singular assignment. He discharged it in a poem which is entitled Σκολιον in the manuscripts, writing with an elegant superiority and delicate humour.

Hiero died in 466, and with his death the hour had struck for the Sicilian tyrants. Pindar, however, soon found the way open to another prince's court. In 474 he had celebrated the victory in the chariot-race of Telesicrates of Cyrene, the most flourishing Greek city in Libya; twelve years later king Arcesilaus IV won with his chariot at Delphi, and the event called forth two poems from Pindar. One (***Pyth. 5***) was intended for performance in Cyrene at the feast of the Dorian Apollo Carneius in celebration of the victory; the other (***Pyth. 4***), the longest of all extant choral lyrics, was sung at a feast in the palace. The victory is hardly mentioned, but the story how Battus came to found the city from Therae leads Pindar to relate at great length the tale of the Argonauts in the manner of choral lyric. At the end of this long ode Pindar sides with the exiled conspirator Damophilus and makes a plea for wise moderation. Such interference is seldom welcome: when Arcesilaus won the chariot-race at Olympia two years later, Pindar received no commission.

In all these vicissitudes friendship with Aegina remained a sure and permanent possession. Again and again Pindar had Aeginetan victors to celebrate, and the last word that we have from him (***Pyth. 8*** in 446) refers to the beloved island. In the concluding section of the ode we find one of those gloomy reflections which often darken the sunlight of Greek thought: 'What is man? The dream of a shadow; no more. But God can send his light upon all the weaknesses of our life, and the heavenly ones can keep the city on the path of freedom.' Freedom Aegina had partly lost already, when in 456 she was forced into the Athenian maritime alliance. The final catastrophe, the expulsion of the Aeginetans in 431, was one which death saved Pindar from experiencing.

Pindar's crown of glory was not without its thorns. The envious grudged him his Sicilian successes: he was traduced as a friend of tyrants, a neglector of his homeland. The rather violent manner in which in the ***Ninth Pythian***—dedicated to a Cyrenean, but sung in Thebes—he drags in an account of his poetical activities on his country's behalf shows how seriously he took reproaches of this sort. But in the last years of his life he must have suffered much more deeply from the political developments. As the days of common danger receded into the past, so the rivalry of Sparta and Athens ate deeper into the vitals of Greece. The battle at Oenophyta (457) confirmed for a decade the oppressive Athenian dominion over Boeotia. Only two epinicia are known from this period. The recovery of Boeotian freedom at Coronea (447) came within Pindar's lifetime. Ancient tradition says that he died in Argos, and it is a happy invention which makes this priest-like poet of beauty breathe his last on the knees of a boy whom he loved.

In the classical period such a poet as Pindar was fated very soon to be considered old-fashioned. He shared this fate with Alcman, Stesichorus and Simonides, as we see from a passage of Eupolis. We can just as easily understand, however, that the Alexandrians took a great interest in the difficult and allusive poet who yet had a deep sense of his creative mission. Here again it was Aristophanes of Byzantium who made the definitive contribution; he divided the lyrical text into cola and edited all that then survived in seventeen books. The *Vita Ambrosiana* gives us the best synopsis of what the Alexandrians had before them. Eleven books were composed of songs connected with worship: first and foremost the ***Hymns to the Gods,*** next the ***Paeans,*** both of these in one book each; then ***Dithyrambs, Processional Hymns*** (***Prosodia***), ***Songs for a Chorus of Maidens*** (***Partheneia***) and ***Songs for Dancing*** (***Hyporchemata***), each of these groups composing two books, except the ***Partheneia,*** which had another book of separate songs for girls added to it: there are obvious difficulties in the subdivision here. The provinces newly won for choral lyric by Simonides are represented by four books of ***Epinicia*** and one each of ***Threnoi*** and ***Encomia.***

A glance at this list shows us how miserably little has survived. We have reason to believe that the same factors which caused tragedy to be represented now only by a small selection were at work in Pindar's case also. The age of the Antonines, with its strong concentration on the requirements of the schools, was content with an edition of Pindar which comprised only the ***Epinicia.*** When Eustathius of Thessalonica was preparing a commentary on Pindar in the twelfth century—the introduction still survives—he justified this limited selection on the ground that the victory-odes were the most intelligible part of Pindar's output.

To some extent our knowledge of Pindar has been helped by the papyrus discoveries, and the larger fragments have given us some impression of his other work. Often, of course, we have to content ourselves with titles and citations in later writers. For one of the hymns these are enough to give us some inkling how much we have lost. In the ***Hymn to Zeus*** written for Thebes a song sung by Apollo (or by the Muses to his lyre) is related, which is said to have been performed at Cadmus' wedding and to have related the creation of the world and the ordering of it by Zeus. When the work was finished (so the song related) Zeus asked the gods if anything was lacking to this beautiful world. They replied: a divine nature to sing its praises. Thus Pindar elaborately displays in mythical form the poet's place in the world, as he saw it and maintained it.

It is of the ***Paeans*** mostly that our knowledge has been advanced by the papyri. We have already mentioned the one with which Pindar stepped into the breach at Delphi in 490. The ***Paean for the Abderites,*** a very difficult poem, implores divine assistance for the Ionian colonists, who were in constant conflict with the Thracian population. Another paean reflects the terror felt in Thebes at the solar eclipse of the 30th April 463. With a disregard of Ionian science Pindar, the lover of light, prays to the rays of the sun, which he calls 'mother of the eyes'. Even Ceos, the home of his rivals Simonides and Bacchylides, had a paean written for it by Pindar, in which he praised the island for its fame in the arts. Two of the dithyrambs were composed for the Athenians. One contained the passage already mentioned in praise of the city. These poems had their own titles: thus one composed for Thebes was entitled ***Descent of Heracles into the Underworld*** or ***Cerberus.*** In the surviving verses Pindar turns against the long-windedness of the old dithyramb, almost certainly under the influence of Lasus. Suidas mentions δραματα τραγικα in his list of Pindar's works: he means of course the dithyrambs.

The remains of the ***Prosodia*** are very scanty, but those of the ***Partheneia*** are much better. Among these were included the ***Daphnephorica,*** sung at Thebes when a staff wreathed in laurel, flowers and ribbons (the κωπω) was carried in procession to Apollo Ismenius. We have appreciable remains of one of these poems (fr. 94 b.), and we know of another, which Pindar composed when his son Daiphantus had the honour to be chosen as a daphnephorus. We can find out very little with certainty about the ***Hyporchemata:*** we do not even know what they were. Ancient interpretations are confused, and they show how much we depend on the classifications and definitions of the old grammarians. There is much uncertainty, so that many things are cited as from scolia, which Aristophanes apparently put under the ***Encomia.*** At all events, poems of the last-named variety were performed at banquets in praise of individuals. Some historical interest attaches to an encomium on the phil-Hellene Alexander, king of Macedon, and a special personal interest to a poem on the beautiful boy Theoxenos of Tenedos. Pederasty is here spiritualized: the beams that dart from the eyes of Theoxenos kindle a flame in the poet's heart. Some remains of the threnoi remind us of the ***Second Olympian*** (addressed to Theron) with its Pythagorean elements of thought: here consolation is sought in the assurance of a happy life hereafter. The Orphic and Pythagorean themes of metempsychosis and judgment after death (fr. 129 f. 133) rub shoulders with the beatification of those dedicated at Eleusis (fr. 137). One fragment (131 b) shows a remarkable juxtaposition of the Homeric notion of the likeness concealed within the body and the belief in an immortal soul proceeding from the gods. We do not know its context, but the verses show that in these realms of religious thought Pindar was no more than an occasional visitor.

Among the surviving fragments scarcely any has so singular an atmosphere as the ***Cerberus**-dithyramb* (fr. 70 b) with its depiction of the wild ecstasy which at the feasts of Dionysus seized even upon the gods. But passages of such individual colouring are the exception. In general the style (taking the word in its widest sense) of the fragments is very similar to that of the ***Epinicia,*** so that we can feel confident that the latter enable us to grasp all the essentials of Pindar's personality as a poet.

The Alexandrians arranged the four books of the ***Epinicia*** according to the festivals: one book each for the great Olympic and Delphic games which recurred every four years and for the smaller Nemean and Isthmian games which were held biennially. The supposition that the Nemeans once brought up the rear of the collection, explains the appearance of alien elements in the third book. The ***Ninth Nemean*** celebrates a victory of Chromius of Aetna at Sicyon, the ***Tenth*** a victory of one Theaeus at the games of Hera in Argos, while the ***Eleventh*** is not even an epinicion, but was written for Aristagoras of Tenedos to celebrate his appointment as prytanis. Apparently in the change from roll to codex the last two books changed places: the ***Isthmians*** came at the end and in this exposed position suffered damage at the closing sections. The ***Olympians*** include one spurious piece—the ***Fifth,*** in which a contemporary of Pindar's, probably a Sicilian poet, sings the praises of Psaumis of Camarina, whose victory in the chariot-race is celebrated in ***Ol. 4.***

A passage such as ***Nem. 4.*** 13 shows that after the celebration the ***Epinicia*** might sometimes be performed by a single singer to the lyre. It is not impossible that some of them were intended from the beginning for solo performance, but it seems unlikely. These songs of victory were sung by a chorus to the accompaniment of flute and lyre, only occasionally on the scene of the success, generally at the celebration held in the victor's city.

There are certain elements which appear in almost every epinicion. The purpose of the strong demanded some statements about the victor, his family, his sporting achievements at other festivals. We are seldom told anything about the course of the contest itself. The Pindar of the 'Wanderers Sturmlied', revelling in the rumble of chariot-wheels and the crack of whips, had no existence outside the mind of the young Goethe.

Another element, varying greatly in extent, but usually taking up a good deal of space, is mythical narrative. The poet and his employer might very well take different views of the relative importance of these two parts, as we see in the story that Simonides' fees were reduced because he had given too much space to the Dioscuri. Several different considerations may govern the introduction of myth. It may have a relevance to the place of the victory—this was particularly common in the odes written for west Greeks, who had not many family myths of their own. It may be prompted by the victor's own circumstances. It may contain an inner meaning which serves as a great example to the victor himself. Choral lyric narrative is essentially different from epic narrative. Such an elaborate passage as the story of the Argonauts in the ***Fourth Pythian*** gives us an especially good opportunity to see its characteristic features. The point of departure is not the beginning of the story, but some later stage in it, from which the poet ranges, or rather jumps, backwards and forwards. The object is not to tell a straightforward story, but to elaborate within the framework of the poem something in the tale which seems important and presents itself to the mind as a separate picture. One cannot forget Pelops standing at night on the seashore and calling the god from the sea (***Ol. 1***), the bold huntress Cyrene, who wins Apollo's heart, so that he goes and takes counsel with the wise Centaur before his cave (***Pyth. 9***) or the young Jason coming down from the mountains and standing in the marketplace of Iolcus like a radiant god among the astonished townsfolk (***Pyth. 4***). The poet is fond of framing his scenes and sections by the archaic device of ring-composition. There are a good many speeches, giving some element of drama. The narratives end as suddenly as they begin, with some brief formal phrase. But with all its changes in tempo and texture, Pindar's narrative is by no means formless; rather it has to be understood in reference to some definite value which the poet is particularly concerned to illustrate.

A third constituent element is that of proverbial wisdom. All the separate poems are shot through with it, and gnomae recur constantly. Usually the poet gives the impression that he is conveying the fruit of his own reflections. Consequently the gnomic elements are closely connected with another constituent, which can therefore only be separated out if we bear this in mind: namely expressions of Pindar's own views, usually on the value and purpose of the poet's calling, but sometimes rising in hymn-like strains to the expression of his religious convictions.

The *Partheneion* of Alcman allows us to see that the individual elements which we have here enumerated were already found in the earliest choral lyric; and when we see how Alcman follows the myth of the sons of Hippocoon with the gnome about the avenging power of the gods, passing immediately to, 'But I sing of the light of Agido . . . ', we can conclude that these sudden transitions were all part of the style. Pindar himself occasionally speaks of his rapid changes of subject as if they were a stylistic feature demanded by the rules of his art. It is striking that his testimony (***Pyth. 10.*** 54; ***11.*** 41) is supported by that of Bacchylides (10. 51) and probably of Stesichorus (fr. 25). In the very nature of the epinicia it was inevitable that the question of their unity should in recent times have become once more a central problem in the interpretation of Pindar. August Boeckh, whose great edition of 1821 laid the foundations of Pindaric research, was the first to look for dominating themes in this poetry whose manner of composition is so hard to grasp. The method was brought into disrepute by the speculations of L. Dissen and others, and the house had to be put in order by A. B. Drachmann. Then for a long time the most fashionable type of interpretation was that which aimed at discovering the associative connections which seemed predominant between the different parts. Wilamowitz' *Pindaros* paved the way for change, and Schadewaldt has recently brought the question of unity back into the foreground.

The problem is as follows: Pindar's ***Epinicia*** give the impression of a sometimes kaleidoscopic mixture of diverse elements, tied together by loose and even wilful transitions. Yet anyone who has any feeling for poetry cannot escape the feeling that in the last resort all this multiplicity is subsumed under a great unity. Now where does this unity reside? The decisive answer has been given by Hermann Fränkel: the epinicion elevates the significant event of victory into the realm of values, the world from which the poet's creation flows. This world of values is displayed and exemplified in its various spheres: in the divine itself, in the tales of the heroes, in the rules of conduct and not least in the poet's own creative activity as an artistic realm in its own right. Once this is understood, we shall not find it difficult to find a unity in Pindar's poetry which is comparable (although distantly so) with the unity of classical works of art. Observations like those of Dornseiff in particular on the peculiarities of his composition—sometimes gliding smoothly, sometimes desultory and abrupt—are entirely justified. On the other hand, the lines of thought emanating from the individual elements are all within a realm provided by the personality of the poet and his way of seeing the world. Thus the unity of these poems lies not in their internal structure, but in the consistent relevance of their constituent parts to that firm world of aristocratic values which Pindar felt to be immovable.

We can only mention the most important of his convictions. A central feature of the aristocratic view of humanity was the firm belief that innate and inherited qualities (φυα) were decisive. 'It is a vain struggle, if one seeks to hide one's inborn character' (***Ol. 13.*** 13). Pindar speaks throughout in the spirit of the aristocracy when he looks down on those who have acquired skill compared with those who have inherited it. The Olympic victor needs a trainer, certainly, but the trainer's job is only to 'sharpen' the inborn abilities (***Ol. 10.*** 20). One who only possesses acquired ability is always a man in darkness, who never walks with a sure foot (***Nem. 3.*** 41).

The direct light of this world of ideas falls first on the myths of the heroes. The characters they depict, with their deeds of supreme bravery, are all illustrations of that noble quality that shows itself also in the hard-won successes achieved in the great games. Very frequently these two realms touch one another, since the heroes were the putative ancestors of the noble houses from which the athletic victors sprang.

Next to the athlete's achievement, and of equal merit, was the poet's. Through it the victory achieved permanence, since the words of the poet elevated his victory into the realm of the noble and valuable. Just as in Homer, the worth of a man is first authenticated by the recognition that it finds in the bestowal of honours and in words of praise. Pindar is conscious of his important office, and speaks of it often and emphatically. 'Noble deeds must perish if none speak of them' (fr. 121). Goethe expressed the same view when in *The Natural Daughter* he puts into Eugenie's mouth the words, 'Das Wesen, wär' es, wenn es nicht erschiene?'

Both these things, however, the victories that come from innate ability and the gift of poetry that defies time, depend on the basic condition of all successful achievement—the blessing bestowed by the gods. In other words, Pindar's outlook on the world is essentially religious.

'From the gods come all possibilities of mortal achievement; by them men become wise and strong of arm and mighty in speech' (***Pyth. 1.*** 41). Zeus is lord and giver of all. Next place to him in the poet's heart is held by the Delphian god, the protector of aristocratic qualities. Pindar's pantheon is not so colourful as Homer's. His gods are less individual: he sees them rather as powers that penetrate the whole universe. Hence we find a great part played by such figures as Tyche, Hesychia, Hora, which represent a crystallization of the divine into particular powers or around particular aspects of human life. It would be wrong to speak of personification. The most impressive expression of this *Weltanschauung* is the proemium of the ***Fifth Isthmian.*** In Hesiod's *Theogony* Theia is the mother of Helios, Selene and Eos: in Pindar she has become the primal source of the world of beauty and splendour, the ultimate, divine basis whence all that shines and gives light derives its magical power, whether it be gold or victory in holy places.

There is another respect in which Pindar's view of the gods differs yet more profoundly from Homer's. The poet himself declares (***Ol. 1.*** 35) that it becomes a singer to speak good of the gods. This involves abandonment of several features of Homer's mythology, and we see how in practice Pindar purified the traditional tales. His suppressing the story of the dismemberment of Pelops and his replacing it by the theme—blameless by contemporary standards—of Poseidon's carrying the boy off provides the best-known example. This procedure is very different from the passionate protest of a Xenophanes or the struggles of Aeschylus to justify the ways of Zeus, but ultimately it is rooted in the same dissatisfaction with the religion of the epics. The poet's attitude to this world of the divine contains an antinomy which is surprising and yet typically Greek. It finds striking expression in the opening of the ***Sixth Nemean:*** the poet is well aware of the impotence of men, which must ever set them apart from the power and certainty of the gods. But he knows the other side of the medal: in spite of everything, power of mind and greatness of soul can make man comparable to the gods. They are two eternally distinct races, yet both are children of the same mother. The ***Eighth Pythian*** also speaks of the two sides of human life. We find there the gloomy dictum that man is only the dream of a shadow; but at once comes the comforting reflection that if light from the gods shines on this troubled existence, it can rise to success and glory. To embody this light in poetry and to impart it thus to men—this for Pindar is the duty and purpose of the poet.

Pindar's language falls essentially within the framework of the literary dialect of choral lyric: that is, it adopts the epic inheritance, displays a Doric colouring (stronger in Pindar than in the two Cean poets of Ionian extraction), and includes Aeolic elements. Our evaluation of the latter depends on the degree of faith that we have in the transmission. The style enjoined by the genre was less binding on Pindar than on an epic poet. He did not let tradition prevent him from the effective deployment of his individual manner of expression. His massive sentence-structure, in which the heavy load of ornament scarcely lets the framework be seen, his renunciation of the antitheses and particles beloved of Greek authors in favour of a wilful violence in stringing together and interlacing his clauses, the weight which he places on the noun, so that the verb in contrast is little more than a colourless prop to the sentence, his wealth of images, aimed at the nature of the thing, not at its sensible properties, and mingling one with another with a head-strong recklessness—all these qualities went into Pindar's creation of that ornate style which has characterized the ode right down into modern times.

Despite all his generic propriety, Pindar is essentially the great individualist. (pp. 190-202)

Albin Lesky, "The Archaic Period," in his A History of Greek Literature, *translated by James Willis and Cornelis de Heer, Methuen & Co. Ltd., 1966, pp. 91-240.*

C. M. Bowra (essay date 1964)

[Bowra, an English critic and literary historian, was considered among the foremost classical scholars of the first half of the twentieth century. He also wrote extensively on modern literature, particularly modern European poetry, in studies noted for their erudition, lucidity, and straightforward style. In addition, Bowra translated Pindar's odes into English and wrote a full-length study of the poet, Pindar *(1964). In the following excerpt from the latter work, he assesses Pindar's poetical personality and vision, paying particular attention to the poet's characteristic mood of "exhilaration and exaltation."]*

[Pindar's] most characteristic mood is of exhilaration and exaltation. There are times indeed, as at the end of ***Pythian 1*** or the beginning of ***Nemean 8,*** when it is pure joy, and this is no doubt what he thought to be the felicity of the gods. But more usually he is too close to some particular issue to attain quite this degree of purity in his mood. Nor indeed would we expect it. Celestial joy tends to be divorced from ordinary feelings because it moves at a superhuman level, but Pindar's notion of the felicity of the gods was largely that they found it in action and relaxation, in exerting their powers and pursuing their loves and their friendships. The delight of action means a great deal to him, even if the action is no more than music and song at a feast. Something well done, in which a man sets the whole of his capacities to work and wins, or some occasion when gnawing fears and anxieties are drowned in success, touches his imagination and sets him to work in his most exalted moods. In these there is perhaps no passion, but there is certainly the emotion of enthralling delight. What Pindar felt is to be seen in his song to the Graces of Orchomenus, especially when he speaks of their universal part in all happy and beautiful things: . . .

For not even the gods govern dances or feasts
Without the holy Graces;
They dispose all things in heaven;
Their thrones are set at the side
Of Pythian Apollo, the golden-bowed,
And they honour the everlasting glory
Of the Father on Olympus.

[(***O.14.*** 8-12)]

Then he proceeds to name them, Aglaia, Euphrosyna, and Thalia—Glory, Delight, and Health—and these are indeed powers dear to him and reflected in the depths of his song. They are manifested in particular actions and achievements, and it is they who give to Pindar his predominant tone. He abandons it when his sense of harmony is broken by the thought of envy or hatred, or when he is too troubled to be sure of himself, but usually, even when he speaks with grave authority, there is a touch of this exaltation in him, alike in his words to Theron about the life after death, his vigorous appreciation of the Argonauts, his admiration for the heroes of Aegina in their bold enterprises, his honour for men or heroes who give all that they have for a cause. In many of Pindar's finest moments untrammelled joy is not in question, but there is nearly always some positive assertion, some vivid claim, which sets doubt and defeat aside and reveals glory in gods or men. It was to this that he responded most readily, and it was central to his whole poetical achievement. He took life very seriously, and for this very reason did not despair of it but found his inspiration in those times of extended effort and enlarged consciousness which he saw both in the past and in the present and knew to be the state in which men come closest to the gods.

Because so much of Pindar's poetry is pitched in a key of exalted excitement and arouses in us a strong response, we do not think of him as a poet of ideas, and this is on the whole right. He certainly does not think it is his task to impart instruction as Hesiod often does, and his method is not that of the bare statement of advice. Nor is he a philosopher in any sense in which either the Greeks or ourselves would understand the word. He has no affinities with Parmenides or Empedocles, and would probably have agreed with Aristotle that each should be called a φυσιολογοσ rather than a poet, and from him this would not be a word of praise. Yet he has his own metaphysics, if we may apply the name to a system which has been closely thought out and remains remarkably consistent on all important points. Pindar early made up his mind on what poetry ought to be and carried out his own precepts for it, and in this coherence of his outlook and his performance, more than in his many maxims, we see the unusual cast of his intelligence. His maxims are indeed usually delightful, often percipient and true, sometimes of a striking beauty and penetration, but their strength is ultimately derived from the contexts in which they are placed and which they summarize in a neat and memorable form. They have their own gnomic appeal, but this would be less impressive if they were not reinforced and illustrated by the much more individual poetry around them. They present conclusions rather than immediate experience, and Pindar does not make too much of them or rely on them for his final, overwhelming flights. Their very impersonality means that they miss some of Pindar's most characteristic effects which come from his uniquely individual approach to any matter that captures his imagination. Moreover, they are for the most part traditional, and though they have been happily refurbished for their new duties, they lack the astonishing freshness, the unpredictable surprises of the themes which they illustrate. Yet Pindar's poetry, like most other Greek poetry, has a strong intellectual element. He is far from indulging in unpremeditated outbursts; he thinks hard about a subject before he writes about it, and puts into it his gathered experience and conclusions, and though his thought is largely imaginative or dramatic or emotional, it is none the less thought. It works more through images than through maxims, more through single examples than through generalizations, but it is active alike in the structure of a poem, the treatment of a myth, the variation of tone, the shift from one theme to another, the adaptation of other outlooks to Pindar's own. It is busy in insight, choice, and decision, and in the end it secures an impressively concentrated result. So far from allowing his senses or his emotions to dominate him and dictate his words, Pindar subjects both to a discriminating scrutiny and relates them to his unifying outlook. They become part of a single system, which is indeed more felt than demonstrated but is none the less present in all his work and reflects his personality at every point.

The personality which permeates Pindar's poetry and which emerges so richly from it is not remote or stiff or self-contained. His art indeed imposes, as he would think right, a distance between itself and us, and this is demanded by the high authority which he claims for himself as the prophet of the Muses and the interpreter of gods to men. But this makes us all the more ready not to take it too easily for granted or to shrink from looking for the essential structure and thought behind the many devices with which they are clothed. It calls for our full attention and a cautious awareness that it is always likely to contain more than it shows on the surface at a first glance. Just because it is like this the poet's personality comes out in its unique qualities, and we know him better than if he had diluted some of his concentration in the interests of simplicity and ease. It is conceivable that, if he has so wished, he might have written in the flowing manner of Simonides, but, if he had, he would have lost his central and most characteristic strength. The man and the poet are inextricably one, and we can see that he had indeed the generous breadth of vision which we expect from a man of the fifth century, even if he is not an Athenian. Pindar accepted without question or reservation the worth and the standards of his own aristocratic society, and when he ventured outside it, what he noted was much less the differences between it and monarchies or democracies than what they had in common. He knew that there might be dangerous discords between them, but he passed them over in his desire to find a bond between all men of his own kind. This gave him an unusual unity of temper and outlook, which lasted through his life and survived even the shocks of war which bore so hard on Thebes and Aegina. He did not question his assumptions or quarrel with his universe. On this sure foundation his human gifts matured without any serious setback or sign of decline, and he was able to put them into his poetry. His warmth in love and friendship, his deep appreciation of noble talents in action and success, his keen eye for the visible world were all brought together by his sense of a single scheme of things in which all that matters on the human stage comes, directly or indirectly, from the gods, from their blood which still flows in the veins of men, and from the strength and the support which they give to those whom they love. His outlook was the ripe product of the aristocratic age in Greece. In it most riddles had been answered, most contradictions solved. The fierce new generation in Athens was asking other, more probing questions and seeking more adventurous goals, but Pindar remained true to his beginnings and kept to the end his faith in their assumptions.

Though Pindar presents a remarkably constant and consistent personality, we can discern a certain growth and development in him and his art, as indeed we might expect from a man who lived to be eighty years old, and we can, without committing ourselves too decisively, divide his career into three periods. The first is from ***Pythian 10*** in 498 to the Persian Wars of 480-479, and though ***Pythian 10*** already displays most of Pindar's methods and mannerisms and reveals without shyness where his personal tastes lie, it has still many qualities of youth. Pindar sees a light shed by the gods on human success and happiness and is primarily concerned with this in whatever form it may take. He is fully conscious that he is a poet and dedicated to a special task, and the mere thought of this almost limits his vision of the actual world. Because it means so much to him he seeks those moments of rapturous joy which come from the gods, and admires those, like his Thessalian hosts, who have no small share of the delightful things of Hellas (***P. 10.*** 19-20). He lives in his imagination, whether it takes him to the happy Hyperboreans at the end of the world or finds abundant satisfaction among men who are descended from Heracles. Even the slaying of the Gorgon by Perseus does not strike him in its more fearsome aspects but is just another instance of what the gods can do for men. The darker sides of life do not trouble him, since he is absorbed in his celestial vision and its brilliant, if momentary, reflections on earth. This is still his spirit in 490, when he falls in love with Thrasybulus or finds in the music of Midas' flute an image by which the gods turn suffering and horror into joy. Even his comparison of Thrasybulus with the heroic Antilochus strikes no very emotional note and indicates that what fascinates Pindar is the likeness of a young man in the present to another young man in the past. It is true that for Midas he develops his later theme that no happiness will last for long, but this is no more than a foil to indicate that after all Midas is indeed happy and fortunate. In ***Olympian 14*** he presents his living vision of the Graces without any of his mature misgivings that they may, for all their enchanting beauty, distort the truth, and so strong is his trust in song that he believes that it can up to a point defeat death. When in ***Pythian 7*** he touches on contemporary events, they are almost forced on him, and he shows no understanding of what lies behind them. He has indeed to mention the ostracism of Megacles, since that is why Megacles has taken part in the Games, but Pindar's real interest in him and his family is that they restored the temple of Apollo at Delphi, where his song is performed. In ***Nemean 5,*** written not long before Salamis, he dwells with loving imagination on the song which the Muses sang at the wedding of Peleus and Thetis, when Apollo played the lyre and the Muses told of the bridegroom and of the love which the gods felt for him. His tone deepens as he tells of Phocus and of Peleus' rejection of Hippolyta, but it is still detached and in its own way distant. In ***Isthmian 6*** his maturing manhood turns to the theme of heroic friendship between Heracles and Telamon, and he has begun to extend his scope and his scale, but he still lives in the past and sees it at work in the present. In this period Pindar's eyes are so fixed on the skies that he does not notice the battle of Marathon or pay much attention to the war between Athens and Aegina. He is so content with his way of life that he does not suspect that the aristocratic system of society is likely to be threatened, as he sees in it an image of divine felicity and concord. Though the scale and the richness of his songs increase steadily, he does not yet put into them all that he has in him or elaborate them with the full range of his genius. His myths are still short and lack the dramatic strength which is to come later. The visionary quality of his songs, their concentration on the gods, their attachment to the actual delight of singing, mean that they have much more light than shadow, and the darker corners of experience have not yet begun to trouble him. For Pindar this was still a secure world, with no menace of barbarian conquest or of destructive rivalry between Greek states. Pindar was free to indulge his youthful fancies and to breathe a serene air in what his imagination discovered.

The Persian Wars mark a decisive turning-point in Pindar's career. That he was deeply troubled by them is abundantly clear from ***Isthmians 5*** and ***8,*** and the spiritual distress through which he has passed has already done much for him by forcing him to face hard realities, including his own personal problems as a Theban in a time when Thebes was hated by most of Greece. They brought into play qualities which he had hitherto felt no need to exercise, and with the coming of peace came a great expansion of his powers and a new phase in his creative activity. He was now famous throughout the Greek world, and the first sign of this was his visit to Sicily in 476, which inspired him to an astonishing productivity and initiated the long series of full-scale works which are his most characteristic achievement. In them he advanced in many ways from his earlier poems. His first sense of delight is now extended and tempered by a keener awareness of the range of human achievement, and with this comes a wider scope of emotional effects and a careful elaboration of his fundamental beliefs on the nature of success and glory and what both imply in the scheme of things. As he turns his mature mind to new subjects his poetry becomes more intricate and more allusive, his myths longer and more intimately associated with his main themes, his structure more complicated as he weaves more threads into richer patterns. Since his patrons are now to be found outside his own aristocratic circle, he finds himself forced to give fresh consideration to much that he has hitherto taken for granted and to fit his new experience into his old views. As his powers find new directions and he himself is honoured in many places, he becomes more confident and more authoritative. In this period we may sometimes miss the old, warm, intimate touch, and feel that he was not personally very interested in Xenophon of Corinth or Theaeus of Argos, and though his poetry has a vaulting splendour, it may at times lack an appeal to the heart. Yet it maintains an astonishing inventiveness as he makes new variations on the traditional themes without repeating himself or seeming to lose interest in his recurrent obligations. He gets more out of his fixed ideas and sentiments and gives them a new colour or a new depth. The challenge of new places and new faces enlarged his outlook and forced on his attention many aspects of human life and divine behaviour which make his conclusions more impressive, and his old concentration on a god-given felicity yields to a complex outlook in which the intricate relations of gods and men inspire a more dramatic, more illuminating, and at times a more troubling sequence of poetical effects. He has unified the two halves of his world, and is equally at home in both, showing how human life takes its meaning from the gods, and how the gods act in their own unconscionable majesty. He speaks with a firm belief in himself and is not likely to admit that he can be wrong, as he gives outspoken counsel to kings and tyrants. Though his candour costs him something, he does not shrink from the consequences, but is prepared to defend himself publicly against his critics. In this period he is most at home and most himself in Aegina, where the aftermath of the Persian Wars fostered a national pride which he assumes to be in some part his own. Towards 460 he feels the threat of danger increasing for it and begins to see that its ancient security is menaced. Yet he keeps his international status, his prophet's detachment, and finds much to praise in the circles where he moves. Even when the Sicilian monarchies had fallen, he could find a royal patron in Cyrene, and he reaches his climax in 462-I with ***Pythian 4,*** which is unmatched among Epinicians both in length and in wealth of narrative and even in the frank courage of his words to the king Arcesilas. This is the master-poet in his heyday, less otherworldly than in his youth and sometimes a little too brilliant to be tender, but bold and magnificent and entirely sure of himself and of his yet unchallenged convictions.

Pindar's third period begins about 460, when at last it was tragically clear to him that Athens was no longer what he had tried to believe but was laying an axe to the root of his world. His sympathy and his love are with Aegina, for whom he strikes a deep note of tenderness in ***Olympian 8, Nemean 8,*** and ***Pythian 8.*** He saw political changes which he condemned and feared, and he was himself not free from attacks in his own home. But despite all the shocks and disasters he kept to his beliefs and put his trust in the gods. His main position, which he had taken for granted, was now open to attack, and though he conceded nothing on the importance of song, he took pains to clarify his place in society. The man who had spoken up to Sicilian tyrants and the king of Cyrene now made more modest claims for himself. At a time when Aegina was in peril from Athens and he felt keenly the harm which untruth can do to all honourable things, he stated what he himself desired: . . .

> Father, Zeus, may such a temper never be mine,
> But may I keep to plain paths of life,
> And when I die,
> Leave to my children a name
> Of which no evil is spoken.
> Men pray for gold, others for land without limit,
> But I to please my townsmen,
> Till I wrap my limbs in earth,
> Praising what should be praised,
> And scattering reproach on wrongdoers.
> [(***N.8.*** 35-39)]

This is almost a confession of defeat. Pindar no longer claims that his causes will necessarily triumph or that he himself will be a Panhellenic figure, but instead of this he is content with winning the approval of his own people and winning a good name such as he gives to others by his songs. He has still some twenty years to live, but he feels that he must prepare himself for the end, at least by shaping his life to a modest pattern and looking to what lies beyond it. In 454-3 he says very much the same thing to his own compatriots: . . .

> God help me to love beauty, yet desire
> What I may have, among men of my age.
> [(***P. 11.*** 50-51)]

He feels that his mature years impose an outlook on him, and that he must conform to it, and he states firmly that his first task is now the love of beauty through song. It is almost a return to his first years when celestial music rang in his head and he gave all his powers to it. Even when his own country is under Athenian domination and he praises those who have fallen in its defence, he clings to this idea and finds consolation in it: . . .

> I shall seek the delight that each day brings
> And in calm of mind come to old age and my
> fated days;
> For all alike we die.
> [(***I.7.*** 40-42)]

Then he contrasts his own modest desires with the flaunting ambition of Athens and says that, though destiny does not give equal justice, such pride will surely be humbled. This mood is still with him in ***Pythian 8*** and informs his calm assessment of a situation in which excited hopes are busy with revival and revenge. From his garnered wisdom he gives advice and comfort. In the end, as in the beginning, what matters most to him is the worth of individual men, which survives national disasters and national triumphs, and this worth is proved through toil and trial. Though the years have dimmed his admiration for power and taught him that much of life is the merest shadow, yet some forms of achievement are still to be valued beyond everything else, and song plays its immemorial task in giving to them the immortal recompense of glory. The poet, who has seen so much and mixed with so many different kinds of men, knows that his own calling is still enviably unique because it comes from the gods. Yet though he is sure of this, he does not boast of it, but prays to Apollo that he himself may respond to the true spirit of song in everything that he says: . . .

> My King, with willing heart I pray
>
> That my eyes may rain melody
> On every step that I take.
> [(***P. 8.*** 67-69)]

With the gods to help him, he is still confident of his calling.

In his long career Pindar wrote for an aristocratic society whose outlook he shared and honoured. Much lay outside his horizon, and though he saw himself as a Panhellenic poet, he was less worthy of the title than Simonides, who had a keener insight into the new forces at work in Greece. Yet just because Pindar's outlook was in some respects narrow and his convictions not open to argument, his vision is all the more piercing. He is always and everywhere a poet. His imagination and his emotions are set to work with an astonishing strength and concentration and brilliance because in certain human events he sees divine powers at work and knows that through them men transcend their habitual limitations and realize their utmost potentialities. His love of mankind and of the physical world which is its home is immeasurably enhanced by the celestial radiance which from time to time illumines it. Often enough gods and men are hopelessly severed, and, as the gods indulge in power and pleasure, men go their own faint and aimless way, but at times the whole situation is transfigured because the gods work in men to make them in some respects like themselves. In bringing them together song has much more to do than simply to announce a fact; it is itself an instrument by which men are made conscious of their closeness to the gods, and the gods are entreated to display their affection to men. With such duties to perform song must indeed have qualities of a very rare kind, and Pindar is confident that he possesses them through his intimate dependence on Apollo and the Muses. His innate, unquestioning pride in his poetical mission means that he gives to it all his gifts and all his efforts. The result is a poetry that by any standards deserves the name because it is based on a radiant vision of reality and fashioned with so subtle, so adventurous, and so dedicated an art that it is worthy to be an earthly counterpart of the songs which Apollo and the Muses sing on Olympus, and which Pindar regards as the archetype of music on those lofty occasions when all discords are resolved and all misgivings obliterated by the power of the life-giving word. (pp. 390-401)

C. M. Bowra, in his Pindar, *Oxford at the Clarendon Press, 1964, 446 p.*

John D. Jump (essay date 1974)

[*In the following excerpt, Jump traces the history of Pindar's influence on English poets from the sixteenth to the eighteenth centuries.*]

In the seventh and sixth centuries before Christ, Greek lyrics, or poems to be sung to the lyre, took two forms. There were monodies, sung by single persons, and choral odes, sung by choirs. If we may judge by the fragments in which their works have come down to us, Alcaeus and Sappho were among the finest monodists. But our main concern is with the choral odes.

These had originated in religious celebrations and were performed at festivals and on other important occasions, human and divine. They normally included four elements: prayers or praise to the gods, stories or myths from the heroic past, moral maxims, and personal references appropriate to the circumstances of the performance. Their tone was grave and dignified.

Naturally, they developed differently in the hands of different poets. Though the extant writings of Alcman and Stesichorus are tantalizingly fragmentary, critics have felt able to speak of the freshness and charm of the former and the heroic temper of the latter. To a third poet, Simonides, is ascribed the shaping of the epinician ode, the choral song in honour of a victory in the Olympic or other games.

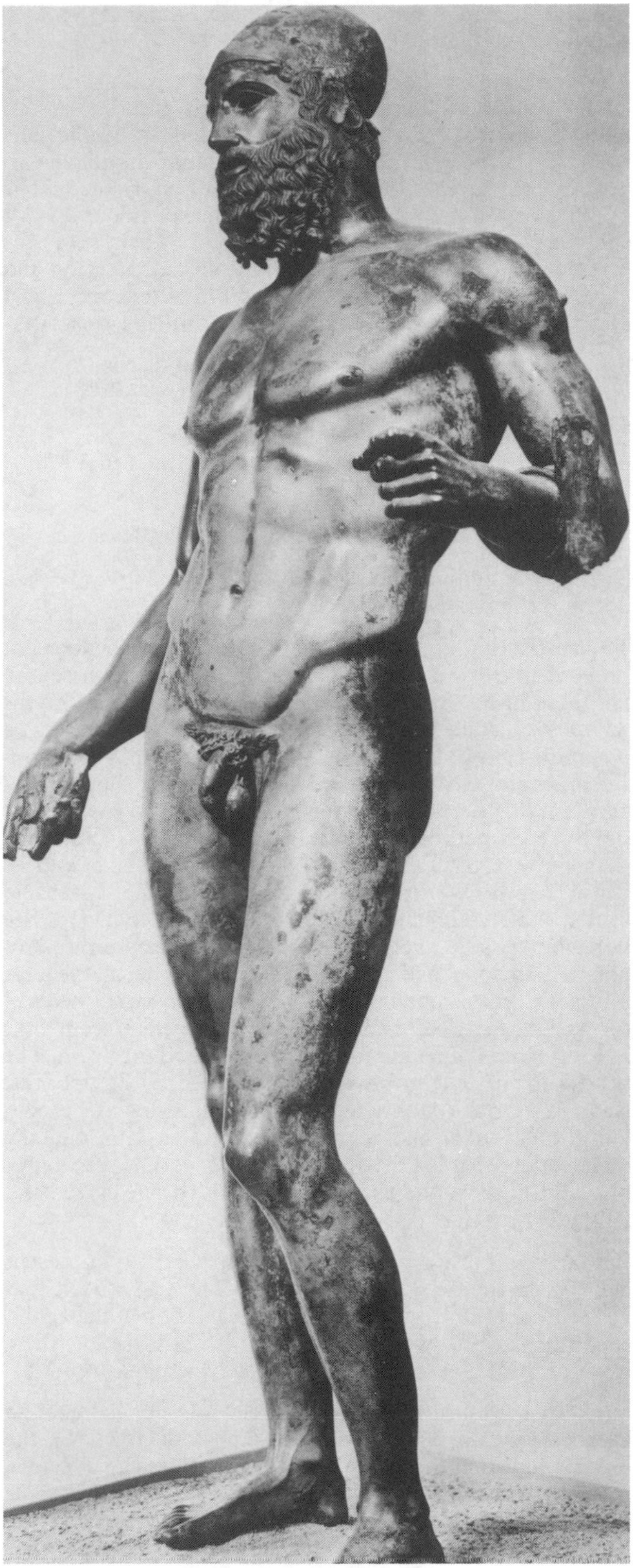

A bronze warrior, 460-440 B.C.

This was to find its greatest exponent in Pindar (518 B.C.-*c.* 438 B.C.).

The games are little more than Pindar's point of departure. From them he invariably proceeds with little or no delay to matters of wider scope and deeper significance. Men win in the games, he believes, because they have natural talent, develop it by hard toil, and enjoy the favour of the gods. Life everywhere owes its splendour to just such high endeavour as they manifest. Their successes bring them exhilaration and exaltation, an extension and enrichment of consciousness, a dazzling glory, and a sort of immortality in the memory of an admiring posterity.

For if any man delights in expense and effort
And sets in action high gifts shaped by the Gods,
And with him his destiny
Plants the glory which he desires,
Already he casts his anchor on the furthest edge
of bliss,
And the Gods honour him.
(***Isthmian VI:*** trans. Bowra)

Seeing this significance in sporting triumphs, Pindar is a deeply religious poet.

The restriction of his immediate subject-matter does not prevent him from displaying considerable enterprise and boldness in his handling of details. He introduces myths which he has chosen for their relevance to his themes or patrons or both. He handles these myths briefly and allusively, often leaving his reader or hearer to supply links between the topics on which he touches and to guess intentions which he does not declare. His boldness and swiftness show, too, in his syntax and in his choice of words. But he always works within regular metrical and stanzaic limits. Thirty-eight of his forty-four epinician odes are written in triads. Each triad consists of three stanzas: strophe, antistrophe, and epode. In any single ode, all the strophes and antistrophes have one and the same metrical form. The metrical form of the epodes differs from this, but it remains the same for all the epodes in the poem. The triadic form, said to have been invented by Stesichorus, was a favourite not only with Pindar but also with his contemporary and rival, Bacchylides. It relates to the dancing which accompanied the singing of an ode; during the strophe and antistrophe the chorus would be in movement, while during the epode it would be at rest.

Pindar was both a painstaking craftsman and an ardent believer in the need for inspiration. The Greeks felt that he sometimes failed to maintain the elevation and magnificence of his best writing. But this did not prevent them from considering him their greatest lyric poet. (pp. 3-5)

Shakespeare's use of the word 'ode' was normal enough in his time and place. Pierre de Ronsard (1524-85), the leading figure in the French group known as the 'Pléiade', had so labelled poems of his own that differed widely from one another in form and in substance. They ranged from a number of miniature pieces, or 'odelettes', written on the model of Anacreon, to fifteen elaborate Pindaric odes, the longest being an 816-line giant addressed to Ronsard's protector, Michel de l'Hospital. Following Ronsard's lead, the English poets of the fifteen-nineties felt free to give the name to almost any sort of lyric.

The first Englishman to claim to have written a Pindaric ode was apparently a poetaster named John Soothern in a volume published in 1584. He certainly plundered the Pindarics of Ronsard, but nothing in his three odes and three 'Odellets' suggests that he knew those of the Greek himself. Indeed, Pindar aroused very little interest in England during the sixteenth century, despite the fact that contemporary Continental interest was lively enough to call for the publication of a whole series of printed editions. The earliest English edition was to appear only at the end of the following century, in 1697.

In a poetical miscellany issued in 1602, the word 'ode' acquires a slightly more definite meaning, being reserved mainly for poems written in complex stanza forms. But Michael Drayton (1563-1631) recognized that the Classical odes had been distinctive in substance as well as in form. In a prose address to his readers he briefly characterizes the transcendently lofty odes of Pindar, the soft and amorous lyrics of Anacreon, and the odes of a mixed kind written by Horace. Nineteen of his own, printed in 1606 and 1619, vary appreciably from one another. Anacreon's influence upon them extends further than the poem in which it is announced, 'An Amouret Anacreontick'; and Horace's pervades almost the entire corpus. But Drayton owes much also to the English tradition. By fusing native and Classical elements—in 'To the Virginian Voyage' and 'His Ballad of Agincourt', for example—he reflects on a smaller scale the important achievement of the English Renaissance playwrights.

On Christmas Day, 1629, John Milton (1608-74) began his great ode 'On the Morning of Christs Nativity'. Though he is known to have studied Pindar closely, Milton did not use the triadic form which Pindar favoured but a monostrophic form such as the Greek had occasionally employed. Four stanzas written in a variant of rime royal introduce the 'Hymn' or 'humble ode' written in twenty-seven stanzas of a type apparently devised by Milton himself. All stanzas, both in 'The Hymn' and in the introduction, end with alexandrines, perhaps under the influence of Milton's 'sage and serious' master, Edmund Spenser. In 'The Hymn' itself, the shifting between shorter and longer lines, with the longer prevailing as each stanza draws to its close, leads up repeatedly to concluding alexandrines of impressive amplitude and weight:

Ring out ye Crystall sphears,
Once bless our human ears,
(If ye have power to touch our senses so)
And let your silver chime
Move in melodious time;
And let the Base of Heav'ns deep Organ blow,
And with your ninefold harmony
Make up full consort to th' Angelike symphony.
(xiii)

In a number of ways the poem reminds us of Pindar. Its rich language and striking imagery, its oblique allusions and swift transitions, and its impassioned lyricism and transcendent loftiness are all characteristics that it shares with the triumphal odes of the Greek.

Similar qualities characterize the Pindaric ode 'To the immortall memorie, and friendship of that noble paire, Sir

Lucius Cary and Sir H. Morison', which Ben Jonson (?1573-1637) wrote about the same time. Jonson contrasts the brief existence which enabled Henry Morison to prove himself an active and worthy soldier, patriot, friend, and son, with the longer career of an unnamed man who after a promising start 'did no good' for the last sixty of his eighty years. Virtuous achievement, not mere duration, gives value to life. Turning to Lucius Cary, the young friend who has outlived Morison, Jonson assures him that the dead man, having 'leap'd the present age', survives in eternity; and that fate, having separated the pair, 'doth so alternate the designe' that while one of them now shines in heaven, the other still brightens the earth

The Turne

It is not growing like a tree
In bulke, doth make man better bee;
Or standing long an Oake, three hundred yeare,
To fall a logge at last, dry, bald, and seare:
A Lillie of a Day,
Is fairer farre, in May,
Although it fall, and die that night;
It was the Plant, and flowre of light.
In small proportions, we just beauties see:
And in short measures, life may perfect bee.

The Counter-turne

Call, noble *Lucius,* then for Wine,
And let thy lookes with gladnesse shine:
Accept this garland, plant it on thy head,
And thinke, nay know, thy *Morison*'s not dead.
He leap'd the present age,
Possest with holy rage,
To see that bright eternall Day:
Of which we *Priests,* and *Poëts* say
Such truths, as we expect for happy men,
And there he lives with memorie; and *Ben*

The Stand

Jonson, who sung this of him, e're he went
Himselfe to rest,
Or taste a part of that full joy he meant
To have exprest,
In this bright *Asterisme*:
Where it were friendships schisme,
(Were not his *Lucius* long with us to tarry)
To separate these twi-
Lights, the *Dioscuri*;
And keepe the one halfe from his *Harry.*
But fate doth so alternate the design,
Whilst that in heav'n, this light on earth must
shine.

This is the third of the four triads that make up the poem. Jonson has given English names to the strophe, antistrophe, and epode: *'The Turne', 'The Counter-turne',* and *'The Stand'.* The metrical form and rhyme-scheme of the turn are identical with those of the counter-turn, and with those of all the other turns and counter-turns in the poem; the metrical form and rhyme-scheme of the stand differ from these but are identical with those of all the other stands in the poem, apart from a slight variation at the beginning of the second. Since the principles governing Greek metres differed from those governing English metres, and since Greek poetry made no use of rhyme, what Jonson offers is not an exact reproduction of what we meet in Pindar. But it is as close an equivalent as the nature of the two languages and poetic traditions allows.

He had precedents in Pindar for letting the sense of the counter-turn or antistrophe in the passage just quoted run uninterruptedly into the stand or epode. But his discipleship to Pindar goes further than this. It appears in the bold imagery, and especially the imagery of light and brightness; in the passing reference to the myth of the Dioscuri, Castor and Polydeuces; in the introduction into the poem of the panegyrist, Ben Jonson, himself; in the weighty moral maxims; in the rapid transitions from topic to topic; and in the deliberately lofty tone. Jonson, however, is the cooler, the less impassioned of the two. We are not surprised to find that in general his odes are more Horatian than Pindaric. Nevertheless, in the example that has concerned us here we have the first close approximation in English to the characteristic achievement of Pindar. Nothing else as close as this was to appear during the seventeenth century.

In the middle of that century Abraham Cowley (1618-67) tried to reproduce Pindar's spirit and manner without imitating his metrical and stanzaic forms. According to Thomas Sprat (1635-1713), the historian of the Royal Society, 'The occasion of his falling on the Pindaric way of Writing was his accidental meeting with *Pindars* Works in a place where he had no other Books to direct him. Having then considered at leisure the height of his Invention and the Majesty of his Style, he try'd immediately to imitate it in *English'.* This was presumably during the years when Cowley was based on Paris in the service of Queen Henrietta Maria, the wife, and after 1649 the widow, of Charles I. His collection of *Pindarique Odes* came out in 1656.

He did not adopt a regular metrical form for these. His lines vary unpredictably in length, his rhymes conform to no set pattern, and his stanzas differ considerably from one another in size. Since his lines are metrical, and since they rhyme, he cannot be considered a writer of free verse like Walt Whitman, Ezra Pound, or D. H. Lawrence. Nevertheless, his irregular metrical verse has seemed to some critics to allow those who use it too much licence. Dr Johnson deplored its widespread influence: 'This lax and lawless versification so much concealed the deficiencies of the barren, and flattered the laziness of the idle, that it immediately overspread our books of poetry; all the boys and girls caught the pleasing fashion, and they that could do nothing else could write like Pindar' (*Lives of the Poets,* 'Abraham Cowley').

Cowley did not originate this freely rhymed and freely metrical verse. Many of his English predecessors had written in it; George Herbert, for example, had handled it with great sensitivity and flexibility to record an intimate personal conflict in 'The Collar'. But Cowley certainly popularized it as the vehicle for rendering what he and others believed to be Pindar's style and manner.

We need not assume, as did many critics in the past, that Cowley discerned no regularity whatsoever in Pindar's poetic forms. His remarks in the 'Preface' to his *Pindarique*

Odes concerning his versions of 'Nemean I' and 'Olympian II' make it clear that, for better or worse, he showed his discipleship by seeking to follow the spirit rather than the letter of his original:

> If a man should undertake to translate *Pindar* word for word, it would be thought that one *Mad man* had translated *another;* as may appear, when he that understands not the *Original,* reads the verbal Traduction of him into *Latin Prose,* than which nothing seems more *Raving.* And sure, *Rhyme,* without the addition of *Wit,* and the *Spirit* of *Poetry* . . . would but make it ten times more *Distracted* than it is in *Prose.* We must consider in *Pindar* the great difference of time betwixt his age and ours, which changes, as in *Pictures,* at least the *Colours* of *Poetry,* the no less difference betwixt the *Religions* and *Customs* of our Countrys, and a thousand particularities of places, persons, and manners, which do but confusedly appear to our Eyes at so great a distance. And lastly, (which were enough alone for my purpose) we must consider that our Ears are strangers to the Musick of his *Numbers,* which sometimes (especially in *Songs* and *Odes*) almost without any thing else, makes an excellent *Poet;* for though the *Grammarians* and *Criticks* have laboured to reduce his Verses into regular feet and measures (as they have also those of the *Greek* and *Latine Comedies*) yet in effect they are little better than *Prose* to our Ears. And I would gladly know what applause our best pieces of *English Poesie* could expect from a *Frenchman* or *Italian,* if converted faithfully, and word for word, into *French* or *Italian Prose.*

Cowley's understanding of Pindar's metre was certainly limited. Indeed, no one in modern times understood it correctly until the nineteenth century. But his refraining from imitating the triadic form was undoubtedly deliberate. He chose to employ a kind of verse that would leave him as free as possible to recreate, both in his two translations and in his numerous original odes, what he took to be the essential qualities of Pindar's poetry: its wild and impulsive character, its frequent, abrupt digressions, its daring images, and its sometimes harsh utterance. But Cowley certainly failed to appreciate Pindar's craftsmanship and control; and, in seeking to accommodate to the taste of his own age what he supposed to be the main Pindaric qualities, he produced poetry that is intelligently conceived, fluent and ingenious, that declaims a little too determinedly, and that sometimes swells with bombast. It is the poetry of a baroque artist of genuine but mediocre talent.

The fourth and last stanza of 'The Resurrection' simultaneously describes the bold poetry Cowley was trying to write and exemplifies the frigid verse which was often the best he could manage:

> Stop, stop, my *Muse,* allay thy vig'orous heat,
> Kindled at a *Hint* so Great.
> Hold thy *Pindarique Pegasus* closely in,
> Which does to *rage* begin,
> And this steep *Hill* would gallop up with violent course,
> 'Tis an unruly, and a *hard-Mouth'd Horse,*
> Fierce, and unbroken yet,
> Impatient of the *Spur* or *Bit.*
> Now *praunces* stately, and anon *flies* o're the place,
> Disdains the *servile Law* of any settled *pace,*
> *Conscious* and *proud* of his own *natural force.*
> 'Twill no *unskilful Touch* endure,
> But flings *Writer* and *Reader* too that *sits* not *sure.*

The lines composing this stanza vary in length from three to six metrical feet. Neither they nor the rhymes form any strictly regular pattern, though there is a tendency for the rhymes to occur in couplets. In metrical and rhyming pattern, as well as in total length, the other three stanzas differ from this and from one another. But these liberties do not enable Cowley to achieve the '*way* and *manner* of speaking' that he ascribed to Pindar. Rhetoric deputizes for passion, and fancy for imagination.

In the second stanza of 'The Muse', he describes how the goddess takes her flight

> Where never *Foot* of *Man,* or *Hoof* of *Beast,*
> The passage prest,
> Where never *Fish* did *fly,*
> And with short silver *wings* cut the low liquid *Sky.*
> Where *Bird* with painted *Oars* did nere
> *Row* through the trackless *Ocean* of the *Air.* . . .

The self-delighting playfulness of this would be appropriate enough in a popular song, but it is far removed from the true Pindaric dignity:

> Joy is the best healer
> Of labours decided, and Songs,
> The Muses' wise daughters,
> Charm her forth by their touch,
> Nor does warm water so drench and soften the limbs
> As praise joined to the harp.
> Longer than actions lives the word,
> Whatsoever, with the Graces' help,
> The tongue picks out from the depths of the mind.
>
> (***Nemean IV***: trans. Bowra)

In 1685 John Dryden (1631-1700) noted the spread of the irregular Pindaric ode. He ascribed this to its 'seeming easiness' but held that hardly anyone apart from Cowley had yet handled it with success. Cowley had 'the warmth and vigour of fancy, the masterly figures, and the copiousness of imagination' which the form requires. But even he fell short in certain respects; 'somewhat of the purity of English, somewhat of more equal thoughts, somewhat of sweetness in the numbers [i.e., the metre], in one word, somewhat of a finer turn and more lyrical verse, is yet wanting.'

> Since Pindar was the prince of lyric poets, let me have leave to say that, in imitating him, our numbers should, for the most part, be lyrical: for variety, or rather where the majesty of thought requires it, they may be stretched to the English heroic of five feet, and to the French Alexandrine of six. But the ear must preside and direct the judgment to the choice of numbers: without the nicety of this, the harmony of Pindaric verse

> can never be complete; the cadency of one line must be a rule to that of the next; and the sound of the former must slide gently into that which follows, without leaping from one extreme into another. It must be done like the shadowings of a picture, which fall by degrees into a darker colour.
>
> ('Preface' to *Sylvae*)

Dryden demonstrates his own feeling for this harmony in 'Threnodia Augustalis' (1685), a poem occasioned by the death of Charles II. Though this was his first Pindaric ode, he had been publishing poetry for more than a quarter of a century and was a highly experienced craftsman. The last of his eighteen irregular stanzas ends not with an ample line of six or seven metrical feet, such as Cowley had favoured, but with a brief, emphatic line of three feet. Yet this short line can easily be heard as extending the four-foot line that precedes it into a seven-foot line which completes the sequence established in the lines of four, five, and six feet which lead up to it. So we have a hint of an ample, resounding conclusion simultaneously with an actual presentation that is compact and epigrammatic. The lines speak of the restoration of English sea-power:

> While starting from his Oozy Bed,
> Th' asserted Ocean rears his reverend Head;
> To View and Recognize his ancient Lord again:
> And with a willing hand, restores
> The *Fasces* of the Main.

The ease and assurance of this ending are characteristic of the mature Dryden.

But Dryden's finest irregular Pindarics are 'To the Pious Memory Of the Accomplisht Young Lady Mrs Anne Killigrew' (1686), 'A Song for St Cecilia's Day, 1687', and 'Alexander's Feast; or The Power of Musique' (1697). The second and third of these were written for two of the annual celebrations of St Cecilia's Day. The saint had a special association with church music, and in particular with the organ, which she was sometimes said to have invented, so the programme on each occasion from 1683 onwards took the form of a church service followed by an entertainment in which an ode, written and composed for the occasion, had an important place. In style, these odes reflect the growing taste of their time for Italian music, which was dignified, emotional, and decorative.

In the central stanzas of the ode of 1687, Dryden puts on a display of virtuosity. His theme is the power of music to 'raise and quell' every human emotion. He starts with the trumpet and drum, suggesting their effect by an impetuous anapaestic metre, by a diction which amplifies the onomatopoeia, and by a series of vigorously martial images. For the flute and lute, he reverts to iambic metre; the lines move gently and unassertively, assonance contributing to the onomatopoeia, until the stanza dies away in the *rallentando* of its long last line. Violins suggest to Dryden almost insanely violent personal passions. After a single iambic line introducing the instruments, he hastens the tempo and switches without a jolt into a plunging trochaic metre, with alliteration pointing important stresses and with onomatopoeia again contributing, this time to evoke the insistency of the music. The whole passage is a copybook illustration of what Dryden meant when he said that in irregular Pindarics 'the ear must preside and direct the judgement to the choice of numbers':

> The TRUMPETS loud Clangor
> Excites us to Arms
> With shrill Notes of Anger
> And mortal Alarms.
> The double double double beat
> Of the thundring DRUM
> Cryes, heark the Foes come;
> Charge, Charge, 'tis too late to retreat.
>
> The soft complaining FLUTE
> In dying Notes discovers
> The Woes of hopeless Lovers,
> Whose Dirge is whisper'd by the warbling LUTE.
>
> Sharp VIOLINS proclaim
> Their jealous Pangs, and Desperation,
> Fury, frantick Indignation,
> Depth of Pains, and height of Passion,
> For the fair, disdainful Dame.

But 'Alexander's Feast' is Dryden's crowning achievement in this kind. It describes how Timotheus by his music sways the emotions of Alexander the Great at a feast celebrating the conquest of Persia. In turns, Alexander supposes himself divine, revels in drinking, pities his fallen enemy Darius, feels love for his mistress Thais, and lusts for revenge against his Persian foes. Though Dryden's lines vary more widely than ever both in length and in metre, his ear and judgement were never more sures. Repetitions of words and phrases, which in isolation could easily seem extravagant, entirely justify themselves in their contexts. The writing is versatile, elegant, serene; at the same time it is virile, bold, even flamboyant.

The fourth stanza starts as Timotheus concludes his 'Praise of *Bacchus*':

> Sooth'd with the Sound the King grew vain;
> Fought all his Battails o'er again;
> And thrice He routed all his Foes; and thrice He slew the slain.
> The Master saw the Madness rise;
> His glowing Cheeks, his ardent Eyes;
> And while He Heav'n and Earth defy'd
> Chang'd his hand, and check'd his Pride.
> He chose a Mournful Muse
> Soft Pity to infuse:
> He sung *Darius* Great and Good,
> By too severe a Fate,
> Fallen, fallen, fallen, fallen,
> Fallen from his high Estate
> And weltring in his Blood:
> Deserted at his utmost Need,
> By those his former Bounty fed:
> On the bare Earth expos'd He lyes,
> With not a Friend to close his Eyes.
>
> With down-cast Looks the joyless Victor sate,
> Revolveing in his alter'd Soul
> The various Turns of Chance below;
> And, now and then, a Sigh he stole;
> And Tears began to flow.

Here again we find Dryden manipulating his metres with conspicuous skill. As elsewhere, alliteration reinforces many of his stresses; the example in the seventh line contributes, along with the simultaneous brief imposition of a trochaic rhythm, to the sharp deceleration and momentary halt which precede the musician's choice of a 'Mournful Muse'. Dryden must have meant the king's flushed review of his past victories to be just a little laughable; 'thrice He slew the slain' forbids us to take it otherwise. In the poem as a whole the extremes through which Alexander passes not only testify to the power of music but also imply a comment upon the conqueror's whole career.

Dryden thought 'Alexander's Feast' his best poem, and many readers have called it the greatest ode in the language. Romantic readers, on the other hand, have often decried it for its lack of 'sincerity', or intimate self-revelation; Elizabeth Barrett Browning, for instance, considered it commonplace. Even Dryden's extraordinary virtuosity has been dismissed as mere craftsmanship. But the life's work of W. H. Auden has taught us not to draw too rigid a line between craftsmanship and art; and when craftsmanship is as superb as Dryden's in 'Alexander's Feast' surely only prejudice can cause us to withhold high praise.

In 1697, 'Alexander's Feast' was sung to a setting by Jeremiah Clarke, which has perished. Some decades later, G. F. Handel composed a setting for it. This has survived and is still performed from time to time.

By writing the poems we have been reviewing, Dryden made the irregular ode an accepted and interesting form. Many took it up during the century that followed the composition of 'Alexander's Feast', believing it a suitable vehicle for dignified themes: 'religious fervor, patriotic zeal, philosophic reflection, and biographical tribute'. But successes were rare. Late in the century, William Cowper had to admit that 'we have few good English odes' (letter dated 4 August 1783).

Our Poets Laureate were among the more frequent users of the form. Throughout the eighteenth century and into the early part of the nineteenth century, they turned out annual Birthday Odes and New Year Odes for royalty. Many of these deliver their stately compliments in the 'lax and lawless versification' of the irregular Pindaric; they were often ridiculed at the time and can excite little interest today. When offering the Laureateship to Thomas Gray in 1757, the Lord Chamberlain tried to tempt him by suggesting that the New Year and Birthday Odes might no longer be required. But Gray refused the offer, and the new Laureate, William Whitehead, dutifully performed the set tasks as his predecessors had done. It was Robert Southey, appointed in 1813, who earned the gratitude of his successors by shifting the emphasis from writing odes 'at stated times and upon stated subjects' to celebrating 'great public events . . . as the spirit moved' (letter dated 5 September 1813).

William Congreve (1670-1729), our most accomplished author of comedies of manners, tried his hand at the irregular Pindaric before reacting against the influence of Cowley and turning to the strict triadic form. No memorable writer had employed it since Ben Jonson, and no other was to do so until Thomas Gray (1716-71) produced 'The Progress of Poesy' and 'The Bard'.

The first of these celebrates the power of poetry and glimpses its operations in the savage state, in Greece, in Rome, and in England. The second tells how a solitary Welsh bard curses the conquering Edward I and foretells the misfortunes which await the king's descendants. He predicts finally the glorious reign of Elizabeth I, whose 'eye proclaims her of the Briton-Line'.

The broad sweep and the patriotic and other important implications of these subjects evidently invited Pindaric treatment; and Gray did not stop at the adoption of the triadic structure. The last epode of 'The Bard' opens with a vision of the literary glories of the Elizabethan age and its successor:

> The verse adorn again
> Fierce War, and faithful Love,
> And Truth severe, by fairy Fiction drest.
> In buskin'd measures move
> Pale Grief, and pleasing Pain,
> With Horrour, Tyrant of the throbbing breast.
> A Voice, as of the Cherub-Choir,
> Gales from blooming Eden bear;
> And distant warblings lessen on my ear,
> That lost in long futurity expire.

The second of these lines echoes a phrase from the first stanza of the introduction to *The Faerie Queene,* and the words 'fairy Fiction' confirm that Gray intends an allusion to Edmund Spenser. In this context, the mention of 'buskin'd [i.e., tragic] measures' and of the feelings which they express inevitably brings Shakespeare to mind. The last four lines similarly suggest Milton, and the 'Gales from blooming Eden' are evidently the 'gentle gales' which blow from Eden in *Paradise Lost,* iv. 153-65. None of the three poets is actually named. Gray, like Pindar, prefers oblique allusions, which give an aloof dignity to his lines. The inversion of three successive clauses in the passage quoted contributes to this same effect, as does the elaborateness of the diction.

The oblique allusions and swift transitions of 'The Bard' have baffled many readers, as have the similar attributes of Pindar's odes. But from the start Gray's regular Pindarics have evoked admiration, even if sometimes reluctant, for their rich diction, their striking imagery, and their consistently lofty tone. The bard's vision of his massacred fellows displays the characteristic qualities:

> Cold is Cadwallo's tongue,
> That hush'd the stormy main:
> Brave Urien sleeps upon his craggy bed:
> Mountains, ye mourn in vain
> Modred, whose magic song
> Made huge Plinlimmon bow his cloud-top'd head.
> On dreary Arvon's shore they lie,
> Smear'd with gore, and ghastly pale:
> Far, far aloof th' affrighted ravens sail;
> The famish'd Eagle screams, and passes by.
> Dear lost companions of my tuneful art,
> Dear, as the light that visits these sad eyes,
> Dear, as the ruddy drops that warm my heart,
> Ye died amidst your dying country's cries—

No more I weep. They do not sleep.
On yonder cliffs, a griesly band,
I see them sit, they linger yet,
Avengers of their native land:
With me in dreadful harmony they join,
And weave with bloody hands the tissue of thy
line.

According to Dr Johnson, however, we have here only 'the puerilities of obsolete mythology'. He protests that when we learn of the deeds attributed to Cadwallo and Modred 'attention recoils from the repetition of a tale that, even when it was first heard, was heard with scorn'. In his view, 'the two Sister Odes' are disfigured 'by glittering accumulations of ungraceful ornaments; they strike, rather than please; the images are magnified by affectation; the language is laboured into harshness. The mind of the writer seems to work with unnatural violence.' Johnson finds 'a kind of cumbrous splendor' in Gray's odes generally.

These include an irregular 'Ode for Music', an elegant mock-ode 'On the Death of a Favourite Cat Drowned in a Tub of Gold Fishes', and an 'Ode on a Distant Prospect of Eton College' that recalls the half-dozen monostrophic odes of Pindar himself. But after Gray little life remained in the strictly Pindaric tradition in England. During subsequent centuries the irregular ode was to attract several distinguished practitioners. These would use it in their own fashions, however, and not in emulation of the Greek lyrist. (pp. 10-25)

John D. Jump, "Classical Models" and "Pindaric Odes," in his The Ode, *Methuen & Co. Ltd., 1974, pp. 1-9, 10-25.*

Aelian (fl. c. 200) describes an encounter between Pindar and the poet Corinna:

When the poet Pindar was competing in Thebes an uncultivated audience fell to his lot and he was five times defeated by Corinna. Pindar reproached their lack of cultivation and called Corinna a sow.

Aelian, quoted in Ancilla to Classical Reading, *by Moses Hadas, 1954.*

M. L. West (essay date 1980)

[In the following excerpt, West gives a brief account of the development of early Greek poetry and provides an assessment of Pindar's artistic stature, focusing in particular on the ode Pythian 1.]

[Early] Greek poetry down to about 500 B.C. is sometimes loosely lumped together as 'lyric'. This is unfortunate, because it implies that that poetry had a unity which it did not have, and because the word 'lyric' has associations which are largely inappropriate. In an ancient context it properly refers to poetry sung or recited to the accompaniment of the lyre. But the rhapsodes who recited epic poetry at least sometimes accompanied themselves on the lyre; while much of the smaller-scale poetry to be reviewed in this chapter was accompanied by the pipes, or not at all. Often we do not know how it was performed.

It is better (though still not completely satisfactory) to divide it into melic poetry, iambic poetry, elegy, and epigram. Melic poetry means simply song, whether solo or choral, and naturally covers a very wide range. Iambic poetry, which sounds like a metrical category, in fact includes more than one kind of verse associated with the *iambos,* a particular sort of entertainment. Elegy is a purely metrical category, comprising verse composed in elegiac couplets; it has none of the mournful associations that the word carries in the context of English literature. Epigram, in this period, stands apart: it is verse not intended for oral delivery but to be written on a physical object as a label. Only later, when the verse inscription comes to be the subject of literary imitation, does it become a department of book literature.

Much of this poetry has survived only in fragments: quotations by later authors and remnants of ancient papyrus copies recovered from Egypt. Complete poems are rare until we come to Pindar in the fifth century. But enough survives for us to trace the main lines of development, and to appreciate the qualities of the principal poets and the justification for the reputations they enjoyed; enough to delight and tantalize us. The continuing publication of papyrus fragments is still adding materially to our knowledge of this area.

Since accounts of Greek literature so often treat epic and 'lyric' as successive stages in its development, the point must be made again that date of first appearance in writing is no reliable guide to date of origin. However old epic poetry may be, song is older. From time immemorial men sang as they brought in the harvest, women as they ground the corn, children in their play, choruses at festivals. Homer himself refers to the singing of paeans to propitiate Apollo in time of danger, harvest songs, and laments for the dead; Circe sings as she weaves. The study of comparative metrics has shown that it is in melic poetry, not epic, that the oldest forms of Greek verse are to be found—forms recognizably related to early Indian, Slavic, and other Indo-European verse forms, and thus going back by a continuous tradition to the remote times when these peoples were together. Epic for its part continued to be composed in the traditional style into the fifth century, that is, for two hundred years after melic and other kinds of poetry had begun to be written down.

By the time this poetry comes into sight, regional traditions have developed, differing from each other in metre, dialect, and probably musical style. But just as epic spread beyond the Ionian area where it reached perfection, so in time other regional styles spilled over local boundaries and were imitated more generally. They had grown too far apart for complete fusion, and they retained elements of their separate identities, particularly in respect of dialect. For example, elegy belonged with epic in the Ionian tradition, and throughout history it was normally composed with an Ionic dialect colouring, wherever the poet happened to come from. Similarly, poetry in the Doric manner is composed by Ionian and Athenian poets with a Doric dialect colouring. The dialect in which Greek literary works were composed always depended more on the genre to which it belonged than on the author's place of origin. The literary dialects were seldom identical with spoken dialects: they were subject to various influences, such as the native speech habits of the writer himself and of all his predecessors in the genre, and archaisms borrowed from the epic language.

The degree to which poetic language was removed from ordinary speech also varied according to genre. The main features which distinguished it before 500 B.C. were the use of old words and grammatical forms, the free addition of ornamental adjectives and adverbs, and the avoidance of words felt to be coarse or undignified. It is in epic that these features are most in evidence; elegy and melic poetry come next on the scale, then spoken iambic verse, some of which does approach the level of colloquial language. What is not characteristic of poetry at this period is any straining after novelty or originality of expression. Indeed, the use of ready-made phrases borrowed from others is almost an essential element in convincing poetic style. The poet's effort is not directed towards expanding the boundaries of art but towards organizing his thoughts and feelings for persuasive presentation; the poetic form in which he expresses them is something given, a familiar, comfortable vessel. Sometimes he achieves originality spontaneously, but he does not officiously strive for it. The result is that this poetry is consistently clear and straightforward; when it is obscure, it is usually because we are ignorant about something that was well known to the original audience, and not because the poet failed to express himself in a natural way.

In our own culture verse that is written to be set to music rarely gives much satisfaction when read on its own. The best poetry is to be found elsewhere. In ancient Greece the situation is quite different. Melody was not considered a substitute for substance. Much of the finest, most profound and most difficult poetry was designed to be sung. Of the music we have only the rhythms, mirrored in the precise, often complex metres of the verse, which repeat themselves from stanza to stanza or in the triadic pattern of strophe, antistrophe, epode, that is, two stanzas with the same melody, a third with a different one, and then the pattern repeated, AABAABAAB . . . In the case of choral song there was often a further aspect to the performance: dancing. A chorus presupposes a definite ceremonial occasion and a sizeable audience. It might be a regular festival with religious associations, or some special event, an emergency supplication to the gods, a wedding or a funeral, a celebration of military or athletic victory. Where dancing was part of the procedure, it was commonly done by the singers. So in reading some texts, we have to bear in mind that they are only part of a whole. We must try to supply in imagination the music, the dancing, the atmosphere of the occasion. (pp. 29-31)

Of the work of Pindar and Bacchylides we have a substantial amount, but in both cases, as it happens, predominantly from their Epinicia, choral odes celebrating sporting victories. They also wrote hymns, paeans, partheneia, convivial songs, and other pieces. Pindar is the greater of the two; also the more uneven and the more difficult. The difficulty lies in his originality (even eccentricity) of metaphor and involution of thought and phrasing. The involution may be illustrated from the ode composed for Hieron's victory in the Olympic horse-race in 476. Pindar decides to make a start by saying that the Olympic games are the greatest of all games. By the time he has wrapped up this simple idea a little, it has become 'water is supreme among liquids; gold is supreme among material possessions; and the Olympics are outstanding among games'. But he is not content with that. What actually comes out is:

> Supreme is water; gold shines
> like a burning fire in the night above all proud wealth;
> but if games are what thou yearnest to sing, my heart,
> seek not, after the sun, another luminary
> through the airy void with greater heat in the day,
> nor shall we call any contest superior to Olympia.
>
> (Pindar, ***Olympian Odes 1***. 1-7)

An untidy little paragraph; but without saying anything extravagant about the games, Pindar has succeeded in investing them with the splendour of water, gold, fire, and the sun.

The athletic record of the victor and his family provides further material, and here involution may become a necessity if the facts are to be accommodated at all compactly in the strict, complex metrical scheme.

> He is tasting contests;
> and to the Amphictionic
> host the Parnassian hollow has proclaimed him
> highest of boys in the circuit race.
> Apollo, sweet men's goal
> and their beginning grows when a god gives speed:
> he must have accomplished this
> by your design; but kinship walks in the steps
> of his father, Olympic victor twice
> in battle-bearing arms of Ares; also
> the deep-meadow contest under the cliffs of Cirrha
> made Phricias master-foot.
>
> (Pindar, ***Pythian Odes 10***. 7-16)

No archaic poet could have written in this contorted way.

Pindar is not much interested in sport for its own sake. The significance of the victory for him is that it manifests the innate quality of the man and his family. The bulk of most odes is taken up by moralizing and myths, as in other kinds of choral poetry. Any myth can be used, and on the slightest pretext. It may have some connection with the victor's ancestry, or his home town, or the games at which he has been successful; it may have no particular relevance, its presence being ostensibly justified as an illustration of some commonplace such as 'there is a time and place for everything'. Pindar's attitude to myth is flexible. He is prepared to adapt it to suit his patrons or his own moral sense. He was not exceptional in this; the Greeks never regarded tradition as sacrosanct, but as raw material for the artist's use.

He does not follow any fixed pattern in constructing an ode, and one is often left with the impression of a suitcase filled rather at random. Yet there are odes which impress as architecture and are thoroughly integrated wholes. Foremost among them is Pindar's masterpiece, the ***First Pythian*** ode. It is worth giving a brief account of this poem, as an indication of what Pindar at his most inspired was able to make out of the epinician form.

It was composed in 470 for Hieron on the occasion of a chariot victory; it was at the same time a celebration of the new town of Etna, which Hieron had founded below the volcano and put in the charge of his son Deinomenes, and of the battle of Cumae in 474, at which he had broken the Etruscan sea power. It is in five triads, Pindar's normal maximum: just a hundred lines as conventionally divided. The first strophe and antistrophe present a wonderful vision of Apollo playing the lyre in heaven for the chorus of Muses. The gods are at peace, Zeus' fiery thunderbolt flickers out, his great eagle is lulled to sleep by the divine music, even Ares, disarmed, drowses contentedly. The epode, with its change of tune, brings a contrast: Zeus' enemies are bewildered by the distant sound of the Muses' song, and especially the many-headed monster Typhon, firmly and painfully confined under the cliffs of Cumae and under Etna. Although it is not said in so many words, Typhon clearly symbolized Hieron's defeated enemies, and the divine concert his present leisure. From Typhon Pindar passes straight to the new town, whose protecting god Zeus is, and to Hieron's athletic victory. In the course of the third triad he recalls Hieron's battles, and his ill health; the myth of Philoctetes comes in briefly as a neat and complimentary parallel. Then he moves on to Deinomenes, with the justification that 'the father's victory is no alien rejoicing to him'. He prays to Zeus that Etna may continue as it has begun, referring explicitly now to the Etruscan calamity at Cumae and his own role as the poet who celebrates Greek victories over barbarians. This state of affairs in the world of men mirrors the divine situation described in the first triad. The final triad consists of admonitions for the young king, and a reference at the end to the lyres that resound for successful rulers takes us back to the start. (pp. 44-7)

M. L. West, "Other Early Poetry," in Ancient Greek Literature *by K. J.and others, edited by K. J. Dover, Oxford University Press, Oxford, 1980, pp. 29-49.*

Frank J. Nisetich (essay date 1980)

[*In the following excerpt from the introduction to his highly praised translation of Pindar's odes, Nisetich provides an overview of the poet's life and times.*]

Pindar's odes, in their original form and purpose, are different from anything modern readers have encountered as poetry before. They are not private, personal, or spontaneous. Pindar received money to compose his poems; he wrote them to be performed by a singing and dancing chorus; and he was required to mention various matters that he might not have mentioned if he were entirely free to follow his inspiration. He certainly had no notion of the kind

A pig is sacrificed before the Olympic games begin, from an Attic red-figured cup, ca. 510 B.C.

of book now in the reader's hands, and yet he speaks often with confidence of the distant future. He implies that the family for which he wrote would keep and prize his work from generation to generation. But within a few centuries of his death his musical notations and choreographical directions vanished from the preserved texts. As choral poetry ceased to be composed and was performed less and less, its peculiar poetic conventions lost their meaning. By the time Alexandrian scholars turned to the study of Pindar, his odes had become what they are to us now—mysterious relics of a distant past.

This, however, is only the beginning. The loss of an audience used to the performance of poetry did not have disastrous consequences for the appreciation of Homer or the Greek dramatists, nor is it the sole cause of modern difficulty with Pindar. The audience of a Homeric recitation had the narrative to rely on. The basic plots of the *Iliad* and the *Odyssey* are still there to guide a modern reader. Indeed, the story is seldom absent from the immediate foreground, and when it retires into the background, it is never absent for long. There is nothing so constant to give readers of Pindar their bearings. The victory celebrated in a Pindaric ode may be the starting or the finishing point, but everything in between varies from one ode to the next. Sometimes the connection between the different parts of an ode and the victory commemorated in it is apparent, at other times it is not. At any rate, the victory does not provide the kind of background that the narrative in Homer provides. It does not fasten the poem down in the same way, if at all. In Homeric recitation, moreover, the poetry itself was unaffected by the circumstances of performance. The poet's personality receded into the background. There was no need for him to interrupt the story with interpretation: his characters would express his insights at dramatic moments, and the narrative itself called for an easy-going, straightforward style. The poet might have an evening, perhaps a succession of evenings, to tell his tale; he would not need to resort to compression in order to accomplish his task.

Comparison of Pindar's odes with the odes of Greek drama is perhaps more to the point. Both were meant to be sung and danced by a chorus. Both are characterized by intense compression of style and by a striving on the poet's part to interpret the meaning of things for the audience. Yet even in an ode by Aeschylus, who is in many ways similar to Pindar, audience and reader always have the dramatic context to help follow the thought. In the *Agamemnon,* for example, the Watchman's opening speech puts us at a specific time and place within a larger narrative. We know that the Trojan War has ended, that Agamemnon will soon come home. No matter how complex the reflections of the chorus after the Watchman has left the stage, his prologue, our own acquaintance with the legend, and the dramatic situation never leave our minds. We may be puzzled by words and phrases whose full meaning will emerge later, but we are never adrift as we are at the opening of a Pindaric ode.

In Pindar there is no single story to give the poem its coherence, as in Homer; there is no dramatic background against which to assess the poet's reflections, as in tragedy. Instead of a dramatic stage where actors and chorus portray a single incident from a recognizable mythic tradition, the scene of a Pindaric performance is a temple or a street or a doorstep or a banquet hall somewhere in archaic Greece. Usually, we cannot even be certain what the scene of performance is, so any impact it may have on the poetry itself may escape us. And what the poet tells us from moment to moment cannot be referred to anything with which we are already familiar, so we must take it as it comes, absorbing it and keeping it in mind as well as we can, if we are to have a background at all.

And we will need a background, for we find as we read that almost anything may happen. We may begin with a solemn invocation, but often it is not directed to a recognizable deity but to an abstraction like "Peace" or "Divineness," or to a city or the song itself or a musical instrument. Ostensibly, the poem was written to celebrate a victory at the athletic games of Greece, but the victor himself does not seem to be the center of attention, at least not as we would expect him to be. The poet, for example, is at pains to display the victor's ancestry. He may go back a hundred years to mention an athletic forebear. He may mention living relatives who also happen to be athletes. In this way, more time may go to the victor's family than to the victor himself. His city may also displace him from the limelight. Yet even more peculiar is the poet's manner of praising the victor, when he gets around to it. To us it seems anything but straightforward. He is inclined, for example, to attack people who do not have the victor's virtues, rather than to praise the victor for having them. Sometimes, when no explicit reference is made to the victor, we are unprepared for such attacks. Thus they give the impression of willful cantankerousness. It is only a step from here to the traditional image of Pindar as a poet who habitually disregards the demands of propriety and relevance.

And then there is the mythic portion of the ode. Here we have narrative, but we are quickly disappointed if we expect anything like the narrative in Homer. The poet moves backward, or backward and forward at once. He may interrupt a myth, dismiss it and start another, totally unrelated to the first, at least as far as we can tell immediately. Careful study of the ode may reveal a connection between the two, but the connection may be in the difference between them, not in their similarity. The proverbial statements that occur in the ode, the poet's moralistic pronouncements or observations, may give us the clue to the way in which we should view the myth or myths in it. In any event, we are forced to read the ode with partial understanding from moment to moment. The poet has created a complex structure where words take on special significance. They derive their full meaning, their full effect, from the total impression made by the ode. Only a second, third, and fourth reading will bring out these extra resonances.

A poet whose style is so compressed, whose manner of proceeding is, at first sight, so unpredictable, might well seem incoherent. Pindar's reputation as the supreme lyric poet of Greece keeps interest in him alive, but many who go to his poems to find the reason for his reputation come away disappointed. Those who read him in translation find him too difficult to understand; those who read him in Greek find that his language impresses even before it communicates, and the odes dissolve into a series of purple passages. Pindar's power and his difficulty combine with the loss of appreciation for the genre in which he worked to create the traditional image of him as a poet beholden to nothing but the laws of his own genius. In times when poetry is in a heroic or tragic mode, Pindar's sublimity is admired and emulated, usually at the expense of poetic coherence; in times when poetry has a quieter voice, preferring irony to celebration, Pindar simply goes out of favor.

He seems to be out of favor now, but the present moment may also be propitious for him. Recent progress in scholarship has begun to revise the traditional image of Pindar as a sublime but incomprehensible poet. Having begun to understand him, we have no need to admire him blindly. But he is not easy to understand. He requires preparation. To begin to appreciate him, we need to know something about the kind of poetry he wrote and the times in which he lived.

PINDAR, THE VICTOR, AND POETRY OF OCCASION

Every Pindaric ode begins with its occasion, someone's victory in one of the Greek athletic festivals. The most prestigious of these were the four after which the four books of Pindar's odes have been named: the Olympian, Pythian, Nemean, and Isthmian games, often called the "great" or pan-Hellenic games, to distinguish them from the innumerable minor athletic festivals held throughout the Greek world. Any Greek could compete at the great games, but in practice participation was limited to those who could afford it, and these, in Pindar's day, were the members of aristocratic families.

No money prizes were given officially at the great games themselves, but victors on their return home found ample rewards for their efforts. To judge from the number of statutes of athletic victors, the number of inscriptions recording their triumphs, and the number of poems written to commemorate them, they did not consider the fleeting moment of glory sufficient: they looked to the future and wanted a place in it. If they competed during Pindar's lifetime and were wise enough to hire him, they were among the thirty-five individuals whose names, with one or two exceptions, we know today only because Pindar celebrated their victories.

Not very much is known in detail about the events surrounding the production of a Pindaric ode. We can only imagine, in a general way, what these events must have been. First was the moment of victory itself. At the four great games the official prize was a crown or garland—of olive at Olympia, laurel at Pytho (Delphi), green parsley at Nemea, and dry parsley at the Isthmos. As the victor advanced to the altar to be crowned by the judges, the criers would announce his name, his father's name, and the name of his city.

After the moment of triumph, the victor might approach the poet and ask him to compose a song virtually impromptu, to be sung by his friends at the site of the games, whether in a procession or at a banquet. But usually, he would ask for a song to be performed on his return home. If this were the case, the poet would have time to compose a more elaborate ode. He would consider the history of the victor's family and city, finding in it something to deepen the significance of the present moment. He might travel with the victor from the site of the games to his native city, composing the ode on the way. On arrival, a chorus of boys or men would be assembled. The poet would instruct them in the movements he wanted them to execute as they sang the ode, explaining, when necessary, the meaning of its more difficult passages. He also wrote the music, usually for harp and flute.

How much time elapsed between the moment the victor was crowned at the games and the moment he witnessed his success being celebrated in song and dance must have varied a great deal. The whole process reached its culmination in performance. When the poet finally left the scene of celebration, he would have provided the victor with a fair copy of the ode itself. At other times, when he did not accompany the victor back from the games, he must have composed the ode at home. He would then send it, complete with directions for performance, to the victor, or he would send it together with a chorus leader who saw to its performance.

None of this is very familiar in modern poetry. The idea that a poet should be hired to celebrate an important event scarcely occurs to anyone. More important, over the last two and a half millennia the link between poetry and music has been severed. Lyric poetry, once a matter involving musical instruments and, in its choral form, intricate dance steps, now involves only a solitary audience reading in silence what the poet wrote without anyone's asking him to write it. Pindar's odes have been reduced from their original splendor to the bare minimum with which all poetry must now make do. But if the only strength of Pindar's odes lay in their instrumentation or in their choreography, they would not have survived. We may feel nostalgia for the missing dance and musical accompaniment, but the essential power of the poetry is still there, in the words.

PINDAR'S LIFE AND TIMES

Pindar was born in Thebes, the main city of Boiotia, in 518 B.C. His earliest extant ode, ***Pythian 10,*** was composed in 498, when he was twenty; his last datable poem, ***Pythian 8,*** was written in 446, when he was seventy-two. Thus his career as a writer of victory odes spans at least fifty-two years.

During the course of his long, productive career, Pindar traveled from one end of the Greek world to the other, celebrating the triumphs of aristocrats and kings. He lived during momentous times and wrote for men who played both large and small roles in the unfolding of events. For this reason it is advisable that a reader have some awareness of historical background. The Persian invasions of the first quarter of the fifth century and the gradual changes that occurred in the Greek world in the twenty-five years or so that followed, mainly as a result of the growing power of Athens, are the two principal developments to keep in mind.

The most famous and powerful patrons of Pindar's art were the Sicilian dynasts Hieron and Theron, both of whom Pindar visited in 476. He had praised Theron fourteen years previously, in ***Pythian 6,*** which celebrates the victory of Theron's brother Xenokrates in the chariot race at Pytho in 490. It is addressed to Xenokrates' son, Thrasyboulos, Theron's nephew, whom Pindar commends by reference to his more famous uncle (line 46). Even while Thrasyboulos and his friends were enjoying Pindar's song at Delphi, a Persian army was on its way to the shores of Greece. Not long afterward the Athenians pushed the invaders into the sea at the battle of Marathon. But by the time Pindar went to Sicily, fourteen years later in 476, the Persians had come again, and Greek Sicily itself had faced an equally ominous threat from another quarter.

A decade after Marathon a second, more formidable barbarian invasion was launched against Greece. In the east, Xerxes attacked by land and sea. In the west, Carthage sent an army against the Greek cities in Sicily. In all likelihood, the two invasions were coordinated. Athens and her allies defeated the Persian fleet at the battle of Salamis. At almost the same time, Theron of Akragas and Gelon of Syracuse, Hieron's older brother, met and defeated the Carthaginian army at the battle of Himera in Sicily. In the following year, a Greek army under Spartan leadership defeated the Persian army at the battle of Plataia.

The battle of Salamis took place in September 480. Some time after that, Pindar was commissioned to write an ode honoring Phylakidas of Aigina for a victory in the *pankration* at the Isthmian games. The poem, ***Isthmian 5,*** mentions the battle of Salamis by name. We can guess with some confidence why Pindar mentioned the battle in this particular ode, written for a citizen of Aigina. After the battle, the Greeks who had fought in it singled out the Aiginetan contingent for its bravery. The allusion to the battle in which his countrymen had distinguished themselves is designed to please the victor.

A similar design accounts for Pindar's mention of the battle of Himera in the first Pythian ode, written for Hieron in 470. Hieron's older brother Gelon had defeated the Carthaginians at Himera in 480. By the time Pindar wrote ***Pythian 1,*** Salamis and Plataia had become examples of Greek bravery for all to emulate. It is to Pindar's credit that he perceived the importance of the battle of Himera, for it determined the survival of Greek culture in Sicily, as the other two battles ensured its survival in the mother country. In ***Pythian 1,*** Pindar places all three battles on a par. Plataia was fought "beneath (Mt.) Kithairon"; Himera was won by the "Deinomenidai" (sons of Deinomenes), Gelon and Hieron:

> I will earn
> the praise of Athens by singing of Salamis,
> and of Sparta by making my theme
> the battles beneath Kithairon
> where the curve-bow Persians strove and were crushed.
> But when I come to the rivery field of Himera
> I will sing of the Deinomenidai, conquerors of the foe.
>
> (75-80)

Pindar is said to have gone to Athens in his youth to learn song and music. In the above lines from ***Pythian 1,*** he praises Athens for her part in the battle of Salamis. Some years later, he wrote a dithyramb for the Athenians. The poem (fragment 76), apparently recalling the role Athens had played in saving Greece from the barbarian enemy, hails her as "the bulwark of Hellas." Pindar's own city Thebes, an enemy of Athens throughout the fifth century, on this occasion reportedly fined Pindar for praising her. Eustathius records the sum of 1,000, Isocrates of 10,000, drachmas. Isocrates adds that the Athenians voted Pindar 10,000 drachmas in recompense for the fine. We hear of another instance of Athenian affection for Pindar from Pausanias, who tells us that the Athenians erected a bronze statue of Pindar seated with his lyre beside him. Exactly when the Athenians erected the statue we cannot tell, nor do we know if it had anything to do with the alleged rivalry between Athens and Thebes—Thebes anxious to punish and Athens to reward Pindar for his Athenian sympathies.

There is probably a trace of historical fantasy operating in much of this, a result of the natural tendency to wonder what Pindar must have felt and experienced, being both a pan-Hellenic and a Theban poet. Thebes had disgraced herself during the invasion of Xerxes. She had capitulated to the invader before the battle of Salamis, and Theban forces had fought alongside the Persians against the Greeks at Plataia. In the course of his career, however, Pindar the Theban poet was called upon to sing of Athens and of at least two Athenian athletes. He also sang, possibly during the period of Theban disgrace, of Thebes and of at least four Theban athletes. Enmity between Thebes and Athens was as intense as it has ever been between any two states. Though it is hard for us to imagine a prominent citizen in one country ever asking a poet from an adversary country to celebrate an event of national significance, that happened in Pindar's case, and not merely because he had acquired a reputation for tact. The great games in which his patrons competed took place during times of declared sacred truce, when all hostilities between Greek states were suspended and the Greeks vied with each other in pursuit of glory, as if they were a single nation, not a hodgepodge of cities ever embroiled in territorial and ideological disputes. The pan-Hellenic character of the games affected the poetry they produced. "One man at a people's bidding" is Pindar's way of describing himself, a private individual with a Hellenic message (***Olympian 13.*** 49).

The war against Persia did not end when Xerxes' vast armies were beaten back. In 478, the Greeks formed a league to guard against yet another threat from the East and to carry on the struggle. Athens became the dominant member of this alliance, known today as the Delian League, because, in the beginning, its headquarters were located on the island of Delos. But as Athens began to use her control over the League to further her own ambitions, what had been a mutual defense alliance of Greek states turned into an Athenian empire. The treasury of the League was eventually transferred from Delos to Athens and used to finance the rebuilding of the Acropolis, pillaged by the Persians. Membership in the League, at one time voluntary, became compulsory. One of the states that wanted out was Aigina, long a rival, at times an open enemy, of Athens. Hostilities between the two date from the end of the sixth century. In 459, war broke out between them again. Aigina was defeated, her fleet dismantled, and she was forced to pay a yearly tribute of thirty talents.

Behind this struggle for power and independence an equally important and bitter ideological struggle was being waged. Athens was a vigorous young democracy. Aigina, visible from the port of Athens and dependent, like her, on the sea for commerce, was ruled by a small number of ancient noble families whose claims to power were hereditary and who traced their ancestry back to the great heroes of the Trojan War and beyond them to Zeus himself. Other Greek cities were ruled by similar if less illustrious oligarchies. The struggle between them and Athens became a struggle not only among cities but also among forms of government and ways of life. When Athens succeeded in imposing her will, she uprooted institutions that displeased her and replaced them with democracies on whose loyalty she felt she could rely. More traditional, conservative states like Thebes, Sparta, and Aigina considered her an aggressor and exporter of revolution. Approximately twenty years after Pindar's death, the Peloponnesian War erupted between Athens with her allies and Sparta with hers. The seeds of destruction had been sown long before.

Already in his last years when the Athenians put an end to Aiginetan independence in 458, Pindar did not live to see the outbreak of the Peloponnesian War in 431. His last poem, ***Pythian 8,*** celebrates an Aiginetan victory. Indeed, a fourth of his odes celebrate victors from Aigina, a fact that must indicate a bond of mutual affection between the poet and the island. His own city, Thebes, suffered with

Aigina in the struggle against Athens, but not as much. For a brief period between 456 and 447 Boiotia was under Athenian domination; Aigina lost her freedom in 458 and did not recover it for over fifty years. Meanwhile her citizens continued to intrigue against Athens, with the result that when war broke out in 431, the Athenians removed them from their homes and brought in a new population. The Aiginetans returned at the end of the war in 403, but they were never again prominent in the life of Greece. Only the magnificent ruins from the temple of Aphaia and the odes of Pindar remain to tell us what they were.

The odes, however, give us a very different view of Greece from what we find in historical descriptions of the fifth century. Even when Pindar names what we would call an historical event it seems to have become no longer a simple event but a paradigm, a model, something to which he can appeal in illustration or defense of a truth whose relevance he wants to press home. At such moments we may feel that history has melded into myth. A more accurate way of describing it would be to say that myth and history are not as distinct from each other in Pindar's mind as they are in ours. The political and ideological sympathy between Thebes and Aigina, for example, appeared to Pindar as a reflection of their mythological relationship: Aigina and Theba, nymphs for whom the two places were named, were both daughters of the river god Asopos in Boiotia, where Thebes was located. Zeus had fallen in love with Aigina and had taken her from her original home in Boiotia to the island of Oinona, which thereafter bore her name. There he made love to her and there she bore him a son, Aiakos, founder of the Aiakid line. Thus when Pindar sang of Aiakid heroes, he could think of them as his remote ancestral cousins, descended from Aigina, sister of Pindar's "mother" Theba. Pindar speaks of these relationships as if they were actual, while we can only take them metaphorically. To Pindar, however, the Aiginetan warriors were what they were at the battle of Salamis because of their descent from the sons of Aiakos, the Aiakidai, who were even imagined to have fought beside them against the Persians. Similarly, a figure like Patroklos belongs, in our view, to a category utterly separate from that in which we place the Greek warriors who died fighting the Persians at the battle of Plataia; the funeral games of Patroklos in the *Iliad* and the funeral games conducted every fifth year in honor of those who fell at Plataia inhabit two different realms in our minds, the one belonging to mythology, the other to history. It was not so for the Greeks. For them, a living and apparent connection existed between what happens now and what happened in the remote past, between history in our sense of the word and myth in the Greek sense—not what was imagined to have happened or was now over, but what had happened and had also become, through poetry, part of a living tradition.

Almost from the moment of their first appearance, then, Pindar's odes have belonged both to poetry and to history. Written in order to preserve the memory and interpret the significance of certain real events, they have an historical emphasis not usually present in poetry. The further we have come in time from the original celebration that gave them birth and of which they were a part, the more their historical aspect has come into prominence. The passage of time has made it easy for us to forget that Pindar's odes are poems; it is tempting to treat them as documents. But, unlike most forms even of occasional poetry, a Pindaric ode did not begin its life as a document until sometime after Pindar had entrusted it to its patron. Up to that moment it was less an interpretation or a recollection of events than an event in and of itself. Because the odes were written for performance, we have in each of them not a record of fifth-century life, but an actual piece of it. (pp. 1-12)

PINDAR'S VICTORY SONGS

Pindar's odes come to us from that nebulous period in the history of Greek literature called The Archaic Age, falling roughly between the epic of Homer and the drama of Aeschylus. In lyric poetry its chief and almost sole representative is Pindar. His contemporary and rival in the art of the victory ode, Bacchylides, was known only from scattered pieces of his poetry until 1897, when the publication of a papyrus discovered in Egypt gave us a substantial portion of his work. Bacchylides' uncle Simonides is the earliest poet who we know wrote victory odes. Of Simonides' work in this genre there remain some titles, a few lines, but nothing complete. One or two of the other poets who composed lyric in the Archaic Age enjoy more renown than the pitiful remains of their work would lead us to expect. Sappho, the most famous, is little more than a ghost. Anacreon's fame is due more to his reflection in later poetry than to the slender substance of his own. The bitter voice of Archilochos speaks with such telling effect at the beginning of the archaic period that he has been called the inventor of personality. Archaic poetry would be more apprehensible to us if it were not mainly in ruins.

Pindar's work, the one edifice left standing among those ruins, is not easy to enter. It would be wise to remain outside a moment, studying its external characteristics. First is the surrounding landscape: the archaic period itself. A working notion of the fundamental habits and predilections of archaic poetry is essential preparation for reading Pindar. Second is the language in which his odes are written. We cannot go into much detail here, but awareness of a few facts will afford the view needed to appreciate the peculiar character of Pindar's work and to assess the degree to which it can be represented in English. This is even more the case with regard to the third external characteristic, the meter of the odes. If there were any way to experience the odes of Pindar as choral poetry, it would be through their rhythmical patterns. The complexities of these are too enormous to permit of anything beyond a brief description of major facts. The facts, however, are exciting in themselves, not only because Pindar was a consummate artist in metric but also because his meters and their laws are mainly a modern rediscovery. The same can be said of the fourth external characteristic, the conventions of the genre. It is only in the last half century that these have come into the light again. Like the meter, they have much to tell us about the original nature of choral song. But they are more important, for while we can forget the original meter when reading a translation, or keep it in the back of our minds as a silent reminder of what has been lost, if we do not recognize the presence and respond to the operation of the conventions of the victory song from moment to moment, we shall miss not only the sound but also the sense of Pindar's poetry. Finally, the more difficult aspects of Pindar's style must be considered, for their misinterpretation, perhaps more than anything, has contributed to the development of a Pindaric tradition in literature that has very little to do with Pindar as he actually was.

THE ARCHAIC PERIOD: PATTERNS OF THOUGHT AND STYLE

There is a scene in the *Iliad* that sets the tone for Pindar and other poets of his era perhaps better than any other: the scene in Book 24, where Achilleus consoles the aged Priam for the death of his son Hektor, killed in hand-to-hand combat by Achilleus himself. To Achilleus, there seems to be very little sweetness or light in human life, and he advises Priam not to miss the little that there is. The temptation to mourn forever must be resisted:

> We'll probe our wounds no more but let them rest,
> though grief lies heavy on us. Tears heal nothing,
> drying so stiff and cold.

The uselessness of sorrow is one reason for putting a limit to it. Another is that its causes lie beyond our control. What has happened to Priam is not singular, it is the rule. Achilleus sees what lies behind his own grief, behind Priam's, behind everyone's:

> This is the way
> the gods ordained the destiny of men,
> to bear such burdens in our lives, while they feel no affliction.

We may observe two tendencies in the way Achilleus proceeds: he does not dwell for long upon the particular but almost immediately sees in it the manifestation of a general truth, and he cannot think of the human condition without at the same time imagining its opposite. His observation, that the gods who feel no sorrow themselves send it in abundance to us, is not a complaint. The phrase "while they (the gods) feel no affliction" has almost the force of a defining epithet. Of course they feel no affliction, for they are gods. The thought of human misery automatically conjures the thought of divine bliss, and vice versa. He goes on:

> At the door of Zeus
> are those two urns of good and evil gifts
> that he may choose for us; and one for whom
> the lightning's joyous king dips in both urns
> will have by turns bad luck and good. But one
> to whom he sends all evil—that man goes
> contemptible by the will of Zeus; ravenous
> hunger drives him over the wondrous earth,
> unresting, without honor from gods or men.

The argument Achilleus is making, that the gods are responsible for everything that happens to us, immediately takes on concrete expression. Achilleus speaks both as a teacher and as a storyteller. What he has to say he says in two ways at once, assertively and mythologically. A little later, when he is urging Priam to eat, he appeals to the example of Niobe in order to strengthen his persuasion. All these tendencies—to see the general behind the particular, to grasp one thing by contrast with its opposite, to trace human vicissitudes to the will of the gods, and to explain, appreciate, or find the right response to a present situation through reference to myth or proverb—remain as dominant forms of thought and style in archaic poetry.

Achilleus does not imagine Zeus sending mortals nothing but good. Some good, yes, or all bad—but never good unalloyed with evil. This too is a dominant feature of archaic poetry: it is steeped in profound pessimism. Like Achilleus, Pindar sees the gods dispensing more evil to men than good, and he urges the man to whom he is speaking to bear up under the circumstances:

> If, Hieron, you understand,
> recall the proverb now:
> the deathless gods
> dole out to death-bound men
> two pains for every good.
> Fools make nothing of either.
> The noble turn both to advantage,
> folding pain within,
> and showing beauty without.
>
> (***Pythian 3.*** 80-83)

Ancient and modern commentators on this passage have accused Pindar of misunderstanding Homer: Homer's two jars, one good and one bad, have apparently become three jars, two bad and one good. Pindar, however, is adapting a traditional image to his own purposes, as he often does. In his lines, the evil is exactly twice the good. The impression of a finer distinction carries over into a much more precise and succinct bit of advice than that given by Achilleus to Priam. Pindar urges Hieron to respond to reality as a wise man would. The conscious decision to suppress what is painful and to put on display what is not takes wisdom to conceive and strength to execute. It involves an acceptance of, and triumph over, pain. And it has an artistic emphasis that is typical of Pindar: Hieron, in arranging the happy and the unhappy elements of his life, is similar to Pindar arranging the light and dark elements of his poem. The artist in words counsels the king to be an artist in character.

Still, we may wonder why this pessimism, characteristic of Homer and early Greek poetry in general, should make so strong an appearance in Pindar's odes, which are written, after all, in order to celebrate a happy event, a success. The answer is that Pindar's odes also *evaluate* success. Pindar sees success against the background of failure and death, as Achilleus saw the happiness of the gods against the background of mortal sorrow and affliction. Though Pindar has been hired to rejoice in someone's behalf, he knows that a simple shout for joy makes little impression in the world and that one man's fortune may provoke another's resentment. The traditional poetic wisdom to which he is heir also puts a very slight premium on human happiness, a still slighter one on human power and understanding. Most happiness is foolish, most understanding unhappy, and those who pride themselves on either may discover that the gods have deceived them. For happiness, finally, is the gods' prerogative. In a world where the gods may take offense at human exultation, it is *dangerous* to exult. Such attitudes come, as it were, to bear on Pindar's poetry from without: they are in the wind, they are the milieu, the ethical assumptions that govern archaic poetry. Sometimes they become explicit, sometimes they remain in the background. But they are always there.

All these habits of mind affect Pindar's style too. If one thing leads him to think of its opposite, he may do so immediately: we will miss the kind of grammatical linkage to which we are accustomed. The figure of litotes is very common: instead of stating something positively ("this man is brave"), Pindar will give us the negative of its counterpart ("he is no coward"). Moments of high emotion will suddenly yield to moments of cautious restraint. The audience would have had to adjust to a dramatic shift, but not to a disconcerting one, for they and the poet shared in the traditional distrust of human happiness. They expected the poet to remind them of it. As the Muses' representative, he should wield authority, interpreting both the present occasion and the myth he has chosen to tell. In addition, the poet's assumption of the role of moral instructor would be a signal to his audience. They would know, for example, that a myth has been concluded when suddenly the poet speaks in his own voice, pronouncing a maxim or even a series of maxims, while we at such moments are liable to feel jolted by an irrelevant intrusion. We do not appreciate, let alone expect, the poet's sage advice or wise counsel, for with us he has lost his ancient authority. Pindar's audience would anticipate his teaching. They would look forward to it, wondering how much he would extract from the occasion in the form of memorable utterances. These might come singly or in clusters of seemingly independent ideas. What is in fact an argument or development of themes will appear as a series of conclusions in several arguments to which we never hear the proofs. The effect is confusing to the eye that scans the page. On the ancient audience, it probably made the double impression of massiveness and speed: massiveness in the juxtaposition of ideas, speed in the omission of the logical steps leading to them.

Pindar, indeed, composes with a maximum of compression. We may remember what Ezra Pound observed about the German word *dichten,* "to compose poetry." Pound gave it a Latin gloss: *condensare,* to condense, to compress. It makes for slow reading, inviting contemplation. If we had the benefit of seeing and hearing a Pindaric ode performed, the connections between its various parts might be more apparent. If we were familiar with the range of truths taken for granted in this kind of poetry (some of them are described above), we would be more adept at supplying the connections that the poet, in his sovereign will to forge ahead, has omitted to spell out. Most important, if we were schooled in the special grammar of the victory ode, its conventions, we would recognize the various signs Pindar employs in moving from theme to theme. But if we were in such command of the genre, we would feel the compression, not the omission, of the thought. It would still be true, however, that archaic poets, and Pindar in particular, place greater emphasis on moving ahead than on smoothing the transitions between one section of the poem and the next. The net effect in Pindar is one of his most distinctive qualities, the pleasing ruggedness described by Dionysius of Halicarnassus. It is due both to Pindar's disposition and to the nature of the victory ode. The meters and the language, as we shall see, are composite things; the same is true of the ode itself: it consists of a number of parts that the poet combines into a whole. Pindar seems to have preferred placing masses solidly together. His rival Bacchylides achieves a greater fluidity in his verse, but also less grandeur.

Another composite entity is the poet's own personality. He is both a private and a public figure. The Archaic Age is an age of wandering bards, itinerant choir-masters hired by towns, tribes, and individuals to conduct choruses of youths or maidens in the celebration of gods and of great events. The earliest remains of choral poetry show us the poet giving a voice to the different members of his choir. In the maiden song composed by Alcman in Sparta during the seventh century, we overhear the girls praising each other's beauty, their talent in the dance, their grace in song. As far as we can tell, the poet's personality has merged with that of his chorus. There is a similar authorial anonymity in one of Pindar's fragments, a *paian* written for the people of Keos. Here the choral voice belongs not to Pindar, but to the island of Keos and its people.

The situation is more complex in the victory ode, which is a choral performance and therefore a more or less public event; but it is composed in honor of an individual. Praise of a god or even of a city invites no one's resentment. Except, perhaps, in unusual political circumstances, there are no problems attending it. But praise of an individual in a public setting is another matter. The introduction of the victor into a choral ode has consequences for the poet too—indeed, especially for him. He and the victor must face the potential resentment of other men and of the gods. By its very nature, then, the victory ode will demand tact. At the same time, it is the duty of the poet to see the significance of the present occasion in all its facets, and to exult for the victor. He should balance exultation with advice, warning both his audience and his patron not to offend the gods. For all this he will need the authority of the Muses who have instilled the power of song in him. The clearest evidence of its presence in him will be his poetic skill. In the victory ode that skill is often taxed most by the composite character of the song itself. It is no accident that Pindar often draws attention to his poetic role and mastery just at those moments when he is making a transition from one section of the ode to another.

The reader will notice, finally, that Pindar is proud of his art and does not hesitate to say so. No doubt his willingness to sing his own praises expresses something about his character, but it is also part of his heritage as a choral poet of the Archaic Age. Alcman, Ibycus, and Bacchylides also proclaim their power in song, and it is not mere egotism for them to do so. Their art, choral poetry, is first of all an event. There is much more involved in it than pen and ink. Indeed, the participation of the chorus, the practice sessions, the execution of dance patterns to express the ode, the playing of music to accompany it, and, not least, the gathering of the audience to hear and see it—that is, the entire occasion, with its various formal and ritual components—all these things make such an impression on the poetry that it tends to merge with them: the medium of the song becomes its subject. The poet will invite the audience to share with him in the genesis of the poem. His skill and inspiration, after all, place a guarantee of permanence on all these things, the only guarantee possible. Hence, the greatness of the poet is not an offensive theme to his audience—it is a legitimate subject of his verse. In Pindar's odes, we have the fullest surviving expression of an age that valued poetry as a gift from the gods. (pp. 21-6)

Frank J. Nisetich, in an introduction to Pindar's Victory Songs, *translated by Frank J. Nisetich, The Johns Hopkins University Press, 1980, pp. 1-77.*

Hugh Lloyd-Jones (lecture date 1982)

[*Lloyd-Jones is an eminent British classical scholar and critic best known for his study of Greek tragedy and religion,* The Justice of Zeus *(1971). In the following lecture, he provides a survey of twentieth-century Pindar scholarship, charting the process by which a growing understanding of Pindar's poetic conventions informed a novel appreciation of the poet's achievement. The critic further places Pindar in historical context and discusses the archaic conception of the universe.*]

By no means every good poet can be credited with a master mind. To deserve such a designation, a poet does not need to have a philosophy, or to have versified the philosophy of others; he does need to have produced a considerable body of verse which communicates a distinctive vision of the world, conveyed with great imaginative power. If this canon is applied with strictness, only great poets will be found to satisfy it.

A discus thrower, from a fifth-century B.C. Panathenaic amphora.

The poet I have chosen to speak about has a name familiar to most educated people. Since the Renaissance several famous poets have imitated him, or have believed that they were doing so; for example Ronsard and Chiabrera, Cowley and Gray, the young Goethe and Hölderlin. There are many translations, including good modern ones by Richmond Lattimore, Maurice Bowra, and recently Frank Nisetich, and much scholarly work has been devoted to Pindaric interpretation. But since the Renaissance comparatively few people with a working knowledge of the Greek language have studied Pindar with serious attention; and among these only a minority would have claimed, stating their honest opinion, that he deserved to be considered as a master mind in the sense that I have just described.

This is partly because Pindar has always had a reputation for being difficult. One cannot deny that he is difficult, but the difficulty has been exaggerated; his style and language, once superficial awkwardnesses have been overcome, are hardly as difficult as those of Sophocles. His text is better preserved than that of any of the great tragedians; and though some of his poems are written in complicated metres, about half are written in dactylo-epitrite, whose main features can be set out in half a page. The main difficulties in the way of literary appreciation lie in the conventions of the genre he writes in; the sometimes abrupt transitions from one topic to another are often hard to grasp and the unity of the poems has proved so hard to comprehend that many scholars have denied that they have any unity at all. We need to learn to read Pindar not only in the sense of how to construe him, but in that of how to view each poem and each part of each poem in the light of the tradition it belongs to; and it is only very lately that scholars have begun to give readers the assistance that they need.

Readers would not have been scared away by Pindar's difficulty if they had been convinced that the effort needed to understand him would be rewarded; but for many years the people best qualified to help them have not encouraged them to make that effort. The great period of German scholarship which ended, roughly speaking, with the fall of the empire did much for the editing of the text and of the extensive ancient commentaries, and for the philological and historical elucidation of Pindaric problems. But its principal figures complained that Pindar's world was strange to modern minds, and that he lacked sympathy with the new science and philosophy that in his time was active in the eastern part of the Greek world. They did not regard him as the equal of the Attic tragedians, who in their view stood for progress while Pindar was the poet of an aristocratic world doomed to rapid extinction. Even Gilbert Murray, whose feeling for poetry strongly responded to Pindar's verse, complained that Pindar was 'a poet and nothing more'; he would not have credited him with being a master mind. A living scholar who has done much for Pindar, Bruno Snell [in his *The Discovery of the Mind,* 1953], writes that in Pindar's time Attic tragedy was requiring that justice should be done on earth, and in consequence was making many demands not only of men but of the gods, but that Pindar kept himself far from any such thoughts, which seemed to him presumptuous.

If a great poet belongs to a world remote from our own and gives expression to its outlook, that is no reason why we should not respond to the greatness of his poetry; it is enough to think of Homer, or of Dante. The notion that, because the world of Pindar's aristocratic patrons was visibly perishing before his death, therefore his poetry is somehow less valuable than that of poets belonging to communities whose prosperity was then beginning scarcely deserves respect. Neither does the complaint that a lyric poet shows no interest in science and philosophy; if Keats reproached Newton with having explained the mystery of the rainbow, shall we refuse to read Keats's poetry on that account? In fact the tragedians see life in terms of the traditional religion scarcely less than Pindar does, for all the play Euripides may make with the new rhetoric and with casual allusions to the new speculations.

Many people are prejudiced against Pindar for political and social reasons. He was an aristocrat, belonging to one of the great clans whose members were spread over different civic communities. His own city, Thebes, belonged to the division of the Greek race called Aeolian, and like most Dorian and Aeolian communities was ruled by an aristocracy; at the time of the Persian invasion of 480, geography determined that Thebes had about as much chance of resisting the invader as Denmark in 1940 or Czechoslovakia in 1945. Many of those who commissioned Pindar to celebrate their victories in the great games were noblemen; some were even monarchs, like the rulers of the Greek colonies in Sicily or in Cyrene. In his poetry, Pindar often stresses the importance of breeding; learning is no use, he says, unless nature has made one apt to learn. A distinguished ancient historian, perhaps not especially skilful in linguistic or aesthetic matters [M. I. Finley], seems to think it morally wrong for anyone to admire Pindar's poetry.

We should not now make the mistake of exaggerating the differences between the Dorian, Aeolian, and Ionian divisions of the Greeks. The poetry of the archaic period, like its art, cut across these barriers; thus Pindar's older contemporary Simonides and his nephew Bacchylides came from the Ionian island of Ceos, but this did not prevent them from investing their choral lyric poetry with the thin patina of West Greek dialect which was customary in a genre belonging traditionally to western Greece. Pindar did not write poems only for individuals; he was sometimes commissioned by communities, including, on more than one occasion, democratic Athens. He often proclaims his sympathy with his patrons of the moment, and several times praises the Dorian institutions observed in Syracuse and Aegina; yet he nowhere, if his text is understood correctly, makes a declaration of political allegiance, as Yeats did when he wrote a poem for General O'Duffy and his Blueshirts. Indeed, W. S. Barrett [in *Journal of Hellenic Studies,* XCIII (1973)] has made it seem probable that in the ***Twelfth Olympian*** he saluted the new régime in Himera which had replaced one controlled by his former patrons, the rulers of Akragas. The truth is that he was not a romantic individualist, like Yeats, but a poet operating within the terms of fixed religious and poetical conventions, and like the tragedians he is concerned less with what is temporary and accidental in human life than with what is permanent and fundamental.

The preponderance in Pindar's extant work of odes written to celebrate athletic victories is due to accident. His poems were collected by the scholars of Alexandria in seventeen books. Only six of these consisted of poems written for men; these were the four books of victory odes for athletes, with one book of enkomia and one of dirges. The remaining eleven books consisted of poems written for the service of the gods, most of them what we should call hymns of one sort or another. Of this large output only the victory odes have survived virtually entire. But we have enough fragments of Pindar's other poems, some from quotations by other authors and others from papyri discovered in the sands of Egypt, to have a very fair notion of their character. It is clear that the religious background, the use of myth, and the general outlook expressed in the victory odes were, like their language, style, and metre, similar to those found in the other poetry of Pindar.

The convention of the victory ode was already established well before the date of the ***Tenth Pythian,*** the earliest poem of Pindar whose date we know. The great poet Simonides, born in 556, more than thirty years before Pindar, must long before then have been an established writer in this genre. Almost all surviving victory odes were written to honour victories won in the four great games held in connection with Panhellenic religious festivals. The Olympic Games at Olympia in the western Peloponnese and the Pythian Games at Delphi were held every four years, and the Nemean Games at Nemea in the Argolid and the Isthmian Games on the Isthmus of Corinth were held every two years. It is generally assumed that each victory ode was performed, with an accompaniment of dance and music created by the poet, by a chorus of men, trained if circumstances permitted by the poet himself; the performance took place either at the scene of the games soon after the victory, or later at the victor's home. Most remarkably, the poet speaks through the chorus in the first person singular, in his own person. This is not the case in all of Pindar's poetry; in his poems for choirs of maidens, for example, the chorus speaks in its own character. The lost poems of which we know most are the paeans, a kind of lyric poem in honour of Apollo or Artemis or both, but occasionally extended to the service of other gods. In some paeans the chorus speaks in its own person, but in others the poet speaks. Was every victory ode performed by a chorus? Till lately it was believed that the lyric narrative poems on epic themes composed by the sixth-century Sicilian poet Stesichorus were performed chorally; but now that we know that several of them had many more than a thousand lines it seems likelier that the poet or another chanted them to the accompaniment of the lyre, as rhapsodes did the poetry of Homer. One of Pindar's victory odes, the ***Fourth Pythian,*** is three hundred lines long, and largely consists of epic narrative; I wonder whether this, and perhaps also other victory odes, was not performed, as Pindar's enkomia must have been, by a single person.

A victory ode normally contains certain recurring elements. It praises a particular victor on a particular occasion, and usually his family and his city also; it usually contains a modicum of general reflection upon human life in relation to the gods, and often the narration of a myth judged to be appropriate to the occasion. But these elements occur in different orders, and are linked together by different methods of transition. Since August Boeckh early in the nineteenth century laid the foundations of modern Pindaric scholarship, the unity of the victory ode has been the subject of much controversy.

For the greater part of that century, most scholars believed in its essential unity. Boeckh himself distinguished between an objective unity determined by the occasion for which the ode was written and a subjective unity dictated by the poet's personal preoccupations. His collaborator Ludolf Dissen introduced the notion of a 'Grundgedanke', or central thought; he and many others did harm by trying to boil down the content of whole poems into painfully trite and jejune summaries. At the end of the century this produced a violent reaction, whose main proponent was Wilamowitz [in his *Pindaros,* 1922]. Sharply rejecting the idea that a victory ode had any unity, he and his followers concentrated on the philological exegesis of the text and on its historical aspect, taking comparatively little interest in the construction of the poems and the poet's art. In 1928 Wolfgang Schadewaldt [in *Der Aufbau des pindarischen Epinikions*] so far modified this trend as to offer a refined version of Boeckh's objective and subjective unity. Objective unity was determined by what Schadewaldt called the 'programme' of the ode, the praise of the victor and his home and family and other historical elements; to these were added the general reflection and the narration of the myth; and upon this material the poet imposed other matter derived from his own thoughts and feelings. A different kind of neo-unitarianism has been advocated by Hermann Fränkel [in his *Early Greek Poetry and Philosophy,* 1975], who found the main content of each ode to lie in its contribution to the general picture of the divine government of the world and the values which it generates that is built up by the poet's work as a whole. In his detailed exposition of Pindaric poems Fränkel has proved one of the best modern critics; but to say that the individual ode, composed for performance on a particular occasion, must be explained in terms of its relation to the entire corpus, like different pieces of a jigsaw puzzle that are given away in different packets of some product, is an odd way of dealing with the specific problem of the poem's unity. Other kinds of neo-unitarianism, based upon a more or less vaguely conceived symbolism, seem to me to have been a good deal less effective.

A new trend started in America during the early sixties, one not unconnected with Milman Parry's work on the Homeric formula, and indeed with the general movement towards 'structuralist' analysis of poetry and other things. In 1962 Elroy R. Bundy [in *Studia Pindarica* I, II] brought out detailed studies of two Pindaric victory odes, the ***Eleventh Olympian*** and the ***First Isthmian.*** He strongly insisted on the importance of understanding the conventions of the epinician genre, showing how often formal devices that conform to standard patterns are used at corresponding places in different poems in order to effect transitions. In several places he and his followers have been able to resolve in terms of such devices problems which earlier scholars had tried to explain by assuming the presence of personal or historical allusions for which there was no independent evidence. For this purpose Bundy invented a formidable technical terminology, oddly recalling the edition published at Wittenberg in 1616 by Erasmus Schmid, who analysed each ode in terms of the categories prescribed in the rhetorical handbooks of the early Roman Empire. As an Ariadne's clue to the unity of the victory ode, Bundy offered the principle that its main purpose is to praise the victor, and that all that it contains ultimately subserves that purpose.

Two years after Bundy's studies there appeared a survey of Pindaric criticism from the time of Boeckh, in which another American scholar, David Young [in *The Minnesota Review,* IV (1964)], forcefully argued for a not dissimilar approach; he later followed it with studies of four odes, contending that each is 'a unified, meaningful work of literary art'. Young objects that Bundy recognizes no unity in the epinician beyond mere linear continuity, and concentrates too narrowly upon the theme of praise. He himself uses his grasp of the traditional themes and the conventional rhetoric of the genre to explain the complex but coherent working-out of each poem's argument. Since then a number of scholars in Europe as well as in America have adopted a similar approach.

The new movement has done a great service to the understanding of Pindar by emphasizing the importance of convention in his art, and so helping to correct the vast damage done by the fatal conjunction of nineteenth-century historicism with nineteenth-century romanticism. The romantics held all poetry, and particularly lyric poetry, to be the spontaneous outpouring of the poet's sincerest feelings; a genuine poet felt an overmastering urge to express in verse his own most deeply held convictions. In many ways they appreciated the Greek tragic and lyric poets better than their eighteenth-century precursors, whose understanding of the poetry of archaic and classical Greece was limited by their preoccupation with the rules of their own classicism; and it was natural that they should assume that the Greek poets were like themselves, gravely underrating the importance of form and convention in their work. Wilamowitz in his famous book on Pindar, published in 1922, when he was 74 years of age, adopted a biographical approach; so did Maurice Bowra as late as 1964 [in his *Pindar*], never doubting that Pindar was a lyric poet like Yeats, expressing his personal attitude to the world and to those with whom he might have dealings. Both relied upon the data furnished by the ancient lives of Pindar and the ancient commentaries upon his work, adding further matter based on modern inference from the actual poems. But as Mary Lefkowitz in particular has shown [in her *The Lives of the Greek Poets,* 1981], little reliance can be placed upon the biographical traditions about the early Greek poets; much of them has no securer basis than jokes from comedy later taken seriously by owlish grammarians or frivolous speculations based upon the poets' actual works. The most solid part of the ancient commentators' evidence for Pindar's life is chronological;

lists of the victors at Olympia and Delphi were available, so that most Olympian and Pythian odes are dated. But the dates of Nemean and Isthmian odes are matter for conjecture; and the attempts made by stylometric methods to guess at the date of poems whose date we do not know have not, so far at least, had very much success.

Romanticism as well as historicism has derived encouragement from the ancient commentators, who seem to operate with a theory of poetic inspiration deriving, in the last resort, from Plato. The poet writes in frenzy, they assume, as though improvising; when he employs the traditional device of apologizing for a digression by saying that in his excitement he has been carried far out of his path, they innocently take his word for it. Since the Renaissance a vast amount of misunderstanding has been fostered by the second ode of Horace's fourth book, in which he warns a would-be imitator of Pindar of the hazards of the attempt, depicting Pindar's verse as a rushing torrent, 'bound by no laws'. In fact Pindar scrupulously obeys many laws, not only those of a strict form and metre, the same pattern of strophe, antistrophe, and epode being repeated many times in the same poem, but the conventions of the genre which it is the great merit of the new movement to have made us properly aware of. In doing so it has placed new weapons in the hands of those who would defend the essential unity of the victory ode, and since it started anti-unitarianism has been very much on the defensive.

But the new trend has its dangers, and we must guard against them. Bundy himself, as I know from talks with him in 1969, six years before his untimely death at only 51, regretted the forbidding dryness of his revolutionary studies, and was planning work which would do better justice to Pindar as a poet. Inevitably his approach has been adopted by a number of those humdrum scholars who are forever on the look-out for a mechanical recipe for getting results, and these have created a dreary scholasticism, treating an ode as a collection of commonplaces strung together by a few stock devices. In fact the commonplaces were originally chosen because of their relation to reality, and both they and the traditional devices are used as the context demands, and are skilfully adapted by the poet according to his needs, so that to talk of 'formulas' in this connection is out of place. The clue to understanding lies, indeed, in the knowledge that above all else the poet aims to praise the victor; but Pindar was a human being writing to please other human beings, and those who wish to understand him will neglect the historical dimension only at their peril. He does honour to the victor by placing the moment of felicity which his triumph gives him in the context of his historical situation against the background of the permanent situation of the world as the gods govern it.

This is not the only danger that confronts the new unitarianism. A second is that of exaggerating the significance, sometimes real enough, of the repetitions of words and ideas within a poem; this is sometimes combined with an exaggerated notion of the importance of symbolism in Pindar's work. A third danger is that of using excessive ingenuity to try to prove the myth narrated in a given poem to be relevant to that poem's theme; in many cases we must be content to observe that the myth illustrates Pindar's view of heroism and its relation to the gods only in a general way. To have unity, a Pindaric ode does not need to have a streamlined unity.

In the light of these considerations, let us consider the recurrent elements of the epinician ode. First, there is the religious background. Pindar is above all else a religious poet, and much of the failure to understand him has been bound up with the failure to understand the Greek religion that pervades his poetry. That failure has encouraged the romantic error of taking Pindar's religion for a personal construction of his own. For a believer in the archaic Greek religion, to praise a mortal man was a hazardous enterprise. The gods are immortal, and alone enjoy true happiness; men are the creatures of a day, and are subject to all the misfortunes which the day may bring. The gods govern the universe, understandably enough, in their own interest, and with little regard for that of men; the various creation-myths make men an accidental or a casual element in the scheme of things. The gods in Pindar's poetry are most vividly realized as individual personalities, and something of the same concreteness invests even the personified abstractions which so often figure in his work. But these gods work through real forces in the world, so that to deny their existence would be pointless, since the reality of the forces which they stand for cannot be denied.

No man can be pronounced fortunate till he is dead; at any moment an unforeseen catastrophe may overwhelm the happiest among mankind. But men may enjoy moments of felicity; these are dependent on the favour of the gods, and come most of all to men descended from the unions with mortal women which the gods allowed themselves during the heroic age. Such men's heroic nature makes them capable of becoming rulers, warriors, athletes, or poets. Nature is vitally important, and without natural aptitude education is in vain. But natural gifts by themselves are not enough; hard labour and endurance are required, and the need for them is quite as strongly stressed as that for natural gifts. Not that even the conjunction of natural ability and strenuous effort can command success; in the last resort, all mortal triumph is dependent on the favour of the gods. The gods may grudge success to any mortal; the divine envy which may make them do so is conceived by Pindar not as mere spite, but as a facet of divine justice, whose workings mortals are not always able to perceive.

Any man who praises other men must remain always conscious of the danger of provoking envy, not only divine but human. Envy is a force which any man who strives after any kind of *areta,* excellence, must fight; of this the man who praises others must remain aware. Hesiod, the greatest Boeotian poet before Pindar, had stressed the community between kings and poets, both of whom derive authority from Zeus, kings directly, but poets through Apollo and the Muses. Conscious of his own *areta* as an inspired poet, Pindar has a deep sense of community with the men of action, rulers, warriors, and athletic victors, whom he praises; like them he has to struggle against envy, not simply that of rivals, but that which any man who praises others has to strive to overcome. If the poet can contrive to vanquish envy and to place the victory in its setting in the world of gods as well as men, then the victor's brief moment of felicity can in a limited but real sense be made eternal.

To the modern mind it may seem strange, even ridiculous, that athletes should be coupled with rulers and warriors as bearers of *areta.* That is not how the archaic Greeks saw the matter. A victory in the games, with their strong religious associations, carried vast prestige; athletes endured arduous training of a kind that fitted them for war as well as triumph in the games. The Aeginetans, for whom Pindar wrote more odes of victory than for any other community, won the prize for valour awarded by the Greek army after Salamis; the Sicilian tyrants, whatever modern moralizers may say about their ideology, saved the Greeks of Sicily from the Carthaginians and Etruscans. Again, the conventional references to the customary fee should not lead us to suppose, as ancient comic poets did in jest and later grammarians in all seriousness, that Pindar and Simonides were especially mercenary. One proof of the noble man's nobility, according to the poetic convention, was his readiness to spend his money generously in assuring that his fame would live.

Yeats lived at a time when there was no generally accepted picture of the world to serve as background for his poetry, so that he was compelled to construct one for himself out of very disparate materials. Pindar, like Dante, inherited the picture of the world fashioned by the religion of his people. The greatest error of romantic criticism has been to treat this as though it were a personal philosophy or religion of the poet's own making; we can see that it is common to him and to other writers in the genre, both to the older Simonides of whom we know little and to the younger Bacchylides of whom we possess large parts of fourteen victory odes. If we make allowances for the differences of genre and avoid the pervasive error of reading ideas into ancient tragedy that are not there, we can see that it is not very different from the religious outlook that we find in Aeschylus or Sophocles.

This romantic misconception has been fostered by the force and clarity of Pindar's many statements in the first person, which give the reader nurtured on romantic verse the irresistible impression of being in contact with a powerful and independent poetic personality. That is in a sense true; but we shall not appreciate Pindar's poetry correctly unless we are aware of how much he has in common with other writers in the same genre, with Greek archaic poetry in general, and with all believers in archaic Greek religion. Presented by a poet whose imagination has grasped its tragic truth with utter honesty and clarity, the austere world of early Greek religion comes across to us in all its beauty and with all its hardness.

Against this backcloth the poet must place the victory won by his client of the moment. The odes commonly start with an elaborate prelude, ultimately deriving, it would seem, from the invocation of deities with which cult-hymns began. Sometimes the poet invokes a god, but more often a personified abstraction, or the hero or heroine who personifies a place; he may address his own Muse, who is about to perform in honour of the victor; he may start with general reflection or with praise of the victory; or he may describe his ode by means of an elaborate simile, likening it to a cup or bowl ceremonially offered by one man to another or to one of the splendid treasuries which wealthy communities built at the great religious centres to contain their dedications.

Nothing is more indicative of the distorting effect exercised by romanticism upon Pindaric criticism than the proneness of critics to assume that the mention of the victory and the enumeration of other victories won by the victor and by other members of his family must have been irksome duties which the poet resented and was eager to get out of the way as soon as possible in order to give expression to his personal preoccupations. In fact the victory is the starting-point and epicentre of the entire poem, and the other victories of the family must be mentioned too, since they help to demonstrate that these men possess that nobility of nature which makes effort fruitful and wins the divine favour which alone can bring success. In the hands of an indifferent poet this part of the poem might indeed turn out monotonous, but Pindar displays the greatest virtuosity in the avoidance of this danger. With typical Greek realism he frequently remarks that not all the members even of the greatest athletic families possess equal gifts; talent often skips a generation or so. What counted for the Greeks was victory, and Pindar has no compunction in imagining the discomfiture of the defeated rivals of the winner. Not that the odes dwell at all frequently on the incidents of the games, despite the poet's fondness for athletic metaphors.

The character and history of the victors, their families, and the civic communities they belonged to stimulate the poet to recall history as well as legend; to the Greeks of his time the boundary between the two was vague and almost non-existent. Naturally the part of the poems dealing with the victors takes on a special interest when they are great personages like Arkesilas, king of Cyrene, Hieron, ruler of Syracuse, Theron, ruler of Akragas, and other members of his family. A poetic convention that is as old as Hesiod allows Pindar to address such people as an equal, and to advise them to persist in their noble ways, advice which the audience knows there is no possibility of their neglecting, any more than Britannia might reject the advice of those who in song urge her to rule the waves.

Most victory odes include the narration of a myth, sometimes short, but sometimes very long. Pindar's narrative technique is masterly; he knows what to leave out, and has a flair for the significant detail. Sometimes it is not easy to perceive the myth's special relevance to the situation; but at other times that relevance is so obvious that one cannot help asking why it is not obvious in every case.

In the ***Third Pythian,*** for instance, the myth has a peculiar aptness. This is not a true victory ode, but a poem of consolation addressed to Hieron, who was suffering from a painful illness. Pindar starts by expressing the wish that he could call back from the dead Chiron, the noble centaur, who taught the great healer Asklepios. He tells how Koronis, when pregnant with Asklepios by Apollo, broke the law of the gods by having intercourse with a mortal; Apollo destroyed her, but as the funeral pyre was about to consume her body, snatched the child from her womb and brought him to Chiron for his education. Some poets might have found it wiser not to mention that in the end Asklepios was persuaded by a great fee to break, like his mother, the law of the gods by raising a man from the dead, so that Zeus destroyed him with the thunderbolt; but Pindar goes on to tell it, as a reminder of man's mortality and fallibility. Later, he recalls to Hieron words of Homer which he interprets to mean that the gods give men two parts of evil for one part of good; even Peleus and Cadmus, the two heroes who married goddesses, met with grievous misfortunes. Human happiness never lasts for long, and a man must adapt himself to whatever fortune the gods send him. Pindar concludes the poem with a reminder that poetry can confer on human triumphs a kind of permanence.

Still more perfect is the applicability of the myth of the ***First Pythian.*** The poem honours a Pythian victory of Hieron's chariot, but also celebrates his foundation of the new city of Aitna, founded on the site of Katane, the modern Catania, as a kingdom for Hieron's son Deinomenes. Very near that city lies the mighty volcano from which it takes its name; beneath it, in the legend, but stretching all the way from Etna to Vesuvius, lies Typhos or Typhoeus, the mightiest of the giants who have challenged Zeus. The poem starts with a solemn invocation of the Apolline instrument, the lyre, and a description of the celestial music played to the gods upon Olympus by Apollo and the Muses. Even the savage war-god yields to that music's spell; but the enemies of Zeus are infuriated by its strains. One such is Typhos, and the poet memorably describes his fiery breath, which only a few years before the poem was written had burst forth in a devastating eruption. Pindar prays that he may never displease Zeus, interprets the Pythian victory of Hieron as a good omen for the new city, and prays to Apollo, lord of Delphi, for its prosperity. All human excellence depends upon the gods, and Pindar prays to them for Hieron's welfare, making allusion to his great achievements. Since Hieron is grievously sick, he is compared with Philoktetes, the hero whose poisoned foot did not prevent him from making a great contribution to the Greek victory over Troy. Now Pindar returns to Aitna and his hopes for it; he prays Zeus to keep off the ever present danger from the barbarous enemies of the Greeks, with an allusion to the glorious victory which Hieron had won at Cumae, near to Vesuvius, four years earlier, and coupling it with the earlier victory of Hieron's brother and predecessor, Gelon, over the Carthaginians and with those of the mainland Greeks over the Persians. So the poet comes to his final praise of Hieron, contrasting the fame won by his nobility and generosity with the ill repute of an earlier Sicilian tyrant, the cruel Phalaris. Happiness and fame are the two greatest things for mortals. In this great poem, the continuing presence of the giant, a natural enemy of the beauty and order which the Olympian gods stand for, brought low by Zeus but living and always to be reckoned with, mirrors the abiding threat to Sicily from the barbarians; the Greeks of Sicily lived a life as precarious as that of modern Israel. It mirrors also the threat to Hieron's dynasty from its enemies; a few years after the performance, Hieron was dead and the rule of his dynasty was at an end. The myth's significance is even wider, for it relates also to man's position in the world; by great exertions he may merit and enjoy the favour of the gods, but its continuance cannot be guaranteed, and nothing that is human lasts for ever.

But in other cases the relevance of a myth is far from obvious. In the ***First Nemean,*** for example, written for the Syracusan general Chromios, Pindar tells how the infant Herakles strangled the snakes sent by Hera to kill him and his brother, and in the ***Eleventh Pythian,*** written for the Theban boy Thrasydaios, he tells the story of the murder of Agamemnon and the revenge of his son Orestes. A myth may be relevant in more than one way; so that any legend about Herakles is appropriate to a Nemean victory, because he founded the Nemean games, and any myth connected with Delphi, like the myth of Orestes, is relevant to a Pythian victory. But another reason why these myths are relevant is that both illustrate the strength that goes with true nobility, and the power and justice of the gods; Heracles and Orestes through their valour triumph against overwhelming odds. Just so when Pindar honours an Aeginetan victor, he always recounts one of the many legends about the great heroes descended from the founder of Aegina, Aiakos; all such stories illustrate the fundamental principles that govern the universe of archaic Greek religion.

Already in the seventh-century Spartan choral poet Alcman we find mythic narrative closely linked with gnomic reflection; either a reflection prompted by the situation may be illustrated by a myth, or else a myth may prompt such a reflection. Taken out of context, Pindar's gnomic reflections might be made to appear as so many commonplaces, despite the striking manner in which they are expressed; but in their proper contexts they do not give that impression, unlike many of the similar reflections in the epinicians of Bacchylides.

Transition between the various elements of the poems is effected by means of various technical devices, most of which Bundy furnished with somewhat alarming technical names. It is important to recognize these and to understand the function they perform; but it is equally important to realize that they are never trotted out mechanically, but are cunningly disposed to suit the context and the requirements of the poet's art. There is absolutely no fixed order for the elements of the victory ode, each poem having not only its own metrical pattern but its own structure with its own particular shape; the claims of certain scholars to have 'created a generalized formal model' cannot be substantiated.

It is precisely when we have made full allowance for the element of convention both in Pindar's picture of the universe and in his literary technique that the power of his poetic genius makes the most profound impression. To grasp what is most distinctive in his art we may start by comparing him with his younger contemporary Bacchylides. Bacchylides has often been unfairly blamed for not having been a Pindar. He is an admirable poet, whose smoother and lighter style has its own special quality, one seen to less advantage in his victory odes than in the brief narrative lyric poems which are termed dithyrambs. One may say of Bacchylides what Eliot says of the early work of Yeats, that 'these are beautiful poems, but only craftsman's work, because one does not feel present in them that particularity which must provide the material for the general truth'. What enables Pindar to seize on that particularity is his unusual power to select the detail that will most vividly bring home the scene he is describing or the truth on which he is insisting. His determination to describe such a detail with absolute precision sometimes results in the choice of a manner of expression so unusual as to seem bizarre. In the ***First Nemean,*** the infant Herakles grasps by the throat the twin serpents sent by Hera; 'and as they choked time breathed the lives out of their dread bodies'. . . . In a [fragmentary] poem in which he describes how Herakles dealt with the man-eating horses of the Thracian king Diomedes, Pindar tells how the hero came to the stables and distracted the attention of the horses by tossing one of their grooms into the manger to be devoured; 'and swiftly a crunching sound rang out through the white bones as they splintered'. . . . (pp. 139-55)

The so-called Longinus says of Ion of Chios and Bacchylides that they are 'impeccable, uniformly beautiful writers in the polished manner', but of Pindar and Sophocles that they 'sometimes set the world on fire with their vehemence, for all that their flame sometimes goes out without reason and they collapse dismally'. These two passages, I suspect, are examples of the kind of thing in Pindar that distressed the gifted rhetorician of the early imperial period; his style, like those of Aeschylus and Sophocles, conserves an element of archaic roughness, displeasing to the taste of periods like the eighteenth century, when 'the polished manner' is in fashion, but seeming to a different kind of criticism to give these authors strength and to preserve them from the facile smoothness which is the excellence of writers of the other kind, but is also the quality that prevents their rising to the greatest heights.

Very often in Pindar the significant detail is beautifully expressed, besides being hit off with an aptitude that contributes to its beauty. The holy island of Apollo in the Aegean, Pindar wrote in his hymn to Zeus, 'mortals call Delos, but the blessed ones on Olympus call the star that shines far off in the dark earth'. . . . Bacchylides could never have imagined how Delos must appear to the gods looking down on earth from heaven. The birth of Athena is a favourite subject of art as well as literature; it was memorably depicted on the eastern pediment of the Parthenon. Pindar in the ***Seventh Olympian*** describes how Hephaistos split his father's skull with his brazen axe and how Athena leapt up, uttering her warcry, 'and Heaven shuddered at her, and Mother Earth'. . . . (p. 155)

In the ***Thirteenth Olympian*** Pindar tells the Corinthian story of Bellerophon, who made many vain attempts to catch the winged horse Pegasus, 'till Pallas brought him a golden bridle, and his dream was changed to waking, and she said, "Are you asleep, prince, son of Aiolos? Come, take this to make horses love you! Sacrifice a white bull to the Tamer, and show him this!" So much as he dozed he heard the maiden say, with her blue aegis in the dark.' After duly sacrificing to Poseidon Bellerophon succeeds; once mounted, he cannot resist showing off in typically Greek fashion, and does a war-dance in the sky. . . . Effects of this kind are not easily appreciated in translation.

Arnold [in the lectures *On Translating Homer,* 1861] wrote of Homer 'that he is eminently rapid; that he is eminently plain and direct, both in the evolution of his thought and in the expression of it, that is both in his syntax and in his words; that he is eminently plain and direct in the substance of his thought, that is in the matter and ideas; and finally, that he is eminently noble.' When one first reads that famous judgement, it seems somewhat paradoxical; how can the notably grand style of Homer, carrying so great a weight of ornament and prone to such elaborate verbal effects, be called rapid, plain, direct? But when one has considered Homer's style with care, distinguishing, so to speak, the flesh from the bones of his poetry, one must acknowledge the justness of the description. Pindar even more obviously carries a great weight of ornament, and has in addition the quality imposed by his resolute search for precision that makes him at times seem almost baroque; yet I contend that Arnold's words are just as true of Pindar as of Homer, as the longer passages I shall now examine are designed to show.

At the end of the ***Fourteenth Olympian,*** an exquisite short poem for a boy victor from Orchomenos, where the Graces had their cult, Pindar remembers the boy's dead father. 'Go, Echo', he writes, 'to the black-walled house of Persephone to bring the glorious news to his father; see Kleodamos and tell him that in Pisa's famous valley his son has crowned his locks with the feathers of splendid prizes.'

In the ***Tenth Nemean,*** for the Argive wrestler Theaios, the myth is placed, unusually, at the end. From a catalogue of Argive legends—Pindar uses the device of *praeteritio,* making a series of brief mentions of stories he does not intend to tell—he comes to the victor and his long list of victories. It is not surprising that this family should produce great athletes, for the victor's ancestor Pamphaes once had the privilege of entertaining the Dioskouroi, Kastor and Polydeukes. In Sparta they share with Hermes and with Herakles the direction of the games, and they take good care of righteous men; the sons of gods may be relied on. Now follows the story of the last battle of the Dioskouroi against their cousins and enemies, the sons of Aphareus, Idas and Lynkeus (55 f.):

> Turn and turn about, they spend one day with their father Zeus, and one beneath the caverns of the earth, in the hollows of Therapna, each fulfilling a fate like the other's; for it was that which Polydeukes chose, rather than to be altogether a god and live in heaven, after Kastor had been slain in battle. Idas, angry over some affair of cattle, had gashed him with the point of his brazen spear. Looking down from Taygetos, Lynkeus saw them seated inside the trunk of an oak; for his was the most piercing eye of all men upon earth. With swift feet they came up at once, and in a moment did the dreadful deed. And the Apharetids suffered sorely at the hands of Zeus; for at once Leda's son came in pursuit; and they took their stand near their father's

> tomb. From it they seized a funeral monument, a wrought stone, and hurled it at the chest of Polydeukes. But they failed to crush him or to drive him back; and darting forward with his swift javelin he drove the bronze into the ribs of Lynkeus. And Zeus hurled upon Idas the sooty thunderbolt, and alone they were burned together; it is hard for men to contend with those whose power is greater.
>
> And quickly back to his mighty brother came the son of Tyndareus, and he found him not yet dead, but breathing in great gasps. Shedding hot tears he groaned, and cried aloud, 'Father, son of Kronos, what release shall there be from sorrow? Grant me too death together with him, lord! A man's honour is gone when he has lost those who belong to him; few among mortals can be trusted in hard times to take a share of labour!' So he spoke, and Zeus came to meet him, and uttered these words, 'You are my son; but this man is mortal seed, sown when the hero came after to your mother. Come, I give you the choice; if you wish to escape death and hated old age, and live on Olympus with me and with Athena and with Ares of the black spear, you have a right to. But if you fight for your brother, and have a mind to share alike in all things, you may live half the time below the earth, and half in the golden halls of heaven.' After that speech he did not hesitate in his decision, but opened the eye of Kastor of the brazen corselet, and made him speak again.

I hope that even that bald rendering, which can give no notion of the greatness of the poetry, can make the reader who does not know the language aware that Pindar, often censured for grandiloquence, is capable of great simplicity and directness. Arnold's words about Homer apply in every detail to this passage.

Pindar's last dated poem is the ***Eighth Pythian,*** performed in 446 BC, when he will have been well over seventy. It was written for a wrestler called Aristomenes from the small island of Aegina, visible from Athens, inhabited by Dorians under aristocratic leadership. Its people had been notably active in trade, in sea voyaging and in war; Pindar seems to have had a special link with them, for he wrote more victory odes for them than for any other people, no less than fourteen out of the fifty whose recipients are known to us. Since Aiakos, son of Zeus by the nymph Aegina, was father both of Peleus, father of Achilles, and of Telamon, father of Ajax, the island could claim some of the greatest fighting heroes of Greek legend; before the battle of Salamis, not far from Aegina, and in legend ruled over by Telamon, their statues were carried round the fleet, and gave great encouragement to the men about to fight. Telamon helped Herakles to conquer Troy in the time of Priam's father, king Laomedon; Achilles, his son Neoptolemos, and Ajax all took part in the siege of Troy described in the *Iliad;* and both wars are depicted in the sculptures from the temple of Aphaia, on Aegina, now in Munich. These sculptures illustrate Pindar's odes for Aeginetan victors, just as those from the temple of Zeus at Olympia illustrate the myth of Pelops narrated in the ***First Olympian,*** for in poem after poem Pindar dwells on the rewarding themes supplied by the glorious deeds of Aiakos' descendants.

At the start of the ***Eighth Pythian,*** Pindar invokes Hesychia, 'Tranquillity'. It is a commonplace of the epinician genre that the victor wins peace, repose, tranquillity as the reward of his mighty labours, so that this choice is natural enough. But that may not be the only reason for it; tranquillity is the opposite of *polypragmosyne,* that readiness to interfere in other people's business that was thought characteristic of the imperialist democracy of Athens. In 446, the year of this poem, Aegina had been for twelve years under Athenian domination; later, after the Peloponnesian War had broken out in 431, the Athenians would expel its entire population.

> Gentle Tranquillity, daughter of Justice who makes cities great, you who hold the keys supreme of counsels and of wars, receive for Aristomenes the honour due to his Pythian victory. For you know how to give and how to take a gentle touch with flawless instinct. But when someone has welded ungentle rancour into his heart, you strike back hard against the power of your enemies, and put their insolence in the bilge. Porphyrion was one who did not realize the folly of provoking you. What one gains is most precious when he from whose house one carries it is willing.
>
> In time violence has been the ruin even of the mighty boaster; Typhos of Cilicia did not escape its consequence, neither did the king of the giants; but they were brought low by the thunder and by the arrows of Apollo, he who received the son of Xenarkes with kindness when he came from Kirrha garlanded with the leaves of Parnassus and with Dorian revelry.

Porphyrion and the king of the giants are the same person; the allusion is to the battle in which the giants challenged the might of the Olympians and were overwhelmed by them, a favourite theme of archaic art and of much poetry, now mostly lost. In the ***First Pythian*** we have found the presence under Etna of Typhos, the most formidable enemy of Zeus, not to be unrelated to the ever-present danger to the Greeks of Sicily from their barbarian enemies. The strong stress laid on the power of self-defence possessed by Tranquillity 'who holds the keys supreme of counsels and of wars' must cause us to wonder whether here too the poet may be glancing at the present situation of the community to which his client belongs; it may be significant that here also Typhos finds a mention.

> Not far from the Graces has fallen the lot of the island of the righteous city, which has a part in the far-famed deeds of glory of the sons of Aiakos; solid has been her fame from the beginning; she is sung of as the nurse of heroes supreme in many victorious contests and in many fierce battles; and the same quality is manifest in her men.

Now Pindar uses a standard device to move from the praise of the victor's city to that of the victor.

> But I have no leisure to dedicate the whole long story with the lyre and with sweet singing, lest

> satiety should come and irk us. Let my art give wings to the matter now in hand, the debt I owe you, boy, the newest of noble things. In your wrestling you follow in the tracks of your mother's brothers; at Olympia you do not shame Theognetos, nor at the Isthmus the victory of Kleitomachos, brave and strong. By bringing glory to the Meidylidai you earn the praise which once the son of Oikles spoke in riddles, when he saw his son and his friends' sons standing fast in battle at seven-gated Thebes, when the Epigonoi came from Argos on that second march.

The son of Oikles is the warrior and prophet Amphiaraos, one of the seven champions who accompanied Adrastos, king of Argos, in his famous and disastrous attempt to restore Polyneikes to the throne of Thebes; and the allusion leads up to the brief myth of the poem. In the next generation Adrastos and the sons of the Seven, known as the Epigonoi, launched a new attack; among them were such heroes as Diomedes and Sthenelos, known from the *Iliad,* and this time the attack met with success.

> Thus he spoke as they fought: 'By nature a valiant spirit from the fathers shines upon the sons. Clearly I see Alkman plying his shield with its sinuous snakes, foremost in the gates of Cadmus. He who suffered in the disaster long ago now enjoys a better omen, the hero Adrastos. But in his own family his fortune will be the opposite; he alone of the Danaan army shall gather the bones of his son, and by a fortune sent from the gods shall return to the broad streets of Abas with his host unscathed.' So spoke Amphiaraos; and I myself rejoice to crown Alkman with flowers and to sprinkle him with song; for he is my neighbour and the guardian of my possessions, and on my way to earth's navel, famed in song, he met me and prophesied by the art belonging to his house.

Amphiaraos belonged to one of the great prophetic families of heroic Greece; he had not been killed, but had been swallowed up by the earth, and in his shrine at Oropos, on the borders of Boeotia and Attica, continued to prophesy. It would seem that Alkman or Alkmaion, like his father, was the object of a hero-cult, that Pindar lived near his shrine and had deposited property there for safekeeping, in accordance with a common practice, and that he believed himself to have received a prophecy from the hero. Perhaps he had a waking vision, but it seems likelier that he dreamed a dream, for at the shrine of Amphiaraos inquirers slept in the sanctuary in the hope of a dream in which they would receive their answers. The simple significance of the myth is made explicit by the poet; it lies in the commonplace, often expressed in victory odes, that nature implants nobility in the sons of noble fathers. In the earlier battle the Seven had all perished, but Adrastos survived, carried to safety by the wonder-horse Arion; in the attack of the Epigonoi all the sons of the Seven survived, but Aigialeus, son of Adrastos, was killed by the defending commander Laodamas, son of Eteokles, who was himself killed by Alkman. As so often, the myth carries a reminder that even the greatest human triumphs are seldom undiluted by an element of sadness.

Now the poet directly addresses Apollo, lord of Delphi:

> You, Far-Darter, lord of the glorious temple that welcomes all in the hollows of Pytho, granted him there the greatest of delights, but first at home in your festival you brought him a gift eagerly to be snatched up, that of the pentathlon. King, I pray you to deign to look upon all my goings according to a harmony! The band of revellers with sweet song has justice standing near; and I pray that the gods grant unstinted favour to your fortunes.

As often, gnomic reflection follows the prayer for divine favour; that prayer is necessary, because without such favour, no success is possible for men.

> For if a man possesses good things that have come without long effort, many think that he is clever among fools and builds up his success by schemes based on right judgements. But such things do not lie within the power of men; it is the god who gives them, now putting one on top and bringing down the other, now the reverse. Enter the contest with right measure in your heart! You have the honours you won at Megara, and in the lowland of Marathon, and with three victories you have prevailed in Hera's games in your own country.

Thus the victor's wins in local games are rapidly dispatched. The Greeks of Pindar's time did not share English notions of sportsmanship.

> Upon four bodies you came down with fierce intent; for them no equally delightful homecoming was decreed in the Pythiad, nor did sweet laughter arouse joy when they returned to their mothers; in dark passages they cower, avoiding their enemies, stung by their disaster.

From the gloom of the defeated Pindar passes to the happiness of the victorious; but he is constantly aware of the dangers that attend all praise of human effort, and comes back immediately to the fragility of human happiness.

> He who has some new glory for his lot, revelling in great luxury, flies on wings given to his mighty deeds by hope. In a moment delight flowers for men, and in a moment it falls to the ground, shaken by a stern decree. Humans are creatures of a day; what is one of them? what is he not? The dream of a shadow. But when the Zeus-given glory comes, a bright radiance lies on men, and life is sweet. Aegina, dear mother, convey this city in freedom with the aid of Zeus and mighty Aiakos and Peleus and valiant Telamon and with Achilles.

Aegina, the eponymous heroine, mother of Aiakos by Zeus, is begged 'to convey this city in freedom'; with her are joined Zeus himself and three of the five mighty heroes of the family. In the light of this we must surely acknowledge that the invocation of Tranquillity and the reminder of the fate met by the barbarous giants who challenged the Olympians, though fitting perfectly the ordinary requirements of an epinician ode to honour the victory of Aristomenes, cannot have been felt by the audience to be irrelevant to the dangerous situation in which Aegina at that time found herself. But the poem is infinitely remote from the political pamphlet against democracy and imperialism which a certain kind of criticism would make of it; it ends with reflections that have the widest possible relevance to the conditions of human life.

Despite the loss of about three-quarters of Pindar's work, the victory odes together with the fragments are enough to justify the claim that he has produced a body of poems that communicate a distinctive vision of the world, conveyed with great imaginative power. Since the victory odes constantly show gods and men in close relation to each other, it may be fortunate that we possess them, rather than, say, four books of hymns of various kinds; for their subject-matter is well calculated to display Pindar's tragic view of human life. Seeing the victor and his circumstances always against the background of archaic Greek religion, and being always aware of the difficulty which a believer in it must find in praising any mortal, Pindar, by using the dark colour of the greater part of men's existence to bring out the brightness of that small part of it which is lit up by what he calls 'the Zeus-given glory', achieves a magnificent chiaroscuro. He is grateful to the gods for all the splendour of the world, and for the occasional favours that they show to men; but he never forgets the precariousness of human life, and knows that men have no right to count on the continuance of such favours. He shows himself aware of one client's sickness, another's exile, the losses in battle suffered by the family of another, the threat to Sicily from the barbarians and to Aegina from the Athenians; he reminds the victors that not even the greatest heroes of the past were exempt from misfortune. In the ***Second Olympian*** and in several of his dirges, Pindar speaks of a happy life in the afterworld granted to certain souls who have lived out three lifetimes without committing an injustice; Peleus, Cadmus, and Achilles are among them. Here the Homeric notion of Elysium as the haven of a fortunate few seems to be combined with beliefs of the sort which Pindar's contemporaries associated with the name of Orpheus; and yet he faces up to a realistic view of the limitations of human life, with complete freedom from illusion and complete absence of false comfort. In the last resort, what makes his poetry so powerful is his power to present, to use Eliot's words once more, 'that particularity which must provide the material for the general truth'; in that respect, and not in that alone, Pindar resembles Dante. (pp. 155-63)

Hugh Lloyd-Jones, "Pindar," in Proceedings of the British Academy, *Vol. LXVIII, 1982, pp. 139-63.*

An excerpt from Abraham Cowley's "The Praise of Pindar" (1656):

Pindar is imitable by none:
The *Phœnix Pindar* is a vast *Species alone.*
Whoe'er but *Dædalus* with waxen Wings could fly,
And neither *sink* too low, nor *soar* too high?
What could he who *follow'd* claim,
But of vain *Boldness* the unhappy Fame,
And by his Fall a *Sea* to name?
Pindar's unnavigable Song
Like a swoln *Flood* from some steep *Mountain* pours along;
The *Ocean* meets with such a *Voice*
From his enlarged *Mouth,* as drowns the *Ocean's* Noise.

Abraham Cowley, in his The Complete Works in Verse and Prose of Abraham Cowley, *edited by Rev. Alexander B. Grossart, AMS Press, 1967.*

Anthony J. Podlecki (essay date 1984)

[*In the following excerpt, Podlecki places Pindar's lyric poetry in the historical and social context of archaic Greece, paying particular attention to his treatment of myth, relation to Athens, and his general values.*]

With the exception of Homer and the dramatists, more of Pindar's work survives than of any Greek poet before Theocritus—forty-five victory odes collected according to the festival at which the victory was won. An even greater proportion of his work has been lost, amounting to thirteen of the seventeen "books" into which the Alexandrian scholar Aristophanes of Byzantiuym (*c.* 200 B.C.) classified his poems. Although all were intended for performance before audiences of varying sizes, some of these categories seem to have been intended primarily for private occasions; thus we hear of an *Hyporcheme,* or dance song, for the Syracusan tyrant Hieron, of *Encomia* or eulogies for Hieron again, for Alexander "Philhellene" of Macedon, and for members of leading families from Corinth and Akragas, for whom Pindar also wrote victory odes. Little survives from the one book of dirges and three of ***Partheneia,*** or maiden songs, but Pindar wrote one poem of the former category for an Athenian of the Alcmeonid house and a maiden song for a Theban whose son was to become a noted general in the Peloponnesian War. Other genres again were commissioned by cities for public occasions and in this "official" category may be placed hymns, paeans (usually to Apollo), dithyrambs (to Dionysus), and *prosodia,* or "processional songs." What has been lost, then, is almost immeasurable, but enough survives to give a clearer picture of Pindar's poetic craft than of any ancient Greek poet save for Homer and the dramatists, and the papyri have shed some additional light, particularly with respect to the paeans.

The victors for whom Pindar composed his odes were normally citizens of the great states—Thebes, Aegina, Sicily, but occasionally, Pindar accepted commissions from cities that were not in the mainstream of events in Greece. ***Paean 2*** was written for the city of Abdera, and Pindar spares no pains in recounting the early history of the city, which Herodotus tells briefly. Around 540 B.C. Harpagus, lieutenant of Cyrus the Great, was systematically reducing the Greek cities of Ionia and adding them to the Persian Empire. He built a siege-mound against the city of Teos and ultimately captured it, but the inhabitants escaped northward to Thrace, where they carved out a location among the Paeonians, a tribe in the region, and resettled an earlier Ionian foundation that the Thracians had overrun. Pindar reminds his Abderite patrons how their ancestors "won by war a land with dower of wealth, and planted prosperity firm, when they had pursued the tribes of the Paeonian warriors beyond Mount Athos, their nurse divine" (vv. 59-63, trans. Sandys). The poem continues with details of other, or perhaps subsequent, encounters: the Abderites facing the enemy before the Thracian mountain Melamphyllon ("Clothed in dark leaves"), their drawing up along the river Nestus and so, though fewer in number, being able to rout the Thracians "on the first of the month" (vv. 75-76). It has been suggested that the poem dates from the mid-470's, when, according to Plutarch (*Life of Cimon* ch. 7), the Persians in the area of Eion on the Strymon were making trouble for the Greek settlements along the Thracian coast; Abdera was then perhaps being threatened by a combined force of Persians and Thracians. It would be unwise, however, to be dogmatic in placing Pindar's poem in just this historical situation, since evidence for the exact sequence of events in Thrace during this period is exceedingly skimpy. At what appears to be the end of the poem, the chorus address the namesake-hero of the city, Abderus: "By thy might, even lead forward our host of fighting horsemen for a final war" (vv. 104-6, Sandys); this seems to be an ominous hint of continuing difficulties with the native tribes. It is mildly surprising to find among the papyrus fragments of the ***Paeans*** one for the citizens of Ceos, a small island off the east coast of Attica, for the Ceians had two writers of choral poetry who were native sons, Simonides and Bacchylides. In fact, however, if Pindar's comments at the beginning of ***Isthmian 1,*** where he alludes to Ceos, "sea-girt, attended by men of the deep," are rightly taken as showing a connection between the two poems, it is likely that they both date from the 450's, when Simonides was already dead and Bacchylides perhaps in exile. Pindar in any case praises his patrons in the grand style when he has the chorus sing "I dwell on this rocky island and am known for successes in the games of Greece, am known too for providing music in abundance" (***Paean 4.*** 21-24), a graceful compliment to the poets with whom he must often have vied for commissions.

Some of the individuals for whom Pindar wrote victory odes also hailed from relatively undistinguished cities. Thus the twenty-four line ***Olympian 14*** was composed for a patron from the neighbouring, not very distinguished Boeotian town of Orchomenos, while ***Olympian 9*** celebrates a victory won by a famous wrestler from the northern city of Opous. Italian, or "Epizephyrian," Locri flits briefly across the pages of fifth-century history as a victim of aggression by Anaxilas, tyrant of Rhegium; the Locrians appealed to and were championed by the Syracusan tyrant Hieron in about 477 B.C., and the danger from Rhegium subsided. Pindar alludes in passing to these events in ***Pythian 2,*** vv. 18-20, where he describes a Locrian maiden standing before her doorway and "gazing in safety" thanks to Hieron's intervention. Besides ***Olympians 10*** and ***11,*** written for a victory gained by a Locrian shortly after this incident, Pindar mentions the remote western town again in a context too fragmentary to be restored satisfactorily (fr. 149 b Snell). These are brief notices of cities far from the centres of power in the Greek world; for the most part, however, Pindar's patrons hailed from states that dominated Greek affairs.

Although no evidence has come down about the procedures by which poets obtained commissions or how much they were paid, it seems reasonable to assume that the transactions were for the most part strictly commercial; citizens even of lesser states who could afford it might avail themselves of Pindar's poetic talents. "There was a time," the poet says rather nostalgically, "when the Muse was not money-grubbing and did not work for hire, nor were the sweet, soft-voiced songs of honey-tongued Terpsichore available for sale with a silver price-tag on their faces" (***Isthmian 2.*** 6 ff.). But even if that happy state ever existed in fact, it has now changed, for as Pindar himself indicates elsewhere, his own Muse has "contracted to provide a silver-plated voice for pay" (***Pythian 11.*** 41-42). So he is not above accepting a commission from a local magistrate from the small island of Tenedos, near Troy, to celebrate not an athletic victory (although the poem has come down as the eleventh of the "Nemean" odes), but his election or appointment to this annual magistracy. Save for the absence of a separate, often lengthy, section devoted to the full-scale development of an appropriate myth, the poem may be taken as a typical and very successful example of the *Epinician,* or victory ode, form. Pindar opens with a salute to the goddess Hestia, Hearth, daughter of Cronos and so a genealogical and cultic equal of her siblings, Zeus and Hera; she, as keeper of the civic hearth and protectress of the magistrates' chamber, is asked to receive Aristagoras, Pindar's patron, into his new office. He and his colleagues for their parts are to "honour you (Hestia) and keep Tenedos on a straight course" (vv. 1-5), a graceful reminder to the victor, and thoroughly in Pindar's manner, that victory brings with it social responsibilities.

In the second stanza Pindar goes on to specify what some of these new duties are: maintaining the full round of public sacrifices and feasts, especially those involving music and poetry, and making sure that the customs of civic hospitality are observed (in poets' language: "the ordinance of Zeus god of Guests is practiced at overflowing tables," vv. 8-9c). Pindar then moves in the third stanza to the "victor's" family and previous successes; he is "blessed for his father Agesilas, blessed too for his wonderful physique and innate fearlessness" but, lest such praise go to his head, "let him remember that he wears mortal flesh and his very last vesture will be of earth" (15-16). In the section devoted to a catalogue of other victories, Pindar is able to mention sixteen successes won by Aristagoras and his kinsmen in local contests in wrestling and the pankration for which Aristagoras "should be praised by the citizens' good reports"; for the absence of prizes in the great panhellenic competitions Pindar offers polite apology: his parents were too fearful of his youthful strength to let him try, but if he had (the poet here offers his "personal opinion"), he would have returned from Delphi or Olympia more successful than his opponents.

In that part of the poem usually devoted to a full-scale myth, Pindar alludes briefly to the victor's descent from the island's hereditary aristocracy, transplants from the

Greek mainland who came as part of the legendary "Aeolian" migration led by Peisander and Orestes, with an admixture of Boeotians from Thebes (33-37). Such historical mythologizing allows the poet to coin one of his beloved maxims: "antique virtues transfer their strength and yield fruit now in one, now in another generation of men" (37-38). The poem ends, as often, with a sobering philosophical reflection. "Zeus offers men no clear sign, but in our manifold desires we embark on schemes bold and brave, for our limbs are bound to the rack of wanton hope, while the streams of foreknowledge lie hidden. But we should hunt only moderate gain. Desires unattained lead to attacks of frenzy" (43-48).

This last in the series of ***Nemean Odes,*** and the two preceding, ***9*** and ***10,*** turn out not to have been composed for victories at the Nemean Games at all. (In the Alexandrian collection, the ***Nemeans*** came last, with some miscellaneous odes added as a kind of appendix; the order of the ***Isthmians*** and ***Nemeans***—with the additional songs—was reversed in a later transcription, and the last part of the manuscript was then damaged, leaving the ***Isthmians*** incomplete.) ***"Nemean" 9*** was composed for a victory at Sicyon at a festival in Apollo's honour, to which Pindar alludes elsewhere (***Nemean 10.*** 43, ***Isthmian 4.*** 28, ***Olympian 13.*** 109). ***"Nemean" 10,*** Pindar's only surviving ode for an Argive patron (scraps remain also of a dithyramb for the Argives), seems to have been composed for a victory in local games in honour of Hera mentioned in vv. 22 ff. of the poem and elsewhere in the odes (***Olympians 7.*** 83, 9. 88, and 13. 107); it is a complex composition and there may be, as we shall see, a particular point to the myths the poet chooses for elaboration. It may be possible to infer from the ninety verses (the mean length of the forty-five poems is seventy-six verses) it contains that the length of a victory ode did not stand in any direct proportion to the importance of the festival or the victor; ***Pythian 7,*** for a victory won at Delphi by the important Athenian figure Megacles is but three stanzas long for a total of eighteen lines. It is an easy assumption that what a customer was willing or able to pay had some effect on the length if not on the elaborateness of the ode, but there may be other factors, which now elude us: the occasion of the poem's performance, the time available to the poet, or whether or not he had himself witnessed the victory. Besides the Sicyonian and Argive festivals that occasioned these "pseudo-Nemean" odes, Pindar refers briefly in his works to victories won by his patrons at competitions in honour of local or panhellenic divinities at Thebes, Orchomenus, Megara, Corinth, Athens (where what must have been relatively minor festivals at Marathon and Eleusis are mentioned separately), Euboea, Aegina, Epidarus, Tegea, Achaean Pallene, Arcadia, Parrhasia, Rhodes and even Sicilian Etna. To honour some of the winners in these major or minor festivals Pindar may have composed odes which were never published for a wider audience. It is in any case clear that we possess only a portion of what must have been an enormous total poetic output.

There can be little doubt, however, that what antiquity judged to be the best of Pindar's victory odes do survive. The collection comprises choral songs commissioned by victors in the four main panhellenic festivals, the Olympic Games, held to honour Zeus near Elis in the western Peloponnese every four years in late summer, the Pythian Games celebrated in Apollo's honour at Delphi in July, also on a four-year cycle, but with two years intervening between them and the Olympics, and, at two-year intervals, the games dedicated to Poseidon at the Corinthian Isthmus, and the Nemean Games to Zeus at Cleonae south of Corinth.

Although by far the largest number commemorate victories in the major events, the chariot and horse race, as well as mens' and boys' pankration (all-in wrestling), pentathlon, foot race, boxing and wrestling, Pindar was not above accepting commissions for the humbler events such as the mule race (***Olympians 5*** and ***6***), and the last in the series of ***Pythians, 12,*** commemorates not an athletic victory but one in the flute-playing contest.

Very little is definitely known, although something can be surmised, about the circumstances under which the odes were performed. The readiest assumption is of a full-dress performance in the victor's home city by a trained chorus of his fellow citizens. For some odes, however, their metrical form, a succession of identical stanzas rather than the usual triad of strophe-antistrophe-epode, and their relatively abbreviated length, suggest that they may have been performed immediately following the victory and as part of the closing ceremonies of the festival itself. At the opening of ***Pythian 6,*** the chorus chant, "Let us approach the temple at the navel of deep-roaring earth" (vv. 3-4), which should probably be taken as referring to an actual procession to Apollo's temple at Delphi. A similar phrase at the beginning of ***Nemean 9,*** however, is not so certainly to be taken literally: "Muses," Pindar has his chorus sing, "we shall join the revel band from Sicyon" (the location of the festival where the victory was won)" . . . to the victor's happy home at Etna" (vv. 1-3). Occasionally the poet provides specific information about the setting in which the work is being performed; "I am drawn by a love-charm to keep touch with the new moon," the Chorus sing at ***Nemean 4,*** v. 35, which seems to refer to a festival to Apollo held at Aegina at the time of the new moon. The victor of ***Olympian 3,*** Theron of Akragas, "propitiously approaches this feast" along with the Dioscuri (vv. 34-35), an apparent reference to the festival of *theoxenia* being celebrated at Akragas in honour of the latter divinities, and a description of a festival in honour of Karneian Apollo in ***Pythian 5*** (vv. 77 ff.), for a victor from Cyrene, may point to that as a setting in which the ode was performed. ***Pythian 11*** is apparently being sung at Apollo's main shrine at Thebes known as the Ismenion (vv. 6-7). ***Olympians 11*** and ***10*** are paired poems of which the former appears to be a short sketch containing Pindar's "promise" and "pledge" to write a full-scale ode, and the latter opens with the pretty conceit of the poet asking the Muse to "tell me where in my mind the victor's name is written, for I forgot I owed him a sweet song" (***Ol. 10.*** 2-4). It is generally assumed that the odes were composed and performed soon after the victories they celebrate, but here and there can be detected signs of revision or delay. ***Isthmian 2,*** although nominally for a victory won by Xenocrates, a member of the ruling house of Akragas, before 476 B.C., refers repeatedly to the victor's other achievements in the past tense (vv. 37 ff.). This suggests that the poem was presented after the victor's death in about 472 B.C. to his son Thrasybulus, whom Pindar mentions elsewhere (***Pythian 6.*** 15), as a kind of retrospective tribute to the whole family's fame. ***Pythian 3,*** although cast in the form of a victory song, is more in the nature of a poetic epistle to Hieron, a gesture of friendship and condolence from the poet to his Syracusan patron on the occasion of the latter's illness. (pp. 203-09)

Pindar establishes lines of contact between the poetic and the real world . . . by his use of certain myths and his modifications of them. The section in which the poet interrupts the business at hand, praise of the victor and his family, and launches into a narrative, often fairly lengthy, of some episode from the very large store of traditional myth is an almost invariable feature of a Pindaric victory ode. Most often, the hero of the myth or the entire episode will have some relevance to the particular circumstances of the victor or his achievement or will be connected to the poet's theme in a more general way; for example, the majority of odes for Aeginetan victors develop some episode from the great cycle of legend surrounding the island's leading mythical clan, that of Aeacus and his descendants. Now the main outlines of all the myths would have been more or less familiar to a contemporary Greek audience, whether of choral poetry or of drama; what they were interested in hearing was how skilful the poet was in his handling of the myths, which segments he had chosen for emphasis, and how he might elaborate them. As a creative artist Pindar did not simply retell his mythical material, he moulded it and infused it with a new life. The myth of Pelops and Tantalus in ***Olympian 1*** is a case in point. Tantalus, in a fit of mad pride, invited the gods to a meal at which he served up his own son Pelops' dismembered limbs; the gods discovered the crime, but not before Demeter had consumed the boy's shoulder, so one made of ivory had to be substituted instead. The poet throws up his hands in mock-horror; "It is fitting for a man," he protests, "to say only good things about divinities" (v. 35), and again, "it is impossible for me to call one of the gods a glutton" (v. 52). Of course, the audience knew the "orthodox" version (if one may call it that), and Pindar in his unique, allusive way gives enough of the standard details to show that he was not only familiar with it, but enjoyed retelling it, so his protests of horror and shock should not be taken too seriously; it is all an elaborate *praeteritio,* a "refusal to mention" what he does in fact tell, almost completely, and a splendid excuse for him to perform a mythographic tour de force and produce a cleverly "laundered" version (which is really not that at all, for Pindar introduces at two places, v. 25 and 41, the detail that Poseidon was "out of control with passion" for the boy Pelops, which surely belies Pindar's claim that he will say only "seemly" or "good" things about the gods).

Another characteristic technique of Pindar's in his mythic narratives is to break up the usual chronology of the received versions and select certain central scenes, which he takes out of their natural place and redeploys, giving them a prominence that better suits his artistic instincts. The Argonautic saga of ***Pythian 4*** is a good example. The lengthy mythic interlude begins in fact somewhere near the end of the story Pindar intends to tell, with the Argonauts on their way from the Black Sea with the Golden Fleece; they call in at Thera, and the sorceress Medea foretells the future founding of Cyrene by a colonist from Thera. This abnormal order has the effect of throwing mythic past and actual present into close association, for the ode honours a contemporary king of Cyrene, Arcesilas. Moreover, the Theraean founder of Cyrene was reputedly himself descended from one of Jason's Argonauts and a woman of Lemnos. Thus Pindar caps his story of the quarrel between Jason and Pelias and the dangerous quest of the Golden Fleece in which it resulted by bringing the expedition to Lemnos: "there in a foreign soil some fated day, maybe, or the night-watches witnessed that seed implanted, from which should spring the glorious light of your high fortune," Pindar can say to his Cyrenaean patron (vv. 254-57, Conway's translation). Once again, Pindar has adapted the myth to suit present circumstances, for the usual version had the Argonauts stop at Lemnos on the way out to the Black Sea and not after their successful venture; Pindar felt free to shift the episodes in a way that would better suit a performance at Cyrene.

It is also his practice to truncate or abridge myths, usually with the plea that he is running out of time; "the rule (*tethmos*) prevents my telling it all at length, and the pressing hours," he says in cutting short his catalogue of the exploits of Heracles and Telamon in ***Nemean 4*** (vv. 33-34) and a similar phrase occurs, again to close off an account of the deeds of these two heroes, at ***Isthmian 6*** (v. 56). But, once again, his protests fool no one; it is simply a poetic *façon de parler* and occurs so often in the odes as to be considered almost a Pindaric mannerism. It is his way of saying, "my sense of what is artistically appropriate or called for by the occasion tells me it is time to pass on to another section of my poem."

It should come as no surprise, then, that his firm grasp of mythic details and his assured mastery in deploying them should sometimes reveal themselves in the way he seems to introduce variations, or even to invent whole episodes, simply to suit some immediate, but ulterior, purpose. Twice in the extant odes (***Olympian 4,*** 8 ff., ***Pythian 1,*** vv. 15 ff.) and again in the fragments (91-93, Snell), he touches on the story of the terrible, hundred-headed monster Typhos, who audaciously attacked Zeus himself but was for his pains cast into Tartarus, from which "rivers of glowing smoke pour forth a lurid stream, and in the dark a red and rolling flood tumbles down boulders to the deep sea's plain in riotous clatter" (***Pythian 1,*** vv. 22-24, Conway's translation); in short, he had become a volcano. This type of explanation of a natural phenomenon was very common in Greek mythology, and the Typho story had been told in these terms at least as early as Hesiod (*Theogony* 859 ff.), but what Pindar does—and he may be responsible for the innovation—is to localize the legend in Sicily: "now the sea-cliffs above Cymae and Sicily press upon his shaggy breast" (vv. 17-19); Typhos has simply been identified as Mt. Etna. This must have been extremely gratifying for Pindar's influential Sicilian host, Hieron of Syracuse, for whom ***Pythian 1*** was written shortly after he had "founded" (in fact, re-settled) a new city at Mt. Etna; no doubt he would have needed little encouragement to see himself as capable of wielding something like Zeus' own power over men and the forces of nature. ***Olympian 6*** was written for a Syracusan victor whose clan, the Iamidai, traced their descent from an important mainland family of professional prophets in Arcadia. Pindar introduces a seemingly novel element into their mythical genealogy by making the eponymous hero of the clan, Iamos, the grandson of Poseidon and a Spartan nymph, not, as another, probably earlier, version has it, of an ancient Arcadian king; according to this innovation mother and child remove to Arcadia and the boy is brought up as the king's foster child, with the connivance of the boy's father, Apollo, who of course had a vested interest in seeing that the widest possible acceptance throughout the Greek world should be given to his descendant's prophetic powers. Now one of the most famous seers of the time of the Persian Wars was a member of this same Iamid clan, Tisamenos, who had become official prophet for the Spartans and had even been accorded the unique honour of Spartan citizenship. The change in the genealogy appears to have the effect of downgrading the victor's Arcadian connection (through his mother he held a secondary citizenship in the Arcadian town of Stymphalos) and enhancing his family's ties with Sparta, but no doubt this kind of *ad hoc* genealogizing was intended as a compliment; it was a feather in the cap of a merely regional aristocrat to ally himself, if only mythologically, with one of the leading powers in Greece. Only one of Pindar's surviving victory odes was composed for an Argive patron, although traces also remain of a dithyramb in the city's honour (fr. 70a, Snell), and here in ***Nemean 10*** the poet introduces some unusual mythic details. Among the heroes of Argos' legendary past he names Amphitryon (v. 13), Heracles' human foster father, who was usually placed at Thebes, sometimes at Mycenae; later in the poem he remarks that the victor's mother came from Tiryns (vv. 37 ff.). It is known that Argos waged war against and ultimately destroyed Mycenae in about 468 B.C., which is also the most plausible date for this ode, and at about the same time Argos was campaigning successfully against a group of her own dissident former citizens, who had taken possession of Tiryns. There can be little doubt that, as several commentators have pointed out, these events are reflected in Pindar's poem. A little harder to explain is the emphasis that the poet places upon the friendly reception given to the Spartan Dioscuri, Castor and Pollux, by the legendary Argive hero Pamphaes (vv. 49 ff.). Although Argos and Sparta were normally at odds with each other through the fifth century, this may reflect a period, as Bowra suggests, when some Argive aristocrats, including perhaps the victor's family, were seeking a rapprochement with Sparta. In ***Isthmian 1,*** for a victor from Thebes, the Theban hero Iolaos and the Spartan hero Castor are closely linked (vv. 16 ff.). This may reflect the close co-operation between Sparta and Thebes in the years after 460 B.C., culminating in the victory of the Peloponnesian League against Athens at the Boeotian town of Tanagra in the early summer of 457 B.C.

"I was trained," Pindar proclaims in an unidentified poem (fr. 198 a Snell), "no stranger to nor ignorant of the Muses, by famous Thebes," and indeed the poet's warm and patriotic affection for his city is manifest in his verses. "Famous" (*klutai*) in the preceding citation is matched by another, *polykleitan,* in fr. 194: for all the city's fame, the poet says his song will exalt the streets shared by gods and men to even greater heights. An ancient commentary notes that in the first poem in his book of ***Dithyrambs,*** Pindar claimed for his city the honour of having invented that verse form (fr. 71) although, as the same commentator observes, he had elsewhere claimed this distinction for Naxos. One of his favourite epithets for cities is *liparos,* "radiant," "sleek," which he uses twice of Thebes, (***Pythian 2.***3, fr. 196), a frequency surpassed only by its triple application to Athens. In the complex "theogony," or generations of the gods, worked out by Hesiod, Zeus' second wife was the moral abstraction Themis, Right, and from this union sprang the "Hours," *Eunomia* or Good Order, Justice, and Peace (*Theogony,* 901-2). In a ***Hymn*** written for Thebes, Pindar retold this edifying story (fr. 30, Snell) and in ***Paean 1*** he again describes how "the Hours, daughters of Themis, came to the city of Thebes, driver of horses" ("lover of the chariot," he calls her at ***Isthmian 8.***22, "of fair chariots," fr. 195); the poet then prays to Apollo to "deck her people long with the blossoms of chaste Eunomia" (fr. 52 a). Bowra maintains that as Pindar uses this personification, which was important in the poetry of Tyrtaeus and Solon, it has political overtones, revealing his preference for a conservative form of government, whether oligarchic or "royal" (all too often, in fact, tyrannical). Pindar describes several other cities in similar, clearly laudatory, terms, and two of these are particularly noteworthy. At the opening of ***Olympian 13,*** for Corinth, he reproduces the full Hesiodic genealogy: the city is "blessed . . . with glorious young men" and in her dwell Eunomia and her sisters, Justice, "secure foundation of cities" and Peace, "trustee of men's wealth, golden children of prudent Themis" (vv. 6-8). Pindar praises the Locrian city of Opous in similar terms in ***Olympian 9:*** "for Themis and her noble daughter, Eunomia the preserver, hold this city a bright jewel in their crown" (vv. 15-16, trans. Conway). Pindar was not being original in applying the term to Opous. Strabo (9. C425) cites the epitaph that the city erected at Thermopylae to commemorate the substantial number of its citizens who along with the Spartans and contingents from other Greek cities were annihilated there by the Persians. The inscription contains an exact synonym, *Lokrôn euthynomôn.* Pindar's use of *eunomia* in connection with particular cities, then, so far from being a code word to designate an aristocratic form of government, as in Tyrtaeus, begins to look like a general honorific epithet that any city might reasonably expect to have applied to it by a poet enlisted to sing its praises. Thus it can be applied even to a legendary figure such as the Eleusinian king Eumolpus, "a wise leader," who is said to rule "with *eunomia* that brings joy to the people" (fr. 346, Lloyd-Jones' restoration), where the term *eunomia* seems to be hardly more than a pale cliché.

Another citation from an ***Hypochreme,*** or dance song, for the Thebans, contains a somewhat different set of political abstractions:

> Let a man find the bright light of Quiet [*Hesychia*] that makes men great by putting the common good of citizens into calm weather, after re-

moving from his heart hateful Faction [*Stasis*],
bestower of poverty and hateful nurse of young
men. (fr. 109, Snell)

Pindar personifies *Hêsychia,* peacefulness or quiet, several times in the poems; for example, at ***Pythian 8,*** vv. 1-2, he addresses her as "benevolent Quiet who brings greatness to cities, daughter of Justice." As a daughter of one of the Hours, then, she is brought down to the second generation of descent, as it were, from Themis. Here, the juxtaposition of *Hêsychia* and *Stasis* is of some interest, for the latter term was one of the important catch-words of fifth-century politics: it could be, and was, used by politicians of any stripe to impugn the motives of their opponents by suggesting that they were promoting factionalism and partisanship at the expense of civic harmony and peace; it occurs again in a Theban context in ***Paean 9,*** where the poet takes a sudden eclipse of the sun as a portent of evil, "a sign of war . . . or destructive stasis" (vv. 13, 15). One of the chief causes of *stasis* was unbridled political ambition, and in a passage from an unknown context quoted, or perhaps paraphrased, by Plutarch Pindar wrote: "courting to excess ambition (*philotimian*) in cities, men set up (*histasin*) manifest suffering" (fr. 210). Polybius, who quotes only the first two lines of the above passage from the ***Hyporcheme*** (4. 31), appears to misinterpret it. He infers that Pindar "agrees in supporting the inaction" the pro-Persian party proposed at the time of the Persian invasion, but commentators have pointed out that the occurrence of the word *Stasis* in the longer citation (which Polybius need not have known, if he was drawing on an anthology), shows that the reference is to the internal politics of Thebes, not to the external stance of a group within the city who espoused "quietism" in the face of the Persian threat. In that case, Polybius may have been wrong about the occasion of the poem, and perhaps it has no connection at all with the events of 480.

A more reliable gauge of Pindar's feelings in that year is the long passage, already cited, from ***Isthmian 8,*** in which Pindar speaks with fervent relief of the passing of the stone of Tantalus, "turned aside from us by some god, an unendurable torment for Greece" (vv. 11-12). The Persian menace has passed, Pindar seems to be saying; in spite of his city's "official" pro-Persian stance, due in large part, perhaps, to the self-interested short-sightedness of families like that of Melissus, the patron of ***Isthmian 4,*** Pindar now breathes a sigh of relief, offering a prayer of thanks not only in his own name, but also on behalf of his countrymen and of all Greece. The name of one of Thebes' important citizens, Aioladas, appears in two ***Partheneia,*** or maiden songs, preserved in a fragmentary state in a papyrus from Oxyrhynchus (659); in the second of these there occurs the passage that alludes to "hateful strife which brooks no opposition" against the family (fr. 94 b, v. 64), but not enough remains of the context to make clear to what the poet is referring.

Of the odes that survive intact, five are for Theban victors. ***Isthmians 3*** and ***4*** were composed for a Melissus, whose family appears to have been on the wrong side at Plataea. After touching on this debacle, "the harsh snowstorm of war," Pindar passes deftly to a more positive tone, still continuing the nature imagery: "but now again, after the winter's murk, the patterned earth has burst into blossom with scarlet roses, by the Gods' designs" (vv. 19-21, Bowra's trans.; a very similar image occurs in ***Isthmian 7*** in an almost identical situation: "But now Poseidon Earthkeeper granted me calm weather after a storm," vv. 37-39). The opening of ***Isthmian 1*** finds Pindar in an expansive mood as he addresses the nymph after whom the city was named: "My Mother, Thêbê of the golden shield." The poem celebrates a victory by one of Pindar's countrymen whose father, Asopodorus, is very probably the cavalry commander of that name who, according to Herodotus (9. 69), distinguished himself in the fighting at Plataea. Midway through the poem there is a reference to "his ancestral land in Orchomenus, which received him when he was driven aground in shipwreck from the immeasurable sea in freezing misfortune" (vv. 35-38). The Scholiasts are uncertain whether Pindar means the victor or his father. The Scholiasts add that Asopodorus himself had been exiled from Thebes and enrolled as a citizen at Orchomenos; it has been suggested that this occurred as an aftermath of the Persian invasion, when the pro-Persian policy of, among others, Asopodorus, proved to be an embarrassment to the resumption of normal relations with the other Greek cities. The trouble, whatever it was, has passed, and "now again," the poet continues, "his innate destiny has brought him to the fine weather of former times" (39-40). Pindar then adds, possibly in a tactful allusion to the family's recantation of its former pro-Persian position, "the man who has known suffering wins too the prize of foresight."

It is easy to see why ***Pythian 11,*** also for a Theban victor, begins with a catalogue of Theban heroines, Semele, and Ino-Leucothoë, the daughters of Cadmus and Harmonia. Commentators have puzzled over why, well over halfway through ***Pythian 9*** for a victor from Cyrene, Pindar suddenly veers off to a laudatory account of the Theban hero Iolaus; they suggest, rather implausibly, that the song was performed at Thebes, although for a Cyrenaean victor. The Scholiast on v. 89 offers a likelier explanation that in addition to his victory at Delphi, the victor had won a prize in the games in honour of Iolaus at Thebes. ***Isthmian 7,*** like ***Pythian 1,*** opens with an invocation of the nymph Thêbê and proceeds to catalogue the glorious deeds of the city's heroic past, the birth of Dionysus and Heracles, the defeat of the Argive "Seven against Thebes," and assistance rendered to Sparta in the capture of Amyklai. A very similar enumeration stood at the beginning of a ***Hymn*** that Pindar composed for the Thebans, which came first in the collected editions of poems of that genre (fr. 29).

For the other cities that in the course of the fifth century were to become closely allied with Thebes, Pindar seems, with one conspicuous exception, to have composed comparatively little. Only one ***Olympian Ode (13)*** survives for a Corinthian patron, but here Pindar sows his praises with a lavish hand. The city is . . . the natural home of the moralized Hours, *Eunomia,* Justice and Peace, and together they will drive out their opponent vice, "Hybris (Insolence), brash-tongued mother of Surfeit" (v. 10). Pindar alludes in passing to the inventions claimed for the city, the dithyramb, horse bridle and a certain kind of decoration for temple roofs; "in her dwells the Muse sweet of breath and in her blossoms Ares with the deadly spears of young warriors" (vv. 22-23), a theme to which the poet returns later when he mentions the "contriving skill of her ancients and her heroes' valour in war" (vv. 50-51). Pindar composed an ***Encomion*** for this same patron. An address to the sacred prostitutes who attended the worshippers in Aphrodite's temple in Acrocorinth (fr. 122) is preserved from it. For a Megarian victor nothing survives but some papyrus shreds of a lost ***Isthmian*** (fr. 6 a). There is no evidence that Pindar composed a victory song for any Spartan patron, but there are references to an ***Hyporcheme*** for that city. The splendid lines in which Sparta is described as "the place where counsels of Elders excel, and spears of young warriors, and choruses, and the Muse and radiant Joy" (fr. 199) also survive (p. 108). "Blessed is Lacedaemon," Pindar began ***Pythian 10,*** and his admiration for the stability of Dorian institutions is clear from his remark that Hieron of Syracuse founded his new city of Etna "in freedom built of heaven's will, within the pattern of the laws of Hyllus" (***Pythian 1,*** vv. 61-62, trans. Conway). A few lines later he alludes to the Spartan achievement at Plataea: "I shall win the reward of thanks . . . at Sparta for the battles before Mt. Cithaeron, in which were felled the Medes with curving bows" (vv. 75-77). A passage in ***Pythian 5*** has been taken as an expression of Pindar's personal pride to be a member of the Aegeids, a Theban clan of which a branch settled in Sparta (vv. 72 ff.).

Almost one-quarter, eleven out of forty-five, of Pindar's surviving victory odes were composed for Aeginetan patrons. His special fondness for the island is clear from the careful finish he gave to many of these poems and the warm praise he heaps on the city's ancient heroes and present inhabitants. His poetic imagination draws a close mythical tie between his own city and Aegina: "It is necessary that one bred in seven-gated Thebes," he insists, "allot the Graces' finest first fruits to Aegina, because these are the twin youngest daughters" of the Boeotian river Asopus (***Isth. 8,*** 17-19). The beginning of a lost ***Isthmian*** for an Aeginetan victor sounds the keynote:

> Famous is the story of Aeacus; famous too is Aegina,
> renowned for her navy. It was under heaven's blessing
> that she was founded by the coming of the Dorian host
> of Hyllus and Aegimius,
> beneath whose rule they dwell.
> They never transgress right, nor yet the justice due to strangers;
> on the sea they are a match for dolphins in prowess, and they are
> wise ministrants of the Muses and of athletic contests.
>
> (***Isth. 9*** [fr. 4], trans. J. E. Sandys)

The city's Doric probity is here emphasized, as at ***Olympian 8:*** "An ordinance of the Immortals placed this sea-girt land as a holy pillar for strangers from everywhere . . . a Dorian people watch over it from Aeacus' time" (vv. 25-30, Bowra's trans.), and mention of the island's great patron-hero, Aeacus, gives Pindar a natural entrée into the world of myth:

> Wide are the avenues of approach, and from every direction, for chroniclers to adorn this famous island, since the Aeacidae gave them a destiny unsurpassed when they showed the way to great achievements, and over land and through seas far and wide flies their name. (***Nemean 6,*** vv. 45-49)

The "chroniclers" mentioned in this passage are storytellers versed in the legends of the past for whom the great mythical families provided abundant and varied materials for their tales. Of these families none was more prolific of heroes with a penchant for adventure than the Aeacidae, and Pindar could turn almost at random to any of their exploits for myths gratifying to his Aeginetan patrons. From the union of Zeus and the nymph Aegina, whose other name was Oenone, was born the peerless Aeacus, "city-ruler for his fatherland of fair name" (***Nemean 7.*** 85), "peerless in might and counsels," whom all the neighbouring heroes longed to see and whose commands they all . . . even those from Athens and Sparta . . . willingly obeyed (***Nemean 8.*** 8-12). Aeacus himself had three sons, one of whom, Phocus, his son by an earlier marriage with a sea nymph, was killed while throwing the discus with his half-brothers Telamon and Peleus; Pindar is aware of the version that his death was not accidental, and that as a result the two brothers left the island, but his sense of propriety, the poet insists, will allow him to do no more than darkly allude to it (***Nemean 5.*** 13 ff.). Peleus in any case left Aegina for Thessaly where he lodged with Acastus, king of Iolkos; there he had the misadventure of having the queen fall in love with him. Unable to seduce him, she lyingly accused him of seducing her. The king's misplaced jealousy would have vented itself disastrously on the hapless Peleus were it not for the timely intervention of the centaur Chiron (***Nemean 4.*** 54 ff., ***5.*** 27 ff.). In retribution, Peleus seized Iolkos (***Nemean 3.*** 34). Aeacus, meanwhile, was invited by the gods Apollo and Poseidon to join them in fashioning a crown of fortifications for Troy; but men—even heroes—are not gods, and so the wall's impregnability was in danger at just that place where Aeacus had built. Apollo, in fact, foresaw and foretold two later breaches in the divine fortifications and, in paradoxical compensation, by Aeacus' own descendants, Telamon in the first and Achilles' son Neoptolemus in the fourth generations (***Olympian 8.*** 31 ff. with Apollo's prophecy at 42-46; more briefly, at ***Isthmian 5.*** 34 ff.). To both of these Trojan expeditions Pindar returns several times. He tells how Telamon and Heracles undertook to punish the Trojan king Laomedon for failure to pay a promised reward to Heracles for an earlier service and mentions in passing their subsidiary exploits against the Meropes on Cos and the giant Alkyoneus (***Isthmian 6.*** 26 ff., ***Nemean 4.*** 25 ff.). As an added enhancement to the Aeacid clan, Pindar relates how, on the eve of the expedition, Heracles had foretold to Telamon the birth of the latter's long prayed for son, Ajax, "the man of might, a most dreaded warrior to the peoples amidst the toils of war" (***Isthmian 6.*** 53-54, Conway's trans). Less flattering to the family's reputation was the tale of how Ajax later lost the award of Achilles' armour and, in a fit of insane rage, attempted unsuccessfully to kill the Greek chiefs, his former colleagues, finally committing suicide in remorse. This was a well-known myth that Pindar, feeling himself unwilling or unable to refashion it as he had done with Pelops' shoulder, at one place simply relegates to "poetic cleverness deceiving and leading astray with words (*mythois*)" (***Nemean 7.*** 23 and ff.), or excuses on grounds that what caused Ajax's death was envy, *phthonos,* which wrongly deprived him of his due: "hateful deceit, companion of flattering words, treacherous of intent, a reproach productive of evil" (***Nemean 8.*** 32-33).

Aeacus' other son, Peleus, had been left at a disadvantage in Iolkos. As compensation, Zeus gave to Peleus the Nereid Thetis for a wife. This incidentally averted the threat that Zeus' pursuit of the lady posed to his own divine supremacy (***Isthmian 8.*** 29 ff.). At the wedding feast Peleus "saw in a circle about him the throned kings of sky and sea, who gave their gifts and revealed to him the power his family should have" (***Nemean 4.*** 66-68 also ***Nemean 5.*** 34 ff). From this marriage was born the mighty Achilles, whose assault on Troy matched his uncle Telamon's. Like his uncle, Achilles engaged in subsidiary adventures that took him against such fearsome opponents as Kyknos, Memnon, Telephus and others. Greek audiences knew these stories from Homer and the Cyclic epics such as the *Aithiopis,* which recounted the attack on the Greek camp at Troy by Memnon and his Ethiopian troops, and from numerous tragedies, now lost. Pindar can give them the merest mention, almost catalogue-fashion (so ***Olympian 2.*** 81 ff., ***Isthmian 5.*** 39 ff., ***8.*** 54 ff.). He can also capture in a vivid phrase the whole sweep of an epic lay or of a scene from a lost play like Aeschylus' *Memnon,* by describing how "Achilles came down to the ground from his chariot and fell on them like a mass of strife when he slew shining Dawn's son with the point of his wrathful spear" (***Nemean 6.*** 50-53). Pindar and, seemingly, his Aeginetan patrons never tired of hearing the adventures of this greatest of Greek heroes, "the Aeacids' warder, who cast light upon Aegina and his own stock" (***Isthmian 8.*** 55-56).

Dates for many of the victories that Pindar's victory songs celebrate have been preserved in the Scholiasts' notes; for others, an approximate chronology can be deduced from other evidence; in a residual number of cases, only a conjectural dating is possible. A relatively firm chronology can be established for the Aeginetan odes, and they in turn help to throw light on the city's status in the Greek world in the first half of the fifth century. Hostilities had broken out between her and Athens a few years before 500 B.C. on the chronological indications given by Herodotus (5. 81 and 89). Fighting, quite serious this time, erupted again in the 480's and the "war against Aegina" gave Themistocles the chance he had been looking for to press for a build-up of Athenian naval strength (7. 144) to challenge the traditional Aeginetan superiority at sea. It was these ships that turned the tide against the Persian fleet in the sea battles off Cape Artemisium in Northern Euboea and in the straits of Salamis in 480 B.C. If aspersions had been cast on the Aeginetans' loyalty to the Greek cause because of the readiness with which they had yielded token submission to Darius' envoys ten years before, the record was now wiped clean and more by the outstanding bravery of Aegina's captains and sailors at Salamis. Herodotus singles out their heroism, both individual and collective, for special mention (8. 93). It is no accident, then, that Pindar's two earliest Aeginetan odes, probably dating from the mid-480's, ***Nemean 5*** and ***Isthmian 6,*** emphasize Aegina's maritime prowess. In ***Nemean 5,*** Pindar imagines his poem as spreading the victor's fame from Aegina to the far corners of the world "on any merchant vessel or in a skiff" (v. 2), and the island itself he calls "land beloved of guests . . . endowed with noble men and famed for ships" (v. 9). Nautical imagery reappears at the close of the poem when Pindar bids his chorus "raise full sail to the mast's yardarm" and re-echo the victor's praises (v. 52). In ***Isthmian 6*** Pindar chooses the myth about the expedition of Heracles and Telamon against Troy, but emphasizes their setting out "in ships" (v. 30) and Heracles' summoning his shipmate "to the voyage" (36). In this poem, Aegina is graced by an epithet unique in Pindar's surviving works, "this city beloved-of-God" (v. 60). By far the most moving of these early odes, however, is ***Isthmian 5,*** which opens with a reference to "ships contending on the sea" (vv. 4-5). Later, Aegina is praised as "this city of good laws" (*eunomon*) which has "proceeded upwards along the pure path of God-given deeds" (vv. 22-23). Pindar notes that "the good warriors among her heroes" have had their fame immortalized in poets' praises (vv. 26-27), and he seems to intend to include Aeginetans of the more recent as well as the mythical past. It is an "illustrious island," and the epithet, *diaprepea* (44), is again unique in Pindar's surviving works. Unlike the walls of Troy, Aegina "has from of old had a battlement of walls to be scaled only by lofty excellence" (44-45). The passage that follows shows where all this apparently unspecific praise is really leading: "Even now could Ajax's city Salamis bear witness that she was kept on an even keel by [Aegina's] sailors in Zeus' murderous hailstorm that brought death to countless men" (vv. 48-50). After opening ***Isthmian 8,*** written probably in 478, with the heartfelt prayer of thanks for the passing of the Persian threat, "Tantalus' stone" (v. 11), Pindar later remarks, "Aeacus' godlike sons, and their children dear to Ares, excelled (*aristeuon*) by their manliness in managing the echoing bronze din of battle" (vv. 26-27). The phrase is as likely to have a specific as a general reference: Pindar perhaps once again has in mind the *aristeia,* or prizes of excellence, won by the Aeginetans for their showing at Salamis.

Nemeans 3 and ***4*** have been placed in the 470's. In both poems Pindar pays his compliments to Aeginetan hospitality, "that Dorian island . . . abounding in guests" (***Nem 3.*** 2-3), "stronghold-seat of the Aeacids, shining a communal light to protect and give justice to strangers" (***Nem. 4.*** 12-13). This same image of the beacon light of rectitude recurs in the earlier poem: "the Aeacids' light firmly fixed and visible afar off shines from there" (***Nem. 3.*** 64). Although the dates and the exact circumstances in which ***Paean 6*** and ***Nemean 7*** were composed remain uncertain, they can reasonably be seen as "paired" poems, and they have on stylistic grounds been assigned to Pindar's middle period, that is, in the 470's or 460's. Although not commissioned for an Aeginetan patron, ***Paean 6*** contains a passage in which Pindar outdoes his former praise of the island: "island of famous name, you dwell in and rule over a Dorian sea, O shining star of Hellenic Zeus!" (vv. 123-26); he then calls on Aegina to reveal the source of her "divine spirit of leadership at sea and her excellence at observing the rights of guests" (130-31). Almighty Zeus, the poet remarks, has bestowed prosperity, *olbos,* on the island (133) but in the light of an earlier reference to the fall of Troy, which the gods could defer but not avert (80-83), this may be more in the nature of a wish than a statement of fact. It was antiquity's view that ***Nemean 7*** was written by Pindar as a recantation of his harsh treatment of Neoptolemus in the ***Paean,*** but even if that were not the case, the two poems seem to stand together as a kind of diptych. Aegina is praised as the "song-loving city of the Aeacids of the clashing spears" (v. 9), but there seems to be a hint of trouble: wise men can foresee the coming storm (17-18). The note of possible danger ahead is sounded again at the end, where the chorus address the hero Heracles and pray for "assistance for mortals against impassable difficulties" (96-97); "may you join and interweave a firmly fixed and happy life" for the victor, "and may their children's children hold forever their present honour and even greater hereafter" (98-101). In ***Nemean 6,*** perhaps dating from the late 460's, Aegina is still "this famous island" and the Aeacids' name "flies far over land and sea" (vv. 46-48), but the nautical imagery once again takes an ominous turn: the wave whirling before the ship sets the sailor's heart to trembling (55-57). ***Nemean 8,*** probably from the same time, opens with lofty praise of Aeacus and puts him in the remarkable position of receiving suppliant delegations even from Sparta and Athens (vv. 11 ff.); this has been taken, perhaps rightly, as an appeal in particular to the latter city to deal equitably with her old enemy, and the comment which follows, "prosperity (*olbos*) engendered with God's help is more abiding for men" (v. 17), may be covert admonition to the Aeginetans. In ***Olympian 8,*** which from evidence the Scholiasts provide can be securely dated to 460 B.C., Aegina's naval glories are once again touched on ("land of long-oared ships") and her justice and hospitality given more than passing praise: "where Right who brings safety, who shares the throne of Zeus of Guests, is honoured outstandingly among men" (vv. 20-23); "some divine ordinance set firm this land as a godlike pillar for strangers of all kinds" (25-27). Then a tone of concern creeps in: "may time in its rise not tire of accomplishing this." The poem closes with a prayer that "Zeus send no contentious spirit of revenge, but may give them a life without woes and make them and their city flourish" (vv. 86-88). The last phrases seem to strike once again a note of apprehension. Within a few years of the performance of this ode, in the summer of 458 B.C., there occurred the "great naval battle" between Athens and Aegina that Thucydides records (1. 105. 2). Other, less reliable sources, indicate that the Aeginetan fleet may have been augmented just before this, and there is archaeological evidence of expansion and strengthening of her south harbour, although the sequence of these events is not certain. If Athens took these developments as threats to her own growing dominance of Aegean maritime affairs, she may have tried to force Aegina to join her military alliance, the so-called Delian League. The inevitable refusal by Aegina would have been enough to goad Athens into retaliating. In any case the confrontation came, and allies of both the belligerents "were present" (so Thucydides), and probably joined in the fighting: Athens and her league members vs. Aegina's supporters in the Peloponnesian League, Corinth and Epidaurus, which had fleets, Megara, and possibly also Thebes and Sparta herself. The Athenian side won, seventy Aeginetan ships were captured, the city itself was invested and a nine-month siege ensued. Aegina was compelled to take down her fortifications, hand over her fleet and become a tribute-paying member of the Delian Alliance. In the last surviving ode for an Aeginetan victory, ***Pythian 8,*** which dates apparently from 446 B.C., the poet hymns Aegina one final time:

> The Graces have been allotted this island-city of justice;
> She has her hand on the excellent deeds of the renowned
> Aeacidae;
> Full and perfect is her repute from of old;
> A subject of songs is her nurture of heroes outstanding in
> numerous contests for prizes and in fast-moving battles;
> In men too she excels.
>
> (vv. 21-27)

But, as Pindar and most Greeks believed, men are "creatures of a day . . . the dream of a shadow" (95-96). The prayer with which Pindar ends, "dear mother Aegina, convey this city on a voyage of freedom," (98-99), was not to be fulfilled.

Pindar's connections with Athens began early, when he was hardly out of his teens. A combination of ancient testimonies places his birth in the Pythian year of the sixty-fifth Olympiad, that is in 518 B.C. and a recently discovered Oxyrhynchus papyrus (2438) records a victory of his at Athens with a dithyramb in either 497-496 or 496-495. He is reported to have studied there with various teachers who are now mere names, Apollodorus and Agathocles, and to have come under the influence of the celebrated dithyrambist Lasus of Hermione. Only two victory odes survive for Athenian patrons, the extremely brief ***Pythian 7*** of 486 B.C. for Megacles of the Alcemonid family, and ***Nemean 2*** for Timodemus of the *deme* or district of Acharnae, probably to be dated about the same time. Besides victory songs, however, Pindar is known to have composed under Athenian sponsorship a ***Paean*** (number ***5*** in the traditional numbering) to be sung by an Athenian choir at a festival to Apollo on Delos. In the paean, the chorus related how the Athenians in the distant past "took and dwelt in Euboea . . . and settled in the Scattered Islands (that is, the Sporades, Siphnos, Seriphos and Skyros) rich in flocks, and held famous Delos" (vv. 35-40). He also composed at least one dithyramb, notorious even in antiquity but replete with problems; a song to be sung in the festival of Oschophoria in honour of Athena Skiras, which celebrated Theseus' return from Crete after his successful encounter with the Minotaur; and a dirge for another Alcmeonid, a certain Hippocrates, who is probably to be identified as brother of Cleisthenes the lawgiver and the father of the Megacles who commissioned ***Pythian 7.*** In ***Pythian 1*** Pindar's chorus sing: "I shall win from the Athenians the favour of recompense for Salamis" (vv.76. 77), the reference seems to be hypothetical, since Pindar goes on in the next phrase to say, in effect, "and recompense from the

Spartans for mentioning Plataea"; the two battles are bracketed simply as prelude to a military victory against the Carthaginians by the Syracusan patrons who commissioned this ode. In ***Paean 2,*** the poet alludes to a more poignant episode of the campaign of resistance to the Persians when the chorus of citizens of Abdera sing, "I am a young city, but I nevertheless saw my mother's mother stricken with enemy fire" (vv. 28-30). Pindar apparently meant the Persian burning of Athens, since she claimed to be founder of Ionian Teos, which in turn colonized Abdera. Pindar then draws a general mortal: "if anyone in aiding friends goes forth fiercely to meet the enemy, his labour wins peace because of his opportune descent to combat" (vv. 30-34). This can, and perhaps should, be taken as a graceful compliment to the Athenians for their single-minded if not single-handed resistance to the Persians in 480.

The brief surviving ode honouring Megacles' chariot victory at Delphi in 486 has been subjected to close scrutiny in an effort to decipher some possible covert message from the poet to the Athenian populace at large. "The fairest prelude is Athens great among cities when laying a foundation of songs for chariots for the wide-ruling race of Alcmeonids; for what country, what house could one name as his dwelling more glorious for Greece to hear? For all cities are visited, Apollo, by the account of Erechtheus' citizens, who made your chamber at divine Pytho a place of wonder" (vv. 1-9). Several points in this first part of the poem call for comment. "Great among cities," *megalopolies,* is an epithet Athens shares with Syracuse (***Pythian 2.*** 1). The poet's use of an architectural metaphor in "foundation" and his mention of the Delphic temple were taken by the Scholiast as alluding to the way that the Alcmeonids had ingratiated themselves with Apollo's oracular shrine by their undertaking, many years before, to rebuild the temple that had been destroyed in a disastrous fire soon after the middle of the sixth century, and then completing the project more lavishly than called for by the terms of the contract. The propaganda value to the Alcmeonid family throughout the Greek world must have been enormous, as Herodotus, who tells the story (5. 62), implies. Pindar, who incorporated into ***Paean 8*** the tradition of a succession of Delphic temples in pre-historic times, would certainly have known of the Alcmeonids' largesse (if it was that). It seems reasonable to suppose that he chose to emphasize it as a well-known link between his patron's family and the site of the victory. In the list of the family's other victories to which Pindar moves at vv. 10 ff., he mentions one at Olympia, almost certainly to be identified with the victory won by this Megacles' grandfather, Alcmeon, which Herodotus mentions (6. 125), probably in 592 B.C. A shadow, as we have already seen, falls across the end of the poem; Pindar's chorus say "I am grieved by the *phthonos,* envy, with which noble deeds are requited" (vv. 14-15). The Scholiast follows the Alexandrian critic Aristarchus in seeing here an allusion to the death of the victor's father, Hippocrates, but most modern scholars prefer to discover a cryptic reference to Megacles' own recent ostracism, an event brought vividly to life by the discovery in 1965 by the German excavators of the Athenian Cerameicus of over 2,200 *ostraka,* painted or inscribed fragments of pottery, bearing Megacles' name. Whatever it is that must temper the victor's joy, Pindar can conclude with a theme to which he frequently reverts: good fortune, for all the richness of its blossoming, is for humans never unalloyed in its effect.

Nemean 2, the other surviving Athenian victory ode, dates from perhaps a year or two after the Megacles poem and is only slightly longer, twenty-five lines compared to eighteen. The victor, one Timodemus from the *deme* Acharnae somewhat north of Athens was "given a straight escort by his destiny along his father's path" and has himself proven an "adornment to great Athens" (vv. 6-8); history preserves no further evidence to identify either son or father, whom Pindar also names, Timonoös (v. 10). To judge from the number and variety of victories listed later in the poem, the family had achieved some prominence in athletic if not political circles. The poet makes one cryptic remark that has not been satisfactorily explained: "It is certainly true that Salamis can nurture a man who is a warrior" (vv. 13-14), and he then goes on to bracket Timodemus' achievement with that of Ajax at Troy. The Scholiasts confessed themselves nonplussed: What does a mythical hero from Salamis have to do with a victor from the northern part of Attica? They quote two first-century B.C. commentators for different explanations, neither of which seems compelling: either the victor's ancestors had originally gone to Salamis as one of the Athenian "cleruchs," or resident Athenian settlers, towards the end of the sixth century, or the family, like those of Cimon, Miltiades, and Alcibiades, traced its descent from the hero Ajax. In a poem of about this same time Pindar alludes to Athens being notable for producing some of the most successful athletic trainers of the day: "a fashioner of athletes should come from Athens" (***Nemean 5.*** 48), and he names two of them, a certain Menander in connection with the foregoing remark, and a man whose family became politically prominent in the next generation, Melesias the celebrated wrestling coach, "a charioteer of skill and strength" (***Nemean 6.*** 66; also 4. 93). He is probably the Melesias whose son, bearing the same name as the historian, Thucydides, later became leader of the conservative aristocratic faction that attempted to obstruct the building programme of Pericles just after mid-century.

Sometime after the great encounters of 480, Pindar accepted a commission from the Athenians for a dithyramb, a poem that brought him fame and fortune in his own lifetime, and that enjoyed a great celebrity in later antiquity. It is best to begin by putting out the facts about this elusive poem, before considering the elaborate stories, for the most part bearing marks of the fabulous, that surround it. It began with an extravagant address to the city: "sleek and violet-crowned and famed in song, support of Hellas, famous Athens, the gods' own city" (fr. 76). These lush praises appear to have made a tremendous impact on the Athenian audience. In a passage in the *Acharnians* (425 B.C.), Aristophanes has his chorus make fun of the Athenians for "sitting up on your bottoms' edge because of the 'crowns,' and if anyone flatters you further by calling Athens 'sleek,' he could earn anything because of 'sleek,' applying a term of honour for sardines!" (vv. 637-40). Pindar's choice of the epithet "violet-crowned" was a particularly felicitous one, for it captures the hue of the special purplish or amethystine glow visible over Mt. Hymettus as the sun is setting and also suggests that Athens has something of the divine about her, since, as A. B. Cook has shown it was common practice to bedeck statues of such joyous divinities as Aphrodite, the Muses and the Graces with wreaths of violets on festal occasions. A possible implication of Aristophanes' joke is that Pindar received some special recompense from the Athenians for this dithyramb, but what exactly it was remains in doubt. Later writers, including the travel writer Pausanias (1. 8. 4), saw a statue of Pindar in front of the Stoa Basileios, the so-called Royal Stoa that has recently been excavated by the Agora archeologists. Pindar was portrayed sitting with lyre in hand, an unrolled book in his lap, and a diadem on his head. The statue is specifically said to have been a reward for the dithyramb under discussion. Extreme caution must be used in disentangling fact from fiction in this whole episode. Our credulity is strained, for example, when we read of the heaping up of honours, reported by writers as respectable as Isocrates (*Antidosis* 166), which included Pindar's designation as Athenian *proxenos,* or honorary consul, in his native city, and a money grant of 10,000 drachmas. This last figure seems inordinately large, although it compares favourably with the ludicrously inflated ten talents said to have been bestowed by the Athenians on Herodotus. A different version reduces Pindar's award to 1,000 drachmas, but complicates the issue by designating it as Athens' payment of the fine imposed upon the poet by his fellow Thebans in a fit of jealous outrage at his lavish praises of a rival city. A further variation has the Athenians pay twice the amount of the fine, which is left unspecified. The *proxenia* should probably be rejected, for it both represents a conventional "reward" and looks like a doublet of the otherwise authenticated *proxenia* held by Pindar for the Delphians (Pindar has also been credited with a proxeny for the Molossians of Epirus, on the slender basis of a cryptic comment in ***Nemean 7,*** vv. 64-65, but the Scholiasts on the passage offer that as only one possible interpretation of Pindar's words); the 1,000 drachma payment is on the surface of it plausible enough and may represent nothing more than the fee specified by Pindar in the first place. The statue remains a possibility, but seems exceedingly unlikely for this early period, when the only other humans so honoured were the so-called tyrannicides Harmodius and Aristogeiton, whose original portrait-group, carried off by Xerxes, was perhaps just at this time in process of being replaced. The Theban fine and Athenian payment of it, whether simply or in twice the amount, has no claim to credibility; it probably represents nothing more than a garbled reminiscence by a later writer of the 1,000 drachma fine imposed by the Athenians on the dramatist Phrynichus, which Herodotus reports (6. 121).

In an additional passage from this same dithyramb, quoted not less than four times by Plutarch, Pindar alluded to the series of sea fights off Cape Artemisium in Northern Euboea, "where the sons of the Athenians laid the bright foundation of freedom." The building metaphor perhaps provides a link with the victory ode for Megacles (***Pythian 7.*** 3), but it is also an apt image for the battles to which Pindar applies it. Herodotus' more sober account can stand as a kind of corrective, for he makes it clear that the engagements with the Persians off Euboea in the early summer of 480 B.C. were at best indecisive—which did not prevent the Athenians' putting up a thanks offering in Artemis' sanctuary there for having "defeated hordes of motley men from Asia." If Artemisium was the "foundation of freedom," Pindar may have gone on to recount the succeeding battles of 480, especially Salamis for he mentioned that victory in ***Pythian 1*** (75 ff.) as being especially likely to win him gratitude and even recompense from the Athenians. It is possible, too, that a scene describing the burning of Athens by the Persians also found a place in the dithyramb, for what has been taken as a reference to this event occurs in ***Paean 2,*** when the chorus of Abderites lament the fact that their "mother's mother" (Abdera's metropolis, Ionian Teos, in theory settled from Athens during the Dark Age migrations) had been "stricken by the enemy's fire" (vv. 28-31). It is difficult to be sure what else the dithyramb contained, but G. Donnay in a brief note in *Revue Belge de Philologie et d'Histoire* (vol. 42, 1964, pp. 205-6) puts forward the attractive theory that some of the otherwise unassigned Theseus fragments belong to it, especially those that related how the Amazons invaded Attica and (a mythical prototype of the Persians in 480) laid siege to the Acropolis. The siege was ultimately terminated through the good offices of the Amazon Antiope, whom Theseus had captured and wed on an earlier expedition to the Black Sea and who became, according to Pindar (fr. 176), the mother of his son Demophon. How much of this Pindar actually touched on in his poem remains matter for speculation, but a glorification of Theseus would certainly have been appropriate in a period that was to culminate in his elevation to the role of patron saint of the Delian League, and Cimon's "discovery" and transferral of his bones to Athens *c.* 474 B.C. Donnay also may be correct in ascribing to a propagandistic purpose the rather odd innovation with which Pindar is credited by Pausanias (7. 2. 7), that the Amazons on their way to invade Attica stopped at Ephesus and founded the famous sanctuary to Artemis there; here was an older and more celebrated "Artemisium" that Pindar may have hinted was a spiritual forerunner of the shrine in Euboea, and there may well be some connection with Ephesus' recent, or impending, entry into the Delian Alliance. Although some editors have also assigned to the Athenian dithyramb a striking fragment in which the chorus call upon a personification of the battle cry "daughter of war, to whom men are offered on behalf of their city in the holy sacrifice of death" (fr. 78), the lines are never cited in connection with the more celebrated Athenian dithyramb, and their basically choriambic rhythm seems to mark them off as metrically distinct from the other fragments.

There was, however, at least one other dithyramb for Athens. Dionysius of Halicarnassus (*On Literary Composition,* 22) preserves a long and flowery excerpt from it.

> Hasten to the dance, Olympian gods,
> And send upon it your renowned grace.
> To the city's navel filled with throngs, smoking
> With sacrifices in sacred Athens
> You proceed, to her splendid, famous agora,
> To receive garlands bound with violets and
> songs like spring flowers.
>
> (fr. 75. 1-6)

The spirit of spring pervades the second part of the excerpt, where Pindar describes the "fragrant, nectared plants," violets and roses, whose blossoms are strewn on the ground or twined in the hair of the revellers, and where the strains of singers and flautists re-echo their songs in honour of Semele, mother of the god whose festival is being celebrated, Dionysus. It is a charming opening of what must have been a very pretty song, although few of the details concerning its performance can be definitely fixed. Mention of the "city's navel" in verse 3 is generally taken to be a reference to the altar of the twelve gods, which, Thucydides reports (6. 54), was erected by the younger Peisistratus, grandson of the tyrant, and which constituted the official centre of the city from which distances to other parts of Attica and even beyond were measured. This is far from proving, however, that the dithyramb was performed in the agora, as some commentators have assumed; the gods of the agora are summoned as a kind of official divine delegation to lend the weight of their authority to the ceremony that is about to take place. A relatively recent suggestion about the poem's occasion of performance maintains that it was written for the festival of Anthesteria, on the basis of a derivation of the term "anthesteria" from *anthea,* blossoms, flowers, and the superabundant allusions in Pindar's verses to the garlands of violets, roses and other spring flowers with which the chorus bedeck themselves and strew their way. This theory, attractive as it may at first sight appear, must be rejected in view of the absence of any good evidence that dithyrambs were performed at the Anthesteria, which, though it was to some extent a harvest festival celebrating the new vintage, also contained a large admixture of a more somber element, the propitiation of dead souls to avert their possibly malevolent intervention during the year to come; it is possible that this latter aspect predominated and that even the "flower" etymology for the name of the festival, though widely accepted even in antiquity, was mistaken, and that the word derives, as Verrall suggested, from a rare, archaic verb meaning "to summon up (the dead souls) by prayer." It seems best, therefore, to return to the older view that Pindar's song was performed at the major festival in honour of Dionysus at which dithyrambic competitions were held, the City Dionysia. A further, perhaps insoluble, difficulty remains in the poet's apparent reference to the chorus' coming into the presence of the god "second" or "a second time" (verse 8). Some have seen this as an autobiographical comment by the poet: this is his second competition at Athens; but in fact such a personal remark is not in keeping with Pindar's style, where the chorus speaks primarily for itself, or at least in some more objective, general way. The phrase, therefore, is likelier to allude to this particular chorus performing for a second time in the festival. (A less likely interpretation has it that they are referring to their place in the Dionysiac procession.)

Some have professed to see a cooling off of the warmth of Pindar's honorific epithets for Athens. In the dithyrambs, of uncertain date, we find "sacred," and "sleek," the latter being applied again to Athens in ***Nemean 4*** and ***Isthmian 2,*** dating perhaps from the 470's; elsewhere Pindar applies this rather extravagant praise also to Thebes, Orchomenos, Olympia, Marathon, and Smyrna. From ***Pythian 7*** for Megacles of 486 B.C. and ***Nemean 2*** of perhaps just slightly later, we noticed two near-synonyms, "a great city," and "great." The Rhodian victor of ***Olympian 7,*** composed in 464 B.C., had won earlier in "rocky" Athens (v. 82, *kranaais,* probably an archaic traditional epithet), and the same rather spare phrase occurs again in ***Olympian 13*** of the same year, for a Corinthian victor, and in ***Nemean 8*** of a few years later; but this is perhaps balanced by the reference in ***Nemean 10*** (date unknown, but perhaps from the 460's) to praise rendered an Argive victor by "sweet Athenian voices" (vv. 33-35).

By 460, however, things have changed. Athens' foreign policy has become much more aggressive, and she is even willing now to challenge Sparta and her allies, among them Pindar's native Thebes and his beloved Aegina, to a test of strength that culminated in hostilities known as the First Peloponnesian War. If the battle alluded to in ***Isthmian 7*** did indeed occur during this war (p. 211), then Pindar's phrases like "hail of blood" and "enemy host" are but thinly veiled indictments of Thebes' opponent, Athens. Bowra may be right to see the myth of Bellerophon's mad, ultimately abortive, attempt to vault to heaven on his winged steed Pegasus as an allegorical attack on Athens' aggrandizing ambition. In 446 B.C. Pindar composed for an Aeginetan victor ***Pythian 8,*** a poem that Wade-Gery termed [in his *Essays in Greek History,* 1958] "passionate, rapt, serene." In a parallel to the Bellerophon myth, and perhaps equally allegorically, Pindar introduces the giants Porphyrion and Typhos to exemplify the futility of naked aggressive force bound to be thwarted in the end by the "higher" moral force of Zeus and the Olympians. In the previous decade, Aegina had unsuccessfully attempted to resist the growing power of Athens' Delian Alliance, had been beaten decisively at sea, besieged, and made to become a tributary member at a sizable annual assessment. The poem opens with an address to "Peace, daughter of Justice, you make cities great" (a similar personification, "Peace, lover of cities" occurs in ***Olympian 4***), and it is perhaps not a coincidence that Pindar adapts the adjective he had previously used of Athens in the poem for Megacles. At the end he prays to the patron goddess of the island, the nymph Aegina, to "convey this city on a voyage of freedom," a prayer made more poignant by the island's state of virtual servitude to Athens.

A substantial proportion of Pindar's surviving odes were composed for Sicilian victors, most of whom were in positions of authority in their cities, either as self-styled *basileis,* "kings," or "monarchs" (whose autocratic power, however, in some cases rested more on brute force than on constitutional validity), or as junior members of these ruling families, or mere courtiers. Pindar's chief purpose is to praise, and the items he mentions most frequently are the obvious external and material features of a royal court: the vast sums spent on socially acceptable and even beneficial projects, buildings and other public works; the lavishness of a wealthy host's hospitality to foreign visitors (especially poets seeking commissions); the magnificence of festivals and other ritual occasions honouring the city's gods; an intense and spare-no-expense drive towards victory in the great Panhellenic games, which brought with it international celebrity. Blended into the grand eulogizing chords, however, are subtler but insistent notes of admonition, tactful urgings to gentleness, moderation and a use of wealth and power for peaceful, genuinely civic, ends. Pindar, it appears, truly saw himself in the role not just of panegyrist, but as a trusted counsellor and in some cases even a real friend of his powerful patrons.

How these themes are interwoven can be seen in two odes composed not for a "king," but for a private although very wealthy citizen of Camarina on the south coast of Sicily. They date probably from the 450's, at any rate well after a troubled period in the earlier part of the century when the city had been several times destroyed and taken over by the tyrants of nearby Gela. Psaumis, the individual whose victory with a mule car at Olympia is being celebrated, may have undertaken some improvements to the city's water supply. In one of the poems Pindar makes special mention of the city's two main rivers, one of which he describes as "swiftly welding together a soaring forest of steadfast dwellings, bringing this people of citizens out of perplexity into the light of day" (***Olympian 5,*** vv. 13-14, after Sandys; the ascription to Pindar has been questioned by some scholars). In the preceding poem, which may in fact have been written for the same victory, the chorus sing, "I praise him for his ready expenditure on horses, for the joy he takes in hospitable entertainment of guests, and for turning with pure mind towards Peacefulness, lover of cities" (***Olympian 4,*** vv. 14-16). The last comment may point, as the Scholiast suggests, to Psaumis steering clear of the factional involvements that had brought troubles upon his city.

Pindar's connection with the ruling family of Akragas, the Emmenidae, dated from at least 490 B.C., when he composed two ***Pythians, 12*** and ***6,*** the former in honour of a flautist who seems to have been employed by the court, and the latter celebrating a chariot victory by Xenocrates, brother of the future tyrant, Theron. The actual victory had been won by Xenocrates' young son and charioteer, Thrasybulus, with whom Pindar seems to have struck up a close friendship; several lines from an after-dinner song in his honour survive (fr. 124, Snell), perhaps written about this time, and his virtues as a drinking companion are alluded to at the close of ***Pythian 6.*** The youth's moderation and disciplined temperament are extolled: "he keeps his wealth reined in intelligently, culls no flowers of unjust or overbearing pride from his youth, but rather wisdom in the Muses' haunts" (vv. 47-49); the poet allows himself a hint of an admonitory tone that will become more pronounced in the later Sicilian odes.

Xenocrates' brother Theron, who became tyrant of Akragas in 488 B.C., won the chariot race at Olympia in 476, and Pindar's celebratory ode, ***Olympian 2,*** opens with a burst of praise: "Proclaim Theron, just in his converse with guests, pillar of Akragas, flower of famous ancestors who guides his city aright" (vv. 6-7). At the close of the poem, Pindar turns back to praise Theron again: "like a friend lavishing benefits with an open hand, his city has not found his equal in 100 years" (vv. 93-94). In spite of "envious babbling that tries to hide good men's fine deeds" (the Scholiast on the immediately preceding passage sees hints of friction with Hieron of Syracuse over the latter's brother, Polyzelus, who had married Theron's daughter and had sought refuge with his father-in-law), it would be as impossible to recount all the joys Theron has given others as to number the sands of the sea (vv. 93-100). Pindar composed another ode, ***Olympian 3,*** for this same victory, which was intended to be performed at a *theoxenia* in the victor's city, a ritual banquet honouring the city's gods. Fittingly, then, Theron and his brother Emmenids are praised for their dutiful observance of religious obligations; by them "more than by any other mortals are hospitable tables laid for the gods, for they keep the rites of the Blessed Ones with pious heart" (vv. 39-41). This theme of discharging religious duties occurred also in an ***Encomium*** for Theron of which only fragments remain: the citizens of Akragas "inhabit a lofty city, raising vast gifts to the gods, and a cloud of wealth ever-flowing surrounds them" (frs. 118-19, Snell). It is touched on once more in ***Isthmian 2,*** a poem composed probably after the deaths of both Theron and Xenocrates, in which the latter is complimented for his "temperament sweet beyond other men's"; he was "revered by the citizens in their dealings with him" and, like Theron, he "welcomed the gods' ritual banquets." His "hospitable table," which he would go to any lengths to replenish, was never wracked by any inclement weather (vv. 36-42).

Pindar's odes for the tyrants of Akragas are, for the most part, on a simpler scale than his more extensive and elaborate series of victory odes that he composed for Hieron of Syracuse and the members of his court. Hieron had taken over from his elder brother Gelon as tyrant of Gela in 485, and when Gelon died in 478 he moved over to succeed him at Syracuse. Unfairly or not, it was reported in the later tradition that Hieron's rule was much harsher than Gelon's had been. Diodorus reports that Gelon was "beloved by all because of his mild rule" and "lived in uninterrupted peace until his death" (11. 67. 3 in Oldfather's translation). The notice is probably over-eulogistic; the people of Camarina, which Gelon had destroyed in 484, would doubtless have expressed different sentiments. Hieron, on the other hand, was "avaricious and violent and, speaking generally, an utter stranger to sincerity and nobility of character" (Diodorus 11. 67. 4, Oldfather). We have no reason to doubt this account of Hieron's unpopularity, and his subjects' criticisms of his rule may help to explain two themes heard frequently in Pindar's odes for his Syracusan patron. The first is a tendency to offer justification of his autocratic position, which must, in Pindar's eyes, be taken more as a sign of the gods' favour than as the result of any innate qualities that the divinely blessed individual may possess. Secondly, there is a tone of admonition to Hieron to live up to the unchallenged power he enjoys; in other words, "right legitimizes might." Pindar opens the resplendent ***Olympian 1,*** written for Hieron's victory in the horse race in 476 B.C., by proclaiming, "We have come to the rich and blessed hearth of Hieron, who wields a sceptre of righteousness in Sicily rich in flocks, where he plucks the crowns of all excellence" (vv. 10-13). Hieron is "King of Syracuse who delights in chariot-racing," where "King," *basileus,* seems to be chosen as an honorific, even a legitimizing, title. The poet then develops the myth of Tantalus and Pelops, and chooses some rather ominous details that are perhaps intended as a kind of moral lesson to Hieron: Tantalus "could not digest his great prosperity (*olbos*), but through greed (*koros*), won destruction, *atê,* for his pride" (vv. 55-57), that is, the everlasting punishment of the rock; the moral of Tantalus', if not Hieron's, story: "if a man thinks that any of his actions go unnoticed by God, he is wrong" (64). At the close of the poem, Pindar returns to his characteristic tempering of praise by advice: "I am confident that I shall never adorn with my song any host with more knowledge of noble ends or more power to achieve them; God has taken upon himself the task of being overseer of your concerns" (vv. 104-7). Similarly, in the consolatory ***Pythian 3*** (*c.* 474 B.C.), Pindar prays for the miracle of health for his "Etnaean host, who holds sway in Syracuse, a King, gentle to his citizens, not grudging the good, a wonderful father to guests" (vv. 69-71). And later, "the fate of blessedness attends you; great destiny looks with favour upon you, if anyone of men, as leader of the people and *tyrannos*" (vv. 84-86), a unique application of this word by Pindar to any of his Sicilian patrons.

Pindar uses "Etnaean" in the above citation because about this time Hieron had embarked on a grandiose scheme to expel the original inhabitants of Catane and resettle it under the name of "Etna," and his brother-in-law and lieutenant, Chromios, has been named overseer. For this individual Pindar wrote two odes, ***Nemeans 1*** and ***9.*** The themes in ***Nemean 1*** are mainly honorific: Zeus'—Olympian and Etnaean Zeus'—blessings on Sicily, "rich with wealthy crowns of cities" and famed for her soldiers and athletes (vv. 15-18). The victor and, by extension, his superior, Hieron, "loves guests"; their "halls lack not experience of foreigners" (vv. 19-23). In ***Nemean 9*** Etna is "new-founded," Chromios' house is "prosperous," his doors again flung open wide to guests (2-3). When Pindar prays to Zeus that the children of the Etnaeans might be awarded "an allotment of sound laws . . . and splendid celebrations by the citizens" (vv. 29-31), we may suspect that this is more admonition than praise; Pindar is tactfully saying to Hieron that now, after the upheavals of founding the city, he must be careful to maintain sound laws, *eunomia,* and to keep the citizens secure. "From labours in youth, with justice in attendance, there comes peace with age . . . wonderful prosperity from the gods" (vv. 44-45). The poem closes with praises of peacefulness, *Hêsychia,* and the various blessings that attend it, like revels and banquets.

In ***Olympian 6*** of 472 B.C., for a Syracusan victor, the poet returns to the theme of the legitimacy of Hieron's rule over the most ancient part of Syracuse, the island of Ortygia, "with pure sceptre and fitting counsels" (vv. 93-94). Hieron's "gentler" virtues are once again underlined: the hereditary priesthood he holds of Demeter and Persephone, the feasts where his name is celebrated with lyre and song, his "lovely deeds of friendliness" (vv. 95-98). The most famous of Pindar's Sicilian odes is ***Pythian 1,*** which celebrated Hieron's chariot victory at Delphi in the summer of 470 B.C. Hieron's enemies are tacitly compared to Typhos, whom Zeus overcame and buried under the crushing weight of Mt. Etna, whose periodic eruptions were poetically conceived, both by Pindar here and elsewhere and by Aeschylus in his *Prometheus Bound,* as the angry exhalations of the once dangerous but now subdued monster; by implication some of Zeus' power in overcoming *his* opponents transfers itself to Hieron. In the central section of the ode, the poet turns to a meditation on the source of all human success, the gods' goodwill; the honour Hieron has won in numerous battles, "such honour as no man in all Hellas has reaped e'er now, a proud and lordly crown of wealth" (vv. 49-50, trans. Conway), is the result not only of his own "enduring soul" (in the brief myth he is likened, in his courage in the face of physical debility, to Philoctetes), but of the "gods' devices" (v. 49). Pindar settles down to the business at hand, the direct but tactful advice his own poetic *sophia* entitles him to dispense to "Etna's King" (v. 60). The new city has been founded in "God-built freedom" (v. 61) and according to the age-old "laws and ordinances of the Dorians"; the poet seems to be saying that antiquity brings legitimacy, as well as a standard by which to measure future performance. Pindar then prays to Zeus Fulfiller for future generations of "citizens and their kings" (68), that with God's help the youthful ruler, Hieron's young son Deinomenes, and his father their "leader" (Pindar uses an unpolitical term, *hagêtêr,* v. 69), may "honour the *damos* and turn them to harmonious peace" (vv. 71-72). The next section recalls the victory won in 474 against the Etruscans at Cymae, where the "Syracusans' leader (*archos,* the same word he had used at the poem's opening of Zeus' eagle) dragged the heavy weight of slavery from Greece" (v. 75). Pindar insists this victory, together with the earlier one against the Carthaginians at Himera in 480, is worthy of mention on an equal footing with Salamis and Plataea. The last part of the poem is a list of injunctions: "Do not relax from doing good: steer your people with the rudder of justice; forge your tongue on the anvil of truth," and so on (90 ff.); in short, leave behind you, Pindar urges, as your share of immortality the reputation of a Croesus rather than of a Phalaris (vv. 94-96).

Whatever the exact nature and occasion of the problematic ***Pythian 2*** (either, as some have thought, Pindar's private offering, which was sent "on approval" for Hieron's long-desired victory in the Olympic chariot-race in 468, or an ode written in the mid-470's to celebrate a victory at Theban games honouring Iolaos), the laudatory central section of the poem echoes many of the themes that have by now become almost commonplace: Hieron combines wealth and wisdom "with free heart" (v. 57); he is the "lord and *prytanis* (the term is applied to Zeus at ***Pythian 6,*** v. 24) of many turreted streets and a host of men" (v. 58) who has won "infinite renown" in battle (vv. 63-64). Pindar also wrote for Hieron two other poems, an ***Encomium*** (fr. 126, Snell) and an ***Hyporcheme,*** in which he is addressed as "founder of Etna, namesake and father of very holy shrines" (fr. 105 a, Snell).

An attempt must be made to summarize some of Pindar's own views about the values that justify human existence. What standards of evaluation did he use in determining what constituted genuine *areta,* "excellence"? From the frequency with which the idea recurs in his work, it is clear that he put a high premium on a special combination of physical and psychological qualities that comes down to a series of variations on the dichotomy of which the

Greeks were so fond, intelligence (word) *vs.* action (deed). Aeacus is "best in hand and counsel" (*cheiri kai boulais aristos,* ***Nem. 8.*** 8); an Aeginetan victor in the myth of ***Olympian 4*** boasts that his swiftness is matched by "hands and heart" (v. 29). Success in battle is achieved by those who are "capable (*dynatoi*) in hands and soul" (***Nem. 9.*** 39). Amphitryon is amazed at Heracles' "spirit and power" (*lêma te kai dynamin,* ***Nem. 1.*** 57). "Strength acts in deed, mind in counsels" (***Nem. 1.*** 26-27), the greatest prizes are won "by daring and strength" (***Pyth. 10.*** 24) and, as a slight modification of this contrast, a victor is said to be like "roaring lions in daring, a fox in cunning" (***Isth. 4.*** 49-51). The poet prays, seemingly in his own person, for "daring and burgeoning power" (***Olymp. 9.*** 82).

The victors who elicit Pindar's highest praise must possess not only physical strength and courage, but good looks. The victor of ***Isthmian 7*** is "wonderful in strength and attractive to look upon, and he possesses an excellence (*areta*) that casts no slight on his nature" (*phya,* v. 22); the father of a newly elected magistrate is "blessed . . . both in his admirable physique and in his innate fearlessness" (***Nem. 11.*** 12). Pindar's use of such terms as "nature," "breeding," "innate," and "inbred" shows how much stock he put in qualities, moral as well as physical, that were inherited rather than acquired. Twice he specifically draws the contrast:

> One with innate grounds for fame [*syngenei. . . eudoxiai*] is a heavyweight,
> but the one who is merely taught them [*didakta*] is obscure and has no assurance in his stride.
> (***Nem. 3.*** 40-42)

> Everything that comes by *phya* (nature, breeding) is best,
> although many men rush forward to win fame by
> skills merely learned [*didaktais . . . aretais*].
> (***Olymp. 9.*** 100-102)

The Aeginetan victor of ***Nemean 6*** "gives manifest proof of what is inborn" (v. 8). In the Dioscuri and their Dorian descendants it is "innate to be good athletes" (***Nem. 10.*** 51), just as the mythical Alcmaeon shares in the "inherited seercraft" of his father Amphiaraus and an earlier ancestor-prophet (***Pyth. 8.*** 60: at ***Nemean 1.*** 28 this craft of foretelling the future is called *syngenes,* hereditary, even among contemporary peoples). Of the Thessalian foot-race winner of ***Pythian 10*** Pindar writes: "his inborn quality trod in the tracks of his father," who had himself won two Olympic victories (vv. 12-13). A Theban victor at Nemea "does not disgrace the manly *areta* born in him" (***Isth. 3.*** 13-14). Elsewhere Pindar praises his victors for demonstrating or living up to *gnêsiais aretais* (***Olymp. 2.*** 11), where the adjective carries two connotations, "legitimate," "genuine," as well as "inborn"; he refers to a man "born for achievement (*phynt' aretai,* ***Olymp. 10.*** 20). "One must walk in straight paths and struggle in accordance with one's nature, *phya,*" the poet declares (***Nem. 1.*** 25).

Pindar's emphasis on the importance of heredity or "breeding" and the fact that so many of his patrons were wealthy (training for the competitions was extremely time-consuming, and raising racehorses was then, as now, an expensive hobby) seem to have predisposed the poet to what have been called "conservative" political attitudes. Several *obiter dicta* seem to confirm this view. In ***Pythian 3,*** a poem for Hieron, he writes "The man of honest speech stands out under any law: in a tyranny, or when the *labros* people rule, or when the wise look after the city" (vv. 86-88). This has generally been taken as a reference to the familiar threefold classification of constitutions, monarchy, democracy, and oligarchy. If this is correct (as seems probable), Pindar appears to be conferring an accolade upon oligarchy by using the epithet "wise"; what is not so clear is whether *labros* as applied to the masses (for that is the meaning that the word Pindar uses, *stratos,* undoubtedly bears, as several parallel passages indicate: ***Pythian 10.*** 8, ***Olympian 5.*** 12, ***Isthmian 1.*** 11) has a critical or pejorative connotation, as some commentators have suggested. Now although *labros* can mean, in certain contexts, something "unruly" or even "wild," there are several passages in Pindar where it seems to have only a quantitative meaning, "abundant," "vast." At ***Olympian 8.*** 36 Pindar refers to "*labron* smoke," a phrase which Sandys translates as "vast columns of smoke," and Pindar uses the term elsewhere of a rock (the manuscript reading at ***Nemean 8.*** 46); in ***Pythian 3*** he applies it to the radiance of a funeral pyre (vv. 39-40), although here it may have the additional implication of "irresistible, devouring." The poem in which the tripartite classification is mentioned was composed for Hieron, and therefore, whatever Pindar's personal preference, he could hardly have adopted a disparaging tone to the first, "tyranny," and he was probably therefore also using a neutral term to describe the remaining constitutional form, democracy. Scholars have likewise assumed that an "exclusivist" attitude to democracy lies behind the poet's remarks in ***Nemean 7,*** that "the vast majority of men have a blind heart" (vv. 23-24). Again, however, the context must be examined to see exactly what Pindar means and what his words may fairly be taken as implying. The comment occurs in a section in which the poet is contrasting the reputations achieved by Odysseus and Ajax respectively, reputations based not on intrinsic worth but, in the case of Odysseus, on the flattering portrait of him painted by Homer; Pindar then goes on to observe that "there is a kind of reverence paid to (Homer's) fabrications"—Pindar says "lies"—"and his winged skill; poetic wisdom can mislead and deceive, *and* the majority of men have a blind heart," that is, ordinary men fall under the spell of poetry, especially of so authoritative a poetic voice as Homer's, and so are ready to accept whatever the poets say (especially about the mythic period in the distant past) as true.

Towards the end of ***Pythian 11,*** Pindar has his chorus, who have now completed their praises to the Theban victor and his family, ascend to a more general level; they pray

> that the gods may grant me to have what is noble (*kalon*),
> striving for what is possible (*ta dynata*) at my time of life.
> For, since I find in a city the "middle" blossoming

with greater prosperity, I reproach the lot of tyrannies,
and I am eager for communal achievements (*xynaisi . . . aretais*)
(vv. 50-53)

It is important to try to determine what exactly Pindar intended by his use of the term *"ta mesa,"* translated above as "the middle." The majority of interpreters have assumed that the word bears a political meaning, and its occurrence in association with the phrase "in the city" seems at first sight to confirm this interpretation. Thus W. J. Slater in his *Lexicon to Pindar* suggests that the phrase means "the middle classes" and Sandys offers "the middle rank". I have quoted above the larger context in which the phrase occurs, because another interpretation seems possible. The word may have here a primarily moral connotation: "the mean," as opposed to the kind of extreme grasping that characterizes a tyrant's ambitions and ultimately hybristic grandioseness. This, I suggest, is the clear implication of including the phrase "middle" between the adjectives "possible" and "common" in the lines that precede and follow. Pindar (or his chorus) prays that he may spend his creative energies on *possible* pursuits; that his ambitions be kept within *moderate* bounds which have a chance of success (unlike those of a tyrant); that they issue in achievements such as ordinary people may aspire to, which will also—for the phrase *xynai aretai* seems to have this further implication—be of benefit to the whole community. Note, too, the similar wording of Bacchylides' *Dithyramb* 1 (*Ode* 15, 53-54): "it *lies in the middle* for all men to obtain straight justice," where Jebb's translation of the phrase in italics is "open before all men." At "Theognis" 678, the phrase *es to meson* has been translated "in the collective interest." The meaning of *ta mesa* at ***Pythian 11.*** 52, then, will be much the same as "one must hunt for only moderate profit" (*kerdeôn . . . metron,* ***Nemean 11.*** 47) and praise of a victor for "pursuing moderate things (*metra*) in his thoughts, holding fast to moderate deeds" (***Isthmian 6.*** 71). A similar phrase is used by an author close to Pindar both in time and temperament, Herodotus. In the discussion allegedly held at Persia preceding Darius' assumption of royal power, the Persian counsellor Otanes argued for turning the government over to the whole body of the Persians, "placing it in the middle" (*es meson . . . katatheinai,* 3. 80). Here, so far from implying "middle classes," or "oligarchy," the term clearly denotes a democratic form of government.

Occasionally, however, Pindar seems to speak directly to his patron's aristocratic preferences. At the end of his earliest poem, ***Pythian 10,*** composed in 498 B.C. for the Aleuad family, the hereditary dynasts of Thessalian Larissa (who were, a score of years later, to collaborate with the invading forces of Xerxes, as Herodotus reports, 7. 6 and 130), the poet remarks, "in good men's hands, born of true blood, the pilotage of cities rests secure" (vv. 71-72, Conway's translation), where the phrase "good men" has a predominantly social connotation. Pindar closes ***Pythian 2*** with a sentiment that sounds very similar: "May it be possible for me to please 'the good' and keep company with them" (v. 96), where the phrase seems to designate the aristocrats, with their whole stock of traditional values.

For all his praise of outstanding physical and moral qualities, Pindar is aware that, however great the advantages a man may have inherited from his aristocratic forbears, success can and often does still elude him; human achievement, then, ultimately depends on an additional, imponderable factor, God's grace. "When, for any deed, a beginning hath been shown by God, straight indeed is the path for pursuing virtue, and fairer are its issues" (Sandys' translation of fr. 108 a Snell); "Zeus, great *aretai* attend mortals from you" (***Isth. 3.*** 4-5); "he who tempers fine the spirit's blade in a man to valour born, may with God's help bring him to high renown" (***Olymp. 10.*** 20-21): "where God is not, that deed is no worse for being passed over in silence" (***Olymp. 9.*** 103-4); "Apollo, for mortals the completion waxes sweet as well as the beginning when a divinity lends support" (***Pyth. 10.*** 10). This can be restated as the unpredictability of Fortune, *Tychê,* in human ventures: "in the outcome of events the winner is Fortune, not Might" (fr. 38).

Victory, when it is achieved, redounds not only to the individual's but also to his city's glory, hence the emphasis already noted on *"xynai aretai,"* communal achievements (***Pythian 11.*** 53), on "that which labour achieves for the common good" (***Pythian 9.*** 93). The victor in the athletic contests "applies a common glory to his city" (***Isthmian 6.*** 69), in a way that parallels the renown, *kleos,* which the war hero's deeds win for the whole "race of citizens" (***Isthmian 7.*** 29). Correspondingly, the poet's praises "erect a common glory" to celebrate the achievement (***Isthmian 1.*** 46). In return, the collective energies of the city are called on to support the athlete's (like the soldier's) exertions: "the whole city fights for noble ends" (***Nemean 5.*** 47).

Given the divine origin of success and the collective benefits that it brings, it is almost sinful for one with outstanding abilities not to develop them to his utmost. "Among mortals, one man is cast down from good results by his empty-headed boasts, while another who devalues his strength too far stumbles and misses glorious results that are properly his; his spirit, *thymos,* has no daring and drags him backward" (***Nemean 11.*** 29-33). Achievements for the common good must be recognized as such, hence the *phthonos,* envy, shown by meaner spirits who could not have done as well, is not only a necessary price to pay, it is, paradoxically, a kind of compliment, a fitting recognition of genuine preeminence. "Honours hang over mortals; for every man there is envy stored up for excellence, whereas the one who has nothing covers his head under black silence" (fr. 94 a, vv. 8-10); "envy is better than pity" (***Pythian 1.*** 85); "prosperity has a corresponding measure of envy" (***Pythian 11.*** 29).

To describe the moment of victory and the consequent popular acclaim Pindar quite often employs an image ablaze with radiance: "*areta* flashes out clearly" (***Isthmian 1.*** 10); "their friendliness and fame blaze forth" (***Pythian 11.*** 45). But over this momentary radiance there hangs a pall cast by a typically Greek consciousness of mortality:

Even if a man have strength and surpass others in looks,
and make an example of his life by excelling in the games,
let him remember that he shrouds limbs that are mortal
and will draw about him a mantle of earth at the end.
(***Nemean 11.*** 13-16)

"We shall all die withal" (***Isthmian 7.*** 42); "there is no escaping from what is allotted" (***Pythian 12.*** 30). Pindar has one of his mythical characters ask,

For men who must die, why should one sit in darkness
nursing a vain and nameless old age,
without a share in any noble deeds?
(***Olympian 1.*** 82-84)

The poet has little ultimate solace to offer against such bleak realism; the particular interests of his patron in ***Olympian 2,*** Theron, perhaps led him to descant upon the "tearless age" of the idyllic Isle of the Blessed Ones, where "ocean breezes waft about, and flowers of gold blaze up, some from glorious trees on the land, others the water nourishes" (vv. 72-73). A much surer reward is the pseudo-immortality conferred upon human achievement by the poet's celebratory verses:

. . . great feats of strength
have only abundant darkness if they lack songs;
but for noble deeds we know a certain kind of mirror:
if with the aid of gold-crowned Memory
they find a reward for labour in the glorious songs of poets.
(***Nemean 7.*** 13-16)

Whenever a man goes to Hades' abode
after doing noble deeds but uncelebrated in song,
he has wasted his breath and has won only a brief pleasure by his toil.
(***Olympian 10.*** 91-93)

The grace of long ago sleeps;
men do not remember
unless it emerges to the high summit of the poet's craft,
yoked to famous strains of verse.
(***Isthmian 7.*** 16-19)

And, more briefly, "a hymn for good deeds makes a man's lot the equal of kings" (***Nemean 4.*** 83-85); "it is only the reputation vaunted in stories and songs that survives and reveals to later ages the life-work of men who are gone" (***Pythian 1.*** 92-94); "*areta* becomes longer-lived through famous songs" (***Pythian 3.*** 114-15).

Indeed, excellence of achievement deserves to be matched by a corresponding excellence of celebratory song, which in its turn assuages and makes worthwhile the efforts expended in winning the prize. Pindar prays the Muses to assist him in "lighting a beacon of songs . . . a crown worthy of the pankration" (***Isthmian 4.*** 43-44). "I rejoice," he remarks at the end of ***Nemean 8,*** "to send forth praise that suits the deed, and a man eases the pain of his labour with songs" (vv. 48-50). (pp. 212-43)

Anthony J. Podlecki, "Pindar and Bacchylides," in his The Early Greek Poets and Their Times, *University of British Columbia Press, 1984, pp. 203-50.*

D. S. Carne-Ross (essay date 1985)

[*Carne-Ross was a noted American classicist and scholar of comparative literature. In the following excerpt from his study* Pindar *(1985), he examines the form and conventions of the victory ode.*]

We have learned from recent studies that the victory ode is a highly disciplined form with its special conventions, its recurrent, expected features. It does not take long to recognize these things, once one has been alerted to their presence and function, and to enjoy the poet's skill in handling them and see how they are used as structural principles of composition. The victory ode, one comes to realize, is more like a classical symphony, or more exactly perhaps a classical sonata, than like any poetry written since the Romantic period. It differs from most modern poetry in this respect too, that it is always occasional, and to understand why Pindar's odes are as they are we must do what we can (it is not much) to picture the occasions they served. So and so has gained a victory in one of the four great games, Olympian, Pythian, Nemean, or Isthmian. His triumph will be celebrated on the evening of the day with a brief traditional or impromptu song, but something more solid and more splendid is needed if the achievement is to be fittingly memorialized. So the victor or his family commission a poet to compose a celebratory ode which

A boy victor of the games, from a fifth-century B.C. bronze.

will be performed later on at home. In due course the great day arrives and we must imagine the whole community united in a state of joyful anticipation, for victory in one of the major games is not simply a family affair but a civic triumph, and the victor will enjoy certain privileges in his township for life. The poet will often be there in person to conduct the performance, or he may have sent the ode and left the performance in the hands of a local chorus master. Several weeks of rehearsal will be needed, for this is a complex, composite art, with intricately patterned words to be danced and sung to the music of flute or lyre. Pindar speaks in his ***Third Olympian*** of "fitting the voice of festal splendor to the Doric sandal." The chorus is composed of young men of the region, trained from earliest youth in the art of choral dancing, as every educated Greek was, and the public too will know more or less what to look for, in the way that a musically literate person knows what to look for in a piece of classical music.

Certain elements must obviously always be included. The victor's name has to be announced, the festival at which he competed and the type of contest he won. Given the close tie binding a man to his family or clan and to his city, they too must receive their due honor. Other features we would not necessarily expect are also required; we will be looking at some of them in the course of this chapter and more closely in the readings of individual poems which follow. Some features we might expect we do not find, or only very sparingly. About the contest itself almost nothing is said, unless there was some special reason for it. Fortunately enough, the genre did not require Pindar to report that "our man was running strongly in second place on the inside track, but then with the final lap. . . ."

Let us look at an ode and see how the poet carries out his commission. He begins ***Pythian 9*** with a poetic equivalent of the actual proclamation of victory made immediately after the contest:

> I long to proclaim him!
> He took the Pythian crown, a bronzeshield runner—
> and the Graces join in my cry
> that garlands Kyrána:
> this fortunate man Telesíkrates.

The job is deftly done in the Greek with four sonorous lines stating the contest (the race in armor), the name of the festival, the victor's name, and the name of his city, Kyrana (Cyrene, in Libya). Four essential elements, and a fifth: the credentials of the poet. He can be trusted to praise the victor fittingly since he is inspired by the Graces, the goddesses who, with the Muses, preside over victory celebration.

Since these and other elements must always be included, the poet has to come up with novel ways of presenting them. Variation plays a crucial role in these poems whose immediate task is always the same. We learn to take pleasure in the poet's skill in ringing the changes on his generic constants, even when the material itself strikes us as out of place in lyric poetry. Take the so-called victory list. A man who scored in one of the great games was likely to have had other victories to his credit; often he came from an athletically successful family, and the poet was required—it would have been part of his commission—to work these various triumphs into the ode. They could not just be slipped in; they had to stand out in bold glorious relief. Nor could they simply be listed—"He won the footrace at A and B and his brother won the boxing match at C," and so forth. The thing had to be done artistically. Pindar seems to have relished the task of composing these victorious catalogues, but although he handles them with great skill they are a feature of the odes which the modern reader has to learn to enjoy. It is a lesson worth learning all the same, for it opens a way not only to aspects of Pindaric and other classical poetry but of our own traditional poetry which, since the Romantic period, we have not been at home with. Milton and Pope, for instance, are not only great poets, they are great poetic craftsmen who delight in and should delight us with their consummate virtuosity. So too Pindar, who displays his virtuosity when he heightens the bare statement "He won in the Nemean games" into this:

> Leaves from the Lion's Field thatched his brow
> the day he won
> in the shadow of the immemorial hills of Phleious.
>
> (***Nemean 6.***42 ff.)

(The Nemean valley, near the town of Phleious, was where Herakles killed the Nemean lion, one of his traditional labors.) Sometimes Pindar is content with kennings which we find at best ingenious, as when he announces that the victor has won "a warm remedy against chilly winds" (***Olympian 9.***97; the prize was a woolen jacket). Often he circumvents our prejudices successfully—in these lines, surely, for a victor in the Athenian games:

> Sweetly
> preludial voices hailed his triumph at Athens
> twice. And their fired earth brought the olive's fruit
> to this brave land of Hera
> in the great jar's patterned hold.
>
> (***Nemean 10.***33 ff.)

The prize was a richly decorated amphora filled with olive oil. The vessel is broken down into its constituent parts—the earth out of which it was made, the fruit of the olive which fills it, the painted round of its circumference. Hera's land is Argos where the victor came from. Pindar is doing here what the poet, Santayana said, must always do, disintegrating "the fictions of common perception into their sensuous elements" and recreating them in poetry's special terms to produce the sudden shock of a thing truly seen. This may seem strangely modern. Too modern for Pindar? Not necessarily. The resources of poetry have always been available to poets, even if criticism has been tardy in coming up with the terms to describe them.

The best-known and most popular feature of the Pindaric ode is the myth, though in fact by no means all odes contain a myth; nine out of the forty-five do not. They provide the occasion for some of the most dazzling poetry in Greek, but like most things in Pindar they have often puzzled his readers. Ancient criticism got us off to a bad start by regularly referring to the myths as "digressions." Two things have in particular been much canvassed, the way in which they are narrated and their relation to the victor. Both questions can best be taken in the context of particular poems, but it will be helpful to try to clear up a few points in advance.

Pindar tells a story not in chronological sequence of events but by presenting a series of lyrical moments or pictures, cutting swiftly from one to another and omitting narrative links in order to achieve the maximum concentration. Often he will start with an exciting moment near the end of the story. In ***Pythian 9,*** after the initial proclamation of the victor, he relates how in the primal days Apollo brought the nymph Kyrana to the place where her future city would arise and there made her his bride. This is the high moment of the myth and hence comes first. Pindar then moves back in time to tell us who Kyrana was, how Apollo first saw her, and after a prophecy about her future he tracks forward again and ends with another account of her marriage with the god. This mode of composition, circular rather than linear and normally regressive, is now known as ring-composition; Kyrana's story begins with her marriage and rounds back to the same event—the ring has closed on itself.

The general purpose of myth, in Pindar's odes as in almost all high Greek poetry and in the archaic poetry of other times and places, is to set the particular, nonrecurrent event—here a victory in the games—in relation to an event in the permanent, paradigmatic world of the gods and heroes which makes it understandable. The bearing of the individual myth on this or that ode has given rise to much discussion, more perhaps than is needed since usually there is a clear enough formal or official link to the athlete whose triumph is being celebrated. The myth may relate directly to him (in ***Olympian 6*** the victor was a prophet, so Pindar tells the story of the founder of his clan who was also a prophet), or to an event in his family history (the myth in ***Nemean 10*** concerns the semidivine heroes Kastor and Polydeukes who were once entertained by an ancestor of the victor; since they were patrons of the games, the family has been athletically successful ever since). Sometimes the myth is related to the victor's homeland (the victor in ***Olympian 7*** came from Rhodes and the myth relates three crucial moments in the island's history), sometimes to the place where the victory was gained (the myth in ***Olympian 3*** describes how Herakles founded the Olympian games). There is naturally more to it than this, and the function of the myth is sometimes genuinely obscure—to us at least. The best course is to look for some general consonance without trying to set up any mechanical point-for-point correspondence, leaving the mind free to ponder the deeper relations which bind the myth to its ode. I spoke of the formal or official connection, but this is sometimes no more than the bone thrown to the dog to allow the burglar to get on with his job undisturbed, to use Eliot's figure. Pindar's finest myths work in strange ways, most wonderfully when they trace the present moment of victory back to the foundational event which brought it about. This event—a sacred marriage between a god and the ancestral heroine of the victor's city it may be, or some great deed of bravery performed by an ancestor—is the origin of today's triumph, the seed from which it grew. And the movement goes two ways, not only from foundational event to present victory but back or rather *down,* from present victory to foundational event, a path to which now lies open. What grants the enormous joy breathing through the odes, before which we stand abashed and awed, is that for a brief stretch of profane time a place here on earth is bathed in the sacred light of the origins. But this leads straight to Pindar's deeps and we are not yet ready to venture into those mysterious regions.

Like myth, gnomic sentences and pithy bits of proverbial wisdom are found, inserted at strategic points, throughout the odes, as in all high Greek poetry; they too are a means of understanding the local and particular in the timeless terms of general truth. Pindar will often introduce his sententiae in the first person. "I will be small among the small, great among the great," he says in ***Pythian 3,*** and goes on to speak of what would happen if the gods should grant him wealth. He is not talking about himself here or inopportunely introducing his financial expectations. In such passages the first person means no more than "one," any man—the "first person indefinite," it has been neatly termed. Another very common and still more neutral function of the first person is to mark a transition from one part of the ode to another. In ***Olympian 8,*** after a passage in praise of the victor, the poet declares: "But I must awaken memory to tell"—and he goes on to praise the man's family. In ***Nemean 10,*** having celebrated the victor's homeland, he protests that there is simply too much to say on the subject:

> Too much for my tongue's telling
> all the fine things this Argive precinct holds!

and turns to the victor himself. The first person singular serves its functional purpose of signaling a new movement even when it seems to record a personal experience requiring attention in its own right.

In addition to these functional usages of the first person, there are many passages where we hear the poet himself in one of his several roles, as participant in and director of the performance (in reality or by convention), and as guest-friend of the victor whose achievement he is eager to praise. Our knowledge of what happened on these ancient occasions is so limited that there is often no way of deciding whether we hear the poet himself or the chorus among whom he is stationed. The bare text does not need to be explicit here since performance would have made the matter plain. There is no difficulty when, at the start of ***Isthmian 1,*** written for a Theban victor, he addresses Theba, ancestral heroine of their city, as "my mother." This is Pindar the Theban poet. But what of ***Nemean 3*** where he begins by speaking of the Muse as "our mother"? We assume that this is a choral utterance, but then the poet distinguishes himself from the chorus by describing them as they stand by the bank of their river waiting for the Muse's voice, or in other words the poet's song. The matter could be pursued (and is being pursued) in much greater detail, but perhaps all that needs be said here is that we should be on our guard against two opposing errors. We should not bluntly say "This is Pindar speaking" whenever we come across a personal pronoun. Nor should we banish him from the odes or be too zealous about finding a strictly epinician function for every personal utterance. When at the end of ***Isthmian 6*** Pindar says of the victor and his father:

> I will give them a draft of the holy water of
>   Dirka
> which the daughters of Memory golden-robed
> made to spring by the walled city of Kadmos

he is doing two things which we should not try to distinguish. He is stating his poetic credentials, a regular epinician element; the victor can be assured that the praise he is getting, drawn from the very source of all poetry, will be of the highest quality. Pindar is also asserting, with proper pride, the sacrality of his poetic calling. Great artists are not always modest little people.

This account of the victory ode has been brief, deliberately so. Pindaric specialists have debated each of the topics here discussed at great length; but I have found that a good many of them are less troublesome than they have been made out to be in the scholarly literature. In any case, the beginner—and the general reader—would be well advised to take them in stride. Moreover, paying undue attention to the conventional and generic can result in underplaying what may be uniquely Pindaric or, in other words, innovative. When a major artist makes use of an existing form he does not simply follow the rules and leave the thing as he found it. He is more likely to reshape it to his own ends. In Bacchylides one senses a modest, somewhat anonymous performer; when you commissioned an ode from him, you probably got more or less what you expected, a finely crafted decently conventional poem. I suspect that the more enterprising people who engaged Pindar's services did so knowing full well that there was no telling what to expect. That was the wonder of the man.

We should master the grammar of choral lyric, learning its rules so well that we internalize them and half "forget" them: in order to leave our attention free for what may be specially even uniquely Pindaric, for the strange and, yes, *difficult* things his poetry has to offer. His reputation as a difficult poet may not, after all, be wholly undeserved; long-standing judgments are seldom quite without foundation. There must be something to Voltaire's gibe (everyone praises Pindar because no one understands him) and to Cowley's claim that if someone translated Pindar word for word "it would be thought that one madman had translated another." Even the *débordements* of the seventeenth- and eighteenth-century Pindarique ode must reflect some quality in the original, something that the Greek scholiasts were pointing to when they censured the poet's metaphors as harsh and dithyrambic. Surely it *is* very odd to say of a victor:

> that evening by Kastalia's fountain
> he flamed with the clamor of the Graces
> (***Nemean 6***.37 f.)

and the oddity is not removed by noting that the verb is here conventional. Pindar's diction is often heightened to a point well beyond the expected hyperbole of praise. He starts one ode (***Olympian 9***) by saying that the brief traditional song hailing the victor does well enough for the immediate occasion but that if his achievement is to be celebrated properly something more is needed. He goes on (I quote from the translation of Frank Nisetich to show that I am not forcing the text to my argument):

> But now
> let the long-range bow of the Muses aim
>   at Zeus himself, lord of crimson lightning,
>   and let its arrows rain upon
> the sacred height of Elis. . . .

Then he turns to the victor's city. Praise her, he cries,

> for her triumphs
>   bursting in bloom
> by Kastalia's stream. . . .
>
> So I make this city blaze,
> fuel to my impetuous song,
> this town I love.

The expression, here and often elsewhere, is not just highly energetic; it is wrought to such a pitch of intensity and excitement that to the outsider it can well appear slightly mad. Consider the way Pindar praises his victors. They paid him to praise them, of course, and expected their poet to tell them and the world at large that by coming in first in the four hundred yards they had done something quite out of the ordinary. One can't help feeling, all the same, that the height at which he chose to pitch it must sometimes have made them wonder if what they had done quite matched the words that the poet had devised. Bacchylides is content to tell his victors that their achievement is "laid up on high with the gods" (ode 9.82 ff.) and that their fame will live on after death (13.63 f.). Sometimes Pindar does not say much more than this even though, being a stronger poet, he says it more powerfully. One victor "has gone to the top of man's endeavor" (***Nemean 3***.20); to another he says "for a mortal there is no further peak to reach" (***Nemean 9***.47). He strikes a stranger, more rapturous note when he says that the victor "casts anchor on the farthest shores of joy" (***Isthmian 6***.12 f.). Stranger still, to our ears, what he says on two occasions: "Do not try to be God" (***Olympian 5***.24, ***Isthmian 5***.14). He is not preaching prudence to his triumphant young men or warning them to go no further but telling them how staggeringly far they have come. They have momentarily entered a condition only just short of the unending felicity of the immortals. In his last and greatest poem he sees a light playing round the victor that is almost unearthly, *aigla diosdotos,* a radiance granted by Zeus.

Pindar's is a world of straddling energy and splendor, so brilliantly lit that to untutored eyes it can seem to glare. He is not hysterical or feverish; you do not have the uncomfortable sense, as you often do with a poet like Tasso, that his temperature is several degrees above normal. His pulse is steady. This is where as a poet he lives and is at home, a world where everything and everyone is *au comble du paraître,* standing before us in the plenitude of their being. Here is a golden wine bowl, *phialan khrusōi pephrikuian.* The verb (*phrissein*) means to shiver or shudder and we should let it carry its full force here. This bowl, as Pindar sees it, is not simply gleaming or glittering with gold, as translators are mostly content to write, but shuddering: *phialam auro horrentem.* Your father would praise you if he were still alive, Pindar tells one victor. But no, what the Greek says is "if he were still warmed by the raging Sun" (***Nemean 4.*** 13 f.). Soldiers in battle "break wounds" (***Nemean 8.*** 29) in the hot flesh of their enemies—"tear," everyone translates. Fire rises from an altar, "kicking the heavens with savory smoke of sacrifice" (***Isthmian 4.*** 66). Most translators prefer to write "lashing" or the like. A constant tendency of our tradition of interpretation from ancient times to today has been to tone down and tame this passionate diction.

I spoke just now of the outsider. The fact is that we are all outsiders with Pindar, in a sense and to a degree that we are not with Homer and the dramatists: outside his genre, outside the occasions for which his poems were composed. We do not of course know anything directly about these occasions; we cannot imagine ourselves part of those small Greek townships bound together (often torn apart) by their intense communal life and far more than normally bound by the burning desire to pay homage to the young athlete home from Delphi or Olympia with his simple but infinitely precious wreath. If by some miracle we could be transported to one of those distant celebrations I suspect we might find the whole thing entirely too much for us. "We would not dare to place ourselves in Renaissance circumstances," Nietzsche once wrote; "our nerves could not support that reality, not to mention our muscles" (*Twilight of the Idols,* IX. 37). Although we are often warned against reading modern attitudes into the classical world, we still tend to assume—it is a lazy assumption—that the senses work in roughly the same way at all times and that despite cultural differences "reality" remains more or less constant. We need something like an archaeology of the emotions or senses to help us to understand the work of other ages, some way of taking the pulse of a period that would explain (to move nearer home) what it was in the world of Elizabeth and James which called for a diction not simply ebullient but constantly straining at the limits of expression ("Enrobe the roaring waters with my silks"—what a way for a merchant to speak of shipwreck!), and only a century later was content with the chastened speech of the age of Queen Anne.

Pindar's occasions have gone beyond recall; his odes remain and they are what concern us. They took fire, we must suppose, from those occasions while themselves greatly contributing to the blaze. As a means of getting a closer hold on this poetry—which in the days before we became grammarians of choral lyric made some people wonder if Pindar was quite in his right mind—I propose to look at a single puzzling feature of his diction which turns up rather often: the way he uses what appears to be the language of love and sexual desire to convey the victor's relation to victory. In the ***First Olympian*** Pindar says, literally, that a racehorse "mingled his master with power [or victory]" (*kratei. . . prosemeixe despotan*). The verb *meignumi,* in its simple or compounded forms, is something of a favorite with Pindar. Meaning mix or mingle, it is used in Greek of various forms of contact or union, including sexual union. What does it mean here? "Brought power unto his master," the Loeb translator, Sandys, thinks; "brought success to his master," Slater agrees. Gildersleeve, the finest Pindaric commentator ("It is hardly possible to go wrong," he wrote, "in pressing Pindar's vocabulary until the blood comes"), has this to say: "The concrete, personal *meignumi* is common in Pindar, and must have its rights of contact. Here, 'brought to victory's embrace.' 'Wedded,' 'clasped,' 'embraced,' 'encircled,' will answer for many cases." Following Gildersleeve's lead, Nisetich gets the sense right though he hardly makes poetry of it: the horse "put his lord in the embrace of power." Victory, it seems, is (like?) an amorous bride.

This erotic diction or imagery is sometimes so clear that it cannot be concealed, though some have tried to dull its force. Of one young athlete Pindar says that he fell twice into the arms of victory and, literally, touched elaborately wrought song (***Nemean 5.***42). Sandys demurely prefers to let him fall into "the lap of victory" and "win" song. Farnell acknowledges "the voluptuous phrase" but is quick to warn us that "it is doubtful whether . . . the amorous idea is vividly present." A more robust commentator, J. B. Bury, says that the boy "enjoyed the embraces of. . . Victory" and suggests that the verb *touch* was "used by poets of the touches of amorous encounters." Nisetich, following this hint or perhaps simply guided by his own instinct, gives us—for the first time, I believe, in translation—what may be the true sense of the Greek:

> You, Euthymenes,
> twice taken into the arms of Victory
> at Aigina, have known the embrace
> of elaborate song.

A few lines later, of another victory, Nisetich translates:

> He vanquished those of his age
> who came against him, at home
> and in the lovely arms of Megara.

(The victor, an Aiginetan, won victory as his bride just as in the myth his ancestor Peleus won Thetis.) The last line is a real recovery. The brown varnish has been scraped off to let us see the startlingly bright colors that were hidden all the time just beneath. The Greek is normally taken to mean that the boy won "in the beautiful-valley-by-the hill of Nisos" (*Nisou . . . en euangkei lophōi*), periphrastic for Megara. But the root element here, *angk-,* means primarily not a valley but anything curved or rounded and it occurred just before in the phrase about the arms of victory (*Nikas en angkōnessi*).

The sexual overtones found in the imagery sometimes pass over into the action of a poem, nowhere so explicitly as in the ***Tenth Pythian,*** composed when Pindar was twenty. The ode sets up a relation between the joy of the festal occasion and the greater joy of the Hyperboreans, that legendary people who live, free from the cares of mortality, "beyond the North Wind." The official point is that no one, not even a victor, can experience that order of well-being. There are, however, a number of similarities between the two worlds which go some way to bridging the gap. The Hyperboreans are described as blessed, *makares;* Thessaly, the victor's home, is also blessed. We see the Hyperboreans enjoying their privileged estate, crowned with golden leaves (the victor is also crowned), as girls dance to the music of flute and lyre and the whole place quivers or trembles with the flash of limbs and the call of the instruments. There is dancing and singing in Thessaly too as the chorus pours forth the poet's lovely song beside the banks of the Peneios and the poet expresses the hope that his ode will make the victor wonderful (*thaēton*) in the eyes of the young men and their elders, an object too of fond concern to girls. "Different loves excite the heart," Pindar goes on, using a verb often used of sexual excitement. The erotic note, the sense that the victor is the focus of markedly sexual attention, is strongly even disconcertingly emphasized by a moment earlier on in the myth. When we first see them, the Hyperboreans are busy with a great sacrifice to Apollo, a hecatomb of asses. The god enjoys the spectacle "and laughs as he sees their beasts' high-cocked presumption" (trans. Bowra). This is the traditional interpretation of the phrase and surely correct, though it has recently been challenged. The ancient critic Didymos censured Pindar for his impropriety here and asked, "What reason is there for Apollo to enjoy the sight of asses in a state of erection?" Perhaps this is, for Pindar, rather blunt. The sexual theme will be treated more finely in a later poem, ***Pythian 9***. . . . He was only twenty at the time, Farnell says in extenuation, "and the Thessalians would not have been shocked." One imagines it would have taken a good deal more to shock those rude Squire Westerns.

The sexual aspect of victory is of course admitted. "The Greek admiration for physical beauty," Bowra allows rather blandly, "was all the more powerful because it had a strong erotic element, and of this of course Pindar was well aware . . . " (*Pindar,* 168). No one denies this but somehow we do not make much of it. Greek poetry has still not been scrubbed quite clean of the decorous neoclassical patina that obscured it for so long, and the effects of centuries of cloistered, clerical study are even more obstructive—that minute, laborious philological labor but for which we could not read the Greek poets at all and which has yet done so much to neutralize the inestimable gift it brought us. Hence even today we tend to blink the fact that those young men who competed naked under the Mediterranean sun must have aroused more than athletic admiration, and that the victor back home must have been the cause of much sexual commotion. Let Pindar speak:

> What a shout as he walked round the ring!
> He was young and beautiful and very beautiful
> the things that he did.
>
> (***Olympian 9.***94)

. . . This is not simply praise. The words are gentle as a caress.

The strong sensual excitement in the odes is however only one aspect of a larger excitement, an intensity of feeling that is present almost everywhere. And victory, however much desired, is not a bride; the "embrace of victory" has to be metaphorical. But a metaphor for what? For something that would otherwise not be fully expressible, the astounding joy which Pindar found in these celebrations and which his task was to recreate and make permanent by his tripartite art—words, music, dance—an art that fits the voice of festal splendor to the Doric sandal. There may be an analogue to what Pindar is doing here in the Christian mystics, unlikely though this may appear. Having to express the otherwise inexpressible felicity of union with the divine, the mystics will draw on the most intense form of earthly experience known to us, the sexual, and use explicitly even grossly erotic terms to describe a joy for which there are no direct words, the *fruitio Dei.* These Greek victors, as Pindar saw them, in the hour of their triumph (flaming with the clamor of the Graces) and later during its celebration at home, tasted a joy beyond any normally granted us, a condition that for a brief space trembles on the border of divinity itself, and yet does so without the dangers, the sinfulness, that in Greek eyes darkened the drive to transcendence. What Nietzsche called "the highest and most illustrious human joys, in which existence celebrates its own transfiguration" (*The Will to Power,* sec. 1051): here is the burden of the odes, their deepest matter, and what makes them really difficult. For they come up against a long-standing, deeply rooted prejudice, in its older, nobler form the conviction that the supreme vision is the tragic, more recently the sense that literature's proper subject is suffering. There is no arguing with these beliefs. At the most, one may ask why joy should not be allowed to express itself as richly in poetry as it does in music. Certainly it does so less often. All the more reason to cherish the poet who put joy at the center of his odes and built for it these ceremonies of praise. "Festal sublimity is a far rarer thing than tragic sublimity," C. S. Lewis once wrote. Rarer, and no less valuable.

To enter this strange world we need all the help we can get. Recent studies of the form of epinician poetry have removed many old barriers to understanding, but they hardly take us beyond the level of technique. The Pindar who once seemed so willful and incoherent may have been replaced by a consummate virtuoso, but has our new grasp of the genre really brought us any closer to Pindar the great poet or given any true substance to that dusty old claim? Wilamowitz' gloomy pronouncement, "His world is quite alien to us," remains as true today as it was sixty years ago. Or would be so, had not help come from an unsuspected quarter. For perhaps a new means of access has opened up, though it has hardly been noticed. I can make the point most quickly by means of a personal experience. A few years ago I gave a small seminar on Pindar and in the introductory class read ***Olympian 7*** (admittedly one of the easier poems), presenting it with a minimum of technicalities and trying so far as possible to let the text speak for itself. At the end of the class someone said, "But why is Pindar supposed to be so difficult?" The person who asked this question was a poet and familiar with the poetry of this century and found that she could take more or less in her stride things which so puzzled earlier readers—the rapid cutting from one theme to another, the ellipses and apparent lack of connections, the brilliant images imbedded in some pretty impenetrable stuff. Recalling this occasion I find myself wondering about the way a Pindaric scholar, Mary R. Lefkowitz, introduced the poet to beginners in her book *The Victory Ode* (1976). One of the poems she chose was ***Olympian 1.*** We had better have the opening lines in front of us; again, I quote the Nisetich translation to show that I am playing fair:

> Water is preeminent and gold, like a fire
> burning in the night, outshines

all possessions that magnify men's pride.
But if, my soul, you yearn
to celebrate great games,
look no further
for any other star
shining through the deserted ether
brighter than the sun, or for a contest
mightier than Olympia—

Professor Lefkowitz examined the opening of the poem carefully and then paused to say this: "As modern readers, rather than ancient listeners, it is only natural that we might feel at this point rather dazed. So much has been suggested in so few words, so many ideas associated that in ordinary life have no logical relation." The ancient audience, Lefkowitz explained, "more accustomed than we to making connections between similar words and actions on first hearing, would have more readily understood the juxtaposition of absolutes in the ode's opening lines." That is, water, gold, sun, Olympian games, all supreme in their own sphere. There are of course different kinds of modern reader. The one I have in mind is a quick-witted person, not perhaps very well instructed but curious and clever enough to get hold of the information he may lack, and quite at home with abrupt juxtapositions and the association of logically unrelated ideas. They are after all part of modern life; our jokes and films are full of them. My modern reader cut his critical teeth on a poem in which someone walking down a London street meets a man called Stetson and exclaims "You who were with me in the ships at Mylae!" and then asks if the corpse he planted in his garden has sprouted. Such a reader is not notably dazed by the opening of Pound's fourth canto:

Palace in smoky light,
Troy but a heap of smouldering boundary stones,
ANAXIFORMINGES! Aurunculeia!
Hear me. Cadmus of Golden Prows!

There are four elements here which Pound juxtaposes, leaving us to work out the relation between them. A ruined city, Troy. The poem has much to say about the rise and fall of cities and the reader has already met Helen *heleptolis,* "destroyer of cities," destroyer of a city called Troy, in the second canto. Next, a sonorous epithet—from Pindar, as it happens: *anaxiforminges,* "[songs] that rule the lyre." It is poetry that told us, long before archaeology, of Troy's fall. Third, Aurunculeia, the name of the bride in a radiant marriage poem by Catullus, representing perhaps (at this stage the reader is simply keeping open a number of possibilities) the creative aspect of sexuality, in contrast to Helen's destructiveness. Fourth, Cadmus, who sailed in pursuit of his abducted sister Europa and founded a new city, Thebes. (Like Menelaos, who sailed in pursuit of abducted Helen; unlike Menelaos, who helped to destroy an old city.) The person quick enough to handle this sort of thing—such people do happily exist—is not, it seems to me, going to make heavy weather of Pindar's illogical associations and compressions and juxtapositions. Far from feeling "rather dazed" by them, he is likely to find himself agreeably challenged and I can imagine him saying, "Hmm, might be this fellow Pindar is worth looking into."

One must be quite clear about the kind and the limits of the help which modern (more properly, modernist) poetry could provide: it could take the reader past the initial obstacles which have caused so much trouble. Then of course he comes up against the differences. The parts of a Pindaric ode are very firmly connected whereas in much twentieth-century poetry the connections may really be missing, suppressed as a matter of poetic strategy. Moreover, Pindar's choral lyric, however much he may have reshaped what he inherited, is a traditional form whose procedures were broadly familiar, while the modern poem aims, in a desperate wager against total noncommunication, to be each time new, spun afresh from its own inner necessities. The similarities, it may be said, are all of the surface. Perhaps so, but they are enough to allow the initial all-important encounter to take place, that first shock of poetic excitement which later study can modify and deepen but never replace. And this can happen without the dulling interposition of learned commentary. Contact once established, the reader can go on to mug up the doctrine of the matter. But he has got the sequence right. It is better, Eliot once said, "to be spurred to acquire the scholarship because you enjoy the poetry, than to suppose that you enjoy the poetry because you have acquired the scholarship."

The surface similarities, though apparently offering only a fragile bridge to Pindar, may however be buttressed by something more solid. There may be a real if remote kinship. Consider a passage like this, a description of medieval Welsh poetry which a critic cites for the light it throws on another great if still too little read modernist poem, *The Anathemata of* David Jones:

> The absence of a centred design, of an architectural quality, is not a weakness in old Welsh poetry, but results quite reasonably from a specific view of composition. English and most Western European creative activity has been conditioned by the inheritance from Greece and Rome of the notion of a central point of interest in a poem, a picture or a play, a nodal region to which everything leads and upon which everything depends. The dispersed nature of the thematic splintering of Welsh poetry is not due to a failure to follow this classical convention. [Welsh poets] were not trying to write poems that would read like Greek temples or even Gothic cathedrals but, rather, like stone circles or the contour-following rings of the forts from which they fought, with hidden ways slipping from one ring to another. (Gwyn Williams, *The Burning Tree,* 1956)

Does not the structural principle in the last sentence (adopted by David Jones in his poem) sound curiously like Pindaric ring-composition? More important, the concept of a centered design, inherited as the writer says from Greece and Rome, is absent not only in Jones's poem: it is absent in Pindar too. It is a *classical* concept, informing a classical masterpiece like the *Oedipus Rex.* Pindar's art, however, is not in this sense classical; it belongs to an earlier world which we have rather recently come to call *archaic.* Since this is a large topic, let me take a single example, the way the archaic writer can move backwards and forwards in time without regard to chronological sequence. This was a stumbling block to older Pindaric scholars. Farnell, for example, says of the myth in ***Nemean 3*** that the poet "shows more than his usual carelessness in respect to the order of events." Pindar is telling how the centaur Kheiron educated Achilles and suddenly "breaks into" this account with a detail about Kheiron's tutelage of another hero, Jason, who belonged to an earlier generation. And yet Pindar seems to put them both on the same temporal plane. He does this sort of thing constantly, often in far more startling ways. Pound and Jones in our day do precisely the same thing. In canto 2, I said, Pound introduces the figure of Helen "destroyer of cities." But look again. It is not Helen who is thus characterized but Eleanor, patroness of troubadour poets in the twelfth century A.D. Pound then goes on—trusting in our ability to make connections between similar-sounding words and names—to relate what Homer, in the eighth century B.C., said about . . . Eleanor.

The disregard of chronological sequence in the modernist masters is part of something larger, something that might open up a directer path to Pindar than any we have had before. The recovery of the archaic, the new feeling in the art and thought of our time for archaic images and structures and modes of thought, has given us access to older, half lost (sometimes wholly lost) worlds, very much including the world of pre-Platonic Greece. Again, a single example must suffice to suggest the kind of kinship we might in consequence enjoy with Pindar. He has a strange and beautiful way of seeing the city as a living, growing thing. The same conception is found already in Hesiod—"Where the city flourishes, the people flower" (*Works and Days,* 227)—but Pindar greatly develops it. The Pindaric city is (like?) a tree. Its roots are the ancestral heroes and their foundational acts, the visible tree is the city's continuing life, its leaves and flowers the city's sons and their achievements. The poet's song waters the roots of the city-tree and ensures that it will continue to bear its heroic blossom. This organic, vegetal conception of the human community finds its richest expression in the great ***Seventh Olympian*** (the poem which made my admirable student wonder why people found Pindar difficult). The poem was written for an athlete from Rhodes and the myth presents three scenes from the legendary history of the island. These scenes are set in receding chronological sequence ("in his pleasant wayward fashion," says Farnell, Pindar "reverses the time-order of events in his mythic world"), each involving an offense or error, in diminishing order of gravity. Only the third scene need concern us here. It takes place in the primal days when Zeus and the other immortals were portioning out the world between them and "Rhodes was not yet visible on the sea's face. The island lay hidden in the salt deeps." It somehow happened that Helios, the Sun, was not present when the lots were cast and thus received no portion. Zeus then proposed another cast but Helios would not have it:

> For he said that within the grey water
> he saw, burgeoning from the bed
> a land very fertile for men and a friend to flocks.

Helios asked that this land, about to lift into the brilliant air, should be his. The gods agreed. And then the island emerged, grew, from the water. In translation we had better say *rose,* for Pindar takes advantage of the fact that in Greek *Rhodos,* Rhodes, is indistinguishable, in the oblique cases which he uses, from *rhodon,* rose:

> From the salt sea
> an island rose
> growing into the light! It is his, the Lord
> of Horses whose breath is fire.
> There Helios lay with Rose [Rhodes]
> and fathered seven wiser sons than earlier men
> from his own wit.

Among the issue of these seven were the three men who founded and named after them the three principal cities into which historical Rhodes was divided. (pp. 13-37)

[Earlier] I quoted Pound expressing his dislike of Pindar, but the Pindar he disliked was the creature of an old misreading. Had he been able to see through to the true Pindar he would have found in him a friend and a master. For Pound too saw the city as a living, growing thing. In the first canto we are shown, mysteriously, through a jumble of fragmentary quotations (the full vision lies far ahead) Aphrodite emerging from the welter of the sea with her crown of city walls—Aphrodite, Love, Amor. The poem presents a series of attempts to build the city, the true city where we "political beings" are at home, not the feverish travesty we endure today. Only much later do we see the process by which the city comes into being. It grows like a tree:

> The roots go down to the river's edge
> and the hidden city moves upward
> white ivory under the bark.
> (Canto 83)

The tree, earliest form of the column; the column that sustains the temple; the temple that stands at the center of the city. Pound puts it more simply, in a pun, in the previous canto: "Let the herbs rise in April abundant." It is a vision very close to Pindar's, but of the two Pound's is the more archaic.

Let me not be misunderstood. I am not saying that Pindar is really quite modern after all. He is nothing of the sort. His poetry is very distant and this distance must be preserved and cherished. For it is not a void, not an obstacle to be overcome, but rather what Gadamer calls a productive distance which, while it separates us from Pindar, can also bring us close to him if we allow it to do so. For this distance is our tradition, a tradition which, however fractured it may be and however lightly Pindar belonged to it, still has some hold on us, can still address us, even when we think to reject it. And we in our turn can address it and establish a relation to what it holds, a relation in which both parties have their rights. We cannot, that is, remove an old work from its time and require it to take up residence here and show its relevance to us. That is a mere vulgarization and laying waste of the past. Nor can we deny our location in the present and transplant ourselves there. That is the naive error of historicism; the most learned among us would cut a very poor figure in fifth-century Thebes. To establish a true relation with a work from the past is to enter into a dialogue with it. The dialogue may first be prompted by curiosity or by chance; or by a sense of need, the sense of something there which is missing here and which we want. Something which has cropped up fragmentarily in the art and thought of our time, in answer to an unspoken need of our time, may exist there more richly. It may perhaps be found in Pindar. (pp. 37-9)

D. S. Carne-Ross, in his Pindar, *Yale University Press, 1985, 195 p.*

Edward Young on Pindar's muse (1728):

Pindar's muse, like Sacharissa, is a stately, imperious, and accomplished beauty; equally disdaining the use of art and the fear of any rival; so intoxicating that it was the highest commendation that could be given an ancient that he was not afraid to taste of her charms. . . .

Edward Young, in his "On Lyric Poetry," in Eighteenth-Century Critical Essays, *edited by Scott Elledge, Cornell University Press, 1961.*

Charles Segal (essay date 1986)

[*Segal is an American classical scholar and critic who has written numerous works on ancient literature, including* Tragedy and Civilization: An Interpretation of Sophocles*(1981). In the following excerpt, he discusses Pindar's use of mythological and political material in* Pythian 4 *and affirms the "transitional status of Pindar between oral and literate composer."*]

The ***Fourth Pythian*** is the longest of Pindar's Epinician Odes and the longest independent choral work extant from classical antiquity. It is unique in the grandeur and richness of its themes, its bold organization of different time frames, and its picturesque detail and elliptical synopsis. By skillfully mixing fulness and brevity, Pindar surrounds the events of the tale with an aura of numinous mystery. By selecting intense moments and rendering their quality of the marvelous through strong metaphors, he impels the hearer or reader to share the imaginative recreation of the mythic past in its elusive beauty and remoteness.

The newly discovered fragments of Stesichorus show us what archaic choral lyric could achieve in extended narration through the pathos of direct discourse and the elaboration of decorative detail in colorful settings. ***Pythian 4*** combines the limpidity, expansiveness, and richness of detail that we can see in Stesichorus' poems on Geryon and on Thebes, in Simonides' Danae fragment, and in Bacchylides' longer odes with Pindar's own peculiar ability to convey the epic wonder of heroic deeds in bold images and powerfully condensed narrative. Even so, earlier choral poetry has nothing comparable to Pindar's great ode. Wilamowitz's characterization of the poem some sixty years ago [in his *Pindaros,* 1922] is still apt: "Dies längste Gedicht ist wahrlich ein seltsames Gebilde, chimaerahaft, wenn man näher zusieht, unrubrizierbar für jeden Systematiker der Poetik."

A work as ambitious as ***Pythian 4*** tends to emerge only late in an artist's career and at the end of long tradition. When Pindar came to compose ***Pythian 4*** in 462 B.C., he had been producing epinicia for over thirty years. Now he brilliantly manages the art of amplification and of silence; he knows the *kairos* of when to expand and when to hasten to his end (247). And he is fully aware of his own supremacy in the art: "To many others," he boasts, "I am a guide in the skill of poetry" (248). Modern critics agree. To quote Farnell [in his *The Works of Pindar,* 1930-32] "The mellow golden diction of the ode shows Pindar at his height as a master-artist of speech."

Medea's prophecy at the beginning springs upon us with an abruptness appropriate to her shadowy western kingdom and the mysterious sea-realm of her tale. Niece of Circe and the granddaughter of Helios, she at once brings into the story the atmosphere of a fabulous world close to the gods. The narrative on either side of her prophecy refers to the Argonauts as half-divine sailors (12) and godlike heroes (58). The first direct speech in the ode comes from her, and it contains her ennobling address, "children of high-spirited mortals and gods". . . . The heroes' varied divine parentage is in fact catalogued at length some hundred and fifty lines later.

Medea is, appropriately, the focal point of the fabulous elements in the ode. Around her play the love-magic of Aphrodite, "mistress of sharpest missiles" (214ff.), the drugs that protect Jason from the fire-breathing bulls (233ff.), and the ominous power of her father, Aeetes. He is given his potent epithet, "wondrous son of Helios," at the moment when he reveals the location of the "brilliant hide" of the Golden Fleece, but he presumably conceals the existence of the dragon that guards it. This creature "surpassed in thickness and length a fifty-oared ship which the blows of iron have completed" (241-46). With this marvelous detail Pindar breaks off his narrative. He has told the myth at great length; "completed," τελεσαν, is an appropriate note on which to close. Shipbuilding also leads into the break-off motif of the journey: "I have far to go on my path" (247); the poem, as it were, returns to land. Now three rapid lines of his summarizing style suffice for the remaining essentials of Jason's tale (249-51) and effect a transition back to the founding of Cyrene with which he had begun some two hundred and forty verses earlier.

In this work Pindar's power of incisive characterization is at its height. The mythical personages reveal themselves at once through their manner of speech and a briefly caught essential gesture or quality: Medea's prophecy has its appropriate vatic mystery (cf. 10f.). Jason is forthright, restrained, and polite. He has the modesty and reverence of the ideal young adult, and he displays an instinctive leadership in the heroic magnificence and ritual expansiveness of entertaining his kinsfolk (129-33). His father Aeson's spontaneous emotion (120-23) contrasts both with Pelias' cautious self-control (96-100, 156-67) and with Aeetes' distant majesty (230). Events are pregnant with their divine meaning as oracles are fulfilled in the day or night appointed by destiny (*moiridion amar,* 255f.). But they also resonate with the feelings that they stir in the participants: the awed silence of the young heroes at the great enterprise awaiting them (57f.); Aeson's tears of fatherly joy; Aeetes' astonishment and chagrin; and the Argonauts' joyful triumph and enthusiastic affection when their leader, no older than themselves, accomplishes the deed that the barbarian king has put to him (238-41). Performing a hopeless task against overwhelming odds: this is the undaunted confidence of youthful energy at its best. The companions, like a winning football team, ecstatically mob their captain, and we want to join in the congratulatory embraces.

Like all of Pindar's great odes, ***Pythian 4*** is a meditation on the relation between the cosmic and the moral order, on kingship and divinity, on the power of eros and the power of song, on the restless energy of superb young heroes and the sage wisdom of just monarchs, on the heroic spirit that would achieve great deeds in an open and exciting world, and on the corrupting and narrowing effect of greed and treachery. Poetics, politics, sexuality, the vocation of a divinely given destiny are all interwoven. By allowing himself the unprecedented breadth of thirteen triads, Pindar brings together in a tour de force epic adventure, foundation legends, love, magic, family conflict, and cosmogonic myths.

I have not argued specifically for the unity of the ode—once a favorite pastime of Pindarists—but it is obvious from my study that I consider the ode a unified whole. This unity derives not from any single element in isolation—an image or a fundamental idea—but from a more complex clustering of interrelated themes, narrative patterns, imagery, verbal echoes, parallelism and contrasts in the form and in the subject matter. The themes of travel, founding cities, kingship, and the fulfilment of a divinely appointed destiny in time are central and interrelated concerns. The model of heroic action underlying these elements is also defined by contrast to trickery, greed, and lack of the moral restraints of shame or respect (*aidōs*).

Pindar begins with the *kōmos,* the formal celebration of the victory for the ruler of a land "good in horses" (*euhippou Kuranas,* 2). The "glory in the horse-racing" at the end of the third strophic system rounds off the first section of the ode in what could be in effect a complete epinician in itself. After this point, Pindar never again mentions the occasion of the poem: King Arcesilaus' Pythian victory in the chariot-race of 462 B.C. Having performed his formal obligations to the genre in the first section, as it were, he allows the myth to expand to unprecedented length.

In its lack of athletic detail ***Pythian 4*** bears some resemblance to ***Pythian 3,*** also addressed to a tyrant and more like a poetic epistle than a victory-ode. The ***Fourth Pythian,*** unlike the Third, however, has the requisite formal features of the full-fledged Epinician, as described by Schadewaldt, Bundy, and Thummer. In ***Pythian 5,*** which celebrates the same victory as the Fourth, Pindar had given a spectacular account of the Delphic victory for the sportsmen (***Pyth. 5.***26-34, 49-53); thus in ***Pythian 4*** he had the liberty to expand his mythical material and to deepen the moral seriousness and grandeur of tone beyond what was often possible in the "standard" epinician. Like Hieron, commissioning the ***First Pythian*** to glorify his new foundation, Aetnaea, Arcesilaus had probably requested a work of proportions appropriate to the magnificence of an occasion of state.

We may speculate whether Pindar also enjoys another kind of freedom, that of a poet who makes increasing use of writing in his mode of composition and perhaps even thinks of literate as well as oral / aural reception for his work. We know too little about the details of either composition or performance to do more than speculate; but there are a few references to reading and writing in the Epinicia that suggest that Pindar at least had the idea of a written text. Pindar seems to think of himself primarily as an oral poet, a public voice bestowing praise and blame in communal gatherings and preserving for the future what is memorable, noble, exemplary, and therefore useful. The complexity of Pindar's style and organization, which both qualitatively and quantitatively mark an enormous step beyond earlier choral narrative (so far as we can judge from the fragments of Alcman, Stesichorus, and Simonides), may also reflect a poet in transition between the oral tradition, with its formulaic elements, and an increasingly literate society.

Among the indications of this transitional status of Pindar between oral and literate composer, I would suggest, is his greater self-consciousness about the craft, artistry, and potential deceptiveness of his poetry. Such concerns are of course expressed as early as Hesiod and Solon, but in Pindar they are more pervasive and more insistent. There is a greater awareness of the careful premeditation and "plotting" that go into the make-up of his work. Such an attitude is perhaps more comprehensible for one who thinks of himself as a writer, the producer of a written text that will be performed by others, rather than as an oral poet who composes and improvises (with whatever amount of premeditation) directly before his audience. The use of writing, I would suggest, was a further catalyst for the growing professionalism of the poet over the course of the sixth century.

Pindar's odes certainly do not look like improvised works; yet he still maintains the direct personal relationship with his audience characteristic of the oral poet, and he still affirms the role of spokesman for communal, collective values. What particularly concerns us here is the other side of this role, the self-awareness of the craft and elaboration behind these productions. Here, perhaps, we have an indication of a new mentality of poetic creation, and one that belongs to the age of tragedy as well as the age of epic, for the tragic poets, too, stand in this intermediate position. They are oral poets who create works to be performed before a live audience, but they are also the producers of a written text.

These subjects take us far beyond the scope of this study. They directly touch the concerns of ***Pythian 4,*** however, in the ode's emphasis (again, hardly unique in the Epinicia) on the notions of clever skill, craft, guile, and drugs (*sophia, mētis, dolos, pharmaka*). Here, as elsewhere (notably in ***Nemeans 7*** and ***8*** and ***Isthmian 4***), Pindar draws analogies between these elements in his mythical actions and his own poetics. In ***Pythian 4*** he is particularly concerned with the ambiguities of his hero, which in turn reflect on the ambiguities of the poetic craft that creates and describes him. At one level the ode masks the ambiguous qualities of guile and magic that lie behind its hero's success and the poet's own techniques of artful persuasion and adornment. At another level the ode not only reveals but also celebrates the process of crafting myths, inventing details, elaborating a persuasive and seductive surface that enables the poet to believe his story and makes us want to believe it too.

Given the occasion, the victory of the King of Cyrene at a panhellenic festival in the Greek homeland, Pindar is careful to bestow eloquent praise on stable monarchy and on the inherited possession of a land through generations of ancestors (***Pyth. 4.*** 256-62). But political affairs in Cyrene had been turbulent and precarious throughout the previous century, and the 460s were no safer for kings and tyrants. At the end of the sixth century Arcesilaus III already had to contend with serious internal dissension—the efforts of the popular faction, led by one Demonax, to revise the constitution, limit regal power, and extend the privileges of full citizenship. Externally, the kingdom, though protected by the vast desert to the east, had to pay tribute to the Persians after the Egyptian conquest of Cambyses. Expelled once in an outbreak of *stasis,* Arcesilaus III managed to return, but did not long survive. Persian intervention, obtained through his mother, the formidable Pheretime, brutally avenged his death and put down the rebels (Herodotus 4.162-67, 200-204).

Battus IV, Arcesilaus' grandson and successor, held together the restored monarchy for some forty years (ca. 510-470). He enriched his kingdom with the lucrative export of silphium, but he still had formally to recognize Persian sovereignty. His successor, Pindar's Arcesilaus (Arcesilaus IV), seems to have ruled until about 440. His reign, like those of his predecessors, was marred by internal dissension; and one of his first undertakings was to suppress a group of discontented citizens. Among those exiled was the Damophilus for whose restoration Pindar pleads in the ode. Around 440 B.C. a democratic faction overthrew the monarchy and brought about Arcesilaus' violent death, extinguishing the Battiad dynasty.

Arcesilaus' reign was still new at the time of his Pythian victory of 462; and, like Hieron in 470, he seems to have taken advantage of the originally religious occasion for political propaganda. Of this function in ***Pythian 4*** there is an indication in Pindar's vivid account of Battus' visit to Delphi and the oracle that announces the succession of Battiad kings (59-66). Herodotus reports a disagreement between Thera and Cyrene on the correct version of the founding legend (4.154). Pindar obviously follows the Cyrenean story, with its strong Delphic legitimization of the ruling dynasty. But, whatever his personal feelings and personal politics, he also shows us, inevitably, how myths of patriarchal succession and domination can be enlisted to support this kind of power. (pp. 4-14)

Charles Segal, in his Pindar's Mythmaking: The Fourth Pythian Ode, *Princeton University Press, 1986, 208 p.*

A boxing victory, with the loser raising a finger to admit defeat.

Anne Burnett (essay date 1987)

[*Burnett is an American classicist noted for her studies of archaic Greek poetry,* Three Archaic Poets: Archilochus, Alcaeus, Sappho*(1983) and* The Art of Bacchylides *(1985). In the following essay, she analyzes the political dimension of Pindar's poetry, paying particular attention to the poet's aristocratic values.*]

Pindar's songs were composed for men at play, but his poetry was political in its impulse and in its function. The men in question were rich and powerful, and their games were a display of exclusive class attributes, vicariously shared by lesser mortals who responded with gratitude and loyalty (for example, ***Pythia 5***.43-44). Victories were counted as princely benefactions (compare ***Olympia 5.***3 and 15, 7.94, 8.87, ***Isthmia 6***.69) and laid up as city treasure like the wealth deposited in the treasuries at Delphi (***Pythia 6***.5). Athletic victory was thus both a manifestation and an enhancement of aristocratic domination, which meant that the poet who praised those who boxed and raced in pan-Hellenic games necessarily praised the social structure that depended on them.

Pindar understood his political function and was proud of it—"I would consort with victors" (***Olympia 1***.115b). He believed in athletic contest as a model for all human life. He believed in the aristocratic system: "Inherited governance of cities lies properly with the nobility" (***Pythia 10***.71-72). He believed also that praise poetry could regulate as well as laud that system, and he believed finally that such poetry was itself incorruptible. Games, song, and princely rulers were all parts of a single brilliant order, and this truth had a linguistic reflection, for the bit that tames a horse, the meter of a poetic line, and the moderation of a ruler were all called by the same name—*metron.* "Measure (*metron*) inheres in everything" (***Olympia 13***.47 and throughout).

As Pindar saw it, there was only one pursuit open to a man, whether he was a prince or a poet or an ordinary citizen, and that was to search out the superlative and try to embody it in his own sort of action. And the search was not difficult because in the world as in song the best—the topmost element in any hierarchy—was plainly marked by its beauty. One could not fail to recognize it because all creation fell into natural categories in which one item had its evident and lovely dominance: water among the elements, gold among the metals, sun among the planets, Olympia among the games, and among men the princely victor (***Olympia 1***.1-7; compare ***Olympia 3***.42-45). "Magnificence takes manifold forms but its extremest peak is reached in princes. Look no higher," he says in praise of a victorious tyrant (***Olympia 1***.113-15). The wealthy aristocrat, winning and spending with splendor, was the "bastion" of his city and also its "eye"—its most beautiful part—because the world was so organized that pragmatic and aesthetic values were in agreement (***Pythia 5***.55-57; compare ***Olympia 14***.1-7, where the Charites are involved alike in wisdom, physical beauty, and social preeminence). Beauty was, in fact, a kind of moral imperative: "If a man be fair himself, and if he act in harmony with his appearance, he mounts to the topmost height of manhood" (***Nemea 3***.19). And for a demonstration of the coincidence of beauty with excellence one had only to look at the games where the aristocracy, through disciplined exertions toward supremacy, discovered to the world its own superlative qualities: the victor was "fair himself, his exploits like his looks" (***Nemea 3***.19). Wealth was a prerequisite, just as strength was (***Pythia 3***.110), but the particular virtue that was put on display was a combination of courage, judgment, desire to please ancestors and gods, and a will to distinguish oneself (***Isthmia 6-10***). This was the best that lay in human nature, and it took a form that was outwardly beautiful, making its appearance in the flesh of blooded horses and the bodies of young victors as lovely as Ganymede (***Olympia 10***.103-5).

At the games aristocrats, the most beautiful of men, vied among themselves in the most beautiful of pastimes to discover the most beautiful embodiments of their own best qualities (compare, for example, ***Olympia 9***.94-100). And since success derived finally from god, the victor's triumph had no danger in it. "All the machinery of mortal excellence comes from god" (***Pythia 1***.41; compare, for example, ***Nemea 9***.45). The victor, his competitors, the spectators, and the world at large were all reminded, precisely through the wreath that was put around his head, "won not without the aid of god" (***Pythia 2***.6-7; compare ***Olympia 6***.79, 8.18, ***Pythia 8***.61-69), of the nonhuman power that defined and reduced even the achievements of victors and kings. This meant that the victory poet did not praise a particular man in his strength; rather, he praised the success (*kudos,* as at ***Olympia 3***.39, 5.7, ***Pythia 4***.66) that was a divine gift bestowed upon one representative of a class of men. Ultimately, he praised god: "I come as a suppliant, O Zeus . . . sighing through Lydian flutes, begging you to deck this city out with deeds of manly virtue" (***Olympia 5***.19, 21-22). Furthermore, his own poetic success, exactly like that of the athlete, was in the same divine hands (***Olympia 9***.27-29, 11.10, ***Pythia 8***.76, ***Nemea 4***.41-43). Only with god's help would he be able to give the beauty of the moment of victory a musical reduplication and, by translating it to the realm of what is remembered, rescue it from the dissolution that necessarily marks all human action.

Athletic contest was thus a metaphor for the test of action which must be accepted by anyone who would give his innate quality its finest outward expression. "Only in trial is the fulness of a man's excellence made plain" (***Nemea 3***.70; compare ***Olympia 4***.22, ***Isthmia 4***.33). The games also represented the natural visibility of excellence: there could be no lying about prizes present or past, for the herald had cried out the names, and so Olympia was "Mistress of Truth" (***Olympia 8***.2; compare phrases in which the games are said to "know" a man, as at ***Olympia 7***.83). And finally the athletic contest figured, in its spectators, the passive recognition and approbation which must be accorded to all the superlatives that cap the world's various priamels. "There is a rule among men that a splendid accomplishment must not fall and be covered in silence" (***Nemea 9***.6). The contest's double demand of action and acclamation defined man's life at its best, whatever his class or profession, and the poet was in the peculiar position of answering both imperatives at once. The act of composing a song was congruent with the act of competing in the games, as the poet made trial of his own powers and put the manifestation of his best in competition with the songs of others. At the same time, his praise of the victor was congruent with the applause of the spectators, though it was a more artful show of admiration. Epinician poetry thus differed from other pursuits, whether athletic, political, or technical, only by being doubly functional and doubly beautiful.

Such was Pindar's largest view of the interaction of politics, contest, and the poetry of praise. About the excellence of the aristocracy he was confident. It was his belief that men were not born equal (***Nemea 7***.5 and 54), that the qualities of temper and strength (***Nemea 1***.57; compare ***Nemea 2***.14-15) lived in the seed of certain families (***Pythia 8***.44; compare ***Olympia 7***.92-93, 9.100, ***Pythia 10***.11-12) where they were present even in infants and children (***Nemea 1***.57, 3.44). This was a universal law—"It is by nature that a noble temper predominates, passing from father to child" (***Pythia 8***.44)—and the only exception Pindar would allow was the possibility that such blood-virtue might lie dormant in a generation of less assertive men (***Nemea 6***.8b-11, ***11***.37-43). Since a man was a single whole ("like the speed of feet, so the strength of arm and the greatness of heart," ***Olympia 4***.28-29; compare ***Olympia 8***.19), one with the native qualities of nobility would use them to fight forward along "direct paths" of open and splendid deeds (***Nemea 1***.25; compare ***Isthmia 5***.22, where the road of action is "pure"), because there was a familial fame (***Nemea 3***.40) and a familial destiny (a *daimon genethlios,* ***Olympia 13***.105; compare ***Isthmia 1***.39, ***Nemea 5***.40) shaping his life. Nevertheless, each noble individual had to "track down" his own inborn virtue (***Nemea 6***.14), and having apprehended it, he had to exert himself because only action had significance, and action was always risky and difficult: "Toil and expenditure ever struggle for excellence in the deed that is wrapped in danger" (***Olympia 5***.16-17; compare ***Olympia 6***.9-10). Whatever the danger, however, it had to be faced because inactivity was like sitting at home by one's mother while others went out to find a cure for death in courageous deeds (***Pythia 4***.185-87; compare ***Olympia 1***.81-84).

Superb powers came from a superb inheritance and that inheritance was an obligation: one could not spot the fair fame of one's family (see especially ***Pythia 6***). The opportunity to exercise such powers, however, came not from one's blood but from god. The grand risk (***Olympia 1***.81, usually called *kairos*), once recognized, had to be taken with a kind of modesty—one was its companion but not its master (***Pythia 4***.287)—and the success that was gained in the end was no more man's creation than the original chance had been, for the beginning and the end of every action was with god. The wealth that naturally belonged to an aristocrat (***Pythia 10***.17) played its part, of course, allowing him to pursue the "wilder ambitions" (***Olympia 2***.54) of contest and war. "If god give soft wealth to me, I can hope to find the height of fame in future time" (***Pythia 3***.110; compare ***Pythia 8***.92). Nevertheless, it was only with divine help that a man might, "with luck from the gods and not betraying his own courage" (***Olympia 8***.67), mix his wealth with inherited virtue and use it in individual risk so that his familial fame should be renewed and revived. "Let him spend in joy, / let him put divinely given qualities to work, then / god will make fair reputation grow for him and he, / with heaven's honors plain, will cast his anchor on / the furthest shores of blessedness" (***Isthmia 6***.10; compare the opening of ***Pythia 5***).

In theory, then, all was well as splendid men, licensed by splendid gods, performed splendid deeds which were given splendid praise by poets who added permanence to this redundancy of perfections. Nevertheless, neither Pindar nor his clients nor his audiences were simpletons, and all knew that imperfections, not to say corruptions, existed in the world. Most particularly did they all know, as Greeks, that one could lie—and lie beautifully if one were a poet (***Olympia 1***.29)—even about beauty. A man could cheat, using power that was either political or poetical, so as to impose a lesser substitute for a natural superlative; he could cover over what was really finest and exhibit something second-rate. This danger existed even inside the sanctified spaces of the great games, and outside in the secular world it was everywhere, menacing statesmen and singers as well as ordinary men. It could touch even the true aristocrat, for all his innate virtue, because especially in a moment of success a man might run mad and, with something other than his ordinary character ("with maddened heart," ***Pythia 2***.26), commit an outrage. He might be in the midst of a fair action and yet, by means of false oaths, flattery, or calumny, he might create something ugly: a city in which the best men did not predominate, a praise poem that aroused only vulgar envy or, if he were a mythic hero, a monster that was neither god nor man nor beast.

Pindar saw these dangers but he also knew, or thought he knew, of elements within the aristocratic culture that would check them. In the first place, nobles moved by a desire for deathless renown (and such a desire was presumably a generic trait with them) could not expect to cheat Time, the eventual judge of all actions (***Olympia 10***.53-55). "The manner of one's life is told forth in the words or songs of after-coming men" (***Pythia 1***.92-94). And in the second place, even if this ideal failed to inhibit them, the actual would, for these men lived in the extreme openness of small and talkative communities. As leaders they were necessarily conspicuous and consequently the true quality of each of their moves, whether clean or sordid, was observable by all. They "walked the road where all could see," with every possession bearing witness to its source (***Olympia 6***.72). Furthermore, their wealth and success made them subject to a prying, envious blame that grudged proper acclamation but made out every misdeed (*phthonos*, ***Pythia 11***.29; *momos*, ***Olympia 6***.74). Neighbors were quick to spread evil tales (***Olympia 1***.47; compare ***Olympia 2***.95), and consequently wealth and success were enjoyable only when a man behaved so as to be well thought of among his fellow citizens (***Pythia 11***.45; compare ***Pythia 11***.28, ***Nemea 8***.38).

Though it had no constituted power the public was thus a kind of check upon the aristocracy, while song itself provided a more far-reaching instrument of scrutiny. In order to be sure of an undying glory, the victor had to entrust his reputation to an epinician poet, for "Though he has wrought fair deeds, if a man go to Hades without song, his panting labor is hollow and his joy brief" (***Olympia 10***.91-93; compare ***Pythia 3***.114, ***Nemea 7***.12). Since the song he (or his family) commissioned would be performed by a multiplicity of singers before a greater number of guests, this was tantamount to his presentation of his good fame to his fellow citizens for their examination. True, only a small number of fellow aristocrats would be present at the poem's single performance, but the young chorus members would certainly repeat its lines throughout the town, so that the song would become a public statement. With it the victor said in effect: "What I have done (which is the same thing as what I am) is here presented to you in the full glare of poetry: I am no Clytemnestra with something to hide, but a man who has gained the force of wealth without violence, one who now uses it in tranquility" (compare ***Pythia 11***, and especially 54-56). The song's production was thus the victor's pledge to his community, his assertion that he did indeed care primarily for its opinion and was in consequence kept from any wrongdoing by the many eyes that were upon him. Before such a number of witnesses the statesman or prince could not afford to give off false sparks, but had to sharpen his tongue on the anvil of truth (***Pythia 1***.87-88). And by extension, though he paid a poet to celebrate his victory, that poet could only commemorate a glory that already existed, one created by impeccable actions of courage and manliness.

This, indeed, is only the narrowest description of song's power of review, because the victory ode offered its client's deeds not just to a local public but to the entire Hellenic community. "I am no statue-maker whose image stands fixed on its base; I go out from Aegina in every ship, a sweet song-cargo" (***Nemea 5***.1-3). The ode, moreover, reached even beyond a man's contemporaries, for it found an audience among the dead: "They listen with underground minds, when great deeds are sprinkled with the soft dewdrops of song" (***Pythia 5***.96-103; compare ***Olympia 8***.77-80). And finally, an epinician was heard in heaven by the gods it so frequently addressed, and this was no conceit but an actuality, for its performance mode was borrowed from the danced songs of magic and worship, its gestures and melodies close to those of cult. Praise poetry was thus the medium through which a great man's actions were, by his own command, tested against the norms of a collective Hellenic morality. The epinician was a "faithful seal" (***Olympia 11***.6) affixed to a life that dared affront an audience of ghosts and daimones as well as the mortal envy of peers and inferiors. Furthermore, because virtue came to fulfillment only "slowly, by way of splendid songs" (***Pythia 3***.114), the ode had an influence that was not merely retrospective. In all the preliminary choices and exercises meant to lead to a desired success, a man had to keep this melodious investigation in mind. His every move had to be of the sort that would lend itself to future celebration by flutes and lyres, and consequently Pindar could say that the "grace" of music acted as an "overseer" in the lives of successful men (*Charis . . . epopteuei,* ***Olympia*** *7*.11).

Success was forever splendid only when it had been sung, and this truth had a negative corollary that gave to music in addition an almost punitive power (symbolically stated in the unfriendly effects of the lyre at ***Pythia 1***.13-14 and of Hesychia at ***Pythia 8***.8-12). Actions that failed or were flawed were deprived of music, for they demanded its opposite, the shadow of silence and forgetfulness (***Nemea 5***.18). Indeed, this condemnation reached even to simple inaction, for Pindar speaks of "the unrecognized silences of things left untried" (***Isthmia 4***.32). Poetry could punish simply by refusing to come into being, thus creating the silence that would suffocate a man's fame. In actuality there was a particular kind of poetry that went further, defying the law by which the unsightly should be suppressed to sing out a verbalized blame, "fattening itself on heavy words of hatred" (***Pythia 2***.55-56). The praise poet was of course debarred by definition from any such practice, but Pindar nevertheless liked to remind his clients, on occasion, that there are times when open blame would be appropriate. He points ostentatiously to the silence to which he has sentenced certain unworthy actions (***Olympia 13***.91, ***Nemea 5***.14b, and so on), thus suggesting that they might have been denounced, and in the case of the tyrant Phalaris he actually finds a way of voicing silence by making his chorus sing, "An evil reputation holds him captive, nor do lyres join the murmuring of young voices to make sweet sound for him" (***Pythia 1***.96). Again and again, with one of his favorite conceits, he describes his own acts of celebration as a form of "attack." He "does battle with" his client's many victories (***Olympia 13***.44); the victor cannot "escape" his song (***Olympia 6***.6), for his words are "arrows" shot at courage (***Olympia 1***.112), and the Muse has put many into his quiver (***Olympia 6***.6, 9.8). All this is arch and playful, but Pindar once shifts his metaphor to become a poet-wolf who might leap from hiding upon his enemy (***Pythia 2***.84-85). Even a praise poet, he warns, could learn to sing another sort of song if goaded by flagrant iniquity.

Since evil or base actions demanded silence, the praise poet in principle would refuse to sing any victory that was tainted or any victor who was beneath the standard of aristocratic virtue. Theoretically he accepted a commission only when he recognized an occasion as one in which the Muse, Memory, Festivity, and Tranquility the daughter of Justice might be willing to join. Epinician poetry thus acted as a censor, ever dividing what was worthy of blame from what was worthy of praise, and Pindar, at any rate, thought it right to continue in this work of discrimination even as he composed his laudatory odes. What he praised, after all, was splendid action crowned by success; it was victory, not the victorious man, that was to be rescued from forgetfulness and fixed in men's memory. The wreath alone was perfect and immortal, whereas the man who wore it was necessarily imperfect and mortal. Other deeds of his might fall far short of the superlative, or he might go madly on into violence and excess, and Pindar did not tire of mentioning these possibilities. His commission might come from a haughty northern nobleman or even from a tyrant with a reputation for cruelty; still, he would presume to offer counsels of moderation, even admonitions aimed at faults, if they seemed appropriate.

Such presumption from a powerless hireling was at the very least rash, but Pindar was encouraged in it by traditions that had long identified poets with prophets, and he also found his own ways of dressing out his negative warnings. In the guise of sympathy, he dared to sing about the physical ailments of Hieron of Syracuse, insisting that he, the harshest tyrant of his time, would have to die exactly as all the rest of mankind dies (***Pythia 3***). The poet would like to bring him the starlight of rescue from death (ll. 72-76), but of course he cannot since even Asclepius was not allowed to reverse the process of dying. Only insofar as Hieron has been a true ruler, gentle to his people, fair to his nobility, and open to strangers (ll. 70-71, this to the man credited with having invented the secret police!) can he hope. And his hope will be no more than what is common to all men: that immortality will come when virtue at last finds its completion in continuing songs (l. 114). Similarly, in the guise of piety, Pindar presumed to insist upon this same tyrant's dependence upon god's aid for his success, and then to suggest that such aid might not be always forthcoming. "It is god who governs your ambitions and has the care of your power and fame, Hieron. As long as he does not abandon you, you may hope for more victories" (***Olympia 1***.106-11). The overt statement is a happy one, but it rests on the ominous assumption that the divine prop might yet be withdrawn. The same suggestion is made to a noble family of Aegina who is reminded with a prayer ("May Time not tire in its support!") that the strength of their island, resting as it does with god, could still crumble and fall like a column (***Olympia 8***.25-30; compare ***Olympia 4***.16, ***13***.25-26 and 105, ***Pythia 5***.117-21).

Those, however, were mere insinuations. For real admonition Pindar borrowed a sophisticated tool from earlier poets: the indirect but inarguable demonstration grounded in myth. Mythic scenes were, after all, generic to choral poetry, and Pindar was liberal with freestanding instantaneous glimpses of familiar figures from the gigantic drama that was always being played just outside of time. Danced by the chorus, such tableaux traditionally served to attach present ephemeral festivities to the world of permanence. They were employed as well by the epinician poets as reinforcement to the thought pattern of an ode, for they could give the super-actuality of fiction to general notions such as the presence of god in the world's order or the inefficacy even of error in the face of fate. To these two uses of myth Pindar added a third. Exploiting the multitude of meanings that each myth contained, he would sometimes bring a story forward in ostensible support of his general praise but load it with an opposite, ominous message as well. In this way he could maintain the suave and laudatory surface of his hymn, and yet produce solemn warnings that seemed to rise directly from the most ancient Hellenic conclusions about the shape of human existence.

The best-known example of the monitory myth occurs in the ***First Olympian*** Ode, where shifting instants from the story of Pelops are being activated. The song is for Hieron, and the mythic demonstration is apparently suited to the tyrant's praised success, since it too culminates in a chariot victory. Nevertheless there is a second strand to the story, one that ends with the eternal punishments of another hero who did not know how to use success. Tantalus, forever tortured by unappeased appetites, was a model for anyone who—like Hieron—had known prosperity far beyond that of others (***Olympia 1***.54-55; 103-5) but could not "digest" his advantages. Forgetting that he was a receiver and not a giver of divine favor, he tried to usurp powers that were not his, and his consequent fall was immediate and cruel. Put this way, the application to Hieron's almost superhuman arrogance is blatant, but Pindar has provided every possible distraction: the hint (via repudiation) of divine cannibalism, the self-conscious proclamation of originality, the glancing erotic reference to Ganymede, and above all a poetic language which, as he reminds us, could charm belief into the unbelievable (l. 31). Here it works to add enchantment to the unpalatable, but nevertheless it is finally the myth itself that lets the poet do his work. Pindar is able to tell the tyrant that tyrannical behavior is dangerous only because myth allows him to do so in signs instead of in words.

The same effect of mythic admonition is achieved in the ***Second Pythian*** Ode, also made for Hieron. Again Pindar chooses the tale of one who stood at the peak of divine favor but forgot that there was an absolute difference between man and god. Ixion, like Tantalus, tried to take prerogatives (sexual, this time, instead of dietary) that were denied him by the constitution of the universe, and he too was given an endless punishment. His adventure signifies the danger and ugliness of ingratitude, and in the ostensible movement of the ode it provides a grotesque foil for the grateful response which the present music offers to the benefactions of Hieron. Ixion's ingratitude created a monster, whereas the thankfulness of Syracuse creates the ode now being sung. As the poem proceeds, however, the parallel between the enormous bliss of Ixion before his misstep and the enormous bliss of Hieron at the present moment induces a sense of discomfort (ll. 58-61). And the result is that when the end of the ode is invaded by beasts representing the various distortions of a healthy public, there is an unspoken indication that Hieron, too, may be about to engender monsters by going beyond the bounds of permitted political aspirations. If he does, he will be almost as conspicuous in his fall as Ixion on his wheel. The passage in which the poet suggests that tyranny and mob rule are a pair of extremes between which lies the admirable mean—rule by the wise (l. 88)—is purposely obscure, but in the final lines the victor is plainly included in a leveling exhortation. The great ruler of Syracuse, the shockingly rich horse-trainer tyrant, must bear the yoke of divine superiority along with the rest of mankind and, like a beast, answer to god's goad (ll. 93-96).

Myth allowed Pindar to object to the misuse of power, but his more characteristic political pressures were positive. In every ode he urged victors and the class that produced them to be in fact the best—to be a literal aristocracy. And in doing so he went beyond exhortation and took up a mode of magical duress, the precedent for which he found in earlier religious poetry. In prayers and hymns petitioners had tried, like sorcerers, to trap a divinity into showing a favorable aspect, using a time-honored method. First they described the god to himself as having the desired quality, using traditional epithets that he could not deny, and then they told him of past actions which he must, in consistency with himself, repeat once more. In this way the god was caught in the inescapable obligations of his own nature, and when the process was carried out simultaneously by a number of worshippers he was bound to respond. (This same idea of prayer as a binding spell is expressed, incidentally, in Donne's Sermon on Psalm 90:14, and Anglicans still, when asking for mercy, say "For thou art the same Lord, whose property is always to have mercy. . . . ")

It was this almost universal technique of prayer that Pindar borrowed, realizing that the victory ode, a secular hymn danced by a number of performers, could exert a like coercion upon its client. Once the magical words of a group of dancers had formally described a man (or a family or a class or a city) as having a certain quality, that subject would be bound in faith to itself to continue in a display of the same. Pindar expressed the purely practical side of this notion when he said that good fame "masters" or "takes control of" a man (***Olympia 6***.10), but he understood as well the more occult force of his chorus. When once he had ritually reminded Hieron of his ideal aspect as a ruler (a lordly first among peers, one who used his wealth in freedom of spirit, bold in youth and wise in maturity), he spoke like the magician who knows that his spell has been properly performed. To the summoned spirit of Hieron's favorable aspect he gave this simple command: "Now BE what you have learned yourself to be!" (***Pythia 2***.72).

Hieron was not the only one thus bound by Pindar's hymns. Victors, and with them their friends and families, were reminded again and again of their innate excellence, of the virtues that grew like plants within their natures (for example, ***Olympia 9***.16), and also of their proper association with such nonviolent world-forces as Good Order, Justice, Tranquility, Truth, and Maturity (for example, ***Olympia 9***.15-16). These repeated descriptions are parallel to the invocation of a true prayer, where the god's particular powers are revived and contained even as he is called ("O thou whose strength it is to . . ."). And having thus invoked his aristocrats, what Pindar urged upon them was the defense of the present order, properly understood. Eunomia, that balanced and peaceful political mode in which the nobles rejoiced, was not their own construction to do with as they pleased. It was instead the gift of the same god who had established music, prophecy, and healing medicines (***Pythia 5***.63-69), and the principles of all four had to be kept congruent. One word, *nomos,* could be used both for a melodic line (***Nemea 5***.25) and for traditional law (***Pythia 1***.62). Another word, *tethmos,* served for the rules that established song (***Olympia*** 7.88, ***13***.29, ***Isthmia 6***.20, ***Nemea 4***.33) and for those that established contest (***Olympia*** 6.69, ***13***.40), as well as for the ancient Doric constitution (***Pythia 1***.64; compare ***Paean 4***.43, where reference is to the Kean customs) and also for the divine favor granted to a city (***Olympia 8***.25). These were not philological accidents but linguistic evidences of the single divine harmony—authoritative and inalterable—that rulers were meant to protect.

Pindar thus urged an active conservatism upon his noble victors, invoking them as powerful but reminding them that they moved within a fixed and transcendent scheme. Certainly they flew as eagles, while lesser men cowered below (***Nemea 3***.81-82), but they occupied a hierarchical position that was superb only when viewed from the ground. Within the cosmos they were at best only imitators of the mighty ones above: a tyrant might drive away enemies and create a new city, but those exploits shrank beside their cosmic doublet wherein Zeus crushed a gigantic chaos monster under a volcano and created the concept of order (***Pythia 1***). Every act of strength and governance was enhanced but also minimized by a like absolute model, a truth most plainly stated in the ***Eighth Isthmian,*** where the present athletic victory, the repulse of the Persians, and even the legendary taking of Troy are all magnified but diminished as well by the example of Zeus in victory over a potential rival. The ascendancy of the nobles was only a lesser projection of the royal and statesmanlike rule of Zeus. It had its limitations, and these Pindar attempted to bind upon it, even as he invoked the nobility at the height of its powers.

The victor class was described to itself as turning its back on unjust violence (***Olympia*** 7.92, ***Pythia 11***.55b; compare ***Pythia 8***.12, where Hesychia thrusts hybris into the bilge). It was reminded that it used wealth only when that wealth came in justice, willingly (***Pythia 5***.4, 14, ***Pythia 3***.105) and as a healthy thing (***Olympia*** 5.25), for noble souls were superior to riches (***Nemea 9***.32). An aristocrat scorned oath breaking, flattery, and calumny. Even more important, he was above envy, which meant that he could recognize and acclaim true superiority. He was not quarrelsome and ready to fight for evil ends, nor was he bent simply on winning—neither *dyseris* nor *philonikos* (from Adrastus' praise of his former enemy at ***Olympia 6***. 19). Consequently he would not disrupt the polity by sordid struggles for dominance. Furthermore, he could not be swayed by bribery or bad counsel but would "orphan the evil tongue of its bright sound, and know / how to hate all acts of selfish violence" (from the description of Damophilus as the ideal citizen at ***Pythia 4***.283). Trained by the games, he would acclaim the opinion that proved to be best in today's political contest, knowing that all played by the same rules, "upholding and resisting policies with moderation, / their tongues in line with their hearts" (of the Aeginetan Phylacids at ***Isthmia 6***.71-72).

An ideal such as this was naturally anti-autocratic and Pindar, when he could, used his chorus to involve the noble community in a public and solemn abjuration of tyranny. Thus at Aegina he caused the citizen singers to renounce with their general voice the kind of conspiracy that could bring undeserved dominance to a cunning man, while they swore to subject one another to a constant, friendly review:

> Falsehood does violence to what is bright
> and offers rotten fame to the obscure.
> Let this never be my way, O father Zeus!
> Let me take the simple paths
> not those of duplicity,
> that when I die I may not leave my sons
> ill-fame. Some pray for gold,
> some for boundless lands,
> but I would wish to please my fellow townsmen,
> then hide my limbs beneath the ground
> as one who praised the man deserving praise
> and sprinkled blame upon iniquity.
> [***Nemea 8***.34-45]

At home in Thebes Pindar bound the citizens even more explicitly in an aristocratic creed hostile to tyranny, giving his chorus these words to sing:

> In city matters I find out the middle way
> that longer flowers with prosperity, for I reject
> the tyrant's lot.
>
> I reach instead towards virtues common to all
> noble men;
> thus the envious are held at bay.
>
> The man who takes the bloom of noble deeds,
> steers his life in quietude
> and turns his back on dire violence
> will have a finer passing into black death
> for offering his sweet continuing race
> this best prize as its inheritance—
> the grace of good repute.
> [***Pythia 11***.52-60]

Statements such as these, solemnly proclaimed in a multiple first-person voice and magically reinforced by choral gesture, were not unlike the oaths sworn in certain ancient sodalities. With them Pindar meant to fix the nobles for whom his odes were made in a common allegiance to traditional aristocratic forms.

Music was necessary to the aristocracy because it was the source of immortalizing glory. This meant that the poet had an enormous influence since, in theory at least, the reserved powers of review, admonition, and exhortation lodged in the epinician ode could not be suppressed. But what kept the poet from simply selling this influence or using his control over princely fame in an unscrupulous fashion? This question clearly troubled Pindar, for his odes are filled not only with pointed self-vindication but also with general meditations on the honesty of song. He knows that even those who have the highest endowments may be open to bribery—Asclepius himself sold his powers unlawfully (***Pythia 3***.54). He blames other men for useless chatter (***Olympia 2***.87), dangerous slander (***Pythia 2***.54-56), or vain croaking boasts (***Olympia 9***.38-39), and he admits that lies may be decked out with elaborate beguilements so as to impose themselves as truth (***Olympia 1***.28b-29). Worse yet, one may commit an act of killing injustice by refusing praise to the deserving and giving it to a lesser man; this, he says, is what the Achaeans (and Homer) did in the case of Ajax and Odysseus (***Nemea*** 7.20; compare ***Nemea 8***.23). Such are the possible perversions of praise, but he, Pindar, feels secure in his profession because true poets, like true aristocrats, are part of the appointed order of things. They too are invested by nature with their special virtue (***Olympia 2***.86), given their opportunities by god-made splendors, and granted success only by the Muses. The man who sings with such a vocation imitates eternal songs that have been shaped in heaven (***Nemea 5***.22-25, ***Isthmia 8***.63-66), and this means that, though his work may be imperfect, it cannot be false. Furthermore, the poet, again like the aristocrat, is driven by his own need for good fame, and he too is scrutinized in the envious openness of small communities. "To make a new song and give it over to trial on the touchstone—that is danger in full!" (***Nemea 8***.20-21; compare ***Pythia 1***.84). When he takes a commission he is thus like a charioteer entering a race (***Olympia 9***.81-82) or an athlete descending into the playing space (***Olympia 8***.54, ***Olympia 13***.93, ***Pythia 2***.44). He needs all his daring (***Olympia 13***.11), for he is engaging his particular excellence in that risky public toil which is man's only means of escaping the nonlife of obscure inaction. In such an endeavor anyone would be a fool to be other than true.

Convinced of such sublimities Pindar could approach even the question of his own pay. True, his compositions were bought, but all work had its natural wage. Shepherds, birdcatchers, and fishermen worked to keep themselves from hunger; poets worked for pay, and the class whose work was contest and war earned its own proper wage, paid in the words that the poets produced (***Isthmia 1***.47; compare ***Nemea*** 7.63, ***Olympia*** 7.16). Pindar's clients did not purchase his praise; rather, their actions—when they were inwrought with virtue—demanded it. Thus in fact he was paying them, not the other way around. The fee covered the rehearsing and costuming of a chorus, presumably leaving something over for the poet to take home, but the duty of acclamation had been imposed directly by the victory. "Crowns laid upon curling heads force this god-made duty upon me . . . and Pisa too bids me to speak" (***Olympia 3***.6-9; compare ***Pythia*** 7.10-13).

The fundamental notion was one of just recompense, often seen as answering light with light. "Wherever god-given brightness comes, a brilliant light lies upon men and a sweet spate of days" (***Pythia 8***.96-97). Every superlative achievement was luminous, as were also youth, wealth, fame, and salvation (***Nemea 8***.34; compare ***Nemea 3***.64, ***3***.84, ***4***.13; youth, ***Nemea*** 7.3; wealth, ***Olympia 2***.55-56; fame, ***Olympia 1***.23; 23; salvation, ***Pythia 3***.75). Especially at the games did innate excellence shine out in each contest (***Isthmia 1***.22; compare ***Nemea 3***.84, 9.42, and ***Isthmia 2***.17, where the victor brings light to his city), and such light could be prolonged indefinitely by the light of superlative poetry (the chorus equals light at ***Olympia 4***.12; compare ***Olympia 9***.22). A victor could lead a portion of song up into the light, reviving the actions of his forefathers (***Isthmia 6***.62; compare ***Olympia 5***.15 where the victor leads his city into light), and he himself could burn bright with the Muses (***Isthmia*** 7.23) because poetry was like a torch (***Isthmia 4***.47) that shone back inextinguishable upon the beam of a fine accomplishment. And light, like air and water, was incorruptible.

As Pindar saw it, the power of poets was checked exactly as the power of princes was: by the divine order that dealt out natural endowments, by the need for good fame and the appetite for glory, by the ready criticism of peers, and by the unseen audience of Time and the Olympians. Poetry, moreover, (at any rate his own) was asked to undergo a further regulation, for Pindar invited the public to scrutinize not just his finished work but also his creative processes. A Pindaric ode presents itself not as a final and impervious object, but rather as a performance under construction. There is a constant wavering between inception and finality, intention and effect. There is a dizzying shift of temporal occasion, which at one point may seem to be the winning of the victory, at another the commissioning of the ode or the instruction of the chorus; sometimes the public performance describes itself, but again the poetic moment may seem to be one of private communion between poet and Muse. And all this is reflected in a hybrid persona, for the frequent "I" of the odes may refer to an "I, poet" (for example, ***Olympia 6***.84, ***Isthmia 1***.1), an "I, poem" (***Nemea 5***.3), an "I, chorus" (***Olympia 14***.18), or a combination of the three (***Olympia 9***.20). And what this mixed "voice of the ode" repeatedly asks is that an audience assumed to be close at hand observe each gesture and test each ingredient in the semimagical praise process.

The ruling fiction is that the song is dynamic; it is taking form before the eyes and ears of the spectators. Furthermore, it is fallible and in need of encouragement and confirmation. "Have I made an idle boast?" (***Pythia 10***.4). "Would anyone call this the work of a Boeotian pig?" (***Olympia 6***.89-90). The negations provoked by questions such as these involve the audience in a kind of complicity in the act of praise. When difficult choices are to be made, listeners may be asked to participate. "Which of your glories, Thebes, would you hear sung?" is the explicit demand at the opening of ***Isthmia 7,*** and the same kind of appeal may be made implicitly, as when the chorus confesses that the praise of a tyrant is more difficult than that of a king (***Pythia 2***.13-18), with the unspoken appeal: How then shall we proceed? Sometimes a song will expose a stress point in its structure, so that the audience will seem to supervise the search for a solution (for example, ***Olympia 13***.40-46b, ***Nemea*** 7.53). Again, an ode may explain that just here a long list of victories might be offered but will not appear because "deep in their hidden hearts men re-sent the praise of others' virtues" (***Pythia 1***.84; compare, for example, ***Pythia 8***.31-32). An alternate motif will be proposed and the listener who has been treated with such comradely courtesy is bound to approve; indeed, the poem's next phase will seem to have originated with him.

These are of course tricks of style, useful for emphasis and also for a kind of irony, a classic technique for involving an audience. Thus, having chosen to evoke the figure of Clytemnestra (as a negative foil to a conspicuous but guiltless victor), the chorus of ***Pythia 11*** pretends to be at a loss. Whirling in its dance it sings, "Friends, I am whirled at a crossroads, though I was going on so well—surely some wind has blown me off course!" (ll. 38-40), which, "translated," means, "Admire the apt unconventionality of our myth and ponder its meaning!" The notion that the audience might catch the dancers in some sort of *faux pas* is a favorite conceit (***Olympia 9***.35-36, ***Pythia 10***.51, ***Nemea 3***.26-27), but it is also an invitation to collaboration, as is the Pindaric habit of making the song describe itself. Having struck up in a mode called the Castorian, a chorus will chant: "I would yoke my victor to a Castorian hymn" (***Isthmia 1***.16). Or alternatively, in the Dorian: "Muse, stand by me as I devise a bright new way to yoke the Dorian mode to the voice of the komos-singer" (***Olympia 3***.4-5). Placing an initial image, the singers say, "I shall place golden columns at this broad porch . . . " (***Olympia 6***.1-3); breaking off a narrative (and perhaps coming to a choreographed halt) the dancers sing: "I come to a stop" (***Nemea 5***.16). Song is action; action is decision, danger, and the grasping of opportunities, and the audience is forced to share the risk with techniques such as these.

Some of these practices are generic, deriving from the self-description of magical operations; a certain number of them are to be found as well in the epinicians of Bacchylides. Nevertheless there is a pervasive assumption of close assistance from an audience that sets Pindar's metapoetical passages apart from others. He insists upon discussing the performance with those who watch it, breaking through its facade so that the inner contrivances are visible. This is of course only one more contrivance, but it expresses Pindar's sense of his political function. He does praise those in power; he must, for that is his profession. Nevertheless he announces with these programmatic appeals that his praise is (or should be) a fully popular affair. His chorus stands as one, but it represents the commonality (it is *idios en koinōi*, ***Olympia 13***.49).

It would be foolish to try to assess the immediate influence of Pindar's political thought. There is no way to know if Thebans and Aeginetans did actually behave according to the civic creeds repeated for them by Pindaric choruses. Nor can anyone say whether Hieron in any way moderated his arrogance after watching the Tantalus example danced out in his halls. Did Arcesilaus, king of Cyrene, in fact try to mix pure virtue with his wealth because his singers had told him he did? The question is ephemeral as well as unanswerable, for he was soon overthrown. Indeed, the continuing events of the fifth century seem to accuse Pindar of bad political prophecy, as city after city saw aristocratic governments (reflections of the eternal harmonies of Apollo's lyre) edged out by what Pindar called the "loud-mouthed mob" (***Pythia 2***.87). Time in its longer reaches, however, makes another sort of judgment. In every generation since his own, certain men have been moved afresh by Pindar's vision of government by men who were both strong and fine. The notion of poetic scrutiny is gone but some still dream—according to the two great Pindaric metaphors—of political rivalry as an open and glorious contest, and of political entities as festive places where Quietude suppresses violence and rejoices in all the forms of graciousness (***Pythia 8***.1-5). (pp. 434-49)

Anne Burnett, "The Scrutiny of Song: Pindar, Politics, and Poetry," in Critical Inquiry, *Vol. 13, No. 3, Spring, 1987, pp. 434-49.*

FURTHER READING

Bundy, Elroy L. *Studia Pindarica* I and II. Berkeley: University of California Press, 1962, 92 p.

Pioneering study of Pindar's *Olympian 11* and *Isthmian 1* odes that fostered a new understanding of the structure and meaning of the victory poem.

Carne-Ross, D. S. "Weaving with Points of Gold: Pindar's *Sixth Olympian.*" *Arion* 3, No. 1 (1976): 5-44.

Detailed discussion of the themes and imagery in *Olympian 6.*

Dodds, E. R. *The Greeks and the Irrational.* Berkeley: University of California Press, 1951, 327 p.

Important examination of Greek culture and religion in the archaic and classical ages, with scattered references to Pindar.

Finley, Jr., John H. "Pindar's Beginnings." In *The Poetic Tradition: Essays on Greek, Latin, and English Poetry,* edited by Don Cameron Allen and Henry T. Rowell, pp. 3-26. Baltimore: The Johns Hopkins Press, 1968.

Places Pindar's early poetic development in historical context.

Finley, M. I. "Silver Tongue." In his *Aspects of Antiquity: Discoveries and Controversies,* pp. 38-43. New York: The Viking Press, 1968.

Negative assessment of Pindar, finding fault with the stylistic difficulty and aristocratic values of the odes.

Gildersleeve, Basil L. "Introductory Essay." In his *Pindar: The Olympian and Pythian Odes,* pp. vii-cxv. London: Macmillan & Co., 1885.

General discussion of Pindar's life, thought, and artistic development.

Goldhill, Simon. "Intimations of Immortality: Fame and Tradition from Homer to Pindar." In his *The Poet's Voice: Essays on Poetics and Greek Literature,* pp. 69-166. Cambridge: Cambridge University Press, 1991.

Study of Homeric epic and Pindar's epinician odes, considering "the development of what is a crucial aspect of the ancient perception of the poet's role—praise, celebration, memorial."

Jaeger, Werner. "The Aristocracy: Conflict and Transformation." In his *Paideia: The Ideals of Greek Culture,* Vol. 1, translated by Gilbert Highet, pp. 185-222. New York: Oxford University Press, 1965.

Discussion of the Greek nobility during the archaic age in which Pindar's social conservatism is emphasized.

Jebb, R. C. "Pindar." *The Journal of Hellenic Studies* III, No. 1 (April 1882): 144-83.

Article seeking to bring about "a closer appreciation of a poet whose charm gains on those who endeavour to see him more clearly in his relation to the life of his day, to its thought and art, and, above all, to the art which he had made his own."

Lefkowitz, Mary R. *The Victory Ode: An Introduction.* Park Ridge, N. J.: Noyes Press, 1976, 186 p.

Line-by-line analysis of six poems by Pindar and Bacchylides, focusing on "the amazing potential of a complex art form . . . and the innovative linguistic talents of two great poets."

———. "Autobiographical Fiction in Pindar." In *Harvard Studies in Classical Philology,* Volume 84, pp. 29-49. Cambridge, Mass.: Harvard University Press, 1980.

Argues that in Pindar's victory odes "the combative tone and 'personal' references express the poet's understanding of the meaning of victory; that in these statements he describes himself as taking a combatant's risks, showing his determination, experiencing his sense of isolation."

Lloyd-Jones, Hugh. "Modern Interpretation of Pindar: The Second Pythian and Seventh Nemean Odes." *The Journal of Hellenic Studies* XCIII (1973): 109-37.

Examination of various critical interpretations of Pindar, maintaining that he is "one of the greatest Greek and also one of the greatest European poets."

Rose, Peter W. "The Myth of Pindar's First *Nemean:* Sportsmen, Poetry, and *Paideia.*" In *Harvard Studies in Classical Philology,* Volume 78, pp. 145-75. Cambridge, Mass.: Harvard University Press, 1974.

Discussion of the relevance of myth to Pindar's victory odes, concentrating on *Nemean 1.*

Young, David C. *Three Odes of Pindar: A Literary Study of Pythian 11, Pythian 3, and Olympian 7.* Leiden: E. J. Brill, 1968, 133 p.

Modifies Elroy L. Bundy's thesis on Pindar (see above) to "advance the understanding of . . . three poems as individual works of the literary art."

CLASSICAL AND MEDIEVAL LITERATURE CRITICISM

INDEXES

Literary Criticism Series
Cumulative Author Index

Literary Criticism Series
Cumulative Topic Index

CMLC Cumulative Nationality Index

CMLC Cumulative Title Index

CMLC Cumulative Critic Index

How to Use This Index

The main references

Calvino, Italo
1923-1985.....CLC 5, 8, 11, 22, 33, 39, 73; SSC 3

list all author entries in the following Gale Literary Criticism series:

CLC = *Contemporary Literary Criticism*
CLR = *Children's Literature Review*
CMLC = *Classical and Medieval Literature Criticism*
DC = *Drama Criticism*
LC = *Literature Criticism from 1400 to 1800*
NCLC = *Nineteenth-Century Literature Criticism*
PC = *Poetry Criticism*
SSC = *Short Story Criticism*
TCLC = *Twentieth-Century Literary Criticism*

The cross-references

See also CANR 23; CA 85-88;
obituary CA 116

list all author entries in the following Gale biographical and literary sources:

AAYA = *Authors & Artists for Young Adults*
AITN = *Authors in the News*
BLC = *Black Literature Criticism*
BW = *Black Writers*
CA = *Contemporary Authors*
CAAS = *Contemporary Authors Autobiography Series*
CABS = *Contemporary Authors Bibliographical Series*
CANR = *Contemporary Authors New Revision Series*
CAP = *Contemporary Authors Permanent Series*
CDALB = *Concise Dictionary of American Literary Biography*
CDBLB = *Concise Dictionary of British Literary Biography*
DA = *DISCovering Authors*
DLB = *Dictionary of Literary Biography*
DLBD = *Dictionary of Literary Biography Documentary Series*
DLBY = *Dictionary of Literary Biography Yearbook*
HW = *Hispanic Writers*
JRDA = *Junior DISCovering Authors*
MAICYA = *Major Authors and Illustrators for Children and Young Adults*
MTCW = *Major 20th-Century Writers*
SAAS = *Something about the Author Autobiography Series*
SATA = *Something about the Author*
WLC = *World Literature Criticism, 1500 to the Present*
YABC = *Yesterday's Authors of Books for Children*

Literary Criticism Series Cumulative Author Index

Anthony, Piers 1934- . . . . **CLC 35**
See also CA 21-24R; CANR 28; DLB 8; MTCW

Antoine, Marc
See Proust, (Valentin-Louis-George-Eugene-) Marcel

Antoninus, Brother
See Everson, William (Oliver)

Antonioni, Michelangelo 1912- . . . . . **CLC 20**
See also CA 73-76

Antschel, Paul 1920-1970. . . . . . . **CLC 10, 19**
See also Celan, Paul
See also CA 85-88; CANR 33; MTCW

Anwar, Chairil 1922-1949 . . . . **TCLC 22**
See also CA 121

Apollinaire, Guillaume . . **TCLC 3, 8, 51; PC 7**
See also Kostrowitzki, Wilhelm Apollinaris de

Appelfeld, Aharon 1932- . . . . **CLC 23, 47**
See also CA 112; 133

Apple, Max (Isaac) 1941-. . . . . **CLC 9, 33**
See also CA 81-84; CANR 19; DLB 130

Appleman, Philip (Dean) 1926- . . . . . **CLC 51**
See also CA 13-16R; CAAS 18; CANR 6, 29

Appleton, Lawrence
See Lovecraft, H(oward) P(hillips)

Apteryx
See Eliot, T(homas) S(tearns)

Apuleius, (Lucius Madaurensis)
125(?)-175(?) . . . . **CMLC 1**

Aquin, Hubert 1929-1977. . . . . **CLC 15**
See also CA 105; DLB 53

Aragon, Louis 1897-1982 . . . . **CLC 3, 22**
See also CA 69-72; 108; CANR 28; DLB 72; MTCW

Arany, Janos 1817-1882. . . . . **NCLC 34**

Arbuthnot, John 1667-1735 . . . . **LC 1**
See also DLB 101

Archer, Herbert Winslow
See Mencken, H(enry) L(ouis)

Archer, Jeffrey (Howard) 1940- . . . . **CLC 28**
See also BEST 89:3; CA 77-80; CANR 22

Archer, Jules 1915- . . . . **CLC 12**
See also CA 9-12R; CANR 6; SAAS 5; SATA 4

Archer, Lee
See Ellison, Harlan

Arden, John 1930- . . . . **CLC 6, 13, 15**
See also CA 13-16R; CAAS 4; CANR 31; DLB 13; MTCW

Arenas, Reinaldo 1943-1990 . . . . **CLC 41**
See also CA 124; 128; 133; HW

Arendt, Hannah 1906-1975 . . . . **CLC 66**
See also CA 17-20R; 61-64; CANR 26; MTCW

Aretino, Pietro 1492-1556 . . . . **LC 12**

Arghezi, Tudor 1880-1967 . . . . **CLC 80**
See also Theodorescu, Ion N.

Arguedas, Jose Maria
1911-1969 . . . . **CLC 10, 18**
See also CA 89-92; DLB 113; HW

Argueta, Manlio 1936-. . . . . **CLC 31**
See also CA 131; HW

Ariosto, Ludovico 1474-1533. . . . . **LC 6**

Aristides
See Epstein, Joseph

Aristophanes
450B.C.-385B.C. . . . . **CMLC 4; DC 2**
See also DA

Arlt, Roberto (Godofredo Christophersen)
1900-1942 . . . . **TCLC 29**
See also CA 123; 131; HW

Armah, Ayi Kwei 1939- . . . . **CLC 5, 33**
See also BLC 1; BW; CA 61-64; CANR 21; DLB 117; MTCW

Armatrading, Joan 1950- . . . . **CLC 17**
See also CA 114

Arnette, Robert
See Silverberg, Robert

Arnim, Achim von (Ludwig Joachim von Arnim) 1781-1831 . . . . **NCLC 5**
See also DLB 90

Arnim, Bettina von 1785-1859. . . . **NCLC 38**
See also DLB 90

Arnold, Matthew
1822-1888 . . . . **NCLC 6, 29; PC 5**
See also CDBLB 1832-1890; DA; DLB 32, 57; WLC

Arnold, Thomas 1795-1842 . . . . . . **NCLC 18**
See also DLB 55

Arnow, Harriette (Louisa) Simpson
1908-1986 . . . . **CLC 2, 7, 18**
See also CA 9-12R; 118; CANR 14; DLB 6; MTCW; SATA 42, 47

Arp, Hans
See Arp, Jean

Arp, Jean 1887-1966. . . . . **CLC 5**
See also CA 81-84; 25-28R; CANR 42

Arrabal
See Arrabal, Fernando

Arrabal, Fernando 1932- . . . **CLC 2, 9, 18, 58**
See also CA 9-12R; CANR 15

Arrick, Fran. . . . . **CLC 30**

Artaud, Antonin 1896-1948 . . . . . **TCLC 3, 36**
See also CA 104

Arthur, Ruth M(abel) 1905-1979. . . . **CLC 12**
See also CA 9-12R; 85-88; CANR 4; SATA 7, 26

Artsybashev, Mikhail (Petrovich)
1878-1927 . . . . **TCLC 31**

Arundel, Honor (Morfydd)
1919-1973 . . . . **CLC 17**
See also CA 21-22; 41-44R; CAP 2; SATA 4, 24

Asch, Sholem 1880-1957 . . . . **TCLC 3**
See also CA 105

Ash, Shalom
See Asch, Sholem

Ashbery, John (Lawrence)
1927- . . . . . . **CLC 2, 3, 4, 6, 9, 13, 15, 25, 41, 77**
See also CA 5-8R; CANR 9, 37; DLB 5; DLBY 81; MTCW

Ashdown, Clifford
See Freeman, R(ichard) Austin

Ashe, Gordon
See Creasey, John

Ashton-Warner, Sylvia (Constance)
1908-1984 . . . . **CLC 19**
See also CA 69-72; 112; CANR 29; MTCW

Asimov, Isaac
1920-1992 . . . . . . **CLC 1, 3, 9, 19, 26, 76**
See also BEST 90:2; CA 1-4R; 137; CANR 2, 19, 36; CLR 12; DLB 8; DLBY 92; JRDA; MAICYA; MTCW; SATA 1, 26, 74

Astley, Thea (Beatrice May)
1925- . . . . **CLC 41**
See also CA 65-68; CANR 11, 43

Aston, James
See White, T(erence) H(anbury)

Asturias, Miguel Angel
1899-1974 . . . . **CLC 3, 8, 13**
See also CA 25-28; 49-52; CANR 32; CAP 2; DLB 113; HW; MTCW

Atares, Carlos Saura
See Saura (Atares), Carlos

Atheling, William
See Pound, Ezra (Weston Loomis)

Atheling, William, Jr.
See Blish, James (Benjamin)

Atherton, Gertrude (Franklin Horn)
1857-1948 . . . . **TCLC 2**
See also CA 104; DLB 9, 78

Atherton, Lucius
See Masters, Edgar Lee

Atkins, Jack
See Harris, Mark

Atticus
See Fleming, Ian (Lancaster)

Atwood, Margaret (Eleanor)
1939- . . . . . **CLC 2, 3, 4, 8, 13, 15, 25, 44; SSC 2**
See also BEST 89:2; CA 49-52; CANR 3, 24, 33; DA; DLB 53; MTCW; SATA 50; WLC

Aubigny, Pierre d'
See Mencken, H(enry) L(ouis)

Aubin, Penelope 1685-1731(?) . . . . **LC 9**
See also DLB 39

Auchincloss, Louis (Stanton)
1917- . . . . **CLC 4, 6, 9, 18, 45**
See also CA 1-4R; CANR 6, 29; DLB 2; DLBY 80; MTCW

Auden, W(ystan) H(ugh)
1907-1973 . . . . . . **CLC 1, 2, 3, 4, 6, 9, 11, 14, 43; PC 1**
See also CA 9-12R; 45-48; CANR 5; CDBLB 1914-1945; DA; DLB 10, 20; MTCW; WLC

Audiberti, Jacques 1900-1965 . . . . . . **CLC 38**
See also CA 25-28R

Auel, Jean M(arie) 1936-. . . . . **CLC 31**
See also AAYA 7; BEST 90:4; CA 103; CANR 21

Auerbach, Erich 1892-1957 . . . . **TCLC 43**
See also CA 118

Augier, Emile 1820-1889 . . . . **NCLC 31**

August, John
See De Voto, Bernard (Augustine)

Baron, David
See Pinter, Harold

Baron Corvo
See Rolfe, Frederick (William Serafino Austin Lewis Mary)

Barondess, Sue K(aufman) 1926-1977 . . . . **CLC 8**
See also Kaufman, Sue
See also CA 1-4R; 69-72; CANR 1

Baron de Teive
See Pessoa, Fernando (Antonio Nogueira)

Barres, Maurice 1862-1923 . . . . **TCLC 47**
See also DLB 123

Barreto, Afonso Henrique de Lima
See Lima Barreto, Afonso Henrique de

Barrett, (Roger) Syd 1946- . . . . **CLC 35**
See also Pink Floyd

Barrett, William (Christopher) 1913-1992 . . . . **CLC 27**
See also CA 13-16R; 139; CANR 11

Barrie, J(ames) M(atthew) 1860-1937 . . . . **TCLC 2**
See also CA 104; 136; CDBLB 1890-1914; CLR 16; DLB 10; MAICYA; YABC 1

Barrington, Michael
See Moorcock, Michael (John)

Barrol, Grady
See Bograd, Larry

Barry, Mike
See Malzberg, Barry N(athaniel)

Barry, Philip 1896-1949 . . . . **TCLC 11**
See also CA 109; DLB 7

Bart, Andre Schwarz
See Schwarz-Bart, Andre

Barth, John (Simmons) 1930- . . . . . . **CLC 1, 2, 3, 5, 7, 9, 10, 14, 27, 51; SSC 10**
See also AITN 1, 2; CA 1-4R; CABS 1; CANR 5, 23; DLB 2; MTCW

Barthelme, Donald 1931-1989 . . . . . . **CLC 1, 2, 3, 5, 6, 8, 13, 23, 46, 59; SSC 2**
See also CA 21-24R; 129; CANR 20; DLB 2; DLBY 80, 89; MTCW; SATA 7, 62

Barthelme, Frederick 1943- . . . . **CLC 36**
See also CA 114; 122; DLBY 85

Barthes, Roland (Gerard) 1915-1980 . . . . **CLC 24**
See also CA 130; 97-100; MTCW

Barzun, Jacques (Martin) 1907- . . . . **CLC 51**
See also CA 61-64; CANR 22

Bashevis, Isaac
See Singer, Isaac Bashevis

Bashkirtseff, Marie 1859-1884 . . . **NCLC 27**

Basho
See Matsuo Basho

Bass, Kingsley B., Jr.
See Bullins, Ed

Bass, Rick 1958- . . . . **CLC 79**
See also CA 126

Bassani, Giorgio 1916- . . . . **CLC 9**
See also CA 65-68; CANR 33; DLB 128; MTCW

Bastos, Augusto (Antonio) Roa
See Roa Bastos, Augusto (Antonio)

Bataille, Georges 1897-1962 . . . . **CLC 29**
See also CA 101; 89-92

Bates, H(erbert) E(rnest) 1905-1974 . . . . **CLC 46; SSC 10**
See also CA 93-96; 45-48; CANR 34; MTCW

Bauchart
See Camus, Albert

Baudelaire, Charles 1821-1867 . . . . **NCLC 6, 29; PC 1**
See also DA; WLC

Baudrillard, Jean 1929- . . . . **CLC 60**

Baum, L(yman) Frank 1856-1919 . . . **TCLC 7**
See also CA 108; 133; CLR 15; DLB 22; JRDA; MAICYA; MTCW; SATA 18

Baum, Louis F.
See Baum, L(yman) Frank

Baumbach, Jonathan 1933- . . . . . . **CLC 6, 23**
See also CA 13-16R; CAAS 5; CANR 12; DLBY 80; MTCW

Bausch, Richard (Carl) 1945- . . . . . . **CLC 51**
See also CA 101; CAAS 14; CANR 43; DLB 130

Baxter, Charles 1947- . . . . **CLC 45, 78**
See also CA 57-60; CANR 40; DLB 130

Baxter, George Owen
See Faust, Frederick (Schiller)

Baxter, James K(eir) 1926-1972 . . . . **CLC 14**
See also CA 77-80

Baxter, John
See Hunt, E(verette) Howard, Jr.

Bayer, Sylvia
See Glassco, John

Beagle, Peter S(oyer) 1939- . . . . **CLC 7**
See also CA 9-12R; CANR 4; DLBY 80; SATA 60

Bean, Normal
See Burroughs, Edgar Rice

Beard, Charles A(ustin) 1874-1948 . . . . **TCLC 15**
See also CA 115; DLB 17; SATA 18

Beardsley, Aubrey 1872-1898 . . . . . **NCLC 6**

Beattie, Ann 1947- . . . . **CLC 8, 13, 18, 40, 63; SSC 11**
See also BEST 90:2; CA 81-84; DLBY 82; MTCW

Beattie, James 1735-1803 . . . . **NCLC 25**
See also DLB 109

Beauchamp, Kathleen Mansfield 1888-1923
See Mansfield, Katherine
See also CA 104; 134; DA

Beauvoir, Simone (Lucie Ernestine Marie Bertrand) de 1908-1986 . . . . **CLC 1, 2, 4, 8, 14, 31, 44, 50, 71**
See also CA 9-12R; 118; CANR 28; DA; DLB 72; DLBY 86; MTCW; WLC

Becker, Jurek 1937- . . . . **CLC 7, 19**
See also CA 85-88; DLB 75

Becker, Walter 1950- . . . . **CLC 26**

Beckett, Samuel (Barclay) 1906-1989 . . . . . . **CLC 1, 2, 3, 4, 6, 9, 10, 11, 14, 18, 29, 57, 59**
See also CA 5-8R; 130; CANR 33; CDBLB 1945-1960; DA; DLB 13, 15; DLBY 90; MTCW; WLC

Beckford, William 1760-1844 . . . . **NCLC 16**
See also DLB 39

Beckman, Gunnel 1910- . . . . **CLC 26**
See also CA 33-36R; CANR 15; CLR 25; MAICYA; SAAS 9; SATA 6

Becque, Henri 1837-1899 . . . . **NCLC 3**

Beddoes, Thomas Lovell 1803-1849 . . . . **NCLC 3**
See also DLB 96

Bedford, Donald F.
See Fearing, Kenneth (Flexner)

Beecher, Catharine Esther 1800-1878 . . . . **NCLC 30**
See also DLB 1

Beecher, John 1904-1980 . . . . **CLC 6**
See also AITN 1; CA 5-8R; 105; CANR 8

Beer, Johann 1655-1700 . . . . **LC 5**

Beer, Patricia 1924- . . . . **CLC 58**
See also CA 61-64; CANR 13; DLB 40

Beerbohm, Henry Maximilian 1872-1956 . . . . **TCLC 1, 24**
See also CA 104; DLB 34, 100

Begiebing, Robert J(ohn) 1946- . . . . . **CLC 70**
See also CA 122; CANR 40

Behan, Brendan 1923-1964 . . . . **CLC 1, 8, 11, 15, 79**
See also CA 73-76; CANR 33; CDBLB 1945-1960; DLB 13; MTCW

Behn, Aphra 1640(?)-1689 . . . . **LC 1**
See also DA; DLB 39, 80, 131; WLC

Behrman, S(amuel) N(athaniel) 1893-1973 . . . . **CLC 40**
See also CA 13-16; 45-48; CAP 1; DLB 7, 44

Belasco, David 1853-1931 . . . . **TCLC 3**
See also CA 104; DLB 7

Belcheva, Elisaveta 1893- . . . . **CLC 10**

Beldone, Phil "Cheech"
See Ellison, Harlan

Beleno
See Azuela, Mariano

Belinski, Vissarion Grigoryevich 1811-1848 . . . . **NCLC 5**

Belitt, Ben 1911- . . . . **CLC 22**
See also CA 13-16R; CAAS 4; CANR 7; DLB 5

Bell, James Madison 1826-1902 . . . **TCLC 43**
See also BLC 1; BW; CA 122; 124; DLB 50

Bell, Madison (Smartt) 1957- . . . . . . **CLC 41**
See also CA 111; CANR 28

Bell, Marvin (Hartley) 1937- . . . . . **CLC 8, 31**
See also CA 21-24R; CAAS 14; DLB 5; MTCW

Bell, W. L. D.
See Mencken, H(enry) L(ouis)

Bellamy, Atwood C.
See Mencken, H(enry) L(ouis)

Bellamy, Edward 1850-1898 ...... **NCLC 4**
See also DLB 12

Bellin, Edward J.
See Kuttner, Henry

Belloc, (Joseph) Hilaire (Pierre)
1870-1953 .... **TCLC 7, 18**
See also CA 106; DLB 19, 100; YABC 1

Belloc, Joseph Peter Rene Hilaire
See Belloc, (Joseph) Hilaire (Pierre)

Belloc, Joseph Pierre Hilaire
See Belloc, (Joseph) Hilaire (Pierre)

Belloc, M. A.
See Lowndes, Marie Adelaide (Belloc)

Bellow, Saul
1915- ...... **CLC 1, 2, 3, 6, 8, 10, 13, 15, 25, 33, 34, 63, 79**
See also AITN 2; BEST 89:3; CA 5-8R; CABS 1; CANR 29; CDALB 1941-1968; DA; DLB 2, 28; DLBD 3; DLBY 82; MTCW; WLC

Belser, Reimond Karel Maria de
1929- .... **CLC 14**

Bely, Andrey .... **TCLC 7**
See also Bugayev, Boris Nikolayevich

Benary, Margot
See Benary-Isbert, Margot

Benary-Isbert, Margot 1889-1979 ... **CLC 12**
See also CA 5-8R; 89-92; CANR 4; CLR 12; MAICYA; SATA 2, 21

Benavente (y Martinez), Jacinto
1866-1954 .... **TCLC 3**
See also CA 106; 131; HW; MTCW

Benchley, Peter (Bradford)
1940- .... **CLC 4, 8**
See also AITN 2; CA 17-20R; CANR 12, 35; MTCW; SATA 3

Benchley, Robert (Charles)
1889-1945 .... **TCLC 1**
See also CA 105; DLB 11

Benedikt, Michael 1935- .... **CLC 4, 14**
See also CA 13-16R; CANR 7; DLB 5

Benet, Juan 1927-................ **CLC 28**

Benet, Stephen Vincent
1898-1943 .... **TCLC 7; SSC 10**
See also CA 104; DLB 4, 48, 102; YABC 1

Benet, William Rose 1886-1950 ... **TCLC 28**
See also CA 118; DLB 45

Benford, Gregory (Albert) 1941-.... **CLC 52**
See also CA 69-72; CANR 12, 24; DLBY 82

Bengtsson, Frans (Gunnar)
1894-1954 .... **TCLC 48**

Benjamin, David
See Slavitt, David R(ytman)

Benjamin, Lois
See Gould, Lois

Benjamin, Walter 1892-1940 ...... **TCLC 39**

Benn, Gottfried 1886-1956......... **TCLC 3**
See also CA 106; DLB 56

Bennett, Alan 1934- .... **CLC 45, 77**
See also CA 103; CANR 35; MTCW

Bennett, (Enoch) Arnold
1867-1931 .... **TCLC 5, 20**
See also CA 106; CDBLB 1890-1914; DLB 10, 34, 98

Bennett, Elizabeth
See Mitchell, Margaret (Munnerlyn)

Bennett, George Harold 1930-
See Bennett, Hal
See also BW; CA 97-100

Bennett, Hal .... **CLC 5**
See also Bennett, George Harold
See also DLB 33

Bennett, Jay 1912-............... **CLC 35**
See also AAYA 10; CA 69-72; CANR 11, 42; JRDA; SAAS 4; SATA 27, 41

Bennett, Louise (Simone) 1919-..... **CLC 28**
See also BLC 1; DLB 117

Benson, E(dward) F(rederic)
1867-1940 .... **TCLC 27**
See also CA 114

Benson, Jackson J. 1930-.......... **CLC 34**
See also CA 25-28R; DLB 111

Benson, Sally 1900-1972 .... **CLC 17**
See also CA 19-20; 37-40R; CAP 1; SATA 1, 27, 35

Benson, Stella 1892-1933......... **TCLC 17**
See also CA 117; DLB 36

Bentham, Jeremy 1748-1832 ..... **NCLC 38**
See also DLB 107

Bentley, E(dmund) C(lerihew)
1875-1956 .... **TCLC 12**
See also CA 108; DLB 70

Bentley, Eric (Russell) 1916-....... **CLC 24**
See also CA 5-8R; CANR 6

Beranger, Pierre Jean de
1780-1857 .... **NCLC 34**

Berger, Colonel
See Malraux, (Georges-)Andre

Berger, John (Peter) 1926- ...... **CLC 2, 19**
See also CA 81-84; DLB 14

Berger, Melvin H. 1927- .... **CLC 12**
See also CA 5-8R; CANR 4; CLR 32; SAAS 2; SATA 5

Berger, Thomas (Louis)
1924- .... **CLC 3, 5, 8, 11, 18, 38**
See also CA 1-4R; CANR 5, 28; DLB 2; DLBY 80; MTCW

Bergman, (Ernst) Ingmar
1918- .... **CLC 16, 72**
See also CA 81-84; CANR 33

Bergson, Henri 1859-1941 .... **TCLC 32**

Bergstein, Eleanor 1938- .... **CLC 4**
See also CA 53-56; CANR 5

Berkoff, Steven 1937-............. **CLC 56**
See also CA 104

Bermant, Chaim (Icyk) 1929- ...... **CLC 40**
See also CA 57-60; CANR 6, 31

Bern, Victoria
See Fisher, M(ary) F(rances) K(ennedy)

Bernanos, (Paul Louis) Georges
1888-1948 .... **TCLC 3**
See also CA 104; 130; DLB 72

Bernard, April 1956- .... **CLC 59**
See also CA 131

Bernhard, Thomas
1931-1989 .... **CLC 3, 32, 61**
See also CA 85-88; 127; CANR 32; DLB 85, 124; MTCW

Berrigan, Daniel 1921-............. **CLC 4**
See also CA 33-36R; CAAS 1; CANR 11, 43; DLB 5

Berrigan, Edmund Joseph Michael, Jr.
1934-1983
See Berrigan, Ted
See also CA 61-64; 110; CANR 14

Berrigan, Ted.................... **CLC 37**
See also Berrigan, Edmund Joseph Michael, Jr.
See also DLB 5

Berry, Charles Edward Anderson 1931-
See Berry, Chuck
See also CA 115

Berry, Chuck.................... **CLC 17**
See also Berry, Charles Edward Anderson

Berry, Jonas
See Ashbery, John (Lawrence)

Berry, Wendell (Erdman)
1934- .... **CLC 4, 6, 8, 27, 46**
See also AITN 1; CA 73-76; DLB 5, 6

Berryman, John
1914-1972 ...... **CLC 1, 2, 3, 4, 6, 8, 10, 13, 25, 62**
See also CA 13-16; 33-36R; CABS 2; CANR 35; CAP 1; CDALB 1941-1968; DLB 48; MTCW

Bertolucci, Bernardo 1940- .... **CLC 16**
See also CA 106

Bertrand, Aloysius 1807-1841 .... **NCLC 31**

Bertran de Born c. 1140-1215 ..... **CMLC 5**

Besant, Annie (Wood) 1847-1933 ... **TCLC 9**
See also CA 105

Bessie, Alvah 1904-1985........... **CLC 23**
See also CA 5-8R; 116; CANR 2; DLB 26

Bethlen, T. D.
See Silverberg, Robert

Beti, Mongo...................... **CLC 27**
See also Biyidi, Alexandre
See also BLC 1

Betjeman, John
1906-1984 .... **CLC 2, 6, 10, 34, 43**
See also CA 9-12R; 112; CANR 33; CDBLB 1945-1960; DLB 20; DLBY 84; MTCW

Bettelheim, Bruno 1903-1990 ...... **CLC 79**
See also CA 81-84; 131; CANR 23; MTCW

Betti, Ugo 1892-1953 .... **TCLC 5**
See also CA 104

Betts, Doris (Waugh) 1932-.... **CLC 3, 6, 28**
See also CA 13-16R; CANR 9; DLBY 82

Bevan, Alistair
See Roberts, Keith (John Kingston)

Beynon, John
See Harris, John (Wyndham Parkes Lucas) Beynon

Bialik, Chaim Nachman
1873-1934 .... **TCLC 25**

Bickerstaff, Isaac
See Swift, Jonathan

Breton, Andre 1896-1966... **CLC 2, 9, 15, 54**
See also CA 19-20; 25-28R; CANR 40; CAP 2; DLB 65; MTCW

Breytenbach, Breyten 1939(?)- .. **CLC 23, 37**
See also CA 113; 129

Bridgers, Sue Ellen 1942- .... **CLC 26**
See also AAYA 8; CA 65-68; CANR 11, 36; CLR 18; DLB 52; JRDA; MAICYA; SAAS 1; SATA 22

Bridges, Robert (Seymour) 1844-1930 .... **TCLC 1**
See also CA 104; CDBLB 1890-1914; DLB 19, 98

Bridie, James..................... **TCLC 3**
See also Mavor, Osborne Henry
See also DLB 10

Brin, David 1950-................ **CLC 34**
See also CA 102; CANR 24; SATA 65

Brink, Andre (Philippus) 1935-..................... **CLC 18, 36**
See also CA 104; CANR 39; MTCW

Brinsmead, H(esba) F(ay) 1922-.... **CLC 21**
See also CA 21-24R; CANR 10; MAICYA; SAAS 5; SATA 18

Brittain, Vera (Mary) 1893(?)-1970 .... **CLC 23**
See also CA 13-16; 25-28R; CAP 1; MTCW

Broch, Hermann 1886-1951....... **TCLC 20**
See also CA 117; DLB 85, 124

Brock, Rose
See Hansen, Joseph

Brodkey, Harold 1930-............ **CLC 56**
See also CA 111; DLB 130

Brodsky, Iosif Alexandrovich 1940-
See Brodsky, Joseph
See also AITN 1; CA 41-44R; CANR 37; MTCW

Brodsky, Joseph .... **CLC 4, 6, 13, 36, 50**
See also Brodsky, Iosif Alexandrovich

Brodsky, Michael Mark 1948- ..... **CLC 19**
See also CA 102; CANR 18, 41

Bromell, Henry 1947-.............. **CLC 5**
See also CA 53-56; CANR 9

Bromfield, Louis (Brucker) 1896-1956 .... **TCLC 11**
See also CA 107; DLB 4, 9, 86

Broner, E(sther) M(asserman) 1930- .... **CLC 19**
See also CA 17-20R; CANR 8, 25; DLB 28

Bronk, William 1918-............. **CLC 10**
See also CA 89-92; CANR 23

Bronstein, Lev Davidovich
See Trotsky, Leon

Bronte, Anne 1820-1849.......... **NCLC 4**
See also DLB 21

Bronte, Charlotte 1816-1855 .... **NCLC 3, 8, 33**
See also CDBLB 1832-1890; DA; DLB 21; WLC

Bronte, (Jane) Emily 1818-1848 .... **NCLC 16, 35**
See also CDBLB 1832-1890; DA; DLB 21, 32; WLC

Brooke, Frances 1724-1789.......... **LC 6**
See also DLB 39, 99

Brooke, Henry 1703(?)-1783......... **LC 1**
See also DLB 39

Brooke, Rupert (Chawner) 1887-1915 .... **TCLC 2, 7**
See also CA 104; 132; CDBLB 1914-1945; DA; DLB 19; MTCW; WLC

Brooke-Haven, P.
See Wodehouse, P(elham) G(renville)

Brooke-Rose, Christine 1926-...... **CLC 40**
See also CA 13-16R; DLB 14

Brookner, Anita 1928-...... **CLC 32, 34, 51**
See also CA 114; 120; CANR 37; DLBY 87; MTCW

Brooks, Cleanth 1906-............ **CLC 24**
See also CA 17-20R; CANR 33, 35; DLB 63; MTCW

Brooks, George
See Baum, L(yman) Frank

Brooks, Gwendolyn 1917- ...... **CLC 1, 2, 4, 5, 15, 49; PC 7**
See also AITN 1; BLC 1; BW; CA 1-4R; CANR 1, 27; CDALB 1941-1968; CLR 27; DA; DLB 5, 76; MTCW; SATA 6; WLC

Brooks, Mel..................... **CLC 12**
See also Kaminsky, Melvin
See also DLB 26

Brooks, Peter 1938-.............. **CLC 34**
See also CA 45-48; CANR 1

Brooks, Van Wyck 1886-1963...... **CLC 29**
See also CA 1-4R; CANR 6; DLB 45, 63, 103

Brophy, Brigid (Antonia) 1929- .... **CLC 6, 11, 29**
See also CA 5-8R; CAAS 4; CANR 25; DLB 14; MTCW

Brosman, Catharine Savage 1934-.... **CLC 9**
See also CA 61-64; CANR 21

Brother Antoninus
See Everson, William (Oliver)

Broughton, T(homas) Alan 1936- ... **CLC 19**
See also CA 45-48; CANR 2, 23

Broumas, Olga 1949-.......... **CLC 10, 73**
See also CA 85-88; CANR 20

Brown, Charles Brockden 1771-1810 .... **NCLC 22**
See also CDALB 1640-1865; DLB 37, 59, 73

Brown, Christy 1932-1981......... **CLC 63**
See also CA 105; 104; DLB 14

Brown, Claude 1937- .... **CLC 30**
See also AAYA 7; BLC 1; BW; CA 73-76

Brown, Dee (Alexander) 1908- .. **CLC 18, 47**
See also CA 13-16R; CAAS 6; CANR 11; DLBY 80; MTCW; SATA 5

Brown, George
See Wertmueller, Lina

Brown, George Douglas 1869-1902 .... **TCLC 28**

Brown, George Mackay 1921-.... **CLC 5, 48**
See also CA 21-24R; CAAS 6; CANR 12, 37; DLB 14, 27; MTCW; SATA 35

Brown, (William) Larry 1951-...... **CLC 73**
See also CA 130; 134

Brown, Moses
See Barrett, William (Christopher)

Brown, Rita Mae 1944-..... **CLC 18, 43, 79**
See also CA 45-48; CANR 2, 11, 35; MTCW

Brown, Roderick (Langmere) Haig-
See Haig-Brown, Roderick (Langmere)

Brown, Rosellen 1939-............ **CLC 32**
See also CA 77-80; CAAS 10; CANR 14

Brown, Sterling Allen 1901-1989 .... **CLC 1, 23, 59**
See also BLC 1; BW; CA 85-88; 127; CANR 26; DLB 48, 51, 63; MTCW

Brown, Will
See Ainsworth, William Harrison

Brown, William Wells 1813-1884 .... **NCLC 2; DC 1**
See also BLC 1; DLB 3, 50

Browne, (Clyde) Jackson 1948(?)-... **CLC 21**
See also CA 120

Browning, Elizabeth Barrett 1806-1861 .... **NCLC 1, 16; PC 6**
See also CDBLB 1832-1890; DA; DLB 32; WLC

Browning, Robert 1812-1889 .... **NCLC 19; PC 2**
See also CDBLB 1832-1890; DA; DLB 32; YABC 1

Browning, Tod 1882-1962 .... **CLC 16**
See also CA 141; 117

Bruccoli, Matthew J(oseph) 1931- .. **CLC 34**
See also CA 9-12R; CANR 7; DLB 103

Bruce, Lenny..................... **CLC 21**
See also Schneider, Leonard Alfred

Bruin, John
See Brutus, Dennis

Brulls, Christian
See Simenon, Georges (Jacques Christian)

Brunner, John (Kilian Houston) 1934- .... **CLC 8, 10**
See also CA 1-4R; CAAS 8; CANR 2, 37; MTCW

Brutus, Dennis 1924-............. **CLC 43**
See also BLC 1; BW; CA 49-52; CAAS 14; CANR 2, 27, 42; DLB 117

Bryan, C(ourtlandt) D(ixon) B(arnes) 1936- .... **CLC 29**
See also CA 73-76; CANR 13

Bryan, Michael
See Moore, Brian

Bryant, William Cullen 1794-1878 .... **NCLC 6**
See also CDALB 1640-1865; DA; DLB 3, 43, 59

Bryusov, Valery Yakovlevich 1873-1924 .... **TCLC 10**
See also CA 107

Buchan, John 1875-1940 .... **TCLC 41**
See also CA 108; DLB 34, 70; YABC 2

Buchanan, George 1506-1582 .... **LC 4**

Buchheim, Lothar-Guenther 1918- ... **CLC 6**
See also CA 85-88

Buchner, (Karl) Georg 1813-1837 .... **NCLC 26**

Cameron, Peter 1959- . . . . . **CLC 44**
See also CA 125

Campana, Dino 1885-1932 . . . . . **TCLC 20**
See also CA 117; DLB 114

Campbell, John W(ood, Jr.)
1910-1971 . . . . . **CLC 32**
See also CA 21-22; 29-32R; CANR 34; CAP 2; DLB 8; MTCW

Campbell, Joseph 1904-1987 . . . . . **CLC 69**
See also AAYA 3; BEST 89:2; CA 1-4R; 124; CANR 3, 28; MTCW

Campbell, (John) Ramsey 1946- . . . . **CLC 42**
See also CA 57-60; CANR 7

Campbell, (Ignatius) Roy (Dunnachie)
1901-1957 . . . . . **TCLC 5**
See also CA 104; DLB 20

Campbell, Thomas 1777-1844 . . . . **NCLC 19**
See also DLB 93

Campbell, Wilfred . . . . . **TCLC 9**
See also Campbell, William

Campbell, William 1858(?)-1918
See Campbell, Wilfred
See also CA 106; DLB 92

Campos, Alvaro de
See Pessoa, Fernando (Antonio Nogueira)

Camus, Albert
1913-1960 . . . . **CLC 1, 2, 4, 9, 11, 14, 32, 63, 69; DC 2; SSC 9**
See also CA 89-92; DA; DLB 72; MTCW; WLC

Canby, Vincent 1924- . . . . . **CLC 13**
See also CA 81-84

Cancale
See Desnos, Robert

Canetti, Elias 1905- . . . . . **CLC 3, 14, 25, 75**
See also CA 21-24R; CANR 23; DLB 85, 124; MTCW

Canin, Ethan 1960- . . . . . **CLC 55**
See also CA 131; 135

Cannon, Curt
See Hunter, Evan

Cape, Judith
See Page, P(atricia) K(athleen)

Capek, Karel
1890-1938 . . . . . **TCLC 6, 37; DC 1**
See also CA 104; 140; DA; WLC

Capote, Truman
1924-1984 . . . . . **CLC 1, 3, 8, 13, 19, 34, 38, 58; SSC 2**
See also CA 5-8R; 113; CANR 18; CDALB 1941-1968; DA; DLB 2; DLBY 80, 84; MTCW; WLC

Capra, Frank 1897-1991 . . . . . **CLC 16**
See also CA 61-64; 135

Caputo, Philip 1941- . . . . . **CLC 32**
See also CA 73-76; CANR 40

Card, Orson Scott 1951- . . . . **CLC 44, 47, 50**
See also CA 102; CANR 27; MTCW

Cardenal (Martinez), Ernesto
1925- . . . . . **CLC 31**
See also CA 49-52; CANR 2, 32; HW; MTCW

Carducci, Giosue 1835-1907 . . . . . **TCLC 32**

Carew, Thomas 1595(?)-1640 . . . . . **LC 13**
See also DLB 126

Carey, Ernestine Gilbreth 1908- . . . . **CLC 17**
See also CA 5-8R; SATA 2

Carey, Peter 1943- . . . . . **CLC 40, 55**
See also CA 123; 127; MTCW

Carleton, William 1794-1869 . . . . . **NCLC 3**

Carlisle, Henry (Coffin) 1926- . . . . . **CLC 33**
See also CA 13-16R; CANR 15

Carlsen, Chris
See Holdstock, Robert P.

Carlson, Ron(ald F.) 1947- . . . . . **CLC 54**
See also CA 105; CANR 27

Carlyle, Thomas 1795-1881 . . . . . **NCLC 22**
See also CDBLB 1789-1832; DA; DLB 55

Carman, (William) Bliss
1861-1929 . . . . . **TCLC 7**
See also CA 104; DLB 92

Carossa, Hans 1878-1956 . . . . . **TCLC 48**
See also DLB 66

Carpenter, Don(ald Richard)
1931- . . . . . **CLC 41**
See also CA 45-48; CANR 1

Carpentier (y Valmont), Alejo
1904-1980 . . . . . **CLC 8, 11, 38**
See also CA 65-68; 97-100; CANR 11; DLB 113; HW

Carr, Emily 1871-1945 . . . . . **TCLC 32**
See also DLB 68

Carr, John Dickson 1906-1977 . . . . . **CLC 3**
See also CA 49-52; 69-72; CANR 3, 33; MTCW

Carr, Philippa
See Hibbert, Eleanor Alice Burford

Carr, Virginia Spencer 1929- . . . . . **CLC 34**
See also CA 61-64; DLB 111

Carrier, Roch 1937- . . . . . **CLC 13, 78**
See also CA 130; DLB 53

Carroll, James P. 1943(?)- . . . . . **CLC 38**
See also CA 81-84

Carroll, Jim 1951- . . . . . **CLC 35**
See also CA 45-48; CANR 42

Carroll, Lewis . . . . . **NCLC 2**
See also Dodgson, Charles Lutwidge
See also CDBLB 1832-1890; CLR 2, 18; DLB 18; JRDA; WLC

Carroll, Paul Vincent 1900-1968 . . . . **CLC 10**
See also CA 9-12R; 25-28R; DLB 10

Carruth, Hayden 1921- . . . . **CLC 4, 7, 10, 18**
See also CA 9-12R; CANR 4, 38; DLB 5; MTCW; SATA 47

Carson, Rachel Louise 1907-1964 . . . **CLC 71**
See also CA 77-80; CANR 35; MTCW; SATA 23

Carter, Angela (Olive)
1940-1992 . . . . . **CLC 5, 41, 76; SSC 13**
See also CA 53-56; 136; CANR 12, 36; DLB 14; MTCW; SATA 66; SATA-Obit 70

Carter, Nick
See Smith, Martin Cruz

Carver, Raymond
1938-1988 . . . **CLC 22, 36, 53, 55; SSC 8**
See also CA 33-36R; 126; CANR 17, 34; DLB 130; DLBY 84, 88; MTCW

Cary, (Arthur) Joyce (Lunel)
1888-1957 . . . . . **TCLC 1, 29**
See also CA 104; CDBLB 1914-1945; DLB 15, 100

Casanova de Seingalt, Giovanni Jacopo
1725-1798 . . . . . **LC 13**

Casares, Adolfo Bioy
See Bioy Casares, Adolfo

Casely-Hayford, J(oseph) E(phraim)
1866-1930 . . . . . **TCLC 24**
See also BLC 1; CA 123

Casey, John (Dudley) 1939- . . . . . **CLC 59**
See also BEST 90:2; CA 69-72; CANR 23

Casey, Michael 1947- . . . . . **CLC 2**
See also CA 65-68; DLB 5

Casey, Patrick
See Thurman, Wallace (Henry)

Casey, Warren (Peter) 1935-1988 . . . **CLC 12**
See also CA 101; 127

Casona, Alejandro . . . . . **CLC 49**
See also Alvarez, Alejandro Rodriguez

Cassavetes, John 1929-1989 . . . . . **CLC 20**
See also CA 85-88; 127

Cassill, R(onald) V(erlin) 1919- . . . **CLC 4, 23**
See also CA 9-12R; CAAS 1; CANR 7; DLB 6

Cassity, (Allen) Turner 1929- . . . . **CLC 6, 42**
See also CA 17-20R; CAAS 8; CANR 11; DLB 105

Castaneda, Carlos 1931(?)- . . . . . **CLC 12**
See also CA 25-28R; CANR 32; HW; MTCW

Castedo, Elena 1937- . . . . . **CLC 65**
See also CA 132

Castedo-Ellerman, Elena
See Castedo, Elena

Castellanos, Rosario 1925-1974 . . . . . **CLC 66**
See also CA 131; 53-56; DLB 113; HW

Castelvetro, Lodovico 1505-1571 . . . . . **LC 12**

Castiglione, Baldassare 1478-1529 . . . **LC 12**

Castle, Robert
See Hamilton, Edmond

Castro, Guillen de 1569-1631 . . . . . **LC 19**

Castro, Rosalia de 1837-1885 . . . . . **NCLC 3**

Cather, Willa
See Cather, Willa Sibert

Cather, Willa Sibert
1873-1947 . . . . . **TCLC 1, 11, 31; SSC 2**
See also CA 104; 128; CDALB 1865-1917; DA; DLB 9, 54, 78; DLBD 1; MTCW; SATA 30; WLC

Catton, (Charles) Bruce
1899-1978 . . . . . **CLC 35**
See also AITN 1; CA 5-8R; 81-84; CANR 7; DLB 17; SATA 2, 24

Cauldwell, Frank
See King, Francis (Henry)

Caunitz, William J. 1933- . . . . . **CLC 34**
See also BEST 89:3; CA 125; 130

Causley, Charles (Stanley) 1917-..... **CLC 7**
See also CA 9-12R; CANR 5, 35; CLR 30; DLB 27; MTCW; SATA 3, 66

Caute, David 1936-............... **CLC 29**
See also CA 1-4R; CAAS 4; CANR 1, 33; DLB 14

Cavafy, C(onstantine) P(eter)...... **TCLC 2, 7**
See also Kavafis, Konstantinos Petrou

Cavallo, Evelyn
See Spark, Muriel (Sarah)

Cavanna, Betty .... **CLC 12**
See also Harrison, Elizabeth Cavanna
See also JRDA; MAICYA; SAAS 4; SATA 1, 30

Caxton, William 1421(?)-1491(?)..... **LC 17**

Cayrol, Jean 1911-............... **CLC 11**
See also CA 89-92; DLB 83

Cela, Camilo Jose 1916-...... **CLC 4, 13, 59**
See also BEST 90:2; CA 21-24R; CAAS 10; CANR 21, 32; DLBY 89; HW; MTCW

Celan, Paul .... **CLC 53**
See also Antschel, Paul
See also DLB 69

Celine, Louis-Ferdinand
.... **CLC 1, 3, 4, 7, 9, 15, 47**
See also Destouches, Louis-Ferdinand
See also DLB 72

Cellini, Benvenuto 1500-1571 .... **LC 7**

Cendrars, Blaise
See Sauser-Hall, Frederic

Cernuda (y Bidon), Luis
1902-1963 .... **CLC 54**
See also CA 131; 89-92; DLB 134; HW

Cervantes (Saavedra), Miguel de
1547-1616 .... **LC 6, 23; SSC 12**
See also DA; WLC

Cesaire, Aime (Fernand) 1913- .. **CLC 19, 32**
See also BLC 1; BW; CA 65-68; CANR 24, 43; MTCW

Chabon, Michael 1965(?)- .... **CLC 55**
See also CA 139

Chabrol, Claude 1930-............ **CLC 16**
See also CA 110

Challans, Mary 1905-1983
See Renault, Mary
See also CA 81-84; 111; SATA 23, 36

Challis, George
See Faust, Frederick (Schiller)

Chambers, Aidan 1934- .... **CLC 35**
See also CA 25-28R; CANR 12, 31; JRDA; MAICYA; SAAS 12; SATA 1, 69

Chambers, James 1948-
See Cliff, Jimmy
See also CA 124

Chambers, Jessie
See Lawrence, D(avid) H(erbert Richards)

Chambers, Robert W. 1865-1933... **TCLC 41**

Chandler, Raymond (Thornton)
1888-1959 .... **TCLC 1, 7**
See also CA 104; 129; CDALB 1929-1941; DLBD 6; MTCW

Chang, Jung 1952-............... **CLC 71**
See also CA 142

Channing, William Ellery
1780-1842 .... **NCLC 17**
See also DLB 1, 59

Chaplin, Charles Spencer
1889-1977 .... **CLC 16**
See also Chaplin, Charlie
See also CA 81-84; 73-76

Chaplin, Charlie
See Chaplin, Charles Spencer
See also DLB 44

Chapman, George 1559(?)-1634...... **LC 22**
See also DLB 62, 121

Chapman, Graham 1941-1989 ...... **CLC 21**
See also Monty Python
See also CA 116; 129; CANR 35

Chapman, John Jay 1862-1933 ..... **TCLC 7**
See also CA 104

Chapman, Walker
See Silverberg, Robert

Chappell, Fred (Davis) 1936-.... **CLC 40, 78**
See also CA 5-8R; CAAS 4; CANR 8, 33; DLB 6, 105

Char, Rene(-Emile)
1907-1988 .... **CLC 9, 11, 14, 55**
See also CA 13-16R; 124; CANR 32; MTCW

Charby, Jay
See Ellison, Harlan

Chardin, Pierre Teilhard de
See Teilhard de Chardin, (Marie Joseph) Pierre

Charles I 1600-1649............... **LC 13**

Charyn, Jerome 1937- .... **CLC 5, 8, 18**
See also CA 5-8R; CAAS 1; CANR 7; DLBY 83; MTCW

Chase, Mary (Coyle) 1907-1981 ...... **DC 1**
See also CA 77-80; 105; SATA 17, 29

Chase, Mary Ellen 1887-1973....... **CLC 2**
See also CA 13-16; 41-44R; CAP 1; SATA 10

Chase, Nicholas
See Hyde, Anthony

Chateaubriand, Francois Rene de
1768-1848 .... **NCLC 3**
See also DLB 119

Chatterje, Sarat Chandra 1876-1936(?)
See Chatterji, Saratchandra
See also CA 109

Chatterji, Bankim Chandra
1838-1894 .... **NCLC 19**

Chatterji, Saratchandra .... **TCLC 13**
See also Chatterje, Sarat Chandra

Chatterton, Thomas 1752-1770 .... **LC 3**
See also DLB 109

Chatwin, (Charles) Bruce
1940-1989 .... **CLC 28, 57, 59**
See also AAYA 4; BEST 90:1; CA 85-88; 127

Chaucer, Daniel
See Ford, Ford Madox

Chaucer, Geoffrey 1340(?)-1400 ..... **LC 17**
See also CDBLB Before 1660; DA

Chaviaras, Strates 1935-
See Haviaras, Stratis
See also CA 105

Chayefsky, Paddy .... **CLC 23**
See also Chayefsky, Sidney
See also DLB 7, 44; DLBY 81

Chayefsky, Sidney 1923-1981
See Chayefsky, Paddy
See also CA 9-12R; 104; CANR 18

Chedid, Andree 1920-............. **CLC 47**

Cheever, John
1912-1982 ...... **CLC 3, 7, 8, 11, 15, 25, 64; SSC 1**
See also CA 5-8R; 106; CABS 1; CANR 5, 27; CDALB 1941-1968; DA; DLB 2, 102; DLBY 80, 82; MTCW; WLC

Cheever, Susan 1943-.......... **CLC 18, 48**
See also CA 103; CANR 27; DLBY 82

Chekhonte, Antosha
See Chekhov, Anton (Pavlovich)

Chekhov, Anton (Pavlovich)
1860-1904 ...... **TCLC 3, 10, 31; SSC 2**
See also CA 104; 124; DA; WLC

Chernyshevsky, Nikolay Gavrilovich
1828-1889 .... **NCLC 1**

Cherry, Carolyn Janice 1942-
See Cherryh, C. J.
See also CA 65-68; CANR 10

Cherryh, C. J. .... **CLC 35**
See also Cherry, Carolyn Janice
See also DLBY 80

Chesnutt, Charles W(addell)
1858-1932 .... **TCLC 5, 39; SSC 7**
See also BLC 1; BW; CA 106; 125; DLB 12, 50, 78; MTCW

Chester, Alfred 1929(?)-1971....... **CLC 49**
See also CA 33-36R; DLB 130

Chesterton, G(ilbert) K(eith)
1874-1936 .... **TCLC 1, 6; SSC 1**
See also CA 104; 132; CDBLB 1914-1945; DLB 10, 19, 34, 70, 98; MTCW; SATA 27

Chiang Pin-chin 1904-1986
See Ding Ling
See also CA 118

Ch'ien Chung-shu 1910-........... **CLC 22**
See also CA 130; MTCW

Child, L. Maria
See Child, Lydia Maria

Child, Lydia Maria 1802-1880 .... **NCLC 6**
See also DLB 1, 74; SATA 67

Child, Mrs.
See Child, Lydia Maria

Child, Philip 1898-1978 .... **CLC 19, 68**
See also CA 13-14; CAP 1; SATA 47

Childress, Alice 1920-.......... **CLC 12, 15**
See also AAYA 8; BLC 1; BW; CA 45-48; CANR 3, 27; CLR 14; DLB 7, 38; JRDA; MAICYA; MTCW; SATA 7, 48

Chislett, (Margaret) Anne 1943-.... **CLC 34**

Chitty, Thomas Willes 1926-....... **CLC 11**
See also Hinde, Thomas
See also CA 5-8R

Chomette, Rene Lucien 1898-1981 .. **CLC 20**
See also Clair, Rene
See also CA 103

Chopin, Kate .... **TCLC 5, 14; SSC 8**
See also Chopin, Katherine
See also CDALBB 1865-1917; DA; DLB 12, 78

Chopin, Katherine 1851-1904
See Chopin, Kate
See also CA 104; 122

Chretien de Troyes
c. 12th cent. - .... **CMLC 10**

Christie
See Ichikawa, Kon

Christie, Agatha (Mary Clarissa)
1890-1976 ...... **CLC 1, 6, 8, 12, 39, 48**
See also AAYA 9; AITN 1, 2; CA 17-20R; 61-64; CANR 10, 37; CDBLB 1914-1945; DLB 13, 77; MTCW; SATA 36

Christie, (Ann) Philippa
See Pearce, Philippa
See also CA 5-8R; CANR 4

Christine de Pizan 1365(?)-1431(?) .... **LC 9**

Chubb, Elmer
See Masters, Edgar Lee

Chulkov, Mikhail Dmitrievich
1743-1792 .... **LC 2**

Churchill, Caryl 1938- .... **CLC 31, 55**
See also CA 102; CANR 22; DLB 13; MTCW

Churchill, Charles 1731-1764......... **LC 3**
See also DLB 109

Chute, Carolyn 1947- .... **CLC 39**
See also CA 123

Ciardi, John (Anthony)
1916-1986 .... **CLC 10, 40, 44**
See also CA 5-8R; 118; CAAS 2; CANR 5, 33; CLR 19; DLB 5; DLBY 86; MAICYA; MTCW; SATA 1, 46, 65

Cicero, Marcus Tullius
106B.C.-43B.C. .... **CMLC 3**

Cimino, Michael 1943- .... **CLC 16**
See also CA 105

Cioran, E(mil) M. 1911- .... **CLC 64**
See also CA 25-28R

Cisneros, Sandra 1954- .... **CLC 69**
See also AAYA 9; CA 131; DLB 122; HW

Clair, Rene .... **CLC 20**
See also Chomette, Rene Lucien

Clampitt, Amy 1920- .... **CLC 32**
See also CA 110; CANR 29; DLB 105

Clancy, Thomas L., Jr. 1947-
See Clancy, Tom
See also CA 125; 131; MTCW

Clancy, Tom .... **CLC 45**
See also Clancy, Thomas L., Jr.
See also AAYA 9; BEST 89:1, 90:1

Clare, John 1793-1864 .... **NCLC 9**
See also DLB 55, 96

Clarin
See Alas (y Urena), Leopoldo (Enrique Garcia)

Clark, Al C.
See Goines, Donald

Clark, (Robert) Brian 1932- .... **CLC 29**
See also CA 41-44R

Clark, Eleanor 1913- .... **CLC 5, 19**
See also CA 9-12R; CANR 41; DLB 6

Clark, J. P.
See Clark, John Pepper
See also DLB 117

Clark, John Pepper 1935- .... **CLC 38**
See also Clark, J. P.
See also BLC 1; BW; CA 65-68; CANR 16

Clark, M. R.
See Clark, Mavis Thorpe

Clark, Mavis Thorpe 1909- .... **CLC 12**
See also CA 57-60; CANR 8, 37; CLR 30; MAICYA; SAAS 5; SATA 8, 74

Clark, Walter Van Tilburg
1909-1971 .... **CLC 28**
See also CA 9-12R; 33-36R; DLB 9; SATA 8

Clarke, Arthur C(harles)
1917- ...... **CLC 1, 4, 13, 18, 35; SSC 3**
See also AAYA 4; CA 1-4R; CANR 2, 28; JRDA; MAICYA; MTCW; SATA 13, 70

Clarke, Austin 1896-1974......... **CLC 6, 9**
See also CA 29-32; 49-52; CAP 2; DLB 10, 20

Clarke, Austin C(hesterfield)
1934- .... **CLC 8, 53**
See also BLC 1; BW; CA 25-28R; CAAS 16; CANR 14, 32; DLB 53, 125

Clarke, Gillian 1937- .... **CLC 61**
See also CA 106; DLB 40

Clarke, Marcus (Andrew Hislop)
1846-1881 .... **NCLC 19**

Clarke, Shirley 1925- .... **CLC 16**

Clash, The .... **CLC 30**
See also Headon, (Nicky) Topper; Jones, Mick; Simonon, Paul; Strummer, Joe

Claudel, Paul (Louis Charles Marie)
1868-1955 .... **TCLC 2, 10**
See also CA 104

Clavell, James (duMaresq)
1925- .... **CLC 6, 25**
See also CA 25-28R; CANR 26; MTCW

Cleaver, (Leroy) Eldridge 1935- .... **CLC 30**
See also BLC 1; BW; CA 21-24R; CANR 16

Cleese, John (Marwood) 1939- ..... **CLC 21**
See also Monty Python
See also CA 112; 116; CANR 35; MTCW

Cleishbotham, Jebediah
See Scott, Walter

Cleland, John 1710-1789 .... **LC 2**
See also DLB 39

Clemens, Samuel Langhorne 1835-1910
See Twain, Mark
See also CA 104; 135; CDALB 1865-1917; DA; DLB 11, 12, 23, 64, 74; JRDA; MAICYA; YABC 2

Cleophil
See Congreve, William

Clerihew, E.
See Bentley, E(dmund) C(lerihew)

Clerk, N. W.
See Lewis, C(live) S(taples)

Cliff, Jimmy .... **CLC 21**
See also Chambers, James

Clifton, (Thelma) Lucille
1936- .... **CLC 19, 66**
See also BLC 1; BW; CA 49-52; CANR 2, 24, 42; CLR 5; DLB 5, 41; MAICYA; MTCW; SATA 20, 69

Clinton, Dirk
See Silverberg, Robert

Clough, Arthur Hugh 1819-1861 .. **NCLC 27**
See also DLB 32

Clutha, Janet Paterson Frame 1924-
See Frame, Janet
See also CA 1-4R; CANR 2, 36; MTCW

Clyne, Terence
See Blatty, William Peter

Cobalt, Martin
See Mayne, William (James Carter)

Coburn, D(onald) L(ee) 1938- ...... **CLC 10**
See also CA 89-92

Cocteau, Jean (Maurice Eugene Clement)
1889-1963 .... **CLC 1, 8, 15, 16, 43**
See also CA 25-28; CANR 40; CAP 2; DA; DLB 65; MTCW; WLC

Codrescu, Andrei 1946- .... **CLC 46**
See also CA 33-36R; CANR 13, 34

Coe, Max
See Bourne, Randolph S(illiman)

Coe, Tucker
See Westlake, Donald E(dwin)

Coetzee, J(ohn) M(ichael)
1940- .... **CLC 23, 33, 66**
See also CA 77-80; CANR 41; MTCW

Coffey, Brian
See Koontz, Dean R(ay)

Cohen, Arthur A(llen)
1928-1986 .... **CLC 7, 31**
See also CA 1-4R; 120; CANR 1, 17, 42; DLB 28

Cohen, Leonard (Norman)
1934- .... **CLC 3, 38**
See also CA 21-24R; CANR 14; DLB 53; MTCW

Cohen, Matt 1942- .... **CLC 19**
See also CA 61-64; CAAS 18; CANR 40; DLB 53

Cohen-Solal, Annie 19(?)- .... **CLC 50**

Colegate, Isabel 1931- .... **CLC 36**
See also CA 17-20R; CANR 8, 22; DLB 14; MTCW

Coleman, Emmett
See Reed, Ishmael

Coleridge, Samuel Taylor
1772-1834 .... **NCLC 9**
See also CDBLB 1789-1832; DA; DLB 93, 107; WLC

Coleridge, Sara 1802-1852 .... **NCLC 31**

Coles, Don 1928- .... **CLC 46**
See also CA 115; CANR 38

Colette, (Sidonie-Gabrielle)
1873-1954 ...... **TCLC 1, 5, 16; SSC 10**
See also CA 104; 131; DLB 65; MTCW

Collett, (Jacobine) Camilla (Wergeland)
1813-1895 .... **NCLC 22**

Cowley, Malcolm 1898-1989 . . . . **CLC 39**
See also CA 5-8R; 128; CANR 3; DLB 4, 48; DLBY 81, 89; MTCW

Cowper, William 1731-1800 . . . . **NCLC 8**
See also DLB 104, 109

Cox, William Trevor 1928- . . . **CLC 9, 14, 71**
See also Trevor, William
See also CA 9-12R; CANR 4, 37; DLB 14; MTCW

Cozzens, James Gould
1903-1978 . . . . **CLC 1, 4, 11**
See also CA 9-12R; 81-84; CANR 19; CDALB 1941-1968; DLB 9; DLBD 2; DLBY 84; MTCW

Crabbe, George 1754-1832 . . . . **NCLC 26**
See also DLB 93

Craig, A. A.
See Anderson, Poul (William)

Craik, Dinah Maria (Mulock)
1826-1887 . . . . **NCLC 38**
See also DLB 35; MAICYA; SATA 34

Cram, Ralph Adams 1863-1942 . . . . **TCLC 45**

Crane, (Harold) Hart
1899-1932 . . . . **TCLC 2, 5; PC 3**
See also CA 104; 127; CDALB 1917-1929; DA; DLB 4, 48; MTCW; WLC

Crane, R(onald) S(almon)
1886-1967 . . . . **CLC 27**
See also CA 85-88; DLB 63

Crane, Stephen (Townley)
1871-1900 . . . . . **TCLC 11, 17, 32; SSC 7**
See also CA 109; 140; CDALB 1865-1917; DA; DLB 12, 54, 78; WLC; YABC 2

Crase, Douglas 1944- . . . . **CLC 58**
See also CA 106

Crashaw, Richard 1612(?)-1649 . . . . . . **LC 24**
See also DLB 126

Craven, Margaret 1901-1980 . . . . **CLC 17**
See also CA 103

Crawford, F(rancis) Marion
1854-1909 . . . . **TCLC 10**
See also CA 107; DLB 71

Crawford, Isabella Valancy
1850-1887 . . . . **NCLC 12**
See also DLB 92

Crayon, Geoffrey
See Irving, Washington

Creasey, John 1908-1973 . . . . **CLC 11**
See also CA 5-8R; 41-44R; CANR 8; DLB 77; MTCW

Crebillon, Claude Prosper Jolyot de (fils)
1707-1777 . . . . **LC 1**

Credo
See Creasey, John

Creeley, Robert (White)
1926- . . . . . **CLC 1, 2, 4, 8, 11, 15, 36, 78**
See also CA 1-4R; CAAS 10; CANR 23, 43; DLB 5, 16; MTCW

Crews, Harry (Eugene)
1935- . . . . **CLC 6, 23, 49**
See also AITN 1; CA 25-28R; CANR 20; DLB 6; MTCW

Crichton, (John) Michael
1942- . . . . **CLC 2, 6, 54**
See also AAYA 10; AITN 2; CA 25-28R; CANR 13, 40; DLBY 81; JRDA; MTCW; SATA 9

Crispin, Edmund . . . . **CLC 22**
See also Montgomery, (Robert) Bruce
See also DLB 87

Cristofer, Michael 1945(?)- . . . . **CLC 28**
See also CA 110; DLB 7

Croce, Benedetto 1866-1952 . . . . . . **TCLC 37**
See also CA 120

Crockett, David 1786-1836 . . . . **NCLC 8**
See also DLB 3, 11

Crockett, Davy
See Crockett, David

Croker, John Wilson 1780-1857 . . **NCLC 10**
See also DLB 110

Crommelynck, Fernand 1885-1970 . . **CLC 75**
See also CA 89-92

Cronin, A(rchibald) J(oseph)
1896-1981 . . . . **CLC 32**
See also CA 1-4R; 102; CANR 5; SATA 25, 47

Cross, Amanda
See Heilbrun, Carolyn G(old)

Crothers, Rachel 1878(?)-1958 . . . . . **TCLC 19**
See also CA 113; DLB 7

Croves, Hal
See Traven, B.

Crowfield, Christopher
See Stowe, Harriet (Elizabeth) Beecher

Crowley, Aleister . . . . **TCLC 7**
See also Crowley, Edward Alexander

Crowley, Edward Alexander 1875-1947
See Crowley, Aleister
See also CA 104

Crowley, John 1942- . . . . **CLC 57**
See also CA 61-64; CANR 43; DLBY 82; SATA 65

Crud
See Crumb, R(obert)

Crumarums
See Crumb, R(obert)

Crumb, R(obert) 1943- . . . . **CLC 17**
See also CA 106

Crumbum
See Crumb, R(obert)

Crumski
See Crumb, R(obert)

Crum the Bum
See Crumb, R(obert)

Crunk
See Crumb, R(obert)

Crustt
See Crumb, R(obert)

Cryer, Gretchen (Kiger) 1935- . . . . . . **CLC 21**
See also CA 114; 123

Csath, Geza 1887-1919 . . . . **TCLC 13**
See also CA 111

Cudlip, David 1933- . . . . **CLC 34**

Cullen, Countee 1903-1946 . . . . . **TCLC 4, 37**
See also BLC 1; BW; CA 108; 124; CDALB 1917-1929; DA; DLB 4, 48, 51; MTCW; SATA 18

Cum, R.
See Crumb, R(obert)

Cummings, Bruce F(rederick) 1889-1919
See Barbellion, W. N. P.
See also CA 123

Cummings, E(dward) E(stlin)
1894-1962 . . . . . . **CLC 1, 3, 8, 12, 15, 68; PC 5**
See also CA 73-76; CANR 31; CDALB 1929-1941; DA; DLB 4, 48; MTCW; WLC 2

Cunha, Euclides (Rodrigues Pimenta) da
1866-1909 . . . . **TCLC 24**
See also CA 123

Cunningham, E. V.
See Fast, Howard (Melvin)

Cunningham, J(ames) V(incent)
1911-1985 . . . . **CLC 3, 31**
See also CA 1-4R; 115; CANR 1; DLB 5

Cunningham, Julia (Woolfolk)
1916- . . . . **CLC 12**
See also CA 9-12R; CANR 4, 19, 36; JRDA; MAICYA; SAAS 2; SATA 1, 26

Cunningham, Michael 1952- . . . . **CLC 34**
See also CA 136

Cunninghame Graham, R(obert) B(ontine)
1852-1936 . . . . **TCLC 19**
See also Graham, R(obert) B(ontine) Cunninghame
See also CA 119; DLB 98

Currie, Ellen 19(?)- . . . . **CLC 44**

Curtin, Philip
See Lowndes, Marie Adelaide (Belloc)

Curtis, Price
See Ellison, Harlan

Cutrate, Joe
See Spiegelman, Art

Czaczkes, Shmuel Yosef
See Agnon, S(hmuel) Y(osef Halevi)

D. P.
See Wells, H(erbert) G(eorge)

Dabrowska, Maria (Szumska)
1889-1965 . . . . **CLC 15**
See also CA 106

Dabydeen, David 1955- . . . . **CLC 34**
See also BW; CA 125

Dacey, Philip 1939- . . . . **CLC 51**
See also CA 37-40R; CAAS 17; CANR 14, 32; DLB 105

Dagerman, Stig (Halvard)
1923-1954 . . . . **TCLC 17**
See also CA 117

Dahl, Roald 1916-1990 . . . . . **CLC 1, 6, 18, 79**
See also CA 1-4R; 133; CANR 6, 32, 37; CLR 1, 7; JRDA; MAICYA; MTCW; SATA 1, 26, 73; SATA-Obit 65

Dahlberg, Edward 1900-1977 . . . **CLC 1, 7, 14**
See also CA 9-12R; 69-72; CANR 31; DLB 48; MTCW

Dale, Colin . . . . **TCLC 18**
See also Lawrence, T(homas) E(dward)

Dale, George E.
See Asimov, Isaac

Daly, Elizabeth 1878-1967 . . . . **CLC 52**
See also CA 23-24; 25-28R; CAP 2

Daly, Maureen 1921- . . . . **CLC 17**
See also AAYA 5; CANR 37; JRDA; MAICYA; SAAS 1; SATA 2

Daniel, Samuel 1562(?)-1619 . . . . **LC 24**
See also DLB 62

Daniels, Brett
See Adler, Renata

Dannay, Frederic 1905-1982 . . . . **CLC 11**
See also Queen, Ellery
See also CA 1-4R; 107; CANR 1, 39; MTCW

D'Annunzio, Gabriele
1863-1938 . . . . **TCLC 6, 40**
See also CA 104

d'Antibes, Germain
See Simenon, Georges (Jacques Christian)

Danvers, Dennis 1947- . . . . **CLC 70**

Danziger, Paula 1944- . . . . **CLC 21**
See also AAYA 4; CA 112; 115; CANR 37; CLR 20; JRDA; MAICYA; SATA 30, 36, 63

Dario, Ruben 1867-1916 . . . . **TCLC 4**
See also CA 131; HW; MTCW

Darley, George 1795-1846 . . . . **NCLC 2**
See also DLB 96

Daryush, Elizabeth 1887-1977 . . . . **CLC 6, 19**
See also CA 49-52; CANR 3; DLB 20

Daudet, (Louis Marie) Alphonse
1840-1897 . . . . **NCLC 1**
See also DLB 123

Daumal, Rene 1908-1944 . . . . **TCLC 14**
See also CA 114

Davenport, Guy (Mattison, Jr.)
1927- . . . . **CLC 6, 14, 38**
See also CA 33-36R; CANR 23; DLB 130

Davidson, Avram 1923-
See Queen, Ellery
See also CA 101; CANR 26; DLB 8

Davidson, Donald (Grady)
1893-1968 . . . . **CLC 2, 13, 19**
See also CA 5-8R; 25-28R; CANR 4; DLB 45

Davidson, Hugh
See Hamilton, Edmond

Davidson, John 1857-1909 . . . . **TCLC 24**
See also CA 118; DLB 19

Davidson, Sara 1943- . . . . **CLC 9**
See also CA 81-84

Davie, Donald (Alfred)
1922- . . . . **CLC 5, 8, 10, 31**
See also CA 1-4R; CAAS 3; CANR 1; DLB 27; MTCW

Davies, Ray(mond Douglas) 1944- . . **CLC 21**
See also CA 116

Davies, Rhys 1903-1978 . . . . **CLC 23**
See also CA 9-12R; 81-84; CANR 4

Davies, (William) Robertson
1913- . . . . **CLC 2, 7, 13, 25, 42, 75**
See also BEST 89:2; CA 33-36R; CANR 17, 42; DA; DLB 68; MTCW; WLC

Davies, W(illiam) H(enry)
1871-1940 . . . . **TCLC 5**
See also CA 104; DLB 19

Davies, Walter C.
See Kornbluth, C(yril) M.

Davis, Angela (Yvonne) 1944- . . . . . . **CLC 77**
See also BW; CA 57-60; CANR 10

Davis, B. Lynch
See Bioy Casares, Adolfo; Borges, Jorge Luis

Davis, Gordon
See Hunt, E(verette) Howard, Jr.

Davis, Harold Lenoir 1896-1960 . . . . **CLC 49**
See also CA 89-92; DLB 9

Davis, Rebecca (Blaine) Harding
1831-1910 . . . . **TCLC 6**
See also CA 104; DLB 74

Davis, Richard Harding
1864-1916 . . . . **TCLC 24**
See also CA 114; DLB 12, 23, 78, 79

Davison, Frank Dalby 1893-1970 . . . **CLC 15**
See also CA 116

Davison, Lawrence H.
See Lawrence, D(avid) H(erbert Richards)

Davison, Peter (Hubert) 1928- . . . . . **CLC 28**
See also CA 9-12R; CAAS 4; CANR 3, 43; DLB 5

Davys, Mary 1674-1732 . . . . **LC 1**
See also DLB 39

Dawson, Fielding 1930- . . . . **CLC 6**
See also CA 85-88; DLB 130

Dawson, Peter
See Faust, Frederick (Schiller)

Day, Clarence (Shepard, Jr.)
1874-1935 . . . . **TCLC 25**
See also CA 108; DLB 11

Day, Thomas 1748-1789 . . . . **LC 1**
See also DLB 39; YABC 1

Day Lewis, C(ecil)
1904-1972 . . . . **CLC 1, 6, 10**
See also Blake, Nicholas
See also CA 13-16; 33-36R; CANR 34; CAP 1; DLB 15, 20; MTCW

Dazai, Osamu . . . . **TCLC 11**
See also Tsushima, Shuji

de Andrade, Carlos Drummond
See Drummond de Andrade, Carlos

Deane, Norman
See Creasey, John

de Beauvoir, Simone (Lucie Ernestine Marie Bertrand)
See Beauvoir, Simone (Lucie Ernestine Marie Bertrand) de

de Brissac, Malcolm
See Dickinson, Peter (Malcolm)

de Chardin, Pierre Teilhard
See Teilhard de Chardin, (Marie Joseph) Pierre

Dee, John 1527-1608 . . . . **LC 20**

Deer, Sandra 1940- . . . . **CLC 45**

De Ferrari, Gabriella . . . . **CLC 65**

Defoe, Daniel 1660(?)-1731 . . . . **LC 1**
See also CDBLB 1660-1789; DA; DLB 39, 95, 101; JRDA; MAICYA; SATA 22; WLC

de Gourmont, Remy
See Gourmont, Remy de

de Hartog, Jan 1914- . . . . **CLC 19**
See also CA 1-4R; CANR 1

de Hostos, E. M.
See Hostos (y Bonilla), Eugenio Maria de

de Hostos, Eugenio M.
See Hostos (y Bonilla), Eugenio Maria de

Deighton, Len . . . . **CLC 4, 7, 22, 46**
See also Deighton, Leonard Cyril
See also AAYA 6; BEST 89:2; CDBLB 1960 to Present; DLB 87

Deighton, Leonard Cyril 1929-
See Deighton, Len
See also CA 9-12R; CANR 19, 33; MTCW

Dekker, Thomas 1572(?)-1632 . . . . **LC 22**
See also CDBLB Before 1660; DLB 62

de la Mare, Walter (John)
1873-1956 . . . . **TCLC 4, 52**
See also CDBLB 1914-1945; CLR 23; DLB 19; SATA 16; WLC

Delaney, Franey
See O'Hara, John (Henry)

Delaney, Shelagh 1939- . . . . **CLC 29**
See also CA 17-20R; CANR 30; CDBLB 1960 to Present; DLB 13; MTCW

Delany, Mary (Granville Pendarves)
1700-1788 . . . . **LC 12**

Delany, Samuel R(ay, Jr.)
1942- . . . . **CLC 8, 14, 38**
See also BLC 1; BW; CA 81-84; CANR 27, 43; DLB 8, 33; MTCW

Delaporte, Theophile
See Green, Julian (Hartridge)

De La Ramee, (Marie) Louise 1839-1908
See Ouida
See also SATA 20

de la Roche, Mazo 1879-1961 . . . . . . **CLC 14**
See also CA 85-88; CANR 30; DLB 68; SATA 64

Delbanco, Nicholas (Franklin)
1942- . . . . **CLC 6, 13**
See also CA 17-20R; CAAS 2; CANR 29; DLB 6

del Castillo, Michel 1933- . . . . **CLC 38**
See also CA 109

Deledda, Grazia (Cosima)
1875(?)-1936 . . . . **TCLC 23**
See also CA 123

Delibes, Miguel . . . . **CLC 8, 18**
See also Delibes Setien, Miguel

Delibes Setien, Miguel 1920-
See Delibes, Miguel
See also CA 45-48; CANR 1, 32; HW; MTCW

DeLillo, Don
1936- . . . . . **CLC 8, 10, 13, 27, 39, 54, 76**
See also BEST 89:1; CA 81-84; CANR 21; DLB 6; MTCW

Author Index

Author Index

Eliot, Alice
See Jewett, (Theodora) Sarah Orne

Eliot, Dan
See Silverberg, Robert

Eliot, George
1819-1880 .... **NCLC 4, 13, 23, 41**
See also CDBLB 1832-1890; DA; DLB 21, 35, 55; WLC

Eliot, John 1604-1690 .... **LC 5**
See also DLB 24

Eliot, T(homas) S(tearns)
1888-1965 ..... **CLC 1, 2, 3, 6, 9, 10, 13, 15, 24, 34, 41, 55, 57; PC 5**
See also CA 5-8R; 25-28R; CANR 41; CDALB 1929-1941; DA; DLB 7, 10, 45, 63; DLBY 88; MTCW; WLC 2

Elizabeth 1866-1941 .... **TCLC 41**

Elkin, Stanley L(awrence)
1930- ... **CLC 4, 6, 9, 14, 27, 51; SSC 12**
See also CA 9-12R; CANR 8; DLB 2, 28; DLBY 80; MTCW

Elledge, Scott..................... **CLC 34**

Elliott, Don
See Silverberg, Robert

Elliott, George P(aul) 1918-1980..... **CLC 2**
See also CA 1-4R; 97-100; CANR 2

Elliott, Janice 1931-.............. **CLC 47**
See also CA 13-16R; CANR 8, 29; DLB 14

Elliott, Sumner Locke 1917-1991 ... **CLC 38**
See also CA 5-8R; 134; CANR 2, 21

Elliott, William
See Bradbury, Ray (Douglas)

Ellis, A. E.......................... **CLC 7**

Ellis, Alice Thomas................ **CLC 40**
See also Haycraft, Anna

Ellis, Bret Easton 1964-........ **CLC 39, 71**
See also AAYA 2; CA 118; 123

Ellis, (Henry) Havelock
1859-1939 .... **TCLC 14**
See also CA 109

Ellis, Landon
See Ellison, Harlan

Ellis, Trey 1962-................. **CLC 55**

Ellison, Harlan 1934-........ **CLC 1, 13, 42**
See also CA 5-8R; CANR 5; DLB 8; MTCW

Ellison, Ralph (Waldo)
1914- .... **CLC 1, 3, 11, 54**
See also BLC 1; BW; CA 9-12R; CANR 24; CDALB 1941-1968; DA; DLB 2, 76; MTCW; WLC

Ellmann, Lucy (Elizabeth) 1956-.... **CLC 61**
See also CA 128

Ellmann, Richard (David)
1918-1987 .... **CLC 50**
See also BEST 89:2; CA 1-4R; 122; CANR 2, 28; DLB 103; DLBY 87; MTCW

Elman, Richard 1934-............. **CLC 19**
See also CA 17-20R; CAAS 3

Elron
See Hubbard, L(afayette) Ron(ald)

Eluard, Paul.................. **TCLC 7, 41**
See also Grindel, Eugene

Elyot, Sir Thomas 1490(?)-1546 ..... **LC 11**

Elytis, Odysseus 1911-......... **CLC 15, 49**
See also CA 102; MTCW

Emecheta, (Florence Onye) Buchi
1944- .... **CLC 14, 48**
See also BLC 2; BW; CA 81-84; CANR 27; DLB 117; MTCW; SATA 66

Emerson, Ralph Waldo
1803-1882 .... **NCLC 1, 38**
See also CDALB 1640-1865; DA; DLB 1, 59, 73; WLC

Eminescu, Mihail 1850-1889 ..... **NCLC 33**

Empson, William
1906-1984 .... **CLC 3, 8, 19, 33, 34**
See also CA 17-20R; 112; CANR 31; DLB 20; MTCW

Enchi Fumiko (Ueda) 1905-1986.... **CLC 31**
See also CA 129; 121

Ende, Michael (Andreas Helmuth)
1929- .... **CLC 31**
See also CA 118; 124; CANR 36; CLR 14; DLB 75; MAICYA; SATA 42, 61

Endo, Shusaku 1923-..... **CLC 7, 14, 19, 54**
See also CA 29-32R; CANR 21; MTCW

Engel, Marian 1933-1985.......... **CLC 36**
See also CA 25-28R; CANR 12; DLB 53

Engelhardt, Frederick
See Hubbard, L(afayette) Ron(ald)

Enright, D(ennis) J(oseph)
1920- .... **CLC 4, 8, 31**
See also CA 1-4R; CANR 1, 42; DLB 27; SATA 25

Enzensberger, Hans Magnus
1929- .... **CLC 43**
See also CA 116; 119

Ephron, Nora 1941-........... **CLC 17, 31**
See also AITN 2; CA 65-68; CANR 12, 39

Epsilon
See Betjeman, John

Epstein, Daniel Mark 1948- .... **CLC 7**
See also CA 49-52; CANR 2

Epstein, Jacob 1956- .... **CLC 19**
See also CA 114

Epstein, Joseph 1937-............. **CLC 39**
See also CA 112; 119

Epstein, Leslie 1938- .... **CLC 27**
See also CA 73-76; CAAS 12; CANR 23

Equiano, Olaudah 1745(?)-1797...... **LC 16**
See also BLC 2; DLB 37, 50

Erasmus, Desiderius 1469(?)-1536.... **LC 16**

Erdman, Paul E(mil) 1932- .... **CLC 25**
See also AITN 1; CA 61-64; CANR 13, 43

Erdrich, Louise 1954-.......... **CLC 39, 54**
See also AAYA 10; BEST 89:1; CA 114; CANR 41; MTCW

Erenburg, Ilya (Grigoryevich)
See Ehrenburg, Ilya (Grigoryevich)

Erickson, Stephen Michael 1950-
See Erickson, Steve
See also CA 129

Erickson, Steve .... **CLC 64**
See also Erickson, Stephen Michael

Ericson, Walter
See Fast, Howard (Melvin)

Eriksson, Buntel
See Bergman, (Ernst) Ingmar

Eschenbach, Wolfram von
See Wolfram von Eschenbach

Eseki, Bruno
See Mphahlele, Ezekiel

Esenin, Sergei (Alexandrovich)
1895-1925 .... **TCLC 4**
See also CA 104

Eshleman, Clayton 1935-........... **CLC 7**
See also CA 33-36R; CAAS 6; DLB 5

Espriella, Don Manuel Alvarez
See Southey, Robert

Espriu, Salvador 1913-1985......... **CLC 9**
See also CA 115; DLB 134

Espronceda, Jose de 1808-1842... **NCLC 39**

Esse, James
See Stephens, James

Esterbrook, Tom
See Hubbard, L(afayette) Ron(ald)

Estleman, Loren D. 1952-.......... **CLC 48**
See also CA 85-88; CANR 27; MTCW

Evan, Evin
See Faust, Frederick (Schiller)

Evans, Evan
See Faust, Frederick (Schiller)

Evans, Marian
See Eliot, George

Evans, Mary Ann
See Eliot, George

Evarts, Esther
See Benson, Sally

Everett, Percival
See Everett, Percival L.

Everett, Percival L. 1956-......... **CLC 57**
See also CA 129

Everson, R(onald) G(ilmour)
1903- .... **CLC 27**
See also CA 17-20R; DLB 88

Everson, William (Oliver)
1912-................... **CLC 1, 5, 14**
See also CA 9-12R; CANR 20; DLB 5, 16; MTCW

Evtushenko, Evgenii Aleksandrovich
See Yevtushenko, Yevgeny (Alexandrovich)

Ewart, Gavin (Buchanan)
1916- .... **CLC 13, 46**
See also CA 89-92; CANR 17; DLB 40; MTCW

Ewers, Hanns Heinz 1871-1943 ... **TCLC 12**
See also CA 109

Ewing, Frederick R.
See Sturgeon, Theodore (Hamilton)

Exley, Frederick (Earl)
1929-1992 .... **CLC 6, 11**
See also AITN 2; CA 81-84; 138; DLBY 81

Eynhardt, Guillermo
See Quiroga, Horacio (Sylvestre)

Ezekiel, Nissim 1924-............. **CLC 61**
See also CA 61-64

Ezekiel, Tish O'Dowd 1943-....... **CLC 34**
See also CA 129

Fagen, Donald 1948-.............. **CLC 26**

Fainzilberg, Ilya Arnoldovich 1897-1937
See Ilf, Ilya
See also CA 120

Fair, Ronald L. 1932- . . . . **CLC 18**
See also BW; CA 69-72; CANR 25; DLB 33

Fairbairns, Zoe (Ann) 1948- . . . . **CLC 32**
See also CA 103; CANR 21

Falco, Gian
See Papini, Giovanni

Falconer, James
See Kirkup, James

Falconer, Kenneth
See Kornbluth, C(yril) M.

Falkland, Samuel
See Heijermans, Herman

Fallaci, Oriana 1930- . . . . **CLC 11**
See also CA 77-80; CANR 15; MTCW

Faludy, George 1913- . . . . **CLC 42**
See also CA 21-24R

Faludy, Gyoergy
See Faludy, George

Fanon, Frantz 1925-1961 . . . . **CLC 74**
See also BLC 2; BW; CA 116; 89-92

Fanshawe, Ann . . . . **LC 11**

Fante, John (Thomas) 1911-1983 . . . **CLC 60**
See also CA 69-72; 109; CANR 23; DLB 130; DLBY 83

Farah, Nuruddin 1945- . . . . **CLC 53**
See also BLC 2; CA 106; DLB 125

Fargue, Leon-Paul 1876(?)-1947 . . . **TCLC 11**
See also CA 109

Farigoule, Louis
See Romains, Jules

Farina, Richard 1936(?)-1966 . . . . **CLC 9**
See also CA 81-84; 25-28R

Farley, Walter (Lorimer)
1915-1989 . . . . **CLC 17**
See also CA 17-20R; CANR 8, 29; DLB 22; JRDA; MAICYA; SATA 2, 43

Farmer, Philip Jose 1918- . . . . **CLC 1, 19**
See also CA 1-4R; CANR 4, 35; DLB 8; MTCW

Farquhar, George 1677-1707 . . . . **LC 21**
See also DLB 84

Farrell, J(ames) G(ordon)
1935-1979 . . . . **CLC 6**
See also CA 73-76; 89-92; CANR 36; DLB 14; MTCW

Farrell, James T(homas)
1904-1979 . . . . **CLC 1, 4, 8, 11, 66**
See also CA 5-8R; 89-92; CANR 9; DLB 4, 9, 86; DLBD 2; MTCW

Farren, Richard J.
See Betjeman, John

Farren, Richard M.
See Betjeman, John

Fassbinder, Rainer Werner
1946-1982 . . . . **CLC 20**
See also CA 93-96; 106; CANR 31

Fast, Howard (Melvin) 1914- . . . . . . **CLC 23**
See also CA 1-4R; CAAS 18; CANR 1, 33; DLB 9; SATA 7

Faulcon, Robert
See Holdstock, Robert P.

Faulkner, William (Cuthbert)
1897-1962 . . . . . **CLC 1, 3, 6, 8, 9, 11, 14, 18, 28, 52, 68; SSC 1**
See also AAYA 7; CA 81-84; CANR 33; CDALB 1929-1941; DA; DLB 9, 11, 44, 102; DLBD 2; DLBY 86; MTCW; WLC

Fauset, Jessie Redmon
1884(?)-1961 . . . . **CLC 19, 54**
See also BLC 2; BW; CA 109; DLB 51

Faust, Frederick (Schiller)
1892-1944(?) . . . . **TCLC 49**
See also CA 108

Faust, Irvin 1924- . . . . **CLC 8**
See also CA 33-36R; CANR 28; DLB 2, 28; DLBY 80

Fawkes, Guy
See Benchley, Robert (Charles)

Fearing, Kenneth (Flexner)
1902-1961 . . . . **CLC 51**
See also CA 93-96; DLB 9

Fecamps, Elise
See Creasey, John

Federman, Raymond 1928- . . . . . . **CLC 6, 47**
See also CA 17-20R; CAAS 8; CANR 10, 43; DLBY 80

Federspiel, J(uerg) F. 1931- . . . . **CLC 42**

Feiffer, Jules (Ralph) 1929- . . . . **CLC 2, 8, 64**
See also AAYA 3; CA 17-20R; CANR 30; DLB 7, 44; MTCW; SATA 8, 61

Feige, Hermann Albert Otto Maximilian
See Traven, B.

Fei-Kan, Li
See Li Fei-kan

Feinberg, David B. 1956- . . . . **CLC 59**
See also CA 135

Feinstein, Elaine 1930- . . . . **CLC 36**
See also CA 69-72; CAAS 1; CANR 31; DLB 14, 40; MTCW

Feldman, Irving (Mordecai) 1928- . . . . **CLC 7**
See also CA 1-4R; CANR 1

Fellini, Federico 1920- . . . . **CLC 16**
See also CA 65-68; CANR 33

Felsen, Henry Gregor 1916- . . . . **CLC 17**
See also CA 1-4R; CANR 1; SAAS 2; SATA 1

Fenton, James Martin 1949- . . . . **CLC 32**
See also CA 102; DLB 40

Ferber, Edna 1887-1968 . . . . **CLC 18**
See also AITN 1; CA 5-8R; 25-28R; DLB 9, 28, 86; MTCW; SATA 7

Ferguson, Helen
See Kavan, Anna

Ferguson, Samuel 1810-1886 . . . . . **NCLC 33**
See also DLB 32

Ferling, Lawrence
See Ferlinghetti, Lawrence (Monsanto)

Ferlinghetti, Lawrence (Monsanto)
1919(?)- . . . . **CLC 2, 6, 10, 27; PC 1**
See also CA 5-8R; CANR 3, 41; CDALB 1941-1968; DLB 5, 16; MTCW

Fernandez, Vicente Garcia Huidobro
See Huidobro Fernandez, Vicente Garcia

Ferrer, Gabriel (Francisco Victor) Miro
See Miro (Ferrer), Gabriel (Francisco Victor)

Ferrier, Susan (Edmonstone)
1782-1854 . . . . **NCLC 8**
See also DLB 116

Ferrigno, Robert 1948(?)- . . . . **CLC 65**
See also CA 140

Feuchtwanger, Lion 1884-1958 . . . . . **TCLC 3**
See also CA 104; DLB 66

Feydeau, Georges (Leon Jules Marie)
1862-1921 . . . . **TCLC 22**
See also CA 113

Ficino, Marsilio 1433-1499 . . . . **LC 12**

Fiedeler, Hans
See Doeblin, Alfred

Fiedler, Leslie A(aron)
1917- . . . . **CLC 4, 13, 24**
See also CA 9-12R; CANR 7; DLB 28, 67; MTCW

Field, Andrew 1938- . . . . **CLC 44**
See also CA 97-100; CANR 25

Field, Eugene 1850-1895 . . . . **NCLC 3**
See also DLB 23, 42; MAICYA; SATA 16

Field, Gans T.
See Wellman, Manly Wade

Field, Michael . . . . **TCLC 43**

Field, Peter
See Hobson, Laura Z(ametkin)

Fielding, Henry 1707-1754 . . . . **LC 1**
See also CDBLB 1660-1789; DA; DLB 39, 84, 101; WLC

Fielding, Sarah 1710-1768 . . . . **LC 1**
See also DLB 39

Fierstein, Harvey (Forbes) 1954- . . . **CLC 33**
See also CA 123; 129

Figes, Eva 1932- . . . . **CLC 31**
See also CA 53-56; CANR 4; DLB 14

Finch, Robert (Duer Claydon)
1900- . . . . **CLC 18**
See also CA 57-60; CANR 9, 24; DLB 88

Findley, Timothy 1930- . . . . **CLC 27**
See also CA 25-28R; CANR 12, 42; DLB 53

Fink, William
See Mencken, H(enry) L(ouis)

Firbank, Louis 1942-
See Reed, Lou
See also CA 117

Firbank, (Arthur Annesley) Ronald
1886-1926 . . . . **TCLC 1**
See also CA 104; DLB 36

Fisher, M(ary) F(rances) K(ennedy)
1908-1992 . . . . **CLC 76**
See also CA 77-80; 138

Fisher, Roy 1930- . . . . **CLC 25**
See also CA 81-84; CAAS 10; CANR 16; DLB 40

Fisher, Rudolph 1897-1934 . . . . **TCLC 11**
See also BLC 2; BW; CA 107; 124; DLB 51, 102

Fisher, Vardis (Alvero) 1895-1968. . . . **CLC 7**
See also CA 5-8R; 25-28R; DLB 9

Frederic, Harold 1856-1898...... **NCLC 10**
See also DLB 12, 23

Frederick, John
See Faust, Frederick (Schiller)

Frederick the Great 1712-1786...... **LC 14**

Fredro, Aleksander 1793-1876..... **NCLC 8**

Freeling, Nicolas 1927-........... **CLC 38**
See also CA 49-52; CAAS 12; CANR 1, 17; DLB 87

Freeman, Douglas Southall
1886-1953.................. **TCLC 11**
See also CA 109; DLB 17

Freeman, Judith 1946-............ **CLC 55**

Freeman, Mary Eleanor Wilkins
1852-1930............ **TCLC 9; SSC 1**
See also CA 106; DLB 12, 78

Freeman, R(ichard) Austin
1862-1943.................. **TCLC 21**
See also CA 113; DLB 70

French, Marilyn 1929-...... **CLC 10, 18, 60**
See also CA 69-72; CANR 3, 31; MTCW

French, Paul
See Asimov, Isaac

Freneau, Philip Morin 1752-1832.. **NCLC 1**
See also DLB 37, 43

Freud, Sigmund 1856-1939....... **TCLC 52**
See also CA 115; 133; MTCW

Friedan, Betty (Naomi) 1921-...... **CLC 74**
See also CA 65-68; CANR 18; MTCW

Friedman, B(ernard) H(arper)
1926-........................ **CLC 7**
See also CA 1-4R; CANR 3

Friedman, Bruce Jay 1930-.... **CLC 3, 5, 56**
See also CA 9-12R; CANR 25; DLB 2, 28

Friel, Brian 1929-........... **CLC 5, 42, 59**
See also CA 21-24R; CANR 33; DLB 13; MTCW

Friis-Baastad, Babbis Ellinor
1921-1970................... **CLC 12**
See also CA 17-20R; 134; SATA 7

Frisch, Max (Rudolf)
1911-1991..... **CLC 3, 9, 14, 18, 32, 44**
See also CA 85-88; 134; CANR 32; DLB 69, 124; MTCW

Fromentin, Eugene (Samuel Auguste)
1820-1876................. **NCLC 10**
See also DLB 123

Frost, Frederick
See Faust, Frederick (Schiller)

Frost, Robert (Lee)
1874-1963.... **CLC 1, 3, 4, 9, 10, 13, 15, 26, 34, 44; PC 1**
See also CA 89-92; CANR 33; CDALB 1917-1929; DA; DLB 54; DLBD 7; MTCW; SATA 14; WLC

Froy, Herald
See Waterhouse, Keith (Spencer)

Fry, Christopher 1907-....... **CLC 2, 10, 14**
See also CA 17-20R; CANR 9, 30; DLB 13; MTCW; SATA 66

Frye, (Herman) Northrop
1912-1991................ **CLC 24, 70**
See also CA 5-8R; 133; CANR 8, 37; DLB 67, 68; MTCW

Fuchs, Daniel 1909-1993........ **CLC 8, 22**
See also CA 81-84; 142; CAAS 5; CANR 40; DLB 9, 26, 28

Fuchs, Daniel 1934-.............. **CLC 34**
See also CA 37-40R; CANR 14

Fuentes, Carlos
1928-...... **CLC 3, 8, 10, 13, 22, 41, 60**
See also AAYA 4; AITN 2; CA 69-72; CANR 10, 32; DA; DLB 113; HW; MTCW; WLC

Fuentes, Gregorio Lopez y
See Lopez y Fuentes, Gregorio

Fugard, (Harold) Athol
1932-.... **CLC 5, 9, 14, 25, 40, 80; DC 3**
See also CA 85-88; CANR 32; MTCW

Fugard, Sheila 1932-............. **CLC 48**
See also CA 125

Fuller, Charles (H., Jr.)
1939-.................. **CLC 25; DC 1**
See also BLC 2; BW; CA 108; 112; DLB 38; MTCW

Fuller, John (Leopold) 1937-....... **CLC 62**
See also CA 21-24R; CANR 9; DLB 40

Fuller, Margaret................. **NCLC 5**
See also Ossoli, Sarah Margaret (Fuller marchesa d')

Fuller, Roy (Broadbent)
1912-1991................. **CLC 4, 28**
See also CA 5-8R; 135; CAAS 10; DLB 15, 20

Fulton, Alice 1952-............... **CLC 52**
See also CA 116

Furphy, Joseph 1843-1912........ **TCLC 25**

Fussell, Paul 1924-............... **CLC 74**
See also BEST 90:1; CA 17-20R; CANR 8, 21, 35; MTCW

Futabatei, Shimei 1864-1909...... **TCLC 44**

Futrelle, Jacques 1875-1912...... **TCLC 19**
See also CA 113

G. B. S.
See Shaw, George Bernard

Gaboriau, Emile 1835-1873...... **NCLC 14**

Gadda, Carlo Emilio 1893-1973.... **CLC 11**
See also CA 89-92

Gaddis, William
1922-........ **CLC 1, 3, 6, 8, 10, 19, 43**
See also CA 17-20R; CANR 21; DLB 2; MTCW

Gaines, Ernest J(ames)
1933-.................. **CLC 3, 11, 18**
See also AITN 1; BLC 2; BW; CA 9-12R; CANR 6, 24, 42; CDALB 1968-1988; DLB 2, 33; DLBY 80; MTCW

Gaitskill, Mary 1954-............ **CLC 69**
See also CA 128

Galdos, Benito Perez
See Perez Galdos, Benito

Gale, Zona 1874-1938............ **TCLC 7**
See also CA 105; DLB 9, 78

Galeano, Eduardo (Hughes) 1940-... **CLC 72**
See also CA 29-32R; CANR 13, 32; HW

Galiano, Juan Valera y Alcala
See Valera y Alcala-Galiano, Juan

Gallagher, Tess 1943-.......... **CLC 18, 63**
See also CA 106; DLB 120

Gallant, Mavis
1922-........... **CLC 7, 18, 38; SSC 5**
See also CA 69-72; CANR 29; DLB 53; MTCW

Gallant, Roy A(rthur) 1924-....... **CLC 17**
See also CA 5-8R; CANR 4, 29; CLR 30; MAICYA; SATA 4, 68

Gallico, Paul (William) 1897-1976... **CLC 2**
See also AITN 1; CA 5-8R; 69-72; CANR 23; DLB 9; MAICYA; SATA 13

Gallup, Ralph
See Whitemore, Hugh (John)

Galsworthy, John 1867-1933.... **TCLC 1, 45**
See also CA 104; 141; CDBLB 1890-1914; DA; DLB 10, 34, 98; WLC 2

Galt, John 1779-1839............ **NCLC 1**
See also DLB 99, 116

Galvin, James 1951-.............. **CLC 38**
See also CA 108; CANR 26

Gamboa, Federico 1864-1939...... **TCLC 36**

Gann, Ernest Kellogg 1910-1991.... **CLC 23**
See also AITN 1; CA 1-4R; 136; CANR 1

Garcia, Cristina 1958-............ **CLC 76**
See also CA 141

Garcia Lorca, Federico
1898-1936.. **TCLC 1, 7, 49; DC 2; PC 3**
See also Lorca, Federico Garcia
See also CA 104; 131; DA; DLB 108; HW; MTCW; WLC

Garcia Marquez, Gabriel (Jose)
1928-.... **CLC 2, 3, 8, 10, 15, 27, 47, 55; SSC 8**
See also Marquez, Gabriel (Jose) Garcia
See also AAYA 3; BEST 89:1, 90:4; CA 33-36R; CANR 10, 28; DA; DLB 113; HW; MTCW; WLC

Gard, Janice
See Latham, Jean Lee

Gard, Roger Martin du
See Martin du Gard, Roger

Gardam, Jane 1928-.............. **CLC 43**
See also CA 49-52; CANR 2, 18, 33; CLR 12; DLB 14; MAICYA; MTCW; SAAS 9; SATA 28, 39

Gardner, Herb.................... **CLC 44**

Gardner, John (Champlin), Jr.
1933-1982..... **CLC 2, 3, 5, 7, 8, 10, 18, 28, 34; SSC 7**
See also AITN 1; CA 65-68; 107; CANR 33; DLB 2; DLBY 82; MTCW; SATA 31, 40

Gardner, John (Edmund) 1926-..... **CLC 30**
See also CA 103; CANR 15; MTCW

Gardner, Noel
See Kuttner, Henry

Gardons, S. S.
See Snodgrass, W(illiam) D(e Witt)

Garfield, Leon 1921-.............. **CLC 12**
See also AAYA 8; CA 17-20R; CANR 38, 41; CLR 21; JRDA; MAICYA; SATA 1, 32

Glasscock, Amnesia
See Steinbeck, John (Ernst)

Glasser, Ronald J. 1940(?)- . . . . **CLC 37**

Glassman, Joyce
See Johnson, Joyce

Glendinning, Victoria 1937- . . . . **CLC 50**
See also CA 120; 127

Glissant, Edouard 1928- . . . . **CLC 10, 68**

Gloag, Julian 1930- . . . . **CLC 40**
See also AITN 1; CA 65-68; CANR 10

Gluck, Louise (Elisabeth)
1943- . . . . **CLC 7, 22, 44**
See also Glueck, Louise
See also CA 33-36R; CANR 40; DLB 5

Glueck, Louise . . . . **CLC 7, 22**
See also Gluck, Louise (Elisabeth)
See also DLB 5

Gobineau, Joseph Arthur (Comte) de
1816-1882 . . . . **NCLC 17**
See also DLB 123

Godard, Jean-Luc 1930- . . . . **CLC 20**
See also CA 93-96

Godden, (Margaret) Rumer 1907- . . . **CLC 53**
See also AAYA 6; CA 5-8R; CANR 4, 27, 36; CLR 20; MAICYA; SAAS 12; SATA 3, 36

Godoy Alcayaga, Lucila 1889-1957
See Mistral, Gabriela
See also CA 104; 131; HW; MTCW

Godwin, Gail (Kathleen)
1937- . . . . **CLC 5, 8, 22, 31, 69**
See also CA 29-32R; CANR 15, 43; DLB 6; MTCW

Godwin, William 1756-1836 . . . . . . **NCLC 14**
See also CDBLB 1789-1832; DLB 39, 104

Goethe, Johann Wolfgang von
1749-1832 . . . . **NCLC 4, 22, 34; PC 5**
See also DA; DLB 94; WLC 3

Gogarty, Oliver St. John
1878-1957 . . . . **TCLC 15**
See also CA 109; DLB 15, 19

Gogol, Nikolai (Vasilyevich)
1809-1852 . . . . . . **NCLC 5, 15, 31; DC 1; SSC 4**
See also DA; WLC

Goines, Donald 1937(?)-1974 . . . . **CLC 80**
See also AITN 1; BLC 2; BW; CA 124; 114; DLB 33

Gold, Herbert 1924- . . . . **CLC 4, 7, 14, 42**
See also CA 9-12R; CANR 17; DLB 2; DLBY 81

Goldbarth, Albert 1948- . . . . **CLC 5, 38**
See also CA 53-56; CANR 6, 40; DLB 120

Goldberg, Anatol 1910-1982 . . . . **CLC 34**
See also CA 131; 117

Goldemberg, Isaac 1945- . . . . **CLC 52**
See also CA 69-72; CAAS 12; CANR 11, 32; HW

Golden Silver
See Storm, Hyemeyohsts

Golding, William G(erald)
1911-1993 . . . . **CLC 1, 2, 3, 8, 10, 17, 27, 58**
See also AAYA 5; CA 5-8R; 141; CANR 13, 33; CDBLB 1945-1960; DA; DLB 15, 100; MTCW; WLC

Goldman, Emma 1869-1940 . . . . **TCLC 13**
See also CA 110

Goldman, Francisco 1955- . . . . **CLC 76**

Goldman, William (W.) 1931- . . . . **CLC 1, 48**
See also CA 9-12R; CANR 29; DLB 44

Goldmann, Lucien 1913-1970 . . . . . . **CLC 24**
See also CA 25-28; CAP 2

Goldoni, Carlo 1707-1793 . . . . **LC 4**

Goldsberry, Steven 1949- . . . . **CLC 34**
See also CA 131

Goldsmith, Oliver 1728-1774 . . . . **LC 2**
See also CDBLB 1660-1789; DA; DLB 39, 89, 104, 109; SATA 26; WLC

Goldsmith, Peter
See Priestley, J(ohn) B(oynton)

Gombrowicz, Witold
1904-1969 . . . . **CLC 4, 7, 11, 49**
See also CA 19-20; 25-28R; CAP 2

Gomez de la Serna, Ramon
1888-1963 . . . . **CLC 9**
See also CA 116; HW

Goncharov, Ivan Alexandrovich
1812-1891 . . . . **NCLC 1**

Goncourt, Edmond (Louis Antoine Huot) de
1822-1896 . . . . **NCLC 7**
See also DLB 123

Goncourt, Jules (Alfred Huot) de
1830-1870 . . . . **NCLC 7**
See also DLB 123

Gontier, Fernande 19(?)- . . . . **CLC 50**

Goodman, Paul 1911-1972 . . . . **CLC 1, 2, 4, 7**
See also CA 19-20; 37-40R; CANR 34; CAP 2; DLB 130; MTCW

Gordimer, Nadine
1923- . . . . **CLC 3, 5, 7, 10, 18, 33, 51, 70**
See also CA 5-8R; CANR 3, 28; DA; MTCW

Gordon, Adam Lindsay
1833-1870 . . . . **NCLC 21**

Gordon, Caroline
1895-1981 . . . . **CLC 6, 13, 29**
See also CA 11-12; 103; CANR 36; CAP 1; DLB 4, 9, 102; DLBY 81; MTCW

Gordon, Charles William 1860-1937
See Connor, Ralph
See also CA 109

Gordon, Mary (Catherine)
1949- . . . . **CLC 13, 22**
See also CA 102; DLB 6; DLBY 81; MTCW

Gordon, Sol 1923- . . . . **CLC 26**
See also CA 53-56; CANR 4; SATA 11

Gordone, Charles 1925- . . . . **CLC 1, 4**
See also BW; CA 93-96; DLB 7; MTCW

Gorenko, Anna Andreevna
See Akhmatova, Anna

Gorky, Maxim . . . . **TCLC 8**
See also Peshkov, Alexei Maximovich
See also WLC

Goryan, Sirak
See Saroyan, William

Gosse, Edmund (William)
1849-1928 . . . . **TCLC 28**
See also CA 117; DLB 57

Gotlieb, Phyllis Fay (Bloom)
1926- . . . . **CLC 18**
See also CA 13-16R; CANR 7; DLB 88

Gottesman, S. D.
See Kornbluth, C(yril) M.; Pohl, Frederik

Gottfried von Strassburg
fl. c. 1210- . . . . **CMLC 10**

Gottschalk, Laura Riding
See Jackson, Laura (Riding)

Gould, Lois . . . . **CLC 4, 10**
See also CA 77-80; CANR 29; MTCW

Gourmont, Remy de 1858-1915 . . . . **TCLC 17**
See also CA 109

Govier, Katherine 1948- . . . . **CLC 51**
See also CA 101; CANR 18, 40

Goyen, (Charles) William
1915-1983 . . . . **CLC 5, 8, 14, 40**
See also AITN 2; CA 5-8R; 110; CANR 6; DLB 2; DLBY 83

Goytisolo, Juan 1931- . . . . **CLC 5, 10, 23**
See also CA 85-88; CANR 32; HW; MTCW

Gozzi, (Conte) Carlo 1720-1806 . . **NCLC 23**

Grabbe, Christian Dietrich
1801-1836 . . . . **NCLC 2**
See also DLB 133

Grace, Patricia 1937- . . . . **CLC 56**

Gracian y Morales, Baltasar
1601-1658 . . . . **LC 15**

Gracq, Julien . . . . **CLC 11, 48**
See also Poirier, Louis
See also DLB 83

Grade, Chaim 1910-1982 . . . . **CLC 10**
See also CA 93-96; 107

Graduate of Oxford, A
See Ruskin, John

Graham, John
See Phillips, David Graham

Graham, Jorie 1951- . . . . **CLC 48**
See also CA 111; DLB 120

Graham, R(obert) B(ontine) Cunninghame
See Cunninghame Graham, R(obert) B(ontine)
See also DLB 98

Graham, Robert
See Haldeman, Joe (William)

Graham, Tom
See Lewis, (Harry) Sinclair

Graham, W(illiam) S(ydney)
1918-1986 . . . . **CLC 29**
See also CA 73-76; 118; DLB 20

Graham, Winston (Mawdsley)
1910- . . . . **CLC 23**
See also CA 49-52; CANR 2, 22; DLB 77

Grant, Skeeter
See Spiegelman, Art

Guillen (y Batista), Nicolas (Cristobal) 1902-1989 . . . . . **CLC 48, 79**
See also BLC 2; BW; CA 116; 125; 129; HW

Guillevic, (Eugene) 1907- . . . . . **CLC 33**
See also CA 93-96

Guillois
See Desnos, Robert

Guiney, Louise Imogen 1861-1920 . . . . . **TCLC 41**
See also DLB 54

Guiraldes, Ricardo (Guillermo) 1886-1927 . . . . . **TCLC 39**
See also CA 131; HW; MTCW

Gunn, Bill . . . . . **CLC 5**
See also Gunn, William Harrison
See also DLB 38

Gunn, Thom(son William) 1929- . . . . . **CLC 3, 6, 18, 32**
See also CA 17-20R; CANR 9, 33; CDBLB 1960 to Present; DLB 27; MTCW

Gunn, William Harrison 1934(?)-1989
See Gunn, Bill
See also AITN 1; BW; CA 13-16R; 128; CANR 12, 25

Gunnars, Kristjana 1948- . . . . . **CLC 69**
See also CA 113; DLB 60

Gurganus, Allan 1947- . . . . . **CLC 70**
See also BEST 90:1; CA 135

Gurney, A(lbert) R(amsdell), Jr. 1930- . . . . . **CLC 32, 50, 54**
See also CA 77-80; CANR 32

Gurney, Ivor (Bertie) 1890-1937 . . . **TCLC 33**

Gurney, Peter
See Gurney, A(lbert) R(amsdell), Jr.

Gustafson, Ralph (Barker) 1909- . . . . **CLC 36**
See also CA 21-24R; CANR 8; DLB 88

Gut, Gom
See Simenon, Georges (Jacques Christian)

Guthrie, A(lfred) B(ertram), Jr. 1901-1991 . . . . . **CLC 23**
See also CA 57-60; 134; CANR 24; DLB 6; SATA 62; SATA-Obit 67

Guthrie, Isobel
See Grieve, C(hristopher) M(urray)

Guthrie, Woodrow Wilson 1912-1967
See Guthrie, Woody
See also CA 113; 93-96

Guthrie, Woody . . . . . **CLC 35**
See also Guthrie, Woodrow Wilson

Guy, Rosa (Cuthbert) 1928- . . . . . **CLC 26**
See also AAYA 4; BW; CA 17-20R; CANR 14, 34; CLR 13; DLB 33; JRDA; MAICYA; SATA 14, 62

Gwendolyn
See Bennett, (Enoch) Arnold

H. D. . . . . . **CLC 3, 8, 14, 31, 34, 73; PC 5**
See also Doolittle, Hilda

Haavikko, Paavo Juhani 1931- . . . . . **CLC 18, 34**
See also CA 106

Habbema, Koos
See Heijermans, Herman

Hacker, Marilyn 1942- . . . . **CLC 5, 9, 23, 72**
See also CA 77-80; DLB 120

Haggard, H(enry) Rider 1856-1925 . . . . . **TCLC 11**
See also CA 108; DLB 70; SATA 16

Haig, Fenil
See Ford, Ford Madox

Haig-Brown, Roderick (Langmere) 1908-1976 . . . . . **CLC 21**
See also CA 5-8R; 69-72; CANR 4, 38; CLR 31; DLB 88; MAICYA; SATA 12

Hailey, Arthur 1920- . . . . . **CLC 5**
See also AITN 2; BEST 90:3; CA 1-4R; CANR 2, 36; DLB 88; DLBY 82; MTCW

Hailey, Elizabeth Forsythe 1938- . . . **CLC 40**
See also CA 93-96; CAAS 1; CANR 15

Haines, John (Meade) 1924- . . . . . **CLC 58**
See also CA 17-20R; CANR 13, 34; DLB 5

Haldeman, Joe (William) 1943- . . . . . **CLC 61**
See also CA 53-56; CANR 6; DLB 8

Haley, Alex(ander Murray Palmer) 1921-1992 . . . . . **CLC 8, 12, 76**
See also BLC 2; BW; CA 77-80; 136; DA; DLB 38; MTCW

Haliburton, Thomas Chandler 1796-1865 . . . . . **NCLC 15**
See also DLB 11, 99

Hall, Donald (Andrew, Jr.) 1928- . . . . . **CLC 1, 13, 37, 59**
See also CA 5-8R; CAAS 7; CANR 2; DLB 5; SATA 23

Hall, Frederic Sauser
See Sauser-Hall, Frederic

Hall, James
See Kuttner, Henry

Hall, James Norman 1887-1951 . . . **TCLC 23**
See also CA 123; SATA 21

Hall, (Marguerite) Radclyffe 1886(?)-1943 . . . . . **TCLC 12**
See also CA 110

Hall, Rodney 1935- . . . . . **CLC 51**
See also CA 109

Halliday, Michael
See Creasey, John

Halpern, Daniel 1945- . . . . . **CLC 14**
See also CA 33-36R

Hamburger, Michael (Peter Leopold) 1924- . . . . . **CLC 5, 14**
See also CA 5-8R; CAAS 4; CANR 2; DLB 27

Hamill, Pete 1935- . . . . . **CLC 10**
See also CA 25-28R; CANR 18

Hamilton, Clive
See Lewis, C(live) S(taples)

Hamilton, Edmond 1904-1977 . . . . . **CLC 1**
See also CA 1-4R; CANR 3; DLB 8

Hamilton, Eugene (Jacob) Lee
See Lee-Hamilton, Eugene (Jacob)

Hamilton, Franklin
See Silverberg, Robert

Hamilton, Gail
See Corcoran, Barbara

Hamilton, Mollie
See Kaye, M(ary) M(argaret)

Hamilton, (Anthony Walter) Patrick 1904-1962 . . . . . **CLC 51**
See also CA 113; DLB 10

Hamilton, Virginia 1936- . . . . . **CLC 26**
See also AAYA 2; BW; CA 25-28R; CANR 20, 37; CLR 1, 11; DLB 33, 52; JRDA; MAICYA; MTCW; SATA 4, 56

Hammett, (Samuel) Dashiell 1894-1961 . . . . . **CLC 3, 5, 10, 19, 47**
See also AITN 1; CA 81-84; CANR 42; CDALB 1929-1941; DLBD 6; MTCW

Hammon, Jupiter 1711(?)-1800(?) . . **NCLC 5**
See also BLC 2; DLB 31, 50

Hammond, Keith
See Kuttner, Henry

Hamner, Earl (Henry), Jr. 1923- . . . **CLC 12**
See also AITN 2; CA 73-76; DLB 6

Hampton, Christopher (James) 1946- . . . . . **CLC 4**
See also CA 25-28R; DLB 13; MTCW

Hamsun, Knut . . . . . **TCLC 2, 14, 49**
See also Pedersen, Knut

Handke, Peter 1942- . . **CLC 5, 8, 10, 15, 38**
See also CA 77-80; CANR 33; DLB 85, 124; MTCW

Hanley, James 1901-1985 . . . **CLC 3, 5, 8, 13**
See also CA 73-76; 117; CANR 36; MTCW

Hannah, Barry 1942- . . . . . **CLC 23, 38**
See also CA 108; 110; CANR 43; DLB 6; MTCW

Hannon, Ezra
See Hunter, Evan

Hansberry, Lorraine (Vivian) 1930-1965 . . . . . **CLC 17, 62; DC 2**
See also BLC 2; BW; CA 109; 25-28R; CABS 3; CDALB 1941-1968; DA; DLB 7, 38; MTCW

Hansen, Joseph 1923- . . . . . **CLC 38**
See also CA 29-32R; CAAS 17; CANR 16

Hansen, Martin A. 1909-1955 . . . . . **TCLC 32**

Hanson, Kenneth O(stlin) 1922- . . . . **CLC 13**
See also CA 53-56; CANR 7

Hardwick, Elizabeth 1916- . . . . . **CLC 13**
See also CA 5-8R; CANR 3, 32; DLB 6; MTCW

Hardy, Thomas 1840-1928 . . . . . **TCLC 4, 10, 18, 32, 48; SSC 2**
See also CA 104; 123; CDBLB 1890-1914; DA; DLB 18, 19; MTCW; WLC

Hare, David 1947- . . . . . **CLC 29, 58**
See also CA 97-100; CANR 39; DLB 13; MTCW

Harford, Henry
See Hudson, W(illiam) H(enry)

Hargrave, Leonie
See Disch, Thomas M(ichael)

Harlan, Louis R(udolph) 1922- . . . . . **CLC 34**
See also CA 21-24R; CANR 25

Harling, Robert 1951(?)- . . . . . **CLC 53**

Harmon, William (Ruth) 1938- . . . . . **CLC 38**
See also CA 33-36R; CANR 14, 32, 35; SATA 65

Helforth, John
See Doolittle, Hilda

Hellenhofferu, Vojtech Kapristian z
See Hasek, Jaroslav (Matej Frantisek)

Heller, Joseph
1923- .... **CLC 1, 3, 5, 8, 11, 36, 63**
See also AITN 1; CA 5-8R; CABS 1; CANR 8, 42; DA; DLB 2, 28; DLBY 80; MTCW; WLC

Hellman, Lillian (Florence)
1906-1984 ...... **CLC 2, 4, 8, 14, 18, 34, 44, 52; DC 1**
See also AITN 1, 2; CA 13-16R; 112; CANR 33; DLB 7; DLBY 84; MTCW

Helprin, Mark 1947- ..... **CLC 7, 10, 22, 32**
See also CA 81-84; DLBY 85; MTCW

Helyar, Jane Penelope Josephine 1933-
See Poole, Josephine
See also CA 21-24R; CANR 10, 26

Hemans, Felicia 1793-1835 ...... **NCLC 29**
See also DLB 96

Hemingway, Ernest (Miller)
1899-1961 .... **CLC 1, 3, 6, 8, 10, 13, 19, 30, 34, 39, 41, 44, 50, 61, 80; SSC 1**
See also CA 77-80; CANR 34; CDALB 1917-1929; DA; DLB 4, 9, 102; DLBD 1; DLBY 81, 87; MTCW; WLC

Hempel, Amy 1951- .... **CLC 39**
See also CA 118; 137

Henderson, F. C.
See Mencken, H(enry) L(ouis)

Henderson, Sylvia
See Ashton-Warner, Sylvia (Constance)

Henley, Beth .... **CLC 23**
See also Henley, Elizabeth Becker
See also CABS 3; DLBY 86

Henley, Elizabeth Becker 1952-
See Henley, Beth
See also CA 107; CANR 32; MTCW

Henley, William Ernest
1849-1903 .... **TCLC 8**
See also CA 105; DLB 19

Hennissart, Martha
See Lathen, Emma
See also CA 85-88

Henry, O.. .... **TCLC 1, 19; SSC 5**
See also Porter, William Sydney
See also WLC

Henryson, Robert 1430(?)-1506(?).... **LC 20**

Henry VIII 1491-1547............. **LC 10**

Henschke, Alfred
See Klabund

Hentoff, Nat(han Irving) 1925- ..... **CLC 26**
See also AAYA 4; CA 1-4R; CAAS 6; CANR 5, 25; CLR 1; JRDA; MAICYA; SATA 27, 42, 69

Heppenstall, (John) Rayner
1911-1981 .... **CLC 10**
See also CA 1-4R; 103; CANR 29

Herbert, Frank (Patrick)
1920-1986 .... **CLC 12, 23, 35, 44**
See also CA 53-56; 118; CANR 5, 43; DLB 8; MTCW; SATA 9, 37, 47

Herbert, George 1593-1633 .... **LC 24; PC 4**
See also CDBLB Before 1660; DLB 126

Herbert, Zbigniew 1924- .... **CLC 9, 43**
See also CA 89-92; CANR 36; MTCW

Herbst, Josephine (Frey)
1897-1969 .... **CLC 34**
See also CA 5-8R; 25-28R; DLB 9

Hergesheimer, Joseph
1880-1954 .... **TCLC 11**
See also CA 109; DLB 102, 9

Herlihy, James Leo 1927- .... **CLC 6**
See also CA 1-4R; CANR 2

Hermogenes fl. c. 175- .... **CMLC 6**

Hernandez, Jose 1834-1886...... **NCLC 17**

Herrick, Robert 1591-1674 .... **LC 13**
See also DA; DLB 126

Herring, Guilles
See Somerville, Edith

Herriot, James 1916- .... **CLC 12**
See also Wight, James Alfred
See also AAYA 1; CANR 40

Herrmann, Dorothy 1941- .... **CLC 44**
See also CA 107

Herrmann, Taffy
See Herrmann, Dorothy

Hersey, John (Richard)
1914-1993 .... **CLC 1, 2, 7, 9, 40**
See also CA 17-20R; 140; CANR 33; DLB 6; MTCW; SATA 25

Herzen, Aleksandr Ivanovich
1812-1870 .... **NCLC 10**

Herzl, Theodor 1860-1904........ **TCLC 36**

Herzog, Werner 1942- .... **CLC 16**
See also CA 89-92

Hesiod c. 8th cent. B.C.- .... **CMLC 5**

Hesse, Hermann
1877-1962 .... **CLC 1, 2, 3, 6, 11, 17, 25, 69; SSC 9**
See also CA 17-18; CAP 2; DA; DLB 66; MTCW; SATA 50; WLC

Hewes, Cady
See De Voto, Bernard (Augustine)

Heyen, William 1940- .... **CLC 13, 18**
See also CA 33-36R; CAAS 9; DLB 5

Heyerdahl, Thor 1914-............ **CLC 26**
See also CA 5-8R; CANR 5, 22; MTCW; SATA 2, 52

Heym, Georg (Theodor Franz Arthur)
1887-1912 .... **TCLC 9**
See also CA 106

Heym, Stefan 1913- .... **CLC 41**
See also CA 9-12R; CANR 4; DLB 69

Heyse, Paul (Johann Ludwig von)
1830-1914 .... **TCLC 8**
See also CA 104; DLB 129

Hibbert, Eleanor Alice Burford
1906-1993 .... **CLC 7**
See also BEST 90:4; CA 17-20R; 140; CANR 9, 28; SATA 2; SATA-Obit 74

Higgins, George V(incent)
1939- .... **CLC 4, 7, 10, 18**
See also CA 77-80; CAAS 5; CANR 17; DLB 2; DLBY 81; MTCW

Higginson, Thomas Wentworth
1823-1911 .... **TCLC 36**
See also DLB 1, 64

Highet, Helen
See MacInnes, Helen (Clark)

Highsmith, (Mary) Patricia
1921- .... **CLC 2, 4, 14, 42**
See also CA 1-4R; CANR 1, 20; MTCW

Highwater, Jamake (Mamake)
1942(?)- .... **CLC 12**
See also AAYA 7; CA 65-68; CAAS 7; CANR 10, 34; CLR 17; DLB 52; DLBY 85; JRDA; MAICYA; SATA 30, 32, 69

Hijuelos, Oscar 1951- .... **CLC 65**
See also BEST 90:1; CA 123; HW

Hikmet, Nazim 1902(?)-1963....... **CLC 40**
See also CA 141; 93-96

Hildesheimer, Wolfgang
1916-1991 .... **CLC 49**
See also CA 101; 135; DLB 69, 124

Hill, Geoffrey (William)
1932- .... **CLC 5, 8, 18, 45**
See also CA 81-84; CANR 21; CDBLB 1960 to Present; DLB 40; MTCW

Hill, George Roy 1921- .... **CLC 26**
See also CA 110; 122

Hill, John
See Koontz, Dean R(ay)

Hill, Susan (Elizabeth) 1942- .... **CLC 4**
See also CA 33-36R; CANR 29; DLB 14; MTCW

Hillerman, Tony 1925-............ **CLC 62**
See also AAYA 6; BEST 89:1; CA 29-32R; CANR 21, 42; SATA 6

Hillesum, Etty 1914-1943 .... **TCLC 49**
See also CA 137

Hilliard, Noel (Harvey) 1929-...... **CLC 15**
See also CA 9-12R; CANR 7

Hillis, Rick 1956-................ **CLC 66**
See also CA 134

Hilton, James 1900-1954......... **TCLC 21**
See also CA 108; DLB 34, 77; SATA 34

Himes, Chester (Bomar)
1909-1984 .... **CLC 2, 4, 7, 18, 58**
See also BLC 2; BW; CA 25-28R; 114; CANR 22; DLB 2, 76; MTCW

Hinde, Thomas .... **CLC 6, 11**
See also Chitty, Thomas Willes

Hindin, Nathan
See Bloch, Robert (Albert)

Hine, (William) Daryl 1936- .... **CLC 15**
See also CA 1-4R; CAAS 15; CANR 1, 20; DLB 60

Hinkson, Katharine Tynan
See Tynan, Katharine

Hinton, S(usan) E(loise) 1950- ..... **CLC 30**
See also AAYA 2; CA 81-84; CANR 32; CLR 3, 23; DA; JRDA; MAICYA; MTCW; SATA 19, 58

Hippius, Zinaida .... **TCLC 9**
See also Gippius, Zinaida (Nikolayevna)

Hiraoka, Kimitake 1925-1970
See Mishima, Yukio
See also CA 97-100; 29-32R; MTCW

Hirsch, E(ric) D(onald), Jr. 1928-... **CLC 79**
See also CA 25-28R; CANR 27; DLB 67; MTCW

Hirsch, Edward 1950- .... **CLC 31, 50**
See also CA 104; CANR 20, 42; DLB 120

Hitchcock, Alfred (Joseph) 1899-1980 .... **CLC 16**
See also CA 97-100; SATA 24, 27

Hoagland, Edward 1932- .... **CLC 28**
See also CA 1-4R; CANR 2, 31; DLB 6; SATA 51

Hoban, Russell (Conwell) 1925- .. **CLC 7, 25**
See also CA 5-8R; CANR 23, 37; CLR 3; DLB 52; MAICYA; MTCW; SATA 1, 40

Hobbs, Perry
See Blackmur, R(ichard) P(almer)

Hobson, Laura Z(ametkin) 1900-1986 .... **CLC 7, 25**
See also CA 17-20R; 118; DLB 28; SATA 52

Hochhuth, Rolf 1931-........ **CLC 4, 11, 18**
See also CA 5-8R; CANR 33; DLB 124; MTCW

Hochman, Sandra 1936-.......... **CLC 3, 8**
See also CA 5-8R; DLB 5

Hochwaelder, Fritz 1911-1986...... **CLC 36**
See also Hochwalder, Fritz
See also CA 29-32R; 120; CANR 42; MTCW

Hochwalder, Fritz................. **CLC 36**
See also Hochwaelder, Fritz

Hocking, Mary (Eunice) 1921- ..... **CLC 13**
See also CA 101; CANR 18, 40

Hodgins, Jack 1938-.............. **CLC 23**
See also CA 93-96; DLB 60

Hodgson, William Hope 1877(?)-1918 .... **TCLC 13**
See also CA 111; DLB 70

Hoffman, Alice 1952-............. **CLC 51**
See also CA 77-80; CANR 34; MTCW

Hoffman, Daniel (Gerard) 1923- .... **CLC 6, 13, 23**
See also CA 1-4R; CANR 4; DLB 5

Hoffman, Stanley 1944-............ **CLC 5**
See also CA 77-80

Hoffman, William M(oses) 1939- ... **CLC 40**
See also CA 57-60; CANR 11

Hoffmann, E(rnst) T(heodor) A(madeus) 1776-1822 .... **NCLC 2; SSC 13**
See also DLB 90; SATA 27

Hofmann, Gert 1931-............. **CLC 54**
See also CA 128

Hofmannsthal, Hugo von 1874-1929 .... **TCLC 11**
See also CA 106; DLB 81, 118

Hogan, Linda 1947- .... **CLC 73**
See also CA 120

Hogarth, Charles
See Creasey, John

Hogg, James 1770-1835.......... **NCLC 4**
See also DLB 93, 116

Holbach, Paul Henri Thiry Baron 1723-1789 .... **LC 14**

Holberg, Ludvig 1684-1754 .... **LC 6**

Holden, Ursula 1921-............. **CLC 18**
See also CA 101; CAAS 8; CANR 22

Holderlin, (Johann Christian) Friedrich 1770-1843 .... **NCLC 16; PC 4**

Holdstock, Robert
See Holdstock, Robert P.

Holdstock, Robert P. 1948-........ **CLC 39**
See also CA 131

Holland, Isabelle 1920- .... **CLC 21**
See also CA 21-24R; CANR 10, 25; JRDA; MAICYA; SATA 8, 70

Holland, Marcus
See Caldwell, (Janet Miriam) Taylor (Holland)

Hollander, John 1929-...... **CLC 2, 5, 8, 14**
See also CA 1-4R; CANR 1; DLB 5; SATA 13

Hollander, Paul
See Silverberg, Robert

Holleran, Andrew 1943(?)-......... **CLC 38**

Hollinghurst, Alan 1954-.......... **CLC 55**
See also CA 114

Hollis, Jim
See Summers, Hollis (Spurgeon, Jr.)

Holmes, John
See Souster, (Holmes) Raymond

Holmes, John Clellon 1926-1988.... **CLC 56**
See also CA 9-12R; 125; CANR 4; DLB 16

Holmes, Oliver Wendell 1809-1894 .... **NCLC 14**
See also CDALB 1640-1865; DLB 1; SATA 34

Holmes, Raymond
See Souster, (Holmes) Raymond

Holt, Victoria
See Hibbert, Eleanor Alice Burford

Holub, Miroslav 1923-............. **CLC 4**
See also CA 21-24R; CANR 10

Homer c. 8th cent. B.C.- .... **CMLC 1**
See also DA

Honig, Edwin 1919-.............. **CLC 33**
See also CA 5-8R; CAAS 8; CANR 4; DLB 5

Hood, Hugh (John Blagdon) 1928- .... **CLC 15, 28**
See also CA 49-52; CAAS 17; CANR 1, 33; DLB 53

Hood, Thomas 1799-1845........ **NCLC 16**
See also DLB 96

Hooker, (Peter) Jeremy 1941-...... **CLC 43**
See also CA 77-80; CANR 22; DLB 40

Hope, A(lec) D(erwent) 1907- .... **CLC 3, 51**
See also CA 21-24R; CANR 33; MTCW

Hope, Brian
See Creasey, John

Hope, Christopher (David Tully) 1944- .... **CLC 52**
See also CA 106; SATA 62

Hopkins, Gerard Manley 1844-1889 .... **NCLC 17**
See also CDBLB 1890-1914; DA; DLB 35, 57; WLC

Hopkins, John (Richard) 1931-...... **CLC 4**
See also CA 85-88

Hopkins, Pauline Elizabeth 1859-1930 .... **TCLC 28**
See also BLC 2; CA 141; DLB 50

Hopley-Woolrich, Cornell George 1903-1968
See Woolrich, Cornell
See also CA 13-14; CAP 1

Horatio
See Proust, (Valentin-Louis-George-Eugene-) Marcel

Horgan, Paul 1903- .... **CLC 9, 53**
See also CA 13-16R; CANR 9, 35; DLB 102; DLBY 85; MTCW; SATA 13

Horn, Peter
See Kuttner, Henry

Hornem, Horace Esq.
See Byron, George Gordon (Noel)

Horovitz, Israel 1939- .... **CLC 56**
See also CA 33-36R; DLB 7

Horvath, Odon von
See Horvath, Oedoen von
See also DLB 85, 124

Horvath, Oedoen von 1901-1938... **TCLC 45**
See also Horvath, Odon von
See also CA 118

Horwitz, Julius 1920-1986......... **CLC 14**
See also CA 9-12R; 119; CANR 12

Hospital, Janette Turner 1942-..... **CLC 42**
See also CA 108

Hostos, E. M. de
See Hostos (y Bonilla), Eugenio Maria de

Hostos, Eugenio M. de
See Hostos (y Bonilla), Eugenio Maria de

Hostos, Eugenio Maria
See Hostos (y Bonilla), Eugenio Maria de

Hostos (y Bonilla), Eugenio Maria de 1839-1903 .... **TCLC 24**
See also CA 123; 131; HW

Houdini
See Lovecraft, H(oward) P(hillips)

Hougan, Carolyn 1943- .... **CLC 34**
See also CA 139

Household, Geoffrey (Edward West) 1900-1988 .... **CLC 11**
See also CA 77-80; 126; DLB 87; SATA 14, 59

Housman, A(lfred) E(dward) 1859-1936 .... **TCLC 1, 10; PC 2**
See also CA 104; 125; DA; DLB 19; MTCW

Housman, Laurence 1865-1959..... **TCLC 7**
See also CA 106; DLB 10; SATA 25

Howard, Elizabeth Jane 1923- ... **CLC 7, 29**
See also CA 5-8R; CANR 8

Howard, Maureen 1930- ..... **CLC 5, 14, 46**
See also CA 53-56; CANR 31; DLBY 83; MTCW

Howard, Richard 1929- ...... **CLC 7, 10, 47**
See also AITN 1; CA 85-88; CANR 25; DLB 5

Howard, Robert Ervin 1906-1936... **TCLC 8**
See also CA 105

Howard, Warren F.
See Pohl, Frederik

Johnson, Benj. F. of Boo
See Riley, James Whitcomb

Johnson, Benjamin F. of Boo
See Riley, James Whitcomb

Johnson, Charles (Richard) 1948- .... **CLC 7, 51, 65**
See also BLC 2; BW; CA 116; CAAS 18; CANR 42; DLB 33

Johnson, Denis 1949- .... **CLC 52**
See also CA 117; 121; DLB 120

Johnson, Diane 1934- .... **CLC 5, 13, 48**
See also CA 41-44R; CANR 17, 40; DLBY 80; MTCW

Johnson, Eyvind (Olof Verner) 1900-1976 .... **CLC 14**
See also CA 73-76; 69-72; CANR 34

Johnson, J. R.
See James, C(yril) L(ionel) R(obert)

Johnson, James Weldon 1871-1938 .... **TCLC 3, 19**
See also BLC 2; BW; CA 104; 125; CDALB 1917-1929; CLR 32; DLB 51; MTCW; SATA 31

Johnson, Joyce 1935- .... **CLC 58**
See also CA 125; 129

Johnson, Lionel (Pigot) 1867-1902 .... **TCLC 19**
See also CA 117; DLB 19

Johnson, Mel
See Malzberg, Barry N(athaniel)

Johnson, Pamela Hansford 1912-1981 .... **CLC 1, 7, 27**
See also CA 1-4R; 104; CANR 2, 28; DLB 15; MTCW

Johnson, Samuel 1709-1784 .... **LC 15**
See also CDBLB 1660-1789; DA; DLB 39, 95, 104; WLC

Johnson, Uwe 1934-1984 .... **CLC 5, 10, 15, 40**
See also CA 1-4R; 112; CANR 1, 39; DLB 75; MTCW

Johnston, George (Benson) 1913- ... **CLC 51**
See also CA 1-4R; CANR 5, 20; DLB 88

Johnston, Jennifer 1930- .... **CLC 7**
See also CA 85-88; DLB 14

Jolley, (Monica) Elizabeth 1923- ... **CLC 46**
See also CA 127; CAAS 13

Jones, Arthur Llewellyn 1863-1947
See Machen, Arthur
See also CA 104

Jones, D(ouglas) G(ordon) 1929- .... **CLC 10**
See also CA 29-32R; CANR 13; DLB 53

Jones, David (Michael) 1895-1974 .... **CLC 2, 4, 7, 13, 42**
See also CA 9-12R; 53-56; CANR 28; CDBLB 1945-1960; DLB 20, 100; MTCW

Jones, David Robert 1947-
See Bowie, David
See also CA 103

Jones, Diana Wynne 1934- .... **CLC 26**
See also CA 49-52; CANR 4, 26; CLR 23; JRDA; MAICYA; SAAS 7; SATA 9, 70

Jones, Edward P. 1950- .... **CLC 76**
See also CA 142

Jones, Gayl 1949- .... **CLC 6, 9**
See also BLC 2; BW; CA 77-80; CANR 27; DLB 33; MTCW

Jones, James 1921-1977 .... **CLC 1, 3, 10, 39**
See also AITN 1, 2; CA 1-4R; 69-72; CANR 6; DLB 2; MTCW

Jones, John J.
See Lovecraft, H(oward) P(hillips)

Jones, LeRoi .... **CLC 1, 2, 3, 5, 10, 14**
See also Baraka, Amiri

Jones, Louis B. .... **CLC 65**
See also CA 141

Jones, Madison (Percy, Jr.) 1925- ... **CLC 4**
See also CA 13-16R; CAAS 11; CANR 7

Jones, Mervyn 1922- .... **CLC 10, 52**
See also CA 45-48; CAAS 5; CANR 1; MTCW

Jones, Mick 1956(?)- .... **CLC 30**
See also Clash, The

Jones, Nettie (Pearl) 1941- .... **CLC 34**
See also CA 137

Jones, Preston 1936-1979 .... **CLC 10**
See also CA 73-76; 89-92; DLB 7

Jones, Robert F(rancis) 1934- .... **CLC 7**
See also CA 49-52; CANR 2

Jones, Rod 1953- .... **CLC 50**
See also CA 128

Jones, Terence Graham Parry 1942- .... **CLC 21**
See also Jones, Terry; Monty Python
See also CA 112; 116; CANR 35; SATA 51

Jones, Terry
See Jones, Terence Graham Parry
See also SATA 67

Jong, Erica 1942- .... **CLC 4, 6, 8, 18**
See also AITN 1; BEST 90:2; CA 73-76; CANR 26; DLB 2, 5, 28; MTCW

Jonson, Ben(jamin) 1572(?)-1637 ...... **LC 6**
See also CDBLB Before 1660; DA; DLB 62, 121; WLC

Jordan, June 1936- .... **CLC 5, 11, 23**
See also AAYA 2; BW; CA 33-36R; CANR 25; CLR 10; DLB 38; MAICYA; MTCW; SATA 4

Jordan, Pat(rick M.) 1941- .... **CLC 37**
See also CA 33-36R

Jorgensen, Ivar
See Ellison, Harlan

Jorgenson, Ivar
See Silverberg, Robert

Josipovici, Gabriel 1940- .... **CLC 6, 43**
See also CA 37-40R; CAAS 8; DLB 14

Joubert, Joseph 1754-1824 .... **NCLC 9**

Jouve, Pierre Jean 1887-1976 ...... **CLC 47**
See also CA 65-68

Joyce, James (Augustine Aloysius) 1882-1941 .... **TCLC 3, 8, 16, 35; SSC 3**
See also CA 104; 126; CDBLB 1914-1945; DA; DLB 10, 19, 36; MTCW; WLC

Jozsef, Attila 1905-1937 .... **TCLC 22**
See also CA 116

Juana Ines de la Cruz 1651(?)-1695 ... **LC 5**

Judd, Cyril
See Kornbluth, C(yril) M.; Pohl, Frederik

Julian of Norwich 1342(?)-1416(?) .... **LC 6**

Just, Ward (Swift) 1935- .... **CLC 4, 27**
See also CA 25-28R; CANR 32

Justice, Donald (Rodney) 1925- .. **CLC 6, 19**
See also CA 5-8R; CANR 26; DLBY 83

Juvenal c. 55-c. 127 .... **CMLC 8**

Juvenis
See Bourne, Randolph S(illiman)

Kacew, Romain 1914-1980
See Gary, Romain
See also CA 108; 102

Kadare, Ismail 1936- .... **CLC 52**

Kadohata, Cynthia .... **CLC 59**
See also CA 140

Kafka, Franz 1883-1924 .... **TCLC 2, 6, 13, 29, 47; SSC 5**
See also CA 105; 126; DA; DLB 81; MTCW; WLC

Kahn, Roger 1927- .... **CLC 30**
See also CA 25-28R; SATA 37

Kain, Saul
See Sassoon, Siegfried (Lorraine)

Kaiser, Georg 1878-1945 .... **TCLC 9**
See also CA 106; DLB 124

Kaletski, Alexander 1946- .... **CLC 39**
See also CA 118

Kalidasa fl. c. 400- .... **CMLC 9**

Kallman, Chester (Simon) 1921-1975 .... **CLC 2**
See also CA 45-48; 53-56; CANR 3

Kaminsky, Melvin 1926-
See Brooks, Mel
See also CA 65-68; CANR 16

Kaminsky, Stuart M(elvin) 1934- ... **CLC 59**
See also CA 73-76; CANR 29

Kane, Paul
See Simon, Paul

Kane, Wilson
See Bloch, Robert (Albert)

Kanin, Garson 1912- .... **CLC 22**
See also AITN 1; CA 5-8R; CANR 7; DLB 7

Kaniuk, Yoram 1930- .... **CLC 19**
See also CA 134

Kant, Immanuel 1724-1804 ...... **NCLC 27**
See also DLB 94

Kantor, MacKinlay 1904-1977 ...... **CLC 7**
See also CA 61-64; 73-76; DLB 9, 102

Kaplan, David Michael 1946- ...... **CLC 50**

Kaplan, James 1951- .... **CLC 59**
See also CA 135

Karageorge, Michael
See Anderson, Poul (William)

Karamzin, Nikolai Mikhailovich 1766-1826 .... **NCLC 3**

Karapanou, Margarita 1946- .... **CLC 13**
See also CA 101

Karinthy, Frigyes 1887-1938 ...... **TCLC 47**

Karl, Frederick R(obert) 1927- ..... **CLC 34**
See also CA 5-8R; CANR 3

Kastel, Warren
See Silverberg, Robert

Kataev, Evgeny Petrovich 1903-1942
See Petrov, Evgeny
See also CA 120

Kataphusin
See Ruskin, John

Katz, Steve 1935- .... **CLC 47**
See also CA 25-28R; CAAS 14; CANR 12; DLBY 83

Kauffman, Janet 1945- .... **CLC 42**
See also CA 117; CANR 43; DLBY 86

Kaufman, Bob (Garnell) 1925-1986 .... **CLC 49**
See also BW; CA 41-44R; 118; CANR 22; DLB 16, 41

Kaufman, George S. 1889-1961 ..... **CLC 38**
See also CA 108; 93-96; DLB 7

Kaufman, Sue .... **CLC 3, 8**
See also Barondess, Sue K(aufman)

Kavafis, Konstantinos Petrou 1863-1933
See Cavafy, C(onstantine) P(eter)
See also CA 104

Kavan, Anna 1901-1968 .... **CLC 5, 13**
See also CA 5-8R; CANR 6; MTCW

Kavanagh, Dan
See Barnes, Julian

Kavanagh, Patrick (Joseph) 1904-1967 .... **CLC 22**
See also CA 123; 25-28R; DLB 15, 20; MTCW

Kawabata, Yasunari 1899-1972 .... **CLC 2, 5, 9, 18**
See also CA 93-96; 33-36R

Kaye, M(ary) M(argaret) 1909- ..... **CLC 28**
See also CA 89-92; CANR 24; MTCW; SATA 62

Kaye, Mollie
See Kaye, M(ary) M(argaret)

Kaye-Smith, Sheila 1887-1956 ..... **TCLC 20**
See also CA 118; DLB 36

Kaymor, Patrice Maguilene
See Senghor, Leopold Sedar

Kazan, Elia 1909- .... **CLC 6, 16, 63**
See also CA 21-24R; CANR 32

Kazantzakis, Nikos 1883(?)-1957 .... **TCLC 2, 5, 33**
See also CA 105; 132; MTCW

Kazin, Alfred 1915- .... **CLC 34, 38**
See also CA 1-4R; CAAS 7; CANR 1; DLB 67

Keane, Mary Nesta (Skrine) 1904-
See Keane, Molly
See also CA 108; 114

Keane, Molly .... **CLC 31**
See also Keane, Mary Nesta (Skrine)

Keates, Jonathan 19(?)- .... **CLC 34**

Keaton, Buster 1895-1966 .... **CLC 20**

Keats, John 1795-1821 ...... **NCLC 8; PC 1**
See also CDBLB 1789-1832; DA; DLB 96, 110; WLC

Keene, Donald 1922- .... **CLC 34**
See also CA 1-4R; CANR 5

Keillor, Garrison .... **CLC 40**
See also Keillor, Gary (Edward)
See also AAYA 2; BEST 89:3; DLBY 87; SATA 58

Keillor, Gary (Edward) 1942-
See Keillor, Garrison
See also CA 111; 117; CANR 36; MTCW

Keith, Michael
See Hubbard, L(afayette) Ron(ald)

Kell, Joseph
See Wilson, John (Anthony) Burgess

Keller, Gottfried 1819-1890 .... **NCLC 2**
See also DLB 129

Kellerman, Jonathan 1949- .... **CLC 44**
See also BEST 90:1; CA 106; CANR 29

Kelley, William Melvin 1937- ...... **CLC 22**
See also BW; CA 77-80; CANR 27; DLB 33

Kellogg, Marjorie 1922- .... **CLC 2**
See also CA 81-84

Kellow, Kathleen
See Hibbert, Eleanor Alice Burford

Kelly, M(ilton) T(erry) 1947- .... **CLC 55**
See also CA 97-100; CANR 19, 43

Kelman, James 1946- .... **CLC 58**

Kemal, Yashar 1923- .... **CLC 14, 29**
See also CA 89-92

Kemble, Fanny 1809-1893 .... **NCLC 18**
See also DLB 32

Kemelman, Harry 1908- .... **CLC 2**
See also AITN 1; CA 9-12R; CANR 6; DLB 28

Kempe, Margery 1373(?)-1440(?) ..... **LC 6**

Kempis, Thomas a 1380-1471 .... **LC 11**

Kendall, Henry 1839-1882 .... **NCLC 12**

Keneally, Thomas (Michael) 1935- ...... **CLC 5, 8, 10, 14, 19, 27, 43**
See also CA 85-88; CANR 10; MTCW

Kennedy, Adrienne (Lita) 1931- .... **CLC 66**
See also BLC 2; BW; CA 103; CABS 3; CANR 26; DLB 38

Kennedy, John Pendleton 1795-1870 .... **NCLC 2**
See also DLB 3

Kennedy, Joseph Charles 1929- ...... **CLC 8**
See also Kennedy, X. J.
See also CA 1-4R; CANR 4, 30, 40; SATA 14

Kennedy, William 1928- ... **CLC 6, 28, 34, 53**
See also AAYA 1; CA 85-88; CANR 14, 31; DLBY 85; MTCW; SATA 57

Kennedy, X. J. .... **CLC 42**
See also Kennedy, Joseph Charles
See also CAAS 9; CLR 27; DLB 5

Kent, Kelvin
See Kuttner, Henry

Kenton, Maxwell
See Southern, Terry

Kenyon, Robert O.
See Kuttner, Henry

Kerouac, Jack ..... **CLC 1, 2, 3, 5, 14, 29, 61**
See also Kerouac, Jean-Louis Lebris de
See also CDALB 1941-1968; DLB 2, 16; DLBD 3

Kerouac, Jean-Louis Lebris de 1922-1969
See Kerouac, Jack
See also AITN 1; CA 5-8R; 25-28R; CANR 26; DA; MTCW; WLC

Kerr, Jean 1923- .... **CLC 22**
See also CA 5-8R; CANR 7

Kerr, M. E. .... **CLC 12, 35**
See also Meaker, Marijane (Agnes)
See also AAYA 2; CLR 29; SAAS 1

Kerr, Robert .... **CLC 55**

Kerrigan, (Thomas) Anthony 1918- .... **CLC 4, 6**
See also CA 49-52; CAAS 11; CANR 4

Kerry, Lois
See Duncan, Lois

Kesey, Ken (Elton) 1935- .... **CLC 1, 3, 6, 11, 46, 64**
See also CA 1-4R; CANR 22, 38; CDALB 1968-1988; DA; DLB 2, 16; MTCW; SATA 66; WLC

Kesselring, Joseph (Otto) 1902-1967 .... **CLC 45**

Kessler, Jascha (Frederick) 1929- .... **CLC 4**
See also CA 17-20R; CANR 8

Kettelkamp, Larry (Dale) 1933- .... **CLC 12**
See also CA 29-32R; CANR 16; SAAS 3; SATA 2

Keyber, Conny
See Fielding, Henry

Keyes, Daniel 1927- .... **CLC 80**
See also CA 17-20R; CANR 10, 26; DA; SATA 37

Khayyam, Omar 1048-1131 ...... **CMLC 11**

Kherdian, David 1931- .... **CLC 6, 9**
See also CA 21-24R; CAAS 2; CANR 39; CLR 24; JRDA; MAICYA; SATA 16, 74

Khlebnikov, Velimir .... **TCLC 20**
See also Khlebnikov, Viktor Vladimirovich

Khlebnikov, Viktor Vladimirovich 1885-1922
See Khlebnikov, Velimir
See also CA 117

Khodasevich, Vladislav (Felitsianovich) 1886-1939 .... **TCLC 15**
See also CA 115

Kielland, Alexander Lange 1849-1906 .... **TCLC 5**
See also CA 104

Kiely, Benedict 1919- .... **CLC 23, 43**
See also CA 1-4R; CANR 2; DLB 15

Kienzle, William X(avier) 1928- .... **CLC 25**
See also CA 93-96; CAAS 1; CANR 9, 31; MTCW

Kierkegaard, Soren 1813-1855 .... **NCLC 34**

Killens, John Oliver 1916-1987 ..... **CLC 10**
See also BW; CA 77-80; 123; CAAS 2; CANR 26; DLB 33

Killigrew, Anne 1660-1685 .... **LC 4**
See also DLB 131

Kim
See Simenon, Georges (Jacques Christian)

Kincaid, Jamaica 1949- .... **CLC 43, 68**
See also BLC 2; BW; CA 125

Larson, Charles R(aymond) 1938- . . . **CLC 31**
See also CA 53-56; CANR 4

Latham, Jean Lee 1902- . . . . **CLC 12**
See also AITN 1; CA 5-8R; CANR 7; MAICYA; SATA 2, 68

Latham, Mavis
See Clark, Mavis Thorpe

Lathen, Emma . . . . **CLC 2**
See also Hennissart, Martha; Latsis, Mary J(ane)

Lathrop, Francis
See Leiber, Fritz (Reuter, Jr.)

Latsis, Mary J(ane)
See Lathen, Emma
See also CA 85-88

Lattimore, Richmond (Alexander)
1906-1984 . . . . **CLC 3**
See also CA 1-4R; 112; CANR 1

Laughlin, James 1914- . . . . **CLC 49**
See also CA 21-24R; CANR 9; DLB 48

Laurence, (Jean) Margaret (Wemyss)
1926-1987 . . **CLC 3, 6, 13, 50, 62; SSC 7**
See also CA 5-8R; 121; CANR 33; DLB 53; MTCW; SATA 50

Laurent, Antoine 1952- . . . . **CLC 50**

Lauscher, Hermann
See Hesse, Hermann

Lautreamont, Comte de
1846-1870 . . . . **NCLC 12**

Laverty, Donald
See Blish, James (Benjamin)

Lavin, Mary 1912- . . . . . . **CLC 4, 18; SSC 4**
See also CA 9-12R; CANR 33; DLB 15; MTCW

Lavond, Paul Dennis
See Kornbluth, C(yril) M.; Pohl, Frederik

Lawler, Raymond Evenor 1922- . . . . **CLC 58**
See also CA 103

Lawrence, D(avid) H(erbert Richards)
1885-1930 . . . . **TCLC 2, 9, 16, 33, 48; SSC 4**
See also CA 104; 121; CDBLB 1914-1945; DA; DLB 10, 19, 36, 98; MTCW; WLC

Lawrence, T(homas) E(dward)
1888-1935 . . . . **TCLC 18**
See also Dale, Colin
See also CA 115

Lawrence of Arabia
See Lawrence, T(homas) E(dward)

Lawson, Henry (Archibald Hertzberg)
1867-1922 . . . . **TCLC 27**
See also CA 120

Lawton, Dennis
See Faust, Frederick (Schiller)

Laxness, Halldor . . . . **CLC 25**
See also Gudjonsson, Halldor Kiljan

Layamon fl. c. 1200- . . . . **CMLC 10**

Laye, Camara 1928-1980 . . . . **CLC 4, 38**
See also BLC 2; BW; CA 85-88; 97-100; CANR 25; MTCW

Layton, Irving (Peter) 1912- . . . . . **CLC 2, 15**
See also CA 1-4R; CANR 2, 33, 43; DLB 88; MTCW

Lazarus, Emma 1849-1887 . . . . **NCLC 8**

Lazarus, Felix
See Cable, George Washington

Lazarus, Henry
See Slavitt, David R(ytman)

Lea, Joan
See Neufeld, John (Arthur)

Leacock, Stephen (Butler)
1869-1944 . . . . **TCLC 2**
See also CA 104; 141; DLB 92

Lear, Edward 1812-1888 . . . . **NCLC 3**
See also CLR 1; DLB 32; MAICYA; SATA 18

Lear, Norman (Milton) 1922- . . . . . . **CLC 12**
See also CA 73-76

Leavis, F(rank) R(aymond)
1895-1978 . . . . **CLC 24**
See also CA 21-24R; 77-80; MTCW

Leavitt, David 1961- . . . . **CLC 34**
See also CA 116; 122; DLB 130

Leblanc, Maurice (Marie Emile)
1864-1941 . . . . **TCLC 49**
See also CA 110

Lebowitz, Fran(ces Ann)
1951(?)- . . . . **CLC 11, 36**
See also CA 81-84; CANR 14; MTCW

le Carre, John . . . . **CLC 3, 5, 9, 15, 28**
See also Cornwell, David (John Moore)
See also BEST 89:4; CDBLB 1960 to Present; DLB 87

Le Clezio, J(ean) M(arie) G(ustave)
1940- . . . . **CLC 31**
See also CA 116; 128; DLB 83

Leconte de Lisle, Charles-Marie-Rene
1818-1894 . . . . **NCLC 29**

Le Coq, Monsieur
See Simenon, Georges (Jacques Christian)

Leduc, Violette 1907-1972 . . . . **CLC 22**
See also CA 13-14; 33-36R; CAP 1

Ledwidge, Francis 1887(?)-1917 . . . **TCLC 23**
See also CA 123; DLB 20

Lee, Andrea 1953- . . . . **CLC 36**
See also BLC 2; BW; CA 125

Lee, Andrew
See Auchincloss, Louis (Stanton)

Lee, Don L. . . . . **CLC 2**
See also Madhubuti, Haki R.

Lee, George W(ashington)
1894-1976 . . . . **CLC 52**
See also BLC 2; BW; CA 125; DLB 51

Lee, (Nelle) Harper 1926- . . . . . . **CLC 12, 60**
See also CA 13-16R; CDALB 1941-1968; DA; DLB 6; MTCW; SATA 11; WLC

Lee, Julian
See Latham, Jean Lee

Lee, Larry
See Lee, Lawrence

Lee, Lawrence 1941-1990 . . . . **CLC 34**
See also CA 131; CANR 43

Lee, Manfred B(ennington)
1905-1971 . . . . **CLC 11**
See also Queen, Ellery
See also CA 1-4R; 29-32R; CANR 2

Lee, Stan 1922- . . . . **CLC 17**
See also AAYA 5; CA 108; 111

Lee, Tanith 1947- . . . . **CLC 46**
See also CA 37-40R; SATA 8

Lee, Vernon . . . . **TCLC 5**
See also Paget, Violet
See also DLB 57

Lee, William
See Burroughs, William S(eward)

Lee, Willy
See Burroughs, William S(eward)

Lee-Hamilton, Eugene (Jacob)
1845-1907 . . . . **TCLC 22**
See also CA 117

Leet, Judith 1935- . . . . **CLC 11**

Le Fanu, Joseph Sheridan
1814-1873 . . . . **NCLC 9**
See also DLB 21, 70

Leffland, Ella 1931- . . . . **CLC 19**
See also CA 29-32R; CANR 35; DLBY 84; SATA 65

Leger, Alexis
See Leger, (Marie-Rene Auguste) Alexis Saint-Leger

Leger, (Marie-Rene Auguste) Alexis Saint-Leger 1887-1975 . . . . **CLC 11**
See also Perse, St.-John
See also CA 13-16R; 61-64; CANR 43; MTCW

Leger, Saintleger
See Leger, (Marie-Rene Auguste) Alexis Saint-Leger

Le Guin, Ursula K(roeber)
1929- . . . . **CLC 8, 13, 22, 45, 71; SSC 12**
See also AAYA 9; AITN 1; CA 21-24R; CANR 9, 32; CDALB 1968-1988; CLR 3, 28; DLB 8, 52; JRDA; MAICYA; MTCW; SATA 4, 52

Lehmann, Rosamond (Nina)
1901-1990 . . . . **CLC 5**
See also CA 77-80; 131; CANR 8; DLB 15

Leiber, Fritz (Reuter, Jr.)
1910-1992 . . . . **CLC 25**
See also CA 45-48; 139; CANR 2, 40; DLB 8; MTCW; SATA 45; SATA-Obit 73

Leimbach, Martha 1963-
See Leimbach, Marti
See also CA 130

Leimbach, Marti . . . . **CLC 65**
See also Leimbach, Martha

Leino, Eino . . . . **TCLC 24**
See also Loennbohm, Armas Eino Leopold

Leiris, Michel (Julien) 1901-1990 . . . **CLC 61**
See also CA 119; 128; 132

Leithauser, Brad 1953- . . . . **CLC 27**
See also CA 107; CANR 27; DLB 120

Lelchuk, Alan 1938- . . . . **CLC 5**
See also CA 45-48; CANR 1

Lem, Stanislaw 1921- . . . . **CLC 8, 15, 40**
See also CA 105; CAAS 1; CANR 32; MTCW

Lemann, Nancy 1956- . . . . **CLC 39**
See also CA 118; 136

Lemonnier, (Antoine Louis) Camille
1844-1913 . . . . **TCLC 22**
See also CA 121

Lively, Penelope (Margaret) 1933- .... **CLC 32, 50**
See also CA 41-44R; CANR 29; CLR 7; DLB 14; JRDA; MAICYA; MTCW; SATA 7, 60

Livesay, Dorothy (Kathleen) 1909- .... **CLC 4, 15, 79**
See also AITN 2; CA 25-28R; CAAS 8; CANR 36; DLB 68; MTCW

Livy c. 59B.C.-c. 17 .... **CMLC 11**

Lizardi, Jose Joaquin Fernandez de 1776-1827 .... **NCLC 30**

Llewellyn, Richard .... **CLC 7**
See also Llewellyn Lloyd, Richard Dafydd Vivian
See also DLB 15

Llewellyn Lloyd, Richard Dafydd Vivian 1906-1983 .... **CLC 80**
See also Llewellyn, Richard
See also CA 53-56; 111; CANR 7; SATA 11, 37

Llosa, (Jorge) Mario (Pedro) Vargas
See Vargas Llosa, (Jorge) Mario (Pedro)

Lloyd Webber, Andrew 1948-
See Webber, Andrew Lloyd
See also AAYA 1; CA 116; SATA 56

Llull, Ramon c. 1235-c. 1316..... **CMLC 12**

Locke, Alain (Le Roy) 1886-1954 .... **TCLC 43**
See also BW; CA 106; 124; DLB 51

Locke, John 1632-1704 .... **LC 7**
See also DLB 101

Locke-Elliott, Sumner
See Elliott, Sumner Locke

Lockhart, John Gibson 1794-1854 .... **NCLC 6**
See also DLB 110, 116

Lodge, David (John) 1935-......... **CLC 36**
See also BEST 90:1; CA 17-20R; CANR 19; DLB 14; MTCW

Loennbohm, Armas Eino Leopold 1878-1926
See Leino, Eino
See also CA 123

Loewinsohn, Ron(ald William) 1937- .... **CLC 52**
See also CA 25-28R

Logan, Jake
See Smith, Martin Cruz

Logan, John (Burton) 1923-1987..... **CLC 5**
See also CA 77-80; 124; DLB 5

Lo Kuan-chung 1330(?)-1400(?)...... **LC 12**

Lombard, Nap
See Johnson, Pamela Hansford

London, Jack........ **TCLC 9, 15, 39; SSC 4**
See also London, John Griffith
See also AITN 2; CDALB 1865-1917; DLB 8, 12, 78; SATA 18; WLC

London, John Griffith 1876-1916
See London, Jack
See also CA 110; 119; DA; JRDA; MAICYA; MTCW

Long, Emmett
See Leonard, Elmore (John, Jr.)

Longbaugh, Harry
See Goldman, William (W.)

Longfellow, Henry Wadsworth 1807-1882 .... **NCLC 2**
See also CDALB 1640-1865; DA; DLB 1, 59; SATA 19

Longley, Michael 1939-........... **CLC 29**
See also CA 102; DLB 40

Longus fl. c. 2nd cent. -........... **CMLC 7**

Longway, A. Hugh
See Lang, Andrew

Lopate, Phillip 1943- .... **CLC 29**
See also CA 97-100; DLBY 80

Lopez Portillo (y Pacheco), Jose 1920- .... **CLC 46**
See also CA 129; HW

Lopez y Fuentes, Gregorio 1897(?)-1966 .... **CLC 32**
See also CA 131; HW

Lorca, Federico Garcia 1898-1936
See Garcia Lorca, Federico

Lord, Bette Bao 1938-............ **CLC 23**
See also BEST 90:3; CA 107; CANR 41; SATA 58

Lord Auch
See Bataille, Georges

Lord Byron
See Byron, George Gordon (Noel)

Lord Dunsany .... **TCLC 2**
See also Dunsany, Edward John Moreton Drax Plunkett

Lorde, Audre (Geraldine) 1934-1992 .... **CLC 18, 71**
See also BLC 2; BW; CA 25-28R; 142; CANR 16, 26; DLB 41; MTCW

Lord Jeffrey
See Jeffrey, Francis

Lorenzo, Heberto Padilla
See Padilla (Lorenzo), Heberto

Loris
See Hofmannsthal, Hugo von

Loti, Pierre .... **TCLC 11**
See also Viaud, (Louis Marie) Julien
See also DLB 123

Louie, David Wong 1954- .... **CLC 70**
See also CA 139

Louis, Father M.
See Merton, Thomas

Lovecraft, H(oward) P(hillips) 1890-1937 .... **TCLC 4, 22; SSC 3**
See also CA 104; 133; MTCW

Lovelace, Earl 1935-............. **CLC 51**
See also CA 77-80; CANR 41; DLB 125; MTCW

Lovelace, Richard 1618-1657........ **LC 24**
See also DLB 131

Lowell, Amy 1874-1925 .... **TCLC 1, 8**
See also CA 104; DLB 54

Lowell, James Russell 1819-1891 .. **NCLC 2**
See also CDALB 1640-1865; DLB 1, 11, 64, 79

Lowell, Robert (Traill Spence, Jr.) 1917-1977 ... **CLC 1, 2, 3, 4, 5, 8, 9, 11, 15, 37; PC 3**
See also CA 9-12R; 73-76; CABS 2; CANR 26; DA; DLB 5; MTCW; WLC

Lowndes, Marie Adelaide (Belloc) 1868-1947 .... **TCLC 12**
See also CA 107; DLB 70

Lowry, (Clarence) Malcolm 1909-1957 .... **TCLC 6, 40**
See also CA 105; 131; CDBLB 1945-1960; DLB 15; MTCW

Lowry, Mina Gertrude 1882-1966
See Loy, Mina
See also CA 113

Loxsmith, John
See Brunner, John (Kilian Houston)

Loy, Mina .... **CLC 28**
See also Lowry, Mina Gertrude
See also DLB 4, 54

Loyson-Bridet
See Schwob, (Mayer Andre) Marcel

Lucas, Craig 1951-................ **CLC 64**
See also CA 137

Lucas, George 1944-.............. **CLC 16**
See also AAYA 1; CA 77-80; CANR 30; SATA 56

Lucas, Hans
See Godard, Jean-Luc

Lucas, Victoria
See Plath, Sylvia

Ludlam, Charles 1943-1987 ..... **CLC 46, 50**
See also CA 85-88; 122

Ludlum, Robert 1927- .... **CLC 22, 43**
See also AAYA 10; BEST 89:1, 90:3; CA 33-36R; CANR 25, 41; DLBY 82; MTCW

Ludwig, Ken...................... **CLC 60**

Ludwig, Otto 1813-1865.......... **NCLC 4**
See also DLB 129

Lugones, Leopoldo 1874-1938 ..... **TCLC 15**
See also CA 116; 131; HW

Lu Hsun 1881-1936 .... **TCLC 3**

Lukacs, George .... **CLC 24**
See also Lukacs, Gyorgy (Szegeny von)

Lukacs, Gyorgy (Szegeny von) 1885-1971
See Lukacs, George
See also CA 101; 29-32R

Luke, Peter (Ambrose Cyprian) 1919- .... **CLC 38**
See also CA 81-84; DLB 13

Lunar, Dennis
See Mungo, Raymond

Lurie, Alison 1926-........ **CLC 4, 5, 18, 39**
See also CA 1-4R; CANR 2, 17; DLB 2; MTCW; SATA 46

Lustig, Arnost 1926-.............. **CLC 56**
See also AAYA 3; CA 69-72; SATA 56

Luther, Martin 1483-1546 .... **LC 9**

Luzi, Mario 1914-................ **CLC 13**
See also CA 61-64; CANR 9; DLB 128

Lynch, B. Suarez
See Bioy Casares, Adolfo; Borges, Jorge Luis

Lynch, David (K.) 1946-........... **CLC 66**
See also CA 124; 129

Lynch, James
See Andreyev, Leonid (Nikolaevich)

Lynch Davis, B.
See Bioy Casares, Adolfo; Borges, Jorge Luis

Lyndsay, SirDavid 1490-1555 .... **LC 20**

Lynn, Kenneth S(chuyler) 1923- .... **CLC 50**
See also CA 1-4R; CANR 3, 27

Lynx
See West, Rebecca

Lyons, Marcus
See Blish, James (Benjamin)

Lyre, Pinchbeck
See Sassoon, Siegfried (Lorraine)

Lytle, Andrew (Nelson) 1902- ...... **CLC 22**
See also CA 9-12R; DLB 6

Lyttelton, George 1709-1773 .... **LC 10**

Maas, Peter 1929- .... **CLC 29**
See also CA 93-96

Macaulay, Rose 1881-1958 ..... **TCLC 7, 44**
See also CA 104; DLB 36

Macaulay, Thomas Babington
1800-1859 .... **NCLC 42**
See also CDBLB 1832-1890; DLB 32, 55

MacBeth, George (Mann)
1932-1992 .... **CLC 2, 5, 9**
See also CA 25-28R; 136; DLB 40; MTCW; SATA 4; SATA-Obit 70

MacCaig, Norman (Alexander)
1910- .... **CLC 36**
See also CA 9-12R; CANR 3, 34; DLB 27

MacCarthy, (Sir Charles Otto) Desmond
1877-1952 .... **TCLC 36**

MacDiarmid, Hugh ..... **CLC 2, 4, 11, 19, 63**
See also Grieve, C(hristopher) M(urray)
See also CDBLB 1945-1960; DLB 20

MacDonald, Anson
See Heinlein, Robert A(nson)

Macdonald, Cynthia 1928- ...... **CLC 13, 19**
See also CA 49-52; CANR 4; DLB 105

MacDonald, George 1824-1905 ..... **TCLC 9**
See also CA 106; 137; DLB 18; MAICYA; SATA 33

Macdonald, John
See Millar, Kenneth

MacDonald, John D(ann)
1916-1986 .... **CLC 3, 27, 44**
See also CA 1-4R; 121; CANR 1, 19; DLB 8; DLBY 86; MTCW

Macdonald, John Ross
See Millar, Kenneth

Macdonald, Ross ..... **CLC 1, 2, 3, 14, 34, 41**
See also Millar, Kenneth
See also DLBD 6

MacDougal, John
See Blish, James (Benjamin)

MacEwen, Gwendolyn (Margaret)
1941-1987 .... **CLC 13, 55**
See also CA 9-12R; 124; CANR 7, 22; DLB 53; SATA 50, 55

Machado (y Ruiz), Antonio
1875-1939 .... **TCLC 3**
See also CA 104; DLB 108

Machado de Assis, Joaquim Maria
1839-1908 .... **TCLC 10**
See also BLC 2; CA 107

Machen, Arthur .... **TCLC 4**
See also Jones, Arthur Llewellyn
See also DLB 36

Machiavelli, Niccolo 1469-1527 ...... **LC 8**
See also DA

MacInnes, Colin 1914-1976 ...... **CLC 4, 23**
See also CA 69-72; 65-68; CANR 21; DLB 14; MTCW

MacInnes, Helen (Clark)
1907-1985 .... **CLC 27, 39**
See also CA 1-4R; 117; CANR 1, 28; DLB 87; MTCW; SATA 22, 44

Mackay, Mary 1855-1924
See Corelli, Marie
See also CA 118

Mackenzie, Compton (Edward Montague)
1883-1972 .... **CLC 18**
See also CA 21-22; 37-40R; CAP 2; DLB 34, 100

Mackenzie, Henry 1745-1831 .... **NCLC 41**
See also DLB 39

Mackintosh, Elizabeth 1896(?)-1952
See Tey, Josephine
See also CA 110

MacLaren, James
See Grieve, C(hristopher) M(urray)

Mac Laverty, Bernard 1942- .... **CLC 31**
See also CA 116; 118; CANR 43

MacLean, Alistair (Stuart)
1922-1987 .... **CLC 3, 13, 50, 63**
See also CA 57-60; 121; CANR 28; MTCW; SATA 23, 50

Maclean, Norman (Fitzroy) 1902-1990
See also CA 102; 132; SSC 13

MacLeish, Archibald
1892-1982 .... **CLC 3, 8, 14, 68**
See also CA 9-12R; 106; CANR 33; DLB 4, 7, 45; DLBY 82; MTCW

MacLennan, (John) Hugh
1907-1990 .... **CLC 2, 14**
See also CA 5-8R; 142; CANR 33; DLB 68; MTCW

MacLeod, Alistair 1936- .... **CLC 56**
See also CA 123; DLB 60

MacNeice, (Frederick) Louis
1907-1963 .... **CLC 1, 4, 10, 53**
See also CA 85-88; DLB 10, 20; MTCW

MacNeill, Dand
See Fraser, George MacDonald

Macpherson, (Jean) Jay 1931- ...... **CLC 14**
See also CA 5-8R; DLB 53

MacShane, Frank 1927- .... **CLC 39**
See also CA 9-12R; CANR 3, 33; DLB 111

Macumber, Mari
See Sandoz, Mari(e Susette)

Madach, Imre 1823-1864 .... **NCLC 19**

Madden, (Jerry) David 1933- .... **CLC 5, 15**
See also CA 1-4R; CAAS 3; CANR 4; DLB 6; MTCW

Maddern, Al(an)
See Ellison, Harlan

Madhubuti, Haki R.
1942- .... **CLC 6, 73; PC 5**
See also Lee, Don L.
See also BLC 2; BW; CA 73-76; CANR 24; DLB 5, 41; DLBD 8

Madow, Pauline (Reichberg) .... **CLC 1**
See also CA 9-12R

Maepenn, Hugh
See Kuttner, Henry

Maepenn, K. H.
See Kuttner, Henry

Maeterlinck, Maurice 1862-1949 ... **TCLC 3**
See also CA 104; 136; SATA 66

Maginn, William 1794-1842 .... **NCLC 8**
See also DLB 110

Mahapatra, Jayanta 1928- .... **CLC 33**
See also CA 73-76; CAAS 9; CANR 15, 33

Mahfouz, Naguib (Abdel Aziz Al-Sabilgi)
1911(?)-
See Mahfuz, Najib
See also BEST 89:2; CA 128; MTCW

Mahfuz, Najib .... **CLC 52, 55**
See also Mahfouz, Naguib (Abdel Aziz Al-Sabilgi)
See also DLBY 88

Mahon, Derek 1941- .... **CLC 27**
See also CA 113; 128; DLB 40

Mailer, Norman
1923- ...... **CLC 1, 2, 3, 4, 5, 8, 11, 14, 28, 39, 74**
See also AITN 2; CA 9-12R; CABS 1; CANR 28; CDALB 1968-1988; DA; DLB 2, 16, 28; DLBD 3; DLBY 80, 83; MTCW

Maillet, Antonine 1929- .... **CLC 54**
See also CA 115; 120; DLB 60

Mais, Roger 1905-1955 .... **TCLC 8**
See also BW; CA 105; 124; DLB 125; MTCW

Maitland, Sara (Louise) 1950- ...... **CLC 49**
See also CA 69-72; CANR 13

Major, Clarence 1936- .... **CLC 3, 19, 48**
See also BLC 2; BW; CA 21-24R; CAAS 6; CANR 13, 25; DLB 33

Major, Kevin (Gerald) 1949- .... **CLC 26**
See also CA 97-100; CANR 21, 38; CLR 11; DLB 60; JRDA; MAICYA; SATA 32

Maki, James
See Ozu, Yasujiro

Malabaila, Damiano
See Levi, Primo

Malamud, Bernard
1914-1986 ...... **CLC 1, 2, 3, 5, 8, 9, 11, 18, 27, 44, 78**
See also CA 5-8R; 118; CABS 1; CANR 28; CDALB 1941-1968; DA; DLB 2, 28; DLBY 80, 86; MTCW; WLC

Malcolm, Dan
See Silverberg, Robert

Malherbe, Francois de 1555-1628 ..... **LC 5**

Mallarme, Stephane
1842-1898 .... **NCLC 4, 41; PC 4**

Mallet-Joris, Francoise 1930- ...... **CLC 11**
See also CA 65-68; CANR 17; DLB 83

Malley, Ern
See McAuley, James Phillip

Mallowan, Agatha Christie
See Christie, Agatha (Mary Clarissa)

Maloff, Saul 1922- . . . . **CLC 5**
See also CA 33-36R

Malone, Louis
See MacNeice, (Frederick) Louis

Malone, Michael (Christopher)
1942- . . . . **CLC 43**
See also CA 77-80; CANR 14, 32

Malory, (Sir) Thomas
1410(?)-1471(?) . . . . **LC 11**
See also CDBLB Before 1660; DA; SATA 33, 59

Malouf, (George Joseph) David
1934- . . . . **CLC 28**
See also CA 124

Malraux, (Georges-)Andre
1901-1976 . . . . . . **CLC 1, 4, 9, 13, 15, 57**
See also CA 21-22; 69-72; CANR 34; CAP 2; DLB 72; MTCW

Malzberg, Barry N(athaniel) 1939- . . . **CLC 7**
See also CA 61-64; CAAS 4; CANR 16; DLB 8

Mamet, David (Alan)
1947- . . . . **CLC 9, 15, 34, 46**
See also AAYA 3; CA 81-84; CABS 3; CANR 15, 41; DLB 7; MTCW

Mamoulian, Rouben (Zachary)
1897-1987 . . . . **CLC 16**
See also CA 25-28R; 124

Mandelstam, Osip (Emilievich)
1891(?)-1938(?) . . . . **TCLC 2, 6**
See also CA 104

Mander, (Mary) Jane 1877-1949 . . . **TCLC 31**

Mandiargues, Andre Pieyre de . . . . **CLC 41**
See also Pieyre de Mandiargues, Andre
See also DLB 83

Mandrake, Ethel Belle
See Thurman, Wallace (Henry)

Mangan, James Clarence
1803-1849 . . . . **NCLC 27**

Maniere, J.-E.
See Giraudoux, (Hippolyte) Jean

Manley, (Mary) Delariviere
1672(?)-1724 . . . . **LC 1**
See also DLB 39, 80

Mann, Abel
See Creasey, John

Mann, (Luiz) Heinrich 1871-1950 . . . **TCLC 9**
See also CA 106; DLB 66

Mann, (Paul) Thomas
1875-1955 . . . . **TCLC 2, 8, 14, 21, 35, 44; SSC 5**
See also CA 104; 128; DA; DLB 66; MTCW; WLC

Manning, David
See Faust, Frederick (Schiller)

Manning, Frederic 1887(?)-1935 . . . **TCLC 25**
See also CA 124

Manning, Olivia 1915-1980 . . . . . . **CLC 5, 19**
See also CA 5-8R; 101; CANR 29; MTCW

Mano, D. Keith 1942- . . . . **CLC 2, 10**
See also CA 25-28R; CAAS 6; CANR 26; DLB 6

Mansfield, Katherine . . . **TCLC 2, 8, 39; SSC 9**
See also Beauchamp, Kathleen Mansfield
See also WLC

Manso, Peter 1940- . . . . **CLC 39**
See also CA 29-32R

Mantecon, Juan Jimenez
See Jimenez (Mantecon), Juan Ramon

Manton, Peter
See Creasey, John

Man Without a Spleen, A
See Chekhov, Anton (Pavlovich)

Manzoni, Alessandro 1785-1873 . . **NCLC 29**

Mapu, Abraham (ben Jekutiel)
1808-1867 . . . . **NCLC 18**

Mara, Sally
See Queneau, Raymond

Marat, Jean Paul 1743-1793 . . . . **LC 10**

Marcel, Gabriel Honore
1889-1973 . . . . **CLC 15**
See also CA 102; 45-48; MTCW

Marchbanks, Samuel
See Davies, (William) Robertson

Marchi, Giacomo
See Bassani, Giorgio

Margulies, Donald . . . . **CLC 76**

Marie de France c. 12th cent. - . . . . **CMLC 8**

Marie de l'Incarnation 1599-1672 . . . . **LC 10**

Mariner, Scott
See Pohl, Frederik

Marinetti, Filippo Tommaso
1876-1944 . . . . **TCLC 10**
See also CA 107; DLB 114

Marivaux, Pierre Carlet de Chamblain de
1688-1763 . . . . **LC 4**

Markandaya, Kamala . . . . **CLC 8, 38**
See also Taylor, Kamala (Purnaiya)

Markfield, Wallace 1926- . . . . **CLC 8**
See also CA 69-72; CAAS 3; DLB 2, 28

Markham, Edwin 1852-1940 . . . . . . **TCLC 47**
See also DLB 54

Markham, Robert
See Amis, Kingsley (William)

Marks, J
See Highwater, Jamake (Mamake)

Marks-Highwater, J
See Highwater, Jamake (Mamake)

Markson, David M(errill) 1927- . . . . **CLC 67**
See also CA 49-52; CANR 1

Marley, Bob . . . . **CLC 17**
See also Marley, Robert Nesta

Marley, Robert Nesta 1945-1981
See Marley, Bob
See also CA 107; 103

Marlowe, Christopher
1564-1593 . . . . **LC 22; DC 1**
See also CDBLB Before 1660; DA; DLB 62; WLC

Marmontel, Jean-Francois
1723-1799 . . . . **LC 2**

Marquand, John P(hillips)
1893-1960 . . . . **CLC 2, 10**
See also CA 85-88; DLB 9, 102

Marquez, Gabriel (Jose) Garcia . . . . . . **CLC 68**
See also Garcia Marquez, Gabriel (Jose)

Marquis, Don(ald Robert Perry)
1878-1937 . . . . **TCLC 7**
See also CA 104; DLB 11, 25

Marric, J. J.
See Creasey, John

Marrow, Bernard
See Moore, Brian

Marryat, Frederick 1792-1848 . . . . **NCLC 3**
See also DLB 21

Marsden, James
See Creasey, John

Marsh, (Edith) Ngaio
1899-1982 . . . . **CLC 7, 53**
See also CA 9-12R; CANR 6; DLB 77; MTCW

Marshall, Garry 1934- . . . . **CLC 17**
See also AAYA 3; CA 111; SATA 60

Marshall, Paule 1929- . . **CLC 27, 72; SSC 3**
See also BLC 3; BW; CA 77-80; CANR 25; DLB 33; MTCW

Marsten, Richard
See Hunter, Evan

Martha, Henry
See Harris, Mark

Martin, Ken
See Hubbard, L(afayette) Ron(ald)

Martin, Richard
See Creasey, John

Martin, Steve 1945- . . . . **CLC 30**
See also CA 97-100; CANR 30; MTCW

Martin, Violet Florence
1862-1915 . . . . **TCLC 51**

Martin, Webber
See Silverberg, Robert

Martindale, Patrick Victor
See White, Patrick (Victor Martindale)

Martin du Gard, Roger
1881-1958 . . . . **TCLC 24**
See also CA 118; DLB 65

Martineau, Harriet 1802-1876 . . . . **NCLC 26**
See also DLB 21, 55; YABC 2

Martines, Julia
See O'Faolain, Julia

Martinez, Jacinto Benavente y
See Benavente (y Martinez), Jacinto

Martinez Ruiz, Jose 1873-1967
See Azorin; Ruiz, Jose Martinez
See also CA 93-96; HW

Martinez Sierra, Gregorio
1881-1947 . . . . **TCLC 6**
See also CA 115

Martinez Sierra, Maria (de la O'LeJarraga)
1874-1974 . . . . **TCLC 6**
See also CA 115

Martinsen, Martin
See Follett, Ken(neth Martin)

Martinson, Harry (Edmund)
1904-1978 . . . . **CLC 14**
See also CA 77-80; CANR 34

McGinniss, Joe 1942- .... **CLC 32**
See also AITN 2; BEST 89:2; CA 25-28R; CANR 26

McGivern, Maureen Daly
See Daly, Maureen

McGrath, Patrick 1950- .... **CLC 55**
See also CA 136

McGrath, Thomas (Matthew)
1916-1990 .... **CLC 28, 59**
See also CA 9-12R; 132; CANR 6, 33; MTCW; SATA 41; SATA-Obit 66

McGuane, Thomas (Francis III)
1939- .... **CLC 3, 7, 18, 45**
See also AITN 2; CA 49-52; CANR 5, 24; DLB 2; DLBY 80; MTCW

McGuckian, Medbh 1950- .... **CLC 48**
See also DLB 40

McHale, Tom 1942(?)-1982 .... **CLC 3, 5**
See also AITN 1; CA 77-80; 106

McIlvanney, William 1936- .... **CLC 42**
See also CA 25-28R; DLB 14

McIlwraith, Maureen Mollie Hunter
See Hunter, Mollie
See also SATA 2

McInerney, Jay 1955- .... **CLC 34**
See also CA 116; 123

McIntyre, Vonda N(eel) 1948- ...... **CLC 18**
See also CA 81-84; CANR 17, 34; MTCW

McKay, Claude .... **TCLC 7, 41; PC 2**
See also McKay, Festus Claudius
See also BLC 3; DLB 4, 45, 51, 117

McKay, Festus Claudius 1889-1948
See McKay, Claude
See also BW; CA 104; 124; DA; MTCW; WLC

McKuen, Rod 1933- .... **CLC 1, 3**
See also AITN 1; CA 41-44R; CANR 40

McLoughlin, R. B.
See Mencken, H(enry) L(ouis)

McLuhan, (Herbert) Marshall
1911-1980 .... **CLC 37**
See also CA 9-12R; 102; CANR 12, 34; DLB 88; MTCW

McMillan, Terry (L.) 1951- ..... **CLC 50, 61**
See also CA 140

McMurtry, Larry (Jeff)
1936- .... **CLC 2, 3, 7, 11, 27, 44**
See also AITN 2; BEST 89:2; CA 5-8R; CANR 19, 43; CDALB 1968-1988; DLB 2; DLBY 80, 87; MTCW

McNally, Terrence 1939- ...... **CLC 4, 7, 41**
See also CA 45-48; CANR 2; DLB 7

McNamer, Deirdre 1950- .... **CLC 70**

McNeile, Herman Cyril 1888-1937
See Sapper
See also DLB 77

McPhee, John (Angus) 1931- ...... **CLC 36**
See also BEST 90:1; CA 65-68; CANR 20; MTCW

McPherson, James Alan
1943- .... **CLC 19, 77**
See also BW; CA 25-28R; CAAS 17; CANR 24; DLB 38; MTCW

McPherson, William (Alexander)
1933- .... **CLC 34**
See also CA 69-72; CANR 28

McSweeney, Kerry .... **CLC 34**

Mead, Margaret 1901-1978 .... **CLC 37**
See also AITN 1; CA 1-4R; 81-84; CANR 4; MTCW; SATA 20

Meaker, Marijane (Agnes) 1927-
See Kerr, M. E.
See also CA 107; CANR 37; JRDA; MAICYA; MTCW; SATA 20, 61

Medoff, Mark (Howard) 1940- ... **CLC 6, 23**
See also AITN 1; CA 53-56; CANR 5; DLB 7

Meged, Aharon
See Megged, Aharon

Meged, Aron
See Megged, Aharon

Megged, Aharon 1920- .... **CLC 9**
See also CA 49-52; CAAS 13; CANR 1

Mehta, Ved (Parkash) 1934- .... **CLC 37**
See also CA 1-4R; CANR 2, 23; MTCW

Melanter
See Blackmore, R(ichard) D(oddridge)

Melikow, Loris
See Hofmannsthal, Hugo von

Melmoth, Sebastian
See Wilde, Oscar (Fingal O'Flahertie Wills)

Meltzer, Milton 1915- .... **CLC 26**
See also AAYA 8; CA 13-16R; CANR 38; CLR 13; DLB 61; JRDA; MAICYA; SAAS 1; SATA 1, 50

Melville, Herman
1819-1891 ...... **NCLC 3, 12, 29; SSC 1**
See also CDALB 1640-1865; DA; DLB 3, 74; SATA 59; WLC

Menander
c. 342B.C.-c. 292B.C. ... **CMLC 9; DC 3**

Mencken, H(enry) L(ouis)
1880-1956 .... **TCLC 13**
See also CA 105; 125; CDALB 1917-1929; DLB 11, 29, 63; MTCW

Mercer, David 1928-1980 .... **CLC 5**
See also CA 9-12R; 102; CANR 23; DLB 13; MTCW

Merchant, Paul
See Ellison, Harlan

Meredith, George 1828-1909 ... **TCLC 17, 43**
See also CA 117; CDBLB 1832-1890; DLB 18, 35, 57

Meredith, William (Morris)
1919- .... **CLC 4, 13, 22, 55**
See also CA 9-12R; CAAS 14; CANR 6, 40; DLB 5

Merezhkovsky, Dmitry Sergeyevich
1865-1941 .... **TCLC 29**

Merimee, Prosper
1803-1870 .... **NCLC 6; SSC 7**
See also DLB 119

Merkin, Daphne 1954- .... **CLC 44**
See also CA 123

Merlin, Arthur
See Blish, James (Benjamin)

Merrill, James (Ingram)
1926- .... **CLC 2, 3, 6, 8, 13, 18, 34**
See also CA 13-16R; CANR 10; DLB 5; DLBY 85; MTCW

Merriman, Alex
See Silverberg, Robert

Merritt, E. B.
See Waddington, Miriam

Merton, Thomas
1915-1968 .... **CLC 1, 3, 11, 34**
See also CA 5-8R; 25-28R; CANR 22; DLB 48; DLBY 81; MTCW

Merwin, W(illiam) S(tanley)
1927- ...... **CLC 1, 2, 3, 5, 8, 13, 18, 45**
See also CA 13-16R; CANR 15; DLB 5; MTCW

Metcalf, John 1938- .... **CLC 37**
See also CA 113; DLB 60

Metcalf, Suzanne
See Baum, L(yman) Frank

Mew, Charlotte (Mary)
1870-1928 .... **TCLC 8**
See also CA 105; DLB 19

Mewshaw, Michael 1943- .... **CLC 9**
See also CA 53-56; CANR 7; DLBY 80

Meyer, June
See Jordan, June

Meyer, Lynn
See Slavitt, David R(ytman)

Meyer-Meyrink, Gustav 1868-1932
See Meyrink, Gustav
See also CA 117

Meyers, Jeffrey 1939- .... **CLC 39**
See also CA 73-76; DLB 111

Meynell, Alice (Christina Gertrude Thompson)
1847-1922 .... **TCLC 6**
See also CA 104; DLB 19, 98

Meyrink, Gustav .... **TCLC 21**
See also Meyer-Meyrink, Gustav
See also DLB 81

Michaels, Leonard 1933- .... **CLC 6, 25**
See also CA 61-64; CANR 21; DLB 130; MTCW

Michaux, Henri 1899-1984 ...... **CLC 8, 19**
See also CA 85-88; 114

Michelangelo 1475-1564 .... **LC 12**

Michelet, Jules 1798-1874 .... **NCLC 31**

Michener, James A(lbert)
1907(?)- .... **CLC 1, 5, 11, 29, 60**
See also AITN 1; BEST 90:1; CA 5-8R; CANR 21; DLB 6; MTCW

Mickiewicz, Adam 1798-1855 ..... **NCLC 3**

Middleton, Christopher 1926- ...... **CLC 13**
See also CA 13-16R; CANR 29; DLB 40

Middleton, Stanley 1919- .... **CLC 7, 38**
See also CA 25-28R; CANR 21; DLB 14

Migueis, Jose Rodrigues 1901- ..... **CLC 10**

Mikszath, Kalman 1847-1910 ..... **TCLC 31**

Miles, Josephine
1911-1985 .... **CLC 1, 2, 14, 34, 39**
See also CA 1-4R; 116; CANR 2; DLB 48

Militant
See Sandburg, Carl (August)

Mill, John Stuart 1806-1873 . . . . . **NCLC 11**
See also CDBLB 1832-1890; DLB 55

Millar, Kenneth 1915-1983 . . . . **CLC 14**
See also Macdonald, Ross
See also CA 9-12R; 110; CANR 16; DLB 2; DLBD 6; DLBY 83; MTCW

Millay, E. Vincent
See Millay, Edna St. Vincent

Millay, Edna St. Vincent
1892-1950 . . . . **TCLC 4, 49; PC 6**
See also CA 104; 130; CDALB 1917-1929; DA; DLB 45; MTCW

Miller, Arthur
1915- . . . . **CLC 1, 2, 6, 10, 15, 26, 47, 78; DC 1**
See also AITN 1; CA 1-4R; CABS 3; CANR 2, 30; CDALB 1941-1968; DA; DLB 7; MTCW; WLC

Miller, Henry (Valentine)
1891-1980 . . . . **CLC 1, 2, 4, 9, 14, 43**
See also CA 9-12R; 97-100; CANR 33; CDALB 1929-1941; DA; DLB 4, 9; DLBY 80; MTCW; WLC

Miller, Jason 1939(?)- . . . . **CLC 2**
See also AITN 1; CA 73-76; DLB 7

Miller, Sue 1943- . . . . **CLC 44**
See also BEST 90:3; CA 139

Miller, Walter M(ichael, Jr.)
1923- . . . . **CLC 4, 30**
See also CA 85-88; DLB 8

Millett, Kate 1934- . . . . **CLC 67**
See also AITN 1; CA 73-76; CANR 32; MTCW

Millhauser, Steven 1943- . . . . **CLC 21, 54**
See also CA 110; 111; DLB 2

Millin, Sarah Gertrude 1889-1968 . . **CLC 49**
See also CA 102; 93-96

Milne, A(lan) A(lexander)
1882-1956 . . . . **TCLC 6**
See also CA 104; 133; CLR 1, 26; DLB 10, 77, 100; MAICYA; MTCW; YABC 1

Milner, Ron(ald) 1938- . . . . **CLC 56**
See also AITN 1; BLC 3; BW; CA 73-76; CANR 24; DLB 38; MTCW

Milosz, Czeslaw
1911- . . . . **CLC 5, 11, 22, 31, 56**
See also CA 81-84; CANR 23; MTCW

Milton, John 1608-1674 . . . . **LC 9**
See also CDBLB 1660-1789; DA; DLB 131; WLC

Minehaha, Cornelius
See Wedekind, (Benjamin) Frank(lin)

Miner, Valerie 1947- . . . . **CLC 40**
See also CA 97-100

Minimo, Duca
See D'Annunzio, Gabriele

Minot, Susan 1956- . . . . **CLC 44**
See also CA 134

Minus, Ed 1938- . . . . **CLC 39**

Miranda, Javier
See Bioy Casares, Adolfo

Miro (Ferrer), Gabriel (Francisco Victor)
1879-1930 . . . . **TCLC 5**
See also CA 104

Mishima, Yukio
. . . . **CLC 2, 4, 6, 9, 27; DC 1; SSC 4**
See also Hiraoka, Kimitake

Mistral, Frederic 1830-1914 . . . . . . **TCLC 51**
See also CA 122

Mistral, Gabriela . . . . **TCLC 2**
See also Godoy Alcayaga, Lucila

Mistry, Rohinton 1952- . . . . **CLC 71**
See also CA 141

Mitchell, Clyde
See Ellison, Harlan; Silverberg, Robert

Mitchell, James Leslie 1901-1935
See Gibbon, Lewis Grassic
See also CA 104; DLB 15

Mitchell, Joni 1943- . . . . **CLC 12**
See also CA 112

Mitchell, Margaret (Munnerlyn)
1900-1949 . . . . **TCLC 11**
See also CA 109; 125; DLB 9; MTCW

Mitchell, Peggy
See Mitchell, Margaret (Munnerlyn)

Mitchell, S(ilas) Weir 1829-1914 . . **TCLC 36**

Mitchell, W(illiam) O(rmond)
1914- . . . . **CLC 25**
See also CA 77-80; CANR 15, 43; DLB 88

Mitford, Mary Russell 1787-1855 . . **NCLC 4**
See also DLB 110, 116

Mitford, Nancy 1904-1973 . . . . **CLC 44**
See also CA 9-12R

Miyamoto, Yuriko 1899-1951 . . . . . **TCLC 37**

Mo, Timothy (Peter) 1950(?)- . . . . . . **CLC 46**
See also CA 117; MTCW

Modarressi, Taghi (M.) 1931- . . . . . . **CLC 44**
See also CA 121; 134

Modiano, Patrick (Jean) 1945- . . . . . **CLC 18**
See also CA 85-88; CANR 17, 40; DLB 83

Moerck, Paal
See Roelvaag, O(le) E(dvart)

Mofolo, Thomas (Mokopu)
1875(?)-1948 . . . . **TCLC 22**
See also BLC 3; CA 121

Mohr, Nicholasa 1935- . . . . **CLC 12**
See also AAYA 8; CA 49-52; CANR 1, 32; CLR 22; HW; JRDA; SAAS 8; SATA 8

Mojtabai, A(nn) G(race)
1938- . . . . **CLC 5, 9, 15, 29**
See also CA 85-88

Moliere 1622-1673 . . . . **LC 10**
See also DA; WLC

Molin, Charles
See Mayne, William (James Carter)

Molnar, Ferenc 1878-1952 . . . . **TCLC 20**
See also CA 109

Momaday, N(avarre) Scott
1934- . . . . **CLC 2, 19**
See also CA 25-28R; CANR 14, 34; DA; MTCW; SATA 30, 48

Monroe, Harriet 1860-1936 . . . . **TCLC 12**
See also CA 109; DLB 54, 91

Monroe, Lyle
See Heinlein, Robert A(nson)

Montagu, Elizabeth 1917- . . . . **NCLC 7**
See also CA 9-12R

Montagu, Mary (Pierrepont) Wortley
1689-1762 . . . . **LC 9**
See also DLB 95, 101

Montagu, W. H.
See Coleridge, Samuel Taylor

Montague, John (Patrick)
1929- . . . . **CLC 13, 46**
See also CA 9-12R; CANR 9; DLB 40; MTCW

Montaigne, Michel (Eyquem) de
1533-1592 . . . . **LC 8**
See also DA; WLC

Montale, Eugenio 1896-1981 . . . **CLC 7, 9, 18**
See also CA 17-20R; 104; CANR 30; DLB 114; MTCW

Montesquieu, Charles-Louis de Secondat
1689-1755 . . . . **LC 7**

Montgomery, (Robert) Bruce 1921-1978
See Crispin, Edmund
See also CA 104

Montgomery, L(ucy) M(aud)
1874-1942 . . . . **TCLC 51**
See also CA 108; 137; CLR 8; DLB 92; JRDA; MAICYA; YABC 1

Montgomery, Marion H., Jr. 1925- . . **CLC 7**
See also AITN 1; CA 1-4R; CANR 3; DLB 6

Montgomery, Max
See Davenport, Guy (Mattison, Jr.)

Montherlant, Henry (Milon) de
1896-1972 . . . . **CLC 8, 19**
See also CA 85-88; 37-40R; DLB 72; MTCW

Monty Python . . . . **CLC 21**
See also Chapman, Graham; Cleese, John (Marwood); Gilliam, Terry (Vance); Idle, Eric; Jones, Terence Graham Parry; Palin, Michael (Edward)
See also AAYA 7

Moodie, Susanna (Strickland)
1803-1885 . . . . **NCLC 14**
See also DLB 99

Mooney, Edward 1951- . . . . **CLC 25**
See also CA 130

Mooney, Ted
See Mooney, Edward

Moorcock, Michael (John)
1939- . . . . **CLC 5, 27, 58**
See also CA 45-48; CAAS 5; CANR 2, 17, 38; DLB 14; MTCW

Moore, Brian
1921- . . . . **CLC 1, 3, 5, 7, 8, 19, 32**
See also CA 1-4R; CANR 1, 25, 42; MTCW

Moore, Edward
See Muir, Edwin

Moore, George Augustus
1852-1933 . . . . **TCLC 7**
See also CA 104; DLB 10, 18, 57

Moore, Lorrie . . . . **CLC 39, 45, 68**
See also Moore, Marie Lorena

Moore, Marianne (Craig)
1887-1972 . . . . **CLC 1, 2, 4, 8, 10, 13, 19, 47; PC 4**
See also CA 1-4R; 33-36R; CANR 3; CDALB 1929-1941; DA; DLB 45; DLBD 7; MTCW; SATA 20

Moore, Marie Lorena 1957-
See Moore, Lorrie
See also CA 116; CANR 39

Moore, Thomas 1779-1852........ **NCLC 6**
See also DLB 96

Morand, Paul 1888-1976.......... **CLC 41**
See also CA 69-72; DLB 65

Morante, Elsa 1918-1985........ **CLC 8, 47**
See also CA 85-88; 117; CANR 35; MTCW

Moravia, Alberto....... **CLC 2, 7, 11, 27, 46**
See also Pincherle, Alberto

More, Hannah 1745-1833 .... **NCLC 27**
See also DLB 107, 109, 116

More, Henry 1614-1687............. **LC 9**
See also DLB 126

More, Sir Thomas 1478-1535 .... **LC 10**

Moreas, Jean.................... **TCLC 18**
See also Papadiamantopoulos, Johannes

Morgan, Berry 1919-.............. **CLC 6**
See also CA 49-52; DLB 6

Morgan, Claire
See Highsmith, (Mary) Patricia

Morgan, Edwin (George) 1920-..... **CLC 31**
See also CA 5-8R; CANR 3, 43; DLB 27

Morgan, (George) Frederick
1922- .... **CLC 23**
See also CA 17-20R; CANR 21

Morgan, Harriet
See Mencken, H(enry) L(ouis)

Morgan, Jane
See Cooper, James Fenimore

Morgan, Janet 1945- .... **CLC 39**
See also CA 65-68

Morgan, Lady 1776(?)-1859...... **NCLC 29**
See also DLB 116

Morgan, Robin 1941-.............. **CLC 2**
See also CA 69-72; CANR 29; MTCW

Morgan, Scott
See Kuttner, Henry

Morgan, Seth 1949(?)-1990 .... **CLC 65**
See also CA 132

Morgenstern, Christian
1871-1914 .... **TCLC 8**
See also CA 105

Morgenstern, S.
See Goldman, William (W.)

Moricz, Zsigmond 1879-1942 ..... **TCLC 33**

Morike, Eduard (Friedrich)
1804-1875 .... **NCLC 10**
See also DLB 133

Mori Ogai .... **TCLC 14**
See also Mori Rintaro

Mori Rintaro 1862-1922
See Mori Ogai
See also CA 110

Moritz, Karl Philipp 1756-1793 ...... **LC 2**
See also DLB 94

Morland, Peter Henry
See Faust, Frederick (Schiller)

Morren, Theophil
See Hofmannsthal, Hugo von

Morris, Bill 1952-................ **CLC 76**

Morris, Julian
See West, Morris L(anglo)

Morris, Steveland Judkins 1950(?)-
See Wonder, Stevie
See also CA 111

Morris, William 1834-1896 .... **NCLC 4**
See also CDBLB 1832-1890; DLB 18, 35, 57

Morris, Wright 1910-... **CLC 1, 3, 7, 18, 37**
See also CA 9-12R; CANR 21; DLB 2; DLBY 81; MTCW

Morrison, Chloe Anthony Wofford
See Morrison, Toni

Morrison, James Douglas 1943-1971
See Morrison, Jim
See also CA 73-76; CANR 40

Morrison, Jim .... **CLC 17**
See also Morrison, James Douglas

Morrison, Toni 1931-..... **CLC 4, 10, 22, 55**
See also AAYA 1; BLC 3; BW; CA 29-32R; CANR 27, 42; CDALB 1968-1988; DA; DLB 6, 33; DLBY 81; MTCW; SATA 57

Morrison, Van 1945- .... **CLC 21**
See also CA 116

Mortimer, John (Clifford)
1923- .... **CLC 28, 43**
See also CA 13-16R; CANR 21; CDBLB 1960 to Present; DLB 13; MTCW

Mortimer, Penelope (Ruth) 1918-.... **CLC 5**
See also CA 57-60

Morton, Anthony
See Creasey, John

Mosher, Howard Frank 1943-...... **CLC 62**
See also CA 139

Mosley, Nicholas 1923-........ **CLC 43, 70**
See also CA 69-72; CANR 41; DLB 14

Moss, Howard
1922-1987 .... **CLC 7, 14, 45, 50**
See also CA 1-4R; 123; CANR 1; DLB 5

Mossgiel, Rab
See Burns, Robert

Motion, Andrew 1952-............ **CLC 47**
See also DLB 40

Motley, Willard (Francis)
1912-1965 .... **CLC 18**
See also BW; CA 117; 106; DLB 76

Mott, Michael (Charles Alston)
1930- .... **CLC 15, 34**
See also CA 5-8R; CAAS 7; CANR 7, 29

Mowat, Farley (McGill) 1921- ..... **CLC 26**
See also AAYA 1; CA 1-4R; CANR 4, 24, 42; CLR 20; DLB 68; JRDA; MAICYA; MTCW; SATA 3, 55

Moyers, Bill 1934- .... **CLC 74**
See also AITN 2; CA 61-64; CANR 31

Mphahlele, Es'kia
See Mphahlele, Ezekiel
See also DLB 125

Mphahlele, Ezekiel 1919-.......... **CLC 25**
See also Mphahlele, Es'kia
See also BLC 3; BW; CA 81-84; CANR 26

Mqhayi, S(amuel) E(dward) K(rune Loliwe)
1875-1945 .... **TCLC 25**
See also BLC 3

Mr. Martin
See Burroughs, William S(eward)

Mrozek, Slawomir 1930-........ **CLC 3, 13**
See also CA 13-16R; CAAS 10; CANR 29; MTCW

Mrs. Belloc-Lowndes
See Lowndes, Marie Adelaide (Belloc)

Mtwa, Percy (?)-................. **CLC 47**

Mueller, Lisel 1924-........... **CLC 13, 51**
See also CA 93-96; DLB 105

Muir, Edwin 1887-1959 .... **TCLC 2**
See also CA 104; DLB 20, 100

Muir, John 1838-1914 .... **TCLC 28**

Mujica Lainez, Manuel
1910-1984 .... **CLC 31**
See also Lainez, Manuel Mujica
See also CA 81-84; 112; CANR 32; HW

Mukherjee, Bharati 1940-......... **CLC 53**
See also BEST 89:2; CA 107; DLB 60; MTCW

Muldoon, Paul 1951-.......... **CLC 32, 72**
See also CA 113; 129; DLB 40

Mulisch, Harry 1927-............. **CLC 42**
See also CA 9-12R; CANR 6, 26

Mull, Martin 1943-............... **CLC 17**
See also CA 105

Mulock, Dinah Maria
See Craik, Dinah Maria (Mulock)

Munford, Robert 1737(?)-1783 .... **LC 5**
See also DLB 31

Mungo, Raymond 1946-........... **CLC 72**
See also CA 49-52; CANR 2

Munro, Alice
1931- .... **CLC 6, 10, 19, 50; SSC 3**
See also AITN 2; CA 33-36R; CANR 33; DLB 53; MTCW; SATA 29

Munro, H(ector) H(ugh) 1870-1916
See Saki
See also CA 104; 130; CDBLB 1890-1914; DA; DLB 34; MTCW; WLC

Murasaki, Lady.................. **CMLC 1**

Murdoch, (Jean) Iris
1919- ...... **CLC 1, 2, 3, 4, 6, 8, 11, 15, 22, 31, 51**
See also CA 13-16R; CANR 8, 43; CDBLB 1960 to Present; DLB 14; MTCW

Murphy, Richard 1927- .... **CLC 41**
See also CA 29-32R; DLB 40

Murphy, Sylvia 1937-............. **CLC 34**
See also CA 121

Murphy, Thomas (Bernard) 1935-... **CLC 51**
See also CA 101

Murray, Albert L. 1916- .... **CLC 73**
See also BW; CA 49-52; CANR 26; DLB 38

Murray, Les(lie) A(llan) 1938- ..... **CLC 40**
See also CA 21-24R; CANR 11, 27

Murry, J. Middleton
See Murry, John Middleton

Murry, John Middleton
1889-1957 .... **TCLC 16**
See also CA 118

Musgrave, Susan 1951- .... **CLC 13, 54**
See also CA 69-72

Norris, Frank
See Norris, Benjamin Franklin, Jr.
See also CDALB 1865-1917; DLB 12, 71

Norris, Leslie 1921- . . . . **CLC 14**
See also CA 11-12; CANR 14; CAP 1; DLB 27

North, Andrew
See Norton, Andre

North, Anthony
See Koontz, Dean R(ay)

North, Captain George
See Stevenson, Robert Louis (Balfour)

North, Milou
See Erdrich, Louise

Northrup, B. A.
See Hubbard, L(afayette) Ron(ald)

North Staffs
See Hulme, T(homas) E(rnest)

Norton, Alice Mary
See Norton, Andre
See also MAICYA; SATA 1, 43

Norton, Andre 1912- . . . . **CLC 12**
See also Norton, Alice Mary
See also CA 1-4R; CANR 2, 31; DLB 8, 52; JRDA; MTCW

Norway, Nevil Shute 1899-1960
See Shute, Nevil
See also CA 102; 93-96

Norwid, Cyprian Kamil
1821-1883 . . . . **NCLC 17**

Nosille, Nabrah
See Ellison, Harlan

Nossack, Hans Erich 1901-1978 . . . . . **CLC 6**
See also CA 93-96; 85-88; DLB 69

Nosu, Chuji
See Ozu, Yasujiro

Nova, Craig 1945-. . . . . **CLC 7, 31**
See also CA 45-48; CANR 2

Novak, Joseph
See Kosinski, Jerzy (Nikodem)

Novalis 1772-1801 . . . . **NCLC 13**
See also DLB 90

Nowlan, Alden (Albert) 1933-1983 . . **CLC 15**
See also CA 9-12R; CANR 5; DLB 53

Noyes, Alfred 1880-1958 . . . . **TCLC 7**
See also CA 104; DLB 20

Nunn, Kem 19(?)- . . . . **CLC 34**

Nye, Robert 1939- . . . . **CLC 13, 42**
See also CA 33-36R; CANR 29; DLB 14; MTCW; SATA 6

Nyro, Laura 1947- . . . . **CLC 17**

Oates, Joyce Carol
1938- . . . . . . **CLC 1, 2, 3, 6, 9, 11, 15, 19, 33, 52; SSC 6**
See also AITN 1; BEST 89:2; CA 5-8R; CANR 25; CDALB 1968-1988; DA; DLB 2, 5, 130; DLBY 81; MTCW; WLC

O'Brien, E. G.
See Clarke, Arthur C(harles)

O'Brien, Edna
1936- . . . **CLC 3, 5, 8, 13, 36, 65; SSC 10**
See also CA 1-4R; CANR 6, 41; CDBLB 1960 to Present; DLB 14; MTCW

O'Brien, Fitz-James 1828-1862. . . **NCLC 21**
See also DLB 74

O'Brien, Flann. . . . . **CLC 1, 4, 5, 7, 10, 47**
See also O Nuallain, Brian

O'Brien, Richard 1942- . . . . **CLC 17**
See also CA 124

O'Brien, Tim 1946-. . . . . **CLC 7, 19, 40**
See also CA 85-88; CANR 40; DLBD 9; DLBY 80

Obstfelder, Sigbjoern 1866-1900. . . **TCLC 23**
See also CA 123

O'Casey, Sean
1880-1964 . . . . **CLC 1, 5, 9, 11, 15**
See also CA 89-92; CDBLB 1914-1945; DLB 10; MTCW

O'Cathasaigh, Sean
See O'Casey, Sean

Ochs, Phil 1940-1976 . . . . **CLC 17**
See also CA 65-68

O'Connor, Edwin (Greene)
1918-1968 . . . . **CLC 14**
See also CA 93-96; 25-28R

O'Connor, (Mary) Flannery
1925-1964 . . . . **CLC 1, 2, 3, 6, 10, 13, 15, 21, 66; SSC 1**
See also AAYA 7; CA 1-4R; CANR 3, 41; CDALB 1941-1968; DA; DLB 2; DLBY 80; MTCW; WLC

O'Connor, Frank. . . . . **CLC 23; SSC 5**
See also O'Donovan, Michael John

O'Dell, Scott 1898-1989. . . . . **CLC 30**
See also AAYA 3; CA 61-64; 129; CANR 12, 30; CLR 1, 16; DLB 52; JRDA; MAICYA; SATA 12, 60

Odets, Clifford 1906-1963 . . . . **CLC 2, 28**
See also CA 85-88; DLB 7, 26; MTCW

O'Doherty, Brian 1934- . . . . **CLC 76**
See also CA 105

O'Donnell, K. M.
See Malzberg, Barry N(athaniel)

O'Donnell, Lawrence
See Kuttner, Henry

O'Donovan, Michael John
1903-1966 . . . . **CLC 14**
See also O'Connor, Frank
See also CA 93-96

Oe, Kenzaburo 1935- . . . . **CLC 10, 36**
See also CA 97-100; CANR 36; MTCW

O'Faolain, Julia 1932- . . . . **CLC 6, 19, 47**
See also CA 81-84; CAAS 2; CANR 12; DLB 14; MTCW

O'Faolain, Sean
1900-1991 . . . . **CLC 1, 7, 14, 32, 70; SSC 13**
See also CA 61-64; 134; CANR 12; DLB 15; MTCW

O'Flaherty, Liam
1896-1984 . . . . **CLC 5, 34; SSC 6**
See also CA 101; 113; CANR 35; DLB 36; DLBY 84; MTCW

Ogilvy, Gavin
See Barrie, J(ames) M(atthew)

O'Grady, Standish James
1846-1928 . . . . **TCLC 5**
See also CA 104

O'Grady, Timothy 1951- . . . . **CLC 59**
See also CA 138

O'Hara, Frank
1926-1966 . . . . **CLC 2, 5, 13, 78**
See also CA 9-12R; 25-28R; CANR 33; DLB 5, 16; MTCW

O'Hara, John (Henry)
1905-1970 . . . . **CLC 1, 2, 3, 6, 11, 42**
See also CA 5-8R; 25-28R; CANR 31; CDALB 1929-1941; DLB 9, 86; DLBD 2; MTCW

O Hehir, Diana 1922- . . . . **CLC 41**
See also CA 93-96

Okigbo, Christopher (Ifenayichukwu)
1932-1967 . . . . **CLC 25; PC 7**
See also BLC 3; BW; CA 77-80; DLB 125; MTCW

Olds, Sharon 1942-. . . . . **CLC 32, 39**
See also CA 101; CANR 18, 41; DLB 120

Oldstyle, Jonathan
See Irving, Washington

Olesha, Yuri (Karlovich)
1899-1960 . . . . **CLC 8**
See also CA 85-88

Oliphant, Margaret (Oliphant Wilson)
1828-1897 . . . . **NCLC 11**
See also DLB 18

Oliver, Mary 1935-. . . . . **CLC 19, 34**
See also CA 21-24R; CANR 9; DLB 5

Olivier, Laurence (Kerr)
1907-1989 . . . . **CLC 20**
See also CA 111; 129

Olsen, Tillie 1913- . . . . . **CLC 4, 13; SSC 11**
See also CA 1-4R; CANR 1, 43; DA; DLB 28; DLBY 80; MTCW

Olson, Charles (John)
1910-1970 . . . . . **CLC 1, 2, 5, 6, 9, 11, 29**
See also CA 13-16; 25-28R; CABS 2; CANR 35; CAP 1; DLB 5, 16; MTCW

Olson, Toby 1937- . . . . **CLC 28**
See also CA 65-68; CANR 9, 31

Olyesha, Yuri
See Olesha, Yuri (Karlovich)

Ondaatje, (Philip) Michael
1943- . . . . **CLC 14, 29, 51, 76**
See also CA 77-80; CANR 42; DLB 60

Oneal, Elizabeth 1934-
See Oneal, Zibby
See also CA 106; CANR 28; MAICYA; SATA 30

Oneal, Zibby . . . . **CLC 30**
See also Oneal, Elizabeth
See also AAYA 5; CLR 13; JRDA

O'Neill, Eugene (Gladstone)
1888-1953 . . . . **TCLC 1, 6, 27, 49**
See also AITN 1; CA 110; 132; CDALB 1929-1941; DA; DLB 7; MTCW; WLC

Onetti, Juan Carlos 1909- . . . . **CLC 7, 10**
See also CA 85-88; CANR 32; DLB 113; HW; MTCW

O Nuallain, Brian 1911-1966
See O'Brien, Flann
See also CA 21-22; 25-28R; CAP 2

Paterson, Katherine (Womeldorf) 1932- .... **CLC 12, 30**
See also AAYA 1; CA 21-24R; CANR 28; CLR 7; DLB 52; JRDA; MAICYA; MTCW; SATA 13, 53

Patmore, Coventry Kersey Dighton 1823-1896 .... **NCLC 9**
See also DLB 35, 98

Paton, Alan (Stewart) 1903-1988 .... **CLC 4, 10, 25, 55**
See also CA 13-16; 125; CANR 22; CAP 1; DA; MTCW; SATA 11, 56; WLC

Paton Walsh, Gillian 1937-
See Walsh, Jill Paton
See also CANR 38; JRDA; MAICYA; SAAS 3; SATA 4, 72

Paulding, James Kirke 1778-1860. . **NCLC 2**
See also DLB 3, 59, 74

Paulin, Thomas Neilson 1949-
See Paulin, Tom
See also CA 123; 128

Paulin, Tom .... **CLC 37**
See also Paulin, Thomas Neilson
See also DLB 40

Paustovsky, Konstantin (Georgievich) 1892-1968 .... **CLC 40**
See also CA 93-96; 25-28R

Pavese, Cesare 1908-1950 .... **TCLC 3**
See also CA 104; DLB 128

Pavic, Milorad 1929- .... **CLC 60**
See also CA 136

Payne, Alan
See Jakes, John (William)

Paz, Gil
See Lugones, Leopoldo

Paz, Octavio 1914- .... **CLC 3, 4, 6, 10, 19, 51, 65; PC 1**
See also CA 73-76; CANR 32; DA; DLBY 90; HW; MTCW; WLC

Peacock, Molly 1947-............. **CLC 60**
See also CA 103; DLB 120

Peacock, Thomas Love 1785-1866 .... **NCLC 22**
See also DLB 96, 116

Peake, Mervyn 1911-1968 .... **CLC 7, 54**
See also CA 5-8R; 25-28R; CANR 3; DLB 15; MTCW; SATA 23

Pearce, Philippa .... **CLC 21**
See also Christie, (Ann) Philippa
See also CLR 9; MAICYA; SATA 1, 67

Pearl, Eric
See Elman, Richard

Pearson, T(homas) R(eid) 1956- .... **CLC 39**
See also CA 120; 130

Peck, John 1941- .... **CLC 3**
See also CA 49-52; CANR 3

Peck, Richard (Wayne) 1934- ...... **CLC 21**
See also AAYA 1; CA 85-88; CANR 19, 38; JRDA; MAICYA; SAAS 2; SATA 18, 55

Peck, Robert Newton 1928-........ **CLC 17**
See also AAYA 3; CA 81-84; CANR 31; DA; JRDA; MAICYA; SAAS 1; SATA 21, 62

Peckinpah, (David) Sam(uel) 1925-1984 .... **CLC 20**
See also CA 109; 114

Pedersen, Knut 1859-1952
See Hamsun, Knut
See also CA 104; 119; MTCW

Peeslake, Gaffer
See Durrell, Lawrence (George)

Peguy, Charles Pierre 1873-1914 .... **TCLC 10**
See also CA 107

Pena, Ramon del Valle y
See Valle-Inclan, Ramon (Maria) del

Pendennis, Arthur Esquir
See Thackeray, William Makepeace

Pepys, Samuel 1633-1703........... **LC 11**
See also CDBLB 1660-1789; DA; DLB 101; WLC

Percy, Walker 1916-1990 .... **CLC 2, 3, 6, 8, 14, 18, 47, 65**
See also CA 1-4R; 131; CANR 1, 23; DLB 2; DLBY 80, 90; MTCW

Perec, Georges 1936-1982 .... **CLC 56**
See also CA 141; DLB 83

Pereda (y Sanchez de Porrua), Jose Maria de 1833-1906 .... **TCLC 16**
See also CA 117

Pereda y Porrua, Jose Maria de
See Pereda (y Sanchez de Porrua), Jose Maria de

Peregoy, George Weems
See Mencken, H(enry) L(ouis)

Perelman, S(idney) J(oseph) 1904-1979 ... **CLC 3, 5, 9, 15, 23, 44, 49**
See also AITN 1, 2; CA 73-76; 89-92; CANR 18; DLB 11, 44; MTCW

Peret, Benjamin 1899-1959 .... **TCLC 20**
See also CA 117

Peretz, Isaac Loeb 1851(?)-1915... **TCLC 16**
See also CA 109

Peretz, Yitzkhok Leibush
See Peretz, Isaac Loeb

Perez Galdos, Benito 1843-1920... **TCLC 27**
See also CA 125; HW

Perrault, Charles 1628-1703 .... **LC 2**
See also MAICYA; SATA 25

Perry, Brighton
See Sherwood, Robert E(mmet)

Perse, St.-John .... **CLC 4, 11, 46**
See also Leger, (Marie-Rene Auguste) Alexis Saint-Leger

Peseenz, Tulio F.
See Lopez y Fuentes, Gregorio

Pesetsky, Bette 1932-............. **CLC 28**
See also CA 133; DLB 130

Peshkov, Alexei Maximovich 1868-1936
See Gorky, Maxim
See also CA 105; 141; DA

Pessoa, Fernando (Antonio Nogueira) 1888-1935 .... **TCLC 27**
See also CA 125

Peterkin, Julia Mood 1880-1961.... **CLC 31**
See also CA 102; DLB 9

Peters, Joan K. 1945-............. **CLC 39**

Peters, Robert L(ouis) 1924-........ **CLC 7**
See also CA 13-16R; CAAS 8; DLB 105

Petofi, Sandor 1823-1849........ **NCLC 21**

Petrakis, Harry Mark 1923-........ **CLC 3**
See also CA 9-12R; CANR 4, 30

Petrov, Evgeny .... **TCLC 21**
See also Kataev, Evgeny Petrovich

Petry, Ann (Lane) 1908- ...... **CLC 1, 7, 18**
See also BW; CA 5-8R; CAAS 6; CANR 4; CLR 12; DLB 76; JRDA; MAICYA; MTCW; SATA 5

Petursson, Halligrimur 1614-1674 .... **LC 8**

Philipson, Morris H. 1926-........ **CLC 53**
See also CA 1-4R; CANR 4

Phillips, David Graham 1867-1911 .... **TCLC 44**
See also CA 108; DLB 9, 12

Phillips, Jack
See Sandburg, Carl (August)

Phillips, Jayne Anne 1952- ..... **CLC 15, 33**
See also CA 101; CANR 24; DLBY 80; MTCW

Phillips, Richard
See Dick, Philip K(indred)

Phillips, Robert (Schaeffer) 1938-... **CLC 28**
See also CA 17-20R; CAAS 13; CANR 8; DLB 105

Phillips, Ward
See Lovecraft, H(oward) P(hillips)

Piccolo, Lucio 1901-1969.......... **CLC 13**
See also CA 97-100; DLB 114

Pickthall, Marjorie L(owry) C(hristie) 1883-1922 .... **TCLC 21**
See also CA 107; DLB 92

Pico della Mirandola, Giovanni 1463-1494 .... **LC 15**

Piercy, Marge 1936- .... **CLC 3, 6, 14, 18, 27, 62**
See also CA 21-24R; CAAS 1; CANR 13, 43; DLB 120; MTCW

Piers, Robert
See Anthony, Piers

Pieyre de Mandiargues, Andre 1909-1991
See Mandiargues, Andre Pieyre de
See also CA 103; 136; CANR 22

Pilnyak, Boris .... **TCLC 23**
See also Vogau, Boris Andreyevich

Pincherle, Alberto 1907-1990 ... **CLC 11, 18**
See also Moravia, Alberto
See also CA 25-28R; 132; CANR 33; MTCW

Pinckney, Darryl 1953- .... **CLC 76**

Pindar 518B.C.-446B.C.......... **CMLC 12**

Pineda, Cecile 1942-.............. **CLC 39**
See also CA 118

Pinero, Arthur Wing 1855-1934 ... **TCLC 32**
See also CA 110; DLB 10

Pinero, Miguel (Antonio Gomez) 1946-1988 .... **CLC 4, 55**
See also CA 61-64; 125; CANR 29; HW

Pinget, Robert 1919- .... **CLC 7, 13, 37**
See also CA 85-88; DLB 83

Raphael, Frederic (Michael) 1931- .... **CLC 2, 14**
See also CA 1-4R; CANR 1; DLB 14

Ratcliffe, James P.
See Mencken, H(enry) L(ouis)

Rathbone, Julian 1935- .... **CLC 41**
See also CA 101; CANR 34

Rattigan, Terence (Mervyn) 1911-1977 .... **CLC 7**
See also CA 85-88; 73-76; CDBLB 1945-1960; DLB 13; MTCW

Ratushinskaya, Irina 1954- .... **CLC 54**
See also CA 129

Raven, Simon (Arthur Noel) 1927- .... **CLC 14**
See also CA 81-84

Rawley, Callman 1903-
See Rakosi, Carl
See also CA 21-24R; CANR 12, 32

Rawlings, Marjorie Kinnan 1896-1953 .... **TCLC 4**
See also CA 104; 137; DLB 9, 22, 102; JRDA; MAICYA; YABC 1

Ray, Satyajit 1921-1992 .... **CLC 16, 76**
See also CA 114; 137

Read, Herbert Edward 1893-1968 .... **CLC 4**
See also CA 85-88; 25-28R; DLB 20

Read, Piers Paul 1941- .... **CLC 4, 10, 25**
See also CA 21-24R; CANR 38; DLB 14; SATA 21

Reade, Charles 1814-1884 .... **NCLC 2**
See also DLB 21

Reade, Hamish
See Gray, Simon (James Holliday)

Reading, Peter 1946- .... **CLC 47**
See also CA 103; DLB 40

Reaney, James 1926- .... **CLC 13**
See also CA 41-44R; CAAS 15; CANR 42; DLB 68; SATA 43

Rebreanu, Liviu 1885-1944 .... **TCLC 28**

Rechy, John (Francisco) 1934- .... **CLC 1, 7, 14, 18**
See also CA 5-8R; CAAS 4; CANR 6, 32; DLB 122; DLBY 82; HW

Redcam, Tom 1870-1933 .... **TCLC 25**

Reddin, Keith .... **CLC 67**

Redgrove, Peter (William) 1932- .... **CLC 6, 41**
See also CA 1-4R; CANR 3, 39; DLB 40

Redmon, Anne .... **CLC 22**
See also Nightingale, Anne Redmon
See also DLBY 86

Reed, Eliot
See Ambler, Eric

Reed, Ishmael 1938- .... **CLC 2, 3, 5, 6, 13, 32, 60**
See also BLC 3; BW; CA 21-24R; CANR 25; DLB 2, 5, 33; DLBD 8; MTCW

Reed, John (Silas) 1887-1920 .... **TCLC 9**
See also CA 106

Reed, Lou .... **CLC 21**
See also Firbank, Louis

Reeve, Clara 1729-1807 .... **NCLC 19**
See also DLB 39

Reid, Christopher (John) 1949- .... **CLC 33**
See also CA 140; DLB 40

Reid, Desmond
See Moorcock, Michael (John)

Reid Banks, Lynne 1929-
See Banks, Lynne Reid
See also CA 1-4R; CANR 6, 22, 38; CLR 24; JRDA; MAICYA; SATA 22, 75

Reilly, William K.
See Creasey, John

Reiner, Max
See Caldwell, (Janet Miriam) Taylor (Holland)

Reis, Ricardo
See Pessoa, Fernando (Antonio Nogueira)

Remarque, Erich Maria 1898-1970 .... **CLC 21**
See also CA 77-80; 29-32R; DA; DLB 56; MTCW

Remizov, A.
See Remizov, Aleksei (Mikhailovich)

Remizov, A. M.
See Remizov, Aleksei (Mikhailovich)

Remizov, Aleksei (Mikhailovich) 1877-1957 .... **TCLC 27**
See also CA 125; 133

Renan, Joseph Ernest 1823-1892 .... **NCLC 26**

Renard, Jules 1864-1910 .... **TCLC 17**
See also CA 117

Renault, Mary .... **CLC 3, 11, 17**
See also Challans, Mary
See also DLBY 83

Rendell, Ruth (Barbara) 1930- .... **CLC 28, 48**
See also Vine, Barbara
See also CA 109; CANR 32; DLB 87; MTCW

Renoir, Jean 1894-1979 .... **CLC 20**
See also CA 129; 85-88

Resnais, Alain 1922- .... **CLC 16**

Reverdy, Pierre 1889-1960 .... **CLC 53**
See also CA 97-100; 89-92

Rexroth, Kenneth 1905-1982 .... **CLC 1, 2, 6, 11, 22, 49**
See also CA 5-8R; 107; CANR 14, 34; CDALB 1941-1968; DLB 16, 48; DLBY 82; MTCW

Reyes, Alfonso 1889-1959 .... **TCLC 33**
See also CA 131; HW

Reyes y Basoalto, Ricardo Eliecer Neftali
See Neruda, Pablo

Reymont, Wladyslaw (Stanislaw) 1868(?)-1925 .... **TCLC 5**
See also CA 104

Reynolds, Jonathan 1942- .... **CLC 6, 38**
See also CA 65-68; CANR 28

Reynolds, Joshua 1723-1792 .... **LC 15**
See also DLB 104

Reynolds, Michael Shane 1937- .... **CLC 44**
See also CA 65-68; CANR 9

Reznikoff, Charles 1894-1976 .... **CLC 9**
See also CA 33-36; 61-64; CAP 2; DLB 28, 45

Rezzori (d'Arezzo), Gregor von 1914- .... **CLC 25**
See also CA 122; 136

Rhine, Richard
See Silverstein, Alvin

R'hoone
See Balzac, Honore de

Rhys, Jean 1890(?)-1979 .... **CLC 2, 4, 6, 14, 19, 51**
See also CA 25-28R; 85-88; CANR 35; CDBLB 1945-1960; DLB 36, 117; MTCW

Ribeiro, Darcy 1922- .... **CLC 34**
See also CA 33-36R

Ribeiro, Joao Ubaldo (Osorio Pimentel) 1941- .... **CLC 10, 67**
See also CA 81-84

Ribman, Ronald (Burt) 1932- .... **CLC 7**
See also CA 21-24R

Ricci, Nino 1959- .... **CLC 70**
See also CA 137

Rice, Anne 1941- .... **CLC 41**
See also AAYA 9; BEST 89:2; CA 65-68; CANR 12, 36

Rice, Elmer (Leopold) 1892-1967 .... **CLC 7, 49**
See also CA 21-22; 25-28R; CAP 2; DLB 4, 7; MTCW

Rice, Tim 1944- .... **CLC 21**
See also CA 103

Rich, Adrienne (Cecile) 1929- .... **CLC 3, 6, 7, 11, 18, 36, 73, 76; PC 5**
See also CA 9-12R; CANR 20; DLB 5, 67; MTCW

Rich, Barbara
See Graves, Robert (von Ranke)

Rich, Robert
See Trumbo, Dalton

Richards, David Adams 1950- .... **CLC 59**
See also CA 93-96; DLB 53

Richards, I(vor) A(rmstrong) 1893-1979 .... **CLC 14, 24**
See also CA 41-44R; 89-92; CANR 34; DLB 27

Richardson, Anne
See Roiphe, Anne Richardson

Richardson, Dorothy Miller 1873-1957 .... **TCLC 3**
See also CA 104; DLB 36

Richardson, Ethel Florence (Lindesay) 1870-1946
See Richardson, Henry Handel
See also CA 105

Richardson, Henry Handel .... **TCLC 4**
See also Richardson, Ethel Florence (Lindesay)

Richardson, Samuel 1689-1761 .... **LC 1**
See also CDBLB 1660-1789; DA; DLB 39; WLC

Richler, Mordecai
1931- .... **CLC 3, 5, 9, 13, 18, 46, 70**
See also AITN 1; CA 65-68; CANR 31; CLR 17; DLB 53; MAICYA; MTCW; SATA 27, 44

Richter, Conrad (Michael)
1890-1968 .... **CLC 30**
See also CA 5-8R; 25-28R; CANR 23; DLB 9; MTCW; SATA 3

Riddell, J. H. 1832-1906 .... **TCLC 40**

Riding, Laura.................... **CLC 3, 7**
See also Jackson, Laura (Riding)

Riefenstahl, Berta Helene Amalia 1902-
See Riefenstahl, Leni
See also CA 108

Riefenstahl, Leni.................. **CLC 16**
See also Riefenstahl, Berta Helene Amalia

Riffe, Ernest
See Bergman, (Ernst) Ingmar

Riley, James Whitcomb
1849-1916 .... **TCLC 51**
See also CA 118; 137; MAICYA; SATA 17

Riley, Tex
See Creasey, John

Rilke, Rainer Maria
1875-1926 .... **TCLC 1, 6, 19; PC 2**
See also CA 104; 132; DLB 81; MTCW

Rimbaud, (Jean Nicolas) Arthur
1854-1891 .... **NCLC 4, 35; PC 3**
See also DA; WLC

Rinehart, Mary Roberts
1876-1958 .... **TCLC 52**
See also CA 108

Ringmaster, The
See Mencken, H(enry) L(ouis)

Ringwood, Gwen(dolyn Margaret) Pharis
1910-1984 .... **CLC 48**
See also CA 112; DLB 88

Rio, Michel 19(?)-................ **CLC 43**

Ritsos, Giannes
See Ritsos, Yannis

Ritsos, Yannis 1909-1990..... **CLC 6, 13, 31**
See also CA 77-80; 133; CANR 39; MTCW

Ritter, Erika 1948(?)-............. **CLC 52**

Rivera, Jose Eustasio 1889-1928... **TCLC 35**
See also HW

Rivers, Conrad Kent 1933-1968...... **CLC 1**
See also BW; CA 85-88; DLB 41

Rivers, Elfrida
See Bradley, Marion Zimmer

Riverside, John
See Heinlein, Robert A(nson)

Rizal, Jose 1861-1896........... **NCLC 27**

Roa Bastos, Augusto (Antonio)
1917- .... **CLC 45**
See also CA 131; DLB 113; HW

Robbe-Grillet, Alain
1922- ...... **CLC 1, 2, 4, 6, 8, 10, 14, 43**
See also CA 9-12R; CANR 33; DLB 83; MTCW

Robbins, Harold 1916-............. **CLC 5**
See also CA 73-76; CANR 26; MTCW

Robbins, Thomas Eugene 1936-
See Robbins, Tom
See also CA 81-84; CANR 29; MTCW

Robbins, Tom............... **CLC 9, 32, 64**
See also Robbins, Thomas Eugene
See also BEST 90:3; DLBY 80

Robbins, Trina 1938-............. **CLC 21**
See also CA 128

Roberts, Charles G(eorge) D(ouglas)
1860-1943 .... **TCLC 8**
See also CA 105; DLB 92; SATA 29

Roberts, Kate 1891-1985 .... **CLC 15**
See also CA 107; 116

Roberts, Keith (John Kingston)
1935- .... **CLC 14**
See also CA 25-28R

Roberts, Kenneth (Lewis)
1885-1957 .... **TCLC 23**
See also CA 109; DLB 9

Roberts, Michele (B.) 1949-........ **CLC 48**
See also CA 115

Robertson, Ellis
See Ellison, Harlan; Silverberg, Robert

Robertson, Thomas William
1829-1871 .... **NCLC 35**

Robinson, Edwin Arlington
1869-1935 .... **TCLC 5; PC 1**
See also CA 104; 133; CDALB 1865-1917; DA; DLB 54; MTCW

Robinson, Henry Crabb
1775-1867 .... **NCLC 15**
See also DLB 107

Robinson, Jill 1936-.............. **CLC 10**
See also CA 102

Robinson, Kim Stanley 1952- ...... **CLC 34**
See also CA 126

Robinson, Lloyd
See Silverberg, Robert

Robinson, Marilynne 1944-........ **CLC 25**
See also CA 116

Robinson, Smokey................. **CLC 21**
See also Robinson, William, Jr.

Robinson, William, Jr. 1940-
See Robinson, Smokey
See also CA 116

Robison, Mary 1949-............. **CLC 42**
See also CA 113; 116; DLB 130

Rod, Edouard 1857-1910 .... **TCLC 52**

Roddenberry, Eugene Wesley 1921-1991
See Roddenberry, Gene
See also CA 110; 135; CANR 37; SATA 45

Roddenberry, Gene................ **CLC 17**
See also Roddenberry, Eugene Wesley
See also AAYA 5; SATA-Obit 69

Rodgers, Mary 1931-............. **CLC 12**
See also CA 49-52; CANR 8; CLR 20; JRDA; MAICYA; SATA 8

Rodgers, W(illiam) R(obert)
1909-1969 .... **CLC 7**
See also CA 85-88; DLB 20

Rodman, Eric
See Silverberg, Robert

Rodman, Howard 1920(?)-1985..... **CLC 65**
See also CA 118

Rodman, Maia
See Wojciechowska, Maia (Teresa)

Rodriguez, Claudio 1934-.......... **CLC 10**
See also DLB 134

Roelvaag, O(le) E(dvart)
1876-1931 .... **TCLC 17**
See also CA 117; DLB 9

Roethke, Theodore (Huebner)
1908-1963 ...... **CLC 1, 3, 8, 11, 19, 46**
See also CA 81-84; CABS 2; CDALB 1941-1968; DLB 5; MTCW

Rogers, Thomas Hunton 1927- ..... **CLC 57**
See also CA 89-92

Rogers, Will(iam Penn Adair)
1879-1935 .... **TCLC 8**
See also CA 105; DLB 11

Rogin, Gilbert 1929-.............. **CLC 18**
See also CA 65-68; CANR 15

Rohan, Koda .... **TCLC 22**
See also Koda Shigeyuki

Rohmer, Eric..................... **CLC 16**
See also Scherer, Jean-Marie Maurice

Rohmer, Sax .... **TCLC 28**
See also Ward, Arthur Henry Sarsfield
See also DLB 70

Roiphe, Anne Richardson 1935- ... **CLC 3, 9**
See also CA 89-92; DLBY 80

Rojas, Fernando de 1465-1541 ...... **LC 23**

Rolfe, Frederick (William Serafino Austin Lewis Mary) 1860-1913...... **TCLC 12**
See also CA 107; DLB 34

Rolland, Romain 1866-1944....... **TCLC 23**
See also CA 118; DLB 65

Rolvaag, O(le) E(dvart)
See Roelvaag, O(le) E(dvart)

Romain Arnaud, Saint
See Aragon, Louis

Romains, Jules 1885-1972 .... **CLC 7**
See also CA 85-88; CANR 34; DLB 65; MTCW

Romero, Jose Ruben 1890-1952 ... **TCLC 14**
See also CA 114; 131; HW

Ronsard, Pierre de 1524-1585........ **LC 6**

Rooke, Leon 1934-............ **CLC 25, 34**
See also CA 25-28R; CANR 23

Roper, William 1498-1578 .... **LC 10**

Roquelaure, A. N.
See Rice, Anne

Rosa, Joao Guimaraes 1908-1967 ... **CLC 23**
See also CA 89-92; DLB 113

Rosen, Richard (Dean) 1949-....... **CLC 39**
See also CA 77-80

Rosenberg, Isaac 1890-1918....... **TCLC 12**
See also CA 107; DLB 20

Rosenblatt, Joe .... **CLC 15**
See also Rosenblatt, Joseph

Rosenblatt, Joseph 1933-
See Rosenblatt, Joe
See also CA 89-92

Rosenfeld, Samuel 1896-1963
See Tzara, Tristan
See also CA 89-92

Saki .... **TCLC 3; SSC 12**
See also Munro, H(ector) H(ugh)

Salama, Hannu 1936- .... **CLC 18**

Salamanca, J(ack) R(ichard) 1922- .... **CLC 4, 15**
See also CA 25-28R

Sale, J. Kirkpatrick
See Sale, Kirkpatrick

Sale, Kirkpatrick 1937- .... **CLC 68**
See also CA 13-16R; CANR 10

Salinas (y Serrano), Pedro 1891(?)-1951 .... **TCLC 17**
See also CA 117; DLB 134

Salinger, J(erome) D(avid) 1919- .... **CLC 1, 3, 8, 12, 55, 56; SSC 2**
See also AAYA 2; CA 5-8R; CANR 39; CDALB 1941-1968; CLR 18; DA; DLB 2, 102; MAICYA; MTCW; SATA 67; WLC

Salisbury, John
See Caute, David

Salter, James 1925- .... **CLC 7, 52, 59**
See also CA 73-76; DLB 130

Saltus, Edgar (Everton) 1855-1921 .... **TCLC 8**
See also CA 105

Saltykov, Mikhail Evgrafovich 1826-1889 .... **NCLC 16**

Samarakis, Antonis 1919- .... **CLC 5**
See also CA 25-28R; CAAS 16; CANR 36

Sanchez, Florencio 1875-1910 ..... **TCLC 37**
See also HW

Sanchez, Luis Rafael 1936- .... **CLC 23**
See also CA 128; HW

Sanchez, Sonia 1934- .... **CLC 5**
See also BLC 3; BW; CA 33-36R; CANR 24; CLR 18; DLB 41; DLBD 8; MAICYA; MTCW; SATA 22

Sand, George 1804-1876 .... **NCLC 2, 42**
See also DA; DLB 119; WLC

Sandburg, Carl (August) 1878-1967 ... **CLC 1, 4, 10, 15, 35; PC 2**
See also CA 5-8R; 25-28R; CANR 35; CDALB 1865-1917; DA; DLB 17, 54; MAICYA; MTCW; SATA 8; WLC

Sandburg, Charles
See Sandburg, Carl (August)

Sandburg, Charles A.
See Sandburg, Carl (August)

Sanders, (James) Ed(ward) 1939- ... **CLC 53**
See also CA 13-16R; CANR 13; DLB 16

Sanders, Lawrence 1920- .... **CLC 41**
See also BEST 89:4; CA 81-84; CANR 33; MTCW

Sanders, Noah
See Blount, Roy (Alton), Jr.

Sanders, Winston P.
See Anderson, Poul (William)

Sandoz, Mari(e Susette) 1896-1966 .... **CLC 28**
See also CA 1-4R; 25-28R; CANR 17; DLB 9; MTCW; SATA 5

Saner, Reg(inald Anthony) 1931- .... **CLC 9**
See also CA 65-68

Sannazaro, Jacopo 1456(?)-1530 ...... **LC 8**

Sansom, William 1912-1976 .... **CLC 2, 6**
See also CA 5-8R; 65-68; CANR 42; MTCW

Santayana, George 1863-1952 ..... **TCLC 40**
See also CA 115; DLB 54, 71

Santiago, Danny .... **CLC 33**
See also James, Daniel (Lewis); James, Daniel (Lewis)
See also DLB 122

Santmyer, Helen Hooven 1895-1986 .... **CLC 33**
See also CA 1-4R; 118; CANR 15, 33; DLBY 84; MTCW

Santos, Bienvenido N(uqui) 1911- ... **CLC 22**
See also CA 101; CANR 19

Sapper .... **TCLC 44**
See also McNeile, Herman Cyril

Sappho fl. 6th cent. B.C.- .... **CMLC 3; PC 5**

Sarduy, Severo 1937-1993 .... **CLC 6**
See also CA 89-92; 142; DLB 113; HW

Sargeson, Frank 1903-1982 .... **CLC 31**
See also CA 25-28R; 106; CANR 38

Sarmiento, Felix Ruben Garcia
See Dario, Ruben

Saroyan, William 1908-1981 ..... **CLC 1, 8, 10, 29, 34, 56**
See also CA 5-8R; 103; CANR 30; DA; DLB 7, 9, 86; DLBY 81; MTCW; SATA 23, 24; WLC

Sarraute, Nathalie 1900- .... **CLC 1, 2, 4, 8, 10, 31**
See also CA 9-12R; CANR 23; DLB 83; MTCW

Sarton, (Eleanor) May 1912- .... **CLC 4, 14, 49**
See also CA 1-4R; CANR 1, 34; DLB 48; DLBY 81; MTCW; SATA 36

Sartre, Jean-Paul 1905-1980 .... **CLC 1, 4, 7, 9, 13, 18, 24, 44, 50, 52; DC 3**
See also CA 9-12R; 97-100; CANR 21; DA; DLB 72; MTCW; WLC

Sassoon, Siegfried (Lorraine) 1886-1967 .... **CLC 36**
See also CA 104; 25-28R; CANR 36; DLB 20; MTCW

Satterfield, Charles
See Pohl, Frederik

Saul, John (W. III) 1942- .... **CLC 46**
See also AAYA 10; BEST 90:4; CA 81-84; CANR 16, 40

Saunders, Caleb
See Heinlein, Robert A(nson)

Saura (Atares), Carlos 1932- .... **CLC 20**
See also CA 114; 131; HW

Saurraute, Nathalie 1900- .... **CLC 80**

Sauser-Hall, Frederic 1887-1961 .... **CLC 18**
See also CA 102; 93-96; CANR 36; MTCW

Saussure, Ferdinand de 1857-1913 .... **TCLC 49**

Savage, Catharine
See Brosman, Catharine Savage

Savage, Thomas 1915- .... **CLC 40**
See also CA 126; 132; CAAS 15

Savan, Glenn .... **CLC 50**

Saven, Glenn 19(?)- .... **CLC 50**

Sayers, Dorothy L(eigh) 1893-1957 .... **TCLC 2, 15**
See also CA 104; 119; CDBLB 1914-1945; DLB 10, 36, 77, 100; MTCW

Sayers, Valerie 1952- .... **CLC 50**
See also CA 134

Sayles, John (Thomas) 1950- .... **CLC 7, 10, 14**
See also CA 57-60; CANR 41; DLB 44

Scammell, Michael .... **CLC 34**

Scannell, Vernon 1922- .... **CLC 49**
See also CA 5-8R; CANR 8, 24; DLB 27; SATA 59

Scarlett, Susan
See Streatfeild, (Mary) Noel

Schaeffer, Susan Fromberg 1941- .... **CLC 6, 11, 22**
See also CA 49-52; CANR 18; DLB 28; MTCW; SATA 22

Schary, Jill
See Robinson, Jill

Schell, Jonathan 1943- .... **CLC 35**
See also CA 73-76; CANR 12

Schelling, Friedrich Wilhelm Joseph von 1775-1854 .... **NCLC 30**
See also DLB 90

Scherer, Jean-Marie Maurice 1920-
See Rohmer, Eric
See also CA 110

Schevill, James (Erwin) 1920- .... **CLC 7**
See also CA 5-8R; CAAS 12

Schiller, Friedrich 1759-1805 .... **NCLC 39**
See also DLB 94

Schisgal, Murray (Joseph) 1926- .... **CLC 6**
See also CA 21-24R

Schlee, Ann 1934- .... **CLC 35**
See also CA 101; CANR 29; SATA 36, 44

Schlegel, August Wilhelm von 1767-1845 .... **NCLC 15**
See also DLB 94

Schlegel, Johann Elias (von) 1719(?)-1749 .... **LC 5**

Schmidt, Arno (Otto) 1914-1979 .... **CLC 56**
See also CA 128; 109; DLB 69

Schmitz, Aron Hector 1861-1928
See Svevo, Italo
See also CA 104; 122; MTCW

Schnackenberg, Gjertrud 1953- ..... **CLC 40**
See also CA 116; DLB 120

Schneider, Leonard Alfred 1925-1966
See Bruce, Lenny
See also CA 89-92

Schnitzler, Arthur 1862-1931 ...... **TCLC 4**
See also CA 104; DLB 81, 118

Schor, Sandra (M.) 1932(?)-1990 ... **CLC 65**
See also CA 132

Schorer, Mark 1908-1977 .... **CLC 9**
See also CA 5-8R; 73-76; CANR 7; DLB 103

Schrader, Paul (Joseph) 1946- . . . . . . **CLC 26**
See also CA 37-40R; CANR 41; DLB 44

Schreiner, Olive (Emilie Albertina) 1855-1920 . . . . . . **TCLC 9**
See also CA 105; DLB 18

Schulberg, Budd (Wilson) 1914- . . . . . . **CLC 7, 48**
See also CA 25-28R; CANR 19; DLB 6, 26, 28; DLBY 81

Schulz, Bruno 1892-1942 . . . . . . **TCLC 5, 51; SSC 13**
See also CA 115; 123

Schulz, Charles M(onroe) 1922- . . . . **CLC 12**
See also CA 9-12R; CANR 6; SATA 10

Schumacher, Ernst Friedrich 1911-1977 . . . . . . **CLC 80**
See also CA 81-84; 73-76; CANR 34

Schuyler, James Marcus 1923-1991 . . . . . . **CLC 5, 23**
See also CA 101; 134; DLB 5

Schwartz, Delmore (David) 1913-1966 . . . . . . **CLC 2, 4, 10, 45**
See also CA 17-18; 25-28R; CANR 35; CAP 2; DLB 28, 48; MTCW

Schwartz, Ernst
See Ozu, Yasujiro

Schwartz, John Burnham 1965- . . . . **CLC 59**
See also CA 132

Schwartz, Lynne Sharon 1939- . . . . . **CLC 31**
See also CA 103

Schwartz, Muriel A.
See Eliot, T(homas) S(tearns)

Schwarz-Bart, Andre 1928- . . . . **CLC 2, 4**
See also CA 89-92

Schwarz-Bart, Simone 1938- . . . . **CLC 7**
See also CA 97-100

Schwob, (Mayer Andre) Marcel 1867-1905 . . . . . . **TCLC 20**
See also CA 117; DLB 123

Sciascia, Leonardo 1921-1989 . . . . . . **CLC 8, 9, 41**
See also CA 85-88; 130; CANR 35; MTCW

Scoppettone, Sandra 1936- . . . . **CLC 26**
See also CA 5-8R; CANR 41; SATA 9

Scorsese, Martin 1942- . . . . **CLC 20**
See also CA 110; 114

Scotland, Jay
See Jakes, John (William)

Scott, Duncan Campbell 1862-1947 . . . . . . **TCLC 6**
See also CA 104; DLB 92

Scott, Evelyn 1893-1963 . . . . **CLC 43**
See also CA 104; 112; DLB 9, 48

Scott, F(rancis) R(eginald) 1899-1985 . . . . . . **CLC 22**
See also CA 101; 114; DLB 88

Scott, Frank
See Scott, F(rancis) R(eginald)

Scott, Joanna 1960- . . . . **CLC 50**
See also CA 126

Scott, Paul (Mark) 1920-1978 . . . . **CLC 9, 60**
See also CA 81-84; 77-80; CANR 33; DLB 14; MTCW

Scott, Walter 1771-1832 . . . . **NCLC 15**
See also CDBLB 1789-1832; DA; DLB 93, 107, 116; WLC; YABC 2

Scribe, (Augustin) Eugene 1791-1861 . . . . . . **NCLC 16**

Scrum, R.
See Crumb, R(obert)

Scudery, Madeleine de 1607-1701 . . . . . **LC 2**

Scum
See Crumb, R(obert)

Scumbag, Little Bobby
See Crumb, R(obert)

Seabrook, John
See Hubbard, L(afayette) Ron(ald)

Sealy, I. Allan 1951- . . . . **CLC 55**

Search, Alexander
See Pessoa, Fernando (Antonio Nogueira)

Sebastian, Lee
See Silverberg, Robert

Sebastian Owl
See Thompson, Hunter S(tockton)

Sebestyen, Ouida 1924- . . . . **CLC 30**
See also AAYA 8; CA 107; CANR 40; CLR 17; JRDA; MAICYA; SAAS 10; SATA 39

Secundus, H. Scriblerus
See Fielding, Henry

Sedges, John
See Buck, Pearl S(ydenstricker)

Sedgwick, Catharine Maria 1789-1867 . . . . . . **NCLC 19**
See also DLB 1, 74

Seelye, John 1931- . . . . **CLC 7**

Seferiades, Giorgos Stylianou 1900-1971
See Seferis, George
See also CA 5-8R; 33-36R; CANR 5, 36; MTCW

Seferis, George . . . . **CLC 5, 11**
See also Seferiades, Giorgos Stylianou

Segal, Erich (Wolf) 1937- . . . . **CLC 3, 10**
See also BEST 89:1; CA 25-28R; CANR 20, 36; DLBY 86; MTCW

Seger, Bob 1945- . . . . **CLC 35**

Seghers, Anna . . . . **CLC 7**
See also Radvanyi, Netty
See also DLB 69

Seidel, Frederick (Lewis) 1936- . . . . . **CLC 18**
See also CA 13-16R; CANR 8; DLBY 84

Seifert, Jaroslav 1901-1986 . . . . . **CLC 34, 44**
See also CA 127; MTCW

Sei Shonagon c. 966-1017(?) . . . . . . **CMLC 6**

Selby, Hubert, Jr. 1928- . . . . . **CLC 1, 2, 4, 8**
See also CA 13-16R; CANR 33; DLB 2

Selzer, Richard 1928- . . . . **CLC 74**
See also CA 65-68; CANR 14

Sembene, Ousmane
See Ousmane, Sembene

Senancour, Etienne Pivert de 1770-1846 . . . . . . **NCLC 16**
See also DLB 119

Sender, Ramon (Jose) 1902-1982 . . . . **CLC 8**
See also CA 5-8R; 105; CANR 8; HW; MTCW

Seneca, Lucius Annaeus 4B.C.-65 . . . . **CMLC 6**

Senghor, Leopold Sedar 1906- . . . . . . **CLC 54**
See also BLC 3; BW; CA 116; 125; MTCW

Serling, (Edward) Rod(man) 1924-1975 . . . . . . **CLC 30**
See also AITN 1; CA 65-68; 57-60; DLB 26

Serna, Ramon Gomez de la
See Gomez de la Serna, Ramon

Serpieres
See Guillevic, (Eugene)

Service, Robert
See Service, Robert W(illiam)
See also DLB 92

Service, Robert W(illiam) 1874(?)-1958 . . . . . . **TCLC 15**
See also Service, Robert
See also CA 115; 140; DA; SATA 20; WLC

Seth, Vikram 1952- . . . . **CLC 43**
See also CA 121; 127; DLB 120

Seton, Cynthia Propper 1926-1982 . . . . . . **CLC 27**
See also CA 5-8R; 108; CANR 7

Seton, Ernest (Evan) Thompson 1860-1946 . . . . . . **TCLC 31**
See also CA 109; DLB 92; JRDA; SATA 18

Seton-Thompson, Ernest
See Seton, Ernest (Evan) Thompson

Settle, Mary Lee 1918- . . . . **CLC 19, 61**
See also CA 89-92; CAAS 1; DLB 6

Seuphor, Michel
See Arp, Jean

Sevigne, Marie (de Rabutin-Chantal) Marquise de 1626-1696 . . . . . . **LC 11**

Sexton, Anne (Harvey) 1928-1974 . . . . **CLC 2, 4, 6, 8, 10, 15, 53; PC 2**
See also CA 1-4R; 53-56; CABS 2; CANR 3, 36; CDALB 1941-1968; DA; DLB 5; MTCW; SATA 10; WLC

Shaara, Michael (Joseph Jr.) 1929-1988 . . . . . . **CLC 15**
See also AITN 1; CA 102; DLBY 83

Shackleton, C. C.
See Aldiss, Brian W(ilson)

Shacochis, Bob . . . . **CLC 39**
See also Shacochis, Robert G.

Shacochis, Robert G. 1951-
See Shacochis, Bob
See also CA 119; 124

Shaffer, Anthony (Joshua) 1926- . . . . **CLC 19**
See also CA 110; 116; DLB 13

Shaffer, Peter (Levin) 1926- . . . . **CLC 5, 14, 18, 37, 60**
See also CA 25-28R; CANR 25; CDBLB 1960 to Present; DLB 13; MTCW

Shakey, Bernard
See Young, Neil

Shalamov, Varlam (Tikhonovich) 1907(?)-1982 . . . . . . **CLC 18**
See also CA 129; 105

Shamlu, Ahmad 1925- . . . . **CLC 10**

Shammas, Anton 1951- . . . . **CLC 55**

Shange, Ntozake
1948- . . . . **CLC 8, 25, 38, 74; DC 3**
See also AAYA 9; BLC 3; BW; CA 85-88; CABS 3; CANR 27; DLB 38; MTCW

Shanley, John Patrick 1950- . . . . **CLC 75**
See also CA 128; 133

Shapcott, Thomas William 1935- . . . **CLC 38**
See also CA 69-72

Shapiro, Jane . . . . **CLC 76**

Shapiro, Karl (Jay) 1913- . . **CLC 4, 8, 15, 53**
See also CA 1-4R; CAAS 6; CANR 1, 36; DLB 48; MTCW

Sharp, William 1855-1905 . . . . **TCLC 39**

Sharpe, Thomas Ridley 1928-
See Sharpe, Tom
See also CA 114; 122

Sharpe, Tom . . . . **CLC 36**
See also Sharpe, Thomas Ridley
See also DLB 14

Shaw, Bernard . . . . **TCLC 45**
See also Shaw, George Bernard

Shaw, G. Bernard
See Shaw, George Bernard

Shaw, George Bernard
1856-1950 . . . . **TCLC 3, 9, 21**
See also Shaw, Bernard
See also CA 104; 128; CDBLB 1914-1945; DA; DLB 10, 57; MTCW; WLC

Shaw, Henry Wheeler
1818-1885 . . . . **NCLC 15**
See also DLB 11

Shaw, Irwin 1913-1984 . . . . **CLC 7, 23, 34**
See also AITN 1; CA 13-16R; 112; CANR 21; CDALB 1941-1968; DLB 6, 102; DLBY 84; MTCW

Shaw, Robert 1927-1978 . . . . **CLC 5**
See also AITN 1; CA 1-4R; 81-84; CANR 4; DLB 13, 14

Shaw, T. E.
See Lawrence, T(homas) E(dward)

Shawn, Wallace 1943- . . . . **CLC 41**
See also CA 112

Sheed, Wilfrid (John Joseph)
1930- . . . . **CLC 2, 4, 10, 53**
See also CA 65-68; CANR 30; DLB 6; MTCW

Sheldon, Alice Hastings Bradley
1915(?)-1987
See Tiptree, James, Jr.
See also CA 108; 122; CANR 34; MTCW

Sheldon, John
See Bloch, Robert (Albert)

Shelley, Mary Wollstonecraft (Godwin)
1797-1851 . . . . **NCLC 14**
See also CDBLB 1789-1832; DA; DLB 110, 116; SATA 29; WLC

Shelley, Percy Bysshe
1792-1822 . . . . **NCLC 18**
See also CDBLB 1789-1832; DA; DLB 96, 110; WLC

Shepard, Jim 1956- . . . . **CLC 36**
See also CA 137

Shepard, Lucius 1947- . . . . **CLC 34**
See also CA 128; 141

Shepard, Sam
1943- . . . . **CLC 4, 6, 17, 34, 41, 44**
See also AAYA 1; CA 69-72; CABS 3; CANR 22; DLB 7; MTCW

Shepherd, Michael
See Ludlum, Robert

Sherburne, Zoa (Morin) 1912- . . . . . . **CLC 30**
See also CA 1-4R; CANR 3, 37; MAICYA; SATA 3

Sheridan, Frances 1724-1766 . . . . **LC 7**
See also DLB 39, 84

Sheridan, Richard Brinsley
1751-1816 . . . . **NCLC 5; DC 1**
See also CDBLB 1660-1789; DA; DLB 89; WLC

Sherman, Jonathan Marc . . . . **CLC 55**

Sherman, Martin 1941(?)- . . . . **CLC 19**
See also CA 116; 123

Sherwin, Judith Johnson 1936- . . . **CLC 7, 15**
See also CA 25-28R; CANR 34

Sherwood, Robert E(mmet)
1896-1955 . . . . **TCLC 3**
See also CA 104; DLB 7, 26

Shiel, M(atthew) P(hipps)
1865-1947 . . . . **TCLC 8**
See also CA 106

Shiga, Naoya 1883-1971 . . . . **CLC 33**
See also CA 101; 33-36R

Shimazaki Haruki 1872-1943
See Shimazaki Toson
See also CA 105; 134

Shimazaki Toson . . . . **TCLC 5**
See also Shimazaki Haruki

Sholokhov, Mikhail (Aleksandrovich)
1905-1984 . . . . **CLC 7, 15**
See also CA 101; 112; MTCW; SATA 36

Shone, Patric
See Hanley, James

Shreve, Susan Richards 1939- . . . . . . **CLC 23**
See also CA 49-52; CAAS 5; CANR 5, 38; MAICYA; SATA 41, 46

Shue, Larry 1946-1985 . . . . **CLC 52**
See also CA 117

Shu-Jen, Chou 1881-1936
See Hsun, Lu
See also CA 104

Shulman, Alix Kates 1932- . . . . . . **CLC 2, 10**
See also CA 29-32R; CANR 43; SATA 7

Shuster, Joe 1914- . . . . **CLC 21**

Shute, Nevil . . . . **CLC 30**
See also Norway, Nevil Shute

Shuttle, Penelope (Diane) 1947- . . . . . **CLC 7**
See also CA 93-96; CANR 39; DLB 14, 40

Sidney, Mary 1561-1621 . . . . **LC 19**

Sidney, Sir Philip 1554-1586 . . . . **LC 19**
See also CDBLB Before 1660; DA

Siegel, Jerome 1914- . . . . **CLC 21**
See also CA 116

Siegel, Jerry
See Siegel, Jerome

Sienkiewicz, Henryk (Adam Alexander Pius)
1846-1916 . . . . **TCLC 3**
See also CA 104; 134

Sierra, Gregorio Martinez
See Martinez Sierra, Gregorio

Sierra, Maria (de la O'LeJarraga) Martinez
See Martinez Sierra, Maria (de la O'LeJarraga)

Sigal, Clancy 1926- . . . . **CLC 7**
See also CA 1-4R

Sigourney, Lydia Howard (Huntley)
1791-1865 . . . . **NCLC 21**
See also DLB 1, 42, 73

Siguenza y Gongora, Carlos de
1645-1700 . . . . **LC 8**

Sigurjonsson, Johann 1880-1919 . . . **TCLC 27**

Sikelianos, Angelos 1884-1951 . . . . **TCLC 39**

Silkin, Jon 1930- . . . . **CLC 2, 6, 43**
See also CA 5-8R; CAAS 5; DLB 27

Silko, Leslie Marmon 1948- . . . . **CLC 23, 74**
See also CA 115; 122; DA

Sillanpaa, Frans Eemil 1888-1964 . . . **CLC 19**
See also CA 129; 93-96; MTCW

Sillitoe, Alan
1928- . . . . **CLC 1, 3, 6, 10, 19, 57**
See also AITN 1; CA 9-12R; CAAS 2; CANR 8, 26; CDBLB 1960 to Present; DLB 14; MTCW; SATA 61

Silone, Ignazio 1900-1978 . . . . **CLC 4**
See also CA 25-28; 81-84; CANR 34; CAP 2; MTCW

Silver, Joan Micklin 1935- . . . . **CLC 20**
See also CA 114; 121

Silver, Nicholas
See Faust, Frederick (Schiller)

Silverberg, Robert 1935- . . . . **CLC 7**
See also CA 1-4R; CAAS 3; CANR 1, 20, 36; DLB 8; MAICYA; MTCW; SATA 13

Silverstein, Alvin 1933- . . . . **CLC 17**
See also CA 49-52; CANR 2; CLR 25; JRDA; MAICYA; SATA 8, 69

Silverstein, Virginia B(arbara Opshelor)
1937- . . . . **CLC 17**
See also CA 49-52; CANR 2; CLR 25; JRDA; MAICYA; SATA 8, 69

Sim, Georges
See Simenon, Georges (Jacques Christian)

Simak, Clifford D(onald)
1904-1988 . . . . **CLC 1, 55**
See also CA 1-4R; 125; CANR 1, 35; DLB 8; MTCW; SATA 56

Simenon, Georges (Jacques Christian)
1903-1989 . . . . **CLC 1, 2, 3, 8, 18, 47**
See also CA 85-88; 129; CANR 35; DLB 72; DLBY 89; MTCW

Simic, Charles 1938- . . . **CLC 6, 9, 22, 49, 68**
See also CA 29-32R; CAAS 4; CANR 12, 33; DLB 105

Simmons, Charles (Paul) 1924- . . . . . **CLC 57**
See also CA 89-92

Simmons, Dan 1948- . . . . **CLC 44**
See also CA 138

Simmons, James (Stewart Alexander)
1933- . . . . **CLC 43**
See also CA 105; DLB 40

Simms, William Gilmore 1806-1870 .... **NCLC 3**
See also DLB 3, 30, 59, 73

Simon, Carly 1945-............... **CLC 26**
See also CA 105

Simon, Claude 1913-....... **CLC 4, 9, 15, 39**
See also CA 89-92; CANR 33; DLB 83; MTCW

Simon, (Marvin) Neil 1927-........... **CLC 6, 11, 31, 39, 70**
See also AITN 1; CA 21-24R; CANR 26; DLB 7; MTCW

Simon, Paul 1942(?)- .... **CLC 17**
See also CA 116

Simonon, Paul 1956(?)- .... **CLC 30**
See also Clash, The

Simpson, Harriette
See Arnow, Harriette (Louisa) Simpson

Simpson, Louis (Aston Marantz) 1923- .... **CLC 4, 7, 9, 32**
See also CA 1-4R; CAAS 4; CANR 1; DLB 5; MTCW

Simpson, Mona (Elizabeth) 1957-... **CLC 44**
See also CA 122; 135

Simpson, N(orman) F(rederick) 1919- .... **CLC 29**
See also CA 13-16R; DLB 13

Sinclair, Andrew (Annandale) 1935- .... **CLC 2, 14**
See also CA 9-12R; CAAS 5; CANR 14, 38; DLB 14; MTCW

Sinclair, Emil
See Hesse, Hermann

Sinclair, Iain 1943-............... **CLC 76**
See also CA 132

Sinclair, Iain MacGregor
See Sinclair, Iain

Sinclair, Mary Amelia St. Clair 1865(?)-1946
See Sinclair, May
See also CA 104

Sinclair, May................. **TCLC 3, 11**
See also Sinclair, Mary Amelia St. Clair
See also DLB 36

Sinclair, Upton (Beall) 1878-1968 .... **CLC 1, 11, 15, 63**
See also CA 5-8R; 25-28R; CANR 7; CDALB 1929-1941; DA; DLB 9; MTCW; SATA 9; WLC

Singer, Isaac
See Singer, Isaac Bashevis

Singer, Isaac Bashevis 1904-1991 .... **CLC 1, 3, 6, 9, 11, 15, 23, 38, 69; SSC 3**
See also AITN 1, 2; CA 1-4R; 134; CANR 1, 39; CDALB 1941-1968; CLR 1; DA; DLB 6, 28, 52; DLBY 91; JRDA; MAICYA; MTCW; SATA 3, 27; SATA-Obit 68; WLC

Singer, Israel Joshua 1893-1944 ... **TCLC 33**

Singh, Khushwant 1915-........... **CLC 11**
See also CA 9-12R; CAAS 9; CANR 6

Sinjohn, John
See Galsworthy, John

Sinyavsky, Andrei (Donatevich) 1925- .... **CLC 8**
See also CA 85-88

Sirin, V.
See Nabokov, Vladimir (Vladimirovich)

Sissman, L(ouis) E(dward) 1928-1976 .... **CLC 9, 18**
See also CA 21-24R; 65-68; CANR 13; DLB 5

Sisson, C(harles) H(ubert) 1914-..... **CLC 8**
See also CA 1-4R; CAAS 3; CANR 3; DLB 27

Sitwell, Dame Edith 1887-1964 .... **CLC 2, 9, 67; PC 3**
See also CA 9-12R; CANR 35; CDBLB 1945-1960; DLB 20; MTCW

Sjoewall, Maj 1935-............... **CLC 7**
See also CA 65-68

Sjowall, Maj
See Sjoewall, Maj

Skelton, Robin 1925-............. **CLC 13**
See also AITN 2; CA 5-8R; CAAS 5; CANR 28; DLB 27, 53

Skolimowski, Jerzy 1938- .... **CLC 20**
See also CA 128

Skram, Amalie (Bertha) 1847-1905 .... **TCLC 25**

Skvorecky, Josef (Vaclav) 1924- .... **CLC 15, 39, 69**
See also CA 61-64; CAAS 1; CANR 10, 34; MTCW

Slade, Bernard................. **CLC 11, 46**
See also Newbound, Bernard Slade
See also CAAS 9; DLB 53

Slaughter, Carolyn 1946-.......... **CLC 56**
See also CA 85-88

Slaughter, Frank G(ill) 1908- ...... **CLC 29**
See also AITN 2; CA 5-8R; CANR 5

Slavitt, David R(ytman) 1935-.... **CLC 5, 14**
See also CA 21-24R; CAAS 3; CANR 41; DLB 5, 6

Slesinger, Tess 1905-1945 .... **TCLC 10**
See also CA 107; DLB 102

Slessor, Kenneth 1901-1971........ **CLC 14**
See also CA 102; 89-92

Slowacki, Juliusz 1809-1849 ..... **NCLC 15**

Smart, Christopher 1722-1771........ **LC 3**
See also DLB 109

Smart, Elizabeth 1913-1986........ **CLC 54**
See also CA 81-84; 118; DLB 88

Smiley, Jane (Graves) 1949- .... **CLC 53, 76**
See also CA 104; CANR 30

Smith, A(rthur) J(ames) M(arshall) 1902-1980 .... **CLC 15**
See also CA 1-4R; 102; CANR 4; DLB 88

Smith, Betty (Wehner) 1896-1972... **CLC 19**
See also CA 5-8R; 33-36R; DLBY 82; SATA 6

Smith, Charlotte (Turner) 1749-1806 .... **NCLC 23**
See also DLB 39, 109

Smith, Clark Ashton 1893-1961 .... **CLC 43**

Smith, Dave.................. **CLC 22, 42**
See also Smith, David (Jeddie)
See also CAAS 7; DLB 5

Smith, David (Jeddie) 1942-
See Smith, Dave
See also CA 49-52; CANR 1

Smith, Florence Margaret 1902-1971 .... **CLC 8**
See also Smith, Stevie
See also CA 17-18; 29-32R; CANR 35; CAP 2; MTCW

Smith, Iain Crichton 1928- .... **CLC 64**
See also CA 21-24R; DLB 40

Smith, John 1580(?)-1631 .... **LC 9**

Smith, Johnston
See Crane, Stephen (Townley)

Smith, Lee 1944-............. **CLC 25, 73**
See also CA 114; 119; DLBY 83

Smith, Martin
See Smith, Martin Cruz

Smith, Martin Cruz 1942-......... **CLC 25**
See also BEST 89:4; CA 85-88; CANR 6, 23, 43

Smith, Mary-Ann Tirone 1944-..... **CLC 39**
See also CA 118; 136

Smith, Patti 1946- .... **CLC 12**
See also CA 93-96

Smith, Pauline (Urmson) 1882-1959 .... **TCLC 25**

Smith, Rosamond
See Oates, Joyce Carol

Smith, Sheila Kaye
See Kaye-Smith, Sheila

Smith, Stevie............. **CLC 3, 8, 25, 44**
See also Smith, Florence Margaret
See also DLB 20

Smith, Wilbur A(ddison) 1933-..... **CLC 33**
See also CA 13-16R; CANR 7; MTCW

Smith, William Jay 1918- .... **CLC 6**
See also CA 5-8R; DLB 5; MAICYA; SATA 2, 68

Smith, Woodrow Wilson
See Kuttner, Henry

Smolenskin, Peretz 1842-1885.... **NCLC 30**

Smollett, Tobias (George) 1721-1771 .. **LC 2**
See also CDBLB 1660-1789; DLB 39, 104

Snodgrass, W(illiam) D(e Witt) 1926- .... **CLC 2, 6, 10, 18, 68**
See also CA 1-4R; CANR 6, 36; DLB 5; MTCW

Snow, C(harles) P(ercy) 1905-1980 .... **CLC 1, 4, 6, 9, 13, 19**
See also CA 5-8R; 101; CANR 28; CDBLB 1945-1960; DLB 15, 77; MTCW

Snow, Frances Compton
See Adams, Henry (Brooks)

Snyder, Gary (Sherman) 1930- .... **CLC 1, 2, 5, 9, 32**
See also CA 17-20R; CANR 30; DLB 5, 16

Snyder, Zilpha Keatley 1927- ...... **CLC 17**
See also CA 9-12R; CANR 38; CLR 31; JRDA; MAICYA; SAAS 2; SATA 1, 28, 75

Soares, Bernardo
See Pessoa, Fernando (Antonio Nogueira)

Sobh, A.
See Shamlu, Ahmad

Sobol, Joshua .... **CLC 60**

Soderberg, Hjalmar 1869-1941 .... **TCLC 39**

Sodergran, Edith (Irene)
See Soedergran, Edith (Irene)

Soedergran, Edith (Irene)
1892-1923 .... **TCLC 31**

Softly, Edgar
See Lovecraft, H(oward) P(hillips)

Softly, Edward
See Lovecraft, H(oward) P(hillips)

Sokolov, Raymond 1941- .... **CLC 7**
See also CA 85-88

Solo, Jay
See Ellison, Harlan

Sologub, Fyodor .... **TCLC 9**
See also Teternikov, Fyodor Kuzmich

Solomons, Ikey Esquir
See Thackeray, William Makepeace

Solomos, Dionysios 1798-1857 ... **NCLC 15**

Solwoska, Mara
See French, Marilyn

Solzhenitsyn, Aleksandr I(sayevich)
1918- ...... **CLC 1, 2, 4, 7, 9, 10, 18, 26, 34, 78**
See also AITN 1; CA 69-72; CANR 40; DA; MTCW; WLC

Somers, Jane
See Lessing, Doris (May)

Somerville, Edith 1858-1949 ...... **TCLC 51**

Somerville & Ross
See Martin, Violet Florence; Somerville, Edith

Sommer, Scott 1951- .... **CLC 25**
See also CA 106

Sondheim, Stephen (Joshua)
1930- .... **CLC 30, 39**
See also CA 103

Sontag, Susan 1933- ... **CLC 1, 2, 10, 13, 31**
See also CA 17-20R; CANR 25; DLB 2, 67; MTCW

Sophocles
496(?)B.C.-406(?)B.C. ... **CMLC 2; DC 1**
See also DA

Sorel, Julia
See Drexler, Rosalyn

Sorrentino, Gilbert
1929- .... **CLC 3, 7, 14, 22, 40**
See also CA 77-80; CANR 14, 33; DLB 5; DLBY 80

Soto, Gary 1952- .... **CLC 32, 80**
See also AAYA 10; CA 119; 125; DLB 82; HW; JRDA

Soupault, Philippe 1897-1990 ...... **CLC 68**
See also CA 116; 131

Souster, (Holmes) Raymond
1921- .... **CLC 5, 14**
See also CA 13-16R; CAAS 14; CANR 13, 29; DLB 88; SATA 63

Southern, Terry 1926- .... **CLC 7**
See also CA 1-4R; CANR 1; DLB 2

Southey, Robert 1774-1843 .... **NCLC 8**
See also DLB 93, 107; SATA 54

Southworth, Emma Dorothy Eliza Nevitte
1819-1899 .... **NCLC 26**

Souza, Ernest
See Scott, Evelyn

Soyinka, Wole
1934- .... **CLC 3, 5, 14, 36, 44; DC 2**
See also BLC 3; BW; CA 13-16R; CANR 27, 39; DA; DLB 125; MTCW; WLC

Spackman, W(illiam) M(ode)
1905-1990 .... **CLC 46**
See also CA 81-84; 132

Spacks, Barry 1931- .... **CLC 14**
See also CA 29-32R; CANR 33; DLB 105

Spanidou, Irini 1946- .... **CLC 44**

Spark, Muriel (Sarah)
1918- .... **CLC 2, 3, 5, 8, 13, 18, 40; SSC 10**
See also CA 5-8R; CANR 12, 36; CDBLB 1945-1960; DLB 15; MTCW

Spaulding, Douglas
See Bradbury, Ray (Douglas)

Spaulding, Leonard
See Bradbury, Ray (Douglas)

Spence, J. A. D.
See Eliot, T(homas) S(tearns)

Spencer, Elizabeth 1921- .... **CLC 22**
See also CA 13-16R; CANR 32; DLB 6; MTCW; SATA 14

Spencer, Leonard G.
See Silverberg, Robert

Spencer, Scott 1945- .... **CLC 30**
See also CA 113; DLBY 86

Spender, Stephen (Harold)
1909- .... **CLC 1, 2, 5, 10, 41**
See also CA 9-12R; CANR 31; CDBLB 1945-1960; DLB 20; MTCW

Spengler, Oswald (Arnold Gottfried)
1880-1936 .... **TCLC 25**
See also CA 118

Spenser, Edmund 1552(?)-1599 .... **LC 5**
See also CDBLB Before 1660; DA; WLC

Spicer, Jack 1925-1965 ...... **CLC 8, 18, 72**
See also CA 85-88; DLB 5, 16

Spiegelman, Art 1948- .... **CLC 76**
See also AAYA 10; CA 125; CANR 41

Spielberg, Peter 1929- .... **CLC 6**
See also CA 5-8R; CANR 4; DLBY 81

Spielberg, Steven 1947- .... **CLC 20**
See also AAYA 8; CA 77-80; CANR 32; SATA 32

Spillane, Frank Morrison 1918-
See Spillane, Mickey
See also CA 25-28R; CANR 28; MTCW; SATA 66

Spillane, Mickey .... **CLC 3, 13**
See also Spillane, Frank Morrison

Spinoza, Benedictus de 1632-1677 .... **LC 9**

Spinrad, Norman (Richard) 1940- ... **CLC 46**
See also CA 37-40R; CANR 20; DLB 8

Spitteler, Carl (Friedrich Georg)
1845-1924 .... **TCLC 12**
See also CA 109; DLB 129

Spivack, Kathleen (Romola Drucker)
1938- .... **CLC 6**
See also CA 49-52

Spoto, Donald 1941- .... **CLC 39**
See also CA 65-68; CANR 11

Springsteen, Bruce (F.) 1949- ...... **CLC 17**
See also CA 111

Spurling, Hilary 1940- .... **CLC 34**
See also CA 104; CANR 25

Squires, (James) Radcliffe
1917-1993 .... **CLC 51**
See also CA 1-4R; 140; CANR 6, 21

Srivastava, Dhanpat Rai 1880(?)-1936
See Premchand
See also CA 118

Stacy, Donald
See Pohl, Frederik

Stael, Germaine de
See Stael-Holstein, Anne Louise Germaine Necker Baronn
See also DLB 119

Stael-Holstein, Anne Louise Germaine Necker Baronn 1766-1817 .... **NCLC 3**
See also Stael, Germaine de

Stafford, Jean 1915-1979 ... **CLC 4, 7, 19, 68**
See also CA 1-4R; 85-88; CANR 3; DLB 2; MTCW; SATA 22

Stafford, William (Edgar)
1914-1993 .... **CLC 4, 7, 29**
See also CA 5-8R; 142; CAAS 3; CANR 5, 22; DLB 5

Staines, Trevor
See Brunner, John (Kilian Houston)

Stairs, Gordon
See Austin, Mary (Hunter)

Stannard, Martin 1947- .... **CLC 44**
See also CA 142

Stanton, Maura 1946- .... **CLC 9**
See also CA 89-92; CANR 15; DLB 120

Stanton, Schuyler
See Baum, L(yman) Frank

Stapledon, (William) Olaf
1886-1950 .... **TCLC 22**
See also CA 111; DLB 15

Starbuck, George (Edwin) 1931- .... **CLC 53**
See also CA 21-24R; CANR 23

Stark, Richard
See Westlake, Donald E(dwin)

Staunton, Schuyler
See Baum, L(yman) Frank

Stead, Christina (Ellen)
1902-1983 .... **CLC 2, 5, 8, 32, 80**
See also CA 13-16R; 109; CANR 33, 40; MTCW

Stead, William Thomas
1849-1912 .... **TCLC 48**

Steele, Richard 1672-1729 .... **LC 18**
See also CDBLB 1660-1789; DLB 84, 101

Steele, Timothy (Reid) 1948- .... **CLC 45**
See also CA 93-96; CANR 16; DLB 120

Steffens, (Joseph) Lincoln 1866-1936 .... **TCLC 20**
See also CA 117

Stegner, Wallace (Earle) 1909-1993 .... **CLC 9, 49**
See also AITN 1; BEST 90:3; CA 1-4R; 141; CAAS 9; CANR 1, 21; DLB 9; MTCW

Stein, Gertrude 1874-1946 .... **TCLC 1, 6, 28, 48**
See also CA 104; 132; CDALB 1917-1929; DA; DLB 4, 54, 86; MTCW; WLC

Steinbeck, John (Ernst) 1902-1968 ...... **CLC 1, 5, 9, 13, 21, 34, 45, 75; SSC 11**
See also CA 1-4R; 25-28R; CANR 1, 35; CDALB 1929-1941; DA; DLB 7, 9; DLBD 2; MTCW; SATA 9; WLC

Steinem, Gloria 1934-............. **CLC 63**
See also CA 53-56; CANR 28; MTCW

Steiner, George 1929-............. **CLC 24**
See also CA 73-76; CANR 31; DLB 67; MTCW; SATA 62

Steiner, K. Leslie
See Delany, Samuel R(ay, Jr.)

Steiner, Rudolf 1861-1925 .... **TCLC 13**
See also CA 107

Stendhal 1783-1842............. **NCLC 23**
See also DA; DLB 119; WLC

Stephen, Leslie 1832-1904 .... **TCLC 23**
See also CA 123; DLB 57

Stephen, Sir Leslie
See Stephen, Leslie

Stephen, Virginia
See Woolf, (Adeline) Virginia

Stephens, James 1882(?)-1950...... **TCLC 4**
See also CA 104; DLB 19

Stephens, Reed
See Donaldson, Stephen R.

Steptoe, Lydia
See Barnes, Djuna

Sterchi, Beat 1949-............... **CLC 65**

Sterling, Brett
See Bradbury, Ray (Douglas); Hamilton, Edmond

Sterling, Bruce 1954-............. **CLC 72**
See also CA 119

Sterling, George 1869-1926 .... **TCLC 20**
See also CA 117; DLB 54

Stern, Gerald 1925- .... **CLC 40**
See also CA 81-84; CANR 28; DLB 105

Stern, Richard (Gustave) 1928-... **CLC 4, 39**
See also CA 1-4R; CANR 1, 25; DLBY 87

Sternberg, Josef von 1894-1969..... **CLC 20**
See also CA 81-84

Sterne, Laurence 1713-1768.......... **LC 2**
See also CDBLB 1660-1789; DA; DLB 39; WLC

Sternheim, (William Adolf) Carl 1878-1942 .... **TCLC 8**
See also CA 105; DLB 56, 118

Stevens, Mark 1951- .... **CLC 34**
See also CA 122

Stevens, Wallace 1879-1955 .... **TCLC 3, 12, 45; PC 6**
See also CA 104; 124; CDALB 1929-1941; DA; DLB 54; MTCW; WLC

Stevenson, Anne (Katharine) 1933- .... **CLC 7, 33**
See also CA 17-20R; CAAS 9; CANR 9, 33; DLB 40; MTCW

Stevenson, Robert Louis (Balfour) 1850-1894 .... **NCLC 5, 14; SSC 11**
See also CDBLB 1890-1914; CLR 10, 11; DA; DLB 18, 57; JRDA; MAICYA; WLC; YABC 2

Stewart, J(ohn) I(nnes) M(ackintosh) 1906- .... **CLC 7, 14, 32**
See also CA 85-88; CAAS 3; MTCW

Stewart, Mary (Florence Elinor) 1916- .... **CLC 7, 35**
See also CA 1-4R; CANR 1; SATA 12

Stewart, Mary Rainbow
See Stewart, Mary (Florence Elinor)

Stifter, Adalbert 1805-1868 ...... **NCLC 41**
See also DLB 133

Still, James 1906-................ **CLC 49**
See also CA 65-68; CAAS 17; CANR 10, 26; DLB 9; SATA 29

Sting
See Sumner, Gordon Matthew

Stirling, Arthur
See Sinclair, Upton (Beall)

Stitt, Milan 1941-................ **CLC 29**
See also CA 69-72

Stockton, Francis Richard 1834-1902
See Stockton, Frank R.
See also CA 108; 137; MAICYA; SATA 44

Stockton, Frank R................ **TCLC 47**
See also Stockton, Francis Richard
See also DLB 42, 74; SATA 32

Stoddard, Charles
See Kuttner, Henry

Stoker, Abraham 1847-1912
See Stoker, Bram
See also CA 105; DA; SATA 29

Stoker, Bram..................... **TCLC 8**
See also Stoker, Abraham
See also CDBLB 1890-1914; DLB 36, 70; WLC

Stolz, Mary (Slattery) 1920-....... **CLC 12**
See also AAYA 8; AITN 1; CA 5-8R; CANR 13, 41; JRDA; MAICYA; SAAS 3; SATA 10, 71

Stone, Irving 1903-1989........... **CLC 7**
See also AITN 1; CA 1-4R; 129; CAAS 3; CANR 1, 23; MTCW; SATA 3; SATA-Obit 64

Stone, Oliver 1946-.............. **CLC 73**
See also CA 110

Stone, Robert (Anthony) 1937- .... **CLC 5, 23, 42**
See also CA 85-88; CANR 23; MTCW

Stone, Zachary
See Follett, Ken(neth Martin)

Stoppard, Tom 1937- ... **CLC 1, 3, 4, 5, 8, 15, 29, 34, 63**
See also CA 81-84; CANR 39; CDBLB 1960 to Present; DA; DLB 13; DLBY 85; MTCW; WLC

Storey, David (Malcolm) 1933- .... **CLC 2, 4, 5, 8**
See also CA 81-84; CANR 36; DLB 13, 14; MTCW

Storm, Hyemeyohsts 1935- .... **CLC 3**
See also CA 81-84

Storm, (Hans) Theodor (Woldsen) 1817-1888 .... **NCLC 1**

Storni, Alfonsina 1892-1938 .... **TCLC 5**
See also CA 104; 131; HW

Stout, Rex (Todhunter) 1886-1975 ... **CLC 3**
See also AITN 2; CA 61-64

Stow, (Julian) Randolph 1935- .. **CLC 23, 48**
See also CA 13-16R; CANR 33; MTCW

Stowe, Harriet (Elizabeth) Beecher 1811-1896 .... **NCLC 3**
See also CDALB 1865-1917; DA; DLB 1, 12, 42, 74; JRDA; MAICYA; WLC; YABC 1

Strachey, (Giles) Lytton 1880-1932 .... **TCLC 12**
See also CA 110; DLBD 10

Strand, Mark 1934- ...... **CLC 6, 18, 41, 71**
See also CA 21-24R; CANR 40; DLB 5; SATA 41

Straub, Peter (Francis) 1943- ...... **CLC 28**
See also BEST 89:1; CA 85-88; CANR 28; DLBY 84; MTCW

Strauss, Botho 1944- .... **CLC 22**
See also DLB 124

Streatfeild, (Mary) Noel 1895(?)-1986 .... **CLC 21**
See also CA 81-84; 120; CANR 31; CLR 17; MAICYA; SATA 20, 48

Stribling, T(homas) S(igismund) 1881-1965 .... **CLC 23**
See also CA 107; DLB 9

Strindberg, (Johan) August 1849-1912 .... **TCLC 1, 8, 21, 47**
See also CA 104; 135; DA; WLC

Stringer, Arthur 1874-1950 .... **TCLC 37**
See also DLB 92

Stringer, David
See Roberts, Keith (John Kingston)

Strugatskii, Arkadii (Natanovich) 1925-1991 .... **CLC 27**
See also CA 106; 135

Strugatskii, Boris (Natanovich) 1933- .... **CLC 27**
See also CA 106

Strummer, Joe 1953(?)- .... **CLC 30**
See also Clash, The

Stuart, Don A.
See Campbell, John W(ood, Jr.)

Stuart, Ian
See MacLean, Alistair (Stuart)

Stuart, Jesse (Hilton) 1906-1984 .... **CLC 1, 8, 11, 14, 34**
See also CA 5-8R; 112; CANR 31; DLB 9, 48, 102; DLBY 84; SATA 2, 36

Sturgeon, Theodore (Hamilton) 1918-1985 .... **CLC 22, 39**
See also Queen, Ellery
See also CA 81-84; 116; CANR 32; DLB 8; DLBY 85; MTCW

Sturges, Preston 1898-1959 .... **TCLC 48**
See also CA 114; DLB 26

Styron, William 1925- .... **CLC 1, 3, 5, 11, 15, 60**
See also BEST 90:4; CA 5-8R; CANR 6, 33; CDALB 1968-1988; DLB 2; DLBY 80; MTCW

Suarez Lynch, B.
See Borges, Jorge Luis

Suarez Lynch, B.
See Bioy Casares, Adolfo; Borges, Jorge Luis

Su Chien 1884-1918
See Su Man-shu
See also CA 123

Sudermann, Hermann 1857-1928 .. **TCLC 15**
See also CA 107; DLB 118

Sue, Eugene 1804-1857 .... **NCLC 1**
See also DLB 119

Sueskind, Patrick 1949- .... **CLC 44**

Sukenick, Ronald 1932- ..... **CLC 3, 4, 6, 48**
See also CA 25-28R; CAAS 8; CANR 32; DLBY 81

Suknaski, Andrew 1942- .... **CLC 19**
See also CA 101; DLB 53

Sullivan, Vernon
See Vian, Boris

Sully Prudhomme 1839-1907 ...... **TCLC 31**

Su Man-shu .... **TCLC 24**
See also Su Chien

Summerforest, Ivy B.
See Kirkup, James

Summers, Andrew James 1942- ..... **CLC 26**
See also Police, The

Summers, Andy
See Summers, Andrew James

Summers, Hollis (Spurgeon, Jr.) 1916- .... **CLC 10**
See also CA 5-8R; CANR 3; DLB 6

Summers, (Alphonsus Joseph-Mary Augustus) Montague 1880-1948 .... **TCLC 16**
See also CA 118

Sumner, Gordon Matthew 1951- .... **CLC 26**
See also Police, The

Surtees, Robert Smith 1803-1864 .... **NCLC 14**
See also DLB 21

Susann, Jacqueline 1921-1974 .... **CLC 3**
See also AITN 1; CA 65-68; 53-56; MTCW

Suskind, Patrick
See Sueskind, Patrick

Sutcliff, Rosemary 1920-1992 ...... **CLC 26**
See also AAYA 10; CA 5-8R; 139; CANR 37; CLR 1; JRDA; MAICYA; SATA 6, 44; SATA-Obit 73

Sutro, Alfred 1863-1933 .... **TCLC 6**
See also CA 105; DLB 10

Sutton, Henry
See Slavitt, David R(ytman)

Svevo, Italo .... **TCLC 2, 35**
See also Schmitz, Aron Hector

Swados, Elizabeth 1951- .... **CLC 12**
See also CA 97-100

Swados, Harvey 1920-1972 .... **CLC 5**
See also CA 5-8R; 37-40R; CANR 6; DLB 2

Swan, Gladys 1934- .... **CLC 69**
See also CA 101; CANR 17, 39

Swarthout, Glendon (Fred) 1918-1992 .... **CLC 35**
See also CA 1-4R; 139; CANR 1; SATA 26

Sweet, Sarah C.
See Jewett, (Theodora) Sarah Orne

Swenson, May 1919-1989 ..... **CLC 4, 14, 61**
See also CA 5-8R; 130; CANR 36; DA; DLB 5; MTCW; SATA 15

Swift, Augustus
See Lovecraft, H(oward) P(hillips)

Swift, Graham 1949- .... **CLC 41**
See also CA 117; 122

Swift, Jonathan 1667-1745 .... **LC 1**
See also CDBLB 1660-1789; DA; DLB 39, 95, 101; SATA 19; WLC

Swinburne, Algernon Charles 1837-1909 .... **TCLC 8, 36**
See also CA 105; 140; CDBLB 1832-1890; DA; DLB 35, 57; WLC

Swinfen, Ann .... **CLC 34**

Swinnerton, Frank Arthur 1884-1982 .... **CLC 31**
See also CA 108; DLB 34

Swithen, John
See King, Stephen (Edwin)

Sylvia
See Ashton-Warner, Sylvia (Constance)

Symmes, Robert Edward
See Duncan, Robert (Edward)

Symonds, John Addington 1840-1893 .... **NCLC 34**
See also DLB 57

Symons, Arthur 1865-1945 .... **TCLC 11**
See also CA 107; DLB 19, 57

Symons, Julian (Gustave) 1912- .... **CLC 2, 14, 32**
See also CA 49-52; CAAS 3; CANR 3, 33; DLB 87; DLBY 92; MTCW

Synge, (Edmund) J(ohn) M(illington) 1871-1909 .... **TCLC 6, 37; DC 2**
See also CA 104; 141; CDBLB 1890-1914; DLB 10, 19

Syruc, J.
See Milosz, Czeslaw

Szirtes, George 1948- .... **CLC 46**
See also CA 109; CANR 27

Tabori, George 1914- .... **CLC 19**
See also CA 49-52; CANR 4

Tagore, Rabindranath 1861-1941 .... **TCLC 3**
See also CA 104; 120; MTCW

Taine, Hippolyte Adolphe 1828-1893 .... **NCLC 15**

Talese, Gay 1932- .... **CLC 37**
See also AITN 1; CA 1-4R; CANR 9; MTCW

Tallent, Elizabeth (Ann) 1954- ..... **CLC 45**
See also CA 117; DLB 130

Tally, Ted 1952- .... **CLC 42**
See also CA 120; 124

Tamayo y Baus, Manuel 1829-1898 .... **NCLC 1**

Tammsaare, A(nton) H(ansen) 1878-1940 .... **TCLC 27**

Tan, Amy 1952- .... **CLC 59**
See also AAYA 9; BEST 89:3; CA 136; SATA 75

Tandem, Felix
See Spitteler, Carl (Friedrich Georg)

Tanizaki, Jun'ichiro 1886-1965 .... **CLC 8, 14, 28**
See also CA 93-96; 25-28R

Tanner, William
See Amis, Kingsley (William)

Tao Lao
See Storni, Alfonsina

Tarassoff, Lev
See Troyat, Henri

Tarbell, Ida M(inerva) 1857-1944 .... **TCLC 40**
See also CA 122; DLB 47

Tarkington, (Newton) Booth 1869-1946 .... **TCLC 9**
See also CA 110; DLB 9, 102; SATA 17

Tarkovsky, Andrei (Arsenyevich) 1932-1986 .... **CLC 75**
See also CA 127

Tartt, Donna 1964(?)- .... **CLC 76**
See also CA 142

Tasso, Torquato 1544-1595 .... **LC 5**

Tate, (John Orley) Allen 1899-1979 .... **CLC 2, 4, 6, 9, 11, 14, 24**
See also CA 5-8R; 85-88; CANR 32; DLB 4, 45, 63; MTCW

Tate, Ellalice
See Hibbert, Eleanor Alice Burford

Tate, James (Vincent) 1943- ... **CLC 2, 6, 25**
See also CA 21-24R; CANR 29; DLB 5

Tavel, Ronald 1940- .... **CLC 6**
See also CA 21-24R; CANR 33

Taylor, Cecil Philip 1929-1981 ..... **CLC 27**
See also CA 25-28R; 105

Taylor, Edward 1642(?)-1729 .... **LC 11**
See also DA; DLB 24

Taylor, Eleanor Ross 1920- .... **CLC 5**
See also CA 81-84

Taylor, Elizabeth 1912-1975 ... **CLC 2, 4, 29**
See also CA 13-16R; CANR 9; MTCW; SATA 13

Taylor, Henry (Splawn) 1942- ...... **CLC 44**
See also CA 33-36R; CAAS 7; CANR 31; DLB 5

Taylor, Kamala (Purnaiya) 1924-
See Markandaya, Kamala
See also CA 77-80

Taylor, Mildred D. .... **CLC 21**
See also AAYA 10; BW; CA 85-88; CANR 25; CLR 9; DLB 52; JRDA; MAICYA; SAAS 5; SATA 15, 70

Taylor, Peter (Hillsman)
1917- ...... **CLC 1, 4, 18, 37, 44, 50, 71; SSC 10**
See also CA 13-16R; CANR 9; DLBY 81; MTCW

Taylor, Robert Lewis 1912- .... **CLC 14**
See also CA 1-4R; CANR 3; SATA 10

Tchekhov, Anton
See Chekhov, Anton (Pavlovich)

Tcherniak, Nathalie 1900-
See Saurraute, Nathalie

Teasdale, Sara 1884-1933 .... **TCLC 4**
See also CA 104; DLB 45; SATA 32

Tegner, Esaias 1782-1846 .... **NCLC 2**

Teilhard de Chardin, (Marie Joseph) Pierre
1881-1955 .... **TCLC 9**
See also CA 105

Temple, Ann
See Mortimer, Penelope (Ruth)

Tennant, Emma (Christina)
1937- .... **CLC 13, 52**
See also CA 65-68; CAAS 9; CANR 10, 38; DLB 14

Tenneshaw, S. M.
See Silverberg, Robert

Tennyson, Alfred
1809-1892 .... **NCLC 30; PC 6**
See also CDBLB 1832-1890; DA; DLB 32; WLC

Teran, Lisa St. Aubin de .... **CLC 36**
See also St. Aubin de Teran, Lisa

Teresa de Jesus, St. 1515-1582 ...... **LC 18**

Terkel, Louis 1912-
See Terkel, Studs
See also CA 57-60; CANR 18; MTCW

Terkel, Studs .... **CLC 38**
See also Terkel, Louis
See also AITN 1

Terry, C. V.
See Slaughter, Frank G(ill)

Terry, Megan 1932- .... **CLC 19**
See also CA 77-80; CABS 3; CANR 43; DLB 7

Tertz, Abram
See Sinyavsky, Andrei (Donatevich)

Tesich, Steve 1943(?)- .... **CLC 40, 69**
See also CA 105; DLBY 83

Teternikov, Fyodor Kuzmich 1863-1927
See Sologub, Fyodor
See also CA 104

Tevis, Walter 1928-1984 .... **CLC 42**
See also CA 113

Tey, Josephine .... **TCLC 14**
See also Mackintosh, Elizabeth
See also DLB 77

Thackeray, William Makepeace
1811-1863 .... **NCLC 5, 14, 22**
See also CDBLB 1832-1890; DA; DLB 21, 55; SATA 23; WLC

Thakura, Ravindranatha
See Tagore, Rabindranath

Tharoor, Shashi 1956- .... **CLC 70**
See also CA 141

Thelwell, Michael Miles 1939- ..... **CLC 22**
See also CA 101

Theobald, Lewis, Jr.
See Lovecraft, H(oward) P(hillips)

Theodorescu, Ion N. 1880-1967
See Arghezi, Tudor
See also CA 116

The Prophet
See Dreiser, Theodore (Herman Albert)

Theriault, Yves 1915-1983 .... **CLC 79**
See also CA 102; DLB 88

Theroux, Alexander (Louis)
1939- .... **CLC 2, 25**
See also CA 85-88; CANR 20

Theroux, Paul (Edward)
1941- .... **CLC 5, 8, 11, 15, 28, 46**
See also BEST 89:4; CA 33-36R; CANR 20; DLB 2; MTCW; SATA 44

Thesen, Sharon 1946- .... **CLC 56**

Thevenin, Denis
See Duhamel, Georges

Thibault, Jacques Anatole Francois
1844-1924
See France, Anatole
See also CA 106; 127; MTCW

Thiele, Colin (Milton) 1920- .... **CLC 17**
See also CA 29-32R; CANR 12, 28; CLR 27; MAICYA; SAAS 2; SATA 14, 72

Thomas, Audrey (Callahan)
1935- .... **CLC 7, 13, 37**
See also AITN 2; CA 21-24R; CANR 36; DLB 60; MTCW

Thomas, D(onald) M(ichael)
1935- .... **CLC 13, 22, 31**
See also CA 61-64; CAAS 11; CANR 17; CDBLB 1960 to Present; DLB 40; MTCW

Thomas, Dylan (Marlais)
1914-1953 .... **TCLC 1, 8, 45; PC 2; SSC 3**
See also CA 104; 120; CDBLB 1945-1960; DA; DLB 13, 20; MTCW; SATA 60; WLC

Thomas, (Philip) Edward
1878-1917 .... **TCLC 10**
See also CA 106; DLB 19

Thomas, Joyce Carol 1938- .... **CLC 35**
See also BW; CA 113; 116; CLR 19; DLB 33; JRDA; MAICYA; MTCW; SAAS 7; SATA 40

Thomas, Lewis 1913- .... **CLC 35**
See also CA 85-88; CANR 38; MTCW

Thomas, Paul
See Mann, (Paul) Thomas

Thomas, Piri 1928- .... **CLC 17**
See also CA 73-76; HW

Thomas, R(onald) S(tuart)
1913- .... **CLC 6, 13, 48**
See also CA 89-92; CAAS 4; CANR 30; CDBLB 1960 to Present; DLB 27; MTCW

Thomas, Ross (Elmore) 1926- ...... **CLC 39**
See also CA 33-36R; CANR 22

Thompson, Francis Clegg
See Mencken, H(enry) L(ouis)

Thompson, Francis Joseph
1859-1907 .... **TCLC 4**
See also CA 104; CDBLB 1890-1914; DLB 19

Thompson, Hunter S(tockton)
1939- .... **CLC 9, 17, 40**
See also BEST 89:1; CA 17-20R; CANR 23; MTCW

Thompson, Jim 1906-1977(?) .... **CLC 69**

Thompson, Judith .... **CLC 39**

Thomson, James 1700-1748 .... **LC 16**

Thomson, James 1834-1882 ...... **NCLC 18**

Thoreau, Henry David
1817-1862 .... **NCLC 7, 21**
See also CDALB 1640-1865; DA; DLB 1; WLC

Thornton, Hall
See Silverberg, Robert

Thurber, James (Grover)
1894-1961 .... **CLC 5, 11, 25; SSC 1**
See also CA 73-76; CANR 17, 39; CDALB 1929-1941; DA; DLB 4, 11, 22, 102; MAICYA; MTCW; SATA 13

Thurman, Wallace (Henry)
1902-1934 .... **TCLC 6**
See also BLC 3; BW; CA 104; 124; DLB 51

Ticheburn, Cheviot
See Ainsworth, William Harrison

Tieck, (Johann) Ludwig
1773-1853 .... **NCLC 5**
See also DLB 90

Tiger, Derry
See Ellison, Harlan

Tilghman, Christopher 1948(?)- ..... **CLC 65**

Tillinghast, Richard (Williford)
1940- .... **CLC 29**
See also CA 29-32R; CANR 26

Timrod, Henry 1828-1867 .... **NCLC 25**
See also DLB 3

Tindall, Gillian 1938- .... **CLC 7**
See also CA 21-24R; CANR 11

Tiptree, James, Jr. .... **CLC 48, 50**
See also Sheldon, Alice Hastings Bradley
See also DLB 8

Titmarsh, Michael Angelo
See Thackeray, William Makepeace

Tocqueville, Alexis (Charles Henri Maurice Clerel Comte) 1805-1859 ..... **NCLC 7**

Tolkien, J(ohn) R(onald) R(euel)
1892-1973 .... **CLC 1, 2, 3, 8, 12, 38**
See also AAYA 10; AITN 1; CA 17-18; 45-48; CANR 36; CAP 2; CDBLB 1914-1945; DA; DLB 15; JRDA; MAICYA; MTCW; SATA 2, 24, 32; WLC

Toller, Ernst 1893-1939 .... **TCLC 10**
See also CA 107; DLB 124

Tolson, M. B.
See Tolson, Melvin B(eaunorus)

Tolson, Melvin B(eaunorus) 1898(?)-1966 . . . . **CLC 36**
See also BLC 3; BW; CA 124; 89-92; DLB 48, 76

Tolstoi, Aleksei Nikolaevich
See Tolstoy, Alexey Nikolaevich

Tolstoy, Alexey Nikolaevich 1882-1945 . . . . **TCLC 18**
See also CA 107

Tolstoy, Count Leo
See Tolstoy, Leo (Nikolaevich)

Tolstoy, Leo (Nikolaevich) 1828-1910 . . . . . . **TCLC 4, 11, 17, 28, 44; SSC 9**
See also CA 104; 123; DA; SATA 26; WLC

Tomasi di Lampedusa, Giuseppe 1896-1957
See Lampedusa, Giuseppe (Tomasi) di
See also CA 111

Tomlin, Lily. . . . . **CLC 17**
See also Tomlin, Mary Jean

Tomlin, Mary Jean 1939(?)-
See Tomlin, Lily
See also CA 117

Tomlinson, (Alfred) Charles 1927- . . . . **CLC 2, 4, 6, 13, 45**
See also CA 5-8R; CANR 33; DLB 40

Tonson, Jacob
See Bennett, (Enoch) Arnold

Toole, John Kennedy 1937-1969 . . . . **CLC 19, 64**
See also CA 104; DLBY 81

Toomer, Jean 1894-1967 . . . . . . **CLC 1, 4, 13, 22; PC 7; SSC 1**
See also BLC 3; BW; CA 85-88; CDALB 1917-1929; DLB 45, 51; MTCW

Torley, Luke
See Blish, James (Benjamin)

Tornimparte, Alessandra
See Ginzburg, Natalia

Torre, Raoul della
See Mencken, H(enry) L(ouis)

Torrey, E(dwin) Fuller 1937-. . . . . . . **CLC 34**
See also CA 119

Torsvan, Ben Traven
See Traven, B.

Torsvan, Benno Traven
See Traven, B.

Torsvan, Berick Traven
See Traven, B.

Torsvan, Berwick Traven
See Traven, B.

Torsvan, Bruno Traven
See Traven, B.

Torsvan, Traven
See Traven, B.

Tournier, Michel (Edouard) 1924- . . . . **CLC 6, 23, 36**
See also CA 49-52; CANR 3, 36; DLB 83; MTCW; SATA 23

Tournimparte, Alessandra
See Ginzburg, Natalia

Towers, Ivar
See Kornbluth, C(yril) M.

Townsend, Sue 1946- . . . . **CLC 61**
See also CA 119; 127; MTCW; SATA 48, 55

Townshend, Peter (Dennis Blandford) 1945- . . . . **CLC 17, 42**
See also CA 107

Tozzi, Federigo 1883-1920. . . . . **TCLC 31**

Traill, Catharine Parr 1802-1899 . . . . **NCLC 31**
See also DLB 99

Trakl, Georg 1887-1914. . . . . **TCLC 5**
See also CA 104

Transtroemer, Tomas (Goesta) 1931- . . . . **CLC 52, 65**
See also CA 117; 129; CAAS 17

Transtromer, Tomas Gosta
See Transtroemer, Tomas (Goesta)

Traven, B. (?)-1969. . . . . **CLC 8, 11**
See also CA 19-20; 25-28R; CAP 2; DLB 9, 56; MTCW

Treitel, Jonathan 1959- . . . . **CLC 70**

Tremain, Rose 1943-. . . . . **CLC 42**
See also CA 97-100; DLB 14

Tremblay, Michel 1942-. . . . . **CLC 29**
See also CA 116; 128; DLB 60; MTCW

Trevanian (a pseudonym) 1930(?)-. . . **CLC 29**
See also CA 108

Trevor, Glen
See Hilton, James

Trevor, William 1928- . . . . **CLC 7, 9, 14, 25, 71**
See also Cox, William Trevor
See also DLB 14

Trifonov, Yuri (Valentinovich) 1925-1981 . . . . **CLC 45**
See also CA 126; 103; MTCW

Trilling, Lionel 1905-1975 . . . . **CLC 9, 11, 24**
See also CA 9-12R; 61-64; CANR 10; DLB 28, 63; MTCW

Trimball, W. H.
See Mencken, H(enry) L(ouis)

Tristan
See Gomez de la Serna, Ramon

Tristram
See Housman, A(lfred) E(dward)

Trogdon, William (Lewis) 1939-
See Heat-Moon, William Least
See also CA 115; 119

Trollope, Anthony 1815-1882 . . **NCLC 6, 33**
See also CDBLB 1832-1890; DA; DLB 21, 57; SATA 22; WLC

Trollope, Frances 1779-1863 . . . . . **NCLC 30**
See also DLB 21

Trotsky, Leon 1879-1940. . . . . **TCLC 22**
See also CA 118

Trotter (Cockburn), Catharine 1679-1749 . . . . **LC 8**
See also DLB 84

Trout, Kilgore
See Farmer, Philip Jose

Trow, George W. S. 1943-. . . . . **CLC 52**
See also CA 126

Troyat, Henri 1911-. . . . . **CLC 23**
See also CA 45-48; CANR 2, 33; MTCW

Trudeau, G(arretson) B(eekman) 1948-
See Trudeau, Garry B.
See also CA 81-84; CANR 31; SATA 35

Trudeau, Garry B.. . . . . **CLC 12**
See also Trudeau, G(arretson) B(eekman)
See also AAYA 10; AITN 2

Truffaut, Francois 1932-1984. . . . . . . **CLC 20**
See also CA 81-84; 113; CANR 34

Trumbo, Dalton 1905-1976 . . . . **CLC 19**
See also CA 21-24R; 69-72; CANR 10; DLB 26

Trumbull, John 1750-1831. . . . . . . **NCLC 30**
See also DLB 31

Trundlett, Helen B.
See Eliot, T(homas) S(tearns)

Tryon, Thomas 1926-1991 . . . . **CLC 3, 11**
See also AITN 1; CA 29-32R; 135; CANR 32; MTCW

Tryon, Tom
See Tryon, Thomas

Ts'ao Hsueh-ch'in 1715(?)-1763. . . . . . . **LC 1**

Tsushima, Shuji 1909-1948
See Dazai, Osamu
See also CA 107

Tsvetaeva (Efron), Marina (Ivanovna) 1892-1941 . . . . **TCLC 7, 35**
See also CA 104; 128; MTCW

Tuck, Lily 1938-. . . . . **CLC 70**
See also CA 139

Tunis, John R(oberts) 1889-1975 . . . **CLC 12**
See also CA 61-64; DLB 22; JRDA; MAICYA; SATA 30, 37

Tuohy, Frank. **CLC 37**
See also Tuohy, John Francis
See also DLB 14

Tuohy, John Francis 1925-
See Tuohy, Frank
See also CA 5-8R; CANR 3

Turco, Lewis (Putnam) 1934- . . . **CLC 11, 63**
See also CA 13-16R; CANR 24; DLBY 84

Turgenev, Ivan 1818-1883 . . . . **NCLC 21; SSC 7**
See also DA; WLC

Turner, Frederick 1943-. . . . . **CLC 48**
See also CA 73-76; CAAS 10; CANR 12, 30; DLB 40

Tusan, Stan 1936-. . . . . **CLC 22**
See also CA 105

Tutu, Desmond M(pilo) 1931-. . . . . . **CLC 80**
See also BLC 3; BW; CA 125

Tutuola, Amos 1920- . . . . **CLC 5, 14, 29**
See also BLC 3; BW; CA 9-12R; CANR 27; DLB 125; MTCW

Twain, Mark . . . . **TCLC 6, 12, 19, 36, 48; SSC 6**
See also Clemens, Samuel Langhorne
See also DLB 11, 12, 23, 64, 74; WLC

Tyler, Anne 1941- . . . . **CLC 7, 11, 18, 28, 44, 59**
See also BEST 89:1; CA 9-12R; CANR 11, 33; DLB 6; DLBY 82; MTCW; SATA 7

Tyler, Royall 1757-1826. . . . . **NCLC 3**
See also DLB 37

Tynan, Katharine 1861-1931 .... **TCLC 3**
See also CA 104

Tytell, John 1939- .... **CLC 50**
See also CA 29-32R

Tyutchev, Fyodor 1803-1873 ..... **NCLC 34**

Tzara, Tristan .... **CLC 47**
See also Rosenfeld, Samuel

Uhry, Alfred 1936-............... **CLC 55**
See also CA 127; 133

Ulf, Haerved
See Strindberg, (Johan) August

Ulf, Harved
See Strindberg, (Johan) August

Unamuno (y Jugo), Miguel de 1864-1936 .... **TCLC 2, 9; SSC 11**
See also CA 104; 131; DLB 108; HW; MTCW

Undercliffe, Errol
See Campbell, (John) Ramsey

Underwood, Miles
See Glassco, John

Undset, Sigrid 1882-1949.......... **TCLC 3**
See also CA 104; 129; DA; MTCW; WLC

Ungaretti, Giuseppe 1888-1970 .... **CLC 7, 11, 15**
See also CA 19-20; 25-28R; CAP 2; DLB 114

Unger, Douglas 1952-............. **CLC 34**
See also CA 130

Unsworth, Barry (Forster) 1930-.... **CLC 76**
See also CA 25-28R; CANR 30

Updike, John (Hoyer) 1932- ...... **CLC 1, 2, 3, 5, 7, 9, 13, 15, 23, 34, 43, 70; SSC 13**
See also CA 1-4R; CABS 1; CANR 4, 33; CDALB 1968-1988; DA; DLB 2, 5; DLBD 3; DLBY 80, 82; MTCW; WLC

Upshaw, Margaret Mitchell
See Mitchell, Margaret (Munnerlyn)

Upton, Mark
See Sanders, Lawrence

Urdang, Constance (Henriette) 1922- .... **CLC 47**
See also CA 21-24R; CANR 9, 24

Uriel, Henry
See Faust, Frederick (Schiller)

Uris, Leon (Marcus) 1924-....... **CLC 7, 32**
See also AITN 1, 2; BEST 89:2; CA 1-4R; CANR 1, 40; MTCW; SATA 49

Urmuz
See Codrescu, Andrei

Ustinov, Peter (Alexander) 1921-.... **CLC 1**
See also AITN 1; CA 13-16R; CANR 25; DLB 13

v
See Chekhov, Anton (Pavlovich)

Vaculik, Ludvik 1926- .... **CLC 7**
See also CA 53-56

Valenzuela, Luisa 1938-........... **CLC 31**
See also CA 101; CANR 32; DLB 113; HW

Valera y Alcala-Galiano, Juan 1824-1905 .... **TCLC 10**
See also CA 106

Valery, (Ambroise) Paul (Toussaint Jules) 1871-1945 .... **TCLC 4, 15**
See also CA 104; 122; MTCW

Valle-Inclan, Ramon (Maria) del 1866-1936 .... **TCLC 5**
See also CA 106; DLB 134

Vallejo, Antonio Buero
See Buero Vallejo, Antonio

Vallejo, Cesar (Abraham) 1892-1938 .... **TCLC 3**
See also CA 105; HW

Valle Y Pena, Ramon del
See Valle-Inclan, Ramon (Maria) del

Van Ash, Cay 1918-.............. **CLC 34**

Vanbrugh, Sir John 1664-1726 ...... **LC 21**
See also DLB 80

Van Campen, Karl
See Campbell, John W(ood, Jr.)

Vance, Gerald
See Silverberg, Robert

Vance, Jack .... **CLC 35**
See also Vance, John Holbrook
See also DLB 8

Vance, John Holbrook 1916-
See Queen, Ellery; Vance, Jack
See also CA 29-32R; CANR 17; MTCW

Van Den Bogarde, Derek Jules Gaspard Ulric Niven 1921-
See Bogarde, Dirk
See also CA 77-80

Vandenburgh, Jane .... **CLC 59**

Vanderhaeghe, Guy 1951- .... **CLC 41**
See also CA 113

van der Post, Laurens (Jan) 1906- ... **CLC 5**
See also CA 5-8R; CANR 35

van de Wetering, Janwillem 1931- .. **CLC 47**
See also CA 49-52; CANR 4

Van Dine, S. S. .... **TCLC 23**
See also Wright, Willard Huntington

Van Doren, Carl (Clinton) 1885-1950 .... **TCLC 18**
See also CA 111

Van Doren, Mark 1894-1972..... **CLC 6, 10**
See also CA 1-4R; 37-40R; CANR 3; DLB 45; MTCW

Van Druten, John (William) 1901-1957 .... **TCLC 2**
See also CA 104; DLB 10

Van Duyn, Mona (Jane) 1921- .... **CLC 3, 7, 63**
See also CA 9-12R; CANR 7, 38; DLB 5

Van Dyne, Edith
See Baum, L(yman) Frank

van Itallie, Jean-Claude 1936-....... **CLC 3**
See also CA 45-48; CAAS 2; CANR 1; DLB 7

van Ostaijen, Paul 1896-1928 ..... **TCLC 33**

Van Peebles, Melvin 1932- ...... **CLC 2, 20**
See also BW; CA 85-88; CANR 27

Vansittart, Peter 1920-........... **CLC 42**
See also CA 1-4R; CANR 3

Van Vechten, Carl 1880-1964 ...... **CLC 33**
See also CA 89-92; DLB 4, 9, 51

Van Vogt, A(lfred) E(lton) 1912-..... **CLC 1**
See also CA 21-24R; CANR 28; DLB 8; SATA 14

Vara, Madeleine
See Jackson, Laura (Riding)

Varda, Agnes 1928- .... **CLC 16**
See also CA 116; 122

Vargas Llosa, (Jorge) Mario (Pedro) 1936- .... **CLC 3, 6, 9, 10, 15, 31, 42**
See also CA 73-76; CANR 18, 32, 42; DA; HW; MTCW

Vasiliu, Gheorghe 1881-1957
See Bacovia, George
See also CA 123

Vassa, Gustavus
See Equiano, Olaudah

Vassilikos, Vassilis 1933-......... **CLC 4, 8**
See also CA 81-84

Vaughn, Stephanie................. **CLC 62**

Vazov, Ivan (Minchov) 1850-1921 .... **TCLC 25**
See also CA 121

Veblen, Thorstein (Bunde) 1857-1929 .... **TCLC 31**
See also CA 115

Vega, Lope de 1562-1635........... **LC 23**

Venison, Alfred
See Pound, Ezra (Weston Loomis)

Verdi, Marie de
See Mencken, H(enry) L(ouis)

Verdu, Matilde
See Cela, Camilo Jose

Verga, Giovanni (Carmelo) 1840-1922 .... **TCLC 3**
See also CA 104; 123

Vergil 70B.C.-19B.C. .... **CMLC 9**
See also DA

Verhaeren, Emile (Adolphe Gustave) 1855-1916 .... **TCLC 12**
See also CA 109

Verlaine, Paul (Marie) 1844-1896 .... **NCLC 2; PC 2**

Verne, Jules (Gabriel) 1828-1905 .... **TCLC 6, 52**
See also CA 110; 131; DLB 123; JRDA; MAICYA; SATA 21

Very, Jones 1813-1880........... **NCLC 9**
See also DLB 1

Vesaas, Tarjei 1897-1970.......... **CLC 48**
See also CA 29-32R

Vialis, Gaston
See Simenon, Georges (Jacques Christian)

Vian, Boris 1920-1959 .... **TCLC 9**
See also CA 106; DLB 72

Viaud, (Louis Marie) Julien 1850-1923
See Loti, Pierre
See also CA 107

Vicar, Henry
See Felsen, Henry Gregor

Vicker, Angus
See Felsen, Henry Gregor

Vidal, Gore
1925- . . . . . **CLC 2, 4, 6, 8, 10, 22, 33, 72**
See also AITN 1; BEST 90:2; CA 5-8R; CANR 13; DLB 6; MTCW

Viereck, Peter (Robert Edwin)
1916- . . . . . **CLC 4**
See also CA 1-4R; CANR 1; DLB 5

Vigny, Alfred (Victor) de
1797-1863 . . . . . **NCLC 7**
See also DLB 119

Vilakazi, Benedict Wallet
1906-1947 . . . . . **TCLC 37**

Villiers de l'Isle Adam, Jean Marie Mathias Philippe Auguste Comte
1838-1889 . . . . . **NCLC 3**
See also DLB 123

Vincent, Gabrielle a pseudonym . . . . . **CLC 13**
See also CA 126; CLR 13; MAICYA; SATA 61

Vinci, Leonardo da 1452-1519 . . . . . **LC 12**

Vine, Barbara . . . . . **CLC 50**
See also Rendell, Ruth (Barbara)
See also BEST 90:4

Vinge, Joan D(ennison) 1948- . . . . . **CLC 30**
See also CA 93-96; SATA 36

Violis, G.
See Simenon, Georges (Jacques Christian)

Visconti, Luchino 1906-1976 . . . . . **CLC 16**
See also CA 81-84; 65-68; CANR 39

Vittorini, Elio 1908-1966 . . . . . **CLC 6, 9, 14**
See also CA 133; 25-28R

Vizinczey, Stephen 1933- . . . . . **CLC 40**
See also CA 128

Vliet, R(ussell) G(ordon)
1929-1984 . . . . . **CLC 22**
See also CA 37-40R; 112; CANR 18

Vogau, Boris Andreyevich 1894-1937(?)
See Pilnyak, Boris
See also CA 123

Vogel, Paula A(nne) 1951- . . . . . **CLC 76**
See also CA 108

Voight, Ellen Bryant 1943- . . . . . **CLC 54**
See also CA 69-72; CANR 11, 29; DLB 120

Voigt, Cynthia 1942- . . . . . **CLC 30**
See also AAYA 3; CA 106; CANR 18, 37, 40; CLR 13; JRDA; MAICYA; SATA 33, 48

Voinovich, Vladimir (Nikolaevich)
1932- . . . . . **CLC 10, 49**
See also CA 81-84; CAAS 12; CANR 33; MTCW

Voltaire 1694-1778 . . . . . **LC 14; SSC 12**
See also DA; WLC

von Daeniken, Erich 1935- . . . . . **CLC 30**
See also von Daniken, Erich
See also AITN 1; CA 37-40R; CANR 17

von Daniken, Erich . . . . . **CLC 30**
See also von Daeniken, Erich

von Heidenstam, (Carl Gustaf) Verner
See Heidenstam, (Carl Gustaf) Verner von

von Heyse, Paul (Johann Ludwig)
See Heyse, Paul (Johann Ludwig von)

von Hofmannsthal, Hugo
See Hofmannsthal, Hugo von

von Horvath, Odon
See Horvath, Oedoen von

von Horvath, Oedoen
See Horvath, Oedoen von

von Liliencron, (Friedrich Adolf Axel) Detlev
See Liliencron, (Friedrich Adolf Axel) Detlev von

Vonnegut, Kurt, Jr.
1922- . . . . . **CLC 1, 2, 3, 4, 5, 8, 12, 22, 40, 60; SSC 8**
See also AAYA 6; AITN 1; BEST 90:4; CA 1-4R; CANR 1, 25; CDALB 1968-1988; DA; DLB 2, 8; DLBD 3; DLBY 80; MTCW; WLC

Von Rachen, Kurt
See Hubbard, L(afayette) Ron(ald)

von Rezzori (d'Arezzo), Gregor
See Rezzori (d'Arezzo), Gregor von

von Sternberg, Josef
See Sternberg, Josef von

Vorster, Gordon 1924- . . . . . **CLC 34**
See also CA 133

Vosce, Trudie
See Ozick, Cynthia

Voznesensky, Andrei (Andreievich)
1933- . . . . . **CLC 1, 15, 57**
See also CA 89-92; CANR 37; MTCW

Waddington, Miriam 1917- . . . . . **CLC 28**
See also CA 21-24R; CANR 12, 30; DLB 68

Wagman, Fredrica 1937- . . . . . **CLC 7**
See also CA 97-100

Wagner, Richard 1813-1883 . . . . . **NCLC 9**
See also DLB 129

Wagner-Martin, Linda 1936- . . . . . **CLC 50**

Wagoner, David (Russell)
1926- . . . . . **CLC 3, 5, 15**
See also CA 1-4R; CAAS 3; CANR 2; DLB 5; SATA 14

Wah, Fred(erick James) 1939- . . . . . **CLC 44**
See also CA 107; 141; DLB 60

Wahloo, Per 1926-1975 . . . . . **CLC 7**
See also CA 61-64

Wahloo, Peter
See Wahloo, Per

Wain, John (Barrington)
1925- . . . . . **CLC 2, 11, 15, 46**
See also CA 5-8R; CAAS 4; CANR 23; CDBLB 1960 to Present; DLB 15, 27; MTCW

Wajda, Andrzej 1926- . . . . . **CLC 16**
See also CA 102

Wakefield, Dan 1932- . . . . . **CLC 7**
See also CA 21-24R; CAAS 7

Wakoski, Diane
1937- . . . . . **CLC 2, 4, 7, 9, 11, 40**
See also CA 13-16R; CAAS 1; CANR 9; DLB 5

Wakoski-Sherbell, Diane
See Wakoski, Diane

Walcott, Derek (Alton)
1930- . . . . **CLC 2, 4, 9, 14, 25, 42, 67, 76**
See also BLC 3; BW; CA 89-92; CANR 26; DLB 117; DLBY 81; MTCW

Waldman, Anne 1945- . . . . . **CLC 7**
See also CA 37-40R; CAAS 17; CANR 34; DLB 16

Waldo, E. Hunter
See Sturgeon, Theodore (Hamilton)

Waldo, Edward Hamilton
See Sturgeon, Theodore (Hamilton)

Walker, Alice (Malsenior)
1944- . . . . . **CLC 5, 6, 9, 19, 27, 46, 58; SSC 5**
See also AAYA 3; BEST 89:4; BLC 3; BW; CA 37-40R; CANR 9, 27; CDALB 1968-1988; DA; DLB 6, 33; MTCW; SATA 31

Walker, David Harry 1911-1992 . . . . **CLC 14**
See also CA 1-4R; 137; CANR 1; SATA 8; SATA-Obit 71

Walker, Edward Joseph 1934-
See Walker, Ted
See also CA 21-24R; CANR 12, 28

Walker, George F. 1947- . . . . . **CLC 44, 61**
See also CA 103; CANR 21, 43; DLB 60

Walker, Joseph A. 1935- . . . . . **CLC 19**
See also BW; CA 89-92; CANR 26; DLB 38

Walker, Margaret (Abigail)
1915- . . . . . **CLC 1, 6**
See also BLC 3; BW; CA 73-76; CANR 26; DLB 76; MTCW

Walker, Ted . . . . . **CLC 13**
See also Walker, Edward Joseph
See also DLB 40

Wallace, David Foster 1962- . . . . . **CLC 50**
See also CA 132

Wallace, Dexter
See Masters, Edgar Lee

Wallace, Irving 1916-1990 . . . . . **CLC 7, 13**
See also AITN 1; CA 1-4R; 132; CAAS 1; CANR 1, 27; MTCW

Wallant, Edward Lewis
1926-1962 . . . . . **CLC 5, 10**
See also CA 1-4R; CANR 22; DLB 2, 28; MTCW

Walpole, Horace 1717-1797 . . . . . **LC 2**
See also DLB 39, 104

Walpole, Hugh (Seymour)
1884-1941 . . . . . **TCLC 5**
See also CA 104; DLB 34

Walser, Martin 1927- . . . . . **CLC 27**
See also CA 57-60; CANR 8; DLB 75, 124

Walser, Robert 1878-1956 . . . . . **TCLC 18**
See also CA 118; DLB 66

Walsh, Jill Paton . . . . . **CLC 35**
See also Paton Walsh, Gillian
See also CLR 2; SAAS 3

Walter, Villiam Christian
See Andersen, Hans Christian

Wambaugh, Joseph (Aloysius, Jr.)
1937- . . . . . **CLC 3, 18**
See also AITN 1; BEST 89:3; CA 33-36R; CANR 42; DLB 6; DLBY 83; MTCW

Ward, Arthur Henry Sarsfield 1883-1959
See Rohmer, Sax
See also CA 108

Wescott, Glenway 1901-1987....... **CLC 13**
See also CA 13-16R; 121; CANR 23; DLB 4, 9, 102

Wesker, Arnold 1932- .... **CLC 3, 5, 42**
See also CA 1-4R; CAAS 7; CANR 1, 33; CDBLB 1960 to Present; DLB 13; MTCW

Wesley, Richard (Errol) 1945-....... **CLC 7**
See also BW; CA 57-60; CANR 27; DLB 38

Wessel, Johan Herman 1742-1785 .... **LC 7**

West, Anthony (Panther)
1914-1987 .... **CLC 50**
See also CA 45-48; 124; CANR 3, 19; DLB 15

West, C. P.
See Wodehouse, P(elham) G(renville)

West, (Mary) Jessamyn
1902-1984 .... **CLC 7, 17**
See also CA 9-12R; 112; CANR 27; DLB 6; DLBY 84; MTCW; SATA 37

West, Morris L(anglo) 1916-..... **CLC 6, 33**
See also CA 5-8R; CANR 24; MTCW

West, Nathanael
1903-1940 .... **TCLC 1, 14, 44**
See also CA 104; 125; CDALB 1929-1941; DLB 4, 9, 28; MTCW

West, Owen
See Koontz, Dean R(ay)

West, Paul 1930- .... **CLC 7, 14**
See also CA 13-16R; CAAS 7; CANR 22; DLB 14

West, Rebecca 1892-1983 .. **CLC 7, 9, 31, 50**
See also CA 5-8R; 109; CANR 19; DLB 36; DLBY 83; MTCW

Westall, Robert (Atkinson)
1929-1993 .... **CLC 17**
See also CA 69-72; 141; CANR 18; CLR 13; JRDA; MAICYA; SAAS 2; SATA 23, 69; SATA-Obit 75

Westlake, Donald E(dwin)
1933- .... **CLC 7, 33**
See also CA 17-20R; CAAS 13; CANR 16

Westmacott, Mary
See Christie, Agatha (Mary Clarissa)

Weston, Allen
See Norton, Andre

Wetcheek, J. L.
See Feuchtwanger, Lion

Wetering, Janwillem van de
See van de Wetering, Janwillem

Wetherell, Elizabeth
See Warner, Susan (Bogert)

Whalen, Philip 1923- .... **CLC 6, 29**
See also CA 9-12R; CANR 5, 39; DLB 16

Wharton, Edith (Newbold Jones)
1862-1937 .... **TCLC 3, 9, 27; SSC 6**
See also CA 104; 132; CDALB 1865-1917; DA; DLB 4, 9, 12, 78; MTCW; WLC

Wharton, James
See Mencken, H(enry) L(ouis)

Wharton, William (a pseudonym)
.... **CLC 18, 37**
See also CA 93-96; DLBY 80

Wheatley (Peters), Phillis
1754(?)-1784 .... **LC 3; PC 3**
See also BLC 3; CDALB 1640-1865; DA; DLB 31, 50; WLC

Wheelock, John Hall 1886-1978 .... **CLC 14**
See also CA 13-16R; 77-80; CANR 14; DLB 45

White, E(lwyn) B(rooks)
1899-1985 .... **CLC 10, 34, 39**
See also AITN 2; CA 13-16R; 116; CANR 16, 37; CLR 1, 21; DLB 11, 22; MAICYA; MTCW; SATA 2, 29, 44

White, Edmund (Valentine III)
1940- .... **CLC 27**
See also AAYA 7; CA 45-48; CANR 3, 19, 36; MTCW

White, Patrick (Victor Martindale)
1912-1990 .. **CLC 3, 4, 5, 7, 9, 18, 65, 69**
See also CA 81-84; 132; CANR 43; MTCW

White, Phyllis Dorothy James 1920-
See James, P. D.
See also CA 21-24R; CANR 17, 43; MTCW

White, T(erence) H(anbury)
1906-1964 .... **CLC 30**
See also CA 73-76; CANR 37; JRDA; MAICYA; SATA 12

White, Terence de Vere 1912-...... **CLC 49**
See also CA 49-52; CANR 3

White, Walter F(rancis)
1893-1955 .... **TCLC 15**
See also White, Walter
See also CA 115; 124; DLB 51

White, William Hale 1831-1913
See Rutherford, Mark
See also CA 121

Whitehead, E(dward) A(nthony)
1933- .... **CLC 5**
See also CA 65-68

Whitemore, Hugh (John) 1936-..... **CLC 37**
See also CA 132

Whitman, Sarah Helen (Power)
1803-1878 .... **NCLC 19**
See also DLB 1

Whitman, Walt(er)
1819-1892 .... **NCLC 4, 31; PC 3**
See also CDALB 1640-1865; DA; DLB 3, 64; SATA 20; WLC

Whitney, Phyllis A(yame) 1903-.... **CLC 42**
See also AITN 2; BEST 90:3; CA 1-4R; CANR 3, 25, 38; JRDA; MAICYA; SATA 1, 30

Whittemore, (Edward) Reed (Jr.)
1919- .... **CLC 4**
See also CA 9-12R; CAAS 8; CANR 4; DLB 5

Whittier, John Greenleaf
1807-1892 .... **NCLC 8**
See also CDALB 1640-1865; DLB 1

Whittlebot, Hernia
See Coward, Noel (Peirce)

Wicker, Thomas Grey 1926-
See Wicker, Tom
See also CA 65-68; CANR 21

Wicker, Tom .... **CLC 7**
See also Wicker, Thomas Grey

Wideman, John Edgar
1941- .... **CLC 5, 34, 36, 67**
See also BLC 3; BW; CA 85-88; CANR 14, 42; DLB 33

Wiebe, Rudy (Henry) 1934-... **CLC 6, 11, 14**
See also CA 37-40R; CANR 42; DLB 60

Wieland, Christoph Martin
1733-1813 .... **NCLC 17**
See also DLB 97

Wieners, John 1934-............... **CLC 7**
See also CA 13-16R; DLB 16

Wiesel, Elie(zer) 1928-..... **CLC 3, 5, 11, 37**
See also AAYA 7; AITN 1; CA 5-8R; CAAS 4; CANR 8, 40; DA; DLB 83; DLBY 87; MTCW; SATA 56

Wiggins, Marianne 1947-.......... **CLC 57**
See also BEST 89:3; CA 130

Wight, James Alfred 1916-
See Herriot, James
See also CA 77-80; SATA 44, 55

Wilbur, Richard (Purdy)
1921- .... **CLC 3, 6, 9, 14, 53**
See also CA 1-4R; CABS 2; CANR 2, 29; DA; DLB 5; MTCW; SATA 9

Wild, Peter 1940-................ **CLC 14**
See also CA 37-40R; DLB 5

Wilde, Oscar (Fingal O'Flahertie Wills)
1854(?)-1900 .... **TCLC 1, 8, 23, 41; SSC 11**
See also CA 104; 119; CDBLB 1890-1914; DA; DLB 10, 19, 34, 57; SATA 24; WLC

Wilder, Billy .... **CLC 20**
See also Wilder, Samuel
See also DLB 26

Wilder, Samuel 1906-
See Wilder, Billy
See also CA 89-92

Wilder, Thornton (Niven)
1897-1975 ...... **CLC 1, 5, 6, 10, 15, 35; DC 1**
See also AITN 2; CA 13-16R; 61-64; CANR 40; DA; DLB 4, 7, 9; MTCW; WLC

Wilding, Michael 1942-........... **CLC 73**
See also CA 104; CANR 24

Wiley, Richard 1944-............. **CLC 44**
See also CA 121; 129

Wilhelm, Kate .... **CLC 7**
See also Wilhelm, Katie Gertrude
See also CAAS 5; DLB 8

Wilhelm, Katie Gertrude 1928-
See Wilhelm, Kate
See also CA 37-40R; CANR 17, 36; MTCW

Wilkins, Mary
See Freeman, Mary Eleanor Wilkins

Willard, Nancy 1936-........... **CLC 7, 37**
See also CA 89-92; CANR 10, 39; CLR 5; DLB 5, 52; MAICYA; MTCW; SATA 30, 37, 71

Williams, C(harles) K(enneth)
1936- .... **CLC 33, 56**
See also CA 37-40R; DLB 5

Williams, Charles
See Collier, James L(incoln)

Williams, Charles (Walter Stansby)
1886-1945 . . . . **TCLC 1, 11**
See also CA 104; DLB 100

Williams, (George) Emlyn
1905-1987 . . . . **CLC 15**
See also CA 104; 123; CANR 36; DLB 10, 77; MTCW

Williams, Hugo 1942- . . . . **CLC 42**
See also CA 17-20R; DLB 40

Williams, J. Walker
See Wodehouse, P(elham) G(renville)

Williams, John A(lfred) 1925- . . . . **CLC 5, 13**
See also BLC 3; BW; CA 53-56; CAAS 3; CANR 6, 26; DLB 2, 33

Williams, Jonathan (Chamberlain)
1929- . . . . **CLC 13**
See also CA 9-12R; CAAS 12; CANR 8; DLB 5

Williams, Joy 1944- . . . . **CLC 31**
See also CA 41-44R; CANR 22

Williams, Norman 1952- . . . . **CLC 39**
See also CA 118

Williams, Tennessee
1911-1983 . . . . . **CLC 1, 2, 5, 7, 8, 11, 15, 19, 30, 39, 45, 71**
See also AITN 1, 2; CA 5-8R; 108; CABS 3; CANR 31; CDALB 1941-1968; DA; DLB 7; DLBD 4; DLBY 83; MTCW; WLC

Williams, Thomas (Alonzo)
1926-1990 . . . . **CLC 14**
See also CA 1-4R; 132; CANR 2

Williams, William C.
See Williams, William Carlos

Williams, William Carlos
1883-1963 . . . . **CLC 1, 2, 5, 9, 13, 22, 42, 67; PC 7**
See also CA 89-92; CANR 34; CDALB 1917-1929; DA; DLB 4, 16, 54, 86; MTCW

Williamson, David (Keith) 1942- . . . . **CLC 56**
See also CA 103; CANR 41

Williamson, Jack . . . . **CLC 29**
See also Williamson, John Stewart
See also CAAS 8; DLB 8

Williamson, John Stewart 1908-
See Williamson, Jack
See also CA 17-20R; CANR 23

Willie, Frederick
See Lovecraft, H(oward) P(hillips)

Willingham, Calder (Baynard, Jr.)
1922- . . . . **CLC 5, 51**
See also CA 5-8R; CANR 3; DLB 2, 44; MTCW

Willis, Charles
See Clarke, Arthur C(harles)

Willy
See Colette, (Sidonie-Gabrielle)

Willy, Colette
See Colette, (Sidonie-Gabrielle)

Wilson, A(ndrew) N(orman) 1950- . . **CLC 33**
See also CA 112; 122; DLB 14

Wilson, Angus (Frank Johnstone)
1913-1991 . . . . **CLC 2, 3, 5, 25, 34**
See also CA 5-8R; 134; CANR 21; DLB 15; MTCW

Wilson, August
1945- . . . . **CLC 39, 50, 63; DC 2**
See also BLC 3; BW; CA 115; 122; CANR 42; DA; MTCW

Wilson, Brian 1942- . . . . **CLC 12**

Wilson, Colin 1931- . . . . **CLC 3, 14**
See also CA 1-4R; CAAS 5; CANR 1, 22, 33; DLB 14; MTCW

Wilson, Dirk
See Pohl, Frederik

Wilson, Edmund
1895-1972 . . . . **CLC 1, 2, 3, 8, 24**
See also CA 1-4R; 37-40R; CANR 1; DLB 63; MTCW

Wilson, Ethel Davis (Bryant)
1888(?)-1980 . . . . **CLC 13**
See also CA 102; DLB 68; MTCW

Wilson, John 1785-1854 . . . . **NCLC 5**

Wilson, John (Anthony) Burgess
1917- . . . . **CLC 8, 10, 13**
See also Burgess, Anthony
See also CA 1-4R; CANR 2; MTCW

Wilson, Lanford 1937- . . . . **CLC 7, 14, 36**
See also CA 17-20R; CABS 3; DLB 7

Wilson, Robert M. 1944- . . . . **CLC 7, 9**
See also CA 49-52; CANR 2, 41; MTCW

Wilson, Robert McLiam 1964- . . . . . **CLC 59**
See also CA 132

Wilson, Sloan 1920- . . . . **CLC 32**
See also CA 1-4R; CANR 1

Wilson, Snoo 1948- . . . . **CLC 33**
See also CA 69-72

Wilson, William S(mith) 1932- . . . . . **CLC 49**
See also CA 81-84

Winchilsea, Anne (Kingsmill) Finch Counte
1661-1720 . . . . **LC 3**

Windham, Basil
See Wodehouse, P(elham) G(renville)

Wingrove, David (John) 1954- . . . . . . **CLC 68**
See also CA 133

Winters, Janet Lewis . . . . **CLC 41**
See also Lewis, Janet
See also DLBY 87

Winters, (Arthur) Yvor
1900-1968 . . . . **CLC 4, 8, 32**
See also CA 11-12; 25-28R; CAP 1; DLB 48; MTCW

Winterson, Jeanette 1959- . . . . **CLC 64**
See also CA 136

Wiseman, Frederick 1930- . . . . **CLC 20**

Wister, Owen 1860-1938 . . . . **TCLC 21**
See also CA 108; DLB 9, 78; SATA 62

Witkacy
See Witkiewicz, Stanislaw Ignacy

Witkiewicz, Stanislaw Ignacy
1885-1939 . . . . **TCLC 8**
See also CA 105

Wittig, Monique 1935(?)- . . . . **CLC 22**
See also CA 116; 135; DLB 83

Wittlin, Jozef 1896-1976 . . . . **CLC 25**
See also CA 49-52; 65-68; CANR 3

Wodehouse, P(elham) G(renville)
1881-1975 . . . **CLC 1, 2, 5, 10, 22; SSC 2**
See also AITN 2; CA 45-48; 57-60; CANR 3, 33; CDBLB 1914-1945; DLB 34; MTCW; SATA 22

Woiwode, L.
See Woiwode, Larry (Alfred)

Woiwode, Larry (Alfred) 1941- . . . **CLC 6, 10**
See also CA 73-76; CANR 16; DLB 6

Wojciechowska, Maia (Teresa)
1927- . . . . **CLC 26**
See also AAYA 8; CA 9-12R; CANR 4, 41; CLR 1; JRDA; MAICYA; SAAS 1; SATA 1, 28

Wolf, Christa 1929- . . . . **CLC 14, 29, 58**
See also CA 85-88; DLB 75; MTCW

Wolfe, Gene (Rodman) 1931- . . . . **CLC 25**
See also CA 57-60; CAAS 9; CANR 6, 32; DLB 8

Wolfe, George C. 1954- . . . . **CLC 49**

Wolfe, Thomas (Clayton)
1900-1938 . . . . **TCLC 4, 13, 29**
See also CA 104; 132; CDALB 1929-1941; DA; DLB 9, 102; DLBD 2; DLBY 85; MTCW; WLC

Wolfe, Thomas Kennerly, Jr. 1931-
See Wolfe, Tom
See also CA 13-16R; CANR 9, 33; MTCW

Wolfe, Tom . . . . **CLC 1, 2, 9, 15, 35, 51**
See also Wolfe, Thomas Kennerly, Jr.
See also AAYA 8; AITN 2; BEST 89:1

Wolff, Geoffrey (Ansell) 1937- . . . . . **CLC 41**
See also CA 29-32R; CANR 29, 43

Wolff, Sonia
See Levitin, Sonia (Wolff)

Wolff, Tobias (Jonathan Ansell)
1945- . . . . **CLC 39, 64**
See also BEST 90:2; CA 114; 117; DLB 130

Wolfram von Eschenbach
c. 1170-c. 1220 . . . . **CMLC 5**

Wolitzer, Hilma 1930- . . . . **CLC 17**
See also CA 65-68; CANR 18, 40; SATA 31

Wollstonecraft, Mary 1759-1797 . . . . . . **LC 5**
See also CDBLB 1789-1832; DLB 39, 104

Wonder, Stevie . . . . **CLC 12**
See also Morris, Steveland Judkins

Wong, Jade Snow 1922- . . . . **CLC 17**
See also CA 109

Woodcott, Keith
See Brunner, John (Kilian Houston)

Woodruff, Robert W.
See Mencken, H(enry) L(ouis)

Woolf, (Adeline) Virginia
1882-1941 . . . . **TCLC 1, 5, 20, 43; SSC 7**
See also CA 104; 130; CDBLB 1914-1945; DA; DLB 36, 100; DLBD 10; MTCW; WLC

Woollcott, Alexander (Humphreys)
1887-1943 . . . . **TCLC 5**
See also CA 105; DLB 29

Woolrich, Cornell 1903-1968 . . . . **CLC 77**
See also Hopley-Woolrich, Cornell George

Wordsworth, Dorothy 1771-1855 . . . . **NCLC 25**
See also DLB 107

Wordsworth, William 1770-1850 . . . . **NCLC 12, 38; PC 4**
See also CDBLB 1789-1832; DA; DLB 93, 107; WLC

Wouk, Herman 1915- . . . . **CLC 1, 9, 38**
See also CA 5-8R; CANR 6, 33; DLBY 82; MTCW

Wright, Charles (Penzel, Jr.) 1935- . . . . **CLC 6, 13, 28**
See also CA 29-32R; CAAS 7; CANR 23, 36; DLBY 82; MTCW

Wright, Charles Stevenson 1932- . . . **CLC 49**
See also BLC 3; BW; CA 9-12R; CANR 26; DLB 33

Wright, Jack R.
See Harris, Mark

Wright, James (Arlington) 1927-1980 . . . . **CLC 3, 5, 10, 28**
See also AITN 2; CA 49-52; 97-100; CANR 4, 34; DLB 5; MTCW

Wright, Judith (Arandell) 1915- . . . . **CLC 11, 53**
See also CA 13-16R; CANR 31; MTCW; SATA 14

Wright, L(aurali) R. 1939- . . . . **CLC 44**
See also CA 138

Wright, Richard (Nathaniel) 1908-1960 . . . . **CLC 1, 3, 4, 9, 14, 21, 48, 74; SSC 2**
See also AAYA 5; BLC 3; BW; CA 108; CDALB 1929-1941; DA; DLB 76, 102; DLBD 2; MTCW; WLC

Wright, Richard B(ruce) 1937- . . . . . . **CLC 6**
See also CA 85-88; DLB 53

Wright, Rick 1945- . . . . **CLC 35**
See also Pink Floyd

Wright, Rowland
See Wells, Carolyn

Wright, Stephen 1946- . . . . **CLC 33**

Wright, Willard Huntington 1888-1939
See Van Dine, S. S.
See also CA 115

Wright, William 1930- . . . . **CLC 44**
See also CA 53-56; CANR 7, 23

Wu Ch'eng-en 1500(?)-1582(?) . . . . **LC 7**

Wu Ching-tzu 1701-1754 . . . . **LC 2**

Wurlitzer, Rudolph 1938(?)- . . . **CLC 2, 4, 15**
See also CA 85-88

Wycherley, William 1641-1715 . . . . **LC 8, 21**
See also CDBLB 1660-1789; DLB 80

Wylie, Elinor (Morton Hoyt) 1885-1928 . . . . **TCLC 8**
See also CA 105; DLB 9, 45

Wylie, Philip (Gordon) 1902-1971 . . . **CLC 43**
See also CA 21-22; 33-36R; CAP 2; DLB 9

Wyndham, John
See Harris, John (Wyndham Parkes Lucas) Beynon

Wyss, Johann David Von 1743-1818 . . . . **NCLC 10**
See also JRDA; MAICYA; SATA 27, 29

Yakumo Koizumi
See Hearn, (Patricio) Lafcadio (Tessima Carlos)

Yanez, Jose Donoso
See Donoso (Yanez), Jose

Yanovsky, Basile S.
See Yanovsky, V(assily) S(emenovich)

Yanovsky, V(assily) S(emenovich) 1906-1989 . . . . **CLC 2, 18**
See also CA 97-100; 129

Yates, Richard 1926-1992 . . . . . **CLC 7, 8, 23**
See also CA 5-8R; 139; CANR 10, 43; DLB 2; DLBY 81, 92

Yeats, W. B.
See Yeats, William Butler

Yeats, William Butler 1865-1939 . . . . **TCLC 1, 11, 18, 31**
See also CA 104; 127; CDBLB 1890-1914; DA; DLB 10, 19, 98; MTCW; WLC

Yehoshua, A(braham) B. 1936- . . . . **CLC 13, 31**
See also CA 33-36R; CANR 43

Yep, Laurence Michael 1948- . . . . . . **CLC 35**
See also AAYA 5; CA 49-52; CANR 1; CLR 3, 17; DLB 52; JRDA; MAICYA; SATA 7, 69

Yerby, Frank G(arvin) 1916-1991 . . . . **CLC 1, 7, 22**
See also BLC 3; BW; CA 9-12R; 136; CANR 16; DLB 76; MTCW

Yesenin, Sergei Alexandrovich
See Esenin, Sergei (Alexandrovich)

Yevtushenko, Yevgeny (Alexandrovich) 1933- . . . . **CLC 1, 3, 13, 26, 51**
See also CA 81-84; CANR 33; MTCW

Yezierska, Anzia 1885(?)-1970 . . . . . **CLC 46**
See also CA 126; 89-92; DLB 28; MTCW

Yglesias, Helen 1915- . . . . **CLC 7, 22**
See also CA 37-40R; CANR 15; MTCW

Yokomitsu Riichi 1898-1947 . . . . . . **TCLC 47**

Yonge, Charlotte (Mary) 1823-1901 . . . . **TCLC 48**
See also CA 109; DLB 18; SATA 17

York, Jeremy
See Creasey, John

York, Simon
See Heinlein, Robert A(nson)

Yorke, Henry Vincent 1905-1974 . . . **CLC 13**
See also Green, Henry
See also CA 85-88; 49-52

Young, Al(bert James) 1939- . . . . **CLC 19**
See also BLC 3; BW; CA 29-32R; CANR 26; DLB 33

Young, Andrew (John) 1885-1971 . . . . **CLC 5**
See also CA 5-8R; CANR 7, 29

Young, Collier
See Bloch, Robert (Albert)

Young, Edward 1683-1765 . . . . **LC 3**
See also DLB 95

Young, Neil 1945- . . . . **CLC 17**
See also CA 110

Yourcenar, Marguerite 1903-1987 . . . . **CLC 19, 38, 50**
See also CA 69-72; CANR 23; DLB 72; DLBY 88; MTCW

Yurick, Sol 1925- . . . . **CLC 6**
See also CA 13-16R; CANR 25

Zabolotskii, Nikolai Alekseevich 1903-1958 . . . . **TCLC 52**
See also CA 116

Zamiatin, Yevgenii
See Zamyatin, Evgeny Ivanovich

Zamyatin, Evgeny Ivanovich 1884-1937 . . . . **TCLC 8, 37**
See also CA 105

Zangwill, Israel 1864-1926 . . . . **TCLC 16**
See also CA 109; DLB 10

Zappa, Francis Vincent, Jr. 1940-
See Zappa, Frank
See also CA 108

Zappa, Frank . . . . **CLC 17**
See also Zappa, Francis Vincent, Jr.

Zaturenska, Marya 1902-1982 . . . . **CLC 6, 11**
See also CA 13-16R; 105; CANR 22

Zelazny, Roger (Joseph) 1937- . . . . . **CLC 21**
See also AAYA 7; CA 21-24R; CANR 26; DLB 8; MTCW; SATA 39, 57

Zhdanov, Andrei A(lexandrovich) 1896-1948 . . . . **TCLC 18**
See also CA 117

Zhukovsky, Vasily 1783-1852 . . . . **NCLC 35**

Ziegenhagen, Eric . . . . **CLC 55**

Zimmer, Jill Schary
See Robinson, Jill

Zimmerman, Robert
See Dylan, Bob

Zindel, Paul 1936- . . . . **CLC 6, 26**
See also AAYA 2; CA 73-76; CANR 31; CLR 3; DA; DLB 7, 52; JRDA; MAICYA; MTCW; SATA 16, 58

Zinov'Ev, A. A.
See Zinoviev, Alexander (Aleksandrovich)

Zinoviev, Alexander (Aleksandrovich) 1922- . . . . **CLC 19**
See also CA 116; 133; CAAS 10

Zoilus
See Lovecraft, H(oward) P(hillips)

Zola, Emile (Edouard Charles Antoine) 1840-1902 . . . . **TCLC 1, 6, 21, 41**
See also CA 104; 138; DA; DLB 123; WLC

Zoline, Pamela 1941- . . . . **CLC 62**

Zorrilla y Moral, Jose 1817-1893 . . **NCLC 6**

Zoshchenko, Mikhail (Mikhailovich) 1895-1958 . . . . **TCLC 15**
See also CA 115

Zuckmayer, Carl 1896-1977 . . . . **CLC 18**
See also CA 69-72; DLB 56, 124

Zuk, Georges
See Skelton, Robin

Zukofsky, Louis 1904-1978 . . . . **CLC 1, 2, 4, 7, 11, 18**
See also CA 9-12R; 77-80; CANR 39; DLB 5; MTCW

Zweig, Paul 1935-1984 . . . . **CLC 34, 42**
See also CA 85-88; 113

Literary Criticism Series Cumulative Topic Index

This index lists all topic entries in the Gale Literary Criticism Series *Classical and Medieval Literature Criticism, Contemporary Literary Criticism, Literature Criticism from 1400 to 1800, Nineteenth-Century Literature Criticism,* and *Twentieth-Century Literary Criticism.*

CMLC Cumulative Nationality Index

CMLC Cumulative Title Index

See "Le Fraisne"
The Friars (Aristophanes) **4**:100
The Frogs (Aristophanes)
See *Batrakhoi*
Furens (Seneca)
See *Hercules furens*
Furies (Aeschylus)
See *Eumenides*
Furious Hercules (Seneca)
See *Hercules furens*
"Ganem, Son to Abou Ayoub, and Known by the Surname of Love's Slave" **2**:14, 36, 38
Gauvain (Chretien de Troyes)
See *Perceval*
De genesi ad litteram (Augustine) **6**:9, 137, 139
De Genesi ad litteram imperfectum (Augustine) **6**:137
De Genesi adversus Manichaeos (Augustine) **6**:137
"Genesis" (*Paraphrase*; *Paraphrase of Genesis*) (Caedmon) **7**:78-9, 82-9, 91-4, 104
"Genesis A" (Caedmon) **7**:84-90
"Genesis B" (Caedmon) **7**:85-6, 91, 93
Genesis of the Gods (Hesiod)
See *Theogony*
Genji Monogatari (*The Tale of Genji*) (Murasaki) **1**:413-76
Georgos (Menander) **9**:250
Gertadés (Aristophanes) **4**:102, 105
Gilgamesh
See *Epic of Gilgamesh*
"Gilgamesh and the Agga of Kish" **3**:336
"Gilgamesh and the Bull of Heaven" **3**:337, 349
"Gilgamesh and the Huluppu Tree" ("Gilgamesh, Enkidu and the Nether World") **3**:326, 337, 349, 362
"Gilgamesh and the Land of the Living" **3**:325, 332-33, 336-37, 349
"Gilgamesh, Enkidu and the Nether World"
See "Gilgamesh and the Huluppu Tree"
Gilgamesh Epic
See *Epic of Gilgamesh*
Gilgamish
See *Epic of Gilgamesh*
The Girl from Samos (Menander)
See *Samia*
The Girl Who Gets Her Hair Cut Short (Menander)
See *Perikeiromenē*
The Girl with Shorn Hair (Menander)
See *Perikeiromenē*
Gita
See *Bhagavad Gītā*
Gīta
See *Bhagavadgīta*
Glaucus Potnieus (Aeschylus) **11**:159, 179
"Goat's Leaf" (Marie de France)
See "Chevrefoil"
The Golden Ass (Apuleius)
See *Asinus aureus*
Gorgias (Plato) **8**:217, 233, 235, 239, 247-48, 255, 264, 266-68, 270, 274, 283, 285-87, 306, 322
De gratia et libero arbitrio (*On Grace and Free Will*) (Augustine) **6**:89, 118, 122
Great Epic
See *Mahābhārata*
Grumpy (Menander)
See *Dyskolos*
"Guigemar" (Marie de France)
See "Lay of Guigemar"
"Guildeluec and Gualadun" (Marie de France)
See "Eliduc"
Guillaume d'Angleterre (*William of England*) (Chretien de Troyes) **10**:137, 139, 142-43, 183, 218, 225, 232
"Guingamor" (Marie de France) **8**:122-23, 126-28, 131
"Gulnare of the Sea" **2**:14, 23
Halieticon/On Fishing (Ovid)
See *Halieutica*
Halieutica (*The Fisherman's Art*; *Halieticon/On Fishing*) (Ovid) **7**:328-29
"Hard Roads to Shu" (Li Po) **2**:131-32, 145, 158, 166
"Hardships of Travel" (Li Po) **2**:139
The Harpist (Menander) **9**:288
"Harrowing of Hell" (Caedmon) **7**:79, 91-2
Hated (Menander)
See *Misoumenos*
"The Hawk and the Owl" (Marie de France) **8**:192, 194
Hazar Afsana
See *Alf Layla wa-Layla*
Heautontimorumenus (*The Man Who Punished Himself*) (Menander) **9**:243, 269
He Clips Her Hair (Menander)
See *Perikeiromenē*
Heliades (Aeschylus) **11**:211
Hell (Dante)
See *Inferno*
"Heng-chiang Lyrics" (Li Po) **2**:161
Hercules furens (*Furens*; *Furious Hercules*; *Mad Hercules*) (Seneca) **6**:340, 342-43, 363, 366, 369-70, 372-73, 379-81, 402-03, 405, 413, 415-17, 422-23, 431-32, 440-41, 446
Hercules oetaeus (*Hercules on Oeta*; *Oetaeus*) (Seneca) **6**:342-44, 363, 366, 370, 377, 379, 381, 414, 417-18, 423, 431-32, 446
Hercules on Oeta (Seneca)
See *Hercules oetaeus*
Hero (Menander) **9**:207, 211, 217, 246, 252
Heroides (*Epistles*; *Epistol**** Heroidum*; *Heroines*; *Letters*; *Letters of the Heroines*) (Ovid) **7**:291-93, 296-97, 299-301, 303, 310-13, 316-19, 321, 329-36, 343-44, 346-47, 355, 376-83, 388, 417, 419-20, 425, 444
Heroines (Ovid)
See *Heroides*
Hikayet-i Oguzname-i Kazan Beg ve Gayri
See *Kitabi-i Dedem Qorkut*
Hiketides (Aeschylus)
See *Suppliants*
Hipparchus (Plato) **8**:305, 311
Hippeis (*The Knights*) (Aristophanes) **4**:38, 43, 46, 60, 62-3, 65, 74, 94, 98-9, 101, 114-15, 126-28, 132, 143, 146, 148, 152, 162-63, 167
Hippias maior (*Hippias Major*) (Plato) **8**:270, 305-06
Hippias Major (Plato)
See *Hippias maior*
Hippias Minor (*Lesser Hippias*) (Plato) **8**:306
Hippolytus (Seneca)
See *Hyppolytus*
Historia Calamitatum (*History of My Troubles*; *Story of Calamities*; *Story of His Misfortunes*) (Abelard) **11**:24, 28, 32, 33, 40, 45, 48, 51, 52, 55, 57-59, 61, 63-66
History of My Troubles (Abelard)
See *Historia Calamitatum*
The History of Rome from Its Foundation (Livy)
See *Ab urbe condita libri*
"The Honeysuckle" (Marie de France)
See "Chevrefoil"
Hortensius (Cicero) **3**:178, 242, 288
"How Basat Killed Goggle-eye" ("The Story of Basat Who Killed Depegöz"; "The Story of Basat Who Kills the One-Eyed Giant") **8**:103, 108-09
"How Prince Urez Son of Prince Kazan was Taken Prisoner" **8**:103
"How Salur Kazan's House was Pillaged"
See "The Plunder of the Home of Salur-Kazan"
"How the Outer Oghuz Rebelled Against the Inner Oghuz and How Beyrek Died" **8**:103
Hrafnkatla
See *Hrafnkel's saga Freysgodi*
Hrafnkel's Saga
See *Hrafnkel's saga Freysgodi*
Hrafnkel's saga Freysgodi (*Hrafnkatla*; *Hrafnkel's Saga*) **2**:74-129
"Hsiang-yang Song" (Li Po) **2**:161
Hundred Names of God (*Cent Noms de Déu*) (Llull) **12**:122, 125
"Hymn" (Caedmon) **7**:84-5, 93-7, 100-01, 103-13
Hymn (Pindar) **12**:355-56
Hymns to the Gods (Pindar) **12**:320
"Hymn to Aphrodite" (Sappho)
See "Ode to Aphrodite"
Hymn to Zeus (Pindar) **12**:276-78, 320
Hypobolimaeus (Menander) **9**:203
Hyporcemata (*Hyporcheme*; *Songs for Dancing*) (Pindar) **12**:320-21, 355-57, 364
Hyporcheme (Pindar)
See *Hyporcemata*
Hyppolytus (*Hippolytus*) (Seneca) **6**:340, 342, 363, 373
Hypsipyle (Aeschylus) **11**:124
I. 3 (Pindar)
See *Isthmian 3*
I. 4 (Pindar)
See *Isthmian 4*
Ibis (Ovid) **7**:327-28, 444
Ichneutai (*The Trackers*) (Sophocles) **2**:289, 338, 388, 408
De ideis (Hermogenes)
See *On Types of Style*
Iliad (*Iliads*; *Ilias*) (Homer) **1**:268-412
Iliads (Homer)
See *Iliad*
Ilias (Homer)
See *Iliad*
De immortalitate animae (Augustine) **6**:68
In Catilinam (*Against Catilina*; *Catilinarians*) (Cicero) **3**:193, 196, 198, 268, 270
In Collation (Eckhart)
See *Rede der Unterscheidungen*
Inferno (*Hell*) (Dante) **3**:1-169
'Ingredientibus' (Abelard)
See *Logica 'Ingredientibus'*
In Pisonem (Cicero) **3**:269, 284
"In Quest of the Tao in An-Ling, I Met Kai Huan Who Fashioned for Me a Register of the Realized Ones; (This Poem) Left Behind As a Present When About to Depart" (Li Po) **2**:175
De interpretatione (Abelard) **11**:63
Introductio (Abelard) **11**:10
In Vatinium (Cicero) **3**:223

Title Index

Title Index

Title Index

Title Index

CMLC Cumulative Critic Index

ISBN 0-8103-2433-4
90000
9 780810 324336